Pro ASP.NET 1.1 in C#:
From Professional to Expert

MATTHEW MACDONALD, EDITOR

K. SCOTT ALLEN
JAMES AVERY
RUSS BASIURA
MIKE BATONGBACAL
MARCO BELLINASO
MATT BUTLER
ANDREAS EIDE
DANIEL CAZZULINO
MICHAEL CLARK
RICHARD CONWAY
ROBERT EISENBERG
BRADY GASTER
JAMES GREENWOOD
KEVIN HOFFMAN
ERIK JOHANSSON
ANGELO KASTROULIS
DAN KENT
SITARAMAN LAKSHMINARAYANAN
DON LEE
CHRISTOPHER MILLER
MATT MILNER
JAN NARKIEWICZ
MATT ODHNER
RYAN O'KEEFE
ANDREW REID
MATTHEW REYNOLDS
ENRICO SABBADIN
BILL SEMPF
DOUG SEVEN
SRINIVASA SIVKUMAR
THIRU THANGARATHINAM
DOUG THEWS

Pro ASP.NET 1.1 in C#: From Professional to Expert

ISBN (pbk): 1-59059-351-0

Printed and bound in the United States of America 9 8 7 6 5 4 3 2 1

Trademarked names may appear in this book. Rather than use a trademark symbol with every occurrence
of a trademarked name, we use the names only in an editorial fashion and to the benefit of the trademark
owner, with no intention of infringement of the trademark.

Lead Editor: Ewan Buckingham
Technical Reviewers: Robert Lair, Jason Lefebvre
Editorial Board: Steve Anglin, Dan Appleman, Ewan Buckingham, Gary Cornell, Tony Davis,
   Jason Gilmore, Chris Mills, Dominic Shakeshaft, Jim Sumser
Associate Publisher: Grace Wong
Copy Edit Manager: Nicole LeClerc
Lead Copy Editor: Mark Nigara
Second Copy Editor: Ami Knox
Production Manager: Kari Brooks-Copony
Compositor: Dina Quan
Second Production Editor: Katie Stence
Proofreader: Linda Seifert
Indexer: Kevin Broccoli
Artist: Kinetic Publishing Services, LLC
Cover Designer: Kurt Krames
Manufacturing Manager: Tom Debolski

Distributed to the book trade in the United States by Springer-Verlag New York, Inc., 233 Spring Street,
6th Floor, New York, NY 10013, and outside the United States by Springer-Verlag GmbH & Co. KG,
Tiergartenstr. 17, 69112 Heidelberg, Germany.

In the United States: phone 1-800-SPRINGER, fax 201-348-4505, e-mail orders@springer-ny.com, or visit
www.springer-ny.com. Outside the United States: fax +49 6221 345229, e-mail orders@springer.de, or
visit www.springer.de.

For information on translations, please contact Apress directly at 2560 Ninth Street, Suite 219, Berkeley,
CA 94710. Phone 510-549-5930, fax 510-549-5939, e-mail info@apress.com, or visit www.apress.com.

The information in this book is distributed on an "as is" basis, without warranty. Although every precaution has been taken in the preparation of this work, neither the author(s) nor Apress shall have any
liability to any person or entity with respect to any loss or damage caused or alleged to be caused directly
or indirectly by the information contained in this work.

The source code for this book is available to readers at www.apress.com in the Downloads section. You will
need to answer questions pertaining to this book in order to successfully download the code.

Contents at a Glance

PART THREE ■ ■ ■ Security

PART FOUR ■ ■ ■ Advanced User Interface

PART FIVE ■ ■ ■ Web Services

Contents

PART ONE ■ ■ ■ Core Concepts

PART TWO ■ ■ ■ Data Access

PART THREE ███ Security

About the Editor

MATTHEW MACDONALD is an author, educator, and MCSD developer. He's a regular contributor to programming journals and the author of over a dozen books about .NET programming, including *ASP.NET: The Complete Reference* (Osborne McGraw-Hill), *Programming .NET Web Services* (O'Reilly), *Beginning ASP.NET in C#: From Novice to Professional* (Apress), and *Microsoft .NET Distributed Applications* (Microsoft Press). In a dimly remembered past life he studied English literature and theoretical physics.

About the
Technical Reviewer

ROBERT LAIR is the president and CEO of Intensity Software, Inc. (www.intensitysoftware.com), which specializes in offering Microsoft .NET solutions including legacy migrations to ASP.NET. In addition to consulting services, Intensity offers .Kicks for .NET, a CICS to ASP.NET migration utility that automates the migration process while maintaining existing business-logic source code. Bob was one of the developers who created the original IBuySpy Store and Web Portal demo applications as well as the NetCOBOL for .NET version of IBuySpy and the QuickStart samples. Bob has been a participating author in a number of books and has written numerous articles on topics related to Microsoft .NET. Bob's personal website is located at www.robertlair.com and his blog is located at www.robertlair.com/blogs/lair.

Acknowledgments

Portions of this book were derived from the following works:

Basiura, et al., *Professional ASP.NET Security* (Chapters 2, 6, 7, 9, 10, 12, 15), Wrox Press, 2002

Basiura, et al., *Professional ASP.NET Web Services* (Chapters 1, 4, 5, 6), Wrox Press, 2001

Butler, et al., *Professional ASP.NET Server Controls: Building Custom Controls with C#* (Chapters 2, 5, 6, 8, 9), Wrox Press, 2002

Gaster, et al., *Fast Track ASP.NET* (Chapters 1 to 6, and 8), Wrox Press, 2002

MacDonald, *Beginning ASP.NET in C#: From Novice to Professional*, Apress, 2005

MacDonald and Johansson, *C# Data Security Handbook* (Chapter 2), Wrox Press, 2003

Odhner, et al., *Professional ASP.NET Performance* (Chapter 3), Wrox Press, 2002

Introduction

ASP.NET is Microsoft's next-generation technology for creating server-side web applications. It's built on the Microsoft .NET Framework, which is a cluster of closely related new technologies that revolutionizes everything from database access to distributed applications. ASP.NET is one of the most important components of the .NET Framework—it's the part that enables you to develop high-performance *web applications* and *web services*.

The traditional concepts involved in creating web applications still hold true in the .NET world. Each web application is made up of web pages. You can render rich HTML and even use JavaScript, create components that encapsulate programming logic, and tweak and tune your applications using configuration settings. However, behind the scenes ASP.NET works quite differently than traditional scripting technologies like classic ASP (Active Service Pages) or PHP (PHP: Hypertext Preprocessor). It's also much more ambitious than JSP (Java Server Pages).

Some of the differences between ASP.NET and earlier web development platforms include:

- ASP.NET features a completely object-oriented programming model, which includes an event-driven, control-based architecture that encourages code encapsulation and code reuse.

- ASP.NET gives you the ability to code in any supported .NET language (including Visual Basic .NET, C#, J#, and many other languages that have third-party compilers).

- ASP.NET is also a platform for building *web services*, which are reusable units of code that other applications can call across platform and computer boundaries. You can use a web service to do everything from web enabling a desktop application to sharing data with a Java client running on UNIX.

- ASP.NET is dedicated to high performance. ASP.NET pages and components are compiled on demand instead of being interpreted every time they're used. ASP.NET also includes a fine-tuned data access model and flexible data caching to further boost performance.

These are only a few in the wide range of features, which include enhanced state management, practical data binding, dynamic graphics, and a robust security model. You'll look at these improvements in detail in this book, and see why both ASP.NET 1.0 and 1.1 have been wildly popular in the web development community.

What Does This Book Cover?

Here is a quick breakdown of what you'll find in this book:

- **Part One: Core Concepts.** You'll begin in Chapter 1 with a look at the overall ASP.NET platform, the .NET Framework, and the promise that they hold. In Chapters 2 and 3, you'll branch out to learn the tools of the trade: the IIS web server software and the Visual Studio .NET design tool. In Chapters 4, 5, 6, and 7, you'll learn the key parts of the ASP.NET infrastructure, like the web-page model, application configuration, state management, and caching. As you learn these core concepts, you'll also take a low-level look at how ASP.NET processes requests and manages the lifetime of your web applications. You'll even learn how to extend the ASP.NET architecture.

- **Part Two: Data Access.** This part tackles one of the core problem domains for all software development—accessing and manipulating data. In Chapters 8 and 9, you'll learn the fundamentals of ADO.NET, which is .NET's new toolkit for interacting with relational databases. In Chapter 10, you'll learn about ASP.NET's set of innovative data bound controls that let you format and present data without writing pages of code. Chapter 11 branches out into more advanced data access techniques, like handling transactions, serving images, and creating complex grids for master/details pages and shopping carts. Finally, Chapters 12 and 13 move beyond the world of databases to show you how to work with XML content and handle ordinary file access.

- **Part Three: Security.** In this part you'll take a look at ASP.NET's rich complement of security features. You'll start with a high-level overview of security concepts in Chapter 14, and then learn the ins and outs of forms authentication (Chapter 15) and Windows authentication (Chapter 16). In Chapter 17, you'll learn how to restrict authenticated users with sophisticated authorization rules. In Chapter 18, you'll go one step further and learn how to protect the data you store in a database as well as the information you send in a URL with encryption.

- **Part Four: Advanced User Interface.** This part shows how you can extend web pages with custom controls. You'll start simply with user controls in Chapter 19, which allow you to reuse segments of the user interface, and continue with more advanced custom server controls in Chapter 20. In Chapter 21, you'll learn how to make your custom controls work well in the design environment. Finally, Chapters 22 and 23 show how you can extend your web applications and web controls with clever client-side scripting techniques and dynamic, handcrafted graphics.

- **Part Five: Web Services.** Web services promise to revolutionize the way functionality is shared across different applications, network environments, and computing platforms. In Chapter 24, you'll start on the ground floor, with examples that show you how to create basic web services, and how to use them in ASP.NET web applications, .NET windows applications, and even legacy ASP applications. In Chapter 25, you'll take a low-level look at the standards that make it all possible, and see how they work. In Chapter 26, you'll learn how to use more advanced techniques to call web services asynchronously, implement secure services, and start working with newer web service standards using the WSE (Web Services Enhancements) toolkit.

Who Is This Book For?

This book is intended as a primer for professional developers who have a reasonable knowledge of server-side web development, and who are considering migrating to ASP.NET. It's assumed that you're already familiar with the syntax of the C# language and object-oriented concepts. However, if you're a seasoned Java or C++ developer, you'll probably be able to pick up everything you need to know about C# along the way.

This book isn't an exhaustive look at every ingredient in the .NET Framework—in fact, such a book would require twice as many pages. Instead, this book aims to provide a lean, intelligent introduction to ASP.NET for professional programmers who don't want to rehash the basics.

This book is also relentlessly practical. You won't learn just learn about *features*, but also the real-world *techniques* that can take your website to the next level. Later chapters are dedicated to cutting-edge topics like custom controls, dynamic graphics, advanced security, and high-performance data access, all with the goal of giving you everything you need to build professional web applications.

What Do You Need to Use This Book?

The main prerequisite for this book is a computer with the .NET Framework installed. In order to run ASP.NET pages, you need Windows 2000 Professional, Windows XP Professional, Windows 2000 Server, or Windows Server 2003. You also need to install the .NET Framework and IIS (Internet Information Services), the web hosting software that's a part of the Windows operating system.

The .NET Framework currently comes in three flavors:

- **The .NET Framework redistributable.** This package includes the full .NET Framework, with everything you need to build, deploy, and run a .NET application. The easiest way to install this is using the Windows Update feature (approximate size: 20 MB).

- **The .NET Framework SDK (Software Development Kit).** This package includes the full .NET Framework plus samples, tutorials, and the ever-important documentation. This package is available for free, and can be downloaded from www.asp.net (approximate size: 130 MB).

- **Visual Studio .NET.** This package includes the .NET Framework SDK along with a rich design environment for writing, testing, and profiling code. Visual Studio .NET is available in several editions, and is available as part of the MSDN Professional or higher subscription programs.

A full copy of Visual Studio .NET is recommended in order for you to use the downloadable code, but it's not essential if you just want to learn the concepts presented in this book. If you aren't afraid of a little hard work and a lot of drudgery, you can create all the examples using a bare-bones text editor, compile them wherever necessary using a command prompt, and view them using an ordinary web browser. You can even use another design tool, like Web Matrix (available for free at www.asp.net). However, this book explains all you need to know to author websites with Visual Studio .NET, which is the favorite tool of most professional developers. Visual Studio .NET offers more debugging tools, better support for component-based development, helpful IntelliSense, and a cleaner code-behind model.

▪**Note** This book includes several examples that use sample SQL Server 2000 databases to demonstrate data access code, security techniques, and web services. If you use other relational database engines the same concepts will apply, but you will need to modify the example code.

ASP.NET 1.0 and 1.1

The .NET Framework is currently available in two versions: the original version 1.0 (released in 2002), and version 1.1 (released in 2003). There are very few noticeable differences between the two versions, as 1.1 mainly consists of minor bug fixes and performance enhancements. You can use this book to program with either version of .NET. Any differences are clearly highlighted in the text.

Visual Studio .NET also exists in two versions. The original version of Visual Studio .NET is designed to work with .NET 1.0, while Visual Studio .NET 2003 adds support for .NET 1.1. Although VS .NET 2002 and VS .NET 2003 are very similar, they use a different format for project and solution files. The downloadable code examples for this book include VS .NET 2003 project files.

Customer Support

We always value hearing from our readers, and we want to know what you think about this book—what you liked, what you didn't like, and what you think we can do better next time. You can send us your comments by e-mail to feedback@apress.com. Please be sure to mention the book title in your message.

Sample Code

To download the sample code, visit the Apress site at www.apress.com, and search for this title. On the book's detail page is a link to the sample code, which is compressed into a single ZIP file. Before you use the code, you'll need to uncompress it using a utility like WinZip. Code is arranged into separate directories by chapter. Before using the code, refer to the accompanying readme.txt file for information about other prerequisites and considerations.

Errata

We've made every effort to make sure that there are no errors in the text or in the code. However, no one is perfect and mistakes do occur. If you find an error in the book, such as a spelling mistake or a faulty piece of code, we would be very grateful to hear about it. By sending in errata, you may save another reader hours of frustration, and you'll be helping us to provide ever-higher quality information. Simply e-mail the problem to support@apress.com, where your information will be checked and posted on the errata page, or used in subsequent editions of the book. You can view errata from the book's detail page.

PART ONE

■ ■ ■

Core Concepts

CHAPTER 1

Introducing ASP.NET

Over ten years ago, Tim Berners-Lee performed the first transmission across HTTP, the Hypertext Transfer Protocol. Since then, HTTP has become exponentially more popular, expanding beyond a small group of computer-science visionaries to the personal and business sectors. Today, it's almost a household world.

When HTTP was first established, developers were faced with the challenge of designing applications that could discover and interact with each other. To help meet these challenges, standards such as HTML and XML were created. HTML established a simple language that could describe how to display rich documents on virtually any computer platform. XML created a set of rules for building platform-neutral data formats that different applications could use to exchange information. These standards guaranteed that the Web could be used by anyone, located anywhere, using any type of computing system.

At the same time, software vendors faced their own challenges. They needed to develop not only language and programming tools that could integrate with the Web, but also entire frameworks that would allow developers to architect, develop, and deploy these applications easily. Major software vendors including IBM, Sun Microsystems, and Microsoft rushed to meet this need with a host of products. The latest stage in this ongoing arms race is .NET, which changes the face of web development dramatically. In .NET, Microsoft has created an integrated suite of components that combine the building blocks of the Web—markup languages and HTTP—with proven object-oriented methodology.

This book introduces ASP.NET web pages and web services. It also focuses on the other corners of the .NET Framework that you'll need in order to build professional web applications, including data access and XML. Using these features, you'll be able to create next-generation websites with the best tools on hand today.

The Evolution of Web Development

Previous server-based web application frameworks relied on scripting languages or proprietary tagging conventions. Most of these web development models just provide clumsy hooks that allow you to trigger applications or run components on the server. They don't provide a modern, integrated framework for web programming.

Overall, most of the web development frameworks that were created before ASP.NET fall into one of two following categories:

- Scripts that are interpreted by a server-side resource

- Separate, tiny applications that are executed by server-side calls

Classic ASP and ColdFusion fall into the first category. You, the developer, are responsible for creating a script file that contains embedded code. The script file is examined by another component, which alternates between rendering ordinary HTML and executing your embedded code. If you've created ASP applications before, you probably know that scripted applications usually execute at a much slower rate than compiled applications. Additionally, scripted platforms introduce other problems, such as the lack of ability to control security settings and inefficient resource usage.

The second approach, used widely by Perl over CGI (Common Gateway Interface), yields an entirely different set of problems. In these frameworks, the web server launches a separate application to handle the client's request. That application executes its code and dynamically creates the HTML that should be sent back to the client. Though these applications execute faster than their scripted counterparts, they tend to require much more memory. The key problem is that the web server needs to create a separate instance of the application for each client request. This model makes these applications much less scalable in environments with large numbers of simultaneous users, unless you code carefully. This type of application can also be quite difficult to write, debug, and integrate with other components.

ASP.NET is far more than a simple evolution of either type of application. Instead, it breaks the trend with a whole new development model. The difference is that ASP.NET is the first web application development platform that's truly integrated with its underlying framework. ASP.NET is *not* an extension or modification to the .NET Framework with loosely coupled hooks into the functionality it provides. Instead, ASP.NET is a portion of the .NET Framework that's managed by the .NET runtime. In essence, ASP.NET blurs the line between *application* development and *web* development by extending the tools and technologies previously monopolized by desktop developers into the web development world.

Why Do We Need a New Version of ASP?

Classic ASP developers sometimes wonder whether they should bother making the change to ASP.NET. Learning a whole new framework isn't trivial, and .NET introduces a slew of new concepts and can pose some serious stumbling blocks.

Overall, classic ASP is an excellent tool for developing web applications using Microsoft technologies. However, as with most development models, ASP contains some fundamental design issues that raise new problems. These problems are described in the following sections.

Spaghetti Code

If you've created applications with ASP, you've probably seen lengthy pages that contain server-side script code intermingled with HTML. Consider the following example, which fills an HTML drop-down list with the results of a database query:

```
<%
  Set dbConn = Server.CreateObject("ADODB.Connection")
  Set rs = Server.CreateObject("ADODB.Recordset")
  dbConn.Open connectionString
%>

<select name="cboAuthors">
  <%
```

```
    rs.Open "SELECT * FROM Authors", dbConn, 3, 3
    Do While Not rs.EOF
  %>
  <option value="<%=rs("au_id")%>"><%=rs("au_lname") & ", " & _
    rs("au_fname")%></option>
  <%
    rs.MoveNext
    Loop
  %>
</select>
```

This example needs an unimpressive 16 lines of code to generate one simple HTML control. But what's worse is the way this style of coding diminishes application performance because it mingles HTML and script. When this page is processed by the ASP ISAPI (Internet Server Application Programming Interface) extension that runs on the web server, the scripting engine needs to switch on and off multiple times just to handle this single request. This increases the amount of time needed to process the whole page and send it to the client.

Another code-related problem occurs if the graphic designers on your web development team need to make changes to a web page's user interface with a WYSIWYG editor. Hopefully, you'll keep a few spare copies of your script code around just in case. Most HTML editors fail to recognize ASP code, and many end up removing the server-side code entirely!

Furthermore, web pages written in this style can easily grow to unmanageable lengths. If you add your own custom COM components to the puzzle (which are needed to supply functionality ASP can't provide), the management nightmare grows. The bottom line is that no matter what approach you take, ASP code tends to become beastly, long, and incredibly difficult to debug—if you can even get ASP debugging working in your environment at all.

In ASP.NET, these problems don't exist. Web pages are written with traditional object-oriented concepts in mind. Your web pages contain controls that can be programmed against in a way similar to desktop applications. This means you don't need to combine a jumble of HTML markup and inline code. If you opt to use the code-behind approach when creating ASP.NET pages, the code and presentation are actually placed in two different files, which simplifies code maintenance and allows you to separate the task of web-page design from the heavy-duty work of web coding.

Script Languages

At the time of its creation, ASP seemed like a perfect solution for desktop developers who were moving to the world of the Web. Rather than requiring programmers to learn a completely new language or methodology, ASP allowed developers to use familiar languages like VBScript on a server-based programming platform. By leveraging the already-popular COM programming model as a backbone, these scripting languages also acted as a convenient vehicle for accessing server components and resources. But even though ASP was easy to understand for developers who were already skilled with scripting languages like VBScript, this familiarity came with a price. Because ASP was based on old technologies that were originally designed for client use, it couldn't perform as well in the new environment of web development.

Performance wasn't the only problem. Every object or variable used in classic ASP script is created as a *variant* data type. As most Visual Basic programmers know, variant data types are weakly typed. They require larger amounts of memory, are late-bound, and result in slower performance. Additionally, the compiler and development tools can't identify them at design time. That made it all but impossible to create a truly integrated IDE that could provide ASP programmers with anything like the powerful debugging, IntelliSense, and error checking found in Visual Basic and Visual C++. And without debugging tools, ASP programmers were hard-pressed to troubleshoot the problems in their scripts.

ASP.NET circumvents all of these problems. For starters, ASP.NET pages and web services are executed within the CLR (common language runtime), so they can be authored in any language that has a CLR-compliant compiler. No longer are you limited to the use of VBScript or JavaScript—instead, you can use modern object-oriented languages like VB .NET and C#.

It's also important to note that ASP.NET pages are not interpreted, but are instead compiled into *assemblies* (the .NET term for any unit of compiled code). This is one of the most significant enhancements to Microsoft's web development model. What actually happens behind the scenes is revolutionary. Even if you create your code in Notepad and copy it directly to a virtual directory on a web server, the application is dynamically compiled as soon as a client accesses it, and cached for future requests. If any of the files are modified after this compilation process, the application is recompiled automatically the next time a client requests it.

The Death of COM

At the 2001 DevelopMentor .NET conference in San Francisco, a few presenters joked that .NET would eventually be the death of COM. Around the same time, a textbook that was written to introduce programmers to the C# language described COM as old and archaic technology. These less-than-subtle clues indicate a very important shift in Microsoft's strategy for distributed enterprise development. Though Microsoft claims undying support for COM, it's obvious that .NET is being touted as the new path for developers. As COM applications wane in popularity and applications are converted to .NET, classic ASP will become a thing of the past. Even though .NET includes robust support for COM interoperability, the sad fact remains that simple, classic ASP applications have no real place in a .NET world.

By the time you finish reading this book, you probably won't miss COM at all. ASP.NET introduces a whole new breed of more robust, scalable, manageable, and efficient web-based applications. By using compiled (rather than interpreted) code, data-bound controls, and a hierarchical library of objects that are accessible to virtually any language (provided a CLR-compliant compiler exists for that language), the .NET Framework provides a welcome step up.

Seven Important Facts About ASP.NET

Throughout the remainder of this book, you'll see virtually every aspect of ASP.NET programming from web controls to security. But before you dive in, you need a little more background. The following sections give you a quick tour of the fundamental building blocks of the .NET world. You'll examine the general architecture of the .NET Framework, and look at how ASP.NET integrates with .NET to provide rich functionality for your web applications.

1. ASP.NET Is Integrated with the .NET Framework

The .NET Framework is divided into an almost painstaking collection of functional parts, with a staggering total of more than 7,000 *types* (the .NET term for classes, structures, interfaces, and other core programming ingredients). Before you can program any type of .NET application, you need a basic understanding of those parts—and an understanding of why things are organized the way that they are.

The massive collection of functionality that the .NET Framework provides is organized in a way that traditional Windows programmers will see as a happy improvement. Each one of the thousands of classes in the .NET Framework is grouped into a logical, hierarchical container called a *namespace*. Different namespaces provide different features. Taken together, the .NET namespaces offer functionality for nearly every aspect of distributed development from message queuing to security. This massive toolkit is called the *class library*.

Interestingly, the way you use the .NET Framework classes in ASP.NET is exactly the same as the way you use them in any other type of .NET application (including a standalone Windows application, a Windows service, a command-line utility, and so on). In other words, .NET gives the exact same tools to web developers that it gives to rich client developers. Imagine a web development framework that gives you access to every system and network resource that desktop developers have taken for granted for years! That framework is ASP.NET.

UNDERSTANDING NAMESPACES

Namespaces play the same role in .NET as they do in Java—they group types based on function, and prevent naming conflicts.

For example, in order to interact with a text box in a web page, you'll use the TextBox class, which is found in the System.Web.UI.WebControls namespace. That means the fully qualified class name in System.Web.UI.WebControls.TextBox. Each period (.) indicates a level of hierarchy. The .NET Framework includes more than one TextBox class (there's also a Windows variant in the System.Windows.Forms namespace), but because these two classes are in separate namespaces, there's no conflict.

When programming with the TextBox and other classes in the System.Web.UI.WebControls namespace, you won't want to use the fully qualified names, because they lead to unnecessarily long lines of code (not to mention cramped fingers). Instead, you'll usually *import* the namespace at the beginning of your code file with the C# using statement. This way, you can use just the class name in your code. When you compile your code, the compiler will search the imported namespaces in order to find the matching class. This shortcut won't slow down the execution of your code, because all the class names are converted into fully qualified names in the compiled code.

Remember, namespaces are logical, not physical containers. The actual compiled files that hold the types from the .NET class library are called *assemblies*. In other words, assemblies are the physical package (EXE or DLL files), while namespaces are a grouping convention used for organization. There is no intrinsic relationship between namespaces and assemblies. A single assembly can contain types in more than one namespace, and two assemblies can contain types that are in the same namespaces.

■**Tip** One of the best resources for learning about new corners of the .NET Framework is the .NET Framework class library reference, which is part of the MSDN Help library reference. If you have Visual Studio .NET installed, you can view the MSDN Help library by selecting Start ➤ Programs ➤ Microsoft Visual Studio .NET ➤ Microsoft Visual Studio .NET Documentation (the exact shortcut depends on your version of Visual Studio .NET). Once you've loaded the help, you can find class reference information grouped by namespace under the Visual Studio .NET ➤ .NET Framework ➤ Reference ➤ Class Library node.

---

2. ASP.NET Is Compiled, Not Interpreted

One of the major reasons for performance degradation in ASP scripts was the fact that all ASP web-page code uses interpreted scripting languages. That means that when your application is executed, a scripting host on the server machine needs to interpret your code and translate it to lower-level machine code, line by line. This process is notoriously slow.

■**Note** In fact, in this case the reputation is a little worse than the reality. Interpreted code is certainly slower than compiled code, but the performance hit isn't so significant that you can't build a professional website using ASP. The same limitations that affect ASP in this area also affect Java applications, because Java is also an interpreted language that is never compiled. This is one of the dramatic differences between Java and the languages you'll use with ASP.NET.

ASP.NET applications are always compiled—in fact, it's impossible to execute C# or VB .NET code without it being compiled first.

ASP.NET applications actually go through two stages of compilation. In the first stage, the C# code you write is compiled into an intermediate language called Microsoft Intermediate Language (MSIL) code, or just IL. This first step is the fundamental reason that .NET can be language-interdependent. Essentially, all .NET languages (including C#, VB .NET, and many more) are compiled into virtually identical IL code. This first compilation step may happen automatically when the page is first requested, or you can perform it in advance (a process known as precompiling). The compiled file with IL code is an assembly.

The second level of compilation happens just before the page is actually executed. At this point, the IL code is compiled into low-level native machine code. This stage is known as *just-in-time* (JIT) compilation, and it takes place in the same way for all .NET applications (including Windows applications, for example). Figure 1-1 shows this two-step compilation process.

.NET compilation is decoupled into two steps in order to offer developers the most convenience and the best portability. Before a compiler can create low-level machine code, it needs to know what type of operating system and hardware platform the application will run on (for example, 32-bit or 64-bit Windows). By having two compile stages, you can create a compiled assembly with .NET code, but still distribute this to more than one different platform.

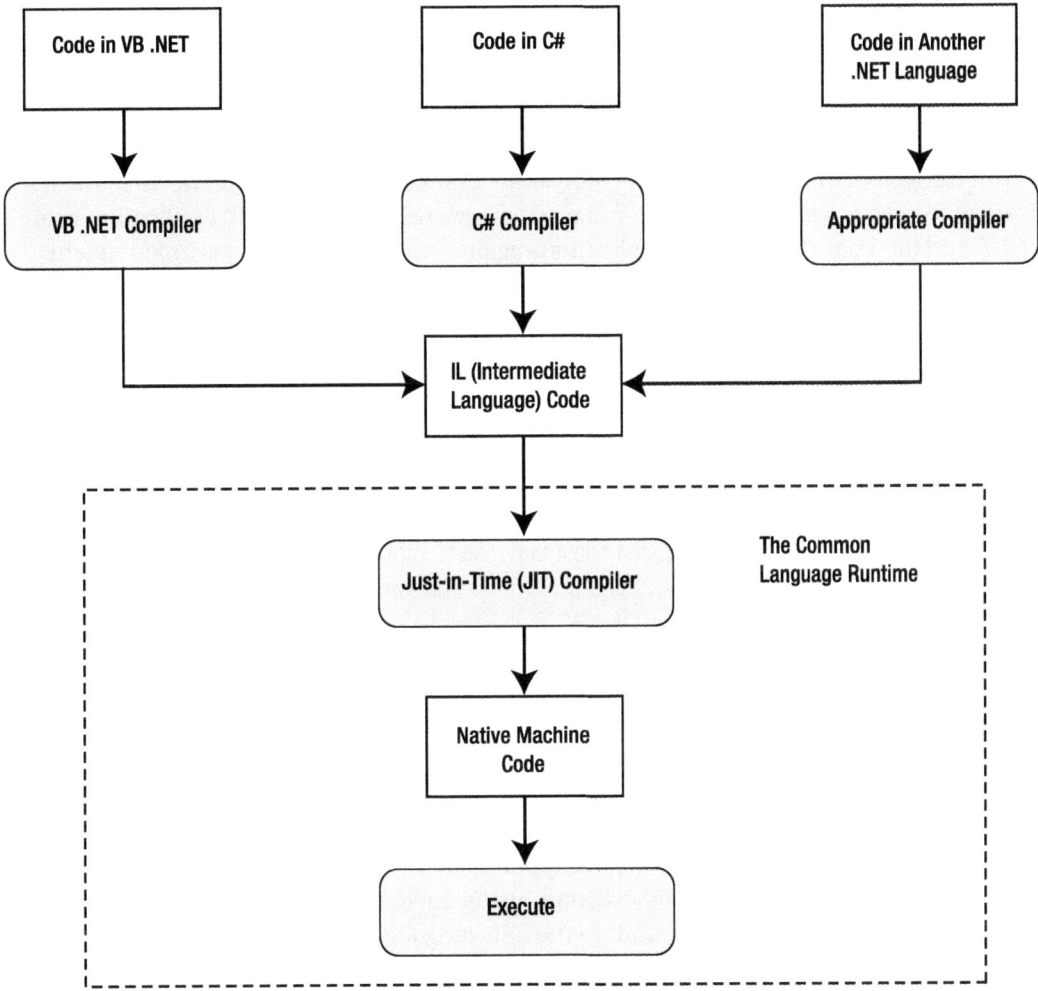

Figure 1-1. *Compilation in an ASP.NET web page*

■**Note** One day soon, this model may even help business programmers deploy applications to non-Microsoft operating systems like Linux. This ambitious goal hasn't quite been realized yet, but if you'd like to try out the first version of .NET for the Linux platform (complete with a work-in-progress implementation of ASP.NET), visit www.go-mono.com and download the latest version of this open-source effort.

Of course, JIT compilation probably wouldn't be that useful if it needed to be performed every time a user requested a web page from your site. Fortunately, ASP.NET applications don't need to be compiled every time a web page or web service is requested. Instead, the MSIL code is created once, and only regenerated when the source is modified. Similarly, the native machine code files are cached in a system directory that has a path like c:\[WinDir]\Microsoft.NET\Framework\[Version]\Temporary ASP.NET Files, where [WinDir] in the Windows directory and [Version] is the version number for the currently installed version of the .NET Framework, like v.1.1.4322 (the version installed with Visual Studio .NET 2003).

With the advent of compiled pages, chances are that you will see a dramatic increase in performance in your web applications. As a test, try reworking a simple ASP application using ASP.NET, and then benchmark your applications against one another. Various independent parties have performed similar tests, and the results come out strongly in favor of ASP.NET.

Note Although benchmarks are often controversial, you can find some interesting information at http://gotdotnet.com/team/compare. Keep in mind that the real issues limiting performance are usually related to specific bottlenecks, like disk access, CPU use, network bandwidth, and so on. In many benchmarks, ASP.NET outperforms other solutions due to its support for performance-enhancing platform features like caching, not because of the speed boost that results from compiled code.

---

3. ASP.NET Is Multilanguage

Though you'll probably opt to use one language over another when you develop an application, that choice won't determine what you can accomplish with your web applications. That's because no matter what language you use, the code is compiled into an intermediate language called IL.

IL is a stepping stone for every managed application. (A *managed application* is any application that's written for .NET, and executes inside the managed environment of the CLR.) In a sense, IL is *the* language of .NET, and it's the only language that the CLR recognizes.

To understand MSIL, it helps to consider a simple example. Take a look at this function, written in C#:

```
namespace HelloWorld
{
    public class TestClass
    {
        private static void Main(string[] args)
        {
            Console.WriteLine("Hello World");
        }
    }
}
```

This code shows the most basic application that's possible in .NET—a simple command-line utility that displays a single, predictable message on the console window.

Now look at it from a different perspective. Here's the IL code for the same class:

```
.method public static void  Main() cil managed
{
  .entrypoint
  .custom instance void [mscorlib]System.STAThreadAttribute::.ctor() =
  ( 01 00 00 00 )
  // Code size        14 (0xe)
  .maxstack  8
  IL_0000:  nop
  IL_0001:  ldstr      "Hello World"
  IL_0006:  call       void [mscorlib]System.Console::WriteLine(string)
  IL_000b:  nop
  IL_000c:  nop
  IL_000d:  ret
} // end of method Module1::Main
```

It's easy enough to take a look at the MSIL for any compiled .NET application. You simply need to run the IL Disassembler, which is installed with Visual Studio .NET and the .NET SDK. Look for the file ildasm.exe in a directory like c:\Program Files\Visual Studio .NET 2003\SDK\ v1.1\Bin. Once you've loaded the program use the File ➤ Open command and select any DLL or EXE that was created with .NET.

If you're patient and a little logical, you can deconstruct the IL code fairly easily and figure out what's happening. The fact that IL is so easy to disassemble can raise privacy and code control issues, but these issues usually aren't of any concern to ASP.NET developers. That's because all ASP.NET code is stored and executed on the server. Because the client never receives the compiled code file, the client has no opportunity to decompile it. If it *is* a concern, consider using an obfuscator that scrambles code to try and make it more difficult to understand. (For example, an obfuscator might rename all variables to have generic, meaningless names like f__a__234.) Visual Studio .NET 2003 includes a scaled-down version of one popular obfuscator, called Dotfuscator.

The following code shows the same console application in VB .NET code.

```
Namespace HelloWorld
    Public Class TestClass
        Private Shared Sub Main(Ars() As String)
            Console.WriteLine("Hello World")
        End Sub
    End Class
End Namespace
```

If you compile this application and look at the IL code, you'll find that every line is identical to the IL code generated from the C# version. Although different compilers can sometimes introduce their own optimizations, as a general rule of thumb no .NET language outperforms any other .NET language, because they all share the same common infrastructure. This infrastructure is formalized in the Common Language Specification, which is described in the sidebar on this page.

It's important to note that IL was recently adopted as an ANSI standard. This adoption could quite possibly spur the adoption of other common language frameworks. The Mono project at www.go-mono.com is an example of one such project.

THE COMMON LANGUAGE SPECIFICATION

The CLS (Common Language Specification) defines the standard properties that all objects must contain in order to communicate with one another in a homogenous environment. In order to allow this communication, the CLR, expects all objects to adhere to a specific set of rules.

The CLS is this set of rules. It defines many laws that all languages must follow, such as keywords, types, primitive types, method overloading, and so on. Any compiler that generates IL code to be executed in the CLR must adhere to all rules governed within the CLS. The CLS gives developers, vendors, and software manufacturers the opportunity to work within a common set of specifications for languages, compilers, and data types. As time goes on, you'll see more CLS-compliant languages and compilers emerge, although there are several so far.

Given these criteria, the creation of a language compiler that generates true CLR-compliant code can be complex. Nevertheless, compilers can exist for virtually any language, and chances are that there may eventually be one for just about every language you'd ever want to use. Imagine—mainframe programmers who loved COBOL in its heyday can now use their knowledge base to create web applications!

4. ASP.NET Runs Inside the Common Language Runtime

Perhaps the most important aspect of ASP.NET to remember is that it runs inside the runtime engine of the CLR. The whole of the .NET Framework—that is, all namespaces, applications, and classes—are referred to as *managed* code. Though a full-blown investigation of the CLR is beyond the scope of this chapter, some of the benefits are as follows:

- **Automatic memory management and garbage collection.** Every time your application instantiates an object, the CLR allocates space on the *managed heap* for that object. However, you never need to clear this memory manually. As soon as your reference to an object goes out of scope (or your application ends), the object becomes available for garbage collection. The garbage collector runs periodically inside the CLR, automatically reclaiming unused memory for inaccessible objects. This model saves you from the low-level complexities of C++ memory handling, and the quirkiness of COM reference counting.

- **Type safety.** When you compile an application, .NET adds information to your assembly that indicates details like the available classes, their members, their data types, and so on. As a result, your compiled code assemblies are completely self-sufficient. Other people can use them without requiring any other support files, and the compiler can verify that every call is valid at runtime. This extra layer of safety completely obliterates low-level errors like the infamous buffer overflow.

- **Extensible metadata.** The information about classes and members is only one of the types of metadata that .NET stores in a compiled assembly. *Metadata* describes your code and allows you to provide additional information to the runtime or other services. For example, this metadata might tell a debugger how to trace your code, or it might tell Visual Studio .NET how to display a custom control at design time. You could also use metadata to enable other runtime services (like web methods or COM+ services).

- **Structured error handling.** If you've ever written any moderately useful Visual Basic or VBScript code, you'll most likely be familiar with the limited resources these languages offer for error handling. With structured exception handling, you can organize your error-handling code logically and concisely. You can create separate blocks to deal with different types of errors. You can also nest exception handlers multiple layers deep.

- **Multithreading.** The CLR provides a pool of threads that various classes can make use of. For example, you can call methods, read files, or communicate with web services asynchronously, without needing to explicitly create new threads.

Figure 1-2 shows a high-level look at the CLR and the .NET Framework.

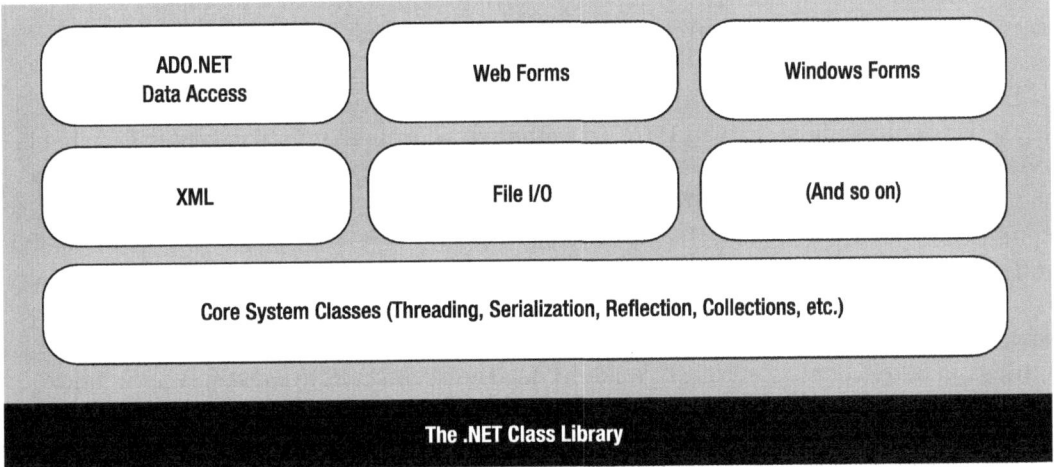

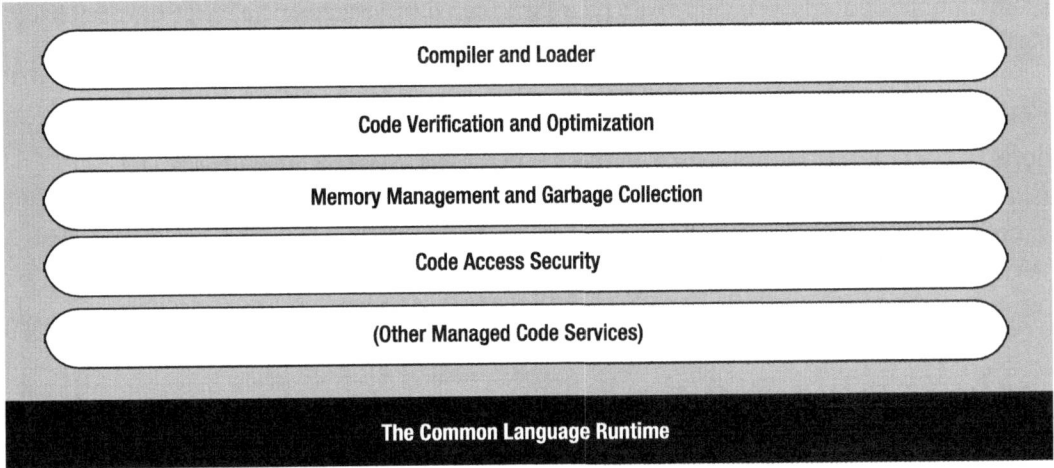

Figure 1-2. *The CLR and .NET Framework*

5. ASP.NET Is Multidevice and Multibrowser

One of the greatest challenges web developers face is the wide variety of browsers they need to support. Different browser brands, versions, and configurations differ in their support of HTML. Web developers need to choose whether they should render their content according to the HTML 3.2 standard, HTML 4.0, or something else entirely (like XHTML 1.0, or even WML for mobile devices). This problem, fueled by the various browser companies, has plagued developers since the World Wide Web Consortium proposed the first version of HTML. Life gets even more complicated if you want to use an HTML extension like JavaScript to create a more dynamic page or provide validation.

ASP.NET addresses this problem in a remarkably intelligent way. Although you can retrieve information about the client browser and its capabilities in an ASP.NET page, ASP.NET actually encourages developers to ignore these considerations and use a rich suite of web server controls. These server controls render their HTML adaptively by taking the client's capabilities into account.

During the page-rendering process, ASP.NET determines the browser's functionality. Each server control adjusts how its HTML is rendered accordingly. In older, less-skilled clients (known as *down-level* clients), the HTML 3.2 standard is used. On the other hand, more capable *up-level* clients will receive HTML 4.0. Some controls even enhance the user interface with a combination of JavaScript and DHTML (Dynamic HTML). For example, ASP.NET's validation controls add client-side JavaScript to show dynamic error messages without the user needing to send the page back to the server for more processing. These features are optional, but they demonstrate how intelligent controls can make the most of cutting-edge browsers without shutting out other clients. Best of all, you don't need any extra coding work to support both types of client.

The future gets even better. Currently, ASP.NET includes a separate toolkit of controls for *smart devices* (like mobile phones, PDAs, and so on). Most smart devices don't support the full HTML standard, but support scaled-down standards like WML or HDML. By using the ASP.NET mobile controls, you can create pages that can be viewed using a range of specialized smart devices.

Note Of course, there's still one wrinkle. You need to create web pages for mobile devices using a different (but similar) set of controls from the one you use to create ordinary web pages. Interestingly, Microsoft's upcoming ASP.NET 2.0 removes this limitation, and gives the current set of controls the ability to render themselves to smart devices.

---

6. ASP.NET Is Object-Oriented

ASP provides a relatively feeble object model. There's a small set of objects, which are really just a thin layer over the raw details of HTTP and HTML. On the other hand, ASP.NET is truly object-oriented. Not only does your code have full access to all objects in the .NET Framework, but you can also exploit all the conventions of an object-oriented programming (OOP) environment. For example, you can create reusable classes, standardize code with interfaces, and bundle together useful functionality in a distributable, compiled component.

One of the best examples of object-oriented thinking in ASP.NET is found in *server-based controls*. Server-based controls are the epitome of encapsulation. Developers can manipulate control objects programmatically, using code to customize their appearance, provide data to display, and even react to events. The low-level HTML details (which can be quite complex), are hidden away behind the scenes. Instead of forcing the developer to write raw HTML manually, the control objects render themselves to HTML when the page is finished rendering. In this way, ASP.NET offers server controls as a way to abstract the low-level details of HTML and HTTP programming.

ASP.NET server-based controls give you remarkable flexibility, fine-grained control, and effortless customization. Best of all, you can embedded a control into a page with a simple control tag.

7. ASP.NET Is Easy to Deploy and Configure

One of the biggest headaches a web developer faces during a development cycle is deploying a completed application to a production server. Not only do the web-page files, databases, and components need to be transferred, but you also need to register components and re-create a slew of configuration settings. ASP.NET simplifies this process considerably.

Every installation of the .NET Framework provides the same core classes. As a result, deploying an ASP.NET application is relatively simple. In most cases, you simply need to copy all the files to a virtual directory on a production server (using an FTP program or even a command-line command like XCOPY). As long as the host machine has the .NET Framework, there are no time-consuming registration steps.

Distributing the components your application uses is just as easy. All you need to do is copy the component assemblies when you deploy your web application. Because all the information about your component is stored directly in the assembly file metadata, there's no need to launch a registration program or modify the Windows registry. As long as you place these components in the correct place (the Bin subdirectory of the web-application directory), the ASP.NET engine automatically detects them and makes them available to your web-page code. Try that with a traditional COM component!

Configuration is another challenge with application deployment, particularly if you need to transfer security information like user accounts and user privileges. ASP.NET makes this deployment process easier by minimizing the dependence on settings in IIS (Internet Information Services). Instead, most ASP.NET settings are stored in a dedicated web.config file. The web.config file is placed in the same directory as your web pages. It contains a hierarchical grouping of application settings stored in an easily readable XML format that you can edit using nothing more than a text editor like Notepad. When you modify an application setting, ASP.NET notices that change, and smoothly restarts the application in a new application domain (keeping the existing application domain alive long enough to finish processing any outstanding requests). The web.config file is never locked, so it can be updated at any time.

Two of the configuration sections in a web.config file—authentication and authorization—are illustrated in the following configuration fragment. These settings, which are extracted from a complete web.config file, demonstrate how easily a web application can be configured to deny anonymous requests.

```
<authentication mode="Windows" />
<authorization>
  <deny users="?" />
</authorization>
```

In this example, the application is configured to use Windows accounts for authentication. Anonymous users (represented with the ? wildcard) are restricted from using the application. As a result, every client must be authenticated before a page can be served. With a little more subtlety, you can block specific users or groups, or restrict specific pages or subdirectories. Best of all, when this web.config file is deployed with the application to the production web server, the security configuration is deployed with it!

In addition to security, ASP.NET includes several other prebuilt services that you can harness through simple web.config settings. These include web-farm-ready session state, custom error pages, and debugging. You'll learn about all of these features in this book.

A Quick Tour of ASP.NET

Now that you've learned about the fundamentals of ASP.NET, it's a great time to take a quick tour and introduce some of the features you'll explore in the coming chapters. In the following sections, you'll get a whirlwind look at web forms, server-based controls, and web services.

HTML Server Controls

The quick and easy way to start your migration path from ASP to ASP.NET is to add runat="server" to your HTML controls. This converts them from standard controls to server controls.

Let's look at a quick example:

```
<input type="text" id="myText" runat="server" />
```

This example is a standard HTML text box. With the addition of the runat="server" attribute, this static piece of HTML becomes a fully functional server-side control that you can manipulate in your code. You can now work with events that it generates, set attributes, and bind controls to data sources.

Note In order to become a server control, your HTML tag must be uniquely identifiable. To accomplish this, make sure you've included the id attribute with a unique name. This is the name you'll use to manipulate the control object.

For example, you can set the text of this text box when the page first loads using the following code:

```
void Page_Load(object sender, EventArgs e)
{
    myText.Value = "Hello World!";
}
```

Technically, this code sets the Value property of the HtmlInputText class. The end result is that a string of text appears in a text box on the HTML page that's rendered and sent to the client.

HTML controls are quick and easy to implement, and they have the same set of attributes that you're used to when working with standard HTML elements on a page. Without these controls, the only way to create dynamic content is by writing the page piecemeal using the Response.Write() command. This approach is awkward, messy, and prone to introducing syntax errors in the page. Letting a server-side control do the work for you is both more elegant and more efficient.

ASP.NET Controls

When ASP.NET was first created, there were two schools of thought. Some ASP.NET developers were most interested in server-side controls that matched the existing set of HTML controls exactly. This approach allows you to create ASP.NET web-page interfaces in dedicated HTML editors, and it provides a quick migration path for existing ASP pages. However, another set of ASP.NET developers saw the promise of something more—rich server-side controls that didn't just emulate individual HTML tags. These controls might render their interface out of dozens of distinct HTML elements, while still providing a simple object-based interface to the programmer. Using this model, developers could work with programmable menus, calendars, data lists, and validators.

After some deliberation, Microsoft decided to provide both models. You've already seen an example of HTML server controls, which map directly to the basic set of HTML tags. Along with these are ASP.NET *web controls*, which provide a higher level of abstraction and more functionality. In most cases, you'll use HTML server-side controls for backward compatibility and quick migration, and web controls for new projects.

ASP.NET control tags always start with the prefix *asp:* followed by the class name. For example, the following snippet creates a text box and a check box:

```
<asp:TextBox id="myASPText" Text="Hello ASP.NET TextBox" runat="server" />
<asp:CheckBox id="myASPCheck" Text="My CheckBox" runat="server" />
```

And again, you can interact with these controls in your code, as follows:

```
myASPText.Text = "New text";
myASPCheck.Text = "Check me!";
```

Notice that the Value property that you saw with the HTML control has been replaced with a Text property. The HtmlInputText.Value property was named to match the underlying value attribute in the HTML <input> tag. However, web server controls don't place the same emphasis on correlating with HTML syntax, so the more descriptive property name Text is used instead.

The ASP.NET family of web controls include complex rendered controls (like the Calendar and DataGrid), along with more streamlined controls (like TextBox, Label, and Button), which map closely to existing HTML tags. In the latter case, the HTML server-side control and the ASP.NET web-control variants provide similar functionality, although the web controls tend to expose a more standardized, streamlined interface. That makes the web controls very easy to learn and it also means they're a natural fit for Windows developers moving to the world of the Web, because many of the property names are similar to the corresponding Windows controls.

> **Note** ASP.NET web controls are still server controls. Technically, server controls identify any ASP.NET control that executes on the server. There are two types of server controls, simpler HTML server controls, and full-fledged web controls.

To show you a quick example of the similarity between HTML server controls and web controls, consider the following ASP.NET web page, which includes both server controls and their HTML server-side equivalents. In this example, the markup for the page (which defines the HTML and includes all the control tags) and the code for the page (which defines what happens on the server in reaction to certain events) are both placed in the same file. This is the simplest approach, but in later chapters we'll use the more robust approach of separating these two pieces into different files.

```
<%@ Page Language="C#" %>
<html>
<head>
  <title>SimpleControls</title>
</head>

  <body>
    <form id="Form1" method="post" runat="server">
      <h3>Web Controls</h3>
      <asp:Label ID="lblArea" Runat="server" /><br>
      <asp:Button ID="cmdOK" Runat="server" /><br>
      <br><br>
      <h3>HTML Server-Side Controls</h3>
      <span id="spnArea" runat="server"/><br>
      <button id="btnOK" runat="server" type="button"/>
    </form>
  </body>
</html>

<script runat="server">
  void Page_Load()
  {
      // Set the text for the ASP.NET web controls.
      lblArea.Text = "this is an asp:label";
      cmdOK.Text = "this is an asp:button";

      // Set the text for the HTML server-side controls.
      // Note that the InnerText property represents text
      // between the start and end tags of this control.
      spnArea.InnerText = "this is an html span";
      btnOK.InnerText = "this is an html button";
  }
</script>
```

The script block at the bottom of this page reacts when the page first loads on the server, and sets the text in all four of these controls. Then the page is rendered to HTML, and sent to the client. Figure 1-3 shows the final result.

■**Note** To test this page, you need to save the code with the extension .aspx, which represents an ASP.NET web page, and place it in a virtual directory on your web server that's hosted by IIS. A *virtual directory* exposes a physical directory to remote clients over a network (or the Internet). For more information about creating virtual directories and configuring them in IIS, refer to the next chapter.

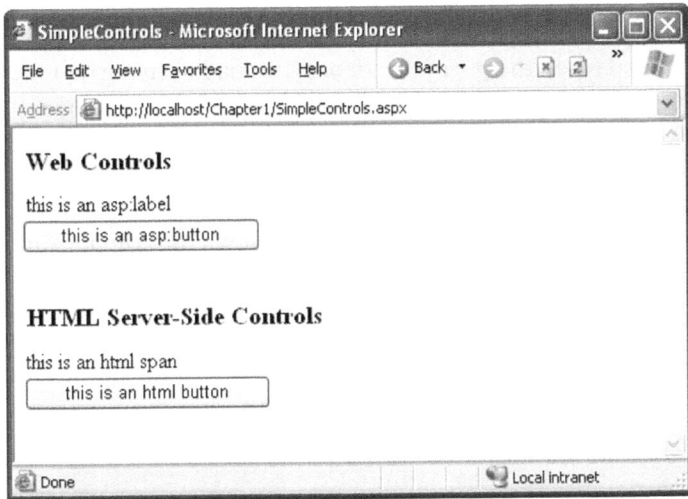

Figure 1-3. *A page that mixes two types of controls*

It's no coincidence that these two types of controls look the same in this example. If you look at the HTML that's sent to the client, you'll find that both sections of the page are virtually identical. That's because the ASP.NET web controls in this example render themselves using the same tags as the HTML server controls. With HTML server controls, it's always obvious what tag will be used in the rendering process. However, with web controls you don't have direct control over the tag or tags that are used. The web control creates its interface based on the properties you've set and the capabilities of the client browser.

■**Note** Along with the built-in ASP.NET controls, it's worth noting that you can also create your own controls for elements of functionality that you want to reuse. You'll consider this topic in much more detail in Part Four.

Web Forms

Web forms are a vital part of what makes up an ASP.NET application. They provide the actual output of a web application—the web pages that clients request and view in their browsers. Although web pages aren't anything new, the concept of web *forms* is something entirely unique to ASP.NET. In essence, each web form is a graphical prototype driven by programming logic. You can place this logic either in the same file as the layout code but enclosed entirely within a <script> block or, ideally, in a separate class in a code-behind file. Either way, the separation of graphical interface from programming logic is very similar to how you create a visual layout for a form in Windows programming and then use event handlers and logic to manipulate that form.

Under the hood, each web form that you create is a class that inherits from the base class System.Web.UI.Page, which is defined in the .NET Framework. You'll learn much more about web pages in the coming chapters. For now, all you need to know is that one of the many features that all web pages include is a built-in Page.Load event, which you can handle to perform initialization. This event is triggered when the page is loaded. (This load occurs when the page is requested by a client—don't make the mistake of assuming a page's lifetime is longer than a single request.)

In a minor revolution, the state of all of the controls on that web form is maintained automatically for you using a mechanism called *view state*. This feature is enabled by default, but you can turn it off if you know you won't need it. This allows you to slim down the size of your pages and increase transmission times if you don't need to use highly dynamic content. Just to demonstrate a little bit about how the ASP.NET web form works and automatic state maintenance, I'll walk you through another quick sample.

Here's the complete code for this example web page:

```
<%@ Page language="C#" %>
<html>
  <head>
    <title>TextBox</title>
  </head>
  <body>
    <form id="TextBox" method="post" runat="server">
      <asp:TextBox id="txtSample" runat="server" />
      <asp:Button id="Button1" runat="server" Text="Button" />
    </form>
  </body>
</html>

<script runat="server">
  void Page_Load()
  {
      if (!Page.IsPostBack)
      {
          Response.Write("This is the first time the page loaded.");
      }
      else
      {
```

```
            Response.Write("You typed [" + txtSample.Text + "] into txtSample.");
        }
    }
</script>
```

This web page uses two ASP.NET controls (a text box and a submit button), and defines an event handler for the Page.Load event. If you request this page, you'll see the interface shown in Figure 1-4.

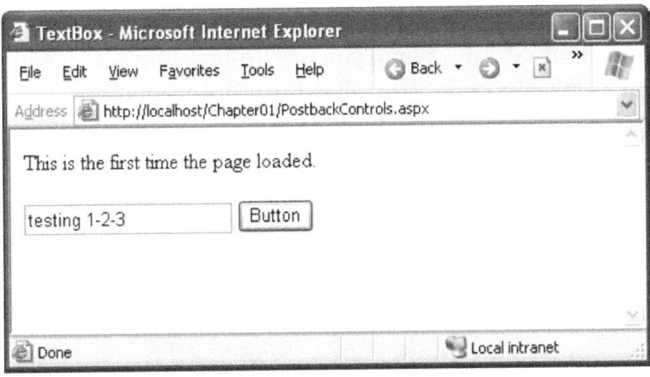

Figure 1-4. *Requesting a page for the first time*

This means that the Page.Load event fired, and the code in the Page_Load() method was triggered. This code evaluated the state of the Page.IsPostBack property, and determined that the value was false, indicating the page is being requested anew. (You'll learn more about postbacks in future chapters. For now, it's enough to just know that a postback is a round-trip to the web server in response to a web form being submitted to the web server.)

Now if you type some text into the text box and click the submit button, you'll see something like the page shown in Figure 1-5.

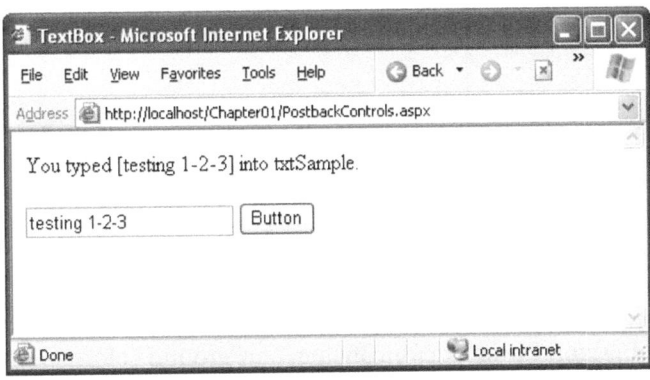

Figure 1-5. *Posting data back to a page*

Notice here that not only is the code able to retrieve the data from the form post without looking up dictionary entries in the Request collection (which is required in classic ASP), but the text box automatically repopulates itself with the text the user supplied before the postback. This means the form behaves in the way users intuitively expect it to behave, even though this behavior isn't necessarily natural in the stateless world of the Web. Under the surface, ASP.NET is taking the state of all of the controls on that form and stuffing that information into a hidden form field automatically. This way, all of that information is sent back to your code when the user clicks the submit button.

Data-Bound Controls

One of the most impressive features of ASP.NET controls is the ability to *bind* data to controls. Using data binding, you can access a data source like a database, read some data, and then insert that data into one or more controls automatically. When you use this approach, you can display all the data you've retrieved with hardly any code. The following example demonstrates data binding.

The first step is to define a web control for displaying the data. Although you can use basic controls like text boxes and labels, these controls can't show all the data in a table of records. On the other hand, the new DataGrid is an all-in-one package that is perfected for shoring tabular information. Here's how you insert a DataGrid into a page:

```
<asp:DataGrid id="MyDataGrid" runat="server"/>
```

Next, you need some code to retrieve the data and bind it to the control. Here's an example of the code you need to retrieve the records from:

```
void Page_Load()
{
    string connectionString =
      "Data Source=localhost;Initial Catalog=Northwind;Integrated Security=SSPI";
    SqlConnection con = new SqlConnection(connectionString);
    SqlCommand cmd = new SqlCommand("SELECT CompanyName, ContactName, " +
      "ContactTitle, City FROM Customers", con);
    con.Open();
    SqlDataReader reader = cmd.ExecuteReader();
    MyDataGrid.DataSource = reader;
    MyDataGrid.DataBind();
    con.Close();
}
```

This code uses ADO.NET (discussed in Part Two of this book) to connect to a database, and retrieve a DataReader with the results from a query. The bolded lines are the only lines that are required to actually display this information, and they use ASP.NET data binding.

Without adding any special formatting to the DataGrid control (and there are a lot of options for doing exactly that), you'll see the bare-bones table in Figure 1-6. On top of this basic representation, you can define values for things like font styling, background colors, header styles, and much more. You can also enable features for column-based sorting, paging (splitting a table over multiple pages), selecting, and editing.

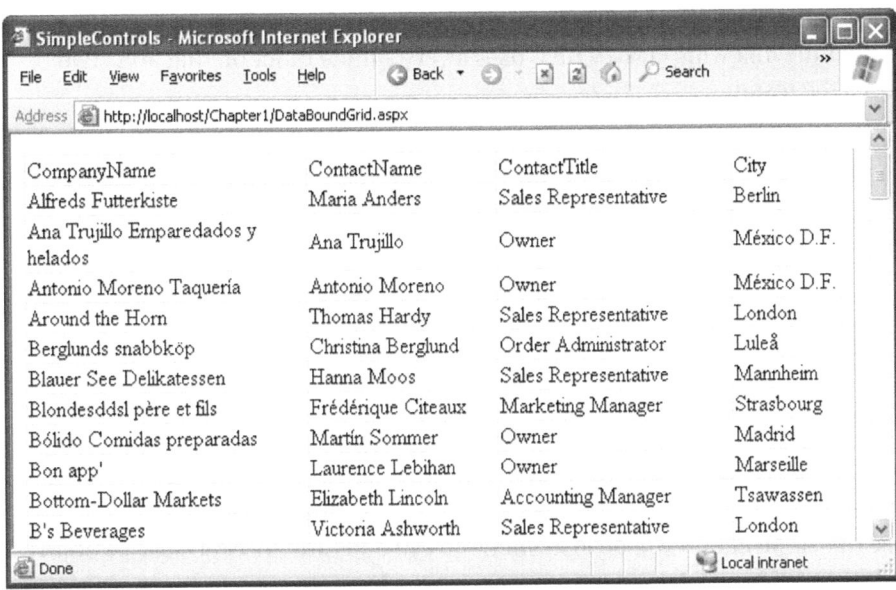

Figure 1-6. *A simple data-bound grid*

Web Services

.NET places a major emphasis on *web services*—reusable units of code that you can call across platform and computer boundaries. In many ways, web services can be seen as a component model for the Internet. Instead of building an application out of locally available components, web services allow you to call methods in a remote component that's hosted on a web server. The most exciting feature of web services is the way they allow you to integrate applications that are written in different programming languages, running on different computers, and developed by completely separate companies or organizations. This is possible due to a solid backbone of XML-based open standards. Though many other software vendors have released web services toolkits (as Microsoft previously did with its own SOAP Toolkit), none come close to the support that's built into .NET.

■**Note** .NET and web services are often confused. It's important to remember that .NET is not web serv-ices and web services don't have to be written in .NET. It's common misconception that the two concepts are synonymous with one another. Though this isn't accurate, there are reasons—both marketing-related and technically justifiable—for the misconception that .NET and web services are interrelated technologies that can't exist without one another.

One of most important functions of web services is to allow you to expose existing func-tionality to clients with a minimum amount of extra effort. In order to make life as easy as possible, ASP.NET web services have their own dedicated file type (with the extension .asmx).

Let's take a look at how an existing code method can be modified so that it's exposed as a web service. Consider the following class, which uses a very simple function that adds two integers and returns the result:

```
public class Calculator
{
    public int Add(int X, int Y)
    {
        return (X + Y);
    }
}
```

The Add() method isn't very sophisticated, but it serves as a good example to show how you create a web service from an existing class method. In general, you can turn any method into a web method provided that the parameters and return value use supported data types and the class is stateless (in other words, the class shouldn't hold any information in member variables, because this information will be lost when the call ends and the web service object is automatically destroyed).

The first step for turning the Add() method into a web service is to create an .asmx file that's linked to this code file. The .asmx file simply contains a single line—a WebService directive that indicates the language you're using, and points to the class you want to expose as a web service, as follows:

```
<%@ WebService Language="C#" Class="Calculator" %>
```

The final step in this process is to modify the class so that the Add() method is exposed as a remotely accessible web method. To accomplish this, you need to flag the Add() method with a WebMethod attribute from the System.Web.Services namespace. Technically, the Web-Method attribute, like all attributes, is a form of *metadata* that adds information to your code. In this case, this information instructs ASP.NET to make this method remotely accessible to web-service calls.

```
using System.Web.Services;
public class Calculator
{
    [WebMethod]
    public int Add(int X, int Y)
    {
        return (X + Y);
    }
}
```

That's it! To deploy the web service, just place the .asmx file in an ASP.NET virtual directory, and place the compiled Calculator code into the Bin subdirectory for the same application.

To use this web service, you'll want to create another application that uses this piece of functionality. For example, you might build an ASP.NET application, a rich .NET Windows client, or even a Visual Basic 6 or Java program that calls the Calculator.Add() method. All of these languages provide easy-to-use frameworks that allow you to call web methods, using little more than a URL that points to the location of the web service.

You can also perform a simple test of the web service without writing a single line of code. All you need to do is request the URL in any web browser. ASP.NET will automatically present an easy-to-use test page that lets you see what methods are available and try them out. Figure 1-7 shows the test page for the Calculator web service, which lists the available web methods.

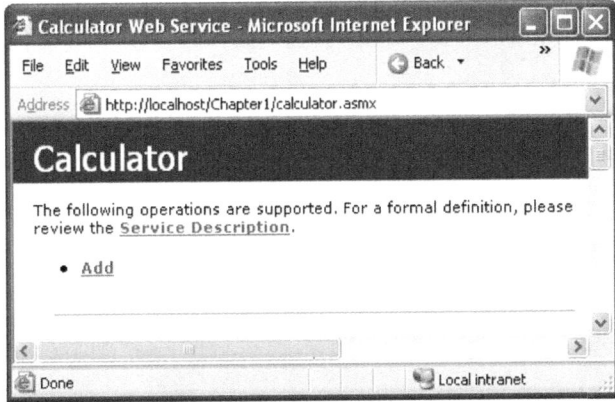

Figure 1-7. *Listing methods in a web service*

If you select the Add() method, you'll see the test page in Figure 1-8. Using this page, you can supply some sample parameter values and click Invoke to run the web method.

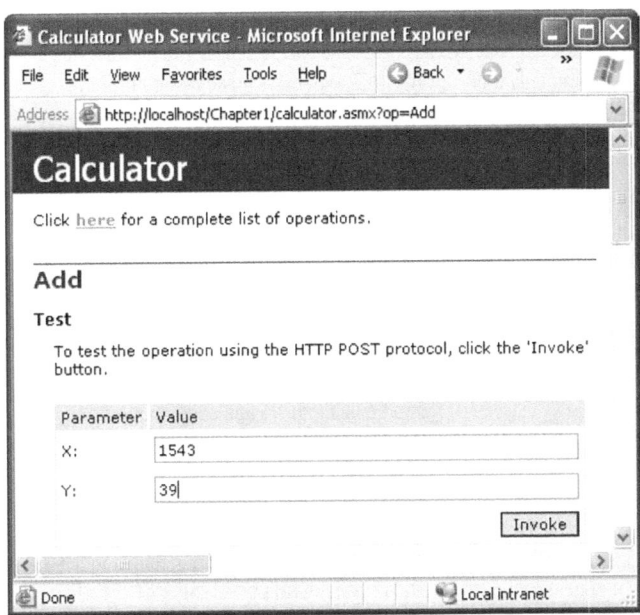

Figure 1-8. *Testing a web method*

Figure 1-9 shows the result you'll receive if you test the Add() web method with the numbers 1543 and 39. The result (1582) is packaged into a neat snippet of XML that can be parsed in any language.

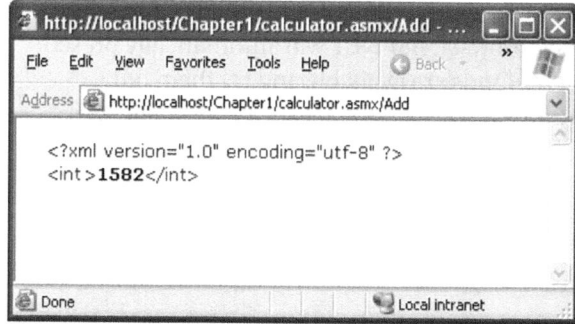

Figure 1-9. *The result of a web-method test*

You'll learn much more about building and using web services in Part Five.

ASP.NET AND CLASSIC ASP COMPARED

There are many differences and similarities between ASP and ASP.NET applications. The following is a quick reference illustrating some of the main comparison points between the two technologies. This should give you a good feeling for how an ASP.NET application compares to a classic ASP application, and it will help you get an idea of what to expect in the first part of this book.

Table 1-1. *ASP vs. ASP.NET*

	Classic ASP	**ASP.NET**
Configuration	Classic ASP is configured using only the options available to you from within the IIS Manager utility.	ASP.NET allows for advanced control over dozens of options via XML configuration files that are automatically made available to all code in ASP.NET pages.
Application events	The global.asa file provides a place to respond to application and session start or stop events. It's written in a scripted language.	The global.asax file provides the traditional application and session start and stop events, and requests begin and end events. This code is compiled.
Pages	Page code is written in line with all user-interface code. The code language is interpreted.	Pages have supporting code and HTML UI elements separated for clarity and easy programming. Supporting code is compiled into an assembly. Page code supports everything the .NET Framework can use, including advanced data and UI caching, COM interop, .NET components, and much more.
Web Services support	There is no native support for XML Web Services. However, you can gain reduced functionality through the Microsoft SOAP Toolkit, which is a separate COM component.	XML Web Services support is native to .NET, and is an integral part of the ASP.NET application model.

	Classic ASP	**ASP.NET**
Controls	All support for "controls" is achieved through server-side includes and COM components that return HTML rendered strings. Using server-side controls is difficult and time-consuming.	.NET provides support for server controls, and completely compiled classes designed to render themselves on an ASP.NET web page output. .NET provides support for user controls, providing a quick, easy, reusable, programmable UI similar to server-side includes. Programmers no longer need to worry about the target browser, because ASP.NET handles browser detection and adapts many controls automatically.
Components	Components can be used from individual ASP pages using COM. Due to limitations of scripting languages, all COM communication is late-bound, thereby reducing performance.	Any native .NET component is easily accessible from any code within an ASP.NET application. Due to compiled nature of ASP.NET, even COM interop is accomplished via faster early-bound calls.
Debugging	Debugging is practically nonexistent in classic ASP applications. If you need any detailed information during the progress of your process execution, you need to find a way to print it out yourself.	Visual Studio .NET can debug local and remote ASP.NET applications, which allows you to step through the execution of the generation of an ASP.NET page and into separate components. You can set breakpoints and monitor variables. You can display diagnostic information in a page in any environment using the Trace class. Trace listeners can write messages from the trace log to virtually any location, including files, event logs, and more.
Session state	Classic ASP has only one way to maintain session state, and even then it provides a slow, single-threaded model.	ASP.NET allows you to maintain session state locally, or remotely via the ASP.NET state service or SQL Server. This allows you to support session state on web farms (installations with multiple web server computers). Session-state access and management is free-threaded, so there are no performance concerns.

Summary

So far, you've only just scratched the surface of the features and frills that are provided in ASP.NET and the .NET Framework. You've taken a quick look at the high-level concepts you need to understand in order to be a competent ASP.NET programmer, and you've taken a quick tour of ASP.NET web pages and web services. As you continue through this book, you'll learn much more about the innovations and revolutions of ASP.NET and the .NET Framework.

CHAPTER 2

■■■

Internet Information Services

A key part of the ASP.NET model is IIS (Internet Information Services), the web-hosting software that's built into most versions of the Windows operating system. Using IIS, you can configure what directories are exposed as *virtual directories*, and are thereby accessible to other clients that make remote calls over the network or the Internet.

Learning to use IIS and the IIS Manager configuration tool is important, and fairly straightforward. In this chapter, you'll read about all the basics, and learn how to create and configure virtual directories.

The ASP.NET Architecture

Like all web applications, a client accesses an ASP.NET application over HTTP, by typing a URL into a browser. However, ASP.NET doesn't directly handle HTTP requests—that's the work of another operating system component called IIS.

When an HTTP request reaches a web request, it's passed up through the network stack of the Windows operating system. If this request is received on a port that's registered with IIS—typically port 80 for an ordinary HTTP request and port 443 for HTTP over SSL (Secure Sockets Layer)—the request is passed along to IIS.

The URL Request

When IIS receives a request, its first step is to examine the requested URL. A typical URL for a web application might take the following format:

```
http://WebServer/OnlineStore/catalog.aspx
```

In this case, the first portion (WebServer) identifies the name of the web-server computer on a local network. The second portion (OnlineStore) identifies the virtual directory where the ASP.NET application is stored. The third portion (catalog.aspx) indicates the requested file. Because this file has the extension .aspx, IIS recognizes that it's a request for an ASP.NET resource, and it passes the request to ASP.NET. Interestingly enough, IIS will pass the request to ASP.NET even if the file doesn't exist. That allows ASP.NET to add extensions that don't actually correspond to physical pages. One example is the trace.axd extension, which allows local developers to see recent debugging output.

Of course, URLs can come in many flavors. If your web server is publicly accessible over the Internet, clients might connect to it using an IP address or a registered domain name.

Here are two examples:

```
http://145.0.5.5/OnlineStore/catalog.aspx
http://www.MyBusiness.com/catalog.aspx
```

Finally, you've no doubt noticed that not all URLs include the portion with the filename. For example, you might make a request like this:

```
http://WebServer/OnlineStore
```

In this case, if OnlineStore is a virtual directory, IIS will search for one of the default documents, and automatically run that. IIS will check first for a Default.htm file, then for Default.asp, index.htm, iisstart.asp, and finally the ASP.NET file Default.aspx. As a result, it's always a good idea to name your home page for a web application Default.aspx. (Of course, you can configure this list of default documents using IIS, as described later in this chapter.)

■**Tip** Even if you don't know the name of the computer you're working on, you can still easily request a local page using the *loopback address*. The loopback address is 127.0.0.1 and the alias is localhost. The loopback address and alias always point to the current computer, and are extremely useful while testing. For example, you can enter `http://localhost/OnlineStore/catalog.aspx` to request an ASP.NET page from the OnlineStore virtual directory on the local computer.

Processing Requests

When IIS receives a request for static content, like an HTML page or a graphic, it serves the file immediately (assuming there aren't any settings that prevent this file from being accessed in the current security context). When an ASP.NET request is made, the process is much different. To make matters even more interesting, the behavior differs between IIS 5 (the version included with Windows 2000 and Windows XP) and IIS 6 (the enhanced web-hosting software that's a part of Windows Server 2003). In this section, you'll take a high-level look at both models.

ASP.NET uses an ISAPI (Internet Server Application Programming Interface) extension to plug into IIS, just like classic ASP. The key difference is that in an ASP application, the ISAPI extension performs all of the script processing. In ASP.NET, the ISAPI extension is really just a dispatcher. It receives the requests, and sends them along to another component—the ASP.NET *worker process*. If the worker process isn't running yet, the ASP.NET ISAPI extension starts it. Typically, you'll have one instance of the worker process running on your web server and handling all your web applications, although IIS 6 gives you the option to run multiple instances in order to take advantage of multiple CPUs. (This technique of running separate web applications on separate CPUs in the same computer is known as a *web garden*.)

The worker process performs a variety of tasks. One of its chief responsibilities is compiling web pages to machine code and caching them on the hard drive. The worker process also hosts the CLR (common language runtime), which is required to execute any .NET code.

Additionally, the worker process manages the lifetime of your web applications. Every time you request a web page or a web service in a new virtual directory (one that hasn't been accessed since IIS was started), the worker process creates a separate *application domain* for the application. Application domains are often described as lightweight processes or logical processes. That's because they enforce application isolation, just like ordinary Win32 processes. That means the code in one web application can't directly access the objects, state information, cached data, or configuration details of another application. Application isolation allows you to run multiple websites without worrying about potential conflicts, buggy code, or security issues. However, because application domains aren't full-fledged processes, but rather logical boundaries enforced by the CLR, they don't incur the same performance overhead.

■**Note** In an ASP.NET application, a web application is comprised of all the ASP.NET web pages, web services, and resources in a virtual directory and its subdirectories. An ASP.NET application also shares a common set of application and session state information, configuration settings, and cached data.

Figure 2-1 shows a high-level look at the ASP.NET execution model in IIS 5. This figure also fills in a few more details, like the file that contains the ASP.NET ISAPI extension (aspnet_isapi.dll) and the worker process (aspnet_wp.exe).

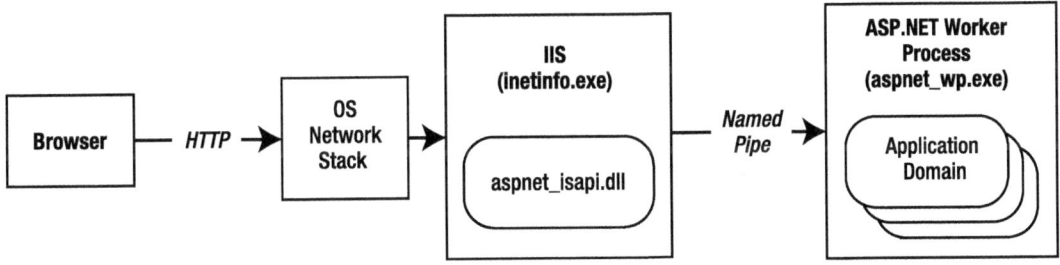

Figure 2-1. *ASP.NET execution in IIS 5*

In IIS 6, the model is conceptually similar, but IIS provides the worker-process host instead of ASP.NET. A kernel-level HTTP listener forwards ASP.NET requests directly to this worker process. A separate service, called WAS (Web Administration Service), starts the worker processes when needed and provides health monitoring. Figure 2-2 shows how these components work together.

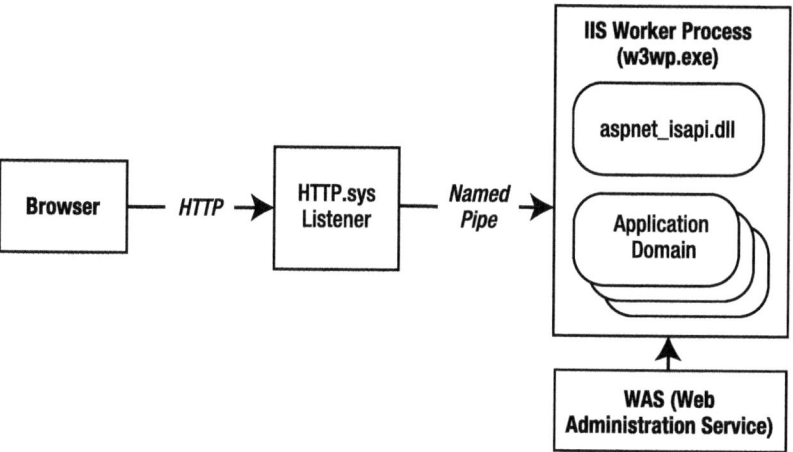

Figure 2-2. *ASP.NET execution in IIS 6*

The IIS 6 worker process is known as an *application pool*, because it can be used to host multiple ASP.NET web applications, just like the ASP.NET worker process. However, you can also create multiple instances of the IIS worker process for different web applications. That allows you to easily configure them to run under different accounts, set different resource usage limits, make use of multiple CPUs, and provide even more robust web application isolation. Of course, the drawback is that these separate instances of the IIS worker process load separate instances of the CLR, which consumes additional memory.

THE CASSINI WEB SERVER

The entire architecture of ASP.NET is designed in a modular, extensible way. One of the interesting possibilities this raises is the ability to host the ASP.NET runtime engine outside of IIS. Using the classes in the System.Web.Hosting namespace, you could quite easily create a custom application that uses ASP.NET to dynamically compile and display ASP.NET pages. Of course, this application would lack many of key features that IIS provides, including the ability to serve remote requests, log traffic, and use SSL encryption. Currently, there isn't any serious competitor to IIS on the Windows platform. Covalent (www.covalent.com) has developed an Apache server for Windows that supports ASP.NET, but it hasn't been widely tested or adopted.

Of course, there are special cases in which you might want to host ASP.NET outside of IIS. One scenario is if you want to test ASP.NET code on a version of Windows that doesn't support IIS (like Windows XP Home). Another scenario is if you want to distribute a stand-alone demonstration version of your software on a CD or through an Internet download. In both of these situations, you don't need a full-fledged web server. Microsoft provides a possible solution with the freely downloadable open-source Cassini web-server example (available for download at www.asp.net/Projects/Cassini/Download).

Cassini isn't a production-level web server, and it's designed to only serve requests that start with http://localhost. However, Cassini does provide a compact, standalone web server that you can distribute on a CD and use to run ASP.NET web applications offline. And if you need more functionality, you can even download and modify the complete C# source code! Cassini is available individually or with the Web Matrix development tool. It supports all versions of Windows 2000, Windows XP, Windows Server 2000, and Windows Server 2003.

> ■**Note** Remember, the worker process isn't limited to a single task. Both the ASP.NET worker process and the IIS worker process run multiple threads at the same time so that they can serve simultaneous requests from different users.

This overview should give you a fairly good understanding of how IIS and ASP.NET work together. However, there's a lot more to learn before you can consider yourself an experienced web administrator. In particular, IIS 6 is a sophisticated program with a slew of powerful options. To learn more about these features, consult the online documentation (one good resource is the Microsoft site `http://www.microsoft.com/windowsserver2003/techinfo/overview/iis.mspx`) or a dedicated book on IIS administration. However, you'll learn enough in this book to create, configure, and test web applications in virtual directories with IIS.

Account Security with the Worker Process

As you've seen, whether you're using IIS 5 or IIS 6, a dedicated worker process executes all ASP.NET code. When you're configuring your system, you need to give careful consideration to the Windows account that's used to run the worker process. Its permissions determine what your code can and cannot do with resources on the server computer. These issues won't affect simple operations like performing calculations and rendering web pages, but they can cause complications when your code needs to read files, write to the event log, and connect to a database.

When ASP.NET is installed with IIS 5, a new Windows user account is created called ASPNET. By default, the ASP.NET worker process runs under this account. The ASPNET account has a set of carefully limited privileges. By default, the ASPNET account won't be allowed to perform tasks like reading the Windows registry, retrieving information from a database, or writing to most locations on the local hard drive. It also won't be able to access other resources on a local network. On the other hand, it will have the permissions that are essential for normal functioning. For example, the ASPNET account *is* allowed to access the c:\[WinDir]\Microsoft.NET\[Version]\Temporary ASP.NET Files directory so that it can compile and cache web pages.

If you're using IIS 6, the worker process runs under the *network service* account. This built-in account has the same limited level of access to resources and objects as members of the Users group. The network service account is similar to the local service account, with the added ability to access network resources.

The limited security settings of the ASPNET and network service accounts are designed to prevent malicious code from damaging your web server. However, you'll probably find that your applications require some additional permissions beyond those given to the ASPNET and network service accounts. You can grant additional permissions to these accounts in the same way that you would grant them to any other Windows user account. However, the process isn't always obvious—so you might want to consult a good handbook about Windows system administration before you take these steps.

Alternatively, you might want to change the account that's used to run the worker process to a different account with the required permissions. You can perform this task in IIS 6 using the IIS Manager (use the Identity tab of the application pool settings). In IIS 5, you need to modify the <processModel> element in the machine.config configuration file, and then restart ASP.NET. This process is described in the next section.

Using the Local System Account in IIS 5

If you're using a computer for development testing only, you can also take advantage of a useful shortcut to give the ASP.NET service greater privileges. Instead of using the ASPNET account, you can configure ASP.NET code so that it runs under the *local system* account. The local system account is a built-in Windows account with administrator-level permissions. Code that runs under this account has the ability to do almost anything on the current computer. Using the local system account is a poor idea on a production system, but it isn't necessarily a bad approach for testing a new web application on a development computer.

■Note Before using the local system account, it's worth reviewing a couple of potential drawbacks. First of all, using the local system account makes developers less conscious of security while they program, which is never a good approach in the threat-conscious world of modern programming. Secondly, it also means you are less aware of what the minimum permissions the application requires, which can complicate deployment.

To change the ASP.NET settings to use the local system account, you need to perform the following steps.

1. Open the machine.config file in the c:\[WinDir]\Microsoft.NET\[Version]\Config directory using Notepad. (If you've installed the .NET Framework 1.1 on a Windows XP computer, this directory will be c:\Windows\Microsoft.NET\v1.1.4322\Config.

2. Search for the text userName="Machine". You'll find this setting in the processModel tag, which looks something like this:

```
<processModel enable="true" ...
  userName="Machine" password="AutoGenerate" ... />
```

3. The userName="Machine" instruction tells ASP.NET to run using the special ASPNET account. Modify this attribute to be userName="System". This tells ASP.NET to use the local system account.

```
<processModel enable="true" ...
  userName="System" password="AutoGenerate" ... />
```

4. Now you must restart the ASP.NET worker process. To do this, you can either reboot the computer, or you can use Task Manager to manually terminate the ASP.NET service. In the latter case, look for the process named aspnet_wp.exe. Select it and click End Process. When it restarts, it will run under the local system account.

Note As you'll discover later in this book, ASP.NET includes its own security model. However, ASP.NET security works in addition to the Windows account security described in this section. Essentially, the account that your code uses sets the maximum permissions that your code can take advantage of. You may still choose to limit the actions you perform based on the current web application user.

Process Recycling

Successful web applications usually have far greater demands placed on them than ordinary desktop applications. Not only do they need to serve dozens, hundreds, or even thousands of simultaneous requests, but they also need to run around the clock without a glitch.

No matter how robust your web application code is, it may run into errors. Perhaps a component you're using isn't releasing memory correctly, and the steady trickle of wasted bytes is gradually accumulating to become a significant waste of resources (a problem known as a *memory leak*). Or perhaps your code is stalled while trying to perform a task and hasn't recovered properly, leaving other requests unattended.

To help guard against these sorts of problems, the ASP.NET worker process performs *process recycling*. It monitors the application domains that are loaded for any signs of potential problems or performance degradation. Parameters that the worker process can use to evaluate an application include the number of requests that have been served and the number of requests that are currently queued, how much memory is used, and the total time the application has been running up to date. When these parameters exceed certain thresholds, the worker process restarts the application in a new application domain (leaving the old application domain alive long enough to finish processing any requests that are left in its queue). Health monitoring and process recycling also take place with IIS 6, but in this case it's the WAS that has the responsibility, not the worker process.

If you want to configure when this type of automatic refresh is performed, you can tweak the settings in the <processModel> element in the computer-wide machine.config configuration file, which is found in the c:\[WinDir]\Microsoft.NET\[Version]\Config directory. Table 2-1 lists these settings.

Note IIS 6 ignores most of the process model settings. However, you can usually configure an equivalent application pool setting using IIS Manager. Table 2-1 indicates the IIS 6 equivalent for each setting, wherever applicable.

Table 2-1. *<processModel> Attributes*

Attribute Setting	Description	IIS 6 Equivalent
enable	Determines whether ASP.NET should run in a separate worker process (true, the default) or in-process with IIS (false). When set to false, all other settings are ignored, and your web applications may be slightly faster (although if one crashes, they may all be affected).	No equivalent setting. The worker process is always a separate process.
timeout	Determines how long the process will run before it's recycled (a new process is created and the old one is terminated). The default value is Infinite, although you can specify a time in the format hr:min:sec.	Use the Recycle Worker Processes setting on the Recycling tab.
idleTimeout	Similar to the timeout setting, but takes effect when the ASP.NET worker process is idle. The default is Infinite.	Use the Idle Timeout setting on the Performance tab.
shutdownTimeout	This sets the amount of time the ASP.NET worker process is given to try to shut down gracefully before it's assumed to be "locked up," and the process is terminated. By default, this value is only 5 seconds.	Use Shutdown Time Limit on the Health tab.
requestLimit	Provides another way to support ASP.NET worker-process recycling. For example, if you notice that the performance of ASP.NET degrades after about 10,000 requests, you can set this value to 10000. After 10,000 requests, a new process will be started to handle the new requests and the old process will be terminated.	Use the Recycle Worker Process setting on the Recycling tab.
requestQueueLimit	This allows the ASP.NET process to be recycled if a certain number of queued requests is detected. This could detect that a thread is blocked or unable to service requests because of an error. The default is a fairly generous 5,000 queued requests.	No equivalent setting.
responseDeadlockInterval	If there are queued requests, and there has not been a response during this interval of time, the worker process is restarted. The default is three minutes, and you can specify times in the hr:min:sec format.	There is no equivalent application pool setting. However, IIS 6 reads this attribute from the Machine.config file and respects it.
memoryLimit	This provides automatic memory recycling if too much memory is used. The default value of 60 isn't a value in megabytes, but a percentage of the total system memory. Memory leaks are almost impossible with managed .NET code, but could still be a problem if you're using legacy COM components that don't properly clean up after themselves.	Use the Memory Recycling setting on the Recycling tab.
logLevel	Configures how ASP.NET logs events. The default is Errors, which only records information about errors that occur. All entries are written to the Windows event log.	No equivalent application pool setting. All errors are logged.

Attribute Setting	Description	IIS 6 Equivalent
clientConnectedCheck	Allows you to configure how often ASP.NET checks if the client is still connected. For example, during a long-running task the client might hit the Refresh button to start a new request, but leave the current request processing. ASP.NET can save some effort by detecting that these requests have been abandoned and then aborting the unneeded work. By default, ASP.NET will check every 5 seconds.	There is no equivalent application pool setting. HTTP.SYS monitors the request queue and removes disconnected requests every 120 seconds.
pingFrequency	Specifies how frequently the ASP.NET ISAPI extension checks to see if the worker process is still running (by sending a simple ping message). If it doesn't respond within a set interval of time (determined by the pingTimeout interval), the worker process is restarted. The default is 30 seconds, and you can specify times in the hr:min:sec format.	Use the Enable Pinging setting on the Health tab.
pingTimeout	Specifies how long the worker process has to respond to a ping message before it is deemed unresponsive and restarted. The default is five seconds, and you can specify times in the hr:min:sec format.	There is no equivalent application pool setting in IIS Manager. However, this setting is configurable if you write your own script. The setting is stored in the metabase as PingResponseInterval.
maxWorkerThreads	Sets the maximum amount of worker threads to be used for the process on a per-CPU basis. For example, if this value is 25, ASP.NET uses 25 threads on a single-processor server, or 50 threads on a two-processor server. The default is 20, which means that ASP.NET can handle 20 simultaneous requests. The value of maxWorkerThreads must be equal to or greater than the minFreeThread attribute setting in the <httpRuntime> configuration section.	There is no equivalent application pool setting. However, IIS 6 reads this attribute from the machine.config file and respects it.
maxIoThreads	Similar to maxWorkerThreads, but this sets the maximum number of threads used for file I/O (reading and writing data to the disk).	There is no equivalent application pool setting. However, IIS 6 reads this attribute from the machine.config file and respects it.

The ASP.NET Execution Model

In the previous chapter, you learned how ASP.NET compiles code on demand. You also took your first look at an ASP.NET web page.

Now that you've learned the basics of IIS and the ASP.NET worker process, it's time to put it all together. Figure 2-3 shows a high-level look at the end-to-end process involved in processing a client's request.

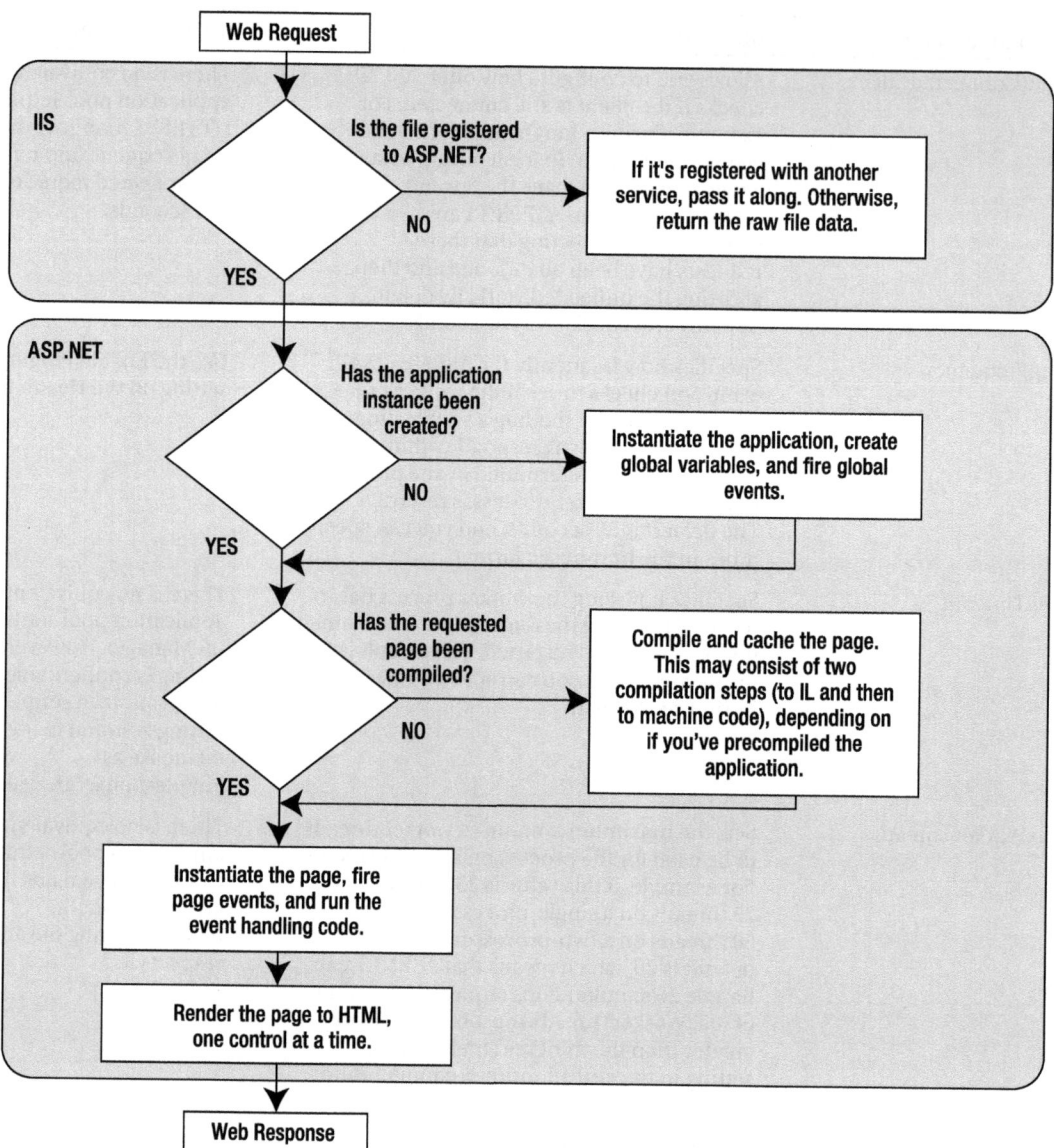

Figure 2-3. *Processing an ASP.NET request from start to finish*

Remember, a client request only represents one interaction with a web application. In the course of using your website in a given session, a user could easily make hundreds of requests. In Chapter 4, you'll learn how ASP.NET manages the life cycle of a page across multiple requests.

Installing IIS

Even though IIS is included with Windows, it's not installed by default. That's because Microsoft recognizes that allowing Internet access to any part of your computer is a security risk, and it's not an operation that should be performed automatically if it's not needed.

■**Note** IIS is only available if your computer is running Windows 2000, Windows 2000 Server, Windows XP Professional, or Windows Server 2003. Each version of Windows has a slightly different version or configuration of IIS. As a general rule of thumb, when you want to publish your website, you should use a server version of Windows to host it. Desktop versions, like Windows 2000 and Windows XP Professional, are fine for development testing, but they implement a connection limit of ten simultaneous users, which makes them much less suitable for real-world use.

The process of configuring IIS depends on the version of Windows that you have installed. The next two sections lead you through the steps you need to perform.

Installing IIS 5

On a Windows 2000, Windows 2000 Server, or Windows XP Professional computer, you can follow these steps to install IIS:

1. Click Start, and select Settings ➤ Control Panel.

2. Choose Add or Remove Programs.

3. Click Add/Remove Windows Components.

4. If Internet Information Services is checked (see Figure 2-4), you already have this component installed. Otherwise, click it and click Next to install the required IIS files. You'll need to have your Windows setup CD handy.

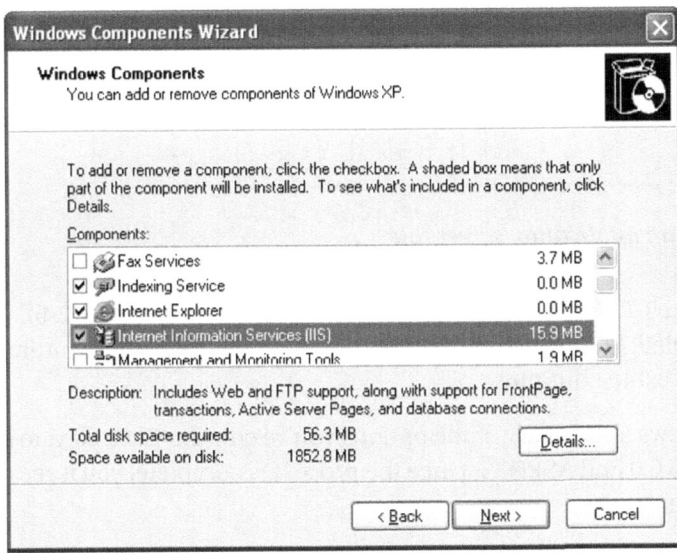

Figure 2-4. *IIS is currently installed*

Installing IIS 6

If you're using Windows Server 2003, you can install IIS through the Add/Remove Windows Components dialog box, but it's more likely that you'll use the Manage Your Server wizard. Here's how it works:

1. Select Add or Remove a Role from the main Manage Your Server window. This launches the Configure Your Server wizard.

2. Click Next to continue past the introductory window. The setup wizard will test your available and enabled network connections and then continue to the next step.

3. Now you choose the roles to enable. Select Application Server (IIS, ASP.NET) from the list as shown in Figure 2-5 and click Next.

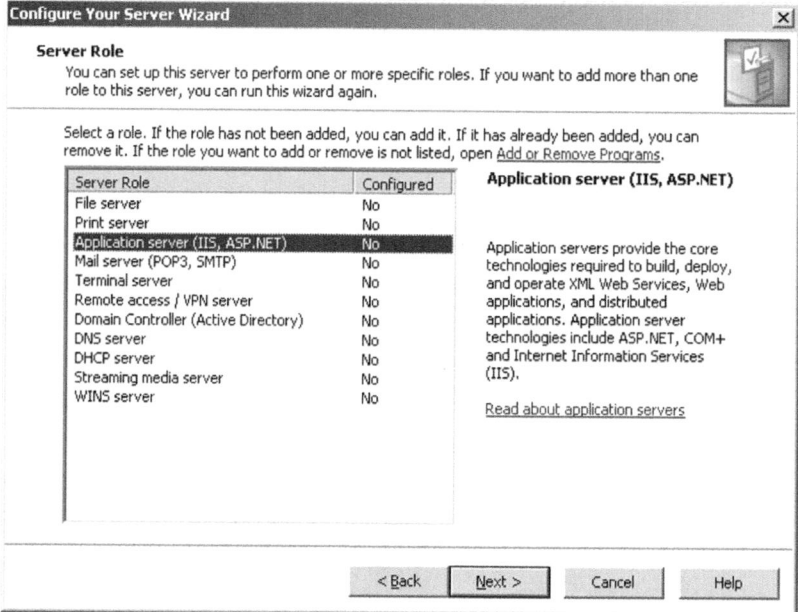

Figure 2-5. *Choosing an application server role*

4. Click the Enable ASP.NET check box on the next window (shown in Figure 2-6). If you don't IIS will be enabled, but it will only be able to serve static content like ordinary HTML pages. Click Next to continue.

5. The next window shows a summary of the options you've chosen. Click Next to continue by installing IIS 6.0 and ASP.NET. Once the process is complete, you'll see a final confirmation message.

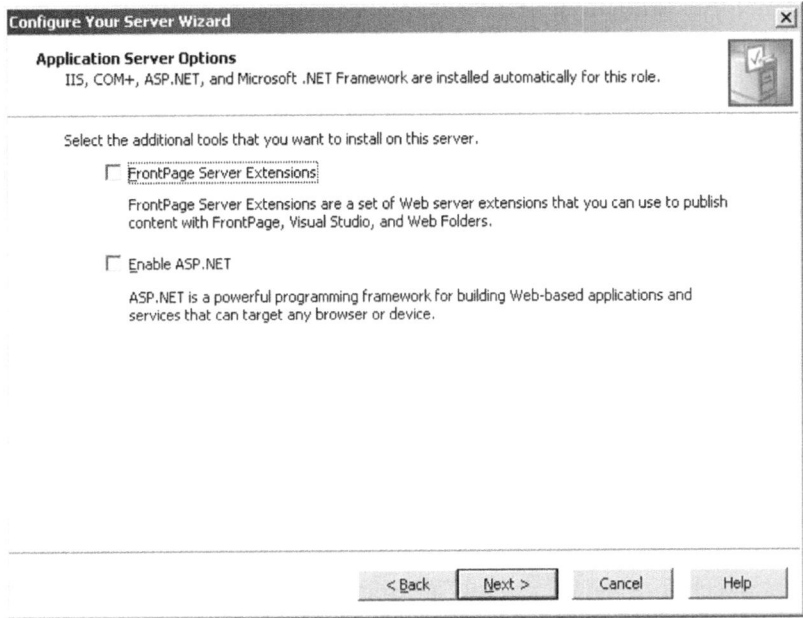

Figure 2-6. *Enabling other services*

Note The rest of this chapter describes website administration with IIS 5, which is usually used when developing a website. However, if you're starting out with IIS 6, you'll still be able to use most of the instructions in this chapter, but you may want to supplement your knowledge with the online help for IIS 6 or a dedicated book about IIS 6 administration.

Managing Websites

When IIS is installed, it automatically creates a directory named c:\Inetpub\wwwroot, which represents your website. Any files in this directory will appear as though they're in the root of your web server.

To add more pages to your web server, you can copy HTML, ASP, or ASP.NET files directly to the c:\Intetpub\wwwroot directory. For example, if you add the file TestFile.html to this directory, you can request it in a browser through the URL http://localhost/TestFile.html. You can even create subdirectories to group together related resources. For example, the c:\Intetpub\wwwroot\MySite\MyFile.html file can be accessed through a browser using the URL http://localhost/MySite/MyFile.html. If you're using Visual Studio .NET to create new web projects, you'll find that it automatically generates new subdirectories in the wwwroot directory. So if you create a web application named WebApplication1, the files will be stored in c:\Inetpub\wwwroot\WebApplication1, and made available through http://localhost/WebApplication1.

Using the wwwroot directory is straightforward, but it makes for poor organization. To properly use ASP or ASP.NET, you should create a new *virtual directory* for each web application you create. With a virtual directory, you can expose any physical directory (on any drive on your computer) on your web server, as though it were located in the c:\Inetpup\wwwroot directory.

To create virtual directories, you need to use the administrative IIS Manager utility. To start it, select Settings ➤ Control Panel ➤ Administrative Tools ➤ Internet Information Services from the Start menu. The next few sections walk you through the steps and explain the settings that you can configure.

Creating a Virtual Directory

When you're ready to create a new website, the first step you'll usually take is to create the physical directory where the pages will be stored (for example, c:\MySite). The second step is to expose this physical directory as a virtual directory through IIS. This means that the website becomes publicly accessible to other computers that connect to your computer over HTTP.

To create a new virtual directory for an existing physical directory, right-click the Default Website item in the IIS tree, and choose New ➤ Virtual Directory from the context menu. A wizard will start to manage the process, as shown in Figure 2-7.

Figure 2-7. *The Virtual Directory Creation wizard*

As you step through the wizard, you'll need to provide three pieces of information: an alias, a directory, and a set of permissions. These settings are described in the following sections.

Alias

The alias is the name a remote client will use to access the files in this virtual directory. For example, if your alias is MyApp and your computer is named MyServer, you can request pages using URLs such as http://MyServer/MyApp/MyPage.aspx.

Directory

The directory is the physical directory on your hard drive that will be exposed as a virtual directory. For example, c:\Intetpub\wwwroot is the physical directory that is used for the root virtual directory of your web server. IIS will provide access to all the allowed file types in this directory.

Permissions

Finally, the wizard asks you to set permissions for your virtual directory, as shown in Figure 2-8. There are several permissions you can set:

- **Read.** This is the most basic permission—it's required in order for IIS to provide any requested files to the user. If this is disabled, the client will not be able to access ASP or ASP.NET pages, or static files like HTML and images. Note that even when you enable read permission, there are several other layers of possible security in IIS. For example, some file types (such as those that correspond to ASP.NET configuration files) are automatically restricted, even if they're in a directory that has read permission.

- **Run scripts.** This permission allows the user to request an ASP or ASP.NET page. If you enable read, but don't allow script permission, the user will be restricted to static file types such as HTML documents. ASP and ASP.NET pages require a higher permission because they could conceivably perform operations that would damage the web server or compromise security.

- **Execute.** This permission allows the user to run an ordinary executable file or CGI application. This is a possible security risk as well, and shouldn't be enabled unless you require it (which you won't for ordinary ASP or ASP.NET applications).

- **Write.** This permission allows the user to add, modify, or delete files on the web server. This permission should never be granted, because it could easily allow the computer to upload and then execute a dangerous script file (or at the least, use up all your available disk space). Instead, use an FTP site, or create an ASP.NET application that allows the user to upload specific types of information or files.

- **Browse.** This permission allows you to retrieve a full list of files in the virtual directory, even if the contents of those files are restricted. Browse is generally disabled, because it allows users to discover additional information about your website and its structure as well as exploit possible security holes. On the other hand, it's quite useful for testing, so you might want to enable it on a development computer.

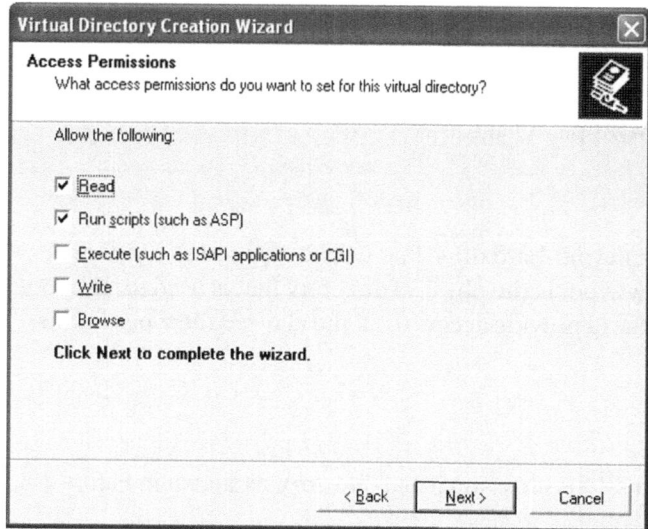

Figure 2-8. *Virtual directory permissions*

To host an ASP.NET application, you only need to enable the read and execute permissions (the first two check boxes). If you're using a development computer that will never act as a live web server, you can allow additional permissions. Keep in mind, however, that this could allow other users on a local network to access and modify files in the virtual directory. You can also change the virtual-directory permissions after you have created the virtual directory.

Virtual Directories and Web Applications

You can manage all the virtual directories on your computer in the Internet Information Service utility by expanding the tree under the Default Website item. You'll notice that items in the tree have three different types of icons:

- **Ordinary folder.** This represents a subdirectory inside another virtual directory. For example, if you create a virtual directory and then add a subdirectory to the physical directory, it will be displayed here.

- **Folders with a globe.** This represents a virtual directory.

- **Package folders.** This represents a virtual directory that is also a web application. By default, when you use the wizard to create a virtual directory, it's also configured as a web application. This means that it will share a common set of resources and run in its own separate application domain.

When you create a virtual directory with the Virtual Directory Creation wizard, it's also configured as a web application. This is almost always what you want. If your virtual directory *isn't* a web application, you won't be able to control its ASP.NET configuration settings, and you won't be able to create a web application in it using Visual Studio .NET.

Folder Settings

IIS makes it easy to configure virtual directories after you've created them. Simply right-click the virtual directory in the list and choose Properties. The Properties window will appear, with its information divided into several tabs. The following sections describe some of the most important settings.

Virtual Directory

The Virtual Directory tab includes options that allow you to change the permissions you set when creating the virtual directory with the wizard. You can also see the local path that corresponds to this virtual directory. If you're looking at the root of a virtual directory, you can set the local path to point to a different physical directory by clicking the Browse button. If you're looking at an ordinary subdirectory *inside* a virtual directory, the local path will be read-only.

Remember, when you create a virtual directory with the wizard, it's also configured as a web application. You can change this by clicking the Remove button next to the application name. Similarly, you can click the Create button to transform an ordinary virtual directory into a full-fledged application. Usually you won't need to perform these tasks, but it's nice to know they are available if you need to make a change. They can come in useful when transplanting an application from one computer to another.

Note Any changes that you make will be automatically applied to all subdirectories. If you want to make a change that will affect all the virtual directories on your server, right-click the Default Website item and choose Properties. The change will be cascaded down to all the subdirectories that are contained in the current virtual directory. If your change conflicts with the custom settings that you've set for a virtual directory, IIS will warn you. It will present a list of the directories that will be affected and give you the chance to specify exactly which ones you want to change and which ones you want to leave as is.

File Mappings

As explained earlier in this chapter, IIS hands off requests for ASP pages to the ASP ISAPI extension, and sends requests for ASP.NET pages to the ASP.NET ISAPI extension. So how does IIS decide who gets what? When ASP.NET is installed, it modifies the IIS metabase to add the mappings for file types that it needs to process. To view these file mappings, click the Configuration button on the Virtual Directory tab. You'll see the window shown in Figure 2-9.

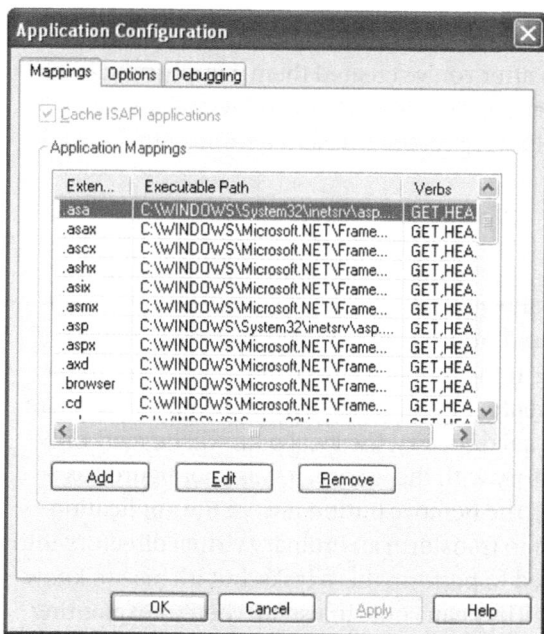

Figure 2-9. *File mappings*

The ASP.NET file mappings are listed in Table 2-2.

Table 2-2. *The ASP.NET File Mappings*

File Extension	Description
.aspx	These are ASP.NET web pages.
.ascx	These are ASP.NET user controls. User controls are similar to web pages, except that they can't be accessed directly. Instead, they must be hosted inside an ASP.NET web page.
.asmx	These are ASP.NET web services, which allow you to expose useful functionality to other applications over HTTP.
.asax	This extension is used for the global application file, which you can use to react to global events, such as when a web application first starts.
.ashx	This extension is used for HTTP handlers, which allow you to process requests without using the full-fledged ASP.NET web-page model.
.axd	This extension is used for the trace.axd application extension, which allows you to view trace messages while debugging.
.rem and .soap	These extensions are used to identify that IIS is hosting an object that can be called by .NET remoting. The remoting technology is similar to web services, but it's a proprietary .NET solution that doesn't have the same features for cross-platform capability.
.cs, .csproj, .vb, .vbproj, .licx, .config, .resx, .webinfo, and .vsdisco	These file types are used by ASP.NET, but they can't be directly requested by clients. However, ASP.NET registers them so that it can explicitly *prevent* users from accessing these files, regardless of the IIS security settings.

Is there any reason that you should explicitly change an ASP.NET file mapping? Probably not. If you have multiple versions of ASP.NET installed at once time, you may want to configure the mappings differently in different directories. That way, each website can use the version of ASP.NET that it was compiled with. However, there's no reason to make this sort of change by hand. Instead, you can use the aspnet_regiis.exe command-line utility (see the "Side-by-Side Execution" sidebar).

In other cases, you might want to add a file mapping. For example, you could specify that the ASP.NET service will handle any requests for GIF images by adding a mapping for the .gif file type that points to the aspnet_isapi.dll file. This would allow you to use ASP.NET security services for GIF file requests. (Note that this sort of change can slow down performance for GIF requests, because these requests will need to trickle through more layers on the server.)

SIDE-BY-SIDE EXECUTION

You'll notice that ASP files are mapped differently than ASP.NET files. For example, .asp requests are handled by c:\[WinDir]\System32\inetsrv\asp.dll, while .aspx requests are handled by c:\[WinDir]\Microsoft.NET\ Framework\[Version]\aspnet_isapi.dll. In other words, ASP.NET doesn't replace ASP. Instead, it runs alongside it, allowing ASP requests to be handled by the existing asp.dll, and providing a new aspnet_isapi.dll for ASP.NET page requests. This design allows both types of applications to be hosted on the same web server with no potential conflict (and little possible integration).

You could also use a similar approach to make sure that .aspx page requests in one virtual directory are handled by a different version of the ASP.NET service than requests in another virtual directory. The easiest way to set this up is to use the aspnet_regiis.exe utility included with the .NET Framework (you'll find it in the c:\[WinDir]\Microsoft.NET\Framework\[Version] directory). The following are a few examples of the tasks you can perform with aspnet_regiis.exe.

If you want a list of all the versions of ASP.NET that are installed on the computer, and the matching ISAPI extension, execute this command:

```
aspnet_regiis -lv
```

To configure a specific virtual directory to use a specific version of ASP.NET, make sure you're using the right version of aspnet_regiis.exe. For example, if you want to configure an application to use ASP.NET 1.1 instead of ASP.NET 1.0, make sure you're using the version of aspnet_regiis.exe that's included with the .NET 1.1 Framework (and in the corresponding version directory). Then, execute a command line like this:

```
aspnet_regiis -s W3SVC/1/ROOT/SampleApp1
```

This command maps the SampleApp1 virtual directory to use the version of ASP.NET that corresponds with the version of aspnet_regiis.exe. The first part of the path, W3SVC/1/ROOT/ identifies the web root of the current computer.

Finally, if you need to migrate all the applications in one fell swoop, you can use the following command:

```
aspnet_regiis -i
```

This command also comes in handy if your IIS file mappings are set incorrectly (for example, you installed IIS after you installed ASP.NET, and so the ASP.NET file mappings were not applied).

Caution You should never remove any of the ASP.NET file-type mappings! If you remove the .aspx or .asmx file types, web pages and web service won't work. Instead of being processed by the ASP.NET service, the raw file will be sent directly to the browser. If you remove other files types like .vb or .config, you'll compromise security. ASP.NET will no longer process requests for these types of files, which means that malicious users will be able to request them through IIS and inspect the code and configuration information for your web application.

Documents

This tab allows you to specify the default documents for a virtual directory. For example, consider the virtual directory http://localhost/MySite. A user can request a specific page in this directory using a URL like http://localhost/MySite/MyPage1.aspx. But what happens if the user simply types http://localhost/MySite into a web browser?

In this case, IIS will examine the list of default documents defined for that virtual directory. It will scan the list from top to bottom, and return the first matching page. Using the list in Figure 2-10, IIS will check first for a Default.htm file, then for default.asp, index.htm, iisstart.asp, and default.aspx. If none of these pages are found, IIS will return the HTTP 404 (page not found) error.

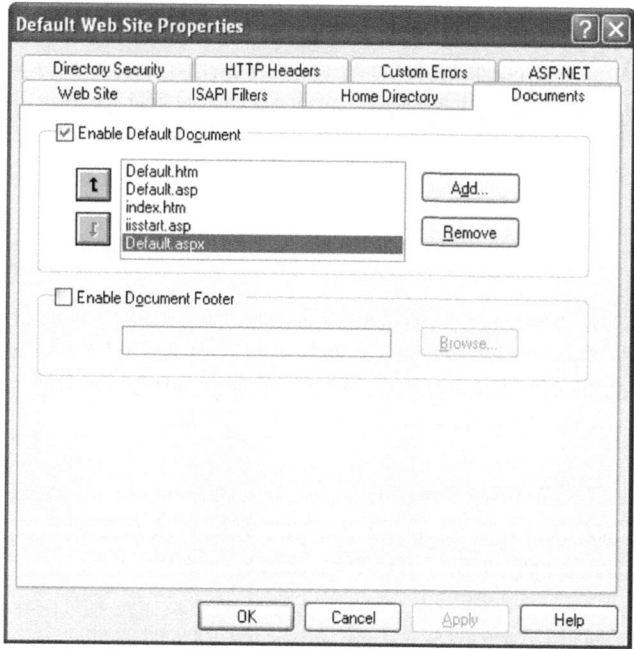

Figure 2-10. *The default document list*

You can configure the default document list by removing entries or adding new ones. Most ASP.NET applications simply use default.aspx as their home page.

Custom Errors

The Custom Errors tab (see Figure 2-11) allows you to specify an error page that will be displayed for specific types of HTTP errors. You can use ASP.NET configuration to replace HTTP errors or application errors with custom messages. However, these techniques won't work if the web request never makes it to the ASP.NET service (for example, if the user requests an HTML file that doesn't exist). In this case, you may want to supplement custom ASP.NET error handling with the appropriate IIS error pages for other generic error conditions.

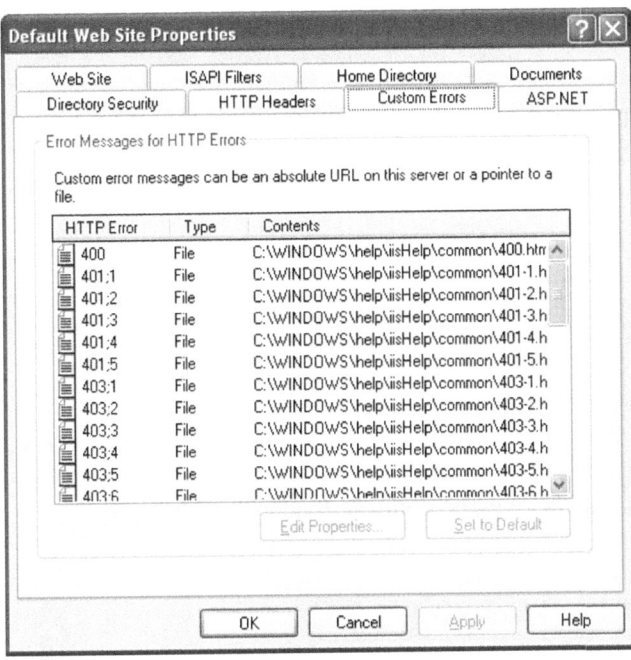

Figure 2-11. *IIS custom errors*

Verifying the ASP.NET Installation

After installing ASP.NET, it's a good idea to test that it's working. All you need to do is create a simple ASP.NET page, request it in a browser, and make sure that it's processed successfully.

To perform this test, create a new physical directory on your computer. Now, use the Create Virtual Directory wizard to expose this directory as a virtual directory named Test. Finally, create a new file in this directory using Notepad. Name this file test.aspx. The filename isn't that important, but the extension *is*. It's the .aspx extension that tells IIS that this file needs to be processed by the ASP.NET engine.

Inside the test.aspx file, paste the following code:

```
<html>
<body>
<h1>The date is <% Response.Write(DateTime.Now.ToLongDateString()) %>
</h1>
</body>
</html>
```

When you request this file in a browser, ASP.NET will load the file, execute the embedded code statement (which retrieves the current date and inserts it into the page), and then return the final HTML page. This example isn't a full-fledged ASP.NET web page, because it doesn't use the web-control model you'll be exploring in the second part of this book. However, it's still enough to test that ASP.NET is working properly. When you enter http://localhost/Test/test.aspx in the browser, you should see a page that looks like the one shown in Figure 2-12.

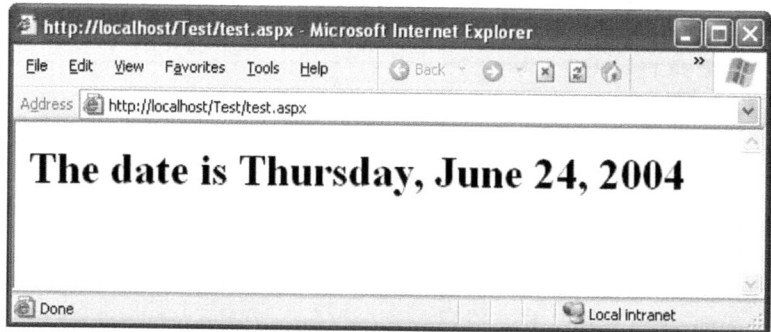

Figure 2-12. *ASP.NET is correctly installed*

If you see only the plain text, as in Figure 2-13, ASP.NET isn't installed correctly. This problem commonly occurs if ASP.NET is installed but the ASP.NET file types aren't registered in IIS. In this case, ASP.NET won't actually process the request. Instead, the raw page will be sent directly to the user, and the browser will only display the content that isn't inside a tag or script block.

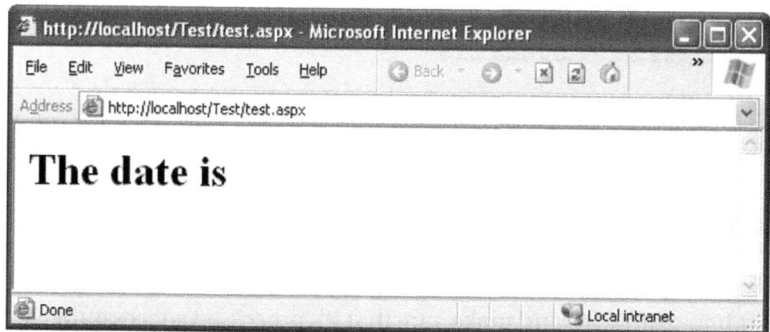

Figure 2-13. *ASP.NET isn't installed or configured correctly*

This problem can usually be solved by repairing your IIS file mappings using the aspnet_regiis.exe utility described earlier. Here's the syntax that you'll need:

```
c:\[WinDir]\Microsoft.NET\Framework\[Version]\aspnet_regiis.exe -i
```

Microsoft provides more detailed information about troubleshooting and aspnet_regiis.exe in a knowledge-base article at http://support.microsoft.com/default.aspx?scid=kb;en-us;325093.

Summary

In this chapter, you took a comprehensive look at the ASP.NET and IIS architecture. You also learned how to create and configure virtual directories, and how to manage multiple versions of ASP.NET on the same server. In the next chapter, you'll get ready to start developing by taking a tour of Visual Studio .NET.

CHAPTER 3

▪▪▪

Visual Studio .NET

Developing with a new language can be daunting. Not only do you need to get accustomed to the syntax of the language itself, but you may also need to master a brand new development tool before you can write a single line of code.

With ASP.NET, you have several choices for developing web applications:

- **Plain text editors like Notepad.** Using a bare-bones text editor, you can write all your ASP.NET code by hand. This approach is appealingly straightforward, but tedious and error-prone for anything other than a simple page. Professional ASP.NET developers rarely go this route.

- **Web Matrix.** This freely downloadable development tool gives you a set of useful design tools, like the ability to lay out a web page by dragging and dropping controls at design time. However, you won't get streamlined debugging features, integrated support for components, or IntelliSense statement completion.

- **Visual Studio .NET.** This professional development tool supports a rich set of design tools, including a legendary set of debugging tools and IntelliSense, which catches errors and offers suggestions as you type. Visual Studio .NET also supports the robust code-behind model, which separates the .NET code you write from the web-page user interface.

Overall, Web Matrix is a compact, elegant tool for building simple websites. Visual Studio .NET is a much more powerful professional-level design tool. It's a must for complex, multilayered applications. To download Web Matrix (and take a look at a concise user guide in PDF format), surf to `www.asp.net`. To learn about Visual Studio .NET, keep reading. This chapter tours the IDE (integrated development environment) and explores several key features. It also introduces the code-behind model for writing ASP.NET web pages and web services.

Note Visual Studio .NET and Web Matrix are the most popular IDEs, but they aren't the only tools you'll find. Other contenders include SharpDevelop (`www.icsharpcode.net/OpenSource/SD`), Dreamweaver MX (`www.macromedia.com`), and even Borland Delphi (`www.borland.com/delphi_net`).

Understanding .NET Development Tools

In many respects all commercial and academic languages share some common and simple characteristics with each other. All languages need to allow developers to do the following:

- Edit human-readable code

- Debug applications or components

- Compile human-readable code into a ready-to-run component

For these reasons, it seems like a sensible approach to produce a single common interface for all languages. Microsoft's solution to this problem is to separate the compiler from the IDE and develop the IDE as a non-language-specific tool. In .NET, this standard IDE is Visual Studio .NET.

The .NET Compilers

In order to create an ASP.NET application, you need two high-level areas of functionality:

- The IDE, which allows a developer to write code

- The compiler, which inspects the developer code and translates it into lower-level code (in this case, IL, or Microsoft Intermediate Language)

.NET separates these two pieces. The compilers include the following:

- The VB .NET compiler (vbc.exe)

- The C# compiler (csc.exe)

- The JScript compiler (jsc.exe)

- The J# compiler (vjc.exe)

If you want to use these compilers manually, you can invoke them from the command line. You'll find all of them in the c:\[WinDir]\Microsoft.NET\[Version] where WinDir is the directory of the operating system (like c:\Windows) and Version is the version number of .NET that you've installed, like v1.1.4322. However, using the .NET compilers is awkward because you need to specify the files you want to compile and the other .NET assemblies they use. You also need to compile your entire application at once, or compile each web page separately. To avoid these headaches, most developers rely on ASP.NET's ability to compile a web page dynamically when it's requested, or they use a development tool that uses the appropriate compiler behind the scenes, like Visual Studio .NET.

The Visual Studio .NET IDE

To those who are used to the previous version of the Visual Studio IDE, it's an obvious choice to use the new VS .NET IDE. After all, it offers all the benefits of the previous version but with significant advancements in operability, syntax, and integration with other languages.

For those who haven't tried Visual Studio before, the reasons to use VS .NET may not be immediately obvious. Some of its advantages include the following:

- **WYSIWYG.** Who writes HTML pages by hand? Using Visual Studio .NET, you can tweak and fine-tune even static HTML content, applying fonts, styles, and even using absolute positioning.

- **Less code to write.** Most applications require a fair bit of standard boilerplate code, and ASP.NET web pages are no exception. For example, when you add a new control to a web page, you also need to define a variable that allows you to manipulate that control in your code. With Visual Studio .NET, these basic tasks are performed for you. Similar automation is provided for connecting to web services.

- **Intuitive coding style.** By default, Visual Studio .NET formats your code as you type, indenting automatically and using color-coding to distinguish elements like comments. These minor differences make code much more readable and less prone to error.

- **Use of a compiled deployment model.** Visual Studio .NET automatically compiles all your web pages, classes, and other code files into a single DLL assembly (containing IL code). This way, you don't need to deploy your source code to the web server—just the web-page user-interface files and the assembly.

- **Multilanguage development.** VS .NET allows you to code in your language or languages of choice using the same interface (IDE) at all times. This common interface allows you to concentrate on the syntax of the code rather than forcing you to learn the peculiarities of a new IDE. Visual Studio .NET provides robust support for several languages, notably C# and VB .NET. When debugging, you can even step from a web page written in one language into a component written in another.

- **Faster development times.** Many of the features in Visual Studio .NET are geared to helping you get your work done faster. Convenience features like powerful search-and-replace and automatic comment and uncomment features, which can temporarily hide a block of code, allow you to work quickly and efficiently.

- **Debugging.** The Visual Studio .NET debugging tools are the best way to track down mysterious errors and diagnose strange behavior. You can execute your code one line at a time, set intelligent breakpoints that you can save for later use, and view current in-memory information at any time.

Visual Studio .NET also has a wealth of features that you won't see in this chapter, including project management, source-code control, and a rich extensibility model.

Tip Visual Studio .NET had a minor facelift from version 2002 to version 2003. However, the features, functionality, and menu organization are virtually unchanged.

Creating a Website in Visual Studio .NET

You start Visual Studio .NET from the Start menu by selecting Programs ➤ Microsoft Visual Studio .NET ➤ Microsoft Visual Studio .NET. When the IDE first loads, it shows an initial start page. You can use various user-specific options from this page, and access online information like recent MSDN articles. But to get right to work, choose File ➤ New Project to create a new Visual Studio .NET project. Visual Studio .NET will then show the New Project dialog box (see Figure 3-1).

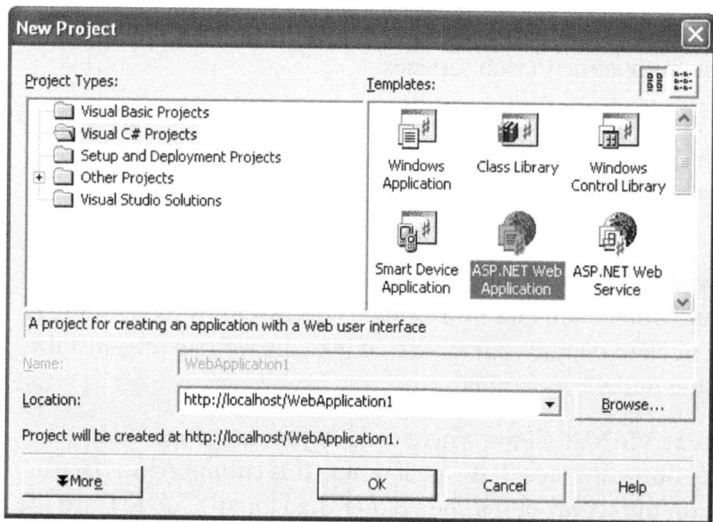

Figure 3-1. *The New Project window*

The New Project window allows you to choose the type of project and the location where it will be stored. You should choose the Visual C# Projects node, and the ASP.NET Web Application template.

■**Note** Visual Studio .NET supports two types of ASP.NET applications: web applications and web service applications. These applications are actually compiled and executed in the exact same way. In fact, you can add web pages to a web service application and web services to an ordinary web application. The only difference is the files that Visual Studio .NET creates by default. In a web application, you'll start with one sample web page in your project, named WebForm1.aspx. In a web service application, you'll start out with a sample web service, named WebService1.aspx.

Visual Studio .NET and Virtual Directories

As you learned in Chapter 2, every web application must be placed inside a virtual directory. In Visual Studio .NET, there are three ways that you can work with virtual directories:

- Create a new virtual directory in c:\Inetpub\wwwroot using Visual Studio .NET.

- Create the virtual directory manually using IIS, and then create a Visual Studio .NET project in that virtual directory.

- Create a new virtual directory inside an existing virtual directory using Visual Studio .NET.

The approach you use is a matter of personal preference. However, the second choice is the most flexible, because you won't be forced into storing all your web projects in the c:\Inetpub\wwwroot directory. To use this approach, simply supply the path to the existing virtual directory when you create the project. For example, if you create a virtual directory http://localhost/MySite and map it to c:\MySite, you can create a web project in this directory by specifying the location http://localhost/MySite.

If you want to create a new virtual directory using only Visual Studio .NET, you must place this virtual directory inside the website root or another virtual directory that already exists. For example, if you specify http://localhost/WebApplication1, then Visual Studio .NET will create the directory c:\Inetpub\wwwroot\WebApplication1, and configure it to be a virtual directory. Or, if you've created the virtual directory http://localhost/MySite and mapped it to c:\MySite, you can use Visual Studio .NET to create the new virtual directory http://localhost/MySite/NewSite. The new virtual directory will be placed inside the first one, so in this case it will map to c:\MySite\NewSite. However, despite the fact that one virtual directory will be nested inside the other, the two virtual directories will not share any characteristics, and they won't be a part of the same web application.

Note When Visual Studio .NET creates a new virtual directory, it automatically configures it to be a web application (much like the IIS Create Virtual Directory wizard does). This means that all the web pages in this directory will have their own configuration settings and memory space, which are requirements for debugging them in Visual Studio .NET.

Projects and Solutions

Visual Studio .NET creates specialized file types for tracking the files and resources that you are writing, running, and debugging together as part of a web application. There are two key VS .NET file types, as follows:

- **Project.** A suite of files and resources that together form a distinct application or library. One example of a project is an ASP.NET website. However, you might create other projects for class libraries (reusable components) or even long-running system services that work in conjunction with your application.

- **Solution.** A grouping of one of more projects. When you create a new project, VS .NET also creates a new solution for that project. You can add additional projects to this solution if you want to debug other components in conjunction with your website. For example, you might want to debug a web application and a custom component, or a web service and a client that uses it.

To track projects, VS .NET creates a file with the extension .csproj (for C# projects). This file uses an XML format, and you can view it with a text editor like Notepad. Its main ingredients are a list of files that are a part of the project, and a list of assemblies you've referenced. Additionally, for ASP.NET projects VS .NET creates a second file with the extension .csproj.webinfo. This file contains a single line of information that identifies the virtual directory path that this application uses.

Tip If you're moving a Visual Studio .NET project to a new virtual directory, you will need to edit the .csproj.webinfo file by hand in order to open the project. Otherwise, an error will occur when you attempt to open the project. The only other solution is to create a new project in the desired location and add all the files from the original project.

To track solutions, VS .NET uses a .sln file. This file is created even if your solution only has a single project. The solution file lists the linked projects. In addition, VS .NET creates an addition solution file with a .suo extension. It contains binary information that includes miscellaneous details like the breakpoints you've set while debugging your code.

Designing a Web Page

To start designing a web page, double-click the web page in the Solution Explorer (start with WebPage1.aspx if you haven't added any additional pages). A blank page will appear in the designer.

Before you begin adding controls, you may want to switch to grid layout, which gives you complete freedom to place controls wherever you want on the page. Select DOCUMENT in the Properties window (or just click the blank web form once), and find the pageLayout property. You have the following two options:

- **FlowLayout.** In a FlowLayout page, elements are positioned line by line, like in a word processor document. To add a control, you need to drag and drop it to an appropriate place. You also need to add spaces and hard returns to position elements the way you want them.

- **GridLayout.** In a GridLayout page, elements can be positioned with absolute coordinates. You can draw controls directly onto the web-form surface. The disadvantage is that the controls won't adjust their position if the page content changes. For example, if you add a significant amount of text to a label control, thereby forcing it to become much larger, it might overwrite another nearby control.

When using GridLayout, Visual Studio .NET positions HTML elements using CSS (Cascading Style Sheets). Often, web developers store CSS information in separate files, but Visual Studio .NET positions each item using *inline styles*, which are specified in the style attribute for the element. For example, the following tag shows an ordinary ASP.NET button. Its position is determined by where it occurs in the HTML markup.

```
<asp:Button id="Button1" runat="server" Text="Submit"></asp:Button>
```

And here's the same tag with positional information in the inline style:

```
<asp:Button id="Button1" runat="server" Text="Submit"
    style="Z-INDEX: 103; LEFT: 287px; POSITION: absolute; TOP: 20px"></asp:Button>
```

These style attributes are passed to the rendered HTML tag, along with any formatting properties that you set.

Tip Although you must choose GridLayout or FlowLayout for the page, you can place controls inside special Grid Layout or Flow Layout panels. This allows you to align some controls relative to one another, but place them at a specific location on the page. (It also allows you to do the converse: align controls absolutely in a Grid Layout box, but have this box change position to accommodate the content on the rest of a FlowLayout page.) You'll find the Grid Layout Panel and Flow Layout Panel in the HTML tab on the toolbox. These controls are actually just <div> tags that use a special attribute to tell Visual Studio .NET how to treat them.

To add controls, choose the control type from the toolbox on the left. Once you've added a control, you can resize it and configure its properties in the Properties window. Every time you add a web control, Visual Studio automatically adds the corresponding tag to your .aspx web-page file. You can switch your view to look at the tags by clicking the HTML button at the bottom of the web-designer window. Click Design to revert back to the graphical web-form designer.

Figure 3-2 shows two views of the same web page that contain a label and a button. One view is in design mode, and the other is in HTML mode.

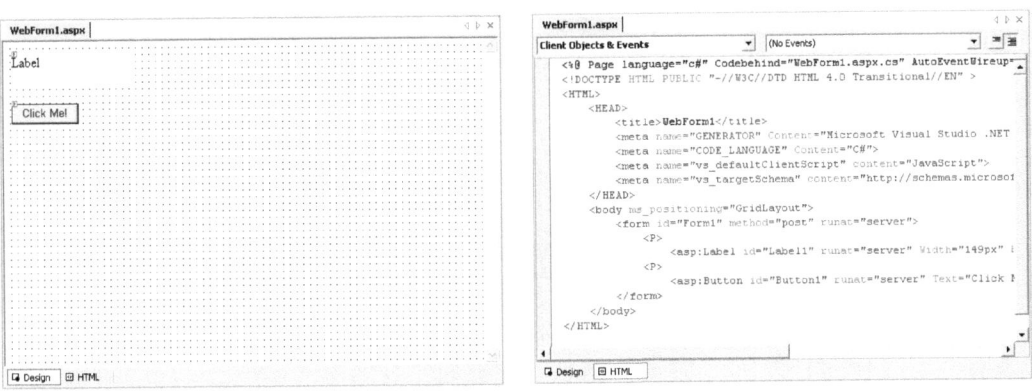

Figure 3-2. *The two modes for editing web pages*

Using the HTML view, you can manually add attributes or rearrange controls. In fact, Visual Studio .NET even provides limited IntelliSense features that automatically complete opening tags and alert you if you use an invalid tag. Generally, you won't need to use the HTML view in Visual Studio .NET. Instead, you can use the design view and configure controls through the Properties window.

To configure a control, click once to select it, or choose it by name in the drop-down list at the top of the Properties window. Then, modify the appropriate properties in the window, such as Text, ID, and ForeColor. These settings are automatically translated to the corresponding ASP.NET control tag attributes and define the initial appearance of your control. Visual Studio .NET even provides special "choosers" (technically known as UITypeEditors) that allow you to select extended properties. For example, you can select a color from a drop-down list that shows you the color, and you can configure the font from a standard font selection dialog box.

Static HTML Tags

By default, when you add an item from the HTML tab of the toolbox, Visual Studio .NET adds a static HTML element, not a server control. If you want to configure the element as a server control so that you can handle events and interact with it in code, you need to right-click it in the web page, and select Run As Server Control. This adds the required runat="server" attribute to the control tag. Alternatively, you could switch to design view and type this in on your own.

Of course, not all HTML elements need to be server controls. For example, you might want to create a simple <div> tag using the Grid Layout Panel or Flow Layout panel items in the HTML tab of the toolbox. Visual Studio .NET provides a valuable style builder for formatting any static HTML element with CSS style properties. To test it out, add one of the panel controls to your web page from the HTML section of the toolbox. Then right-click the panel and choose Build Style. The Style Builder dialog box (shown in Figure 3-3) will appear, with options for configuring the colors, font, layout, and border for the element. As you configure these properties, the web page HTML will be updated to reflect your settings.

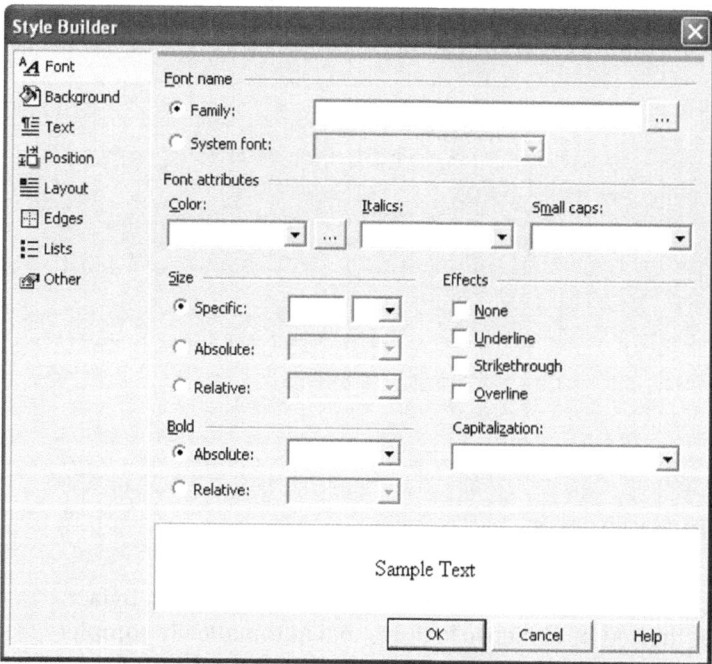

Figure 3-3. *Building HTML styles*

Writing Code

Some of Visual Studio .NET's most welcome enhancements appear when you start to write the code that supports your user interface. To start coding, you need to switch to the code-behind view. To switch back and forth, you can use two buttons that are placed just above the Solution Explorer window. The tooltips identify these buttons as View Code and View Designer, respectively. When you switch to code view, you'll see the page class for your web page. You'll learn more about code-behind later in this chapter.

ASP.NET is event-driven, and everything in your web-page code takes place in response to an event. To create a simple event handler for the Button.Click event, double-click the button in design view. Visual Studio .NET will add this event handler to your page class:

```
private void Button1_Click(object sender, System.EventArgs e)
{
}
```

According to .NET convention, all events use two parameters. The first parameter is used to pass a reference to the object that fired the event (in this case, the Button control). The second parameter is used to pass an object with any additional information. If additional information isn't required, an empty EventArgs object is used, as in this example.

For example, consider a web page with a button and a label control named Label1. You can add this line of code to modify the label when the button is clicked, and display the current date and time:

```
private void Button1_Click(object sender, System.EventArgs e)
{
    Label1.Text = "Current time: " + DateTime.Now.ToLongTimeString();
}
```

To test this page out, select Debug ➤ Start from the menu. Your page will be compiled to a DLL assembly with IL code, and then Visual Studio .NET will launch your default browser, with the URL set to your page. At this point, the request will be passed to IIS, which will then invoke ASP.NET and load the CLR (common language runtime). ASP.NET will compile the page to native machine code, and execute it.

To test your event-handling logic, click the button on the page. The page will then be submitted back to ASP.NET, which will run your event-handling code and return a new HTML page with the data (as shown in Figure 3-4).

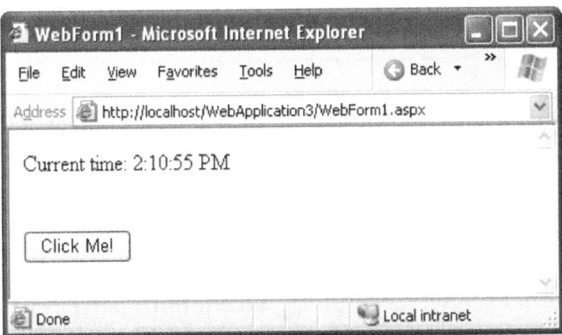

Figure 3-4. *Testing a simple web page*

The Visual Studio .NET IDE

Now that you've created a basic website, it's a good time to take a tour of the different parts of the VS .NET interface. Figure 3-5 identifies each part of the Visual Studio .NET window, and Table 3-1 describes each one.

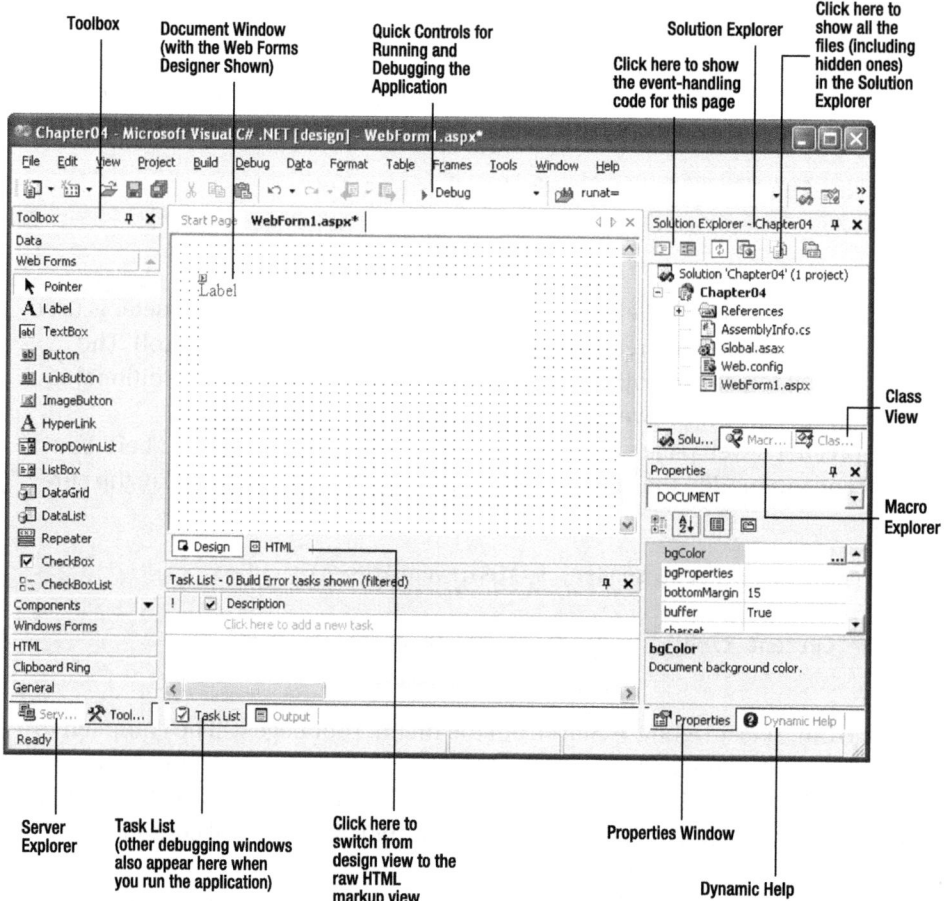

Figure 3-5. *The Visual Studio .NET interface*

Table 3-1. *Visual Studio .NET windows*

Windows	Description
Solution Explorer	Lists the files that are a part of this project. Also allows you to work with several projects (each of which can be in any supported language) simultaneously, which make up a single solution. The Solution Explorer also provides access to project management code-storage software such as Visual SourceSafe, and allows you to add references to other components you need to use.
Toolbox	Shows ASP.NET's built-in server controls, and any third-party controls or custom controls that you build yourself and add to the Toolbox. Controls can be written in any language and used in any language.

Windows	Description
Dynamic Help and Search	Allows you to search for any help within documents or help files. The Dynamic Help window suggests related topics based on your current statement while you're writing code.
Server Explorer	Allows access to databases, system services, message queues, and other server-side resources.
Properties	Allows you to configure the currently selected element, whether it's a file in the Solution Explorer or a control on the design surface of a web form.
Task List	Serves two purposes. First, it reports on errors that Visual Studio .NET has detected in your code but that you haven't resolved yet. Second, it lists comments that start with a predefined moniker so that you can keep track of portions of code that you want to change and also jump to the appropriate position quickly.
Document	Allows you to design a web page by dragging and dropping, and to edit the code files you have within your Solution Explorer. Also supports non-ASP.NET file types, like static HTML and XML files.
Macro Explorer	Allows you to see all the macros you've created, and execute them. Macros are an advanced VS .NET feature that allow you to automate time-consuming tasks. VS. NET exposes a rich extensibility model and you can write a macro using pure .NET code.
Class View	Shows a different view of your application that is organized to show all the classes you've created (and their methods, properties, and events).

Tip The Visual Studio .NET interface is highly configurable. You can drag the various windows and dock them to different sides of the main VS .NET window. Also, some windows on the side automatically slide into and out of view as you move your mouse. If you want to freeze these windows in place, just click the thumbtack icon in the top-right corner of the window.

Solution Explorer

The Solution Explorer is, at its most basic, a visual filing system. It allows you to see the items that are in your project. Some of these items correspond to physical files, but this correspondence isn't exact. For example, the Solution Explorer also includes logical items like assembly references and web references.

It's important to remember that the Solution Explorer only shows files that you have created as part of your project. That means it omits files that may be in the same directory, but aren't a part of the project. Also, there are certain files that are a part of a project but are hidden by default. To see any of these files, you need to right-click the project name in the Solution Explorer and select Show All Files. Figure 3-6 compares two views of the Solution Explorer for a simple web project with only one web page. The expanded view shows the Bin directory where compiled code is stored, the .cs code-behind file where you write your event handlers for web-page events, and the .resx resource file where Visual Studio .NET stores localizable information.

■**Tip** When you're using the Show All Files feature, you can quickly add files to your project by right-clicking the file in the Solution Explorer and choosing Include in Project. You can also right-click existing project files and choose Exclude from Project to remove them from the project without deleting them from the directory.

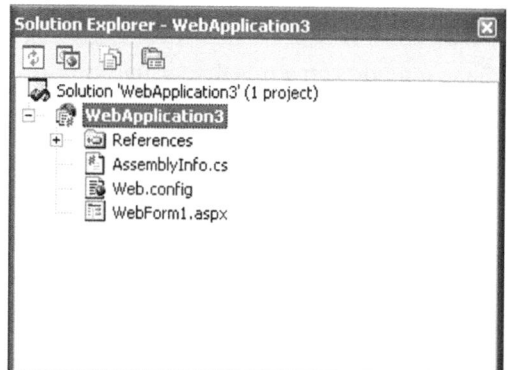
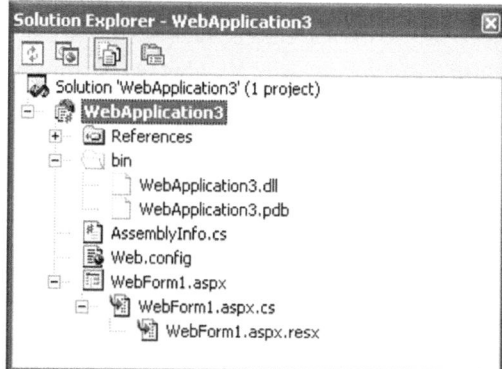

Figure 3-6. *Showing all files in the Solution Explorer*

Table 3-2 lists all the file types that you're likely to see in an ASP.NET project in Visual Studio .NET.

Table 3-2. *ASP.NET File Types*

File	Description
Ends with .aspx	These are ASP.NET web pages (the .NET equivalent of the .asp file in an ASP application). They contain the user interface and, optionally, the underlying application code. Users request or navigate directly to one of these pages to start your web application.
Ends with .ascx	These are ASP.NET user controls. User controls are similar to web pages, except that they can't be accessed directly. Instead, they must be hosted inside an ASP.NET web page. User controls allow you to develop an important piece of the user interface and reuse it in as many web forms as you want without repetitive code. You'll learn about user controls in Chapter 19.
Ends with .asmx	These are ASP.NET web services. Web services work differently than web pages, but they still share the same application resources, configuration settings, and memory.
web.config	This is the XML-based configuration file for your ASP.NET application. It includes settings for customizing security, state management, memory management, and much more.
global.asax	This is the global application file (the .NET equivalent of the global.asa file in an ASP application). You can use this file to define global variables and react to global events, such as when a web application first starts.

File	Description
Ends with .disco or .vsdisco	These are discovery files that are used to advertise the web services a web application provides.
Ends with .cs	These are code-behind files that contain C# code. They allow you to separate the application from the user interface of a web page. The code-behind model is introduced in this chapter, and used extensively in this book.
Ends with .resx	These files are used to store localization information (like text in multiple languages), and binary information that you add to the web page at design time.
Ends with .sln, .suo, .vbproj, and .csproj	These files are used by Visual Studio .NET to group together projects (a collection of files in a web application) and solutions (a collection of projects that you're developing or testing at once). These files are only used during development and should not be deployed to a web server. However, even if you *do* inadvertently copy these files to a web server, the default ASP.NET security settings will prevent a user from viewing them.

In addition, your web application can contain other resources that aren't ASP.NET file types. For example, your virtual directory can hold image files, HTML files, or CSS files. These resources might be used in one of your ASP.NET web pages, or they can be used independently.

Visual Studio .NET distinguishes between different file types. When you right-click a file in the list, a context menu appears with the menu options that apply for that file type. For example, if you right-click a web page, you'll have the option of building it and launching it in a browser window.

File Management

Using the Solution Explorer, you can remove, rename, rearrange, and add files. To get information about a file, select it in the Solution Explorer. You can then read various pieces of information in the Properties window. For example, the Build Action property describes what will happen when you run the web application in Visual Studio .NET (typically, it will compile the file). The File Name property allows you to rename files without leaving the IDE.

When you first create a web application, you'll begin with one web page called Web-Form1.aspx. You can add additional web pages by right-clicking your project in the Solution Explorer and selecting Add ➤ Add New Item. You can add various different types of files to your project, including web forms, web services, standalone components, resources you want to track like bitmaps and text files, and even ordinary HTML files. You can also copy files that already exist into your project by selecting Add ➤ Add Existing Item. Use the Add ➤ New Folder to create a new subdirectory inside your web application. You can then drag web pages and other files into or out of this directory.

To delete a file, just select it in the Solution Explorer and press the Delete key.

■**Tip** Usually, when you create a new web application, you'll want to delete the WebForm1.aspx file immediately, and then add a new file with the name you want. If you simply rename WebForm1.aspx, Visual Studio .NET will keep using the old name for the web-page class, which probably isn't what you want. However, when you create a new file, the name you enter is used for the filename and the web-page class name.

The Solution Explorer also controls and checks for project management events such as when another process changes a file in a project you currently have open. When this occurs, Visual Studio .NET will notify and give you the option to refresh the file.

Adding Assembly References

The Solution Explorer also shows all the assembly references that are configured for your project. These are the .NET assemblies that contain classes you might want to use. By default, every Visual Studio .NET web project references the assemblies in Table 3-3.

Table 3-3. *Default Project References for an ASP.NET Project*

Assembly	Description
System.dll	Includes the core set of .NET data types, common exception types, and numerous other fundamental building blocks.
System.Data.dll	Includes the data container classes for ADO.NET, along with the four ADO.NET data providers you use to connect to different databases.
System.Drawing.dll	Includes classes representing colors, fonts, and shapes. Also includes the GDI+ drawing logic you need to build graphics on the fly.
System.Web.dll	Includes the core ASP.NET types, including classes for building web forms.
System.Xml.dll	Includes .NET classes for reading, writing, searching, transforming, and validating XML.

These assemblies that Visual Studio .NET references by default don't represent the entire .NET Framework. For example, if you want to gain access to COM+ services like transactions, you'll need to add a reference to the System.EnterpriseServices.dll assembly. Similarly, if you develop your own components, or want to use a custom third-party component, you'll also need to add an assembly reference. To add a reference, follow these steps:

1. Right-click the References item in the Solution Explorer and choose Add Reference.

2. In the Add Reference window, select the component you want to use. If the component isn't located in the centralized component registry on your computer (known as the global assembly cache, or GAC), you'll need to click the Browse button and select the DLL file from the appropriate directory.

3. Click OK to add the reference to your web project.

Remember, assemblies can contain more than one namespace: For example, the System.Web.dll assembly includes classes in the System.Web namespace and the System.Web.UI namespace.

If you look at the code for a web-page class, you'll notice that Visual Studio .NET imports a lengthy number of core .NET namespaces. Here's the code you'll see:

```
using System;
using System.Collections;
using System.ComponentModel;
using System.Data;
using System.Drawing;
using System.Web;
using System.Web.SessionState;
using System.Web.UI;
using System.Web.UI.WebControls;
using System.Web.UI.HtmlControls;
```

Adding a reference isn't the same as importing the namespace with the using statement. The using statement allows you to use the classes in a namespace without typing the long, fully qualified class names. However, if you're missing a reference, it doesn't matter what using statements you include—the classes won't be available. For example, if you import the System.Web.UI namespace, you can write Page instead of System.Web.UI.Page in your code. But if you haven't added a reference to the System.Web.dll assembly that contains these classes, you still won't be able to access the classes in the System.Web.UI namespace.

Document Window

The document window is the portion of VS .NET that allows you to edit various types of files using different designers. Some of the designers include the following:

- Source code (text) editor

- CSharp editor

- Visual Basic editor

- HTML/XML editor

- XML Schema editor

- IEXPLORE.EXE (web-page viewer)

- Binary editor

- Resource editor

Each file type has a default editor. To find out a file's default editor simply click that file in the Solution Explorer and right-click your mouse button, and then select Open With from the pop-up menu. The default editor will have the word Default alongside it.

Depending on the applications you've installed, you may see additional designers that plug in to Visual Studio .NET. For example, if you've installed FrontPage 2003, you'll have the option of editing web pages with a FrontPage designer (which actually opens your web page in a standalone FrontPage window).

Toolbox

The Toolbox works in conjunction with the document window. Its primary use is providing the controls that you can drag onto the design surface of a web form. However, it also allows you to store code and HTML snippets.

The content of the Toolbox depends on the current designer you're using as well as the project type. For example, when designing a web page you'll see the set of tabs described in Table 3-4. Each tab contains a group of buttons. You can only see one tab at a time. To view a tab, click the heading and the buttons will slide into view.

Table 3-4. *Toolbox Tabs for an ASP.NET Project*

Tab	Description
Data	These components allow you to connect to a database. They're nonvisual, but because they're in the toolbox you can drag them onto a web form and configure them at design time, without using any code.
Web Forms	This tab includes the rich web server controls that are the heart of ASP.NET's web form model.
HTML	This tab allows you to drag and drop static HTML elements. If you want, you can also use this tab to create server-side HTML controls—just drop a static HTML element onto a page, right-click it, and choose Run as Server Control.
Clipboard Ring	Shows you items that you have recently cut or copied from the Document Window that contain text, such as programming code and HTML. You can click one of these items to paste it directly from the Toolbox.
General	Provides a repository for code snippets and control objects. Just drag and drop them here, and pull them off when you need to use them later.

You can customize both the tabs and the items in each tab. To modify the tab groups, right-click a tab heading and select Rename Tab, Add Tab, or Delete Tab. To add an item right-click the blank space on the toolbox and choose Add/Remove Items. You can also drag items from one tab group to another.

Figure 3-7 shows an example of the clipboard ring, which shows recently copied text while you're editing code. By default, each item shows the beginning of the text block. You can also give any of these items descriptive names—just right-click the item and select Rename.

Finally, one other interesting technique is to create your own mini-composite controls by adding groups of control objects to the General tab. For example, you might select a group of controls on a web form, drag it onto the General tab, and then drag it to a new page later on. Figure 3-8 shows an example.

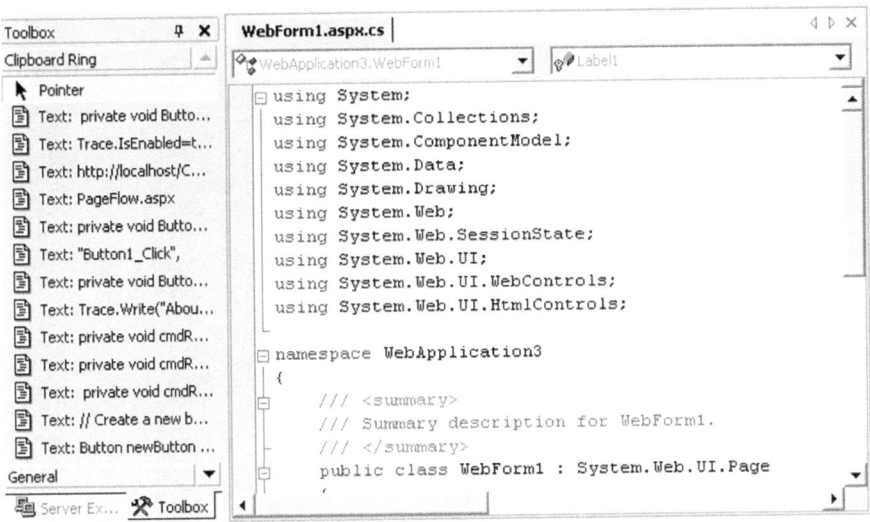

Figure 3-7. *Using the Clipboard Ring tab*

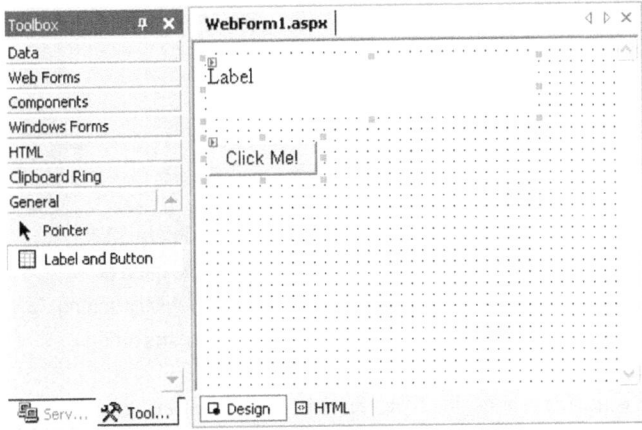

Figure 3-8. *Dragging and dropping an object to the General tab*

Dynamic Help and Search

Dynamic Help is a Visual Studio .NET service that runs while you code. It examines your current task, selections, and nearby code to determine what information is most useful. It provides this information in a Dynamic Help window (typically at the bottom-right corner of the IDE). Figure 3-9 shows what you might see while working with the CheckBox control on an ASP.NET web form.

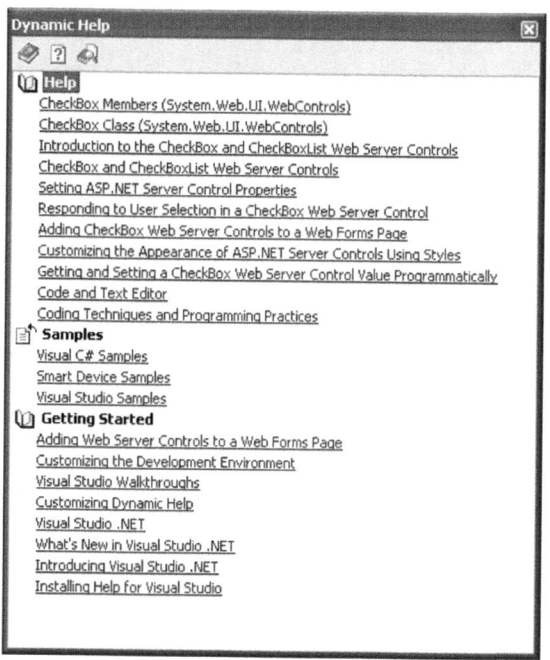

Figure 3-9. *Dynamic Help when the current keyword is CheckBox*

DYNAMIC HELP BEHIND THE SCENES

Dynamic Help provides a sort of "super context-sensitive help" that incorporates much more information than the user's current window. Unfortunately, it's hard to tell exactly what's taking place in the mind of VS .NET when it uses Dynamic Help. To take a look behind the scenes, you need to modify a registry setting in the key HKEY_CURRENT_USER\Software\Microsoft\VisualStudio\7.0\Dynamic Help. Look for the string setting Display Debug Output in Retail and set it to YES.

When you run Visual Studio.NET after making this change, the Dynamic Help window will include additional information after the list of topics. (If the Dynamic Help window isn't currently displayed, just press Ctrl+F1.) This information is the list of the criteria that Visual Studio .NET is currently using to select what links should be displayed.

Task List

The Task List window keeps a list of error information, to-do tasks, and other code annotations. Each entry in the Task List consists of a text description and, optionally, a link that leads you to a specific line of code somewhere in your project. You can use the task window to keep track of issues or changes you need to make, and Visual Studio .NET also uses it to flag syntax errors.

With the default Visual Studio .NET settings, the Task List appears automatically whenever you build a project that has errors, but is not shown when you first create an application. To display it at any time, select View ➤ Show Tasks ➤ All.

Tasks are grouped into one of four different types, as listed in Table 3-5.

Table 3-5. *Task Types*

Task Type	Description
Comment	These tasks represent special comments in your code that are preceded with a predefined comment token (typically TODO, HACK, and UNDONE). You can also define your own custom token tags.
Build Errors	These are syntax errors that Visual Studio .NET discovers when you build your project. To remove these entries from the list, simply fix the error and rebuild the solution.
User	These are entries you've placed in the Task List by simply clicking the Click Here to Add a New Task option. This is the only type of task that doesn't have a link to a specific line of code.
Shortcut	These are links to important places in your code. To add a shortcut to a line of code, just find the relevant code line in the designer window, right-click it, and select Add Task List Shortcut from the context menu. Code lines that have been marked with a shortcut have a blue ribbon displayed in the margin next to them.

To try out the task list, move somewhere in your code and enter the comment marker (//) followed by the word TODO (which is commonly referred to as a *token tag*). Now type in some descriptive text.

Here's an example:

```
// TODO: Replace this hard-coded value with a configuration file setting.
string FileName = @"c:\myfile.txt"
```

Next, view the Task List by selecting View ➤ Show Tasks ➤ All. Because your comment uses the recognized token tag TODO, it automatically appears in the list (as shown in Figure 3-10).

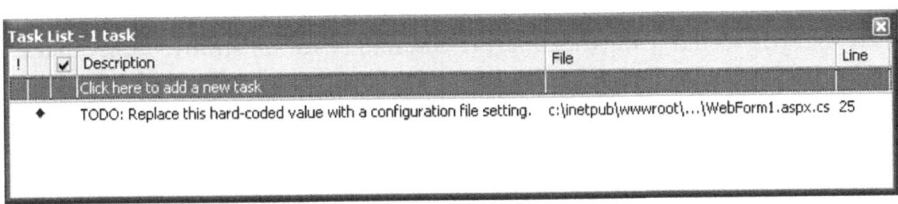

Figure 3-10. *Keeping track of tasks*

To move to the line of code, double-click the new task entry. Notice how if you remove the comment, the task entry is automatically removed as well.

There are three built-in token tags—HACK, TODO, and UNDONE. However, you can add more. Simply select Tools ➤ Options. In the Options dialog box, navigate to the Environment ➤ Task List tab. You'll see a list of comment tokens, which you can modify, remove, and add to. Figure 3-11 shows this window with a new ASP comment token that you could use to keep track of sections of code that have been migrated from classic ASP pages.

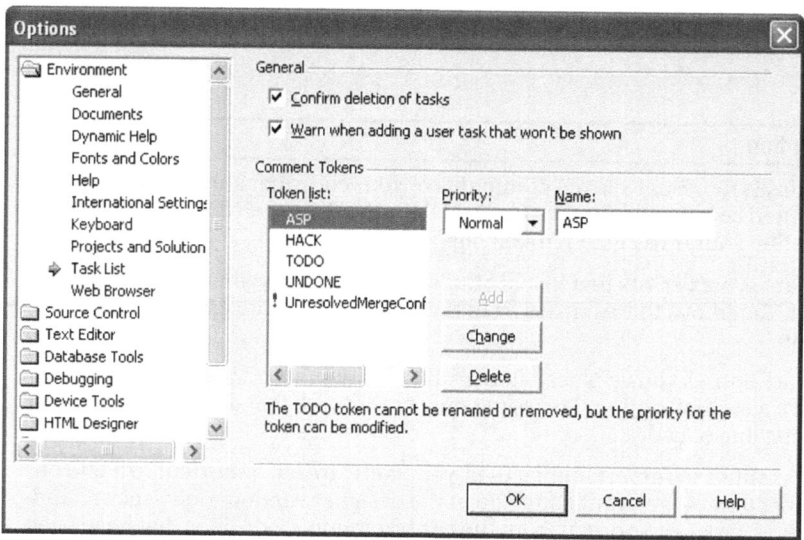

Figure 3-11. *Adding a new comment token*

Server Explorer

The Server Explorer provides a tree that allows you to explore various types of services on the current computer (and other servers on the network). It's similar to the Computer Management administrative tool. Typically, you'll use the Server Explorer to learn about available event logs, message queues, performance counters, system services, and SQL Server databases on your computer.

The Server Explorer is particularly noteworthy because it doesn't just provide a way for you to browse server resources; it also allows you to interact with them. For example, you can create databases, execute queries, and write stored procedures using the Server Explorer in much the same way that you would using the Enterprise Manager administrative utility that's included with SQL Server. To find out what you can do with a given item, right-click it. Figure 3-12 shows a screenshot where the Server Explorer window shows the databases in a local SQL Server, and allows you to retrieve all the records in the selected table.

IntelliSense and Outlining

As you program with Visual Studio .NET, you'll become familiar with its many timesaving conveniences. The following sections outline the most important features you'll use.

Outlining

Outlining allows Visual Studio .NET to "collapse" a subroutine, block structure, or region to a single line. It allows you to see the code that interests you, while hiding unimportant code. To collapse a portion of code, click the minus box next to the first line. Click the box again (which will now have a plus symbol) to expand it (see Figure 3-13).

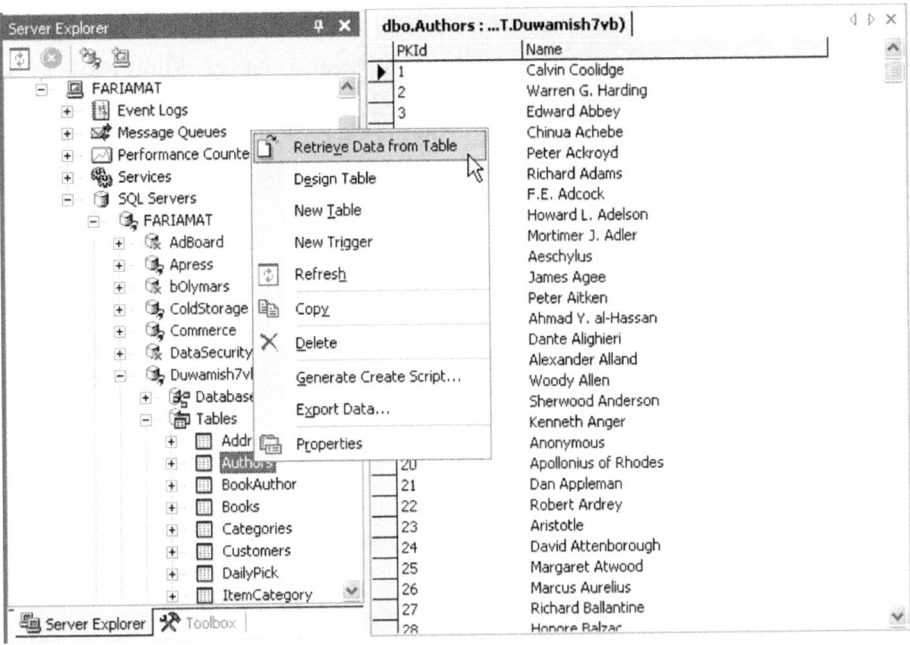

Figure 3-12. *Querying data in a database table*

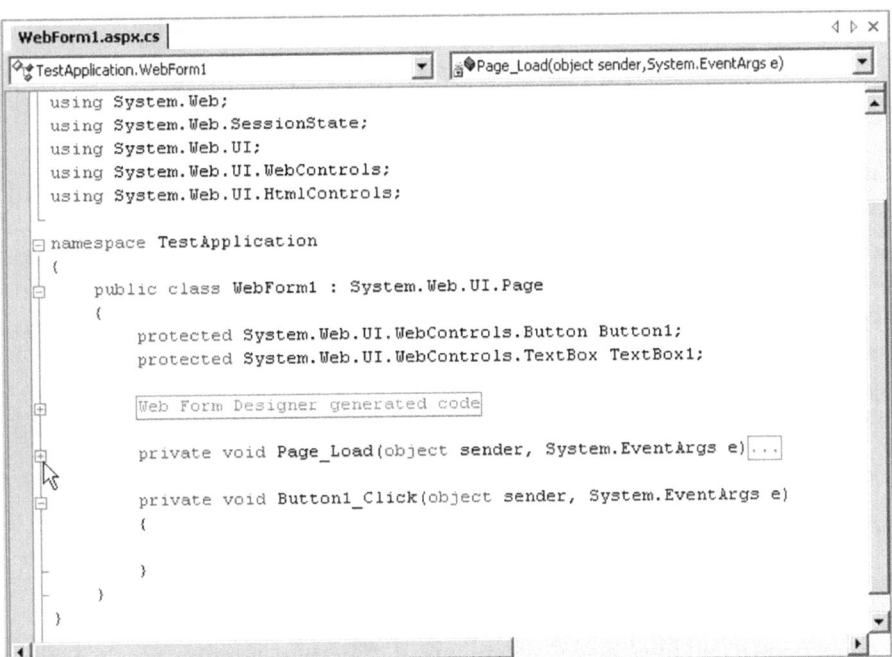

Figure 3-13. *Collapsing code*

You can hide any section of code that you want. Simply select the code, right-click the selection, and choose Outlining ➤ Hide Selection.

Member List

Visual Studio .NET makes it easy for you to interact with controls and classes. When you type a class or object name, it pops up a list of available properties and methods (see Figure 3-14). It uses a similar trick to provide a list of data types when you define a variable, or to provide a list of valid values when you assign a value to an enumeration.

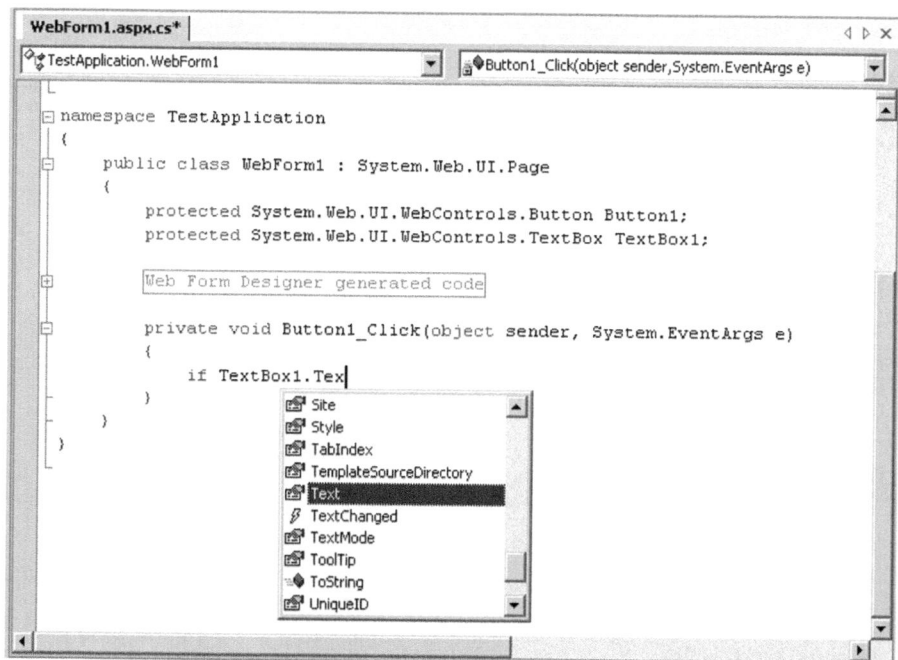

Figure 3-14. *IntelliSense at work*

Visual Studio .NET also provides a list of parameters and their data types when you call a method or invoke a constructor. This information is presented in a tooltip above the code and is shown as you type. Because the .NET class library makes heavy use of function overloading, these methods may have multiple different versions. When they do, Visual Studio .NET indicates the number of versions and allows you to see the method definitions for each one by clicking the small up and down arrows in the tooltip. Each time you click the arrow, the tooltip displays a different version of the overloaded method (see Figure 3-15).

Error Underlining

One of the code editor's most useful features is error underlining. Visual Studio .NET is able to detect a variety of error conditions, such as undefined variables, properties or methods, invalid data-type conversions, and missing code elements. Rather than stopping you to alert you that a problem exists, the VS .NET editor quietly underlines the offending code. You can hover your mouse over an underlined error to see a brief tooltip description of the problem (see Figure 3-16).

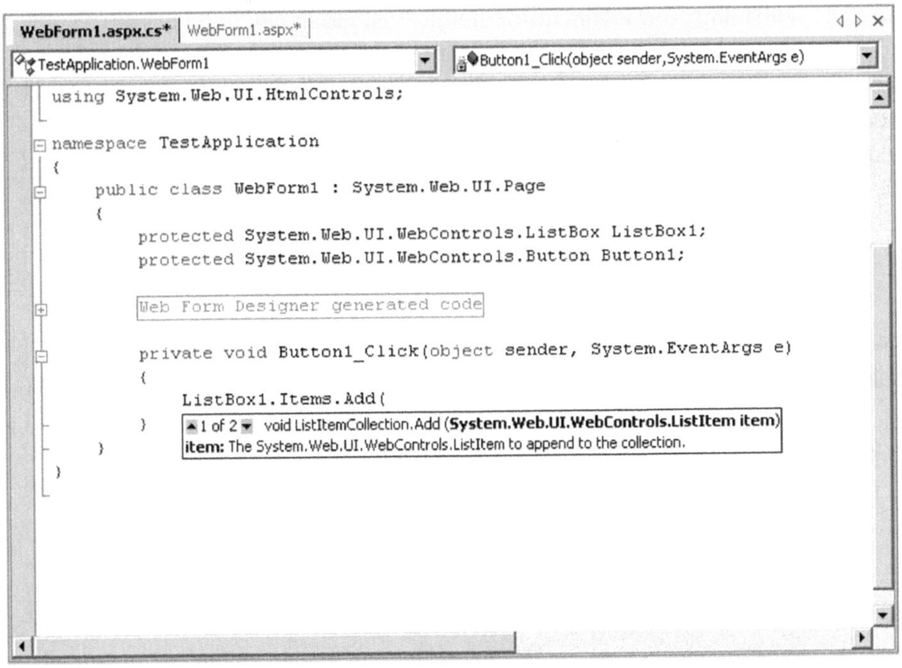

Figure 3-15. *IntelliSense with overloaded methods*

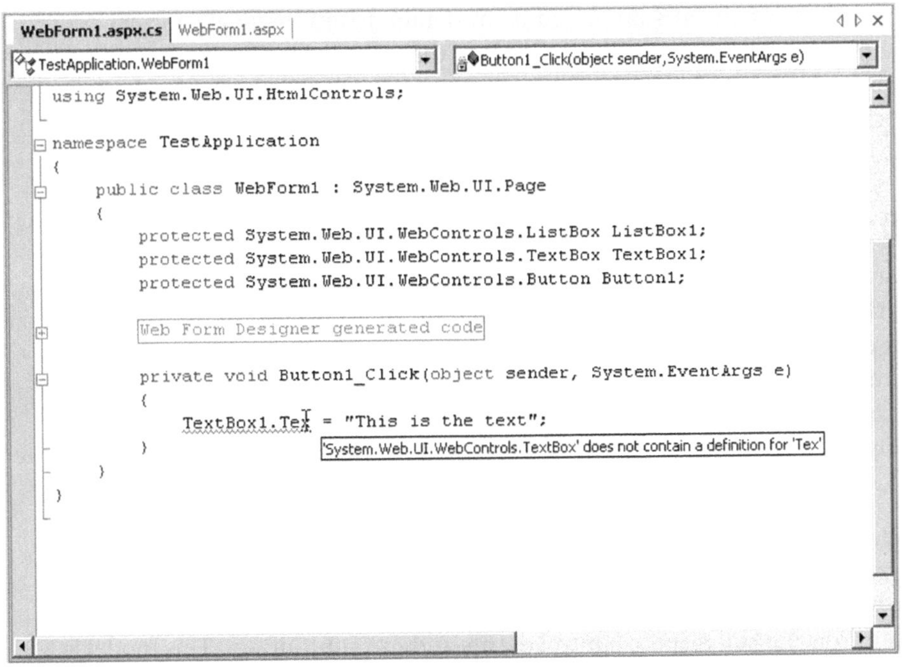

Figure 3-16. *Highlighting errors at design time*

Visual Studio .NET won't flag your errors immediately. Instead, it will quickly scan through your code as soon as you try to compile it, and mark all the errors it finds. If your code contains at least one error, Visual Studio .NET will ask you whether it should continue. At this point, you'll almost always decide to cancel the operation and fix the problems Visual Studio .NET has reported. (If you choose to continue, you'll actually wind up using the last compiled version of your application, because the .NET compilers can't build an application that has errors.)

Note You may find that as you fix errors and rebuild your project, you discover more problems. That's because Visual Studio .NET doesn't check for all types of errors at once. When you try to compile your application, Visual Studio .NET scans for basic problems like unrecognized class names. If these problems exist, they can easily mask other errors. On the other hand, if your code passes this basic level of inspection, Visual Studio .NET checks for more subtle problems like trying to use an unassigned variable.

Auto Format and Color

Visual Studio .NET also provides some cosmetic conveniences. It automatically colors your code, making comments green, keywords blue, and normal code black. The result is much more readable code. You can even configure the colors Visual Studio .NET uses by selecting Tools ➤ Options and then choosing the Environment ➤ Fonts and Colors section.

In additional, Visual Studio .NET is configured by default to automatically format your code. This means you can type your code lines freely without worrying about tabs and positioning. As soon as you insert a closing brace (the curly "}" bracket), Visual Studio .NET applies the "correct" indenting.

The Code-Behind Model

So far, you've learned how to design simple web pages, and you've taken a tour of the Visual Studio .NET interface. But before you get to serious coding, it's important to understand a little more about the underpinnings of the ASP.NET code model. In this section, you'll learn about your different options for using code to program a web page, and how ASP.NET events wire up to your code.

ASP.NET supports three different models for coding web pages and web services. They are as follows:

- **Inline code.** This model is the closest to traditional ASP. All the code and the HTML is stored in a single .aspx file. The code is embedded in one or more script blocks. However, even though the code is in a script block, it doesn't need to be executed sequentially. You can still react to control events and use subroutines. This model is popular for coding simple web pages.

- **Code-behind.** This model separates each ASP.NET web page into two files: a .aspx markup file with the HTML and control tags, and a .cs code file with the source code for the page. This model provides better organization, and the separation of the user interface from programmatic logic is keenly important when building complex pages.

- **Compiled code-behind.** This model is the same as the code-behind model, except that the source-code file is precompiled into a DLL assembly before it's deployed to the web server. This model has the same benefits as the code-behind model, with a few minor improvements, including a simplified deployment model and faster execution for the first web request (because ASP.NET only needs to perform one additional compilation step instead of two the first time the web application is used).

In .NET 1.0 and 1.1, the design tool you choose determines the model you use. Web Matrix is designed with the straightforward inline code model in mind. Visual Studio .NET uses the compiled code-behind model exclusively. With Visual Studio .NET, all the web pages, web services, and utility classes you create are compiled into a single DLL assembly. This assembly is placed in the Bin subdirectory of your web application directory. ASP.NET is hard-coded to look in this subdirectory, examine all the assemblies, and make all the classes available automatically.

Note Technically, you can follow the inline code model and write script blocks in a web page even if you're using Visual Studio .NET. However, if you take this approach you're effectively sidestepping Visual Studio .NET, and you won't have the benefit of features like statement completion, error checking, and debugging.

How Code-Behind Files Are Connected to Pages

Every .aspx page starts with a Page directive. This Page directive specifies the language for the page, and it also tells ASP.NET where to find the associated code (unless you're using inline code, in which case the code is contained in the same file).

There are two ways that you can specify where to find the associated code. If you're using code-behind files with source-code files, you use the Src and the Inherits attribute. The Src attribute names the file that has the source code for the web page. The Inherits attribute names the class that has the code for the page. Here's an example:

```
<%@ Page Language="CS" Inherits="SamplePage" Src="SamplePage.cs" %>
```

In this example, the code for your web page is in a class named SamplePage, and this class is in a text file named SamplePage.cs in the same virtual directory. ASP.NET will compile this file to IL automatically the first time any web page is requested in this virtual directory.

If you're using precompiled web-page classes, the process is slightly simpler. Instead of specifying the source-code file and the class, you only need to specify the class. Here's an example:

```
<%@ Page Language="CS" Inherits="SamplePage" %>
```

In this case, ASP.NET will find the SamplePage class, provided it's in one of the DLL assemblies in the Bin directory. You don't need to worry about the name of the assembly, because ASP.NET automatically examines all the assemblies in the Bin directory.

Visual Studio .NET uses precompilation. However, it also introduces one additional wrinkle. It adds the Codebehind attribute. The Codebehind attribute references the source-code file, much like the Src attribute. However, there is a key difference. ASP.NET doesn't pay any attention to the Codebehind attribute (and the linked file doesn't even need to be present). Instead, this information is used exclusively by Visual Studio .NET so it can load up the correct code file for editing in the design environment.

```
<%@ Page Language="CS" Inherits="SamplePage" Codebehind="SamplePage.aspx.cs" %>
```

Notice that Visual Studio .NET uses a slightly unusual naming syntax for the source-code file. It has the full name of the corresponding web page, complete with the .aspx extension, followed by the .cs extension at the end. This is just a matter of convention, and it avoids a problem if you happen to create two different code-behind file types (for example, a web page and a web service) with the same name.

Note You can use either "c#" or "CS" to set the Language attribute in the Page directive. Both values indicate that the page uses C# code.

When you compile a web application in Visual Studio .NET, all the classes (including web pages, web services, and other classes in separate files), are compiled into one DLL file. The csc.exe compiler is used behind the scenes.

How Control Tags Are Connected to Page Variables

Visual Studio .NET is careful to keep both the .aspx markup file (with the control tags) and the .cs file (with the source code) synchronized. Each time you add a control to the web page, Visual Studio .NET declares the control in the Page class. For example, if you add a text box named txtInput to a web page, Visual Studio .NET adds this tag to the .aspx file:

```
<asp:TextBox id="txtInput" runat="server"/>
```

At the same time, Visual Studio .NET adds the following member variable declaration in your custom page class, as shown here:

```
protected System.Web.UI.TextBox txtInput;
```

When ASP.NET creates the web page at runtime, it exposes the TextBox object through the txtInput variable, because it recognizes that the ID attribute in the control tag matches the variable name. If these names didn't match, the member variable would simply be left as it is (a null reference that doesn't point to anything). For that reason, Visual Studio .NET is careful to keep the names synchronized. For example, if you rename the control in design view, Visual Studio .NET updates both the .aspx file and .cs file. However, you shouldn't modify the variable declarations by hand, or you will disrupt this link.

Tip In rare cases, Visual Studio .NET won't add the control declaration to your page class. One example is the server-side <form> tag. ASP.NET requires every web page to use this tag, but there isn't much that you can accomplish with it in your code. However, now that you understand how ASP.NET connects control tags to member variables, you can add your own declaration for the HtmlForm control, as long as you make sure the names match. You can then manipulate its properties in your code.

Control variables must *always* be declared with the public or protected accessibility keyword. That's because of the way ASP.NET uses inheritance in the web-page model. The following three layers are at work:

1. First, there is the Page class from the .NET class library. This class defines the basic functionality that allows a web page to host other controls, render itself to HTML, and provide access to the traditional ASP objects such as Request, Response, and Session.

2. Second, there is your code-behind class (for example, HelloWorldPage). This class inherits from the Page class to acquire the basic set of ASP.NET web-page functionality.

3. Finally, the .aspx page (for example, HelloWorldPage.aspx) inherits the code from the custom form class you created. This allows it to combine the user interface with the code that supports it.

Protected variables act like private variables with a key difference—they are accessible to derived classes. In other words, using protected variables in your code-behind class ensures that the variables are accessible in the derived page class. This allows ASP.NET to connect your control variables to your control tags at runtime.

How Events Are Connected to Event Handlers

Most of the code in an ASP.NET web page is placed inside event handlers that react to web control events. Using Visual Studio .NET, there are three ways to add an event handler to your code:

- **Type it in by hand.** In this case, you add the method directly to the page class. You must specify the appropriate parameters so that the signature of the event handler exactly matches the signature of the event you want to handle. You'll also need to add code to connect the event handler to the appropriate event when the page first loads.

- **Double-click a control in design view.** In this case, Visual Studio .NET will create an event handler for that control's default event. For example, if you double-click the page, it will create a Page.Load event handler. If you double-click a button or input control, it will create an event handler for the click or change event.

- **Choose the event from the Properties window.** Just select the control and click the lightning bolt in the Properties window. You'll see a list of all the events provided by that control. Double-click in the box next to the event you want to handle, and Visual Studio .NET will automatically generate the event handler in your page class.

The second and third options are the most convenient. The third option is the most flexible, because it allows you to select a method in the page class that you've already created. Just select the event in the Properties window and click the drop-down arrow at the right. You'll see a list that includes all the methods in your class that match the signature this event requires. You can then choose a method from the list to connect it. Figure 3-17 shows an example where the Button.Click event is connected to the Button_Click() method in your page class. The only limitation of this technique is that it only applies to web controls, not server-side HTML controls.

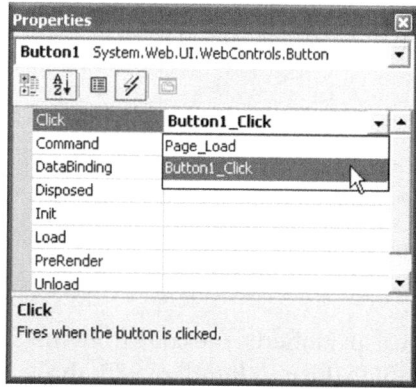

Figure 3-17. *Attaching an event handler*

It's important to understand that once you've created an event handler, you still need to connect the event handler to the appropriate event. In Visual Studio .NET, this task is performed when the page is initialized. When you use Visual Studio .NET to attach an event handler (either by double-clicking a control or using the Properties window), Visual Studio .NET generates the code you need and adds it to the page class. This code is inserted in a special collapsible region titled Web Form Designer generated code. In order to see this code in your web page, you need to expand it by clicking the plus symbol next to this region title.

Here's what you'll see:

```
#region Web Form Designer generated code
override protected void OnInit(EventArgs e)
    {
    //
    // CODEGEN: This call is required by the ASP.NET Web Forms Designer.
    //
    InitializeComponent();
    base.OnInit(e);
}

/// <summary>
/// Required method for Designer support - do not modify
/// the contents of this method with the code editor.
```

```
/// </summary>
private void InitializeComponent()
{
    this.Load += new System.EventHandler(this.Page_Load);
}
#endregion
```

In this example, the automatically generated code attaches a single event handler for the Page.Load event. As you insert more controls and attach more event handlers, you'll see additional lines added to the InitializeComponent() method.

Tip Now that you understand how Visual Studio .NET connects events, you'll understand the source of a very common problem. If you create an event handler and then remove the method, you'll receive a compile-time error because the delegate code still remains—it just points to a method that doesn't exist. To remedy this problem, you simply need to remove the line that attempts to attach the event handler, which is where the problem occurs.

UNDERSTANDING DELEGATES

To connect event handlers, Visual Studio .NET uses a code construct called *delegates*. A delegate is a type that defines the signature of a method (in other words, the return value and the list of parameters that method uses). In the previous example, System.EventHandler is a delegate in the .NET class library. It defines a signature with no return value, and two parameters, as shown here:

```
private void Function(object sender, System.EventArgs e)
```

Using a delegate type, you can create a delegate variable. The delegate variable acts like a function pointer, except it can only point to functions that match the delegate signature. In the previous example, a new delegate variable is created with the new keyword, pointing to the this.Page_Load() method.

Once you've created and assigned a delegate variable, you can use it to subscribe to an event. To accomplish this, you need to use the += operator. If you accidentally use just the = operator, a compile-time error will occur. That's because setting a delegate in this fashion would remove all the other event listeners, preventing any other event handlers from receiving the event. For that reason, it's not allowed.

All these steps—creating the delegate variable, assigning it, and using it to register for the event—are accomplished in a single line of code in the initialization section of the page, as follows:

```
this.Load += new System.EventHandler(this.Page_Load);
```

As you'll see in the following chapters, there are some cases in which you'll want to attach event handlers dynamically using delegate code, rather than relying on Visual Studio .NET. In addition, in Part Four you'll see how to define your own delegates and use them to raise events from custom controls.

Using AutoEventWireup Instead of Delegates

Visual Studio .NET connects all event handlers explicitly, using delegate code. To signal this fact to ASP.NET, it adds the AutoEventWireup attribute to the Page directive, and sets it to false, as shown here:

```
<%@ Page Language="CS" Inherits="SamplePage" Codebehind="SamplePage.aspx.cs"
    AutoEventWireup="false" %>
```

This attributes suggests that there is another way to connect control events, and indeed there is. In fact, Web Matrix uses a different approach, as do most developers who code web forms by hand using a simple text editor. This approach is *automatic event wireup*, and it has two basic principles:

- All page event handlers are connected automatically based on the name of the event handler. In other words, the Page_Load() method is automatically called when the page loads.

- All control event handlers are connected using attributes in the control tag. The attribute has the same name as the event, prefixed by the word "On".

For example, if you want to handle the ServerClick event of the Convert button, you simply need to set the OnServerClick attribute in the control tag with the name of the event handler you want to use. Here's the change you need:

```
<input type="submit" value="OK" id="Convert"
  OnServerClick="Convert_ServerClick" runat="server">
```

ASP.NET controls always use this syntax, and they give the attribute the event name preceded by the word "On". For example, if you want to handle an event named ServerChange, you'd set an attribute in the control tag named OnServerChange. Additionally, because ASP.NET must connect the event handlers, the derived Page class must be able to access the code-behind class. That means your event handlers must be declared with the protected or public keyword. When you connect event handlers using delegate code, you don't have this restriction.

Project Settings

There are several types of project-wide settings that you can configure. One of the most important is setting your *start page*. The start page isn't necessarily the page that users will start with when they use the application—that depends on the URL that they use. Instead, the start page is the page that Visual Studio .NET will launch automatically when you launch your application inside the development environment. To set a start page, right-click the page in the Solution Explorer and select Set as Start Page.

To access the full set of project properties, right-click your project in the Solution Explorer and select Properties (or select Project ➤ Properties from the menu). The window shown in Figure 3-18 will appear.

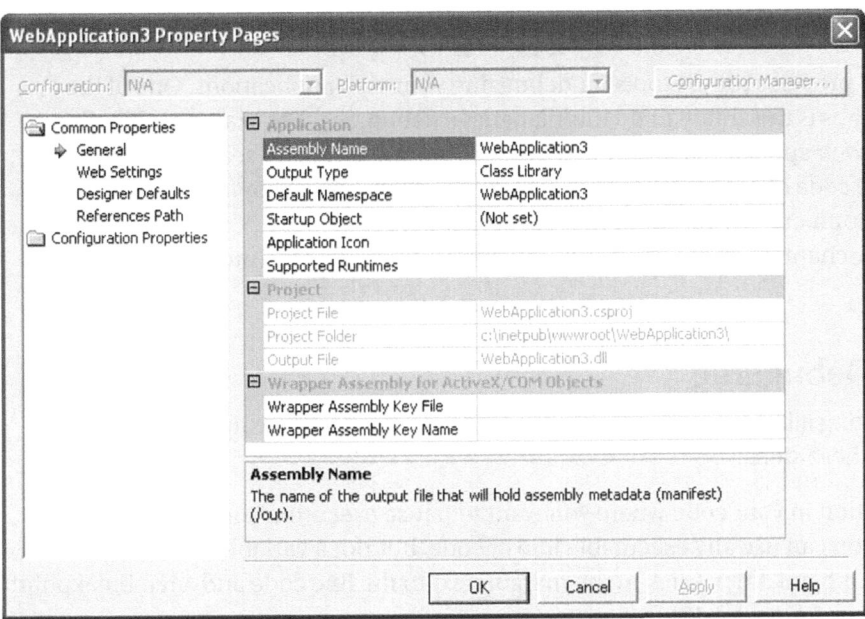

Figure 3-18. *Project properties*

There are two groups of project settings: Common Properties, which always apply, and Configuration Properties, which are tied to a specific configuration mode (for example, release mode or debug mode). You can choose the current configuration mode from a drop-down list in the toolbar.

Some common settings include

- The Assembly Name setting in the General tab specifies the name of the DLL file that VS .NET generates and places in the Bin directory. Remember, the name of this file doesn't have any effect on the user. However, it might be important for code versioning and deployment policies.

- The Output Type setting in the General tab will always be Class Library. That's because a web application is not a standalone executable, but a DLL that the ASP.NET engine loads in response to a user request.

- The Default Namespace setting in the General tab specifies the namespace that Visual Studio .NET will use when you add new web pages or classes to your project. No matter what the default, you can always change the name of the namespace in these files after you generate them.

- The Page Layout setting in the Designer Defaults tab sets the default type of alignment (Grid or Flow Layout) that Visual Studio .NET will use when you add new pages.

Visual Studio .NET Debugging

Visual Studio .NET provides robust tools for debugging your web applications. One of the most exciting features is the ability to do multilanguage debugging. For example, this allows you to create a C# web application that calls a VB .NET component, and seamlessly step through the source code of both applications. This is one of the most remarkable advantages of the shared development environment that VS .NET provides.

In the next few chapters, you'll learn about the basic debugging techniques in Visual Studio .NET.

Single-Step Debugging

Single-step debugging allows you to execute your code one line at a time. It's incredibly easy to use. Just follow these steps:

1. Find a location in your code where you want to pause execution, and start single-stepping (you can use any executable line of code, but not a variable declaration, comment, or blank line). Click in the margin next to the line code and a red breakpoint will appear (see Figure 3-19).

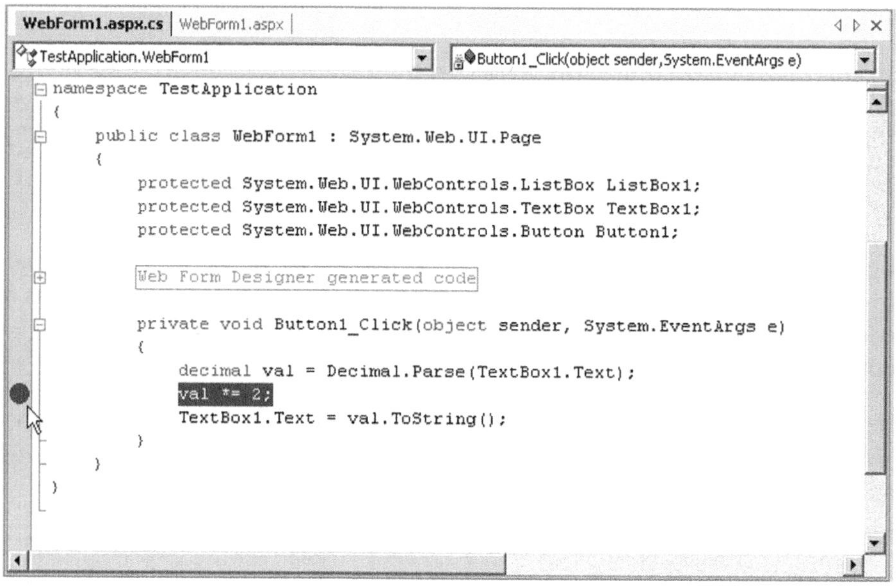

Figure 3-19. *Setting a breakpoint*

2. Now start your program as you would ordinarily. When the program reaches your breakpoint, execution will pause, and you'll be switched back the Visual Studio .NET code window. The breakpoint statement won't be executed.

3. At this point, you have several options. You can execute the current line by pressing F11. The following line in your code will be highlighted with a yellow arrow, indicating that this is the next line that will be executed. You can continue like this through your program, running one line at a time by pressing F11, and following the code's path of execution. Or, you can exit break mode and resume running your code by pressing F5.

Note Instead of using shortcut keys like F11 and F5, you can use the buttons in the Visual Studio .NET Debug toolbar. Alternatively, you can right-click the code window and choose an option from the context menu.

4. Whenever the code is in break mode, you can hover over variables to see their current contents (see Figure 3-20). This allows you to verify that variables contain the values you expect.

5. You can also use any of the commands listed in Table 3-6 while in break mode. These commands are available from the context menu by right-clicking the code window, or by using the associated hot key.

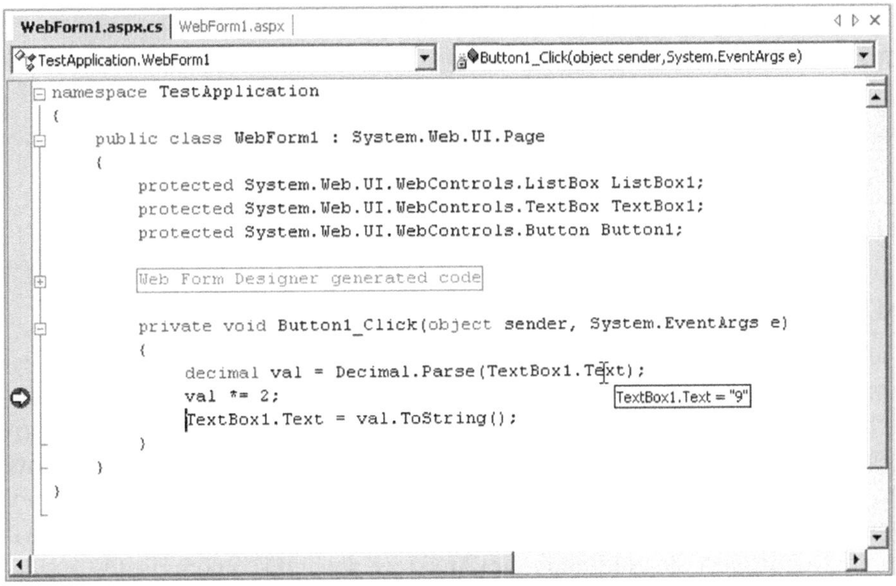

Figure 3-20. *Viewing variable contents in break mode*

Table 3-6. *Commands Available in Break Mode*

Command (Hot Key)	Description
Step Into (F11)	Executes the currently highlighted line and then pauses. If the currently highlighted line calls a procedure, execution will pause at the first executable line inside the method or function (which is why this feature is called stepping "into").
Step Over (F10)	The same as Step Into, except that it runs procedures as though they are a single line. If you press Step Over while a procedure call is highlighted, the entire procedure will be executed. Execution will pause at the next executable statement in the current procedure.

Continued

Table 3-6. *Continued*

Command (Hot Key)	Description
Step Out (Shift+F11)	Executes all the code in the current procedure, and then pauses at the statement that immediately follows the one that called this method or function. In other words, this allows you to step "out" of the current procedure in one large jump.
Continue (F5)	Resumes the program and continues to run it normally without pausing until another breakpoint is reached.
Run to Cursor	Allows you to run all the code up to a specific line (where your cursor is currently positioned). You can use this technique to skip a time-consuming loop.
Set Next Statement	Allows you to change the path of execution of your program while debugging. It causes your program to mark the current line (where your cursor is positioned) as the current line for execution. When you resume execution, this line will be executed, and the program will continue from that point.
Show Next Statement	Moves focus to the line of code that is marked for execution. This line is marked by a yellow arrow. The Show Next Statement command is useful if you lose your place while editing.

You can switch your program into break mode at any point by clicking the pause button in the toolbar or selecting Debug ➤ Break All.

Advanced Breakpoints

Choose Debug ➤ Windows ➤ Breakpoints to see a window that lists all the breakpoints in your current project. The Breakpoints window provides a hit count, showing you the number of times a breakpoint has been encountered (see Figure 3-21). You can jump to the corresponding location in code by double-clicking a breakpoint. You can also use the Breakpoints window to disable a breakpoint without removing it. That allows you to keep a breakpoint to use in testing later, without leaving it active. Breakpoints are automatically saved with the Visual Studio .NET project files, although they aren't used when you compile the application in release mode.

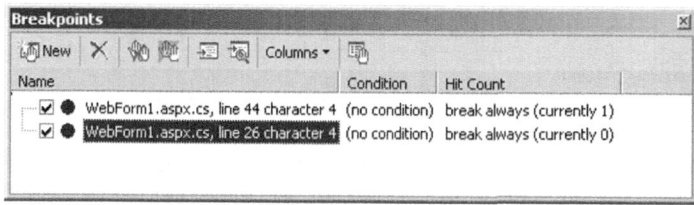

Figure 3-21. *The Breakpoints window*

Visual Studio .NET allows you to customize breakpoints so they only occur if certain conditions are true. To customize a breakpoint, right-click it and select Breakpoint Properties. In the window that appears you can take one of the following actions:

- Click the Condition button to set an expression. You can choose to break when this expression is true or when it has changed since the last time the breakpoint was hit.

- Click the Hit Count button to create a breakpoint that only pauses after a breakpoint has been hit a certain number of times (for example, at least 20), or a specific multiple of times (for example, every fifth time).

Variable Watches

In some cases, you might want to track the status of a variable without switching into break mode repeatedly. In this case, it's more useful to use the Autos, Locals, and Watch windows, which allow you track variables across an entire application. These windows are described in Table 3-7.

Table 3-7. *Variable Watch Windows*

Window	Description
Locals	Automatically displays all the variables that are in scope in the current procedure. This offers a quick summary of important variables.
Autos	Automatically displays variables that VS .NET determines are important for the current code statement. For example, this might include variables that are accessed or changed in the previous line.
Watch	Displays variables you have added. Watches are saved with your project, so you can continue tracking a variable at a later time. To add a watch, right-click a variable in your code and select Add Watch, or double-click the last row in the Watch window and type in the variable name.

Each row in the Locals, Autos, and Watch windows provides information about the type or class of the variable and its current value. If the variable holds an object instance, you can expand the variable and see its private members and properties. For example, in the Locals window you'll see the this variable, which is a reference to the current page class. If you click the plus (+) box next to this, a full list will appear that describes many page properties (and some system values), as shown in Figure 3-22.

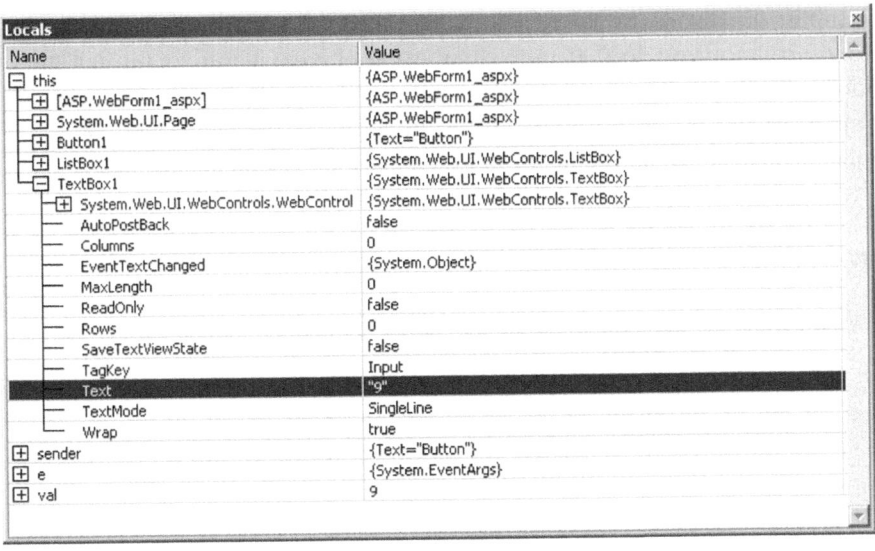

Figure 3-22. *Viewing the current page class in the Locals window*

If you are missing one of the Watch windows, you can show it manually by selecting it from the Debug ➤ Windows submenu.

Tip The Watch, Locals, and Autos windows allow you to change simple variables while your program is in break mode. Just double-click the current value in the Value column, and type in a new value. This allows you to simulate scenarios that are difficult or time consuming to re-create manually, or test specific error conditions.

Resource Checking

Resource checking allows you to get additional types of information while your project is in debug mode. For example, the Call Stack window allows you to view the position your code is in with relation to other methods that are still open and unfinished. (For example, if method A() calls method B(), while B() is executing there are two methods on the stack.)

To display the call stack select Debug ➤ Windows ➤ Call Stack. Figure 3-23 shows an example in which the Page_Load() event handler has called a method named A(), which in turn called a method named B().

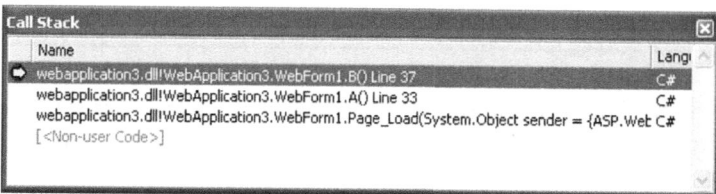

Figure 3-23. *The call stack*

The default call stack display includes the assembly name, class name, and line number, although you can simplify the display by right-clicking the Call Stack window and clearing the checkmarks next to information you don't want to show. Another great feature of the call stack is the ability to double-click any method and move instantly to that part of the code.

Another type of resource checking is found in the Modules window (select Debug ➤ Windows ➤ Modules). This window shows the EXEs and DLLs loaded that are currently serving the code that you're running. Figure 3-24 shows an example.

Name	Path	Order	Version
mscorlib.dll	c:\windows\microsoft.net\framewor...	1	1.1.4322.573
system.web.dll	c:\windows\assembly\gac\system.w...	2	1.1.4322.573
system.dll	c:\windows\assembly\gac\system\1....	3	1.1.4322.573
system.enterpriseservices.dll	c:\windows\assembly\gac\system.e...	4	1.1.4322.573
system.enterpriseservices.thunk.dll	c:\windows\assembly\gac\system.e...	5	1.1.4322.573
system.data.dll	c:\windows\assembly\gac\system.d...	6	1.1.4322.573
system.drawing.dll	c:\windows\assembly\gac\system.dr...	7	1.1.4322.573
system.xml.dll	c:\windows\assembly\gac\system.x...	8	1.1.4322.573
system.web.regularexpressions.dll	c:\windows\assembly\gac\system.w...	9	1.1.4322.573

Figure 3-24. *The currently loaded modules*

One benefit of this window is being able to verify what version of a DLL file your code is actually using.

The other resource-checking windows are more specialized. For example, if you're writing multithreaded code, you can examine and control threads in the program you're debugging (select Debug ➤ Windows ➤ Threads). The Threads window allows you to set the active thread, or temporarily disable a thread you don't want to execute. Another interesting option is the disassembly view, which shows the current machine code for a method (select Debug ➤ Windows ➤ Disassembly).

Debugging Problems

In order to debug a web application with Visual Studio .NET, you must meet a few specific requirements. If these requirements aren't met, you'll receive an "unable to start debugging" error message when you attempt to start the application. This error signals that Visual Studio .NET was able to compile the web application, but can't execute it in debug mode.

Unfortunately, a dizzying range of different problems can cause this error. The following are some possible causes:

- IIS (Internet Information Services), the Windows component that hosts web applications, isn't installed or is installed incorrectly.

- The user running Visual Studio .NET isn't a member of the Debugger Users group for the web server.

- The user running Visual Studio .NET doesn't have permission to debug the ASP.NET process. For example, if the ASP.NET process is running under the local system account, the user must have administrator privileges to debug it.

- The web application doesn't have a web.config file, or the web.config file doesn't enable debugging.

- You have more than one version of ASP.NET installed, and the IIS mapping for the current virtual directory is for a version of ASP.NET that doesn't match the version of Visual Studio .NET you're using.

The first step that you should take when diagnosing this error is to verify that IIS and ASP.NET are installed correctly. Try to run your application by selecting Debug ➤ Start Without Debugging from the Visual Studio .NET menu. If your web application still doesn't execute properly, or a blank or garbled page appears, you may need to repair IIS mapping, as described in Chapter 2. If your web application *does* run properly, continue with the following steps to enable debugging.

The next step is to verify that the virtual directory exists and is correctly configured in IIS. Problems can occur if you've changed the virtual directory settings or removed it. To investigate in more detail, start the IIS Manager utility by selecting Settings ➤ Control Panel ➤ Administrative Tools ➤ Internet Information Services from the Start menu. Find the virtual directory you're using, right-click it, and choose Properties.

First, verify that the virtual directory is configured as web application. If you see the Remove button in the Application Settings section, the directory is configured correctly.

If you see the Create button instead, the directory isn't configured correctly. Click Create to designate the virtual directory as a web application, and then try to run your web application in Visual Studio .NET.

Finally, if the problem persists, you should check that you have a correctly configured web.config file. The web.config file should follow the structure shown here:

```
<configuration>
    <system.web>
        <compilation defaultLanguage="c#" debug="true" >
    <!- Other settings omitted. ->
    </system.web>
</configuration>
```

By default, Visual Studio .NET adds the compilation tag to the automatically generated web.config file with the debug setting set to true.

For more information, refer to the Microsoft white paper at http://msdn.microsoft.com/library/en-us/vsdebug/html/vxtbshttpservererrors.asp, which describes these steps and some other troubleshooting steps for remote servers.

Extending Visual Studio .NET

Visual Studio .NET is a highly extensible application. In fact, it's far more customizable than any previous version, allowing you to write .NET-based add-ins in any language and write managed macros using VB .NET (but not C#) code. In this final section, you'll take a quick tour of a few of the many extensibility options.

Creating Macros

One of the most exciting "frills" of the new Visual Studio .NET development environment is its powerful macro and add-in framework. This framework, known as the Visual Studio .NET Automation model, provides almost 200 objects that give you unprecedented control over the IDE, including the ability to access and manipulate the current project hierarchy, the collection of open windows, and the integrated debugger. One of the most convenient and flexible Automation tools is the macro facility.

The simplest macro is a keystroke recording. To create a simple keystroke macro, select Tools ➤ Macros ➤ Record Temporary Macro from the Visual Studio .NET menu, and type in the appropriate keystrokes. Once you're finished, click the stop button on the floating macro toolbar. You can now replay the recorded macro (with the Ctrl+Shift+P shortcut key).

■**Note** Visual Studio only allows one recorded macro, which is overwritten every time you record a new one. To make a temporary macro permanent, you'll need to cut and paste the code into a different subroutine.

A good way to start learning about macros is to use the record facility, and then look at the code it generates. Select Tool ➤ Macros ➤ Macro Explorer to see a window that shows a tree of macro modules, and the macros they contain (as shown in Figure 3-25). Each macro corresponds to a VB .NET subroutine. (Unfortunately, C# is, as of yet, not supported.) To edit the macro you just created, right-click the TemporaryMacro subroutine in the RecordingModule and select Edit.

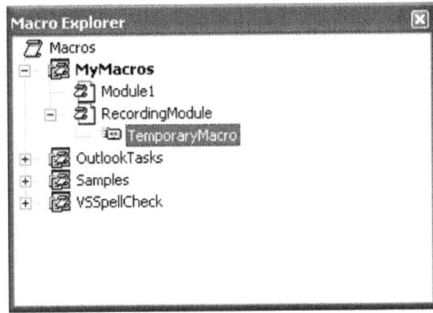

Figure 3-25. *The Macro Explorer*

Macro code makes heavy use of a special DTE (design-time environment) object model. The DTE hierarchy provides the core features that allow you to interact with every aspect of the IDE. Some of the ingredients at your fingertips include the following:

- Window objects (used to close, rearrange, or otherwise manipulate open windows)

- Document objects (used to edit text)

- Solution and project objects (used to manage the underlying files and project collection)

- Tool-window objects (used to configure the IDE's interface)

- Debugging objects (used for tasks like creating breakpoints and halting execution)

- Event objects (used to react to IDE events)

- Code-manipulation objects (used to analyze your project's code constructs)

For example, the following macro automatically displays a list of all the files in the project that have been modified but not saved. The list is shown in the Output window.

```
Sub ListModifiedDocuments()
    Dim win As Window = DTE.Windows.Item(Constants.vsWindowKindCommandWindow)
    Dim target As Object

    ' If the current window window is an Output window, use it. Otherwise, use a
    ' helper function find and activate the window.
    If (DTE.ActiveWindow Is win) Then
        target = win.Object
    Else
        target = GetOutputWindowPane("Modified Documents")
        target.clear()
    End If
```

```
' Loop through all the open documents, and if unsaved changes are detected,
' write the document name to the output window.
Dim doc As Document
For Each doc In DTE.Documents
    If Not doc.Saved Then
        target.OutputString(doc.Name & "   " & doc.FullName & _
            Microsoft.VisualBasic.Constants.vbCrLf)
    End If
Next
End Sub
```

Figure 3-26 shows the result of running this macro.

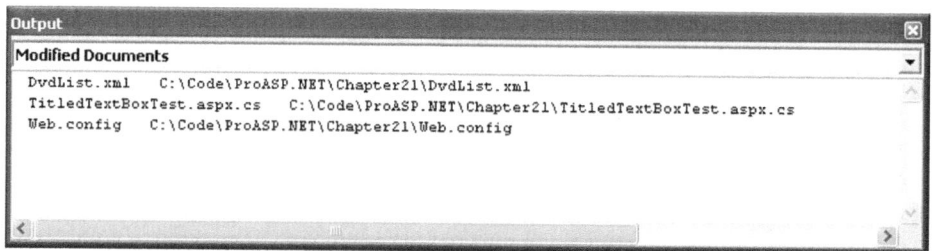

Figure 3-26. *Detecting changed documents*

This is only one of several dozen useful macros that are included in the Samples macro project, which is included with Visual Studio .NET 2003 (and the code download for this chapter).

■**Tip** You can download a wide array of useful Visual Studio .NET macros and add-ins from `http://msdn.microsoft.com/vstudio/downloads/samples`. These samples can do everything from automating the build process to integrating with Outlook and spell-checking the text in your user interface! In addition, a number of simpler macros are included with Visual Studio .NET 2003 (look for the Samples macro project).

Extending Dynamic Help

One of the most remarkable aspects of Dynamic Help is the way you can extend it to show additional links and help topics that you've created. These techniques can be used for any VS .NET installation, but they are most useful for the following types of people:

- Component developers who want to provide integrated support for their add-ins.

- Project managers who want to provide links for coding conventions and internal processes directly in VS .NET.

- Instructors who want to equip classroom computers with links to handouts, projects, or other information.

Adding a new topic to the Dynamic Help list is as simple as copying a file into a directory. The directory depends on where Visual Studio .NET is installed. Typically, this directory is c:\Program Files\Microsoft Visual Studio .NET 2003\Common7\IDE\HTML\XMLLinks\1033. The number 1033 is the LCID (locale identifier) for English-language systems. If you have installed an international version of VS .NET, this number will differ.

Initially, there will only be a couple of files in this directory that correspond to the default Dynamic Help categories. To add new links, you simply need to add a new XML file into this directory. No registry changes or other modifications are required, which makes it easy to install a VS .NET help extension with a typical product setup. On the other hand, because help extensions are file-based, you have to be careful to choose a file name that won't conflict with another vendor. Try to incorporate your company and product name (as in ACME_CustomWidget.xml).

At its simplest, a help extension file looks something like this:

```
<?xml version="1.0" encoding="utf-8" ?>
<DynamicHelp xmlns="http://msdn.microsoft.com/vsdata/xsd/vsdh.xsd"
  xmlns:xsi="http://www.w3.org/2000/10/XMLSchema-instance"
  xsi:schemaLocation="http://msdn.microsoft.com/vsdata/xsd/vsdh.xsd">
  <Context>
    <Keywords>
      <KItem Name="VS.Ambient" />
    </Keywords>
    <Links>
      <LItem URL="http://www.apress.com"
        LinkGroup="GettingStarted">Apress Website</LItem>
    </Links>
  </Context>
</DynamicHelp>
```

This help file includes the following ingredients:

- A root <DynamicHelp> element that contains all the information.

- A <Context> element, which contains all the links and their context information.

- A <Keywords> element, which sets the scope of the links. The <Keywords> element can contain one or more <KItem> elements. If any one of these <KItem> elements corresponds to a keyword that the Dynamic Help system is currently generating, the topics will be added to the window. The previous example uses VS.Ambient, which is always emitted by the Dynamic Help system when Visual Studio is running.

- A <Links> element, which specifies one or more hyperlinks (as <LItem> elements) to add to the window. In the previous example, one link is added. It displays the text "Apress Website."

This is the bare minimum amount of information you need. It you leave out any of these tags, your file will be ignored. Save this file into the XML help extension directory, and restart Visual Studio. You will see the link appear in the Getting Started group in the Dynamic Help window (see Figure 3-27). If you click it, a window with the Apress home page will appear.

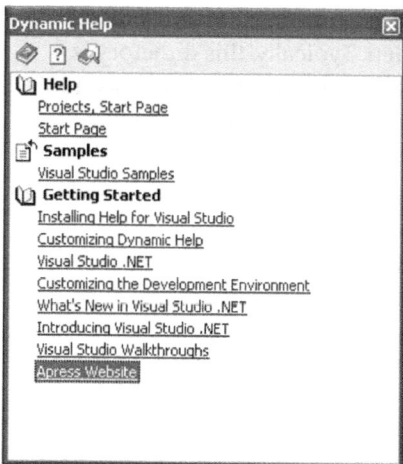

Figure 3-27. *Extending Dynamic Help*

Customizing VS .NET Using Template Policy

When you create a project for the first time, Visual Studio .NET always supplies a few predefined files (unless you choose a blank solution). Visual Studio .NET creates these files based on a template definition.

The following is the list of some of the project templates that are available when developing in C#:

- Windows Application

- Class Library

- Windows Control Library

- ASP.NET Web Application

- ASP.NET Web Service

- Web Control Library

- Console Application

- Windows Service

You can also set up your own templates using an *enterprise template policy*. Template policy allows software architects and teams to give a common look and feel to each of their projects when they are first created. For example, if your team has common components that they use with every project, then you can create a specialized template that automatically includes references to these components. Templates aren't limited to defining the set of initial files—they can also define behavior and options for menus, toolbars, and so on. You can configure what options the Visual Studio .NET environment provides. Best of all, the rules mechanism is set using an XML file, which can be copied onto other computers with VS .NET at any time.

To learn about Visual Studio .NET policy, it helps to try a simple example. In this example, you'll create a new policy document that disables a single menu option.

First, look in the directory C:\Program Files\Microsoft Visual Studio .NET 2003\ EnterpriseFrameworks\Policy for the following two files:

- **DAP.tdl.** This file contains the default template policy.

- **VSIDE.tdl.** This file contains all the possible policy items that are available.

Begin by copying the default document DAP.tdl and renaming it to MyPolicy.tdl. Now open it using Notepad. You'll see that it contains formatted XML content. This XML document controls the menu and interface definitions for VS .NET.

Search in the MyPolicy.tdl file for the following element:

```
<ID>projVBProject</ID>
```

Once you have found it, immediately type the following lines below it:

```
<ID>projCSharpProject</ID>
<CONSTRAINTS>
    <MENUCONSTRAINTS>
        <MENUCONSTRAINT>
            <ID>menuProject.NewFolder</ID>
            <ENABLED>0</ENABLED>
        </MENUCONSTRAINT>
    </MENUCONSTRAINTS>
</CONSTRAINTS>
```

By adding these lines, you've effectively defined a rule that prevents a developer from creating a new folder within a C# project. This rule is defined simply by adding the <MENUCONSTRAINTS> element at the right position within the policy template. The reason this rule is limited to C# projects is because the rule is placed in the policy template section with the ID projCSharpProject.

You'll also notice the ID for the menu is menuProject.NewFolder. This name refers to another section later in the same policy template file. If you search for this section, you'll see that it contains this text:

```
<MENU>
    <ID>menuProject.NewFolder</ID>
    <CMDID>245</CMDID>
    <GUID>{5EFC7975-14BC-11CF-9B2B-00AA00573819}</GUID>
</MENU>
```

Essentially, this section links the menuProject.NewFolder item to a specific GUID and ID that represent the feature you want to disable.

To see this at work, load VS .NET and create a simple C# project (any type). Then right-click your mouse on the project name and select Add. You'll see the full list of options for creating files and directories. That's because by default VS .NET uses the DAP.tdl template, which still allows the New Folder menu item to be enabled.

Now select the project name in the Solution Explorer, and find the Policy File property in the Properties window (see Figure 3-28). Set this file to be the newly copied policy template you have created (MyPolicy.tdl).

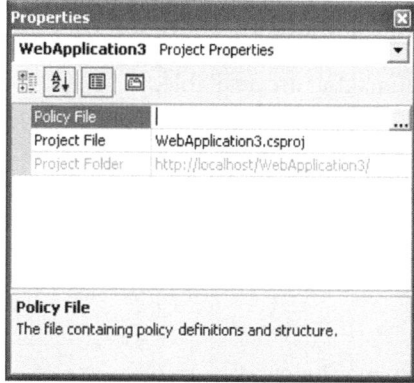

Figure 3-28. *Applying a new policy*

When you enter a new policy document, you'll be prompted to reload the solution. When you do, the new policy will come into effect. To see what this has accomplished, right-click the project name. You'll find that the menu option for New Folder has now been disabled according to the new policy.

■**Tip** Clearly, enterprise templates provide an advanced and detailed set of features. You can learn more about how to implement templates and their rules at `http://msdn.microsoft.com/vstudio/teamsystem/templates`.

Summary

This chapter considered the role that VS .NET can play in helping you develop your web applications. At the same time that you explored its rich design-time environment, you also learned about how it works behind the scenes with the new code-behind model, and how to extend it with time-saving features like macros. If you're interested in learning more about how to customize Visual Studio .NET, you may be interested in *Inside Visual Studio .NET* (Microsoft Press), which covers macros and more advanced extensibility features. In the next two chapters, you'll jump into full-fledged ASP.NET coding with an examination of web pages and server controls.

CHAPTER 4

The ASP.NET Page

Most developers who are familiar with classic ASP consider a page to be the HTML and ASP code contained in a single ASP file. The page processing for ASP files is pretty simple—the ASP ISAPI extension interprets code blocks and executes them piece by piece, starting at the top of the file and moving down to the bottom. Occasionally, classic ASP pages are a little more complex, and they use subroutines, include files, and COM components to extend their reach. However, the page processing in ASP always uses a straightforward, linear model.

ASP.NET pages (officially called *web forms*) are quite a bit different. They are more sophisticated in terms of the functionality they provide, but they are actually much simpler and more elegant in terms of the coding model they expose to the developer. Essentially, web forms allow you to create a web application using the same control-based interfaces and event-based logic as a Windows application.

This chapter provides an in-depth introduction to web forms. You'll learn what they are, how they work, and how to make them work for you. You'll also get an in-depth first look at the page-processing life cycle and the ASP.NET server-side control model.

Page Processing

One of the key goals of ASP.NET is to create a model that lets web developers rapidly develop web forms in the same way that Windows developers can build made-to-measure windows in a desktop application. Of course, web applications are far different from traditional rich client applications. There are two key stumbling blocks:

- **Web applications only execute on the server.** For example, suppose you create a form that allows the user to select a product record and update its information. The user performs these tasks in the browser, but in order for you to perform the required operations (like updating the database), your code needs to run on the web server. ASP.NET handles this divide with a technique called *postback*, which sends the page (and all user-supplied information) back to the server whenever certain actions are performed. Once ASP.NET receives the page, it can then fire the corresponding server-side events to notify your code.

- **Web applications are stateless.** In other words, before the rendered HTML page is sent to the user, your web-page objects are destroyed and all client-specific information is discarded. This model lends itself well to highly scalable, heavily trafficked applications, but it makes it difficult to create a seamless user experience. ASP.NET includes several tools to help you bridge this gap, notably including the new *view state* mechanism, which automatically embeds information about the page in a hidden field in the rendered HTML.

In the following sections, you'll learn about both the postback and view state features. Together, these mechanisms help to abstract the underlying HTML and HTTP details, allowing the developer to work in terms of objects and events.

HTML Forms

If you're familiar with HTML, you know that the simplest way to send client-side data back to the server is using a <form> tag. Inside the <form> tag, you can place other <input> tags to represent basic UI ingredients like buttons, text boxes, list boxes, check boxes, and radio buttons.

For example, here's a form tag with a submit button, two check boxes, a text box, and a button, for a total of five <input> tags:

```
<html>
    <head>
        <title>Programmer Questionnaire</title>
    </head>
    <body>
        <form method="post" action="page.aspx">
            <p>Enter your first name: 
            <input type="text" name="FirstName"/><br>
            Enter your last name: 
            <input type="text" name="LastName"/><p>
            <p>You program with:<br>
               
            <input type="checkbox" name="C"/>C#<br>
               
            <input type="checkbox" name="VB"/>VB .NET<br><br>
            <input type="submit" value="Submit" id="OK"/>
            </p>
        </form>
    </body>
</html>
```

Figure 4-1 shows what this basic page looks like in a web browser.

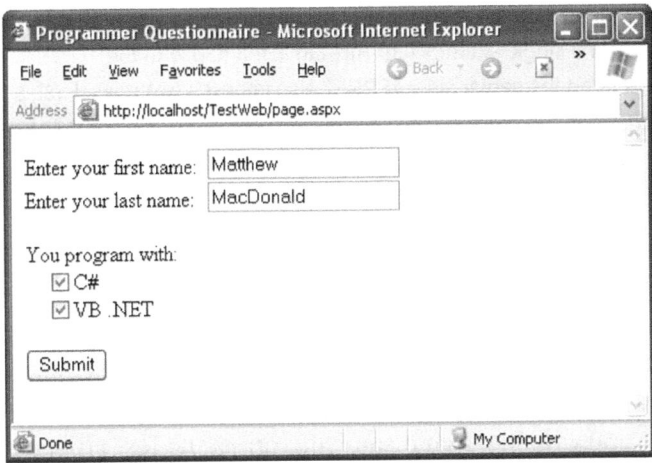

Figure 4-1. *A simple HTML form*

When the user clicks the submit button, the browser collects the current value of each control, and pastes it together in a long string. This string is then sent pack to the page indicated in the <form> tag (in this case, page.aspx) using an HTTP POST operation.

In this example, that means the web server might receive a request with this string of information:

```
FirstName=Matthew&LastName=MacDonald&C=on&VB=on
```

The browser follows certain rules when constructing this string. For example, check boxes are left out unless they are checked, in which case the browser supplies the text "on" for the value. For the complete lowdown on the HTML forms standard, which is supported in every current browser, surf to www.w3.org/TR/REC-html40/interact/forms.html.

Virtually all server-side programming frameworks add a layer of abstraction over the raw form data. They parse this string and expose it in a more useful way. For example, JSP, ASP, and ASP.NET all allow you to retrieve the value of a form control using a thin object layer. In ASP and ASP.NET, you can look up values by name in the Request.Form collection. Here's an example in ASP.NET:

```
string firstName = Request.Form["FirstName"];
```

This thin veneer over the actual POST message is helpful, but it's still a long way from a true object-oriented framework. That's why ASP.NET goes another leap further. When a page is posted back to ASP.NET, it extracts the values, populates the Form collection (for backward compatibility with ASP code), and then configures the corresponding control objects. That means you can use the following much more intuitive syntax to retrieve information:

```
string firstName = txtFirstName.Text;
```

This code also has the benefit of being typesafe. In other words, if you're retrieving the state of the check box, you'll receive a Boolean true or false value, instead of a string with the word "on".

■**Note** In ASP.NET, all controls are placed inside a single <form> tag. This tag is marked with the runat="server" attribute, which allows it to work on the server side. ASP.NET also imposes two rules. First, a web form can only contain a single server-side form tag. Second, the <form> tag always posts back to the original page. As you'll see in this chapter, that's the bare minimum requirement for ASP.NET's new view state mechanism.

Dynamic Interfaces

Clearly, the control model makes life easier for retrieving form information. What's even more remarkable is how it simplifies your life when you need to *add* information to a page. Almost all web-control properties are readable and writable. That means you can set the Text property of a text box just as easily as you can read it.

For example, consider what happens if you want to update a piece of text on a web page to reflect some information the user has entered earlier. In classic ASP, you would need to find a convenient place to insert a script block that would write the raw HTML. Here's an example that displays a brightly colored welcome message:

```
string message = "<span style=\"color:Red\">Welcome " +
  FirstName + " " + LastName + "</span>";
Response.Write(message);
```

On the other hand, life is much neater when you define a Label control:

```
<asp:Label id="lblWelcome" runat="server" />
```

Now you can simply set its properties:

```
lblWelcome.Text = "Welcome " + FirstName + " " + LastName;
lblWelcome.ForeColor = Color.Red;
```

This code has several key advantages. First of all, it's much easier to write (and to write without errors). The savings seems fairly minor in this example, but they are much more dramatic when you consider a complete ASP.NET page that needs to dynamically render complex blocks of HTML that contain anchors, images, and styles.

Control-based code is also much easier to place inside a page. You can write your ASP.NET code wherever the corresponding action takes place. On the other hand, in classic ASP you need to worry about where the content appears on the page, and arrange your script blocks code appropriately. If a page has several dynamic regions, it can quickly become a tangled mess of script blocks that don't show any clear relation or organization.

Another, subtler but equally dramatic advantage to the control model is the way that it insulates you from the low-level HTML details. Not only does this allow you to write code without learning the quirks and idiosyncrasies of HTML, but it also allows your pages to support a wider range of browsers. Because the control renders itself, it has the ability to tailor its output to support different browsers, enhanced client-side features, or even HTML variants used in mobile platforms (like WML). Essentially, your code is no longer tightly coupled to the HTML standard.

■**Tip** Dynamic interface isn't limited to configuring controls. You can actually add completely new controls programmatically. In fact, there are several portal frameworks built on ASP.NET that build their entire interface dynamically based on user preferences. You'll learn about these techniques throughout this book.

The ASP.NET Event Model

Classic ASP uses a linear processing model. That means code on the page is processed from start to finish, and executed in order. Because of this model, classic ASP developers need to write a considerable amount of messy code even for simple pages. A classic example is a web page that has three different submit buttons, for three different operations. In this case, your script code has to carefully distinguish which button was pressed when the page is submitted, and execute the right action using conditional logic.

ASP.NET provides a refreshing change with its new *event-driven* model. In this model, you add controls to a web form, and then decide what events you want to respond to. Each event handler is wrapped up in a discrete method, which keeps the page code tidy and organized. This model is nothing new, but until the advent of ASP.NET it's been the exclusive domain of windowed UI programming in rich client applications.

So how do ASP.NET events work? It's actually surprisingly straightforward. Here's a brief outline:

1. Your page runs for the first time. ASP.NET creates page and control objects, the initialization code executes, and then the page is rendered to HTML and returned to the client. The page objects are also released from server memory.

2. At some point, the user does something that triggers a postback, like clicking a button. At this point, the page is submitted with all the form data.

3. ASP.NET intercepts the returned page, and re-creates the page objects, taking care to return them to the state they were in the last time the page was sent to the client.

4. Next ASP.NET checks what operation triggered the postback, and it raises the appropriate events (like Button.Click), which your code can react to. Typically, at this point you'll perform some server-side operation (such as updating a database or reading data from a file), and then modify the control objects to display new information.

5. The modified page is rendered to HTML and returned to the client. The page objects are released from memory. If another postback occurs, ASP.NET repeats the process in steps 2 through 4.

In other words, ASP.NET doesn't just use the form data to configure the control objects for your page. It also uses it to decide what events to fire. For example, if it notices the text in a text box has changed since the last postback, it raises an event to notify your page. It's up to you whether you want to respond to this event.

Keep in mind that since HTML is completely stateless, and all state made available by ASP.NET is reconstituted, the event-driven model is really emulation. ASP.NET performs quite a few tasks in the background in order to support this model, as you'll see in the following sections. The beauty of this concept is that the beginner programmer need not be familiar with the underpinnings of the system to take advantage of server-side events.

Note Many ASP programmers have been taught virtually since birth that round-trips are bad (because they consume server resources and additional bandwidth and cause time delays), and that the number of round-trips an application performs should be reduced at all cost. While, in general, that concept still holds true in that you should never needlessly create round-trips, the advanced functionality, ease of programming, and reduction in programming time created by this new way of page processing far outweighs the slight delays in processing that occur.

Automatic Postbacks

Of course, there's one gap in the event system described so far. Windows developers have long been accustomed to a rich event model that lets your code react to mouse movements, key presses, and the minutest control interactions. But in ASP.NET, client actions happen on the client side and server processing takes place on the web server. That means there's always a certain amount of overhead involved with responding to an event. For that reason, events that fire very rapidly (like a mouse move event) are completely impractical in the world of ASP.NET.

Note If you want to accomplish a certain UI effect, you might handle rapid events like mouse movements with client-side JavaScript (or, better yet, you might use a custom ASP.NET control that already has these smarts built in, like some sort of pop-up menu). However, all your business code must execute in the secure, feature-rich server environment.

If you're familiar with HTML forms, you know that there is one basic way to submit a page—by clicking a submit button. If you're using the standard HTML server controls, this is still your only option. However, once the page is posted back, ASP.NET can fire other events at the same time (namely events that indicate that the value in an input control has been changed).

Clearly, this isn't enough to build a rich web form. Fortunately, ASP.NET web controls extend this model with an *automatic postback* feature. With this feature, input controls can fire different events, and your server-side code can respond immediately. For example, you can trigger a postback when the user clicks a check box, changes the selection in a list, or changes the text in a text box and then moves to another field. These events still aren't as fine-grained as events in a Windows application, but they are a significant step up from the submit button.

Automatic Postbacks "Under the Hood"

In order to use automatic postback, you simply need to set the AutoPostBack property of a web control to true (the default is false, which ensures optimum performance if you don't need to react to a change event). When you do, ASP.NET uses the client-side abilities of JavaScript to bridge the gap between client-side and server-side code.

Here's how it works. If you create a web page that includes one or more web controls that are configured to use AutoPostBack, ASP.NET adds a JavaScript function to the rendered HTML page named __doPostBack(). When called, it triggers a postback, posting the page back to the web server with all the form information.

In order to support the __doPostBack() function, ASP.NET also adds two additional hidden input fields that are used to pass information back to the server. This information consists of the ID of the control that raised the event, and any additional information that might be relevant. These fields are initially empty, as shown here:

```
<input type="hidden" name="__EVENTTARGET" value="" />
<input type="hidden" name="__EVENTARGUMENT" value="" />
```

The __doPostBack() function has the responsibility for setting these values with the appropriate information about the event, and then submitting the form. A sample __doPostBack() function is shown here:

```
<script language="javascript">
<!-
    function __doPostBack(eventTarget, eventArgument) {
        var theform = document.Form1;
        theform.__EVENTTARGET.value = eventTarget;
        theform.__EVENTARGUMENT.value = eventArgument;
        theform.submit();
    }
// ->
</script>
```

Remember, ASP.NET generates the __doPostBack() function automatically. This code grows lengthier as you add more AutoPostBack controls to your page, because the event data must be set for each control.

Finally, any control that has its AutoPostBack property set to true is connected to the __doPostBack() function using the onClick or onChange attributes. These attributes indicate what action the browser should take in response to the client-side JavaScript events onClick and onChange.

The following example shows the tag for a list control named lstCountry, which posts back automatically. Whenever the user changes the selection in the list, the client side onChange event fires. The browser then calls the __doPostBack() function, which sends the page back to the server.

```
<select id="lstCountry" onchange="__doPostBack('lstBackColor','')"
 language="javascript">
```

In other words, ASP.NET automatically changes a client-side JavaScript event into a server-side ASP.NET event, using the __doPostBack() function as an intermediary. If you're a seasoned ASP developer, you may have manually created a solution like this for traditional ASP web pages. ASP.NET handles these details for you automatically, simplifying life a great deal.

■ **Tip**   Remember, ASP.NET includes two control models: the bare-bones HTML server controls and the more fully functional web controls. Automatic postback is only available with web controls.

View State

The final ingredient in the ASP.NET model is the new *view state* mechanism. View state solves another problem that occurs due to the stateless nature of HTTP—lost changes.

Every time your page is posted back, you receive all the information that the user has entered in any <input> controls in the <form> tag. ASP.NET then loads the web page in its original state (based on the layout and defaults that you've defined), and tweaks the page according to this new information. The problem is that in a dynamic web form, there's a lot more that your code might change. For example, you might programmatically change the color of a heading, modify a piece of static text, hide or show a panel of controls, or even bind a full table of data to a grid. All of these actions change the page from its initial state. However, none of them are reflected in the form data that's posted back. That means this information will be lost after every postback. Traditionally, statelessness has been overcome with the use of simple cookies, session-based cookies, and various other work-arounds. All of these mechanisms require homemade (and sometimes painstaking) measures.

In order to deal with this limitation, ASP.NET has devised its own integrated state serialization mechanism. Essentially, once your page code has finished running (and just before the final HTML is rendered and sent to the client), ASP.NET examines all the properties of all the controls on your page. If any of these properties has been changed from its initial state, ASP.NET makes a note of this information in a name/value collection. Finally, ASP.NET takes all the information it has amassed, and then serializes it as a Base64 string. (A Base64 string ensures that there aren't any special characters that wouldn't be valid HTML.) The final string is inserted in the <form> section of the page as a new hidden field.

When the page is posted back, ASP.NET follows these steps:

1. ASP.NET re-creates the page and control objects based on its defaults. Thus, the page has the same state that it had when it was first requested.

2. Next, ASP.NET deserializes the view state information, and updates all of the controls. This returns the page to the state it was in before it was sent to the client the last time.

3. Finally, ASP.NET adjusts the page according to the posted back form data. For example, if the client has entered new text in a text box or made a new selection in a list box, that information will be in the Form collection and ASP.NET will use it to tweak the corresponding controls. After this step, the page reflects the current state as it appears to the user.

4. Now your event-handling code can get involved. ASP.NET triggers the appropriate events, and your code can react to change the page, move to a new page, or perform a completely different operation.

Using view state is a great solution because server resources can be freed after each request, thereby allowing for scalability to support hundreds or thousands of requests without bogging the server down. However, there is still a price. Because view state is stored in the page, it results in a larger total page size. This affects the client doubly, because the client not only needs to receive a larger page, but the client also needs to send the hidden view-state data back to the server with the next postback. Thus, it takes longer both to receive and post the page. For simple pages, this overhead is minimal, but if you configure complex, lengthy controls such as the DataGrid, the view state information can grow to a size where it starts to exert a toll. In these cases, you can disable view state for a control by setting its EnableViewState property to false. However, this step means you need to reinitialize the control with each postback.

■**Note** It is absolutely essential to your success as an ASP.NET programmer that you remember that the web form is re-created with *every* round trip. It does not persist or remain in memory longer than it takes to render a single request.

You should also keep in mind that ASP.NET only uses view state with page and control properties. ASP.NET doesn't take the same steps with member variables and other data you might use. However, as you'll learn later in this book, you can place other types of data into view state and retrieve this information manually at a later time.

Figure 4-2 shows an end-to-end look at page requests that puts all these concepts together.

View State "Under the Hood"

If you look at the rendered HTML for an ASP.NET page, you can easily find the hidden input field with the view state information. The following example shows a page that uses a simple Label web control, and sets it with a dynamic "Hello World" message.

```
<html>
    <head>
        <title>Hello World Page</title>
    </head>
    <form name="Form1" method="post" action="WebForm1.aspx" id="Form1">
        <input type="hidden" name="__VIEWSTATE" value="dDwtNjI3MTUONjQyO3Q8O2w8aTwx
Pjs+O2w8dDw7bDxpPDM+Oz47bDxOPHA8cDxsPFRleHQ7PjtsPEhlbGxvIHdvcmxkOz4+Oz47O3Pj47P
j47Pkok6aaj8gigzgzEq7J850q107nn" />
        <input type="submit" name="Button1" value="Button" id="Button1" />
        <span id="Label1">Hello world</span>
    </form>
</html>
```

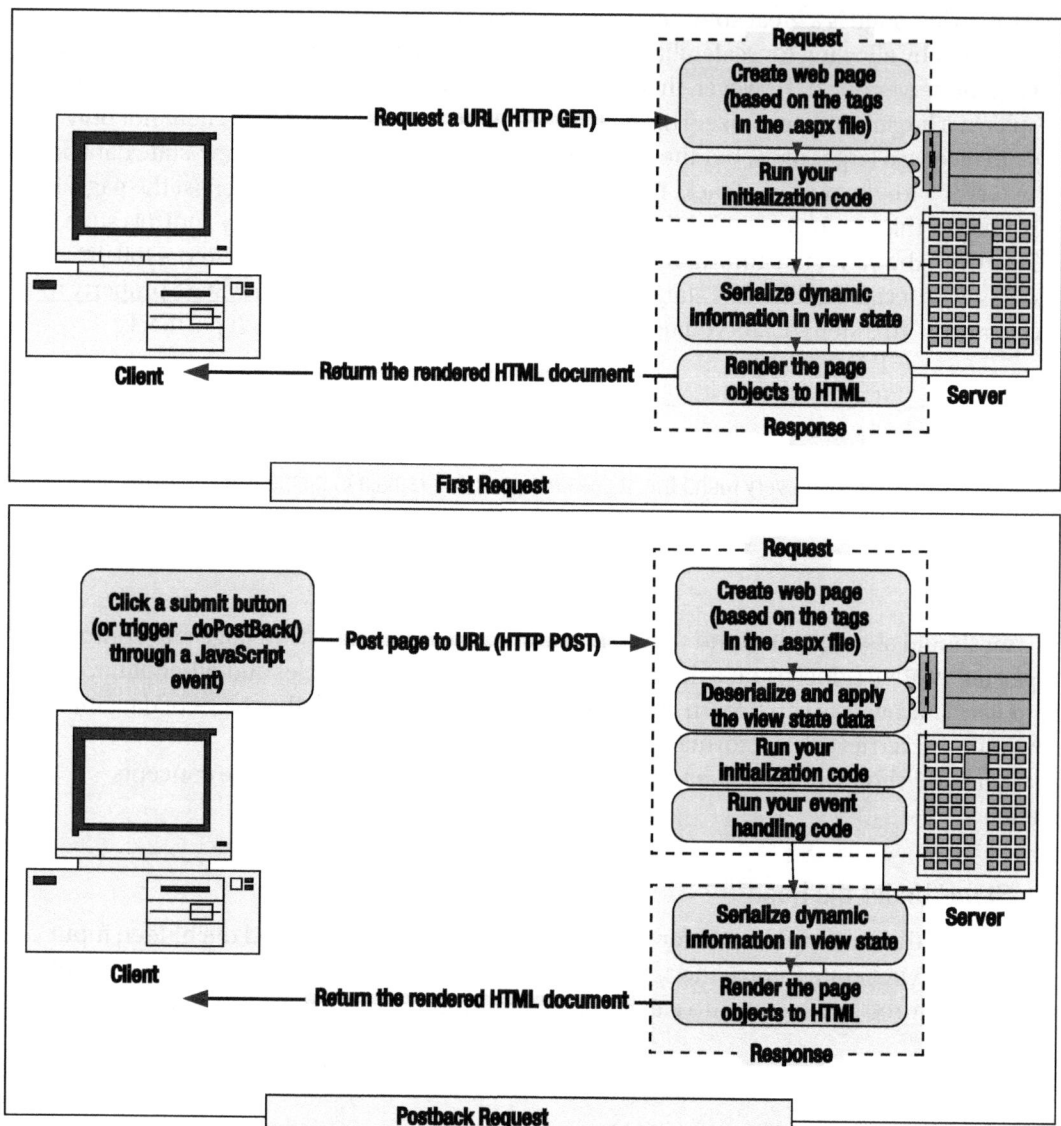

Figure 4-2. *ASP.NET page requests*

As you can see, the string isn't human readable—it just looks like a string of random characters. However, it's important to note that a user who is willing to go to a little work can interpret this data quite easily. Here's a snippet of .NET code that does the job, and writes the decoded information to a debug window:

```
// viewStateString contains the view state information.
// Convert the Base64 string to an ordinary array of bytes
// representing ASCII characters.
byte[] stringBytes = Convert.FromBase64String(viewStateString);
```

```
// Deserialize and display the string.
string decodedViewState = System.Text.Encoding.ASCII.GetString(stringBytes);
Debug.WriteLine(decodedViewState);
```

Here's the resulting string from the Hello World example:

```
t<-627154642;t<;l<i<1>;>;l<t<;l<i<3>;>;l<t<p<p<l<Text;>;l<Helloworld;>>;>;;>;>>;>>;
>J$i&#rgNÍ+2|gJ5;9g
```

As you can see, the control text is clearly visible (along with some special characters that .NET uses to represent lists and other structures). This means that, in its default implementation, view state isn't a good place to store sensitive information that the client shouldn't be allowed to see—that sort of data should stay on the server. Additionally, you shouldn't make decisions based on view state that could compromise your application if the client tampers with the view state data.

Fortunately, it's possible to tighten up view state security quite a bit. You can enable automatic hash codes to prevent view state tampering, and even encrypt it to prevent it from being decoded. These techniques raise hidden fields from a clumsy work-around to a much more robust and respectable piece of infrastructure. You'll learn about both of these techniques in Chapter 7.

Web Forms Processing Stages

On the server-side, the processing of an ASP.NET web form takes place in stages. At each stage, various events are raised. This allows your page to plug into the processing flow at any stage and respond however you like.

The following list shows the major stages in the process flow of an ASP.NET page:

- Page framework initialization

- User code initialization

- Validation

- Event handling

- Cleanup

Remember, these stages occur independently for each web request. Figure 4-3 shows the order in which these stages unfold. There are more stages than listed here, but those are typically used for programming your own ASP.NET controls, and aren't handled directly by the page.

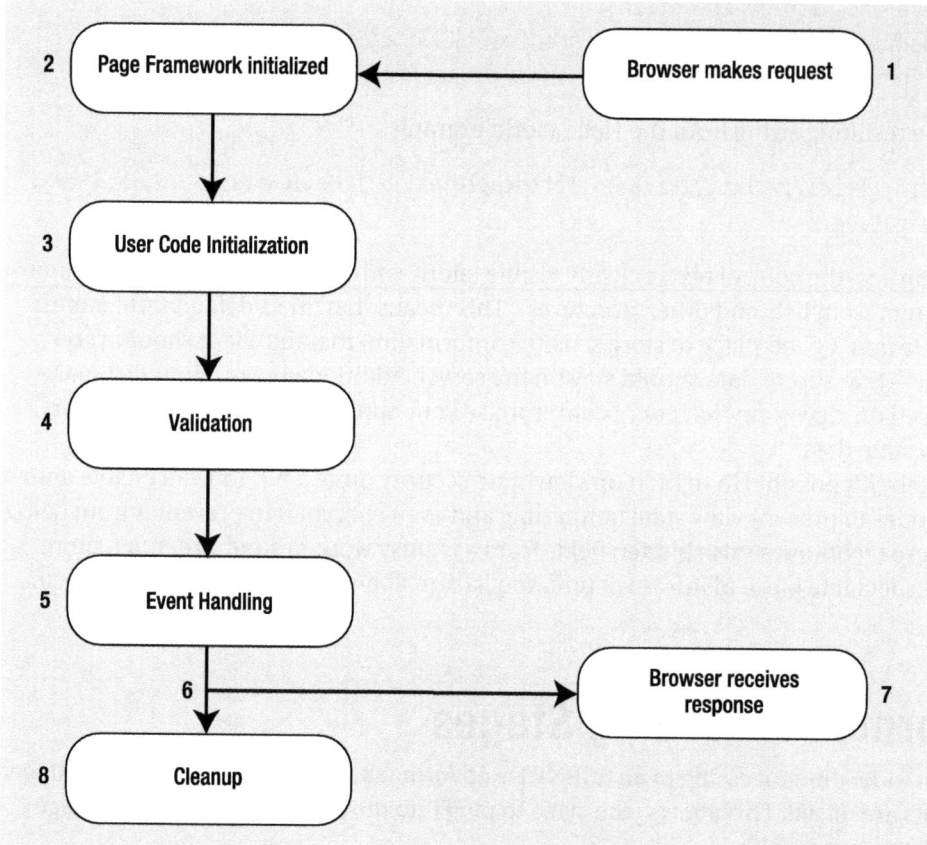

Figure 4-3. *ASP.NET page life cycle*

In the next few sections you'll learn about each stage, and then examine a simple web page example.

Page Framework Initialization

This is the stage in which ASP.NET first creates the page. It generates all the controls that you have defined with tags in the .aspx web page. In addition, if the page is not being requested for the first time (in other words, if it's a postback), ASP.NET deserializes the view state information and applies it to all the controls.

At this stage, the Page.Init event fires. However, this event is rarely handled by the web page, because it's still too early to perform page initialization. That's because the control objects may not be created yet, and the view state information isn't loaded.

User Code Initialization

At this stage of the processing, the Page.Load event is fired. Most web pages handle this event to perform any required initialization (like filling in dynamic text or configuring controls).

The Page.Load *always* fires, regardless of whether or not the page is being requested for the first time, or whether it is being requested as part of a postback. Fortunately, ASP.NET provides a way to allow programmers to distinguish between the first time the page is loaded, and all subsequent loads. Why is this important? First, since view state is maintained automatically, you only have to fetch your data from a dynamic data source on the first page load. On a postback, you can simply sit back, relax, and let ASP.NET restore the control properties for you from the view state. This can provide a dramatic performance boost if the information is expensive to re-create (for example, if you need to query it from a database). There are also other scenarios, such as edit forms and drill-down pages, in which you need the ability to display one interface on a page's first use, and a different interface on subsequent loads.

To determine the current state of the page, you can check the static Page.IsPostBack property, which will be false the first time the page is requested. Here's an example:

```
if (!Page.IsPostBack)
{
    // It's safe to initialize the controls for the first time.
    FirstName.Text = "Enter your name here";
}
```

Note IsPostBack is a static property of the Page class. It always returns the information based on the current page. You can also use the instance IsPostBack (as in this.IsPostBack), which returns the same value. Which approach you use is simply a matter of preference.

Validation

ASP.NET introduces new validation controls that can automatically validate other user input controls and display error messages. These controls fire after the page is loaded, but before any other events take place. However, the validation controls are for the most part self-sufficient, which means you don't need to respond to the validation events. Instead, you can just examine whether or not the page is valid (using the Page.IsValid property) in another event handler. The next chapter discusses the validator controls in more detail.

Event Handling

At this point, the page is fully loaded and validated. ASP.NET will now fire all the events that have taken place since the last postback. For the most part, ASP.NET events are of two types:

- **Immediate response events.** These include clicking a submit button, or clicking some other button, image region, or link in a rich web control that triggers a postback by calling the __doPostBack() JavaScript function.

- **Change events.** These include changing the selection in a control or the text in a text box. These events fire immediately for web controls if AutoPostBack is set to true. Otherwise, they fire the next time the page is posted back.

As you can see, ASP.NET's event model is still quite different than a traditional Windows environment. In a Windows application, the form state is resident in memory, and the application runs continuously. That means you can respond to an event immediately. In ASP.NET, everything occurs in stages, and as a result events are sometimes batched together.

For example, imagine you have a page with a submit button and a text box that doesn't post back automatically. You change the text in the text box and then click the submit button. At this point, ASP.NET raises all of the following events (in this order):

- Page.Init

- Page.Load

- TextBox.TextChanged

- Button.Click

- Page.PreRender

- Page.Unload

Remembering this bit of information can be essential in making your life as an ASP.NET programmer easier. There is a downside and an upside to the event-driven model. The upside is that the event model provides a higher level of abstraction, which keeps your code clear of boilerplate code for maintaining state. The downside is that it's easy to forget that the event model is really just an emulation. This can lead you to make an assumption that doesn't hold true (such as expecting information to remain in member variables) or a design decision that won't perform well (such as storing vast amounts of information in view state).

Cleanup

The page cleanup is a two-stage affair. First, the Page.PreRender event fires just before the page is rendered to HTML. At this point, the page and control objects are still available, so you can perform last-minute steps like storing additional information in view state. After the page has been rendered, the real cleanup begins and the Page.Unload event is fired. At this point, the page objects are still available, but the final HTML is already rendered and can't be changed.

Remember, the .NET Framework has a garbage collection service that runs periodically to release memory tied to objects that are no longer referenced. If you have any unmanaged resources to release, you should make sure you do this explicitly in the cleanup stage or, even better, before. When the garbage collector collects the page, the Page.Disposed event fires. This is the end of the road for the web page.

A Page Flow Example

No matter how many times people tell me how something works, I tend to never be satisfied until I've actually seen it, or broken it trying to find out (unfortunately, I tend to do this more often than see it). To satisfy your curiosity, you can build a sample web-form test that illustrates the flow of processing. About the only thing this example won't illustrate is validation (which is discussed in the next chapter).

To try this out, start by creating a new web form named PageFlow.aspx. If you're using Visual Studio .NET, you simply need to drag two controls onto the design surface from the Web Forms section of the toolbox. This generates a server-side <form> tag with the two control tags that you need in the .aspx file. Next, select the Label control. Using the Properties window, set the ID property to lblInfo and the EnableViewState property to false.

Here's the complete markup for the .aspx file:

```
<%@ Page language="c#" Codebehind="PageFlow.aspx.cs"
    AutoEventWireup="false" Inherits="PageFlow" %>
<HTML>
    <HEAD>
        <title>PageFlow</title>
    </HEAD>
    <body>
        <form id="PageFlow" method="post" runat="server">
            <P>
                <asp:Label id="lblInfo" runat="server" EnableViewState="False">
                </asp:Label>
            </P>
            <P>
            <asp:Button id="Button1" runat="server"
              Text="Button"></asp:Button>
            </P>
        </form>
    </body>
</HTML>
```

So far the code-behind class contains a basic skeleton with declarations for the two web controls you added:

```
public class PageFlow : System.Web.UI.Page
{
    protected System.Web.UI.WebControls.Label lblInfo;
    protected System.Web.UI.WebControls.Button Button1;

    // (Designer code omitted.)
}
```

The next step is to add your event handlers. When you're finished, the code-behind file will hold five event handlers that respond to different events, including Page.Init, Page.Load, Page.PreRender, Page.Unload, and Button.Click.

In Visual Studio .NET, you can add all your event handlers using the Properties window. This ensures that Visual Studio .NET generates the event handler *and* the delegate code that's needed to wire it up to the event, as described in Chapter 3. To add an event handler, select the object from the drop-down list at the top of the Properties window. (For example, select PageFlow to connect event handlers for the Page class events.) Then, click the lightning bolt to see the list of events. To add a new event handler, double-click in the empty box next to the event. Visual Studio .NET will insert the method declaration for the event handler—you just need to insert the code that responds to the event.

Figure 4-4 shows the Properties window after all the event handlers have been created for the Page class events.

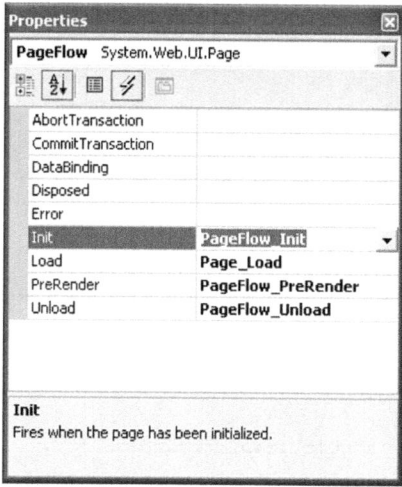

Figure 4-4. *ASP.NET order of operations*

In the PageFlow example, each event handler simply adds to the text in the Text property of the label. Here's the page class code with all the event handlers:

```
public class PageFlow : System.Web.UI.Page
{
    protected System.Web.UI.WebControls.Label lblInfo;
    protected System.Web.UI.WebControls.Button Button1;

    // (Designer code omitted.)

    private void Page_Load(object sender, System.EventArgs e)
    {
        lblInfo.Text += "Page.Load event handled.<br>";
        if (Page.IsPostBack)
        {
            lblInfo.Text +=
              "<b>This is the second time you've seen this page.</b><br>";
        }
    }

    private void PageFlow_Init(object sender, System.EventArgs e)
    {
        lblInfo.Text += "Page.Init event handled.<br>";
    }

    private void Button1_Click(object sender, System.EventArgs e)
    {
        lblInfo.Text += "Button1.Click event handled.<br>";
    }
```

```
private void PageFlow_PreRender(object sender, System.EventArgs e)
{
    lblInfo.Text += "Page.PreRender event handled.<br>";
}

private void PageFlow_Unload(object sender, System.EventArgs e)
{
    // This text never appears because the HTML is already
    // rendered for the page at this point.
    lblInfo.Text += "Page.Unload event handled.<br>";
}
}
```

Note that when the code adds this text, it also uses embedded HTML tags like <b> (to bold the text) and
 (to insert a line break). Another option would be to create separate label controls, and configure the style-related properties of each one.

■**Note** In this example, the EnableViewState property of the label is set to false. This ensures that the text is cleared every time the page is posted back, and the text that's shown only corresponds to the most recent batch of processing. If you left EnableViewState set to true, the list would grow longer with each postback, showing you all the activity that's happened since you first requested the page.

Figure 4-5 shows the ASP.NET page after clicking the button, which triggers a postback and the Button1.Click event. Note that even though this event caused the postback, Page.Init and Page.Load were both raised first.

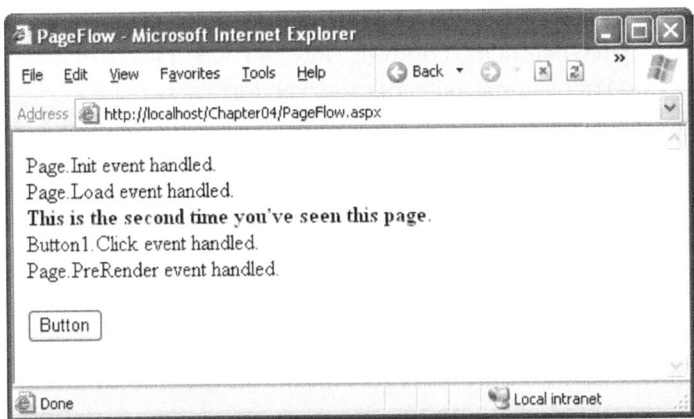

Figure 4-5. *ASP.NET order of operations*

The Page as a Control Container

In order to render a page, the web form needs to collaborate with all its constituent controls. Essentially, the web form renders itself and then asks all of the controls on the page to render themselves. In turn, each of those controls can contain child controls; each of them are also responsible for their own rendering code. As these controls render themselves, the page assembles the generated HTML into a complete page. This process may seem a little complex at first, but it allows for an amazing amount of power and flexibility in creating rich user interface experiences on the Web.

When ASP.NET first creates a page (in response to an HTTP request), it inspects the .aspx file. For each control tag it finds, it creates and configures a control object, and then it adds this control as a *child control* of the page. You can examine the Page.Controls collection to find all the child controls on the page.

Showing the Control Tree

Here's an example that looks for controls. Each time it finds a control, the code uses the Reponse.Write() command to write the control class type and control ID to the end of the rendered HTML page, as shown here:

```
// Every control derives from System.Web.UI.Control, so you can use
// that as a base class to examine all controls.
foreach (Control control in Page.Controls)
{
    Response.Write(control.GetType().ToString() + " - <b>" +
        control.ID + "</b><br>");
}
// Separate this content from the rest of the page with a horizontal line.
Response.Write("<hr>");
```

To test this code, you can add it to the Page.Load event handler. In this case, the rendered content will be written at the top of the page before the controls. However, when you run it, you'll notice some unexpected behavior. For example, consider the web form shown in Figure 4-6, which contains several controls, some of which are organized into a box using the Panel web control. It also contains two lines of static HTML text.

Here's the .aspx markup code for the page:

```
<%@ Page language="c#" Codebehind="Controls.aspx.cs" AutoEventWireup="false"
    Inherits="Chapter3.Controls" %>
<HTML>
    <HEAD>
        <title>Controls</title>
    </HEAD>
    <body>
        <P><i>This is static HTML (not a web control).</i></P>
```

```
            <form id="Controls" method="post" runat="server">
                <asp:panel id="MainPanel" runat="server" Height="112px">
                <P><asp:Button id="Button1" runat="server" Text="Button1"/>
                <asp:Button id="Button2" runat="server" Text="Button2"/>
                <asp:Button id="Button3" runat="server" Text="Button3"/></P>
                <P><asp:Label id="Label1" runat="server" Width="48px">
                  Name:</asp:Label>
                <asp:TextBox id="TextBox1" runat="server"></asp:TextBox></P>
                </asp:panel>
                <P><asp:Button id="Button4" runat="server" Text="Button4"/></P>
            </form>
            <P><i>This is static HTML (not a web control).</i></P>
        </body>
</HTML>
```

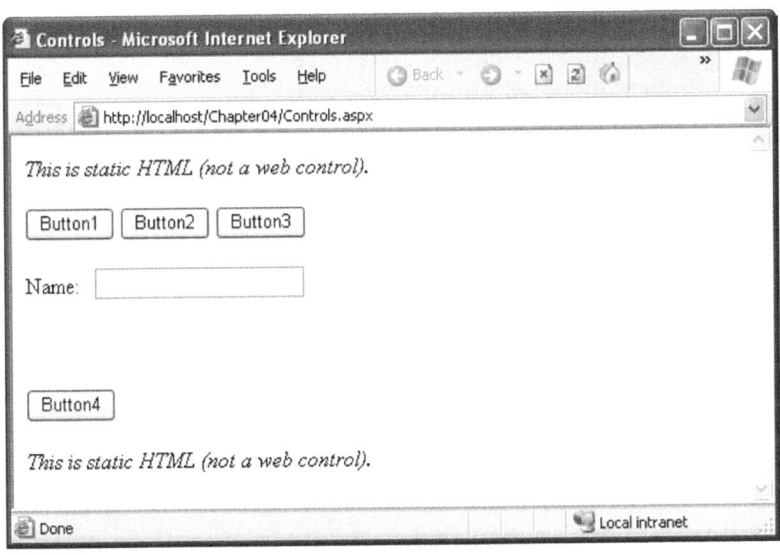

Figure 4-6. *A sample web page with multiple controls*

When you run this page, you won't see a full list of controls. Instead, you'll see a list that names only three controls, as shown in Figure 4-7.

There are two factors at work here. First, ASP.NET models the *entire* page using control objects, including elements that don't correspond to server-side content. For example, if you have one server control on a page, ASP.NET will create a LiteralControl that represents all the static content before the control, and another LiteralControl that represents the content after it. Depending on how much static content you have and how you break it up in between other controls, you may end up with multiple LiteralControl objects.

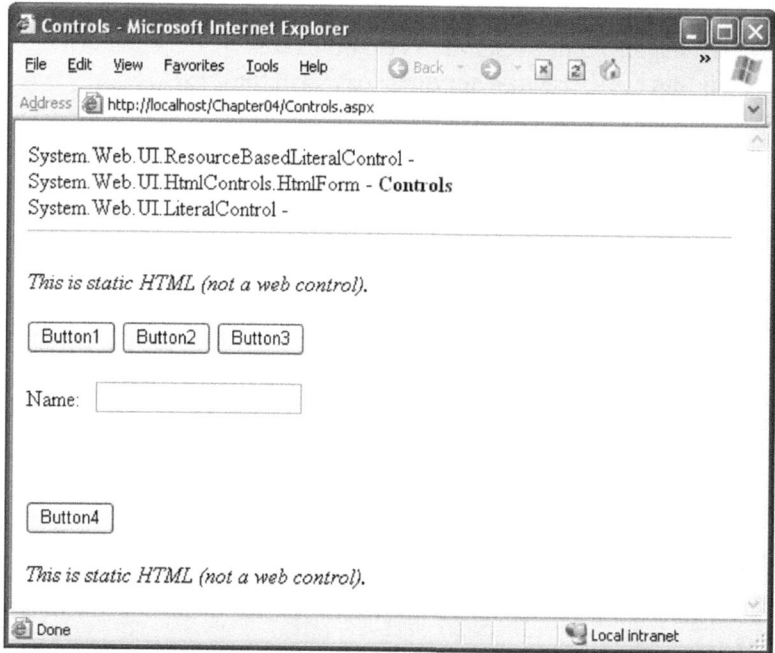

Figure 4-7. *Controls on the top layer of the page*

LiteralControl objects don't provide much in the way of functionality. For example, you can't set style-related information like colors and font. They also don't have a unique server-side ID. However, you can manipulate the content of a LiteralControl using its Text property. The following code rewrites the earlier example so that it checks for literal controls and, if present, it casts the base Control object to the LiteralControl type so that it can extract the associated text.

```
foreach (Control control in Page.Controls)
{
    Response.Write(control.GetType().ToString() + " - <b>" +
      control.ID + "</b><br>");

    if (control is LiteralControl)
    {
        // Display the literal content (whitespace and all).
        Response.Write("*** Text: "+((LiteralControl)control).Text + "<br>");
    }
}
Response.Write("<hr>");
```

This example still suffers from a problem. You now understand the unexpected new content, but what about the missing content—namely, the other control objects on the page?

To answer this question, you need to understand that ASP.NET renders a page *hierarchically*. It only directly renders the top level of controls. If these controls contain other controls, they provide their own Controls properties, which provide access to their child controls. In the example page, as in all ASP.NET web forms, all the controls are nested inside the <form> tag. This means that you need to inspect the Controls collection of the HtmlForm class to get information about the server controls on the page.

However, life isn't necessarily this straightforward. That's because there's no limit to how many layers of nested controls you can use. To really solve this problem and display all the controls on a page, you need to create a recursive routine that can tunnel through the entire control tree.

The following code shows the complete solution:

```
public class Controls : System.Web.UI.Page
{
    // (Designer code omitted.)

    private void Page_Load(object sender, System.EventArgs e)
    {
        // Start examining all the controls.
        DisplayControl(Page.Controls, 0);

        // Add the closing horizontal line.
        Response.Write("<hr>");
    }

    private void DisplayControl(ControlCollection controls, int depth)
    {
        foreach (Control control in controls)
        {
            // Use the depth parameter to indent the control tree.
            Response.Write(new String('-', depth * 4) + "> ");

            // Display this control.
            Response.Write(control.GetType().ToString() + " - <b>" +
              control.ID + "</b><br>");

            if (control.Controls != null)
            {
                DisplayControl(control.Controls, depth + 1);
            }
        }
    }
}
```

Figure 4-8 shows the new result—a hierarchical tree that shows all the controls on the page, and their nesting.

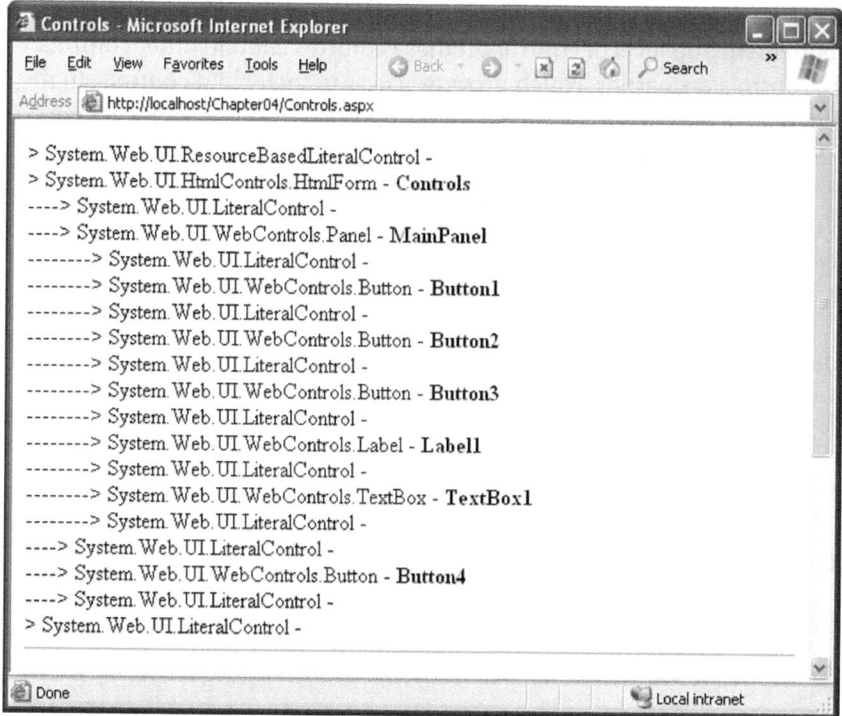

Figure 4-8. *A tree of controls on the page*

Dynamic Control Creation

Using the Controls collection, you can create a control and add it to a page programmatically. Here's an example that generates a new button and adds it to a Panel on the page:

```
private void Page_Load(object sender, System.EventArgs e)
{
    // Create a new button object.
    Button newButton = new Button();

    // Assign some text and an ID so you can retrieve it later.
    newButton.Text = "* Dynamic Button *";
    newButton.ID = "newButton";

    // Add the button to a Panel.
    Panel.Controls.Add(newButton);
}
```

You can execute this code in any event handler. However, because the page is already created, this code always adds the new control at the end of the collection. In this example, that means the new button will end up at the bottom of the Panel.

To get more control over where a dynamically added control is positioned, you can use a PlaceHolder. A PlaceHolder is a control that has no purpose except to house other controls. If you don't add any controls to the Controls collection of the PlaceHolder, it won't render anything in the final web page. However, Visual Studio .NET gives a default representation that looks like an ordinary label at design time, so you can position it exactly where you want. That way, you can add a dynamic control in between other controls.

```
// Add the button to a PlaceHolder.
PlaceHolder1.Controls.Add(newButton);
```

When using dynamic controls, you must remember that they will only exist until the next postback. ASP.NET will not re-create a dynamically added control. If you need to re-create a control multiple times, you should perform the control creation in the Page.Load event handler. This has the additional benefit of allowing you to use view state with your dynamic control. Even though view state is normally restored *before* the Page.Load event, if you create a control in the handler for the Page.Load event, ASP.NET will apply any view state information that it has after the Page.Load event handler ends. This process is automatic.

If you want to interact with the control later, you should give it a unique ID. You can use this ID to retrieve the control from the Controls collection of its container. You could find the control using recursive searching logic, as demonstrated in the control tree example, or you can use the static Page.FindControl() method, which searches the entire page for the control with the ID you specify. Here's an example that searches for the dynamically added control with the FindControl() method, and removes it:

```
private void cmdRemove_Click(object sender, System.EventArgs e)
{
    // Search for the button, no matter what level it's at.
    Button foundButton = (Button)Page.FindControl("newButton");

    // Remove the button.
    if (foundButton != null)
    {
        foundButton.Parent.Controls.Remove(foundButton);
    }
}
```

Dynamically added controls can handle events. All you need to do is attach an event handler (in much the same was as Visual Studio .NET does). You *must* perform this task in your Page.Load event handler. As you learned earlier, all control-specific events are fired after the Page.Load event. If you wait any longer, the event handler will be connected after the event has already fired, and you won't be able to react to it any longer.

```
// Attach an event handler to the Button.Click event.
newButton.Click += new System.EventHandler(this.Button_Click);
```

The following example demonstrates all these concepts (see Figure 4-9). It generates a dynamic button. When you click this button, the text in a label is modified. Two other buttons allow you to dynamically remove or re-create the button.

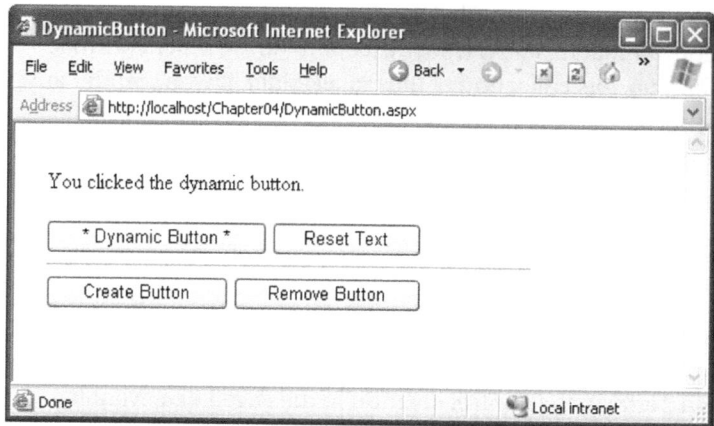

Figure 4-9. *Handling an event from a dynamically added control*

Dynamic control creation is particularly powerful when you combine it with user controls (reusable blocks of user interface that can combine a group of controls and HTML). You'll learn more about user controls in Chapter 19.

The Page Class

Now that you've explored the page life cycle and learned how a page contains controls, it's worth pointing out that the page itself is also instantiated as a type of control object. In fact, all web forms are actually instances of the ASP.NET Page class, which is found in the System.Web.UI namespace.

You may have already figured this out by noticing that every code-behind class explicitly derives from System.Web.UI.Page. This means that every web form you create is equipped with an enormous amount of out-of-the-box functionality. The static FindControl() method and the IsPostBack property are two examples you've seen so far. In addition, deriving from the Page class gives your code the following extremely useful properties:

- Session

- Application

- Cache

- Request

- Response

- Server

- User

- Trace

Many of these properties correspond to intrinsic objects that you could use in classic ASP web pages. However, in classic ASP you accessed this functionality through built-in objects that were available at all times. In ASP.NET, each of these built-in objects actually corresponds to a Page property that exposes an instance of a full-featured class.

The following sections introduce these objects.

Session, Application, and Cache

The Session object is an instance of the System.Web.SessionState.HttpSessionState class. It's designed to store any type of user-specific data that needs to persist between web-page requests. The Session object provides a dictionary-style access to a set of name/value pairs that represent the user's data for that session. Session state is often used to maintain things such as the user's name, the user's ID, a shopping cart, or various other elements that are discarded when a given user is no longer accessing pages on the website.

The Application object is an instance of the System.Web.HttpApplicationState class. Like the Session object, it's also a name/value dictionary of data. However, this data is global to the entire application.

Finally, the Cache object is an instance of the System.Web.Caching.Cache class. It also stores global information, but it provides a much more scalable storage mechanism because ASP.NET can remove objects if server memory becomes scarce. Like the other state collections, it's essentially a name/value collection of objects, but you can also set specialized expiration policies and dependencies for each item.

Deciding how to implement state management is one of the key challenges of programming a web application. You'll learn much more about all these types of state management in Chapter 7.

Request

The Request object is an instance of the System.Web.HttpRequest class. This object represents the values and properties of the HTTP request that caused your page to be loaded. It contains all of the URL parameters and all other information sent by a client. Much of the information provided by the Request object is wrapped by higher-level abstractions (like the ASP.NET web-control model), so it isn't nearly as important as it was in classic ASP. However, you might still use the Request object to find out what browser the client is using, or to set and examine cookies.

Table 4-1 describes some of the more common properties of the Request object.

Table 4-1. *HttpRequest Properties*

Property	Description
ApplicationPath and PhysicalPath	ApplicationPath gets the ASP.NET application's virtual directory (URL), while PhysicalPath gets the "real" directory.
Browser	Provides a link to an HttpBrowserCapabilities object, which contains properties describing various browser features, such as support for ActiveX controls, cookies, VBScript, and frames. This replaces the BrowserCapabilities component that was sometimes used in ASP development.
ClientCertificate	An HttpClientCertificate object that gets the security certificate for the current request, if there is one.

Continued

Table 4-1. *Continued*

Property	Description
Cookies	Gets the collection cookies sent with this request. Cookies are discussed in Chapter 7.
Form	Represents the collection of form variables that were posted back to the page. In almost all cases, you'll retrieve this information from control properties instead of using this collection.
Headers and ServerVariables	Provides a name/value collection of HTTP headers and server variables. You can get the low-level information you need if you know the corresponding header or variable name.
IsAuthenticated and IsSecureConnection	Returns true if the user has been successfully authenticated and if the user is connected over SSL (Secure Sockets Layer).
QueryString	Provides the parameters that were passed along with the query string. In Chapter 7, you'll see how you can use the query string to transfer information between pages.
Url and UrlReferrer	Provides a Url object that represents the current address for the page, and the page where the user is coming from (the previous page that linked to this page).
UserAgent	A string representing the browser type. Internet Explorer provides the value "MSIE" for this property.
UserHostAddress and UserHostName	Gets the IP address and the DNS name of the remote client. You could also access this information through the ServerVariables collection. However, this information may not always be available.
UserLanguages	Provides a sorted string array that lists the client's language preferences. This can be useful if you need to create multilingual pages.

Response

The Response object is an instance of the System.Web.HttpResponse class and it represents the web server's response to a client request. In classic ASP, the Response object was the only way to programmatically send HTML text to the client. Now server-side controls have nested, object-oriented methods for rendering themselves. All you have to do is set their properties. As a result, the Response object doesn't play nearly as central a role.

The HttpResponse does still provide some important functionality—namely cookie features and the Redirect() method. The Redirect() method allows you to send the user to another page. Here's an example:

```
// You can redirect to a file in the current directory.
Response.Redirect("newpage.aspx");

// You can redirect to another website.
Response.Redirect("http://www.prosetech.com");
```

The Redirect() method requires a round-trip. Essentially, it sends a message to the browser that instructs it to request a new page. If you want to transfer the user to another page in the same web application, you can use a faster approach with the Server.Transfer() method.

A list of common HttpResponse members is provided in Table 4-2.

Table 4-2. *HttpResponse Members*

Member	Description
BufferOutput	When set to true (the default), the page isn't sent to the client until it's completely rendered and ready to send, as opposed to being sent piecemeal.
Cache	References an HttpCachePolicy object that allows you to configure output caching. Caching is discussed later in this book.
Cookies	The collection of cookies sent with the response. You can use this property to add additional cookies.
IsClientConnected	A Boolean value indicating whether or not the client is still connected to the server. If it isn't, you might want to stop a time-consuming operation.
Write(), BinaryWrite(), and WriteFile()	These methods allow you to write text or binary content directly to the response stream. You can even write the contents of a file. These methods are de-emphasized in ASP.NET, and shouldn't be used in conjunction with server controls.
Redirect()	This method transfers the user to another page in your application or a different website.

Server

The Server object is an instance of the System.Web.HttpServerUtility class. It provides a handful of miscellaneous helper methods and properties, as listed in Table 4-3.

Table 4-3. *HttpServerUtility Methods*

Method	Description
MachineName	A property representing the computer name of the computer on which the page is running. This is the name the web-server computer uses to identify itself to the rest of the network.
CreateObject()	Creates an instance of the COM object that is identified by its programmatic ID (progID). This is included for backward compatibility, because it will generally be easier to interact with COM objects using .NET's support for COM interop, which provides strongly typed interaction.
HtmlEncode() and HtmlDecode()	Changes an ordinary string into a string with legal HTML characters (and back again).
UrlEncode() and UrlDecode()	Changes an ordinary string into a string with legal URL characters (and back again).
MapPath()	Returns the physical file path that corresponds to a specified virtual file path on the web server.
Transfer()	Transfers execution to another web page in the current application. This is similar to the Response.Redirect() method, but faster. It cannot be used to transfer the user to a site on another web server, or to a non-ASP.NET page (like an HTML page or an ASP page).

The Transfer() is the quickest way to redirect the user to another page in your application. When you use this method, a round-trip is not involved. Instead, the ASP.NET engine simply loads the new page and begins processing it. As a result, the URL that's displayed in the client's browser won't change.

```
// You can transfer to a file in the current web application.
Server.Transfer("newpage.aspx");

// You can't redirect to another website.
// This attempt will cause an error.
Server.Transfer ("http://www.prosetech.com");
```

The MapPath() method is another useful method. For example, imagine you want to load a file named info.txt from the current virtual directory. Instead of hard-coding the path, you can use Request.ApplicationPath() to get the current relative virtual directory, and Server.MapPath() to convert this to an absolute physical path. Here's an example:

```
string physicalPath = Server.MapPath(Request.ApplicationPath + "/info.txt"));

// Now open the file.
StreamReader reader = new StreamReader(physicalPath);
// (Process the file here.)
reader.Close()
```

HTML and URL Encoding

The Server class also includes a set of methods that change ordinary strings into a representation that can safely be used as part of a URL or displayed in a web page. For example, imagine you want to display this text on a web page:

```
To bold text use the <b> tag.
```

If you try to write this information to a page or place it inside a control, you would end up with this instead:

```
To bold text use the tag.
```

Not only will the text "<b>" not appear, but the browser will interpret it as an instruction to make the text that follows bold. To circumvent this automatic behavior, you need to convert potential problematic values to their special HTML equivalents. For example < becomes < in your final HTML page, which the browser displays as the < character. Table 4-4 lists some special characters that need to be encoded.

Table 4-4. *Common HTML Entities*

Result	Description	Encoded Entity
	Nonbreaking space	
<	Less-than symbol	<
>	Greater-than symbol	>

Result	Description	Encoded Entity
&	Ampersand	&
"	Quotation mark	"

Here's an example that circumvents the problem using the Server.HtmlEncode() method:

```
Label1.Text = Server.HtmlEncode("To bold text use the <b> tag.")
```

You also have the freedom to use HtmlEncode for some input, but not for all of it if you want to insert a combination of text that could be invalid and HTML tags. Here's an example:

```
Label1.Text = "To <b>bold</b> text use the ";
Label1.Text += Server.HtmlEncode("<b>") + " tag.";
```

Note Some controls circumvent this problem by automatically encoding tags. (The Label web control is not one of them. Instead, it gives you the freedom to insert HTML tags as you please.) For example, the basic set of HTML server controls include both an InnerText and InnerHtml tag. When you set the contents of a control using InnerText, any illegal characters are automatically converted into their HTML equivalents. However, this won't help if you want to set a tag that contains a mix of embedded HTML tags and encoded characters.

The HtmlEncode() method is particularly useful if you're retrieving values from a database, and you aren't sure if the text is valid HTML. You can use the HtmlDecode() method to revert the text to its normal form if you need to perform additional operations or comparisons with it in your code. Similarly, the UrlEncode() method changes text into a form that can be used in a URL, escaping spaces and other special characters. This step is usually performed with information you want to add to the query string, as described in Chapter 7.

It's worth noting that the HtmlEncode() method won't convert spaces to nonbreaking spaces. This means that if you have a series of space characters, the browser will only display a single space. Although this doesn't invalidate your HTML, it may not be the effect you want. To change this behavior, you can manually replace spaces with nonbreaking spaces using the String.Replace() method. Just make sure you perform this step after you encode the string, not before, or the nonbreaking space character sequence (&nbps;) will be replaced with character entities and treated as ordinary text.

```
// Encode illegal characters.
line = server.HtmlEncode(line);

// Replace spaces with nonbreaking spaces.
line = line.Replace(" ", " ");
```

Similarly, the HtmlEncode() method won't convert line breaks into the <br> tag. This means that hard returns will be ignored unless you specifically insert <br> tags.

■**Note** The issue of properly encoding input is important for more than just ensuring properly displayed data. If you try to display data that has embedded <script> tags, you could inadvertently end up executing a block of JavaScript code on the client. The final section of this chapter has more about this danger, and the ASP.NET request validation feature, which prevents it.

User

The User object represents information about the user making the request of the web server, and allows you to test that user's role membership.

The User object always implements System.Security.Principal.IPrincipal. The specific class depends on the type of authentication that you're using. For example, you can authenticate a user based on Windows account information using IIS, or through cookie-based authentication with a dedicated login page. However, it's important to realize that the User object only provides useful information if your web application is performing some sort of authentication that restricts anonymous users.

Part Three of this book deals with security in detail.

Trace

The Trace object is a general-purpose tracing tool (and an instance of the System.Web.TraceContext class). It allows you to write information to a log that is scoped at the page level. This log has detailed timing information so that not only can you use the Trace object for debugging, but you can also use it for performance monitoring and timing. Additionally, the trace log also shows a compilation of miscellaneous information, grouped into several sections. Table 4-5 describes all the information you'll see.

Table 4-5. *Trace Log Information*

Section	Description
Request Details	This section includes some basic information about the request context, including the current session ID, the time the web request was made, and the type of web request and encoding.
Trace Information	This section shows the different stages of processing the page went through before being sent to the client. Each section has additional information about how long it took to complete, as a measure from the start of the first stage (From First) and as a measure from the start of the previous stage (From Last). If you add your own trace messages (a technique described shortly), they will also appear in this section.
Control Tree	The control tree shows you all the controls on the page, indented to show their hierarchy, similar to the control-tree example earlier in this chapter. One useful feature of this section of the Viewstate column, which tells you how many bytes of space are required to persist the current information in the control. This can help you gauge whether enabling control state could have an effect on page transmission times.

Section	Description
Session State and Application State	These sections display every item that is in the current session or application state. Each item is listed with its name, type, and value. If you're storing simple pieces of string information, the value is straightforward. If you're storing an object, .NET calls the objects ToString() method to get an appropriate string representation. For complex objects, the result may just be the class name.
Cookies Collection	This section displays all the cookies that are sent with the response, and the content and size of each cookie in bytes. Even if you haven't explicitly created a cookie, you'll see the ASP.NET_SessionId cookie, which contains the current session ID. If you're using forms-based authentication, you'll also see the security cookie.
Headers Collection	This section lists all the HTTP headers associated with the request.
Forms Collection	This section lists the posted-back form information.
QueryString Collection	This section lists the variables and values submitted in the query string.
Server Variables	This section lists all the server variables and their contents.

Tip Tracing complements Visual Studio .NET debugging. In many cases, debugging is the best approach for solving problems while you are coding a web application, while tracing gives you an easier option if you need to troubleshoot problems that appear while the application is running on a web server. However, tracing provides a few services that debugging doesn't (at least not as easily), such as showing you the amount of information in view state and the time taken to process the page on the server. Tracing also works regardless of whether you build your application in debug mode (with the debug symbols) or release mode.

There are two ways to enable tracing. You can set the Trace.IsEnabled property to true at any point in your code, as follows:

```
Trace.IsEnabled = true;
```

Usually, you'll do this in the Page.Load event handler. Another option is to use the Trace attribute in the Page directive:

```
<%@ Page language="c#" Codebehind="PageFlow.aspx.cs" AutoEventWireup="false"
    Inherits="PageFlow" Trace="true" %>
```

By default, trace messages are listed in the order they were generated. Alternatively, you can specify that messages should be sorted by category, using the TraceMode attribute in the Page directive, as follows:

```
<%@ Page language="c#" Codebehind="PageFlow.aspx.cs" AutoEventWireup="false"
    Inherits="PageFlow" Trace="true" TraceMode="SortByCategory" %>
```

or the TraceMode property of the Trace object in your code:

```
Trace.TraceMode = TraceMode.SortByCategory;
```

Figure 4-10 shows a partial listing of trace information with the PageFlow example demonstrated earlier.

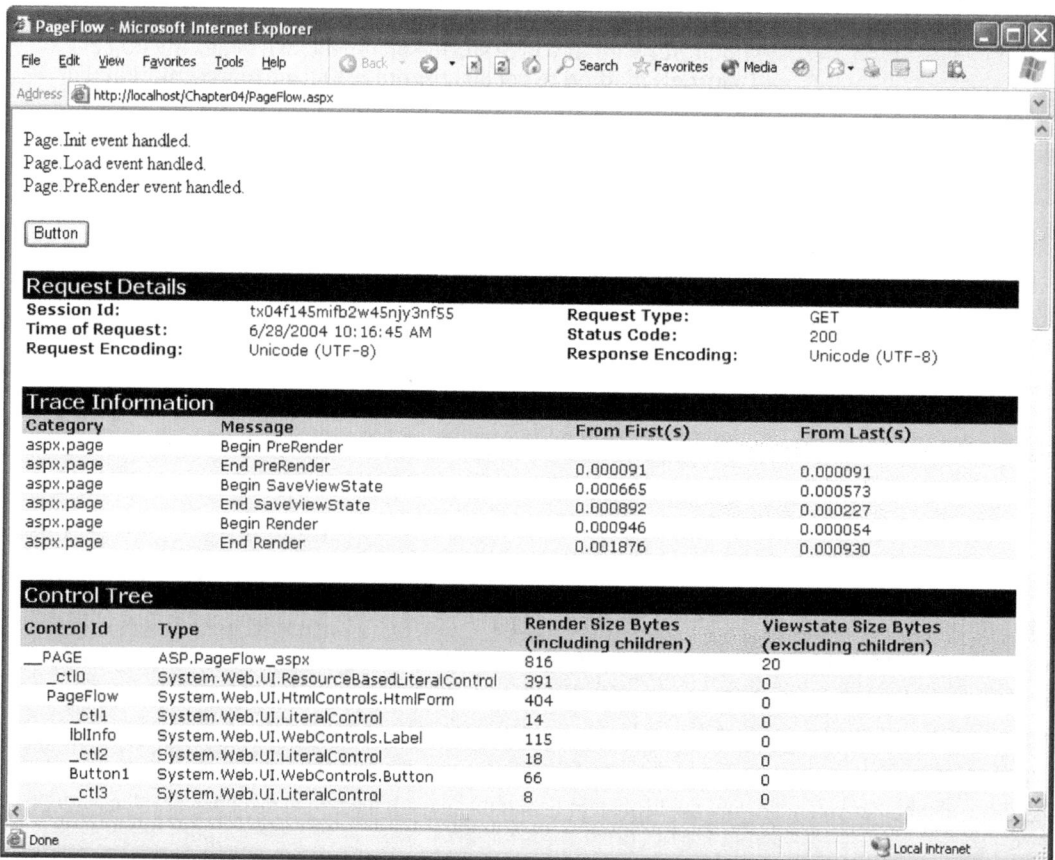

Figure 4-10. *Basic trace information*

■ **Tip** Trace information is appended to the end of your HTML page. However, if you use absolute positioning with CSS style properties (grid layout mode in Visual Studio .NET), you'll notice that tracing messages are displayed on top of your other HTML content. To solve this problem, you can use application-level tracing, as described later in this section.

You can also write your own information to the trace log (the portion of the trace log that appears in the Trace Information section) using the Trace.Write() or Trace.Warn() methods. These methods are equivalent. The only difference is that Warn() displays the message in red lettering, which makes it easier to distinguish them from other messages in the list.

Here's a code snippet that writes a trace message when the user clicks a button:

```
private void Button1_Click(object sender, System.EventArgs e)
{
    // You can supply just a message, or include a category label,
```

```
    // as shown here.
    Trace.Write("Button1_Click", "About to update the label.");
    lblInfo.Text += "Button1.Click event handled.<br>";
    Trace.Write("Button1_Click", "Label updated.");
}
```

When you write trace messages, they are automatically sent to all trace listeners. However, if you've disabled tracing for the page, the messages are simply ignored. Tracing messages are automatically HTML encoded. This means tags like <br> and <b> are displayed as text, not interpreted as HTML.

Figure 4-11 shows the new entries in the log.

Trace Information

Category	Message	From First(s)	From Last(s)
aspx.page	Begin ProcessPostData Second Try		
aspx.page	End ProcessPostData Second Try	0.000096	0.000096
aspx.page	Begin Raise ChangedEvents	0.000172	0.000076
aspx.page	End Raise ChangedEvents	0.000220	0.000049
aspx.page	Begin Raise PostBackEvent	0.000267	0.000046
Button1_Click	About to update the label.	0.000331	0.000064
Button1_Click	Label updated.	0.000389	0.000058
aspx.page	End Raise PostBackEvent	0.000442	0.000053
aspx.page	Begin PreRender	0.000489	0.000047
aspx.page	End PreRender	0.000550	0.000061
aspx.page	Begin SaveViewState	0.001134	0.000584
aspx.page	End SaveViewState	0.001308	0.000174
aspx.page	Begin Render	0.001360	0.000052
aspx.page	End Render	0.002212	0.000852

Figure 4-11. *Writing custom trace messages*

By default, tracing is enabled on a page-by-page basis. This isn't always convenient. In some cases, you want to collect trace statistics for a page, and then view them later. ASP.NET supports this approach with application-level tracing.

To enable application-level tracing, you need to modify the web.config configuration file. Look for the <trace> element and enable it as shown here:

```
<configuration>
    <system.web>
        <trace enabled="true" requestLimit="10" pageOutput="false"
         traceMode="SortByTime" localOnly="true" />
    </system.web>
</configuration>
```

When you enable application-level tracing, you won't see the trace information on the page. Instead, to view tracing information you must request the trace.axd application extension in your web application's root directory. This extension doesn't correspond to an actual file—instead, ASP.NET automatically intercepts the request and provides a list of the most recent collected trace requests (as shown in Figure 4-12), provided you're making the request from the local machine or have enabled remote tracing. You can see the detailed information for any request by clicking the View Details link.

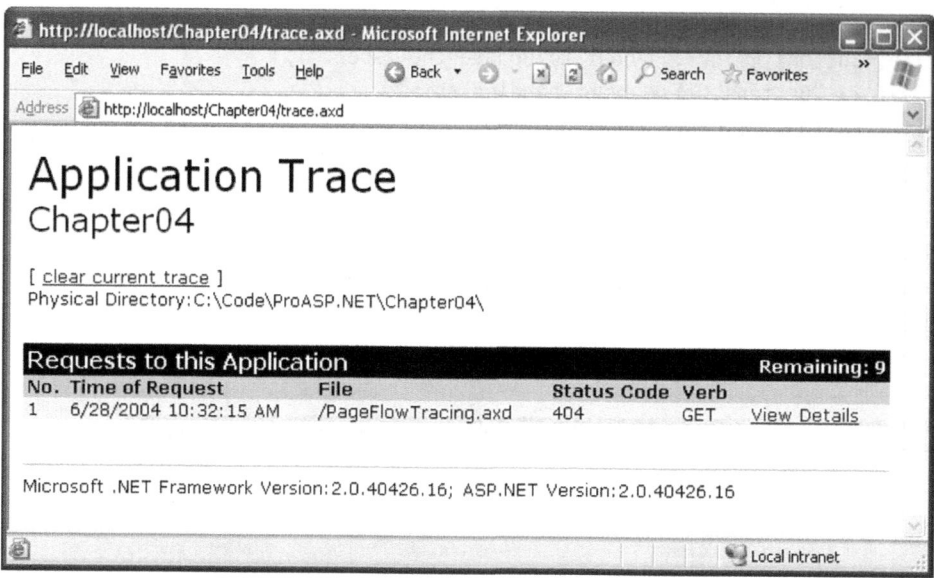

Figure 4-12. *Traced application request*

The full list of tracing options in the web.config <trace> element is described in Table 4-6.

Table 4-6. *Tracing Options*

Attribute	Values	Description
Enabled	true, false	Turns application-level tracing on or off.
requestLimit	Any integer (for example, 10)	This is the number of HTTP requests for which tracing information will be stored. Unlike page-level tracing, this allows you to collect a batch of information from multiple requests. When the maximum is reached, the information for the oldest request is abandoned every time a new request is received.
pageOutput	true, false	Determines whether tracing information will be displayed on the page (as it is with page-level tracing). If you choose false, you'll still be able to view the collected information by requesting trace.axd from the virtual directory where your application is running.
traceMode	SortByTime, SortByCategory	Determines the sort order of trace messages.
localOnly	true, false	Determines whether tracing information will be shown only to local clients (clients using the same computer) or can be shown to remote clients as well. By default, this is true and remote clients cannot see tracing information.

Accessing the HTTP Context in Another Class

Over the last several sections, you've seen how the Page class exposes a significant number of useful features that let you retrieve information about the current HTTP context. These details are available because they're provided as properties of the Page class. But what if you want to retrieve this information from inside another class, one that doesn't derive from Page?

Fortunately, there's another way to get access to all the HTTP context information. You can use the System.Web.HttpContext class. This class exposes a static property called Current, which returns an instance of the HttpContext class that represents all the information about the current request and response. It provides the same set of built-in ASP.NET objects as properties.

For example, here's how you would write a trace message from another component that doesn't derive from Page, but is being used by a web page as part of a web request:

```
HttpContext.Current.Trace.Write("This message is from DB Component");
```

If you want to perform multiple operations, it may be slightly faster to retrieve a reference to the current context and then reuse it:

```
HttpContext current = HttpContext.Current;
current.Trace.Write("This is message 1");
current.Trace.Write("This is message 2");
```

Script Injection Attacks

Often, developers aren't aware of the security vulnerabilities they introduce in a page. That's because many common dangers—including script injection and SQL injection (which you'll confront in Chapter 8)—are surprisingly easy to stumble into. In order to minimize these risks, technology vendors like Microsoft strive to find ways to integrate safety checks into the programming framework itself, thereby insulating application programmers.

One attack to which web pages are commonly vulnerable is a *script injection* attack. A script injection attack occurs when malicious tags or script code are submitted by a user (usually through a simple control like a text box), and then rendered into an HTML page later on. Although this rendering process is intended to *display* the user-supplied data, it actually *executes* the script. A script injection attack can have any of a number of different effects from trivial to significant. If the user-supplied data is stored in a database and inserted later into pages used by other people, the attack may affect the operation of the website for all users.

The basic technique for a script injection attack is for the client to submit content with embedded scripting tags. These scripting tags can include <script>, <object>, <applet>, and <embed>. Although the application can specifically check for these tags and use HTML encoding to replace the tags with harmless HTML entities, that basic validation often isn't performed.

Request Validation

Script injection attacks are a concern of all web developers, whether they are using ASP.NET, ASP, or other web development technologies. However, ASP.NET 1.1 introduces a new feature designed to automatically combat script injection attacks, called *request validation*. Request validation checks the posted form input, and raises an error if any potentially malicious tags (like <script>) are found. In fact, request validation disallows any nonnumeric tags, including HTML tags (like <b> and <img>), and tags that don't correspond to anything (like <asdf>).

To test the new script validation features, you can create a simple web page like the one shown in Figure 4-13. This simple example contains a text box and a button.

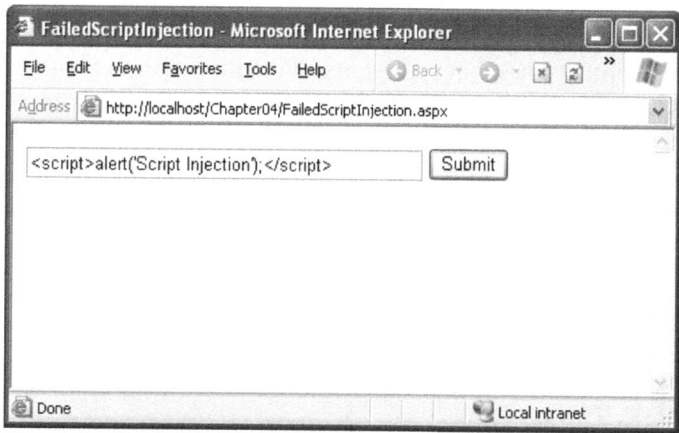

Figure 4-13. *Testing a script injection attack*

Now, try to enter a block of content with a script tag, and then click the button. ASP.NET will detect the potentially dangerous value, and generate an error. If you're running the code locally, you'll see the rich error page with detailed information, as shown in Figure 4-14. (If you're requesting the page remotely, you'll see only a generic error page.)

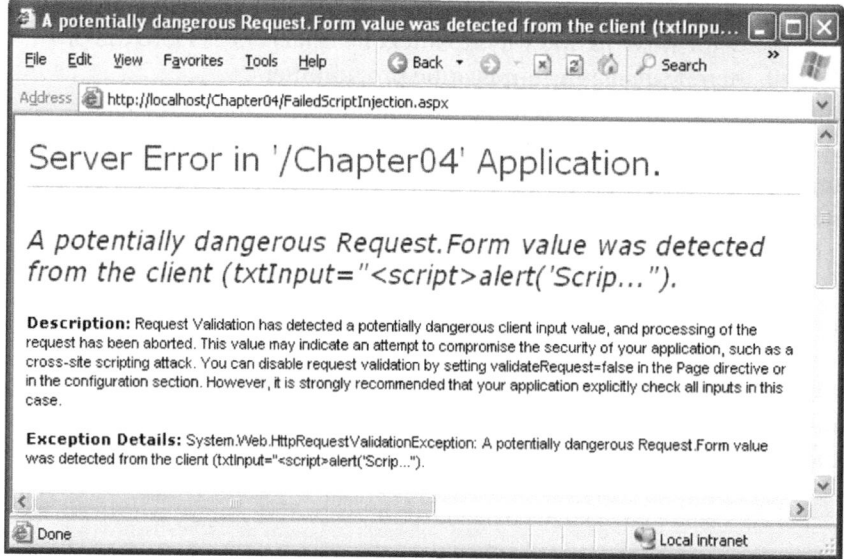

Figure 4-14. *A failed script injection attack*

Note In .NET 1.0, ASP.NET does not perform request validation. As a result, your web-page code must validate or encode user input before displaying it. You'll see this technique in action a little later in this chapter.

Disabling Request Validation

Of course, in some situations the request validation rules are just too restrictive. For example, you might have an application where users have a genuine need to specify HTML tags (for example, when they enter an auction listing or a for-sale advertisement) or a block of XML data. In these situations, you need to specifically disable script validation using the validateRequest Page directive, as shown here:

```
<%@ Page validateRequest="false" ...  %>
```

You can also disable request validation for an entire web application by modifying the web.config file. Add or set the validateRequest attribute of the <pages> element, as shown here:

```
<configuration>
  <system.web>
    <!-- Other settings omitted. -->
    <pages validateRequest="false" />
  </system.web>
</configuration>
```

Now, consider what happens if you attempt to display the user-supplied value in a label with this code:

```
private void cmdSubmit_Click(object sender, System.EventArgs e)
{
    lblInfo.Text = "You entered: " + txtInput.Text;
}
```

If a malicious user enters the text <script>alert('Script Injection');</script>, the returned web page will execute the script, as shown in Figure 4-15.

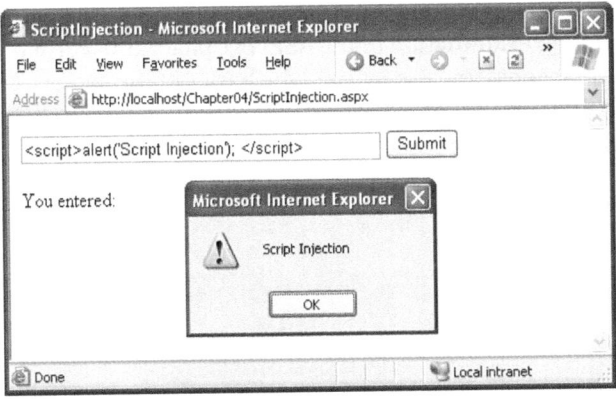

Figure 4-15. *A successful script injection attack*

Keep in mind that the script in a script injection attack is always executed on the client end. However, that doesn't mean it's limited to a single user. In many situations, user-supplied data is stored in a location like a database and can be viewed by other users. For example, if a user supplied a script block for a business name when adding a business to a registry, another user who requests a full list of all businesses in the registry will be affected.

To prevent a script injection attack from happening when request validation is turned off (or in .NET 1.0), you need to explicitly encode the content before you display it using the Server object, as described earlier in this chapter.

Here's a rewritten version of the Button.Click event handler that doesn't suffer from the same susceptibility to script injection attacks:

```
private void cmdSubmit_Click(object sender, System.EventArgs e)
{
    lblInfo.Text = "You entered: " + Server.HtmlEncode(txtInput.Text);
}
```

Figure 4-16 shows the result of an attempted script injection attack on this page.

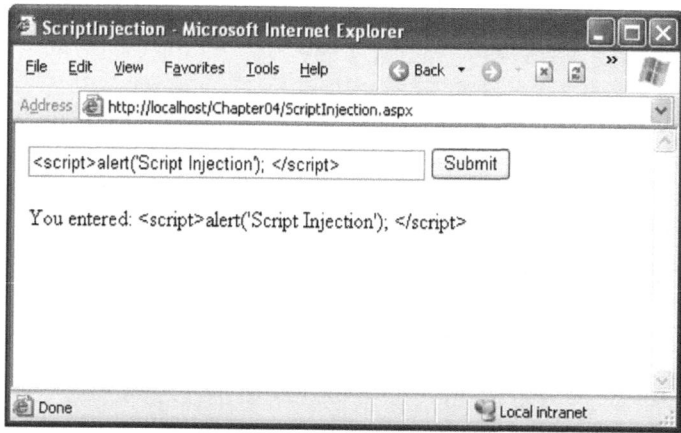

Figure 4-16. *A disarmed script injection attack*

Summary

In this chapter you've walked through a detailed examination of the ASP.NET page, and learned what it is, and how it really works behind the scenes. You also learned the basics of the server-control model, and took a close look at the System.Web.UI.Page class. In the next chapter, you'll take a closer look at the web controls that ASP.NET gives you to build sophisticated pages.

CHAPTER 5

■■■

ASP.NET Controls

ASP.NET server controls are a fundamental part of the ASP.NET architecture. Essentially, server controls are classes in the .NET Framework that represent visual elements on a web form. Some of these classes are relatively straightforward, and map closely to a specific HTML tag. Other controls are much more ambitious abstractions that render a more complex visual representation out of multiple HTML elements.

In this chapter, you'll learn about the different types of ASP.NET server controls, and how they're related. You'll also learn how to use validation controls to ensure that the user input matches standard or user-defined rules before a web page is submitted to the server.

ASP.NET Server Controls

ASP.NET offers many different server controls, which can be grouped in the following categories:

- **HTML server controls**. These are classes that wrap the standard HTML tags and are declared with the runat="server" attribute. Apart from this attribute, the declaration for an HTML server control remains exactly the same. Two examples include HtmlAnchor (for the <a> tag) and HtmlSelect (for the <select> tag). However, you can turn any HTML tag into a server control. If there isn't a direct corresponding class, ASP.NET will simply use the HtmlGenericControl class.

- **ASP.NET web form controls**. These classes duplicate the functionalities of the basic HTML tags, but have a more consistent and meaningful set of properties and methods that make it easier for the developer to declare and access them. Some examples are the HyperLink, ListBox, and Button controls. In addition, there are several other types of ASP.NET controls (templated controls, rich controls, and validation controls) that are commonly considered to be special types of web controls.

- **ASP.NET rich controls**. These advanced controls have the ability to generate quite a lot of HTML markup and even client-side JavaScript to create the interface. The most significant example that's included in the .NET Framework is the Calendar control, but there are others, as you'll see later in this chapter.

- **ASP.NET templated controls**. These controls are designed to deal with repeating content and are particularly useful in data-binding scenarios when you need to show a full table of information. These controls work by repeating a template that you define for every item in the data source. Some of them allow you to use different templates for displaying the records, editing, or highlighting them, and some provide support for advanced features like sorting and pagination.

- **ASP.NET validation controls**. This set of controls allows you to easily validate an associated input control against several standard or user-defined rules. For example, you can specify that the input can't be empty, it must be a number, it must be greater than a certain value, and so on. If validation fails, you can prevent page processing or allow these controls to show inline error messages in the page.

- **ASP.NET mobile controls**. This is a set of controls that resembles the web controls but is customized to support mobile clients such as personal digital assistants (PDA), smart phones, and so on, by generating HTML 3.2 or WML 1.1 according to the client type. The result is that when you create a page using these controls, the page can be rendered in several completely different ways depending on the device that's accessing the page. For this reason, you can consider them as adaptive controls. (This concept is also used in ordinary web controls on a lesser scale. They can generate HTML 4 and JavaScript code or plain HTML 3.2 code according to the client browser's capabilities.)

You'll see most of these controls in this chapter, but some (such as templated controls) won't be explored until later chapters. The mobile controls aren't covered in this book, although you can learn more from Derek Ferguson's *Mobile .NET* (Apress, 2001).

The Server Control Hierarchy

All server controls derive from the base Control class in the System.Web.UI namespace. This is true whether you're using HTML server controls, web controls, or creating your own custom controls. It also applies to the Page class from which all web forms derive. Figure 5-1 illustrates the main branches of this inheritance chain.

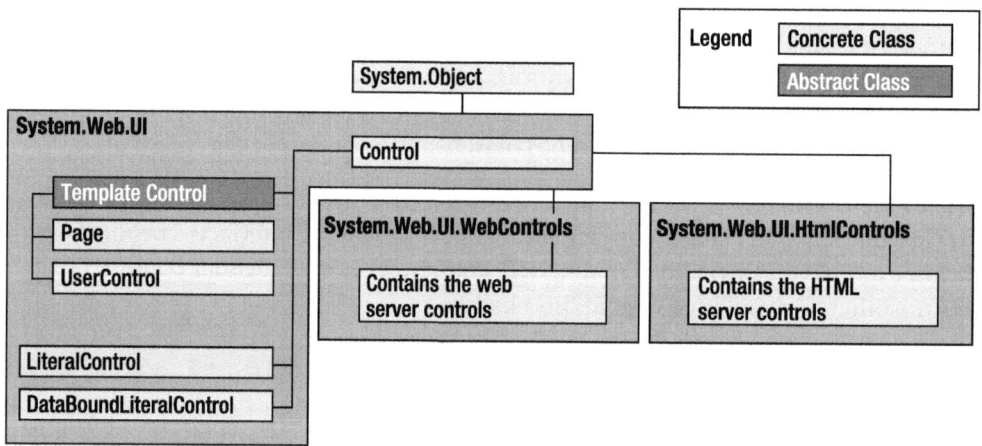

Figure 5-1. *Server control inheritance*

Because all controls derive from the base Control class, you have a basic common denominator that you can use to manipulate any control on the page, even if you don't know the specific control type. (For example, you could use this technique to loop through all the controls on the page and hide each one by setting the Visible property to false.) Table 5-1 and Table 5-2 describe the most commonly used members of the Control class.

Table 5-1. *Control Class Properties*

Property	Description
ClientID	Returns the identifier of the control, which is a unique name created by ASP.NET at the time the page is instantiated.
Controls	Returns the collection of child controls on the page. This is the "first level" of controls, some of which may be container controls that contain additional child controls of their own.
EnableViewState	Returns or sets a Boolean value indicating whether the control should maintain its state across postbacks of its parent page. This property is true by default.
ID	Returns or sets the identifier of the control. In practice, this is the name through which you can access the control from the server-side scripts or the code-behind class.
Page	Returns a reference to the parent Page.
Parent	Returns a reference to the control's parent, which can be the page or another container control.
Visible	Returns or sets a Boolean value indicating whether the control should be rendered or not. If false, the control isn't just made invisible on the client—instead, the corresponding HTML code is not generated and is not sent to the client at all.

Table 5-2. *Control Class Methods*

Method	Description
DataBind()	Binds the control and all of its child controls to the specified data source or expression. You'll learn about data binding in Part Two.
FindControl()	Searches for a child control with a specific name in the current control and all contained controls. If the child control is found, the method returns a reference of general type Control. You can then cast this control to the proper type.
HasControls()	Returns a Boolean value indicating whether this control has any child controls. The control must be a container tag to have child controls (such as a <div> tag).
Render()	Writes the HTML output for the control based on its current state. You don't call this method directly. Instead, ASP.NET calls it when the page is being rendered.

HTML Server Controls

In this section you'll learn about the HTML server controls, which are defined in the namespace System.Web.UI.HtmlControls. Overall, there are 17 distinct HTML server control classes. They're split into separate categories based on whether they are input controls (in which case they derive from HtmlInputControl) or can contain other controls (in which case they derive from HtmlContainerControl). Figure 5-2 shows the inheritance hierarchy.

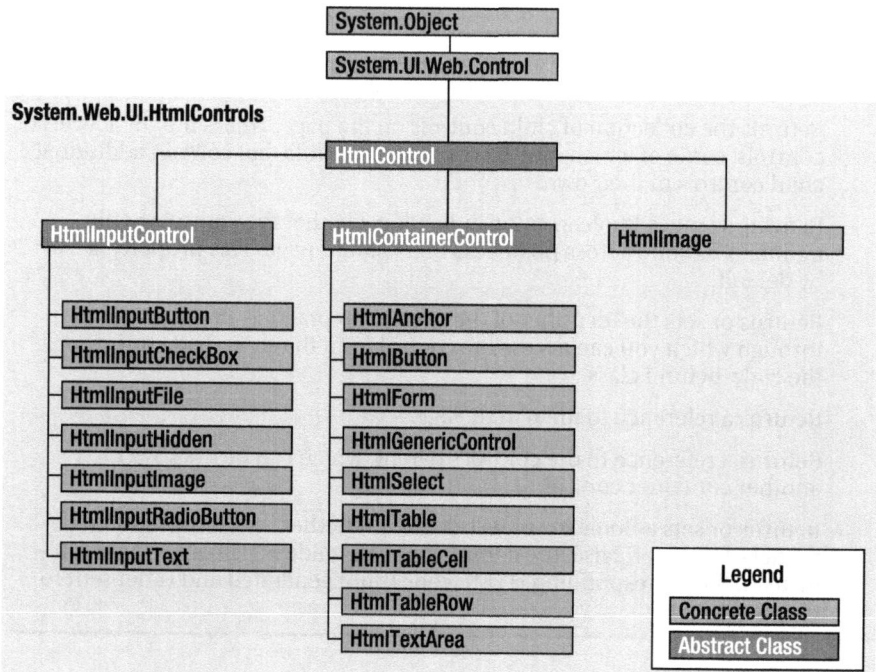

Figure 5-2. *HTML server controls*

The HtmlControl Class

All of the HTML server controls derive from the base class HtmlControl. Table 5-3 shows the properties that the HtmlControl class adds to the base Control class.

Table 5-3. *HtmlControl Properties*

Attributes	Allows you to access or add attributes in the control tag. You can use this collection to add attributes that are not exposed by specific properties. (For example, you could add the onFocus attribute to a text box and specify some JavaScript code to configure what happens when the text box gets focus in the page.)
Disabled	Returns or sets the control's disabled state. If true, the control is usually rendered as a "grayed-out" control and is not usable.
Style	Returns a collection of Cascading Style Sheet (CSS) attributes that are applied to the control. In the web page you set this property as a semicolon-delimited list of style:value attributes. In Visual Studio .NET, you can set this information using a designer by right-clicking the control and selecting Build Style.
TagName	Returns the control's tag name, such as "a", "img", and so on.

The HtmlContainerControl Class

Any HTML tag that has both an opening and a closing tag can contain other HTML content or controls. One example is the anchor tag, which usually wraps text or an image with the tags <a>...</a>. Many other HTML tags also work as containers, including everything from the <div> tag (which allows you to format a block of content) to the lowly <b> tag (which applies bold formatting). These tags don't map to specific HTML server control classes, but you can still use them with the runat="server" attribute. In this case, you interact with them using the HtmlGenericControl class, which itself derives from HtmlContainerControl.

To support containment, the HtmlContainerControl class adds the two additional properties shown in Table 5-4.

Table 5-4. *HtmlContainerControl Properties*

Property	Description
InnerHtml	Returns or sets the HTML text inside the opening and closing tags. When you use this property, all characters are left as is. That means you can embed HTML markup (bolding text, adding line breaks, and so on).
InnerText	Returns or sets the text inside the opening and closing tags. When you use this property, any characters that would be interpreted as special HTML syntax (like the < angle bracket) are automatically replaced with the HTML entity equivalents.

The HtmlInputControl Class

The HTML input controls allow for user interaction. These include the familiar graphical widgets like check boxes, text boxes, buttons, and list boxes. All of these controls are generated with the <input> tag. The type attribute indicates the type of input control, as in <input type="text"> (a text box), <input type="submit"> (a submit button), and <input type="file"> (controls for uploading a file).

Server-side input controls derive from HtmlInputControl, which adds the properties shown in Table 5-5.

Table 5-5. *HtmlInputControl Properties*

Property	Description
Name	Gets the unique identifier name for the HtmlInputControl.
Type	Gets the type of an HtmlInputControl. For example, if this property is set to "text", the HtmlInputControl is a text box for data entry.
Value	Gets or sets the value associated with an input control. The value associated with a control depends on the type of control. For example, in a text box this property contains the text entered in the control. For buttons, this defines the text on the button.

The HTML Server Control Classes

Table 5-6 lists all of the available HTML server controls and the specific properties and events that each one adds to the base class. As noted earlier, the declaration of HTML server controls on the page is the same as what you use for normal static HTML tags, with the addition of the runat="server" attribute. It is this attribute that allows ASP.NET to process them and translate them into instances of the corresponding .NET class. For this reason, the HTML server controls are a good option if you're converting your existing HTML or ASP page to an ASP.NET web form.

Table 5-6. *HTML Server Control Classes*

Tag Declaration	.NET Class	Specific Members
<a runat="server">	HtmlAnchor	Href, Target, Title, Name, ServerClick event
<button runat="server">	HtmlButton	CausesValidation, ServerClick event
<form runat="server">	HtmlForm	Name, Enctype, Method, Target
<img runat="server">	HtmlImage	Align, Alt, Border, Height, Src, Width
<input type="button" runat="server">, <input type="reset" runat="server">, <input type="submit" runat="server">	HtmlInputButton	Name, Type, Value, CausesValidation, ServerClick event
<input type="checkbox" runat="server">	HtmlInputCheckBox	Checked, Name, Type, Value, ServerClick event
<input type="file" runat="server">	HtmlInputFile	Accept, MaxLength, Name, PostedFile, Size, Type, Value
<input type="hidden" runat="server">	HtmlInputHidden	Name, Type, Value, ServerChange event
<input type="image" runat="server">	HtmlInputImage	Align, Alt, Border, Name, Src, Type, Value, CausesValidation, ServerClick event
<input type="radio" runat="server">	HtmlInputRadioButton	Checked, Name, Type, Value, ServerChange event
<input type="text" runat="server">, <input type="password" runat="server">	HtmlInputText	MaxLength, Name, Type, Value, ServerChange event
<select runat="server">	HtmlSelect	Multiple, SelectedIndex, Size, Value, DataSource, DataTextField, DataValueField, Items (collection), ServerChange event
<table runat="server">, <td runat="server">	HtmlTable	Align, BgColor, Border, BorderColor, CellPadding, CellSpacing, Height, NoWrap, Width, Rows (collection)
<th runat="server">	HtmlTableCell	Align, BgColor, Border, BorderColor, ColSpan, Height, NoWrap, RowSpan, Valign, Width

Tag Declaration	.NET Class	Specific Members
<tr runat="server">	HtmlTableRow	Align, BgColor, Border, BorderColor, Height, Valign, Cells (collection)
<textarea runat="server">	HtmlTextArea	Cols, Name, Rows, Value, ServerChange event
Any other HTML tag with the runat="server" attribute	HtmlGenericControl	None

The meaning of most of the HTML server control properties is quite obvious, because they match the underlying HTML tag attributes. This means there's no need to focus on each individual control. In the next few sections, you'll get an overview of some common techniques for using controls, and dig a little deeper into their events and the common object model.

Setting Style Attributes and Other Properties

The following example shows how you can configure a standard HtmlInputText control (which represents the <input type="text"> tag). To read or set the current text in the text box, you use the Value property. If you want to configure the style information, you need to add new CSS style attributes using the Style collection. Finally, if you want to set other attributes that aren't exposed by any properties, you need to use the Attributes collection. This example uses the Attributes collection to associate some simple JavaScript code—showing an alert message box with the current value of the text box—to the client-side onFocus event of the control.

```
private void Page_Load(object sender, System.EventArgs e)
{
    // Only perform the initialization the first time the page is requested.
    // After that, this information is tracked in view state.
    if (!Page.IsPostBack)
    {
        // Set the style attributes to configure appearance.
        TextBox1.Style["font-size"] = "20px";
        TextBox1.Style["color"] = "red";

        // Use a slightly different but equivalent syntax
        // for setting a style attribute.
        TextBox1.Style.Add("background-color", "lightyellow");

        // Set the default text.
        TextBox1.Value = "<Enter e-mail address here>";

        // Set other nonstandard attributes.
        TextBox1.Attributes["onfocus"] = "alert(TextBox1.value)";
    }
}
```

> **Note** Remember to create an HTML server control in Visual Studio .NET, and then drag the control from the HTML group on the toolbox. Then right-click the control and select Run as Server Control to add the required runat="server" attribute.

If you request the page, the following HTML code will be returned for the text box:

```
<input name="TextBox1" id="TextBox1" type="text"
style="WIDTH:410px;HEIGHT:46px;font-size:20px;color:red;
background-color:lightyellow;" size="63" value="<Enter e-mail address here>"
onfocus="alert(TextBox1.value)" />
```

Notice that the CSS style attribute also includes some information that wasn't explicitly set in the code. Instead, Visual Studio .NET added this information to the control tag when the control was resized in the development environment.

Figure 5-3 shows the resulting page when focus changes to the text box.

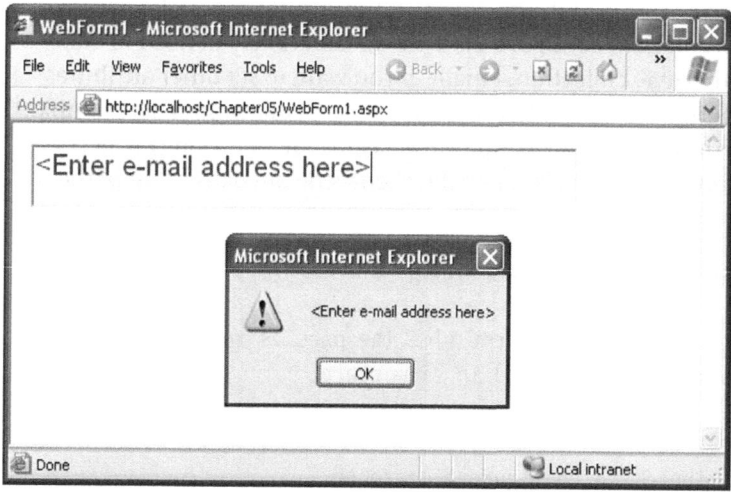

Figure 5-3. *Testing HTML server controls*

> **Tip** Remember that C# is a case-sensitive language, so the control textbox1 is not the same as TextBox1. If the names don't match you'll receive a runtime error because textbox1 does not refer to a control on the page.

This process of control interaction is essentially the same for all HTML server controls. Style properties and attributes are always set in the same way. The only difference is that some controls expose additional properties that you can use. For example, the HtmlAnchor control exposes an Href property that lets you set the target page for the link.

Programmatically Creating Server Controls

There are situations in which you don't know in advance how many text boxes, radio buttons, table rows, or other controls you need because this might depend on the number of records stored in a database, or on the user's input. In classic ASP, the only way to handle this challenge would be with a server-side script that programmatically creates the required HTML code. This approach is highly error-prone, because it's easy to forget to close a tag or include an important attribute. It also results in horrendously confusing code, particularly if you need to dynamically build complex tables or other structures.

With ASP.NET, this problem no longer exists. You can create instances of the HTML server controls, set their properties with the object-oriented approach used in the last example, then simply add them to the Controls collection of the containing page. This technique was introduced in the last chapter, and it applies equally well to HTML server controls and web controls.

For example, the following code dynamically creates a table with five rows and four cells per row, sets their colors and text, and shows all this on the page. The interesting detail is that there are no control tags declared in the .aspx file. Instead, everything is generated programmatically.

```
private void Page_Load(object sender, System.EventArgs e)
{
    // Create a new HtmlTable object.
    HtmlTable table1 = new HtmlTable();

    // Set the table's formatting-related properties.
    table1.Border = 1;
    table1.CellPadding = 3;
    table1.CellSpacing = 3;
    table1.BorderColor = "red";

    // Start adding content to the table.
    HtmlTableRow row;
    HtmlTableCell cell;
    for (int i=1; i<=5; i++)
    {
        // Create a new row and set its background color.
        row = new HtmlTableRow();
        row.BgColor = (i%2==0 ? "lightyellow" : "lightcyan");

        for (int j=1; j<=4; j++)
        {
            // Create a cell and set its text.
            cell = new HtmlTableCell();
            cell.InnerHtml = "Row: " + i.ToString() +
              "<br>Cell: " + j.ToString();
```

```
        // Add the cell to the current row.
        row.Cells.Add(cell);
    }

    // Add the row to the table.
    table1.Rows.Add(row);
}

// Add the table to the page.
this.Controls.Add(table1);
}
```

In this example, there are two nested loops. The outer loop creates a row. The inner loop then creates the cells, and adds them to the Cells collection of the current row. When the inner loop ends, the code adds the entire row to the Rows collection of the table. The final step occurs when the outer loop is finished, and the code adds the completed table to the Controls collection of the page.

Figure 5-4 shows the resulting page.

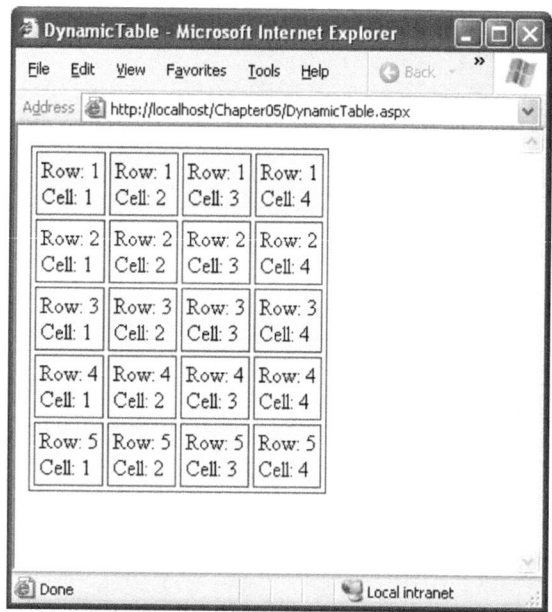

Figure 5-4. *A dynamically generated table*

This example used a table because it gave a good opportunity to show how child controls (cells and rows) are added to the Controls collection of the parent, but of course this mechanism works with any other server control.

Handling Server-Side Events

HTML server controls provide a sparse event model with two possible events: ServerClick and ServerChange. The ServerClick is simply a click that is processed on the server side.

It's provided by most button controls, and it allows your code to take immediate action. This action might override the expected behavior. For example, if you intercept the click event of a hyperlink control (the <a> element), the user won't be redirected to a new page unless you provide extra code to forward the request.

The ServerChange event responds when a change has been made to a text or selection control. This event doesn't occur until the page is posted back (for example, after the user clicks a submit button). At this point, the ServerChange event occurs for all changed controls, followed by the appropriate ServerClick.

Table 5-7 shows which controls provide a ServerClick event, and which ones provide a ServerChange event.

Table 5-7. *HTML Control Events*

Event	Controls That Provide It
ServerClick	HtmlAnchor, HtmlForm, HtmlButton, HtmlInputButton, HtmlInputImage
ServerChange	HtmlInputText, HtmlInputCheckBox, HtmlInputRadioButton, HtmlInputHidden, HtmlSelect, HtmlTextArea

The ServerClick Event and the HtmlInputFile Control

The next example presents a simple test of the ServerClick event on a web page that allows the user to upload a file. This web page includes three controls: the HtmlInputFile control that allows the user to choose a file to upload from the local computer, the HtmlInputButton button for submitting the page, and a server-side <div> tag (which is represented as an instance of HtmlGenericControl) to display result information.

> **Note** In order for this code to work, the account that is used to run the ASP.NET worker process must have rights to the directory you're using. Otherwise, a SecurityException will be thrown when your web page attempts to access the file system. You can modify the permissions for a directory and control that is allowed to access it by right-clicking the directory, selecting Properties, and choosing the Security tab. If you are using the default ASP.NET settings with IIS 5, you need to grant read and write permissions to the ASPNET account. Alternatively, you might find it easier to modify the account that ASP.NET uses so you don't need to change these permissions at all. For more information, refer to Chapter 2, which explains how to configure the account used for ASP.NET applications.

Here's the .aspx control tags you need for this example:

```
<form id="Form1" method="post" runat="server" enctype="multipart/form-data">
    Select a file to upload:<br>
    <P><INPUT id="Uploader" type="file" name="File1" runat="server"></P>
    <P><INPUT id="cmdUpload" type="button" value="Upload" name="Button1"
        runat="server"></P>
    <DIV id="lblStatus" runat="server"></DIV>
</form>
```

As shown in this example, the form must have the enctype attribute set to multipart/form-data in order to handle the uploading of a file. When the button is pressed, the form is posted back to the server, and ASP.NET raises the cmdUpload.ServerClick event. In this example, the ServerClick event is received by an event handler named cmdUpload_ServerClick().

All .NET events provide two arguments. The first is a reference to the control that generated the event (which is useful if you have multiple controls handled by the same server-side event handler). The second is an object that provides any additional information specific to the control. In the case of the ServerClick event, this object is of type EventArgs, which means the event doesn't supply any information. If it does, the second parameter will use a class that derives from EventArgs and includes additional properties.

Here's the event-handling code for the ServerClick event:

```
private void cmdUpload_ServerClick(object sender, System.EventArgs e)
{
    // Check if a file was submitted.
    if (Uploader.PostedFile.ContentLength != 0)
    {
        try
        {
            if (Uploader.PostedFile.ContentLength > 1064)
            {
                // This exceeds the size limit you want to allow,.
                // You should check the size to prevent a denial of
                // service attack that attempts to fill up your
                // web server's hard drive.
                // You might also want to check the amount of
                // remaining free space.
                lblStatus.InnerText = "Too large. This file is not allowed";
            }
            else
            {
                // Retrieve the physical directory path for the Upload
                // subdirectory.
                string destDir = Server.MapPath("./Upload");

                // Extract the filename part from the full path of the
                // original file.
                string fileName = System.IO.Path.GetFileName(
                  Uploader.PostedFile.FileName);

                // Combine the destination directory with the filename.
                string destPath = System.IO.Path.Combine(destDir, fileName);

                // Save the file on the server.
                Uploader.PostedFile.SaveAs(destPath);
                lblStatus.InnerText = "Thanks for submitting your file";
            }
```

```
        }
        catch (Exception err)
        {
            lblStatus.InnerText = err.Message;
        }
    }
}
```

In the example, if a file has been posted to the server and isn't too large, the file is saved using the HttpPostedFile.SaveAs() method. To determine the physical path you want to use, the code combines the destination directory (Upload) with the name of the posted file, using the static utility methods of the Path class. You'll learn more about the Path class and file processing in Chapter 13.

Figure 5-5 shows the page after the file is uploaded.

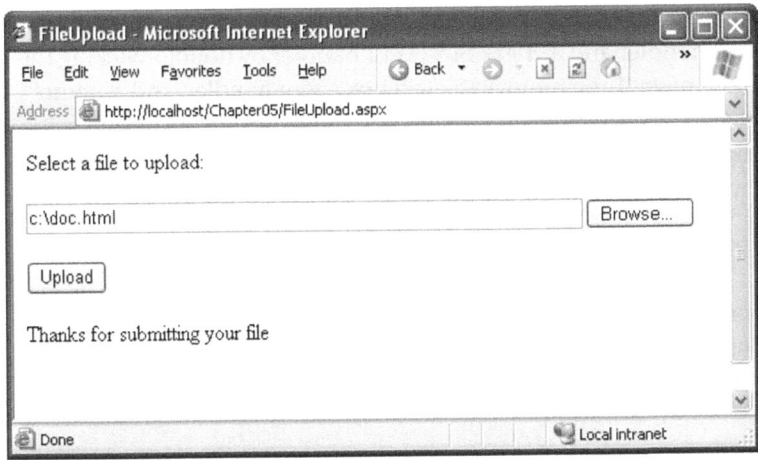

Figure 5-5. *Uploading a file*

■**Note** By default the maximum size of the uploaded file is 4 MB. If you try to upload a bigger file you'll get a runtime error. To change this restriction, modify the maxRequestLength attribute of the <httpRuntime> setting in the application's web.config file. The size is specified in KB, so <httpRuntime maxRequestLength="8192"/> sets the maximum file size to 8 MB.

The ServerChange Event

The ServerChange event occurs when the form is posted back and ASP.NET detects that the content or the state of a control has changed. To see this event in action, consider the following example, which includes a text box, list box, and check box.

Here are the controls on the page:

```
<form id="Form1" method="post" runat="server">
    <select runat="server" ID="List1" size="5" multiple Name="List1">
        <option>Option 1</option>
```

```
        <option>Option 2</option>
    </select>
    <br>
    <input type="text" runat="server" ID="Textbox1" Size="10"
    Name="Textbox1"><br>
    <input type="checkbox" runat="server" ID="Checkbox1" Name="Checkbox1">Option
    text<br>
    <input type="submit" runat="server" ID="Submit1" Name="cmdSubmit"
    value="Submit Query">
</form>
```

Note that this code declares two list items for the list box, and includes the multiple attribute. This means that the user will be able to select multiple items by holding down the Ctrl key while selecting items.

The text box and the check box are attached to the same event handler, while the list box uses a separate event handler with different code. The easiest way to set this up in Visual Studio .NET is to create a text box event handler and a check box event handler by double-clicking the text box and the check box on the page. Then remove the text box event handler, and rename the check box event handler to Ctrl_ServerChange(). Finally, you must modify the delegate code that Visual Studio .NET has generated in the hidden designer region of the web page so that both events use the new method name, as shown here:

```
private void InitializeComponent()
{
    this.Textbox1.ServerChange += new EventHandler(Ctrl_ServerChange);
    this.Checkbox1.ServerChange += new EventHandler(Ctrl_ServerChange);
    ...
}
```

Note Visual Studio .NET provides a greater level of design-time support for events with web controls. When working with web controls, you can attach event handlers using a special event view in the Properties windows—you just need to click the lightning bolt icon. With HTML server controls, this facility isn't available, although you can still coax Visual Studio .NET into generating an event handler for the control's default event by double-clicking it.

The actual event-handler code is quite straightforward. It simply casts the sender object to a Control type, reads its ID property, and writes a message declaring that the event was detected, as shown here:

```
private void Ctrl_ServerChange(object sender, System.EventArgs e)
{
    Response.Write("<li>ServerChange detected for " +
        ((Control)sender).ID + "</li>");
}
```

The event handler for the list box writes a similar message, but it also cycles through the control's Items collection, and writes the value of all the selected items to the client, as follows:

```
private void List1_ServerChange(object sender, System.EventArgs e)
{
    Response.Write("<li>ServerChange detected for List1. " +
      "The selected items are:</li><br>");
    foreach (ListItem li in List1.Items)
    {
        if (li.Selected)
            Response.Write("  - " + li.Value + "<br>");
    }
}
```

Finally, the submit button handles the ServerClick event, as shown here:

```
private void Submit1_ServerClick(object sender, System.EventArgs e)
{
    Response.Write("<li>ServerClick detected for Submit1.</li>");
}
```

As an added bonus, when the page is created the event handler for the Page.Load event adds another three items to the list box, provided the page is being requested for the first time. This shows how easy it is to programmatically add list items.

```
private void Page_Load(object sender, System.EventArgs e)
{
    if (!Page.IsPostBack)
    {
        List1.Items.Add("Option 3");
        List1.Items.Add("Option 4");
        List1.Items.Add("Option 5");
    }
}
```

To test this page, request it in the browser, select some items in the list box, type some characters in the text box, select the check box, and click the submit button to generate a postback. You should end up with something similar to what's shown in Figure 5-6.

Note that the order of change events is nondeterministic, and you shouldn't rely on these events occurring in any set order. However, you're likely to see events raised in the order in which the controls are declared. The only detail of which you're guaranteed is that all the change events fire before the ServerClick event that triggered the postback.

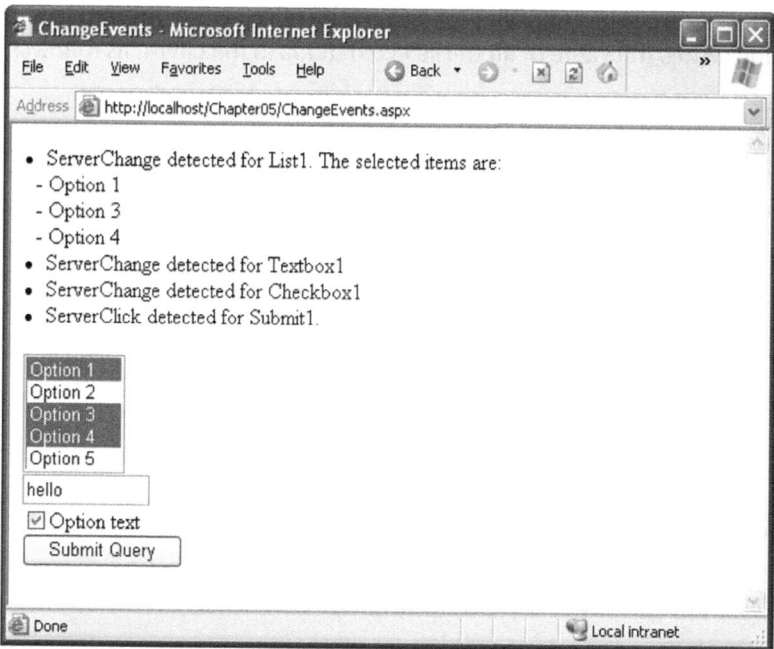

Figure 5-6. *Detecting change events*

ASP.NET Web Form Controls

HTML server controls provide a relatively fast way to migrate to ASP.NET, but not necessarily the best way. For one thing, the names of HTML controls and their attributes are not always intuitive, and they don't have the same design-time support for attaching event handlers. The HTML controls also have certain limitations, such as the fact that style properties must be set through CSS syntax (which is more difficult than setting a direct property), and the fact that change events can't be raised until the page is posted back in response to another action. Finally, HTML server controls can't provide user interface elements that aren't already defined in the HTML standard. If you want to create some sort of aggregate control that uses a combination of HTML elements to render a complex interface, you're on your own.

To address these issues, ASP.NET provides a higher-level web-control model. All web controls are defined in the System.Web.UI.WebControl namespace and derive from the WebControl base class, which provides a more abstract, consistent model than the HTML server controls. Web controls also enable additional features, such as automatic postback. But the really exciting part is that there are also many extended controls that don't just map a single HTML tag, but instead generate more complex output made up of several HTML tags and JavaScript code. Examples include lists of check boxes, radio buttons, calendars, editable grids, and so on. In this section you'll see most of these controls.

Figure 5-7 shows the inheritance hierarchy for web-server controls.

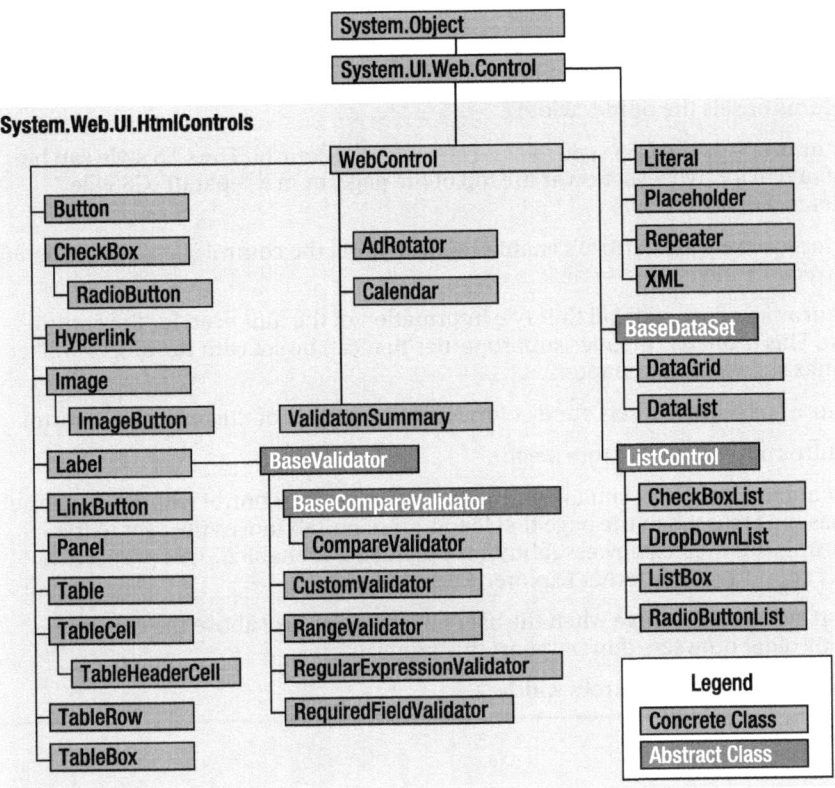

Figure 5-7. *Web-server controls*

The WebControl Base Class

All of the web controls inherit from the WebControl class. The WebControl class also derives from Control. As a result, many of its properties and methods—such as Controls, Visible, FindControl()—are similar to those of the HTML server controls. However, the WebControl class adds the properties shown in Table 5-7. Many of these properties wrap the CSS style attributes, such as the foreground or background color, the font, height, width, and so on. These properties allow you to configure the appearance of a web control much more easily (and with less chance of error).

Table 5-7. *WebServer Class Properties*

Property	Description
AccessKey	Returns or sets the keyboard shortcut that allows the user to quickly navigate to the control. For example, if set to "A" the user can move the focus to this control by pressing Ctrl+A. This property is only supported in Internet Explorer.
BackColor	Returns or sets the background color.
BorderColor	Returns or sets the border color.
BorderStyle	One of the values from the BorderStyle enumeration, including Dashed, Dotted, Double, Groove, Ridge, Inset, Outset, Solid, and None.

Continued

Table 5-7. *Continued*

Property	Description
BorderWidth	Returns or sets the border width.
CssClass	Returns or sets the CSS style to associate with the control. The CSS style can be defined in a <style> section at the top of the page, or in a separate .CSS file referenced by the page.
Enabled	Returns or sets the control's enabled state. If false, the control is usually rendered grayed out and is not usable.
Font	Returns an object with all the style information of the font used for the control's text. This property includes subproperties that can be set with the object-walker syntax shown in this chapter.
ForeColor	Returns or sets the foreground color; for example, that of the text of the control.
Height	Returns or sets the control's height.
TabIndex	A number that allows you to control the tab order. The control with a TabIndex of 0 has the focus when the page first loads. Pressing Tab moves the user to the control with the next lowest TabIndex, provided it is enabled. This property is only supported in Internet Explorer 4.0 and higher.
ToolTip	Displays a text message when the user hovers the mouse above the control. Many older browsers don't support this property.
Width	Returns or sets the control's width.

Basic Web Control Classes

ASP.NET includes a web control that duplicates each HTML server control and provides the same functionality. These web controls inherit from WebControl and add their own properties and events. Table 5-8 summarizes these core controls and their specific members.

Table 5-8. *Basic Web Control Classes*

ASP.NET Tag Declaration	Generated HTML	Specific Members
<asp:Button>	<input type="submit"/> or <input type="button"/>	CommandArgument, CommandName, Text, CausesValidation, Click event, Command event
<asp:CheckBox>	<input type="checkbox"/>	AutoPostBack, Checked, Text, TextAlign, CheckedChanged event
<asp:HyperLink>	<a>...</a>	ImageUrl, NavigateUrl, Target, Text
<asp:Image>	<img/>	AlternateText, ImageAlign, ImageUrl
<asp:ImageButton>	<input type="image"/>	CommandArgument, CommandName, CausesValidation, Click event, Command event
<asp:Label>	...	Text
<asp:LinkButton>	<a><img/></a>	CommandArgument, CommandName, Text, CausesValidation, Click event, Command event

ASP.NET Tag Declaration	Generated HTML	Specific Members
<asp:Panel>	<div>...</div>	BackImageUrl, HorizontalAlign, Wrap
<asp:RadioButton>	<input type="radio"/>	AutoPostBack, Checked, GroupName, Text, TextAlign, CheckedChanged event
<asp:Table>	<table>...</table>	BackImageUrl, CellPadding, CellSpacing, GridLines, HorizontalAlign, Rows (collection)
<asp:TableCell>	<td>...</td>	ColumnSpan, HorizontalAlign, RowSpan, Text, VerticalAlign, Wrap
<asp:TableRow>	<tr>...</tr>	Cells (collection), HorizontalAlign, VerticalAlign
<asp:TextBox>	<input type="test"/> or <input type="test"/> or <textarea>...</textarea>	AutoPostBack, Columns, MaxLength, ReadOnly, Rows, Text, TextMode, Wrap, TextChanged event

The properties of web controls are all fairly intuitive. One of the goals of web controls is to make it easier to set a control's attributes through properties with consistent names, without having to worry about the details of how they translate to HTML code (although having a good knowledge of HTML certainly helps). For this reason, this chapter won't describe and show examples for each and every type of control. Instead, you'll walk through a general discussion that's useful for every control.

To start highlighting some of the key differences between HTML server controls and web controls, consider the following web-control tag:

```
<asp:TextBox runat="server" ID="Textbox1" Text="This is a test"
  ForeColor="red" BackColor="lightyellow" Width="250px"
  Font-Name="Verdana" Font-Bold="True" Font-Size="20" />
```

Web controls are always declared on the page with the syntax <asp:controlname>, with the asp: prefix that makes them immediately recognizable as being different from the HTML controls. But this example also demonstrates a more dramatic difference—the way that style information is specified.

Essentially, this tag generates a text box control with a width of 250 pixels, a red foreground color, and a light yellow background. The text is displayed with font Verdana of size 20 and rendered in bold. The differences between the previous declaration and the respective declaration of a HTML tag are the following:

- The control is declared using its class name (TextBox) instead of the HTML tag name (input).

- The default content is set with the Text property, instead of a less obvious Value attribute.

- The style attributes (colors, width, and font) are set by direct properties, instead of being grouped together in a single style attribute.

Web controls also have two special restrictions:

- Every control declaration must have a corresponding closing tag, or the empty element /> syntax at the end of the opening tag to maintain XHTML compliance. If you don't close the tag you'll get a runtime error. Breaking this rule when working with HTML server controls has no adverse affect.

- All web controls must be declared within a server-side form tag (and there can be only one server-side form per page), even if they don't cause a postback. Otherwise you'll get a runtime error. This rule is not necessary when working with HTML server controls, provided you don't need to handle postbacks.

If you request a page with this tag, you'll see that the control is translated into the following HTML tag when the page is rendered:

```
<input name="Textbox1" type="text" value="This is a test" id="Textbox1"
style="color:Red;background-color:LightYellow;font-family:Verdana;
font-size:20pt;font-weight:bold;width:250px;" />
```

Units

All the properties that use measurements, including BorderWidth, Height, and Width, require the Unit structure, which combines a numeric value with a type of measurement (pixels, percentage, and so on). This means that when you set these properties in a control tag, you must make sure to append px (for pixel) or % (for percentage) to the number to indicate the type of unit.

Here's an example with a Panel control that is 300 pixels wide, and has a height equal to 50 percent of the current browser window:

```
<asp:Panel Height="300px" Width="50%" id="pnl" runat="server" />
```

If you're assigning a unit-based property through code, you need to use one of the static methods of the Unit type. Use Pixel() to supply a value in pixels, and Percentage() to supply a percentage value.

```
// Convert the number 300 to a Unit object
// representing pixels, and assign it.
pnl.Height = Unit.Pixel(300);

// Convert the number 50 to a Unit object
// representing percent, and assign it.
pnl.Width = Unit.Percentage(50);
```

You could also manually create a Unit object and initialize it using one of the supplied constructors and the UnitType enumeration. This requires a few more steps, but allows you to easily assign the same unit to several controls.

```
// Create a Unit object.
Unit myUnit = new Unit(300, UnitType.Pixel);
```

```
// Assign the Unit object to several controls or properties.
pnl.Height = myUnit;
pnl.Width = myUnit;
```

Enumerated Values

Enumerations are used heavily in the .NET class library to group together a set of related constants. For example, when you set a control's BorderStyle property, you can choose one of several predefined values from the BorderStyle enumeration. In code, you set an enumeration using the dot syntax:

```
ctrl.BorderStyle = BorderStyle.Dashed;
```

In the .aspx file, you set an enumeration by specifying one of the allowed values as a string. You don't include the name of the enumeration type, which is assumed automatically.

```
<asp:TextBox BorderStyle="Dashed" Text="Border Test" id="txt"
 runat="server" />
```

Colors

The Color property refers to a Color object from the System.Drawing namespace. Color objects can be created in several different ways:

- **Using an ARGB (alpha, red, green, blue) color value.** You specify each value as integer.

- **Using a predefined .NET color name.** You choose the correspondingly named read-only property from the Color class. These properties include all the HTML colors.

- **Using an HTML color name.** You specify this value as a string using the ColorTranslator class.

To use these any of techniques, you must import the System.Drawing namespace, as follows:

```
using System.Drawing;
```

The following code shows several ways to specify a color in code.

```
// Create a color from an ARGB value.
int alpha = 255, red = 0, green = 255, blue = 0;
ctrl.ForeColor = Color.FromARGB(alpha, red, green, blue);

// Create a color using a .NET name.
ctrl.ForeColor = Color.Crimson;

// Create a color from an HTML code.
ctrl.ForeColor = ColorTranslator.FromHtml("Blue");
```

When defining a color in the .aspx file, you can use any one of the known color names, as follows:

```
<asp:TextBox ForeColor="Red" Text="Test" id="txt" runat="server" />
```

Refer to the MSDN document for a full list of color names. Alternatively, you can use a hexadecimal color number (in the format #<red><green><blue>), as shown here:

```
<asp:TextBox ForeColor="#ff50ff" Text="Test"
    id="txt" runat="server" />
```

Fonts

The Font property actually references a full FontInfo object, which is defined in the System.Drawing namespace. Every FontInfo object has several properties that define a font's name, size, and style. Even though the WebControl.Font property is read-only, you can modify all of the FontInfo properties (shown in Table 5-9).

Table 5-9. *FontInfo Properties*

Property	Description
Name	A string indicating the font name (such as "Verdana").
Names	An array of strings with font names, which are ordered by preference.
Size	The size of the font as a FontUnit object. This can represent an absolute or relative size.
Bold, Italic, Strikeout, Underline, and Overline	Boolean properties that either apply the given style attribute or ignore it.

In code, you can assign values to the various font properties as shown here:

```
ctrl.Font.Name = "Verdana";
ctrl.Font.Bold = true;
```

You can also set the size using the FontUnit type:

```
// Specifies a relative size.
ctrl.Font.Size = FontUnit.Small;

// Specifies an absolute size of 14 pixels.
ctrl.Font.Size = FontUnit.Point(14);
```

In the .aspx file, you need to use a special *object walker* syntax to specify object properties such as font. The object walker syntax uses a hyphen (-) to separate properties. For example, you could set a control with a specific font (Tahoma) and font size (40 point) like this:

```
<asp:TextBox Font-Name="Tahoma" Font-Size="40" Text="Size Test" id="txt"
 runat="server" />
```

or with a relative size, as follows:

```
<asp:TextBox Font-Name="Tahoma" Font-Size="Large" Text="Size Test"
 id="txt" runat="server" />
```

Of course, in the world of the Internet font names are just recommendations. If a given font isn't present on a client's computer, the browser attempts to substitute a similar font. (For more information on this font substitution process, refer to the CSS specification at www.w3.org/TR/REC-CSS2/fonts.html.)

If you want to provide a list of possible fonts, you can use the FontInfo.Names property instead of the FontInfo.Name property. The Names property accepts an array of names that will be rendered as an ordered list (with greatest preference given to the names at the top of the list).

Tip The Names and Name property are kept synchronized, and setting either one affects the other. When you set the Names property, the Name property is automatically set to the first item in the array you used for the Names property. If you set the Name property, the Names property is automatically set with an array containing a single item. Therefore, you should only use the Name property or the Names property, but not both at once.

Handling Web Control Events

Server-side events work in much the same way as the server events of the HTML server controls. Instead of the ServerClick events, there is a Click event, and instead of the generic ServerChange events there are specific events such as CheckedChanged (for the RadioButton and CheckButton) and TextChanged (for the TextBox), but the behavior remains the same.

The key difference is that web controls support the AutoPostBack feature described in the previous chapter, which uses JavaScript to capture a client-side event and trigger a postback. ASP.NET receives the posted-back page, and raises the corresponding server-side event immediately.

To watch these events in action, it helps to create a simple event tracker application (see Figure 5-8). All this application does is add a new entry to a list control every time one of the events it's monitoring occurs. This allows you to see the order in which events are triggered and the effect of using automatic postback.

In this demonstration, all control change events are handled by the same event handler, which simply adds a new message to a list box and scrolls to the end.

```
private void CtrlChanged(Object sender, EventArgs e)
{
    string ctrlName = ((Control)sender).ID;
    lstEvents.Items.Add(ctrlName + " Changed");

    // Select the last item to scroll the list so the most recent
    // entries are visible.
    lstEvents.SelectedIndex = lstEvents.Items.Count - 1;
}
```

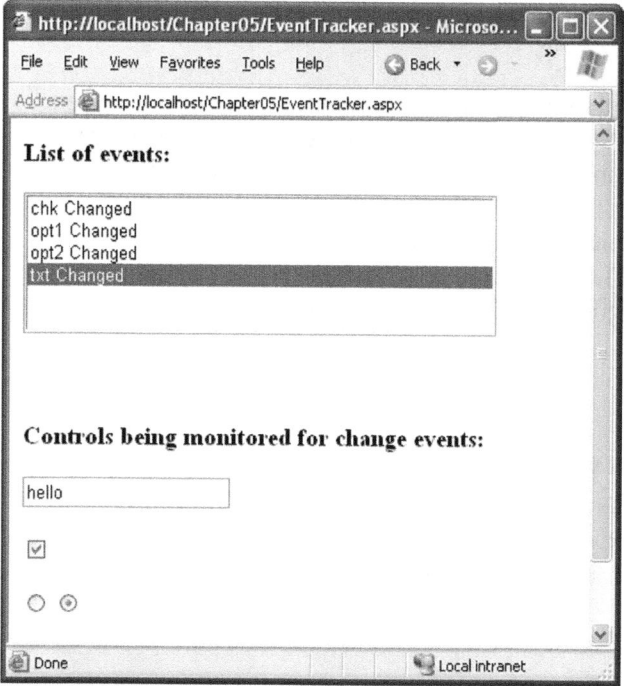

Figure 5-8. *The event tracker*

■Note Automatic postback isn't always a good thing. Posting the page back to the server interrupts the user for a brief amount of time. If the page is large, the delay may be more than a noticeable flicker. If the page is long and the user has scrolled down to the bottom of the page, the user will lose the current position when the page is refreshed and the view is returned to the top of the page. Because of these idiosyncrasies, it's a good idea to evaluate whether you really need postback, and to refrain from using it for minor cosmetic reasons.

The ServerClick Event and the HtmlInputImage Control

In the examples you've looked at so far, the second event parameter has always been used to pass an empty System.EventArgs object. This object doesn't contain any additional information—it's just a glorified placeholder.

One control that does send extra information is the ImageButton control. It sends a special ImageClickEventArgs object (from the System.Web.UI namespace) that provides X and Y properties representing the location where the image was clicked. Using this additional information, you can create a server-side image map. For example, here's the code that simply displays the location where the image was clicked and checks if it was over a predetermined region of the picture:

```
private void ImageButton1_Click(object sender,
  System.Web.UI.ImageClickEventArgs e)
{
    lblResult.Text = "You clicked at (" + e.X.ToString() +
      ", " + e.Y.ToString() + "). ";

    if ((e.Y < 100) && (e.Y > 20) && (e.X > 20) && (e.X < 275))
    {
        lblResult.Text += "You clicked on the button surface.";
    }
    else
    {
        lblResult.Text += "You clicked the button border.";
    }
}
```

The sample web page shown in Figure 5-9 puts this feature to work with a simple graphical button. Depending on whether the user clicks the button border or the button surface, the web page displays a different message.

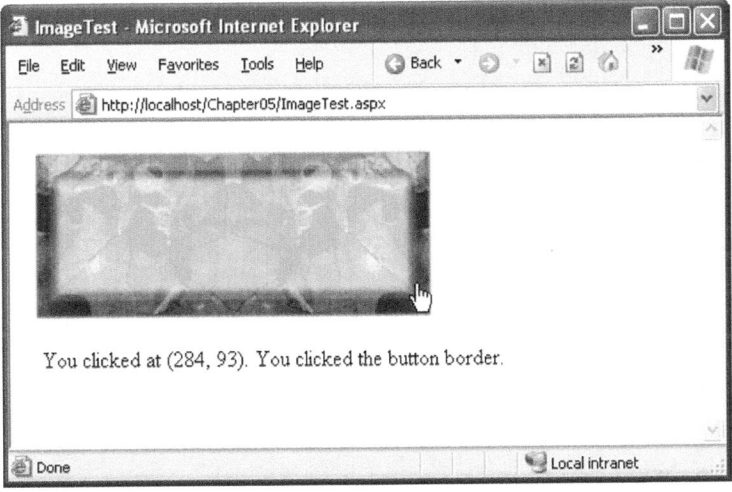

Figure 5-9. *Using an ImageButton control*

The ASP.NET List Controls

The list controls are a specialized group of web controls that generate list boxes, drop-down lists, and other repeating controls that can be either bound to a data source (such as a database or a hard-coded collection of values) or programmatically filled with items. These controls (shown in Table 5-10) range from simple server-side versions of the HTML <select> tag to advanced table-based controls that you can use to show complex, formatted grids and reports.

Table 5-10. *List Controls*

Control	Description
<asp:DropDownList>	This renders a drop-down list populated by a collection of <asp:ListItems> objects. In HTML, it is rendered by a <select> tag with the size="1" attribute.
<asp:ListBox>	A list box list populated by a collection of <asp:ListItems> objects. In HTML, it is rendered by a <select> tag with the size="x" attribute, where x is the number of visible items.
<asp:CheckBoxList>	Its items are rendered as check boxes, aligned in a table with one or more columns.
<asp:RadioButtonList>	Like the <asp:CheckBoxList>, but the items are rendered as radio buttons.
<asp:Repeater>	Repeats a custom template for each item in the data source. It has no predefined layout, and it only generates the code specified in the template.
<asp:DataList>	Repeats a custom template for each item in the data source, but has a predefined template that renders the items in a table with one or more columns. It has a built-in support for editable and selectable rows.
<asp:DataGrid>	A grid that shows the items of the data source in predefined or template columns. It has a built-in support for editable and selectable rows, automatic and custom pagination, and much more.

The last three controls are advanced controls that can only be bound to a data source, and cannot be filled programmatically. You'll learn about these controls in Part Two of this book, but they won't be covered in the rest of this chapter.

The ListControl Class

The list controls support the same base properties and methods as other web controls. In addition, the basic list controls (DropDownList, ListBox, CheckBoxList, and RadioButtonList) all inherit from the System.Web.UI.WebControls.ListControl class, which exposes the properties in Table 5-11.

Table 5-11. *ListControl Class Properties*

Member	Description
AutoPostBack	If true, the form is automatically posted back when the user changes the current selection.
Items	Returns a collection of ListItem items (the items can also be added declaratively by adding the <asp:ListItem> tag).
SelectedIndex	Returns or sets the index of the selected item. For lists with multiple selectable items, you should loop through the collection of Items and check the Selected property of each ListItem instead.
SelectedItem	Returns a reference to the first selected ListItem. For lists with multiple selectable items, you should loop through the collection of Items and check the Selected property of each ListItem instead.

Member	Description
DataSource	You can set this property to an object that contains the information you want to display (such as a DataSet, DataTable, or collection). When you call DataBind(), the list will be filled based on that object.
DataMember	Used in conjunction with data binding when the data source contains more than one table (such as when the source is a DataSet). The DataMember identifies which table you want to use.
DataTextField	Used in conjunction with data binding to indicate which property or field in the data source should be used for the text of each list item.
DataValueField	Used in conjunction with data binding to indicate which property or field in the data source should be used for the value attribute of each list item (which isn't displayed, but can be read programmatically for future reference).
DataTextFormatString	Sets the formatting string used to render the text of the list item (according to the DataTextField property).

In addition, the ListControl control class also defines a SelectedIndexChanged event, which fires when the user changes the current selection.

By default, the RadioButtonList and CheckBoxList render their interfaces by creating multiple option buttons or check boxes. Both of these classes add a few more properties that allow you to manage the layout of these repeated items, as described in Table 5-12.

Table 5-12. *Added RadioButtonList and CheckBoxList Properties*

RepeatLayout	Specifies whether the check boxes or radio buttons will be rendered in a table (the default option), or inline. The values are Table and Flow, respectively.
RepeatDirection	Specifies whether the list of controls will be rendered horizontally or vertically.
RepeatColumn	Sets the number of columns, in case RepeatLayout is set to Table.
CellPadding, CellSpacing, and TextAlign	If RepeatLayout is Table, these properties configure the spacing and alignment of the cells of the layout table.

Using the ASP.NET List Controls

The basic list controls (DropDownList, ListBox, CheckBoxList, and RadioButtonList) don't need to be bound to a data source in order to be filled with information.

Here's an example page that declares an instance of every basic list control, adds items to each of them, and sets a few other properties:

```
<form runat="server">
    <asp:ListBox runat="server" ID="Listbox1" SelectionMode="Multiple" Rows="5">
        <asp:ListItem Selected="true">Option 1</asp:ListItem>
        <asp:ListItem>Option 2</asp:ListItem>
    </asp:ListBox>
    <br><br>
    <asp:DropDownList runat="server" ID="DropdownList1">
```

```
        <asp:ListItem Selected="true">Option 1</asp:ListItem>
        <asp:ListItem>Option 2</asp:ListItem>
    </asp:DropDownList>
    <br><br>
    <asp:CheckBoxList runat="server" ID="CheckboxList1" RepeatColumns="3" >
        <asp:ListItem Selected="true">Option 1</asp:ListItem>
        <asp:ListItem>Option 2</asp:ListItem>
    </asp:CheckBoxList>
    <br>
    <asp:RadioButtonList runat="server" ID="RadiobuttonList1"
     RepeatDirection="Horizontal" RepeatColumns="2">
        <asp:ListItem Selected="true">Option 1</asp:ListItem>
        <asp:ListItem>Option 2</asp:ListItem>
    </asp:RadioButtonList>
    <asp:Button runat="server" Text="Submit"/>
</form>
```

When the page is loaded for the first time, the event handler for the Page.Load event adds three more items to each list control, as shown here:

```
private void Page_Load(object sender, System.EventArgs e)
{
    if (!Page.IsPostBack)
    {
        for (int i=3; i<=5; i++)
        {
            Listbox1.Items.Add("Option " + i.ToString());
            DropdownList1.Items.Add("Option " + i.ToString());
            CheckboxList1.Items.Add("Option " + i.ToString());
            RadiobuttonList1.Items.Add("Option " + i.ToString());
        }
    }
}
```

When the submit button is clicked, the selected items of each control are displayed on the page. For the controls with a single selection (the DropDownList and RadioButtonList), this is just a matter or accessing the SelectedItem property. For the other controls that allow multiple selections, you must cycle through all the items in the Items collection and check whether the ListItem.Selected property is true. Here's the code that does both of these tasks:

```
private void Button1_Click(object sender, System.EventArgs e)
{
    Response.Write("<b>Selected items for Listbox1:</b><br>");
    foreach (ListItem li in Listbox1.Items)
    {
        if (li.Selected) Response.Write("- " + li.Text + "<br>");
    }

    Response.Write("<b>Selected item for DropdownList1:</b><br>");
```

```
Response.Write("- " + DropdownList1.SelectedItem.Text + "<br>");

Response.Write("<b>Selected items for CheckboxList1:</b><br>");
foreach (ListItem li in CheckboxList1.Items)
{
    if (li.Selected) Response.Write("- " + li.Text + "<br>");
}

Response.Write("<b>Selected item for RadiobuttonList1:</b><br>");
Response.Write("- " + RadiobuttonList1.SelectedItem.Text + "<br>");
}
```

To test the page, load it, select one or more items in each control, and then click the button. You should get something like what's shown in Figure 5-10.

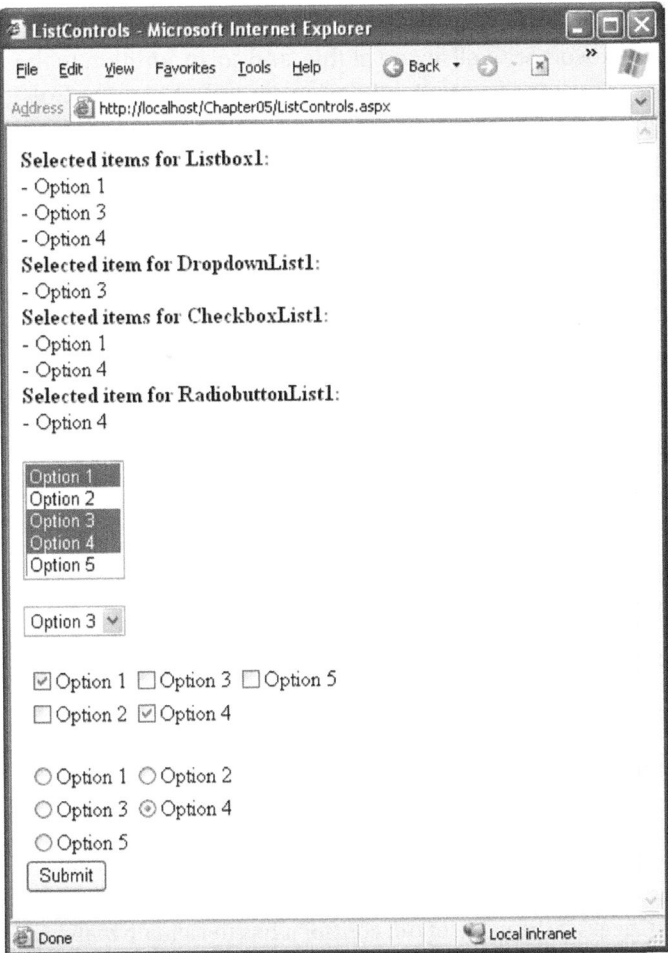

Figure 5-10. *Checking for selected items in the list controls*

The ASP.NET Input Validation Controls

One of the most common uses for web pages (and the reason that the HTML form tags were first created) is to collect data. Often, a web page will ask a user for some information, and then store it in a back-end database. In almost every case, this data must be *validated* to ensure that you don't store useless, spurious, or contradictory information that might cause later problems.

Ideally, the validation of the user input should be done on the client side so that the user is immediately informed that there's something wrong with the input *before* the form is posted back to the server. If this pattern is implemented correctly, it saves server resources and gives the user faster feedback. However, regardless of whether or not client-side validation is performed, the form's data must also be validated on the server side. Otherwise a shrewd attacker could hack the page by removing the client-side JavaScript that validates the input, saving the new page, and using it to submit bogus data.

Writing validation code by hand is a lengthy task, especially because the model for client-side programming (typically JavaScript) and server-side programming (in our case, ASP.NET) are quite different. The developers at Microsoft are well aware of this, and so, in addition to the set of HTML and web controls, they also developed a set of *validation controls*. These controls can be declared on a web form, and then bound to any other input control. Once bound to an input control, the validation control performs automatic client-side *and* server-side validation. If the corresponding control is empty, doesn't contain the correct data type, or doesn't adhere to the specified rules, the validator will prevent the page from being posted back altogether.

The Validation Controls

ASP.NET includes six validation controls. These controls all perform a good portion of the heavy lifting for you, thereby streamlining the validation process and saving you from having to write tedious code. Even better, the validation controls are flexible enough to work with the custom rules you define, which makes your code more reusable and modular. Table 5-13 briefly summarizes each validator.

Table 5-13. *The Validation Controls*

Validation Control	Description
<asp:RequiredFieldValidator>	Checks that the control it has to validate is not empty when the form is submitted.
<asp:RangeValidator>	Checks that the value of the associated control is within a specified range. The value and the range can be numerical—a date or a string.
<asp:CompareValidator>	Checks that the value of the associated control matches a specified comparison (less than, greater than, and so on) against another constant value or control.
<asp:RegularExpressionValidator>	Checks if the value of the control it has to validate matches the specified regular expression.
<asp:CustomValidator>	Allows you to specify any client-side JavaScript validation routine and its server-side counterpart to perform your own custom validation logic.
<asp:ValidationSummary>	Shows a summary with the error messages for each failed validator on the page.

It's important to note that you can use more than one validator for the same control. For example, you could use a validator to ensure that an input control is not empty, and another to ensure that it contains data of a certain type. In fact, if you use the RangeValidator, CompareValidator, or RegularExpressionValidator, validation will automatically succeed if the input control is empty, because there is no value to validate. If this isn't the behavior you want, you should add an additional RequiredFieldValidator to the control. This ensures that two types of validation will be performed, effectively restricting blank values.

While you can't validate RadioButton or CheckBox controls, you can validate the TextBox (the most common choice), ListBox, DropDownList, RadioButtonList, HtmlInputText, HtmlTextArea, HtmlSelect, and HtmlInputFile. When validating a list control, the property that is being validated is the Value property of the selected ListItem object. Remember, the Value property is a hidden attribute that stores a piece of information in the HTML page for each list item, but it isn't displayed in the browser. If you don't use the Value attribute, you can't validate the control (validating the text of the selection isn't a supported option).

Technically, every control class has the option of designating one property that can be validated using the ValidationProperty attribute. For example, if you create your own control class named FancyTextBox, here's how you would designate the Text property as property that supports validation:

```
[ValidationProperty("Text")]
public class FancyTextBox : WebControl
{...}
```

You'll learn more about how attributes work with custom controls in Chapter 21.

The Validation Process

You can use the validation controls to verify a page automatically when the user submits it, or verify it manually in your code. The first approach is the most common.

When using automatic validation, the user receives a normal page and begins to fill in the input controls. When finished, the user clicks a button to submit the page. Every button has a CausesValidation property, which can be set to true or false. What happens when the user clicks the button depends on the value of the CausesValidation property.

- If CausesValidation is false, ASP.NET will ignore the validation controls, the page will be posted back, and your event-handling code will run normally.

- If CausesValidation is true (the default), ASP.NET will automatically validate the page when the user clicks the button. It does this by performing the validation for each control on the page. If any control fails to validate, ASP.NET will return the page with some error information, depending on your settings. Your click-event-handling code may or may not be executed—meaning that you'll have to specifically check in the event handler whether the page is valid or not.

Based on this description, you'll realize that validation happens automatically when certain buttons are clicked. It doesn't happen when the page is posted back due to a change event (like choosing a new value in an AutoPostBack list) or if the user clicks a button that has CausesValidation set to false. However, you can still validate one or more controls manually, and then make a decision in your code based on the results.

In browsers that support it (currently only Internet Explorer 5.0 and above), ASP.NET will automatically add code for client-side validation. In this case, when the user clicks on a CausesValidation button, the same error messages will appear without the page needing to be submitted and returned from the server. This increases the responsiveness of the application. However, if the page validates successfully on the client side, ASP.NET will still revalidate it when it's received at the server. By performing the validation at both ends, your application can be as responsive as possible, but still remain secure.

Figure 5-11 shows a page that uses validation with several text boxes, and ends with a validation summary. In the following section, you'll learn about how you can use the different validators that are used in this example.

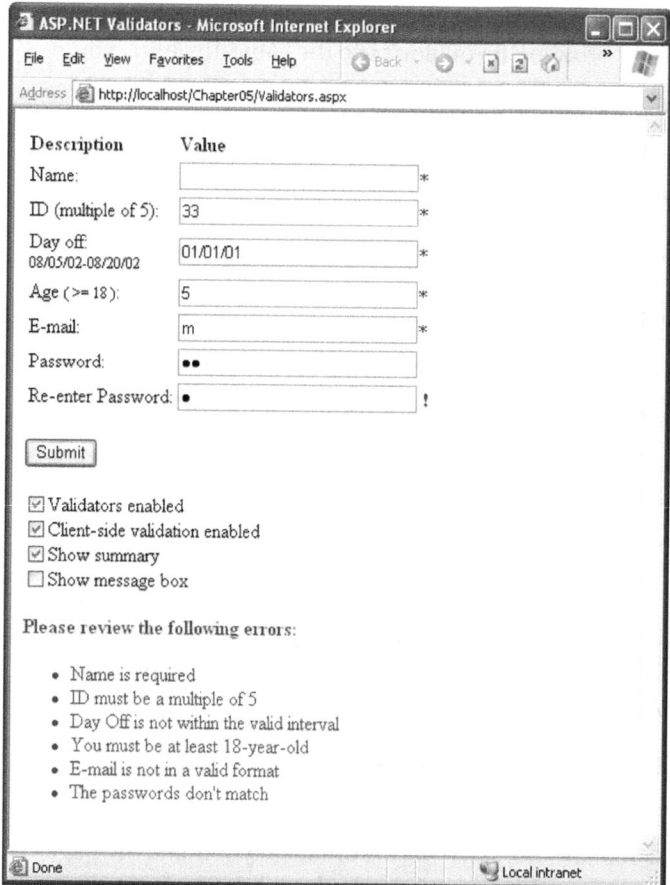

Figure 5-11. *Validating a sample page*

■**NOTE** The validation controls only emit client-side JavaScript for Internet Explorer browsers. They require roundtrips on Netscape, Opera, and other browsers. Part of the problem is the way IIS determines whether a browser is up-level or not (see Chapter 20), and part of the problem is the use of non-standard JavaScript code in the validation routines. For a discussion of the problem and links to third-party controls that address it, you can read the article at http://aspnet.4guysfromrolla.com/articles/051204-1.aspx.

The BaseValidator Class

The validation control classes are found in the System.Web.UI.WebControls namespace and inherit from the BaseValidator class. This class defines the basic functionality for a validation control. Its properties are described in Table 5-14.

Table 5-14. *BaseValidator Members*

Member	Description
ControlToValidate	Indicates the input control to validate.
Display	Indicates how the error message will be shown. If Static, the space required to show the message will be calculated and added to the space layout in advance. If Dynamic, the page layout will dynamically change to show the error string. Be aware that although the dynamic style could seem useful, if your layout is heavily based on table structures it could change quite a bit if multiple strings are dynamically added, and this could confuse the user.
EnableClientScript	A Boolean property that specifies whether the client-side validation will be done or not. It is true by default.
Enabled	A Boolean property that allows the user to enable or disable the validator. When the control is disabled it does not validate anything. This property is usually used programmatically to change the enabled state according to the current page state, or according to another application's settings.
ErrorMessage	Error string that will be shown in the errors summary by the ValidationSummary control, if present.
Text	The error text that will be displayed in the validator control if the attached input control fails its validation.
IsValid	This property is also usually read or set only from script code (or the code-behind class) to determine whether the associated input control's value is valid or not. This property can be checked on the server after a postback, but if the client-side validation is active and supported by the client browser the execution won't get to the server if the value isn't valid. (In other words, you check this property just in case the client-side validation did not run.) Remember that you can also read the Page.IsValid property to know in a single step if all the input controls are in a valid state. Page.IsValid returns true only if all the contained controls are valid.
Validate()	This method revalidates the control and updates the IsValid property accordingly. The web page calls this method when a page is posted back by a CausesValidation control. You can also call it programmatically (for example, if you programmatically set the content of an input control and you want to check its validity).

In addition, the BaseValidator class has other properties such as BackColor, Font, ForeColor, and others that are inherited (and in some case overridden) from the base class Label (and the classes it inherits from, such as WebControl and Control). Every derived validator adds its own specific properties, which you'll see in the following sections.

The RequiredFieldValidator Control

The simplest available control is RequiredFieldValidator, whose only work is to ensure that the associated control is not empty. For example, the control will fail validation if a linked text box doesn't contain any content (or just contains spaces). Alternatively, instead of checking for blank values you can specify a default value using the InitialValue property. In this case, validation fails if the content in the control matches this InitialValue (indicating that the user hasn't changed it in any way).

Here is an example of a typical RequiredFieldValidator:

```
<asp:TextBox runat="server" ID="Name" />
<asp:RequiredFieldValidator runat="server"
  ControlToValidate="Name" ErrorMessage="Name is required"
  Display="dynamic">*
</asp:RequiredFieldValidator>
```

The validator declared here will show an asterisk (*) character if the Name text box is empty. This error text appears when the user tries to submit the form by clicking a button that has CausesValidation set to true. It also occurs on the client side in IE 5.0 or above as soon as the user tabs to a new control, thanks to the client-side JavaScript.

If you want to place a specific message next to the validated control, you should replace the * with an error message. (You don't need to use the ErrorMessage property. The ErrorMessage is only required if you want to show the summary of all the errors on the page using the ValidationSummary control, which you'll see later in this chapter.) Alternatively, for a nicer result, you could use an HTML <img> tag to use a picture (like the common "!" sign inside a yellow triangle) with a tooltip for the error message. You'll see this approach later in this chapter as well.

The RangeValidator Control

The RangeValidator control verifies that an input value falls within a predetermined range. It has three specific properties: Type, MinimumValue, and MaximumValue. The last two define the range of valid values, while Type defines the type of the data that will be typed into the input control and validated. The available values are Currency, Date, Double, Integer, and String.

The following example checks that the date entered falls within August 5 and August 20 (encoded in the form mm/dd/yyyy, so if your web server uses different regional settings, you'll have to change the date format):

```
<asp:TextBox runat="server" ID="DayOff" />
<asp:RangeValidator runat="server" Display="dynamic"
  ControlToValidate="DayOff" Type="Date"
  ErrorMessage="Day Off is not within the valid interval"
  MinimumValue="08/05/2002" MaximumValue="08/20/2002">*
</asp:RangeValidator>
```

The CompareValidator Control

The CompareValidator compares a value in one control with a fixed value or, more commonly, a value in another control. For example, this allows you to check that two text boxes have the same data, or that a value in one text box doesn't exceed a maximum value established in another.

Like the RangeValidator control, the CompareValidator provides a Type property that specifies the type of data you are comparing. It also exposes the ValueToCompare and ControlToCompare properties, which allow you to compare the value of the input control with a constant value or the value of another input control, respectively. You use only one of these two properties.

The Operator property allows you to specify the type of comparison that you want to do. The available values are Equal, NotEqual, GreaterThan, GreaterThanEqual, LessThan, LessThanEqual, and DataTypeCheck. The DataTypeCheck value forces the validation control to check that the input is of valid data type (specified through the Type property), without performing any additional comparison.

The following example compares an input with a constant value in order to ensure that the specified age is greater than or equal to 18:

```
<asp:TextBox runat="server" ID="Age" />
<asp:CompareValidator runat="server" Display="dynamic"
  ControlToValidate="Age" ValueToCompare="18"
  ErrorMessage="You must be at least 18 years old"
  Type="Integer" Operator="GreaterThanEqual">*
</asp:CompareValidator>
```

The next example compares the input values in two password text boxes to ensure that their value is the same:

```
<asp:TextBox runat="server" TextMode="Password" ID="Password" />
<asp:TextBox runat="server" TextMode="Password" ID="Password2" />
<asp:CompareValidator runat="server"
  ControlToValidate="Password2" ControlToCompare="Password"
  ErrorMessage="The passwords don't match"
  Type="String" Display="dynamic">
  <img src="imgError.gif" border="0" alt="The passwords don't match">
</asp:CompareValidator>
```

This example also demonstrates another useful technique. The previous examples have used an asterisk (*) to indicate errors. However, this control tag uses an <img> tag to show a small image file of an exclamation mark instead.

The RegularExpressionValidator Control

The RegularExpressionValidator control is a very powerful tool in the ASP.NET developer's toolbox. It allows you to validate text by matching against a pattern defined in a *regular expression*. You simply need to set the regular expression in the ValidationExpression property.

Regular expressions are a very powerful tool—they allow you to specify complex rules that specify which characters and in what sequence (position and number of occurrences) they are allowed in the string. For example, the following control checks that the text input in the text box is a valid e-mail address:

```
<asp:TextBox runat="server" ID="Email" />
<asp:RegularExpressionValidator runat="server"
  ControlToValidate="Email" ValidationExpression=".*@.{2,}\..{2,}"
  ErrorMessage="E-mail is not in a valid format" Display="dynamic">*
</asp:RegularExpressionValidator>
```

The expression .*@.{2,}\..{2,} specifies that the string that it's validating must begin with a number of characters (.*), then it must contain an @ character, at least two more characters (the domain name), a period (escaped as \.), and finally, at least two more characters for the domain extension. For example, marco@apress.com is a valid e-mail address, while marco@apress or marco.apress.com would fail validation. The proposed expression is quite simple in reality. Using a more complex regular expression, you could check that the domain name is valid, that the extension is not made up (see www.icann.org for a list of allowed domain name extensions), and so on. However, regular expressions obviously don't provide any way to check that a domain actually exists or is online.

Table 5-15 summarizes the commonly used syntax constructs (modifiers) for regular expressions.

Table 5-15. *Metacharacters for Matching Single Characters*

Character Escapes	Description
Ordinary characters	Characters other than .$^{[(|)*+?\ match themselves.
\b	Matches a backspace.
\t	Matches a tab.
\r	Matches a carriage return.
\v	Matches a vertical tab.
\f	Matches a form feed.
\n	Matches a newline.
\	If followed by a special character (one of .$^{[(|)*+?\), this character escape matches that character literal. For example, \+ matches the + character.

In addition to single characters, you can specify a class or a range of characters that can be matched in the expression. For example, you could allow any digit or any vowel in any position, and exclude all the other characters. The metacharacters in Table 5-16 accomplish this.

Table 5-16. *Metacharacters for Matching Types of Characters*

Character Class	Description
.	Matches any character except \n.
[aeiou]	Matches any single character specified in the set.
[^aeiou]	Matches any character not specified in the set.
[3-7a-dA-D]	Matches any character specified in the specified ranges (in the example the ranges are 3–7, a–d, A–D).
\w	Matches any word character; that is, any alphanumeric character or the underscore (_).
\W	Matches any nonword character.
\s	Matches any whitespace character (space, tab, form-feed, newline, carriage return, or vertical feed).
\S	Matches any nonwhitespace character.
\d	Matches any decimal character.
\D	Matches any nondecimal character.

Using more advanced syntax, you can specify that a certain character or class of characters must be present at least once, or between two and six times, and so on. The quantifiers are placed just after a character or a range of characters, and allow you to specify how many times the preceding character must be matched (see Table 5-17).

Table 5-17. *Quantifiers*

Quantifier	Description
*	Zero or more matches
+	One or more matches
?	Zero or one matches
{N}	N matches
{N,}	N or more matches
{N,M}	Between N and M matches

To demonstrate these rules with another easy example, consider the following regular expression:

```
[aeiou]{2,4}\+[1-5]*
```

A string that correctly matches this expression must start with two to four vowels, have a + sign, and terminate with zero or more digits between one and five. Many more expression modifiers are detailed in the .NET Framework documentation.

A few common (and useful) regular expressions are shown in Table 5-18.

Table 5-18. *Commonly Used Regular Expressions*

Content	Regular Expression	Description
Email address[1]	\S+@\S+\.\S+	Check for an @, dot (.), and only allow nonwhitespace characters.
Password	\w+	Any sequence of word characters (letter, space, or underscore).
Specific-length password	\w{4,10}	A password that must be at least four characters long, but no longer than ten characters.
Advanced password	[a-zA-Z]\w{3,9}	As with the specific-length password, this regular expression will allow four to ten total characters. The twist is that the first character must fall in the range of a–z or A–Z (that is to say, it must start with a nonaccented ordinary letter).
Another advanced password	[a-zA-Z]\w*\d+\w*	This password starts with a letter character, followed by zero or more word characters, a digit, and then zero or more word characters. In short, it forces a password to contain a number somewhere inside it. You could use a similar pattern to require two numbers or any other special character.
Limited-length field	\S{4,10}	Like the password example, this allows four to ten characters, but it allows special characters (asterisks, ampersands, and so on).
Social Security number	\d{3}-\d{2}-\d{4}	A sequence of three, two, then four digits, with each group separated by a dash. A similar pattern could be used when requiring a phone number.

The CustomValidator Control

If the validation controls described so far are not flexible or powerful enough for you, and if you need more advanced or customized validation, then the CustomValidator control is what you're looking for. The CustomValidator allows you to execute your custom client-side and server-side validation routines. You can associate these routines with the control so that validation is performed automatically. If the validation fails, the Page.IsValid property to false, as occurs with any other validation control.

The client-side and server-side validation routines for the CustomValidator are declared similarly. They both take two parameters: a reference to the validator, and a custom argument object. This object provides a Value property that contains the current value of the associated input control (the value you have to validate), and an IsValid property through which you

---

1. There are many different ways to validate e-mail addresses with regular expressions of varying complexity. See www.4guysfromrolla.com/webtech/validateemail.shtml for a discussion of the subject and numerous examples.

specify whether the input value is valid. If you want to check that a number is a multiple of five, for example, you could use a client-side JavaScript validation routine like this:

```
<script language="JavaScript">
  function EmpIDClientValidate(ctl, args)
  {

    // the value is a multiple of 5 if the module by 5 is 0
    args.IsValid=(args.Value%5 == 0);
  }
</script>
```

To associate this code with the control so that it's performed automatically, you simply need to set the ClientValidationFunction to the name of the function (in this case, EmpIDClientValidate).

Next, when the page is posted back, ASP.NET fires the CustomValidator.ServerValidate event. You handle this event to perform the same task using C# code. And while the JavaScript logic is optional, you must make sure you include a server-side validation routine to ensure the validation is performed even if the client is using a down-level browser (or tampers with the web page HTML).

Here's the C# server-side equivalent of the validation routine shown earlier:

```
private void EmpIDServerValidate(object sender, ServerValidateEventArgs args)
{
    try
    {
        args.IsValid = (int.Parse(args.Value)%5 == 0);
    }
    catch
    {
        // An error is most likely caused by non-numeric data.
        args.IsValid = false;
    }
}
```

Finally, here's an example CustomValidator tag that uses these routines:

```
<asp:TextBox runat="server" ID="EmpID" />
<asp:CustomValidator runat="server" ControlToValidate="EmpID"
  ClientValidationFunction="EmpIDClientValidate"
  ErrorMessage="ID must be a multiple of 5" Display="dynamic">*
</asp:CustomValidator>
```

The ValidationSummary Control

The ValidationSummary control doesn't perform any validation. Instead, it allows you to show a summary of all the errors in the page. This summary displays the ErrorMessage value of each failed validator. The summary can be shown in a client-side JavaScript message box (if the ShowMessageBox property is true), or on the page (if the ShowSummary property is true).

You can set both ShowMessageBox and ShowSummary to true to show both types of summaries, since they are not exclusive. If you choose to display the summary on the page, you can choose a style with the DisplayMode property (possible values are SingleParagraph, List, and BulletList). Finally, you can set a title for the summary with the HeaderText property.

The control declaration is straightforward:

```
<asp:ValidationSummary runat="server" ID="ValidationSum"
  ShowSummary="true" DisplayMode="BulletList"
  HeaderText="<b>Please review the following errors:</b>"
/>
```

Figure 5-12 shows an example with a validation summary that shows a bulleted summary on the page and in a message box.

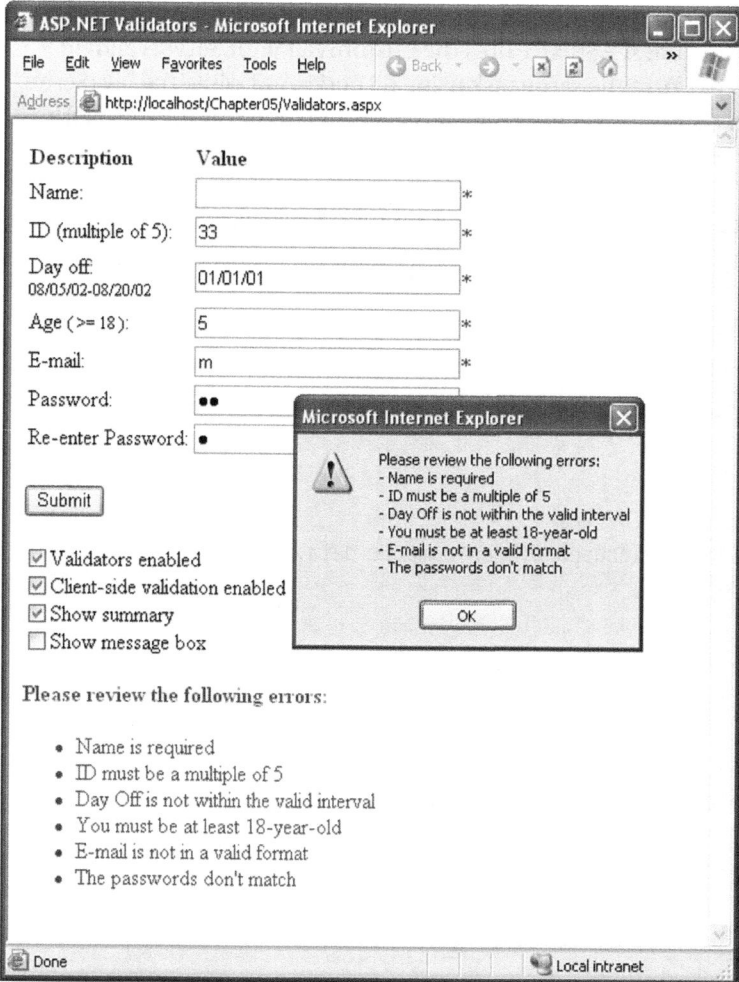

Figure 5-12. *The validation summary*

Using the Validators Programmatically

As with all other server controls, you can programmatically read and modify the properties of a validator. To access all the validators on the page, you can iterate over the Validators collection of the current page.

In fact, this technique is already demonstrated in the sample page shown in Figures 5-11 and 5-12. This page provides four check boxes that allow you to test the behavior of the validators with different options. When a check box is selected it causes a postback. The event handler iterates over all the validators, and updates them according to the new options, as shown here:

```
private void Options_Changed(object sender, System.EventArgs e)
{
    foreach (BaseValidator valCtl in Page.Validators)
    {
        valCtl.Enabled=EnableValidators.Checked;
        valCtl.EnableClientScript = EnableClientSide.Checked;
    }
    ValidationSum.ShowMessageBox = ShowMsgBox.Checked;
    ValidationSum.ShowSummary = ShowSummary.Checked;
}
```

You can use a similar technique to perform custom validation. The basic idea is to add a button with CausesValidation set to false. When this button is clicked, manually validate the page or just specific validators using the Validate() method. Then examine the IsValid property and decide what to do.

The next example uses this technique. It examines all the validation controls on the page by looping through the Page.Validators collection. Every time it finds a control that hasn't validated successfully, it retrieves the invalid value from the input control and adds it to a string. At the end of this routine, it displays a message that describes which values were incorrect. This technique adds a feature that wouldn't be available with automatic validation, which uses the static ErrorMessage property. In that case, it isn't possible to include the actual incorrect values in the message.

```
private void cmdOK_Click(Object sender, EventArgs e)
{
    // Validate the page.
    this.Validate();

    if (!this.IsValid)
    {
        string errorMessage = "<b>Mistakes found:</b><br>";

        // Create a variable to represent the input control.
        TextBox ctrlInput;

        // Search through the validation controls.
        foreach (BaseValidator ctrl in this.Validators)
        {
```

```
            if (!ctrl.IsValid)
            {
                errorMessage += ctrl.ErrorMessage + "<br>";
                ctrlInput = (TextBox)this.FindControl(ctrl.ControlToValidate);
                errorMessage += " * Problem is with this input: ";
                errorMessage += ctrlInput.Text + "<br>";
            }
        }
        lblMessage.Text = errorMessage;
    }
}
```

This example uses an advanced technique: the Page.FindControl() method. It's required because the ControlToValidate property is just a string with the name of a control, not a reference to the actual control object. To find the control that matches this name (and retrieve its Text property), you need to use the FindControl() method. Once the code has retrieved the matching text box, it can perform other tasks such as clearing the current value, tweaking a property, or even changing the text box color.

The ASP.NET Rich Controls

Rich controls are web controls that model complex user interface elements. Although there isn't a strict definition for rich controls, the term is commonly used to describe web controls that have an object model that is decoupled from the underlying HTML representation. A typical rich control can often be programmed as a single object (and defined in a single simple tag), but renders itself with a complex sequence of HTML elements and may even use JavaScript code.

ASP.NET includes three rich controls:

- **Calendar.** A calendar that displays and allows you to move through months and days, and to select a date or a range of days.

- **AdRotator.** A banner ad control that displays one out of a set of images based on a predefined scheduled that's saved in an XML file.

- **Xml.** Takes an XML file and an XSLT stylesheet file as input, and displays the resulting HTML in a browser.

The Calendar Control

This control creates a functionally rich and good-looking calendar box that shows one month at a time. The user can move from month to month, select a date, and even select a range of days (if multiple selection is allowed). The Calendar control has many properties that, taken together, allow you to change almost every part of this control. For example, you can fine-tune the foreground and background colors, font, title, format of the date, the currently selected date, and so on. The Calendar also provides events that enable you to react when the user changes the current month (VisibleMonthChanged), when the user selects a date (SelectionChanged), and when the Calendar is about to render a day (DayRender).

The following Calendar tag sets a few basic properties:

```
<asp:Calendar runat="server" ID="Calendar1"
  ForeColor="red" BackColor="lightyellow" />
```

The most important Calendar event is SelectionChanged, which fires every time a user clicks a date. Here's a basic event handler that responds to the SelectionChanged event and displays the selected date:

```
private void Calendar1_SelectionChanged(object sender, EventArgs e)
{
    lblDates.Text = "You selected" + Calendar1.SelectedDate.ToLondDateString());
}
```

■**Note** Every user interaction with the calendar triggers a postback. This allows you to react to the selection event immediately, and it allows the Calendar to re-render its interface, thereby showing a new month or newly selected dates. The Calendar does not use the AutoPostBack property.

You can also allow users to select entire weeks or months as well as single dates, or you can render the control as a static calendar that doesn't allow selection. The only fact that you must remember is that if you allow month selection, the user can also select a single week or a day. Similarly, if you allow week selection, the user can also select a single day. The type of selection is set through the Calendar.SelectionMode property. You may also need to set the Calendar.FirstDayOfWeek property to configure how a week is selected. (For example, if you set FirstDayOfWeek to the enumerated value Monday, weeks will be selected from Monday to Sunday.)

When you allow multiple date selection (by setting Calendar.SelectionMode to something other than Day), you need to examine the SelectedDates property instead of the SelectedDate property. SelectedDates provides a collection of all the selected dates, which you can examine as shown here:

```
private void Calendar1_SelectionChanged(object sender, EventArgs e)
{
    lblDates.Text = "You selected these dates:<br>";
    foreach (DateTime dt in Calendar1.SelectedDates)
    {
        lblDates.Text += dt.ToLongDateString() + "<br>";
    }
}
```

Finally, by handling the DayRender event, you can completely change the appearance of the cell being rendered. The DayRender event is extremely powerful. Besides allowing you to tailor what dates are selectable, it also allows you to configure the cell where the date is located through the e.Cell property. (The Calendar is really a sophisticated HTML table.)

For example, you could highlight an important date or even add extra controls or HTML content in the cell. Here's an example that changes the background and foreground colors of the weekend days, and also makes them nonclickable so that the user can't choose those days:

```
private void Calendar1_DayRender(object sender, DayRenderEventArgs e)
{
    if (e.Day.IsWeekend)
    {
        e.Cell.BackColor = System.Drawing.Color.Green;
        e.Cell.ForeColor = System.Drawing.Color.Yellow;
        e.Day.IsSelectable = false;
    }
}
```

The result is shown in Figure 5-13.

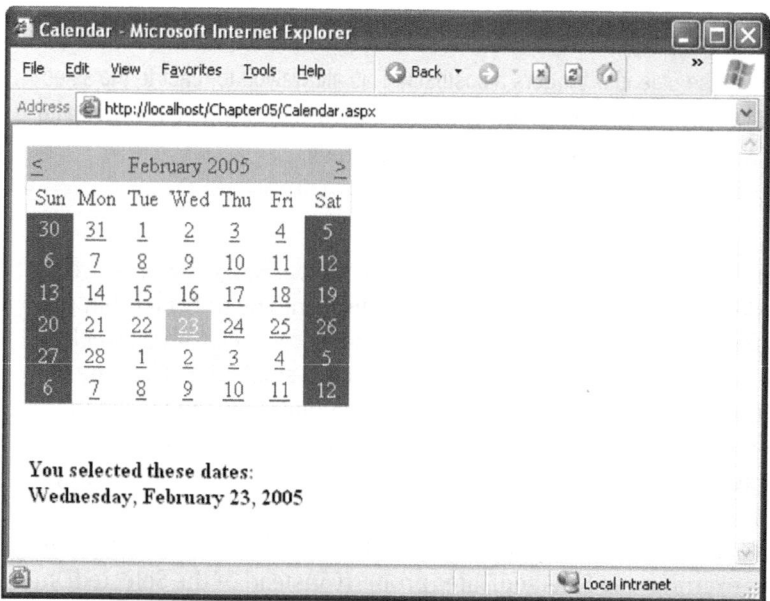

Figure 5-13. *The Calendar control*

Tip If you're using a design tool like Visual Studio .NET, you can even set an entire related color scheme using the built-in designer. Simply right-click the control on your design page and select Auto Format. You'll be presented with a list of predefined formats that set various style properties.

The AdRotator Control

The AdRotator control is the ASP.NET version of the ASP Ad Rotator component. It randomly selects advertisement banners as specified by an external XML schedule file.

Before creating the control, it makes sense to define the XML schedule file. Here's an example:

```
<Advertisements>
  <Ad>
    <ImageUrl>hdr_logo.gif</ImageUrl>
    <NavigateUrl>http://www.apress.com</NavigateUrl>
    <AlternateText>Apress - The Author's Press</AlternateText>
    <Impressions>20</Impressions>
    <Keyword>books</Keyword>
  </Ad>
  <Ad>
    <ImageUrl>javaOne.gif</ImageUrl>
    <NavigateUrl>http://www.sun.com</NavigateUrl>
    <AlternateText>Java from Sun</AlternateText>
    <Impressions>20</Impressions>
    <Keyword>Java</Keyword>
  </Ad>
  <!- More ads can go here. ->
</Advertisements>
```

Each <Ad> element has a number of other important properties that configure the link, the image, and the frequency, as described in Table 5-19.

Table 5-19. *Advertisement File Elements*

Element	Description
ImageUrl	The image that will be displayed. This can be a relative link (a file in the current directory) or a fully qualified Internet URL.
NavigateUrl	The link that will be followed if the user clicks the banner.
AlternateText	The text that will be displayed instead of the picture if it cannot be displayed. This text will also be used as a tooltip in some newer browsers.
Impressions	A number that sets how often an advertisement will appear. This number is relative to the numbers specified for other ads. For example, a banner with the value 10 will be shown twice as often as the banner with the value 5.
Keyword	A keyword that identifies a group of advertisements. This can be used for filtering. For example, you could create ten advertisements, and give half of them the keyword "Retail" and the other half the keyword "Computer." The web page can then choose to filter the possible advertisements to include only one of these groups.

The actual AdRotator class only provides a limited set of properties. You specify both the appropriate advertisement file in the AdvertisementFile property and the type of window that the link should follow in the Target property. You can also set the KeywordFilter property so that the banner will be chosen from entries that have a specific keyword.

Here's an example that opens the link for an advertisement in a new window:

```
<asp:AdRotator runat="server" AdvertisementFile="Ads.xml" Target="_blank" />
```

Figure 5-14 shows the ad rotator control. Try refreshing the page. When you do, you'll see that a new advertisement is randomly selected each time.

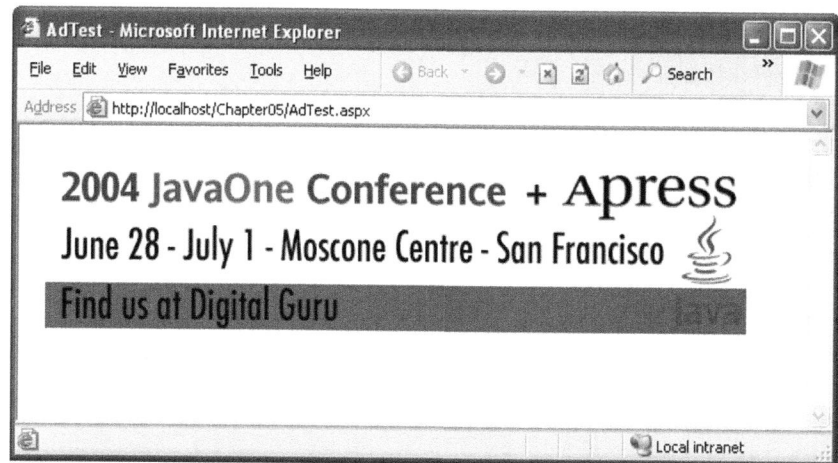

Figure 5-14. *The AdRotator control*

Additionally, you can react to the AdRotator.AdCreated event. This occurs when the page is being created, and an image is randomly chosen from the file. This event provides you with information about the image that you can use to customize the rest of your page.

The event-handling code for this example simply configures a HyperLink control so that it corresponds with the randomly selected advertisement in the AdRotator:

```
protected void Ads_AdCreated(Object sender, AdCreatedEventArgs e)
{
    // Synchronize the Hyperlink control.
    lnkBanner.NavigateUrl = e.NavigateUrl;

    // Synchronize the text of the link.
    lnkBanner.Text = "Click here for information about our sponsor: ";
    lnkBanner.Text += e.AlternateText;
}
```

The Xml Control

The Xml control is essentially very simple. It takes source XML content and transforms it using an XSLT *stylesheet*.

■**Note** An XSLT stylesheet contains the instructions needed to transform a specific XML markup language to another text-based markup language. When you're using the XML control, you'll need to use an XSLT stylesheet that transforms XML to HTML.

First, consider the following sample XML file (available in the code download as Products.xml) that defines a simple hierarchy or categories and products:

```
<?xml version="1.0"?>
<Products>
  <Category title="DVD">
    <Product title="Matrix" />
    <Product title="The Gladiator" />
  </Category>
  <Category title="Books">
    <Product title="Fast Track to ASP.NET" />
    <Product title="ASP.NET Website Programming" />
    <Product title="Beginning C#" />
  </Category>
</Products>
```

Now let's look at the transformation file (available for download as Products.xslt) that renders the category's title in bold and then lists the child products one on each line:

```
<?xml version="1.0"?>
<xsl:stylesheet xmlns:xsl="http://www.w3.org/1999/XSL/Transform" version="1.0">
<xsl:template match="/Products">
  <xsl:for-each select="Category">
    <b><xsl:value-of select="@title"/></b><br/>
    <xsl:for-each select="Product">
      -<xsl:value-of select="@title"/><br/>
    </xsl:for-each>
  </xsl:for-each>
</xsl:template>
</xsl:stylesheet>
```

Using the Xml control, you can apply this stylesheet to the XML file and display the result. All you need is a single tag that sets the DocumentSource and TransformSource properties, as shown here:

```
<asp:Xml runat="server"
  DocumentSource="Products.xml" TransformSource="Products.xslt" />
```

Figure 5-15 shows the result.

If you compare this to what developers had to go through with ASP and the MSXML component to achieve similar results, it's obvious that ASP.NET offers a simpler, quicker, and more intuitive solution.

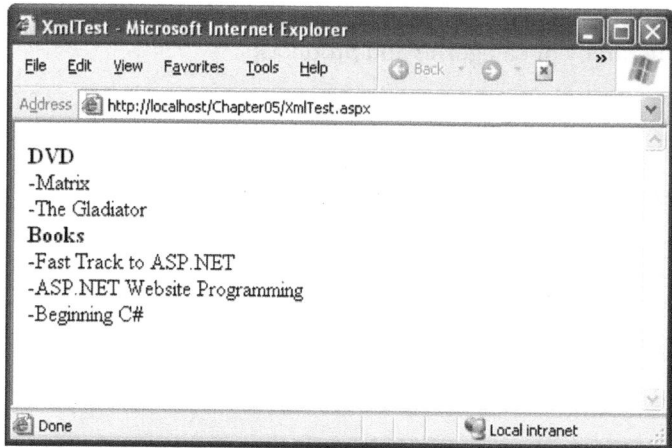

Figure 5-15. *The Xml control*

■**Note** You don't need to use separate files to use the Xml control. Instead of using the DocumentSource property, you can assign an XmlDocument object to the Document property, or a string containing the XML content to the DocumentContent property. Similarly, you can supply the XSLT information by assigning an XslTransform object to the Transform property. These techniques are useful if you need to supply XML and XSLT data programmatically (for example, if you extract it from a database record). Chapter 12 explores XML in much more detail.

GETTING MORE RICH CONTROLS

The Internet contains many hubs for control sharing. One such location is Microsoft's own ASP.NET website (www.asp.net), which provides a control gallery where developers can submit their own ASP.NET web controls. Some of these controls are free (at least in a limited version), while others require a purchase.

In addition, Microsoft's Internet Explorer team has developed its own toolkit of controls for the ASP.NET platform. The Internet Explorer controls correspond to a few standards seen in the Windows world, including a Toolbar control with a collection of graphical buttons, a TreeView control that displays a hierarchy of items (as used in Windows Explorer to show directories), and MultiPage and TabStrip controls, which are often used together to provide a set of tabbed "pages." The user can display a different set of controls (contained in one page in a MultiPage control) by clicking a different button on the TabStrip control.

The Internet Explorer controls can send HTML output for any current browser, but they shine when used with Internet Explorer 5.5 or later, in which case they use special DHTML code automatically to create a more responsive and dynamic user interface. You can download the Internet Explorer controls from http://msdn.microsoft.com/archive/en-us/samples/internet/welcome.asp (which includes C# source code). You can see the Internet Explorer Web control documentation at http://msdn.microsoft.com/workshop/WebControls/webcontrols_entry.asp.

Microsoft does not officially support the Internet Explorer controls. Notably, they will not be supported in the forthcoming ASP.NET 2.0 (although their functionality will be integrated into a similar set of built-in web controls).

Summary

In this chapter you learned the basics of almost every server control available when programming with ASP.NET, including HTML server controls, web controls, list controls, validation controls, and rich controls. You've learned how to use ASP.NET controls from your web-page code, access their properties, and handle their server-side events. You've also learned how to validate potentially problematic user input with the validation controls. In the next chapter, you'll learn how pages come together to form web applications.

CHAPTER 6

ASP.NET Applications

In traditional desktop programming, an *application* is an executable file with related support files. For example, a typical Windows application consists of a main executable file (EXE), supporting components (typically DLLs), and other resources like databases and configuration files. An ASP.NET application follows a much different model.

On the most fundamental level, an ASP.NET application is a combination of files, pages, handlers, modules, and executable code that can be invoked from a virtual directory (and its subdirectories) on a web server. In this chapter, you'll learn why this distinction exists and take a closer look at how an ASP.NET application is configured and deployed. You'll also learn how to use components and HTTP handlers with an ASP.NET application.

Anatomy of an ASP.NET Application

The difference between ASP.NET applications and other rich client applications makes a lot of sense when you consider the ASP.NET execution model. Unlike a Windows application, the end user never runs an ASP.NET application directly. Instead, a user launches a browser like Internet Explorer and makes a request for a specific URL (like http://www.mysite.com/mypage.aspx) over HTTP.

As you learned in Chapter 2, this HTTP request is received by the IIS (Internet Information Services) web server, which recognizes that the user is calling a part of an ASP.NET application. IIS 5 has no concept of separate applications—it simply passes the request to the ASP.NET worker process. However, the ASP.NET worker process carefully segregates code execution into different application domains based on the virtual directory. Web pages and web services that are hosted in the same virtual directory (or one of its subdirectories) execute in the same *application domain*. Web pages and web services in different virtual directories execute in separate application domains.

Tip Remember that IIS 6 gives you an additional layer of applications separation by allowing you to have different ASP.NET applications or groups of applications hosted by separate instances of the IIS worker process. However, within the bounds of each IIS worker process the same rules apply. ASP.NET applications in separate virtual directories are hosted in distinct application domains. IIS 6 uses the term *application pool* to describe this situation. In IIS 5, all ASP.NET applications are essentially tied to the same application pool.

An application domain is the .NET equivalent to a process—it's a boundary enforced by the CLR (common language runtime) that ensures that one application can't influence (or see the in-memory data) of another. The following characteristics are a direct result of the application domain model:

- All the web pages and web services in a single web application share the same in-memory resources, like global application data, per-user session data, and cached data. This information isn't directly accessible to other ASP.NET or ASP applications.

- All the web pages and web services in a single web application share the same core configuration settings. However, some configuration settings can be customized in individual subdirectories of the same virtual directory. For example, you can only set one authentication mechanism for a web application, no matter how many subdirectories it has. However, you can set different authorization rules in each directory to fine-tune who is allowed to access different groups of pages.

- All web applications raise global application events at various stages (when the application domain is first created, when it's released, and so on). You can attach event handlers that react to these global application events using code in the global.asax file in your application's virtual directory.

In other words, the virtual directory is the basic grouping structure that delimits an ASP.NET application. You can create a legitimate ASP.NET application with a single web page (.aspx file) or web service (.asmx file). However, ASP.NET applications can include all of the following ingredients:

- **Web pages (.aspx files).** These are the cornerstones of any ASP.NET application.

- **Web services (.asmx files).** These allow you to share useful functions with applications on other computers and other platforms.

- **Code-behind files.** Depending on the code model you're using, you may also have separate source-code files. If you're using Visual Studio .NET, source-code files are compiled into a single DLL before they're used.

- **A configuration file (web.config).** This file contains a slew of application-level settings that configure everything from security to debugging and state management.

- **Global.asax.** This file contains event handlers that react to global application events (such as when the application is first being started).

- **Other components.** These are compiled assemblies that contain separate components you've developed, or third-party components with useful functionality. Components allow you to separate business and data access logic, and create custom controls.

Of course, a virtual directory can hold a great deal of additional resources that ASP.NET web applications will *use*, including stylesheets, images, XML files, and so on. In addition, you can extend the ASP.NET model by developing specialized components known as HTTP handlers and HTTP modules, which can plug into your application and take part in the processing of ASP.NET web requests.

Note It's possible to have file types that are owned by different ISAPI extensions in the same virtual directory. One example is if you mingle .aspx and .asp files. A more complex example would be if you mapped .aspx web page files to version 1.1 of ASP.NET and .asmx web service files to version 1.0. In these examples, the virtual directory corresponds to more than one application. These applications just happen to be accessible through the same virtual web directory. However, each application is mediated by a different ISAPI extension.

Application Lifetime

ASP.NET uses a *lazy initialization* technique for creating application domains. This means that the application domain for a web application is created the first time a request is received for a page or web service in that application.

An application domain can shut down for a variety of reasons, including if the web server itself is shut down. But, more commonly, applications restart themselves in new application domains in response to error conditions or configuration changes. For example, depending on the settings in the computer-wide machine.config file, an ASP.NET application may be periodically recycled when certain thresholds are reached. This model is designed to keep an application healthy, and detect characteristics that could indicate a problem has developed. Depending on your machine.config settings, application domains may be recycled based on the length of time the application domain has been running, the number of queued requests, or the amount of memory used (as described Chapter 2).

ASP.NET automatically recycles application domains when you change the application. One example is if you modify the web.config file. Another example is if you replace an existing web page file or DLL assembly file. In both of these cases, ASP.NET starts a new application domain to handle all future requests, and keeps the existing application domain alive long enough to finish handling any outstanding requests (including queued requests).

Tip ASP.NET 1.1 added a new method that you can use to programmatically shut down a web application domain. (The application will restart itself automatically the next time it receives a request.) To shut down the current application, simply use the static HttpRuntime.UnloadAppDomain() method. This technique is rarely used, but it can be useful if you're hosting a number of applications on the same server, and some are used only infrequently. In this case, the memory overhead of keeping the application domain alive may outweigh the increased speed of serving subsequent requests into the application.

Application Updates

As you've already learned, ASP.NET applications are compiled into a single DLL resource file before they are executed. This DLL file is stored in the Bin subdirectory of the virtual directory, along with any other compiled .NET components that your web application is using. When the application is executed, it's the ASP.NET engine that loads your web application DLL.

The most remarkable feature of the ASP.NET execution model is the fact that you can update your web application without needing to restart the web server and without worrying about harming existing clients. That means you can add, replace, or delete files in the virtual directory or Bin subdirectory at any time. ASP.NET then performs the same transition to a new application domain that it performs when you modify the web.config configuration file.

Being able to update any part of an application at any time, without interrupting existing requests, is a powerful feature. However, it's important to understand the architecture that makes it possible. Many developers make the mistake of assuming that it's a feature of the CLR that allows ASP.NET to seamlessly transition to a new application domain. But in reality, the CLR always locks assembly files when it executes them. To get around this limitation, ASP.NET doesn't actually use the ASP.NET files in the virtual directory. Instead, it uses another technique, called *shadow copy* during the compilation process to create a copy of your files in c:\[WinDir]\Microsoft.NET\[Version]\Temporary ASP.NET Files. The ASP.NET worker process loads the assemblies from this directory, which means that these assemblies are locked and the versions in the Bin directory aren't.

The second part of the story is ASP.NET's ability to detect when you change the original files. This detail is fairly straightforward—it simply relies on the ability of the Windows operating system to track directories and files and send immediate change notifications. ASP.NET maintains an active list of all assemblies loaded within a particular application's application domain and uses monitoring code to watch for changes and acts accordingly.

Note ASP.NET can use files that are stored in the GAC (global assembly cache), a computer-wide repository of assemblies that includes staples like the assemblies for the entire .NET Framework class library. You can also put your own assemblies into the GAC, but web applications are usually simpler to deploy, and more straightforward to manage, if you rely on the Bin directory instead.

The Global.asax Application File

The global.asax file allows you to write event handlers that react to global events. Users never request the global.asax file directly. Instead, the global.asax file executes its code automatically in response to certain application events. The global.asax file provides a similar service to the global.asa file in classic ASP applications.

You write the code in a global.asax file in a similar way to a web form. The difference is that the global.asax doesn't contain any HTML or ASP.NET tags. Instead, it contains methods with specific, predefined names. For example, the following global.asax file reacts to the Application.EndRequest event, which happens just before the page is sent to the user.

```
<script language="C#" runat="server">
    protected void Application_OnEndRequest()
    {
        Response.Write("<hr>This page was served at " +
          DateTime.Now.ToString());
    }
</script>
```

This event handler writes a footer at the bottom of the page with the date and time that the page was created. Because it reacts to the Application.EndRequest event, it executes every time a page is requested after all of the event-handling code in that page has finished.

As with web forms, you can also separate the content of the global.asax file into two files, one that declares the file and the other that contains the code. In this case, the global.asax file only contains a single line, with a directive that indicates the class name with the corresponding code:

```
<%@ Application Codebehind="Global.cs" Inherits="Global" %>
```

The code-behind class won't inherit from Page, because it doesn't represent a web form. Instead, it inherits from the System.Web.HttpApplication class. Here's an example:

```
public class Global : System.Web.HttpApplication
{
    protected void Application_OnEndRequest()
    {
        Response.Write("This page was served at " +
          DateTime.Now.ToString());
    }
}
```

The global.asax file is optional, but a web application can have no more than one global.asax file, and it must reside in the root directory of the application, not a subdirectory. Visual Studio .NET automatically creates a global.asax file every time you create a new web project. The class in this automatically generated global.asax file includes empty event handlers for the most commonly used application events. You simply need to insert your code in the appropriate method.

It's worth noting that application event handlers aren't attached in the same way as ordinary control events. The usual way to attach an application event handler is just to use the recognized method name. For example, if you create a protected method named Application_OnEndRequest(), ASP.NET automatically calls this method when the Application.EndRequest event occurs. To understand why this works, you need to realize that ASP.NET creates a pool of application objects when your application domain is first loaded, and uses one to serve each request. This pool varies in size depending on the system and the number of available threads, but it typically ranges from 1 to 100 instances. Each request gets exclusive access to one of these application objects, and when the request ends, the object is reused. As different stages in application processing occur, ASP.NET calls the corresponding method, which triggers your code. Of course, if your methods have the wrong name, your implementation won't get called—instead your code will simply be ignored.

If you don't want to use the predefined method names, you can use delegate code to wire up event handlers when the global application class is first created, as with a web form. In fact, in an odd Visual Studio .NET quirk, if you attach a global event handler using the event view in the Properties window, Visual Studio .NET creates a new private event-handling method and attaches it with delegate code. To try this out, click the lightning bolt icon in the Properties window while working with the global.asax file, and then double-click one of the event names.

■**Note** The global application class that's used by the global.asax file should always be stateless. That's because application objects are reused for different requests as they become available. If you set a value in a member variable in one request, it might reappear in another request. However, there's no way to control how this happens, or which request gets which instance of the application object. To circumvent this issue, don't use member variables. If you need to store data in server memory for multiple requests, you should rely on other mechanisms like the Session, Application, and Cache collections.

Application Events

There are two types of events:

- Events that always occur for every request. These include request-related and response-related events.

- Events that occur only under certain conditions.

The required events unfold in this order:

1. **Application_BeginRequest().** This method is called at the start of every request, including requests for non-web-form files like web services.

2. **Application_AuthenticateRequest().** This method is called just before authentication is performed. This is a jumping off point for creating your own authentication logic, as demonstrated later in this book.

3. **Application_AuthorizeRequest().** After the user is authenticated (identified), it's time to determine the user's permissions. You can use this method to assign special privileges.

4. **Application_ResolveRequestCache().** This method is commonly used in conjunction with output caching. With output caching (described in Chapter 7), the rendered HTML of a web form is reused, without executing any of your code. However, this event handler still runs.

5. At this point, the request is handed off to the appropriate handler. For example, for a web form request this is the point when the page is compiled (if necessary), and instantiated.

6. **Application_AcquireRequestState().** This method is called just before session-specific information is retrieved for the client and used to populate the Session collection.

7. **Application_PreRequestHandlerExecute().** This method is called before the appropriate HTTP handler executes the request.

8. At this point, the appropriate handler executes the request. For example, if it's a web form request, the event-handling code for the page is executed and the page is rendered to HTML.

9. **Application_PostRequestHandlerExecute().** This method is called just after the request is handled.

10. **Application_ReleaseRequestState().** This method is called when the session-specific information is about to be serialized from the Session collection so that it's available for the next request.

11. **Application_UpdateRequestCache().** This method is called just before information is added to the output cache. For example, if you've enabled output caching for a web page, ASP.NET will insert the rendered HTML for the page into the cache at this point.

12. **Application_EndRequest().** This method is called at the end of the request, just before the objects are released and reclaimed. It's a suitable point for cleanup code.

Figure 6-1 shows the process of handling a single request.

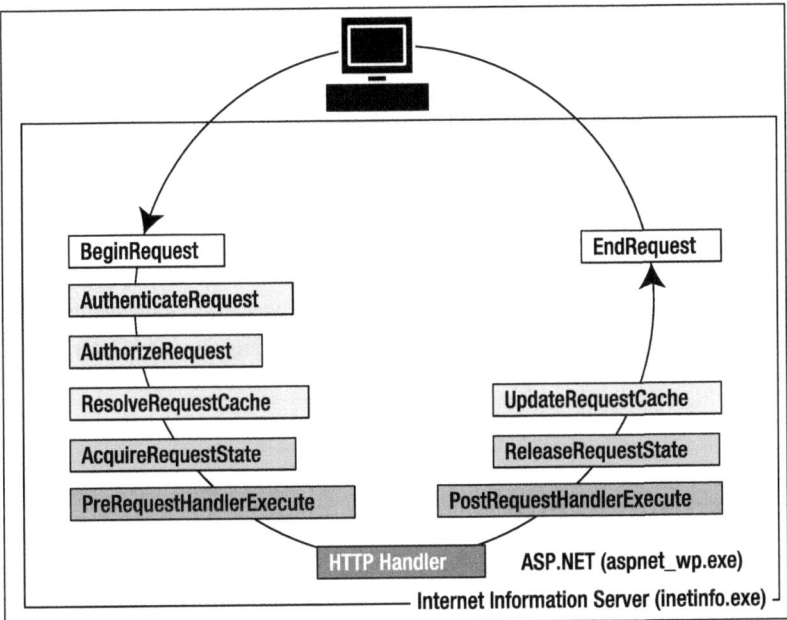

Figure 6-1. *The application events*

There is also a smaller set of events that don't fire with every request. These include the following:

- **Application_Start().** This method is invoked when the application first starts up and the application domain is created. This event handler is a useful place to provide application-wide initialization code. For example, at this point you might load and cache data that will not change throughout the lifetime of an application, such as navigation trees, static product catalogs, and so on.

- **Session_Start().** This method is invoked each time a new session begins. This is often used to initialize user-specific information. Sessions are discussed with state management in Chapter 7.

- **Application_Error().** This method is invoked whenever an unhandled exception occurs in the application.

- **Session_End().** This method is invoked whenever the user's session ends. A session ends when your code explicitly releases it, or when it times out after there have been no more requests received within a given timeout period (typically 20 minutes). This method is typically used to clean up any related data.

- **Application_End().** This method is invoked just before an application ends. The end of an application can occur because IIS is being restarted, or because the application is transitioning to a new application domain in response to updated files or the process recycling settings.

- **Application_Disposed().** This method is invoked some time after the application has been shut down, and the .NET garbage collector is about to reclaim the memory it occupies. This point is too late to perform critical cleanup, but you can use it as a last-ditch failsafe to verify that critical resources are released.

Application events are commonly used to perform application initialization, cleanup, usage logging, profiling, and troubleshooting. However, there's no reason to assume that your application will need to use global application events. Many ASP.NET applications don't use the global.asax file at all.

Tip The global.asax file isn't the only place where you can respond to global web application events. You can also create custom modules that participate in the processing of web requests, as discussed later in this chapter.

Demonstrating Application Events

The following example web application uses a global.asax file that responds to the Application_Error method. It intercepts the error, and displays some information about it in a predefined format. This code uses the Response object, which is provided as a built-in property of the HttpApplication class, just like it is a built-in property of the Page class.

```
public class Global : System.Web.HttpApplication
{
    protected void Application_Error(Object sender, EventArgs e)
    {
        Response.Write("<font face=\"Tahoma\" size=\"2\" color=\"red\">");
        Response.Write("Oops! Looks like an error occurred!!<hr></font>");
        Response.Write("<font face=\"Arial\" size=\"2\">");
        Response.Write(Server.GetLastError().Message.ToString());
        Response.Write("<hr>"+Server.GetLastError().ToString());
        Server.ClearError();
    }
}
```

To test this application event handler, you need to create another web page that causes an error. Here's an example that generates an error by attempting to divide by zero when a page loads:

```csharp
public class DivideByZero : Page
{
    // (Designer code omitted.)

    private void Page_Load(object sender, EventArgs e)
    {
        int i = 0;
        int j = 1;
        int k = j/i;
    }
}
```

If you request this page, you'll see the display shown in Figure 6-2.

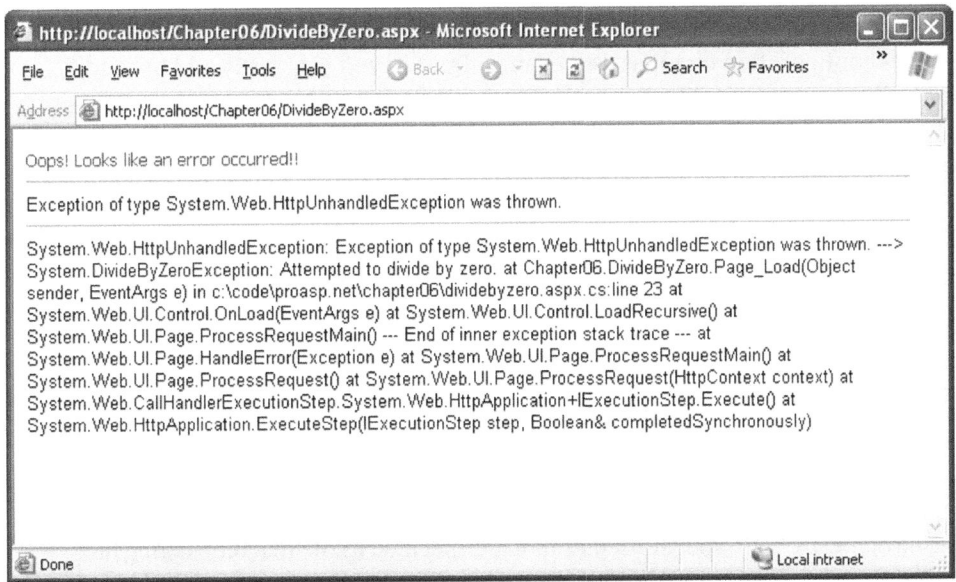

Figure 6-2. *Catching an unhandled error*

Typically, you wouldn't use the Application_Error() method to control the appearance of a web page, because it doesn't give you enough flexibility to deal with different types of errors (without coding painstaking conditional logic). Instead, you would probably configure custom error pages using the web.config file (as described in the next section). However, Application_Error() might be extremely useful if you want to log an error for future reference, or even send an e-mail about it to a system administrator. In fact, in many events you'll need to use techniques like this because the Response object won't be available. Two examples include the Application_Start() and Application_End() methods.

ASP.NET Configuration

Configuration in ASP.NET is managed with XML configuration files. All of the information needed to configure an ASP.NET application's core settings, as well as the custom settings specific to your own application, is stored in these configuration files.

The ASP.NET configuration files have several advantages over traditional ASP configuration:

- **They are never locked.** As described in the beginning of this chapter, you can update configuration settings at any point, and ASP.NET will smoothly transition to a new application domain.

- **They are easily accessed and replicated.** Provided you have the appropriate network rights, you can modify a configuration file from a remote computer (or even replace it by uploading a new version via FTP). You can also copy a configuration file and use it to apply identical settings to another application or another web server that runs the same application in a web farm scenario.

- **They are easy to edit and understand.** The settings in the configuration files are human-readable, which means they can be edited and understood without needing a special configuration tool. In ASP.NET 2.0, Microsoft will introduce a graphical tool that automates configuration changes. But even without it, you can easily add or modify settings using a text editor like Notepad or using Visual Studio .NET.

With ASP.NET, you don't need to worry about configuring the IIS metabase or restarting the web server. However, there are still a few tasks that you can't perform with a web.config file. For example, you can't create or remove a virtual directory. Similarly, you can't change file mappings. If you want the ASP.NET service to process requests for additional file types (such as HTML, or a custom file type you define), you must use IIS Manager, as described in Chapter 2.

The Machine.config File

The configuration starts with a file named machine.config that resides in the directory c:\[WinDir]\Microsoft.NET\Framework\[Version]\Config. This configuration file is quite lengthy (approximately 200 KB), and it configures the behavior of ASP.NET and the CLR on the current computer. Some of the ASP.NET-specific details that are specified in the machine.config file include the supported language compilers, the HTTP handler classes that serve different types of files, and the different types of mobile devices that are supported for adaptive rendering.

Most of the settings in the machine.config are essentially plumbing that you never need to touch. There are two common exceptions, as discussed in the following sections.

<processModel>

This section allows you to configure how the ASP.NET worker process recycles application domains, and the Windows account it executes under, which determines its privileges. If you're using IIS 6 (the version included with Windows 2003 Server) many of these settings are ignored, and you can configure similar settings through the IIS Manager utility.

Chapter 2 has more information about the <processModel> element.

\<machineKey\>

This section allows you to set the server-specific key used for encrypting data and creating digital signatures. Ordinarily, the \<machineKey\> element takes this form:

```
<machineKey validationKey="autogenerate" decryptionKey="autogenerate"
  validation="SHA1" />
```

The autogenerate value indicates that ASP.NET will create and store machine-specific keys. Ordinarily, this is the best approach. However, if you're running a web farm, you need to modify the \<machineKey\> section on every computer to ensure that each one uses the same key. Otherwise, if a user issues multiple requests and different server computers handle these requests, a problem may occur retrieving session data, validating view state information in a page, or using forms authentication. This problem occurs because a web server using one key can't decode the information encoded by another web server using a different key.

To resolve this problem, you need to define the key explicitly in the machine.config file. Here's an example of a \<machineKey\> element with the two key attributes defined:

```
<machineKey
  validationKey="61EA54E0059153320112321149A2EEB317586824B265326CCDB3AD9ABDBE9D
6F24B0625547769E835539AD3882D3DA88896EA531CC7AFE664866BD5242FC2B05D"
  decryptionKey="61EA54E0059153320112321149A2EEB317586824B265337AF"
  validation="SHA1" />
```

The validationKey value can be between 40 and 128 characters long. It is strongly recommended that you use the maximum length key available. The decryptionKey value can be either 16 or 48 characters long. If 16 characters are defined, standard DES (Data Encryption Standard) encryption is used. If 48 characters are defined, Triple DES (or 3DES) will be used. (This means that DES is applied three times consecutively.) 3DES is much more difficult to break than DES so it is recommended that you always use 48 characters for the decryptionKey. If either the length of either of the keys is outside the allowed values, ASP.NET will return a page with an error message when requests are made to the application.

It doesn't make much sense to create the validation and decryption keys on your own. If you do, they're likely to be not sufficiently random, which makes them more subject to certain types of attacks. A better approach is to generate a strong, random key using code and the .NET Framework cryptography classes (from the System.Security.Cryptography namespace).

Here's a generic code routine called CreateMachineKey() that creates a random series of bytes using a cryptographically strong random number generator. The CreateMachineKey() method accepts a single parameter that specifies the number of characters to use. The result is returned in hexadecimal format, which is required for the machine.config file.

```
public static string CreateMachineKey(int length)
{
    // Create a byte array.
    byte[] random = new byte[length/2];

    // Create a cryptographically strong random number generator.
    RNGCryptoServiceProvider rng = new RNGCryptoServiceProvider();
```

```
    // Fill the byte array with random bytes.
    rng.GetBytes(random);

    // Create a StringBuilder to hold the result once it is
    // converted to hexadecimal format.
    System.Text.StringBuilder machineKey = new
      System.Text.StringBuilder(length);

    // Loop through the random byte array and append each value
    // to the StringBuilder.
    for (int i = 0; i < random.Length; i++)
    {
        machineKey.Append(String.Format("{0:X2}", random[i]));
    }
    return machineKey.ToString();
}
```

You can use this function in a web form to create the keys you need. For example, the following snippet of code creates a 48-character decryption key and a 128-character validation key, and displays the values in two separate text boxes:

```
txtDecryptionKey.Text = CreateMachineKey(48);
txtValidationKey.Text = CreateMachineKey(128);
```

You can then copy the information and paste it into the machine.config file for each computer in the web farm. This is much more convenient and a more secure approach than creating keys by hand. You'll learn much more about the cryptography classes in the System.Security.Cryptography namespace in Chapter 18.

Note In .NET 1.1, you have the added ability to automatically generate different keys for each application. This ensures better security on hosting servers that host multiple web applications. To use this feature, supply a value of "AutoGenerate,IsolateApps" for the validationKey and encryptionKey attributes. You can also hard-code application-specific keys by using the <machineKey> element in the web.config file for the application.

The Web.config File

Every web application inherits the settings from the machine.config file. In addition, you can apply application-specific settings. For example, you might want to set a specific method for authentication, a type of debugging, a default language, or custom error pages. However, it's important to understand that you can't override every setting from the machine.config file. There are certain settings, like the process model settings and the machine key, that can't be changed on a per-application basis. In addition, if your web.config sets application-specific options, you must place the web.config file in the root virtual directory of your application.

The entire content of an ASP.NET configuration file is nested in a root <configuration> element. This element contains a <system.web> element, which is used for ASP.NET settings. Inside the <system.web> element are separate elements for each aspect of configuration.

Here's the basic skeletal structure of the web.config file:

```
<?xml version="1.0" encoding="utf-8" ?>
<configuration>
    <system.web>
        <!-- Configuration sections go here. -->
    </system.web>
</configuration>
```

ASP.NET uses a multilayered configuration system that allows you to use different settings for different parts of your application. To use this technique, you need to create additional subdirectories inside your virtual directory. These subdirectories can contain their own web.config files with additional settings. ASP.NET uses *configuration inheritance* so that each subdirectory acquires the settings from the parent directory.

For example, consider the web request http://localhost/A/B/C/MyPage.aspx, where A is the root directory for the web application. In this case, multiple levels of settings come into play:

1. The default machine.config settings are applied first.

2. If there is a web.config file in the application root A, these settings are applied next.

3. If there is a web.config file in the subdirectory B, these settings are applied next.

4. If there is a web.config file in the subdirectory C, these settings are applied last.

In this sequence (shown in Figure 6-3), it's important to note that although you can have an unlimited number of subdirectories, the settings that applied in step 1 and step 2 have special significance. That's because there are certain settings that can only be applied at the machine.config level (like the Windows account used to execute code), and there are other settings that can only be applied at the application root level (like the type of authentication your web application uses).

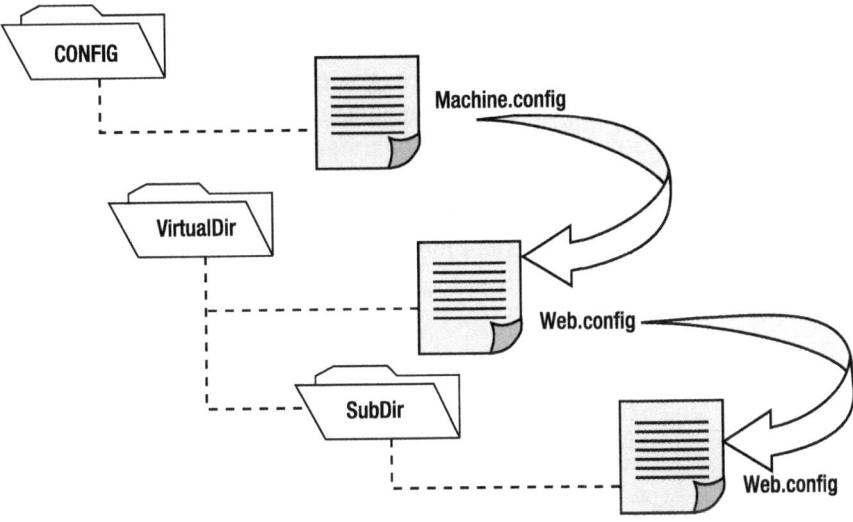

Figure 6-3. *Configuration inheritance*

In this way, subdirectories can specify just a small set of settings that differ from the rest of the web application. One reason you might want to use multiple directories in an application is to apply different security settings. Files that need to be secured would then be placed in a special directory with a web.config file that defines more stringent security settings than the root virtual directory.

If settings conflict, the settings from a web.config in a nested directory always override the settings inherited from the parent. However, there is one exception. You can designate specific *locked* sections that can't be changed. This technique is described in the next section.

Using <location> Elements

The <location> element is an extension that allows you to specify more than one group of settings in the same configuration file. You use the path attribute of the <location> element to specific the subdirectory or file to which the settings should be applied.

For example, the following web.config file uses the <location> element to create two groups of settings—one for the current directory, and one that only applies to files in the subdirectory named Secure:

```
<configuration>
    <system.web>
        <!-- Basic configuration settings go here. -->
    </system.web>

    <location path="/Secure">
        <system.web>
            <!-- Configuration settings for the Secure subdirectory go here. -->
        </system.web>
    </location>
</configuration>
```

This web.config file essentially plays the role of two configuration files. It has the same result as if you had split the settings into two separate web.config files, and placed one in the Secure subdirectory.

There's no limit to how many different location elements you can use in a single configuration file. However, the <location> element isn't used often, because it's usually easier to manage and update configuration settings when they are separated into distinct files. But there is one scenario where the <location> element gives you functionality you can't get any other way. This occurs when you want to lock specific settings so they can't be overridden.

To understand how this technique works, consider the next example. It defines two groups of settings, and sets the allowOverride attribute of the <location> tag to false on one group, as shown here:

```
<configuration>
    <system.web>
        <!-- Unprotected configuration settings go here. -->
    </system.web>
    <location allowOverride="false" >
        <system.web>
            <!-- Locked configuration settings go here. -->
```

```
        </system.web>
    </location>
</configuration>
```

In this case, you can't override any of the settings in the <location> section. If you try to, ASP.NET will generate an unhandled exception when you request a page in the web application.

The allowOverride attribute of the <location> element is primarily useful for web-hosting companies who want to make sure that certain settings can't be changed. In this case, the administrator will modify the machine.config file on the web server and use the <location> element to lock down specific sections.

Tip When you lock settings in the machine.config file, you have two choices. First, you can lock the settings for all applications by omitting the path attribute of the <location> tag. Second, you can lock settings for a specific application, by setting the path attribute to the appropriate web application name.

Configuration Settings

The <system.web> element contains all the ASP.NET-specific configuration settings. These settings are used to configure various aspects of your web application, and enable services like security, state management, and tracing.

Table 6-1 lists the basic child elements that the <system.web> element can contain and their purpose. This list is not complete and is only here to give you a rough idea of the scope of ASP.NET configuration.

Table 6-1. *Configuration Sections*

Element	Purpose
authentication	This element determines how you will verify a client's identity when the client requests a page. This is set at the application level.
authorization	This element controls which clients have access to the resources within the web application or current directory.
browserCaps	This element controls the settings of the browser capabilities component. Typically, this is only set at the machine.config level.
clientTarget	This element contains a list of aliased names for specific user-agent strings, allowing you to name specific browsers such as "opera" and "ie5" and so on. Typically, this is only set at the machine.config level.
compilation	This element contains all of the configuration settings pertinent to the compilation of the ASP.NET application. It allows the definition of recognized compilers that will be used automatically to compile script blocks or uncompiled code-behind files with source code. Typically, this is only set at the machine.config level.
customErrors	This element allows you to set specific redirect URLs that should be used when specific (or default) errors occur. For example, this element could be used to redirect the user to a friendly replacement for the dreaded "404 page not found" error.

Continued

Table 6-1. *Continued*

Element	Purpose
identity	Controls the security identity of the ASP.NET application. You can use this setting to cause the web application to temporarily assume the identity of another Windows account, and its permissions and restrictions. Typically, this is set at the application level.
pages	Provides a way to give default configuration information for page behavior properties. Typically, this is only set at the machine.config level.
sessionState	Configures the various options for maintaining session state for the application, such as whether to maintain it at all, and where to maintain it (SQL, a separate Windows service, and so on). This is set at the application level.
webServices	Controls the many settings used for web services. This allows you to tweak the various protocol and configuration settings for communicating with any web service contained within the application. Typically, this is only set at the machine.config level.

When you create a web application project in Visual Studio .NET, a default web.config file is created for you, including comments that help you figure out what information goes where. Here's the skeletal structure of a typical web.config file (without the comments):

```xml
<?xml version="1.0" encoding="utf-8" ?>
<configuration>
  <system.web>
    <compilation
        defaultLanguage="c#"
        debug="true"
    />
    <customErrors
      mode="Off"
    />
    <authentication mode="Forms">
      <forms name="MyApp" path="/"
        loginUrl="/MyApp/Login.aspx"
        protection="All" timeout="30">
      </forms>
    </authentication>
    <trace
      enabled="false"
      requestLimit="10"
      pageOutput="false"
      traceMode="SortByTime"
      localOnly="true"
    />
    <sessionState
      mode="InProc"
```

```
      stateConnectionString="tcpip=127.0.0.1:42424"
      sqlConnectionString="data source=127.0.0.1;user id=sa;password="
      cookieless="false"
      timeout="20"
    />
    <globalization
      requestEncoding="utf-8"
      responseEncoding="utf-8"
    />
  </system.web>
  <!-- LOCAL APPLICATION SETTINGS -->
  <appSettings>
    <add key="MyAppFullName" value="My Really Nice Website"/>
  </appSettings>
</configuration>
```

You can include as few or as many configuration sections as you want. For example, if you need to specify special error settings, you could add just the <customError> section and leave out the others. If you create an ASP.NET web application project in Visual Studio .NET, a web.config file is created for you with a basic structure that includes all the important sections. Visual Studio .NET adds comments to each section that describe the purpose and syntax of various options. XML comments are bracketed with the <!-- and --> character sequences, as shown here:

```
<!-- This is the format for an XML comment. -->
```

Note Like all XML documents, the web.config file is case-sensitive. Every setting uses camel case, and starts every setting with a lowercase letter. That means you cannot write <CustomErrors> instead of <customErrors>.

The following sections give a brief overview of each section.

<configuration>

<configuration> is the root element that contains all of the configuration details. Every web.config file *must* have a configuration element. The <configuration> element can contain several other subelements, but in an ASP.NET application you're only likely to see two: <system.web> and <appSettings>.

<system.web>

<system.web> acts as a container for the predefined ASP.NET-specific settings, many of which are detailed in the following sections.

Note The configuration file architecture is a .NET standard, and other types of applications (like Windows applications) can also use configuration files. For that reason, the root <configuration> element isn't tailored to web application settings. Instead, web application settings are contained inside the dedicated <system.web> section

---

<compilation>

The <compilation> element configures all of the compilation settings for a given ASP.NET application. The following is a list of some of the more commonly used attributes that can be placed on the <compilation> element:

- **debug.** Specifies whether to compile release binaries or debug binaries. The default is false.

- **defaultLanguage.** Specifies the default programming language to be used when dynamically compiling. Can be any language defined by the compilers tag (see the following list). The default is VB .NET.

- **explicit.** Indicates the state of the Visual Basic .NET explicit compile option. The default is true.

- **strict.** Indicates the state of the Visual Basic .NET strict compile option. This switch, in VB .NET, prevents typecasting data in which data loss would occur. Thus, only type conversions in which the type is widened are allowed.

- **tempDirectory.** Indicates the directory to use for file storage during compilation.

In addition to these attributes, there are some subelements that can be added beneath a compilation element to further configure compilation settings. These include the following:

- **<compilers>.** This element is used to configure the compilers used for the ASP.NET application. This allows you to specify different or new compilers to compile the source code for the ASP.NET application so that your ASP.NET application can take advantage of Perl, or even COBOL for .NET.

- **<assemblies>.** This element is used to tell the ASP.NET application which assemblies should be automatically referenced when code is compiled dynamically.

If you're using Visual Studio .NET, neither of these settings have an effect, because Visual Studio .NET handles the first stage of compilation (to IL code), not ASP.NET.

<customErrors>

This element allows you to configure the behavior of your application in response to various HTTP errors. For example, the dreaded 404 error can be redirected to a page that prints a user-friendly error message to the users of your web application by creating a section like this:

```
<customErrors defaultRedirect="standarderror.aspx" mode="remoteonly">
   <error statuscode="404" redirect="filenotfound.htm"/>
</customErrors>
```

In this example, if the error is code 404 (file not found), it will redirect the user to filenotfound.htm. If any other error occurs (including an HTTP error or an unhandled .NET exception in the web page), the user will be redirected to the page standarderror.aspx. Because the error mode is set to remoteonly, local administrators will see the actual error message rather than being redirected. Remote clients will only see the custom error page.

The following is a list of the modes supported for the mode attribute:

- **on.** Indicates that custom errors are enabled. If no defaultRedirect attribute is supplied, users will see a generic error.

- **off.** Custom errors are disabled. This allows full error details to be displayed.

- **remoteonly.** Custom errors are shown only to remote clients while full detailed errors are displayed to local clients.

Keep in mind that the custom error settings you define in a configuration file only come into effect if ASP.NET is handling the request. For example, if you request the nonexistent page whateverpage.aspx in an application with the previous settings shown, you'll be redirected to filenotfound.aspx, because the .aspx file extension is registered to the ASP.NET service. However, if you request the nonexistent page whateverpage.html, ASP.NET will not process the request, and the default redirect setting specified in IIS will be used. Typically, this means that the user will see the page c:\[WinDir]\Help\IISHelp\common\404b.htm. You could change the set of registered ASP.NET file types to include .html and .htm files, but this will slow down performance for these file types (and give additional work to the ASP.NET worker process).

■**Note** What happens if an error occurs in the error page itself? If an error occurs in custom error page (in this case, DefaultError.aspx), ASP.NET will not be able to handle it. It will not try to re-forward the user to the same page. Instead, it will display the normal client error page with the generic message.

<authentication>

This section configures the authentication system for your application. This element has an attribute named mode that allows you to configure the mode of authentication for the application or directory. It can be any of the following:

- **Windows.** Windows authentication will be used, which means IIS will authenticate the request by comparing the supplied user credentials against a Windows user account. Windows authentication includes all forms of IIS authentication, including Basic, Digest, Integrated Windows authentication (NTLM/Kerberos), or digital certificates.

- **Forms.** Forms authentication will be used, which means ASP.NET will track authorized users by maintaining a special cookie. This cookie is only sent to the user after the user has logged in to the system through a custom login web page.

- **Passport.** Microsoft Passport authentication will be used, which means the Passport servers will authenticate the user, attach a cookie, and redirect the request back to your website.

- **None.** The application will not use any built-in authentication system. However, you can still respond to authentication events and perform your own custom authentication steps.

There are several possibilities available when building authentication and authorization schemes. Which scheme you decide to use depends on the needs of your application and the demands of your environment. For example, you won't use Windows authentication if you know that the users of your site will not be able to transmit Windows security information (perhaps because they are behind firewalls, using non-Windows computers, and so on). On the other hand, you might want to secure an administrative web interface so that only internal users can access it. In this case, using Windows authentication might be a better choice than forms authentication, because you won't have to create a login page.

There is quite a bit to learn about the authentication services that ASP.NET provides for programmers. You'll look at security in depth in Part Three.

<trace>

This element configures the tracing system. As you learned in Chapter 4, tracing allows you to display standard diagnostic information and custom debugging messages on the web page itself. Using the trace settings in the configuration file, you can enable or disable tracing for an entire web application.

Additionally, you can use the <trace> section to direct the trace output to somewhere other than the web page. You can also define *trace listeners*, which are objects that listen for, collect, and then route various messages. For example, the .NET Framework includes a listener that you can use to log the trace to a text file. You can use this listener with the following configuration settings:

```
<trace enabled="true" requestLimit="10" pageOutput="false">
   <listeners>
      <add name="TraceListener"
          type="System.Diagnostics.TextWriterTraceListener, System"
          initializeData="TraceListener.log"/>
   </listeners>
</trace>
```

This section adds a new listener. This listener is simply a class that inherits from the abstract base class TraceListener, which is found in the System.Diagnostics namespace. As usual in .NET configuration files, when you specify a type, you use the fully qualified name of the class, followed by a comma, and then the name of the assembly in which that type can be found (without the extension .dll, which is automatically assumed). If the assembly isn't in the application's Bin directory, or the GAC (global assembly cache), ASP.NET will generate an error.

You can easily create your own trace listener by inheriting from the TraceListener class. However, there are three classes that have already implemented the most commonly needed types of logging: the DefaultTraceListener (for displaying messages in the Output window while debugging), the TextWriterTraceListener (for writing messages to a text file), and the EventLogTraceListener (for writing messages to the Windows event log).

<sessionState>

This section configures session state management. Unlike classic ASP, there are several options for maintaining session state in an ASP.NET application. The default mode is InProc, which indicates that the ASP.NET session state is to be maintained locally. It can also be maintained remotely by the ASP.NET state service, which is a Windows service that you can run on a remote server. This helps facilitate maintaining accurate session state across multiple machines in a web farm. Alternatively, the session state can be maintained by SQL Server.

You'll learn much more about session state, and the advantages and disadvantages of different session stores, in Chapter 7.

<globalization>

This section is used for configuring the text encoding format of the text sent to and received from users of the website. By default, utf-8 is used, which is the standard one-byte ASCII encoding most of us are familiar with. This allows for characters that require more than a single byte to be encoded properly.

<appSettings>

You add custom settings to a web.config file in a special element called <appSettings>. Note that the <appSettings> element is nested in the root <configuration> element, not the <system.web> element, which contains the other groups of predefined settings.

Here's where the <appSettings> section fits in to the web.config file:

```
<?xml version="1.0" encoding="utf-8" ?>
<configuration>
    <appSettings>
        <!-- Custom application data goes here. -->
    </appSettings>
    <system.web>
        <!-- Configuration settings go here. -->
    </system.web>
</configuration>
```

The custom settings that you add are written as simple string variables. There are several reasons that you might want to use a special web.config setting. Often, you'll want the ability to record hard-coded but changeable information for connecting to external resources, like database connection strings, file paths, and web service URLs. Because the configuration file can be modified at any time, this allows you to update the configuration of an application as its physical deployment characteristics change without needing to recompile it.

Custom settings are entered using an <add> element that identifies a unique variable name (the key) and the variable contents (the value). The following example adds two new custom configuration settings:

```
<?xml version="1.0" encoding="utf-8" ?>
<configuration>
  <system.web>
  ...
  </system.web>

  <appSettings>
    <add key="websitename" value="My New Website"/>
    <add key="welcomemessage" value="Welcome to my new Website, friend!"/>
  </appSettings>
</configuration>
```

Once you've added this information, .NET makes it extremely easy to retrieve it in your web-page code. You simply need to use the ConfigurationSettings class from the System.Configuration namespace. It exposes a property called AppSettings, which contains a dynamically built collection of available application settings for the current directory. For example, if the ASP.NET page class referencing the AppSettings collection is at a location such as http://localhost/MyApp/MyDirectory/MySubDirectory, it is possible that the AppSettings collection contains settings from three different web.config files. The AppSettings collection makes that hierarchy seamless to the page that's using it.

To use the ConfigurationSettings class, it helps to first import the System.Configuration namespace so you can refer to the class without needing to use the long fully qualified name, as shown here:

```
using System.Configuration;
```

Next, you simply need to retrieve the value by name. The following example fills two labels using the custom application information:

```
public class Welcome : Page
{
    protected Label lblSiteName;
    protected Label lblWelcome;

    private void Page_Load(object sender, EventArgs e)
    {
        lblSiteName.Text =
          ConfigurationSettings.AppSettings["websitename"];
        lblWelcome.Text =
          ConfigurationSettings.AppSettings["welcomemessage"];
    }
}
```

Figure 6-4 shows the test web page in action.

Figure 6-4. *Retrieving custom application settings*

An error won't occur if you try to retrieve a value that doesn't exist. If you suspect this could be a problem, make sure to test for a null reference before retrieving a value.

Note Values in the <appSettings> element of a configuration file are available to any class in your application, or any component that your application uses, whether it's a web form class, a business logic class, a data access class, or something else. In all these cases, you use the ConfigurationSettings class in exactly the same way.

.NET Components

A well-designed web application written for ASP.NET will include separate components, which may be organized into distinct data and business tiers. Once you've created these components, you can use them from any ASP.NET web page or web service seamlessly.

There is one important distinction between the code in ASP.NET files (like web pages and web services) and the code that's in a separate component. If required, ASP.NET files are compiled on demand. The same behavior doesn't take place with components. Instead, you need to compile the source code for the component to a DLL file before you can use it in a web page.

There are two ways you can create a component:

- Code it by hand in one or more .cs text files, and then compile it with the csc.exe command-line compiler. This is the same compiler used to compile C# code in web pages and web services.

- Use Visual Studio .NET, and start a new Class Library project. Visual Studio .NET will compile your class library project when you build the project.

To assist in debugging, you can add your component project and ASP.NET web application project to the same Visual Studio .NET solution. This allows you to easily modify both the web application and the component code at the same time, and single-step from a web page event handler into a method in your component. To set this up, create your web application first. Then, select File ➤ Add Project ➤ New Project, and select the Class Library project type (see Figure 6-5). Notice that when you create a class library project, you don't specify a virtual directory. Instead, you choose a physical directory on your local hard drive where the source files will be stored.

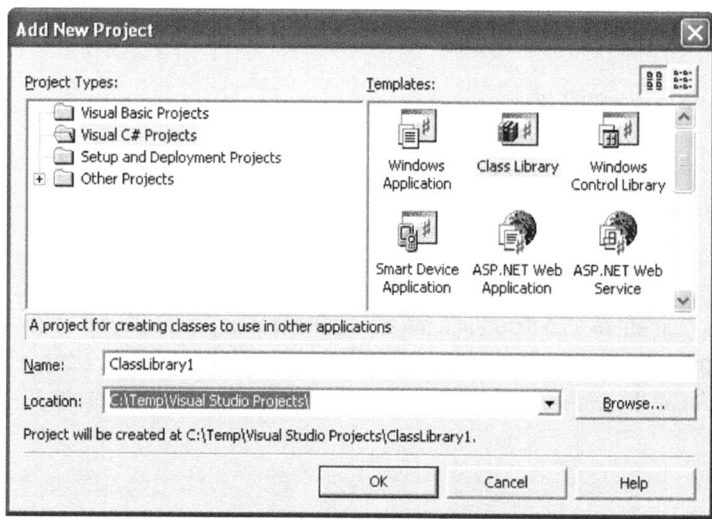

Figure 6-5. *Adding a class library project to a solution*

Creating a Component

The next example demonstrates a simple component that reads a random Sherlock Holmes quote from an XML file. (This XML file is available on the Internet and freely reusable via the GNU Public License.) The component consists of two classes—a Quotation class that represents a single quote, and a SherlockQuotes class that allows you to read a random quote. Both of these classes are placed in the SherlockLib namespace.

The first listing shows the SherlockQuotes class, which loads an XML file containing quotes in the QEL (Quotation Exchange Language XML dialect) when it's instantiated. The SherlockQuotes class provides a public GetRandom() quote method that the web page code can use.

```
using System;
using System.Xml;

namespace SherlockLib
{
    public class SherlockQuotes
    {
        private XmlDocument quoteDoc;
```

```
        private int quoteCount;
        public SherlockQuotes(string fileName)
        {
            quoteDoc = new XmlDocument();
            quoteDoc.Load(fileName);
            quoteCount = quoteDoc.DocumentElement.ChildNodes.Count;
        }

        public Quotation GetRandomQuote()
        {
            int i;
            Random x = new Random();
            i = x.Next(quoteCount-1);
            return new Quotation( quoteDoc.DocumentElement.ChildNodes[i] );
        }
    }
}
```

Each time a random quotation is obtained, it is stored in a Quotation object. The listing for the Quotation class is shown here:

```
using System;
using System.Xml;

namespace SherlockLib
{
    public class Quotation
    {
        private string qsource;
        public string Source
        {
            get {return qsource;}
            set {qsource = value;}
        }

        private string date;
        public string Date
        {
            get {return date;}
            set {date = value;}
        }

        private string quotation;
        public string QuotationText
        {
            get {return quotation;}
            set {quotation = value;}
        }
```

```
    public Quotation(XmlNode quoteNode)
    {
      if ( (quoteNode.SelectSingleNode("source")) != null)
        qsource = quoteNode.SelectSingleNode("source").InnerText;
      if ( (quoteNode.Attributes.GetNamedItem("date")) != null)
        date = quoteNode.Attributes.GetNamedItem("date").Value;
      quotation = quoteNode.FirstChild.InnerText;
    }
  }
}
```

Using a Component

Using the component in an actual ASP.NET page is easy. If you're working without Visual Studio .NET, all you need to do is compile the code to a DLL file and copy the DLL file into the application's Bin directory. ASP.NET automatically monitors this directory, and makes all of its classes available to any web page in the application.

Here's the code you might use to compile this component, assuming the source code is stored in two files:

```
csc /t:library /r:System.Xml.dll Quotation.cs SherlockQuotes.cs
    /out:SherlockLib.dll
```

The /t:library parameter indicates that you want to create a DLL assembly instead of an EXE assembly. The compiled assembly will have the name SherlockLib.dll. The /r parameter specifies any dependent assemblies you use. The compilation process is the same as the one used with web pages.

Tip For the full list of compilation options that you can use with csc.exe, consult the MSDN document or execute the command csc /?.

In Visual Studio .NET, you can compile your component by right-clicking the project in the Solution Explorer and choosing Build. To indicate that your web application needs to use this component, you can add an assembly reference. This allows Visual Studio .NET to provide its usual syntax checking and IntelliSense. Otherwise, it will interpret your attempts to use the class as mistakes and refuse to compile your code.

To add a reference, right-click the name of your web application project in the Solution Explorer and choose Add Reference. The Add Reference dialog box (shown in Figure 6-6) includes three tabs:

- **.NET.** This allows you to add a reference to a .NET assembly. You can choose from the list of .NET assemblies, or you can use a custom assembly by clicking the Browse button and finding the corresponding DLL file.

- **COM.** This allows you to add a reference to a legacy COM component. Once again, you can choose from a list of known components, or browse to the specific file you want to use. When you add a reference to a COM component, .NET automatically creates an intermediary wrapper class known as an *interop assembly*. You use the interop assembly in your .NET code, and the interop assembly interacts with the legacy component.

- **Projects.** This allows you to add a reference to a .NET assembly that's already in the current solution. This tab is similar to using the .NET tab, but you don't need to browse to the specific file—Visual Studio .NET automatically shows a list of eligible projects.

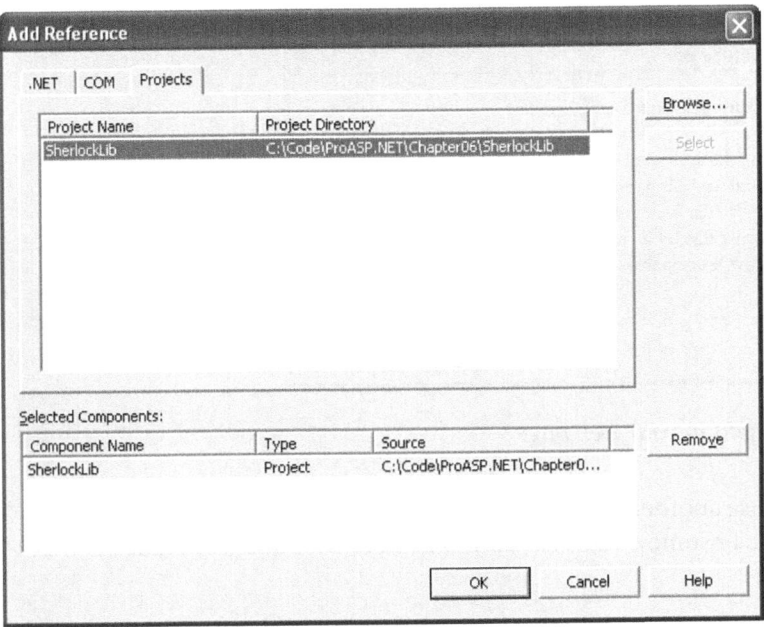

Figure 6-6. *Adding a reference to SherlockLib.dll*

Once you add the reference, the corresponding DLL file will be automatically copied to the Bin directory of your current project. You can verify this by checking the Full Path property of the reference in the Properties window, or just browsing to the directory in Windows Explorer. The nice thing is that this file will automatically be overwritten with the most recent compiled version of the assembly every time you run the project.

Now you might want to import the SherlockLib namespace to make its classes more readily available, as shown here:

```
using SherlockLib;
```

Finally, you can use the class in your web-page code just as you would use a class from the .NET Framework. Here's an example that displays the quotation information on a web page:

```
private void Page_Load(object sender, System.EventArgs e)
{
    // Put user code to initialize the page here.
    SherlockQuotes quotes = new
```

```
        SherlockQuotes(Server.MapPath("./sherlock-holmes.xml"));
    Quotation quote = quotes.GetRandomQuote();
    Response.Write("<b>" + quote.Source + "</b> (<i>" + quote.Date + "</i>)");
    Response.Write("<blockquote>" + quote.QuotationText + "</blockquote>");
}
```

When you run this application, you'll see something like what's shown in Figure 6-7. Every time you refresh the page, you'll see a different quote.

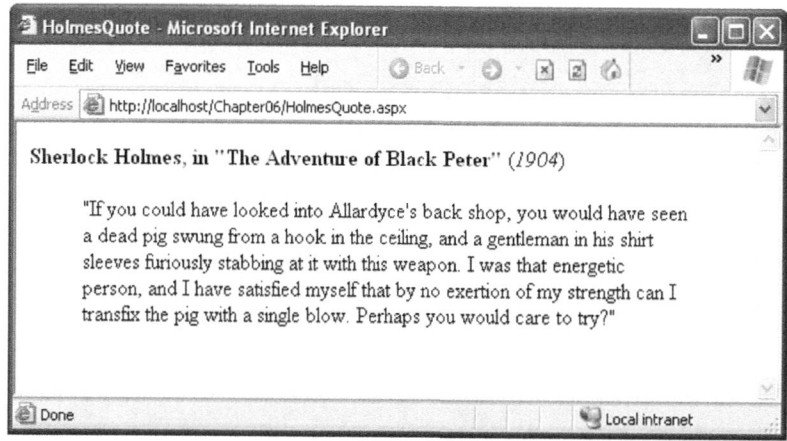

Figure 6-7. *Using the component in your web page*

It really is that easy. To use another component, either from your own business tier, or from a third-party developer, or somewhere else, all you need to do is add a reference to that assembly.

Tip ASP.NET also allows you to use assemblies with custom controls just as easily as you use assemblies with custom components. This allows you to bundle reusable user-interface output and functionality into self-contained packages so that they can be used over and over again within the same or multiple applications. Part Four has more information about this technique.

Extending the HTTP Pipeline

As explained earlier, the pipeline of application events isn't limited to requests for .aspx web forms. It also applies if you request web services, or even create your own handlers to deal with custom file types.

Why would you want to create your own handler? For the most part, you won't. However, there are cases in which it's convenient to use a lower-level interface that still provides access to useful objects like Response and Request but doesn't use the full control-based web form model. One example is if you want to create a web resource that dynamically renders a custom graphic (a technique demonstrated in Chapter 23). In this situation, you simply need to receive a request, check the URL parameters, and then return raw image data as a JPEG or GIF file. By avoiding the full web control model, you save some overhead, because ASP.NET does not need to go through as many steps (such as creating the web-page objects, persisting view state, and so on).

ASP.NET makes scenarios like these remarkably easy through its pluggable architecture. You can "snap in" new handlers for specialized file types just by adding configuration settings. But first, you need to take a closer look at the HTTP pipeline.

HTTP Handlers and HTTP Modules

Every request into an ASP.NET application is handled by a specialized component known as an *HTTP handler*. The HTTP handler is the backbone of the ASP.NET request processing framework. ASP.NET uses different HTTP handlers to serve different file types. For example, the handler for web pages creates the page and control objects, runs your code, and renders the final HTML. The handler for web services has a slightly simpler task—it simply deserializes the SOAP message and invokes the corresponding code.

All HTTP handlers are defined in the <httpHandlers> section of a configuration file. The core set of HTTP handlers is defined in the machine.config file. Here's an excerpt of that file:

```
<httpHandlers>
    <add verb="*" path="trace.axd" type="System.Web.Handlers.TraceHandler"/>
    <add verb="*" path="*.config" type="System.Web.HttpForbiddenHandler"/>
    <add verb="*" path="*.cs" type="System.Web.HttpForbiddenHandler"/>
    <add verb="*" path="*.aspx" type="System.Web.UI.PageHandlerFactory"/>

    ...
</httpHandlers>
```

Inside the <httpHandlers> section you can place <add> elements that register new handlers and <remove> elements to unregister existing handlers. In this example, four classes are registered. All requests for trace.axd are handed to the TraceHandler, which renders an HTML page with a list of all the recently collected trace output (as described in Chapter 4). Requests for files that end in .config or .cs are handled by the HttpForbiddenHandler, which always generates an exception informing the user that these file types are never served. And files ending in .aspx are handled by the PageHandlerFactory. In this case, PageHandlerFactory isn't actually an HTTP handler. Instead, it's a factory class that will create the appropriate HTTP handler. This extra layer allows the factory to create a different handler or configure the handler differently depending on other information about the request.

ASP.NET also uses another ingredient in page processing, called *HTTP modules*. HTTP modules participate in the processing of a request by handling application events, much like the global.asax file. A given request can flow through multiple HTTP modules, but it always ends with a single HTTP handler. Figure 6-8 shows how the two interact.

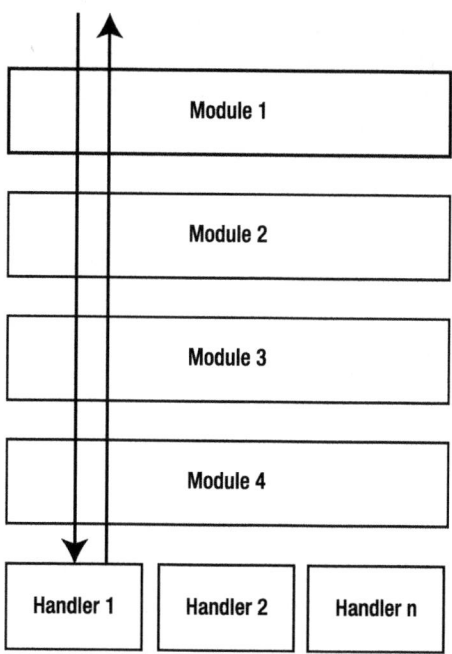

Figure 6-8. *The ASP.NET request processing architecture*

ASP.NET uses a core set of HTTP modules to enable platform features like caching, authentication, and error pages. HTTP modules can be added or removed with <add> and <remove> tags in the <httpModules> section of a configuration file. Here's an excerpt showing some of the HTTP modules that are defined in the machine.config file:

```
<httpModules>
    <add name="OutputCache" type="System.Web.Caching.OutputCacheModule"/>
    <add name="Session" type="System.Web.SessionState.SessionStateModule"/>
    <add name="WindowsAuthentication"
        type="System.Web.Security.WindowsAuthenticationModule"/>
    <add name="FormsAuthentication"
        type="System.Web.Security.FormsAuthenticationModule"/>
    ...
</httpModules>
```

One of the benefits of HTTP modules and HTTP handlers is that they provide an extensible architecture that allows you to easily plug in your own handlers and modules. In the past, developers who need these sort of features were forced to author their own ISAPI extensions (which play the same role as HTTP handlers) or ISAPI filters (which play the same role as HTTP modules). Both of these components are dramatically more complex to create.

Note ISAPI extensions and filters plug directly into IIS. HTTP handlers and modules play the same role, but they plug into ASP.NET. For example, imagine you create and register a custom HTTP handler. When the client issues a request for that file type, it will flow first from IIS to ASP.NET (through the ASP.NET ISAPI extension). Then ASP.NET will create and execute your handler. As a result, your handlers and modules never interact with IIS.

Creating a Custom HTTP Handler

If you want to work at a lower level than the web form model to support a specialized form of processing, you can implement your own HTTP handler.

To create a custom HTTP handler, you simply need to author a class that implements the IHttpHandler interface. This class should be part of a standalone DLL assembly (a class library project in Visual Studio .NET). The IHttpHandler requires your class to implement two members, which are shown in Table 6-2.

Table 6-2. *IHttpHandler Members*

Member	Description
ProcessRequest()	ASP.NET calls this method when a request is received. It's where the HTTP handlers perform all the processing. You can access the intrinsic ASP.NET objects (like Request, Response, and Server) through the HttpContext object that's passed to this method.
IsReusable	After ProcessRequest() finishes its work, ASP.NET checks this property to determine whether a given instance of an HTTP handler can be reused. If you return true, the HTTP handler object can be reused for another request of the same type current. If you return false, the HTTP handler object will simply be discarded.

The following code shows one of the simplest possible HTTP handlers you can create. It simply returns a fixed block of HTML with a message.

```
using System;
using System.Web;

namespace HttpExtensions
{
    public class SimpleHandler : IHttpHandler
    {
        public void ProcessRequest(System.Web.HttpContext context)
        {
```

```
            HttpResponse response = context.Response;
            response.Write("<html><body><h1>Rendered by the SimpleHandler") ;
            response.Write("</h1></body></html>") ;
        }

        public bool IsReusable
        {
            get {return true;}
        }
    }
}
```

■ Note When you create a class library project in Visual Studio .NET, it doesn't automatically reference the System.Web.dll assembly, which contains the bulk of the ASP.NET classes. In order to use types like IHttpHandler and HttpContext, you need to add a reference to this assembly (right-click the project name in the Solution Explorer, choose Add Reference, and find the assembly in the list in the .NET tab).

Configuring a Custom HTTP Handler

Before you can use your HTTP handler, you need to compile it and register it with ASP.NET. You can perform the compilation by hand or using Visual Studio .NET, just like with any other component. Then copy the HTTP handler component to the Bin directory of the web application where you want to use it so that it's readily available. If you're using Visual Studio .NET, you can accomplish this step just by adding a reference to the component with the HTTP handler class in your web application.

Next, you need to alter the web.config file for the web application so that it registers your HTTP handler. Here's an example:

```
<httpHandlers>
    <add verb="*" path="test.simple"
        type="HttpExtensions.SimpleHandler,HttpExtensions" />
</httpHandlers>
```

When you register an HTTP handler, you specify three important details. The verb attribute indicates whether the request is an HTTP POST or HTTP GET request (use * for all requests). The path attribute indicates the file extension that will invoke the HTTP handler. In this example, the web.config section links the SimpleHandler class to the filename test.simple. Finally, the type attribute identifies the HTTP handler class. This identification is made up of two portions. First is the fully qualified class name (in this example, HttpExtensions.Simple-Handler). That portion is followed by a comma and the name of the DLL assembly that contains the class (in this example, HttpExtensions.dll). Note that the .dll extension is always assumed, and you don't include it in the name.

After you've completed all these steps, the HTTP handler still won't work. If you request test.simple, you'll receive an HTTP file not found error. The problem is that the .simple extension is not recognized by IIS. This means that by default it's handled by IIS on its own, not by ASP.NET. IIS default behavior simply checks for a file with that name and, if it exists, IIS returns the raw data from the file.

To change this behavior, you need to add an IIS file mapping for your application. Here's what you need to do:

1. Start IIS Manager (select Settings ➤ Control Panel ➤ Administrative Tools ➤ Internet Information Services from the Start menu).

2. Select the virtual directory for the web application where you want to use the HTTP handler.

3. Right-click the virtual directory, and select Properties.

4. In the Virtual Directory tab, click the Configuration button. The Application Configuration dialog box will appear.

5. In the Mappings tab there is a list of all the currently configured mappings. Click Add to add a new mapping.

6. Now you must map the extension to the ASP.NET ISAPI extension. First, click Browse and find the aspnet_isapi.dll. This is found in a directory like c:\[WinDir]\ Microsoft.NET\Framework\[Version]. Then, specify the extension name (.simple in this example). Finally, clear the Check That File Exists check box, because this application extension doesn't correspond to a physical file. A fully configured mapping is shown in Figure 6-9.

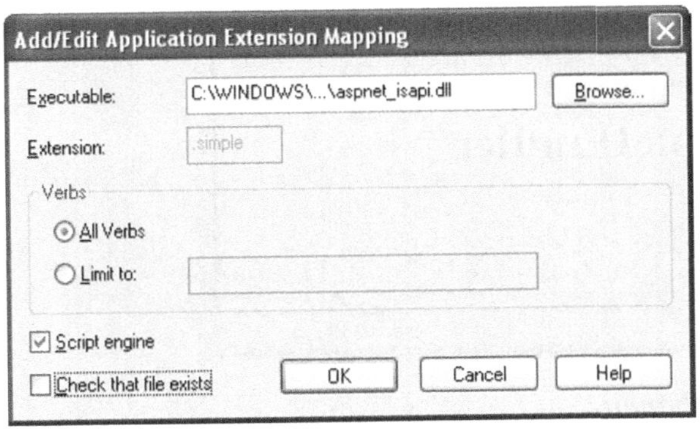

Figure 6-9. *Mapping a new file type*

7. Click OK to save the mapping. You'll see the mapping appear in the list, as shown in Figure 6-10.

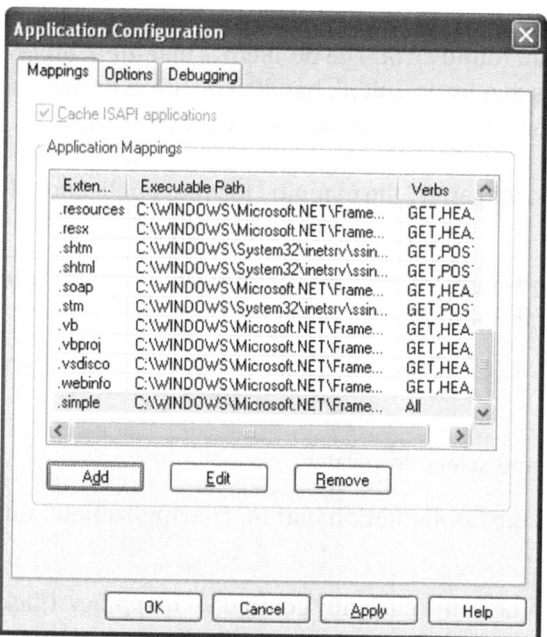

Figure 6-10. *The new mapping*

8. Click OK again to close the Application Configuration dialog box.

That's it! Now if you request test.simple, you'll see the HTML shown in Figure 6-11.

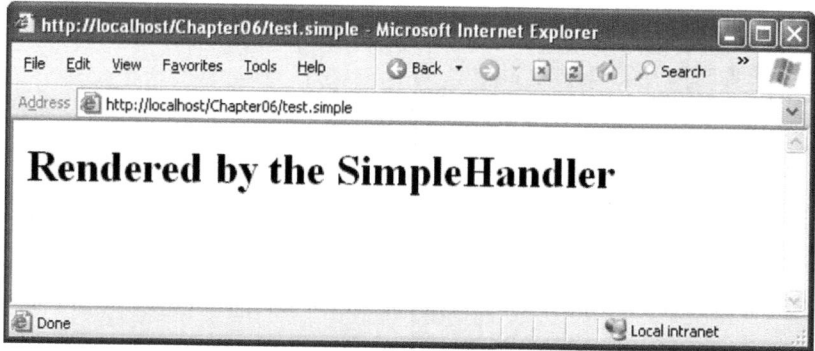

Figure 6-11. *Running a custom HTTP handler*

Registering HTTP Handlers Without Configuring IIS

Instead of using a web.config or machine.config file, ASP.NET provides an alternate approach for registering HTTP handlers—you can use the recognized extension .ashx. All requests that end in .ashx are automatically recognized as requests for a custom HTTP handler.

Visual Studio .NET doesn't directly support the .ashx file type, but you can still create and edit a .ashx file by hand. The .ashx file is a text file that contains a single line with a WebHandler directive. This WebHandler directive indicates the class that should be exposed through this file. Here's an example:

```
<%@ WebHandler Language="C#" Class="HttpExtensions.SimpleHandler" %>
```

If you save this as the file simple.ashx, whenever the client requests simple.ashx your custom web handler will be executed. Best of all, the .ashx file type is registered in IIS, so you don't need to perform any IIS configuration.

Note The WebHandler directive can point to any class that's in one of the assemblies in the Bin directory, even if it's not a part of the main web application project. For example, in this example the HttpExtensions.SimpleHandler class is used from the HttpExtensions.dll assembly.

Whether you use a configuration file or an .ashx file is mostly a matter of preference. However, .ashx files are usually used for simpler extensions that are designed for a single web application. Configuration files also give you a little more flexibility. For example, you can register an HTTP handler to deal with all requests that end with a given extension, whereas an .ashx file only servers a request with a specific filename. Also, you can register an HTTP handler for multiple applications (by registering it in the web.config file and installing the assembly in the GAC). To achieve the same affect with an .ashx file, you need to copy the .ashx file to each virtual directory.

Creating an Advanced HTTP Handler

In the previous example, the HTTP handler simply returns a block of static HTML. However, you can create much more imaginative handlers. For example, you might read data that's been posted to the page or that's supplied in the query string, and use that to customize your rendered output. Here's a more sophisticated example that displays the source code for a requested file. It uses the file I/O support that's found in the System.IO namespace.

```
using System;
using System.Web;
using System.IO;

namespace HttpExtensions
{
    public class SourceHandler : IHttpHandler
    {
        public void ProcessRequest(System.Web.HttpContext context)
        {
```

```
            // Make the HTTP context objects easily available.
            HttpResponse response = context.Response;
            HttpRequest request = context.Request;
            HttpServerUtility server = context.Server;

            response.Write("<html><body>");

            // Get the name of the requested file.
            string file = request.QueryString["file"];
            try
            {
                // Open the file and display its contents one line at a time.
                response.Write("<b>Listing " + file + "</b><br>");
                StreamReader r = File.OpenText(
                  server.MapPath(Path.Combine("./", file)));
                string line = "";
                while (line != null)
                {
                    line = r.ReadLine();

                    if (line != null)
                    {
                        // Make sure tags and other special characters are
                        // replaced by their corresponding HTML entities so that
                        // they can be displayed appropriately.
                        line = server.HtmlEncode(line);

                        // Replace spaces and tabs with nonbreaking spaces
                        // to preserve whitespace.
                        line = line.Replace(" ", " ");
                        line = line.Replace(
                          "\t", "     ");

                        // A more sophisticated source viewer might apply
                        // color coding.
                        response.Write(line + "<br>");
                    }
                }
                r.Close();
            }
            catch (Exception err)
            {
                response.Write(err.Message);
            }
            response.Write("</html></body>");
        }
```

```
    public bool IsReusable
    {
        get {return true;}
    }
  }
}
```

This code simply finds the requested file, reads its content, and uses a little string substitution (for example, replacing spaces with nonbreaking spaces and line breaks with the <br> element) and HTML encoding to create a representation that can be safely displayed in a browser. You'll learn more about techniques for reading and manipulating files in Chapter 12.

Next, you can map the handler to a file extension, as follows:

```
<httpHandlers>
    <add verb="*" path="source.simple"
        type="HttpExtensions.SourceHandler,HttpExtensions"/>
</httpHandlers>
```

To test this handler, you can use the following URL:

```
http://localhost/Chapter06/source.simple?file=HolmesQuote.aspx.cs
```

The HTTP handler will then show the source code for the .cs file, as shown in Figure 6-12.

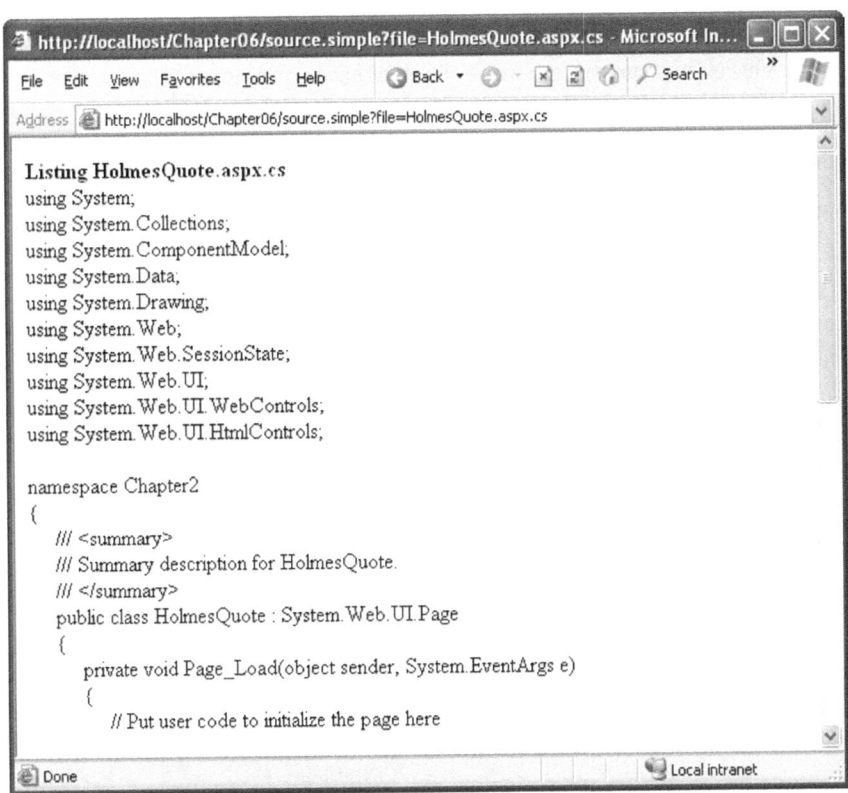

Figure 6-12. *Using a more sophisticated HTTP handler*

Based on this example, you can probably imagine a variety of different ways you can use HTTP handlers. For example, you could render a custom image, perform an ad hoc database query, or return some binary data. These examples extend the ASP.NET architecture, but bypass the web-page model. The result is a leaner, more efficient component.

You can also create HTTP handlers that work *asynchronously*. This means they create a new thread to do their work, instead of using one of the ASP.NET worker threads. This improves scalability in situations where you need to perform a task that takes a long amount of time, but isn't CPU-intensive. A classic example is waiting to read an extremely slow network resource. ASP.NET only allows a fixed set of worker threads to run at one time (typically 25), so once this limit is reached additional requests will be queued, even if the computer has available CPU time. With asynchronous handlers, additional requests can be accepted, because the handler creates a new thread to process each request rather than using the worker process. Of course, there is a risk with this approach. Namely, if you create too many threads for the computer to manage efficiently, or if you try to do too much CPU-intensive work at once, the performance of the entire web server will be adversely affected. Asynchronous HTTP handlers are beyond the scope of this book, but you can read an excellent introduction from MSDN Magazine at http://msdn.microsoft.com/msdnmag/issues/03/06/Threading.

HTTP HANDLERS AND SESSION STATE

By default, HTTP handlers do not have access to client-specific session state. That's because HTTP handlers are generally used for lower-level tasks, and skipping the steps needed to serialize and retrieve session state information achieves a minor increase in performance. However, if you *do* need access to session state information, you simply need to implement one of the following two interfaces:

- IRequiresSessionState

- IReadOnlySessionState

If you only require read-only access to session state, you should implement the IRequiresSessionState interface. If you need to modify or add to session information, you should implement the IReadOnlySessionState interface. You should never implement both at the same time.

These two interfaces are just marker interfaces and do not contain any methods. That means you don't need to write any extra code to enable session support. For example, if you want to use read-only session state with the SimpleHandler class, you would declare it in this way:

```
public class SimpleHandler : IHttpHandler, IReadOnlySessionState
{...}
```

To actually access the Session object, you'll need to work through the HttpContext object that's submitted to the ProcessRequest() method. It provides a Session property.

Creating a Custom HTTP Module

It's just as easy to create custom HTTP modules as custom HTTP handlers. You simply need to author a class that implements the System.Web.IHttpModule interface. You can then register your module by adding it to the <httpModules> section of the web.config file. However, you don't need to configure IIS to use your HTTP modules. That's because modules are automatically used for every web request.

So how does an HTTP module plug itself into the ASP.NET request processing pipeline? It does it in the exact same way as the global.asax file. Essentially, when an HTTP module is created, it registers to receive specific global application events. For example, if the module is concerned with authentication, it will register itself to receive the authentication events. Whenever those events occur, ASP.NET invokes all the interested HTTP modules. The HTTP module wires up its events with delegate code in the Init() method.

The IHttpModule interface defines the two methods shown in Table 6-3.

Table 6-3. *IHttpModule Members*

Member	Description
Init()	This method allows an HTTP module to register its event handlers to receive the events of the HttpApplication object. This method provides the current HttpApplication object for the request as a parameter.
Dispose()	This method gives an HTTP module an opportunity to perform any clean up before the object gets garbage collected.

The following class is a custom HTTP module that handles the event HttpApplication.AuthenticateRequest and then logs the user information to a new entry in the Windows event log using the EventLog class from the System.Diagnostics namespace. In order to use this example, the account used to run ASP.NET code must have permission to write to the event log.

```
using System;
using System.Web;
using System.Diagnostics;

namespace HttpExtensions
{
    public class LogUserModule : IHttpModule
    {
        public void Init(HttpApplication httpApp)
        {
            // Attach application event handlers.
            httpApp.AuthenticateRequest += new EventHandler(OnAuthentication);
        }

        private void OnAuthentication(object sender, EventArgs a)
        {
            // Get the current user identity.
            string name = HttpContext.Current.User.Identity.Name;
```

```
        // Log the user name.
        EventLog log = new EventLog();
        log.Source = "Log User Module";
        log.WriteEntry(name + " was authenticated.");
    }

    public void Dispose()
    {}
  }
}
```

Now you can register the module with the following information in the web.config file:

```
<httpModules>
    <add name="LogUserModule"
        type="HttpExtensions.LogUserModule,HttpExtensions" />
</httpModules>
```

To test this module, request another page in the web application. Then check the entry in the Windows application event log. (To view the log, select Programs ➤ Administrative Tools ➤ Event Viewer from the Start menu.) Figure 6-13 shows the logged messages.

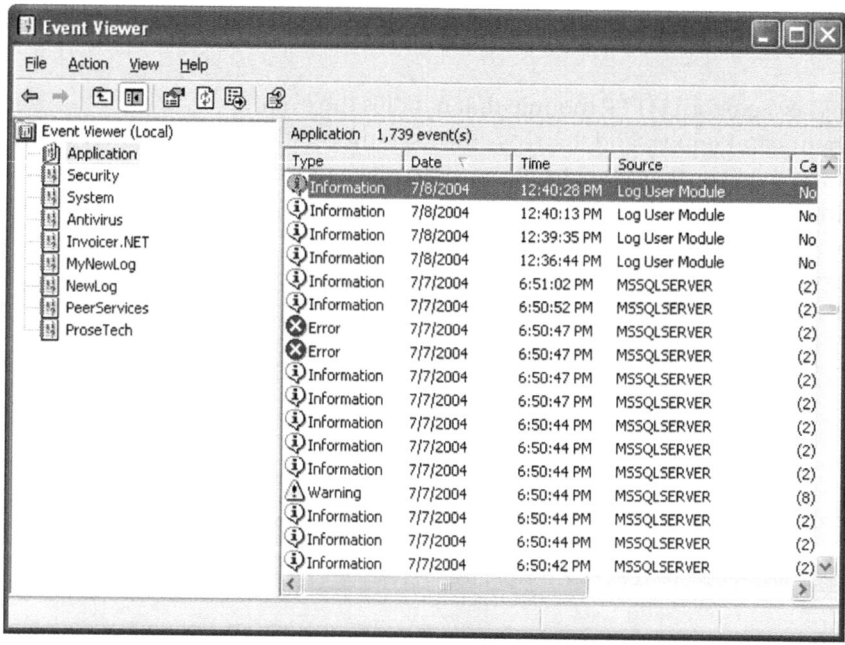

Figure 6-13. *Logging messages with an HTTP module*

In Part Four, you'll see a more detailed example that uses an HTTP module to perform custom authentication.

HANDLING EVENTS FROM OTHER MODULES

The previous example shows how you can handle application events in a custom HTTP module. However, there are some global events that aren't provided by the HttpApplication class, but are still quite important. These include events raised by other HTTP modules, like the events fired to start and end a session.

Fortunately, you can wire up to these events in the Init() event, you just need a slightly different approach. The HttpApplication class provides a collection of all the modules that are a part of the current HTTP pipeline through the Modules collection. You can retrieve a module by name, and then use delegate code to connect an event handler.

For example, if you want to connect an event handler named OnSessionStart() to the SessionStateModule.Start event, you could use code like this for the Init() method in your HTTP module:

```
public void Init(HttpApplication httpApp)
{
    SessionStateModule sessionMod = httpApp.Modules["Session"];
    sessionMod.Start += new EventHandler(OnSessionStart);
}
```

Extending the Configuration File Structure

As you've seen, ASP.NET uses a modular, highly extensible model. Not only can you extend the HTTP pipeline with HTTP handlers and HTTP modules, but you can also extend the structure of the web.config and machine.config configuration files with your own custom sections.

Earlier in this chapter, you learned how you can use the <appSettings> element to store custom information that your application uses. There are two significant limitations to the <appSettings> element. First, it doesn't provide a way to store structured information, such as lists or groups of related settings. Second, it doesn't give you the flexibility to deal with different types of data. Instead, the <appSettings> element is limited to single strings. Fortunately, you can extend the structure of the configuration file with arbitrary XML. You can then create a more specialized class that's able to read this information and convert it into the data type you want.

For example, imagine you want to store several database-specific settings in your web.config files. These settings indicate the connection string to use when connecting to the database, and the query to execute. Although you could enter this information using separate <appSettings> elements, you'd face a few problems. In the configuration file, there wouldn't be any indication that these two settings are related, which could lead to problems if one is updated and the other isn't. Furthermore, if you need to define a connection string and table for multiple different databases, you wouldn't have any way to group this information into separate sections. (If you add duplicate entries into the <appSettings> section, an error occurs.)

If you don't need to fit your information into the limiting structure of the <appSettings> section, it's fairly easy to come up with a solution. Here's one example that defines two connections using nested <Connection> elements. Each <Connection> element defines two pieces of related information using attributes.

```
<DatabaseConnections>
    <Connection connectionString="..." tableName="..." />
    <Connection connectionString="..." tableName="..." />
</DatabaseConnections>
```

Once you've created an XML extension for the web.config file, you need to create a class that can interpret it. ASP.NET uses dedicated classes called *section handlers* to process the information in a configuration file. If you want to add your own XML content, you need to create your own section handler.

Before you create the section handler, it makes sense to define a class that represents the structure information you want to retrieve. The following DbConnectionConfigSection class plays that role. It represents a single <Connection> tag, and provides the connection string and table name information.

```
public class DbConnectionConfigSection
{
    private string connectionString;
    public string ConnectionString
    {
        get {return connectionString;}
    }

    private string tableName;
    public string TableName
    {
        get {return tableName;}
    }

    public DbConnectionConfigSection(string connectionString, string tableName)
    {
        this.connectionString = connectionString;
        this.tableName = tableName;
    }
}
```

Typically, you'll place this class and the section handler class in a separate DLL assembly, just as you did when creating custom HTTP handlers and HTTP modules. You must then copy the compiled assembly into the Bin directory of the web application where you want to use it (or just add a reference in Visual Studio .NET).

Section handlers are ordinary classes that implement the interface IConfigurationSectionHandler from the System.Configuration namespace. The IConfigurationSectionHandler interface defines a single method named Create(), which examines a section of the configuration file and returns the data you need.

Here's the basic structure for a section handler that reads the <DatabaseConnections> section of the configuration file:

```
public class DbConnectionConfigSectionHandler : IConfigurationSectionHandler
{
    public virtual object Create(object parent, object configContext,
```

```
    XmlNode section)
  { ... }
}
```

The most important parameter of the Create() method is the XmlNode, which contains a set of objects representing the section of configuration data you need to process. In this case, that section is the <DatabaseConnections> element with all the nested <Connection> elements.

When the processing is complete, the Create() method can return any type of object. This gives you the ability to convert the configuration file XML into any data type or custom object. In this example, the Create() method needs to create an array of DbConnectionConfigSection objects, one for each <Connection> element it finds.

To perform its work, the Create() method loops through the child nodes of the current node, retrieving the data it needs. It makes use of another helper method that we've added to the DbConnectionConfigSectionHandler class, called GetStringValueOfAttribute(), which retrieves the text of a specific, named attribute. The Create() method calls GetStringValueOfAttribute() to extract the value of the connectionString attribute, and then the value of the tableName attribute. These two pieces of information are used to create a new DbConnectionConfigSection instance, which is stored in the array.

Here's the complete code:

```
public virtual object Create(object parent, object configContext,
  XmlNode section)
{
    // Check that there is at least one <Connection> element.
    if (section.ChildNodes.Count > 0)
    {
        // Create the array of the right size to hold the data
        // from all the <Connection> elements.
        DbConnectionConfigSection[] connections =
          new DbConnectionConfigSection[section.ChildNodes.Count];

        // Examine each <Connection> element.
        for (int i = 0; i < section.ChildNodes.Count; i++)
        {
            // Get the attributes from the current <Connection>.
            string connectionString = GetStringValueOfAttribute(
              section.ChildNodes[i], "connectionString");
            string tableName = GetStringValueOfAttribute(
              section.ChildNodes[i], "tableName");

            // Add the DbConnectionConfigSection object to the array.
            connections[i] = new DbConnectionConfigSection(
              connectionString, tableName);
        }
        // Return the array with all the data.
        return connections;
    }
    else
```

```
    {
        return null;
    }
}
```

The code for the GetStringValueOfAttribute() method is fairly straightforward, although it uses XML processing, which you haven't considered up until this point. The code simply attempts to filter out the named attribute, and returns an exception if it isn't present. (You'll learn much more about XML processing in Chapter 12, which deals with the XML classes like XmlNode.)

```
public string GetStringValueOfAttribute(XmlNode node, string attribute)
{
    XmlNode match = node.Attributes.RemoveNamedItem(attribute);
    if (match == null)
    {
        throw new ConfigurationException("Attribute required: " + attribute);
    }
    else
    {
        return match.Value;
    }
}
```

Once you've completed and compiled your section handler, you need to register it in a configuration file. When you register the section handler, you specifically indicate which section it will be used to process. ASP.NET keeps track of this information, and when you access that portion of the configuration file programmatically, it automatically uses your section handler to process it.

The following web.config file registers the DbConnectionConfigSectionHandler, and indicates that it will process the <DatabaseConnections> element in the <system.web> element. Note that the value of the connectionString attribute is split over several lines, which introduces extra line-break characters you don't want. These line breaks are used to fit the margins of the pages of this book. In the downloadable examples, you'll see that the connectionString value is entered on a single, continuous line.

```
<?xml version="1.0" encoding="utf-8" ?>
<configuration>
    <configSections>
        <sectionGroup name="system.web">
            <section name="DatabaseConnections"
    type="ConfigExtension.DbConnectionConfigSectionHandler, ConfigExtension" />
        </sectionGroup>
    </configSections>
```

```
    <system.web>
        <DatabaseConnections>
            <Connection
             connectionString="Data Source=localhost;Initial Catalog=Pubs;
Integrated Security=SSPI"
              tableName="Publishers" />
            <Connection
             connectionString="Data Source=localhost;Initial Catalog=Northwind;
Integrated Security=SSPI"
              tableName="Customers" />
        </DatabaseConnections>

        <!-- Other ASP.NET settings go here. -->
    </system.web>
</configuration>
```

Section handlers are always registered using a <configSections> element, which is contained in the root <configuration> element.

The final step is to create a simple test page that retrieves the information from the <DatabaseConnection> section. To accomplish this, you use the GetConfig() method of the HttpContext object. You specify the location of the section using a pathlike syntax, and ASP.NET decides automatically which section handler to use.

```
object config = Context.GetConfig("system.web/DatabaseConnections");
```

Of course, it's still up to you to convert the configuration data to the appropriate type of object. In this case, you need to cast the object to an array of DbConnectionConfigSection instances.

```
if (config != null)
{
    DbConnectionConfigSection[] connections =
      (DbConnectionConfigSection[])config;

    ...
```

Now you can loop through the array and display the information for each database connection in a web page, as shown here:

```
    ...
    foreach (DbConnectionConfigSection con in connections)
    {
        lblInfo.Text += "Retrieved a connection with...<br>" +
          "<b>Connection:</b> " + con.ConnectionString +
          "<br><b>Table:</b> " + con.TableName + "<br><br>";
    }
}
```

Figure 6-14 shows the displayed data.

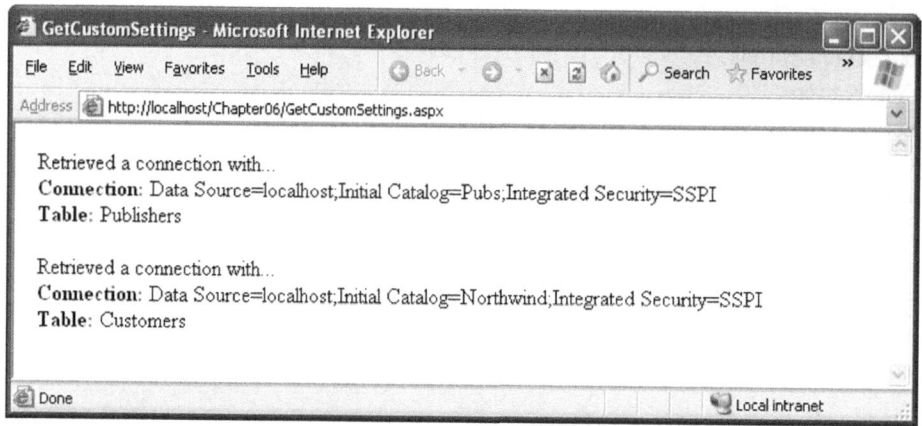

Figure 6-14. *Retrieving configuration data with a custom section handler*

Deploying ASP.NET Applications

To run your web application, a web server needs exactly two things:

- Your application and configuration files

- A virtual directory

A typical ASP.NET website consists of web pages (.aspx), code-behind files (.cs) or compiled assemblies (.dll), and a few miscellaneous details, such as image files and ordinary HTML files. To deploy these applications, you simply need to copy all the files to a new directory on the web server. How you transfer these files depends on the Internet hosting service you're using. Usually, you'll need to use an FTP program to upload the files to a designated area. However, if both your computer and the web server are on the same internal network, you might just use Windows Explorer or the command prompt to copy files.

Once the files are in place, you can follow the steps described in Chapter 2 to expose the new directory as a virtual directory. In the case of a commercial provider, this step will be completed as soon as you subscribe and won't need any work on your part.

If your web application uses a web.config file, you should make sure debug mode isn't enabled in the deployed version. To do so, find the debug attribute in the compilation tag if it is present, and set it to false, as follows:

```
<configuration>
  <system.web>
    <!-- Other settings omitted. -->
    <compilation defaultLanguage="cs" debug="false" />
  </system.web>
<configuration>
```

When debugging is enabled, the compiled ASP.NET web-page code will be larger and execute more slowly. Additionally, temporary compilation files won't be deleted automatically. For that reason, debugging should only be used while testing your web application.

Deploying a Visual Studio .NET Project

ASP.NET web applications can be deployed in much the same way regardless of the tool you use to create them. However, if you're using Visual Studio .NET to create web applications, there are a number of files that you *won't* need to transfer to the web server. Here's a list of files that you can safely ignore:

- **All .cs files.** Visual Studio .NET compiles all your code to a DLL assembly. There's no need for you to deploy the source, because it won't be used.

- **All .resx files.** By default, each web page will have a .resx file to store binary and localizable data. This data is also compiled into the web application assembly, so it doesn't need to be deployed separately.

- **The .csproj, .webinfo, and .sln files.** Visual Studio .NET uses these to track the files that are in the project, as well as various debugging and build settings. They have no effect on the application at runtime.

- **The .pdb files in the Bin directory.** These files help when debugging your web application.

You should also ignore the .vsdisco and global.asax files that Visual Studio .NET generates automatically, unless your web application uses them.

The only files that you *do* need to deploy are the .aspx web pages, the web.config file, the DLL files in the Bin directory, and any other resources you use (like image files, HTML files, and so on).

Note Before you deploy an application that was created in Visual Studio .NET, make sure that you compile the code in release mode. Otherwise, your web application performance will suffer. To compile a web application in release mode, select Release from the Solution Configurations drop-down list on the toolbar. Then start the application (or just right-click the project in the Solution Explorer and choose Rebuild).

Other Configuration Steps

The simple model of deployment that you've seen so far is often called *zero-touch deployment*, because you don't need to manually configure web server resources. (It's also sometimes called *XCopy deployment*, because transferring websites is as easy as copying directories.) However, some applications are more difficult to set up on a web server. Here are some common factors that will require additional configuration steps:

- **Databases.** If your web application uses a database, you'll need to transfer the database to the web server. You can do this by generating a SQL script that will automatically create the database and load it with data. Alternatively, you could back up the database and then restore it on the web server. In either case, an administrator needs to use a database management tool.

- **Alternate machine.config settings.** You can control the settings for your web application in the web.config file that you deploy. However, problems can occur if your web application relies on settings in the machine.config that aren't present on the web server.

- **Windows account permissions.** Usually, a web server will run web-page code under a restricted account like the local ASPNET account. This account might not be allowed to perform the tasks you rely on, like writing to files or the Windows event log. In this case, an administrator needs to specifically grant the permissions you need to the ASPNET account.

- **IIS security settings.** If your website uses SSL encryption or Windows authentication, the virtual directory settings may need to be tweaked in IIS Manager. This typically requires the help of an administrator.

- **IIS file mappings.** If you need to change the file types that are registered to the IIS (perhaps to enable a custom HTTP handler) you also need to use IIS Manager. On the other hand, you don't need any extra steps to use a custom HTTP module.

To solve these problems in the most effective way, it helps to work with an experienced Windows administrator. That's especially true if the web server is using IIS 6 (the version of IIS provided with Windows 2003). IIS 6 provides a number of configuration options, and allows every web application on a server to run under a different Windows account. This ensures that your website can be granted the exact permission set it requires without affecting any other web application.

Summary

In this chapter, you took a closer look at what constitutes an ASP.NET application. After learning more about the life cycle of an application, you learned how to code global application event handlers with the global.asax file, and how to set application configuration with the web.config file. Finally, you learned how to use separately compiled components in your web pages, and how to extend the HTTP pipeline with your own handlers and modules.

CHAPTER 7

■ ■ ■

State Management

No web application framework, no matter how advanced, can change the fact that HTTP is a stateless protocol. After every web request, the client disconnects from the server, and the ASP.NET engine discards the page objects. This architecture ensures that web applications can scale up to serve thousands of simultaneous requests without running out of server memory. The drawback is that your code needs to use other techniques to store information in between web requests and retrieve it when needed.

In this chapter, you'll see how to use all the different types of ASP.NET state management.

ASP.NET State Management

ASP.NET includes a variety of different options for state management. It features the same Session and Application state collections as traditional ASP (with a few enhancements), and an entirely new view state model. ASP.NET even includes a caching system that allows you to retain information without sacrificing server scalability. Each state management choice has a different lifetime, scope, performance overhead, and level of support.

Table 7-1 and Table 7-2 show an at-a-glance comparison of your state management options.

Table 7-1. *State Management Options Compared (Part 1)*

	View State	Query String	Custom Cookies
Allowed Data Types	All serializable .NET data types.	A limited amount of string data.	String data.
Storage Location	A hidden field in the current web page.	The browser's URL string.	The client's computer (in memory or a small text file, depending on its lifetime settings).
Lifetime	Retained permanently for postbacks to a single page.	Lost when the user enters a new URL or closes the browser. However, can be stored in a bookmark.	Set by the programmer. It can be used in multiple pages and can persist between visits.
Scope	Limited to the current page.	Limited to the target page.	The whole ASP.NET application.

Continued

Table 7-1. *Continued*

	View State	**Query String**	**Custom Cookies**
Security	By default it's insecure, although you can use page directives to enforce encryption and hashing.	Clearly visible and easy for the user to modify.	Insecure, and can be modified by the user.
Performance Implications	Storing a large amount of information will slow transmission, but will not affect server performance.	None, because the amount of data is trivial.	None, because the amount of data is trivial.
Typical Use	Page-specific settings.	Sending a Product ID from a catalog page to a details page.	Personalization preferences for a website.

Table 7-2. *State Management Options Compared (Part 2)*

	Session State	**Application State**	**Caching**
Allowed Data Types	All serializable .NET data types. Nonserializable types are supported if you are using the default in-process state service.	All .NET data types.	All .NET data types.
Storage Location	Server memory.	Server memory.	Server memory.
Lifetime	Times out after a predefined period (usually 20 minutes, but can be altered globally or programmatically).	The lifetime of the application (typically, until the server is rebooted).	Depends on the expiration policy you set, but may possibly be released early if server memory becomes scarce.
Scope	The whole ASP.NET application.	The whole ASP.NET application. Unlike most other types of methods, application data is global to all users.	The same as application state (global to all users and all pages).
Security	Very secure, because data is never transmitted to the client.	Very secure, because data is never transmitted to the client.	Very secure, because data is never transmitted to the client.
Performance Implications	Storing a large amount of information can slow down the server severely, especially if there are a large number of users at once, because each user will have a separate copy of session data.	Storing a large amount of information can slow down the server, because this data will never time out and be removed.	Storing a large amount of information may force out other, more useful cached information. However, ASP.NET has the ability to remove items early to ensure optimum performance.
Typical Use	Storing items in a shopping basket.	Storing any type of global data.	Storing data retrieved from a database.

All of these state management systems (with the exception of the query string, which is really a way of transferring information, not maintaining it) work in the same way. In addition, you can use back-end server-side resources to store information. The most common example is one or more tables in a database. The drawback with using server-side resources is that they tend to slow down performance and can hurt scalability. For example, opening a connection to a database or reading information from a file takes time. In many cases, you can salvage these approaches by using caching to supplement your state management system.

View State

View state should be your first choice for storing information within the bounds of a single page. View state is used natively by the ASP.NET web controls. It allows them to retain their properties in between postbacks. You can add your own data to the view state collection using a built-in page property called ViewState. The type of information you can store includes simple data types and your own custom objects.

Like most types of state management in ASP.NET, view state relies on a *dictionary collection*, where each item is indexed with a unique string name. For example, consider this code:

```
ViewState["Counter"] = 1;
```

This places the value 1 (or rather, an integer that contains the value 1) into the ViewState collection, and gives it the descriptive name Counter. If there is currently no item with the name Counter, a new item will be added automatically. If there is already an item indexed under the name Counter, it will be replaced.

When retrieving a value, you use the key name. You also need to cast the retrieved value to the appropriate data type. This extra step is required because the ViewState collection stores all items as generic objects, which allows it to handle many different data types.

Here's the code that retrieves the counter from view state and converts it to an integer:

```
int counter;
if (ViewState["Counter"] != null)
{
    counter = (int)ViewState["Counter"];
}
```

If you attempt to look up a value that isn't present in the collection, you'll receive a NullReferenceException. To defend against this possibility, you should check for a null value before you attempt to retrieve and cast data that may not be present.

Note ASP.NET provides many collections that use the exact same dictionary syntax. This includes the collections you'll use for session and application state as well as those used for caching and cookies. You'll see several of these collections in this chapter.

A View State Example

The following code demonstrates a page that uses view state. It allows the user to save a set of values (all the text that's displayed in all the text boxes of a table), and restore it later. This example uses recursive logic to dig through all child controls, and it uses the control ID for the view state key, because this is guaranteed to be unique in the page.

Here's the complete code:

```csharp
public class ViewStateTest : System.Web.UI.Page
{
    // (Designer code omitted.)

    private void cmdSave_Click(object sender, System.EventArgs e)
    {
        // Save the current text.
        SaveAllText(Table1.Controls, true);
    }

    private void SaveAllText(ControlCollection controls, bool saveNested)
    {
        foreach (Control control in controls)
        {
            if (control is TextBox)
            {
                // Store the text using the unique control ID.
                ViewState[control.ID] = ((TextBox)control).Text;
            }

            if ((control.Controls != null) && saveNested)
            {
                SaveAllText(control.Controls, true);
            }
        }
    }

    private void cmdRestore_Click(object sender, System.EventArgs e)
    {
        // Retrieve the last saved text.
        RestoreAllText(Table1.Controls, true);
    }

    private void RestoreAllText(ControlCollection controls, bool saveNested)
    {
        foreach (Control control in controls)
        {
            if (control is TextBox)
            {
                if (ViewState[control.ID] != null)
```

```
            ((TextBox)control).Text = (string)ViewState[control.ID];
        }
        if ((control.Controls != null) && saveNested)
        {
            RestoreAllText(control.Controls, true);
        }
    }
}
}
```

Figure 7-1 shows the page in action.

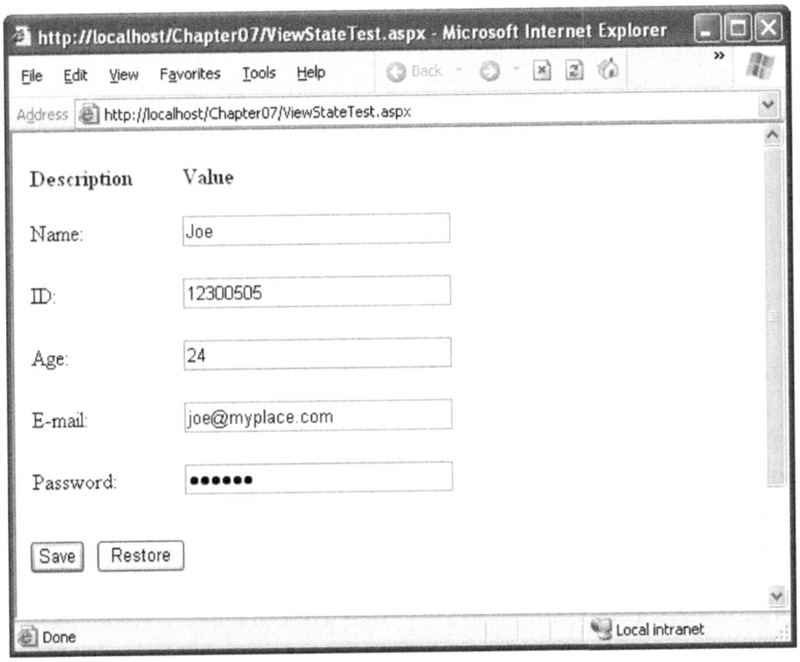

Figure 7-1. *Saving and restoring text using view state*

Storing Objects in View State

You can store your own objects in view state just as easily as you store numeric and string types. However, in order to store an item in view state, ASP.NET must be able to convert it into a stream of bytes so that it can be added to the hidden input field in the page. This process is called *serialization*. If your objects aren't serializable (and by default they're not), you'll receive an error message when you attempt to place them in view state.

To make your objects serializable, you need to add the Serializable attribute before your class declaration. For example, here's an exceedingly simple Customer class:

```
[Serializable]
public class Customer
{
    public string FirstName;
```

```
    public string LastName;

    public Customer(string firstName, string lastName)
    {
        FirstName = firstName;
        LastName = lastName;
    }
}
```

Because the Customer class is marked as serializable, it can be stored in view state:

```
// Store a customer in view state.
Customer cust = new Customer("Marsala", "Simons");
ViewState["CurrentCustomer"] = cust;
```

Remember, when using custom objects, you'll need to cast your data when you retrieve it from view state.

```
// Retrieve a customer from view state.
Customer cust;
cust = (Customer)ViewState["CurrentCustomer"];
```

Once you understand this principle, you'll also be able to determine what .NET objects can be placed in view state. You simply need to find the class information in the MSDN Help. Find the class you're interested in and examine the documentation. If the class declaration is preceded with the Serializable attribute, the object can be placed in view state. If the Serializable attribute isn't present, the object isn't serializable, and you won't be able to store it in view state. However, you will still be able to use other types of state management, like session state, which is described later in this chapter.

The following example rewrites the page shown earlier to use the Hashtable class. The Hashtable class is a serializable dictionary collection that's provided in the System.Collections namespace. Because it's serializable, it can be stored in view state without a hitch. To demonstrate this technique, the page stores all the control information for the page in the hashtable, and then adds the hashtable to the view state for the page. When the user clicks the Display button, the hashtable is retrieved, and all the information it contains is displayed in a label.

```
public class ViewStateObjects : System.Web.UI.Page
{
    // (Designer code omitted.)

    // This will be created at the beginning of each request.
    Hashtable textToSave = new Hashtable();

    private void cmdSave_Click(object sender, System.EventArgs e)
    {
```

```
        // Put the text in the Hashtable.
        SaveAllText(Table1.Controls, true);

        // Store the entire collection in view state.
        ViewState["ControlText"] = textToSave;
    }

    private void SaveAllText(ControlCollection controls, bool saveNested)
    {
        foreach (Control control in controls)
        {
            if (control is TextBox)
            {
                // Add the text to a collection.
                textToSave.Add(control.ID, ((TextBox)control).Text);
            }
            if ((control.Controls != null) && saveNested)
            {
                SaveAllText(control.Controls, true);
            }
        }
    }

    private void cmdDisplay_Click(object sender, System.EventArgs e)
    {
        if (ViewState["ControlText"] != null)
        {
            // Retrieve the hashtable.
            Hashtable savedText = (Hashtable)ViewState["ControlText"];

            // Display all the text by looping through the hashtable.
            lblResults.Text = "";
            foreach (DictionaryEntry item in savedText)
            {
                lblResults.Text += (string)item.Key + " = " +
                  (string)item.Value + "<br>";
            }
        }
    }
}
```

Figure 7-2 shows the result of a simple test, after entering some data, saving it, and retrieving it.

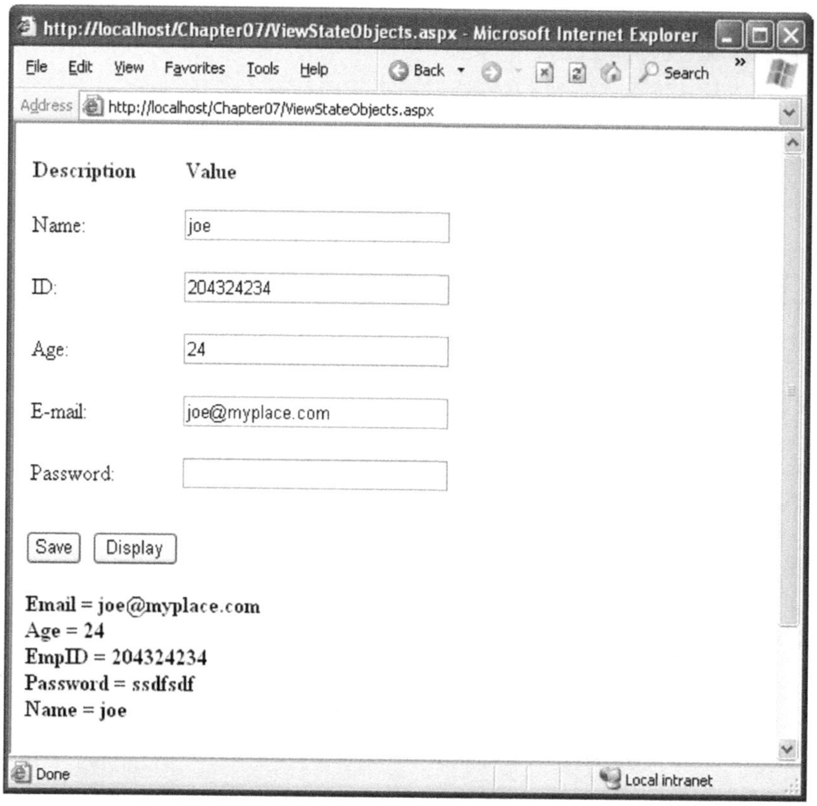

Figure 7-2. *Retrieving an object from view state*

Retaining Member Variables

Unlike control properties, member variables that you add to your web-page classes are never saved in view state. Interestingly, you can work around this limitation using view state.

There are two basic approaches. The first is to create a property procedure that wraps view state access. For example, in the previous web page you could provide the control text hashtable as a property like this:

```
private Hashtable ControlText
{
    get
    {
        if (ViewState["ControlText"] != null)
        { return (Hashtable)ViewState["ControlText"]; }
        else
        { return new Hashtable(); }
    }
    set {ViewState["ControlText"] = value;}
}
```

Now the rest of your page code can freely use the ControlText property, without worrying about how it's being retrieved.

The other approach is to save all your member variables to view state when the Page.PreRender event occurs, and retrieve them when the Page.Load event occurs. That way, all your other event handlers can use the member variables normally.

Keep in mind when you use either of these techniques that you must be careful not to store needless amounts of information. If you store unnecessary information in view state, it will enlarge the size of the final page output, and can thus slow down page transmission times.

Assessing View State

View state is ideal because it doesn't take up any memory on the server, and doesn't impose any arbitrary usage limits (like a timeout). So what might force you to abandon view state for another type of state management? Here are three possible reasons:

- You need to store mission-critical data that the user cannot be allowed to tamper with. (An ingenious user could modify the view state information in a postback request.) In this case, consider session state. Or consider using the countermeasures described in the next section. They aren't bulletproof, but they will *greatly* increase the effort an attacker would need in order to read or modify view state data.

- You need to store information that will be used by multiple pages. In this case, consider session state, cookies, or the query string.

- You need to store an extremely large amount of information, and you don't want to slow down page transmission times. In this case, consider using a database, or possibly session state.

The amount of space used by view state depends on the number of controls, their complexity, and the amount of dynamic information. If you want to profile the view state usage of a page, just turn on tracing by adding the Trace attribute to the page directive, as shown here:

```
<%@ Page Language="c#" Trace="true" ... %>
```

Look for the Control Tree section. Although it doesn't provide the total view state used by the page, it does indicate the view state used by each individual control in the Viewstate Size Bytes column (see Figure 7-3). Don't worry about the Render Size Bytes column, which simply reflects the size of the rendered HTML for the control.

To improve the transmission times of your page, it's a good idea to eliminate view state when it's not needed. Although you can disable view state at the application and page level, it makes most sense to disable it on a per-control basis. There are three instances in which you won't need view state for a control:

- The control never changes. For example, a button with static text doesn't need view state.

- The control is repopulated in every postback. For example, if you have a label that shows the current time, and you set the current time in the Page.Load event handler, it doesn't need view state.

- The control is an input control, and it only changes due to user actions. After each postback, ASP.NET will populate your input controls using the submitted form values. This means that the text in a text box or the selection in a list box won't be lost, even if you don't use view state.

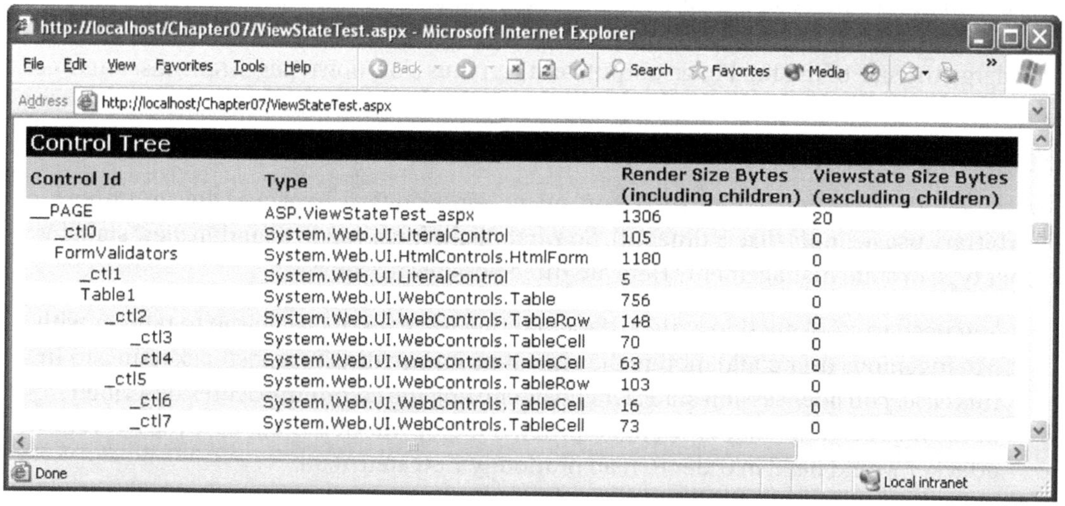

Figure 7-3. *Determining the view state used in a page*

■**Tip** Remember that view state applies to *all* the values that change, not just the text displayed in the control. For example, if you dynamically change the colors used in a label, you'll need to use view state even if you don't dynamically set the text. Technically, it's the control's responsibility to use view state, so it is possible to create a server control that doesn't retain certain values even if view state is enabled. This might be used to optimize performance in certain scenarios.

To turn off view state for a single control, set the EnableViewState property of the control to false. To turn off view state for an entire page and all its controls, set the EnableViewState property of the page to false, or use the EnableViewState attribute in the page directive, as shown here:

```
<%@ Page Language="c#" EnableViewState="false" ... %>
```

Even when you disable view state for the entire page, you'll still see the hidden view state tag with a small amount of information. That's because ASP.NET always stores the control hierarchy for the page at a minimum, even if view state is disabled. There's no way to remove this last little fragment of data.

Making View Sate Secure

As described in earlier chapters, view state information is stored in a single Base64 encoded string that looks like this:

```
<input type="hidden" name="__VIEWSTATE" value="dDw3NDg2NTI5MDg70z4="/>
```

Because this value isn't formatted as clear text, many ASP.NET programmers assume that their view state data is encrypted. It isn't. A clever hacker could reverse-engineer this string and examine your view state data in a matter of seconds, as demonstrated in Chapter 4.

If you want to make view state more secure, you have two choices. First, you can make sure that the view state information is tamper-proof by instructing ASP.NET to use a *hash code*. You do this by adding the EnableViewStateMAC attribute to the Page directive in your .aspx file, as shown here:

```
<%@ Page EnableViewStateMAC="true" %>
```

A hash code is a cryptographically strong checksum. When you set the EnableViewStateMAC, ASP.NET calculates the checksum and adds it to the view state data. When the page is posted back, ASP.NET recalculates the checksum and ensures that it matches. If a malicious user changes the view state data, ASP.NET will be able to detect the change, and it will reject the postback.

Even when you use hash codes, the view state data will still be readable. To prevent users from getting any view state information, you can enable view state *encryption*. In this case, you need to find the <machineKey> tag in the machine.config file. (Remember that the machine.config file is found in a directory like c:\[WinDir]\Microsoft.NET\[Version]\Config.) Set the validation attribute to 3DES, which stands for Triple DES encryption, as follows:

```
<configuration>
   <system.web>
      <!- Other settings omitted. ->
      <machineKey validation="3DES" />
   </system.web>
</configuration>
```

Make sure you also set the EnableViewStateMAC attribute for the page, as described earlier, because these settings work in conjunction. Now the view state information for the page will be completely encrypted.

When hashing or encrypting data, ASP.NET uses the computer-specific key defined in the machine.config file. Because no one else has this key, no user will be able to generate a fake hash code or decrypt encrypted view state information.

Tip Don't encrypt view state data if you don't need to. The encryption will impose a performance penalty, because the web server needs to perform the encryption and decryption with each postback.

Transferring Information with the Query String

One of the most significant limitations with view state is that it's tightly bound to a specific page. If the user navigates to another page, this information is lost. There are several solutions to this problem, and the best approach depends on your requirements. One common approach is to pass information using a query string in the URL. This approach is commonly found in search engines. For example, if you perform a search on the Google website, you'll be redirected to a new URL that incorporates your search parameters. Here's an example:

```
http://www.google.ca/search?q=organic+gardening
```

The query string is the portion of the URL after the question mark. In this case, it defines a single variable named ask, which contains the string "organic+gardening".

The advantage of the query string is that it's very lightweight and doesn't exert any kind of burden on the server. There are some limitations, however:

- Information is limited to simple strings, which must contain URL-legal characters.

- Information is clearly visible to the user and by anyone else who cares to eavesdrop on the Internet.

- The enterprising user might decide to modify the query string and supply new values, which your program won't expect and can't protect against.

- Many browsers impose a limit on the length of a URL (usually from 1 to 2 KB). For that reason, you can't place a large amount of information in the query string and still be assured of compatibility with most browsers.

Adding information to the query string is still a useful technique. It's particularly well suited in database applications where you present the user with a list of items that correspond to records in a database, like products. The user can then select an item and be forwarded to another page with detailed information about the selected item. One easy way to implement this design is to have the first page send the item ID to the second page. The second page then looks that item up in the database, and displays the detailed information. You'll notice this technique in e-commerce sites like Amazon.com.

Using the Query String

To store information in the query string, you need to place it there yourself. Unfortunately, there is no collection-based way to do this. Typically, this means using a special HyperLink control, or a Response.Redirect() statement like the one shown here.

```
// Go to newpage.aspx. Submit a single query string argument
// named recordID and set to 10.
int recordID = 10;
Response.Redirect("newpage.aspx?recordID=" + recordID.ToString());
```

Multiple parameters can be sent as long as they're separated with an ampersand (&).

```
// Go to newpage.aspx. Submit two query string arguments:
// recordID (10) and mode (full).
Response.Redirect("newpage.aspx?recordID=10&mode=full");
```

The receiving page has an easier time working with the query string. It can receive the values from the QueryString dictionary collection exposed by the built-in Request object, as shown here:

```
string ID = Request.QueryString["recordID"];
```

Note that information is always retrieved as a string, which can then be converted to another simple data type. Values in the QueryString collection are indexed by the variable name.

Note Unfortunately, ASP.NET does not expose any mechanism to automatically verify or encrypt query string data. This facility could work in almost exactly the same way as the view state protection. Without these features, query string data is easily subject to tampering. In Chapter 18, you'll take a closer look at the .NET cryptography classes, and learn how you can use them to build a truly secure query string.

URL Encoding

One potential problem with the query string is using characters that aren't allowed in a URL. The list of characters that are allowed in a URL is much shorter than the list of allowed characters in an HTML document. All characters must be alphanumeric, or one of a small set of special characters, including $-_.+!*'(),. Some browsers tolerate certain additional special characters (Internet Explorer is notoriously lax), but many do not.

If you're concerned that the data you want to store in the query string may not consist of URL-legal characters, you should use URL encoding. With URL encoding, special characters are replaced by escaped character sequences starting with the percent sign (%), followed by a two-digit hexadecimal representation. For example, the space becomes %20.

You can use the methods of the HttpServerUtility class to encode your data automatically. For example, here's how you would encode a string of arbitrary data for use in the query string. This replaces all the nonlegal characters with escaped character sequences:

```
string productName = "Flying Carpet";
Response.Redirect("newpage.aspx?productName=" + Server.UrlEncode(productName));
```

And here's how you could decode the same information:

```
string ID = Server.UrlDecode(Request.QueryString["recordID"]);
```

Custom Cookies

Custom cookies provide another way that you can store information for later use. Cookies are small files that are created on the client's hard drive (or, if they're temporary, in the web browser's memory). One advantage of cookies is that they work transparently without the user being aware that information needs to be stored. They also can be easily used by any page in your application, and even retained in between visits, which allows for truly long-term storage. They suffer from some of the same drawbacks that affect query strings. Namely, they're limited to simple string information, and they're easily accessible and readable if the user finds and opens the corresponding file. These factors make them a poor choice for complex or private information or large amounts of data.

Some users disable cookies on their browsers, which will cause problems for web applications that require them. For the most part, cookies are widely adopted because so many sites use them. However, they can limit your potential audience, and they aren't suited for the embedded browsers used with mobile devices.

Before you can use cookies, you should import the System.Net namespace so you can easily work with the appropriate types, as shown here:

```
using System.Net;
```

Cookies are fairly easy to use. Both the Request and Response objects (which are provided through Page properties) provide a Cookies collection. The important trick to remember is that you retrieve cookies from the Request object, and you set cookies using the Response object.

To set a cookie, just create a new System.Net.HttpCookie object. You can then fill it with string information (using the familiar dictionary pattern) and attach it to the current web response, as follows:

```
// Create the cookie object.
HttpCookie cookie = new HttpCookie("Preferences");

// Set a value in it.
cookie["LanguagePref"] = "English";

// Add it to the current web response.
Response.Cookies.Add(cookie);
```

A cookie added in this way will persist until the user closes the browser and will be sent with every request. To create a longer-lived cookie, you can set an expiration date, as shown here:

```
// This cookie lives for one year.
cookie.Expires = DateTime.Now.AddYears(1);
```

Cookies are retrieved by cookie name using the Request.Cookies collection, as shown here:

```
HttpCookie cookie = Request.Cookies["Preferences"];

// Check to see if a cookie was found with this name.
// This is a good precaution to take,
// because the user could disable cookies,
// in which case the cookie will not exist.
string language;
if (cookie != null)
{
    language = cookie["LanguagePref"];
}
```

The only way to remove a cookie is by replacing it with a cookie that has an expiration date that has already passed. The following code demonstrates this technique:

```
HttpCookie cookie = new HttpCookie("LanguagePref");
cookie.Expires = DateTime.Now.AddDays(-1);
Response.Cookies.Add(cookie);
```

> **Note** You'll find that some other ASP.NET features use cookies. Two examples are session state (which allows you to temporarily store user-specific information in server memory) and forms security (which allows you to restrict portions of a website, and force users to access it through a login page).

Session State

Session state is the heavyweight of state management. It allows information to be stored in one page and accessed in another, and it supports any type of object, including your own custom data types. Best of all, session state uses exactly the same collection syntax as view state. The only difference is the name of the built-in page property, which is Session.

Every client that accesses the application has a different session and a distinct collection of information. Session state is ideal for storing information like the items in the current user's shopping basket when the user browses from one page to another. But session state doesn't come for free. Though it solves many of the problems associated with other forms of state management, it forces the web server to store additional information in memory. This extra memory requirement, even if it is small, can quickly grow to performance-destroying levels as hundreds or thousands of clients access the site.

Session Architecture

Session management is not a part of the HTTP standard. As a result, ASP.NET needs to go to extra work to track session information and bind it to the appropriate response.

ASP.NET tracks each session using a unique 120-bit identifier. ASP.NET uses a proprietary algorithm to generate this value, thereby guaranteeing (statistically speaking) that the number is unique, and that it's random enough so that a malicious user can't reverse-engineer or guess what session ID a given client will be using. This ID is the only piece of information that is transmitted between the web server and the client. When the client presents the session ID, ASP.NET looks up the corresponding session, retrieves the serialized data from the state server, converts it to live objects, and places these objects into a special collection so they can be accessed in code. This process takes place automatically.

> **Note** Every time you make a new request, ASP.NET generates a new session ID until you actually use session state to store some information. This behavior achieves a slight performance enhancement—in short, why bother to save the session ID if it's not being used?

At this point you're probably wondering where ASP.NET stores session information, and how it serializes and deserializes it. In classic ASP, the session state is implemented as a free-threaded COM object that's contained in the asp.dll library. In ASP.NET, the programming interface is nearly identical, but the underlying implementation is quite a bit different.

As you saw in Chapter 6, when ASP.NET handles an HTTP request it flows through a pipeline of different modules, which can react to application events. One of the modules in this chain is the SessionStateModule (in the System.Web.SessionState namespace). The SessionStateModule generates the session ID, retrieves the session data from external state providers, and binds the data to the call context of the request. It also saves the session state information when the page is finished processing. However, it's important to realize that the SessionStateModule doesn't actually *store* the session data. Instead, the session state is persisted in external components, which are named *state providers*. Figure 7-4 shows this interaction.

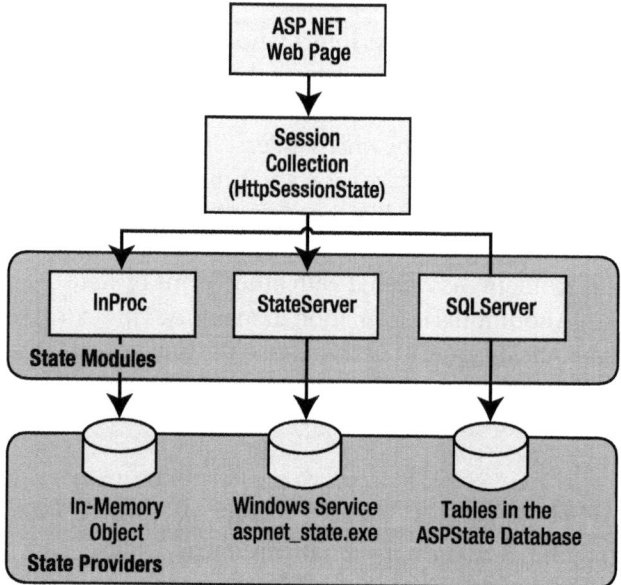

Figure 7-4. *ASP.NET session state architecture*

Session state is another example of ASP.NET's pluggable architecture. A state provider is any class that implements the IStateClientManager interface, which means that you can customize how session state works simply by building (or purchasing) a new .NET component. ASP.NET includes three different prebuilt state providers, which allow you to store information in process, in a separate service, or in a SQL Server database.

The final ingredient in the puzzle is how the cookie is tracked from one request to the next. In order for session state to work, the client needs to present the appropriate session ID with each request. There are two ways this can be accomplished:

- **Using cookies.** In this case, the session ID is transmitted in a special cookie (named "ASP.NET_SessionId"), which ASP.NET creates automatically when the session collection is used. This is the default, and it's also the same approach that was used in earlier versions of ASP.

- **Using modified URLs.** In this case, the session ID is transmitted in a specially modified (or "munged") URL. This is a new feature in ASP.NET that allows you to create applications that use session state with clients that don't support cookies.

You'll learn more about how to configure cookieless sessions and different session state providers later in this chapter.

Using Session State

You can interact with session state using the System.Web.SessionState.HttpSessionState class, which is provided in an ASP.NET web page as the built-in Session object. The syntax for adding items to the collection and retrieving them is basically the same as for adding items to the view state of a page.

For example, you might store a DataSet in session memory like this:

```
Session["ds"] = ds;
```

You can then retrieve it with an appropriate conversion operation:

```
ds = (DataSet)Session["ds"];
```

Session state is global to your entire application for the current user. Session state can be lost in several ways:

- If the user closes and restarts the browser.

- If the user accesses the same page through a different browser window, although the session will still exist if a web page is accessed through the original browser window. Browsers differ on how they handle this situation.

- If the session times out due to inactivity. By default, a session times out after 20 idle minutes.

- If the programmer ends the session by calling Session.Abandon().

In the first two cases, the session actually remains in memory, because the web server has no idea that the client has closed the browser or changed windows. The session will linger in memory, remaining inaccessible, until it eventually expires.

In addition, session state will be lost when the application domain is re-created. This process happens transparently when you update your web application or change a configuration setting. The application domain may also be recycled periodically to ensure application health, as described in Chapter 2. If this behavior is causing a problem, you can store session state information out of process, as described in the next section. With out-of-process state storage, the session information is retained even when the application domain is shut down.

Table 7-3 describes the methods and properties of the HttpSessionState class.

Table 7-3. *HttpSessionState Members*

Member	Description
Count	The number of items in the current session collection.
IsCookieless	Identifies whether this session is tracked with a cookie, or using modified URLs.
IsNewSession	Identifies whether this session was just created for the current request. If there is currently no information in session state, ASP.NET won't bother to track the session or create a session cookie. Instead, the session will be re-created with every request.

Continued

Table 7-3. *Continued*

Member	Description
Mode	Provides an enumerated value that explains how ASP.NET stores session state information. This storage mode is determined based on the web.config configuration settings discussed later in this chapter.
SessionID	Provides a string with the unique session identifier for the current client.
StaticObjects	Provides a collection of read-only session items that were declared by <object runat=server> tags in the global.asax. Generally, this technique isn't used, and is a holdover from ASP programming that is included for backward compatibility.
Timeout	The current number of minutes that must elapse before the current session will be abandoned, provided that no more requests are received from the client. This value can be changed programmatically, giving you the chance to make the session collection longer term when required for more important operations.
Abandon()	Cancels the current session immediately and releases all the memory it occupied. This is a useful technique in a logoff page to ensure that server memory is reclaimed as quickly as possible.
Clear()	Removes all the session items, but doesn't change the current session identifier.

Configuring Session State

You can configure session state through the <sessionState> element in the web.config file for your application, as shown here:

```xml
<?xml version="1.0" encoding="utf-8" ?>
<configuration>
    <system.web>
        <!-- Other settings omitted. -->

        <sessionState
            mode="InProc"
            stateConnectionString="tcpip=127.0.0.1:42424"
            sqlConnectionString="data source=127.0.0.1;user id=sa"
            cookieless="false"
            timeout="20"
        />
    </system.web>
</configuration>
```

The session attributes are described in the following sections.

Mode

The mode session state settings allow you to configure what session state provider is used to store session state information between requests. The following sections explain your different options.

Off

This setting disables session state management for every page in the application. This can provide a slight performance improvement for websites that are not using session state.

InProc

InProc is similar to how session state was stored in previous versions of ASP. It instructs ASP.NET to store information in the current application domain. This provides the best performance, but the least durability. If you restart your server, the state information will be lost.

Generally, InProc is the best option for most websites. The one most notable exception is in a web farm scenario. In order to allow session state to be shared between servers, you must use the out-of-process or SQL Server state service. But before you use either of these mechanisms, keep in mind that more considerations will apply:

- When using the StateServer of SqlServer modes, the objects you store in session state must be serializable. Otherwise, ASP.NET will not be able to transmit the object to the state service or store it in the database.

- If you're hosting ASP.NET on a web farm you'll also need to take some extra configuration steps to make sure all the web servers are in sync. Otherwise, one might encode information in session state differently than another, which will cause a problem if the user is routed from one server to another during a session. The solution is to modify the <machineKey> section of the machine.config file so it's consistent across all servers. For more information, refer to Chapter 6.

- If you aren't using the in-process state provider, the SessionStateModule.End event won't be fired, and any event handlers for this event in the global.asax file or an HTTP module will be ignored.

StateServer

With this setting, ASP.NET will use a separate Windows service for state management. Even if you run this service on the same web server, it will be loaded outside the main ASP.NET process, which gives it a basic level of protection if the ASP.NET process needs to be restarted. The cost is the increased time delay imposed when state information is transferred between two processes. If you frequently access and change state information, this can make for a fairly unwelcome slowdown.

When using the StateServer setting, you need to specify a value for the stateConnectionString setting. This string identifies the TCP/IP address of the computer that is running the StateServer service and its port number (which is defined by ASP.NET and doesn't usually need to be changed). This allows you to host the StateServer on another computer. If you don't change this setting, the local server will be used (set as address 127.0.0.1).

Of course, before your application can use the service, you need to start it. The easiest way to do this is to use the Microsoft Management Console. Select Start ➤ Programs ➤ Administrative Tools ➤ Computer Management (you can also access the Administrative Tools group through the Control Panel). Then select the Services and Applications ➤ Services node. Find the service called ASP.NET State in the list, as shown in Figure 7-5.

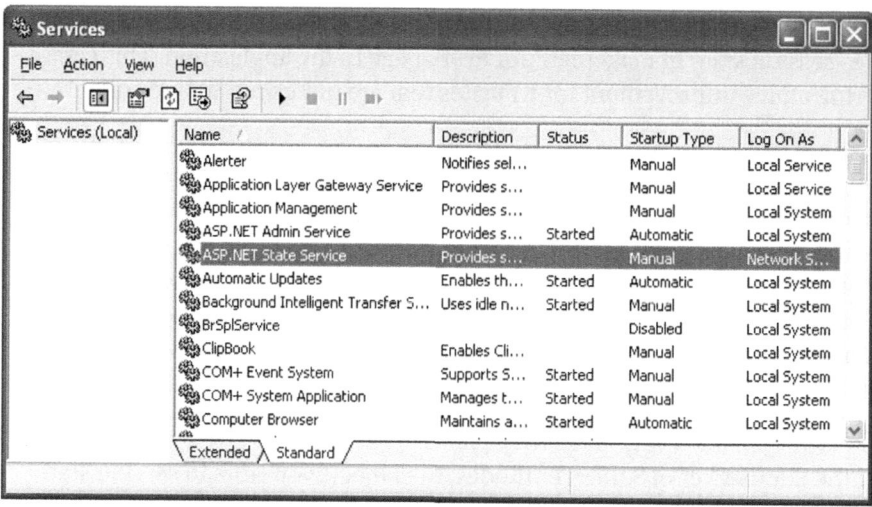

Figure 7-5. *The ASP.NET state service*

Once you find the service in the list, you can manually start and stop it by right-clicking it. Generally, you'll want to configure Windows to automatically start the service. Right-click it, select Properties, and modify the Startup Type setting to Automatic, as show in Figure 7-6.

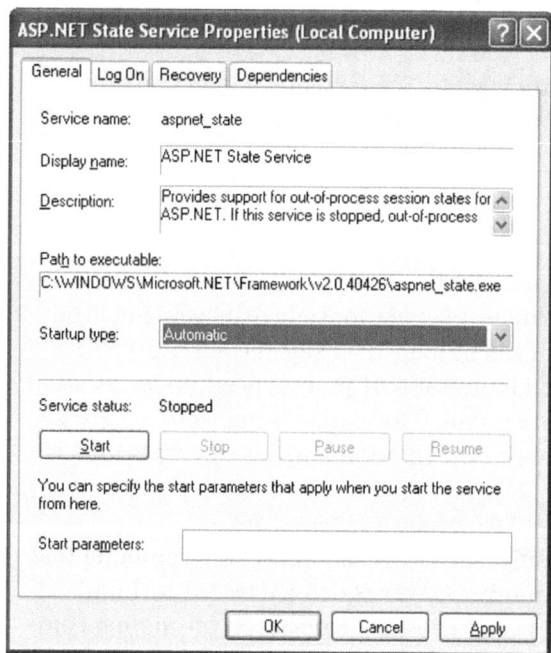

Figure 7-6. *Service properties*

SqlServer

This setting instructs ASP.NET to use an SQL Server database to store session information, as identified by the sqlConnectionString attribute. This is the most resilient state store, but also the slowest by far. To use this method of state management, you'll need to have a server with SQL Server installed.

When setting the sqlConnectionString, you follow the same sort of pattern you use with ADO.NET data access (which is described in Part Two). Generally, you'll need to specify a data source (the server address) and a user ID and password, unless you're using SQL integrated security.

In addition, you need to install the special stored procedures and temporary session databases. These stored procedures take care of storing and retrieving the session information. ASP.NET includes a Transact-SQL script for this purpose called InstallSqlState.sql. It's found in the c:\[WinDir]\Microsoft.NET\Framework\[Version] directory. You can run this script using an SQL Server utility like OSQL.exe or Query Analyzer. It only needs to be performed once. If you decide to change your state service, you can use UninstallSqlState.sql to remove the state tables.

The session state timeout still applies for SQL Server state management. That's because the InstallSqlState.sql script also creates a new SQL Server job named ASPState_Job_DeleteExpiredSessions. As long as the SQLServerAgent service is running, this job will be executed every minute.

Additionally, the state tables will be removed every time you restart SQL Server, no matter what the session timeout. That's because when you use InstallSqlState, the state tables are created in the tempdb database, which is a temporary storage area. If this isn't the behavior you want, you can use the InstallPersistSqlState.sql and UninstallPersistSqlState.sql scripts instead of InstallSqlState.sql and UninstallSqlState.sql. In this case, the state tables are created in the ASPState database, and are permanent.

Cookieless

You can set the cookieless setting to true or false (the default), as follows:

```
<sessionState cookieless="false" ... />
```

When set to true, the session ID will automatically be inserted into the URL. When ASP.NET receives a request, it will remove the ID, retrieve the session collection, and forward the request to the appropriate directory. A munged URL is shown here:

```
http://localhost/WebApplication/(amfvyc55evojk455cffbq355)/Page1.aspx
```

Because the session ID is inserted in the current URL, relative links also automatically gain the session ID. In other words, if the user is currently stationed on Page1.aspx and clicks a relative link to Page2.aspx, the relative link includes the current session ID as part of the URL. The same is true if you call Response.Redirect() with a relative URL, as shown here:

```
Response.Redirect("Page2.aspx");
```

The only real limitation of cookieless state is that you cannot use absolute links, because they will not contain the session ID. For example, this statement causes the user to lose all session information:

```
Response.Redirect("http://localhost/WebApplication/Page2.aspx");
```

Timeout

Another important session state setting in the web.config file is the timeout. This specifies the number of minutes that ASP.NET will wait, without receiving a request, before it abandons the session.

```
<sessionState timeout="20" ... />
```

This setting represents one of the most important compromises of session state. A difference of minutes can have a dramatic effect on the load of your server and the performance of your application. Ideally, you will choose a timeframe that is short enough to allow the server to reclaim valuable memory after a client stops using the application, but long enough to allow a client to pause and continue a session without losing it.

You can also programmatically change the session timeout in code. For example, if you know a session contains an unusually large amount of information, you may need to limit the amount of time the session can be stored. You would then warn the user and change the timeout property. Here's a sample line of code that changes the timeout to ten minutes:

```
Session.Timeout = 10;
```

Application State

Application state allows you to store global objects that can be accessed by any client. Application state is based on the System.Web.HttpApplicationState class, which is provided in all web pages through the built-in Application object.

Application state is very similar to session state. It supports the same type of objects, retains information on the server, and uses the same dictionary-based syntax. A common example with application state is a global counter that tracks how many times an operation has been performed by all of the web application's clients.

For example, you could create a global.asax event handler that tracks how many sessions have been created or how many requests have been received into the application. Or you can use similar logic in the Page.Load event handler to track how many times a given page has been requested by various clients. Here's an example of the latter:

```
private void Page_Load(Object sender, EventArgs e)
{
    int count = (int)Application["HitCounterForOrderPage"];
    count++;
    Application["HitCounterForOrderPage"] = count;
    lblCounter.Text = count.ToString();
}
```

Once again, application state items are stored as objects, so you need to cast them when you retrieve them from the collection. Items in application state never time out. They last until the application or server is restarted, or the application domain refreshes itself (due to automatic process-recycling settings, or an update to one of the pages or components in the application).

Application state isn't often used, because it's generally inefficient. In the previous example, the counter would probably not keep an accurate count, particularly in times of heavy traffic. For example, if two clients requested the page at the same time, you could have a sequence of events like this:

1. User A retrieves the current count (432).

2. User B retrieves the current count (432).

3. User A sets the current count to 433.

4. User B sets the current count to 433.

In other words, one request isn't counted because two clients access the counter at the same time. To prevent this problem, you need to use the Lock() and Unlock() methods, which explicitly allow only one client to access the Application state collection at a time, as follows:

```
private void Page_Load(Object sender, EventArgs e)
{
    // Acquire exclusive access.
    Application.Lock();

    int count = (int)Application["HitCounterForOrderPage"];
    count++;
    Application["HitCounterForOrderPage"] = count;

    // Release exclusive access.
    Application.Unlock();

    lblCounter.Text = count.ToString();
}
```

Unfortunately, all other clients requesting the page will now be stalled until the Application collection is released. This can drastically reduce performance. Generally, frequently modified values are poor candidates for application state. In fact, application state is rarely used in the .NET world because its two most common uses have been replaced by easier, more efficient methods:

• In the past, application state was used to store application-wide constants, such as a database connection string. As you saw in Chapter 6, this type of constant can now be stored in the web.config file, which is generally more flexible because you can change it easily without needing to hunt through web-page code or recompile your application.

• Application state can also be used to store frequently used information that is time-consuming to create, such as a full product catalog that requires a database lookup. However, using application state to store this kind of information raises all sorts of problems about how to check if the data is valid and how to replace it when needed. It can also hamper performance if the product catalog is too large. A similar but much more sensible approach is to store frequently used information in the ASP.NET cache. Many uses of application state can be replaced more efficiently with caching.

Application state information is always stored in process. That means that you can use any .NET data types. However, it also introduces the same two limitations that affect in-process session state. Namely, you can't share application state between the servers in a web farm, and you will always lose your application state information when the application domain is restarted.

Caching

ASP.NET has taken some dramatic steps forward with caching. Many developers who first learn about caching see it as a bit of a frill, but nothing could be further from the truth. Used intelligently, caching could provide a twofold, threefold, or even tenfold performance improvement by retaining important data for just a short period of time.

In ASP.NET, there are really two types of caching. Your applications can and should use both types, because they complement each other:

- **Data caching** is carried out manually in your code. To use data caching, you store important pieces of information that are time-consuming to reconstruct (such as a DataSet retrieved from a database) in the cache. Other pages can check for the existence of this information, and use it, thereby bypassing the steps ordinarily required to retrieve it. Data caching is conceptually the same as using application state, but it's much more server-friendly because items will be removed from the cache automatically when it grows too large and performance could be affected. Items can also be set to expire automatically.

- **Output caching** is the simplest type of caching. It stores a copy of the final rendered HTML page that is sent to the client. The next client that submits a request for this page doesn't actually run the page. Instead, the final HTML output is sent automatically. The time that would have been required to run the page and its code is completely reclaimed.

Additionally, you can use fragment caching, which is really a specialized type of output caching. Fragment caching stores and reuses the compiled HTML output of a user control on a page. Thus, when the page is requested some code may be executed, but the code for the appropriate user control isn't.

Data Caching

Data caching is the most flexible type of caching, but it also forces you to take specific additional steps in your code to implement it. The basic principle of data caching is that you add items that are expensive to create to a special built-in collection object (called Cache). This object works much like the Application object. It's globally available to all requests from all clients in the application. There are only two differences:

- **The Cache object is thread-safe.** This means that you don't need to explicitly lock or unlock the Cache collection before adding or removing an item. However, the objects in the Cache collection will still need to be thread-safe themselves. For example, if you create a custom business object, more than one client could try to use that object at once, which could lead to invalid data. There are various ways to code around this limitation. One easy approach that you'll see in this chapter is just to make a duplicate copy of the object if you need to work with it in a web page.

- **Items in the Cache collection are removed automatically.** ASP.NET will remove an item if it expires, if one of the objects or files it depends on is changed, or if the server becomes low on memory. This means you can freely use the cache without worrying about wasting valuable server memory, because ASP.NET will remove items as needed. But because items in the cache can be removed, you always need to check if a cache object exists before you attempt to use it. Otherwise, you'll run into a NullReferenceException.

As with application state, the cache object is stored in process, which means it doesn't persist if the application domain is restarted and it can't be shared between computers in a web farm. This behavior is by design, because the cost of allowing multiple computers to communicate with an out-of-process cache mitigates some of its performance benefit. It makes more sense for each web server to have its own cache.

As with the Application and Session collections, you can add an item to the Cache collection just by assigning to a new key name:

```
Cache["key"] = item;
```

However, this approach is generally discouraged because it does not allow you to have any control over the amount of time the object will be retained in the cache. A better approach is to use the Insert() method.

The four versions of the Insert() method are shown in Table 7-4.

Table 7-4. *The Insert() Method Overloads*

Overload	Description
Cache.Insert(key, value);	Inserts an item into the cache under the specified key name, using the default priority and expiration. This is the same as using the indexer-based collection syntax and assigning to a new key name.
Cache.Insert(key, value, dependencies);	Inserts an item into the cache under the specified key name, and using the default priority and expiration. The last parameter contains a CacheDependency object that links to other files or cached items, and allows the cached item to be invalidated when these change.
Cache.Insert(key, value, dependencies, absoluteExpiration, slidingExpiration);	Inserts an item into the cache under the specified key name, using the default priority and the indicated sliding or absolute expiration policy (you cannot set both at once). This is the most commonly used version of the Insert() method.
Cache.Insert(key, value, dependencies, absoluteExpiration, slidingExpiration, priority, onRemoveCallback);	Allows you to configure every aspect of the cache policy for the item, including expiration, dependencies, and priority. In addition, you can submit a delegate that points to a method you want invoked when the item is removed.

The most important choice you make when inserting an item into the cache is the expiration policy. ASP.NET allows you to set a sliding expiration or an absolute expiration policy, but you cannot use both at the same time. If you want to use an absolute expiration, set the slidingExpiration parameter to TimeSpan.Zero. To set a sliding expiration policy, set the absoluteExpiration parameter to DateTime.Max.

With sliding expiration, ASP.NET waits for a set period of inactivity to dispose of a neglected cache item. For example, if you use a sliding expiration period of ten minutes, the item will only be removed if it is not used over a ten-minute period. Sliding expiration works well when you have information that is always valid, but may not be in high demand, such as historical data or a product catalog. This information doesn't expire because it's no longer valid, but shouldn't be kept in the cache if it isn't doing any good.

Here's an example that stores an item with a sliding expiration policy of ten minutes, with no dependencies:

```
Cache.Insert("MyItem", obj, null,
             DateTime.MaxValue, TimeSpan.FromMinutes(10));
```

■**Note** The similarity between caching with absolute expiration and session state is no coincidence. When you use the in-process state server for session state, it actually uses the cache behind the scenes! The session state information is stored in a private slot and given an expiration policy to match the timeout value. The session state item is not accessible through the Cache object.

Absolute expirations are best when you know the information in a given item can only be considered valid for a specific amount of time, such as a stock chart or weather report. With absolute expiration, you set a specific date and time when the cached item will be removed.

Here's an example that stores an item for exactly 60 minutes:

```
Cache.Insert("MyItem", obj, null,
             DateTime.Now.AddMinutes(60), TimeSpan.Zero);
```

When you retrieve an item from the cache, you must always check for a null reference. That's because ASP.NET can remove your cached items at any time. One way to handle this is to add special methods that re-create the items as needed. Here's an example:

```
private DataSet GetCustomerData()
{
    if (Cache["CustomerData"] != null)
    {
        // Return the object from the cache.
        return (DataSet)Cache["CustomerData"];
    }
    else
    {
        // Re-create the item and insert it into the cache.
        DataSet customers = QueryCustomerDataFromDatabase();
        Cache.Insert("CustomerData", customers);
```

```
        return customers;
    }
}

private DataSet QueryCustomerDataFromDatabase()
{
    // (Code to query the database goes here.)
}
```

Now you can retrieve the DataSet elsewhere in your code using the following syntax, without worrying about the caching details.

```
DataGrid1.DataSource = GetCustomerData();
```

For an even better design, move the QueryDataFromDatabase() method to a separate component using the techniques demonstrated in the previous chapter.

There's no method for clearing the entire data cache, but you can enumerate through the collection using the DictionaryEntry class. This gives you a chance to retrieve the key for each item, and allows you to empty the class using code like that shown here:

```
foreach(DictionaryEntry item in Cache)
{
    Cache.Remove(objItem.Key.ToString());
}
```

or you can retrieve a list of cached items, as follows:

```
string itemList = "";
foreach (DictionaryEntry item in Cache)
{
    itemList += objItem.Key.ToString() + " ";
}
```

This code is rarely used in a deployed application, but is extremely useful while testing your caching strategies.

A Simple Cache Test

The following page presents a simple caching test. An item is cached for 30 seconds and reused for requests in that time. The page code always runs (because the page itself isn't cached), checks the cache, and retrieves or constructs the item as needed. It also reports whether the item was found in the cache.

```
public class SimpleCacheTest : Page
{
    protected label lblInfo;
    // (Designer code omitted.)

    private void Page_Load(Object sender, EventArgs e)
    {
        if (this.IsPostBack)
```

```
    {
        lblInfo.Text += "Page posted back.<br>";
    }
    else
    {
        lblInfo.Text += "Page created.<br>";
    }

    if (Cache["TestItem"] == null)
    {
        lblInfo.Text += "Creating TestItem...<br>";
        DateTime testItem = DateTime.Now;

        lblInfo.Text += "Storing TestItem in cache ";
        lblInfo.Text += "for 30 seconds.<br>";
        Cache.Insert("TestItem", testItem, null,
                    DateTime.Now.AddSeconds(30), TimeSpan.Zero);
    }
    else
    {
        lblInfo.Text += "Retrieving TestItem...<br>";
        DateTime testItem = (DateTime)Cache["TestItem"];
        lblInfo.Text += "TestItem is '" + testItem.ToString();
        lblInfo.Text += "'<br>";
    }

    lblInfo.Text += "<br>";
    }
}
```

Figure 7-7 shows the result after the page has been loaded and posted back several times in the 30-second period.

Cache Priorities

You can also set a priority when you add an item to the cache. The priority only has an effect if ASP.NET needs to perform *cache scavenging,* which is the process of removing cached items early because memory is becoming scarce. In this situation, ASP.NET will look for underused items that haven't yet expired. If it finds more than one similarly underused item, it will compare the priorities to determine which one to remove first. Generally, you would set a higher cache priority for items that take more time to reconstruct in order to indicate its heightened importance.

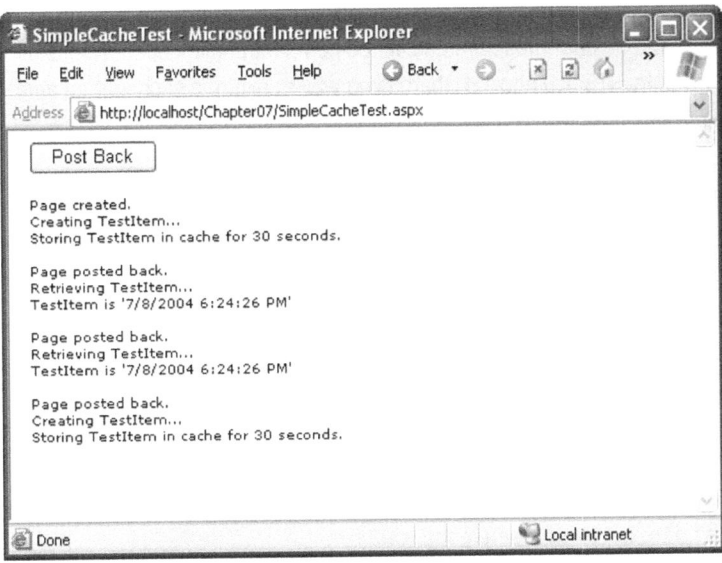

Figure 7-7. *Retrieving data from the cache*

To assign a cache priority, you choose a value from the CachePriority enumeration. Table 7-5 lists all the values.

Table 7-5. *Values of the CachePriority Enumeration*

Value	Description
High	These items are the least likely to be deleted from the cache as the server frees system memory.
AboveNormal	These items are less likely to be deleted than Normal priority items.
Normal	These items have the default priority level. They are deleted only after Low or BelowNormal priority items have been removed.
BelowNormal	These items are more likely to be deleted than Normal priority items.
Low	These items are the most likely to be deleted from the cache as the server frees system memory.
NotRemovable	These items will ordinarily not be deleted from the cache as the server frees system memory.

Caching with Dependencies

You can also specify that a cache item will expire automatically when another cache item expires or when a file is modified. This logic is referred to as a cache dependency, because your cached item is dependent on another resource, and is only valid while that resource remains unchanged.

■**Note** In the upcoming ASP.NET 2.0, it will be possible to create cached items that have dependencies on tables in a SQL Server database. However, in .NET 1.0 and 1.1, there is no way to expire a cached item automatically when information changes in a database.

To create a cache dependency, you need to create a CacheDependency object, and then use it when adding the dependent cached item. For example, the following code creates a cached item that will automatically be evicted from the cache when an XML file is changed.

```
// Create a dependency for the ProductList.xml file.
CacheDependency prodDependency = new CacheDependency(
  Server.MapPath("ProductList.xml"));

// Add a cache item that will be dependent on this file.
Cache.Insert("ProductInfo", prodInfo, prodDependency);
```

CacheDependency monitoring begins as soon as the object is created. If the XML file changes before you have added the dependent item to the cache, the item will expire immediately once it's added.

The CacheDependency object provides several different constructors. You've already seen how it can make a dependency based on a file by using the filename constructor. You can also specify a directory that needs to be monitored for changes, or you can use a constructor that accepts an array of strings that represent multiple files and directories.

Yet another constructor accepts an array of filenames and an array of cache keys. The following example uses this constructor to create an item that is dependent on another item in the cache:

```
Cache["Key1"] = "Cache Item 1";

// Make Cache["Key2"] dependent on Cache["Key1"].
string[] dependencyKey = new string[1];
dependencyKey[0] = "Key1";
CacheDependency dependency = new CacheDependency(null, dependencyKey);

Cache.Insert("Key2", "Cache Item 2", dependency);
```

Next, when Cache["Key 1"] changes or is removed from the cache, Cache["Key 2"] will automatically be dropped.

Figure 7-8 shows a simple test page that is included with the online samples for this chapter. It sets up a dependency, modifies the file, and allows you to verify that the cache item has been dropped from the cache.

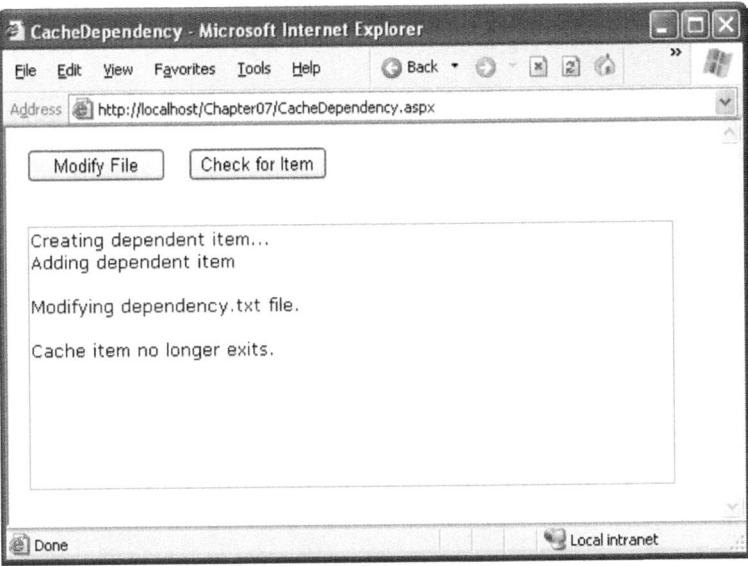

Figure 7-8. *Testing cache dependencies*

The Item Removed Callback

ASP.NET also allows you to write a callback method that will be triggered when an item is removed from the cache. This might be useful if you need to clean up other related resources (like a temporary file on the hard drive). However, you shouldn't use this callback to re-create the item and reinsert the removed item back into the cache. Not only will this waste time generating data that might not be immediately required, but it will thwart ASP.NET's attempt to reduce memory usage when server resources are scarce.

You can place the method that handles the callback in your web-page class, or you can use a static method in another accessible class. However, you should keep in mind that this code won't be executed as part of a web request. That means you can't interact with web-page objects or notify the user.

The following example uses a cache callback to make two interdependent items—a feat that wouldn't be possible with dependencies alone. Two items are inserted in the cache, and when either one of those items is removed, the item-removed callback removes the other.

```
public class CacheCallbackTest : System.Web.UI.Page
{
    protected System.Web.UI.WebControls.Label lblInfo;
    protected System.Web.UI.WebControls.Button cmdRemove;
    protected System.Web.UI.WebControls.Button cmdCheck;
    // (Designer code omitted.)
```

```
private void Page_Load(object sender, System.EventArgs e)
{
    if (!this.IsPostBack)
    {
        lblInfo.Text += "Creating items...<br>";
        string itemA = "item A";
        string itemB = "item B";
        Cache.Insert("itemA", itemA, null, DateTime.Now.AddMinutes(60),
          TimeSpan.Zero, CacheItemPriority.Default,
          new CacheItemRemovedCallback(ItemRemovedCallback));
        Cache.Insert("itemB", itemB, null, DateTime.Now.AddMinutes(60),
          TimeSpan.Zero, CacheItemPriority.Default,
          new CacheItemRemovedCallback(ItemRemovedCallback));
    }
}

private void cmdCheck_Click(object sender, System.EventArgs e)
{
    string itemList = "";
    foreach(DictionaryEntry item in Cache)
    {
        itemList += item.Key.ToString() + " ";
    }
    lblInfo.Text += "<br>Found: " + itemList + "<br>";
}

private void cmdRemove_Click(object sender, System.EventArgs e)
{
    lblInfo.Text += "<br>Removing itemA.<br>";
    Cache.Remove("itemA");
}

private void ItemRemovedCallback(string key, object value,
  CacheItemRemovedReason reason)
{
    // This fires after the request has ended, when the
    // item is removed.

    // If either item has been removed, make sure
    // the other item is also removed.
    if (key == "itemA" || key == "itemB")
    {
        Cache.Remove("itemA");
        Cache.Remove("itemB");
    }
}
}
```

Figure 7-9 shows a test of this page.

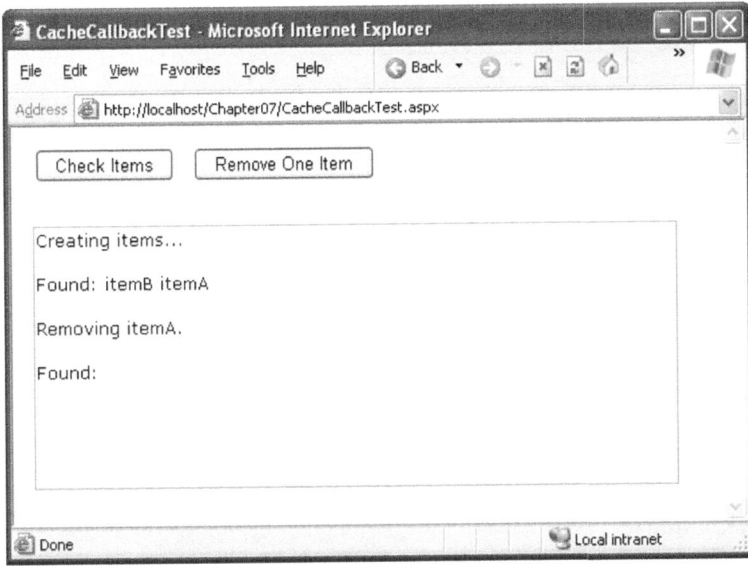

Figure 7-9. *Testing a cache callback*

The callback also provides your code with additional information, including the removed item and the reason it was removed. Possible reasons are shown in Table 7-6.

Table 7-6. *Values for the CacheItemRemovedReason Enumeration*

Value	Description
DependencyChanged	Removed because a file or key dependency changed.
Expired	Removed because it expired (according to its sliding or absolute expiration policy).
Removed	Removed programmatically by a Remove method call or by an Insert method call that specified the same key.
Underused	Removed because ASP.NET decided it wasn't important enough and wanted to free memory.

Output Caching

To see output caching in action, you can create a simple page that displays the current time of day. This page is shown in Figure 7-10.

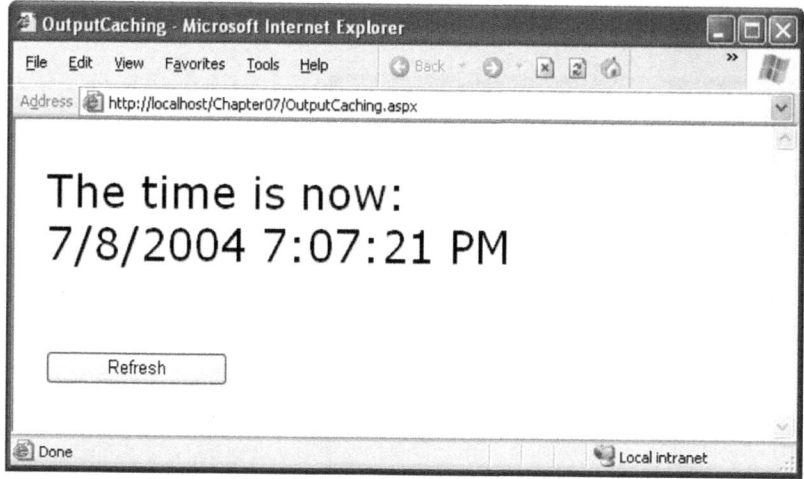

Figure 7-10. *Caching an entire page*

The code for this task is elementary:

```
public class OutputCaching : Page
{
    protected Label lblDate;
    // (Designer code omitted.)

    private void Page_Load(Object sender, EventArgs e)
    {
        lblDate.Text = "The time is now:<br>";
        lblDate.Text += DateTime.Now.ToString();
    }
}
```

There are two ways to cache an ASP.NET page. The most common approach is to insert the OutputCache directive at the top of your .aspx file, as shown here:

```
<%@ OutputCache Duration="20" VaryByParam="None" %>
```

The Duration attribute instructs ASP.NET to cache the page for 20 seconds. The VaryByParam attribute is also required, but you'll learn about its effect a little later.

When you run the test page, you'll discover some interesting behavior. The first time you access the page, the current date will be displayed. If you refresh the page a short time later, however, the page will not be updated. Instead, ASP.NET will automatically send the cached HTML output to you until it expires in 20 seconds. When the cached page expires, ASP.NET will run the page code again, generate a new cached copy, and use that for the next 20 seconds.

Twenty seconds may seem like a trivial amount of time, but in a high-volume site, it can make a dramatic difference. For example, you might cache a page that provides a list of products from a catalog. By caching the page for 20 seconds, you limit database access for this page to three operations per minute. Without caching, the page will try to connect to the database once for each client, and could easily make dozens of requests in the course of a minute.

Of course, just because you request that a page should be stored for 20 seconds doesn't mean that it actually will be. The page could be evicted out of the cache early if the system finds that memory is becoming scarce. This allows you to use caching freely, without worrying too much about hampering your application by using up vital memory.

Tip When you recompile a cached page, ASP.NET will automatically remove the page from the cache. This prevents problems where a page isn't properly updated because the older, cached version is being used. However, you might still want to disable caching while testing your application. Otherwise, you may have trouble using variable watches, breakpoints, and other debugging techniques, because your code will not be executed if a cached copy of the page is available.

Caching and the Query String

One of the main considerations in caching is deciding when a page can be reused and when information must be accurate up to the latest second. Developers, with their love of instant gratification (and lack of patience), generally tend to overemphasize the importance of real-time information. You can usually use caching to efficiently reuse slightly stale data without a problem, and with a considerable performance improvement.

Of course, sometimes information needs to be dynamic. One example is if the page uses information from the current user's session to tailor the user interface. In this case, full page caching just isn't appropriate (although fragment caching may help). Another example is if the page is receiving information from another page through the query string. In this case, the page is too dynamic to cache—or is it?

Our current example sets the VaryByParam attribute to None, which effectively tells ASP.NET that you only need to store one copy of the cached page, which is suitable for all scenarios. If the request for this page adds query string arguments to the URL, it makes no difference—ASP.NET will always reuse the same output until it expires. You can test this by adding a query string parameter manually in the browser window (such as ?a=b).

Based on this experiment, you might assume that output caching isn't suitable for pages that use query string arguments. But ASP.NET actually provides another option. You can set the VaryByParam attribute to "*" to indicate that the page uses the query string, and to instruct ASP.NET to cache separate copies of the page for different query string arguments, as shown here:

```
<%@ OutputCache Duration="20" VaryByParam="*" %>
```

Now when you request the page with additional query string information, ASP.NET will examine the query string. If the string matches a previous request, and a cached copy of that page exists, it will be reused. Otherwise, a new copy of the page will be created and cached separately.

To get a better idea how this process works, consider the following series of requests:

1. You request a page without any query string parameter, and receive page copy A.

2. You request the page with the parameter ProductID=1. You receive page copy B.

3. Another user requests the page with the parameter ProductID=2. That user receives copy C.

4. Another user requests the page with ProductID=1. If the cached output B has not expired, it's sent to the user.

5. The user then requests the page with no query string parameters. If copy A has not expired, it's sent from the cache.

You can try this out on your own, although you might want to lengthen the amount of time that the cached page is retained to make it easier to test.

Caching with Specific Query String Parameters

Setting VaryByParam="*" allows you to use caching with dynamic pages that vary their output based on the query string. This approach could be extremely useful for a product detail page, which receives a product ID in its query string. With vary-by-parameter caching, a separate page could be stored for each product, thereby saving a trip to the database. However, to gain performance benefits you might have to increase the cached output lifetime to several minutes or longer.

Of course, there are some potential problems with this technique. Pages that accept a wide range of different query string parameters (such as a page that receives numbers for a calculation, client information, or search keywords) just aren't suited to output caching. The possible number of variations is enormous, and the potential reuse is very low. Though these pages will be evicted from the cache when the memory is needed, they could inadvertently force other more important information out of the cache first, or slow down other operations.

In many cases, setting VaryByParam to the wildcard asterisk (*) is unnecessarily vague. It's usually better to specifically identify an important query string variable by name. Here's an example:

```
<%@ OutputCache Duration="20" VaryByParam="ProductID" %>
```

In this case, ASP.NET will examine the query string looking for the ProductID parameter. Requests with different ProductID parameters will be cached separately, but all other parameters will be ignored. This is particularly useful if the page may be passed additional query string information that it doesn't use. ASP.NET has no way to distinguish the "important" query string parameters without your help.

You can specify several parameters, as long as you separate them with semicolons, as follows:

```
<%@ OutputCache Duration="20" VaryByParam="ProductID;CurrencyType" %>
```

In this case, query string will cache separate versions provided the query string differs by ProductID or CurrencyType.

> **Note** Output caching works well with pages that only vary based on server-side data (for example, the data in a database), and the data in query string. However, output caching doesn't work if the page output depends on user-specific information like session data or cookies. Output caching also won't work with event-driven pages that use forms. In these cases, events will be ignored, and a static page will be re-sent with each postback, effectively disabling the page. To avoid these problems, use fragment caching instead to cache a portion of the page, or use data caching to cache specific information.

Custom Caching Control

Varying by query string parameters isn't the only option when storing multiple cached versions of a page. ASP.NET also allows you to create your own procedure that decides whether to cache a new page version or reuse an existing one. This code examines whatever information is appropriate, and then returns a string. ASP.NET uses this string to implement caching. If your code generates the same string for different requests, ASP.NET will reuse the cached page. If your code generates a new string value, ASP.NET will generate a new cached version, and store it separately.

One way you could use custom caching is to cache different versions of a page based on the browser type. That way, Netscape browsers will always receive Netscape-optimized pages, and Internet Explorer users will receive IE-optimized HTML. To set up this sort of logic, you start by adding the OutputCache directive to the pages that will be cached. Use the VaryByCustom attribute to specify a name that represents the type of custom caching you're creating. The following example uses the name "Browser" because pages will be cached based on the client browser:

```
<%@ OutputCache Duration="10" VaryByParam="None" VaryByCustom="browser" %>
```

Next, you need to create the procedure that will generate the custom caching string. This procedure must be coded in the global.asax application file (or its code-behind file), and must use the following syntax:

```
public override string GetVaryByCustomString(
  HttpContext context, string arg)
{
    // Check for the requested type of caching.
    if (arg == "browser")
    {
        // Determine the current browser.
        string browserName;
        browserName = Context.Request.Browser.Browser;
        browserName += Context.Request.Browser.MajorVersion.ToString();
```

```
        // Indicate that this string should be used to vary caching.
        return browserName;
    }
    else
    {
        base.GetVaryByCustomString(context, arg)
    }
}
```

The GetVaryByCustomString() function passes the VaryByCustom name in the arg parameter. This allows you to create an application that implements several different types of custom caching in the same function. Each different type would use a different VaryByCustom name (such as "Browser," "BrowserVersion," or "DayOfWeek"). Your GetVaryByCustomString() function would examine the VaryByCustom name, and then return the appropriate caching string. If the caching strings for different requests match, ASP.NET will reuse the cached copy of the page. Or to look at it another way, ASP.NET will create and store a separate cached version of the page for each caching string it encounters.

Interestingly, the base implementation of the GetVaryByCustomString() already includes the logic for browser-based caching. That means you don't need to code the method shown previously. The base implementation of GetVaryByCustomString() creates the cached string based on the browser name and major version number. If you want to change how this logic works (for example, to vary based on name, major version, and minor version), you could override the GetVaryByCustomString() method, as in the previous example.

Note Varying by browser is an important technique for cached pages that use browser-specific features. For example, if your page generates client-side JavaScript that's not supported by all browsers, you should make the caching dependent on the browser version. Of course, it's still up to your code to identify the browser and choose what JavaScript to render. You'll learn more about adaptive pages and JavaScript in Part Four.

The OutputCache directive has a third attribute that you can use to define caching. This attribute, VaryByHeader, allows you to store separate versions of a page based on the value of an HTTP header received with the request. You can specify a single header or a list of headers separated by semicolons. This technique could be used with multilingual sites to cache different versions of a page based on the client browser language, as follows:

```
<%@ OutputCache Duration="20" VaryByParam="None"
    VaryByHeader="Accept-Language" %>
```

Caching with the HttpCachePolicy Class

Using the OutputCache directive is generally the preferred way to cache a page, because it separates the caching instruction from the rest of your code. The OutputCache directive also makes it easy to configure several advanced properties in one line.

However, there is one other choice: You can write code that uses the built-in special Response.Cache property, which provides an instance of the System.Web.HttpCachePolicy class. This object provides properties that allow you to turn on caching for the current page.

In the following example, the date page has been rewritten so that it automatically enables caching when the page is first loaded. This code enables caching with the SetCacheability() method, which specifies that the page will be cached on the server, and that any other client can use the cached copy of the page. The SetExpires() method defines the expiration date for the page, which is set to be the current time plus 60 seconds.

```
private void Page_Load(Object sender, EventArgs e)
{
    // Cache this page on the server.
    Response.Cache.SetCacheability(HttpCacheability.Public);

    // Use the cached copy of this page for the next 60 seconds.
    Response.Cache.SetExpires(DateTime.Now.AddSeconds(60));

    // This additional line ensures that the browser can't
    // invalidate the page when the user clicks the Refresh button
    // (which some rogue browsers attempt to do).
    Response.Cache.SetValidUntilExpires(true);

    lblDate.Text = "The time is now:<br>" + DateTime.Now.ToString();
}
```

Fragment Caching

In some cases, you may find that you can't cache an entire page, but you would still like to cache a portion that is expensive to create and doesn't vary. One way to implement this sort of scenario is to use data caching to store just the underlying information used for the page. Another option is to use fragment caching.

To implement fragment caching, you need to create a user control for the portion of the page you want to cache. You can then add the OutputCache directive to the user control. The result is that the page will not be cached, but the user control will. User controls are discussed in Chapter 19.

Fragment caching is conceptually the same as page caching. There is only one catch—if your page retrieves a cached version of a user control, it cannot interact with it in code. For example, if your user control provides properties, your web-page code cannot modify or access these properties. When the cached version of the user control is used, a block of HTML is simply inserted into the page. The corresponding user control object is not available.

Summary

State management is the art of retaining information between requests. Usually, this information is user-specific (like a list of items in a shopping cart, a user name, or an access level), but sometimes it's global to the whole application (like usage statistics that track site activity). Because ASP.NET uses a disconnected architecture, you need to explicitly store and retrieve state information with each individual request. The approach that you choose for storing this data can have a dramatic effect on the performance, scalability, and security of your application.

PART TWO

Data Access

CHAPTER 8

■ ■ ■

ADO.NET Fundamentals

A large number of computer applications—both desktop and web applications—are *database-driven*. These data-driven applications are largely concerned with the retrieval, display, and modification of data.

Retrieving and processing data seems like a fairly straightforward task, but over the last decade data access technologies have changed repeatedly. Developers have moved from simple client applications that use single-user local databases to multiuser client-server systems that rely on centralized databases on a dedicated server. In the last few years, a new *disconnected data* model has gained ground, and it's designed for distributed and web applications that exchange data over the Internet.

The technologies and tools to access and work with data have changed as well. If you've worked with Microsoft languages for some time, you've most likely heard of (and possibly used) an alphabet soup of data access technologies that includes ODBC, DAO, RDO, RDS, and ADO. All of these older (but still in use) technologies weren't originally designed for distributed applications and loosely coupled networks like the Internet. As a result, they were sometimes awkward to use in web applications.

Now the .NET Framework introduces a completely new data access technology. This data access technology is ADO.NET, which consists of a set of managed classes specifically designed to manage disconnected data. The small miracle of ADO.NET is that it allows you to write more or less the same data access code in web applications that you write for client-server desktop applications, or even single-user applications that connect to a local database.

In this chapter, you'll get your first look at ADO.NET. You'll learn about the architecture of ADO.NET, and what comprises an ADO.NET data provider. You'll also learn how to use ADO.NET to open a connection, execute direct SQL statements, and retrieve the results of a query.

The ADO.NET Architecture

ADO.NET uses a multilayered architecture that revolves around a few key concepts, like Connection, Command, and DataSet objects. However, the ADO.NET architecture is quite a bit different from classic ADO.

One of the key differences between ADO and ADO.NET is how they deal with the challenge of different data sources. In ADO, programmers always use a generic set of objects, no matter what the underlying data source is. For example, if you want to retrieve a record from an Oracle database, you use the exact same Connection class that you would use to tackle the same task with SQL Server. This isn't the case in ADO.NET, which introduces a new data provider model.

ADO.NET Data Providers

A *data provider* is a set of ADO.NET classes that allow you to access a specific database, execute SQL commands, and retrieve data. Essentially, a data provider is a bridge between your application and a data source.

The classes that make up a data provider include the following:

- **Connection.** You use this object to establish a connection to a data source.

- **Command.** You use this object to execute SQL commands and stored procedures.

- **DataReader.** This object provides fast read-only, forward-only access to the data retrieved from a query.

- **DataAdapter.** This object performs two tasks. First, you can use it to fill a DataSet (a disconnected collection of tables and relationships) with information extracted from a data source. Second, you can use it to apply changes to a data source, according to the modifications you've made in a DataSet.

ADO.NET doesn't include generic data provider objects. Instead, it includes different data providers specifically designed for different types of data sources. Each data provider has a specific implementation of the Connection, Command, DataReader, and DataAdapter classes that's optimized for a specific RBDMS (relational database management system). For example, if you need to create a connection to a SQL Server database, you'll use a Connection class named SqlConnection.

Note This book uses generic names for provider-specific objects. In other words, instead of discussing the SqlConnection and OracleConnection object, I'll talk in generic terms about all Connection objects. Just keep in mind that there really isn't a Connection object—it's just convenient shorthand for referring to all the provider-specific Connection objects, which work in a standardized fashion.

One of the key underlying ideas of the ADO.NET provider model is that it's *extensible*. In other words, developers can create their own providers for proprietary data sources. In fact, there are numerous proof-of-concepts examples available that show how you can easily create custom ADO.NET providers to wrap nonrelational data stores, like the file system or a directory service. Some third-party vendors also sell custom providers for .NET.

The .NET Framework 1.1 is bundled with a small set of four providers. These providers include the following:

- **SQL Server provider.** Provides optimized access to an SQL Server database (version 7.0 or later).

- **OLE DB provider.** Provides access to any data source that has an OLE DB driver. This includes SQL Server databases prior to version 7.0.

- **Oracle provider.** Provides optimized access to an Oracle database (version 8i or later).

- **ODBC provider.** Provides access to any data source that has an ODBC driver.

Note The Oracle and ODBC provider weren't included with the original .NET 1.0 release. However, even if you have the older version of .NET, you can still download these providers as separate standalone packages from http://msdn.microsoft.com/downloads.

Figure 8-1 shows the layers of the ADO.NET provider model.

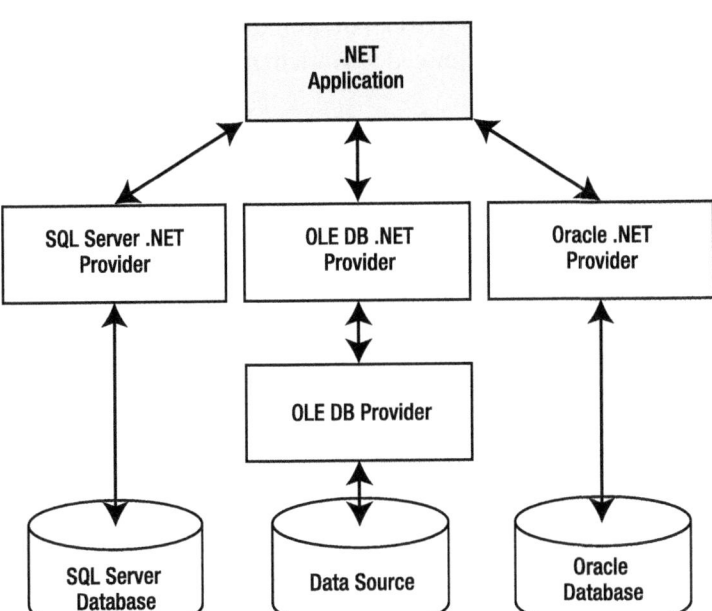

Figure 8-1. *The ADO.NET architecture*

When choosing a provider, you should first try to find one that's customized for your data source. If you can't find a suitable provider, you can use the OLE DB provider, as long as you have an OLE DB driver for your data source. The OLE DB technology has been around for many years as a part of ADO, so most data sources provide an OLE DB driver (including SQL Server, Oracle, Access, MySQL, and many more). In the rare situation when you can't find a dedicated .NET provider or an OLE DB driver, you can fall back on the ODBC provider, which works in conjunction with an ODBC driver.

Tip Microsoft includes the OLE DB provider with ADO.NET so that you can use your existing OLE DB drivers. However, if you can find a provider that's customized specifically for your data source, you should use it instead. For example, you can connect to SQL Server database using either the SQL Server provider or the OLE DB provider, but the first approach will perform best.

Standardization in ADO.NET

At first glance, it might seem that ADO.NET offers a fragmented model, because it doesn't include a generic set of objects that can work with multiple different types of databases. As a result, if you change from one RDBMS to another, you'll need to modify your data access code to use a different set of classes.

But even though different .NET data providers use different classes, all providers are *standardized* in the same way. More specifically, each provider is based on the same set of interfaces and base classes. For example, every Connection object implements the IDbConnection interface, which defines core methods like Open() and Close(). This standardization guarantees that every Connection class is guaranteed to work in the same way, and exposes the same set of core properties and methods.

Behind the scenes, different providers use completely different low-level calls and APIs. For example, the SQL Server provider uses the proprietary TDS (Tabular Data Stream) protocol to communicate with the server. The benefits of this model aren't immediately obvious, but they are significant:

- Because each provider uses the same interfaces, you can still write generic data access code (with a little more effort) by coding against the interfaces instead of the provider classes.

- Because each provider is implemented separately, it can make use of proprietary optimizations. (This is different than the ADO model, where every database call needs to filter through a common layer before it reaches the underlying database driver.) In addition, custom providers can add nonstandard features that aren't included in other providers (like SQL Server's ability to perform an XML query).

ADO.NET also has another layer of standardization: the DataSet. The DataSet is an all-purpose container for data that you've retrieved from one or more tables in a data source. The DataSet is completely generic—in other words, custom providers don't define their own custom versions of the DataSet class. No matter which data provider you use, you can extract your data and place it into a disconnected DataSet in the same way. That makes it easy to separate data *retrieval* code from data *processing* code. If you change the underlying database, you will need to change the data retrieval code, but if you use the DataSet and your information has the same structure you won't need to modify the way you process that data.

Disconnected Data

In a typical ADO application, you connect to the database, create a Recordset, display the information, and then abandon the Recordset and close the connection. While the connection is open, you have a "live" (or cursor-based) connection with the database. This live connection allows you to make immediate updates and you can even see the changes made by other users in real time. Unfortunately, database servers can only provide a limited number of connections before they reject connection requests. The longer you keep a connection open, the greater the chance becomes that another user will be prevented from accessing the database. In a poorly written program, the database connection is kept open while other tasks are being performed. But even in a well-written program using ADO, the connection must be kept open until all the data is processed and the Recordset is no longer needed.

ADO.NET has an entirely different philosophy. In ADO.NET you still create a connection to a database, but you can't use a cursor. Instead, you must immediately fill a DataSet object with a *copy* of the information drawn from the database. If you change the information in the DataSet, the information in the corresponding table in the database isn't changed. That means you can easily process and manipulate the data without worry, because you aren't using a valuable database connection. If necessary, you can reconnect to the original data source, and apply all your DataSet changes in a single batch operation.

Web Applications and the DataSet

A common misconception is that the DataSet is required to ensure scalability in a web application. Now that you understand the ASP.NET request processing architecture, you can probably see that this isn't the case. A web application only runs for a matter of seconds (if that long). That means that even if your web application uses direct cursor-based access, the lifetime of the connection is so short that it won't significantly reduce scalability, except in the mostly highly trafficked web applications.

In fact, the DataSet makes much more sense with distributed applications that use a rich Windows client. In this scenario, the clients can retrieve a DataSet from the server (perhaps using a web service), work with their DataSet objects for a long period of time, and only reconnect to the system when they need to update the data source with the batch of changes they've made. This allows the system to handle a much larger number of concurrent users than it would be able to if each client maintained a direct connection. It also allows you to efficiently share resources by caching data on the server and pooling connections between client requests.

The DataSet also acts as a neat package of information for rich client applications that are only intermittently connected to your system. For example, consider a traveling sales associate who needs to enter order information or review information about sales contacts on a laptop. Using the DataSet, an application on the user's laptop can store disconnected data locally and serialize it to an XML file. This allows the sales associate to build new orders using the cached data, even when no Internet connection is available. The new data can be submitted later when the user reconnects to the system.

So where does all this leave ASP.NET web applications? Essentially, you have two choices. You can use the DataSet, or you can use direct commands to bypass the DataSet altogether. Generally speaking, you'll bypass the DataSet when adding, inserting, or updating records. However, you won't avoid the DataSet completely. In fact, when you *retrieve* records you'll probably want to use the DataSet, because it supports a few indispensable features. In particular, the DataSet allows you to use *data binding* to display your information in advanced data controls like the DataGrid and DataList. For that reason, many web applications retrieve data into the DataSet, but perform direct updates using straightforward commands.

XML Integration

The DataSet also provides native XML serialization. You don't need to even be aware of this fact to enjoy its benefits, such as being able to easily serialize a DataSet to a file or transmit the DataSet to another application through a web service. At its best, this feature allows you to share your data with clients written in different programming languages and running on other operating systems.

The XML integration in the DataSet also allows you to access the information in the DataSet as an XML document *at any time.* You can even modify values, remove rows, and add new records by modifying the XML without losing any information. This deep XML integration isn't required for a typical self-contained web application. In fact, if you modify relational data through an XML model, you can run into several types of problems that you won't face using the DataSet object directly, like data type conversion problems and errors with duplicated data or violated relationships. Where the DataSet support for XML really shines is if you need to exchange the information in the DataSet with other applications and business processes.

Is ADO Really Worse Than ADO.NET?

With ADO, you can code around many scalability problems, with extra effort. Nothing stops you from releasing a connection after every database operation, and storing data in other objects. You can even use ADO's disconnected Recordset, in which case the connection is released almost as quickly as it is with ADO.NET programming.

However, it's well known that developers rarely take the high road. If a solution can be easily designed in the "greedy connection" style and appears to work well in its initial testing phase, there is rarely time to think twice. Developers may not realize the hidden vulnerabilities, or expect the increased user load. And when the problem occurs, it's too late to resolve it easily. In a sense, ADO.NET is a form of quality control that forces developers to work according to Microsoft's best practices.

Table 8-1 summarizes some of the core differences between ADO and ADO .NET.

Table 8-1. *ADO vs. ADO.NET*

Feature	ADO	ADO.NET
Fast read-only access	Uses a Recordset with a live connection.	Uses a DataReader with a live connection.
Disconnected access	Uses one or more disconnected Recordset objects, each of which contains the results of a query as a single table.	Uses a DataSet that can be filled with multiple DataTable objects using multiple queries. DataSets also contain additional information (like relations and column data types).
Disconnected data updates	Difficult to control, error-proof, and optimize.	Far richer set of features for handling conflicts, tracking changes, and increasing performance through stored procedures.
Transport of disconnected data	Rowset requires COM marshaling, which usually cannot easily cross a firewall.	DataSet is sent as plain XML. This requires more bytes, but allows the DataSet to pass over firewalls, and even be received and interpreted by components running on other platforms.

Feature	ADO	ADO.NET
Support for relations	Not provided. Join queries can be used to create a composite rowset.	Provided natively through DataRelation objects, which relate more than one DataTable in a DataSet.
Data navigation	Uses the MoveNext() or MovePrevious() method of the Recordset.	DataReaders use the Read() method; DataSets are collection-based and support foreach iteration.
Cursor support	Supports client-side (disconnected) and server-side cursors, including dynamic cursors that refresh the Rowset when other clients make changes.	Supports a read-only cursor through the DataReader and DataAdapter. Server-side cursors are not supported.
Concurrency issues	Can be minimized (at the cost of scalability) using pessimistic locking and direct updates.	Can be minimized using direct updates. However, pessimistic locking is not supported.
Data types	Limited to COM standard.	Can be as rich as needed, simply by creating additional .NET structures.
Performance	Good, but intermediate OLE DB layer is always required.	Better with native providers, and slightly poorer with legacy OLE DB drivers.
XML data representation	Provided in later versions of ADO as an add-on.	Provided natively. More configurable, but still not 100 percent flexible.

Fundamental ADO.NET Classes

There are two types of objects in ADO.NET: *connection-based* and *content-based*.

- **Connection-based objects.** These are the data provider objects like Connection, Command, DataAdapter, and DataReader. They execute SQL statements, connect to a database, or fill a DataSet. The connection-based objects are specific to the type of data source.

- **Content-based objects.** These objects are really just "packages" for data. They include the DataSet, DataColumn, DataRow, DataRelation, and several others. They are completely independent of the type of data source, and are found in the System.Data namespace.

In the rest of this chapter, you'll learn about the first level of ADO.NET—the connection-based objects, including the Connection, Command, and DataReader. You won't learn about the higher-level DataAdapter yet, because the DataAdapter is designed for use with the DataSet, and is discussed in the next chapter. (Essentially, the DataAdapter is a group of related Command objects that help you synchronize a DataSet with a data source.)

■**Note** An ADO.NET provider is simply a set of ADO.NET classes (with an implementation of the Connection, Command, DataAdapter, and DataReader) that's distributed in a class library assembly. Usually, all the classes in the data provider use the same prefix. For example, the prefix Oracle is used for the ADO.NET Oracle provider, and it provides an implementation of the Connection object named OracleConnection.

The ADO.NET classes are grouped into several namespaces. Each provider has its own namespace, and generic classes like the DataSet are stored in the System.Data namespaces. Table 8-2 lists the namespaces.

Table 8-2. *The ADO.NET Namespaces*

Namespace	Description
System.Data	Contains the key data container classes that model columns, relations, tables, datasets, rows, views, and constraints. In addition, contains the key interfaces that are implemented by the connection-based data objects.
System.Data.Common	Contains base, mostly abstract classes that implement some of the interfaces from System.Data and define the core ADO.NET functionality. Data providers inherit from these classes to create their own specialized versions.
System.Data.OleDb	Contains the classes used to connect to an OLE DB provider, including OleDbCommand, OleDbConnection, and OleDbDataAdapter. These classes support most OLE DB providers, but not those that require OLE DB version 2.5 interfaces.
System.Data.SqlClient	Contains the classes you use to connect to a Microsoft SQL Server database, including SqlDbCommand, SqlDbConnection, and SqlDBDataAdapter. These classes are optimized to use the TDS (Tabular Data Stream) interface to SQL Server.
System.Data.OracleClient	Contains the classes required to connect to an Oracle database (version 8.1.7 or later), including OracleCommand, OracleConnection, and OracleDataAdapter. These classes are using the optimized Oracle Call Interface (OCI).
System.Data.Odbc	Contains the classes required to connect to most ODBC drivers. These classes include OdbcCommand, OdbcConnection, and OdbcDataAdapter. ODBC drivers are included for all kinds of data sources, and are configured through the Data Sources icon in the Control Panel.
System.Data.SqlTypes	Contains structures that match the native data types in SQL Server. These classes aren't required, but provide an alternative to using standard .NET data types, which require automatic conversion.

The Connection Class

The Connection class allows you to establish a connection to the data source that you want to interact with. Before you can do anything else (including retrieving, deleting, inserting, or updating data), you need to establish a connection.

The core Connection properties and methods are specified by the IDbConnection interface, which all Connection classes implement.

Connection Strings

When you create a Connection object, you need to supply a *connection string*. The connection string is a series of name/value settings separated by semicolons (;). The order of these settings is unimportant, as is the capitalization. Taken together, they specify the basic information needed to create a connection.

Although connection strings vary based on the RDBMS and provider you are using, a few pieces of information are almost always required. This information includes the following:

- **The server where the database is located.** In the examples in this book, the database server is always located on the same computer as the ASP.NET application, so the loopback alias localhost is used instead of a computer name.

- **The database you want to use.** The examples in this book use the Northwind database, which is installed by default with most editions of SQL Server.

- **How the database should authenticate you.** The Oracle and SQL Server providers give you the choice of supplying authentication credentials or logging in as the current user. The latter choice is usually best, because you don't need to place password information in your code or configuration files.

For example, here's the connection string you would use to connect to the Northwind database on the current computer using integrated security (which uses the currently logged-in Windows user to access the database):

```
string connectionString = "Data Source=localhost;Initial Catalog=Northwind;" +
  "Integrated Security=SSPI";
```

If integrated security isn't supported, the connection must indicate a valid user and password combination. For a newly installed SQL Server database, the sa (system administrator) account is usually present. Here's a connection string that uses this account:

```
string connectionString = "Data Source=localhost;Initial Catalog=Northwind;" +
  "user id=sa;password=opensesame";
```

If you're using the OLE DB provider, your connection string will still be similar, with the addition of a provider setting that identifies the OLE DB driver. For example, the following connection string can be used to connect to an Oracle database through the MSDAORA OLE DB provider:

```
string connectionString = "Data Source=localhost;Initial Catalog=Sales;" +
  "user id=sa;password=;Provider=MSDAORA";
```

And here's an example that connects to an Access database file:

```
string connectionString = "Provider=Microsoft.Jet.OLEDB.4.0;" +
  @"Data Source=C:\DataSources\Northwind.mdb";
```

Tip If you're using a database other than SQL Server, you might need to consult the data provider documentation (or the .NET Framework class library reference) to determine the supported connection string values. For example, most databases support the Connect Timeout setting, which sets the number of seconds to wait for a connection before throwing an exception. (The SQL Server default is 15 seconds.)

When you create a Connection object, you can pass the connection string as a constructor parameter. Alternatively, you can set the ConnectionString property by hand, as long as you do it before you attempt to open the connection.

Testing a Connection

Once you've chosen your connection string, managing the connection is easy—you simply use the Open() and Close() methods. You can use the following code in the Page.Load event handler to test a connection and write its status to a label (as shown in Figure 8-2).

```
// Create the connection object.
string connectionString = "Data Source=localhost;Initial Catalog=Northwind;" +
  "Integrated Security=SSPI";
SqlConnection con = new SqlConnection(connectionString);

try
{
    // Try to open the connection.
    con.Open();
    lblInfo.Text = "<b>Server Version:</b> " + con.ServerVersion;
    lblInfo.Text += "<br><b>Connection Is:</b> " + con.State.ToString();
}
catch (Exception err)
{
    // Handle an error by displaying the information.
    lblInfo.Text = "Error reading the database. ";
    lblInfo.Text += err.Message;
}
finally
{
    // Either way, make sure the connection is properly closed.
    // Even if the connection wasn't opened successfully,
    // calling Close() won't cause an error.
    con.Close();
    lblInfo.Text += "<br><b>Now Connection Is:</b> ";
    lblInfo.Text +=  con.State.ToString();
}
```

Figure 8-2 shows the results of running this code.

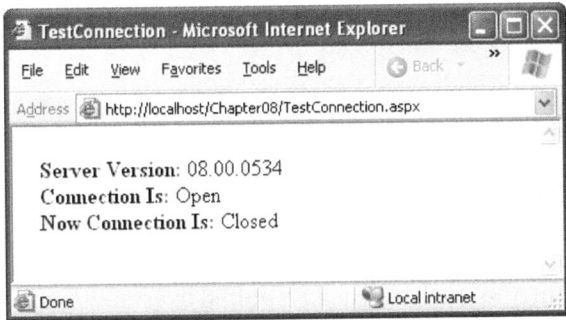

Figure 8-2. *Testing a connection*

Connections are a limited server resource. This means that it's imperative that you open the connection as late as possible, and release it as quickly as possible. In the previous code sample, an exception handler is used to make sure that even if an unhandled error occurs, the connection will be closed in the finally block. If you don't use this design and an unhandled exception occurs, the connection will remain open until the garbage collector disposes the SqlConnection object.

An alternate approach is to wrap your data access code in a using block. The using statement declares that you are using a disposable object for a short period of time. As soon as the using block ends, the CLR releases the corresponding object immediately by calling its Dispose() method. Interestingly, calling the Dispose() method of a Connection object is equivalent to calling Close(). That means you can rewrite the earlier example in the following more compact form:

```
// Create the connection object.
string connectionString = "Data Source=localhost;Initial Catalog=Northwind;" +
  "Integrated Security=SSPI";
SqlConnection con = new SqlConnection(connectionString);

using (con)
{
    con.Open();
    lblInfo.Text = "<b>Server Version:</b> " + con.ServerVersion;
    lblInfo.Text += "<br><b>Connection Is:</b> " + con.State.ToString();
}
lblInfo.Text += "<br><b>Now Connection Is:</b> ";
lblInfo.Text +=  con.State.ToString();
```

The best part is that you don't need to write a finally block—the using statement releases the object you're using even if you exit the block as the result of an unhandled exception.

■**Note** The Connection object also includes a BeginTransaction() method that starts a transaction and returns a Transaction object you can use to commit operations or roll them back. You'll learn more about transactions in Chapter 11.

Connection Pooling

Acquiring a connection takes a short, but definite amount of time. In a web application in which requests are being handled efficiently, connections will be open and closed endlessly as new requests are processed. In this environment, the small overhead required to establish a connection can become significant and limit the scalability of the system.

One solution is *connection pooling*. Connection pooling is the practice of keeping a permanent set of open database connections to be shared by sessions that use the same data source. This avoids the need to create and destroy connections all the time. Connection pools in ADO.NET are completely transparent to the programmer, and your data access code doesn't need to be altered. When a client requests a connection by calling Open(), it's served directly from the available pool, rather than re-created. When a client releases a connection by calling Close() or Dispose(), it's not discarded but returned to the pool to the serve the next request.

ADO.NET does not include a connection pooling mechanism. However, most ADO.NET providers implement some form of connection pooling. The SQL Server and Oracle data providers implement their own efficient connection pooling algorithms. These algorithms are implemented entirely in managed code and—in contrast to some popular misconceptions—do not use COM+ enterprises services. In order for a connection to be reused with the SQL Server or Oracle, the connection string matches exactly. If it differs even slightly, a new connection will be created in a new pool.

■**Tip** SQL Server and Oracle and connection pooling use a full-text match algorithm. That means any minor change in the connection string will thwart connection pooling, even if the change is simply to reverse the order of parameters or add an extra blank space at the end. For this reason, it's imperative that you don't hardcode the connection string in different web pages. Instead, you should store the connection string in one place—preferably the <appSettings> section of the web.config file.

With both the SQL Server and Oracle providers, connection pooling is enabled and used automatically. However, you can also use connection string parameters to configure pool size settings. These parameters are shown in Table 8-3.

Here's an example connection string that sets a minimum pool size:

```
string connectionString = "Data Source=localhost;Initial Catalog=Northwind;" +
  "Integrated Security=SSPI;Min Pool Size=10";
SqlConnection con = new SqlConnection(connectionString);
```

```
// Get the connection from the pool (if it exists)
// or create the pool with 10 connections (if it doesn't).
con.Open();

// Return the connection to the pool.
con.Close();
```

Table 8-3. *Connection Pooling Settings*

Setting	Description
Max Pool Size	The maximum number of connections allowed in the pool (defaults to 100). If the maximum pool size has been reached, any further attempts to open a connection are queued until a connection becomes available. (An error is raised if the Connection.Timeout value elapses before a connection becomes available.)
Min Pool Size	The minimum number of connections always retained in the pool (defaults to 0). This number of connections will be created when the first connection is opened, leading to a minor delay for the first request.
Pooling	When true (the default), the connection is drawn from the appropriate pool, or if necessary, is created and added to the appropriate pool.
Connection Lifetime	Specifies a time interval in seconds. If a connection is returned to the pool and its creation time is older than the specified lifetime, it will be destroyed. The default is 0, which disables this behavior. This feature is useful when you want to recycle a large number of connections at once.

The Command and DataReader Classes

The Command class allows you to execute any type of SQL statement. Although you can use a Command to perform *data-definition* tasks (like creating and altering databases, tables, and indexes), you're much more likely to perform *data-manipulation* tasks (like retrieving and updating the records in a table).

The provider-specific Command classes implement standard functionality, just like the Connection classes. In this case, the IDbCommand interface defines the core set of Command methods that are used to execute a command over an open connection.

Command Basics

Before you can use a command, you need to choose the command type, set the command text, and bind the command to a connection. You can perform this work by setting the corresponding properties (CommandType, CommandText, and Connection), or you can pass the information you need as constructor arguments.

The command text can be a SQL statement, a stored procedure, or the name of a table. It all depends on the *type* of command you're using. There are three types of commands, as listed in Table 8-4.

Table 8-4. *Values for the CommandType Enumeration*

Value	Description
CommandType.Text	The command will execute a direct SQL statement. The SQL statement is provided in the CommandText property. This is the default value.
CommandType.StoredProcedure	The command will execute a stored procedure in the data source. The CommandText property provides the name of the stored procedure.
CommandType.TableDirect	The command will query all the records in the table. The CommandText is the name of the table from which the command will retrieve the records. (This option is included for backward compatibility with certain OLE DB drivers only. It is not supported by the SQL Server Data provider, and it won't perform as well as a carefully targeted query.)

For example, here's how you would create a Command object that represents a query:

```
SqlCommand cmd = new SqlCommand();
cmd.Connection = con;
cmd.CommandType = CommandType.Text;
cmd.CommandText = "SELECT * FROM Employees";
```

And here's a more efficient way using one of the Command constructors. Note that you don't need to specify the CommandType, because CommandType.Text is the default.

```
SqlCommand cmd = new SqlCommand("SELECT * FROM Employees", con);
```

Alternatively, to use a stored procedure you would use code like this:

```
SqlCommand cmd = new SqlCommand("GetEmployees", con);
cmd.CommandType = CommandType.StoredProcedure;
```

These examples simply define a command object; they don't actually execute it. The Command object provides three methods that you can use to perform the command, depending on whether you want to retrieve a full result set, a single value, or just execute a nonquery command. These methods are listed in Table 8-5.

Table 8-5. *Command Methods*

Method	Description
ExecuteNonQuery()	Executes non-SELECT commands, such as SQL commands that insert, delete, or update records. The returned value indicates the number of rows affected by the command.
ExecuteScalar()	Executes a SELECT query and returns the value of the first field of the first row from the rowset generated by the command. This method is usually used when executing an aggregate SELECT command that uses functions such as COUNT() or SUM() to calculate a single value.
ExecuteReader()	Executes a SELECT query and returns a DataReader object that wraps a read-only forward-only cursor.

The DataReader Class

A DataReader allows you to read the data returned by a SELECT command one record at a time, in a forward-only, read-only stream. This is sometimes called a *firehose cursor*. Using a DataReader is the simplest way to get to your data, but it lacks the sorting and relational abilities of the disconnected DataSet described in the next chapter. However, the DataReader provides the quickest possible no-nonsense access to data.

Table 8-6 lists the core methods of the DataReader.

Table 8-6. *DataReader Methods*

Method	Description
Read()	Advances the row cursor to the next row in the stream. This method must also be called before reading the first row of data. (When the DataReader is first created, the row cursor is positioned just before the first row.) The Read() method returns true if there's another row to be read, or false if it's on the last row.
GetValue()	Returns the value stored in the field with the specified column name or index, within the currently selected row. The type of the returned value is the closest .NET match to the native value stored in the data source. If you access the field by index and pass an invalid index that refers to a nonexistent field, you will get an IndexOutOfRangeException exception. You can also access the same value by name, which is slightly less efficient because the DataReader must perform a lookup to find the column with the specified name.
GetValues()	Saves the values of the current row into an array. The number of fields that are saved depends on the size of the array you pass to this method. You can use the DataReader.FieldCount property to determine the number of fields in a row, and you can use that information to create an array of the right size if you want to save all the fields.
GetInt32(), GetChar(), GetDateTime(), GetXxx()	These methods return the value of the field with the specified index in the current row, with the data type specified in the method name. Note that if you try to assign the returned value to a variable of the wrong type, you'll get an InvalidCastException exception.
NextResult()	If the command that generated the DataReader returned more than one rowset, this method moves the pointer to the next rowset (just before the first row).
Close()	Closes the reader. If the originator command ran a stored procedure that returned an output value, that value can only be read from the respective parameter after the reader has been closed.

The ExecuteReader() Method and the DataReader

The following example creates a simple query command to return all the records from the Employees table in the Northwind database. The command is created when the page is loaded:

```
private void Page_Load(object sender, System.EventArgs e)
{
    // Create the Command and the Connection.
```

```
string connectionString = "Data Source=localhost; " +
   "Initial Catalog=Northwind;Integrated Security=SSPI";
SqlConnection con = new SqlConnection(connectionString);
string sql = "SELECT * FROM Employees";
SqlCommand cmd = new SqlCommand(sql, con);
...
```

■Note This SELECT query uses the * wildcard to retrieve all the fields, but in real-world code you should only retrieve the fields you really need in order to avoid consuming time to retrieve data that you'll never use. It's also a good idea to limit the records returned with a WHERE clause if you don't need all the records.

The connection is then opened, and the command is executed through the ExecuteReader() method, which returns a SqlDataReader, as follows:

```
...
// Open the Connection and get the DataReader.
con.Open();
SqlDataReader reader = cmd.ExecuteReader();
...
```

Once you have the DataReader you can cycle through its records by calling the Read() method in a while loop. This moves the row cursor to the next record (which, for the first call, means to the first record). The Read() method also returns a Boolean value indicating whether there are more rows to read. In the following example the loop continues until Read() returns false, at which point the loop ends gracefully.

The information for each record is then joined into a single large string. In order to ensure that these string manipulations performed quickly, a StringBuilder (from the System.Text namespace) is used instead of ordinary string objects.

```
...
// Cycle through the records, and build the HTML string.
StringBuilder htmlStr = new StringBuilder("");
while (reader.Read())
{
    htmlStr.Append("<li>");
    htmlStr.Append(reader["TitleOfCourtesy"]);
    htmlStr.Append(" <b>");
    htmlStr.Append(reader.GetString(1));
    htmlStr.Append("</b>, ");
    htmlStr.Append(reader.GetString(2));
    htmlStr.Append(" - employee from ");
    htmlStr.Append(reader.GetDateTime(6).ToString("d"));
    htmlStr.Append("</li>");
}
...
```

This code reads the value of the TitleOfCourtesy field by accessing the field by name through the Item indexer. Because the Item property is the default indexer, you don't need to explicitly include the Item property name when you retrieve a field value. Next, the code reads the LastName, and FirstName fields by calling GetString() with the field index (1 and 2 in this case). Finally, the code accesses the HireDate field by calling GetDateTime() with a field index of 6. All of these approaches are equivalent and included to show the supported variation.

Note In this example, the StringBuilder ensures a dramatic increase in performance. If you use the + operator to concatenate strings instead, this operation would destroy and create a new string object every time. This operation is noticeably slower, especially for large strings. The StringBuilder object avoids this problem by allocating a buffer of memory for characters.

The final step is to close the reader and the connection, and show the generated text in a server control:

```
...
reader.Close();
con.Close();
HtmlContent.Text = htmlStr.ToString();
}
```

If you run the page, you'll see the output shown in Figure 8-3.

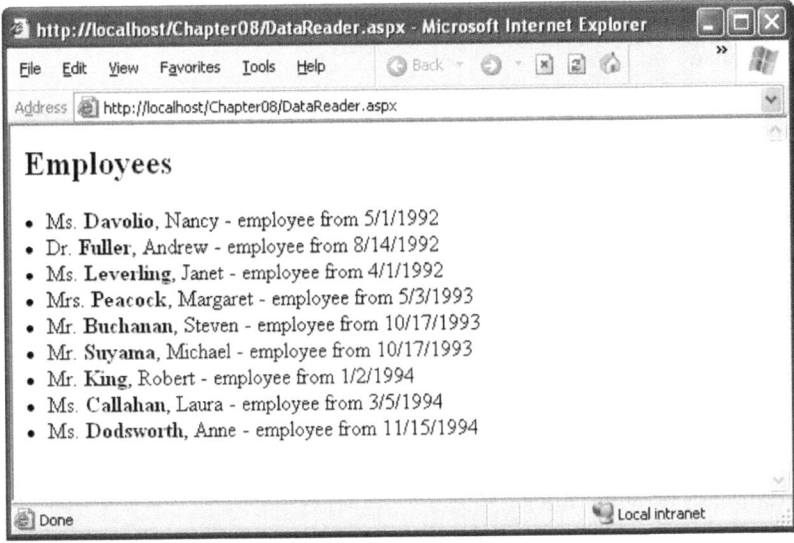

Figure 8-3. *Retrieving results with a DataReader*

CommandBehavior

The ExecuteReader() method has an overloaded version that takes one of the values from the CommandBehavior enumeration as a parameter. One useful value is CommandBehavior.CloseConnection. When you pass this value to the ExecuteReader() method, the DataReader will close the associated connection as soon as you close the DataReader.

Using this technique, you could rewrite the code as follows:

```
SqlDataReader reader = cmd.ExecuteReader(CommandBehavior.CloseConnection);

// (Build the HTML string here.)

// No need to close the connection. You can simply close the reader.
reader.Close();
HtmlContent.Text = htmlStr.ToString();
```

This behavior is particularly useful if you retrieve a DataReader in one method and need to pass it to another method to process it. If you use the CommandBehavior.CloseConnection value, the connection will be automatically closed as soon as the second method closes the reader.

Another possible value is CommandBehavior.SingleRow, which can improve the performance of the query execution when you're retrieving only a single row. For example, if you are retrieving a single record using its unique primary key field (CustomerID, ProductID, and so on), you can use this optimization. You can also use Command.Behavior.SequentialAccess to read part of a binary field at a time, which reduces the memory overhead for large binary fields. You'll see this technique at work in Chapter 11.

The other values are less frequently used, and aren't covered here. You can refer to the .NET documentation for a full list.

Processing Multiple Result Sets

The command you execute doesn't have to return a single result set. Instead, it can execute more than one query, and return more than one result set as part of the same command. This is useful if you need to retrieve a large amount of related data, such as a list of products and product categories which, taken together, represent a product catalog.

There are two ways that a command can return more than one result set:

- If you're calling a stored procedure, it may use multiple SELECT statements.

- If you're using a straight text command, you may be able to batch multiple commands by separating commands with a semicolon (;). Not all providers support this technique, but the SQL Server database provider does.

Here's an example of a string that defines a batch of three select statements:

```
string sql = @"SELECT TOP 5 * FROM Employees;" +
  "SELECT TOP 5 * FROM Customers;SELECT TOP 5 * FROM Suppliers";
```

This string contains three queries. Together, they return the first five records from the Employees table, the first five from the Customers table, and the first five from the Suppliers table.

Processing these results is fairly straightforward. Initially, the DataReader will provide access to the results from the Employees table. Once you've finished using the Read() method to read all these records, you can call NextResult() to the next result set. When there are no more result sets, this method returns false.

You can even cycle through all the available result sets with a while loop, although in this case you must be careful not to call NextResult() until you finish reading the first result set.

Here's an example:

```
// Cycle through the records and all the rowsets,
// and build the HTML string.
StringBuilder htmlStr = new StringBuilder("");
int i = 0;
do
{
    htmlStr.Append("<h2>Rowset: ");
    htmlStr.Append(i.ToString());
    htmlStr.Append("</h2>");

    while (reader.Read())
    {
        htmlStr.Append("<li>");
        // Get all the fields in this row.
        for (int field = 0; field < reader.FieldCount; field++)
        {
            htmlStr.Append(reader.GetName(field).ToString());
            htmlStr.Append(": ");
            htmlStr.Append(reader.GetValue(field).ToString());
            htmlStr.Append("   ");
        }
        htmlStr.Append("</li>");
    }
    htmlStr.Append("<br><br>");
    i++;
} while (reader.NextResult());

// Close the DataReader and the Connection.
reader.Close();
con.Close();

// Show the generated HTML code on the page.
HtmlContent.Text = htmlStr.ToString();
```

Note that in this case all the fields are accessed using the generic GetValue() method, which takes the index of the field to read. That's because the code is designed generically to read all the fields of all the returned result sets, no matter what query you use. However, in a realistic database application, you would almost certainly know which tables to expect as well as the corresponding table and field names.

Figure 8-4 shows the page output.

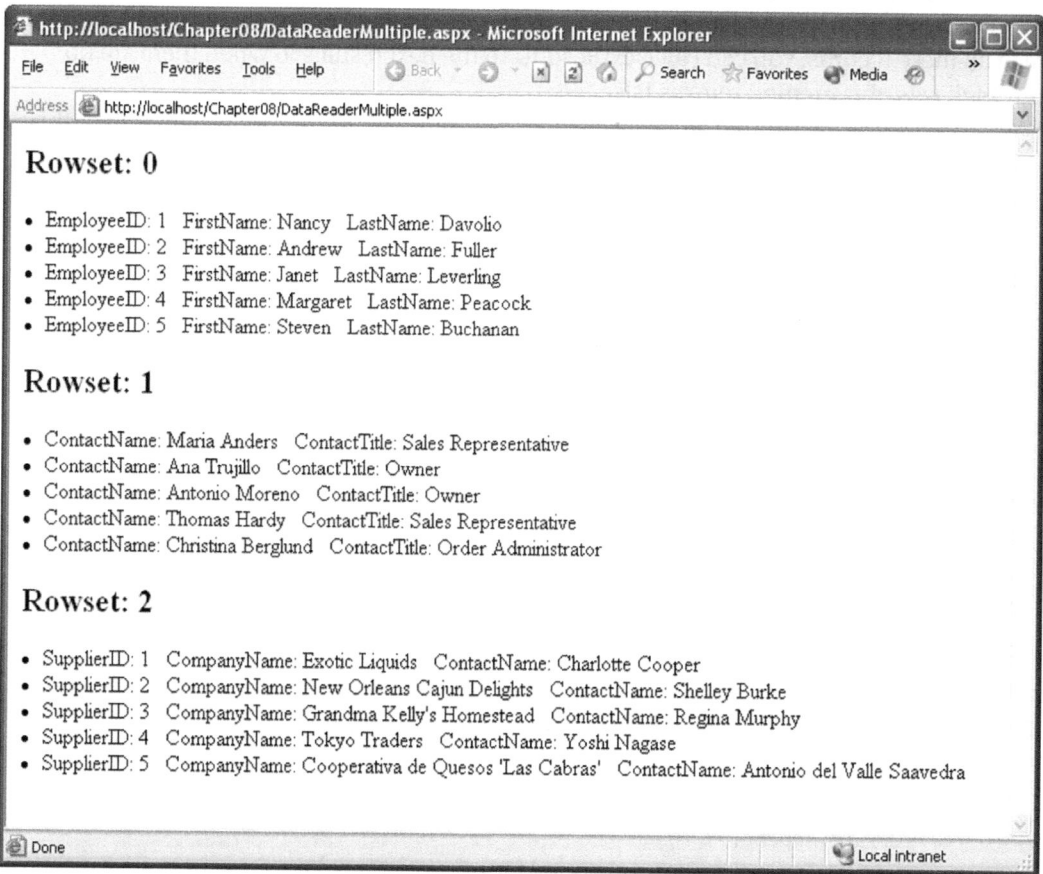

Figure 8-4. *Retrieving multiple result sets*

You don't always need to go to the work of stepping through each record. If you're willing to show the data exactly as it is, with no extra processing or formatting, you can bind the DataReader to the DataGrid control in a single line. Here's the code you would use:

```
// Specify the data source.
DataGrid1.DataSource = reader;

// Fill the DataGrid with all the records in the DataReader.
DataGrid1.DataBind();
```

You'll learn much more about data binding and how to customize it in later chapters.

The ExecuteScalar() Method

The ExecuteScalar() method returns the value stored in the first field of the first row of a result set generated by the command's SELECT query. This method is usually used to execute a query that only retrieves a single field, perhaps calculated by a SQL aggregate function such as COUNT() or SUM().

The following procedure shows how you can get (and write on the page) the number of records in the Employees table with this approach:

```
string connectionString = "Data Source=localhost; " +
  "Initial Catalog=Northwind;Integrated Security=SSPI";
SqlConnection con = new SqlConnection(connectionString);
string sql = " SELECT COUNT(*) FROM Employees ";
SqlCommand cmd = new SqlCommand(sql, con);

// Open the Connection and get the COUNT(*) value.
con.Open();
int numEmployees = (int)cmd.ExecuteScalar();
con.Close();

// Display the information.
HtmlContent.Text += "<br>Total employees: <b>" +
  numEmployees.ToString() + "</b><br>";
```

The code is fairly straightforward, but it's worth noting that you must cast the returned value to the proper type because ExecuteScalar() returns an object.

The ExecuteNonQuery() Method

The ExecuteNonQuery() method is used to execute commands that don't return a result set, such as INSERT, DELETE, and UPDATE. The ExecuteNonQuery() method returns a single piece of information—the number of affected records.

Here's an example that uses a DELETE command by dynamically building an SQL string:

```
SqlConnection con = new SqlConnection(connectionString);
string sql = "DELETE FROM Employees WHERE EmployeeID = " + empID.ToString();
SqlCommand cmd = new SqlCommand(sql, con);

try
{
    con.Open();
    int numAff = cmd.ExecuteNonQuery();
    HtmlContent.Text += string.Format("<br>Deleted <b>{0}</b> record(s)<br>",
      numAff);
}
catch (SqlException exc)
{
    HtmlContent.Text += string.Format("<b>Error:</b> {0}<br><br>", exc.Message);
}
finally
{
    con.Close();
}
```

SQL Injection Attacks

So far, all the examples you've seen have used hard-coded values. That makes the examples simple, straightforward, and relatively secure. It also means they aren't that realistic, and they don't demonstrate one of the most serious risks for web applications that interact with a database—*SQL injection attacks.*

In simple terms, SQL injection is the process of passing SQL code into an application, in a way that was not intended or anticipated by the application developer. This may be possible due to the poor design of the application, and it only affects applications that use SQL string building techniques to create a command using user-supplied values.

Consider the example shown in Figure 8-5. In this example, the user enters a customer ID, and the DataGrid shows all the rows for that customer. In a more realistic example the user would also need to supply some sort of authentication information like a password. Or, the user ID might be based on a previous login screen, and the text box would allow the user to supply additional criteria like a date range or the name of a product in the order.

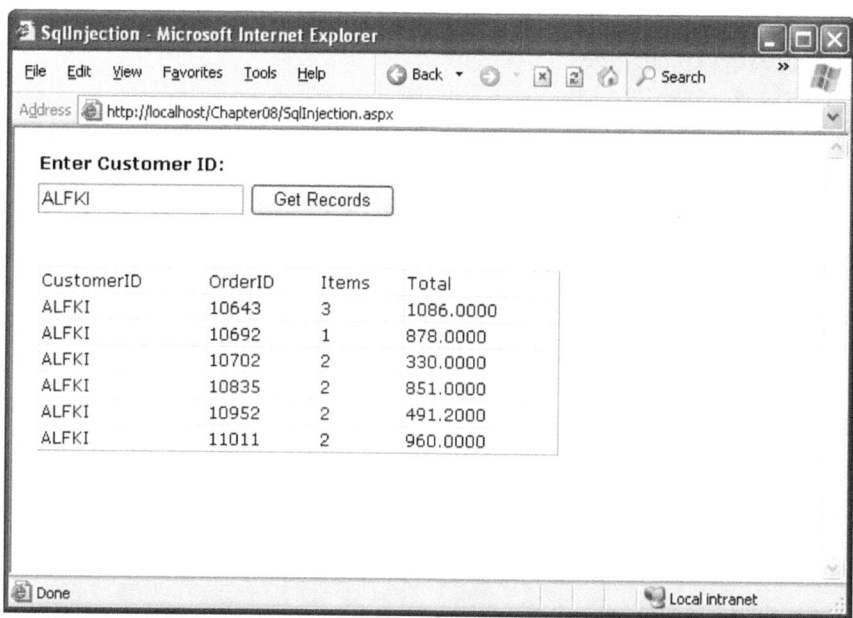

Figure 8-5. *Retrieving orders for a single customer*

The problem is how this command is executed. In this example, the SQL statement is built dynamically using string building technique. The value from the txtID text box is simply pasted into the middle of the string. Here's the code:

```
string connectionString = "Data Source=localhost;Initial Catalog=Northwind;" +
  "Integrated Security=SSPI";
SqlConnection con = new SqlConnection(connectionString);
string sql =
  "SELECT Orders.CustomerID, Orders.OrderID, COUNT(UnitPrice) AS Items, " +
  "SUM(UnitPrice * Quantity) AS Total FROM Orders " +
```

```
    "INNER JOIN [Order Details] " +
    "ON Orders.OrderID = [Order Details].OrderID " +
    "WHERE Orders.CustomerID = '" + txtID.Text + "' " +
    "GROUP BY Orders.OrderID, Orders.CustomerID";
SqlCommand cmd = new SqlCommand(sql, con);

con.Open();
SqlDataReader reader = cmd.ExecuteReader();
DataGrid1.DataSource = reader;
DataGrid1.DataBind();
reader.Close();
con.Close();
```

In this example, a user might try to tamper with the SQL statement. Often, the first goal of such an attack is to receive an error message. If the error isn't handled properly and the low-level information is exposed to the attacker, that information can be used to launch a more sophisticated attack.

For example, imagine what happens if the user enters the following text into the text box:

```
ALFKI' OR '1'='1
```

Now consider the complete SQL statement that this creates:

```
SELECT Orders.CustomerID, Orders.OrderID, COUNT(UnitPrice) AS Items,
    SUM(UnitPrice * Quantity) AS Total FROM Orders
    INNER JOIN [Order Details]
    ON Orders.OrderID = [Order Details].OrderID
    WHERE Orders.CustomerID = 'ALFKI' OR '1'='1'
    GROUP BY Orders.OrderID, Orders.CustomerID
```

This statement returns all the order records. Even if the order wasn't created by ALFKI, it's still true that 1=1 for every row. The result is that instead of seeing the specific information related to the current Customer ID, all the information is exposed to the attacker, as shown in Figure 8-6. If the information shown on the screen is very sensitive, such as social security numbers, date of birth, or credit card information, this could be an enormous problem! In fact, simple SQL injection attacks exactly like this are often the source of problems that affect major e-commerce companies. Often, the vulnerability doesn't occur in a text box, but appears in the query string (which can be used to pass a database value like a unique ID from a list page to a details page).

More sophisticated attacks are possible. For example, the malicious user could simply comment out the rest of your SQL statement by adding two hyphens (--). This attack is specific to SQL Server, but equivalent exploits are possible in MySQL with the hash (#) symbol and Oracle with the semicolon (;). Or the attacker could use a batch command to execute an arbitrary SQL command. With the SQL Server provider, the attacker simply needs to supply a semicolon followed by a new command. This exploit allows the user to delete the contents of another table, or even use the SQL Server xp_cmdshell system stored procedure to execute an arbitrary program at the command line.

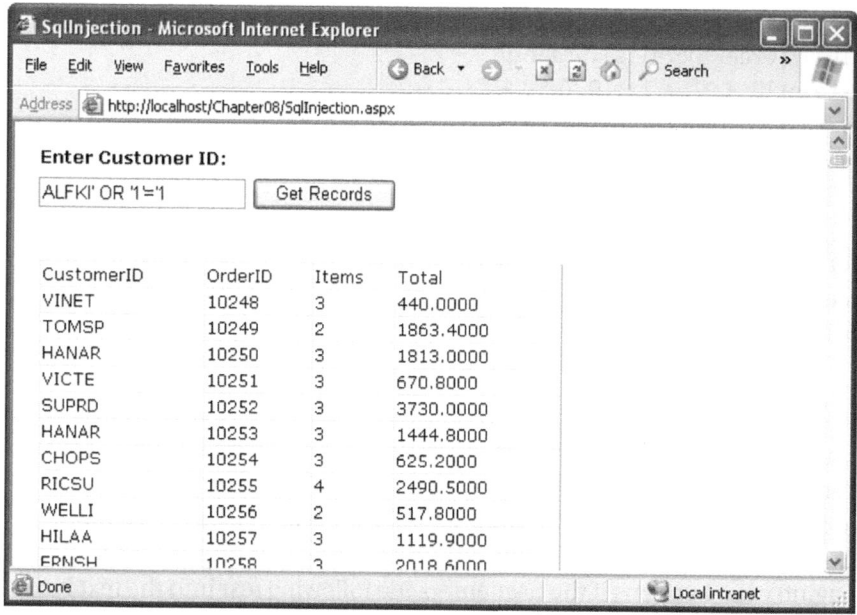

Figure 8-6. *A SQL injection attack that shows all rows*

Here's what the user would need to enter in the text box for a more sophisticated SQL injection attack to delete all the rows in the Customers table:

```
ALFKI'; DELETE * FROM Customers--
```

So how can you defend against SQL injection attacks? There are a few good guidelines to keep in mind. First, it's a good idea to use the TextBox.MaxLength property to prevent overly long entries if they aren't needed. That reduces the chance of a large block of script being pasted in where it doesn't belong. In addition, you should restrict the information given by error messages. If you catch a database exception, you should only report a generic message like "Data source error" rather than display the information in the Exception.Message property, which may indicate system vulnerabilities.

More importantly, you should take care to remove special characters. For example, you can convert all single quotation marks to two quotation marks, thereby ensuring that they won't be confused with the delimiters in your SQL statement:

```
string ID = txtID.Text().Replace("'", "''");
```

Of course, this introduces headaches if your text values really should contain apostrophes. It also suffers from the fact that some SQL injection attacks are still possible. Replacing apostrophes prevents a malicious user from closing a string value prematurely. However, if you're building a dynamic SQL statement that includes numeric values, an SQL injection attack just needs a single space. This vulnerability is often (and dangerously) ignored.

An even better approach is to use a parameterized command or a stored procedure, which performs its own escaping and is impervious to SQL injection attacks. These techniques are described in the following sections.

> **Tip** Another good idea is to restrict the permissions of the account used to access the database so that it doesn't have the right to access other databases or execute extended system stored procedures. However, this can't remove the problem of SQL script injection, because the process you use to connect to the database will almost always require a broader set of privileges than the ones you would allocate to any single user. By restricting the account, you could prevent an attack that deletes a table, for example, but you probably can't prevent an attack that steals someone else's information.

Using Parameterized Commands

A parameterized command is simply a command that uses placeholders in the SQL text. The placeholders indicate dynamically supplied values, which are then sent through the Parameters collection of the Command object.

For example, this SQL statement:

```
SELECT * FROM Customers WHERE CustomerID = 'ALFKI'
```

would become something like this:

```
SELECT * FROM Customers WHERE CustomerID = @CustID
```

The placeholders are then added separately and automatically encoded.

The syntax for using parameterized commands differs slightly for different providers. With the SQL Server provider, parameterized commands used named placeholders (with unique names). With the OLE DB provider, each hard-coded value is replaced with a question mark. In either case, you need to supply a Parameter object for each parameter, which you insert the Command.Parameters collection. With the OLE DB provider, you must make sure that you add the parameters in the same order that they appear in the SQL string. This isn't a requirement with the SQL Server provider, because the parameters are matched to the placeholders based on their name.

The following example rewrites the query to remove the possibility of an SQL injection attack:

```
string connectionString = "Data Source=localhost;Initial Catalog=Northwind;" +
  "Integrated Security=SSPI";
SqlConnection con = new SqlConnection(connectionString);
string sql =
  "SELECT Orders.CustomerID, Orders.OrderID, COUNT(UnitPrice) AS Items, " +
  "SUM(UnitPrice * Quantity) AS Total FROM Orders " +
  "INNER JOIN [Order Details] " +
  "ON Orders.OrderID = [Order Details].OrderID " +
  "WHERE Orders.CustomerID = @CustID " +
  "GROUP BY Orders.OrderID, Orders.CustomerID";
SqlCommand cmd = new SqlCommand(sql, con);
cmd.Parameters.Add("@CustID", txtID.Text);

con.Open();
SqlDataReader reader = cmd.ExecuteReader();
```

```
DataGrid1.DataSource = reader;
DataGrid1.DataBind();
reader.Close();
con.Close();
```

If you try to perform the SQL injection attack against this revised version of the page, you'll find it returns no records. That's because there are no order items that contain a customer ID value that equals the text string ALFKI' OR '1'='1. This is exactly the behavior you want.

Calling Stored Procedures

Parameterized commands are just a short step from commands that call full-fledged stored procedures.

A stored procedure, of course, is a batch of one or more SQL statements that are stored in the database. Stored procedures are similar to functions in that they are well-encapsulated blocks of logic that can accept data (through input parameter) and return data (through result sets and output parameters). Stored procedures have a great many benefits, as follows:

- **They are easier to maintain.** For example, you can optimize the commands in a stored procedure without recompiling the application that uses it.

- **They allow you to implement more secure database usage.** For example, you can allow the Windows account that runs your ASP.NET code to use certain stored procedures, but restrict access to the underlying tables.

- **They can improve performance.** Because a stored procedure batches together multiple statements, you can get a lot of work done with just one trip to the database server. If your database is on another computer, this reduces the total time to perform a complex task dramatically.

Note SQL Server version 7 and later precompile all SQL commands, including off-the-cuff SQL statements. That means you gain the benefit of compilation regardless of whether you are using stored procedures or not. However, stored procedures still tend to increase the performance benefits, because they limit the variation in SQL statements, thereby ensuring that a single compiled execution plan can be reused more often and more effectively. Also, because the database code is contained in the database, not the client, it's easier for a database administrator to fine-tune indexes and locks, and employ other optimization strategies.

Here's the SQL code needed to create a stored procedure for inserting a single record into the Employees table. This stored procedure isn't in the Northwind database initially, so you'll need to add it into the database (using a tool like Enterprise Manager or Query Analyzer) before you use it.

```
CREATE PROCEDURE InsertEmployee
@TitleOfCourtesy varchar(25),
@LastName       varchar(20),
```

```
@FirstName        varchar(10),
@EmployeeID       int OUTPUT
AS

INSERT INTO Employees
  (TitleOfCourtesy, LastName, FirstName, HireDate)
  VALUES (@TitleOfCourtesy, @LastName, @FirstName, GETDATE());

SET @EmployeeID = @@IDENTITY
GO
```

This stored procedure takes in three parameters for the employee's title of courtesy, last name, and first name. It returns the ID of the new record through the output parameter called @EmployeeID, which is retrieved after the INSERT statement using the @@IDENTITY function. This is one example of a simple task that a stored procedure can make much easier. Without using a stored procedure, it's quite awkward to try to determine the automatically generated identity value of a new record you've just inserted.

Next, you can create a SqlCommand to wrap the call to the stored procedure. This command takes the same three parameters as inputs, and uses @@IDENTITY to get and then return the ID of the new record. Here is the first step, which creates the required objects and sets the InsertEmployee as the command text:

```
string connectionString = "Data Source=localhost;Initial Catalog=Northwind;" +
  "Integrated Security=SSPI";
SqlConnection con = new SqlConnection(connectionString);

// Create the command for the InsertEmployee stored procedure.
SqlCommand cmd = new SqlCommand("InsertEmployee", con);
cmd.CommandType = CommandType.StoredProcedure;
```

Now you need to add the stored procedure's parameters to the Command.Parameters collection. When you do, you need to specify the exact data type and length of the parameter, so that it matches the details in the database.

Here's how it works for a single parameter:

```
cmd.Parameters.Add(new SqlParameter("@TitleOfCourtesy", SqlDbType.NVarChar, 25));
cmd.Parameters["@TitleOfCourtesy"].Value = title;
```

The first line creates a new SqlParameter object, sets its name, type, and size in the constructor, and adds it to the Parameters collection. The second line assigns the value for the parameter, which will be sent to the stored procedure when you execute the command.

Note Some providers include an overload to the Parameter.Add() method that allows you to create a parameter object without specifying the data type. However, this approach usually requires some degree of *reflection*, which means the data provider must query the data source to find out the parameter details. The best-performing approach is to specify the data type details in full, even though they make for tedious code.

Now you can add the next two parameters in a similar way:

```
cmd.Parameters.Add(new SqlParameter("@LastName", SqlDbType.NVarChar, 20));
cmd.Parameters["@LastName"].Value = lastName;
cmd.Parameters.Add(new SqlParameter("@FirstName", SqlDbType.NVarChar, 10));
cmd.Parameters["@FirstName"].Value = firstName;
```

The last parameter is an output parameter, which allows the stored procedure to return information to your code. Although this Parameter object is created in the same way, you must make sure that you specify it is an output parameter by setting its Direction property to Output. You don't need to supply a value.

```
cmd.Parameters.Add(new SqlParameter("@EmployeeID", SqlDbType.Int, 4));
cmd.Parameters["@EmployeeID"].Direction = ParameterDirection.Output;
```

Finally, you can open the connection and execute the command with the ExecuteNonQuery() method. When the command is completed, you can read the output value, as shown here:

```
con.Open();
try
{
    int numAff = cmd.ExecuteNonQuery();
    HtmlContent.Text += String.Format(
      "Inserted <b>{0}</b> record(s)<br>", numAff);

    // Get the newly generated ID.
    empID = (int)cmd.Parameters["@EmployeeID"].Value;
    HtmlContent.Text += "New ID: " + empID.ToString();
}
finally
{
    con.Close();
}
```

The next section demonstrates this code with a small but fully functional database component.

A Database Component

In professional applications, database code is not embedded directly in the client, but encapsulated in a dedicated class. To perform a database operation, the client creates an instance of this class, and calls the appropriate method.

When creating a data class, you should follow the basic guidelines listed in this section. This will ensure that you create a well-encapsulated, optimized database component that can be executed in a separate process if needed, and even used in a load-balancing configuration with multiple servers.

- Open the database connection in every method call, and close it before the method ends. Connections should never be held open between client requests, and the client should have no control over how connections are acquired or when they are released. If the client does have this ability, it introduces the possibility that a connection might not be closed as quickly as possible, or might be inadvertently left open, which hampers scalability.

- Use error handling to make sure the connection is closed even if the SQL command generates an exception. Remember, connections are a finite resource, and using them for even a few extra seconds can have a major overall effect on performance.

- Follow stateless design practices: accept all the information needed for a method in its parameters, and return all the retrieved data through the return value. If you create a class that maintains state, it cannot be easily implemented as a web service or used in a load-balancing scenario. Also, if the database component is hosted out of process, each method call has a measurable overhead, and using multiple calls to set properties will take much longer than invoking a single method with all the information as parameters.

- Don't let the client specify connection string information. This poses security risks, raises the possibility that an out-of-date client will fail, and compromises the ability of connection pooling, which requires matching connection strings.

- Don't connect with the client's user ID. Introducing any variability into the connection string will thwart connection pooling, as you'll learn later in this chapter. Instead, rely on role-based security or a ticket-based system whereby you authenticate the user and prevent his from attempting to perform a restricted operation. This model is also faster than trying to perform a database query under an invalid security account, and waiting for an error.

- Don't let the client use wide-open queries. Every query should judiciously select only the columns it needs. Also, you should restrict the results with a WHERE clause whenever possible. For example, when retrieving order records you might impose a minimum date range (or an SQL clause like TOP 1000). Without these safeguards, your application may work well at first, but will slow down as the database grows and clients perform large queries, which can tax both the database and the network.

For examples of good custom data classes, refer to Microsoft's platform samples, including the ASP.NET E-commerce Starter Kit (downloadable at www.asp.net, select the Starter Kits tab). The design is actually quite simple. A separate class is used for every database table, and the common database access methods like inserting, deleting, and modifying a record are all wrapped in separate stateless methods. Every database call uses a dedicated stored procedure. Figure 8-7 shows this carefully layered design.

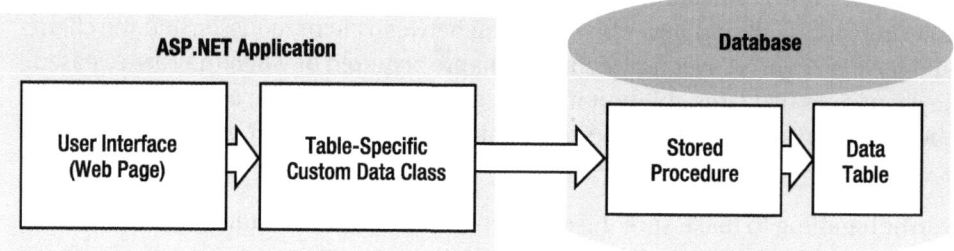

Figure 8-7. *Layered design with a database class*

A Sample Database Component

The following example demonstrates a simple database component. Rather than placing the database code in the web page, it follows a much better design practice of separating the code into a distinct class that can be used in multiple pages. This class can then be compiled as part of a separate component if needed. Additionally, the connection string is retrieved from the <appSettings> section of the web.config file, rather than being hard-coded.

The data component actually consists of two classes—a data package class that wraps a single record of information, and a database utility class that performs the actual database operations with ADO.NET code.

The Data Package

In order to make it easier to shuffle information to the Northwind database and back, it makes sense to create an EmployeeDetails class that provides all the fields as public properties. Here's the full code for this class:

```
public class EmployeeDetails
{
    private int employeeID;
    public int EmployeeID
    {
        get {return employeeID;}
        set {employeeID = value;}
    }

    private string firstName;
    public string FirstName
    {
        get {return firstName;}
        set {firstName = value;}
    }

    private string lastName;
    public string LastName
    {
```

```
        get {return lastName;}
        set {lastName = value;}
    }

    private string titleOfCourtesy;
    public string TitleOfCourtesy
    {
        get {return titleOfCourtesy;}
        set {titleOfCourtesy = value;}
    }

    public EmployeeDetails(int employeeID, string firstName, string lastName,
        string titleOfCourtesy)
    {
        this.employeeID = employeeID;
        this.firstName = firstName;
        this.lastName = lastName;
        this.titleOfCourtesy = titleOfCourtesy;
    }
}
```

Note that this class doesn't include all the information that's in the Employees table, in order to make the example more concise.

The Stored Procedures

Before you can start coding the data access logic, you need to make sure you have the set of stored procedures that you need to retrieve, insert, and update information. The following code listing shows the five stored procedures that are needed:

```
CREATE PROCEDURE InsertEmployee
@EmployeeID      int OUTPUT
@FirstName       varchar(10),
@LastName        varchar(20),
@TitleOfCourtesy varchar(25),
AS
INSERT INTO Employees
  (TitleOfCourtesy, LastName, FirstName, HireDate)
  VALUES (@TitleOfCourtesy, @LastName, @FirstName, GETDATE());
SET @EmployeeID = @@IDENTITY
GO

CREATE PROCEDURE DeleteEmployee
@EmployeeID      int
AS
DELETE FROM Employees WHERE EmployeeID = @EmployeeID
GO
```

```
CREATE PROCEDURE GetAllEmployees
AS
SELECT EmployeeID, FirstName, LastName, TitleOfCourtesy FROM Employees
GO


CREATE PROCEDURE CountEmployees
AS
SELECT COUNT(EmployeeID) FROM Employees
GO


CREATE PROCEDURE GetEmployee
@EmployeeID        int
AS
SELECT FirstName, LastName, TitleOfCourtesy FROM Employees
  WHERE EmployeeID = @EmployeeID
GO
```

The Data Utility Class

Finally, you need the utility class that performs the actual database operations. This class uses the stored procedures that were shown in the previous section.

In this example, the data utility class is named EmployeeDB. It encapsulates all the data access code and database-specific details. Here's the basic outline:

```csharp
public class EmployeeDB
{
    private string connectionString;
    public EmployeeDB()
    {
        // Get connection string from web.config.
        connectionString = ConfigurationSettings.AppSettings["ConnectionString"];
    }

    public int InsertEmployee(EmployeeDetails emp)
    { ... }
    public void DeleteEmployee(int employeeID)
    { ... }
    public EmployeeDetails GetEmployee()
    { ... }
    public EmployeeDetails[] GetEmployees()
    { ... }
    public int CountEmployees()
    { ... }
}
```

Note You may have noticed that the EmployeeDB class uses instance methods, not static methods. That's because even though the EmployeeDB class doesn't store any state from the database, it does store the connection string as a private member variable. Because this is an instance class, the connection string can be retrieved every time the class is created, rather than every time a method is invoked. This method makes the code a little clearer, and allows it to be slightly faster. However, the benefit is fairly small, so you can use static methods just as easily in your database components.

Each method uses the same careful approach, relying exclusively on a stored procedure to interact with the database. Here's the code for inserting a record:

```
public int InsertEmployee(EmployeeDetails emp)
{
    SqlConnection con = new SqlConnection(connectionString);
    SqlCommand cmd = new SqlCommand("InsertEmployee", con);
    cmd.CommandType = CommandType.StoredProcedure;
    cmd.Parameters.Add(new SqlParameter("@FirstName", SqlDbType.NVarChar, 10));
    cmd.Parameters["@FirstName"].Value = emp.FirstName;
    cmd.Parameters.Add(new SqlParameter("@LastName", SqlDbType.NVarChar, 20));
    cmd.Parameters["@LastName"].Value = emp.LastName;
    cmd.Parameters.Add(new SqlParameter("@TitleOfCourtesy",
      SqlDbType.NVarChar, 25));
    cmd.Parameters["@TitleOfCourtesy"].Value = emp.TitleOfCourtesy;
    cmd.Parameters.Add(new SqlParameter("@EmployeeID", SqlDbType.Int, 4));
    cmd.Parameters["@EmployeeID"].Direction = ParameterDirection.Output;

    try
    {
        con.Open();
        cmd.ExecuteNonQuery();
        return (int)cmd.Parameters["@EmployeeID"].Value;
    }
    catch (SqlException err)
    {
        // Replace the error with something less specific.
        // You could also log the error now.
        throw new ApplicationException("Data error.");
    }
    finally
    {
        con.Close();
    }
}
```

As you can see, the method accepts data using the EmployeeDetails package. (Another option would be the disconnected data object discussed in the next chapter.) Any errors are caught and the sensitive internal details are not returned to the web page code. This prevents the web page from providing information that could lead to possible exploits. This would also be an ideal place to call another method in a logging component to report the full information in an event log or another database.

The GetEmployee() and GetEmployees() methods return the data using the EmployeeDetails package. The GetEmployees() method adds EmployeeDetails to a dynamically sized ArrayList collection, which provides a handy Add() method. But to ensure type safety, the final collection is converted to a strongly typed array before it's returned to the caller.

```
public EmployeeDetails GetEmployee(int employeeID)
{
    SqlConnection con = new SqlConnection(connectionString);
    SqlCommand cmd = new SqlCommand("GetEmployee", con);
    cmd.CommandType = CommandType.StoredProcedure;
    cmd.Parameters.Add(new SqlParameter("@EmployeeID", SqlDbType.Int, 4));
    cmd.Parameters["@EmployeeID"].Value = employeeID;

    try
    {
        con.Open();
        SqlDataReader reader = cmd.ExecuteReader(CommandBehavior.SingleRow);

        // Get the first row.
        reader.Read();
        EmployeeDetails emp = new EmployeeDetails(
          (int)reader["EmployeeID"], (string)reader["FirstName"],
          (string)reader["LastName"], (string)reader["TitleOfCourtesy"]);
        reader.Close();
        return emp;
    }
    catch (SqlException err)
    {
        throw new ApplicationException("Data error.");
    }
    finally
    {
        con.Close();
    }
}

public EmployeeDetails[] GetEmployees()
{
    SqlConnection con = new SqlConnection(connectionString);
    SqlCommand cmd = new SqlCommand("GetAllEmployees", con);
    cmd.CommandType = CommandType.StoredProcedure;
```

```
    // Create a collection for all the employee records.
    ArrayList employees = new ArrayList();

    try
    {
        con.Open();
        SqlDataReader reader = cmd.ExecuteReader();
        while (reader.Read())
        {
            EmployeeDetails emp = new EmployeeDetails(
            (int)reader["EmployeeID"], (string)reader["FirstName"],
            (string)reader["LastName"], (string)reader["TitleOfCourtesy"]);
            employees.Add(emp);
        }
        reader.Close();
        return (EmployeeDetails[])employees.ToArray(typeof(EmployeeDetails));
    }
    catch (SqlException err)
    {
        throw new ApplicationException("Data error.");
    }
    finally
    {
        con.Close();
    }
}
```

Finally, the DeleteEmployee() and CountEmployees() methods fill in the last two ingredients:

```
public void DeleteEmployee(int employeeID)
{
    SqlConnection con = new SqlConnection(connectionString);
    SqlCommand cmd = new SqlCommand("DeleteEmployee", con);
    cmd.CommandType = CommandType.StoredProcedure;
    cmd.Parameters.Add(new SqlParameter("@EmployeeID", SqlDbType.Int, 4));
    cmd.Parameters["@EmployeeID"].Value = employeeID;

    try
    {
        con.Open();
        cmd.ExecuteNonQuery();
    }
    catch (SqlException err)
    {
        throw new ApplicationException("Data error.");
```

```
        }
        finally
        {
            con.Close();
        }
    }

    public int CountEmployees()
    {
        SqlConnection con = new SqlConnection(connectionString);
        SqlCommand cmd = new SqlCommand("CountEmployees", con);
        cmd.CommandType = CommandType.StoredProcedure;

        try
        {
            con.Open();
            return (int)cmd.ExecuteScalar();
        }
        catch (SqlException err)
        {
            throw new ApplicationException("Data error.");
        }
        finally
        {
            con.Close();
        }
    }
}
```

Testing the Component

Now it's a simple matter to create a test page to use this database component. As with any other component, you must begin by adding a reference to the component assembly. Then you can import the namespace it uses to make it easier to use the EmployeeDetails and EmployeeDB classes. The only step that remains is to write the code that interacts with the classes. In this example, the code takes place in the Page.Load event handler.

First, the code retrieves and writes the number and the list of employees by using a private WriteEmployeesList() method that translates the details to HTML. Next, the code adds a record and lists the table content again. Finally, the code deletes the added record and shows the content of the Employees table one more time.

Here's the complete page code:

```
public class ComponentTest : System.Web.UI.Page
{
    protected System.Web.UI.WebControls.Literal HtmlContent;
    // (Designer code omitted.)
```

```csharp
    // Create the database component so it's available anywhere on the page.
    private EmployeeDB db = new EmployeeDB();

    private void Page_Load(object sender, System.EventArgs e)
    {
        WriteEmployeesList();

        int empID = db.InsertEmployee(
          new EmployeeDetails(0, "Mr.", "Bellinaso", "Marco"));
          HtmlContent.Text += "<br>Inserted 1 employee.<br>";

        WriteEmployeesList();

        db.DeleteEmployee(empID);
        HtmlContent.Text += "<br>Deleted 1 employee.<br>";

        WriteEmployeesList();
    }

    private void WriteEmployeesList()
    {
        StringBuilder htmlStr = new StringBuilder("");

        int numEmployees = db.CountEmployees();
        htmlStr.Append("<br>Total employees: <b>");
        htmlStr.Append(numEmployees.ToString());
        htmlStr.Append("</b><br><br>");

        EmployeeDetails[] employees = db.GetEmployees();
        foreach (EmployeeDetails emp in employees)
        {
            htmlStr.Append("<li>");
            htmlStr.Append(emp.EmployeeID);
            htmlStr.Append(" ");
            htmlStr.Append(emp.TitleOfCourtesy);
            htmlStr.Append(" <b>");
            htmlStr.Append(emp.FirstName);
            htmlStr.Append("</b>, ");
            htmlStr.Append(emp.LastName);
            htmlStr.Append("</li>");
        }
        htmlStr.Append("<br>");
        HtmlContent.Text += htmlStr.ToString();
    }
}
```

Figure 8-8 shows the page output.

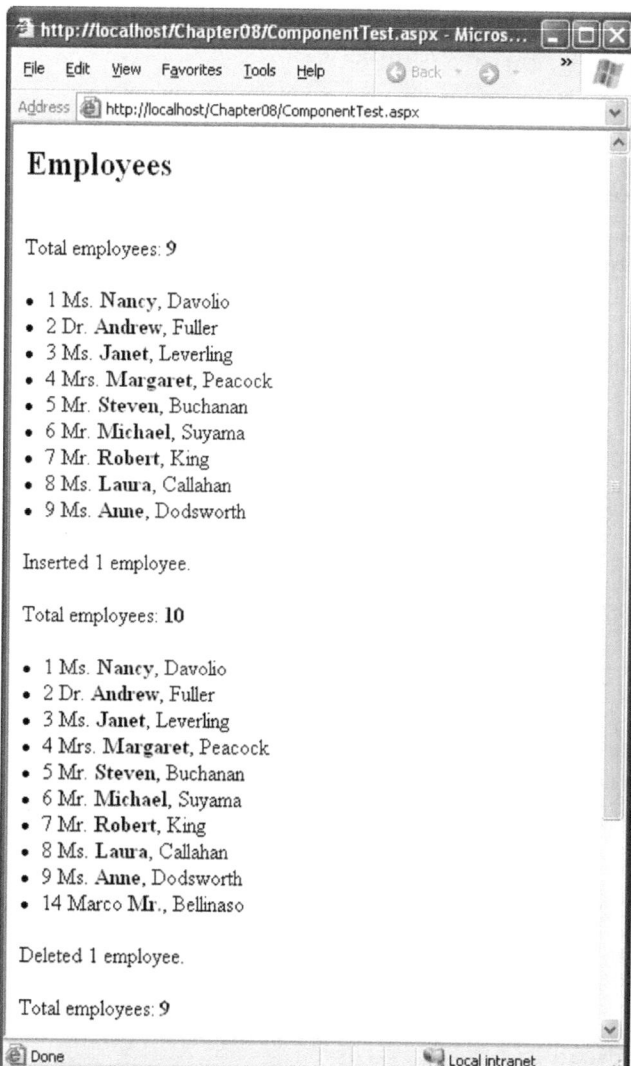

Figure 8-8. *Using a database component*

Summary

In this chapter, you learned about the first level of database access with ADO.NET: connected access. In many cases, using simple commands and quick read-only cursors to retrieve results provides the easiest and most efficient way to write data access code for a web application.

However, there is a whole range of issues that might make you want something more. In the next chapter, you'll learn how the disconnected DataSet gives you more flexibility for navigating your data, binding it to controls, and filtering and sorting it.

CHAPTER 9

■■■

Disconnected Data

In the previous chapter, you had a first look at ADO.NET, and examined connection-based data access. When using this approach, data ceases to have anything to do with the data source the moment it is retrieved. It's up to your code to track user actions, store information, and determine when a new command should be generated and executed.

With *disconnected data*, the information you retrieve is stored in a special container—a DataSet object. The DataSet is more capable than the traditional Recordset of ADO programming (and much more than a glorified array of information). Its key benefit is that it stores a significant amount of schema information, like column constraints, relations, and other details specific to the data source. It also stores the versioning information that's required to track changes. It's largely because of this additional information that you can modify the information in the disconnected DataSet, reconnect, and commit your changes to the data source without having to write individual SQL commands for each operation.

Of course, this convenience isn't without drawbacks, such as concurrency issues. Depending on how your application is designed, an entire batch of changes may be submitted at once. A single error (such as trying to update a record that another user has updated in the meantime) can derail the entire update process. With studious coding you can protect your application from these problems—but it requires additional effort.

On the other hand, there are some additional reasons that you might want to use ADO.NET's disconnected access model and the DataSet. Some of the scenarios in which a DataSet is easier to use than a DataReader include the following:

- When you need a convenient package to send the data to another component (for example, if you're sharing information with other components or distributing it to clients through a web service).

- When you need a convenient file format to serialize the data to disk (the DataSet includes built-in functionality that allows you to save it to an XML file).

- When you want to navigate backward and forward through a large amount of data. For example, you could use a DataSet to support a paged list control that shows a subset of information at time. The DataReader, on the other, can only move in one direction: forward.

- When you want to navigate among several different tables. The DataSet can store all these tables, and information about the relations between them, thereby allowing you to create easy master-detail pages without needing to query the database more than once.

- If you want to use data binding with user interface controls. You can use a DataReader for data binding, but because the DataReader is a forward-only cursor, you can't bind your data to multiple controls. You also won't have the ability to apply custom sorting and filtering criteria, like you can with the DataSet.

- If you want to manipulate the data as XML.

In this chapter, you'll learn about how to retrieve data into a DataSet and use a DataSet to perform updates. You'll also see how to retrieve data from multiple tables and create relationships between these in-memory data tables, how to sort and filter data, and how to search for specific records.

The DataSet Classes

The DataSet is the heart of disconnected data access, and one of the key features of ADO.NET. The DataSet contains two important ingredients: a collection of zero or more tables (exposed through the Tables property), and a collection of zero or more relationships that you can use to link tables together (exposed through the Relationships property). Figure 9-1 shows the basic structure of the DataSet.

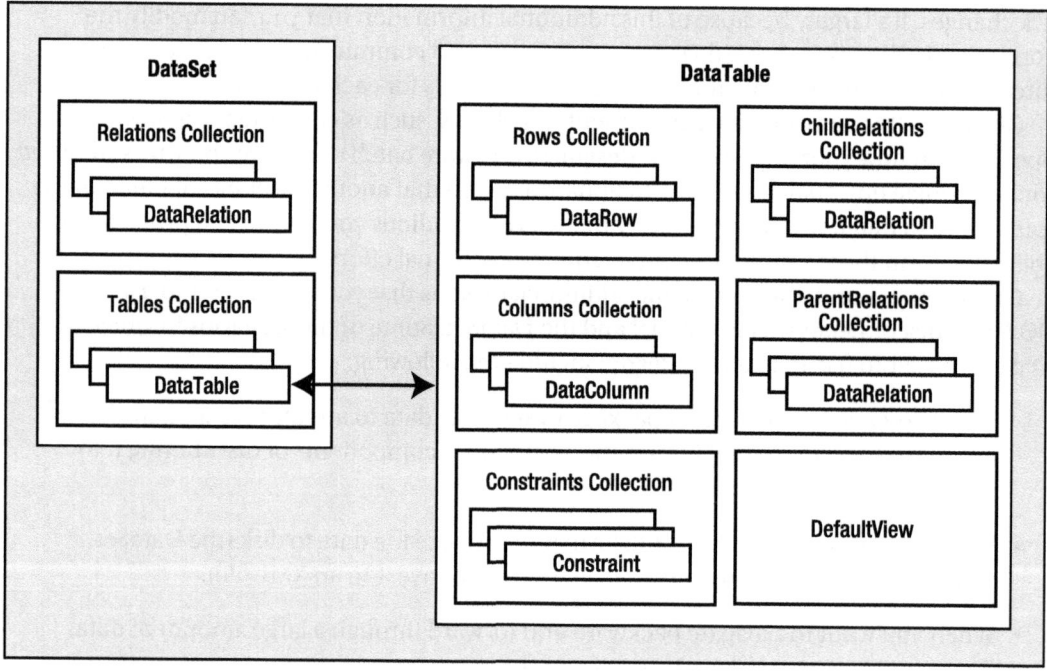

Figure 9-1. *Dissecting the DataSet*

Note Occasionally, novice ADO.NET developers make the mistake of assuming that the DataSet should contain all the information from a given table in the data source. This is not the case. For performance reasons, you will probably use the DataSet to work with a small subset of the total information in the data source. Also, the tables in the DataSet do not need to map directly to tables in the data source. A single table can retrieve include the results of a query on one table, or the results of a JOIN query that combines data from more than one linked table.

As you can see in Figure 9-1, each individual record is represented as a DataRow object. In order to manage disconnected changes, the DataSet tracks versioning information for every DataRow. When you edit the value in a row, the original value is kept in memory, and the row is marked as changed. When you add or delete a row, the row is marked as added or deleted.

Always remember that the data in the data source is not touched at all when you work with the DataSet objects. Instead, all of the changes are made locally to the DataSet in memory. The DataSet never retains any type of connection to a data source. If you want to extract records from a database and use them to fill a table in a DataSet, you need to use another ADO.NET object: a DataAdapter. The DataAdapter also allows you to update the data source according to the changes you make in the DataSet.

Table 9-1 shows the DataSet methods that are used to manage disconnected data.

Table 9-1. *DataSet Version-Tracking Methods*

Method	Description
HasChanges()	Indicates whether the DataSet has rows that have been changed since the DataSet was first loaded or since the last call to AcceptChanges(). An overloaded version of the method allows you to check only for rows with a specified state (only added, deleted, or modified rows).
GetChanges()	Gets a DataSet with tables that contains rows marked as changed, or only the rows with a specified state (added, deleted, or modified). This method is primarily useful if you want to save the DataSet to a file or transmit it to another component, and you only want to store or send information that corresponds to data modifications.
AcceptChanges()	Accepts the changes in all of the tables of the DataSet. This means that any modified row flags are reset to their original unchanged state and deleted rows are removed permanently. Note that this does not mean that the data source is updated. On the contrary, if you call AcceptChanges() before passing the DataSet to the DataAdapter.Update() method, Update() won't find any rows marked as changed and so it won't update anything.
RejectChanges()	Reverses all the changes made on the DataSet since the DataSet was loaded, or since the last call to AcceptChanges(). Essentially, this method rolls back all rows to their original values.

The DataSet also has methods that can write and read XML data and schemas, and methods you can use to quickly clear and duplicate data. Table 9-2 outlines these methods. You'll learn more about XML in Chapter 11.

Table 9-2. *DataSet XML and Miscellaneous Methods*

Method	Description
GetXml() and GetXmlSchema()	Returns a string with the data (in XML markup) or schema information for the DataSet. The schema information is the structural information such as the number of tables, their names, columns, data types, and relationships.
WriteXml() and WriteXmlSchema()	Persists the data and schema represented by the DataSet to a file or a stream in XML format.
ReadXml() and ReadXmlSchema()	Creates the tables in a DataSet based on an existing XML document or XML schema document. The XML source can be a file or any other stream.
Clear()	Empties all the data from the tables. However, this method leaves the schema and relationship information intact.
Copy()	Returns an exact duplicate of the DataSet, with the same set of tables, relationships, and data.
Clone()	Returns an DataSet with the exact same structure (tables and relationships), but no data.
Merge()	Takes another DataSet as input and merges it into the current DataSet, adding any new tables and merging any existing tables.

The DataTable Class

As you can see in Figure 9-1, each item in the DataSet.Tables collection is a DataTable. The DataTable contains its own collections—the Columns collection of DataColumn objects (which describe the name and data type of each field), and the Rows collection of DataRow objects (which contain the actual data in each record).

The DataTable also provides methods such as Clear(), AcceptChanges(), and RejectChanges(), which have the same meaning as the identically named methods of the DataSet class, but only affect a single table. Finally, the DataTable also provides a NewRow() method that creates a DataRow object representing a new record, with the appropriate column structure (schema) for the table. Once you've finished configuring the values of each field, you can add the DataRow object to the DataTable.Rows collection.

The DataRow Class

Each DataRow object represents a single record in a table that's been retrieved from the data source. The DataRow is the container for the actual field values. You can access them by field name, as in myRow["FieldNameHere"]. The DataRow class exposes methods like AcceptChanges() and RejectChanges() that act on that particular row. It also includes the members listed in Table 9-3. You'll see all of these methods and properties in action in the examples later in this chapter.

Table 9-3. *DataRow Members*

Member	Description
BeginEdit(), EndEdit(), and CancelEdit()	These methods start the edit mode, save changes, and abandon the changes, respectively. Using these methods, you can make a series of related changes and then either commit or cancel the changes before saving the row and switching back to normal mode.
Delete()	The row is marked as deleted, but it is not removed from the DataTable.Rows collection or from the data source until you call the DataAdapter.Update() method. Note that this method is very different from calling the Remove() or RemoveAt() methods of the DataTable.Rows collection, because Remove() and RemoveAt() remove the DataRow object from the Rows collection entirely, rather than marking the row as deleted. That means when you call the DataAdapter.Update() method the record won't be deleted from the data source.
GetChildRows()	This method returns an array of DataRow objects that represent this row's related child rows. In order for this to work, the current DataRow must be contained in a parent table that has a defined relationship with a child table in the same DataSet. The method takes the name of the relationship of a DataRelation object.
GetParentRow() and GetParentRows()	These methods return the related parent row for the current row. In order for this to work, the current DataRow must be in a child table that has a defined relationship with a parent table in the same DataSet.
RowState	This property returns a value indicating whether the row has been changed, deleted, inserted, or is unchanged since it was first created or last updated.

The DataView Class

A DataView defines a view onto a DataTable object—in other words, a representation of the data in a DataTable that can include custom filtering and sorting settings. To allow you to configure these settings, the DataView has properties such as Sort and RowFilter. These properties allow you to choose what data you'll see through the view. However, they don't affect the actual data in the DataTable. For example, if you filter a table to hide certain rows, those rows will remain in the DataTable, but they won't be accessible through the DataView.

The DataView is particularly useful in data-binding scenarios. It allows you to show just a subset of the total data in a table, without needing to process or alter that data if you need it for other tasks.

Every DataTable has a default DataView associated with it, although you can create multiple DataView objects to represent different views onto the same table. The default DataView is provided through the DataTable.DefaultView property.

The DataAdapter Class

The DataAdapter serves as a bridge between a single DataTable in the DataSet and the data source. It contains all of the available commands for querying and updating the data source.

The DataAdapter provides three key methods, as listed in Table 9-4.

Table 9-4. *DataAdapter Methods*

Method	Description
Fill()	Adds a DataTable to a DataSet by executing the query in the SelectCommand. If your query returns multiple result sets, this method will add multiple DataTable objects at once. You can also use this method to add data to an existing DataTable.
FillSchema()	Adds a DataTable to a DataSet by executing the query in the SelectCommand and retrieving schema information only. This method doesn't add any data to the DataTable. Instead, it simply preconfigures the DataTable with detailed information about column names, data types, primary keys, and unique constraints.
Update()	Examines all the changes in a single DataTable, and applies this batch of changes to the data source by executing the appropriate InsertCommand, UpdateCommand, and DeleteCommand operations.

In order to enable the DataAdapter to edit, delete, and add rows, you need to specify Command objects for the UpdateCommand, DeleteCommand, and InsertCommand properties of the DataAdapter. In order to use the DataAdapter to fill a DataSet, you must set the SelectCommand.

Figure 9-2 shows how a DataAdapter and its Command objects work together with the data source and the DataSet.

Filling a DataSet

In the following example, you'll see how to retrieve data from a SQL Server table and use it to fill a DataTable object in the DataSet. You'll also see how to display the data with a Repeater control, or by programmatically cycling through the records and displaying them one by one. All the logic takes place in the event handler for the Page.Load event.

First, the code creates the connection and defines the text of the SQL query:

```
string connectionString = "Data Source=localhost;Initial Catalog=Northwind;" +
  "Integrated Security=SSPI";
SqlConnection con = new SqlConnection(connectionString);
string sql = "SELECT * FROM Employees";
```

The next step is to create a new instance of the SqlDataAdapter class that will retrieve the employee list. Although every DataAdapter supports four Command objects, only one of these (the SelectCommand) is required to fill a DataSet. To make life even easier, you can create the Command object you need and assign it to the DataAdapter.SelectCommand property in one step. You just need to supply a Connection object and query string in the DataAdapter constructor, as shown here:

```
SqlDataAdapter da = new SqlDataAdapter(sql, con);
```

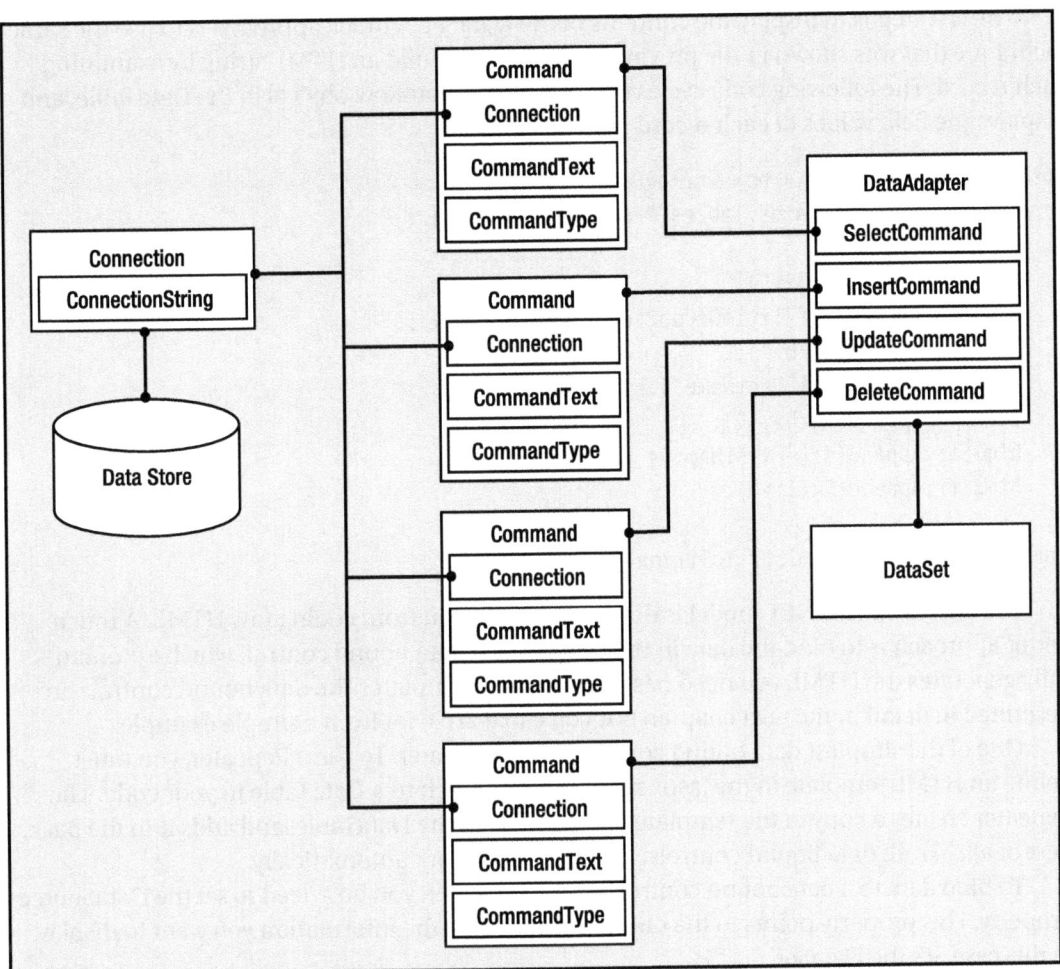

Figure 9-2. *How the DataAdapter interacts with the data source*

Now you need to create a new, empty DataSet, and use the DataAdapter.Fill() method to execute the query and place the results in a new DataTable in the DataSet. At this point, you can also specify the name for the table. If you don't, a default name (like "Table") will be used automatically. In the following example, the table name corresponds to the name of the source table in the database, although this is not a requirement.

```
DataSet ds = new DataSet();
da.Fill(ds, "Employees");
```

Note that this code doesn't open the connection by calling Connection.Open(). Instead, the DataAdapter opens and closes the linked connection automatically when you call the Fill() method. As a result, the only line of code that you should consider placing in a exception-handling block is the call to DataAdapter.Fill(). Alternatively, you can also open and close the connection manually. If the connection is open when you call Fill(), the DataAdapter will use that connection and won't close it automatically. This approach is useful if you want to perform multiple operations with the data source in quick succession, and you don't want to incur the additional overhead of repeatedly opening and closing the connection each time.

The last step is to display the contents of the DataSet. A quick approach is to use the same technique that was shown in the previous chapter, and build an HTML string by examining each record. The following code cycles through all the DataRow objects in the DataTable, and displays the field values of each record in a bulleted list:

```
StringBuilder htmlStr = new StringBuilder("");
foreach (DataRow dr in ds.Tables["Employees"].Rows)
{
    htmlStr.Append("<li>");
    htmlStr.Append(dr["TitleOfCourtesy"].ToString());
    htmlStr.Append(" <b>");
    htmlStr.Append(dr["LastName"].ToString());
    htmlStr.Append("</b>, ");
    htmlStr.Append(dr["FirstName"].ToString());
    htmlStr.Append("</li>");
}
HtmlContent.Text = htmlStr.ToString();
```

Of course, the ASP.NET model is designed to save you from coding raw HTML. A much better approach is to bind the data in the DataSet to a data bound control, which automatically generates the HTML you need based on a single template. The data bound controls are described in detail in the next chapter, but you can learn a lot from a simple example.

One of the simplest data bound controls is the Repeater. To use a Repeater, you must define an HTML template in the .aspx markup, and bind it to a DataTable in your code. The Repeater creates a copy of the template for each row in the DataTable, and adds it to the page. Best of all, like all data bound controls, it performs its work automatically.

To bind data to a data bound control like the Repeater, you first need to set the DataSource property. This property points to the object that contains the information you want to display. In this case, it's the DataSet.

```
Repeater1.DataSource = ds;
```

Because data bound controls can only bind to a single table (not the entire DataSet), you also need to explicitly specify what table you want to use. You can do that by setting the DataMember property to the appropriate table name, as shown here:

```
Repeater1.DataMember = "Employees";
```

Finally, once you've defined where the data is, you need to call the control's DataBind() method to copy the information from the DataSet into the control. If you forget this step, the control will remain empty, and the information will not appear on the page.

```
Repeater1.DataBind();
```

■**Note** When you bind a DataSet to a control, no data objects are stored in view state. The data control only stores enough information to show the data that's currently displayed. If you need to interact with a DataSet over multiple postbacks, you'll need to store it in the ViewState collection manually (which will greatly increase the size of the page), or the Session or Cache objects.

The Repeater itself is a *template-based* control, which means you define how it should display each record by writing a template in the HTML portion of the page (in the .aspx markup file). For example, if you want to show three fields in a bulleted list, you could declare the Repeater using this tag:

```
<asp:Repeater runat="server" ID="Repeater1">
  <HeaderTemplate><h2>Repeater</h2></HeaderTemplate>
  <ItemTemplate>
    <li>
      <%# DataBinder.Eval(Container.DataItem, "TitleOfCourtesy") %>
      <b><%# DataBinder.Eval(Container.DataItem, "LastName") %></b>,
      <%# DataBinder.Eval(Container.DataItem, "FirstName") %>
    </li>
  </ItemTemplate>
</asp:Repeater>
```

The <ItemTemplate> tag contains the HTML skeleton of the template. In this case, the template defines a bulleted list (using the <li> tag), adds some bold formatting (with the <b> tag), and adds three data-binding expressions to extract field values from the current row. (You'll learn much more about templates and data-binding expressions in Chapter 10.)

The Repeater is a bare-bones control. It simply loops through each row in the bound data, applies the data-binding expressions, and then inserts the HTML into the page. Other data bound controls that you'll see in the next chapter, like the DataList and DataGrid, include many more frills.

Note that the Repeater extracts the same information and uses the same tags that were used to create the output with the foreach code. In fact, if you use both approaches you'll get two identical outputs, as shown in Figure 9-3. The only difference is how much code you need to write, and where you put it.

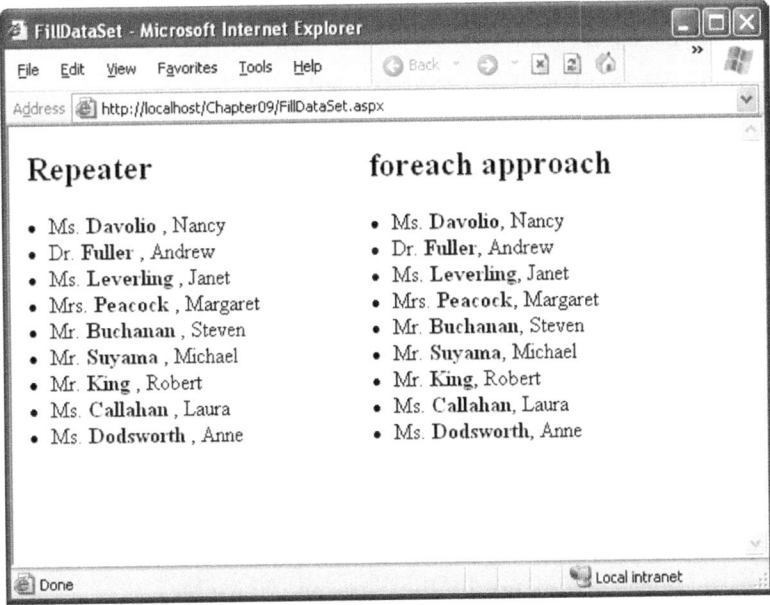

Figure 9-3. *Two ways to display the records in a DataTable*

Working with Multiple Tables and Relationships

The next example shows a more advanced use of the DataSet that, in addition to providing disconnected data, also uses table relationships. This example demonstrates how to retrieve some records from the Categories and Products tables of the Northwind database, and how to create a relationship between them so that it's easy to navigate from a category record to all of its child products and create a simple report.

The first step is to initialize the ADO.NET objects and declare the two SQL queries (for retrieving categories and products), as shown here:

```
// Create the Connection, DataAdapter, and DataSet.
string connectionString = "Data Source=localhost;Initial Catalog=Northwind;" +
  "Integrated Security=SSPI";
SqlConnection con = new SqlConnection(connectionString);

string sqlCat = "SELECT CategoryID, CategoryName FROM Categories";
string sqlProd = "SELECT ProductName, CategoryID FROM Products";

SqlDataAdapter da = new SqlDataAdapter(sqlCat, con);
DataSet ds = new DataSet();
```

Next, the code executes both queries, adding two tables to the DataSet. Note that the connection is explicitly opened at the beginning and closed after the two operations, ensuring the best possible performance.

```
try
{
    con.Open();

    // Fill the DataSet with the Categories table.
    da.Fill(ds, "Categories");

    // Change the command text and retrieve the Products table.
    // You could also use another DataAdapter object for this task.
    da.SelectCommand.CommandText = sqlProd;
    da.Fill(ds, "Products");
}
finally
{
    con.Close();
}
```

In this example, the same DataAdapter is used to fill both tables. This technique is perfectly legitimate, and it makes sense in this scenario because you don't need to reuse the DataAdapter to update the data source. However, if you were using the DataAdapter both to query data *and* commit changes, you probably wouldn't use this approach. Instead, you would use a separate DataAdapter for each table so that you could make sure each DataAdapter has the appropriate insert, update, and delete commands for the corresponding table.

At this point you have a DataSet with two tables. These two tables are linked in the Northwind database by a relationship against the CategoryID field. This field is the primary key for the Categories table, and the foreign key in the Products table. Unfortunately, ADO.NET does not provide any way to read a relationship from the data source and apply it to your DataSet automatically. Instead, you need to manually create a DataRelation that represents the relationship.

A relationship is created by defining a DataRelation object and adding it to the DataSet.Relations collection. When you create the DataRelation, you specify three constructor arguments: the name of the relationship, the DataColumn for the primary key in the parent table, and the DataColumn for the foreign key in the child table.

Here's the code you need for this example:

```
// Define the relationship between Categories and Products.
DataRelation relat = new DataRelation("CatProds",
  ds.Tables["Categories"].Columns["CategoryID"],
  ds.Tables["Products"].Columns["CategoryID"]);

// Add the relationship to the DataSet.
ds.Relations.Add(relat);
```

Once you've retrieved all the data, you can loop through the records of the Categories table, and add the name of each category to the HTML string:

```
StringBuilder htmlStr = new StringBuilder("");
// Loop through the category records and build the HTML string.
foreach (DataRow row in ds.Tables["Categories"].Rows)
{
    htmlStr.Append("<b>");
    htmlStr.Append(row["CategoryName"].ToString());
    htmlStr.Append("</b><ul>");
    ...
```

REFERENTIAL INTEGRITY AND THE DATARELATION

When you add a relationship to a DataSet, you are bound by the rules of referential integrity. For example, you can't delete a parent record if there are linked child rows, and you can't create a child record that references a nonexistent parent. This can cause a problem if your DataSet only contains partial data. For example, if you have a full list of customer orders, but only a partial list of customers, it could appear that an order refers to a customer that doesn't exist just because that customer record isn't in your DataSet. One way to get around this problem is to create a DataRelation without creating the corresponding constraints. To do so, use the DataRelation constructor that accepts the Boolean createConstraints parameter and set it to false, as shown here:

```
DataRelation relat = new DataRelation("CatProds",
  ds.Tables["Categories"].Columns["CategoryID"],
  ds.Tables["Products"].Columns["CategoryID"], false);
```

Another approach is to disable all types of constraint checking (including unique value checking) by setting the DataSet.EnableConstraints property to false before you add the relationship.

Here's the interesting part. Inside this block, you can access the related product records for the current category by calling the DataRow.GetChildRows() method. Once you have this array of product records, you can loop through it using a nested foreach loop. This is far simpler than the code you'd need to look up this information in a separate object or execute multiple queries with traditional connection-based access.

The following piece of code demonstrates this approach, retrieving the child records and completing the outer foreach loop:

```
...
// Get the children (products) for this parent (category).
DataRow[] childRows = row.GetChildRows(relat);

// Loop through all the products in this category.
foreach (DataRow childRow in childRows)
{
  htmlStr.Append("<li>");
  htmlStr.Append(childRow["ProductName"].ToString());
  htmlStr.Append("</li>");
}
htmlStr.Append("</ul>");
}
```

The last step is to display the HTML string on the page:

```
HtmlContent.Text = htmlStr.ToString();
```

The code for this example is now complete. If you run the page, you'll see the output shown in Figure 9-4.

■**Tip** A common question for new ADO.NET programmers is when to use JOIN queries and when to use DataRelation objects. The most important consideration is whether you plan to update the retrieved data. If you do, using separate tables and a DataRelation object always offers the most flexibility. If not, you could use either approach, although the JOIN query may be more efficient because it only involves a single round-trip across the network, while the DataRelation approach often requires two to fill the separate tables.

Searching for Specific Rows

The DataTable provides a useful Select() method that allows you to retrieve an array of DataRow objects based on an SQL expression. The expression you use with the Select() method plays the same role as the WHERE clause in an SELECT statement.

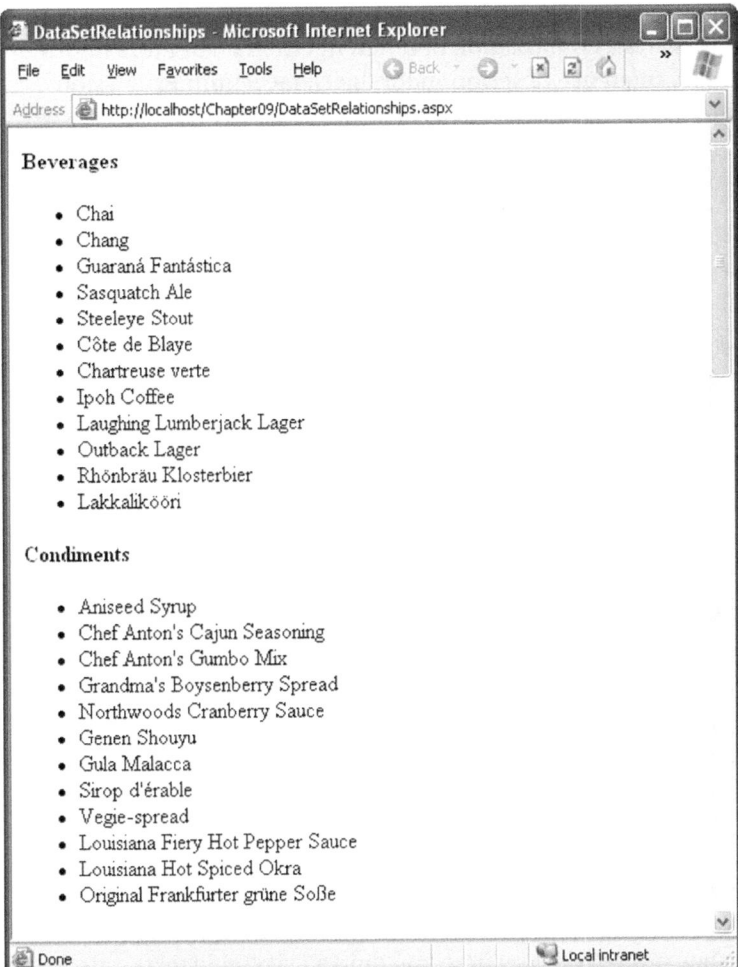

Figure 9-4. *A list of products in each category*

For example, the following code retrieves all the products that are marked as discontinued:

```
// Get the children (products) for this parent (category).
DataRow[] matchRows = DataSet.Tables["Products"].Select("Discontinued = 0")

// Loop through all the discontinued products and generate a bulleted list.
htmlStr.Append("</b><ul>");
foreach (DataRow row in childRows)
{
    htmlStr.Append("<li>");
    htmlStr.Append(row["ProductName"].ToString());
    htmlStr.Append("</li>");
}
htmlStr.Append("</ul>");
```

In this example, the Select() statement uses a fairly simple filter string. However, you're free to use more complex operators and a combination of different criteria. For more information, refer to the MSDN class library reference description for the DataColumn.Expression property, or refer to Table 9-5 and the discussion about filter strings later in this chapter.

■Note There is one potential caveat with the Select() method—it doesn't support a parameterized condition. As a result, it's open to SQL injection attacks. Clearly, the SQL injection attacks that a malicious user could perform in this situation are fairly limited, because there's no way to get access to the actual data source or execute additional commands. However, a carefully written value could still trick your application into returning extra information from the table. If you create a filter expression with a user-supplied value, you might want to iterate over the DataTable manually to find the rows you want, instead of using the Select() method.

The DataView Class

A DataView object represents a view of the data of a particular DataTable, and it enables you to sort and filter rows. Although you can use the DataView to work with a select group of rows programmatically, it's more commonly used for displaying data in a data bound control. In the following examples, you'll see how to create some grids that display records sorted by different fields, and filtered against a given expression.

Data Sorting with a DataView

It's important to note that every DataTable includes a default DataView object that's provided through the DataTable.DefaultView property. Every time you bind a DataTable to a control, this default DataView is used automatically. The default DataView doesn't apply any sort order or filter out any rows. If you want to tweak these settings, you can either configure the default DataView or create your own.

To demonstrate the DataView, the next example uses a page with three DataGrid controls. The DataGrid is the most fully featured of the data-binding controls, and it can create an automatic display for your data without requiring any templates. You'll learn much more about how the DataGrid works in Chapter 10, but the following example provides a quick introduction.

Here's the way you declare a DataGrid on the page:

```
<asp:DataGrid runat="server" ID="Datagrid1" />
```

When the page loads, it binds the same DataTable to each of the grids. However, it uses three different views, each of which sorts the results using a different field.

The code begins by retrieving the list of employees into a DataSet:

```
// Create the Connection, DataAdapter, and DataSet.
string connectionString = "Data Source=localhost;Initial Catalog=Northwind;" +
  "Integrated Security=SSPI";
```

```
SqlConnection con = new SqlConnection(connectionString);
string sql =
  "SELECT TOP 5 EmployeeID, TitleOfCourtesy, LastName, FirstName FROM Employees";

SqlDataAdapter da = new SqlDataAdapter(sql, con);
DataSet ds = new DataSet();

// Fill the DataSet.
da.Fill(ds, "Employees");
```

The next step is to fill the grids by binding the DataTable. To bind the first grid, you can simply use the DataTable directly, which uses the default DataView and displays all the data. For the other two grids, you must create a new DataView object. You can then set its Sort property explicitly.

```
// Bind the original data to #1.
Datagrid1.DataSource = ds.Tables["Employees"];

// Sort by last name and bind it to #2.
DataView view2 = new DataView(ds.Tables["Employees"]);
view2.Sort = "LastName";
Datagrid2.DataSource = view2;

// Sort by first name and bind it to #3.
DataView view3 = new DataView(ds.Tables["Employees"]);
view3.Sort = "FirstName";
Datagrid3.DataSource = view3;
```

Sorting a grid is simply a matter of setting the DataView.Sort property to a valid sorting expression. This example sorts by each view using a single field, but you could also sort by multiple fields, by specifying a comma-separated list. Here's an example:

```
view2.Sort = "LastName, FirstName";
```

The sort is according to the data type of the column. Numeric and date columns are ordered from smallest to largest. String columns are sorted alphanumerically without regard to case, assuming the DataTable.CaseSensitive property is false (the default). Columns that contain binary data cannot be sorted. You can also use the ASC and DESC attributes to sort in ascending or descending order.

Once you've bound the grids, you still need to trigger the data-binding process that copies the values from the DataTable into the control. You can do this for each control separately, or for the entire page by calling Page.DataBind(), as in this example:

```
Page.DataBind();
```

Figure 9-5 shows the resulting page.

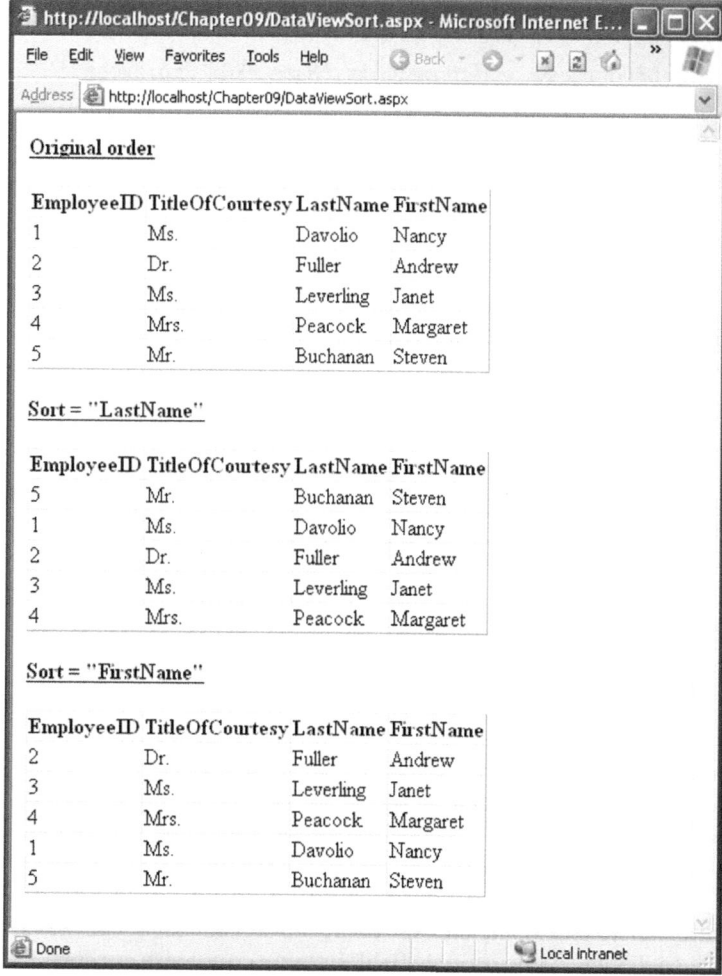

Figure 9-5. *Grids sorted in different ways*

Data Filtering with a DataView

You can also use a DataView to apply custom filtering, so that only certain rows are included in the display. To accomplish this feat, you use the RowFilter property. The RowFilter property acts like a WHERE clause in a SQL query. Using it, you can limit results using logical operators (such as <, >, and =) and a wide range of criteria. Table 9-5 lists the most common filter operators.

Table 9-5. *Filter Operators*

Operator	Description
<, >, <=, and >=	Performs comparison of more than one value. These comparisons can be numeric (with number data types), or alphabetic dictionary comparisons (with string data types).
<> and =	Performs equality testing.
NOT	Reverses an expression. Can be used in conjunction with any other clause.

Operator	Description
BETWEEN	Specifies an inclusive range. For example, "Units BETWEEN 5 AND 15" selects rows that have a value in the Units column from 5 to 15.
IS NULL	Tests the column for a null value.
IN(a,b,c)	A short form for using an OR clause with the same field. Tests for equality between a column and the specified values (a, b, and c).
LIKE	Performs pattern matching with string data types.
+	Adds two numeric values, or concatenates a string.
-	Subtracts one numeric value from another.
*	Multiplies two numeric values.
/	Divides one numeric value by another.
%	Finds the modulus (the remainder after one number is divided by another).
AND	Combines more than one clause. Records must match all criteria to be displayed.
OR	Combines more than one clause. Records must match at least one of the filter expressions to be displayed.

The following example page includes three DataGrid controls. Each one is bound to the same DataTable, but with different filter settings.

```
string connectionString = "Data Source=localhost;Initial Catalog=Northwind;" +
  "Integrated Security=SSPI";
SqlConnection con = new SqlConnection(connectionString);
string sql = "SELECT ProductID, ProductName, UnitsInStock, UnitsOnOrder, " +
  Discontinued FROM Products";

SqlDataAdapter da = new SqlDataAdapter(sql, con);
DataSet ds = new DataSet();
da.Fill(ds, "Products");

// Filter for the Chocolade product.
DataView view1 = new DataView(ds.Tables["Products"]);
view1.RowFilter = "ProductName = 'Chocolade'";
Datagrid1.DataSource = view1;

// Filter for products that aren't on order or in stock.
DataView view2 = new DataView(ds.Tables["Products"]);
view2.RowFilter = "UnitsInStock = 0 AND UnitsOnOrder = 0";
Datagrid2.DataSource = view2;

// Filter for products starting with the letter P.
DataView view3 = new DataView(ds.Tables["Products"]);
view3.RowFilter = "ProductName LIKE 'P%'";
Datagrid3.DataSource = view3;

this.DataBind();
```

Running the page will fill the three grids as shown in Figure 9-6.

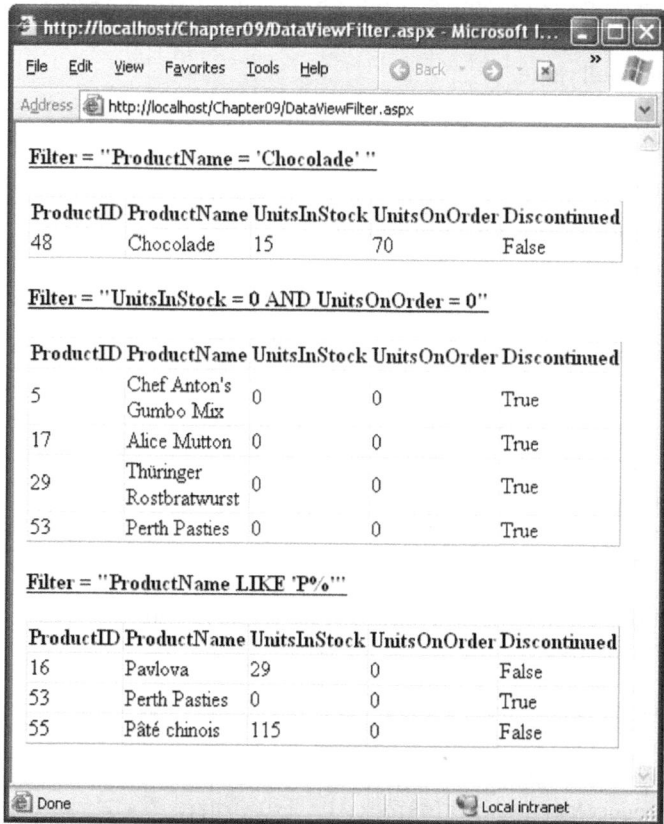

Figure 9-6. *Grids filtered in different ways*

■**Tip** The DataView also includes a RowStateFilter property that you can use to filter a DataTable so that it shows rows in a specific row state (inserted, deleted, modified, or unchanged). By default, this property is set to show all rows except those that have been marked as deleted. You'll learn more about DataSet versioning later in this chapter.

Advanced Data Filtering with Relationships

The DataView allows for some surprisingly complex filter expressions. One of its little-known features is the ability to filter rows based on relationships. For example, you could display categories that contain more than 20 products, or customers that have made a certain number of total purchases. In both of these examples, you need to filter one table based on the information in a related table.

To create this sort of filter string, you need to combine two ingredients:

- A table relationship that links two tables.

- An aggregate function like AVG(), MAX(), MIN(), or COUNT(). This function acts on the data in the related records.

For example, suppose you've filled a DataSet with the Categories and Products tables, and defined this relationship:

```
// Define the relationship between Categories and Products.
DataRelation relat = new DataRelation("CatProds",
  ds.Tables["Categories"].Columns["CategoryID"],
  ds.Tables["Products"].Columns["CategoryID"]);

// Add the relationship to the DataSet.
ds.Relations.Add(relat);
```

You can now filter the display of the Categories table using a filter expression based on the Products table. For example, imagine you only want to show category records that have at least one product worth more than $50 . To accomplish this you use the COUNT() function, along with the name of the table relationships (CatProds). Here's the filter string you need:

```
MAX(Child(CatProds).UnitPrice) > 50
```

And here's the code that applies this filter string to the DataView:

```
DataView view1 = new DataView(ds.Tables["Categories"]);
view1.RowFilter = "MAX(Child(CatProds).UnitPrice) > 50";
Datagrid1.DataSource = view1;
```

The end result is that the DataGrid only shows the categories that have a product worth more than $50.

Calculated Columns

In addition to the fields retrieved from the data source, you can add *calculated columns*. Calculated columns are ignored when retrieving and updating data. Instead, they represent a value that's computed using a combination of existing values. To create a calculated column, you simply create a new DataColumn object (specifying its name and type) and set the Expression property. Finally, you add the DataColumn to the Columns collection of the DataTable using the Add() method.

As an example, here's a column that uses string concatenation to combine the first and last name into one field:

```
DataColumn fullName = new DataColumn(
  "FullName", typeof(string),
  "TitleOfCourtesy + ' ' + LastName + ', ' + FirstName");
ds.Tables["Employees"].Columns.Add(fullName);
```

■**Tip** Of course, you can also execute a query that creates calculated columns. However, that approach makes it more difficult to update the data source later on, and it creates more work for the data source. For that reason, it's often a better solution to create calculated columns in the DataSet.

You can also create a calculated column that incorporates information from related rows. For example, you might add a column in a Categories table that indicates the number of related product rows. In this case, you need to make sure you first define the relationship with a DataRelation object. You also need to use a SQL aggregate function like AVG(), MAX(), MIN(), or COUNT().

Here's an example that creates three calculated columns, all of which use aggregate functions and table relationships:

```
string connectionString = "Data Source=localhost;Initial Catalog=Northwind;" +
    "Integrated Security=SSPI";
SqlConnection con = new SqlConnection(connectionString);
string sqlCat = "SELECT CategoryID, CategoryName FROM Categories";
string sqlProd = "SELECT ProductName, CategoryID, UnitPrice FROM Products";
SqlDataAdapter da = new SqlDataAdapter(sqlCat, con);
DataSet ds = new DataSet();

try
{
    con.Open();
    da.Fill(ds, "Categories");
    da.SelectCommand.CommandText = sqlProd;
    da.Fill(ds, "Products");
}
finally
{
    con.Close();
}

// Define the relationship between Categories and Products.
DataRelation relat = new DataRelation("CatProds",
  ds.Tables["Categories"].Columns["CategoryID"],
  ds.Tables["Products"].Columns["CategoryID"]);
// Add the relationship to the DataSet.
ds.Relations.Add(relat);

// Create the calculated columns.
DataColumn count = new DataColumn(
  "Products (#)", typeof(int), "COUNT(Child(CatProds).CategoryID)");
DataColumn max = new DataColumn(
  "Most Expensive Product", typeof(decimal), "MAX(Child(CatProds).UnitPrice)");
```

```
DataColumn min = new DataColumn(
  "Least Expensive Product", typeof(decimal), "MIN(Child(CatProds).UnitPrice)");

// Add the columns.
ds.Tables["Categories"].Columns.Add(count);
ds.Tables["Categories"].Columns.Add(max);
ds.Tables["Categories"].Columns.Add(min);

// Show the data.
DataGrid1.DataSource = ds.Tables["Categories"];
DataGrid1.DataBind();
```

Figure 9-7 shows the resulting page.

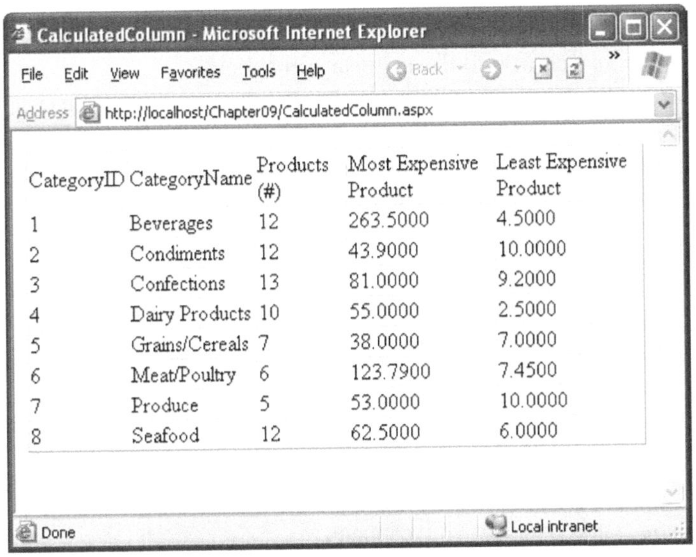
CalculatedColumn - Microsoft Internet Explorer
File Edit View Favorites Tools Help
Back
Address http://localhost/Chapter09/CalculatedColumn.aspx
CategoryID CategoryName Products (#) Most Expensive Product Least Expensive Product
1 Beverages 12 263.5000 4.5000
2 Condiments 12 43.9000 10.0000
3 Confections 13 81.0000 9.2000
4 Dairy Products 10 55.0000 2.5000
5 Grains/Cereals 7 38.0000 7.0000
6 Meat/Poultry 6 123.7900 7.4500
7 Produce 5 53.0000 10.0000
8 Seafood 12 62.5000 6.0000
Done
Local intranet

Figure 9-7. *Showing calculated columns*

■ **Note** Keep in mind that these examples simply demonstrate convenient ways to filter and aggregate data. These operations are only part of *presenting* your data properly. The other half of the equation is proper formatting. In the following chapter, you'll learn a lot more about the DataGrid so that you can show currency values in the appropriate format and customize other details like color, sizing, column order, and fonts. For example, by setting the format you can change 4.5000 to the more reasonable display value, $4.50.

Modifying the DataSet

So far, all the examples have simply filled a DataSet and used its records to produce some sort of report. However, the DataSet also gives you the ability to edit, delete, and add rows.

The following examples demonstrate how to manipulate the rows in a DataTable, handle DataTable changes, cancel or accept edited values, and retrieve the original values. All the examples use the data from the Employees table in the Northwind database. None of these examples includes the code needed to query the database, because you've already seen that code in detail in the earlier examples.

Editing Rows

You can edit the value of a field by simply accessing the field and setting a new value. Here's an example that changes the TitleOfCourtesy value for the first row:

```
table1.Rows[0]["TitleOfCourtesy"] = "Mrs.";
```

Note that the Rows collection is zero-based, as are all .NET collections. If you didn't want to access a row by position, you could loop through the entire collection of rows and search for a record that interests you. Or you could use the Select() method discussed earlier to retrieve a reference to the DataRow objects that match the criteria you specify.

You can also make multiple changes at once by invoking the BeginEdit() and EndEdit() methods of the DataRow. While you're in edit mode, the DataSet won't perform its normal error checking to ensure that constraints aren't violated. Once the data is in a valid state again, you can call EndEdit() to commit the changes (or you can use CancelEdit() to reverse all your operations). Here's an example:

```
// Edit two fields in the second row, but cancel the changes.
DataTable myTable = ds.Tables["Employees"];
myTable.Rows[1].BeginEdit();
myTable.Rows[1]["TitleOfCourtesy"] = "Mr.";
myTable.Rows[1]["FirstName"] = "Andy";
myTable.Rows[1].CancelEdit();

// Edit two fields in the third row, and confirm the changes.
myTable.Rows[2].BeginEdit();
myTable.Rows[2]["LastName"] = "Thompson";
myTable.Rows[2]["FirstName"] = "Jenny";
myTable.Rows[2].EndEdit();
```

The BeginEdit(), EndEdit(), and CancelEdit() methods are useful if you have to edit more than one field in the same row and want to be able to cancel the changes to all the fields should you find some invalid conditions in other fields.

Adding Rows

To add a new row to the DataTable, you must first create a new DataRow object by calling the DataTable.NewRow() method. All DataRow objects are not created equally. The NewRow() method returns a DataRow that has the schema (columns) of its parent table.

Once you've created the new row you can set the values for each field, and then add the DataRow object to the DataTable.Rows collection. The code is fairly straightforward:

```
DataRow newRow = table1.NewRow();
newRow["TitleOfCourtesy"] = "Mr.";
newRow["LastName"] = "Bellinaso";
newRow["FirstName"] = "Marco";
ds.Tables["Employees"].Rows.Add(newRow);
```

Note that this code doesn't specify a value for the EmployeeID field, because that value is defined as a unique autoincrementing number in SQL Server. As a result, it needs to be generated by the data source when you perform the update with the DataAdapter.

Deleting Rows

Deleting a row is the simplest editing task. All you have to do is call the DataRow.Delete() method. For example, this code removes the third row:

```
table1.Rows[2].Delete();
```

Now if you bind a table to the row it will no longer be displayed. However, you must remember that row is actually still in the Rows collection. It's just flagged as a deleted row. This means that if you iterate through the Rows collection, you'll still find the deleted row, although you'll receive an error if you try to access its data. To understand more about how deleted rows work, you need to understand more about DataSet versioning, as described in the next section.

Tip It is possible to "undelete" a row and restore it back to your DataSet. All you need to is call the DataRow.RejectChanges() method, which restores the DataRow to its original state. Of course, this technique won't work once you commit your changes to the DataSet and the row is removed permanently.

DataRow Versioning

When you change, delete, or insert rows, you modify the contents of the DataSet object, but your changes don't affect the original data source. To make a lasting change, you need to reconnect and use the DataAdapter to apply your modifications. But how does the DataAdapter determine what changes need to be made?

ADO.NET approaches the disconnected data challenge by using a versioning system. It stores additional information about the original values for all fields, and it flags rows that have been deleted, changed, or inserted since the last operation.

When a row is edited, added, or deleted, its RowState property is changed. The possible values for the RowState property are those of the DataRowState enumeration, and are summarized in Table 9-6.

Table 9-6. *Values of the DataRowState Enumeration*

Value	Description
Unchanged	The row has not been changed since the table was created or last updated.
Added	The row has been added since the table was created or last updated.

Continued

Table 9-6. *Continued*

Value	Description
Modified	The row has been modified since the table was created or last updated.
Deleted	The row has been deleted since the table was created or last updated.
Detached	This row is not a part of any table. One example is a row that has been created with the NewRow() method, but hasn't been added to the Rows collection yet.

Note that when you call the AcceptChanges() or RejectChanges() method on a DataRow, DataTable, or DataSet, the state of the rows is reset to Unchanged. Usually, you won't use the AcceptChanges() method directly. However, the DataAdapter needs to call AcceptChanges() after it finished updating the data source so that your DataSet reflects the newly updated information. Similarly, you won't use RejectChanges() unless you are working with disconnected data that you never intend to synchronize with a data source, or you are correcting a problem by abandoning your earlier edits.

As explained earlier, when you call RejectChanges(), the fields are rolled back to their original values. But how does this automatic rollback work? It's possible because each field stores both the original and current value. By default, when you retrieve information from a field in the DataRow object, you retrieve the current value. However, you can use an optional parameter with the DataRow indexer to retrieve another version. This optional parameter is a value from the DataRowVersion enumeration, which is described in Table 9-7.

Table 9-7. *Values of the DataRowVersion Enumeration*

Value	Description
Original	The value that was in the column when the row was created or last committed in the DataTable.
Proposed	The value that is in the column after a call to BeginEdit(), but before the call to EndEdit() or CancelEdit().
Current	The current value of the field.

Here's an example that can retrieve the original value for a DataRow field:

```
string originalValue = row["LastName", DataRowVersion.Original].ToString();
```

Storing this additional information doesn't just allow you to reverse your changes. It also allows the DataAdapter to use the original information to locate the row it needs to update. By default, a DataAdapter prevents updates if the values of the record in the data source don't match the original values in your DataSet. If this anomaly occurs, it means someone else has committed a change since you last queried the data source.

Displaying Version Information

You can create a simple test page to show the row version information. The next example fills a DataTable with three records and performs a few edits. It then filters out specific types of changes (addition, deletions, and modifications), and displays them in separate DataGrids, along with the original data. Figure 9-8 shows the test page.

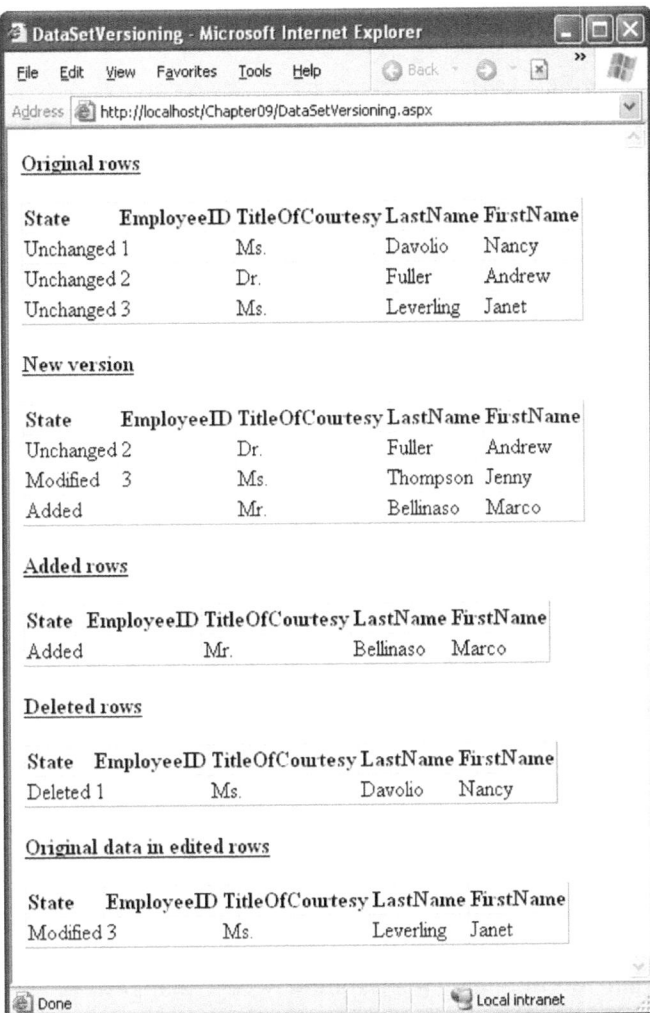

Figure 9-8. *Testing DataRow versioning*

The code for this example is quite straightforward. Here's an excerpted version that omits the code for creating and filling the DataSet:

```
// (Create and fill the DataSet here.)
// (Make some changes here.)

// Bind the edited data to grid #2.
Datagrid2.DataSource = table;
Datagrid2.DataBind();

// Bind the added rows to grid #3.
DataView view3 = new DataView(table);
view3.RowStateFilter = DataViewRowState.Added;
Datagrid3.DataSource = view3;
Datagrid3.DataBind();
```

```
// Bind the deleted rows to grid #4.
DataView view4 = new DataView(table);
view4.RowStateFilter = DataViewRowState.Deleted;
Datagrid4.DataSource = view4;
Datagrid4.DataBind();

// Show the original data from the edited rows in grid #5.
DataView view5 = new DataView(table);
view5.RowStateFilter = DataViewRowState.ModifiedOriginal;
Datagrid5.DataSource = view5;
Datagrid5.DataBind();
```

For the full code, refer to the online code for this chapter.

Updating the Data in the Data Source

In the last chapter you saw how you can use the Command object to execute INSERT, DELETE, and UPDATE statements, or to call stored procedures that modify the data in the database. The DataSet provides a different approach. As you've seen in this chapter, you can make multiple changes to the data in the DataSet, delete existing rows, and insert new rows. All of these changes affect the in-memory DataSet objects, but they don't alter the physical data source. However, once you've made all the changes you need, you can perform a batch update that applies all the changes from the DataSet to the data source. The object that takes care of this step is the DataAdapter.

Essentially, all the DataAdapter really does is scan through the DataSet, examining the RowState property for each DataRow. If it finds a modified row, it applies the change using the UpdateCommand. If it finds a deleted row, it deletes it from the data source using the DeleteCommand. If it finds a new row, it adds it with the InsertCommand. As each update is made, ADO.NET refreshes the appropriate row by calling the DataRow.AcceptChanges() method. For example, once the DataAdapter updates a modified row, it calls AcceptChanges, which then changes the RowState of that row to Unchanged, and sets its Original value to the new value.

Some other criteria need to be met in order for the update process to succeed:

- In the case of a delete or update operation, ADO.NET needs to be able to find the original row. This means that your SELECT query should include at least one unique column (or a combination of columns that are unique when taken together).

- In the case of an insert, your SELECT query must include all the columns that are required for a new row (that is, all required columns that don't have default values). Otherwise, the information specified for the new DataRow object will be insufficient to create the row in the data source, and an error will occur.

The following examples update the data in the database. In order to make these changes without altering the standard Northwind tables, these examples use a table named Employee2 that provides an EmployeeID, TitleOfCourtesy, LastName, and FirstName field. This allows you to test the updating abilities of ADO.NET without touching the original data in the

Employees table. Of course you can create the Employees2 table wherever you want, even in a different database, or with a different table name—all you have to change is the connection string and the SELECT query.

Autogenerating Update Commands

The examples so far have only defined one command for the DataAdapter—the SelectCommand that's used to retrieve rows. When updating a data source, you need to supply an InsertCommand, DeleteCommand, and UpdateCommand, provided you expect to perform these operations.

■**Note** If you know you won't perform a specific type of operation, you don't need to supply the corresponding command. For example, if you know your DataSet doesn't contain any deleted rows, you don't need to supply a DeleteCommand for your DataAdapter. However, if the DataAdapter discovers a deleted row during its update procedure and it doesn't have a DeleteCommand, it will throw an exception.

To save effort, many providers include a CommandBuilder object that can automatically generate the logic for inserting, deleting, and updating records. The CommandBuilder examines the SelectCommand you've created, and it generates matching insert, delete, and update commands that use the same fields.

For example, here's the code you need to create the update logic for a SqlDataAdapter using the SqlCommandBuilder:

```
SqlDataAdapter da = new SqlDataAdapter(sql, con);

// Create the CommandBuilder based on the DataAdapter.
SqlCommandBuilder cb = new SqlCommandBuilder(da);

// Retrieve an updated DataAdapter with the autogenerated logic.
da = cb.DataAdapter;
```

Now the only step left is to call the DataAdapter.Update() method. When you call this method, you specify the name of the table that has the changes you want to apply to the data source:

```
int rowsAffected = da.Update(ds, "Employees");
```

The Update() method returns the total number of records that were changed, inserted, and deleted. As with the Fill() method, the Update() method opens the connection if it's not already open, performs all its work, and then closes the connection. Unlike the Fill() method, the Update() method executes a series of distinct commands, one for each record it needs to update, insert, or delete.

To understand how the automatically generated commands work, it's important to dig into the Command objects in more detail. The following snippet of code retrieves the CommandText of the three command objects, turns it into formatted HTML, and then displays it on a page.

```
StringBuilder str = new StringBuilder("");
str.Append("<hr><b>InsertCommand:</b><br>");
str.Append(cmdBuilder.GetInsertCommand().CommandText);
str.Append("<br><br>");
str.Append("<b>UpdateCommand:</b><br>");
str.Append(cmdBuilder.GetUpdateCommand().CommandText);
str.Append("<br><br>");
str.Append("<b>DeleteCommand:</b><br>");
str.Append(cmdBuilder.GetDeleteCommand().CommandText);
str.Append("<hr>");
CommandsText.Text = str.ToString();
```

The following page (shown in Figure 9-9) retrieves data for a DataSet, makes some changes, and updates the database. It also displays the automatically generated commands that are used by the CommandBuilder.

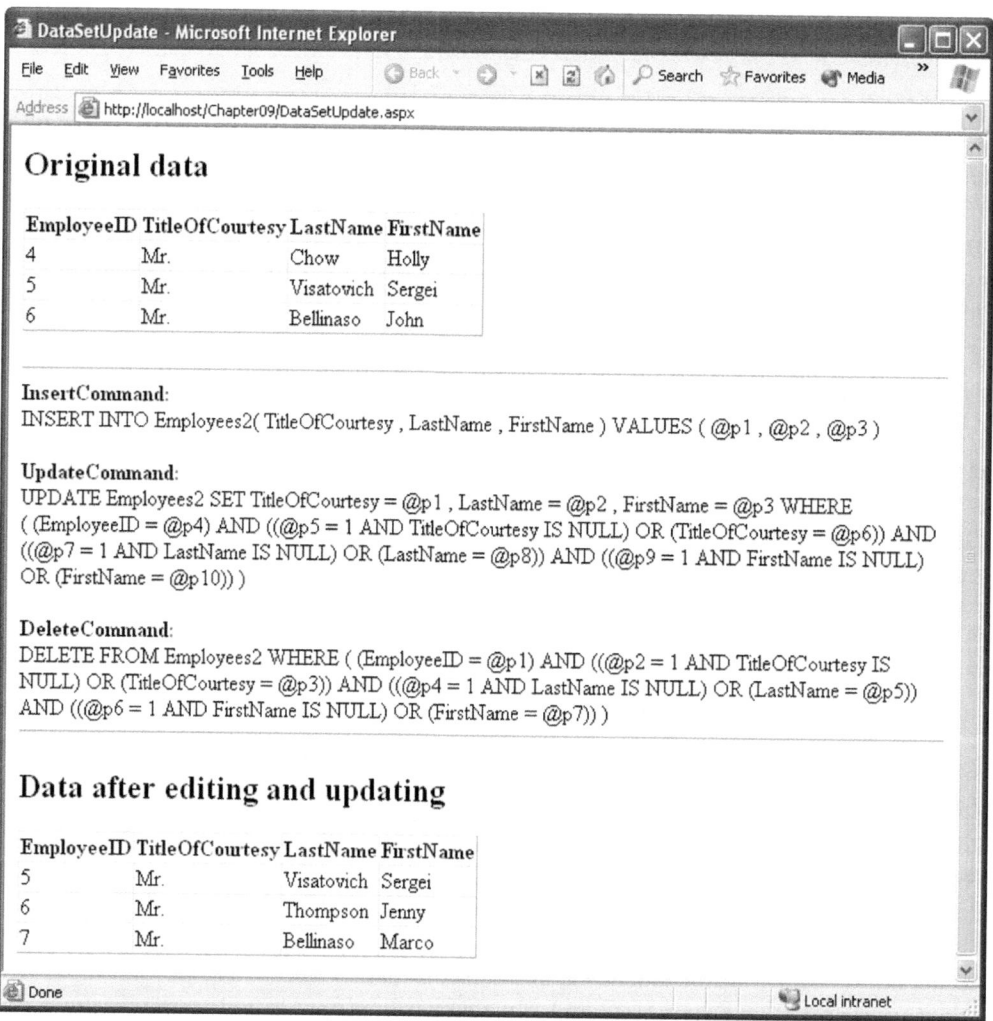

Figure 9-9. *Updating the data source*

Looking at this example, you can determine that one record has been changed, one has been deleted, and one has been added. (The number of total records is still the same, but looking at the IDs helps you to figure out what happened to which rows.) You can also see the text of the commands that were generated by the CommandBuilder, which you'll explore in the next section.

Limits of the CommandBuilder

The CommandBuilder object may seem great at first, but it definitely isn't the solution for every situation. Specifically, the following conditions must be met to be able to use a CommandBuilder:

- The SELECT query can't retrieve data as a result of a JOIN operation. All the data must come from a single table.

- The source data table can't contain calculated columns.

- All of the operations must be performed through dynamic SQL. Stored procedures aren't used.

- Your DataTable must include primary key information in order to update or insert a row.

- The table and column names cannot contain any special characters. These special characters include a period (.), a single or double quotation mark (' or "), a space, or any nonalphanumeric character. This is true regardless of whether you enclosed table and column names in brackets ([]). Though the data source may understand this syntax, the CommandBuilder does not.

Besides these limitations, there's the additional problem that automatically generated commands perform poorly when updating and deleting records in many situations. To understand why, you need to take a closer look at the automatically generated command text. Here's the command used to insert a record in the Employees2 table:

```
UPDATE Employees2 SET TitleOfCourtesy = @p1, LastName = @p2, FirstName = @p3
WHERE (
(EmployeeID = @p4) AND
((@p5 = 1 AND TitleOfCourtesy IS NULL) OR (TitleOfCourtesy = @p6)) AND
((@p7 = 1 AND LastName IS NULL) OR (LastName = @p8))
AND ((@p9 = 1 AND FirstName IS NULL) OR (FirstName = @p10)) )
```

By analyzing the autogenerated Command objects, you'll discover several important facts:

- They are parameterized SQL statements that use inline parameters.

- The parameter values are drawn from current or original values of the appropriate DataRow object.

- When matching a row for DELETE or UPDATE operations, ADO.NET searches for an exact match. For example, in the Employees table it isn't satisfied with a record that has the same unique EmployeeID field, unless all the other columns also match.

The last point is particularly important, because it can have serious performance implications. Because ADO.NET tries to match every field, the query size grows according to the number of fields. If your DataSet has 40 columns, there will be 40 conditions in the WHERE clause of your query, which results in more data to send across the network, and more work for the data source to perform. In addition, if the data row has been changed by another row in the meantime, the record update will fail, and the DataAdapter will stop its batch process and throw a DBConcurrencyException.

Note This type of optimistic concurrency may be the behavior you want, or you might choose to use a looser approach. One example is *last-in-wins* concurrency, in which subsequent edits always overwrite earlier edits. To execute a last-in-wins command, you would use a WHERE clause that matches the record using its unique primary key field and nothing else. You'll see an example of this technique later in this chapter. In either case, you should always use exception-handling logic when you call the Update() method to deal with the possibility for failed updates.

To escape from these problems, or to implement the better performance of stored procedures, you'll need to code the update logic manually. You'll see an example of this approach shortly, but first the next section will show you how to gracefully handle update problems.

NULL VALUES AND QUERIES

There's one other quirk you'll notice in the automatically generated update logic. That's the way the commands deal with null (empty) values.

Null values require extra care. You can't select a record that contains null values simply by using an ordinary condition. Instead, you need to test the field using the IS NULL syntax.

For example, to select a non-nullable column, the following syntax works perfectly well:

```
WHERE TitleOfCourtesy = @p5
```

However, if TitleOfCourtesy can contain a null value, you'll have to use the more circuitous logic shown here instead:

```
WHERE TitleOfCourtesy = @p5 OR
  ((TitleOfCourtesy IS NULL) AND (@p5 IS NULL )))
```

This evaluates true if it matches a non-null value, or if it matches a record that has a null value and the parameter is also null.

Data Conflicts and Update Events

As you've learned, ADO.NET maintains information in the DataSet about the current and the original value of every piece of information in the DataSet. When updating a row, ADO.NET searches for a row that matches every original field exactly, and then updates it with the new values. If another user has changed even a single field in the same record, the DataAdapter won't be able to find the original record to make the update. Instead, the DataAdapter throws a DBConcurrencyException.

This exception should always be caught and handled, even if only to show an error message, as follows:

```
try
{
    da.Update(ds, "Employees");
}
catch (DBConcurrencyException dbexc)
{
    lblInfo.Text = ("Update error in row with ID = " +
      dbexc.Row["EmployeeID"].ToString());
}
```

Unfortunately, this exception derails the entire update process. That means if your DataSet contains 15 changed records and an exception occurs trying to update the second one, the DataAdapter won't even attempt to deal with the remaining 13.

There is an easier way to handle these potential problems—you can respond to the DataAdapter.RowUpdated event. This event occurs after every individual insert, update, or delete operation, but before an exception is thrown. It gives you the chance to examine the results, note any errors, and prevent an error from occurring.

The first step is to create an appropriate event handler for the DataAdapter.RowUpdated event, as follows:

```
private void OnRowUpdated(Object sender, SqlRowUpdatedEventArgs e)
{
    // Check if any records were affected.
    // If no records were affected, the statement didn't execute as expected.
    if (e.RecordsAffected < 1)
    {
        // Find out the type of failed error.
        switch (e.StatementType)
        {
            case StatementType.Delete:
                lstErrors.Items.Add("Not deleted: " + e.Row["au_id"]);
                break;
            case StatementType.Insert:
                lstErrors.Items.Add("Not inserted: " + e.Row["au_id"]);
```

```
            break;
        case StatementType.Update:
            lstErrors.Items.Add("Not updated: " + e.Row["au_id"]);
            break;
    }

    // Using the SqlRowUpdatedEventArgs class, you can tell ADO.NET
    // to ignore the problem and keep updating the other rows.
    e.Status = UpdateStatus.SkipCurrentRow;
}
]
```

The SqlRowUpdatedEventArgs object provides this event handler with information about the row that ADO.NET just attempted to modify (e.Row), the type of modification (e.StatementType), and the result (e.RecordsAffected). In this example, errors are detected, and information about the unsuccessfully updated rows is added to a list control. Now that the problem has been noted, the e.Status property can be set to UpdateStatus.SkipCurrentRow to instruct ADO.NET to continue updating other changed rows in the DataSet.

Remember, this event occurs while the DataAdapter is in mid-update and using a live database connection. For that reason, you should not try to perform anything too complicated or time-consuming in this event handler. Instead, quickly log or display the errors and continue.

Now that the event handler has been created, you need to attach it to the DataSet before your perform the update. You connect this event the same way you connect the web control events:

```
// Connect the event handler.
adapter.RowUpdated += new OleDbRowUpdatedEventHandler(OnRowUpdated);

// Perform the update and check how many rows are changed.
int rowsAffected = adapter.Update(dsPubs, "Authors");
```

Rows that are skipped will remain in the DataSet, with the row status and versioning information they had before you began the update. You can execute the Update() method again to make another attempt updating the data. You can also use the DataTable.GetErrors() method to retrieve an array of DataRow objects that failed to be updated. You can then log or display information about these failed changes.

Using Custom Commands and Stored Procedures

It's not much more difficult to use a custom command—the only difference is that your code will become a fair bit longer. Custom commands enable a great deal of customization, flexibility, and increased performance, and they allow you to use stored procedures. However, they require more code. It's always a good idea to separate this code into a separate component to make it easier to maintain and reuse.

The following code rewrites the earlier update example to use custom commands that rely on stored procedures. Additionally, it improves the design of the application by moving the data access code into a separate database component, as in the previous chapter.

Unlike the component in the previous chapter, it doesn't require you to create a custom data package class (like EmployeeDetails). That's because this component uses the DataSet objects to transmit information.

The database component consists of the single class outlined here:

```
public class Employee2DB
{
    private string connectionString;

    public Employee2DB()
    {
        // Get connection string from web.config.
        connectionString = ConfigurationSettings.AppSettings["ConnectionString"];
    }

    public DataTable GetAllEmployees()
    { ... }
    public DataTable UpdateEmployeeBatch(DataTable dt)
    { ... }
}
```

You'll notice that both the GetAllEmployees() method and the UpdateEmployeeBatch() method use the DataTable object instead of the complete DataSet. That's because these methods only deal with a single table. You could still use a complete DataSet that contains a single DataTable, but this approach gives you more flexibility. For example, the client application could call GetAllEmployees() to retrieve the Employees table and then add that to an existing DataSet, which might contain other DataTable objects that were generated by other methods in the database component.

Finally, note that the UpdateEmployeeBatch() method accepts a DataTable (which contains the changes that need to be applied to the DataSet), and *returns* a DataTable. That's because once the update process is complete, the DataTable is updated so that it corresponds to the data source. For example, all the DataRow objects are reset to have DataRowState.Unchanged, and the original value of each field is updated to match the current value. (Alternatively, error information is set in the DataRow.RowError property if the row wasn't successfully updated.)

Note Technically speaking, you don't need to return the updated DataTable. That's because of the way .NET passes object references. When you pass the DataTable to the UpdateEmployeeBatch() method, that method receives a copy of the memory address that points to the DataTable object. When the data source is updated, this one and only DataTable object is updated automatically. In other words, the calling code's DataTable is always modified. If you want to change this behavior, you could use the DataTable.Copy() method in UpdateEmployeeBatch(), and then update the data source using the copy of the DataTable. In any case, returning a reference to the DataTable is a good decision because it clearly indicates that the DataTable changes.

You've already seen several examples that create and fill a DataSet. For that reason, the following example doesn't show the code for GetAllEmployees() method (although you can study it in the downloadable examples).

The next few sections take a piece-by-piece look at the code you'll use for the UpdateEmployeeBatch() method.

The Command for Inserting a Row

The first step is to create the command for inserting records. This command uses the following stored procedure:

```
CREATE PROCEDURE InsertEmployee2
@TitleOfCourtesy       varchar(25),
@LastName              varchar(20),
@FirstName             varchar(10),
@EmployeeID            int OUTPUT
AS
INSERT INTO Employees2
  (TitleOfCourtesy, LastName, FirstName)
  VALUES (@TitleOfCourtesy, @LastName, @FirstName);
SET @EmployeeID = @@IDENTITY
GO
```

This stored procedure takes the title of courtesy, last name, and first name as inputs, and has an output parameter with the ID of the new record. The command is created and associated to the DataAdapter.InsertCommand as follows:

```
SqlConnection con = new SqlConnection(connectionString);
SqlDataAdapter da = new SqlDataAdapter();
da.InsertCommand = new SqlCommand("InsertEmployee2", con);
```

Next, you need to specify that the command executes a stored procedure, and not a SQL statement:

```
da.InsertCommand.CommandType = CommandType.StoredProcedure;
```

Now you can create the first parameter, as follows:

```
SqlParameter insParam1 = new SqlParameter("@TitleOfCourtesy",
  SqlDbType.NVarChar, 25);
insParam1.SourceColumn = "TitleOfCourtesy";
insParam1.SourceVersion = DataRowVersion.Current;
```

The first line is similar to the code you saw when using stored procedures in the last chapter. However, the properties set in the last two lines are new. The SourceColumn property sets the name of the column in the DataTable that provides the value for this parameter. The SourceVersion specifies whether you want to take the original or current value. The SourceVersion is set to DataRowVersion.Current by default, but this example specifies it anyway to make the code clearer and more maintainable.

The code to insert the LastName and FirstName parameters follows the same pattern:

```
SqlParameter insParam2 = new SqlParameter("@LastName",
  SqlDbType.NVarChar, 20);
insParam2.SourceColumn = "LastName";
insParam2.SourceVersion = DataRowVersion.Current;
SqlParameter insParam3 = new SqlParameter("@FirstName",
  SqlDbType.NVarChar, 10);
insParam3.SourceColumn = "FirstName";
insParam3.SourceVersion = DataRowVersion.Current;
```

The final parameter is an output parameter that retrieves the newly generated ID. That means you need to specify the matching column and set the Direction property to ParameterDirection.Output. This ensures that the new ID is inserted in the appropriate DataRow after the command is executed.

```
SqlParameter insParam4 = new SqlParameter("@EmployeeID",
  SqlDbType.Int, 4);
insParam4.SourceColumn = "EmployeeID";
insParam4.Direction = ParameterDirection.Output;
```

Finally, you must add all the parameters to the InsertCommand:

```
da.InsertCommand.Parameters.Add(insParam1);
da.InsertCommand.Parameters.Add(insParam2);
da.InsertCommand.Parameters.Add(insParam3);
da.InsertCommand.Parameters.Add(insParam4);
```

The Command for Updating a Row

The command for updating a row uses the stored procedure shown here:

```
CREATE PROCEDURE UpdateEmployee2
@EmployeeID             int,
@TitleOfCourtesy        varchar(25),
@LastName               varchar(20),
@FirstName              varchar(10)
AS
UPDATE Employees2
  SET TitleOfCourtesy = @TitleOfCourtesy,
  LastName = @LastName,
  FirstName = @FirstName
  WHERE EmployeeID = @EmployeeID
GO
```

You should notice that the UPDATE statement in the UpdateEmployee2 stored procedure is quite a bit different than the dynamically generated UPDATE statement that the CommandBuilder created. The most important difference is that the stored procedure version finds the employee record to update by matching one field—the unique EmployeeID. As a result, the DataAdapter will be able to update the record even if the record has been changed since it was last retrieved by the web page. This type of concurrency strategy is called *last-in wins* concurrency, and it often makes sense for web-page code because the amount of time between reading a record and updating it is very short.

The code for creating the command is extremely similar to the example for inserting a record. Here it is in its entirety:

```
da.UpdateCommand = new SqlCommand("UpdateEmployee2", con);
da.UpdateCommand.CommandType = CommandType.StoredProcedure;
SqlParameter updParam1 = new SqlParameter("@EmployeeID", SqlDbType.Int, 4);
updParam1.SourceColumn = "EmployeeID";
updParam1.SourceVersion = DataRowVersion.Original;
SqlParameter updParam2 = new SqlParameter("@TitleOfCourtesy",
  SqlDbType.NVarChar, 25);
updParam2.SourceColumn = "TitleOfCourtesy";
updParam2.SourceVersion = DataRowVersion.Current;
SqlParameter updParam3 = new SqlParameter("@LastName",
  SqlDbType.NVarChar, 20);
updParam3.SourceColumn = "LastName";
updParam3.SourceVersion = DataRowVersion.Current;
SqlParameter updParam4 = new SqlParameter("@FirstName",
  SqlDbType.NVarChar, 10);
updParam4.SourceColumn = "FirstName";
updParam4.SourceVersion = DataRowVersion.Current;

// Add the parameters.
da.UpdateCommand.Parameters.Add(updParam1);
da.UpdateCommand.Parameters.Add(updParam2);
da.UpdateCommand.Parameters.Add(updParam3);
da.UpdateCommand.Parameters.Add(updParam4);
```

Conceptually, the only difference between the code for inserting and the code for updating a record is the EmployeeID parameter. This parameter is an input parameter like the others, but in this case its SourceVersion property is set to DataRowVersion.Original instead of DataRowVersion.Current. This ensures that even if you've changed the ID, you can still use the original ID to locate the record. In this example, the ID can't be changed because it's an autoincrement value generated by the database, but that's not always the case.

The Command for Deleting a Row

Finally, records can be removed with the help of this stored procedure:

```
CREATE PROCEDURE DeleteEmployee2
@EmployeeID int
AS
DELETE FROM Employees2
  WHERE EmployeeID = @EmployeeID
GO
```

The DeleteCommand is like the UpdateCommand in that it has an EmployeeID parameter that takes the original value of the EmployeeID field. However, it's much shorter because that's the only parameter it has in its Parameters collection. Here is the complete code:

```
da.DeleteCommand = new SqlCommand("sp_DeleteEmployee2", conn);
da.DeleteCommand.CommandType = CommandType.StoredProcedure;
SqlParameter delParam1 = new SqlParameter("@EmployeeID", SqlDbType.Int, 4);
delParam1.SourceColumn = "EmployeeID";
delParam1.SourceVersion = DataRowVersion.Original;
da.DeleteCommand.Parameters.Add(delParam1);
```

As with the update command, the delete command deletes the matching row, even if other fields have been changed in the meantime, unlike the commands that are automatically generated by the CommandBuilder.

This completes the code that you need to create and configure the commands in the UpdateEmployeeBatch() method. The only remaining step is to use the DataAdapter to update the submitted DataTable, as shown here:

```
// Update the data source.
try
{
    da.Update(dt);
}
catch
{
    throw new ApplicationException("Data error.");
}
return dt;
```

Testing the Component

It's a simple matter to revise the earlier test page to use the new database component. As with any other component, you must begin by adding a reference to the component assembly. Then, you can import the namespace it uses to make it easier to use the Employee2DB classes. The only step that remains is to write the code that interacts with the classes.

In this example, the code takes place in the Page.Load event handler, as shown here:

```
private void Page_Load(object sender, System.EventArgs e)
{
    // Create the component.
    Employee2DB db = new Employee2DB();

    // Get the data and display it.
    DataTable table1 = db.GetAllEmployees();
    Datagrid1.DataSource = table1;
    Datagrid1.DataBind();

    // (Code for editing the DataTable goes here.)
```

```
    // Update the data source and display the updated DataTable.
    table1 = db.UpdateEmployeeBatch(table1);
    Datagrid2.DataSource = table1;
    Datagrid2.DataBind();
}
```

Figure 9-10 shows the new page. Now, the command text is simply the name of the corresponding stored procedure. However, the web-page code works just as easily, and is quite a bit simpler. Overall, the component-based approach is easier to maintain, reuse, extend, and troubleshoot.

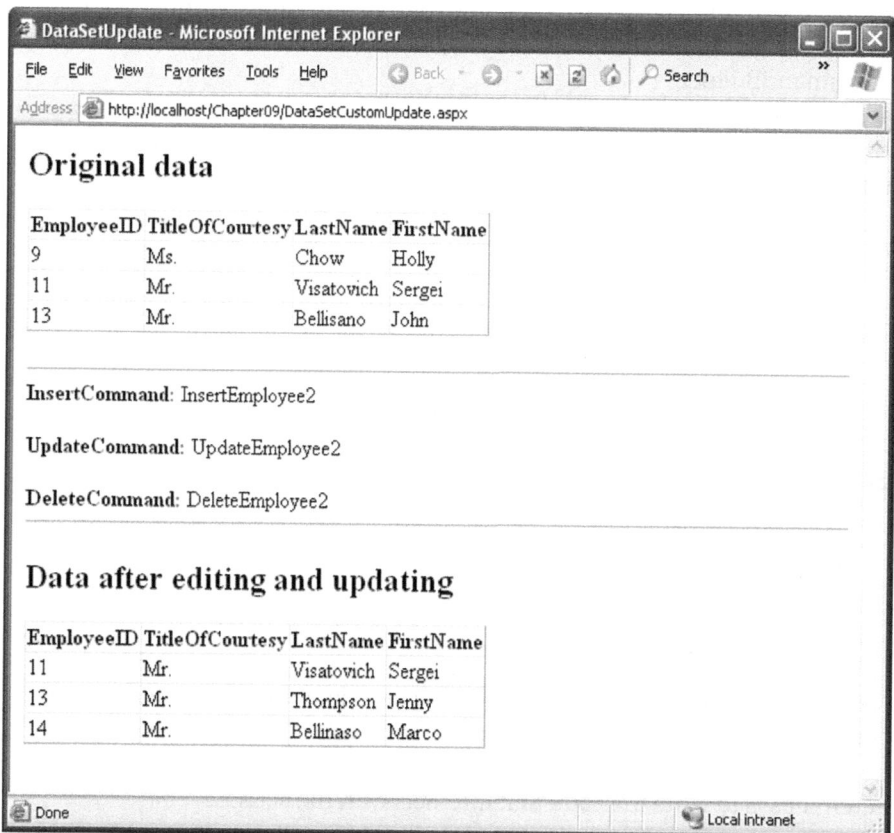

Figure 9-10. *Updating the data source with stored procedures*

Summary

In this chapter, you've taken an in-depth look at the DataSet, and how it stores multiple tables and relationships. You've also learned how to use the DataAdapter to retrieve information and commit changes, either with automatically generated logic or your custom commands.

In the next chapter, you'll continue working with the DataSet. You'll learn how to use it to display tailored data views in the ASP.NET data bound controls.

■ ■ ■

CHAPTER 10

Data Binding

Almost every web application has to deal with data from some kind of data store, whether it's a database, an XML file, structured file, or something else. Retrieving this data is only part of the challenge—a modern application also needs a convenient, flexible, and attractive way to show the data.

Fortunately, ASP.NET web controls can help you create advanced reports. Most web controls support a feature called data binding, which allows them to automatically show the information in a data object like the DataSet. In many cases, you can define the representation of data on a page declaratively—in other words, you can configure the layout, formatting, and colors used in your tables by adding controls and setting their properties, styles, and templates in the .aspx markup, without needing to write a line of code.

In this chapter you'll learn about the simple data bound controls such as ListBox and CheckBoxList (which were introduced earlier in Part One). Next, you'll study the new and more advanced controls including the Repeater, DataList, and DataGrid. These controls make it much easier to deal with common data access scenarios like creating data reports and record editors.

Data Binding Fundamentals

Essentially, data binding is a feature that allows you to associate a data source to a control and have that control automatically display your data. In ASP.NET, most web controls (including TextBox, LinkButton, and Image, and many more) support *single value* data binding. That means you can bind a control property to a data source, but the control can only display a single value. The property you bind doesn't need to represent something directly visible on the page. For example, not only can you bind the text of hyperlink by setting the Hyperlink.Text property, but you can also bind the NavigateUrl property to specify the target destination of the link.

Certain web controls support *repeated value* binding, and can render a set of items in a list, a drop-down list, a grid or a fully customized layout. The data source for a control designed for repeated binding is specified through the DataSource property. When you set the DataSource property, you create the logical link from the server control to the data object that contains the data to render. However, this doesn't directly fill the control with that data. To do that you must call the control's DataBind() method.

Data Structures Supported for Data Binding

Different data structures can be used as data sources for data bound controls as long as they implement the ICollection interface or one of its derivatives. The following list summarizes many of these data classes:

- All in-memory collection classes, such as Collection, ArrayList, Hashtable, and Dictionary.

- An ADO.NET DataView, which is a filtered view built on the top of a DataTable object.

- An ADO.NET DataTable object, which contains the data for a single table. When you bind a DataTable directly, you are actually using the DataView provided through the DataTable.DefaultView property.

- And ADO.NET DataSet object, which contains an in-memory collection of DataTable objects retrieved from the data store. If you use a DataSet, you must specify the name of the DataTable you want to use in the destination control's DataMember property.

- An ADO.NET DataReader object, which provides connection-based, forward-only, and read-only access to the database. This approach is slightly faster than binding a DataSet, but it doesn't allow you to configure sorting and filter settings, and it doesn't work if you need to bind more than one control to the same table, or if you want to cache the data for a future request.

- Any other custom object that implements the ICollection interface.

Controls That Support Repeated Binding

As you'll see shortly, many controls support single-value data binding. However, the most interesting and useful controls are those that support a repeated-value binding. These controls are summarized in the following list:

- All controls that render themselves using the <select> tag, including the HtmlSelect, ListBox, and DropDownList controls.

- The CheckBoxList and RadioButtonList controls, which render each child item with a separate check box or radio button.

- The Repeater control, which repeats the specified template for every item in the data source. The Repeater control has no default layout, so all the content it outputs must be specified using templates.

- The DataList control, which represents each item in the data source in a separate row of a <table> (by default). The DataList also has several templates that allow you to specify how to render the header, footer, and the actual item section. It has built-in support for deleting, editing, and selecting items.

- The DataGrid control, which is by far the most advanced and complex data bound control. It's used to create fully featured grids of data with support for record editing, selection, and deletion, plus automatic and custom pagination. The DataGrid can automatically generate the columns needed to display all the fields in the data source, and it allows you to specify templates to create customized column display. As with the DataList, the DataGrid renders data inside the rows of an HTML <table> tag.

The last three controls in the list are designed exclusively for data binding. They can't be used without an associated data source, and therefore can't be filled by hand (although you could create and fill a DataTable object by hand, and then use that as a data source). These controls have been designed specifically for rendering complex data, and they do their job very well. After a quick tour of basic data binding, you'll focus on these controls for the rest of the chapter.

Single Value Binding

The controls that support single-value data binding allow you to bind some of their properties to a special *data binding expression*. This expression is entered in the .aspx markup portion of the page (not the code-behind field), and enclosed between the <%# and %> delimiters. Here's an example:

```
<%# expression_goes_here %>
```

This may look like a script block, but it isn't. If you try to write any code inside this tag, you will receive an error. The only thing you can add is valid data binding expressions. For example, if you have a public or protected variable on your page named EmployeeName, you could write the following:

```
<%# EmployeeName %>
```

When you call the DataBind() method for the page, this text will be replaced with the current value that's defined for the EmployeeName variable.

The source for single-value data binding can include the value of a property, member variable, or return value of a function (as long as the property, member variable, or function has an accessibility of protected or public). It can also be any other expression that can be evaluated at runtime, such as a reference to another control's property, calculation using operators and literal values, and so on. The following data binding expressions are all valid:

```
<%# GetUserName(ID) %>
<%# 1 + (2 * 20) %>
<%# "John " + "Smith" %>
<%# Request.Browser.Browser %>
```

Note Data binding expressions also have a key limitation—they don't support Visual Studio .NET features like IntelliSense and syntax checking. In other words, if you write a data binding expression with invalid syntax or one that tries to bind to a nonexistent property, you won't realize the problem until you launch the page and receive a runtime error.

You can place your data binding expressions just about anywhere on the page, but usually you'll assign a data binding expression to a property in the control tag. Here's an example page that uses several data binding expressions:

```
<html>
  <body>
    <form method=post runat="server">
      <asp:Image runat="server" ImageUrl='<%# FilePath %>' /><br>
      <asp:Label runat="server" Text='<%# FilePath %>' /><br>
      <asp:TextBox runat="server" Text='<%# GetFilePath() %>' /><br>
      <asp:HyperLink runat="server" NavigateUrl='<%# LogoPath.Value %>'
        Font-Bold="True" Text="Show logo"/><br>
      <input type="hidden" runat="server" ID="LogoPath" value="apress.gif">
      <b><%# FilePath %></b><br>
      <img src="<%# GetFilePath() %>">
    </form>
  </body>
</html>
```

As you can see, not only can you bind the Text property of a Label and a TextBox, but you can also use other properties like the ImageUrl of an Image, the NavigateUrl property of a HyperLink, and even the src attribute of a static HTML <img> tag. You can also put the binding expression elsewhere in the page without binding to any property or attribute. For example, in the previous web page, there's a binding expression placed between the <b> and </b> tags. When it's processed, the resulting text will be rendered on the page and rendered in bold type. You can even place the expression outside the <form> section, as long as you don't try to insert a server-side control there.

The expressions in this sample page refer to a FilePath property, a GetFilePath() function, and the Value property of a server-side hidden field that's declared on the same page. In order to complete this page, you need to define these ingredients in script blocks or in the code-behind class, as shown here:

```
protected string GetFilePath()
{
    return "apress.gif";
}
protected string FilePath
{
    get { return "apress.gif"; }
}
```

In this example, the property and function simply return only a hard-coded string. However, you can also add just about any C# code to generate the value for the data binding expression dynamically.

It's important to remember that the data binding expression does not directly set the property it's bound to. It simple defines a connection between the control's property and some other piece of information. In order to cause the page to evaluate the expression, run the appropriate code, and assign the appropriate value, you must call the DataBind() method of the containing page, as shown here:

```
private void Page_Load(object sender, System.EventArgs e)
{
    this.DataBind();
}
```

Tip When calling the DataBind() method, you can use either the current page instance, as in this.DataBind(), or the name of the class, as in Page.DataBind(). Both approaches are equivalent.

Figure 10-1 shows what you'll see when you run this page.

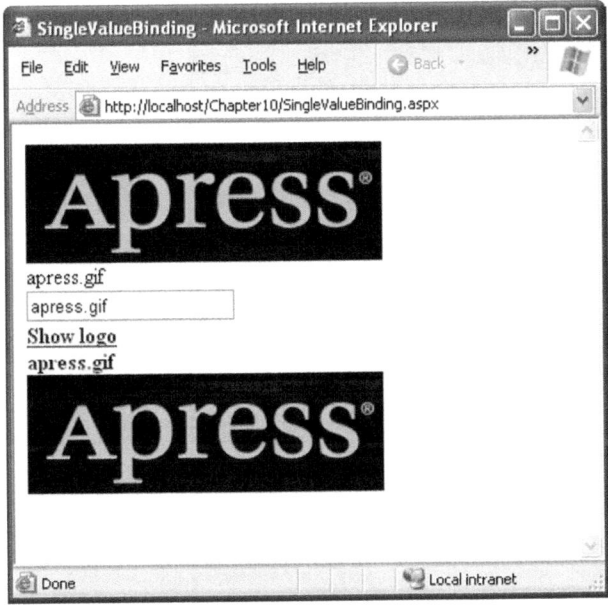

Figure 10-1. *Single-value data binding in various controls*

You'll see data binding expressions and single-value binding again when you create templates for more advanced controls like the Repeater, DataList, and DataGrid later in this chapter.

Simple Controls for Repeated-Value Binding

The HtmlSelect, ListBox, DropDownList, CheckBoxList, and RadioButtonList controls support repeated-value data binding, which allows them to bind to an entire list of information. These controls all provide the same properties to support data binding, as listed in Table 10-1.

Table 10-1. *Data Properties for List Controls*

Property	Description
DataSource	This property takes the data object that contains the data to display.
DataTextField	This property names the field of the data source from which the control retrieves the values to show.
DataValueField	This property names the field of the data source from which the control retrieves the values to use for the value attribute of the underlying HTML tag. This information won't appear in the page, but it will remain stored with the list item so you can retrieve it later. The primary use of this field is to store a unique ID or primary key field so you can use it later to retrieve more data if the user selects this item.

All of the list controls are essentially the same. The only differences are the way they render themselves in HTML, and whether or not they support multiple selection. Figure 10-2 shows a test page that displays all the different list controls, along with some text that displays the current selection for the controls.

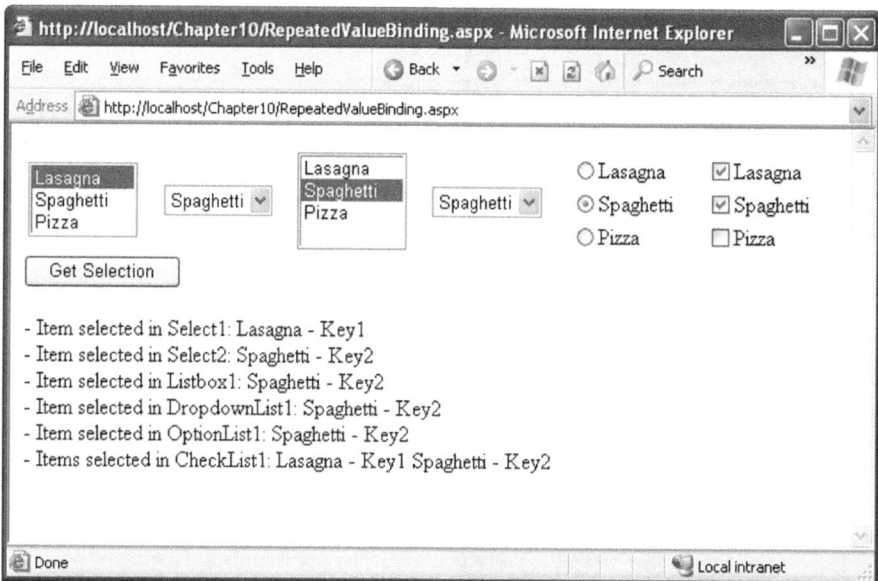

Figure 10-2. *Repeated-value data binding in list controls*

The controls are declared as follows:

```
<select runat="server" ID="Select1" size="3"
  DataTextField="Key" DataValueField="Value" />
<select runat="server" ID="Select2"
  DataTextField="Key" DataValueField="Value" />
<asp:ListBox runat="server" ID="Listbox1" Size="3"
  DataTextField="Key" DataValueField="Value" />
<asp:DropDownList runat="server" ID="DropdownList1"
  DataTextField="Key" DataValueField="Value" />
```

```
<asp:RadioButtonList runat="server" ID="OptionList1"
  DataTextField="Key" DataValueField="Value"/>
<asp:CheckBoxList runat="server" ID="CheckList1"
  DataTextField="Key" DataValueField="Value" />
<br><br>
<asp:Literal runat="server" ID="Result" EnableViewState="False"/>
```

The last control, the Literal control, is used to display information about the selected items. Its EnableViewState attribute is set to false so that its content will be cleared after every postback.

When the page loads for the first time, the code creates a data source and assigns it to all of the list controls. In this example, the data object is a Hashtable collection, which contains a series of strings. The Value of the Hashtable collection item returns the actual item text (which is used for the DataTextField), while the Key of the Hashtable collection item returns the key under which the item is indexed.

Here's the code for creating and binding the collection:

```
private void Page_Load(object sender, System.EventArgs e)
{
    if (!Page.IsPostBack)
    {
        // Create the data source.
        Hashtable ht = new Hashtable(3);
        ht.Add("Lasagna", "Key1");
        ht.Add("Spaghetti", "Key2");
        ht.Add("Pizza", "Key3");

        // Set the DataSource property for the controls.
        Select1.DataSource = ht;
        Select2.DataSource = ht;
        Listbox1.DataSource = ht;
        DropdownList1.DataSource = ht;
        CheckList1.DataSource = ht;
        OptionList1.DataSource = ht;

        // Bind the controls.
        Page.DataBind();
    }
}
```

When the user clicks the button, the code adds the name and values of all of the selected items to the label. Here's the code that accomplishes this task:

```
private void cmdGetSelection_Click(object sender, System.EventArgs e)
{
    Result.Text += "- Item selected in Select1: " +
      Select1.Items[Select1.SelectedIndex].Text + " - " + Select1.Value + "<br>";
    Result.Text += "- Item selected in Select2: " +
      Select2.Items[Select2.SelectedIndex].Text + " - " + Select2.Value + "<br>";
    Result.Text += "- Item selected in Listbox1: " + Listbox1.SelectedItem.Text +
```

```
              " - " + Listbox1.SelectedItem.Value + "<br>";
    Result.Text += "- Item selected in DropdownList1: " +
        DropdownList1.SelectedItem.Text + " - " +
        DropdownList1.SelectedItem.Value + "<br>";
    Result.Text += "- Item selected in OptionList1: " +
        OptionList1.SelectedItem.Text + " - " +
        OptionList1.SelectedItem.Value + "<br>";
    Result.Text += "- Items selected in CheckList1: ";
    foreach (ListItem li in CheckList1.Items)
    {
        if (li.Selected)
            Result.Text += li.Text + " - " + li.Value + " ";
    }
}
```

Binding to a DataReader

The previous example used a Hashtable as the data source. Basic collections certainly aren't the only kind of data source you can use with list data binding. Instead, you can use DataTable and DataReader objects, which allow information to be displayed from a database.

For example, imagine you want to fill a list box with the full name of all of the employees contained in the Employees table of the Northwind database. Figure 10-3 shows the result you want to produce.

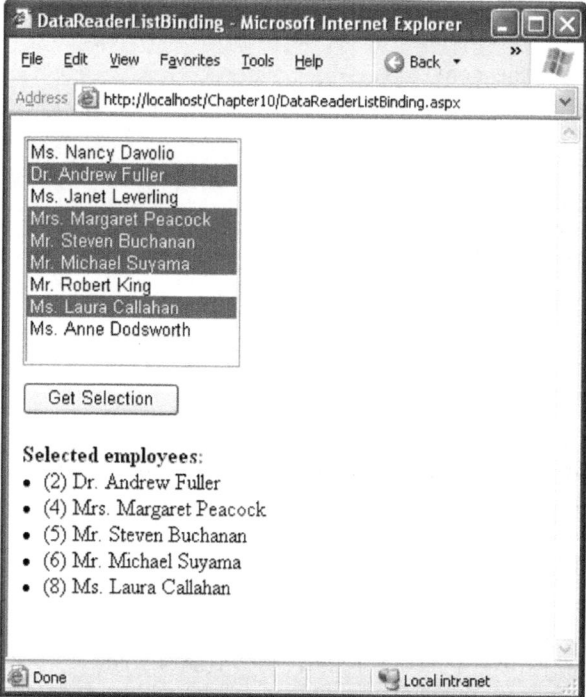

Figure 10-3. *Data binding with a DataReader*

The information in this example includes each person's title of courtesy, first name, and last name, which are stored in three separate fields. Unfortunately, the DataTextField property only expects the name of a single field. There's no way you can use data binding to concatenate these three pieces of data and create a value for the DataTextField. However, you can solve this issue with an easy but powerful trick—using a calculated column. You simply need to modify the SELECT query so that it creates a calculated column that consists of the information in the three fields. You can then use this column for the DataTextField. The SQL command that you need to accomplish this is as follows:

```
SELECT EmployeeID, TitleOfCourtesy + ' ' +
  FirstName + ' ' + LastName As FullName FROM Employees
```

The data-bound list box is declared on the page as follows:

```
<asp:ListBox runat="server" ID="Listbox1" Size="10" SelectionMode="Multiple"
  DataTextField="FullName" DataValueField="EmployeeID"/>
```

When the page loads, it retrieves the records from the database and binds them to the list control. This example uses a DataReader as the data source, as shown here:

```
private void Page_Load(object sender, System.EventArgs e)
{
    if (!Page.IsPostBack)
    {
        // Create the Command and the Connection.
        string connectionString = "Data Source=localhost;" +
          "Initial Catalog=Northwind;Integrated Security=SSPI";
        SqlConnection con = new SqlConnection(connectionString);
        SqlCommand cmd = new SqlCommand(sql, con);

        // Open the connection and get the DataReader.
        con.Open();
        SqlDataReader reader = cmd.ExecuteReader();

        // Bind the DataReader to the list.
        Listbox1.DataSource = reader;
        Listbox1.DataBind();

        // Close the DataReader and the Connection.
        reader.Close();
        con.Close();
    }
}
```

The previous code sample creates a connection to the database, creates the command that will select the data, opens the connection, and executes the command that returns the DataReader. The returned DataReader is bound to the list box, and finally the DataReader and the connection are both closed. Note that the DataBind() method of the page or the control must be called *before* the connection is closed. It's not until you call this method that the actual data is extracted.

The last piece of this example is the code for determining the selected items. As in the previous example, this code is quite straightforward:

```
private void cmdGetSelection_Click(object sender, System.EventArgs e)
{
    Result.Text += "<b>Selected employees:</b>";
    foreach (ListItem li in Listbox1.Items)
    {
        if (li.Selected)
            Result.Text += String.Format("<li>({0}) {1}</li>", li.Value, li.Text);
    }
}
```

If you want to use a DropDownList, a CheckListBox or a RadioButtonList instead of a ListBox, you only need to change the control declaration. The rest of the code that sets up the data binding remains exactly the same.

The Repeater Control

The Repeater control is the simplest and most flexible of the rich data controls. The Repeater allows you to completely define the layout that it will produce and the way it will format the data. The Repeater does not create any HTML tags that you don't explicitly declare in the template. You can declare templates that contain static HTML, web controls, binding expressions, and so on. When you set the Repeater.DataSource property and call the DataBind() method, the Repeater walks through the data source's collection of items, and processes the template for each one, adding the rendered HTML to the page.

Because of its simplicity, the Repeater is an ideal data binding control to explore first. It's also a good choice if you need completely flexible data binding that doesn't put your records into a basic table.

The ItemTemplate

The Repeater supports several templates, but only the ItemTemplate is required. The other templates are optional. The next example uses the ItemTemplate to create a simple list of employees. It demonstrates how a template is structured and what you need to do to access the data bound information. Figure 10-4 shows what the example web page looks like.

The Repeater is declared as follows:

```
<asp:Repeater runat="server" ID="Repeater1">
  <ItemTemplate>
    <li>
    <%# ((DbDataRecord)Container.DataItem)["TitleOfCourtesy"] %>
    <b><%# ((DbDataRecord)Container.DataItem)["LastName"] %></b>,
    <%# ((DbDataRecord)Container.DataItem)["FirstName"] %>
    </li>
  </ItemTemplate>
</asp:Repeater>
```

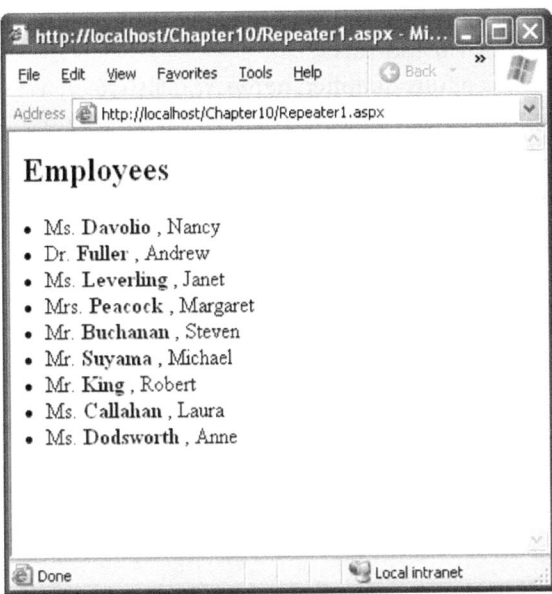

Figure 10-4. *Using the Repeater to show an employee list*

You'll notice that the Repeater contains a nested <ItemTemplate> tag, which represents a single template.

Tip Different ASP.NET controls differ in how they handle nested tags. Often, nested tags represent child controls that you want to add to a container control like a Panel. In other cases, nested tags map to control-specific properties. The <ItemTemplate> tag is an example of the latter—it allows you to define a block of HTML that's used to set the Repeater.ItemTemplate property. You'll learn much more about control serialization and how templated controls work behind the scenes in Part Four when you develop your own.

The <ItemTemplate> tag plays an important role. It defines the HTML that will be repeated for each item in the data source. In this example, the HTML includes minimal formatting (just enough to create a bulleted list), and three data binding expressions that will retrieve the title of courtesy, first name, and last name from the record that's currently being processed. These data binding expressions take a slightly different format than the ones you saw before. Instead of binding directly to the field you're interested in, these expressions need to filter through the Container.DataItem property. The Container is a RepeaterItem object that represents the data in the record that's currently being processed. The Container object has a property named DataItem, which provides the corresponding data object. By accessing Container.DataItem, you are actually accessing the current record from the DataReader that's about to be bound to the Repeater control. You can extract the values from its fields by name and then show them on the page.

In order to bind to the Container.DataItem, you must cast the object to the appropriate type. For a DataReader, this type is DbDataRecord, which is defined in the System.Data.Common namespace. If you were binding to a DataTable, the type of a single item would be DataRowView. These are the most commonly used types of data sources when working with the Repeater, DataList, and DataGrid controls.

In order to use the DbDataRecord without using a fully qualified name, you also need to import the System.Data.Common namespace into the .aspx page. You accomplish this with the following Import directive, which you can add right after the Page directive:

```
<%@ Import Namespace="System.Data.Common" %>
```

Note It may seem a little awkward that you need to cast the data item to use your data binding expression, but it's for a good reason. The Repeater needs to support a wide range of data sources, and the only way this is possible is if it uses an extra, more generic layer of RepeaterItem objects. This gives you the flexibility to bind the Repeater to a DataReader or a DataSet. In the next section, you'll see how to simplify this code with the DataBinder class.

The code in the Page.Load event handler creates the DataReader and binds it to the Repeater. This is basically the same process that was demonstrated in the previous example. The only real difference between these two examples is the SELECT statement, which now retrieves multiple columns from the Employees table. Here is the modified code:

```
private void Page_Load(object sender, System.EventArgs e)
{
    if (!Page.IsPostBack)
    {
        // Create the Command and the Connection.
        string connectionString = "Data Source=localhost;" +
          "Initial Catalog=Northwind;Integrated Security=SSPI";
        SqlConnection con = new SqlConnection(connectionString);
        string sql =
          "SELECT FirstName, LastName, TitleOfCourtesy FROM Employees";
        SqlCommand cmd = new SqlCommand(sql, con);

        // Open the connection and get the DataReader.
        con.Open();
        SqlDataReader reader = cmd.ExecuteReader();

        // Bind the Reader to the Repeater.
        Repeater1.DataSource = reader;
        Repeater1.DataBind();

        // Close the DataReader and the Connection.
        reader.Close();
        con.Close();
    }
}
```

When you use templates, you shift your data display code from your web-page logic into a template. For even better separation, you can combine this approach with a database component. That way, the only responsibility the web page has is to coordinate how the other parts of your application work together. It simply retrieves the data from the component and links it to the appropriate controls.

Note If you attempt to bind a field that isn't present in your result set, you'll receive a runtime error. If you retrieve additional fields that are never bound to any template, no problem will occur.

The DataBinder.Eval() Method

One disadvantage of the binding syntax used in the previous example is that if you change the data source type, you must also change the cast to the proper item type in the expression. For example, if you update your code to use a DataSet instead of a DataReader, the page will no longer work, even though the same fields are present in the DataRowView as in the DbDataRecord.

If you want to avoid this, and use the same syntax for any data source you use, you can use the static Eval() method of the System.Web.UI.DataBinder class, which automatically casts the object to the proper type and returns the value. It uses .NET reflection, a runtime inspection mechanism that allows code to examine type metadata at runtime. In this case, reflection allows the DataBinder to examine any object and access its properties by name, regardless of the type.

You can use the Eval() method as follows:

```
<%# DataBinder.Eval(Container.DataItem, "TitleOfCourtesy") %>
```

This code returns the value of the data source's TitleOfCourtesy field.

The Eval() method is slightly slower than the direct cast method, because of the reflection process. However, this overhead is unlikely to add much time to the processing of a request. The Eval() method also adds the extremely useful ability to format data fields on the fly. In order to use this feature, you must use the overloaded version of the Eval() method that accepts an additional format string parameter.

Format strings are generally made up of a placeholder and format indicator, which are wrapped inside curly brackets. A typical format string looks something like this:

```
"{0:C}"
```

In this case, the 0 represents the value that will be formatted, and the letter indicates a predetermined format style. In this case, C means currency format, which formats a number as a dollar figure (so 3400.34 becomes $3,400.34). To use this format string when data binding, you could use code like this:

```
DataBinder.Eval(Container.DataItem, "Price", "{0:C}")
```

Some of the other formatting options for numeric values are shown in Table 10-2.

Table 10-2. *Numeric Format Strings*

Type	Format String	Example
Currency	{0:C}	$1,234.50
		Brackets indicate negative values: ($1,234.50). Currency sign is locale-specific: (?1,234.50).
Scientific (Exponential)	{0:E}	1.234.50E+004
Percentage	{0:P}	45.6%
Fixed Decimal	{0:F?}	Depends on the number of decimal places you set. {0:F3} would be 123.400. {0:F0} would be 123.

Other examples can be found in the MSDN Help. For date or time values, there is also an extensive list. For example, if you want to write the BirthDate value in the format month/day/year (as in 12/30/05), you would use the following expression:

```
<%# DataBinder.Eval(Container.DataItem, "BirthDate", "{0:MM/dd/yy}") %>
```

Some more examples are shown in Table 10-3.

Table 10-3. *Time and Date Format Strings*

Type	Format String	Example
Short Date	{0:d}	M/d/yyyy
		(for example: 10/30/2005)
Long Date	{0:D}	dddd, MMMM dd, yyyy
		(for example: Monday, January 30, 2005)
Long Date and Short Time	{0:f}	dddd, MMMM dd, yyyy HH:mm aa
		(for example: Monday, January 30, 2005 10:00 AM)
Long Date and Long Time	{0:F}	dddd, MMMM dd, yyyy HH:mm:ss aa
		(for example: Monday, January 30, 2005 10:00:23 AM)
ISO Sortable Standard	{0:s}	yyyy-MM-dd HH:mm:ss
		(for example: 2005-01-30 10:00:23)
Month and Day	{0:M}	MMMM dd
		(for example: January 30)
General	{0:G}	M/d/yyyy HH:mm:ss aa (depends on locale-specific settings)
		(for example: 10/30/2002 10:00:23 AM)

The format characters are not specific to ASP.NET and data binding expressions. They can be used in VB .NET, C#, and all the other .NET languages as parameters for many methods. For example, the Decimal and DateTime types expose their own ToString() methods, which accept a format string.

Other Templates

As mentioned earlier, the ItemTemplate is not the only template supported by the Repeater, although it is the only one that is required. Table 10-4 lists the other optional templates.

Table 10-4. *Optional Repeater Templates*

Template	Description
HeaderTemplate	Determines the HTML for the report's header, and goes before any data bound item. For example, it can be used to open a <table> tag to create a tabular layout. It cannot use any data binding expressions.
AlternatingItemTemplate	This is the template that describes the representation of odd items (with a 0-based index). If not specified, all the items will be rendered as defined by the ItemTemplate.
SeparatorTemplate	Defines the HTML that goes between two consecutive items. It cannot contain data binding expressions.
FooterTemplate	Defines the HTML that concludes the report after all the data has been displayed. For example, it can be used to close a <table> tag opened in the HeaderTemplate. It cannot contain data binding expressions.

Figure 10-5 shows an example that defines a Repeater with several optional templates. It uses templates to create a header and footer, and to alternate the text between dark blue and italic maroon.

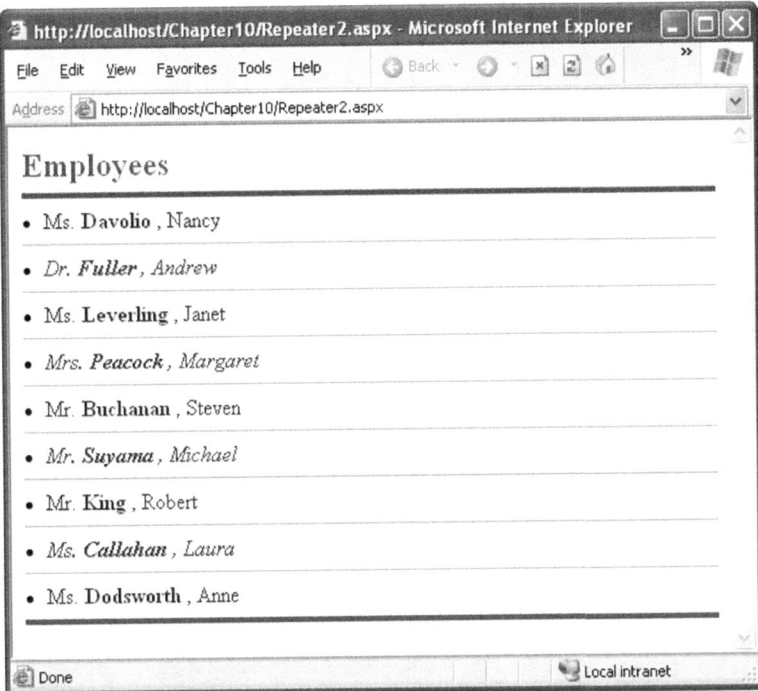

Figure 10-5. *A Repeater with multiple templates*

The following code defines the control and all its templates:

```
<asp:Repeater runat="server" ID="Repeater1">
  <HeaderTemplate>
    <font color="red" size=5"><b>Employees</b></font>
    <hr size="4" color="red">
  </HeaderTemplate>
  <ItemTemplate>
    <li>
    <font name="Verdana" color="darkblue">
    <%# DataBinder.Eval(Container.DataItem, "TitleOfCourtesy") %>
    <b><%# DataBinder.Eval(Container.DataItem, "LastName") %></b>,
    <%# DataBinder.Eval(Container.DataItem, "FirstName") %>
    </font>
    </li>
  </ItemTemplate>
  <AlternatingItemTemplate>
    <li>
    <font name="Courier" color="Maroon"><i>
    <%# DataBinder.Eval(Container.DataItem, "TitleOfCourtesy") %>
    <b><%# DataBinder.Eval(Container.DataItem, "LastName") %></b>,
    <%# DataBinder.Eval(Container.DataItem, "FirstName") %>
    </i></font>
    </li>
  </AlternatingItemTemplate>
  <SeparatorTemplate>
    <hr size="1" noshade>
  </SeparatorTemplate>
  <FooterTemplate>
    <hr size="4" color="red">
  </FooterTemplate>
</asp:Repeater>
```

The HeaderTemplate defines the report's title and a thick line. The ItemTemplate writes the employee's title of courtesy, first, and last names. The AlternatingItemTemplate shows the same information with a different font. The SeparatorTemplate only declares a thin line. Finally, the FooterTemplate declares a thick line, like the header. The code that retrieves the source DataReader and binds it to the Repeater remains unchanged from the previous example.

The Repeater's Events

The Repeater controls allow you to handle the following server-side events in addition to the events inherited from the Control class. Table 10-5 lists the events.

Table 10-5. *Repeater Events*

Event	Description
ItemCommand	Occurs when a button defined in a Repeater template is clicked. The RepeaterItemEventArgs has properties, such as CommandArgument, that return the button's argument; CommandName returns the button's name; and CommandSource returns a reference to the clicked button itself.
ItemCreated	Occurs when a new item is created. The event is raised for any type of templated item, and you can determine its type by reading the ItemType property of a RepeaterItemEventArgs argument. This event can be used to customize the item's appearance to highlight a specific value. For example, you might want to render the name of people who are no longer employed by your company in red, or render employees hired in the last month in bold. These details require conditional logic, and so they can't be specified in the template with a simple data binding expression.
ItemDataBound	Occurs when an item is bound to the control, but before it is rendered on the page. You can handle this event to change the format of a value before it is rendered. This event is not raised for the header, footer, and other parts of the control that are not bound.

In the next example, you'll see practical use of the ItemCommand event. Later in the chapter, you'll see how to use the ItemCreated event with the DataGrid control.

The ItemCommand Event

The ItemCommand event is required to solve a particular problem that occurs when you use ASP.NET controls in a template. The problem is that if you add a control to a template, the Repeater actually creates multiple copies of that control, one for each data item. Unfortunately, you don't have a reference to these newly created button control objects, and you can't connect any event handlers to their Button.Click events. As a result, you can't wire up the code that reacts to these events.

The way to resolve this problem is to use an event from the Repeater, *not* the contained button. The ItemCommand event serves this purpose, because it fires whenever any button is clicked. This process, where a control event in a template is turned into an event in the containing control, is called *event bubbling*.

■**Note** The Repeater isn't the only control to use event bubbling. You'll also need to use it with the same ItemCommand event in a DataList and DataGrid.

The next example extends the previous example by adding a button on the left side of each item. When this button is clicked, the page displays further information about the selected employee, such as the employee's title, address, and so on.

Figure 10-6 shows the resulting page. In this example, the page has been loaded and one of the buttons in the Repeater has been clicked, causing the page to post back and add the information for the selected record at the top of the page.

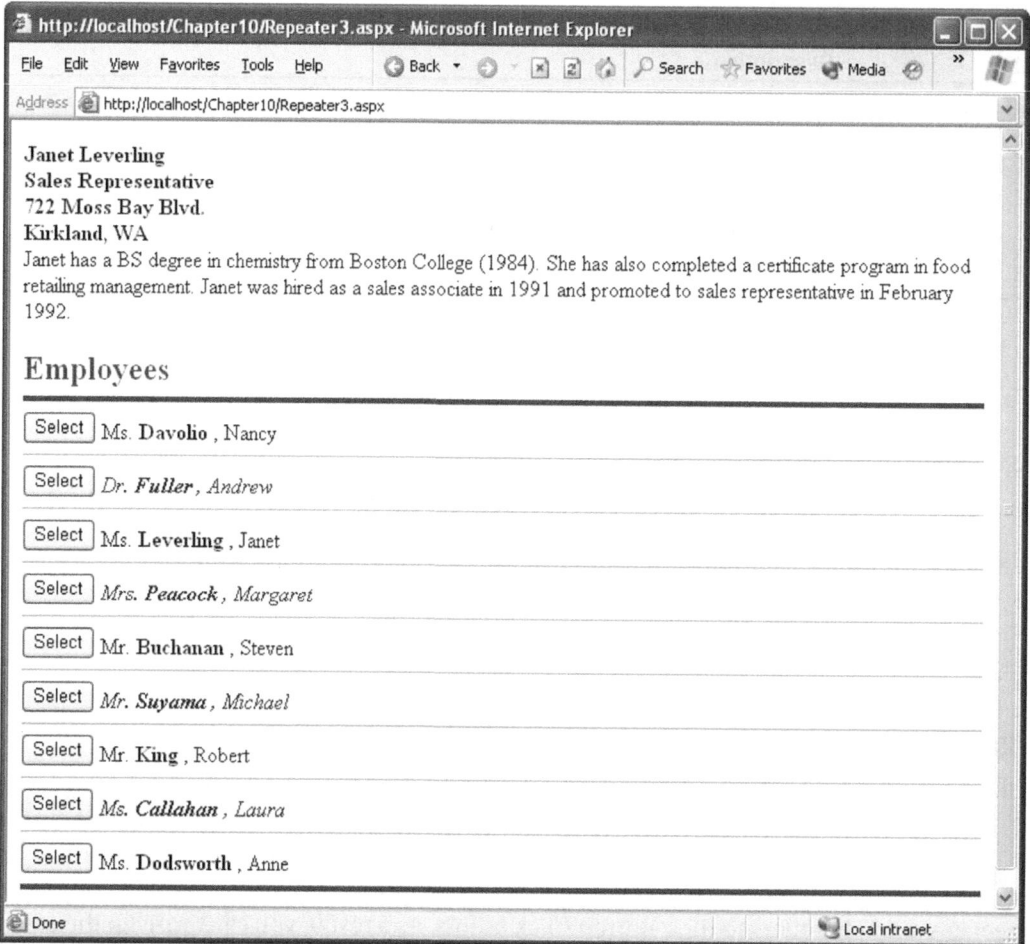

Figure 10-6. *A Repeater that raises the ItemCommand event*

> ■**Note** If there is more than a screenful of employees, you'll have to scroll down to find the employee that you want, and then scroll back up to see the data. This isn't a very practical design for actual use, but here the objective is to demonstrate the Repeater and keep the code as short as possible. In a real-world application, you would probably put the details on another page, or use two frames side by side so that the list of employees can be maintained without being refreshed and independently scrolled, as you'll see in master/detail pages in the next chapter.

To create this page, the first step is to declare the Button web control in the ItemTemplate and the AlternatingItemTemplate sections. Here are the revised templates:

```
<ItemTemplate>
  <asp:Button runat="server" Text="Select" CommandName="Select"
  CommandArgument='<%# DataBinder.Eval(Container.DataItem, "EmployeeID") %>'
  ID="Button1"/>
```

```
  <font name="Verdana" color="darkblue">
  <%# DataBinder.Eval(Container.DataItem, "TitleOfCourtesy") %><b>
  <%# DataBinder.Eval(Container.DataItem, "LastName") %></b>,
  <%# DataBinder.Eval(Container.DataItem, "FirstName") %></font>
</ItemTemplate>
<AlternatingItemTemplate>
  <asp:Button runat="server" Text="Select" CommandName="SelectAlternating"
    CommandArgument='<%# DataBinder.Eval(Container.DataItem, "EmployeeID") %>'
    ID="Button2"/>
  <font name="Courier" color="Maroon"><i>
  <%# DataBinder.Eval(Container.DataItem, "TitleOfCourtesy") %><b>
  <%# DataBinder.Eval(Container.DataItem, "LastName") %></b>,
  <%# DataBinder.Eval(Container.DataItem, "FirstName") %></i></font>
</AlternatingItemTemplate>
```

Note that this template assigns a different string to the CommandName property of the buttons defined in the two templates. This allows you to distinguish which button was pressed when the ItemCommand event is raised. You simply need to read the CommandName property of the RepeaterItemEventArgs, which is passed to the ItemCommand event. More importantly, the template binds the Button.CommandArgument property to the EmployeeID field of the data source so that you'll know which employee's details you need to display by reading the RepeaterItemEventArgs.CommandArgument property.

Here's the event handler that handles the button click, retrieves additional information, and displays it at the top of the page:

```
private void Repeater1_ItemCommand(object source,
  System.Web.UI.WebControls.RepeaterCommandEventArgs e)
{
    // Create a command to get the full details for the
    // selected record.
    string sql = "SELECT * FROM Employees WHERE EmployeeID = " +
      e.CommandArgument;
    SqlConnection con = new SqlConnection(connectionString);
    SqlCommand cmd = new SqlCommand(sql, con);

    // Display the full record details.
    con.Open();
    SqlDataReader reader = cmd.ExecuteReader(CommandBehavior.SingleRow);
    StringBuilder str = new StringBuilder();
    reader.Read();
    str.Append("<b>");
    str.Append(reader["FirstName"].ToString());
    str.Append(" ");
    str.Append(reader["LastName"].ToString());
    str.Append("<br>");
    str.Append(reader["Title"].ToString());
    str.Append("<br>");
    str.Append(reader["Address"].ToString());
```

```
str.Append("<br>");
str.Append(reader["City"].ToString());
str.Append(", ");
str.Append(reader["Region"].ToString());
str.Append("</b><br>");
str.Append(reader["Notes"].ToString());
MoreInfo.Text = str.ToString();

reader.Close();
con.Close();

// Set the ForeColor According to the CommandName.
MoreInfo.ForeColor = (e.CommandName == "Select" ?
System.Drawing.Color.DarkBlue : System.Drawing.Color.Maroon);
}
```

This procedure extracts the ID of the clicked employee, and uses it as parameter for a SQL query. The code then connected to the data source, creates a DataReader, and reads some of the fields from the first and only record of the DataReader. The code then shows the information in the label that's defined above the Repeater. The label is assigned a foreground color according to the clicked button's CommandName property so that the color is different if the button's parent item is an alternate item or not.

To make a more robust implementation of the same test page, you would replace the dynamic text of the query with a parameterized command in order to prevent SQL injection attacks that could be made by tampering with the page. You would probably also want to retrieve the Employee data from a database component instead of directly in the page. Chapter 8 shows examples of both of these techniques, which can plug into this example quite easily.

The DataList Control

While the Repeater control simply repeats a template and doesn't do much else, the DataList control offers built-in support for editing and selecting items, and it allows you to specify styles for the items through its properties. This spares you the need to code all the formatting directly in the template using raw HTML.

By default, each data bound item in a DataList is rendered within a row of a table structure. You can change the RepeatLayout property to Flow and have each item rendered within a <span> tag instead, but you'll most likely use the default table-based approach. This provides a nicer layout as well as the ability to assign colors to the rows, have rows of the same width, and so on. The RepeatColumns and the RepeatDirection properties also affect the layout of the control. These properties get or set the number of columns of the DataList in which the templated items will be rendered, and the direction with which the items will appear (horizontal or vertical).

For example, imagine you are displaying the number from 1 to 9. You could create a single column DataList like this:

1
2
3
. . .

Or you could create a three-column DataList with a RepeatDirection.Horizontal layout:

1	2	3
4	5	6
7	8	9

You could just as easily create the same three-column display with a RepeatDirection.Vertical layout:

1	4	7
2	5	8
3	6	9

In these examples, each item consists of a single data value (the number). But as with the Repeater control, each item in a DataList can include a combination of multiple data fields, HTML, controls, and so on.

Figure 10-7 shows a DataList that displays the same information shown by the Repeater control example, with a slightly different layout.

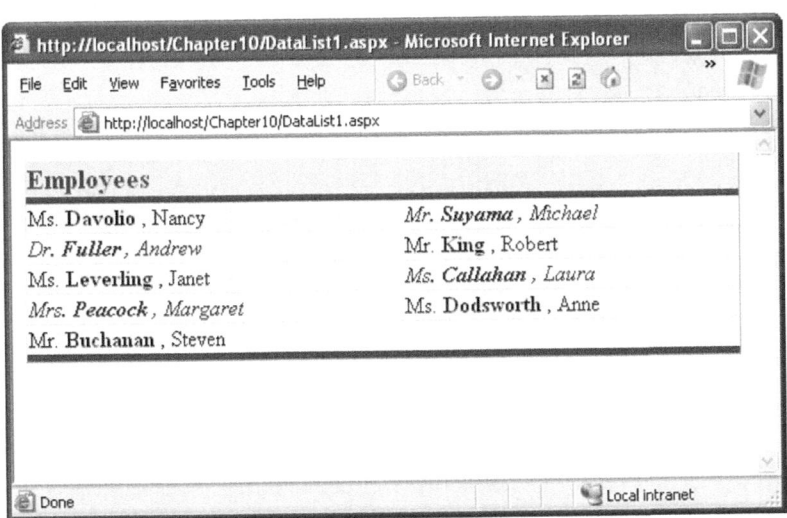

Figure 10-7. *A formatted DataList*

This DataList uses different styles to set the formatting for the templates. To set the styles of the various templates you use the HeaderStyle, ItemStyle, AlternatingItemStyle, SeparatorStyle, SelectedItemStyle, EditItemStyle, and FooterStyle properties. Each of these styles is relative to a template.

The styles are not simple single-value properties. Instead, they expose a Style object that provides properties such as ForeColor, BackColor, Font, and so on, which allow you to change almost any setting of the item's appearance. And if you don't want to hardcode all the appearance settings in the web page, you can set the CssClass property of the style object reference to a stylesheet class defined in the <style> section of an external CSS file.

Tip Visual Studio .NET makes it easier than ever to set DataList formatting. You can configure all the subproperties of each style (like the Font, BackColor, and ForeColor) by expanding the appropriate style properties in the Properties window. For example, to configure the font of the header, expand the HeaderStyle property to show the nested Font property, and set that. Another approach is to click the AutoFormat link at the bottom of the Properties window, which allows you to apply a consistent set of styles to the DataList at once by choosing from a list of presets.

The following code shows the declaration of a DataList control, complete with style settings (the initial portion) and templates:

```
<asp:DataList runat="server" ID="Datalist1"
  Width="100%"
  GridLines="Horizontal"
  RepeatColumns="2"
  HeaderStyle-Font-Size="15"
  HeaderStyle-Font-Bold="true"
  HeaderStyle-ForeColor="Red"
  HeaderStyle-BackColor="Yellow"
  HeaderStyle-BorderColor="Red"
  HeaderStyle-BorderWidth="5"
  FooterStyle-BorderColor="Red"
  FooterStyle-BorderWidth="5"
  ItemStyle-BackColor="LightCyan"
  ItemStyle-ForeColor="DarkBlue"
  AlternatingItemStyle-BackColor="LightYellow"
  AlternatingItemStyle-ForeColor="Maroon"
  AlternatingItemStyle-Font-Italic="true">
  <HeaderTemplate>
    Employees
  </HeaderTemplate>
  <ItemTemplate>
    <%# DataBinder.Eval(Container.DataItem, "TitleOfCourtesy") %>
    <b><%# DataBinder.Eval(Container.DataItem, "LastName") %></b>,
    <%# DataBinder.Eval(Container.DataItem, "FirstName") %>
  </ItemTemplate>
  <FooterTemplate></FooterTemplate>
</asp:DataList>
```

This DataList displays items in two vertical columns, because the DataList.RepeatColumns property is set to 2 and the RepeatDirection is RepeatDirection.Vertical (the default).

Note that this tag doesn't define a separate AlternatingItemTemplate template, although the DataList does support this template. Instead, this example simply defines some of the

AlternatingItemStyle properties so that the alternating item is formatted differently. The DataList control will take care of using the right styles for the even and odd rows of the table.

Also note that this tag doesn't use the SeparatorTemplate. Instead, it sets the GridLines properties to Horizontal so that the DataList will automatically display lines around the rows. If you want to define different separators (such as a separator image or something else), the SeparatorTemplate is still available. Finally, the FooterTemplate does not contain anything, but its BorderWidth property is set to 5 so it's displayed with a thick closing border line. The Page.Load event handler remains unchanged from the last example, except for the minor change that the code now binds to a DataList control, not a Repeater.

Selecting Items

Selecting a row means that the user can highlight or change the appearance of a row by clicking some sort of button or link. When the user clicks the button, not only will the row change its appearance, but your code will have the opportunity to handle the event and show detailed information in a separate label (a technique demonstrated earlier with the Repeater control).

The DataList control doesn't create any controls that allow the user to select a row. However, it does have built-in support for rendering selected rows with a different style. Figure 10-8 shows an example where the user can select items in a DataList, and the full record information is displayed in another control.

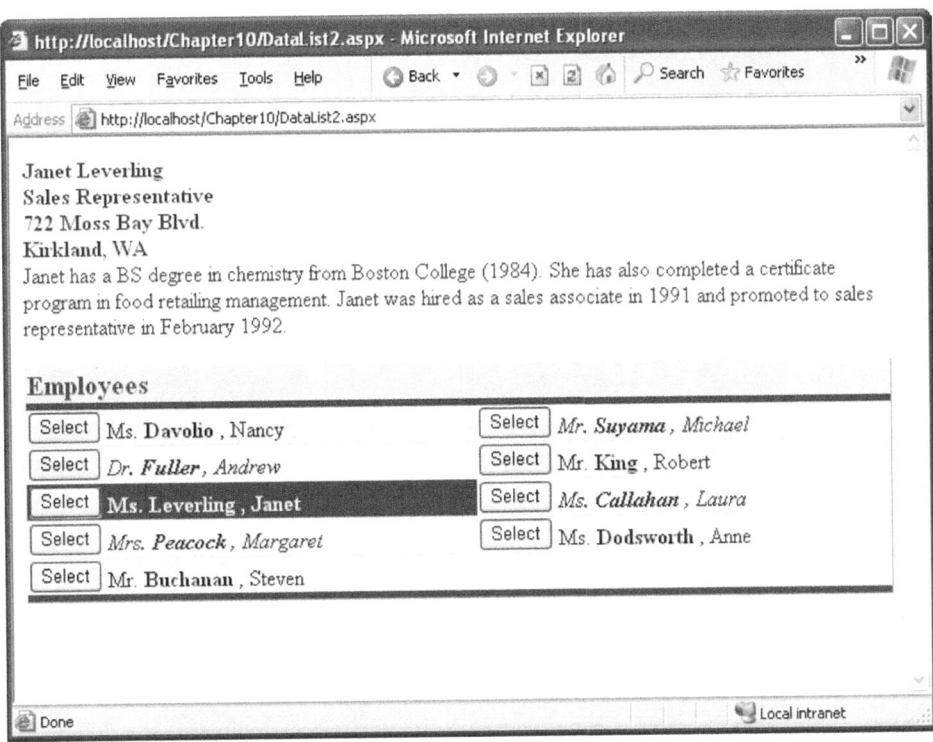

Figure 10-8. *Selection with a DataList*

This example is very similar to the earlier page that demonstrated selection with the Repeater. The difference here is that you can declaratively specify how to represent a selected row through the SelectedItemStyle properties. The DataList also defines a specific event for receiving notification about selection, called SelectedIndexChanged, which fires when the select button is clicked. You still need to create a Button or LinkButton control that triggers the event. However, if you set the Button.CommandName property to the text string Select, the DataList will raise the SelectedIndexChanged event automatically before it raises the generic ItemCommand event. (You might still want to use the ItemCommand event to handle events from buttons that have a different CommandName property, and aren't designed for record selection. This distinction helps you organize your code more effectively.).

There are a slew of minor changes that you need to make to enable selection with the DataList. First, you need to make sure you define a different style for selected items. Otherwise, the selected item will be rendered in the same way as ordinary items. You can specify this formatting by configuring the SelectedItemStyle in the Properties window, or you can add style attributes to the control tag by hand. Here's an example that specifies that selected items should be rendered in bold, using yellow text on a red background:

```
<asp:DataList runat="server" ID="Datalist1"
...
   SelectedItemStyle-ForeColor="Yellow"
   SelectedItemStyle-BackColor="Red"
   SelectedItemStyle-Font-Bold="true"
... />
```

You also need to revise the ItemTemplate so that it includes the selection button, as shown here:

```
<ItemTemplate>
   <asp:Button runat="server" Text="Select" CommandName="Select" />
   <%# DataBinder.Eval(Container.DataItem, "TitleOfCourtesy") %>
   <b><%# DataBinder.Eval(Container.DataItem, "LastName") %></b>,
   <%# DataBinder.Eval(Container.DataItem, "FirstName") %>
</ItemTemplate>
```

When the SelectionIndexChanged event fires, the DataList will provide you with information about which row was selected, so you don't need to explicitly pass this information through the CommandArgument. However, to make your life easier, you should indicate which property represents the unique primary key for the table. To do this, set the DataList.DataKeyField property with the field name. Once you take this step, you have the ability to retrieve the key for a specific row at any time from the DataList.DataKeys collection. In this case, the key field is the EmployeeID:

```
<asp:DataList runat="server" ID="Datalist1"
  DataKeyField="EmployeeID"
... />
```

■**Note** The DataKeyField must be present in the data source, but it doesn't need to be displayed in the DataList template. Even if it's not displayed, the DataList will quietly keep track of the ID for each item. This is another advantage of using the DataKeyField.

Finally, make sure that you only fill the control the first time the page is created. When the page is posted back, the contents of the control will be re-created automatically through view state. If you rebind the control in the Page.Load event handler on every postback, you'll inadvertently erase the selection information before the SelectedIndexChanged event can fire, and no action will be taken.

Now you can define the event handler for the SelectedIndexChanged event. Here's the code you'll need to determine what item is selected and display the related information:

```
private void Datalist1_SelectedIndexChanged(object sender, System.EventArgs e)
{
    // Retrieve the unique ID for the selected row.
    // Note that this item must be explicitly cast to the
    // appropriate data type (in this case, an integer).
    int empID = (int)Datalist1.DataKeys[Datalist1.SelectedIndex];

    // Create a query for this record.
    string sql = "SELECT * FROM Employees WHERE EmployeeID = " +
      empID.ToString();

    // (Command to connect to the database and build the HTML string omitted.)

    // Set the ForeColor according to the ItemType.
    ListItemType lit = Datalist1.Items[Datalist1.SelectedIndex].ItemType;
    MoreInfo.ForeColor = (lit == ListItemType.Item ?
      System.Drawing.Color.DarkBlue : System.Drawing.Color.Maroon);
}
```

This event handler first retrieves the selected item's key by accessing the DataKeys collection at the index specified in the DataList.SelectedIndex property. This property is automatically set to the index of the selected row when the select button is clicked. It can also be set programmatically at any time.

■**Tip** If you want to deselect the item that's currently selected, set the SelectedIndex property to -1.

The event handler uses the key of the selected item to retrieve the record for the respective employee. It then displays the retrieved information in a label. It also sets the label's foreground color according to whether the selected item is or is not an alternate item, as in the previous example. To make this determination, the code needs to read the ItemType property of the item from the DataList.Items collection.

Editing Items

The DataList control also has built-in support for editing items. To take advantage of this feature, you need to define an EditItemTemplate and declare the input controls that will be shown when the user presses the Edit button. The editing mechanism is very similar to the selection mechanism—you create the edit button, and the DataList takes over automatically when the button is clicked.

Figure 10-9 shows the DataList during the editing of an item.

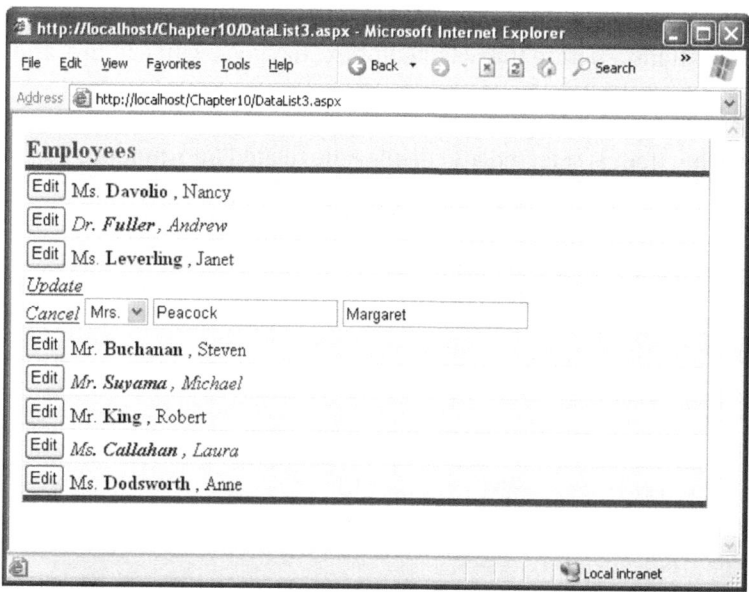

Figure 10-9. *Editing with the DataList*

To support editing, you need to organize your code in a slightly different way. That's because you need to bind the DataList to your data source at several different times. These include the following:

- When the page is first created

- When the user begins an edit

- When the user cancels an edit

- When the user commits an edit

To support this design it makes sense to move your data binding code to a separate private method. In this example, the method is named BindList(). Once you place your data binding code into a separate method, you can call it any time the grid needs to be bound. For example, when the Page.Load event fires you can use this compact logic:

```
private void Page_Load(object sender, System.EventArgs e)
{
    if (!Page.IsPostBack)
```

```
        BindList();
}

private void BindList()
{
    // (Data access and data binding code goes here.)
}
```

With this structure in place, you're ready to add the editing logic.

Initiating an Edit

To allow the user to start editing, you must add a new button to the ItemTemplate section with the CommandName property set to Edit.

```
<ItemTemplate>
    <asp:Button runat="server" Text="Edit" CommandName="Edit" ID="Button1" />
    <%# DataBinder.Eval(Container.DataItem, "TitleOfCourtesy") %>
    <b><%# DataBinder.Eval(Container.DataItem, "LastName") %></b>,
    <%# DataBinder.Eval(Container.DataItem, "FirstName") %>
</ItemTemplate>
```

This button will raise the DataList.EditCommand event. When this event fires, you simply need to set the EditIndex to the appropriate row and bind the DataList to update the display:

```
private void Datalist1_Edit(Object sender, DataListCommandEventArgs e)
{
    Datalist1.EditItemIndex = (int)e.Item.ItemIndex;
    BindList();
}
```

■Tip To turn on editing mode for a row, you simply set the DataList.EditItemIndex. You could do this programmatically in response to another control event, which means you could use a different set of controls (rather than a dedicated edit button) to start editing mode, if need be. You'll notice that the DataList only allows one row to be edited at a time. However, you could work around this limitation by adding edit controls to the ordinary ItemTemplate. In this case, all the rows would be editable all the time.

The EditItemTemplate

When you rebind the DataList, it will automatically render the row that's in edit mode using the EditItemTemplate. To create this template, you need to include a set of input controls, one for each field that the user can modify. In addition, the EditItemTemplate also needs to contain two additional buttons, one for committing the edit and one for canceling the edit. If these buttons have their CommandName property set to Cancel and Update, respectively, they will raise the DataList.CancelCommand and DataList.UpdateCommand events. (If you choose a different CommandName, these buttons will only raise the generic ItemCommand event.)

Here's the template used for the current example:

```
<EditItemTemplate>
  <asp:LinkButton runat="server" Text="Update"
  CommandName="Update" ID="Linkbutton1" /><br>
  <asp:LinkButton runat="server" Text="Cancel"
  CommandName="Cancel" ID="Linkbutton2" />
  <asp:DropDownList runat="server" ID="EditTitle"
  SelectedIndex=
'<%# GetSelectedTitle(DataBinder.Eval(Container.DataItem, "TitleOfCourtesy")) %>'
  DataSource='<%# TitlesOfCourtesy %>' />
  <asp:TextBox runat="server" ID="EditLastName"
  Text='<%# DataBinder.Eval(Container.DataItem, "LastName") %>' />
  <asp:TextBox runat="server" ID="EditFirstName"
  Text='<%# DataBinder.Eval(Container.DataItem, "FirstName") %>' />
</EditItemTemplate>
```

This template uses two text boxes to edit the last and first name, and a drop-down list that allows the user to pick a title of courtesy from a limited selection of possible titles. To create this list, you need to resort to a little trick. The problem is that you can't assign the data source for the list by setting the DataSource property at runtime, because the DropDownList is only created when the DataList switches a row into editing mode. This happens after the EditItem event is fired. However, you can set the DataSource property declaratively to a data binding expression that points to a custom property. This custom property can then return a suitable data source with the available titles of courtesy.

Here's the definition for the TitlesOfCourtesy property in the web page class:

```
public string[] TitlesOfCourtesy
{
  get {
    return new string[4]{"]{"Mr.", "Dr.", "Ms.", "Mrs."};
  }
}
```

■**Note**   This list of titles of courtesy is by no means complete. There are also "Miss," "Lord," "Lady," "Sir," "None," and so on. For a real-world application the titles could come from a database table or configuration file.

This step ensures that the drop-down list is populated, but it doesn't solve the related problem of making sure the right title is selected in the list for the current value. Once again, the EditItem event occurs too early. You could handle the ItemCreated event, detect when the item being created is of type EditItem, find the child DropDownList control, and select the item that represents the current title of courtesy. Although this approach would work, a much simpler approach is to declaratively bind the SelectedIndex to a custom method that takes the current title and returns the index of that value. In this example, the GetSelectedTitle() method performs this task. It takes a title as input and returns the index of the respective value in the array returned by TitlesOfCourtesy:

```
private int GetSelectedTitle(object title)
{
    return Array.IndexOf(TitlesOfCourtesy, title.ToString());
}
```

This code searches the array using the static Array.IndexOf() method. Note that you must explicitly cast the title to a string. That's because the DataBinder.Eval() method returns an object, not a string, and that value is passed to the GetSelectedTitle() method.

Tip To make an even more interesting EditItemTemplate, you could add validator controls to verify input values, as discussed in Chapter 5.

Canceling and Committing the Edit

Canceling the edit process is quite straightforward. It's all about setting the DataList.EditItemIndex property. If this property is set to -1, no row will be placed in edit mode, and the EditItemTemplate will not be rendered when you rebind the grid.

```
private void Datalist1_Cancel(Object sender, DataListCommandEventArgs e)
{
    Datalist1.EditItemIndex = -1;
    BindList();
}
```

Updating the data source with the new values is a bit trickier, but not difficult. The information that you need to update the record is as follows: the ID of the record to modify, the new title for courtesy, and the first and last names. You can retrieve the ID from the DataKeys collection, as demonstrated earlier in the row selection example. Here's the code you need:

```
private void Datalist1_Update(Object sender, DataListCommandEventArgs e)
{
    // Get the ID of the record to update.
    int empID = (int)Datalist1.DataKeys[e.Item.ItemIndex];
    ...
```

For the other values, you need to retrieve a reference to the corresponding input controls. You can then read their current content. To retrieve the input controls, you must use the FindControl() method of the item that's currently being edited. FindControl() searches all the contained control objects, looking for the control with the specified name. It then returns the corresponding control object, which you can cast to the appropriate type (DropDownList or a TextBox in this example) so that you can read the properties you need.

```
...
// Get the references to the edit controls.
 DropDownList title = (DropDownList)e.Item.FindControl("EditTitle");
 TextBox lastName = (TextBox)e.Item.FindControl("EditLastName");
 TextBox firstName = (TextBox)e.Item.FindControl("EditFirstName");
 ...
```

Once you have this data, you can build a SQL UPDATE command, and execute it as demonstrated over the previous two chapters. In this example, a parameterized command is used to remove the possibility of SQL injection attacks.

```
...
// Create the Connection and the Command.
string sql = @"UPDATE Employees SET TitleOfCourtesy = @TitleOfCourtesy, " +
  "LastName = @LastName, FirstName = @FirstName " +
  "WHERE EmployeeID = @EmployeeID";
SqlConnection con = new SqlConnection(connectionString);
SqlCommand cmd = new SqlCommand(sql, con);

// Create the required parameters.
cmd.Parameters.Add(new SqlParameter("@TitleOfCourtesy",
  SqlDbType.NVarChar, 25));
cmd.Parameters["@TitleOfCourtesy"].Value = title.SelectedItem.Text.Trim();
cmd.Parameters.Add(new SqlParameter("@LastName", SqlDbType.NVarChar, 20));
cmd.Parameters["@LastName"].Value = lastName.Text.Trim();
cmd.Parameters.Add(new SqlParameter("@FirstName", SqlDbType.NVarChar, 10));
cmd.Parameters["@FirstName"].Value = firstName.Text.Trim();
cmd.Parameters.Add(new SqlParameter("@EmployeeID", SqlDbType.Int, 4));
cmd.Parameters["@EmployeeID"].Value = empID;

// Execute the Command.
try
{
    con.Open();
    cmd.ExecuteNonQuery();
}
finally
{
    con.Close();
}
...
```

As a last step, you must stop the editing mode by setting EditItemIndex to -1 and rebind the DataList.

```
...
// Stop the editing and rebind the list.
Datalist1.EditItemIndex = -1;
BindList();
}
```

Deleting Items

The DataList control supports yet another special value for the CommandName property of its buttons—Delete. The DataList raises the DeleteCommand event when a Delete button is clicked. Your event handler can then retrieve the ID of the record to delete from the DataKeys collection, and executes a SQL DELETE statement that passes that ID as parameter. Because the code is so similar to the code of previous samples, it isn't shown here.

Loading Templates Dynamically

All the templates used so far have been hard-coded in the .aspx page. However, in some situations you may want to load a template dynamically at runtime. For example, you may want to vary the appearance or editing capabilities of a DataList depending on the type of user (administrator, guest, manager, and so on) who is currently using the application. In this case, you can define the code for different template versions in different files (or even in other data sources, like a database record). You can then load this information at runtime.

The following example allows the user to choose a layout mode by selecting one of two radio buttons. Depending on which option is selected, a different template is loaded dynamically. Figure 10-10 shows both views.

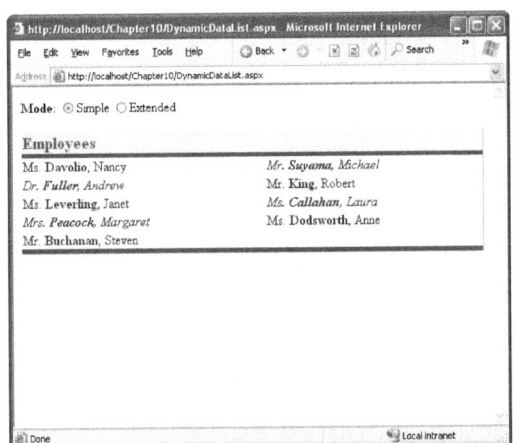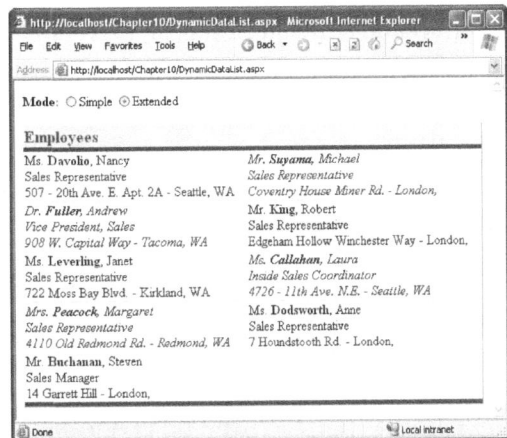

Figure 10-10. *Loading templates dynamically*

The page loads one of two template file every time the page is loaded or posted back, using the Page.LoadTemplate() method. The template object is then assigned to the DataList.ItemTemplate property.

```
private void Page_Load(object sender, System.EventArgs e)
{
    // Decide which template to use.
    string templateFile = (SimpleMode.Checked ?
      "DataList_SimpleTemplate.ascx" : "DataList_ExtTemplate.ascx");
```

```
    // Load the item template.
    Datalist1.ItemTemplate = Page.LoadTemplate(templateFile);

    // Bind the DataList.
    BindList();
}
```

The first template file, DataList_SimpleTemplate.ascx, contains a simplified version of the ItemTemplate, as shown in the earlier examples. You must also add a Control directive to specify the use of the C# language.

```
<%@ Control Language="C#" %>
<%# DataBinder.Eval(
  ((DataListItem)Container).DataItem, "TitleOfCourtesy") %>
<b><%# DataBinder.Eval(
  ((DataListItem)Container).DataItem, "LastName") %></b>,
<%# DataBinder.Eval( ((DataListItem)Container).DataItem, "FirstName") %>
```

Note that this template needs to cast the Container object to DataListItem in order to access the DataItem property that exposes the data for each item. That's because the template is defined outside the DataList.

The second template, DataList_ExtTemplate.ascx, is similar. It merely adds some extra data, namely the content of the Address, City, and Region fields of the current record. Here is its complete code:

```
<%@ Control Language="C#" %>
<%# DataBinder.Eval(
  ((DataListItem)Container).DataItem, "TitleOfCourtesy") %>
<b><%# DataBinder.Eval(
  ((DataListItem)Container).DataItem,"LastName") %></b>,
<%# DataBinder.Eval( ((DataListItem)Container).DataItem, "FirstName") %><br>
<%# DataBinder.Eval( ((DataListItem)Container).DataItem, "Title") %><br>
<%# DataBinder.Eval( ((DataListItem)Container).DataItem, "Address") %> -
<%# DataBinder.Eval( ((DataListItem)Container).DataItem, "City") %>,
<%# DataBinder.Eval( ((DataListItem)Container).DataItem, "Region") %>
```

You can now load the page and switch from simple to extended mode and vice versa.

Tip You can use dynamic template files with the Repeater control, too. The code for this approach is almost exactly the same, except that in the template file you must cast the Container object to the RepeaterItem type instead of the DataListItem type.

The DataGrid Control

The DataGrid control is by far the most advanced control for creating reports and data editing pages. It supports the same features as the DataList does, including templated items and styles, dynamically loaded templates, and events for selecting, editing, and deleting an item. In addition, it has built-in support for paginating items, sorting, and displaying data in a grid with multiple columns.

The DataGrid is the only one of the rich data list controls that can render a basic view of your data without forcing you to define any templates or styles. To try this out, you can define the DataGrid with the simple tag shown here:

```
<asp:DataGrid runat="server" ID="DataGrid1" />
```

You can then connect to your data source, perform a query, and bind the results to the DataGrid as shown here:

```
DataGrid1.DataSource = reader;
DataGrid.DataBind();
```

This DataGrid will automatically build a table that has one column for each field in the data source, and one row for each item (with an extra row for the column titles). Figure 10-11 shows this default representation.

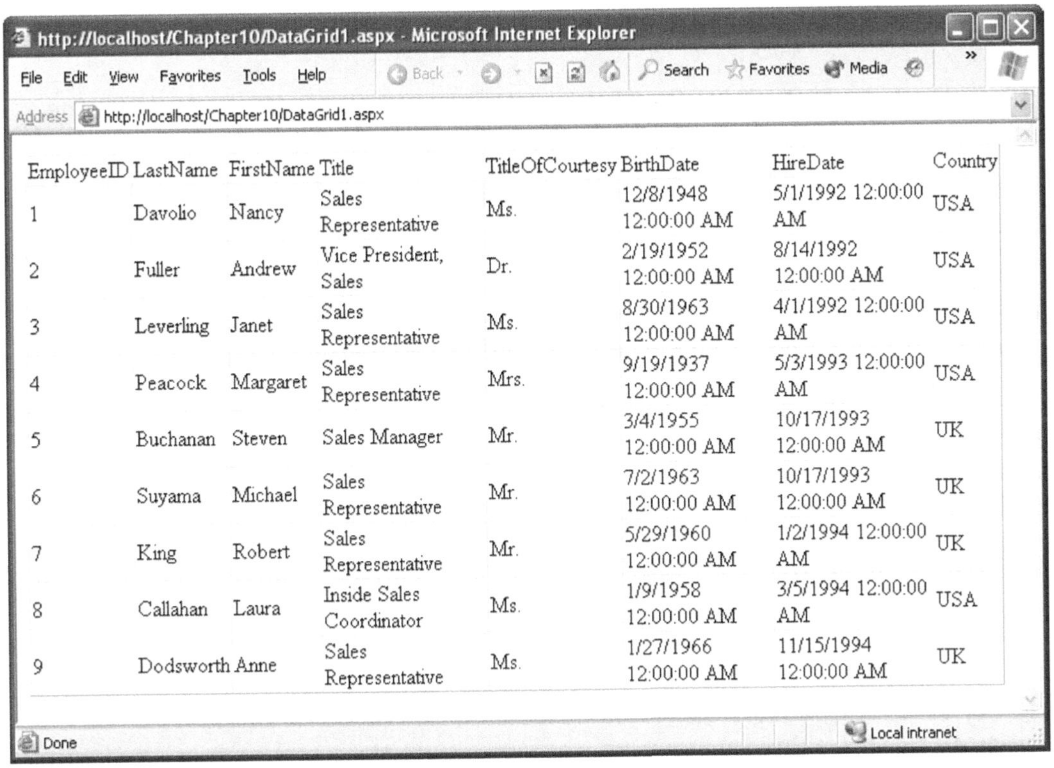

Figure 10-11. *The bare-bones DataGrid*

Clearly, this DataGrid lacks a few niceties (like clearer common titles and a better format for date values so that they don't show the irrelevant time portion). In the next section, you'll learn how easy it is to configure these details.

Defining Columns

You won't always want the DataGrid control to automatically create all the columns for you. It's much more likely that you'll want to show only certain fields, configure the field order, and control how each field is displayed. In order to do this, you must first set the DataGrid.AutoGenerateColumns property to false. Once you take this step, the DataGrid will not render any default columns. It's up to you to define them all.

To define DataGrid columns, you add them in a <Columns> section of the DataGrid control tag. Each column can be any of several different types, including the following:

- **BoundColumn.** This column displays text from a field in the DataSource.

- **ButtonColumn.** This column displays a command button for each item in the list.

- **EditCommandColumn.** This column displays editing buttons for each item in the list.

- **HyperlinkColumn.** This column displays its contents (a field from the data source or static text) as a hyperlink.

- **TemplateColumn.** This column allows you to specify multiple fields, custom controls, and anything you would normally put in template for a DataList control.

For example, here's the definition for a single data bound column. It sets the text in the header, the width, and the field of data that will be displayed.

```
<asp:BoundColumn HeaderText="ID" ItemStyle-Width="30px"
  DataField="EmployeeID" />
```

The next example creates a DataGrid that includes four bound columns, one for the ID, title of courtesy, last name, and first name of the employee. Additionally, it defines several style settings (which are very similar to the style settings used by the DataList).

```
<asp:DataGrid runat="server" ID="Datagrid1"
  AutoGenerateColumns="False"
  Width="100%"
  HeaderStyle-Font-Size="10"
  HeaderStyle-Font-Bold="true"
  HeaderStyle-ForeColor="Red"
  HeaderStyle-BackColor="Yellow"
  HeaderStyle-BorderColor="Red"
  HeaderStyle-BorderWidth="5"
  ItemStyle-BackColor="LightCyan"
  ItemStyle-ForeColor="DarkBlue"
  AlternatingItemStyle-BackColor="LightYellow"
  AlternatingItemStyle-ForeColor="Maroon"
  AlternatingItemStyle-Font-Italic="true">
<Columns>
  <asp:BoundColumn HeaderText="ID" ItemStyle-Width="30px"
    DataField="EmployeeID" />
  <asp:BoundColumn HeaderText="Title" ItemStyle-Width="50px"
    DataField="TitleOfCourtesy" />
```

```
    <asp:BoundColumn HeaderText="Last Name"
      ItemStyle-Width="150px" DataField="LastName" />
    <asp:BoundColumn HeaderText="First Name" DataField="FirstName" />
  </Columns>
</asp:DataGrid>
```

When you bind the data to this DataGrid, you'll see the much more interesting (although somewhat garish) page shown in Figure 10-12.

Tip Each column also provides a DataFormatString property you can use to configure the appearance of numbers and dates using the format strings described earlier in Table 10-2 and Table 10-3.

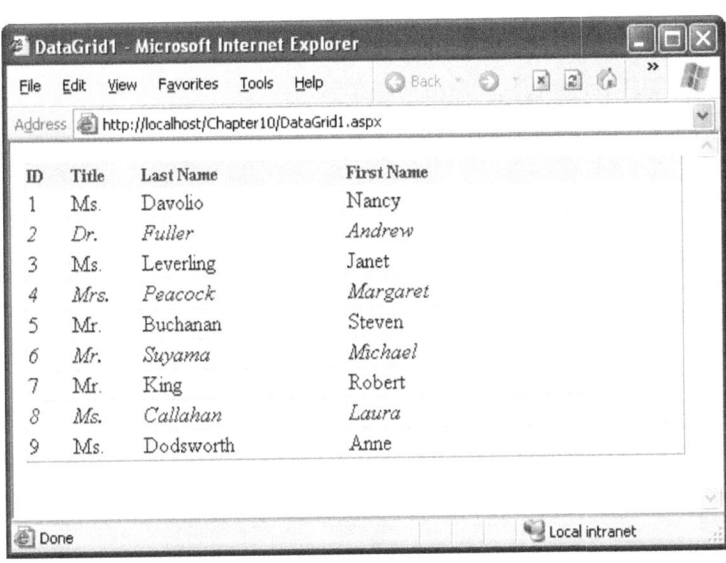

Figure 10-12. *A formatted DataGrid*

When setting style properties, you can use two similar syntaxes (and you'll see both of them in this chapter). First, you can use the object-walker syntax to indicate the extended style properties as tag attributes. Here's an example:

```
<asp:DataGrid runat="server" ID="Datagrid1"
  ItemStyle-ForeColor="DarkBlue" ... />
  ...
</asp:DataGrid>
```

Alternatively, you can add nested tags, as shown here:

```
<asp:DataGrid runat="server" ID="Datagrid1" ...>
  <ItemStyle ForeColor="DarkBlue" ... />
  ...
</asp:DataGrid>
```

Both of these approaches are equivalent. However, there's one other decision you make when setting style properties. You can specify global style properties that affect every column in the grid (as in the previous examples), or you can define column-specific styles. To create a column-specific style, you need to add style attributes or a nested tag inside the appropriate column tag. This technique is most often used to define specific column widths, as shown here:

```
<asp:DataGrid runat="server" ID="Datagrid1" ...>
  <Columns>
    <asp:BoundColumn HeaderText="ID" ItemStyle-Width="30px"
      DataField="EmployeeID" />
    ...
  </Columns>
</asp:DataGrid>
```

Or equivalently, with a nested tag:

```
<asp:DataGrid runat="server" ID="Datagrid1" ...>
  <Columns>
    <asp:BoundColumn HeaderText="ID" DataField="EmployeeID">
      <ItemStyle Width="30px">
    </asp:BoundColumn>
    ...
  </Columns>
</asp:DataGrid>
```

There's no reason you should code the style properties or the columns by hand, because Visual Studio .NET includes tools for automating both processes. To set style properties, you can use the Properties window. You can apply global styles by modifying the style properties (like ItemStyle, AlternatingItemStyle, HeaderStyle, and so on). You can even set a combination of styles using a preset theme by clicking the Auto Format link in the Properties window, and then tweaking those styles. Figure 10-13 shows the Auto Format dialog box with the preset styles you can choose.

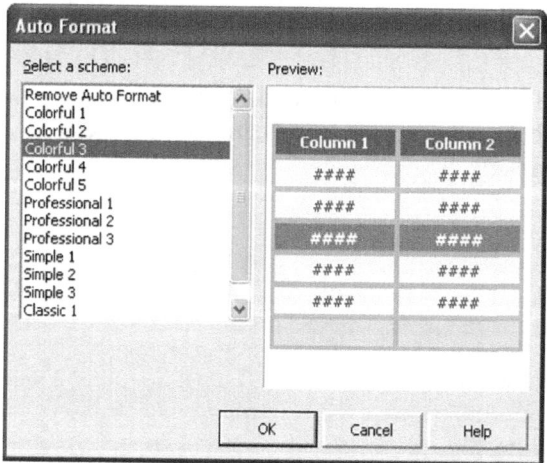

Figure 10-13. *Automatically formatting a DataGrid*

Configuring columns and column-specific styles is just as easy. You simply need to click the ellipsis (. . .) next to the Columns property in the Properties window. Alternatively, you can click the Property Builder link and select the Columns tab on the left. Either way, you'll see the designer shown in Figure 10-14, which allows you to define new columns and set their properties. Select the Format tab to fine-tune the appearance of each row, column, and header with styles, and the Borders tab to change to overall look of the table borders.

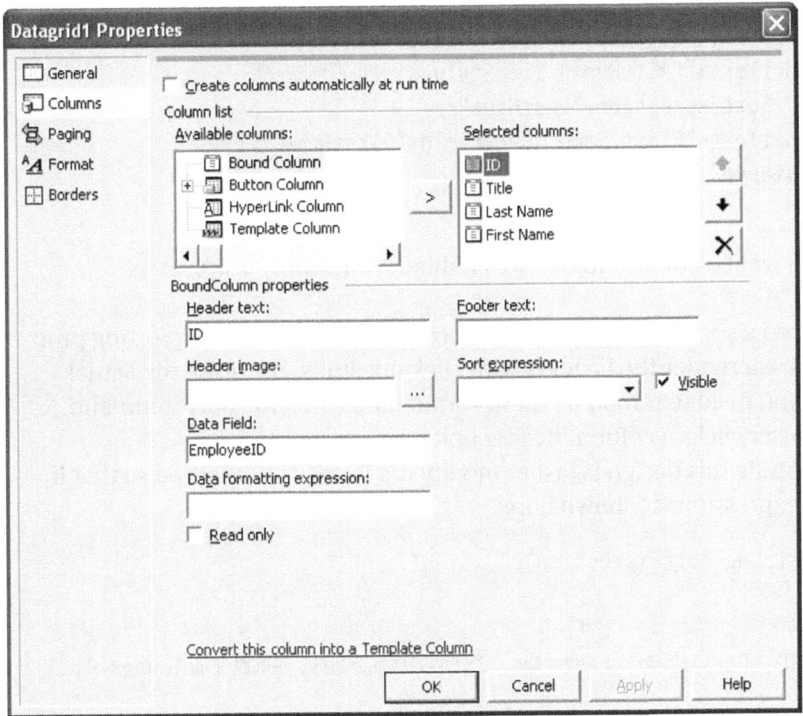

Figure 10-14. *Configuring DataGrid columns at design time*

Tip One useful feature of the DataGrid is the ability to hide individual columns. For example, you could allow the user to set certain preferences that configure the display to be either verbose or streamlined with only a few important columns. This differs from the DataList, which contains all its information in a single cell and cannot be dynamically configured. To hide a column, use the Columns collection for the DataGrid. For example, setting gridAuthors.Columns[2].Visible to false would hide the third column (columns are numbered starting at zero). Hidden columns are left out of the generated HTML entirely.

Sorting Rows

The sort feature is one of the enhancements of the DataGrid over the DataList control. In order to enable it, you must set the DataGrid.AllowSorting property to true. Next, you need to define a SortExpression for each column that can be sorted. This sort expression is essentially the same as the ORDER BY clause in a SQL query. It can include a single field or a list of comma-separated fields, optionally with the word ASC or DESC added after the column name to sort in ascending or descending order.

The amended markup for the declaring the columns is shown here:

```
<Columns>
  <asp:BoundColumn HeaderText="ID" ItemStyle-Width="30px" DataField="EmployeeID"
  SortExpression="EmployeeID"/>
  <asp:BoundColumn HeaderText="Title" ItemStyle-Width="50px"
  DataField="TitleOfCourtesy" SortExpression="TitleOfCourtesy"/>
  <asp:BoundColumn HeaderText="Last Name" ItemStyle-Width="150px"
  DataField="LastName" SortExpression="LastName"/>
  <asp:BoundColumn HeaderText="First Name" DataField="FirstName"
  SortExpression="FirstName"/>
</Columns>
```

Note that if you don't want a column to be sort-enabled, you simply don't set its SortExpression property.

Once you've associated a sort expression with the column and set the AllowSorting property to true, the DataGrid will render the headers with clickable links. However, the actual sorting is still up to you. You need to rebind the new, sorted data when the SortCommand event is raised when the user clicks a column header link

The easiest way to handle this design is just to modify the BindGrid() method so that it accepts an optional sort expression, as shown here:

```
private void BindGrid(string sortExpression)
{
    string sql =
      "SELECT EmployeeID, FirstName, LastName, TitleOfCourtesy FROM Employees ";
    if (sortExpression != "")
      sql += " ORDER BY " + sortExpression;

    // (Now execute the slightly modified query.)
}
```

The next step is to add the event handler for the SortCommand event. In this event handler, you need to call BindGrid() and pass the sort expression for the selected column.

```
private void Datagrid1_SortCommand(object source,
  System.Web.UI.WebControls.DataGridSortCommandEventArgs e)
{
    BindGrid(e.SortExpression);
}
```

Although this approach works, it isn't the best approach if you expect the data to be sorted frequently, because each sorting operation requires another trip to the database. Here's a case where you can realize some real benefits by using the DataSet instead of the DataReader. If you use a DataSet, you can simply store it somewhere (such as in the Session, Cache, or ViewState collections). You can then retrieve the DataSet on subsequent postbacks, and just update the sorting order by changing the Sort property of the DataView. The next example demonstrates this technique, and uses caching to ensure that the page is very scalable.

The first step that you need to perform is to make sure the sort order is stored in view state. This ensures that the sort information is always available, even if the page is posted back later due to another page event.

```
private void Datagrid1_SortCommand(object source,
  System.Web.UI.WebControls.DataGridSortCommandEventArgs e)
{
    ViewState["SortExpression"] = e.SortExpression;
    BindGrid();
}
```

Next, you must revise the BindGrid() method. Here's the code that you need to implement the same solution in a much more efficient way—by caching the DataSet for a fixed amount of time:

```
private void BindGrid()
{
    DataSet ds;
    // Check the cache.
    if (Cache["Employees"] != null)
    {
        ds = (DataSet)Cache["Employees"];
    }
    else
    {
        // Create the DataSet.
        ds = CreateDataSet();

        // Cache the DataSet for five minutes.
        Cache.Insert("Employees", ds, null, DateTime.Now.AddMinutes(5),
          TimeSpan.Zero);
    }

    // Retrieve the default view for the DataSet.
    DataView dv = ds.Tables["Employees"].DefaultView;

    // Set the sort order.
    dv.Sort = (string)ViewState["SortExpression"];

    // Bind the grid.
    Datagrid1.DataSource = dv;
    Datagrid1.DataBind();
}

private DataSet CreateDataSet()
{
    string sql =
      "SELECT EmployeeID, FirstName, LastName, TitleOfCourtesy FROM Employees ";
    SqlConnection con = new SqlConnection(connectionString);
```

```
    SqlDataAdapter da = new SqlDataAdapter(sql, con);
    DataSet ds = new DataSet();
    da.Fill(ds, "Employees");
    return ds;
}
```

If you load the page and click the header link of the Last Name column the rows should be sorted as shown in Figure 10-15. The page works exactly as it did with the previous design, but now the database is only queried once, and the DataSet information is reused for all the postbacks that occur over the next five minutes, from any client who accesses this page.

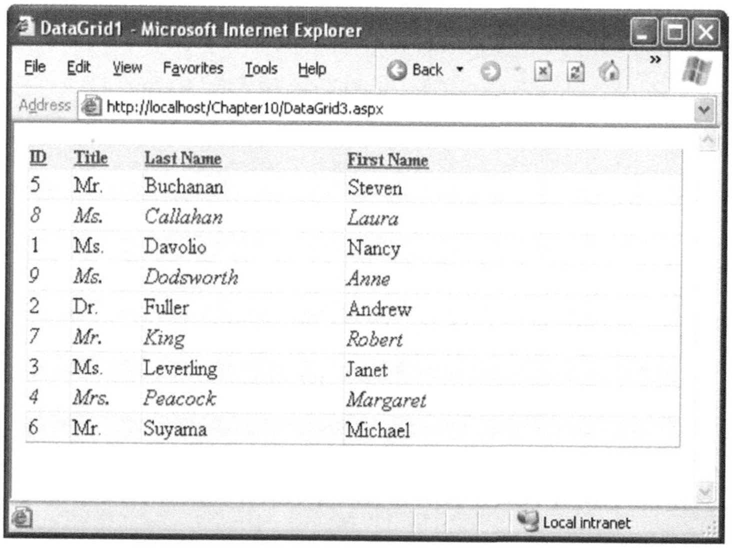

Figure 10-15. *Sorting the DataGrid*

Selecting Rows

The DataGrid allows you to select rows similarly to the way you did with the DataList control. The first step is to declare a new column of type ButtonColumn. This automatically creates a button or link button in every row. You should set the CommandName of the ButtonColumn to Select so that the DataGrid will recognize that its clicks should raise the SelectedIndexChanged event.

```
<asp:ButtonColumn CommandName="Select" ItemStyle-Width="20px"
  Text="<img border=0 src=message.gif>" />
```

Note that this tag sets the new column's Text property to an <img> tag. This will generate an image link. Otherwise, the DataGrid will generate a standard text hyperlink or a push button, depending on the value of the ButtonType property.

Next, you need to define the style for the selected item so that it can be distinguished from the ordinary style. You can add these attributes to the DataGrid control tag:

```
SelectedItemStyle-ForeColor="Yellow" SelectedItemStyle-BackColor="Red"
SelectedItemStyle-Font-Bold="true"
```

The event handler for the SelectedIndexChanged simply needs to rebind the DataGrid. In this example, it also displays a message about which item was selected:

```
private void Datagrid1_SelectedIndexChanged(object sender, System.EventArgs e)
{
    // Extract the ID of the selected row.
    int empID = (int)Datagrid1.DataKeys[Datagrid1.SelectedIndex];
    MoreInfo.Text = "You selected record #<b> " + empID.ToString() + "</b>.";

    // Rebind the DataGrid.
    BindGrid();
}
```

Figure 10-16 shows the result of running this page and clicking the image link at the far right of the grid.

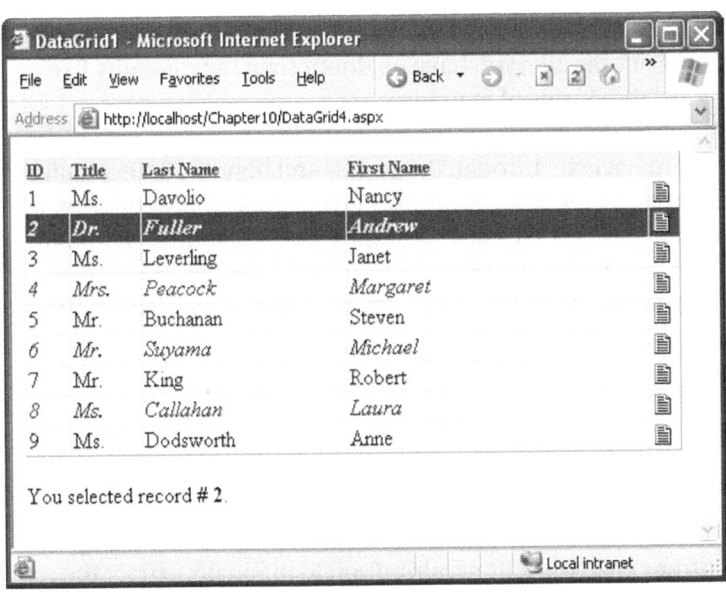

Figure 10-16. *Selection with a DataGrid*

Note that there is still an issue to solve. To see this problem in action, select a row, and then sort the data by any column. You'll see that the selection will remain, but it will shift to a new item that has the same index as the previous item. In other words, if you select the second row and perform a sort, the second row will still be selected in the new page, even though this isn't the record you selected! The only way to solve this problem is to programmatically deselect the selected row every time a header link is clicked. Here's the statement you need to add to the event handler for the DataGrid.SortCommand event to take this extra precaution:

```
DataGrid.SelectedIndex = -1;
```

Tip You don't need to create a new column to support row selection. Instead, you can turn an existing column into a link. To do so, change the existing column into a ButtonColumn and set DataTextField to the field you want to use. This field will be underlined and turned into a link that, when clicked, will select the row. This technique is commonly used to allow users to select rows in a table by the unique ID value.

Paging Records

All the examples of repeated-value binding that you've seen so far show all of the records of the data source on a single web page. However, this isn't always ideal in real-world situations. Connecting to a data source that contains hundreds or even thousands of records would produce an extremely large page that would take a prohibitively long amount of time to render and transmit to the client browser.

Most websites that display data in tables or lists support record *pagination*, which means showing a fixed number of records per page and providing links to navigate to the previous or next pages to display other records. For example, you have no doubt seen functionality like this in search engines that can return thousands of matches.

If you want to support paging with the DataList or the Repeater controls, you need to create a pager bar (a bar with the links to navigate through the pages) and handle all the required details yourself, taking care to retrieve just the records for the current page in your queries. It's perfectly possible, but not convenient. The good news is that the DataGrid control has built-in support for pagination. You can use simple pagination by setting a few DataGrid properties, or you can customize the way the pagination works for a more efficient and scalable solution. In the following sections, you'll see both of these techniques in action, and learn about the benefits and disadvantages of each one.

Automatic Paging

By setting a few properties and handling an event you can make the DataGrid control manage the paging for you. The DataGrid will create the links to jump to the previous or next pages, and display the records for the current page without requiring you to manually extract the records by yourself. Before discussing the advantages and disadvantages of this approach, let's see what you need to get this working.

The DataGrid provides several properties designed specifically to support standard and custom pagination. These properties are listed in Table 10-6.

Table 10-6. *Paging Members of the DataGrid*

Property	Description
AllowPaging	Enables or disables the paging of the bound records. It is false by default.
CurrentPageIndex	Gets or sets the zero-based index of the currently displayed page, if the pagination is enabled.
PagerStyle	Gets the style properties of the grid's pager.

(Continued)

Table 10-6. *Paging Members of the DataGrid (Continued)*

Property	Description
PageSize	Gets or sets the number of items to display on a single page of the grid. The default value is 10.
PageIndexChanged event	Occurs when one of the page selection elements is clicked.

■**Note** In order to use automatic paging, the data source must implement ICollection. The DataSet is a valid choice, but the DataReader won't work.

Here's an example of a DataGrid control declaration that sets some of these paging related properties:

```
<asp:DataGrid runat="server" ID="Datagrid1"
  AllowPaging="true"
  PageSize="3"
  PagerStyle-HorizontalAlign="Right"
  PagerStyle-PageButtonCount="4"
  PagerStyle-Mode="NumericPages"
  PagerStyle-BackColor="Beige"
  PagerStyle-ForeColor="Red"
  ...
</asp:DataGrid>
```

In addition to AllowPaging (which is essential to enable the pagination), you need to specify the PageSize, which specifies the number of rows that will be rendered on each page.

The PagerStyle property returns an object with numerous subproperties that allow you to tweak the appearance of the pager, including the foreground and background colors, the font, the border color and size, and so on. Most importantly, however, the PagerStyle object has a Mode property that allows you to specify how to render the links to the other pages of records. The Mode property can be set to NextPrev or NumericPages (the two values of the DataGridPagerStyle enumeration).

- With a Mode of NextPrev, the grid will render only two links for jumping to the previous and next page. If you choose this option, you can also define the text for the two links through the NextPageText and PrevPageText properties.

- With a Mode of NumericPages, the grid will render as many links to other pages as specified by the PagerStyle.PageButtonCount property. If that number of links is not enough to link to every page of the grid, the pager will display ellipsis links (. . .) that when pressed display the previous or next set of page links.

The two images below show how the pager's links are represented according to these properties:

PageStyle.Mode = NextPrev   PageStyle.Mode = NumericPages

< Prev Next >   1 2 3 ...

Having defined the new properties, you need to handle the PageIndexChanged event as shown here:

```
protected void Datagrid1_PageChanged(Object sender,
  DataGridPageChangedEventArgs e)
{
    // Deselect the currently selected row.
    Datagrid1.SelectedIndex = -1;

    // Change the current page and rebind.
    Datagrid1.CurrentPageIndex = e.NewPageIndex;
    BindGrid();
}
```

In the PageIndexChanged event handler, you must set the DataGrid.CurrentPageIndex property to the new page index. You can get the desired page index from the NewPageIndex property of the DataGridPageChangedEventArgs event argument. Next, you must call the BindGrid() method that rebinds the data source to the grid. You don't need to change the code in the BindGrid() method—you can use the exact same version as in the earlier examples. The DataGrid control automatically takes care of extracting only the records for the current page from the bound data source.

Figure 10-17 shows the DataGrid with three records per page, and with the navigation links in the pager bar.

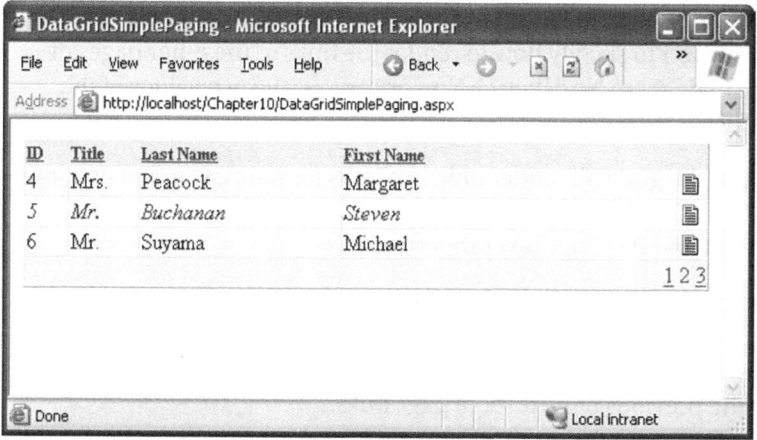

Figure 10-17. *Paging with a DataGrid*

The automatic pagination works fine and it's quick to set up, but it has some drawbacks. First, it doesn't support the DataReader or simple data objects like the ArrayList. Instead, you need to use the disconnected DataSet.

A more significant problem is the fact that the data must be rebound every time the user changes the current page. The DataGrid requires the full DataSet (including the rows it won't display), so that it can independently calculate which items of the data source to actually display according to its CurrentPageIndex and PageSize properties. This operation of requerying the database and filling a DataSet is expensive. Fortunately, you can make automatic paging much more efficient by implementing the exact same caching strategy that was used in the DataGrid selection example. This allows you to reuse the same DataSet object for multiple requests. Of course, storing the DataSet in the cache may not be the ideal solution if you're using paging to deal with an extremely large query. In this case, the amount of memory required to keep the full DataSet in the cache is prohibitively large. That's when custom pagination enters the scene.

Custom Pagination

Custom pagination requires you to take care of extracting and binding only the current page of records for the DataGrid. The DataGrid no longer selects the rows that should be displayed automatically. However, the DataGrid still offers the pager bar with the autogenerated links that allows the user to navigate through the pages.

Although custom pagination is more complex than automatic pagination, it also allows you to minimize the bandwidth usage and avoid storing a large DataSet object in server-side memory. On the other hand, most custom pagination strategies requery the database with each postback, which means you may be creating more work for the database.

Tip To determine whether custom pagination is better than automatic paging with caching, you need to evaluate the way you use data. The larger the amount of data the DataGrid is using, the more likely you'll need to use custom pagination. On the other hand, the slower the database server and the heavier its load, the more likely you'll want to reduce repeated calls by caching the full DataSet. Ultimately, you may need to profile your application to determine the optimum paging strategy.

To enable custom pagination, you need to set the DataGrid.AllowCustomPaging property to true in addition to setting the AllowPaging property to true. If you set AllowCustomPaging to true but fail to set AllowPaging to true, you will not be able to use paging.

In order to have the DataGrid create the correct number of page links for you, it must know the total number of records and the number of records per page. The records-per-page value is set with the PageSize property, as in the last sample. The total number of pages is a little trickier.

When using automatic pagination, the total number of records is automatically determined by the DataGrid based on the number of records in the data source. In custom paging, you must explicitly set the total number using the VirtualItemCount property. The following procedure shows how you can retrieve the number of records of the Employees table and set the VirtualItemCount property programmatically:

```
private void SetGridItemCount()
{
    // Create the Command and the Connection.
    string sql = "SELECT COUNT(*) FROM Employees";
    SqlConnection con = new SqlConnection(connectionString);
    SqlCommand cmd = new SqlCommand(sql, con);
    con.Open();

    // Execute the command and use the return value for the
    // VirtualItemCount property.
    Datagrid1.VirtualItemCount = (int)cmd.ExecuteScalar();
    con.Close();
}
```

This example uses the COUNT() aggregate function to calculate the number of records in the table, and returns that information using the ExecuteScalar() method of the Command object. In the custom paging example, the SetGridItemCount() procedure is only executed when the page loads for the first time, and not as a consequence of a postback. Of course, you can change this behavior if you know that other users may add or delete rows in the meantime.

The code of the PageIndexChanged does not change at all. All it does it set the DataGrid.CurrentPageIndex property and call BindGrid() to retrieve and bind the data to the control. However, the code in the BindGrid() method does change. Instead of retrieving a DataSet with all the records, it must retrieve only the records for the current page. To accomplish this feat, this example uses a stored procedure named GetEmployeesByPage. This stored procedure copies all the employee records into a temporary table that has one additional column—a unique autoincrementing ID that will number each row. Next, the stored procedure retrieves a selection from that table that corresponds to the requested page of data, using the supplied @PageNumber and @PageSize parameters.

Here's the complete stored procedure code:

```
CREATE PROCEDURE GetEmployeesByPage
@PageNumber  int, @PageSize  int
AS
-- create a temporary table with the columns we are interested in
CREATE TABLE #TempEmployees
(
  ID               int IDENTITY PRIMARY KEY,
  EmployeeID       int,
  LastName         nvarchar(20),
  FirstName        nvarchar(10),
  Title            nvarchar(30),
  TitleOfCourtesy  nvarchar(25),
  Address          nvarchar(60),
  City             nvarchar(15),
  Region           nvarchar(15),
  Country          nvarchar(15),
  Notes            ntext
)
```

```
-- fill the temp table with all the employees
INSERT INTO #TempEmployees
(
  EmployeeID, LastName, FirstName, Title, TitleOfCourtesy,
  Address, City, Region, Country, Notes
)
SELECT
  EmployeeID, LastName, FirstName, Title, TitleOfCourtesy,
  Address, City, Region, Country, Notes
FROM
  Employees ORDER BY EmployeeID ASC

-- declare two variables to calculate the range of records
-- to extract for the specified page
DECLARE @FromID int
DECLARE @ToID int
-- calculate the first and last ID of the range of records we need
SET @FromID = ((@PageNumber - 1) * @PageSize) + 1
SET @ToID = @PageNumber * @PageSize

-- select the page of records
SELECT * FROM #TempEmployees WHERE ID >= @FromID AND ID <= @ToID
GO
```

> **Note** This stored procedure uses a SQL Server–specific approach. Other databases might have other possible optimizations. For example, Oracle databases allow you to use the ROWNUM operator in the WHERE clause of a query to return a range of rows. For example, the query SELECT * FROM Employees WHERE ROWNUM > 100 AND ROWNUM < 200 retrieves the page of rows from 101 to 199.

The BindGrid() method uses the stored procedure, in conjunction with a DataReader, to get the required records:

```
private void BindGrid()
{
    // Define a Command that uses the stored procedure.
    SqlConnection con = new SqlConnection(connectionString);
    SqlCommand cmd = new SqlCommand("GetEmployeesByPage", con);
    cmd.CommandType = CommandType.StoredProcedure;
    cmd.Parameters.Add(new SqlParameter("@PageNumber", SqlDbType.Int, 4));
    cmd.Parameters["@PageNumber"].Value = Datagrid1.CurrentPageIndex + 1;
    cmd.Parameters.Add(new SqlParameter("@PageSize", SqlDbType.Int, 4));
    cmd.Parameters["@PageSize"].Value = Datagrid1.PageSize;
```

```
    // Open the Connection and get the DataReader.
    con.Open();
    SqlDataReader reader = cmd.ExecuteReader();

    // Bind the DataReader to the DataGrid.
    Datagrid1.DataSource = reader;
    Datagrid1.DataBind();

    // Clean up.
    reader.Close();
    con.Close();
}
```

When you run this page, you'll see that the output is exactly the same as the output generated by the previous page using automatic pagination, and the pager controls work the same way.

Custom Pager Bar

If you don't like the default pager bar, you can implement your own. You can use any control you want, such as a text box where the user can type the index of the page and a button to submit the request and load the new page. You would still handle an event on the server where you would set the DataGrid.CurrentPageIndex property. The code for extracting and binding the records for the current page would remain exactly the same. In fact, this code does not depend on the pager style, but only on the PageSize and CurrentPageIndex properties of the DataGrid.

Incidentally, this is the very same approach that you would use if you wanted to implement the pagination for the Repeater or DataList controls. The only difference is that they don't have the pagination-specific properties and you would need to make the current index and the page size information persistent in other ways, such as by saving these values in the ViewState collection.

Templated Columns

So far, the examples have used the DataGrid control to show data in using separate bound columns for each field. If you want to place multiple values in the same cell (like you can with the DataList), or have the unlimited ability to customize the content in a cell by adding HTML tags and server controls, you should use a TemplateColumn.

The TemplateColumn allows you to define a completely customized template for a column. In the template you can declare as many data binding expressions as you want, and you can bind these expressions to controls of any type and to different properties and methods in the page exactly as demonstrated with the Repeater and the DataList controls earlier in the chapter.

To create an example, imagine you need a DataGrid that displays the ID, title of courtesy and city in different columns, along with a customized column that provides the full employee's name and yet another one that displays a check box indicating whether the employee is located in a particular country (in this example, the USA). Figure 10-18 shows the output that's needed.

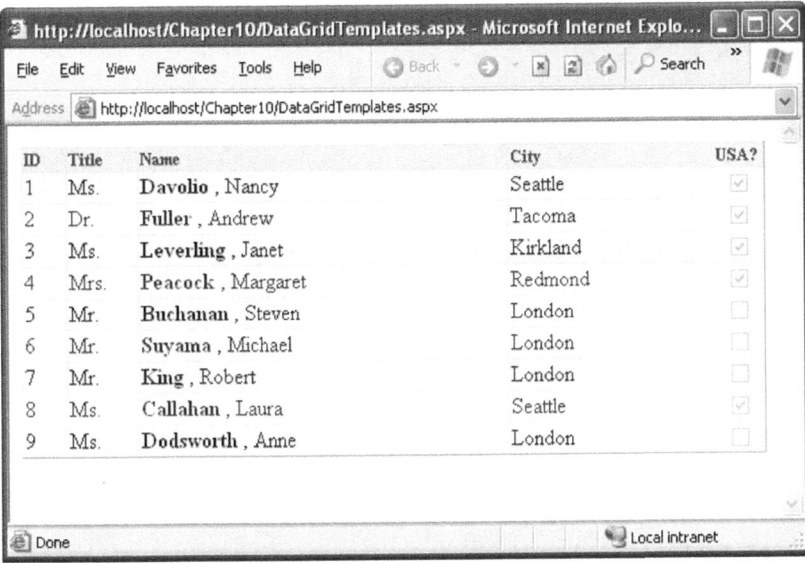

Figure 10-18. *Templated columns with a DataGrid*

Here's how you declare the columns in this example:

```
<Columns>
  <asp:BoundColumn DataField="EmployeeID" HeaderText="ID">
    <ItemStyle Width="30px"></ItemStyle>
  </asp:BoundColumn>
  <asp:BoundColumn DataField="TitleOfCourtesy" HeaderText="Title">
    <ItemStyle Width="50px"></ItemStyle>
  </asp:BoundColumn>
  <asp:TemplateColumn HeaderText="Name">
    <ItemTemplate>
      <b><%# DataBinder.Eval(Container.DataItem, "LastName") %></b>,
      <%# DataBinder.Eval(Container.DataItem, "FirstName") %>
    </ItemTemplate>
  </asp:TemplateColumn>
  <asp:BoundColumn DataField="City" HeaderText="City">
    <ItemStyle Width="150px"></ItemStyle>
  </asp:BoundColumn>
  <asp:TemplateColumn HeaderText="USA?">
    <ItemStyle HorizontalAlign="Center" Width="35px"></ItemStyle>
    <ItemTemplate>
      <asp:CheckBox runat="server" Enabled="false"
      Checked=
'<%# DataBinder.Eval(Container.DataItem, "Country").ToString() == "USA" %>'
      ID="Checkbox1"/>
    </ItemTemplate>
  </asp:TemplateColumn>
</Columns>
```

COMPARING TEMPLATE OPTIONS

The DataGrid doesn't support quite as many templates as the DataList. The following table compares the different template options provided by the ASP.NET data controls.

DataList	DataGrid (TemplateColumn)	Repeater
AlternatingItemTemplate	HeaderTemplate	ItemTemplate
EditItemTemplate	ItemTemplate	AlternatingItemTemplate
HeaderTemplate	EditItemTemplate	SeparatorTemplate
ItemTemplate SelectedItemTemplate SeparatorTemplate FooterTemplate	FooterTemplate	FooterTemplate

Note that the ItemTemplate is placed inside the <TemplateColumn> section. You'll see shortly that you can add other templates to the column, such as an EditItemTemplate that's used when the row is being edited. The fourth column declares a CheckBox control and sets its Checked property to a data binding expression that returns true if the employee's country is USA. Note that to do the comparison, the code must cast the object returned by DataBinder.Eval() to a string. Also note that the check box is disabled (it will be rendered in gray) so that the user can't modify its state.

Editing and Deleting Rows

Earlier in the chapter you saw how the DataList control has built-in support for editing and deleting items. The DataGrid offers this support as well, in a very similar way. In the next sample page, you'll see how to modify the previous page to make the grid editable, as shown in Figure 10-19.

The events to handle are exactly the same as those of the DataList control, and occur when the user presses the button or link to start editing (EditCommand), to cancel the editing mode (CancelCommand), to update the record with the new values (UpdateCommand), or to delete the row (DeleteCommand). Unlike the DataList control, these buttons are not defined using <asp:Button> tags. Instead, they are defined through a couple of special DataGrid columns that are designed for exactly this purpose—the EditCommandColumn and the ButtonColumn.

Declaring the Columns

The EditCommandColumn is used exclusively for managing the editing process. The ButtonColumn is more flexible. If you set its CommandName property to Delete, it raises the DeleteCommand event. Otherwise, you can respond to the generic ItemCommand event to perform some other task.

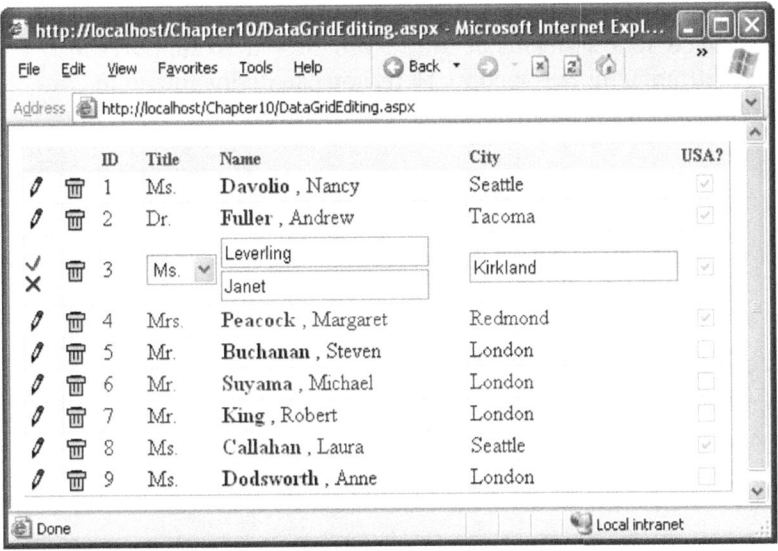

Figure 10-19. *Editing with the DataGrid*

Here's how these columns are declared:

```
<asp:EditCommandColumn ItemStyle-Width="25px"
  EditText="<img border=0 alt='Edit record' src=Edit.gif>"
  CancelText="<img border=0 alt='Cancel changes' src=Cancel.gif>"
  UpdateText="<img border=0 alt='Accept changes'  src=OK.gif>" />
<asp:ButtonColumn ItemStyle-Width="25px" ButtonType="LinkButton"
  Text="<img border=0 src=Delete.gif>" CommandName="delete" />
```

Note that the EditCommandColumn has the CancelText and UpdateText properties that define the text. In this example, the only text that's used is an HTML <img> tag that shows a specific image with a tooltip. The Cancel and Update links won't appear until the row is switched into edit mode, at which point they will appear automatically.

Many of the existing columns in the DataGrid need some changes to support editing. In the remainder of this section, you'll take a look at each column. First is the EmployeeID column. Because this is a unique, automatically generated ID value, you don't want to allow it to be edited. Fortunately, you can disable editing for this column by setting the ReadOnly property of the column to true:

```
<asp:BoundColumn HeaderText="ID" ItemStyle-Width="30px"
  DataField="EmployeeID" ReadOnly="true" />
```

Next is the column that displays the title of courtesy. In the previous page this was defined as a BoundColumn, but when the BoundColumns are in editing mode they create simple text box controls and don't allow much customization. If you want to limit the user's choices to a few titles by using a drop-down list (as demonstrated with the editable DataList example earlier in the chapter), you need to use a TemplateColumn instead.

The TemplateColumn contains two templates. The ItemTemplate section just declares a basic data binding expression that displays the title of courtesy in the cell. To support the editing you must also add an EditItemTemplate section. Here, you can define the input controls—in this case the drop-down list that's bound to the TitlesOfCourtesy property of the web page.

```
<asp:TemplateColumn HeaderText="Title" ItemStyle-Width="50px">
  <ItemTemplate>
    <%# DataBinder.Eval(Container.DataItem, "TitleOfCourtesy") %>
  </ItemTemplate>
  <EditItemTemplate>
    <asp:DropDownList runat="server" ID="EditTitle"
      DataSource='<%# TitlesOfCourtesy %>'
      SelectedIndex='<%# GetSelectedTitle(
      DataBinder.Eval(Container.DataItem, "TitleOfCourtesy")) %>'
    />
  </EditItemTemplate>
</asp:TemplateColumn>
```

The fifth column is declared, like the previous one, through a TemplateColumn column that displays the values for the LastName and FirstName fields in normal mode, and creates two text boxes bound to the same two fields in editing mode:

```
<asp:TemplateColumn HeaderText="Name">
  <ItemTemplate>
    <b><%# DataBinder.Eval(Container.DataItem, "LastName") %></b>,
    <%# DataBinder.Eval(Container.DataItem, "FirstName") %>
  </ItemTemplate>
  <EditItemTemplate>
    <asp:TextBox runat="server" ID="EditLastName"
      Text='<%# DataBinder.Eval(Container.DataItem, "LastName") %>' />
    <asp:TextBox runat="server" ID="EditFirstName"
      Text='<%# DataBinder.Eval(Container.DataItem, "FirstName") %>' />
  </EditItemTemplate>
</asp:TemplateColumn>
```

The next column is a BoundColumn column that's bound to the City field. If you don't set its ReadOnly property to true, the user will be able to edit the column using an ordinary text box when the row is in edit mode. This default behavior is fine in this case, so the column needs no changes.

The last column is the check box. It also remains unchanged. Because it's a TemplateColumn without an EditItemTemplate, it won't support editing and will be treated as read-only.

Performing the Update

The code that handles the server-side events for the editing and the deletion of a row is very similar to the code used for the DataList example. First, you need to create a parameterized UPDATE command that can commit the changes:

```
private void Datagrid1_Update(Object sender, DataGridCommandEventArgs e)
{
    // Create the UPDATE command.
    string sql = @"UPDATE Employees SET TitleOfCourtesy = @TitleOfCourtesy, " +
        "LastName = @LastName, FirstName = @FirstName, City = @City " +
        "WHERE EmployeeID = @EmployeeID";
    SqlConnection con = new SqlConnection(connectionString);
    SqlCommand cmd = new SqlCommand(sql, con);
    ...
```

Next, you need to retrieve the data from the current record. For the input controls that are defined in the templates, you can use the FindControl() method, as with the DataList example. You can also retrieve the unique EmployeeID from the DataKeys collection.

```
...
    // Get the ID of the record to update.
    int empID = (int)Datagrid1.DataKeys[e.Item.ItemIndex];
    // Get the references to the edit controls.
    DropDownList title = (DropDownList)e.Item.FindControl("EditTitle");
    TextBox lastName = (TextBox)e.Item.FindControl("EditLastName");
    TextBox firstName = (TextBox)e.Item.FindControl("EditFirstName");
    ...
```

Getting the information from the City field is a little trickier. You can't use the FindControl() method for the text box that's used to edit the city because the DataGrid automatically creates that text box, and you don't know its name. In this case, the solution is to use the Item property of the DataGridCommandEventArgs object that's passed to the UpdateCommand event. The DataGridCommandEventArgs.Item object represents the item that's being edited, and it exposes a Cells collection. You can access the cell that has the text box input control by index number. Because this cell only contains one control, you can easily retrieve the first control by using the Cell.Controls collection and retrieving the object in position 0. You can then cast this to a TextBox, and retrieve the value the user has entered.

Here's the code that accomplishes this task:

```
...
    TextBox city = (TextBox)e.Item.Cells[5].Controls[0];
    string cityText = city.Text.Trim();
    ...
```

Tip This approach can be problematic if there's a change in the layout, such as if you add or remove columns, and the column with index 5 is no longer the column for the city. If you plan to change the order or number of the columns, and don't want to be forced to update the rest of your code, you should use template columns instead. That way, you declare the input controls explicitly, and you can use the FindControl() method to retrieve a reference to the control using only its name.

Now you have all the information you need to set the command parameters, as shown here:

```
...
// Add the required parameters.
cmd.Parameters.Add(new SqlParameter("@TitleOfCourtesy", SqlDbType.NVarChar,
    25));
cmd.Parameters["@TitleOfCourtesy"].Value = title.SelectedItem.Text.Trim();
cmd.Parameters.Add(new SqlParameter("@LastName", SqlDbType.NVarChar, 20));
cmd.Parameters["@LastName"].Value = lastName.Text.Trim();
cmd.Parameters.Add(new SqlParameter("@FirstName", SqlDbType.NVarChar, 10));
cmd.Parameters["@FirstName"].Value = firstName.Text.Trim();
cmd.Parameters.Add(new SqlParameter("@City", SqlDbType.NVarChar, 15));
cmd.Parameters["@City"].Value = cityText;
cmd.Parameters.Add(new SqlParameter("@EmployeeID", SqlDbType.Int, 4));
cmd.Parameters["@EmployeeID"].Value = empID;
...
```

The final step is to execute the command and rebind the grid:

```
...
try
{
    con.Open();
    cmd.ExecuteNonQuery();
}
finally
{
    con.Close();
}

// Stop the editing process and rebind the grid.
Datagrid1.EditItemIndex = -1;
BindGrid();
}
```

Advanced Customization

If the template columns are not enough for you, you can resort to the ItemCreated event. This event, mentioned earlier during the discussion about the Repeater control, is raised when a part of the grid (the header, footer, pager, or a normal, alternate, or selected item) is being created. It allows you to customize the cell by adding or removing child controls, changing colors and alignment, and so on.

The following example handles the ItemCreated event and sets the colors according to the following rules:

- The item's background color is set to pink and the foreground color is set to maroon if the title of courtesy is a title for a female—in this case Ms. or Mrs.

- The item's background color is set to dark blue and the foreground color is set to light cyan if the title of courtesy is Mr.

- For other generic titles such as Dr., the item is rendered with the background color specified by the DataGrid.BackColor property.

Here is the complete code for the ItemCreated event handler that implements these rules:

```
private void Datagrid1_ItemCreated(Object sender, DataGridItemEventArgs e)
{
    if (e.Item.ItemType == ListItemType.Item ||
      e.Item.ItemType == ListItemType.AlternatingItem)
    {

        // Get the title of courtesy for the item that's being created.
        string title = ((DataRowView)
          e.Item.DataItem)["TitleOfCourtesy"].ToString();

        // If the title of courtesy is "Ms.", "Mrs.", or "Mr.",
        // change the item's colors.
        if (title == "Ms." || title == "Mrs.")
        {
          e.Item.BackColor = System.Drawing.Color.LightPink;
          e.Item.ForeColor = System.Drawing.Color.Maroon;
        }
        else if (title == "Mr.")
        {
          e.Item.BackColor = System.Drawing.Color.LightCyan;
          e.Item.ForeColor = System.Drawing.Color.DarkBlue;
        }
    }
}
```

First, the code checks if the item being created is an item or an alternate item. If not, it means that the item is another interface element, like the pager, footer, or header, and the procedure does nothing. If the item is of the right type, the code extracts the TitleOfCourtesy field from the data bound item and compares it to some hard-coded string values. Figure 10-20 shows the resulting page.

This isn't the most useful example of using the ItemCreated event, but it demonstrates how you can handle the event and read all the important information for the item. You could use much more imaginative formatting to change the way the pager's links are represented, add new buttons to the pager or header, render values that you want to highlight with special fonts and colors, create total and subtotal rows, and more.

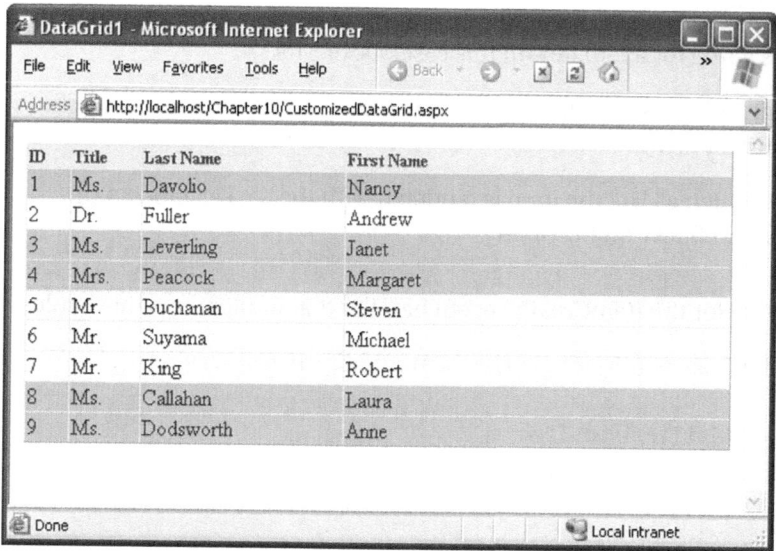

Figure 10-20. *Customizing the DataGrid*

Summary

In this chapter, you've looked at the ASP.NET data bound controls in detail, and at data binding expressions in general. Most of the chapter was dedicated to exploring the three most powerful data bound controls: the Repeater, DataList, and DataGrid controls. Along the way, you've seen some advanced examples, such as dynamically loading templates, using the cache, creating custom pagination, and fine-tuning the display with the ItemCreated event. In the next chapter, you'll tackle some more advanced topics in ADO.NET.

Advanced ADO.NET

ADO.NET is a rich data access technology, and one of the key features of the .NET Framework. Over the previous three chapters, you've seen how to use ADO.NET to execute connected commands and maintain disconnected data. You've also learned how to prevent SQL injection attacks, work with stored procedures, navigate table relationships, sort and filter records, and create dedicated database components. These concepts give you the solid underpinnings that you need to use ADO.NET in a web page.

However, ADO.NET still has a slew of advanced features and tricks that can be quite useful when you're dealing with data in a real-world application. In this chapter, you'll continue your exploration of ADO.NET in three areas:

- **Advanced data access.** You'll learn how to take charge of transactions and deal with images and binary data.

- **Advanced DataSets.** You'll learn how to control column mapping and build strongly typed DataSet classes.

- **Advanced grids.** You'll see more examples that work with the ASP.NET data controls to create master/detail lists and support multiple selection. You'll also learn how to create a shopping cart from scratch.

All of these sections build on the concepts you've learned in the previous three chapters. By the time you finish this chapter, you'll be well on your way to becoming an ADO.NET guru.

Transactions

A *transaction* is a set of operations that must either succeed or fail as a unit. The goal of a transaction is to ensure that data is always in a valid, consistent state.

For example, consider a transaction that transfers $1,000 from account A to account B. Clearly there are two operations:

- It should deduct $1000 from account A.

- It should add $1000 to account B.

Suppose that an application successfully completes step 1, but, due to some error, step 2 fails. This leads to an inconsistent data, because the total amount of money in the system is no longer accurate. A full $1,000 has gone missing.

Transactions help to avoid these types of problems by ensuring that changes are only committed to a data source if *all* the steps are successful. So in our example, if step 2 fails, then the changes made by step 1 will not be committed to the database. This ensures that the system stays in one of its two valid states—the initial state (with no money transferred), and the final state (with money debited from one account and credited to another).

Transactions are characterized by four properties popularly called *ACID properties*. ACID is an acronym that represents the following concepts:

- **Atomic.** All steps in the transaction should succeed or fail together. Unless *all* the steps from a transaction complete, a transaction is not considered completed.

- **Consistent.** The transaction takes the underlying database from one stable state to another.

- **Isolated.** Every transaction is an independent entity. One transaction should not affect any other transaction running at the same time.

- **Durable.** Changes that occur during the transaction are permanently stored on some media, typically a hard disk, before the transaction is declared successful. Logs are maintained so that the database can be restored to a valid state even if a hardware or network failure occurs.

Note that even though these are ideal characteristics of a transaction, they aren't always absolutely attainable. One problem is that in order to ensure isolation, the RDBMS (relational database management system) needs to lock data so that other users can't access it while the transaction is in progress. The more locks you use, and the coarser these locks are, the greater the chance that a user won't be able to perform another task while the transactions are underway. In other words, there's often a trade-off between user concurrency and isolation.

Transactions and ASP.NET Applications

There are actually three basic transaction types that you can use in an ASP.NET web application. They are as follows (from least to most overhead):

- **Stored procedure transactions.** These transactions take place entirely in the database. Stored procedure transactions offer the best performance, because they only need a single round-trip to the database. The drawback is that you also need to write the transaction logic using SQL statements (which may be not so easy as using pure C#).

- **Client-initiated (ADO.NET) transactions.** These transactions are controlled programmatically by your ASP.NET web-page code. Under the covers, they use the same commands as a stored-procedure transaction, but your code uses a set of ADO.NET objects that wrap these details. The drawback is that extra round-trips are required to the database to start and commit the transaction.

- **COM+ transactions.** These transactions are handled by the COM+ runtime, based on declarative attributes that you add to your code. COM+ transactions use a two-stage commit protocol, and always incur extra overhead. They also require that you create a separate serviced component class. COM+ components are generally only a good choice if your transaction spans multiple transaction-aware resource managers, because COM+ includes built-in support for distributed transactions. For example, a single COM+ transaction can span interactions in a SQL Server database *and* an Oracle database. COM+ transactions are not covered in this chapter, although you will see them briefly with web services in Part Five.

Even though ADO.NET provides good support for transactions, you should not always use transactions. In fact, every time you use any kind of transaction, you automatically incur some overhead. Also, transactions involve some kind of locking of table rows. Thus, the unnecessary use of transactions may harm the overall scalability of your application.

When implementing a transaction, the following practices can be followed in order to achieve the best results:

- Keep transactions as short as possible.

- Avoid returning data with a SELECT query in the middle of a transaction. Ideally, you should return the data before the transaction starts.

- If you do retrieve records, fetch only the rows that are required so as not to lock too many resources and keep performance as good as possible.

- Wherever possible, write transactions within stored procedures instead of using ADO.NET transactions.

- Avoid transactions that combine multiple independent batches of work. Put separate batches into separate transactions.

- Avoid updates that affect a large range of records if at all possible.

Tip As a rule of thumb, use a transaction only when your operation requires one. For example, if you are simply selecting records from a database, or firing a single query, you will not need a transaction. On the other hand, if you are inserting an Order record in conjunction with a series of related OrderItem records, you might well want to use a transaction. In general, a transaction is never required for single-statement commands like individual UPDATE, DELETE, or INSERT statements, because these are inherently transactional.

Stored Procedure Transactions

If possible, the best place to put a transaction is in stored procedure code. This ensures that the server-side code is always in control, which makes it impossible for a client to accidentally hold a transaction open too long, and potentially cause problems for other client updates. It also ensures the best possible performance, because all actions can be executed at the data source without requiring any network communication. Generally, the shorter the span of a transaction, the better the concurrency of the database, and the fewer the number of database requests that will be serialized (put on hold while a temporary record lock is in place).

Stored procedure code varies depending on the database you are using, but most RDBMSs support the SQL statement BEGIN TRANSACTION. Once you start a transaction, all subsequent statements are considered part of the transaction. You can end the transaction with the COMMIT or ROLLBACK statement. If you don't, the transaction will be automatically rolled back.

Here's a pseudocode example that performs a fund transfer between accounts. It's a simplified version that allows an account to be set to a negative balance:

```
CREATE Procedure TransferAmount
(
  @Amount Money
  @ID_A int
  #ID_B int
)
AS
  BEGIN TRANSACTION
    UPDATE Accounts SET Balance = Balance + @Amount WHERE AccountID = @ID_A
    UPDATE Accounts SET Balance = Balance - @Amount WHERE AccountID = @ID_B
  IF (@@ERROR > 0)
    ROLLBACK
  ELSE
    COMMIT
```

Note In SQL Server, a stored procedure can also perform a distributed transaction (one that involves multiple data sources, and is typically hosted on multiple servers). By default, every transaction begins as a local transaction, but if you access a database on another server, the transaction is automatically upgraded to a distributed transaction governed by the Windows DTC (Distributed Transaction Coordinator) service.

Client-Initiated ADO.NET Transactions

Most ADO.NET data providers include support for database transactions. Transactions are started through the Connection object by calling the BeginTransaction() method. This method returns a provider-specific Transaction object that's used to manage the transaction. All Transaction classes implement the IDbTransaction interface. Examples include SqlTransaction, OleDbTransaction, OracleTransaction, and so on.

The Transaction class provides two key methods:

- **Commit().** This method identifies that the transaction is complete and that the pending changes should be stored permanently in the data source.

- **Rollback().** This method indicates that a transaction was unsuccessful. Pending changes are discarded and the database state remains unchanged.

Typically, you use Commit() at the end of your operation. However, if any exception is thrown along the way you should call Rollback().

Here's an example that inserts two records into the Employees table:

```
string connectionString = "Data Source=localhost;Initial Catalog=Northwind;" +
  "Integrated Security=SSPI";
SqlConnection con = new SqlConnection(connectionString);

SqlCommand cmd1 = new SqlCommand(
  "INSERT INTO Employees (LastName, FirstName) VALUES ('Joe','Tester')");
SqlCommand cmd2 = new SqlCommand(
  "INSERT INTO Employees (LastName, FirstName) VALUES ('Harry','Sullivan')");
SqlTransaction tran = null;

try
{
    // Open the connection and create the transaction.
    con.Open();
    tran = con.BeginTransaction();

    // Enlist two commands in the transaction.
    cmd1.Transaction = tran;
    cmd2.Transaction = tran;

    // Execute both commands.
    cmd1.ExecuteNonQuery();
    cmd2.ExecuteNonQuery();

    // Commit the transaction.
    tran.Commit();
}
catch
{
    // In the case of error, roll back the transaction.
    tran.Rollback();
}
finally
{
    con.Close();
}
```

Note that it's not enough to create and commit a transaction. You also need to explicitly enlist each Command object to be part of the transaction by setting the Command.Transaction property to the Transaction object. If you try to execute a command that isn't a part of the current transaction while the transaction is underway, you'll receive an error. However, in the future this object model might allow providers to support more than one simultaneous transaction on the same connection.

■**Tip** Instead of using separate command objects, you could also execute the same object twice, and just modify its CommandText property in between (if it's a dynamic SQL statement) or the value of its parameters (if it's a parameterized command). For example, if your command inserts a new record, you could use this approach to insert two records in the same transaction.

To test the rollback features of a transaction, you can insert the following line just before the Commit() method is called in the previous example:

```
throw new ApplicationException();
```

This raises an exception, which will trigger a rollback and ensure that neither record is committed to the database.

Although an ADO.NET transaction revolves around the Connection and Transaction objects, the underlying commands aren't different from a stored procedure transaction. For example, when you call BeginTransaction() with the SQL Server provider, it sends a BEGIN TRANSACTION command to the database.

■**Tip** A transaction should be completed as quickly as possible (started as late as possible and finished as soon as possible). Also, an active transaction puts locks on the various resources involved, so you should only select the rows you really require.

Isolation Levels

The *isolation level* determines how sensitive a transaction is to changes made by other in-progress transactions. For example, by default when two transactions are running independently of one another, records inserted by one transaction are not visible to the other transaction until the first transaction is committed.

The concept of isolation levels is closely related to the concept of locks, because by determining the isolation level for a given transaction you determine what types of locks are required. *Shared locks* are locks that are placed when a transaction wants to read data from the database. No other transactions can modify the data while shared locks exist on a table, row, or range. However, more than one user can use a shared lock to read the data simultaneously. *Exclusive locks* are the locks that prevent two or more transactions modifying data simultaneously. An exclusive lock is issued when a transaction needs to update data and no other locks are already held. No other user can read or modify the data while an exclusive lock is in place.

■**Note** SQL Server actually has several types of locks that work together to help prevent deadlocks and other situations. For more information, refer to the information about locking in the SQL Server Books Online help, which is installed with SQL Server.

In a SQL Server stored procedure, you can set the isolation level using the SET TRANSACTION ISOLATION LEVEL command. In ADO.NET, you can pass a value from the IsolationLevel enumeration to the Connection.BeginTransaction() method. Possible values are listed in Table 11-1.

Table 11-1. *Values of the IsolationLevel Enumeration*

Value	Description
ReadUncommitted	No shared locks are placed, and no exclusive locks are honored. This type of isolation level is appropriate when you want to work with all the data matching certain conditions, irrespective of whether it's committed or not. Dirty reads are possible, but performance is increased.
ReadCommitted	Shared locks are held while the data is being read by the transaction. This avoids dirty reads, but the data can be changed before a transaction completes. This may result in nonrepeatable reads or phantom rows. This is the default isolation level used by SQL Server.
RepeatableRead	In this case, shared locks are placed on all data that is used in a query. This prevents others from modifying the data and it also prevents nonrepeatable reads. However, phantom rows are possible.
Serializable	A range lock is placed on the data you use, thereby preventing other users from updating or inserting rows that would fall in that range. This is the only isolation level that removes the possibility of phantom rows. However, it has an extremely negative effect on user concurrency, and is rarely used in multiple user scenarios.

The isolation levels in Table 11-1 are arranged from the least degree of locking to the highest degree of locking. The default, ReadCommitted, is a good compromise for most transactions. Table 11-2 summarizes the locking behavior for different isolation levels.

Table 11-2. *Isolation Levels Compared*

Isolation Level	Dirty Read	Nonrepeatable Read	Phantom Data	Concurrency
Read uncommitted	Yes	Yes	Yes	Best
Read committed	No	Yes	Yes	Good
Repeatable read	No	No	Yes	Poor
Serializable	No	No	No	Very poor

UNDERSTANDING THE QUIRKS IN TRANSACTIONS

Table 11-2 shows some of the phenomena that you might observe depending on your transaction isolation settings.

A *dirty read* is a condition when a transaction reads data that has yet to be committed. Consider a case where transaction A inserts some records into the table, but is still in progress. Transaction B reads these records. Now, if transaction A rolls back, transaction B will continue using the invalid data that's been discarded. If transaction B makes a decision or inserts new records based on this information, it's possible that the database won't remain in a valid state.

A *nonrepeatable read* occurs when data changes after you read it, while in a transaction. Consider a case where transaction A reads a record from a table. Transaction B then alters or deletes the records, and commits the changes. Now, if transaction A tries to re-read the record, it will either be a different version, or will not be available at all. Such a condition is called a nonrepeatable read.

Phantom rows are a special form of nonrepeatable read. Suppose that transaction A has some criteria for record selection. Initially, transaction A has, say, 100 rows matching these criteria. Now transaction B inserts some rows that match the selection criteria of transaction A. If transaction A executes the selection query again, it will receive a different set of rows than in the previous case. The rows added in this way are called phantom rows.

It's important to note that quirks like dirty reads, nonrepeatable reads, and phantom rows are not necessarily a problem, depending on the type of task you are performing. At worst, they will lead you to make assumptions based on data that isn't yet committed or has changed since you last read it. However, they don't harm the integrity of the data that's already stored in the database.

Savepoints

Whenever you roll back a transaction, it nullifies the effect of every command that you've executed since you started the transaction. But what happens if you only want to roll back *part* of an ongoing transaction? SQL Server handles this with a feature called *savepoints*.

Savepoints are markers that act like a bookmark. You mark a certain point in the flow of transaction, and then you can roll back to that point. You set the savepoint using the Transaction.Save() method. Note that the Save() method is available only for the SqlTransaction class, because it's not a part of the standard IDbTransaction interface.

Here's a conceptual look at how you use a savepoint:

```
// Start the transaction.
SqlTransaction tran = con.BeginTransaction();

// (Enlist and execute some commands inside the transaction.)

// Mark a savepoint.
tran.Save("CompletedInsert");

// (Enlist and execute some more commands inside the transaction.)
```

```
// If needed, roll back to the savepoint.
tran.Rollback("CompletedInsert");

// Commit or roll back the transaction.
tran.Commit();
```

Note how the Rollback() method is used with the savepoint name as a parameter. If you want to roll back the whole transaction, simply omit this parameter.

■**Note** Once you roll back to a savepoint, all the savepoints defined after that save point are lost. You must set them again if they are needed.

Nested Transactions

Savepoints allow a transaction to be arranged as a sequence of actions that can be rolled back individually. Nested transactions play essentially the same role as savepoints—they allow you to start smaller transactions inside a larger transaction that can be committed or rolled back individually. To initiate nested transactions, you must call the Begin () method of the transaction object. This returns a new Transaction object, which you can use just like the original transaction object.

The implementation of nested transactions is up to the data source. Some data sources, like SQL Server, don't properly support nested transactions. In SQL Server, rolling back a nested transaction actually rolls back the entire transaction. For that reason, the Begin() method isn't provided for the SqlTransaction class. Instead, you can use savepoints for similar functionality.

Using Transactions with a DataAdapter

The examples so far have used transactions with direct commands. However, you can also use transactions with the DataAdapter. Unfortunately, the DataAdapter doesn't expose a Transaction property. However, you can accomplish the same functionality by setting the Transaction property of the UpdateCommand, InsertCommand, and DeleteCommand before you begin the update. This way, all the batch operations that the DataAdapter performs will be executed as part of a single transaction.

Here's how you would organize your code:

```
SqlTransaction tran = null;
try
{
    con.Open();
    tran = con.BeginTransaction();

    // Enlist the commands in the transaction.
    da.UpdateCommand.Transaction = tran;
    da.InsertCommand.Transaction = tran;
    da.DeleteCommand.Transaction = tran;
```

```
    // Perform the update.
    da.Update(ds, "Employees");

    // Commit the transaction.
    tran.Commit();
}
catch
{
    // In the case of error, roll back the transaction.
    tran.Rollback();
}
finally
{
    con.Close();
}
```

Serving Images from a Database

The data examples in the last chapter retrieved text, numeric, and date information. However, databases often have the additional challenge of storing binary data like pictures. For example, you might have a Products table that contains pictures of each item in a binary field. Retrieving this data in an ASP.NET web page is fairly easy, but displaying it is not as simple.

The basic problem is that in order to show an image in an HTML page, you need to add an insert tag that links to a separate image file through the src attribute. Here's an example:

```
<img src="myfile.gif" />
```

Unfortunately, this isn't much help if you need to show image data dynamically. Although you can set the src attribute in code, there's no way to set the image *content* programmatically. You could first save the data to an image file on the web server's hard drive, but that approach would be dramatically slower, waste space, and raise the possibility of concurrency errors if multiple requests are being served at the same time and they are all trying to write the same file.

There are two ways to solve this problem. One approach is to store all your images in separate files. Then your database record simply needs to store the filename, and you can bind the filename to a server-side image. This is a perfectly reasonable solution, but it doesn't help in situations where you want to store images in the database so you can take advantage of the abilities of the RDBMS to cache data, log usage, and back up everything.

In these situations, the solution is to use a separate ASP.NET resource that returns the binary data directly. You can then make use of this binary data in other web pages in controls. The following sections will develop this solution piece by piece.

Tip As a general rule of thumb, storing images in a database works well as long as the images are not enormous (for example, over 50 MB), and do not need to be frequently edited by other applications.

Displaying Binary Data

ASP.NET isn't restricted to returning HTML content. In fact, you can use the
Response.BinaryWrite() method to return raw bytes, and completely bypass the web-page
model.

The following page uses this technique with the pub_info table in the pubs database
(another standard database that's included with SQL Server). It retrieves the logo field, which
contains binary image data. The page then writes this data directly to the page, as shown here:

```
private void Page_Load(object sender, System.EventArgs e)
{
    string connectionString =
        "Data Source=localhost;Initial Catalog=pubs;Integrated Security=SSPI";
    SqlConnection con = new SqlConnection(connectionString);
    string SQL = "SELECT logo FROM pub_info WHERE pub_id='1389'";
    SqlCommand cmd = new SqlCommand(SQL, con);

    try
    {
        con.Open();
        SqlDataReader r = cmd.ExecuteReader();
        if (r.Read())
        {
            byte[] bytes = (byte[])r["logo"];
            Response.BinaryWrite(bytes);
        }
        r.Close();
    }
    finally
    {
        con.Close();
    }
}
```

Figure 11-1 shows the result. It doesn't appear terribly impressive (the logo data isn't that
remarkable), but you could easily use the same technique with your own database, which can
include much richer and larger images.

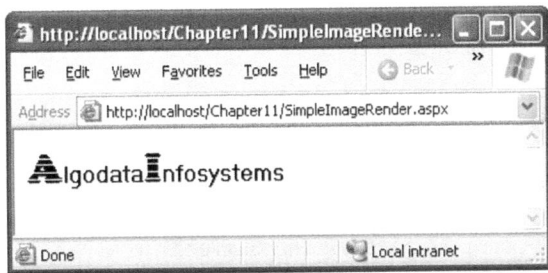

Figure 11-1. *Displaying an image from a database*

When you use BinaryWrite(), you are stepping away from the web-page model. If you add other controls to your web page, they won't appear. Similarly, Response.Write() won't have any effect, because you are no longer creating an HTML page. Instead, you're retuning image data. You'll see how to solve this problem and optimize this approach in the following sections.

Reading Binary Data Efficiently

Binary data can easily grow to large sizes. However, if you're dealing with a large image file, the example shown previously will demonstrate woefully poor performance. The problem is that it uses the DataReader, which loads a single record into memory at a time. This is better than the DataSet (which loads the entire result set into memory at once), but it still isn't ideal if the field size is large.

There's no good reason to load an entire 2 MB picture into memory at once. A much better idea would be to read it piece by piece, and then write each chunk to the output stream using Response.BinaryWrite(). Fortunately, the DataReader has a sequential access feature that supports this design. To use sequential access, you simply need to supply the CommandBehavior.SequentialAccess value to the Command.ExecuteDataReader() method. Then you can move through the row one block at a time, using the DataReader.GetBytes() method.

When using sequential access, there are a couple limitations to keep in mind. First, you must read the data as a forward-only stream. Once you've read a block of data, you automatically move ahead in the stream, and there's no going back. Second, you must read the fields in the same order that they are returned by your query. For example, if your query returns three columns, the third of which is a binary field, you must return the values of the first and second fields before accessing the binary data in the third field. If you access the third field first, you will not be able to access the first two fields.

Here's how you would revise the earlier page to use sequential access:

```
private void Page_Load(object sender, System.EventArgs e)
{
    string connectionString =
      "Data Source=localhost;Initial Catalog=pubs;Integrated Security=SSPI";
    SqlConnection con = new SqlConnection(connectionString);
    string SQL = "SELECT logo FROM pub_info WHERE pub_id='1389'";
    SqlCommand cmd = new SqlCommand(SQL, con);

    try
    {
        con.Open();
        SqlDataReader r =
          cmd.ExecuteReader(CommandBehavior.SequentialAccess);

        if (r.Read())
        {
            int bufferSize = 100;                  // Size of the buffer.
            byte[] bytes = new byte[bufferSize];   // The buffer of data.
            long bytesRead;                        // The number of bytes read.
            long readFrom = 0;                     // The starting index.
```

```
            // Read the field 100 bytes at a time.
            do
            {
                bytesRead = r.GetBytes(0, readFrom, bytes, 0, bufferSize);
                Response.BinaryWrite(bytes);
                readFrom += bufferSize;
            } while (bytesRead == bufferSize);
        }
        r.Close();
    }
    finally
    {
        con.Close();
    }
}
```

The GetBytes() method returns a value that indicates the number of bytes that were retrieved. If you need to determine the total number of bytes in the field, you simply need to pass a null reference instead of a buffer when you call the GetBytes() method.

Integrating Images with Other Content

The Reponse.BinaryWrite() method creates a bit of a challenge if you want to integrate image data with other controls and HTML. That's because when you use BinaryWrite() to return raw image data, you lose the ability to add any additional HTML content.

To attack this problem, you need to create another page that calls your image-generating code. The best way to do this is to replace your image-generating page with a dedicated HTTP handler that generates image output. This way, you save the overhead of the full ASP.NET web form model, which you aren't using anyway. HTTP handlers were first introduced in Chapter 5.

Creating the HTTP handler you need is quite easy. You simply need to implement the IHttpHandler interface and implement the ProcessRequest() method. The HTTP handler will retrieve the ID of the record you want to display from the query string.

Here's the complete HTTP handler code:

```
public class ImageFromDB : IHttpHandler
{
    string connectionString;

    public ImageFromDB()
    {
        // Get connection string from web.config.
        connectionString = ConfigurationSettings.AppSettings["ConnectionString"];
    }

    public void ProcessRequest(HttpContext context)
    {
        // Get the ID for this request.
        string id = context.Request.QueryString["id"];
```

```csharp
        if (id == null) throw new ApplicationException("Must specify ID.");

        // Create a parameterized command for this record.
        SqlConnection con = new SqlConnection(connectionString);
        string SQL = "SELECT logo FROM pub_info WHERE pub_id=@ID";
        SqlCommand cmd = new SqlCommand(SQL, con);
        cmd.Parameters.Add("@ID", id);

        try
        {
            con.Open();
            SqlDataReader r =
              cmd.ExecuteReader(CommandBehavior.SequentialAccess);

            if (r.Read())
            {
                int bufferSize = 100;               // Size of the buffer.
                byte[] bytes = new byte[bufferSize];  // The buffer.
                long bytesRead;                     // The # of bytes read.
                long readFrom = 0;                  // The starting index.

                // Read the field 100 bytes at a time.
                do
                {
                    bytesRead = r.GetBytes(0, readFrom, bytes, 0, bufferSize);
                    context.Response.BinaryWrite(bytes);
                    readFrom += bufferSize;
                } while (bytesRead == bufferSize);
            }
            r.Close();
        }
        finally
        {
            con.Close();
        }
    }

    public bool IsReusable
    {
        get { return true; }
    }
}
```

Once you've created the HTTP handler, you need to register it in the web.config file, as shown here:

```
<httpHandlers>
  <add verb="GET" path="ImageFromDB.ashx"
    type="Chapter11.ImageFromDB, Chapter11" />
</httpHandlers>
```

Now you can retrieve the image data by requesting the HTTP handler URL, with the ID of the row that you want to retrieve. Here's an example:

```
ImageFromDB.ashx?ID=1389
```

To show this image content in another page, you simply need to set the src attribute of an image to this URL, as shown here:

```
<img src="ImageFromDB.ashx?ID=1389"/>
```

Figure 11-2 shows a page that shows multiple controls and logo images. It uses the following ItemTemplate:

```
<ItemTemplate>
  <table border='1'><tr><td>
    <img
src='ImageFromDB.ashx?ID=<%# DataBinder.Eval(Container.DataItem, "pub_id")%>'
/>
    </td></tr></table>
  <b><%# DataBinder.Eval(Container.DataItem, "pub_name") %></b>
  <br>
  <%# DataBinder.Eval(Container.DataItem, "city") %>,
  <%# DataBinder.Eval(Container.DataItem, "state") %>,
  <%# DataBinder.Eval(Container.DataItem, "country") %>
  <br><br>
</ItemTemplate>
```

This current HTTP handler approach works very well if you want to build a detail page with information about a single record. For example, you could show a list of publishers, and then display the image for the appropriate publisher when the user makes a selection. However, this solution isn't as efficient if you want to show image data for every publisher at once, such as in a list control. The approach still works, but it will be inefficient because it uses a separate request to the HTTP handler (and hence a separate database connection) to retrieve each image. You can solve this problem by creating an HTTP handler that checks for image data in the cache before retrieving it from the database. Before you bind the DataGrid, you would then perform a query that returns all the records with their image data, and load each image into the cache.

Figure 11-2. *Displaying database images in ASP.NET web page*

DataSet Mapping

By default, when you use the DataAdapter to fill a DataSet, the column names that are used in the DataSet correspond to the column names defined in the data source. This isn't necessarily a problem, since you can easily tailor the display of column names in a control. For example, in a DataGrid you can set the HeaderText. However, it can be a problem when the database changes, and your application can no longer find the fields it expects. Compounding this problem is the fact that field names can't be checked at compile time. Thus, an invalid name will lead to a runtime error, which may lurk unnoticed or prove more difficult to diagnose.

There is more than one approach to reducing this risk. For example, you can use column ordinals (index numbers) instead of column names. Another possibility is to use some sort of mapping. With ADO.NET, there are two places that you can implement mapping: at the query level, or in the DataAdapter.

The SQL language provides a basic ability to change column names using the AS keyword. For example, the following query selects three columns from the Categories table, and renames two of them.

```
SELECT CategoryID AS ID, CategoryName AS Category, Description
  FROM Categories
```

This technique is useful if you are following good design practices and placing your query in a view or stored procedure in the database. Then, if column names change, you can simply update the corresponding view or stored procedure, and the client application will continue to work seamlessly.

The AS keyword isn't perfect, though. The most obvious drawback is that you can only use the AS keyword in a query. If the client tries to update the data source using the same column names, the update will fail. Once again, this isn't a problem if you are working through an intermediate layer of stored procedures, which can always be adjusted to work with the new column names. But if you haven't taken this precaution, you may need another way to add a new layer in between your database and your client code.

In ADO.NET, this trick is column mapping. The basic principle is to apply a list of column transformations to the DataAdapter object. When you fill a DataSet using the DataAdapter, it automatically renames the source columns, and uses the names you've configured. Even better, when you update the data source using the DataAdapter, it applies the same transformation in reverse, ensuring that the correct columns are modified in the data source.

Here's an example:

```
// Create the new mapping.
DataTableMapping map;
map = adapter.TableMappings.Add("Categories", "Categories");

// Define column mappings.
map.ColumnMappings.Add("CategoryID", "ID");
map.ColumnMappings.Add("CategoryName", "Name");
map.ColumnMappings.Add("Description", "Description");

// Fill the DataSet.
adapter.Fill(ds, "Categories");
```

You may notice that the DataAdapter mappings also give you the opportunity to map table names. However, this isn't very useful, because the table name is never drawn from the data source; instead, it's supplied as a parameter for the Fill() method. In the previous example, the table name "Categories" is mapped to the DataTable named "Categories"—in other words the name is not changed. However, this step is still required. If no parameter is specified, the default name ("Table") is used.

Of course, nothing prevents you from using table mappings if you like. In the example below, the Fill() method actually creates a table in the DataSet named CategoryList, *not* Categories.

```
// Create the new mapping.
DataTableMapping map;
map = adapter.TableMappings.Add("Categories", "CategoryList");
```

```
// (Column mapping code omitted.)

// Fill the DataSet.
adapter.Fill(ds, "Categories");
```

One case in which table mapping can be useful is if you have a stored procedure or batch query that returns multiple result sets. In this case, a number will automatically be added to the table name for each subsequent result set, as in Categories, Categories1, Categories2, and so on. By adding a DataTableMapping object for each of these tables, you can correct this behavior:

```
// Create a mapping for a table that returns a list of categories
// and a list of products.
DataTableMapping map;
adapter.TableMappings.Add("Results", "Categories");
adapter.TableMappings.Add("Results1", "Products");

// Fill the DataSet (using a stored procedure that
// returns multiple result sets).
adapter.Fill(ds, "Results");
```

The DataAdapter provides a special MissingMappingAction property that governs how it behaves if you don't supply column and table mappings. It takes one of the MissingMappingAction values described in Table 11-3.

Table 11-3. *Values for the MissingMappingAction Enumeration*

Value	Description
Passthrough	If there is any column that doesn't have a mapping, the data source column name is used. This is the default.
Error	If there is any column that doesn't have a mapping, an exception is thrown.
Ignore	All columns that don't have a mapping are ignored, and not added to the DataSet.

It's also worth noting that index-based lookup is faster than name-based lookup. Microsoft suggests that an optimized application steer clear of column names and use only index values. This also gives you a chance to provide a higher level of type safety by using numeric constants or enumerations. Here's an example that you might place in a data component:

```
public enum DBFields
{
    CategoryID = 0, CategoryName = 2, Description = 3
}
```

The client application now has less chance to make a mistake, provided one of the enumerated values is used. However, you need to ensure that the column index in the enumeration is correct, which can be a headache if the database changes frequently.

```
// Display the ID.
Console.WriteLine(row[DBFields.CategoryID]);
```

Typed DataSets

There's another possible approach to the problem of weakly typed column names. Using the tools included with Visual Studio .NET or the .NET SDK, you can generate a strongly typed data set. This strongly typed DataSet consists of a series of specialized classes derived from the base DataSet, DataTable, and DataRow objects.

A typed DataSet provides two advantages when compared with ordinary data classes:

- The information about the schema of the DataSet is already "hard-coded" into the DataSet. This means that the DataSet is preinitialized with information about the tables, columns, and data types you want to retrieve. As a result, when you execute a query to retrieve the actual information, it will execute slightly faster. (When you fill a blank DataSet, the data provider actually performs two steps. First, it retrieves the bare minimum schema information, and then it executes the query.)

- You can access table names and field values using strongly typed property names instead of field-name lookup. This allows you to catch errors (such as using the wrong field name, table name, or data type) at compile time instead of at runtime.

The second point is particularly interesting. It allows you to change code like this:

```
lblResult.Text = "Category Name: " +
  (string)ds.Tables["Categories"].Rows[0]["CategoryName"];
```

into code like the following:

```
lblResult.Text = "Category Name: " + ds.Categories.Rows[0].CategoryName;
```

Both of these statements retrieve the value of the CategoryName field in the first row of a Categories table. However, the second version has a variety of advantages. If you make a minor mistake entering the name of the table or the field, the problem will be caught as soon as you try to compile your code. But when you use the string-based collection lookup, you won't realize the problem until your code is executed. Furthermore, the strongly typed approach allows you to use Visual Studio .NET IntelliSense to find the appropriate field or table name. Clearly, a typed DataSet provides a much richer design-time and debugging experience.

The typed DataSet also has its drawbacks, including the fact that you'll need to manage another source-code file or assembly reference for your project. Using a generic DataSet relieves you of this task, and sidesteps any possible versioning problems if the data source changes. However, in an ASP.NET application these considerations aren't very significant. All the code executes on the web server, so you don't need to worry about client deployment issues,

There are two ways to create a typed DataSet: by using the visual tools integrated into Visual Studio .NET or by using the command-line xsd.exe utility. In both cases, your starting point should be an XML schema document (XSD) that defines the data structure for the

DataSet. The easiest way to create this file correctly is simply to create a short utility that creates a DataSet, and then uses the FillSchema() method for the appropriate tables, and then uses the WriteXmlSchema() method to save the schema to disk. (You'll learn more about XML schemas in the next chapter.)

Here's a simple console application that you can use to create a schema with the information for two tables in the Northwind database—Categories and Products.

```
public class CreateSchemaFile
{
    static string connectionString = "Data Source=localhost;" +
        "Initial Catalog=Northwind;Integrated Security=SSPI";

    static string categorySQL = "SELECT * FROM Categories";
    static string productSQL = "SELECT * FROM Products";

    public static void Main()
    {
        // Create ADO.NET objects.
        SqlConnection con = new SqlConnection(connectionString);
        SqlCommand com = new SqlCommand(categorySQL, con);
        SqlDataAdapter adapter = new SqlDataAdapter(com);

        // When creating the DataSet, it's important to name it,
        // because this name will be used as the strongly typed
        // DataSet class name.
        DataSet ds = new DataSet("NorthwindDataSet");

        // Execute the command.
        try
        {
            con.Open();
            adapter.FillSchema(ds, SchemaType.Mapped, "Categories");

            // Modify the command and re-execute it.
            adapter.SelectCommand.CommandText = productSQL;
            adapter.FillSchema(ds, SchemaType.Mapped, "Products");
        }
        catch (Exception err)
        {
            Console.WriteLine(err.ToString());
        }
        finally
        {
            con.Close();
```

```
        }
        ds.WriteXmlSchema(@"c:\Northwind.xsd");
    }
}
```

Using this schema, you can create a typed DataSet using Visual Studio .NET or the xsd.exe tool. The next two sections consider both of these approaches.

Creating a Typed DataSet in Visual Studio .NET

To create a typed DataSet in Visual Studio .NET, open a project, right-click the project in the Solution Explorer, and choose Add Existing Item from the Add menu. Then browse to the XSD file you created in the previous step.

Visual Studio .NET provides two display modes to examine and configure the XSD file. You can look at it as raw XML, or you can view it as a DataSet, which provides a tabular diagram where you can easily modify data types and add relations. Figure 11-3 shows an example of this view, with the Categories and Products table definitions.

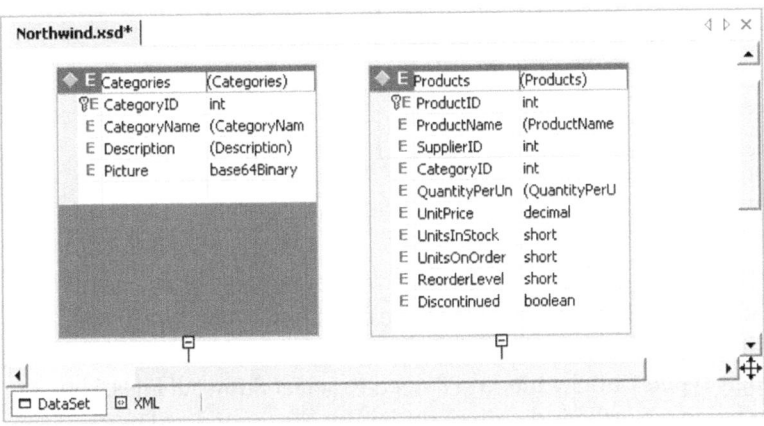

Figure 11-3. *Configuring a DataSet schema*

You can use the Visual Studio .NET designer to modify the type restrictions that will be applied to various fields. However, you shouldn't edit the column names, because this will create a typed DataSet that references nonexistent fields.

You can also define relationships. In the categories and products example, you have two choices. You could revise the earlier example so that the application creates a DataRelation object and adds it to the DataSet before it writes the schema file. This way, the schema file will have a record of the relationship between the two tables. Another approach is to add the relationship using Visual Studio .NET. To accomplish this, right-click the parent CategoryID field and choose Add ➤ New Relation. You can then specify the child and parent columns. Figure 11-4 shows the custom Visual Studio .NET window that allows you to configure the relation and add the implied constraints.

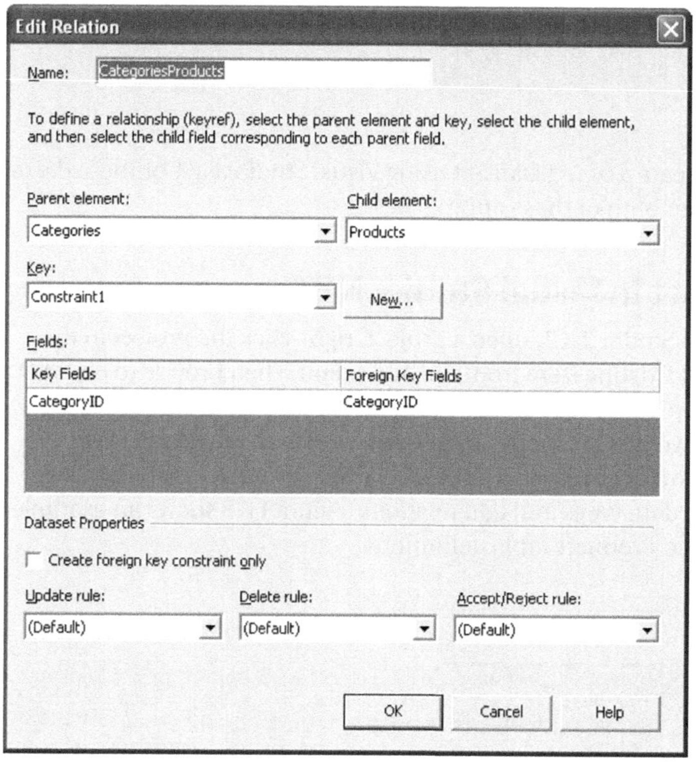

Figure 11-4. *Adding a relationship*

Finally, to generate the DataSet, right-click the designer window and select the Generate DataSet check box. You can also select Preview DataSet to see the names, data types, and structure that will be used for the various data objects.

To actually see the strongly typed DataSet file, you'll need to select Show All Files from the Project menu. Then, you'll find a Northwind.cs item under the Northwind.xsd node (see Figure 11-5).

Creating a Typed DataSet with XSD.exe

You can also create a typed DataSet from an XSD document using a command-line utility that's included with the .NET Framework. To do so, use the following command line:

```
xsd Northwind.xsd /d /l:CS /n:Northwind
```

The /d switch specifies that you want source code for a DataSet to be created, while the /l switch specifies that the utility should use the C# language (which is the default). The /n parameter specifies the namespace for the generated types (the default is Schemas).

The resulting file will have the name Northwind.cs. You can add this file to an existing project, or compile it to an assembly using the csc.exe command-line compiler, as shown here:

```
csc /t:library Northwind.cs /r:System.dll /r:System.Data.dll
```

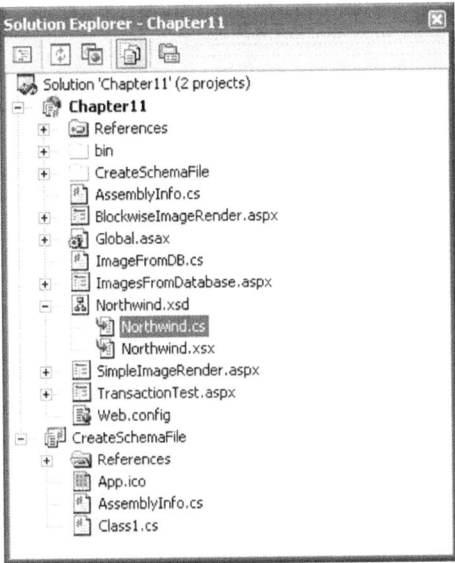

Figure 11-5. *The typed DataSet code file*

Dissecting the Typed DataSet

The strongly typed DataSet consists of specialized classes that derive from the generic data container classes like DataRow, DataTable, and DataSet. These derived classes add strongly typed property access, helper methods for creating records and finding records, typecasting code, and exception handling.

Following is the (somewhat shortened) code from the strongly typed CategoriesDataTable class, which inherits from the base DataTable. It provides strongly typed access to the DataColumns for this table (CategoryIDColumn, CategoryNameColumn, and so on), and strongly typed access to the data as a collection of CategoriesRow objects. It also provides several helper methods, including a strongly typed version of the AddRow() method named AddCategoriesRow() and a FindByCategoryID() method that allows you to search for a row by CategoryID.

```
public class CategoriesDataTable : DataTable, IEnumerable
{
    private DataColumn columnCategoryID;
    private DataColumn columnCategoryName;
    private DataColumn columnDescription;
    private DataColumn columnPicture;

    // (Code to initialized variables and columns omitted.)

    internal DataColumn CategoryIDColumn {
        get { return this.columnCategoryID; } }
    internal DataColumn CategoryNameColumn {
        get { return this.columnCategoryName; } }
    internal DataColumn DescriptionColumn {
```

```
            get { return this.columnDescription; } }
        internal DataColumn PictureColumn {
            get { return this.columnPicture; } }


        public CategoriesRow this[int index] {
            get { return ((CategoriesRow)(this.Rows[index])); }
        }


        public CategoriesRow NewCategoriesRow() {
            return ((CategoriesRow)(this.NewRow()));
        }


        public void AddCategoriesRow(CategoriesRow row) {
            this.Rows.Add(row);
        }


        public CategoriesRow AddCategoriesRow(string CategoryName,
                        string Description, System.Byte[] Picture) {
            CategoriesRow rowCategoriesRow = ((CategoriesRow)(this.NewRow()));
            rowCategoriesRow.ItemArray = new object[] { null, CategoryName,
                                        Description, Picture};
            this.Rows.Add(rowCategoriesRow);
            return rowCategoriesRow;
        }


        public CategoriesRow FindByCategoryID(int CategoryID) {
            return ((CategoriesRow)(this.Rows.Find(new object[] {
                    CategoryID})));
        }
    }
}
```

The CategoriesRow class derives from DataRow and provides strongly typed access to all the fields in the row (CategoryID, CategoryName, and so on). Here's the excerpted code:

```
public class CategoriesRow : DataRow
{
    private CategoriesDataTable tableCategories;
    // (Initialization code ommitted.)

    public int CategoryID {
        get { return
            ((int)(this[this.tableCategories.CategoryIDColumn])); }
        set { this[this.tableCategories.CategoryIDColumn] = value; }
    }
    public string CategoryName {
        get { return
            ((string)(this[this.tableCategories.CategoryNameColumn])); }
        set { this[this.tableCategories.CategoryNameColumn] = value; }
```

```
    }
    public string Description {
        get {
            try {
                return
                    ((string)(this[this.tableCategories.DescriptionColumn])); }
            catch (InvalidCastException e) {
                throw new StrongTypingException(
                    "Cannot get value because it is DBNull.", e); }
        }
        set { this[this.tableCategories.DescriptionColumn] = value; }
    }

    public bool IsDescriptionNull() {
        return this.IsNull(this.tableCategories.DescriptionColumn);
    }
    public void SetDescriptionNull() {
        this[this.tableCategories.DescriptionColumn] =
            System.Convert.DBNull;
    }
}
```

Using the Typed DataSet

Once you've created the typed DataSet, you can write strongly typed code that uses it. This
code can fill the DataSet in exactly the same way (using a DataAdapter). However, once you've
created the DataSet, you can examine tables and fields with more efficient and elegant
strongly typed syntax.

The following example creates an instance of the typed NorthwindDataSet, fills it with the
Categories and Products information, and then iterates over the tables, building an HTML
string that will be displayed on the page. The strongly typed portions are highlighted in bold.

```
private void Page_Load(object sender, System.EventArgs e)
{
    // Create the Connection, DataAdapter, and DataSet.
    string connectionString = "Data Source=localhost;" +
      "Initial Catalog=Northwind;Integrated Security=SSPI";
    SqlConnection con = new SqlConnection(connectionString);
    string sqlProducts = "SELECT * FROM Products";
    string sqlCategories = "SELECT * FROM Categories";

    // Create the strongly typed DataSet.
    NorthwindDataSet ds = new NorthwindDataSet();

    // Fill the DataSet.
    SqlDataAdapter da = new SqlDataAdapter(sqlCategories, con);
    da.Fill(ds.Categories);
```

```
    da.SelectCommand.CommandText = sqlProducts;
    da.Fill(ds.Products);

    // Build the HTML string.
    StringBuilder htmlStr = new StringBuilder("");
    foreach (NorthwindDataSet.CategoriesRow row in ds.Categories)
    {
        htmlStr.Append("<b>");
        htmlStr.Append(row.CategoryName);
        htmlStr.Append("</b><br><i>");
        htmlStr.Append(row.Description);
        htmlStr.Append("</i><br>");

        // Get the related product rows.
        // Note that this code uses the helper method GetProductsRows()
        // instead of the generic GetChildRows().
        // The advantage is you don't need to specify the relationship name.
        NorthwindDataSet.ProductsRow[] products = row.GetProductsRows();
        foreach (NorthwindDataSet.ProductsRow child in products)
        {
            htmlStr.Append("<li>");
            htmlStr.Append(child.ProductName);
            htmlStr.Append("</li>");
        }
        htmlStr.Append("<br><br>");
    }

    // Show the generated HTML.
    lblOutput.Text = htmlStr.ToString();
}
```

The result is shown in Figure 11-6.

The strongly typed data classes also provide helper methods that you can use for common data tasks. For example, if you've defined a relationship for tables in the DataSet, dedicated methods are automatically added for retrieving parent and child rows. The web page shown in Figure 11-6 uses a CategoriesDataTable.GetProductsRows() method to retrieve all the products in a given category. You don't even need to specify the relationship name.

Some of the other helper methods that strongly typed DataSet classes include are methods for editing (for example, the CategoriesDataTable.NewCategoriesRow() and CategoriesDataTable.AddCategoriesRow() methods), and searching based on the primary key information (for example, the CategoriesDataTable.FindByCategoryID() method).

■**Tip** Remember that thanks to inheritance the strongly typed DataSet really *is* a DataSet. That means you can seamlessly cast the NorthwindDataSet class to the DataSet class, and use ordinary string-based field and table lookup. However, the reverse is not true—you can't cast an ordinary DataSet to the NorthwindDataSet type.

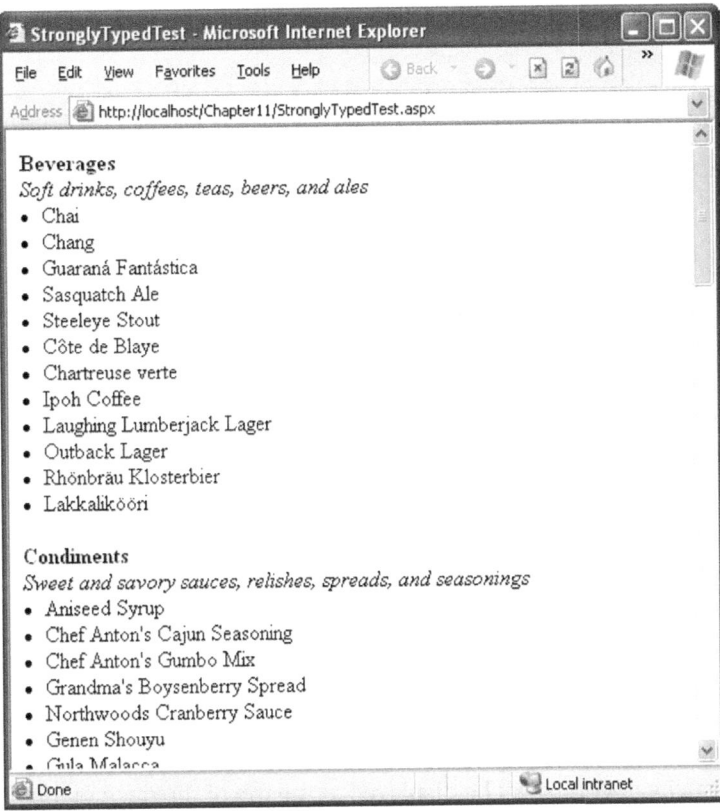

Figure 11-6. *Displaying output with a typed DataSet*

Advanced Grids

ASP.NET's DataGrid control is a remarkably powerful tool. In fact, it far outclasses the nearest Windows equivalent (the System.Windows.Forms.DataGrid control). With a little creativity, you can build entire web pages with little more than a combination of DataGrid controls.

The following sections walk through a few advanced DataGrid examples, and demonstrate several common application patterns along the way, including master/detail lists, frames, and multiple selection.

A Parent/Child View

A common requirement in any application is to allow the user to browse to specific information through a parent/child (also known as a master/details) list. For example, you might want to see the order items belonging to a specific order, the orders made by a specific customer, or the products in a specific category. Although you can implement this design using a variety of controls, it's quite easy to build a basic interface using two DataGrid controls—one for the parent records, and one for the child records that are related to the currently selected parent.

To implement the two-DataGrid design, you have several possible approaches. They include putting

- Both DataGrid controls on the same web page. This is the most straightforward approach from a coding perspective, but it gives you the least flexibility for controlling how the data is displayed. For example, if you scroll down the page the first DataGrid will disappear from view.

- Each DataGrid control on a separate web page. When an item is selected in the first DataGrid, navigate to the second page. This is also easy to code, but it is probably more awkward for the user to navigate.

- Each DataGrid control on a separate web page, and creating an HTML frames page that shows both of them. This gives you more flexibility in the display, but it also forces you to use a little client-side JavaScript to synchronize the two pages.

- Each DataGrid control on a separate web page, and embedding a server-side <iframe> tag on one page that shows the second page. The <iframe> tag is a frame that you can position anywhere in another web page. The drawback is that it isn't supported in all browsers.

The first and second approaches don't require any explanation. You'll see the fourth approach (the <iframe>) at work later in Part Four. In this example, you'll start out by using the third approach to create an ordinary frames page.

In this example, a list of product categories will be displayed at the top of the page in the uppermost frame. Underneath this frame, another frame will show a list of all products in the current category.

The first step is to create the frames page. This doesn't need to be an ASP.NET page because it contains nothing more than a frames declaration. Here's what the page contains:

```
<HTML>
  <HEAD>
    <TITLE>MasterDetails</TITLE>
  </HEAD>
  <frameset rows="50%,50%">
    <frame name="master" src="Master.aspx" target="_self">
    <frame name="details" src="Details.aspx" target="_self">
  </frameset>
</HTML>
```

Because this example requires that two pages access information from the same database, it makes good sense to use a database component to centralize the data access logic. Additionally, because both pages will retrieve similar information separately, the database component should take extra care to store the DataSet in the cache. You won't examine the database component code here, because the code is similar to the examples you've already seen. However, you can see the full code with the downloadable samples.

The last step is to build both pages. When the master page loads, it fills the DataGrid with a list of categories:

```
private void Page_Load(object sender, System.EventArgs e)
{
    // Create the database component.
    NorthwindDB db = new NorthwindDB();

    gridMaster.DataSource = db.GetCategoriesProductsDataSet();
    gridMaster.DataMember = "Categories";
    gridMaster.DataBind();
}
```

Figure 11-7 shows the result.

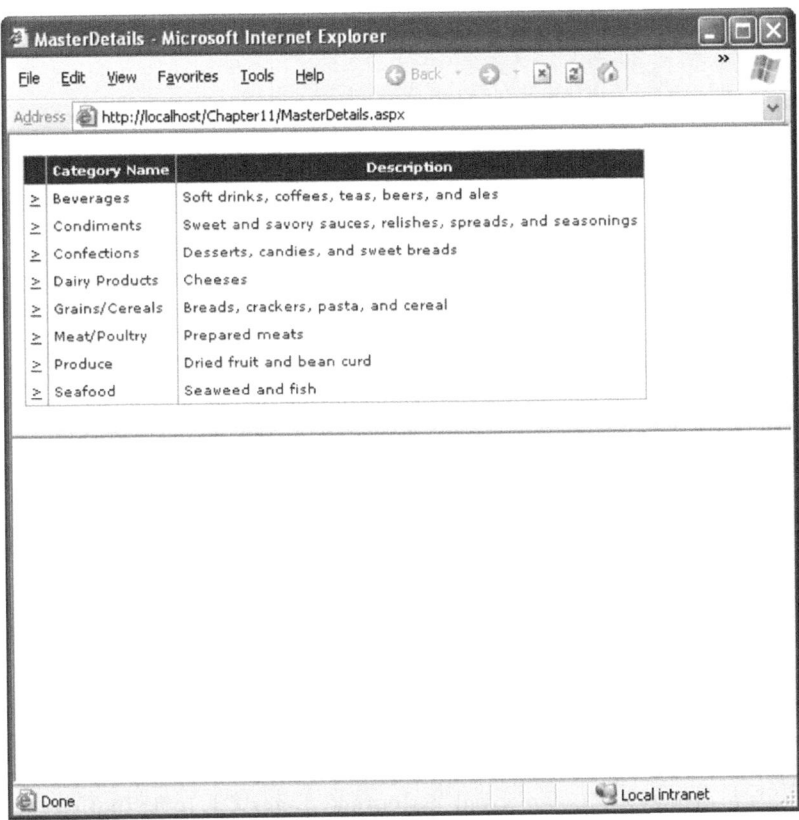

Figure 11-7. *The master list of categories*

The tricky part happens when a category is selected in the DataGrid. At this point, the master page needs to perform two tasks. First, it needs to set aside the CategoryID information so the second page can access it. If you were navigating from one page to the other, you would probably pass the information through the query string. In this case, however, you need to use another object. The Session collection is the most reasonable choice, as it has scope over both pages, is limited to the current user, and is semipermanent. Another reasonable choice is a custom cookie.

The second challenge for the master page is triggering the browser to refresh the second frame. Unfortunately, because the two pages are entirely separate, there's no server-side way to accomplish this. Instead, you need to resort to writing a short JavaScript block that will perform the task as soon as the master page is returned to the client. (As a result, the browser actually updates each frame separately, one after the other.) You add this script to the page using the Page.RegisterStartupScript() method, which you'll take a closer look at in Chapter 22.

Here's the complete code for the SelectedIndexChanged event handler:

```
private void gridMaster_SelectedIndexChanged(object sender, System.EventArgs e)
{
    Session["SelectedCategory"] = gridMaster.DataKeys[gridMaster.SelectedIndex];

    // Use JavaScript to trigger the redirect in the other frame.
    string frameScript = "<script language='javascript'>" +
      "window.parent.frames(1).location='Details.aspx';" + "</script>";
    Page.RegisterStartupScript("FrameScript", frameScript);
}
```

The details page can then retrieve the selected category information (if it exists), and bind its own DataGrid. The page actually retrieves the full DataSet with the full list of products, but it adjusts the RowFilter of the associated DataView so that only the records that match the selected CategoryID will be shown.

```
private void Page_Load(object sender, System.EventArgs e)
{
    if (Session["SelectedCategory"] != null)
    {
        NorthwindDB db = new NorthwindDB();
        DataSet ds = db.GetCategoriesProductsDataSet();

        DataView view = ds.Tables["Products"].DefaultView;
        view.RowFilter = "CategoryID =" + Session["SelectedCategory"].ToString();
        gridDetails.DataSource = view;
        gridDetails.DataBind();
    }
}
```

Figure 11-8 shows the result of selecting a category. Note that you can scroll down through the product list without losing the category list, thanks to the use of frames.

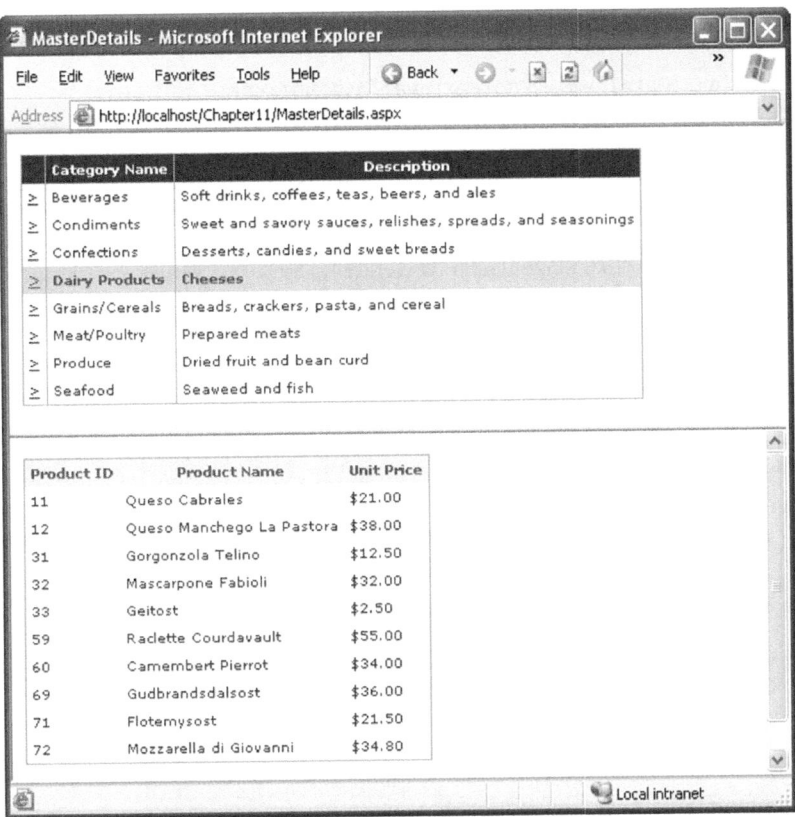

Figure 11-8. *The products list for the selected category*

A Parent/Child/Detail View

Another common data-driven idiom is the list/details view. With this pattern, you present the user with a list of records. When the user selects a record, you show the full details in another control. For example, you could extend the previous example by giving the user the ability to select an individual product, as shown in Figure 11-9.

Creating this example is easy—you simply need to handle the SelectedIndexChanged event of the second DataGrid. You could then extract the related information and display it any ASP.NET controls. However, a quick trick is to display the detailed information in a DataList. This allows you to define the format with a simple template, and support editing abilities if you need them.

Here's the template that's used in to show the details of the selected item in the DataList:

```
<ItemTemplate>
  <b><%# DataBinder.Eval(Container.DataItem, "ProductID") %>
  - <%# DataBinder.Eval(Container.DataItem, "ProductName") %></b><br><br>
  <b>Quantity Per Unit:</b>
  <%# DataBinder.Eval(Container.DataItem, "QuantityPerUnit") %><br>
  <b>Units in Stock:</b>
  <%# DataBinder.Eval(Container.DataItem, "UnitsInStock") %><br>
  <b>Units on Order:</b>
```

```
<%# DataBinder.Eval(Container.DataItem, "UnitsOnOrder") %><br>
<b>Reorder Level:</b>
<%# DataBinder.Eval(Container.DataItem, "ReorderLevel") %><br><br>
</ItemTemplate>
```

To bind the data to the DataList and show a single record, this example uses the following code to respond to the SelectedIndexChanged event of the products DataGrid:

```
private void gridDetails_SelectedIndexChanged(object sender, System.EventArgs e)
{
    NorthwindDB db = new NorthwindDB();
    DataSet ds = db.GetCategoriesProductsDataSet();
    DataView view = new DataView(ds.Tables["Products"]);
    view.RowFilter = "ProductID =" +
        gridDetails.DataKeys[gridDetails.SelectedIndex].ToString();
    listDetail.DataSource = view;
    listDetail.DataBind();
}
```

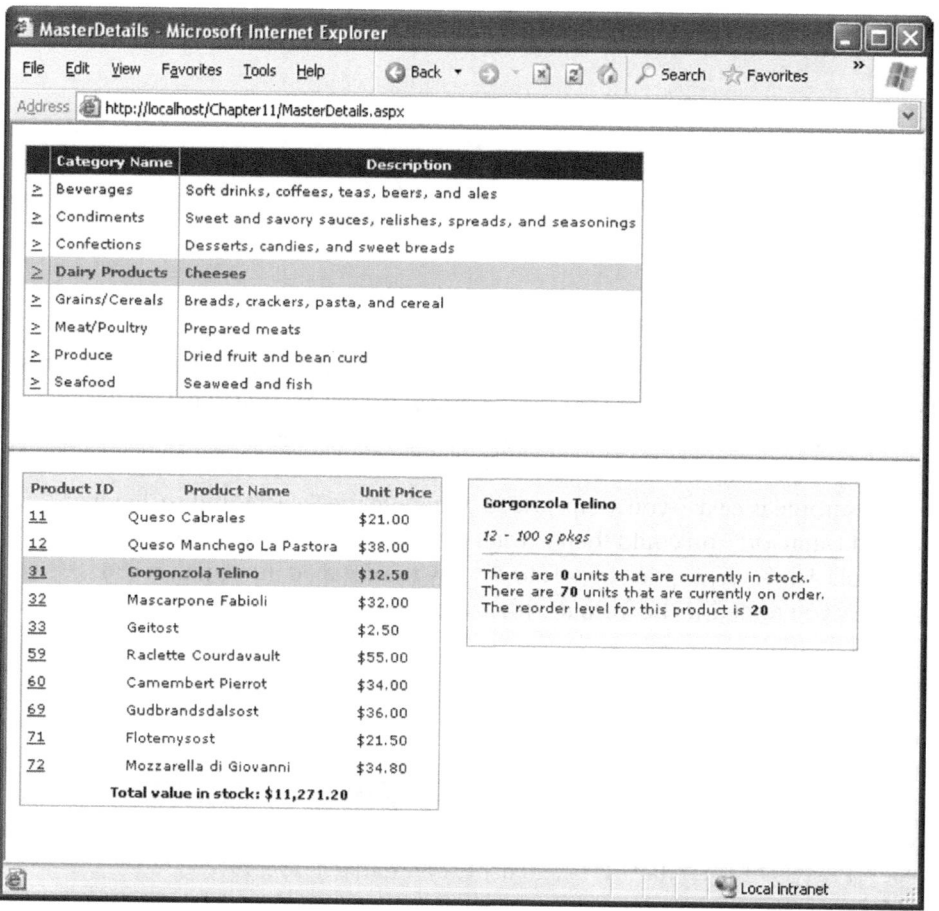

Figure 11-9. *The product defaults for the selected product*

Summaries in the DataGrid

Although the prime purpose of a DataGrid is to show a set of records, you can also add some more interesting information, like summary data. The first step is to add the footer row by setting the DataGrid.ShowFooter property to true. This displays a shaded footer row (which you can customize freely), but it doesn't show any data. To take care of that task, you need to handle the ItemCreated or ItemDataBound events of the DataGrid.

Consider the earlier example, which shows a list of products. A simple summary row could display the total or average product price. You can calculate this information and set it in a member variable just before you bind the grid.

The next example uses the summary row to display the total value of all the in-stock products for the currently selected category. The first step is to calculate this total manually when the page first loads and the data are retrieved. This information is then stored in a private valueInStock member variable so that it can be inserted into the DataGrid when the summary row is rendered.

```
private decimal valueInStock = 0;
private void Page_Load(object sender, System.EventArgs e)
{
    if (Session["SelectedCategory"] != null)
    {
        DataSet ds = db.GetCategoriesProductsDataSet();
        DataView view = ds.Tables["Products"].DefaultView;
        view.RowFilter = "CategoryID =" + Session["SelectedCategory"].ToString();

        // The easiest way to calculate the total value for
        // the displayed records is to work through the DataView,
        // not the DataTable. That's because the DataView will
        // include only the rows in the apporopriate category.
        foreach (DataRowView rowView in view)
        {
            DataRow row = rowView.Row;
            valueInStock +=
                (short)row["UnitsInStock"] * (decimal)row["UnitPrice"];
        }

        // Bind the grid.
        gridDetails.DataSource = view;
        gridDetails.DataBind();
    }
}
```

To actually display the calculated total value, you need to handle the ItemCreated event, and wait until the footer row is generated. When the footer row arrives, you simply access the corresponding cells and insert the summary data, as shown here:

```
private void gridDetails_ItemCreated(object sender,
    System.Web.UI.WebControls.DataGridItemEventArgs e)
{
    // Check if this item is a footer.
```

```
    ListItemType itemType = e.Item.ItemType;
    if ((itemType == ListItemType.Footer))
    {
        // Set the first cell to span over the entire row.
        e.Item.Cells[0].ColumnSpan = 3;
        e.Item.Cells[0].HorizontalAlign = HorizontalAlign.Center;

        // Remove the unneeded cells.
        e.Item.Cells.RemoveAt(2);
        e.Item.Cells.RemoveAt(1);

        // Add the text.
        e.Item.Cells[0].Text = "Total value in stock: " +
            valueInStock.ToString("C");
    }
}
```

The summary row has the same number of columns as the rest of the grid. As a result, if you want your text to be displayed over multiple cells (as it is in this example), you need to configure cell spanning by setting the ColumnSpan property of the appropriate cell. In this example, the first cell spans over three columns (itself, and the next two on the right). The final result is shown in Figure 11-10.

A Parent/Child View in a Single Table

The previous example developed a parent/child page using two DataGrid controls. This gives you the flexibility to show the child records for just the currently selected parent record. However, there are some situations in which you want to create a parent/child report that shows all the records from the child table, organized by parent. For example, you could use this to create a complete list of products organized by category. The next example demonstrates how you show a complete, subgrouped product list in a single grid.

The basic technique is to create a DataGrid for the parent table that contains an embedded DataGrid for each row. These child DataGrids are inserted into the parent DataGrid using a TemplateColumn. The only trick is that you can't bind the child DataGrids at the same time that you bind the parent DataGrid, because the parent rows haven't been created yet. Instead, you need to wait for the DataGrid.ItemDataBound event to fire in the parent.

In this example, the parent DataGrid defines two columns, both of which are the TemplateColumn type. The first column combines the category name and category description:

```
<asp:TemplateColumn HeaderText="Category">
  <ItemStyle VerticalAlign="Top" Width="20%"></ItemStyle>
  <ItemTemplate>
    <br>
    <b><%# DataBinder.Eval(Container.DataItem, "CategoryName") %></b>
    <br><br>
    <%# DataBinder.Eval(Container.DataItem, "Description" ) %>
    <br>
  </ItemTemplate>
</asp:TemplateColumn>
```

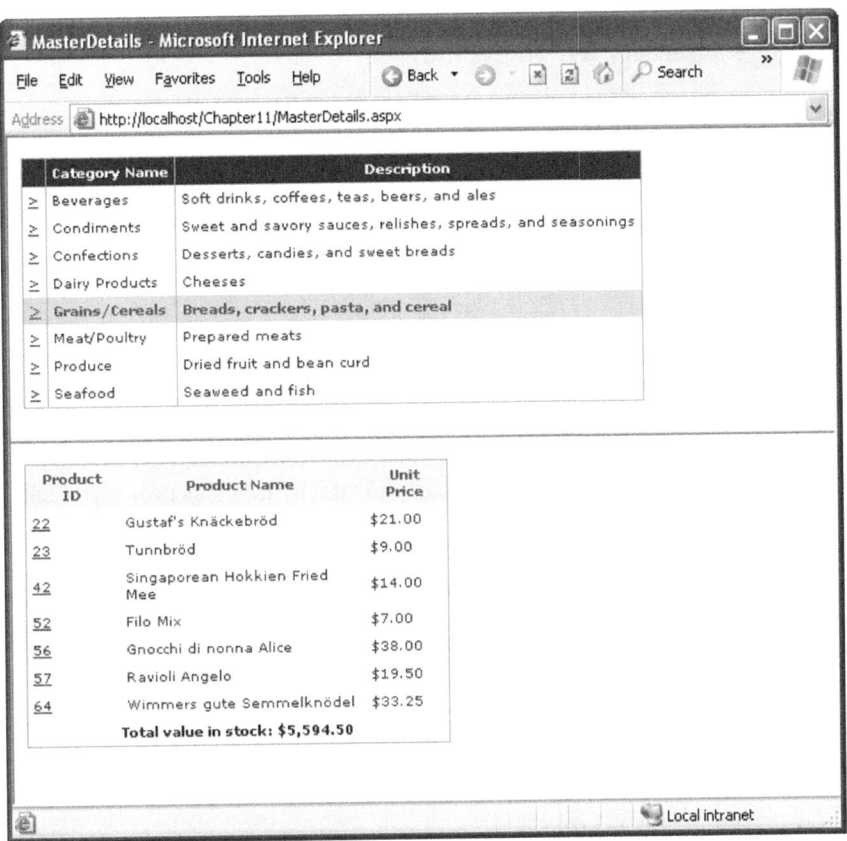

Figure 11-10. *Adding a summary row*

The second column contains an embedded DataGrid of products, with two bound columns. Here's an excerpted listing that omits the style-related attributes:

```
<asp:TemplateColumn HeaderText="Products">
  <ItemStyle VerticalAlign="Top"></ItemStyle>
  <ItemTemplate>
    <asp:DataGrid runat="server">
      <Columns>
        <asp:BoundColumn DataField="ProductName"
          HeaderText="Product Name"></asp:BoundColumn>
        <asp:BoundColumn DataField="UnitPrice"
          HeaderText="Unit Price" DataFormatString="{0:C}"></asp:BoundColumn>
      </Columns>
    </asp:DataGrid>
  </ItemTemplate>
</asp:TemplateColumn>
```

Now all you need to do is fill in the code. When the page first loads, you bind the parent DataGrid, as shown here:

```
private NorthwindDB db = new NorthwindDB();
private void Page_Load(object sender, System.EventArgs e)
{
    if (!Page.IsPostBack)
    {
        gridMaster.DataSource = db.GetCategoriesProductsDataSet();
        gridMaster.DataMember = "Categories";
        gridMaster.DataBind();
    }
}
```

This part of the code is typical. The trick is to bind the child DataGrids. If you leave out this step, the child DataGrids won't appear.

To bind the child DataGrids, you need to react to the DataGrid.ItemDataBound event, which fires every time a row is generated and bound to parent DataGrid. At this point, you can retrieve the child DataGrid control from the second column, and bind it to the product information. To ensure that you only show the products in the current category, you must also retrieve the CategoryID field for the current item and use it to construct a filter expression you can apply to the DataView. Here's the code you need:

```
private void gridProducts_ItemDataBound(object sender,
 System.Web.UI.WebControls.DataGridItemEventArgs e)
{
    // Look for DataGrid items.
    if (e.Item.ItemType == ListItemType.Item ||
      e.Item.ItemType == ListItemType.AlternatingItem)
    {
        // Retrieve the DataGrid control in the second column.
        DataGrid gridChild = (DataGrid)e.Item.Cells[1].Controls[1];

        // Retrieve the DataSet. This DataSet is cached,
        // so performance will not suffer.
        // You could also store it in a page-level variable when the Page.Load
        // event fires so that it's available for the duration of the request.
        DataSet ds = db.GetCategoriesProductsDataSet();

        // Filter the view to only show products in the current category.
        DataView view = ds.Tables["Products"].DefaultView;
        view.RowFilter = "CategoryID='" + gridMaster.DataKeys[e.Item.ItemIndex]
            + "'";

        // Bind the grid.
        gridChild.DataSource = ds.Tables["Products"];
        gridChild.DataBind();
    }
}
```

The resulting grid, with the parent DataGrid and the child DataGrids, is shown in Figure 11-11.

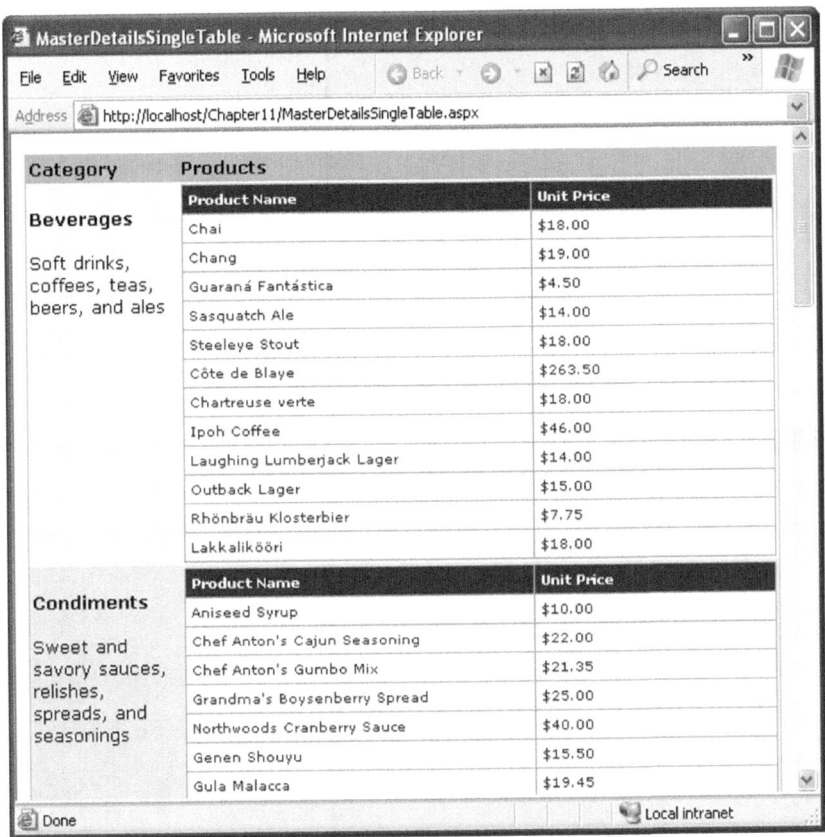

Figure 11-11. *A parent grid with embedded child grids*

Building a Shopping Cart

Shopping carts are a hallmark of e-commerce websites. They allow users to select a batch of items for an upcoming purchase. With the rich DataGrid control, you can build a simple shopping with remarkable ease. But before you begin, you need to consider a few basic design principles that go into creating a good shopping cart implementation.

- Unlike most of the examples you've seen, the shopping cart is not directly tied to an ADO.NET data object. Instead, you need to create your own classes to model the shopping cart information.

- A shopping cart is usually accessed on multiple pages. For that reason, it's natural to place the shopping cart into session state.

- A basic shopping cart example requires two data bound controls—one to show the product catalog, and one to show the shopping cart items. To add items from the catalog, the user must click some sort of button or link in the row.

In the following sections, you'll go through the steps needed to build a complete shopping cart framework that revolves around a single test page. Figure 11-12 shows the final result.

Figure 11-12. *A shopping cart*

The Shopping Cart Classes

In theory, you could use the DataRow and DataTable objects to represent a shopping cart. However, because the shopping cart information doesn't directly correspond to a table in the database, the process would be awkward and counterintuitive. A better approach is to design your own classes designed for representing the shopping cart and its items.

The first ingredient you need is a class to represent individual shopping cart items. This class needs to track the product information, along with the number of units the user wants to order. Here's a ShoppingCartItem class that fills this role:

```
public class ShoppingCartItem
{
    private int productID;
    public int ProductID
    {
        get {return productID;}
    }

    private string productName;
    public string ProductName
    {
        get {return productName;}
    }

    private decimal unitPrice;
    public decimal UnitPrice
    {
        get {return unitPrice;}
    }

    private int units;
    public int Units
    {
        get {return units;}
        set {units = value;}
    }

    public decimal Total
    {
        get {return Units * UnitPrice;}
    }

    public ShoppingCartItem(int productID,
      string productName, decimal unitPrice, int units)
    {
        this.productID = productID;
        this.productName = productName;
        this.unitPrice = unitPrice;
        this.units = units;
    }
}
```

You'll notice two interesting details about this class. First, its properties are almost all read-only. None of the shopping cart item information can be changed once the item is created, with the exception of the number of desired units. The second interesting detail is the Total property. This property doesn't map to a private member variable—instead it's calculated based on the unit price and the number of desired units. It's the class equivalent of a calculated column. This property is a great help when you bind a ShoppingCartItem to a control, because it allows you to easily show the total price of each line.

■**Note** When designing a class that you intend to use with a data bound control, you *must* use property procedures rather than public member variables. For example, if you were to implement the UnitPrice information using a public member variable instead of a property procedure, you wouldn't be able to bind to it and display that information in a data-bound control.

Of course a shopping cart is a *collection* of zero or more shopping cart items. To create the shopping cart, you can use a standard .NET collection class, like the ArrayList. In fact, that approach will work perfectly well in this example. However, a more robust approach is to create your own strongly typed collection class. A strongly typed collection class is a collection that is designed to work with a specific type of object. While the ArrayList can be used to store strings, numbers, shopping cart items, and any other type of .NET object in the same collection, a strongly typed collection restricts the items you can add to one specific type. If you attempt to add other data types, the error is caught immediately at compile time.

Creating a strongly typed collection is easy because you can derive from the System.Collections.CollectionBase class to acquire the basic functionality you need. Essentially, the CollectionBase wraps an ordinary ArrayList, which is exposed through the protected variable List. However, this ArrayList isn't directly accessible to other classes. Instead, your custom class must add methods like Add(), Remove(), Insert(), and so on, which allow other classes to use the collection. Here's the trick—even though the internal ArrayList isn't typesafe, the collection methods that you create are, which prevents errors and ensures that the collection contains the correct type of object.

Here's a strongly typed ShoppingCart collection that only accepts ShoppingCartItem instances:

```
public class ShoppingCart : CollectionBase
{
    public ShoppingCartItem this[int index]
    {
        get {return((ShoppingCartItem)List[index]);}
        set {List[index] = value;}
    }

    public int Add(ShoppingCartItem value)
    {
        return(List.Add(value));
    }

    public int IndexOf(ShoppingCartItem value)
    {
        return(List.IndexOf(value));
    }
```

```
public void Insert(int index, ShoppingCartItem value)
{
    List.Insert(index, value);
}

public void Remove(ShoppingCartItem value)
{
    List.Remove(value);
}

public bool Contains(ShoppingCartItem value)
{
    return(List.Contains(value));
}
}
```

Notice that the ShoppingCart doesn't implement ICollection, which is a requirement for data binding. It doesn't need to, because the CollectionBase class it inherits from already does.

At this point, you're ready to use the ShoppingCart and ShoppingCartItem classes in an ASP.NET web page. Optionally, you might want to consider adding the Serializable attribute before the class declaration of both classes so that the objects can be serialized into view state or an out-of-process session state provider if required, as described in Chapter 7.

The Test Page

The next step is to create and configure the DataGrid controls for showing the product and shopping cart information. In this example, there are two separate DataGrid controls—one for showing the product catalog, and another for showing the contents of the current contents of the shopping cart. The DataGrid for the product information has a fairly straightforward structure. It uses several BoundColumn tags that display fields from the bound table (with the correct numeric formatting), and one ButtonColumn that allows the user to select the row. The ButtonColumn is displayed as a hyperlink with the text Add.

Here are the definitions for all the DataGrid columns that are used to display the product catalog:

```
<Columns>
  <asp:BoundColumn DataField="ProductID" HeaderText="ID"></asp:BoundColumn>
  <asp:BoundColumn DataField="ProductName"
   HeaderText="Product Name"></asp:BoundColumn>
  <asp:BoundColumn DataField="UnitPrice" HeaderText="Unit Price"
   DataFormatString="{0:C}"></asp:BoundColumn>
  <asp:ButtonColumn Text="Add..." CommandName="Select"></asp:ButtonColumn>
</Columns>
```

When this page first loads, it queries the database component to get the full list of products. Then it binds the product list to the DataGrid. The code that performs this work is shown here:

```
private NorthwindDB db = new NorthwindDB();
private DataSet ds;
private ShoppingCart cart;

private void Page_Load(object sender, System.EventArgs e)
{
    // Update the product list.
    ds = db.GetCategoriesProductsDataSet();
    gridProducts.DataSource = ds.Tables["Products"];
    gridProducts.DataBind();

    // Check for the shopping cart. If it doesn't
    // exist, create a new cart and make it available.
    if (Session["Cart"] == null)
    {
        cart = new ShoppingCart();
    }
    else
    {
        cart = (ShoppingCart)Session["Cart"];
    }
}
```

You'll notice that the initialization code performs one other task when the page loads—it
checks for a ShoppingCart object in session state. If it doesn't exist, the initialization code creates a new empty cart. Either way, the cart is assigned to a private member variable so it can
be accessed in other event handlers (without needing to retrieve it from session state and cast
the object reference each time).

No matter what other events happen, the shopping cart is bound just before the page is
rendered. At this point, the current ShoppingCart object is reinserted into the Session collection in case there have been any changes to it during the page processing.

```
private void Page_PreRender(object sender, System.EventArgs e)
{
    // Store the shopping cart.
    Session["Cart"] = cart;

    // Show the shopping cart in the grid.
    gridCart.DataSource = cart;
    gridCart.DataBind();
}
```

So what can happen in the meantime between the Page.Load and the Page.PreRender
events? One possibility is that the user clicks one of the Add links in the products DataGrid.
In this case, the SelectedIndexChanged event fires and a series of steps take place.

First, the code retrieves the DataRow for the selected product, as follows:

```
private void gridProducts_SelectedIndexChanged(object sender, System.EventArgs e)
{
    // Get the full record for the one selected row.
    DataRow[] rows = ds.Tables["Products"].Select(
      "ProductID=" +
      gridProducts.DataKeys[gridProducts.SelectedIndex].ToString());
    DataRow row = rows[0];
    ...
```

Next, the code searches to see if this product is already in the cart. If it is, the Units property of the corresponding ShoppingCartItem is incremented by 1, as shown here:

```
    ...
    // Search to see if an item of this type is already in the cart.
    Boolean inCart = false;
    foreach (ShoppingCartItem item in cart)
    {
        // Increment the number count.
        if (item.ProductID == (int)row["ProductID"])
        {
            item.Units += 1;
            inCart = true;
            break;
        }
    }
    ...
```

If the item isn't in the cart, a new ShoppingCartItem object is created and added to the collection, as follows:

```
    ...
    // If the item isn't in the cart, add it.
    if (!inCart)
    {
        ShoppingCartItem item = new ShoppingCartItem(
          (int)row["ProductID"], (string)row["ProductName"],
          (decimal)row["UnitPrice"], 1);
        cart.Add(item);
    }
    ...
```

Finally, the selected index is cleared so that the product row doesn't become highlighted. The act of selection is now complete.

```
    ...
    // Don't keep the item selected in the product list.
    gridProducts.SelectedIndex = -1;
}
```

Notice that the DataGrid that displays the shopping cart information binds directly to the ShoppingCart collection. Creating this DataGrid is fairly straightforward. You can use BoundColumn tags in the same way that you would with a table, except now the DataField identifies the name of one of the properties in the ShoppingCartItem class. Here are the bound columns used in the DataGrid for the shopping cart details:

```
<asp:BoundColumn DataField="ProductID" HeaderText="ID"></asp:BoundColumn>
<asp:BoundColumn DataField="ProductName" HeaderText="Product Name">
  </asp:BoundColumn>
<asp:BoundColumn DataField="UnitPrice" HeaderText="Unit Price"
  DataFormatString="{0:C}"></asp:BoundColumn>
<asp:BoundColumn DataField="Total" HeaderText="Total"
  DataFormatString="{0:C}"></asp:BoundColumn>
```

The column for displaying the Units property is slightly different. It uses a TemplateColumn. The template uses a text box, which displays the number of desired units, and allows the user to edit this number.

```
<asp:TemplateColumn HeaderText="Units">
  <HeaderStyle Width="5px"></HeaderStyle>
  <ItemTemplate>
    <asp:TextBox runat="server" Font-Size="XX-Small" Width="31px"
      Text='<%# DataBinder.Eval(Container, "DataItem.Units") %>'>
    </asp:TextBox>
  </ItemTemplate>
</asp:TemplateColumn>
```

If a user does decide to change the number of units for an item, the change must be committed by clicking an Update link in another column:

```
<asp:ButtonColumn Text="Update"></asp:ButtonColumn>
```

When the user clicks the Update link, the DataGrid.ItemCommand event fires. At this point, the code finds the corresponding ShoppingCartItem instance, and updates the Units property (or removes the item entirely if the count has reached 0). Here's the code that performs this task:

```
private void gridCart_ItemCommand(object source,
  System.Web.UI.WebControls.DataGridCommandEventArgs e)
{
    // The first control in a template column is always a blank LiteralControl.
    // The text box is the second control.
    TextBox txt =
      (TextBox)gridCart.Items[e.Item.DataSetIndex].Cells[3].Controls[1];
    try
    {
        // Update the appropriate cart item.
        int newCount = int.Parse(txt.Text);
        if (newCount > 0)
        {
```

```
        cart[e.Item.DataSetIndex].Units = newCount;
      }
      else if (newCount == 0)
      {
        cart.RemoveAt(e.Item.DataSetIndex);
      }
    }
    catch
    {
      // Ignore invalid (nonnumeric) entries.
    }
}
```

Invalid entries are simply ignored using an exception handler. Another option is to use a CompareValidator validation control to prevent the user from entering negative numbers or text.

As written, this example is fairly powerful and it's a reasonable starting point to creating a shopping cart for a highly professional application. One change you might want to consider is creating dedicated methods in the ShoppingCart class to handle tasks like searching for items, changing the number of units for an item, and so on. You might also want to store the shopping cart information in a database so that it persists permanently between visits. In this case, a good approach would be to cache the shopping cart in session state. This ensures that the user can use your website without your code needing to constantly requery the database. However, if this user returns after the session has expired, your shopping cart code can retrieve the information from the database and repopulate the session. This approach is used in many e-commerce web applications to create permanent shopping carts.

Multiple Selection

Another refinement you might want to add to this example is to allow the product list to support multiple selection (similar to the way files are selected in a Hotmail inbox). The basic approach is to create a template column that includes a CheckBox control. When the user clicks another button (like submit), you can loop over all the items in the DataGrid, and check the state of the check box in each item. If the state is checked, you would then add that item to the shopping cart.

Summary

ADO.NET is, along with ASP.NET, one of the core ingredients of the .NET Framework. Understanding its subtleties is the key to writing scalable, data-driven applications.

In this chapter, you explored advanced ADO.NET topics like transactions, images, and typed DataSets. You also learned how to build better data bound grids, and design a shopping cart system. To continue your exploration of ADO.NET, you can read one of the many dedicated books. One good choice is David Sceppa's *Microsoft ADO.NET (Core Reference)* (Microsoft Press).

...

CHAPTER 12

XML

Ever since XML (Extensible Markup Language) first arrived on the scene in the late 1990s, it has been the focus of intense activity and over-enthusiastic speculation. Now XML is beginning to come of age, and is being steadily integrated into different applications, problem domains, and industries. Based on nothing but ordinary text, XML offers a means of sharing data between just about any two applications, whether they're new or old, written in different languages, built by distinct companies, or even hosted on different operating systems.

Microsoft's .NET Framework makes heavy use of XML, and gives ASP.NET applications a rich set of features for using and manipulating XML data. In this chapter, you'll learn how to convert DataSet information into XML, how to work with XML in streams and strings, and how to retrieve XML data from a query, transform it, and display the results in a web page.

When Does XML Make Sense?

The question that every new ASP.NET developer asks (and many XML proponents don't answer) is how and when should XML be used in an ASP.NET web application. There are a few core scenarios:

- You need to use data that's already stored in XML. This situation might occur if you want to exchange data with another existing application, and if it uses a specific flavor of XML.

- You want to use XML to store your data and open up the possibilities of future integration. Because you use XML, you know other third-party applications can be designed that will read this data in the future.

- You want to use a technology that depends on XML. For example, web services (discussed in Part Five) use other standards that are all based on XML.

This chapter addresses the first two scenarios. The third scenario involves a higher-level model that's built on top of the low-level XML infrastructure. In other words, you don't need to directly manipulate XML to use web services—instead, you can work through an abstraction of objects. Similarly, you don't need to manipulate XML to read information from ASP.NET configuration files, use the DataSet, or rely on other .NET Framework features that have XML underpinnings. In all these situations, XML is quietly at work, and you gain the benefits of XML without needing to deal with it by hand.

XML makes most sense in *application integration* scenarios. However, there's no reason you can't use an XML format to store your own proprietary data. If you do, you'll gain a few minor conveniences, such as the ability to use .NET classes to read XML data from a file. When storing complex, highly structured data, the convenience of using these classes rather than designing your own custom format and writing your own custom file-parsing logic is significant. It will also make it easier for other developers to understand the system you've created, and to reuse or enhance your work.

Note One of the most important concepts developers must understand is that there are two decisions when deciding how to store data—choosing the way data will be structured (the format), and choosing the way data will be stored (the physical data store). XML is a choice of format, not a choice of storage. This means that if you decide to store data in an XML format, you still need to decide whether that XML will be inserted into a database field, a file, or just kept in memory in a string or some other type of object.

An Introduction to XML

In its simplest form, the XML specification is a set of guidelines, defined by the World Wide Web Consortium (W3C), for describing structured data in plain text. Like HTML, XML is a markup language based on tags within angled brackets. As with HTML, the textual nature of XML makes the data highly portable and broadly deployable. In addition, XML documents can be created and edited in any standard text editor.

Unlike HTML, XML does not have a fixed set of tags; rather, it is a metalanguage that allows for the creation of *other* markup languages. In other words, XML sets out a few simple rules for naming and ordering elements, and you create your own data format with your own custom elements.

For example, the following document shows a custom XML format that stores a product catalog. It starts with some generic product catalog information, followed by a product list with itemized information about two products, as follows:

```xml
<?xml version="1.0" ?>
<productCatalog>
    <catalogName>Acme Fall 2003 Catalog</catalogName>
    <expiryDate>2004-01-01</expiryDate>
    <products>
        <product id="1001">
            <productName>Magic Ring</productName>
            <productPrice>342.10</productPrice>
        </product>
        <product id="1002">
            <productName>Flying Carpet</productName>
            <productPrice>982.99</productPrice>
        </product>
    </products>
</productCatalog>
```

This example uses elements like <productCatalog>, <product>, and <catalogName> to indicate the document structure. However, you're free to use whatever element names describe your data best.

It's because of this flexibility that XML has become extremely successful. Of course, flexibility also has drawbacks. Because XML doesn't define any standard data formats, it's up to you to create data formats that represent product catalogs, invoices, customer lists, and so on. Different companies can easily store similar data using completely different tag names and structures. And even though any application can parse XML data, the writer and the reader of that data still need to agree on a common set of tags and structure in order for the reader to be able to *interpret* that data and extract meaningful information.

Usually, third-party organizations define standards for particular problem domains and industries. For example, if you need to store a mathematical equation in XML, you'll probably choose the MathML format, which is an XML-based format that defines a specific set of tags and a specific structure. Similarly, hundreds more standard XML formats exist for real estate listings, music notation, legal documents, patient records, vector graphics, and much more. Creating a robust, usable XML format takes some experience, so it's always best to use a standardized, agreed-upon, XML-based markup language when possible.

The Advantages of XML

When XML was first introduced, its success was partly due to its simplicity. The rules of XML are much shorter and simpler than the rules of its predecessor, SGML, and simple XML documents are human readable. However, in the intervening years many other supporting standards have been added to the XML mix, and as a result, using XML in a professional application isn't simple at all.

Note Although XML is human-readable in theory, it's often difficult to understand complex documents, and only computer applications, not developers, can read many types of XML.

But if anything, XML is much more useful today than it ever was before. The benefits of using XML in a modern application include

- **Adoption.** XML is ubiquitous. A large majority of companies are using XML to store data, or actively considering it. Whenever data needs to be shared, XML is automatically the first (and often the only) choice that's examined.

- **Extensibility and flexibility.** XML imposes no rules about data semantics and does not tie companies into proprietary networks, unlike EDI (Electronic Data Interchange). As a result, XML can fit any type of data, and is cheaper to implement.

- **Related standards and tools.** Another reason for XML's success is the tools (such as parsers) and the surrounding standards (such as XML Schema, XPath, and XSLT), which help in creating and processing XML documents. As a result, programmers in nearly any language have readymade components for reading XML, verifying that XML is valid, verifying XML against a set of rules (known as a schema), searching XML, and transforming one format of XML into another.

XML acts like the glue that allows different systems to work together. It helps to standardize business processes and transactions between organizations. But XML is not just suited for data exchange between companies. Many programming tasks today are all about *application integration*—web applications integrate multiple web services, e-commerce sites integrate legacy inventory and pricing systems, intranet applications integrate existing business applications. All of these applications are held together by the exchange of XML documents.

Well-Formed XML

XML is a fairly strict standard. This strictness is designed to preserve broad compatibility. HTML, on the other hand, is much more lenient. As a result, it's quite possible to create an HTML web page with errors that will be successfully rendered in one browser but interpreted differently in another. When it comes to storing business data, this type of error could cause catastrophic problems.

To prevent this sort of problem, all XML parsers perform a few basic quality checks. If an XML document does not meet these standards, it's rejected outright. If the XML document does follow these rules, it's deemed to be *well formed*. Well-formed XML isn't necessarily correct XML—for example, it could still contain incorrect data—but an XML processor can parse it.

To be considered well formed, an XML document must meet these criteria:

- Every start tag must have an end tag.

- An empty element must end with />.

- Elements can never overlap. In other words, <person><firstName></firstName> </person> is valid, but <person><firstName></person></firstName> is not.

- An element cannot have two elements with the same name because there will be no way to distinguish them from each other. However, you can have elements with the same name in different places. For example, you can place a <name> element inside multiple <product> elements and a separate <customer> element.

- A document can only have one root element.

- All attributes must have quotes around the value.

- The document must not contain illegal characters.

- Comments and processing instructions can't be placed inside tags.

Tip To quickly test if an XML document is well formed, try opening it in Internet Explorer. If there is an error, Internet Explorer will report a message and flag the offending line.

XML Namespaces

As the XML standard gained ground, dozens of XML markup languages (often called *XML grammars*) were created, and many of them are specific to certain industries, processes, and types of information. In many cases, it becomes important to extend one type of markup with additional company-specific elements, or even create XML documents that combine several different XML grammars. This poses a problem. First, what happens if you need to combine two XML grammars that use elements with the same names? How do you tell them apart? A related, but more typical problem occurs when an application needs to distinguish between XML grammars in a document. For example, consider an XML document that has order-specific information using a standard called OrderML, and client-specific information using a standard called ClientML. This document is sent to an order-fulfillment application that's only interested in the OrderML details. How can it quickly filter out the information that it needs, and ignore the unrelated details?

The solution is the XML Namespaces standard. The core idea behind this standard is that every XML markup language has its own namespace, which is used to uniquely identify all related elements. Technically, namespaces *disambiguate* elements by making it clear what markup language they belong to.

All XML namespaces use URIs (Universal Resource Identifiers). Typically, these URIs look like a web page URL. For example, http://www.mycompany.com/mystandard is a typical name for a namespace. Though the namespace looks like it points to a valid location on the Web, this isn't required (and shouldn't be assumed). URIs are used for XML namespaces because they are more likely to be unique. Usually, if you create a new XML language, you'll use a URI that points to a domain or website you control. That way, you can be sure that no one else is likely to use that URI. However, the namespace doesn't need to be a URI—any sequence of text is acceptable.

Tip Namespace names must match exactly. If you change the capitalization in part of a namespace, add a trailing / character, or modify any other detail, it will be interpreted as a different namespace by the XML parser.

To specify that an element belongs to a specific namespace, you simply need to add the xmlns attribute to the start tag, and indicate the namespace. For example, the element shown here is part of the http://mycompany/OrderML namespace. If you don't take this step, the element will not be a part of any namespace.

```
<order xmlns="http://mycompany/OrderML"></order>
```

It would be cumbersome if you needed to type in the full namespace URI every time you wrote an element in an XML document. Fortunately, when you assign a namespace in this fashion, it becomes the default namespace for all child elements. For example, in the XML document shown here, the <order> and <orderItem> elements are both placed in the http://mycompany/OrderML namespace, as follows:

```
<?xml version="1.0"?>
<order xmlns="http://mycompany/OrderML">
    <orderItem>...</orderItem>
    <orderItem>...</orderItem>
</order>
```

You can declare a new namespace for separate portions of the document. The easiest way to deal with this is to use *namespace prefixes*. Namespace prefixes are short character sequences that you can insert in front of a tag name to indicate its namespace. You define the prefix in the xmlns attribute by inserting a colon (:) followed by the characters you want to use for the prefix.

Here's an order document that uses namespace prefixes to map different elements into two different namespaces:

```xml
<?xml version="1.0"?>
<ord:order xmlns:ord="http://mycompany/OrderML"
 xmlns:cli="http://mycompany/ClientML">
    <cli:client>
        <cli:firstName>...</cli:firstName>
        <cli:lastName>...</cli:lastName>
    </cli:client>

    <ord:orderItem>...</ord:orderItem>
    <ord:orderItem>...</ord:orderItem>
</ord:order>
```

Namespace prefixes are simply used to map an element to a namespace. The actual prefix you use isn't important as long as it remains consistent.

XML Schemas

A good part of the success of the XML standard is due to its remarkable flexibility. Using XML, you can create exactly the markup language you need. This flexibility also raises a few problems. With developers around the world using your XML format, how do you ensure that everyone is following the rules?

The solution is to create a formal document that states the rules of your custom markup language, which is called a *schema*. These rules won't include syntactical details (like the requirement to use angle brackets or properly nest tags) because these requirements are already a part of the basic XML standard. Instead, the schema document will list the logical rules that pertain to your type of data. They include the following:

- **Document vocabulary.** This determines what element and attribute names are used in your XML documents.

- **Document structure.** This determines where tags can be placed, and can include rules specifying that certain tags must be placed before, after, or inside others. You can also specify how many times an element can occur.

- **Supported data types.** This allows you to specify whether data is ordinary text, or must be able to be interpreted as numeric data, date information, and so on.

- **Allowed data ranges.** This allows you to set constraints that restrict numbers to certain ranges, or that only allow specific values.

The XML Schema standard defines the rules you need to follow for creating a schema document. The following is an XML schema that defines the rules for the product catalog document shown earlier:

```xml
<?xml version="1.0"?>
<xsd:schema xmlns:xsd="http://www.w3.org/2001/XMLSchema">
    <xsd:element name="productCatalog">
        <xsd:complexType>
            <xsd:sequence>
                <xsd:element name="catalogName" type="xsd:string"/>
                <xsd:element name="expiryDate" type="xsd:date"/>

                <xsd:element name="products">
                    <xsd:complexType>
                        <xsd:sequence>
                            <xsd:element name="product"
                              type="product" maxOccurs="unbounded" />
                        </xsd:sequence>
                    </xsd:complexType>
                </xsd:element>
            </xsd:sequence>
        </xsd:complexType>
    </xsd:element>

    <xsd:complexType name="product">
        <xsd:sequence>
            <xsd:element name="productName" type="xsd:string"/>
            <xsd:element name="productPrice" type="xsd:decimal"/>
            <xsd:element name="inStock" type="xsd:boolean"/>
        </xsd:sequence>
        <xsd:attribute name="id" type="xsd:integer"/>
    </xsd:complexType>
</xsd:schema>
```

Every schema document is an XML document that begins with a root <schema> element. Inside the <schema> element are two types of definitions—the <element> element, which defines the structure the target document must follow, and one or more <complexType> elements, which define smaller data structures that are used to define the document structure.

The <element> tag is really the heart of the schema, and it's the starting point for all validation. In this example, the <element> tag identifies that the product catalog must begin with a root element named <productCatalog>. Inside the <productCatalog> element is a sequence of three elements. The first, <catalogName>, contains ordinary text. The second, <expiryDate>, includes text that fits the rules for date representation, as set out in the schema standard. The final element, <products>, contains a list of <product> elements.

Each <product> element is a complex type, and the type is defined with the <complexType> element at the end of the document. This <product> complex type consists of a sequence of three elements with product information. They must store this information as text (<productName>), a decimal value (<productPrice>), and a Boolean value (<inStock>), respectively.

Note A full discussion of XML Schema is beyond the scope of this book. However, if you want to learn more you can consider the excellent online tutorials at http://www.w3schools.com/schema, or the standard itself at http://www.w3.org/XML/Schema.

Working with XML in ASP.NET

The .NET Framework makes use of XML internally in many situations, and it allows you to manipulate XML data with a set of classes in the System.Xml namespace (and other namespaces that begin with System.Xml). These types fully support the XML DOM (Document Object Model) Level 2 Core, as defined by the W3C. It also adds classes and methods that make it easier to read and write XML documents, navigate through nodes, attributes, and elements, and query, transform, and manipulate XML data in various ways.

Writing XML Files

The .NET Framework provides two different approaches for writing XML data to a file:

- You can build the document in memory using the XmlDocument class, and write it to a file when you're finished by calling the Save() method. The XmlDocument represents XML using a tree of node objects.

- You can write the document directly to a stream using the XmlTextWriter. This outputs data as you write it, node by node.

The XmlDocument is a good choice if you need to perform other operations on XML content after you create it, like searching it, transforming it, or validating it. It's also the only way to write an XML document in a nonlinear way, because it allows you to insert new nodes anywhere. However, the XmlTextWriter provides a much simpler and better performing model for writing directly to a file, because it doesn't store the whole document in memory at once.

Tip Both the XmlDocument and the XmlTextWriter can be used to create XML data that isn't stored in a file. Both of these classes allow you to write information to any stream, and the XmlDocument allows you to retrieve the raw XML as string data. Using techniques like these, you could build an XML document, and then insert it into another storage location like a text-based field in a database table.

The next web-page example shows how to use the XmlTextWriter to create a well-formed XML file. The first step is to create a private WriteXML() method that will handle the job. It begins by creating an XmlTextWriter object, and passing the physical path of the file you want to create as a constructor argument:

```
private void WriteXML()
{
    string xmlFile = Server.MapPath("DvdList.xml");
    XmlTextWriter writer = new XmlTextWriter(xmlFile, null);
    ...
```

The XmlTextWriter has properties such as Formatting and Indentation, which allow you to specify whether the XML data will be automatically indented with the typical hierarchical structure, and to indicate the number of spaces to use as indentation. You can set these two properties as follows:

```
    ...
    writer.Formatting = Formatting.Indented;
    writer.Indentation = 3;
    ...
```

Tip Remember, in a datacentric XML document, whitespace is almost always ignored. But by adding indentation, you create a file that is easier for a human to read and interpret, so it can't hurt.

Now you're ready to start writing the file. The WriteStartDocument() method writes the XML declaration with version 1.0 (<?xml version="1.0"?>), as follows:

```
    writer.WriteStartDocument();
```

The WriteComment() method writes a comment. You can use it to add a message with the date and time of creation:

```
    writer.WriteComment("Created @ " + DateTime.Now.ToString());
```

Next, you need to write the real content—the elements, attributes, and so on. This example builds an XML document that represents a DVD list, with information such as the title, director, price, and a list of actors for each DVD. These records will be child elements of a parent <DvdList> element, which must be created first:

```
    writer.WriteStartElement("DvdList");
```

Now you can create the child nodes. The following code opens a new <DVD> element:

```
    writer.WriteStartElement("DVD");
```

Now the code writes two attributes, representing the ID and the related category. This information is added to the start tag of the <DVD> element.

```
...
writer.WriteAttributeString("ID", "1");
writer.WriteAttributeString("Category", "Science Fiction");
...
```

The next step is to add the elements with the information about the DVD inside the <DVD> element. These elements won't have child elements of their own, so you can write them and set their values more efficiently with a single call to the WriteElementString() method. WriteElementString() accepts two arguments: the element name and its value (always as string), as shown here:

```
...
// Write some simple elements.
writer.WriteElementString("Title", "The Matrix");
writer.WriteElementString("Director", "Larry Wachowski");
writer.WriteElementString("Price", "18.74");
...
```

Next is a child <Starring> element that lists one or more actors. Because this element contains other elements, you need to open it and keep it open with the WriteStartElement() method. Then you can add the contained child elements, as shown here:

```
...
writer.WriteStartElement("Starring");
writer.WriteElementString("Star", "Keanu Reeves");
writer.WriteElementString("Star", "Laurence Fishburne");
...
```

At this point the code has written all the data for the current DVD. The next step is to close all of the opened tags, in reverse order. To do so you just call the WriteEndElement() method once for each element you've opened. You don't need to specify the element name when you call WriteEndElement(). Instead, each time you call WriteEndElement() it will automatically write the closing tag for the last opened element.

```
...
// Close the <Starring> element.
writer.WriteEndElement();

// Close the <DVD> element.
writer.WriteEndElement();
...
```

Now let's create another <DVD> element using the same approach:

```
...
writer.WriteStartElement("DVD");

// Write a couple of attributes to the <DVD> element.
writer.WriteAttributeString("ID", "2");
writer.WriteAttributeString("Category", "Drama");
```

```
    // Write some simple elements.
    writer.WriteElementString("Title", "Forrest Gump");
    writer.WriteElementString("Director", "Robert Zemeckis");
    writer.WriteElementString("Price", "23.99");

    // Open the <Starring> element.
    writer.WriteStartElement("Starring");

    // Write two elements.
    writer.WriteElementString("Star", "Tom Hanks");
    writer.WriteElementString("Star", "Robin Wright");

    // Close the <Starring> element.
    writer.WriteEndElement();

    // Close the <DVD> element.
    writer.WriteEndElement();
    ...
```

Quite straightforward, isn't it? To complete the document, you simply need to close the <DvdList> item, with yet another call to WriteEndElement(). You can then close the XmlTextWriter, as shown here:

```
    ...
    writer.WriteEndElement();
    writer.Close();
}
```

To try out this code, call the WriteXML() procedure form Page.Load event handler. It will generate an XML file named DvdList.xml in the current folder.

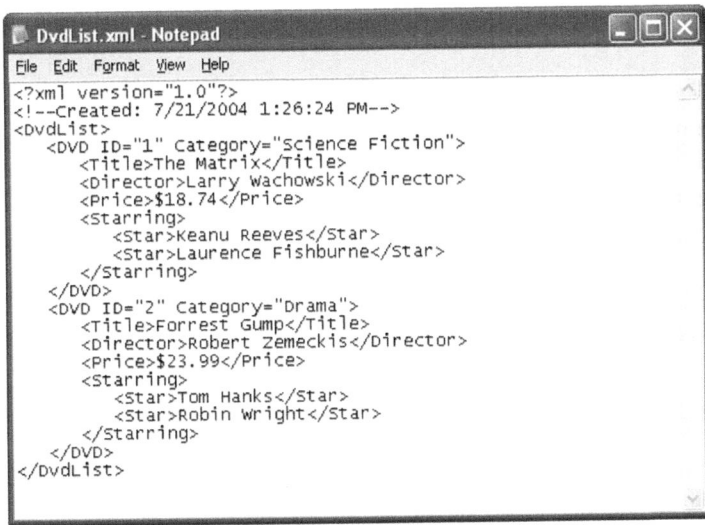

Figure 12-1. *A dynamically created XML document*

■Note Keep in mind that when you use the XmlTextWriter to create an XML file, you face all the limitations that you face when writing any other type of file in a web application. In other words, you need to take safeguards (like generating unique filenames) to ensure that two different clients don't run the same code and try to write the same file at once. The next chapter has more information about file access, and dealing with these types of problems.

Reading and Navigating XML Files

There are several ways to read and navigate the content of a XML file. These include the following:

- You can load the document using the XmlDocument class mentioned earlier. This holds all the XML data in memory once you call Load() to retrieve it from a file or stream. It also allows you to modify that data and save it back to the file at a later point. The XmlDocument class implements the full XML DOM.

- You can load the document into an XPathNavigator (which is located in the System.Xml.XPath namespace). Like the XmlDocument, the XPathNavigator holds the entire XML document in memory. However, it offers a slightly faster, more streamlined model than the XML DOM, along with enhanced searching features. Unlike the XmlDocument, it doesn't provide the ability to make changes and save them.

- You can read the document one node at a time using the XmlTextReader class. This is the least expensive approach in terms of sever resources, but it forces you to examine the data sequentially from start to finish.

The following sections demonstrate each of these different approaches to load the DVD list XML document.

Using the XML DOM

The following example is a simple web page that reads the DVDList.xml document and displays a list of elements, using different levels of indenting to show the overall structure. Figure 12-2 shows the final web page.

The XmlDocument stores information as a tree of nodes. A node is the basic ingredient of an XML file and can be an element, an attribute, a comment, or a value in an element. A separate XmlNode object represents each node, and nodes are grouped together in collections.

You can retrieve the first level of nodes through the XmlDocument.ChildNodes property. In this example, that property provides access to the <DvdList> element. The <DvdList> element contains other child nodes, and these nodes contain still more nodes, and the actual values. In order to drill down through all the layers of the tree, you need to use recursive logic, as shown in this example.

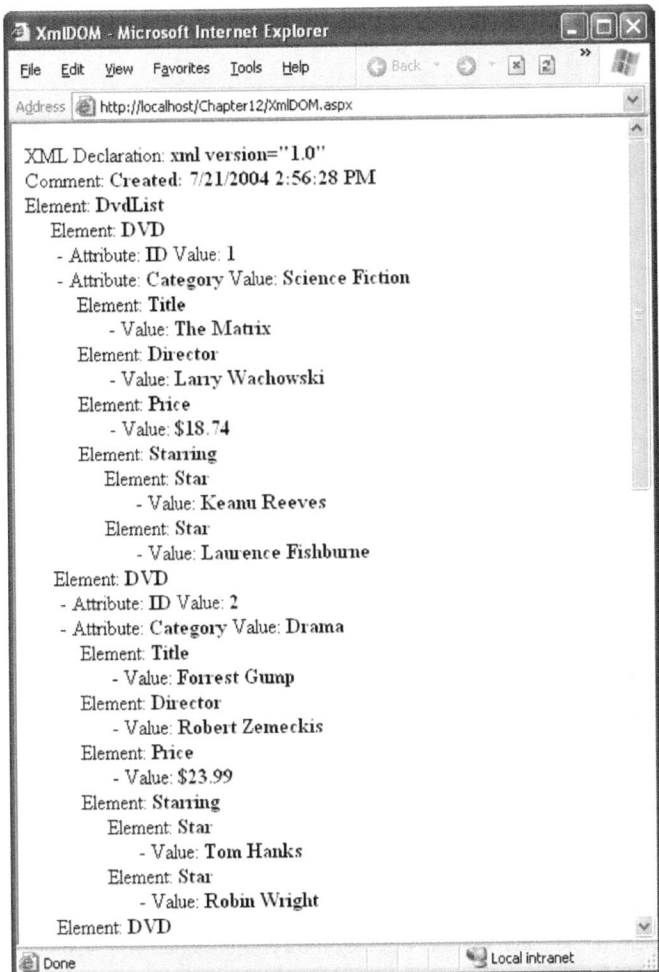

Figure 12-2. *Retrieving information from an XML document*

When the example page loads, it creates an XmlDocument object and calls the Load() method, which retrieves the XML data from the file. It then call a recursive function named GetChildNodesDescr(). GetChildNodesDescr() takes an XmlNodeList object as an input and the index of the nesting level. It then returns the string with the content for that node and all its child nodes and attributes.

```
private void Page_Load(object sender, System.EventArgs e)
{
    string xmlFile = Server.MapPath("DvdList.xml");

    // Load the XML file in a XmlDocument.
    XmlDocument doc = new XmlDocument();
    doc.Load(xmlFile);

    // Write the description text.
    XmlText.Text = GetChildNodesDescr(doc.ChildNodes, 0);
}
```

THE XMLDOCUMENT AND USER CONCURRENCY

In a web application, it's extremely important to pay close attention to how your code accesses the file system. If you aren't careful, a web page that reads data from a file can become a disaster under heavy user loads. The problem occurs when two users access a file at the same time. If the first user hasn't taken care to open a shareable stream, the second user will receive an error.

You'll learn more about these issues in the next chapter. However, all of this raises an excellent question—how does the XmlDocument.Load() method open a file? To find the answer, you need to dig into the IL code of the .NET Framework. What you'll find is that several steps actually unfold to load an XML document into an XmlDocument object. First, the path you supply is examined by an XmlUrlResolver and passed to an XmlDownloadResolver, which determines whether it needs to make a web request (if you've supplied a URL) or can open a FileStream (if you've supplied a path). If it can use the FileStream, it explicitly opens the FileStream with shareable reads enabled. As a result, if more than one user loads the file with the XmlDocument.Load() method at once on different threads, no conflict will occur.

When the Page.Load event handler calls GetChildNodesDescr(), it passes an XmlNodeList object that represents the first level of nodes. (The XmlNodeList contains a collection of XmlNode objects, one for each node.) The code also passes 0 as the second argument of GetChildNodesDescr() to indicate that this is the first level of the structure. The string returned by the GetChildNodesDescr() method is then shown on the page using a Literal control.

Tip What if you want to create an XmlDocument and fill it based on XML content you've drawn from another source, like a field in a database table? In this case, instead of using the Load() method you would use LoadXml(), which accepts a string that contains the content of the XML document.

The interesting part is the GetChildNodesDescr() method. It first creates a string with three spaces for each indentation level that it will later use as a prefix for each line added to the final HTML text:

```
private string GetChildNodesDescr(XmlNodeList nodeList, int level)
{
    string indent = "";
    for (int i=0; i<level; i++)
      indent += "     ";
    ...
```

Next, the GetChildNodesDescr function cycles through all of the child nodes of the XmlNodeList. For the first call, these nodes include the XML declaration, the comment, and the <DvdList> element. An XmlNode object exposes properties such as NodeType, which identifies the type of item (for example, Comment, Element, Attribute, CDATA, Text, EndElement, Name, and Value). The code checks for node types that are relevant in this example, and adds that information to the string, as shown here:

```
...
StringBuilder str = new StringBuilder("");
foreach (XmlNode node in nodeList)
{
    switch(node.NodeType)
    {
        case XmlNodeType.XmlDeclaration:
            str.Append("XML Declaration: <b>");
            str.Append(node.Name);
            str.Append(" ");
            str.Append(node.Value);
            str.Append("</b><br>");
            break;
        case XmlNodeType.Element:
            str.Append(indent);
            str.Append("Element: <b>");
            str.Append(node.Name);
            str.Append("</b><br>");
            break;
        case XmlNodeType.Text:
            str.Append(indent);
            str.Append(" - Value: <b>");
            str.Append(node.Value);
            str.Append("</b><br>");
            break;
        case XmlNodeType.Comment:
            str.Append(indent);
            str.Append("Comment: <b>");
            str.Append(node.Value);
            str.Append("</b><br>");
            break;
    }
...
```

Note that not all types of nodes have a name or a value. For example, for an element such as Title, the Name is Title, but the Value is empty, because it's stored in the following Text node.

Next, the code checks if the current node has any attributes (by testing if its Attributes collection is null). If it does, they are processed with a nested foreach loop:

```
...
if (node.Attributes != null)
{
    foreach (XmlAttribute attrib in node.Attributes)
    {
        str.Append(indent);
        str.Append(" - Attribute: <b>");
        str.Append(attrib.Name);
        str.Append("</b> Value: <b>");
```

```
                str.Append(attrib.Value);
                str.Append("</b><br>");
            }
        }
    ...
```

Lastly, if the node has child nodes (according to its HasChildNodes property), the code recursively calls the GetChildNodesDescr function, passing to it the current node's ChildNodes collection, and the current indent level plus 1, as shown here:

```
    ...
      if (node.HasChildNodes)
          str.Append(GetChildNodesDescr(node.ChildNodes, level+1));
    }
    return str.ToString();
}
```

When the whole process is finished, the outer foreach block is closed, and the function returns the content of the StringBuilder object.

Using the XPathNavigator

The XPathNavigator works in a similar way to the XmlDocument class. It loads all the information into memory, and then allows you to move through the nodes. The key difference is that it uses a cursor-based approach that allows you to use methods like MoveToNext() to move through the XML data. An XPathNavigator can only be positioned on one node a time.

You can create an XPathNavigator from an XmlDocument using the XmlDocument.CreateNavigator() method. Here's an example:

```
private void Page_Load(object sender, System.EventArgs e)
{
    string xmlFile = Server.MapPath("DvdList.xml");

    // Load the XML file in an XmlDocument.
    XmlDocument doc = new XmlDocument();
    doc.Load(xmlFile);

    // Create the navigator.
    XPathNavigator xnav = doc.CreateNavigator();
    XmlText.Text = GetXNavDescr(xnav, 0);
}
```

In this case, the returned object is passed to the GetXNavDescr() recursive method, which returns the HTML code that represents the XML structure, as in the previous example.

The code of the GetXNavDescr() method is a bit different from the GetChildNodesDescr() method in the previous example, because it takes an XPathNavigator object that is positioned on a single node, and not a collection of nodes. That means you don't need to loop through any collections. Instead, you can simply examine the information for the current node, as follows:

```
private string GetXNavDescr(XPathNavigator xnav, int level)
{
    string indent = "";
    for (int i=0; i<level; i++)
      indent += "     ";
    StringBuilder str = new StringBuilder("");
    switch(xnav.NodeType)
    {
        case XPathNodeType.Root:
            str.Append("<b>ROOT</b>");
            str.Append("<br>");
            break;
        case XPathNodeType.Element:
            str.Append(indent);
            str.Append("Element: <b>");
            str.Append(xnav.Name);
            str.Append("</b><br>");
            break;
        case XPathNodeType.Text:
            str.Append(indent);
            str.Append(" - Value: <b>");
            str.Append(xnav.Value);
            str.Append("</b><br>");
            break;
        case XPathNodeType.Comment:
            str.Append(indent);
            str.Append("Comment: <b>");
            str.Append(xnav.Value);
            str.Append("</b><br>");
            break;
    }
    ...
```

Note that the values for the NodeType property are almost the same, except for the enumeration name, which is XPathNodeType instead of XmlNodeType. That's because the XPathNavigator uses a smaller, more streamlined set of nodes. One of the nodes it doesn't support is the XmlDeclaration node type.

The function checks if the current node has any attributes. If so, it moves to the first one with a call to MoveToFirstAttribute(), and loops through all the attributes until the MoveToNextAttribute() method returns false. At that point it returns to the parent node, which is the node originally referenced by the object. Here's the code that carries this out:

```
    ...

    if (xnav.HasAttributes)
    {
        xnav.MoveToFirstAttribute();
        do {
```

```
            str.Append(indent);
            str.Append(" - Attribute: <b>");
            str.Append(xnav.Name);
            str.Append("</b> Value: <b>");
            str.Append(xnav.Value);
            str.Append("</b><br>");
        } while (xnav.MoveToNextAttribute());

        // Return to the parent.
        xnav.MoveToParent();
    }
    ...
```

The function does a similar thing with the child nodes by moving to the first one with MoveToFirstChild(), and recursively calling itself until MoveToNext() returns false, at which point it moves back to the original node, as follows:

```
    ...
    if (xnav.HasChildren)
    {
        xnav.MoveToFirstChild();
        do {
            str.Append(GetXNavDescr(xnav, level+1));
        } while (xnav.MoveToNext());

        // Return to the parent.
        xnav.MoveToParent();
    }
    return str.ToString();
}
```

This code produces almost exactly the same output as shown in Figure 12-2.

Searching an XML Document

In some situations, you don't need to process the entire XML document. Instead, you need to extract a single piece of information. If you know the element name, you can use the XmlDocument.GetElementsByTagName() method, which searches an entire document and returns a XmlNodeList that contains all the matching XmlNode objects.

For example, the following code retrieves the title of each DVD in the document:

```
// Load the XML file.
string xmlFile = Server.MapPath("DvdList.xml");
XmlDocument doc = new XmlDocument();
doc.Load(xmlFile);

// Find all the <Title> elements anywhere in the document.
StringBuilder str = new StringBuilder();
XmlNodeList nodes = doc.GetElementsByTagName("Title");
```

```
foreach (XmlNode node in nodes)
{
    str.Append("Found: <b>");

    // Show the text contained in this <Title> element.
    str.Append(node.ChildNodes[0].Value);
    str.Append("</b><br>");
}
XmlText.Text = str.ToString();
```

Figure 12-3 shows the result of running this code in a web page.

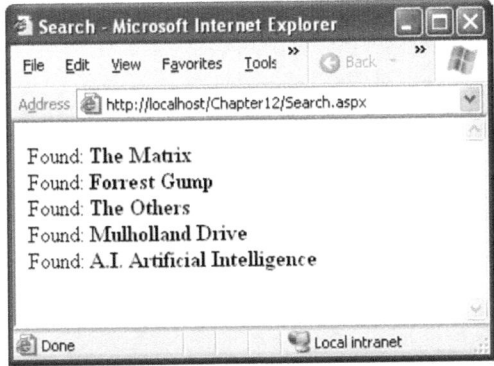

Figure 12-3. *Searching for information in an XML document*

You can also search portions of an XML document by using the method XmlElement.GetElementsByTagName() on a specific element. In this case, the XmlDocument searches all the descendant nodes looking for a match. In order to use this method, first retrieve an XmlNode that corresponds to an element, and then cast this object to an XmlElement. The following example demonstrates how to use this technique to find the stars of a specific movie:

```
// Load the XML file.
string xmlFile = Server.MapPath("DvdList.xml");
XmlDocument doc = new XmlDocument();
doc.Load(xmlFile);

// Find all the <Title> elements anywhere in the document.
StringBuilder str = new StringBuilder();
XmlNodeList nodes = doc.GetElementsByTagName("Title");
foreach (XmlNode node in nodes)
{
    str.Append("Found: <b>");

    // Show the text contained in this <Title> element.
    string name = node.ChildNodes[0].Value;
    str.Append(name);
```

```
    str.Append("</b><br>");

    if (name == "Forrest Gump")
    {
        // Find the stars for just this movie.
        // First you need to get the parent node
        // (which is the <DVD> element for the movie).
        XmlNode parent = node.ParentNode;

        // Then you need to search down the tree.
        XmlNodeList childNodes =
          ((XmlElement)parent).GetElementsByTagName("Star");
        foreach (XmlNode childNode in childNodes)
        {
            str.Append("    Found Star: ");
            str.Append(childNode.ChildNodes[0].Value);
            str.Append("<br>");
        }
    }
}
}
XmlText.Text = str.ToString();
```

Figure 12-4 shows the result of this test.

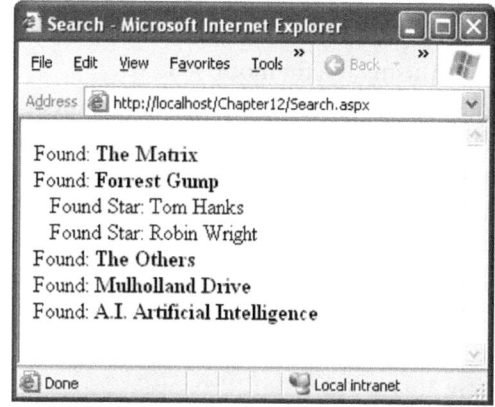

Figure 12-4. *Searching portions of an XML document*

The code that you've seen so far assumes that none of the elements have a namespace. More sophisticated XML documents will always include a namespace, and may even have several of them. In this situation, you can use the overload of the method XmlDocument.GetElementsByTagName(), which requires a namespace name as a string argument, as shown here:

```
// Retrieve all <order> elements in the OrderML namespace.
XmlNodeList nodes = doc.GetElementsByTagName("order",
  "http://mycompany/OrderML");
```

Additionally, you can supply an asterisk (*) for the element name if you wish to match all tags in the specified namespace:

```
// Retrieve all elements in the OrderML namespace.
XmlNodeList nodes = doc.GetElementsByTagName("*",
  "http://mycompany/OrderML");
```

Searching an XML Document with XPath

The GetElementsByTagName() method is fairly limited. It only allows you to search based on the name of an element. You can't filter based on other criteria, like the value of the element or attribute content. XPath is a much more powerful standard that allows you to retrieve the portions of a document that interest you.

XPath uses a pathlike notation. For example, the path / identifies the root of an XML document, and /DvdList identifies the root <DvdList> element. The path /DvdList/DVD selects every <DVD> element inside the <DvdList>. Finally, the period (.) always selects the current node. In addition, the path // is a relative path that searches for nodes anywhere in the document.

These ingredients are enough to build many basic templates, although the XPath standard also defines special selection criteria that can filter out only the nodes you are interested in. Table 12-1 provides an overview of XPath characters.

Table 12-1. *Basic XPath Syntax*

Expression	Meaning
/	Starts an absolute path from the root node. /DvdList/DVD selects all <DVD> elements that are children of the root <DvdList> element.
//	Starts a relative path that select nodes anywhere. //DVD/Title selects all the <Title> elements that are children of a <DVD> element.
@	Selects an attribute of a node. /DvdList/DVD/@ID selects the attribute named ID from the <DVD> element.
*	Selects any element in the path. /DvdList/DVD/* selects all the nodes in the <DVD> element (which include <Title>, <Director>, <Price>, and <Starring> in this example).
|	Combines multiple paths. /DvdList/DVD/Title|/DvdList/DVD/Director selects both the <Title> and <Director> element in the <DVD> element.
.	Indicates the current (default) node.
..	Indicates the parent node. If the current node is <Title>, then .. refers to the <DVD> node.
[]	Define selection criteria that can test a contained node or attribute value. /DvdList/DVD[Title='Forrest Gump'] selects the <DVD> elements that contain a <Title> element with the indicated value. /DvdList/DVD[@ID='1'] selects the <DVD> elements with the indicated attribute value. You can use the keyword and to combine criteria.

Continued

Table 12-1. *Continued*

Expression	Meaning
starts-with	This function retrieves elements based on what text a contained element starts with. /DvdList/DVD[starts-with(Title, 'P')] finds all <DVD> elements that have a <Title> element that contains text that starts with the letter P.
position	This function retrieves elements based on position. /DvdList/DVD[position()=2] selects the second <DVD> element.
count	This function counts the number of elements with the matching name. count(DVD) returns the number of <DVD> elements.

To execute an XPath expression in .NET, you can use the Select() method of the XPathNavigator, or the SelectNodes() or SelectSingleNode() method of the XmlDocument class. The following code uses this technique to retrieve specific information:

```
// Load the XML file.
string xmlFile = Server.MapPath("DvdList.xml");
XmlDocument doc = new XmlDocument();
doc.Load(xmlFile);

// Retrieve the title of every science-fiction movie.
XmlNodeList nodes =
  doc.SelectNodes("/DvdList/DVD/Title[../@Category='Science Fiction']");

// Display the titles.
StringBuilder str = new StringBuilder();
foreach (XmlNode node in nodes)
{
    str.Append("Found: <b>");

    // Show the text contained in this <Title> element.
    str.Append(node.ChildNodes[0].Value);
    str.Append("</b><br>");
}
XmlText.Text = str.ToString();
```

The results are shown in Figure 12-5.

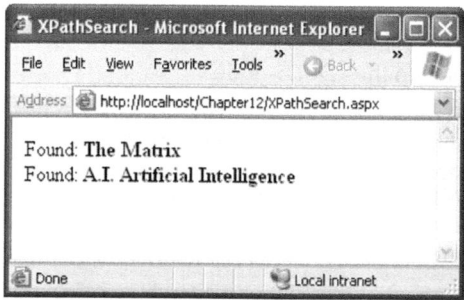

Figure 12-5. *Extracting information with XPath*

Using the XmlTextReader

Reading an XML file with an XmlTextReader object is the simplest approach, but it also provides the least flexibility. The file is read in sequential order, and you can't freely move to the parent, child, and sibling nodes as you can with XmlDocument and XPathNavigator. Instead, you read a node at a time from a stream. For this reason, the code is in a single nonrecursive method, which is more straightforward. It also makes it easy to scan through an entire XML document until you find the node that interests you.

The following code starts off by loading the source file in an XmlTextReader object. It then begins a loop that moves through the document one node at time. To move from one node to the next, you call the XmlTextReader.Read() method. This method returns true until it moves past the last node, at which point it returns false. This is very similar to the approach used by the DataReader class, which is used to retrieve query results from a database.

Here's the code you need:

```
private void ReadXML()
{
    string xmlFile = Server.MapPath("DvdList.xml");

    // Create the reader.
    XmlTextReader reader = new XmlTextReader(xmlFile);
    StringBuilder str = new StringBuilder();

    // Loop through all the nodes.
    while (reader.Read())
    {
        switch(reader.NodeType)
        {
            case XmlNodeType.XmlDeclaration:
                str.Append("XML Declaration: <b>");
                str.Append(reader.Name);
                str.Append(" ");
                str.Append(reader.Value);
                str.Append("</b><br>");
                break;
            case XmlNodeType.Element:
                str.Append("Element: <b>");
                str.Append(reader.Name);
                str.Append("</b><br>");
                break;
            case XmlNodeType.Text:
                str.Append(" - Value: <b>");
                str.Append(reader.Value);
                str.Append("</b><br>");
                break;
        }
        ...
```

After handling the types of nodes you're interested in, the next step is to check if the current node has attributes. There is no Attributes collection for the XmlTextReader, but there is an AttributeCount property that returns the number of attributes. You can continue moving the cursor forward to the next attribute until MoveToNextAttribute() returns false.

```
...
if (reader.AttributeCount > 0)
{
    while(reader.MoveToNextAttribute())
    {
        str.Append(" - Attribute: <b>");
        str.Append(reader.Name);
        str.Append("</b> Value: <b>");
        str.Append(reader.Value);
        str.Append("</b><br>");
    }
}
}


// Close the reader and show the text.
reader.Close();
XmlText.Text = str.ToString();
}
```

In the last two lines the procedure concludes by flushing the content in the buffer and closing the reader. When using the XmlTextWriter, it's imperative that you finish your task and close the reader as soon as possible, because it retains a lock on the file, unlike the XmlDocument, which loads all the information into memory when you call the Load() method.

If you run this code now, you'll see a web page that's quite similar to the earlier examples with the XmlDocument and XPathNavigator.

The XmlTextReader also provides additional methods that help make reading XML even faster and more convenient if you know what structure to expect. For example, you can use MoveToContent(), which skips over irrelevant nodes like comments, whitespace, and the XML declaration, and stops on the declaration of the next element.

You can also use the ReadStartElement() method, which reads a node and performs basic validation at the same time. When you call ReadStartElement(), you specify the name of the element that you expect to appear next in the document. The XmlTextReader calls MoveToContent(), and then verifies that the current element has the name you've specified. If it doesn't, an exception is thrown. You can also use ReadEndElement() to skip over whitespace and read the closing tag for the element.

Finally, if you want to read an element that only contains text data, you move over the start tag, content, and end tag using the ReadElementString(), and specifying the element name. The data you want is returned as a string.

Here's the code that extracts data from the XML list using this more streamlined approach:

```
// Create the reader.
string xmlFile = Server.MapPath("DvdList.xml");
XmlTextReader reader = new XmlTextReader(xmlFile);
```

```
StringBuilder str = new StringBuilder();
reader.ReadStartElement("DvdList");

// Read all the <DVD> elements.
while (reader.Read())
{
    if ((reader.Name == "DVD") && (reader.NodeType == XmlNodeType.Element))
    {
        reader.ReadStartElement("DVD");
        str.Append("<ul><b>");
        str.Append(reader.ReadElementString("Title"));
        str.Append("</b><li>");
        str.Append(reader.ReadElementString("Director"));
        str.Append("</li><li>");
        str.Append(String.Format("{0:C}",
        Decimal.Parse(reader.ReadElementString("Price"))));
          str.Append("</li></ul>");
    }
}
// Close the reader and show the text.
reader.Close();
XmlText.Text = str.ToString();
```

Figure 12-6 shows the result.

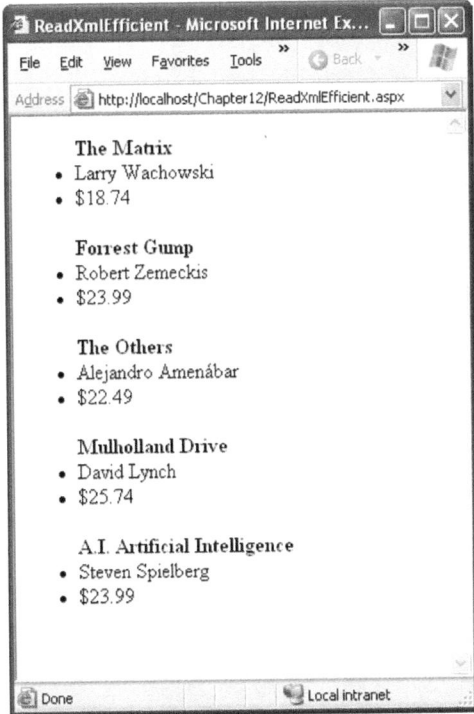

Figure 12-6. *Efficient XML reading*

Validating XML Files

So far you've seen a number of strategies for reading and parsing XML data. If you try to read invalid XML content using any of these approaches, you'll receive an error. In other words, all of these classes require well-formed XML. However, none of the examples you've seen so far have validated the XML to see that it follows any application-specific rules.

As described at the beginning of this chapter, XML formats are commonly codified with an XML schema that lays out the required structure and data types. For the DVD list document, you create an XML schema that looks like this:

```xml
<?xml version="1.0" ?>
<xs:schema id="DvdList" xmlns="" xmlns:xs="http://www.w3.org/2001/XMLSchema"
  xmlns:msdata="urn:schemas-microsoft-com:xml-msdata">
    <xs:element name="DvdList">
        <xs:complexType>
            <xs:sequence maxOccurs="unbounded">
                <xs:element name="DVD" type="DVDType" />
            </xs:sequence>
        </xs:complexType>
    </xs:element>

    <xs:complexType name="DVDType">
        <xs:sequence>
            <xs:element name="Title" type="xs:string" />
            <xs:element name="Director" type="xs:string"  />
            <xs:element name="Price" type="xs:decimal"  />
            <xs:element name="Starring" type="StarringType" />
        </xs:sequence>
        <xs:attribute name="ID" type="xs:integer" />
        <xs:attribute name="Category" type="xs:string" />
    </xs:complexType>

    <xs:complexType name="StarringType">
        <xs:sequence maxOccurs="unbounded">
            <xs:element name="Star" type="xs:string"/>
        </xs:sequence>
    </xs:complexType>
</xs:schema>
```

This schema defines two complex types, representing the list of stars (named StarringType) and the list of DVDs (named DVDType). The structure of the document is defined using an <element> tag.

To validate an XML document against a schema, you use the XmlValidatingReader class. This class is based on the XmlTextReader, but includes the ability to verify that the document follows the rules specified in an XSD schema file. The XmlValidatingReader throws an exception (or raises an event) to indicate errors as you move through the XML file.

The first step when performing validation is to import the System.Xml.Schema name-space, which contains types like XmlSchema and XmlSchemaCollection.

```
using System.Xml.Schema;
```

The following example shows how you can create an XmlValidatingReader that uses the DvdList.xsd file, and use it to verify that the XML in DvdList.xml is valid:

```
string xmlFile = Server.MapPath("DvdList.xml");
string xsdFile = Server.MapPath("DvdList.xsd");

// Open the XML file.
XmlTextReader r = new XmlTextReader(xmlFile);

// Create the validating reader.
XmlValidatingReader vr = new XmlValidatingReader(r);
vr.ValidationType = ValidationType.Schema;

// Add the XSD file to the validator.
XmlSchemaCollection schemas = new XmlSchemaCollection();
schemas.Add("", xsdFile);
vr.Schemas.Add(schemas);

// Read through the document.
while (vr.Read())
{
    // Process document here.
    // If an error is found, an exception will be thrown.
}
vr.Close();
```

Using the current file, this code will succeed, and you'll be able to access the current node through the XmlValidatingReader object in the same way that you could with the XmlTextReader. However, consider what happens if you make the minor modification shown here.

```
<DVD ID="A" Category="Science Fiction">
```

Now when you try to validate the document, an XmlSchemaException (from the System.Xml.Schema namespace) will be thrown, alerting you to the invalid data type—the letter "A" in an attribute that is designated for integer values.

Instead of catching errors, you can react to the ValidationEventHandler event. If you react to this event, you'll be provided with information about the error, but no exception will be thrown. To connect an event handler to this event, create a new ValidationEventHandler dele-gate and assign it to the XmlValidatingReader.ValidationEventHandler event just before you start to read the XML file.

```
// Connect to the method named MyValidateHandler.
vr.ValidationEventHandler += new ValidationEventHandler(ValidateHandler);
```

The event handler receives a ValidationEventArgs class, which contains the exception, a message, and a number representing the severity:

```
private void ValidateHandler(Object sender, ValidationEventArgs e)
{
    lblInfo.Text += "Error: " + e.Message + "<br>";
}
```

To try out validation, you can use the XmlValidation.aspx page in the online samples. This page allows you to validate a valid DVD list as well as another version with incorrect data and an incorrect tag. Figure 12-7 shows the result of a failed validation attempt.

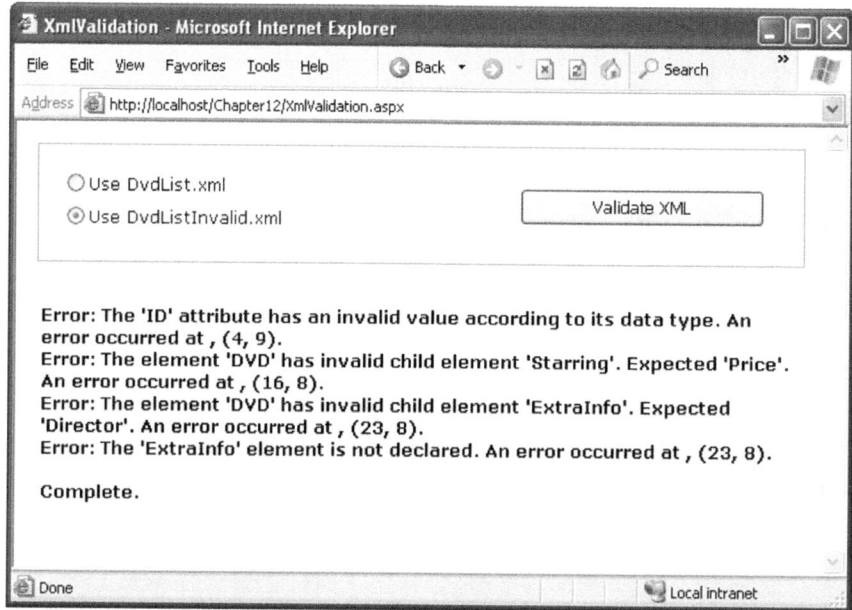

Figure 12-7. *The validation test page*

Transforming XML Files

Another related XML standard is XSL (Extensible Stylesheet Language), which is an XML-based language for creating stylesheets. *Stylesheets* are special documents that can be used (with the help of an XSLT processor) to convert your XML documents into other documents. For example, you can use an XSLT stylesheet to transform one type of XML to a different XML structure. Or you could use a stylesheet to convert your data-only XML into another text-based document like an HTML page, as you'll see with the next example.

Before you can perform a transformation, you need to create an XSL stylesheet that defines how the conversion should be applied. XSL is a complex standard—in fact, it can be considered a genuine language of its own with conditional logic, looping structures, and more.

■**Note** A full discussion of XSLT is beyond the scope of this book. However, if you want to learn more you can consider a book like Jeni Tennison's *Beginning XSLT* (Apress, 2004), the excellent online tutorials at `http://www.w3schools.com/xsl`, or the standard itself at `http://www.w3.org/Style/XSL/`.

To transform the DVD list into HTML, you'll use the simple stylesheet shown here:

```
<xsl:stylesheet xmlns:xsl="http://www.w3.org/1999/XSL/Transform" version="1.0">
  <xsl:template match="/">
    <html>
    <body>
      <xsl:apply-templates select="//DVD" />
    </body>
    </html>
  </xsl:template>

  <xsl:template match="DVD">
    <hr/>
    <h3><u><xsl:value-of select="Title" /></u></h3>
    <b>Price: </b> <xsl:value-of select="Price" /><br/>
    <b>Director: </b> <xsl:value-of select="Director" /><br/>
    <xsl:apply-templates select="Starring" />
  </xsl:template>

  <xsl:template match="Starring">
    <b>Starring:</b><br />
    <xsl:apply-templates select="Star" />
  </xsl:template>

  <xsl:template match="*">
    <li><xsl:value-of select="." /></li>
  </xsl:template>
</xsl:stylesheet>
```

Every XSL file has a root <stylesheet> element. The <stylesheet> element can contain one or more templates (the sample file has four). In this example, the first <template> element searches for the root element. When it finds it, it outputs the tags necessary to start an HTML page, and then uses the <apply-templates> command to branch off and perform processing for any contained <DVD> elements, as follows:

```
  <xsl:template match="/">
    <html>
    <body>
      <xsl:apply-templates select="//DVD" />
    </body>
    </html>
  </xsl:template>
```

Each time the <DVD> tag is matched, a horizontal line is added, and a heading is created. Information about the <Title>, <Price>, and <Director> is extracted and written to the page using the <value-of> command. Here's the full template:

```
<xsl:template match="DVD">
  <hr/>
  <h3><u><xsl:value-of select="Title" /></u></h3>
  <b>Price: </b> <xsl:value-of select="Price" /><br/>
  <b>Director: </b> <xsl:value-of select="Director" /><br/>
  <xsl:apply-templates select="Starring" />
</xsl:template>
```

Using this template and the XslTransform class (contained in the System.Xml.Xsl namespace) you can transform the DVD list into formatted HTML. Here's the code that performs this transformation and saves the result to a new file:

```
string xslFile = Server.MapPath("DvdList.xsl");
string xmlFile = Server.MapPath("DvdList.xml");
string htmlFile = Server.MapPath("DvdList.htm");
XslTransform transf = new XslTransform();
transf.Load(xslFile);
transf.Transform(xmlFile, htmlFile);
```

Of course, in a dynamic web application you'll want to transform the XML file and return the resulting code directly, without generating an HTML file. To do this you have to create an XPathNavigator for the source XML file. You can then pass the XPathNavigator to the XslTranform.Transform() method, which returns an XmlTextReader that you can use to access the transformed output.

The following code demonstrates this technique:

```
// Create an XPathDocument.
XPathDocument xdoc = new XPathDocument(new XmlTextReader(xmlFile));

// Create an XPathNavigator.
XPathNavigator xnav = xdoc.CreateNavigator();

// Transform the XML.
XmlTextReader reader = transf.Transform(xnav, null);
```

Once you have an XmlTextReader for the output, you can move to the beginning of the stream, and render the text to the response stream:

```
reader.MoveToContent();
Response.Write(reader.ReadOuterXml());
reader.Close();
```

Figure 12-8 shows the resulting page.

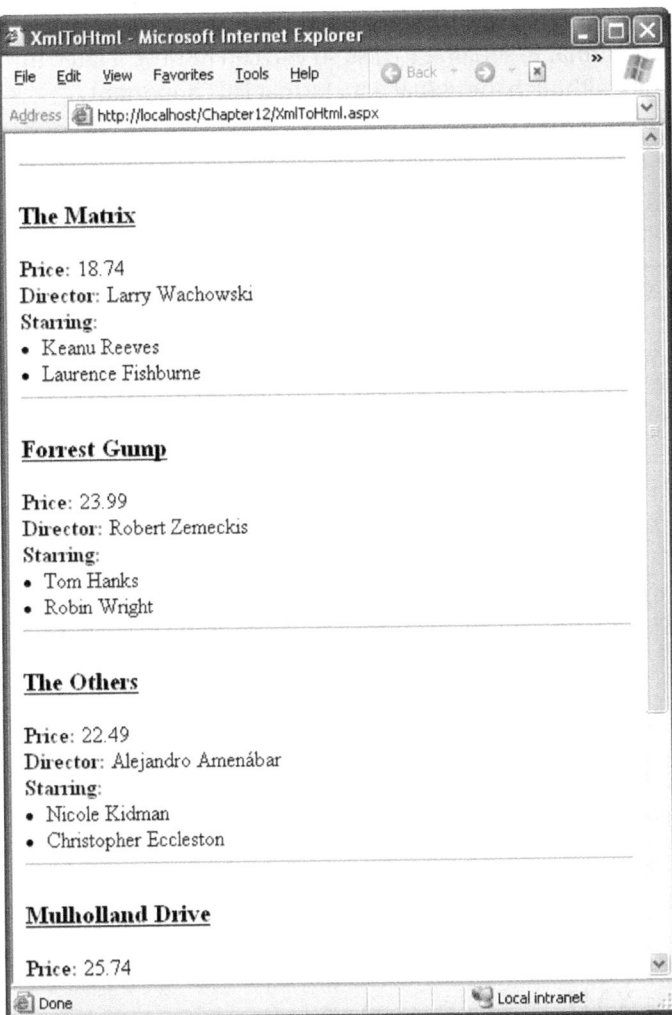

Figure 12-8. *Transforming XML to HTML*

■**Note** In some cases you might want to combine transformed HTML output with other content and web controls. In this case, you can use the Xml control. This Xml control displays the result of an XSL transformation on a discrete portion of a page. Best of all, you simply need to set the XML input and the transform—you don't need to manually initiate the conversion. For more information, refer to Chapter 5, which demonstrates how to use this control.

XML and ADO.NET

The DataSet has the built-in intelligence to convert its collection of tables and rows into an XML document. There are several reasons you might use this functionality. For example, you might want to share data with another application on another platform. You might event want to send this data to another component as part of an XML web-services request (as discussed in Part Five). Or you might simply use the XML format to serialize to disk so you can retrieve it later. In this case, you still use the same methods, although the actual data format isn't important.

Table 12-2 lists all the XML methods of the DataSet.

Table 12-2. *DataSet Methods for Using XML*

Method	Description
GetXml()	Retrieves the XML representation of the data in the DataSet as a single string.
WriteXml()	Writes the contents of the DataSet to a file or a TextWriter, XmlWriter, or Stream object. You can choose a write mode that determines if change tracking information and schema information is also written to the file.
ReadXml()	Reads XML data from a file or a TextReader, XmlReader, or Stream object, and uses it to populate the DataSet.
GetXmlSchema()	Retrieves the XML schema for the DataSet XML as a single string. No data is returned.
WriteXmlSchema()	Writes just the XML schema describing the structure of the DataSet to a file or a TextWriter, XmlWriter, or Stream object. You can choose to include the schema at the beginning of the document.
ReadXmlSchema()	Reads an XML schema from a file or a TextReader, XmlReader, or Stream object, and uses it to configure the structure of the DataSet.
InferXmlSchema()	Reads an XML document with DataSet contents from a file or a TextReader, XmlReader, or Stream object, and uses it to infer what structure the DataSet should have. This is an alternate approach to using the ReadXmlSchema() method, but it doesn't guarantee that all the data type information is preserved.

Converting the DataSet to XML

Using the XML methods of the DataSet is quite straightforward, as you'll see in the next example. This example uses two DataGrid controls on a page. The first DataSet is filled directly from the Employees table of the Northwind database. (The code isn't shown here because it's very similar to what you've seen over the previous chapters.) The second DataSet is filled using XML.

Here's how it works. Once the DataSet has been created, you can generate an XML schema file describing the structure of the DataSet, and an XML file containing the contents of every row. The easiest approach is to use the WriteXmlSchema() and the WriteXml() methods of the DataSet. These methods provide several overloads, including a version that lets you write data directly to a physical file. When you write the XML data, you can choose between several slightly different formats by specifying an XmlWriteMode. You can indicate that you want to save both the data and the schema in a single file (XmlWriteMode.WriteSchema), only the data (XmlWriteMode.IgnoreSchema), or the data with both the current and the original values (XmlWriteMode.DiffGram).

Here's the code that you need to save a DataSet to an XML file:

```
string xmlFile = Server.MapPath("Employees.xml");
ds.WriteXml(xmlFile, XmlWriteMode.WriteSchema);
```

This code creates an Employees.xml file in the current folder.

Now you can perform the reverse step by creating a new DataSet object, and filling it with the data contained in the XML file using the DataSet.ReadXml() method as follows:

```
DataSet dsXml = new DataSet("Northwind");
dsXml.ReadXml(xmlFile);
```

The DataSet you have at this point is the same as any other DataSet. You can edit, add, or delete rows. You can also bind it to the second DataGrid, as shown here:

```
DataGrid2.DataSource = dsXml;
DataGrid2.DataMember = "Employees";
DataGrid2.DataBind();
```

When you run the page, you'll see that the grid filled with the data retrieved directly from the database and the one loaded from the XML file are identical, as shown in Figure 12-9.

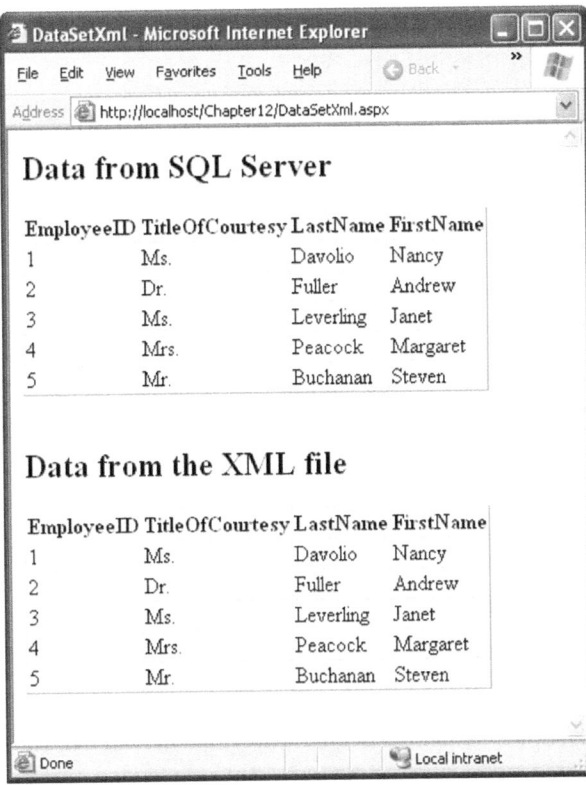

Figure 12-9. *Retrieving a DataSet from XML*

If you want to see the structure of the generated Employees.xml file, you can open it in Internet Explorer, as shown in Figure 12-10. Notice how the first part contains the schema that describes the structure of the table (name, type, and size of the fields), followed by the data itself.

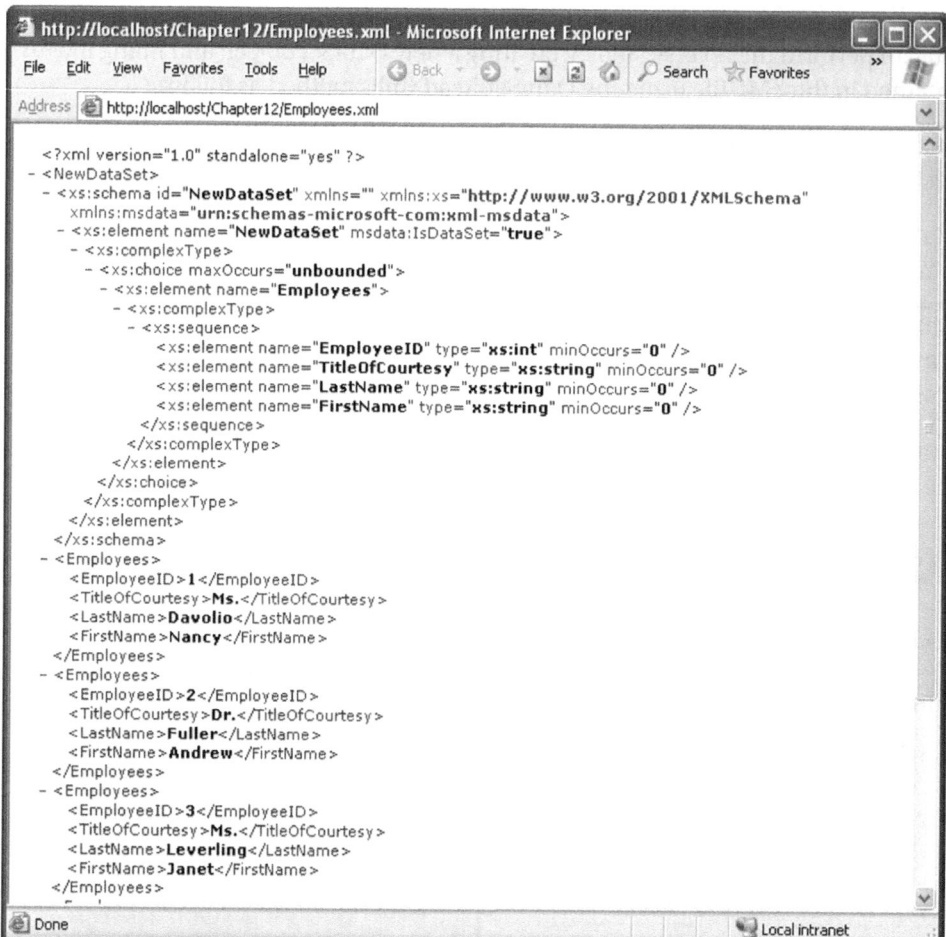

Figure 12-10. *Examining the DataSet XML*

The DataSet XML follows a predefined format that follows a few simple rules:

- The root document element is the DataSet.DataSetName (for example, Northwind).

- Each row in every table is contained in a separate element, using the name of the table. The example with one table means that there are multiple <Employees> elements.

- Every field in the row is contained as a separate tag in the table row tag. The value of the field is stored as text inside the tag.

Unfortunately, the DataSet doesn't make it possible for you to alter the overall structure. If you need to convert the DataSet to another form of XML, you need to manipulate it by using an XSLT or loading it into an XmlDocument object.

Accessing a DataSet as XML

Another option provided by the DataSet is the ability to access it through an XML interface. This allows you to perform XML-specific tasks (like hunting for a tag or applying an XSL transformation) with the data you've extracted from a database. To do so, you create an XmlDataDocument that wraps the DataSet. When you create the XmlDataDocument, you supply the DataSet you want as a parameter, as follows:

```
XmlDataDocument dataDocument = new XmlDataDocument(myDataSet) ;
```

Now you can look at the DataSet in two different ways. Because XmlDataDocument inherits from XmlDocument class, it provides all the same properties and methods for examining nodes and modifying content. You can use this XML-based approach to deal with your data, or you can manipulate the DataSet through the XmlDataDocument.DataSet property. In either case, the two views are kept automatically synchronized—when you change the DataSet, the XML is updated immediately, and vice versa.

For example, consider the pubs database, which includes a table of authors. Using the XmlDataDocument, you could examine a list of authors as an XML document, and then apply an XSL transformation with the help of the Xml web control. Here's the complete code you'd need:

```
// Create the ADO.NET objects.
SqlConnection con = new SqlConnection(connectionString);
string SQL = "SELECT * FROM authors WHERE city='Oakland'";
SqlCommand cmd = new SqlCommand(SQL, con);
SqlDataAdapter adapter = new SqlDataAdapter(cmd);
DataSet ds = new DataSet("AuthorsDataSet");
DataSet ds = new DataSet("AuthorsDataSet");

// Retrieve the data.
con.Open();
adapter.Fill(ds, "AuthorsTable");
con.Close();

// Create the XmlDataDocument that wraps this DataSet.
XmlDataDocument dataDoc = new XmlDataDocument(ds) ;

// Display the XML data (with the help of an XSLT) in the XML web control.
XmlControl.Document = dataDoc ;
XmlControl.TransformSource = "authors.xslt" ;
```

Here's the XSL stylesheet that does the work of converting the XML data into read-to-display HTML:

```
<?xml version="1.0" encoding="UTF-8" ?>
<xsl:stylesheet xmlns:xsl="http://www.w3.org/1999/XSL/Transform" version="1.0">
  <xsl:template match="AuthorsDataSet">
    <h1>The Author List</h1>
      <xsl:apply-templates select="AuthorsTable"/>
    <i>Created through XML and XSLT</i>
  </xsl:template>
```

```
    <xsl:template match="AuthorsTable">
      <p><b>Name: </b><xsl:value-of select="au_lname"/>,
      <xsl:value-of select="au_fname"/><br/>
      <b>Phone: </b> <xsl:value-of select="phone"/></p>
    </xsl:template>
</xsl:stylesheet>
```

The processed data, in HTML form, is shown in Figure 12-11.

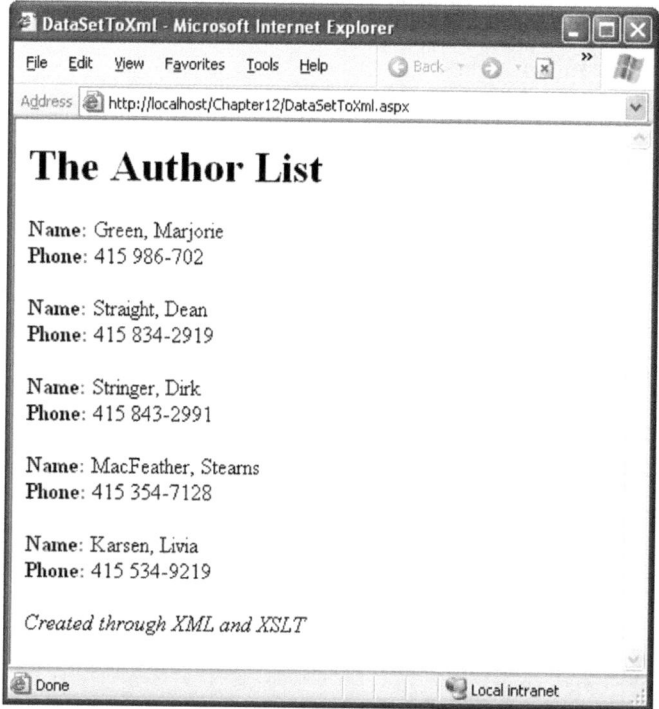

Figure 12-11. *Displaying the results of a query through XML and XSLT*

Remember that when you interact with your data as XML, all the customary database-oriented concepts like relationships and unique constraints go out the window. The only reason you should interact with your DataSet as XML is if you need to perform an XML-specific task. You shouldn't use XML manipulation to replace the approaches used in earlier chapters to update data. In most cases, you'll find it easier to use advanced controls like the DataList and DataGrid, rather than creating a dedicated XSL stylesheet to transform data into the HTML you want to display.

Executing an XML Query

SQL Server 2000 provides built-in support for XML. You can execute any query, and return the results as an XML fragment by adding the FOR XML clause to your query. This feature is completely separate from the XML features of the DataSet. However, it gives you another way to retrieve data from one or more tables in a database and work with it as XML.

Note An XML fragment contains valid XML syntax, but isn't necessarily a valid document of its own. Usually, this is because there is no root element. An XML document requires all elements to be nested in a single root element.

The FOR XML clause supports a specialized syntax that allows you to specify the exact structure and naming of the resulting document. However, this syntax does conform to any XML standard, and it's notoriously messy. As a result, XML queries often use of the two default XML representations that SQL Server provides. The first is FOR XML AUTO.

For example, if you execute this query:

```
SELECT FirstName, LastName FROM Employees FOR XML AUTO
```

you'll receive results like this:

```
<Employees FirstName="Nancy" LastName="Davolio"/>
<Employees FirstName="Andrew" LastName="Fuller"/>
<Employees FirstName="Janet" LastName="Leverling"/>
...
```

As you can see, each record is a separate element, with all the fields as attributes. The other easy option is FOR XML AUTO, ELEMENTS. Here's an example:

```
SELECT FirstName, LastName FROM Employees FOR XML AUTO, ELEMENTS
```

In this case, the data you'll receive uses separate elements for each row and each field, as shown here:

```
<Employees>
  <FirstName>Nancy</FirstName>
  <LastName>Davolio</LastName>
</Employees>
<Employees>
  <FirstName>Andrew</FirstName>
  <LastName>Fuller</LastName>
</Employees>
<Employees>
  <FirstName>Janet</FirstName>
  <LastName>Leverling</LastName>
</Employees>
...
```

Tip You can also fine-tune the format in much more painstaking detail using the FOR XML EXPLICIT syntax. For example, this allows you to convert some fields to attributes and others to elements. Refer to the SQL Server Books Online for more information. Unfortunately, the FOR XML query syntax is specific to SQL Server, and isn't supported by other database products.

To perform an XML query, you must use the SqlCommand.ExecuteXmlReader() method. This method returns an XmlReader with the results of your query as an XML fragment. You can move through the XmlReader one node at a time in a forward-only direction in the exact same way that you use the XmlTextReader. In fact, XmlTextReader derives from XmlReader.

Here's the code needed to retrieve and display a customer list on a web page:

```
// Define the command.
string customerQuery =
  "SELECT FirstName, LastName FROM Employees FOR XML AUTO, ELEMENTS";
SqlConnection con = new SqlConnection(connectionString);
SqlCommand com = new SqlCommand(customerQuery, con);

// Execute the command.
StringBuilder str = new StringBuilder();
try
{
    con.Open();
    XmlReader reader = com.ExecuteXmlReader();

    while (reader.Read())
    {
        // Process each employee.
        if ((reader.Name == "Employees") &&
          (reader.NodeType == XmlNodeType.Element))
        {
            reader.ReadStartElement("Employees");
            str.Append(reader.ReadElementString("FirstName"));
            str.Append(" ");
            str.Append(reader.ReadElementString("LastName"));
            str.Append("<br>");
            reader.ReadEndElement();
        }
    }
    reader.Close();
}
finally
{
    con.Close();
}
XmlText.Text = str.ToString();
```

Of course, life gets much more interesting when you combine an XML query with some of the other standards you've seen in this chapter, like XPath searching or XSLT transformation. These techniques aren't for everyone, but they do give you the ability to transform your data into virtually any XML representation. You might use these techniques with web services (as described in Part Five) to return records from a database in an XML format and provide them to a non-.NET client, without needing to perform the conversion manually in your code.

Summary

In this chapter, you've had a taste of ASP.NET's XML features. The class libraries for interacting with XML are available to any .NET application, whether it's a Windows application, web application, or a simple command-line tool. They provide one of the most fully featured toolkits for working with XML and other standards like XPath, XML Schema, and XSLT.

XML is a vast topic, and there is much more to cover, such as advanced navigation, search and selection techniques, validation, and serialization. If you want to learn more about XML in .NET, you may want to refer to the upcoming *Pro .NET XML* (Apress, 2005). But remember that you should only use XML where it's warranted. XML is a great tool for persisting file-based data in a readable format, and sharing information with other application components and services. However, it doesn't replace the core data management techniques you've seen in previous chapters.

CHAPTER 13

Files and Streams

Most web applications rely heavily on databases to store information. Databases are unmatched in multiuser scenarios. They handle simultaneous access without a hitch, and they support caching and low-level disk optimizations that guarantee blistering performance. Quite simply, a RDBMS (relational database management system) offers the most robust and best-performing storage for data.

Of course, most web developers inevitably face a scenario where they need to access data in other locations, such as the file system. Common examples include reading information produced by another application, writing a quick-and-dirty log for testing purposes, and creating a management page that allows administrators to upload files and view what's currently on the server. In this chapter, you'll learn how to use the classes in the System.IO namespace to get file system information, work with file paths as string, write and read files, and serialize objects.

File and Directory Classes

The simplest level of file access just involves retrieving information about existing files and directories, and performing typical file system operations such as copying files and creating directories. These tasks don't involve actually opening or writing a file (both of which are tasks you'll learn about toward the end of this chapter).

The .NET Framework provides four basic classes for retrieving file system information. They are all located in the System.IO namespace (and, incidentally, can be used in desktop applications in the exact same way that they are used in web applications). They include the following:

- **Directory and File.** These classes provide static methods that allow you to retrieve information about any files and directories that are visible from your server.

- **DirectoryInfo and FileInfo.** These classes use similar instance methods and properties to retrieve the same sort of information.

Both of these classes provide similar methods and properties. The key difference is that you need to create a DirectoryInfo or FileInfo object before you can use any methods, whereas the static methods of the Directory and File classes are always available. Typically, the Directory and File classes are more convenient for one-off tasks. On the other hand, if you need to retrieve several pieces of information, it's better to create DirectoryInfo and FileInfo objects. That way you don't need to keep specifying the name of the directory or file each time you call a method. It's also faster. That's because the FileInfo and DirectoryInfo classes perform their security checks once—when you create the object instance. The Directory and File classes perform a security check every time you invoke a method.

The Directory and File Classes

The Directory and File classes provide a number of useful methods. Tables 13-1 and 13-2 tell the whole story. Note that every method takes the same parameter: a fully qualified path name identifying the directory or file you want the operation to act on. A few methods, like Delete(), have optional parameters.

Table 13-1. *Directory Methods*

Method	Description
CreateDirectory()	Creates a new directory. If you specify a directory inside another nonexistent directory, ASP.NET will thoughtfully create *all* the required directories.
Delete()	Deletes the corresponding empty directory. To delete a directory along with its contents (subdirectories and files), add the optional second parameter of true.
Exists()	Returns true or false to indicate if the specified directory exists.
GetCreationTime(), GetLastAccessTime(), and GetLastWriteTime()	Returns a DateTime object that represents the time the directory was created, accessed, or written to. Each "Get" method has a corresponding "Set" method, which isn't shown in this table.
GetDirectories(), GetFiles(), and GetLogicalDrives()	Returns an array of strings, one for each subdirectory, file, or drive in the specified directory (depending on which method you're using). This method can accept a second parameter that specifies a search expression (like "ASP*.*"). Drive letters are in the format "c:\".
GetParent()	Parses the supplied directory string and tells you what the parent directory is. You could do this on your own by searching for the \ character (or, more generically, the Path.DirectorySeparatorChar), but this function makes life a little easier.
GetCurrentDirectory() and SetCurrentDirectory()	Allows you to set and retrieve the current directory, which is useful if you need to use relative paths instead of full paths. Generally, these functions shouldn't be relied on and aren't necessary.
Move()	Accepts two parameters: the source path and the destination path. The directory and all its contents can be moved to any path, as long as it's located on the same drive.

Table 13-2. *File Methods*

Method	Description
Copy()	Accepts two parameters: the fully qualified source filename and the fully qualified destination file name. To allow overwriting, add the optional third parameter set to true.
Delete()	Deletes the specified file, but doesn't throw an exception if the file can't be found.

Method	Description
Exists()	Indicates true or false whether a specified file exists.
GetAttributes() and SetAttributes()	Retrieves or sets an enumerated value that can include any combination of the values from the FileMode enumeration.
GetCreationTime(), GetLastAccessTime(), and GetLastWriteTime()	Returns a DateTime object that represents the time the file was created, accessed, or last written to. Each "Get" method has a corresponding "Set" method, which isn't shown in this table.
Move()	Accepts two parameters: the fully qualified source filename and the fully qualified destination filename. You can move a file across drives, and even rename it while you move it (or rename it without moving it).
Create() and CreateText()	Creates the specified file and returns a FileStream object that you can use to write to it. CreateText() performs the same task, but returns a StreamWriter object that wraps the stream.
Open(), OpenRead(), OpenText(), and OpenWrite()	Opens a file (provided it exists). OpenRead() and OpenText() open a file in read-only mode, returning a FileStream or StreamReader. OpenWrite() opens a file in write-only mode, returning a FileStream.

■**Tip** The only feature that the File class lacks (and the FileInfo class provides) is the ability to retrieve the size of a specified file.

The File and Directory methods are completely intuitive. For example, here's the code you could use to write a dynamic list displaying the name of each file in the current directory:

```
string directoryName = @"c:\Temp";

// Retrieve the list of files, and display it in the page.
string[] fileList = Directory.GetFiles(ftpDirectory);
foreach (string file in fileList)
{
    lstFiles.Items.Add(file);
}
```

In this example, the string with the file path c:\Temp is preceded by a @ character. This tells C# to interpret the string exactly as written. Without this character, C# would assume the directory separation character (\) indicates the start of a special character sequence. Another option is to use the escaped character sequence \\, which C# reads as a single literal slash. In this case, you would write the path as c:\\Temp.

Because the list of files is simply an ordinary list of strings, it can easily be bound to a list control, resulting in the following more efficient syntax for displaying the files on a page:

```
string directoryName = @"c:\Temp";
lstFiles.DataSource = Directory.GetFiles(ftpDirectory);
lstFiles.DataBind();
```

■**Note** In order for this code to work, the account that is used to run the ASP.NET worker process must have rights to the directory you're using. Otherwise, a SecurityException will be thrown when your web page attempts to access the file system. You can modify the permissions for a directory, and control who is allowed to access it by right-clicking the directory, selecting Properties, and choosing the Security tab. Alternatively, you might find it easier to modify the account that ASP.NET uses so you don't need to change these permissions at all. For more information, refer to Chapter 2, which explains how to configure the account used for ASP.NET applications.

The DirectoryInfo and FileInfo Classes

The DirectoryInfo and FileInfo classes mirror the functionality in the Directory and File classes. In addition, they make it easy to walk through directory and file relationships. For example, you can easily retrieve the FileInfo objects of files in a directory represented by a DirectoryInfo object.

Note that while the Directory and File classes only expose methods, DirectoryInfo and FileInfo provide a combination of properties and methods. For example, while the File class had separate GetAttributes() and SetAttributes() methods, the FileInfo class exposes a read-write Attributes property.

Another nice thing about the DirectoryInfo and FileInfo classes is that they share a common set of properties and methods because they derive from the common FileSystemInfo base class. Table 13-3 describes the members they have in common.

Table 13-3. *DirectoryInfo and FileInfo Members*

Member	Description
Attributes	Allows you to retrieve or set attributes using a combination of values from the FileAttributes enumeration.
CreationTime, LastAccessTime, and LastWriteTime	Allows you to set or retrieve the creation time, last-access time, and last-write time, using a DateTime object.
Exists	Returns true or false depending on whether the file or directory exists. In other words, you can create FileInfo and DirectoryInfo objects that don't actually correspond to current physical directories, although you obviously won't be able to use properties like CreationTime and methods like MoveTo().
FullName, Name and Extension	Returns a string that represents the fully qualified name, the directory or filename (with extension), or the extension on its own, depending on which property you use.
Delete()	Removes the file or directory, if it exists. When deleting a directory, it must be empty or you must specify an optional parameter set to true.
Refresh()	Updates the object so it's synchronized with any file system changes that have happened in the meantime (for example, if an attribute was changed manually using Windows Explorer).

Member	Description
Create()	Creates the specified directory or file.
MoveTo()	Copies the directory and its contents or the file. For a DirectoryInfo object, you need to specify the new path; for a FileInfo object you specify a path and filename.

In addition, the FileInfo and DirectoryInfo classes have a couple of unique members, as indicated in Tables 13-4 and 13-5.

Table 13-4. *Unique DirectoryInfo Members*

Member	Description
Parent, and Root	Returns a DirectoryInfo object that represents the parent or root directory.
CreateSubdirectory()	Creates a directory with the specified name in the directory represented by the DirectoryInfo object. It also returns a new DirectoryInfo object that represents the subdirectory.
GetDirectories()	Returns an array of DirectoryInfo objects that represent all the subdirectories contained in this directory.
GetFiles()	Returns an array of FileInfo objects that represent all the files contained in this directory.

Table 13-5. *Unique FileInfo Members*

Member	Description
Directory	Returns a DirectoryInfo object that represents the parent directory.
DirectoryName	Returns a string that identifies the name of the parent directory.
Length	Returns a long (64-bit integer) with the file size in bytes.
CopyTo()	Copies a file to the new path and filename specified as a parameter. It also returns a new FileInfo object that represents the new (copied) file. You can supply an optional additional parameter of true to allow overwriting.
Create() and CreateText()	Creates the specified file and returns a FileStream object that you can use to write to it. CreateText() performs the same task, but returns a StreamWriter object that wraps the stream.
Open(), OpenRead(), OpenText(), and OpenWrite()	Opens a file (provided it exists). OpenRead() and OpenText() open a file in read-only mode, returning a FileStream or StreamReader. OpenWrite() opens a file in write-only mode, returning a FileStream.

When you create a DirectoryInfo or FileInfo object, you specify the full path in the constructor, as shown here:

```
DirectoryInfo myDirectory = new DirectoryInfo(@"c:\Temp");
FileInfo myFile = new FileInfo(@"c:\Temp\readme.txt");
```

When you create a new DirectoryInfo or FileInfo object, you'll receive an exception if the path you used isn't properly formed (for example, if it contains illegal characters). However, the path doesn't need to correspond to a real physical file or directory. If you're not sure, you can use Exists to check if your directory or file really exists.

If the file or directory doesn't exist, you can always use a method like Create() to create it. Here's an example:

```
// Define the new directory and file.
DirectoryInfo myDirectory = new DirectoryInfo(@"c:\Temp\Test");
FileInfo myFile = new FileInfo(@"c:\Temp\Test\readme.txt");

// Now create them. Order here is important.
// You can't create a file in a directory that doesn't exist yet.
myDirectory.Create();
FileStream stream = myFile.Create();
stream.Close();
```

The FileInfo and DirectoryInfo objects retrieve information from the file system the first time you query a property. They don't check for new information on subsequent use. This could lead to inconsistency if the file changes in the meantime. If you know or suspect that file system information has changed for the given object, you should call the Refresh() method to retrieve the latest information.

Working with Attributes

The Attributes property of the FileInfo and DirectoryInfo classes represent the file system attributes for the file or directory. Because every file and directory can have a combination of attributes, the Attributes property contains a combination of values from the FileAttributes enumeration. These values are listed in Table 13-6.

Table 13-6. *Values for the FileAttributes Enumeration*

Value	Description
Archive	The item is archived. Applications can use this attribute to mark files for backup or removal, although it's really just a holdover from older DOS-based operating systems.
Compressed	The item is compressed.
Device	Not currently used. Reserved for future use.
Directory	The item is a directory.
Encrypted	This item is encrypted. For a file, this means that all data in the file is encrypted. For a directory, this means that encryption is the default for newly created files and directories.
Hidden	This item is hidden, and thus is not included in an ordinary directory listing. However, you can still see it in Windows Explorer.
Normal	This item is normal and has no other attributes set. This attribute is valid only if used alone.
NotContentIndexed	This item will not be indexed by the operating system's content indexing service.

Value	Description
Offline	This file is offline, and not currently available.
ReadOnly	This item is read-only.
ReparsePoint	This file contains a reparse point, which is a block of user-defined data associated with a file or a directory in an NTFS file system.
SparseFile	The file is a sparse file. Sparse files are typically large files whose data are mostly zeros. This item is only supported on NTFS file systems.
System	The item is part of the operating system or is used exclusively by the operating system.
Temporary	This item is temporary, and can be deleted when the application is no longer using it.

To find out all the attributes a file has, you can enumerate over the values in the Attributes property, as shown here:

```
foreach (FileAttributes attribute in myFile.Attributes)
{ ... }
```

You can also call the ToString() method of the Attributes property. This returns a string with a comma-separated list of attributes:

```
// This displays a string in the format "ReadOnly, Archive, Encrypted"
lblInfo.Text = myFile.Attributes.ToString();
```

When testing for a single specific attribute, you need to use bitwise arithmetic. For example, consider the following faulty code:

```
if (myFile.Attributes == FileAttributes.ReadOnly)
{ ... }
```

This test only succeeds if the read-only attribute is the *only* attribute for the current file. This is rarely the case. If you want to successfully check if the file is read-only, you need this code instead:

```
if ((myFile.Attributes & FileAttributes.ReadOnly) == FileAttributes.ReadOnly)
{ ... }
```

This test succeeds because it filters out just the read-only attribute. Essentially, the Attributes setting is made up (in binary) of a series of ones and zeros, such as 00010011. Each 1 represents an attribute that is present, while each 0 represents an attribute that is not. When you use the & operator with an enumerated value, it automatically performs a *bitwise and* operation, which compares each individual digit against each digit in the enumerated value. For example, if you combine a value of 00100001 (representing an individual file's archive and read-only attributes) with the enumerated value 00000001 (which represents the read-only flag), the resulting value will be 00000001. It will only have a 1 where it can be matched in both values. You can then test this resulting value against the FileAttributes.ReadOnly enumerated value using the equals sign.

Similar logic allows you to verify that a file does *not* have a specific attribute:

```
if ((myFile.Attributes & FileAttributes.ReadOnly) =! FileAttributes.ReadOnly)
{ ... }
```

When setting an attribute, you must also use bitwise arithmetic. In this case, it's needed to ensure that you don't inadvertently wipe out the other attributes that are already set.

```
// This adds just the read-only attribute.
myFile.Attributes = myFile.Attributes | FileAttributes.ReadOnly;

// This removes just the read-only attribute.
myFile.Attributes = myFile.Attributes & ~FileAttributes.ReadOnly;
```

■**Note** Some attributes can't be set programmatically. For example, the Encrypted attributed is only set by the operating system if you are using EFS (Encrypting File System) to encrypt files.

Filter Files with Wildcards

The DirectoryInfo and Directory objects both provide a way to search the current directories for files or directories that match a specific filter expression. These search expressions can use the standard ? and * wildcards. The ? wildcard represents any single character, while the * wildcard represents any sequence of zero or more characters.

For example, the following code snippet retrieves the names of all the files in the c:\temp directory that have the extension .txt. The code then iterates through the retrieved FileInfo collection of matching files and displays the name and size of each one.

```
DirectoryInfo dir = new DirectoryInfo(@"c:\temp");

// Get all the files with the .txt extesion.
FileInfo[] files = dir.GetFiles("*.txt");

// Process each file.
foreach FileInfo file in files
{ ... }
```

You can use a similar technique to retrieve directories that match a specified search pattern by using the overloaded DirectoryInfo.GetDirectories() method.

The GetFiles() and GetDirectories() methods only search the current directory. If you want to perform a search through all the contained subdirectories, you'd need to use recursive logic.

Retrieving File Version Information

File version information is the information you see when you look at the properties of an executable file or DLL in Windows Explorer. Version information commonly includes a version number, the company that produced the component, trademark information, and so on.

The FileInfo and File classes don't provide a way to retrieve file version information. However, you can retrieve it quite easily using the static GetVersionInfo() method of the System.Diagnostics.FileVersionInfo class. Here's an example that uses this technique to get a string with the complete version information, and displays it in a label:

```
string filename = @"c:\Windows\explorer.exe";
FileVersionInfo info = FileVersionInfo.GetVersionInfo(fileName);
lblInfo.Text = info.FileVersion;
```

Table 13-7 lists all the properties you can use.

Table 13-7. *FileVersionInfo Properties*

Property	Description
FileVersion, FileMajorPart, FileMinorPart, FileBuildPart, FilePrivatePart	Typically, a version number is displayed as [MajorNumber].[MinorNumber].[BuildNumber] .[Private PartNumber]. These properties allow you to retrieve the complete version as a string (FileVersion) or each individual component as a number.
FileName	Gets the name of the file that this instance of FileVersionInfo describes.
OriginalFilename	Gets the name the file was created with.
InternalName	Gets the internal name of the file, if one exists.
FileDescription	Gets the description of the file.
CompanyName	Gets the name of the company that produced the file.
ProductName	Gets the name of the product this file is distributed with.
ProductVersion, ProductMajorPart, ProductMinorPart, ProductBuildPart, ProductPrivatePart	These properties allow you to retrieve the complete product version as a string (ProductVersion) or each individual component as a number.
IsDebug	Gets a Boolean value that specifies whether the file contains debugging information or is compiled with debugging features enabled.
IsPatched	Gets a Boolean value that specifies whether the file has been modified and is not identical to the original shipping file of the same version number.
IsPreRelease	Gets a Boolean value that specifies whether the file is a development version, rather than a commercially released product.
IsPrivateBuild	Gets a Boolean value that specifies whether the file was built using standard release procedures.
IsSpecialBuild	Gets a Boolean value that specifies whether the file is a special build.
SpecialBuild	If IsSpecialBuild is true, this property contains a string that specifies the how the build differs from an ordinary build.
Comments	Gets the comments associated with the file.

Continued

Table 13-7. *Continued*

Property	Description
Language	Gets the default language string for the version info block.
LegalCopyright	Gets all copyright notices that apply to the specified file.
LegalTrademarks	Gets the trademarks and registered trademarks that apply to the file.

Determining Space Usage

The DirectoryInfo class doesn't provide any property for determining total size information. However, you can calculate the size of all the files in a particular directory quite easily by adding up the FileInfo.Length contribution of each one.

Before you take this step, you need to decide whether or not to include subdirectories in the total. The following method lets you use either approach:

```
private static long GetDirectorySize(DirectoryInfo directory,
 bool includeSubdirectories)
{
    long totalSize = 0;

    // Add up each file.
    FileInfo[] files = directory.GetFiles();
    foreach (FileInfo file in files)
    {
        totalSize += file.Length;
    }

    // Add up each subdirectory, if required.
    if (includeSubdirectories)
    {
        DirectoryInfo[] dirs = directory.GetDirectories();
        foreach (DirectoryInfo dir in dirs)
        {
            totalSize += CalculateDirectorySize(dir, true);
        }
    }
    return totalSize;
}
```

Unfortunately, the .NET Framework doesn't include any managed API for retrieving drive information. That means there's no way to calculate the amount of free space that's available. If you need this functionality, you must import the unmanaged Win32 API function GetDiskFreeSpaceEx(), which is declared in kernel32.dll, as shown here:

```
[DllImport("kernel32.dll", EntryPoint="GetDiskFreeSpaceExA" )]
private static extern long GetDiskFreeSpaceEx(
    string lpDirectoryName, out long lpFreeBytesAvailableToCaller,
    out long lpTotalNumberOfBytes, out long lpTotalNumberOfFreeBytes);
```

This function returns the amount of used space, the amount of free space, and the amount of available free space as output arguments. Here's an example of how you might use it:

```
long result, totalBytes, freeBytes, availableBytes;
result = GetDiskFreeSpaceEx("c:", out availableBytes, out totalBytes,
    out freeBytes);

if (result != 0)
{
    lblInfo.Text = "Total Bytes: " + totalBytes.ToString() + "<br>";
    lblInfo.Text += "Free Bytes: " + freeBytes.ToString() + "<br>";
    lblInfo.Text += "Available Bytes: " + availableBytes.ToString();
}
```

The Path Class

If you're working with files, you're probably also working with file and directory paths. Path information is stored as an ordinary string, which can lead to a number of problems ranging from minor headaches to serious security breaches.

For example, imagine you write the following block of code to add a filename to a path:

```
DirectoryInfo dirInfo = new DirectoryInfo(@"c:\temp\");
string file = "test.txt";
string path = dirInfo.FullName + @"\" + file;
```

At first, this code appears to work correctly. However, a problem occurs with the last line if you try to process the root directory. Here's an example of the error:

```
DirectoryInfo dirInfo = new DirectoryInfo(@"c:\");
string file = "test.txt";
string path = dirInfo.FullName + @"\" + file;
```

The problem here is that the FullName property never returns a trailing backslash. For example, c:\temp\ becomes just c:\temp. However, there's one exception—the root directory c:\, which always includes a trailing backslash. As a result, this seemingly logical code generates the nonsensical path c:\\test.txt, and fails.

The proper solution is to use the System.IO.Path class, which provides static helper methods that perform common path manipulation tasks. In this case, the Combine() method neatly solves the problem and works with any directory and file, as follows:

```
DirectoryInfo dirInfo = new DirectoryInfo(@"c:\");
string file = "test.txt";
string path = Path.Combine(dirInfo.FullName, file);
```

Minor hiccups like this are bothersome, but they aren't serious. A more significant problem is the security risk of a *canonicalization error*. Canonicalization errors are a specific type of application error that can occur when your code assumes that user-supplied values will always be in a standardized form. Canonicalization errors are low-tech but quite serious, and they usually have the result of allowing a user to perform an action that should be restricted.

One infamous type of canonicalization error is SQL injection, whereby a user submits incorrectly formatted values to trick your application into executing a modified SQL command. (SQL injection was covered in detail in Chapter 8). Other forms of canonicalization problems can occur with file paths and URLs.

For example, consider the following method that returns file data from a fixed document directory:

```
FileInfo file = new FileInfo(Server.MapPath("Documents\\" + txtBox.Text));
// (Read the file and display it in another control).
```

This code looks simple enough. It concatenates the user-supplied filename with the Documents path, thereby allowing the user to retrieve data from any file in this directory. The problem is that filenames can be represented in multiple formats. Instead of submitting a valid filename, an attacker can submit a qualified filename like "..\filename". The concatenated path of WebApp\Documents\..\filename will actually retrieve a file from the parent of the Documents directory (WebApp). A similar approach will allow the user to specify any filename on the web application drive. Because the web service is only limited according to the restrictions of the ASP.NET worker process, the user may be allowed to download a sensitive server-side file.

The fix for this code is fairly easy. Once again, you can use the Path class. This time, you use the GetFileName() method to extract just the final filename portion of the string, as shown here:

```
filename = Path.GetFileName(filename);
FileInfo file = new FileInfo(Server.MapPath(
  Path.Combine("Documents", txtBox.Text));
```

This ensures that the user is constrained to the correct directory. If you are dealing with URLs, you can work similar magic with the System.Uri type. For example, here's how you might remove query string arguments from a URI, and make sure it refers to a given server and virtual directory:

```
string uriString = "http://www.wrongsite.com/page.aspx?cmd=run";

Uri uri = new Uri(uriString);
string page = System.IO.Path.GetFileName(uri.AbsolutePath)
// page is now just "page.aspx"

Uri baseUri = new Uri("http://www.rightsite.com")
uri = new Uri(baseUri, page)
// uri now stores the path http://www.rightsite.com/page.aspx.
```

Table 13-8 lists the methods of the Path class.

Table 13-8. *Path Methods*

Methods	Description
Combine()	Combines a path with a filename or a subdirectory.
ChangeExtension()	Modifies the current extension of the file in a string. If no extension is specified, the current extension will be removed.
GetDirectoryName()	Returns all the directory information, which is the text between the first and last directory separators (\).
GetFileName()	Returns just the filename portion of a path.
GetFileNameWithoutExtension()	This method is similar to GetFileName(), but it omits() the extension from the returned string.
GetFullPath()	This method has no effect on an absolute path, and it changes a relative path into an absolute path using the current directory. For example, if c:\Temp\ is the current directory, calling GetFullPath() on a filename such as test.txt returns c:\Temp\test.txt.
GetPathRoot()	Retrieves a string with the root (for example, "C:\"), provided that information is in the string. For a relative path, it returns a null reference.
HasExtension()	Returns true if the path ends with an extension.
IsPathRooted()	Returns true if the path is an absolute path and false if it's a relative path.

Although the Path class contains methods for drilling down the directory structure (adding subdirectories to directory paths), it doesn't provide any methods for going back up (removing subdirectories from directory paths). However, you can work around this limitation by using the Combine() method with relative path "..", which means "move one directory up." For good measure, you can also use the GetFullPath() method on the result to return it to normal form.

Here's an example:

```
string path = @"c:\temp\subdir";

path = Path.Combine(path, "..");
// path now contains the string "c:\temp\subdir\.."

path = Path.GetFullPath(path);
// path now contains the string "c:\temp"
```

Note In most cases, an exception will be thrown if you supply a path that contains illegal characters to one of these methods. However, path names that contain a wildcard character (* or ?) will not cause the methods to throw an exception.

A File Browser

Using the concepts you've learned so far, it's quite straightforward to put together a simple file-browsing application. Rather than iterating through collections of files and directories manually, this example handles everything using the DataList, DataGrid, and some data binding code.

Figure 13-1 shows this program in action as it displays the contents of the c:\Documents and Settings directory.

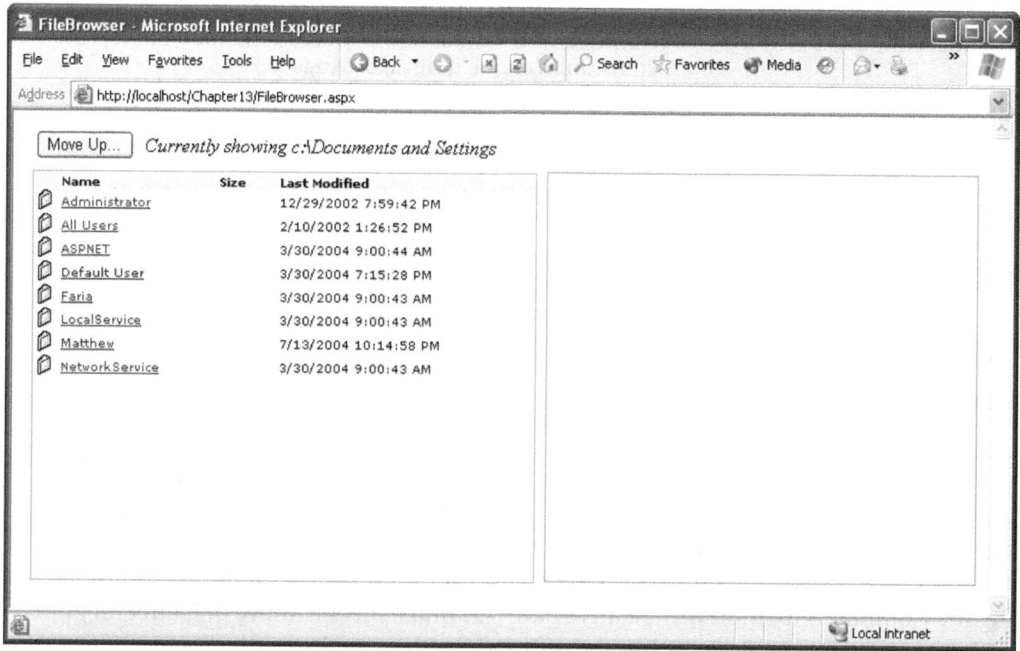

Figure 13-1. *Browing the file system*

The directory listing is actually built using two separate DataGrid controls, one on top of the other. The topmost DataGrid shows the directories, while the DataGrid underneath shows files. The only visible difference to the user is that the directories don't display length information, and have a folder icon next to the name. The ShowHeader property of the second DataGrid is set to false so that the two grids blend into each other fairly seamlessly. And because the DataGrid controls are stacked in a panel that uses flow layout, as the list of directories grows, the list of files moves down the page to accommodate it.

Technically, you could handle the directory and file listing using one DataGrid object. That's because all FileInfo and DirectoryInfo objects have a common parent—the FileSystemInfo object. However, in this grid you want to show the size in bytes of each file. Because the DirectoryInfo object doesn't provide a Length property, trying to bind to it in a more generic list of FileSystemInfo objects would cause an error.

> **Note** There's another equally effective solution to this problem. You could create a single DataGrid, but not bind directly to the FileInfo.Length property. Instead, you would bind to a method in the page class that examines the current data object, and return either the length (for FileInfo objects) or a blank string (for DirectoryInfo objects).

Here's the declaration for the DataGrid control that provides the file list, without the formatting-specific style properties:

```
<asp:DataGrid id="gridDirList" runat="server" AutoGenerateColumns="False"
 Width="418px" GridLines="None" CellPadding="0" CellSpacing="1"
 DataKeyField="FullName">
  <Columns>
    <asp:TemplateColumn>
      <ItemTemplate>
        <img src="folder.jpg" />
      </ItemTemplate>
    </asp:TemplateColumn>
    <asp:ButtonColumn DataTextField="Name" HeaderText="Name">
    </asp:ButtonColumn>
    <asp:BoundColumn HeaderText="Size"></asp:BoundColumn>
    <asp:BoundColumn DataField="LastWriteTime"
     HeaderText="Last Modified"></asp:BoundColumn>
  </Columns>
</asp:DataGrid>
```

This grid binds to an array of DirectoryInfo objects, and displays the Name, Size, and LastWriteTime properties. In addition, the FullName property is designated as the DataGrid.DatKeyField so that you can return the full path after the user clicks one of the directories. You'll also notice that one of the columns doesn't actually display any information—that's the BoundColumn for length that displays header text, but it doesn't link to any data field.

The DataGrid for the files follows immediately after. Here's the slightly shortened control tag:

```
<asp:DataGrid id="gridFileList" runat="server" AutoGenerateColumns="False"
 Width="417px" GridLines="None" CellPadding="0" CellSpacing="1"
 DataKeyField="FullName">
  <SelectedItemStyle BackColor="#C0FFFF"></SelectedItemStyle>
  <Columns>
    <asp:BoundColumn></asp:BoundColumn>
    <asp:ButtonColumn DataTextField="Name" CommandName="Select">
    </asp:ButtonColumn>
    <asp:BoundColumn DataField="Length"></asp:BoundColumn>
    <asp:BoundColumn DataField="LastWriteTime"></asp:BoundColumn>
  </Columns>
</asp:DataGrid>
```

Note that the DataGrid for displaying files must define a SelectedItemStyle because it supports file selection.

The next step is to write the code that fills these controls. The star of the show is a private method named ShowDirectoryContents(), which retrieves the contents of the current folder and binds the two DataGrid controls. Here's the complete code:

```
private void ShowDirectoryContents(string path)
{
    // Define the current directory.
    DirectoryInfo dir = new DirectoryInfo(path);

    // Get the DirectoryInfo and FileInfo objects.
    FileInfo[] files = dir.GetFiles();
    DirectoryInfo[] dirs = dir.GetDirectories();

    // Show the directory listing.
    lblCurrentDir.Text = "Currently showing " + path;
    gridFileList.DataSource = files;
    gridDirList.DataSource = dirs;
    Page.DataBind();

    // Clear any selection.
    gridFileList.SelectedIndex = -1;

    // Keep track of the current path.
    ViewState["CurrentPath"] = path;
}
```

When the page first loads, it calls this method to show the root virtual web directory (typically c:\Inetpub\wwwroot).

```
private void Page_Load(object sender, System.EventArgs e)
{
    if (!Page.IsPostBack)
    {
        ShowDirectoryContents(Server.MapPath("\\"));
    }
}
```

You'll notice that the ShowDirectoryContents() method stores the currently displayed directory in view state. That allows the Move Up button to direct the user to a directory that's one level above the current directory:

```
private void cmdUp_Click(object sender, System.EventArgs e)
{
    string path = (string)ViewState["CurrentPath"];
    path = Path.Combine(path, "..");
```

```
    path = Path.GetFullPath(path);
    ShowDirectoryContents(path);
}
```

To move down through the directory hierarchy, the user simply needs to click a directory link. This is raised as a DataGrid.ItemCommand event. The event handler then displays the new directory:

```
private void gridDirList_ItemCommand(object source,
 System.Web.UI.WebControls.DataGridCommandEventArgs e)
{
    // Get the selected directory.
    string dir = (string)gridDirList.DataKeys[e.Item.ItemIndex];

    // Now refresh the directory list to
    // show the selected directory.
    ShowDirectoryContents(dir);
}
```

But what happens if a user selects a file from the second DataGrid? Because the CommandName for this column is "Select" the DataGrid.SelectedIndexChanged event is raised. The code then retrieves the full file path, creates a new FileInfo object, and binds it to a DataList that uses a template to display several pieces of information about the file. Figure 13-2 shows the result.

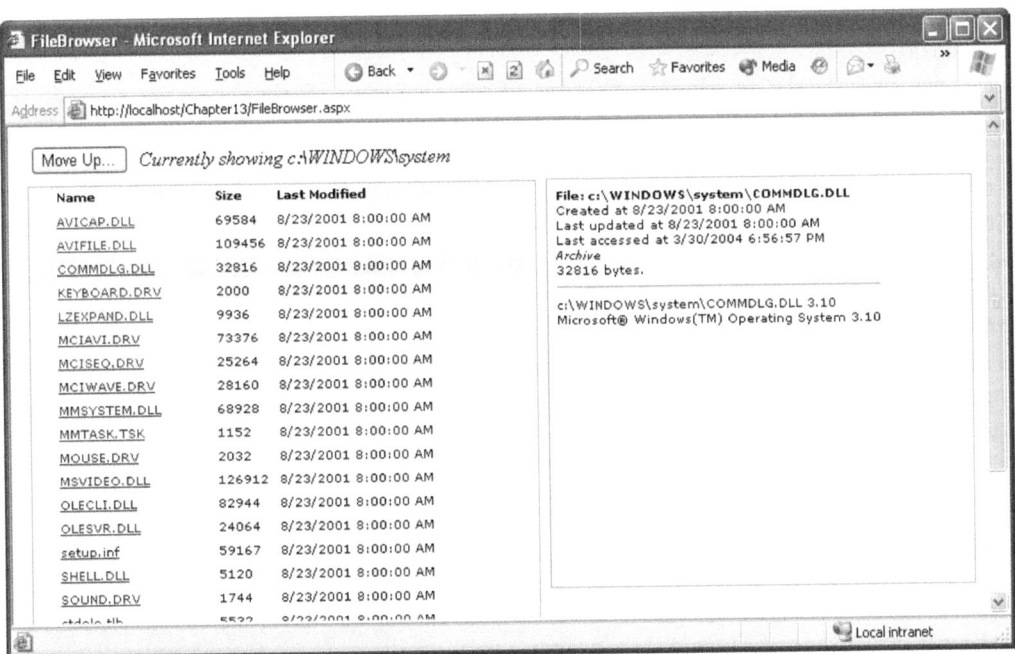

Figure 13-2. *Examine a file*

Here's the code that binds the file information to the DataList when an item is selected in the DataGrid:

```
private void gridFileList_SelectedIndexChanged(object sender, System.EventArgs e)
{
    // Get the selected file.
    string file = (string)gridFileList.DataKeys[gridFileList.SelectedIndex];

    // The DataList shows a collection (or list) of items.
    // To accommodate this design, you must add the file
    // to a collection of some sort.
    ArrayList files = new ArrayList();
    files.Add(new FileInfo(file));

    // Now show the selected file.
    listFile.DataSource = files;
    listFile.DataBind();
}
```

The DataList uses an ItemTemplate to define what properties should be shown and how they should be formatted. Here's what the ItemTemplate looks like:

```
<asp:DataList id="listFile" runat="server">
  <ItemTemplate>
    <b>File:
    <%# DataBinder.Eval(Container.DataItem, "FullName") %></b><br>
    Created at
    <%# DataBinder.Eval(Container.DataItem, "CreationTime") %><br>
    Last updated at
    <%# DataBinder.Eval(Container.DataItem, "LastWriteTime") %><br>
    Last accessed at
    <%# DataBinder.Eval(Container.DataItem, "LastAccessTime") %><br>
    <i><%# DataBinder.Eval(Container.DataItem, "Attributes") %></i><br>
    <%# DataBinder.Eval(Container.DataItem, "Length") %> bytes.
    <hr>
    <%# GetVersionInfoString(DataBinder.Eval(Container.DataItem, "FullName")) %>
  </ItemTemplate>
</asp:DataList>
```

The data binding expressions are fairly straightforward. The only one that needs any expression is the GetVersionInfoString() method. This method is coded inside the page class. It creates a new FileVersionInfo object for the file, and uses that to extract the version information and product name.

```
protected string GetVersionInfoString(object path)
{
    FileVersionInfo info = FileVersionInfo.GetVersionInfo((string)path);
    return info.FileName + " " + info.FileVersion + "<br>" +
    info.ProductName + " " + info.ProductVersion;
}
```

Of course, most developers have FTP tools and other utilities that make it easier to manage files on a web server. However, this page provides an excellent example of how to use the .NET file and directory management classes. With a little more work, you could transform it into a full-featured administrative tool for a web application.

Streams

The .NET Framework uses a *stream* model in several areas of the framework. Streams are an abstraction that allow you to treat different data sources in the similar way—as a stream of ordered bytes. All .NET stream classes derive from the base System.IO.Stream class. Streams are used to represent data in a memory buffers, data that's being retrieved over a network connection, and data that's being retrieved from or written to a file.

Here's how you create a new file and write an array of bytes to it through a FileStream:

```
FileStream fileStream = null;
try
{
    fileStream = new FileStream(fileName, FileMode.Create);
    fileStream.Write(bytes);
}
finally
{
    if (fileStream != null) fileStream.Close();
}
```

In this example, the FileMode.Create value is specified in the FileStream constructor to indicate that you want to create a new file. You can use any of FileMode values described in Table 13-9.

Table 13-9. *Values of the FileMode Enumeration*

Value	Description
Append	Opens the file if it exists and seeks to the end of the file, or creates a new file.
Create	Specifies that the operating system should create a new file. If the file already exists, it will be overwritten.
CreateNew	Specifies that the operating system should create a new file. If the file already exists, an IOException is thrown.
Open	Specifies that the operating system should open an existing file.
OpenOrCreate	Specifies that the operating system should open a file if it exists; otherwise, a new file should be created.
Truncate	Specifies that the operating system should open an existing file. Once opened, the file will be truncated so that its size is zero bytes.

And here's how you can open a FileStream and read its contents into a byte array:

```
FileStream fileStream = null;
try
{
    fileStream = new FileStream(fileName, FileMode.Open);
    byte[] dataArray = new byte[fileStream.Length];

    for(int i = 0; i < fileStream.Length; i++)
    {
        dataArray[i] = fileStream.ReadByte();
    }
}
finally
{
    if (fileStream != null) fileStream.Close();
}
```

On their own, streams aren't that useful. That's because they work entirely in terms of single bytes and byte arrays. .NET includes a more useful higher-level model of writer and reader objects that fills the gaps. These objects wrap stream objects, and allow you to write more complex data, including common data types like integers, strings, and dates. You'll see readers and writers at work in the following sections.

Tip Whenever you open a file through a FileStream, remember to call the FileStream.Close() method when you're finished. This releases the handle on the file and makes it possible for someone else to access the file. In addition, because the FileStream class is disposable, you can use it with the using statement, which ensures that the FileStream is closed as soon as the block ends.

Text Files

You can write to a file and read from a file using the StreamWriter and StreamReader classes in the System.IO namespace. When creating these classes, you simply pass the underlying stream as a constructor argument. For example, here's the code that you need to create a StreamWriter using an existing FileStream:

```
FileStream fileStream = new FileStream(@"c:\myfile.txt", FileMode.Create);
StreamWriter w = new StreamWriter(fileStream);
```

You can also use one of the static methods included in the File and FileInfo classes, like CreateText() or OpenText(). Here's an example that uses this technique to get a StreamWriter:

```
StreamWriter w = File.CreateText(@"c:\myfile.txt");
```

This code is equivalent to the earlier example.

Once you have the StreamWriter, you can use the Write() or WriteLine() method to add information into the file. Both of these methods are overloaded so that they can write many simple data types, including strings, integers, and other numbers. These values are essentially all converted into strings when they're written to a file, and they must be converted back into the appropriate types manually when you read the file. To make this process easier, you should put each separate piece of information on a separate line by using WriteLine() instead of Write(), as shown here:

```
w.WriteLine("This file generated by ASP.NET");  // Write a string.
w.WriteLine(42);                                 // Write a number.
```

When you finish with the file, you must make sure you close it. Otherwise, the changes may not be properly written to disk, and the file could be locked open. At any time, you can also call the Flush() method to make sure all data is written to disk, as the StreamWriter will perform some in-memory caching of your data to optimize performance (which is usually exactly the behavior you want).

```
// Tidy up.
w.Flush();
w.Close();
```

When reading information, you use the Read() or ReadLine() method of the StreamReader. The Read() method reads a single character, or the number of characters you specify, and returns the data as a char or char array. The ReadLine() method returns a string with the content of an entire line. ReadLine() starts at the first line, and advances the position to the end of the file, one line at a time.

Here's a code snippet that opens and reads the file created in the previous example:

```
StreamReader r = File.OpenText(@"c:\myfile.txt");
string inputString;
inputString = r.ReadLine();    // = "This file generated by ASP.NET"
InputString = r.ReadLine();    // = "42"
```

ReadLine() returns a null reference when there is no more data in the file. This means that you can read all the data in a file using code like this:

```
// Read and display the lines from the file until the end
// of the file is reached.
string line;
do
{
    line = r.ReadLine();
    if (line != null)
    {
        // (Process the line here.)
    }
} while (line != null);
```

Tip You can also use the ReadToEnd() method to read the entire content of the file and return it as a single string.

TEXT ENCODING

There is more than one way to represent a string in binary form, depending on the encoding you use. The most common encodings include the following:

- **ASCII**. Encodes each character in a string using 7 bits. ASCII-encoded data can't contain extended Unicode characters. When using ASCII encoding in .NET, the bits will be padded and the resulting byte array will have one byte for each character.

- **Full Unicode (or UTF-16)**. Represents each character in a string using 16 bits. The resulting byte array will have two bytes for each character.

- **UTF-7 Unicode**. Uses 7 bits for ordinary ASCII characters and multiple 7-bit pairs for extended characters. This encoding is primarily for use with 7-bit protocols such as mail, and it isn't regularly used.

- **UTF-8 Unicode**. Uses 8 bits for ordinary ASCII characters and multiple 8-bit pairs for extended characters. The resulting byte array will have one byte for each character (provided there are no extended characters).

.NET provides a class for each type of encoding in the System.Text namespace. When using the StreamReader and StreamWriter, you can specify the encoding that you want to use a constructor argument, or simply use the default UTF-8 encoding.

Here's an example that creates a StreamWriter that uses ASCII encoding:

```
FileStream fileStream = new FileStream(@"c:\myfile.txt", FileMode.Create);
StreamWriter w = new StreamWriter(fileStream, System.Text.Encoding.ASCII);
```

Binary Files

You can also write to a binary file. Binary data uses space more efficiently, but also creates files that aren't readable. If you open a binary file in Notepad, you'll see a lot of extended characters (politely known as gibberish).

To open a file for binary writing, you need to create a new BinaryWriter class. The class constructor accepts a stream, which you can create by hand or retrieve using the File.OpenWrite() method. Here's the code to open the file c:\binaryfile.bin for binary writing:

```
BinaryWriter w = new BinaryWriter(File.OpenWrite(@"c:\binaryfile.bin"));
```

.NET concentrates on stream objects, rather than the source or destination for the data. This means that you can write binary data to any type of stream, whether it represents a file or some other type of storage location, using the same code. In addition, writing to a binary file is almost the same as writing to a text file, as you can see here:

```
string str = "ASP.NET Binary File Test";
int integer = 42;
w.Write(str);
w.Write(integer);
```

```
w.Flush();
w.Close();
```

Unfortunately, when you read data you need to know the data type you want to retrieve. To retrieve a string, you use the ReadString() method. To retrieve an integer, you must use ReadInt32(), as follows:

```
BinaryReader r = new BinaryReader(File.OpenRead(@"c:\binaryfile.bin"));
string str;
int integer;
str = r.ReadString();
integer = r.ReadInt32();
```

Note There's no easy way to jump to a location in a text or binary file without reading through all the information in order. While you can use methods like Seek() on the underlying stream, you need to specify an offset in bytes. This involves some fairly involved calculations to determine variable sizes. If you need to store a large amount of information and move through it quickly, you need a dedicated database, not a binary file.

Making Files Safe for Multiple Users

Although it's fairly easy to create a unique filename, what happens in the situation where you really do need to access the same file to server multiple different requests? Although this situation isn't ideal (and often indicates that a database-based solution would work better), there are some techniques you can use to defend yourself.

One approach is to open your files with sharing, which allows multiple processes to access the same file at the same time. To use this technique, you need to use the four-parameter FileStream constructor that allows you to select a FileMode. Here's an example:

```
FileStream fs = new FileStream(fileName, FileMode.Open, FileAccess.Read,
  FileShare.Read);
```

This statement allows multiple users to open the file for reading at the same time. However, no one will be able to update the file.

Tip Another technique that works well if multiple users need to access the same data, especially if this data is frequently used and not excessively large, is to load the data into Application state or the Cache (as described in Chapter 7). That way the data can be accessed by multiple users simultaneously without a hitch. Of course, this approach may not suit your needs if another process is responsible for creating or periodically updating the file, in which case you can't be sure the data you've cached is up to date.

It is possible to have multiple users open the file in read-write mode by specifying a different FileAccess value (like FileAccess.Write or FileAccess.ReadWrite). In this case, Windows will dynamically lock small portions of the file when you write to them (or you can use the FileStream.Lock() method to lock down a range of bytes in the file). If two users try to write to the same locked portion at once, an exception can occur. Because web applications have high concurrency demands, this technique is not recommended, and is extremely difficult to implement properly. It also forces you to use low-level byte-offset calculations, where it is notoriously easy to make small, aggravating errors.

So what is the solution when multiple users need to update a file at once? One option is to create separate user-specific files for each request. Another option is to tie the file to some other object and use locking. Both techniques are explained in the following sections.

Creating Unique Filenames

One solution for dealing with user-concurrency headaches with files is to avoid the conflict altogether by using different files for different users. For example, imagine you want to store a user-specific log. To prevent the chance for an inadvertent conflict if two web pages try to use the same log, you can use the following two techniques:

- Create a user-specific directory for each user.

- Add some additional information to the filename, like a timestamp, GUID (global unique identifier), or random number. This reduces the chance of duplicate filenames to a vanishingly small possibility.

The following sample page demonstrates this technique. It defines a method for creating filenames that are statistically guaranteed to be unique. In this case, the filename incorporates a GUID value.

Here's the private method that generates a new unique filename:

```
private string GetFileName()
{
    // Create a unique filename.
    string fileName = "user." +
    Guid.NewGuid().ToString();

    // Put the file in the current web application path.
    return Path.Combine(Request.PhysicalApplicationPath, fileName);
}
```

Note A GUID is a 128-bit integer. GUID values are tremendously useful in programming because they're statistically unique. In other words, you can create GUID values continuously with little chance of ever creating a duplicate. For that reason, GUIDs are commonly used to uniquely identify queued tasks, user sessions, and other dynamic information. They also have the advantage over sequential numbers in the fact that they can't easily be guessed. The only disadvantage is that GUIDs are long and almost impossible to remember (for an ordinary human being). GUIDs are commonly represented in strings as a series of lower-case hexadecimal digits, like 382c74c3-721d-4f34-80e5-57657b6cbc27.

Using the GetFileName() method, you can create a safer logging application that writes information about the users actions to a text file. In this example, all the logging is performed by calling a Log() method, which then checks for the filename, and assigns a new one if the file hasn't been created yet. The text message is then added to the file, along with the date and time information.

```
private void Log(string message)
{
    // Check for the file.
    FileMode mode;
    if (ViewState["LogFile"] == null)
    {
        // First, create a unique user-specific filename.
        ViewState["LogFile"] = GetFileName();

        // The log file must be created.
        mode = FileMode.Create;
    }
    else
    {
        // Add to the existing file.
        mode = FileMode.Append;
    }

    // Write the message.
    // A using block ensures the file is automatically closed,
    // even in the case of error.
    string fileName = (string)ViewState["LogFile"];
    using (FileStream fs = new FileStream(fileName, mode))
    {
        StreamWriter w = new StreamWriter(fs);
        w.WriteLine(DateTime.Now);
        w.WriteLine(message);
        w.Close();
    }
}
```

For example, a log message is added every time the page is loaded, as shown here:

```
private void Page_Load(object sender, System.EventArgs e)
{
    if (!Page.IsPostBack)
    {
        Log("Page loaded for the first time.");
    }
    else
    {
```

```
        Log("Page posted back.");
    }
}
```

The last ingredient is two button event handlers that allow you to delete the log file, or show its contents, as follows:

```
private void cmdRead_Click(object sender, System.EventArgs e)
{
    if (ViewState["LogFile"] != null)
    {
        string fileName = (string)ViewState["LogFile"];
        using (FileStream fs = new FileStream(fileName, FileMode.Open))
        {
            StreamReader r = new StreamReader(fs);

            // Read line by line (allows you to add
            // line breaks to the web page).
            string line;
            do
            {
                line = r.ReadLine();
                if (line != null)
                {
                    lblInfo.Text += line + "<br>";
                }
            } while (line != null);
            r.Close();
        }
    }
}

private void cmdDelete_Click(object sender, System.EventArgs e)
{
    if (ViewState["LogFile"] != null)
    {
        File.Delete((string)ViewState["LogFile"]);
    }
}
```

Figure 13-3 shows the web page displaying the log contents.

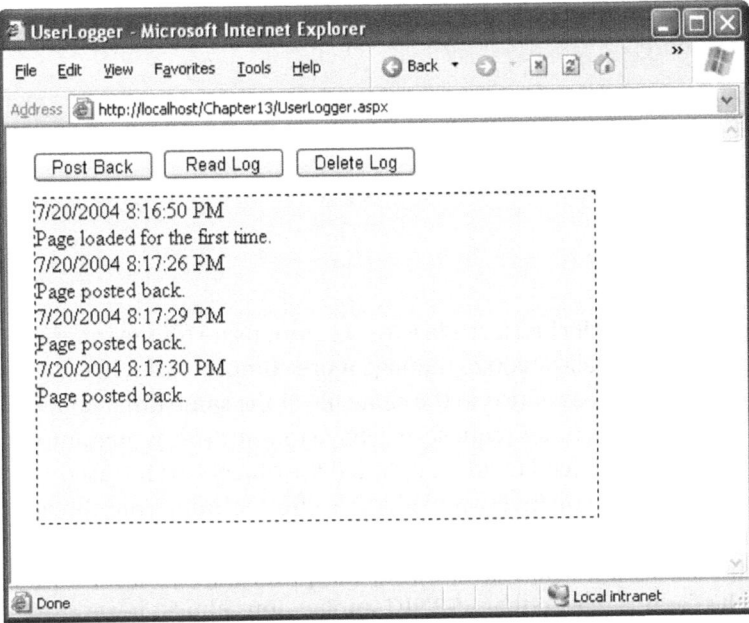

Figure 13-3. *A safer way to write a user-specific log*

Locking File Access Objects

Of course, in some cases you *do* need to update the same file in response to actions taken by multiple different users. One approach is to use *locking*. The basic technique is to create a separate class that performs all the work of retrieving the data. Once you've defined this class, you can create a single global instance of it and add it to the Application collection. Now you can use the C# lock statement to ensure that only one thread can access this object at a time (and hence only one thread can attempt to open the file at once).

For example, imagine you create the following Logger class, which updates a file with log information when you call the LogMessage() method, as shown here:

```
public class Logger
{
    public void LogMessage()
    {
        // (Open the file and update it.)
    }
}
```

You can respond to the HttpApplication.Start event in the global.asax file to create a global instance of the Logger class, as follows:

```
protected void Application_Start(Object sender, EventArgs e)
{
    Application["Logger"] = new Logger();
}
```

Now if you want to ensure that you have exclusive access to the Logger object, you would use the lock statement, as shown here:

```
Logger log = (Logger)Application["Logger"];
lock (log)
{
    // Update the file safely.
    log.LogMessage(myMessage);
}
```

Keep in mind that this approach is really just a crude way to compensate for the inherit limitations of a file-based system. It won't allow you to manage more complex tasks, like having individual users read and write pieces of text in the same file at the same time. Additionally, while a file is locked for one client, other requests will have to wait. This is guaranteed to slow down application performance and lead to an exception if the object isn't released before the second client times out. Unless you invest considerable effort refining your threading code (for example, you can use classes in the System.Threading namespace to test if an object is available, and take alternative action if it isn't), this technique is only suitable for very small-scale web applications. It's for this reason that ASP.NET applications almost never use file-based logs—instead, they write to the Windows event log or a database.

Serialization

There's one more technique that can be used to store data in a file—*serialization*. Serialization is a higher-level model that's built on .NET streams. Essentially, serialization allows you to convert an entire live object into a series of bytes, and write those bytes into a stream object like the FileStream. You can then read those bytes back at a later time to re-create the original object.

In order for serialization to work, your object must all meet the following criteria:

- The object must have a Serializable attribute preceding the class declaration.

- All the public and private variables of the class must be serializable.

- If the class derives from another class, all parent classes must also be serializable.

Here's a serializable class that you could use to store log information:

```
[Serializable()]
public class LogEntry
{
    private string message;
    private DateTime date;

    public string Message
    {
        get {return message;}
        set {message = value;}
    }
```

```
    public string DateTime
    {
        get {return date;}
        set {date = value;}
    }

    public LogEntry(string message)
    {
        this.message = message;
        this.date = DateTime.Now;
    }
}
```

Tip In some cases, a class might contain data that shouldn't be serialized. For example, you might have a large field you can recalculate or re-create easily, or you might have some sensitive data that could pose a security request. In these cases, you can add a NonSerialized attribute before the appropriate variable to indicate it shouldn't be persisted. When you re-create the class, nonserialized variables will return to their default values.

You may remember serializable classes from earlier in this book. Classes need to be serializable in order to be stored in the view state for a page or put into an out-of-process session state store. In those cases, you let .NET serialize the object for you automatically. However, you can also manually serialize a serializable object and store it in a file or another data source of your choosing (like a binary field in a database).

To convert a serializable object into a stream of bytes, you need to use a class that implements the IFormatter interface. The .NET Framework includes two such classes: BinaryFormatter, which serializes an object to a compact binary representation, and SoapFormatter, which uses the SOAP XML format, and results in a longer text-based message. The BinaryFormatter class is found in the System.Runtime.Serialization.Formatters.Binary namespace, while SoapFormatter is found in the System.Runtime.Serialization.Formatters.Soap namespace. (In order to use SoapFormatter, you also need to add a reference to the assembly System.Runtime.Serialization.Formatters.Soap.dll.) Both methods serialize all the private and public data in a class, along with the assembly and type information needed to ensure that the object can be deserialized exactly.

To create a simple example, let's consider what you need to do to rewrite the logging page shown earlier to use object serialization instead of writing data directly to the file. The first step is to change the Log() method so that it creates a LogEntry object and uses the BinaryFormatter to serialize it into the existing file, as follows:

```
private void Log(string message)
{
    // Check for the file.
    FileMode mode;
    if (ViewState["LogFile"] == null)
```

```
    {
        ViewState["LogFile"] = GetFileName();
        mode = FileMode.Create;
    }
    else
    {
        mode = FileMode.Append;
    }

    // Write the message.
    string fileName = (string)ViewState["LogFile"];
    using (FileStream fs = new FileStream(fileName, mode))
    {
        // Create a LogEntry object.
        LogEntry entry = new LogEntry(message);

        // Create a formatter.
        BinaryFormatter formatter = new BinaryFormatter();

        // Serialize the object to a file.
        formatter.Serialize(fs, entry);
    }
}
```

The last step is change the code that fills the label with the complete log text. Instead of reading the raw data, it now deserializes each saved instance using the BinaryFormatter, as shown here:

```
private void cmdRead_Click(object sender, System.EventArgs e)
{
    if (ViewState["LogFile"] != null)
    {
        string fileName = (string)ViewState["LogFile"];
        using (FileStream fs = new FileStream(fileName, FileMode.Open))
        {
            // Create a formatter.
            BinaryFormatter formatter = new BinaryFormatter();

            // Get all the serialized objects.
            while (fs.Position < fs.Length)
            {
                // Deserialize the object from the file.
                LogEntry entry = (LogEntry)formatter.Deserialize(fs);

                // Display its information.
                lblInfo.Text += entry.Date.ToString() + "<br>";
                lblInfo.Text += entry.Message + "<br>";
            }
```

```
        }
    }
}
```

So exactly what information is stored when an object is serialized? Both the BinaryFormatter and the SoapFormatter use a proprietary .NET serialization format that includes information about the class, the assembly that contains the class, and all the data stored in the class member variables. Although the binary format isn't completely interpretable, here's the result of displaying it as ordinary ASCII text:

```
"\0'\0\0\0????'\0\0\0\0\0\0\0\f'\0\0\0GChapter13, Version=1.0.1725.39368,
Culture=neutral, PublicKeyToken=null''\0\0\0'Chapter13.LogEntry
'\0\0\0\amessage'date'\0\r'\0\0\0''\0\0\0Page loaded for the first time.'?C?Dn?\b\v"
```

The SoapFormatter produces more readily interpretable output, although it stores the exact same information (in a less compact form). The assembly information is compressed into a namespace string, and the data is enclosed in separate elements:

```
<SOAP-ENV:Envelope xmlns:xsi="http://www.w3.org/2001/XMLSchema-instance"
 xmlns:xsd="http://www.w3.org/2001/XMLSchema"
 xmlns:SOAP-ENC="http://schemas.xmlsoap.org/soap/encoding/"
 xmlns:SOAP-ENV="http://schemas.xmlsoap.org/soap/envelope/"
 xmlns:clr="http://schemas.microsoft.com/soap/encoding/clr/1.0"
 SOAP-ENV:encodingStyle="http://schemas.xmlsoap.org/soap/encoding/">
  <SOAP-ENV:Body>
    <a1:LogEntry id="ref-1"
     xmlns:a1=
"http://schemas.microsoft.com/clr/nsassem/Chapter13/Chapter13%2C%20Version
%3D1.0.1725.39300%2C%20Culture%3Dneutral%2C%20PublicKeyToken%3Dnull">
        <message id="ref-3">Page loaded for the first time.</message>
        <date>2004-09-21T22:50:04.8677568-04:00</date>
    </a1:LogEntry>
  </SOAP-ENV:Body>
</SOAP-ENV:Envelope>
```

Clearly, this information is only suitable for .NET-only applications. However, it provides the most convenient, compact way to store the contents of an entire object.

Summary

In this chapter, you learned how to use the .NET classes for retrieving file system information. You also examined how to work with files and how to serialize objects. Along the way you learned how data binding can work with the file classes, how to plug security holes with the Path class, and how to deal with file contention in multiuser scenarios.

PART THREE

■■■

Security

CHAPTER 14

The ASP.NET Security Infrastructure

Website security is an issue that we all have to deal with, whether we need to protect sensitive data, authenticate users, or just provide basic personalization and customization features. In all of these scenarios, there is the need for an underlying framework that can provide basic security functionality, such as identifying a user and determining a user's permissions to access a specific resource.

In the past, there have been a limited number of options and programmers have often had to painstakingly build their own security infrastructure to get the functionality they need. Of course, there is always the option of purchasing a separate product that provides a security framework, such as Microsoft's Site Server or Commerce Server 2000 (which not only handles security, personalization, and customization, but also content management). However, purchasing such a product can mean spending considerable sums of money, more administration and maintenance needs, and more hardware requirements.

An ideal solution is to use a programming framework that provides built-in security features, such as ASP.NET and the .NET Framework. They provide a security infrastructure that includes classes for handling authentication, role-based authorization, impersonation, encryption, and code-access security. Best of all, the .NET security features are extensible, giving you a basic foundation you can extend to create custom security solutions.

This chapter provides a roadmap to the security features in ASP.NET. In later chapters, you'll dig deeper into each of the topics covered in this chapter. Here, you'll get a quick introduction to the key features of .NET security. You'll see how the .NET authentication providers and authorization modules work, and you'll learn how the user's security context is represented with identity and principal objects.

ASP.NET Security Processes

ASP.NET provides the functionality needed for several key security processes. These include the following:

- **Authentication.** Authentication asks the question "Who goes there?" It determines the identity of the user that is accessing your site.

- **Authorization.** Authorization asks the question "What is your clearance level?" In other words, is the user who is accessing your site authorized to use the resource they are requesting?

- **Impersonation.** Impersonation allows a user to assume the identity of another user to perform certain actions. By default, ASP.NET websites don't use any impersonation, and all code executes under the identity of a fixed Windows account.

- **Encryption.** Encryption scrambles data so that it can't be understood by others. Encryption can be used to have a secure exchange of information between a client browser and a web server, or it can allow you to store information in a database or in a file so that it can't be easily read by malicious users.

The following sections explore each of these topics.

Authentication

Authentication is the process of discovering a user's identity, and ensuring the authenticity of this identity. The process of authentication is analogous to checking in at a conference registration table. First, you provide some credentials to prove your identity (such as a driver's license or a passport). Once your identity is verified with this information, you are issued a conference badge that you carry with you when you are at the conference. Anyone you meet at the conference can immediately determine your identity by looking at your badge, which typically contains basic identity information, such as your first and last name. This whole process is an example of authentication. Once your identity is established, you are given a *token* that identifies you so that everywhere you go within a particular area, your identity is known.

In an ASP.NET application, authentication is implemented through one of four possible authentication systems:

- Windows authentication

- Forms authentication

- Passport authentication

- A custom authentication process

In each of these, the user provides credentials when logging in. The user's identity is tracked in different ways depending on the type of authentication. For example, the Windows operating system uses a 96-bit number called a SID (security identifier) to identify each logged on user. In ASP.NET forms authentication, the user is given a forms authentication ticket, which is a combination of values that are encrypted and placed in a cookie.

All authentication does is allow the application to identify who a user is on each request. This works very well for personalization and customization, because you can use the identity information to render user-specific messages on the web pages, alter the appearance of the website, add custom content based on user preferences, and so on. However, on its own authentication isn't enough to restrict the tasks that a user is allowed to perform based on that user's identity. For that, you need authorization, as described in the next section.

Authorization

Authorization is the process of determining the rights and restrictions assigned to an authenticated user. In the conference analogy, authorization is the process of being granted permission to a particular type of session, such as the keynote speech. At most conferences it is possible to purchase different types of access, such as full access, pre-conference only, or exhibition hall only. That means that if you want to attend the keynote address at Microsoft's Professional Developer Conference to hear what Bill Gates has to say, you must have the proper permissions (the correct conference pass). As you enter the keynote presentation hall, a member of staff will look at your conference badge. Based on the information on the badge, the staff member will let you pass or will tell you that you cannot enter. This is an example of authorization. Depending on information related to your identity, you are either granted or denied access to the resources you ask for.

The conference example is a case of *role-based authorization*—authorization being based on the role or group the user belongs to, not who the user is. In other words, you are authorized to enter the room for the keynote address based on the role (type of pass), not your specific identity information (first and last name). In many cases, role-based authorization is preferable because it's much easier to implement. If the staff member needed to consult a list with the name of each allowed guest, the process of authorization would be much more awkward. The same is true in a web application, although the roles are more likely to be managers, administrators, guests, salespeople, clients, and so on.

In a web application, different types of authorization happen at different levels. For example, at the topmost level your code can examine the user identity and decide whether or not to continue with a given operation. On a lower level, you can configure ASP.NET to deny access to specific web pages or directories for certain users or roles. At an even lower level, when your code performs various tasks like connecting to a database, opening a file, writing to an event log, and so on, the Windows operating system checks the permissions of the Windows account that's executing the code. In most situations, you won't rely on this bottommost level, because your code will always run under a fixed account. In IIS 5, this is the account named ASPNET. In IIS 6, this is the fixed network service account. (In both cases, you can override the default account, as described in Chapter 2.)

There are sound reasons for using a fixed account to run ASP.NET code. In almost all applications, the rights allocated to the user don't match the rights needed by your application, which works on behalf of the user. Generally, your code needs a broader set of permissions to perform incidental tasks, and you won't want to give these permissions to every user who might access your web application. For example, your code may need to create a log record when a failure occurs, even though the current user isn't allowed to directly write to the Windows Event log, file, or database. Similarly, ASP.NET applications always require rights to the c:\[WinDir]\Microsoft.NET\[Version]\Temporary ASP.NET Files directory to create and cache a compiled machine language version of your web pages. Finally, you might want to use an authentication system that has nothing to do with Windows. For example, an e-commerce application might verify user e-mail addresses against a server-side database. In this case, the user's identity doesn't correspond to a Windows account.

In a few rare cases, you'll want to give your code the ability to temporarily assume the identity of the user. This type of approach is much more common when creating ASP.NET applications for local networks where users already have a carefully defined set of Windows privileges. In this case, you need to supplement your security arsenal with impersonation, as described in the next section.

Impersonation

Impersonation is the process of executing code in the context of another user identity. By default, all ASP.NET code is executed using a fixed machine-specific account (typically ASPNET). To execute code using another identity, you can use the built-in impersonation capabilities of ASP.NET. You can use a predefined user account, or you can assume the user's identity, if the user has already been authenticated using a Windows account.

There are two basic reasons that you might want to use impersonation:

- To give each web application different permissions. In IIS 5, the default account that's specified in the machine.config file is used for all web applications on the computer. If you want to give different web applications different permissions, you can use impersonation to designate different Windows accounts for each application.

- To make use of existing Windows user permissions. For example, consider an application that retrieves information from various files that already have user-specific or group-specific permissions set. Rather than code the authorization logic in your ASP.NET application, you can use impersonation to assume the identity of the current user. That way, Windows will perform the authorization for you, checking permissions as soon as you attempt to access a file.

These two scenarios are fundamentally different. In the first scenario, impersonation is used to define a single specific account. In this case, no matter what user accesses the application, and no matter what type of user-level security you use, the code will run under the account you've set. In the second scenario, the users must be authenticated by IIS. The web page code will then execute under the identity of the appropriate user. You'll learn more about these options in Chapter 16.

Encryption

Encryption is the process of scrambling data so that it's unreadable by other users. Encryption in ASP.NET is a completely separate feature from authentication, authorization, and impersonation. It can be used in combination with these features, or on its own.

There are two ways that you might want to use encryption in a web application:

- To protect communication (data over the wire). For example, you might want to make sure that an eavesdropper on the public Internet can't read a credit card number that's used to purchase an item on your e-commerce site. The industry standard approach to this problem is to use SSL (Secure Sockets Layer). SSL isn't implemented by ASP.NET. Instead, it's a feature provided by IIS. Your web-page (or web-service) code is identical whether SSL is used or not.

- To protect permanent information (data in a database or in a file). For example, you might want to store a user credit card in a database record for future use. Although you could store this data in plain text and assume the web server won't be compromised, this is never a good idea. Instead, you should use the encryption classes that are provided with .NET to manually encrypt data before you store it.

It's worth noting that the .NET encryption classes aren't directly tied to ASP.NET. In fact, you can use them in any type of .NET application. You'll learn how to take control of custom encryption in Chapter 18.

Pulling It All Together

So, how do authentication, authorization, and impersonation all work together in a web application?

When a user first comes to your website, they are anonymous. In other words, your application doesn't know (and doesn't care) who they are. Unless you authenticate them, this is the way it stays.

By default, anonymous users can access any ASP.NET web page. But when a user requests a web page that doesn't permit anonymous access, several steps take place (as shown in Figure 14-1):

1. The request is sent to the web server. Since the user identity is not known at this time, the user is asked to log in (using a custom web page, or a browser-based login dialog box). The specific details of the login process depend on the type of authentication you're using.

2. The user provides their credentials, which are then verified, either by your application (in the case of forms authentication) or automatically by IIS (in the case of Windows authentication).

3. If the user credentials are legitimate, the user is granted access to the web page. If their credentials are not legitimate, then the user is prompted to log in again, or they are redirected to a web page with an "access denied" message.

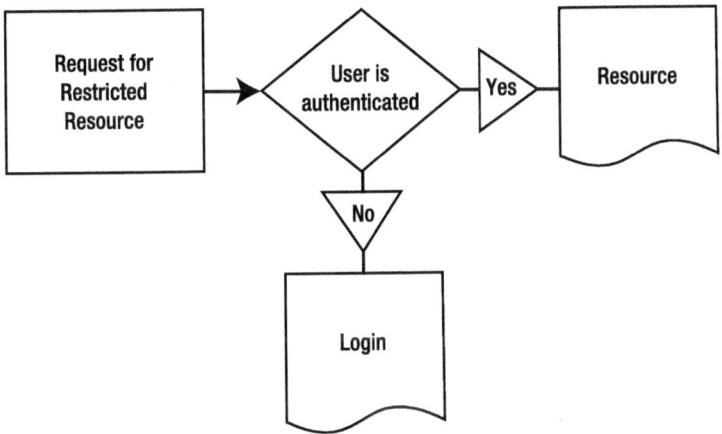

Figure 14-1. *Requesting a web page that requires authentication*

When a user requests a secure web page that only allows specific users or users in specific roles, the process is similar, but an extra step takes place (see Figure 14-2):

1. The request is sent to the web server. Since the user identity is not known at this time, the user is asked to log in (using a custom web page, or a browser-based login dialog box). The specific details of the login process depend on the type of authentication you're using.

2. The user provides their credentials, which are verified with the application. This is the authentication stage.

3. The authenticated user's credentials or roles are compared to the list of allowed users or roles. If the user is in the list, then they are granted access to the resource; otherwise, access is denied.

4. Users who have access denied are either prompted to log in again, or they are redirected to a web page with an "access denied" message.

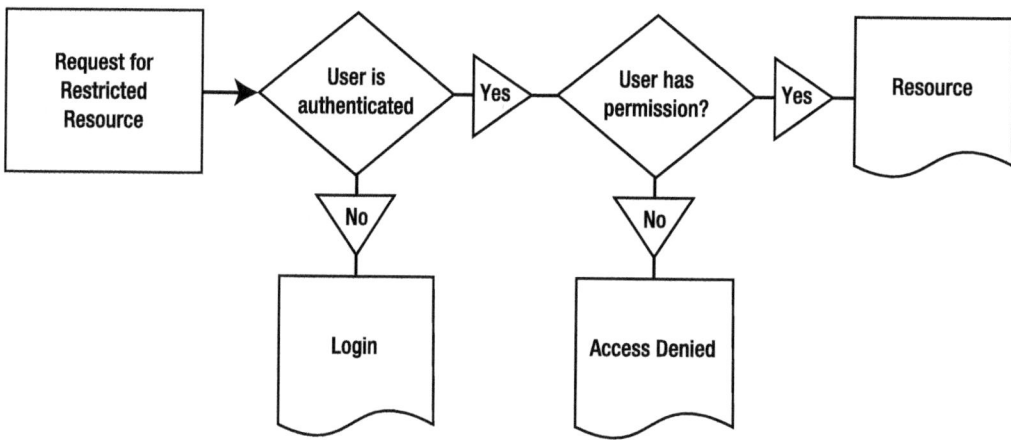

Figure 14-2. *Requesting a web page that requires authentication and authorization*

Authentication

Because web applications use the stateless HTTP protocol, no information is retained for the user between requests. As a result, the user must be authenticated and authorized at the beginning of each request. ASP.NET handles this by firing global application events. Authentication modules can handle these events to perform user authentication. Not all requests require authentication or authorization. However, the related events always fire.

The two primary events you need to deal with are the AuthenticateRequest and AuthorizeRequest events. These aren't the only events that fire, but these are the most useful. Figure 14-3 shows the order of security-related application events.

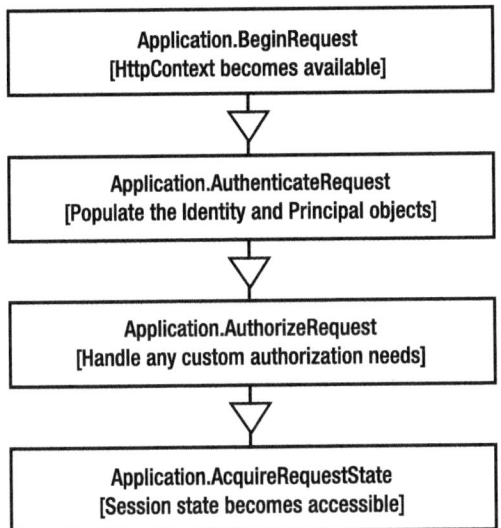

Figure 14-3. *Security-related application events*

■**Note** Session state is not accessible until *after* the authorization and authentication events have fired. This prevents you from storing user identity information in session state. Instead, other mechanisms must be used.

The AuthenticateRequest event is raised by the HttpApplication object when a request requires authentication. Once the user is authenticated (typically supplying some sort of user credentials like a cookie with user information), the next step is to make sure the user identity information is readily available for the rest of the page processing cycle. To accomplish this, a new object with user information must be created and attached to the User property of the current HttpContext.

The AuthorizeRequest event is raised after the user has been authenticated in the AuthenticateRequest event. Authorization modules use AuthorizeRequest to check whether the user is authorized for the resource they are requesting.

You can handle the security events in the global.asax file. However, usually you won't handle these events unless you're specifically creating a custom authentication or authorization system. Instead, you'll use an HTTP module that responds to these events and performs the authentication and authorization automatically.

The Built-In Authentication Modules

Authentication is implemented in ASP.NET through the use of specialized HTTP modules. You choose which authentication module you want to use with the <authentication> element in the web.config configuration file. All authentication modules implement the IHttpModule interface, which provides access to application events (as explained in Chapter 6). This allows them to handle the HttpApplication.AuthenticateRequest event. Each module also exposes its own Authenticate event that you can handle in the global.asax file.

> **Note** The <authentication> element can only be used in the web.config that is in the root directory of an application. Attempting to use it in a subdirectory will cause an error. This means that only one authentication type can be defined for each application. However, different subdirectories can define different authorization rules.

There are three core authentication modules provided with ASP.NET:

- FormsAuthenticationModule
- WindowsAuthenticationModule
- PassportAuthenticationModule

The following sections briefly describe each module.

The FormsAuthenticationModule

The FormsAuthenticationModule uses forms authentication, which allows you to design your own login pages, write your own authentication logic, but rely on ASP.NET to track user and role information using an encrypted cookie. The FormsAuthenticationModule is active when the <authorization> element is set as follows:

```
<authentication mode="Forms" />
```

Chapter 15 explores forms authentication in more detail.

The WindowsAuthenticationModule

The WindowsAuthenticationModule works in conjunction with IIS to perform Windows authentication. This module is active when the <authentication> element in the web.config file is set as follows:

```
<authentication mode="Windows" />
```

Chapter 16 explores Windows authentication in more detail.

The PassportAuthenticationModule

The PassportAuthenticationModule is active when the <authentication> element in the web.config file is set as follows:

```
<authentication mode="Passport" />
```

The PassportAuthenticationModule provides a wrapper for Microsoft's Passport authentication service. When using Passport, users are authenticated using the information in Microsoft's Passport database (the same technology that powers the free Hotmail e-mail system). The advantage of Passport is that you can make use of existing user credentials (such as e-mail address and password), without forcing users to go through a separate registration process. The disadvantage is that you need to enter into a licensing agreement with Microsoft, and pay a yearly fee based on use.

ASP.NET doesn't include full support for Passport authentication. In order to use it successfully, you'll need to download and install the Passport .NET SDK on your web server. This book doesn't cover Passport, but you can learn more (and download the SDK) at `www.microsoft.com/net/services/passport`.

Authorization

Once a user is authenticated, information like the user's name and security context is automatically made available through the web page User object. You can use this information to implement authorization. There are several possible places to put your authorization rules:

- **In the web.config file.** You can define authorization rules that selectively prevent or allow access to specific files or directories. This approach provides a coarse-grained level of authorization—for example, there's no way to allow only certain portions of a web page.

- **In your code.** You can use the User object to determine the current user and the current user's roles. Based on this information, you can tailor what actions your code performs or allows.

- **Using impersonation.** With impersonation, your web page code can assume the identity of the authenticated user. Windows will then perform the required authorization checks whenever you access a protected resource, like a file, database, or registry item. However, your code will need to be prepared to handle the security exceptions that could occur if users attempt to access a resource that they do not have the right to access.

Note User-specific impersonation only works with Windows authentication. If you use forms authentication, the user identity doesn't correspond to a Windows account, so there's no way for your code to impersonate it.

You'll learn more about authorization in Chapter 17. But first, the following sections introduce the security objects that represent user information.

The Security Context

Regardless of the authentication schema chosen, ASP.NET uses the same underlying framework to represent user and role information. Users who log in to a web application are granted a *principal* and an *identity* based on the credentials they have provided. The principal object represents the current security context of the user. It allows you to perform role-based authorization, and it provides a reference to the corresponding identity object. The identity object provides user information like the user name.

The IPrincipal Interface

All principal objects implement the IPrincipal interface, which defines a core set of functionality. When you access the User property of the current web page (System.Web.UI.Page) or from the current HTTP context (HttpContext.Current), you're accessing an IPrincipal object that represents the security context of the current user.

The IPrincipal interface defines a single property named Identity, which retrieves an IIdentity object that provides information about the current user. The IPrincipal interface also defines a single method named IsInRole(), which allows you to test whether the current user is a member of a specific role.

Here's an example that uses the IsInRole() method to test whether the current user is a member of a role named Admin:

```
if (HttpContext.Current.User.IsInRole("Admin"))
{
    // (Do something.)
}
```

When using Windows authentication or forms authentication, the principal object is created automatically. However, it's also possible to create a principal object on the fly, with user and role information that you extract from another location, like a custom database. You'll see examples of both techniques in later chapters.

The IIdentity Interface

Like the IPrincipal interface, the IIdentity interface is used to provide consistency no matter what authentication scheme you use. All Identity objects must implement IIdentity.

The IIdentity interface defines the basic information needed to represent the current user. At a minimum, this includes the following three read-only properties:

- **AuthenticationType.** Returns the type of authentication used as a string (Forms, Passport, NTLM [NT LAN Manager], or a custom authentication type).

- **IsAuthenticated.** Returns a Boolean value that indicates whether the user has been authenticated (true) or is anonymous (false).

- **Name.** Returns the name of the current user as a string.

You can access the IIdentity object that represents the current user through the IIPrincipal object. Here's an example that uses this technique to check whether the user has been authenticated:

```
if (HttpContext.Current.User.Identity.IsAuthenticated)
{
    lblUserName.Text = HttpContext.Current.User.Identity.Name +
      " is logged in";
}
```

The type of identity object depends on the type of authentication used. All in all, there are four identity classes included in the .NET Framework:

- **System.Web.Security.FormsIdentity.** Represents a user that's logged on using forms authentication.

- **System.Security.Principal.WindowsIdentity.** Represents a Windows user account.

- **System.Web.Security.PassportIdentity.** Provides a class to be used by the PassportAuthenticationModule.

- **System.Security.Principal.GenericIdentity.** Represents a generic user identity. (You can use this to create identities if you're creating a custom authentication system.)

Secure Sockets Layer

SSL (Secure Sockets Layer) technology is used to encrypt communication over the HTTP protocol. SSL is supported by a wide range of browsers, and ensures that information exchanged between a client and a web server can't be easily deciphered by an eavesdropper. SSL is important for hiding sensitive information like credit card numbers and confidential company details, but it's also keenly important with user authentication. For example, if you create a login page where the user submits a password and user ID, you must use SSL to encrypt this information. Otherwise, a malicious user could intercept the user credentials and use them to log on to the system at a later date.

SSL is not a part of ASP.NET. Instead, it's provided by IIS. Because SSL operates underneath HTTP, using SSL does not change the way you deal with HTTP requests. All the encryption and decryption work is taken care of by the SSL capabilities of the web server software (in this case, IIS). The only difference is that the URL for addresses protected by SSL begins with https:// rather than http://. SSL traffic also flows over a different port (typically web servers use port 443 for SSL requests and port 80 for normal requests).

In order for a server to support SSL connections, it must have an installed X.509 certificate (the name X.509 was chosen to correspond with the X.500 directory standard). To implement SSL, you need to purchase a certificate, install it, and configure IIS appropriately. We'll cover these steps in the following sections.

Understanding Certificates

Before sending sensitive data, a client must decide whether to trust a website. *Certificates* were designed to serve this purpose, by making it possible to partially verify a user's identity. Certificates can be installed on any type of computer, but they are most often found on web servers.

With certificates, an organization purchases a certificate from a known certificate authority (CA) and installs it on their web server. The client implicitly trusts the certificate authority, and is therefore willing to trust certificate information signed by the CA. This model works well because it is unlikely that a malicious user will go to the expense of purchasing and installing a falsified certificate. The CA also retains information about each registered user. However, a certificate does not in any way ensure the trustworthiness of the server, the safety of the application, or the legitimacy of the business. In this way, certificates are fundamentally limited in scope.

The certificate itself contains certain identifying information. It is signed with the certificate authority's private key to guarantee that it is authentic and has not been modified. The industry-standard certificate type, known as x.509v3, contains the following basic information:

- The holder's name, organization, and address

- The holder's public key, which will be used to negotiate a secure SSL session key for encrypting communication

- The certificate's validation dates

- The certificate's serial number

In addition, a certificate might also include business-specific information, like the certificate holder's industry, the length of time they have been in business, and so on.

The two biggest certificate authorities are listed here:

- **Thawte.** www.thawte.com

- **Verisign.** www.verisign.com

If you don't need the identity validation function of certificate authorities (for example, if your certificates will only be used on a local intranet), you can create and use your own certificates, and configure all clients to trust them. This requires Active Directory and Certificate Server (which is a built-in part of Windows 2003 Server and Windows 2000 Server). For more information, consult a dedicated book about Windows network administration.

Understanding SSL

As described in the last section, every certificate includes a public key. A public key is part of an *asymmetric key pair*. The basic idea is that the public key is freely provided to anyone who's interested. The corresponding private key is kept carefully locked away, and is only available to the server. The interesting twist is that anything that's encrypted with one of the keys is decipherable with the other. That means a client can retrieve the public key, and use it to encode a secret message that can only be decrypted with the corresponding private key. In other words, the client can create a message that only the server can read.

This process is called *asymmetric encryption*, and it's a basic building block of SSL. An important principle of asymmetric encryption is that you can't determine a private key by analyzing the corresponding public key. To do so would be computationally expensive (even more difficult than cracking one of the encrypted messages). However, asymmetric encryption also has its limitations—namely it's much slower and generates much larger messages than symmetric encryption.

Symmetric encryption is the type of encryption that most people are intuitively familiar with. It uses the same secret key to encrypt a message as to decrypt it. The drawback with symmetric encryption is that both parties need to know the secret value in order to have a conversation. However, you can't transmit this information over the Internet, because a malicious user might intercept it, and then be able to decipher the following encrypted conversation. The great trick of SSL is to combine asymmetric and symmetric encryption.

Asymmetric encryption is used to manage the initial key exchange—in other words, to agree on a secret value. Then, this secret value is used to symmetrically encrypt all subsequent messages, which ensures the best possible performance.

The whole process works like this:

1. The client sends a request to connect to the server.

2. The server signs its certificate and sends it to the client. This concludes the handshake portion of the exchange.

3. The client checks whether the certificate was issued by a CA it trusts. If so, it proceeds to the next step. In a web-browser scenario, the client may warn the user with an ominous sounding message if it does recognize the CA, and allow the user to decide whether to proceed.

4. The client compares the information in the certificate with the information received from the site (including its domain name and its public key). The client also verifies that the server-side certificate is valid, has not been revoked, and is issued by a trusted CA. Then the client accepts the connection.

5. The client tells the server what encryption keys it supports for communication.

6. The server chooses the strongest shared key length, and informs the client.

7. Using the indicated key length, the client randomly generates a symmetric encryption key. This will be used for the duration of the transaction between the server and the client. It ensures optimum performance, because symmetric encryption is much faster than asymmetric encryption.

8. The client encrypts the session key using the server's public key (from the certificate), and then it sends the encrypted session key to the server.

9. The server receives the encrypted session key and decrypts it using its private key. Both the client and server now have the shared secret key, and they can use it to encrypt all communication for the duration of the session.

You'll notice that the symmetric key is generated randomly, and only used for the duration of a session. This limits the security risk. First of all, it's harder to break encrypted messages using cryptanalysis, because messages from other sessions can't be used. Secondly, even if the key is determined by a malicious user, it will only remain valid for the course of the session.

Another interesting point is the fact that the client must generate the symmetric key. This is because the client has the server's public key, which can be used to encrypt a message that only the server can read. The server does not have corresponding information about the client, and thus cannot yet encrypt a message. This also means that if the client supplies a weak key, the entire interaction could be compromised. For example, older versions of the Netscape browser used a weak random number generator to create the symmetric key. This would make it much easier for a malicious user to guess the key.

Installing Certificates in IIS

When deploying an application, you will probably want to purchase certificates from a genuine certificate authority like VeriSign (see, for example, www.verisign.com). This is particularly the case with websites and Internet browsers, which recognize a limited number of certificate authorities automatically. If you use a test certificate to encrypt communication with a secured portion of a website, for example, the client browser will display a warning that the certificate is not from a known certificate authority.

IIS Manager allows you to create a certificate request automatically. First, start IIS Manager. Expand the Web Sites group, and right-click your website item (often titled Default Web Site) and choose Properties. Under the Directory Security tab, you'll find a Server Certificate button (see Figure 14-4).

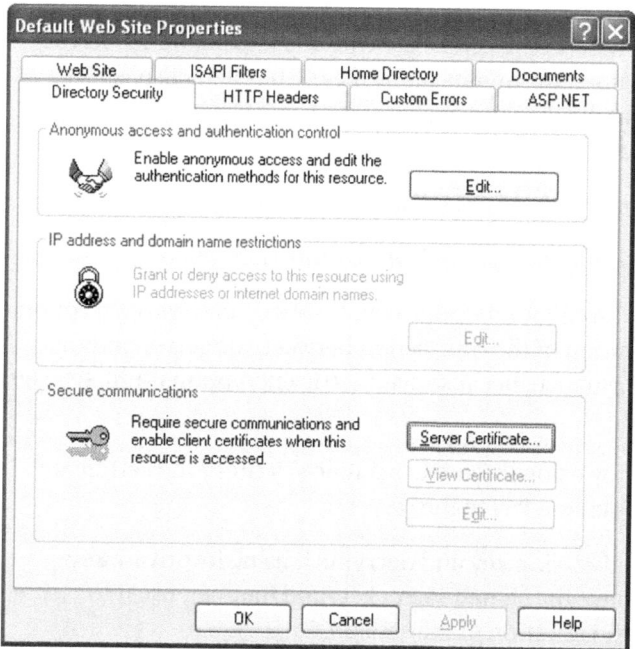

Figure 14-4. *Configuring directory security*

Click the Server Certificate button to start a Web Server Certificate wizard (see Figure 14-5). This wizard requests some basic organization information, and generates a request file. You'll also need to supply a bit length for the key—the higher the bit length, the stronger the key.

The generated file can be saved as a text file, but it must ultimately be e-mailed to a certificate authority. A sample (slightly abbreviated) request file is shown here:

```
Webmaster: administrator@certificatecompany.com
Phone: (555) 555-5555
Server: Microsoft Key Manager for IIS Version 4.0

Common-name: www.yourcompany.com
Organization: YourOrganization
```

```
-----BEGIN NEW CERTIFICATE REQUEST-----
MIIB1DCCAToCAQAwgZMxCzAJBgNVBAYTAlVTMREwDwYDVQQIEwhOZXcgWW9yazEQ
MA4GA1UEBxMHQnVmZmFsbzEeMBwGA1UEChMVVW5pdmVyc2l0eSBhdCBCdWZmYWxv
MRwwGgYDVQQLExNSZXNlYXJjaCBGb3VuZGF0aW9uMSEwHwYDVQQDExh3d3cucmVz
ZWFyY2guYnVmZmFsby5lZHUwgZ8wDQYJKoZIhvcNAQEBBQADgY0AMIGJAoGBALJO
hbsCagHN4KMbl7uzOGwvcjJeWH8JqIUFVFi352tnoA15PZfCxW18KNtFeBtrbOpf
-----END NEW CERTIFICATE REQUEST-----
```

The certificate authority will return a certificate that you can install according to their instructions. By convention, you should run all SSL communication over port 443, and serve normal web traffic over port 80.

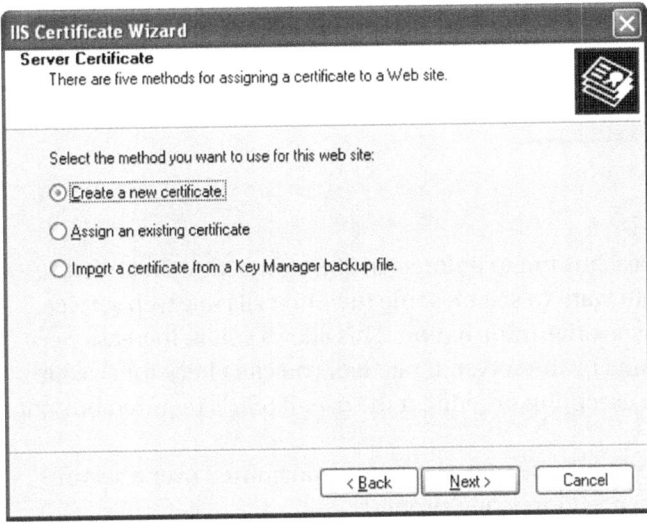

Figure 14-5. *Creating a server certificate request*

Encoding Information with SSL

Once you've installed the certificate, it's fairly easy to use SSL communication. The only other step is to modify your request to use a URL that starts with https:// instead of the http:// prefix. Typically, this means tweaking a Response.Redirect() statement in your code. Because all the encryption and decryption occurs just before the message is sent (or immediately after it is retrieved), your application does not need to worry about deciphering the data manually, manipulating byte arrays, using the proper character encoding, and so on.

At the server side, you can also enforce SSL connections, so that it is impossible to interact with a web service without encrypting communication. Simply right-click the website in IIS Manager, and select the Directory Security tab. In the Secure Communications section, click the Edit button (which is only available after a certificate is installed). Then, choose Require Secure Channel (see Figure 14-6).

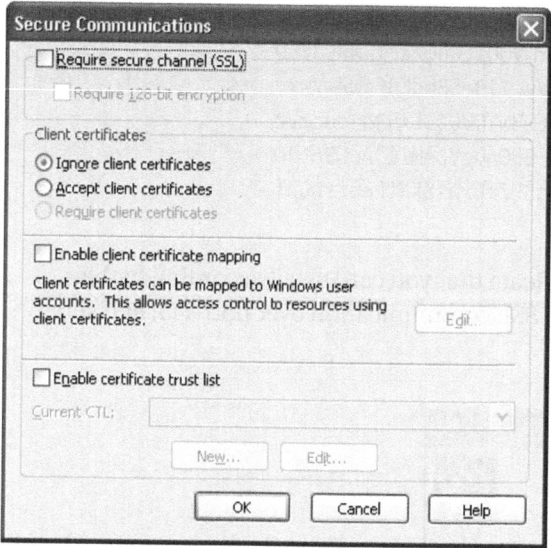

Figure 14-6. *Enforcing SSL access*

Keep in mind that there are good reasons not to enforce an SSL connection for an entire virtual directory. For example, you might want to secure some method calls in a web service, but not secure others that don't return sensitive information. This allows you to increase performance and reduce the work performed by the server. If needed, you can check for a secure connection in your code, and throw an exception or redirect the user if SSL is required but not present.

Here's an example that checks whether the current request is transmitted over a secure connection using the HttpRequest.IsSecureConnection property.

```
if (Request.IsSecureConnection)
{
    // (Application code goes here.)
}
else
{
    // Redirect with https to ensure the page is accessed over SSL.
    Response.Redirect("https://www.mySite.com/account.asmx");
}
```

■**Note** A common mistake is to use localhost or any other aliases for the server host name in an SSL connection. This will not work, because the client attempts to verify that the CN (Common Name) part of the Subject name of the server certificate matches the host name found in the HTTP request during the handshake portion of the SSL exchange.

With SSL, all traffic will be encrypted, not just the sensitive data. For this reason, many web servers use a hardware accelerator to improve the performance of encryption with SSL.

Note Remember, SSL is not tied to ASP.NET in any way. If you want to learn more about SSL, consult a book dedicated to security and IIS.

Summary

With ASP.NET, programmers finally have a comprehensive, full-featured set of security tools. As with many other features in the world of ASP.NET, the presence of a security framework simply means that there is less work for you to do to implement a variety of authentication and authorization scenarios.

The .NET Framework provides three different types of authentication providers, including Windows authentication and forms authentication. Additionally, ASP.NET also includes all of the necessary interfaces and classes you need to build your own authentication and authorization system. In the following chapters, you'll learn about all of these features.

CHAPTER 15

Forms Authentication

If you've ever authenticated users with ASP 3.0, you've probably created your own custom authentication system. One approach is to create a login page that stores some user credentials in session state or in a cookie. You can then check for this information on subsequent requests to identify the user. Although this is a sound overall approach, it's tedious to implement it correctly. Even worse, you need to build it into every new ASP application you create.

Fortunately, ASP.NET includes an authentication module and associated classes that can take care of all the basic plumbing of cookie-based authentication. This system is called *forms authentication*, because users are authenticated by entering their user credentials in a custom HTML login form.

In this chapter, you'll learn how to use and extend forms authentication to meet common web application scenarios.

Introducing Forms Authentication

Forms authentication is a *ticket-based* (also called token-based) system. That means when a user logs in, the user receives a ticket with basic user information. This information is stored in an encrypted cookie that's attached to the response so that it's automatically submitted on each subsequent request.

When the user requests a web page that is not available to anonymous users, ASP.NET automatically checks for the required cookie with the ticket information. If the cookie isn't present, or if the data it contains is invalid or has expired, ASP.NET automatically redirects the user to the login page. The URL of the original request is preserved so that the user can be redirected back to that page after being authenticated.

The login page contains a form for users to enter their credentials (for example, a user name and password). If the details that the user enters are correct, the authentication ticket is created, inserted into a cookie, and attached to the response. The user is then redirected to the originally requested page. Figure 15-1 shows the end-to-end flow.

Of course, many of these steps are optional or configurable. For example, you can always redirect the user to a specific page after logging in, or you can use authentication simply for personalization scenarios, in which case you might make the login process optional. A great part of the strength of forms authentication is its flexibility and customizability.

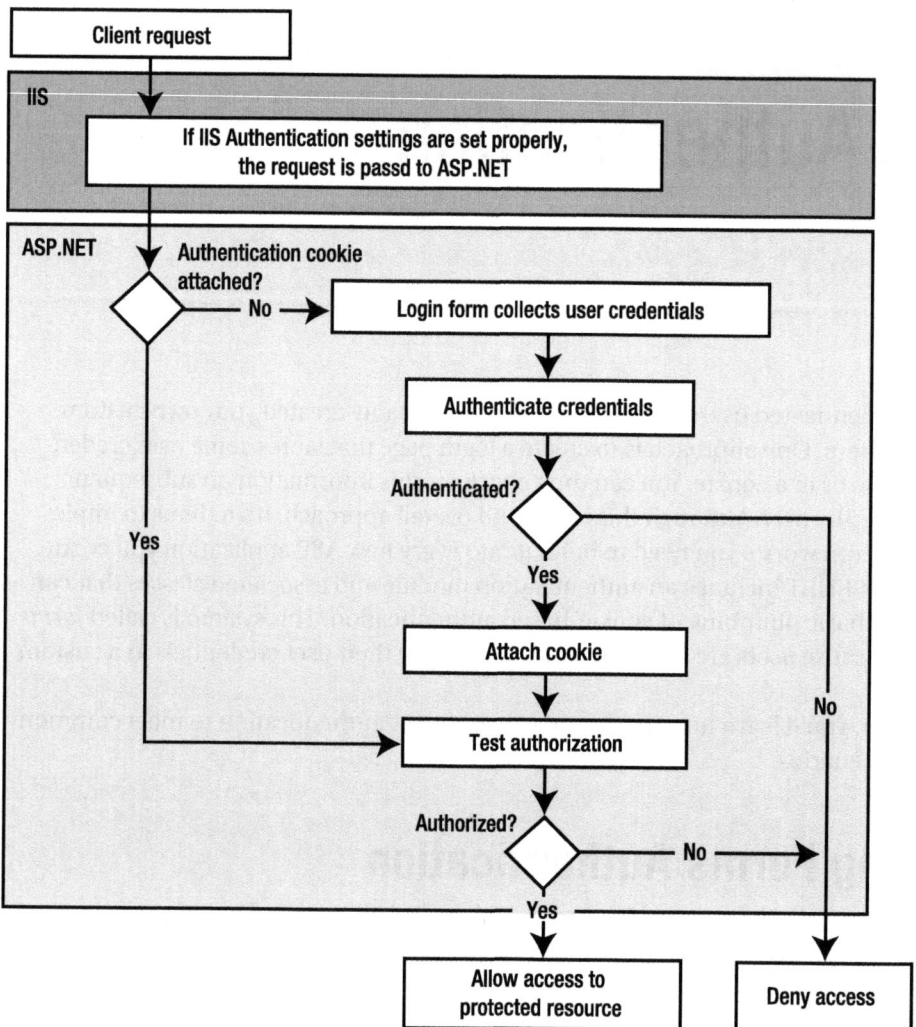

Figure 15-1. *The forms authentication process*

Why Use Forms Authentication?

Cookie authentication is an attractive option for web developers for a number of reasons:

- You have full control over the authentication code.

- You have full control over the appearance of the login form.

- It works for users with any browser.

- It allows you to decide how to store user information.

Let's look at each of these in turn.

Controlling the Authentication Code

Because forms authentication is implemented entirely within ASP.NET, you have complete control over how authentication is performed. You don't need to rely on any external systems, as you do with Windows or Passport authentication. As you will see later in the chapter, you can customize the behavior of forms authentication, adjusting it to suit your needs.

Controlling the Appearance of the Login Form

You have the same degree of control over the appearance of forms authentication as you do over its functionality. You can format the login form in any way you like.

This flexibility in appearance is not available to the other authentication methods. Windows authentication needs the browser to collect credentials, while Passport authentication requires that users leave the website and visit the Passport site to enter their credentials.

Working with a Range of Browsers

Forms authentication uses standard HTML as its user interface, so it can be used by all browsers. Because you can format the login form in any way you like, you can even use forms authentication with browsers that do not use HTML, such as those used in mobile devices. To do this, you would need to detect the browser being used and provide a form in the correct format for the device (such as WML for mobile phones).

Storing User Information

Forms authentication stores user information in the web.config file by default but, as you will see later in the chapter, you can store the information anywhere and anyway you like. You just need to create the code that accesses the data store and retrieves the required information. A common example is to store the user information in a custom database.

This flexibility in the storage of user information also means that you can control how user accounts are created and administered, and attach additional information to user accounts. ASP.NET doesn't include dedicated classes for these tasks—instead, it's up to you to use the ADO.NET classes to connect to the database and retrieve the corresponding information. However, this process is quite straightforward.

Note In the upcoming ASP.NET 2.0, ASP.NET will simplify life by including APIs for storing personalized data and registering users. These features will save even more time when building these parts of your web application.

By comparison, Windows authentication (discussed in the next chapter) is much less flexible. It requires that you set up a Windows user account for each user you want to authenticate. This is obviously a problem if you want to serve large numbers of users or if you want to register users programmatically. It also doesn't allow you to store additional information about users. Instead, you have to store this information separately. Passport authentication has similar limitations. Although Passport stores more user information, it doesn't allow you to add custom information, and it doesn't allow you to take part in user registration or account management.

Why Would You *Not* Use Forms Authentication?

So far, you've considered the reasons that make forms authentication an attractive choice for user authentication. However, there are also downsides to forms authentication:

- You have to create the user interface for users to log in.

- You have to maintain a catalog with user credentials.

- You have to take additional precautions against the interception of network traffic.

The following sections explore these issues.

Creating Your Own Login Interface

As mentioned earlier, forms authentication gives you complete control over the interface that users use to log in to your web application. Along with its benefits, this approach also brings extra work, because you have to create the login page. Other forms of authentication supply some prebuilt portions. If you're using Windows authentication, a standard dialog box is provided by the browser. In Passport authentication, the user interface of the Passport site is always used for logging in.

Creating the login page for forms authentication doesn't require a lot of work. However, it's worth nothing that forms authentication is a toolkit for building an authentication system, rather than an all-in-one system that's complete and ready to use.

Maintaining User Details

When you use forms authentication, you are responsible for maintaining the details of the users who access your system. The most important details are the credentials that the user uses to log in to the system. Not only do you need to devise a way to store them, but you also need to ensure that they are stored securely and backed up in case of system failure.

These considerations don't apply to most other types of authentication. In Windows authentication, user credentials are stored by the underlying operating system. Windows uses a variety of techniques to keep them secure automatically so that you don't need to perform any work of your own. In Passport authentication, the credentials are stored securely on Passport servers.

Interception of Network Traffic

When a user enters credentials for forms authentication, the credentials are sent from the browser to the server in plain text format. This means that anyone intercepting them will be able to read them. This is obviously an insecure situation.

The usual solution to this problem is to use SSL (as described in the previous chapter). You don't need to use SSL for the entire application—instead, you simply need to use it for requests to the login page. The information in the cookie is encrypted, so it's extremely difficult for an attacker to get any information from it. In addition, the cookie only contains the user name, user roles, and additional personalization information that you include. It won't include the password that was used for authentication.

Other authentication mechanisms don't require this extra work. With Windows authentication, you can use a protocol that automatically enforces a secure login process (with the caveat that this is not supported by all browsers and all network environments). With Passport authentication, the login process is handled transparently by the Passport servers, which always use SSL.

Why Not Implement Cookie Authentication Yourself?

Cookie authentication is, on the surface, a fairly straightforward system. You might wonder why you shouldn't just implement it yourself using cookies or session variables.

The answer is the same reason developers don't implement a number of features in ASP.NET—ranging from session state to the web control framework. Not only does ASP.NET save you the trouble, but it also provides an implementation that's secure, well tested, and extensible. Some of the advantages provided by ASP.NET's implementation of forms authentication include the following:

- Security of the authentication cookie.

- Forms authentication is a well-tested system.

- Integration with the .NET security classes.

Keeping the Authentication Cookie Secure

Although cookie authentication seems simple, if it's not implemented correctly you can be left with an insecure system. On their own, cookies are not a safe place to store sensitive information, because a malicious user can easily view and edit cookie data. If your authentication is based on unprotected cookies, attackers will have an easy time compromising your system.

By default, the forms authentication module encrypts its authentication information before placing it in a cookie. It also attaches a hash code, and validates the cookies when they return to the server to verify that no changes have been made. The combination of these two processes makes these cookies very secure, and saves you from needing to write your own security code. Most examples of homemade cookie authentication are far less secure.

Forms Authentication Is Well Tested

Forms authentication is an integral part of ASP.NET, so it has already been used in a number of web applications and websites. Because so many people use the same system, flaws are quickly discovered, publicized, and solved. As long as you keep up to date with patches, you have a high level of protection. On the other hand, if you create your own cookie authentication system, you do not have the advantage of this widespread testing. The first time you'll notice a vulnerability will probably be when your system is compromised.

Integration with the ASP.NET Security Framework

All types of ASP.NET authentication use a consistent framework. Forms authentication is fully integrated with this security framework. For example, it populates the security context (IPrincipal) object and user identity (IIdentity) objects, as it should. This makes it easy to customize the behavior of forms authentication.

The Ingredients of Forms Authentication

Forms authentication is implemented through the following set of classes:

- **FormsAuthenticationModule.** This is the HTTP module that does the background work of dealing with the authentication ticket with each page request.

- **FormsAuthentication.** This class provides static methods and properties that you use when building the login page. For example, once the user is authenticated you can call FormsAuthentication.RedirectFromLoginPage() to send the user back to the originally requested page.

- **FormsIdentity.** This class is an implementation of IIdentity that is specific to forms authentication. The key addition to the FormsIdentity class is the Ticket property, which exposes the authentication ticket. This allows you to store and retrieve additional information in the ticket.

- **FormsAuthenticationTicket.** This class represents the user information that will be encrypted and stored in the authentication cookie.

All of the classes that comprise the forms authentication API are in the System.Web.Security namespace.

Implementing Forms Authentication

To implement forms authentication at its simplest, you must take the following steps:

- Configure forms authentication in the web.config file.

- Restrict anonymous access for a web page, a subdirectory, or the entire application.

- Create a login form to enable users to enter their credentials.

These steps are described in the following sections.

■Note The cookie is encrypted with a machine-specific key that's defined in the machine.config file. Usually, this detail isn't important. However, in a web farm you need to make sure that all servers use the same key so that one server can decrypt the cookie created by another. Refer to Chapter 6 for more information.

Configuring Forms Authentication

In order to use forms authentication, you need to set up the web.config correctly. The first step is to set up the <authentication> element to activate forms authentication, as shown here:

```
<configuration>
    <system.web>
        <!-- Other settings omitted. -->
        <authentication mode="Forms"/>
    </system.web>
</configuration>
```

This tells ASP.NET to load the forms authentication and use it to handle the authentication events like Application_AuthenticateRequest.

Since forms authentication does the work of authentication rather than handing it off to another system (as Windows and Passport authentication do), you have the ability to control several additional details. To do this, you must add the <forms> element inside the <authentication> element:

```
<configuration>
    <system.web>
        <!-- Other settings omitted. -->
        <authentication mode="Forms">
            <forms name="MyAppCookie"
                   loginUrl="login.aspx"
                   protection="All"
                   timeout="30"
                   path="/" />
        </authentication>
    </system.web>
</configuration>
```

These settings are described in Table 15-1. They all supply default values and do not need to be set explicitly.

Table 15-1. *Form Authentication Settings*

Attribute	Description
Name	The name of the HTTP cookie to use for authentication (defaults to .ASPXAUTH). If multiple applications are running on the same web server, you should give each application's security cookie a unique name.
loginUrl	Defines which page the user should be redirected to in order to log in to the application. This could be a page in the root folder of the application or it could be in a subdirectory. The default value is default.aspx.
protection	The type of encryption and validation used for the security cookie (can be All, None, Encryption, or Validation). Validation ensures that the cookie isn't changed during transit by adding a MAC (message authentication code) that can't be faked without significant computational effort (roughly equivalent to breaking an encrypted message using a brute force approach). Encryption ensures that the contents of the cookie are scrambled with a machine-specific key so as to be unreadable by other users. The default value is All, which is recommended.

Continued

Table 15-1. *Continued*

Attribute	Description
timeout	The number of minutes before the cookie expires. ASP.NET will refresh the cookie when it receives a request, as long as half of the cookie's lifetime has expired. The expiry of cookies is a significant concern. If they expire too often, users will have to log in often, and the usability of your application may suffer. If they expire too seldom, you run a greater risk of cookies being stolen and misused. The default value is 30.
path	The path for cookies issued by the application. The default value (\) is recommended, because case-mismatches can prevent the cookie from being sent with a request.

As explained in Table 15-1, you can disable cookie validation and encryption. However, it's reasonable to ask why you would want to remove this protection. The only case in which you might make this choice is if you are not authenticating users for security reasons, but simply identifying users for personalization purposes. In these cases, where it does not really matter if a user impersonates another user, you might decide that the overhead of encrypting, decrypting, and validating the authentication cookies could adversely affect performance without bringing any benefits. Think very carefully before taking this approach, however—it should only be done in situations where it really does not matter if the authentication system is subverted.

Adding Credentials in the web.config File

Forms authentication gives a lot of flexibility in how you store user credentials. One simple approach that's usable in small-scale scenarios is to store them in the web.config file. To store credentials in the web.config, you need to insert a <credentials> element inside the <forms> element, as shown here:

```
<authentication mode="Forms">
  <forms name="MyAppCookie"
    loginUrl="login.aspx"
    timeout="30"
    path="/"
    protection="All">

    <credentials passwordFormat="Clear">
      <user name="dan" password="openSesame" />
      <user name="jenny" password="secret" />
    </credentials>

  </forms>
</authentication>
```

The passwordFormat attribute of the <credentials> tag tells ASP.NET if you have used a hashing algorithm to protect user passwords (which is a technique you'll learn about later in this chapter). This example uses Clear, which indicates that passwords are not hashed and are entered in the web.config file in plain text. The other possible options are MD5 and SHA1, which are two popular hashing algorithms.

Denying Access to Anonymous Users

As mentioned earlier, you do not need to restrict access to pages in order to use authentication. It is perfectly possible to use authentication purely for personalization, so that anonymous users view the same pages as authenticated users (but see slightly different, personalized content). However, in order to demonstrate the redirection functionality of forms authentication, it's useful to create an example that denies access to anonymous users. This will force ASP.NET to redirect anonymous users to the login page.

Authorization is described in detail in Chapter 17. For now, you'll only use the simple technique of denying access to all unauthenticated users. To do this, you must use the <authorization> element of the web.config to add a new authorization rule, as shown here:

```
<configuration>
    <system.web>
        <!-- Other settings omitted. -->
        <authorization>
            <deny users="?" />
        </authorization>
    </system.web>
</configuration>
```

The question mark (?) is a wildcard character that matches all anonymous users. By including this rule in your web.config file, you specify that anonymous users are not allowed. Every user must be authenticated, and every user request will require the security cookie. If you request a page in the application directory now, ASP.NET will detect that the request isn't authenticated, and attempt to redirect the request to the login page (which will probably cause an error, unless you've already created this page).

Tip Unlike the <authentication> element, the <authorization> element is not limited to the web.config in the root of the web application. Instead, it can be used in any subdirectory, thereby allowing you to set different authorization settings for different groups of pages. You'll learn much more about authorization in Chapter 17.

Creating the Login Page

Once you have configured forms authentication and set up a simple authorization rule to require users to log in, the next step is to build the login form.

The two essential parts of a login form are as follows:

- Controls that allow the user to enter user credentials (usually user name and password).

- Code that checks the user credentials. If the credentials are correct, this code should create an authentication ticket and persist it in an authentication cookie. It could also redirect the user to another page.

Figure 15-2 shows a basic login page.

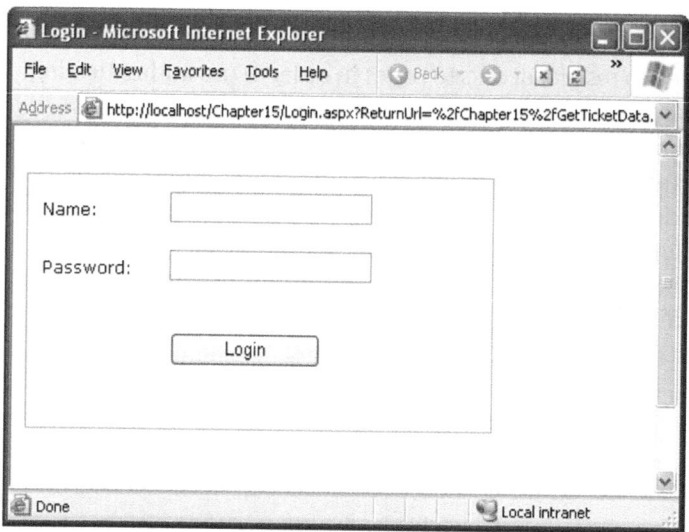

Figure 15-2. *A simple login page*

Tip ASP.NET keeps track of the originally requested page by adding an additional query string parameter with its name. You can see that parameter in the example in Figure 15-2.

This login page consists of a simple assortment of ASP.NET controls, including labels, two text boxes, validation controls, and a button. Here are all the controls that are defined for the page:

```
<form id="Form1" method="post" runat="server">
  <DIV>
    <P>
      Name:
      <asp:TextBox id="txtName" runat="server"
       Width="152px"></asp:TextBox><BR>
      <asp:RegularExpressionValidator id="RegularExpressionValidator1"
       runat="server" ErrorMessage="Contains invalid characters."
       ControlToValidate="txtName" ValidationExpression="[a-z|A-Z|0-9]*"
       Display="Dynamic"></asp:RegularExpressionValidator>
      <asp:RequiredFieldValidator id="RequiredFieldValidator1"
       runat="server" ErrorMessage="Required." ControlToValidate="txtName"
       Display="Dynamic"></asp:RequiredFieldValidator><BR>

      Password:
      <asp:TextBox id="txtPassword" runat="server" Width="152px"
       TextMode="Password"></asp:TextBox><BR>
      <asp:RegularExpressionValidator id="RegularExpressionValidator2"
       runat="server" ErrorMessage="Contains invalid characters."
       ControlToValidate="txtPassword"
```

```
    ValidationExpression="[a-z|A-Z|0-9|!£$%&amp;amp;*@?]*"
    Display="Dynamic"></asp:RegularExpressionValidator>
    <asp:RequiredFieldValidator id="RequiredFieldValidator2"
    runat="server" ErrorMessage="Required."
    ControlToValidate="txtPassword"
    Display="Dynamic"></asp:RequiredFieldValidator></P><P>
    <asp:Button id="cmdLogin" runat="server"
    Text="Login"></asp:Button></P><P>
    <asp:Label id="lblStatus" runat="server"
    ForeColor="#C00000" ></asp:Label>
  </P>
 </DIV>
</form>
```

The validation controls serve two purposes. First, two RequiredFieldValidator controls ensure that both the user name and password boxes are filled in. Second, two RegularExpressionValidator controls ensure that there aren't any invalid characters in the user name or the password. For example, the user-name field is set up to accept only upper and lowercase letters and digits using this expression:

```
ValidationExpression="[a-z|A-Z|0-9]*">
```

The password field accepts the same characters along with some special characters, as defined by this expression:

```
ValidationExpression="[a-z|A-Z|0-9|!£$%&amp;*@?]*">
```

Note that the HTML entity & is used to indicate that the ampersand (&) character is allowed in the password.

Figure 15-3 shows an example of what you'll see if you enter invalid information in the user-name text box.

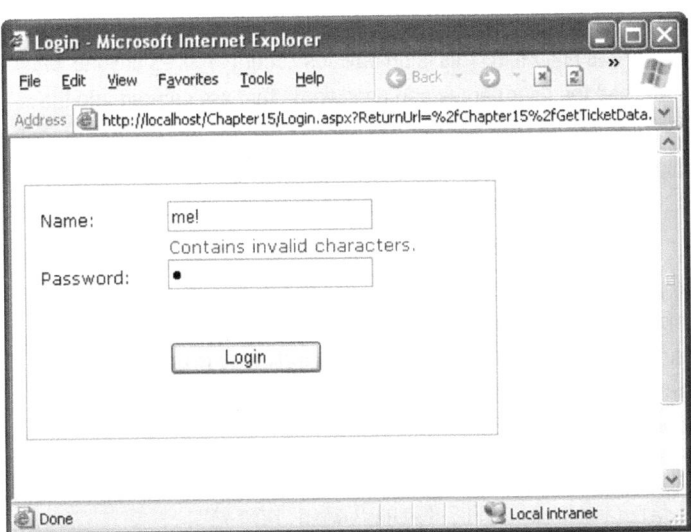

Figure 15-3. *Validation in the login page*

The next step is to create the code that responds when the login button is clicked. First, make sure you've imported the System.Web.Security namespace so that you can access the FormsAuthentication class easily by adding this line at the beginning of your code file:

```
using System.Web.Security;
```

Here's the full code you need to respond to the button click:

```
private void cmdLogin_Click(object sender, System.EventArgs e)
{
    // Check if the control values are valid.
    if (Page.IsValid)
    {
        // Check if the user credentials correspond with a user.
        if (FormsAuthentication.Authenticate(txtName.Text,
            txtPassword.Text))
        {
            // Log the user in, create the cookie,
            // and redirect to the original page.
            FormsAuthentication.RedirectFromLoginPage(txtName.Text, false);
        }
        else
        {
            // Show an error message.
            lblStatus.Text = "Try again.";
        }
    }
}
```

Note Because forms authentication uses standard HTML forms for the entry of credentials, the user name and password are sent over the network as plain text. This is an obvious security risk as anyone who intercepts the network traffic will be able to read the user names and passwords that are entered into the login form. For this reason, it is strongly recommended that the traffic between the browser and the server is encrypted using SSL (as described in Chapter 14), at least while the user is accessing the login page.

The FormsAuthentication class provides two methods that are used in this example. The Authenticate() method checks the specified user name and password against those stored in the web.config and returns a Boolean value indicating whether a match was found. Remember that the methods of FormsAuthentication are static, so you do not need to create an instance of FormsAuthentication to use them—you simply access them through the name of the class, as shown here:

```
if (FormsAuthentication.Authenticate(txtName.Text, txtPassword.Text)) ...
```

If a match is found for the supplied credentials, you can use the RedirectFromLoginPage() method:

```
FormsAuthentication.RedirectFromLoginPage(txtName.Text, false);
```

This method performs several tasks at once:

1. It creates an authentication ticket for the user.

2. It encrypts the information from the authentication ticket.

3. It creates a cookie to persist the encrypted ticket information.

4. It adds the cookie to the HTTP response, sending it to the client.

5. It redirects the user back to the originally requested page.

The second parameter of RedirectFromLoginPage() indicates whether a persistent cookie should be created. Persistent cookies are stored on the user's hard drive and can be reused for later visits. Persistent cookies are described later in this chapter.

Finally, if Authenticate() returns false, an error message is displayed on the page. Feedback like this is always useful. However, make sure it doesn't compromise your security. For example, it's all too common for developers to create login pages that provide separate error messages depending on whether the user has entered a user name that isn't recognized or a correct user name with the wrong password. This is usually not a good idea. If a malicious user is trying to guess a user name and password, the user's chances increase considerably if your application gives this sort of specific feedback.

Logging Out

Logging a user out of forms authentication is as simple as calling the method FormsAuthentication.SignOut(). You can create a Log Out button and add this code, as shown here:

```
private void cmdLogOut_Click(object sender, System.EventArgs e)
{
  // Remove the authentication cookie.
  FormsAuthentication.SignOut();
}
```

When you call the SignOut() method, the authentication cookie is removed. Depending on the application, you may want to redirect the user to another page when the user logs out. If the user requests another restricted page, the request will be redirected back to the login page.

Tip In a sophisticated application, your login page might not actually be a page at all. Instead, it might be a separate portion of the page—either a distinct HTML frame or a separately coded user control. Using these techniques (which are described in Part Four), you can keep a login and logout control visible on every page.

The FormsAuthentication Class

The Authenticate(), RedirectFromLoginPage(), and SignOut() methods are the most commonly used members of the FormsAuthentication class. But there are also several more members you can use, as outlined in Table 15-2.

Table 15-2. *Members of the FormsAuthentication Class*

Member	Description
FormsCookieName	A read-only property that provides the name of the forms authentication cookie.
FormsCookiePath	A read-only property that provides the path set for the forms authentication cookie.
Authenticate()	Checks a user name and password against a list of accounts that can be entered in the web.config file.
RedirectFromLoginPage()	Logs the user in to an ASP.NET application by creating the cookie, attaching it to the current response, and redirecting the user to the page that was originally requested.
SignOut()	Logs the user out of the ASP.NET application by removing the current authentication cookie. The user will be treated as anonymous on subsequent requests.
SetAuthCookie()	Logs the user in to an ASP.NET application by creating and attaching the forms authentication cookie. Unlike the RedirectFromLoginPage() method, it doesn't forward the user back to the initially requested page.
GetAuthCookie()	Creates the authentication cookie but doesn't attach it to the current response. Instead, it returns a cookie object. You can then perform additional cookie customization, and add the cookie to the response manually.
GetRedirectUrl()	Provides the URL of the originally requested page. You could use this with SetAuthCookie() to log a user into an application and make a decision in your code whether to redirect to the requested page or use a more suitable default page.
Decrypt()	Extracts the encrypted information that was in an authentication cookie and creates a FormsAuthenticationTicket object.
Encrypt()	Takes the information from a FormsAuthenticationTicket and encrypts it so that it's ready for writing to an authentication cookie.
RenewTicketIfOld()	Allows you to extend the lifetime of the authentication ticket cookie.
HashPasswordForStoringInConfigFile()	Encrypts a string of text using the specified algorithm (SHA1 or MD5). This hashed value provides a secure way to store an encrypted password in a file or database.

These members become particularly useful as you create more customized solutions that build on forms authentication, as you'll see in the rest of this chapter.

The FormsAuthenticationTicket Class

As explained earlier, the authentication ticket is the information that is encrypted and persisted as an HTTP cookie between requests. The ticket is what allows the forms authentication module to verify that the user has been authenticated. ASP.NET represents the information in the ticket using the FormsAuthenticationTicket class, which you can access in other web pages, provided the user has been authenticated.

It's important to clarify the difference between an instance of FormsAuthenticationTicket and the authentication cookie. An instance of FormsAuthenticationTicket contains the cookie information in an unencrypted format. You can access this information through a set of properties. When the cookie is created, the information in the authentication ticket is encrypted and converted to a long string of data. When an authentication cookie returns to the server, ASP.NET decrypts the information automatically and uses it to re-create the FormsAuthenticationTicket object so that you can access it.

Table 15-3 lists the information you can extract from the FormsAuthenticationTicket.

Table 15-3. *Properties of the FormsAuthenticationTicket Class*

Property	Description
Name	Provides the user name of the user who the ticket is for.
IssueDate	Provides a DateTime object that shows when the cookie was originally created (the time when the user was first authenticated).
Expiration	Provides a DateTime object that represents the expiry date and time of the cookie.
Expired	Returns a Boolean value that is true if the expiry date has already passed.
IsPersistent	Returns a Boolean value that is true if the cookie is set up to persist after the user closes the browser (as configured in the <forms> element in the web.config file). By default, authentication cookies expire when the browser is closed.
CookiePath	Indicates the path the cookie was issued for (as configured in the <forms> element in the web.config file).
UserData	Allows you to add additional information to the ticket that will be persisted in the authentication cookie between requests, and retrieve it later. As demonstrated later in this chapter, this technique offers a useful way of securely persisting information for a user.
Version	Indicates the version of the forms authentication cookie, presumably in case of changes to the forms authentication process in the future. At present, this property returns the value 1 (in both .NET 1.0 and 1.1).

Once the user has logged in, you can retrieve the current ticket object from the current FormsIdentity. You can retrieve the current FormsIdentity from the User property of the web page (or from the static HttpContext.Current.User property in another class). However, before you can access the Ticket property, you need to test if the User object really is a FormsIdentity object, and cast it accordingly. The User property simply returns an object that implements IIdentity, and the IIdentity interface doesn't define the Ticket property you need.

The following code extracts user-specific information and displays it in a label:

```
private void Page_Load(object sender, System.EventArgs e)
{
    StringBuilder htmlString = new StringBuilder();

    // Has the request been authenticated?
    if (Request.IsAuthenticated)
    {
        // Display generic identity information.
        // This is always available, regardless of the type of
        // authentication.
        htmlString.Append("<h3>Generic User Information</h3>");
        htmlString.Append("<b>Name: </b>");
        htmlString.Append(User.Identity.Name);
        htmlString.Append("<br><b>Authenticated With: </b>");
        htmlString.Append(User.Identity.AuthenticationType);
        htmlString.Append("<br><br>");

        // Was forms authentication used?
        if (User.Identity is FormsIdentity)
        {
            // Get the ticket.
            FormsAuthenticationTicket ticket =
             ((FormsIdentity)User.Identity).Ticket;

            htmlString.Append("<h3>Ticket User Information</h3>");
            htmlString.Append("<b>Name: </b>");
            htmlString.Append(ticket.Name);
            htmlString.Append("<br><b>Issued at: </b>");
            htmlString.Append(ticket.IssueDate);
            htmlString.Append("<br><b>Expires at: </b>");
            htmlString.Append(ticket.Expiration);
            htmlString.Append("<br><b>Cookie version: </b>");
            htmlString.Append(ticket.Version);
        }
        // Display the information.
        lblInfo.Text = htmlString.ToString();
    }
}
```

Figure 15-4 shows the resulting page.

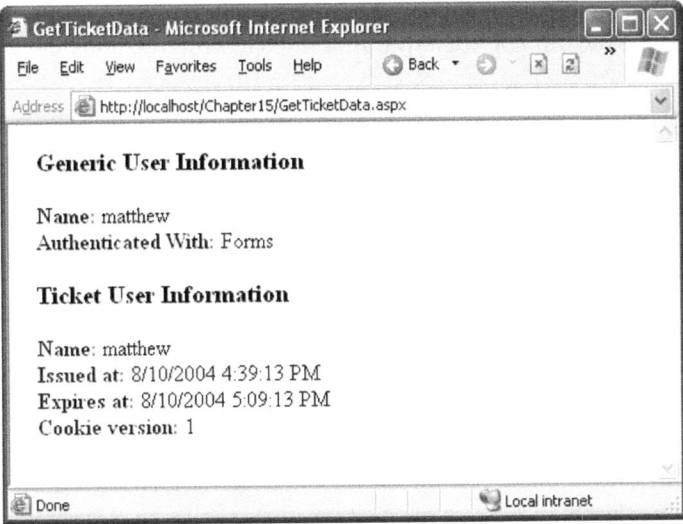

Figure 15-4. *Displaying ticket information*

Persisting the Authentication Cookie

The examples you've seen so far have used a nonpersistent authentication cookie to maintain the authentication ticket between requests. This means that if the user closes the browser, the cookie is immediately removed. This is a sensible step that ensures security. It's particularly important with shared computers to prevent another user from using a previous user's ticket. Nonpersistent cookies also make *session hijacking* attacks (where a malicious user gains access to the network and steals another user's cookie) more difficult and more limited.

Despite the increased security risks of using persistent authentication cookies, there are situations when it is appropriate to use them. If you are performing authentication for personalization rather than to control access to restricted resources, you may decide that the usability advantages of not requiring the users to log in for every visit outweigh the increased danger of unauthorized use.

Once you have made the decision to use persistent cookies, implementing them is very easy. You simply need to supply a value of true rather than false for the second parameter of the RedirectFromLoginPage() or SetAuthCookie() methods of the FormsAuthentication class. Here's an example:

```
FormsAuthentication.RedirectFromLoginPage(User nameTextBox.Text,true);
```

By default, persistent cookies do not expire unless the FormsAuthentication.SignOut() method is used. Persistent cookies are not affected by the timeout attribute that is set in the <forms> element of the web.config. If you want the persistent cookie to eventually expire some time in the future, you have to use the GetAuthCookie() method of FormsAuthentication, set the expiry date and time, and then write the cookie to the HTTP response yourself.

The following example rewrites the code that authenticates the user when the Login button is pressed. It creates a persistent cookie, but goes to additional steps to limit the cookies lifespan to ten days:

```
private void cmdLogin_Click(object sender, System.EventArgs e)
{
    if (Page.IsValid)
    {
        if (FormsAuthentication.Authenticate(txtName.Text,
            txtPassword.Text))
        {
            // Create a new authentication cookie.
            HttpCookie formsCookie;
            formsCookie = FormsAuthentication.GetAuthCookie(
             txtName.Text, true);

            // Set the expiry date of the authentication cookie.
            formsCookie.Expires = DateTime.Now.AddDays(10);

            // Add the cookie to the HTTP response.
            Response.Cookies.Add(formsCookie);

            // Redirect the user back to the originally requested URL.
            Response.Redirect(FormsAuthentication.GetRedirectUrl(
             txtName.Text, true));
        }
        else
        {
            // Show an error message.
            lblStatus.Text = "Try again.";
        }
    }
}
```

The code for checking the credentials is exactly the same in this scenario. The only difference is that the authentication cookie isn't added automatically. Instead, it's created with a call to GetAuthCookie(), which returns a new instance of HttpCookie, as shown here:

```
HttpCookie formsCookie;
formsCookie = FormsAuthentication.GetAuthCookie(txtName.Text, true);
```

Once you've created the authentication cookie, you can retrieve the current date and time (using the DateTime.Now static property), add ten days to it (using the DateTime.AddDays() method), and use this value as the expiry date and time of the cookie:

```
formsCookie.Expires = DateTime.Now.AddDays(10);
```

Next, you have to add the cookie to the HTTP response:

```
Response.Cookies.Add(formsCookie);
```

Finally, you can redirect the user back to the originally requested URL, which you can obtain by using the GetRedirectUrl() method:

```
Response.Redirect(FormsAuthentication.GetRedirectUrl(txtName.Text, true));
```

The end result is a cookie that will persist beyond the closing of the browser but which will expire after ten days, at which point the user will need to reenter credentials to log in to the website.

Advanced Credential Storage

The simple login page examples shown so far use the web.config file to store user credentials. While this provides a simple way to demonstrate forms authentication, it's not suitable for most web applications. There are a number of issues, including the following:

- Potential lack of security. Even though users aren't able to directly request the web.config file, you may still prefer to use a storage medium where access can be secured more effectively. As long as this information is stored on the web server, passwords are accessible to any administrator, developer, or tester who has access.

- No reliable way to programmatically add or remove users. This means you can't create the typical registration page used in e-commerce applications.

- No support for adding additional user-specific information. For example, you might want to store information like addresses, credit cards, personal preferences, and so on.

- Poor performance with large numbers of users. The web.config file is just a file, and it can't provide the efficient caching and multiuser access of a database.

For these reasons, it's common to store user credentials in other locations. In this section, you'll learn how to accomplish this feat. But first, you need to learn how to protect password information with a cryptographic technique called *hashing*.

Hashing Passwords for Storage

A hash code is a cryptographically strong checksum that acts like a digital fingerprint. A hash algorithm takes an arbitrary amount of data (as a large block of binary information), and uses it to generate a small hash code that is unique to that information. The process can be represented by the following equation:

```
Hash = HashAlgorithmFunction(Data)
```

All cryptographic hash algorithms must be:

- **One-way.** As you might expect, it should completely impossible to re-create the document from the hash, because the hash will not include all the information that was in the document. It is also computationally unfeasible to determine anything about the information just by examining the hash.

- **Collision resistant.** If the hashing algorithm is sound and uses a cryptographically strong key, it is computationally impractical to create another document that generates an identical hash. This behavior is important in a wide variety of circumstances. For example, you wouldn't want a client to create an altered version of a contract that still has the same hash code.

It's for these reasons that hashes are referred to as cryptographically strong checksums. Like checksums, hashes provide a small value that represents a much larger block of data. However, with a typical checksum such as the CRC (Cyclical Redundancy Check), which is commonly used in file systems, it's quite easy to create another document that generates an identical checksum. In the case of a hash code, this is all but impossible.

You've already learned a little about hashing in Chapter 7 with secure view state. When you set the EnableViewStateMAC attribute of the Page directive to true, ASP.NET automatically adds a digitally signed hash code to the view state information. That way, it will detect if this information is changed in any way before the page is posted back. Similarly, ASP.NET uses a hash code with the authentication cookie to make sure its information can't be undetectably modified.

Hashing has other uses, like allowing you to compare two blocks of data. (For example, you could generate hashes for two files, and compare the hashes to quickly identify if the files contain the same content.) Hashing is also handy for storing information you do not need to access directly, but that you simply need to compare with another piece of data. By hashing the new data with the same algorithm as the old data, you can compare the hashes. If the hashes match, the two sets of original data match, too. This technique can be very usefully applied to passwords. In fact, most modern operating systems store user passwords as hashes. Storing hashes rather than the original password makes it extremely difficult for malicious users to steal passwords and use them to exploit other systems or launch later attacks. Even if the password hashes are stolen, a brute-force, password-cracking attack is required to get the passwords. If the passwords are strong, this process will take a very long time.

The downside to hashing passwords is that, once hashed, the original passwords cannot be recovered, even by the person who generated the hashes. This means that if a user forgets a password, the application cannot simply retrieve it, because all you have is the hash. An alternate step is to replace the user's password with a new randomly generated value or prompt the user to reset it if this occurs.

It's important to consider the advantages and disadvantages of hashing passwords for each application. If it's important to be able to recover the actual passwords, hashing is not an option. However, since there are other ways to deal with users who have forgotten their passwords, hashing is often an attractive way to guard against password theft. Fortunately, .NET includes classes that help you compute hashes very easily.

Hashing Passwords for the web.config

As you saw earlier, you can store user credentials in the <credentials> element of the web.config. The passwordFormat attribute allows you to set what sort of hashing should be applied. The previous example used Clear to indicate that no hashing is in use. If you use one of the other possible values, SHA1 or MD5, the password you supply to the

FormsAuthentication.Authenticate() method will be hashed using the appropriate algorithm and the hash will be compared to the hashed value stored for the user in the web.config.

The following <authentication> section is equivalent to the example used before, with the same passwords now converted into SHA1 hashes:

```
<authentication mode="Forms">
  <forms name="DansApplication"
    loginUrl="login.aspx"
    timeout="30"
    path="/"
    protection="All">
    <credentials passwordFormat="SHA1">
      <user name="dan"
        password="E5E9FA1BA31ECD1AE84F75CAAA474F3A663F05F4" />
      <user name="jenny"
        password="17618F01A3A21B911C925BCB525A1D21ABD30673" />
    </credentials>
  </forms>
</authentication>
```

The best part is that you don't need to make any change to the login code. Instead, the existing login page works exactly as it did before!

Creating Password Hashes

The only challenge you need to solve is how to generate the hashed passwords and get them into the web.config in the first place. There is no automated way to insert hashed passwords into the web.config, but .NET does give you an easy way to calculate the hash codes for a string value with the HashPasswordForStoringInConfigFile() method of the FormsAuthentication class.

When you call HashPasswordForStoringInConfigFile(), you pass in the password text and a string that specifies the hashing algorithm to use (SHA1 or MD5). The method returns a string that contains the hashed password.

■**Tip** The .NET Framework includes other, more fully featured classes for encryption and hashing in the System.Security.Cryptography namespace. However, the HashPasswordForStoringInConfigFile() is more convenient to use, because it automatically converts your string data into a binary array (which is required to hash it), and then converts the binary information in the hash to an XML-friendly string.

Using the HashPasswordForStoringInConfigFile() method, it's quite easy to build a simple web form that generates hash values. Figure 15-5 shows one such page. In this example, the hash is placed in a text box so that it can be easily copied and pasted in your configuration file.

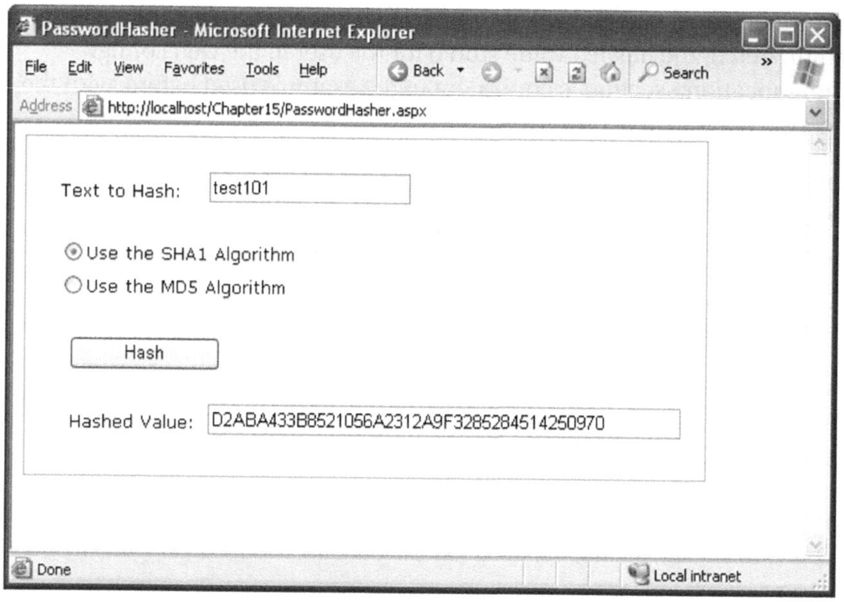

Figure 15-5. *Hashing a password*

Here's the code that computes and displays the hash:

```
private void cmdHash_Click(Object sender, EventArgs e)
{
    string algorithm = "";

    if (optSHA1.Checked)
    {
        algorithm = "SHA1";
    }
    else
    {
        algorithm = "MD5";
    }

    txtHash.Text = FormsAuthentication.HashPasswordForStoringInConfigFile(
                txtPassword.Text, algorithm);
}
```

Unfortunately, you're still left with the manual step of copying the hash code and editing the web.config file by hand. There's no way to avoid this, because .NET doesn't include any classes for writing to configuration files. Trying to open and edit the web.config file using the System.IO classes is a bad idea. You could run into serious trouble with this approach if multiple users are registering themselves at once, and multiple worker threads are trying to update the web.config file simultaneously. Another problem is that each time the web.config file is changed, the entire application is restarted. As a result, frequent registration will reduce performance and lose caching and application state information. It will also lose session state information if you are using the in-process session state store.

A better solution is to use the HashPasswordForStoringInConfigFile() method for creating the hash, and then store the password hash in another location, like a database.

Using Other Credentials Stores

When using forms authentication, you can store credentials wherever you like. You just have to write your own code for checking the credentials of users when they log in and use that code instead of the FormsAuthentication.Authenticate() method that you've been using up until now.

In the following sections, you'll see examples that store credentials in a structured XML file and in a database. To make this customization more logical and consistent, these examples begin by creating an interface that can represent any credential store.

An Interface for Credential Stores

No matter what credential store you use, you typically perform the same function—checking user information to see if it's present and accurate. Since these stores perform the same function, it would be nice if you could switch between credential stores easily. This would improve the flexibility and reusability of your code. For example, if you start with a website with a small number of users, an XML file on the server or an Access database might be sufficient. As the site grows, you may need to move to a full-fledged server-side database that uses stored procedures to authenticate users. If the code for accessing the credential stores is implemented in a consistent way, this changeover will be easy.

A good way of standardizing code is to define an interface for the shared functionality, and then implement this interface in the classes that contain the specific code. This is the approach used in this example.

The following interface shows the starting point—a definition for an Authenticate() method that accepts a user identifier and a password. This example assumes that the user credentials are string based, which is logical because the user will typically submit this information in text-based input controls like the text box.

```
public interface ICredentialStore
{
    bool Authenticate(string userName, string password);
}
```

Every class that implements ICredentialStore must provide an Authenticate() method that matches this signature. Before you create a custom implementation, it's worth considering the simple example where the authentication mechanism uses the FormsAuthentication class to validate user information against the user list in the web.config file.

Here's what you need to create this store:

```
public class DefaultCredentialStore : ICredentialStore
{
    public bool Authenticate(string userName, string password)
    {
        return FormsAuthentication.Authenticate(userName, password);
    }
}
```

All this class does is hand off the real work to the FormsAuthentication.Authenticate() method. To use this with the example developed earlier, you simply need to tweak a couple of lines in the authentication code that runs when the user attempts to log in:

```
private void cmdLogin_Click(object sender, System.EventArgs e)
{
    if (Page.IsValid)
    {
        // Create the class that represents the credential store.
        ICredentialStore store = new DefaultCredentialStore();

        if (store.Authenticate(txtName.Text,
            txtPassword.Text))
        {
            FormsAuthentication.RedirectFromLoginPage(txtName.Text, false);
        }
        else
        {
            lblStatus.Text = "Try again.";
        }
    }
}
```

You could create a credential store interface that requires a lot more functionality, such as the ability to add users to the store or change the details of a user. This would allow you to further standardize the way that registration pages and other parts of your application work, and make it even easier to adapt to different credential stores in the future. All in all, the ICredentialStore interface is a simple example of how you can keep your security options open.

Storing Credentials in an XML File

The web.config file doesn't allow you to store additional tags or data in the <credentials> section. This means that you can't user-specific information other than user names and passwords. To resolve this problem, you could add the user information to a different section of the web.config, and create a custom section handler for the configuration file (as described in Chapter 6). However, an easier approach is to place your user credentials into a separate XML file. This allows you to continue to use the small-scale XML-based approach of the web.config file, but you can add the ability to store additional information.

You can use any schema that you would like for your XML users file—that is the advantage of using your own file rather than web.config. For this example, the file is structured like this:

```
<?xml version="1.0" encoding="utf-8" ?>
<users passwordFormat="SHA1" >
  <user userName="dan"
   password="E5E9FA1BA31ECD1AE84F75CAAA474F3A663F05F4">
  </user>
  <user userName="jenny"
   password="17618F01A3A21B911C925BCB525A1D21ABD30673">
  </user>
</users>
```

As you can see, this example uses hashed passwords to provide increased security. In fact, it uses the passwordFormat attribute of the <users> element in exactly the same way as that of the <credentials> element in the web.config. This isn't a requirement, but it makes sense to follow this convention so that your proprietary system will be easy to understand.

Unlike the web.config, the format of your file is flexible. You can add additional information for users inside <user> tags. For example, you could include e-mail addresses as shown here:

```xml
<?xml version="1.0" encoding="utf-8" ?>
<users passwordFormat="SHA1" >
  <user userName="dan"
   password="E5E9FA1BA31ECD1AE84F75CAAA474F3A663F05F4">
  <email>daniel@apress.com</email>
  </user>
  <user userName="jenny"
   password="17618F01A3A21B911C925BCB525A1D21ABD30673">
  <email>jenny@apress.com</email>
  </user>
</users>
```

Now that you have created the XML file of users, it's time to create the class that will perform the credential checking.

The first step is to indicate that this class implements ICredentialStore

```
public class XmlCredentialStore : ICredentialStore
```

It also makes sense to define a simple constructor that initializes the location of the XML file to use:

```
private string usersFile;
public XmlCredentialStore(string usersFile)
{
    usersFile = usersFile;
}
```

The next step is to code the Authenticate() method. This method begins by creating an XmlDocument object and loading the XML user list into it. At this point, the code also creates an XmlNamespaceManager, which is needed later when using an XPath expression to find a matching user element.

```
public bool Authenticate(string userName, string password)
{
    // Create the XML document object.
    XmlDocument usersXml = new XmlDocument();

    // Create a namespace manager for the document (you need it later).
    XmlNamespaceManager namespaceManager =
      new XmlNamespaceManager(usersXml.NameTable);

    // The XML document might fail to load, so error handling
    // makes sense.
    try
```

```
    {
        usersXml.Load(usersFile);
    }
    catch (Exception error)
    {
        // You could not load the XML file so the user can't be
        // authenticated. Another option is to throw some sort of
        // exception to alert the web page.
        return false;
    }
    ...
```

If an error occurs while loading the XML file, the Authenticate() method returns false to indicate that the user could not be authenticated. This is a safe option for security. Another option is to throw a new exception to alert the code that called Authenticate() and let it deal with error handling. This allows the web page to show a specific error message.

The next step is to locate the <users> node in the XML file, and extract the passwordFormat attribute. This indicates the hashing algorithm that you want to use when checking the password against the XML file.

```
    ...
    XmlNode users = usersXml.GetElementsByTagName("users")[0];
    string hashingAlgorithm = users.Attributes["passwordFormat"].Value;
    ...
```

Next, the code defines a new string variable, named passwordToCompare, which will hold the password value you want to compare to the password information in the XML file. If the hashing algorithm specified in the passwordFormat attribute is not blank and is not set to Clear, the specified algorithm is used in conjunction with the HashPasswordForStoringInConfigFile() method. Otherwise, the code just uses the original value of the password for passwordToCompare.

```
    ...
    string passwordToCompare;
    if ((hashingAlgorithm != null) && (hashingAlgorithm != "Clear"))
    {
        // If a hashing algorithm is specified, hash the password.
        passwordToCompare =
         FormsAuthentication.HashPasswordForStoringInConfigFile(
         password, hashingAlgorithm);
    }
    else
    {
        // Otherwise, use the plain text of the password.
        passwordToCompare = password;
    }
    ...
```

The next step is to search the XML document for a <user> element that has the correct user name and password attributes. To do this, you must use an XPath expression with this form:

```
descendant::user[@userName='[UserName]' and @password='[Password]']
```

Here's the code you need:

```
...
// Get the root node.
XmlNode root = usersXml.DocumentElement;

// Create an XPath expression to match a user node
// with the correct user name and password.
string userXPath = "descendant::user[@userName='" + userName +
  "' and @password='" + passwordToCompare + "']";

// Find the matching user node.
XmlNode matchingUser =
  root.SelectSingleNode(userXPath, namespaceManager);
...
```

Something worth noting here is that the code uses user-supplied values to build a dynamic expression. It would be a good idea to harden this system so that malicious users can't use carefully chosen user names and passwords in order to alter the way the XPath expression works. For example, consider what happens if the user enters this value as the user name:

```
dan' or password='
```

In this case, the XPath expression will be subverted and will match any node when the user name is dan. This is obviously not desirable. There are a number of options to prevent this possibility, including explicitly checking for characters like the apostrophe, or preventing them from being entered in the first place. For example, the validator controls on the login page explicitly reject anything other than alphanumeric characters. Another way to tighten security is to check that the retrieved value really does match the value you expected. The code in this example performs this last sanity check to make sure that a matching node exists, and that it *really* has the expected password and user-name information.

```
...
if (matchingUser != null)
{
    // Perform the final sanity check.
    if ((matchingUser.Attributes["userName"].Value == userName) &&
      (matchingUser.Attributes["password"].Value == passwordToCompare))
    {
        return true;
    }
    else
    {
```

```
                return false;
        }
    }
    else
    {
        return false;
    }
}
```

You now have an XML implementation of ICredentialStore that you can use in the same way as the DefaultCredentialStore class shown earlier.

To use the XML credential store, you simply need to change one line in the login code from the earlier example. Replace this:

```
ICredentialStore store = new DefaultCredentialStore();
```

with this:

```
ICredentialStore store = new XmlCredentialStore("users.xml");
```

Storing Credentials in a Database

If your application has a large number of users, a relational database such as SQL Server is probably the best place to store user information. A database provides good scalability, and gives you the option to easily share the user information between several web servers in a web farm. Database servers can comfortably deal with a large number of users' details without significant performance problems, and they are designed to handle multiple concurrent requests.

The next example creates a DatabaseCredentialStore class that implements ICredentialStore, and provides user authentication in the same way as the XmlCredentialStore class used in the previous example. This class requires a database with a Users table that has the structure and records shown in Figure 15-6. You can easily insert additional user-specific information by adding more columns to this table.

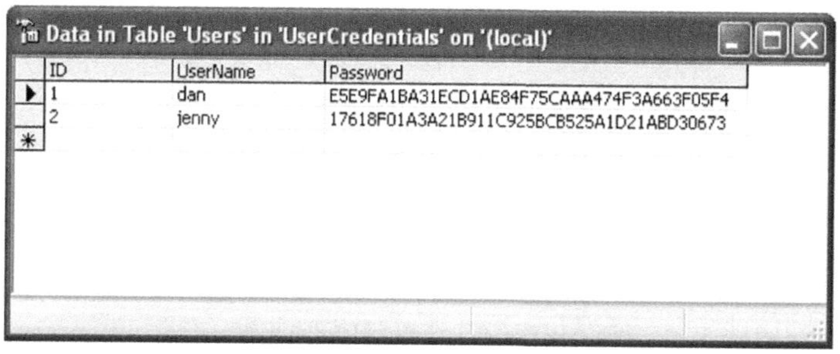

Figure 15-6. *The Users table*

Here's the complete code for the DatabaseCredentialSource class:

```
public class DatabaseCredentialStore : ICredentialStore
{
    // The name of the application setting in the web.config with the
    // connection string.
    string connectionSetting;

    // The type of hashing algorithm (MD5, SHA1, or Clear).
    string hashingAlgorithm;

    public DatabaseCredentialStore(string connectionStringSettingName,
      string hashingAlgorithm)
    {
        this.connectionSetting = connectionStringSettingName;
        this.hashingAlgorithm = hashingAlgorithm;
    }

    public bool Authenticate(string userName, string password)
    {
        string passwordToCompare;
        if ((hashingAlgorithm != null) && (hashingAlgorithm != "Clear"))
        {
            // If a hashing algorithm is specified, hash the password.
            passwordToCompare =
              FormsAuthentication.HashPasswordForStoringInConfigFile(
                password, hashingAlgorithm);
        }
        else
        {
            // Otherwise, use the plain text of the password.
            passwordToCompare = password;
        }

        // Retrieve the connection string from the configuration file.
        SqlConnection con = new SqlConnection(
          ConfigurationSettings.AppSettings[connectionSetting]);

        // Create a parameterized command to prevent SQL injection attacks.
        string query =
          "SELECT UserName, Password FROM Users WHERE UserName = @UserName";
        SqlCommand cmd = new SqlCommand(query, con);
        cmd.Parameters.Add("@UserName", userName);

        // Retrieve the matching record.
        bool isAuthenticated = false;
```

```
        try
        {
            con.Open();

            // The assumption here is that user names must be unique,
            // and they should be enforced by an index in the database.
            SqlDataReader matchingUser =
              cmd.ExecuteReader(CommandBehavior.SingleRow);

            // Default behavior of SELECT is not case sensitive,
            // so it's up to you to perform a case-sensitive comparison.
            if (matchingUser.Read())
            {
                if (((string)matchingUser["Password"] == passwordToCompare)
                  && ((string)matchingUser["UserName"] == userName))
                    isAuthenticated = true;
            }
            matchingUser.Close();
        }
        catch (Exception error)
        {
            return false;
        }
        finally
        {
            con.Close();
        }

        return isAuthenticated;
    }
}
```

One important fact to note is that you must always compare the user name and password text in your code. You can't simply rely on the WHERE clause of the SQL query. The reason for this is that many database servers perform a case-insensitive match when they use SELECT. For example, in SQL Server, the behavior of matching and sorting is determined by the collation that is active for the column involved. The default collation for text columns is case insensitive. Therefore, it's wise to take extra precautions in your code.

To use the DatabaseCredentialStore, you need to add the connection string to your web.config file, as shown here:

```
<configuration>
  <system.web>
    <!-- Other configuration settings here. -->
  </system.web>
  <appSettings>
    <add key="CredentialConnectionString"
      value="Data Source=localhost;Initial Catalog=UserCredentials;
```

```
Integrated Security=SSPI" />
  </appSettings>
</configuration>
```

Then you can modify your login code to use the DatabaseCredentialStore instead of another ICredentialStore object:

```
ICredentialStore store = new DatabaseCredentialStore(
  "CredentialConnectionString", "SHA1");
```

■Note The simple examples shown here demonstrate how you can use forms authentication with a variety of credential stores. You might just as easily decide to tie forms authentication to Active Directory, an LDAP directory, a web service, or something entirely different. As long as you provide code to check the credentials, you can use whatever data store you like.

Adding Information to the Authentication Ticket

The primary purpose of the authentication ticket is to allow the forms authentication module to identify the user. However, the authentication ticket also supports the storage of additional information. This provides a useful way to securely keep track of user-specific information without using any extra server resources. Instead, the appropriate information is stored in an encrypted authentication ticket that the user sends back to the server with each request.

To add information to the ticket, you use the UserData property of the FormsAuthenticationTicket. This property is a string of data that is encrypted along with the rest of the ticket. If you want to store another type of data, you need to convert this data to a string. Similarly, if you want to store multiple values you need to determine your own system for separating them. One approach is to use the StreamReader and StreamWriter classes from the System.IO namespace to write distinct pieces of data to a single string, but separate each one with a line feed. Another choice is to stitch the string together as a series of smaller strings with a custom separator character, and split the string into an array of smaller strings based on this separator using the String.Split() method.

Adding User-Specific Data to the Credential Store

Usually, when you add user-specific data, you'll first retrieve it from some other permanent storage location, like a file or database. Now that you've learned how to use other credential stores, you've cleared the way to store user-specific information along with the user-name and password details. For example, you could enhance the Users table in the previous example with an EmailAddress column, retrieve it in your login code, and then attach it to the authentication ticket.

To implement this design in a consistent way, it makes sense to extend the ICredentialStore interface so that it returns the string of user-specific data:

```
public interface ICredentialStore
{
    bool Authenticate(string userName, string password);
```

```
  bool Authenticate(string userName, string password,
    out string userData);
}
```

If a given credential store doesn't provide user-specific data, you can simply return a null value for the userData parameter.

```
public class DefaultCredentialStore : ICredentialStore
{
    public bool Authenticate(string userName, string password)
    {
        return FormsAuthentication.Authenticate(userName, password);
    }

    public bool Authenticate(string userName, string password,
      out string userData)
    {
        userData = null;

        // Pass the call on to the other version of the
        // Authenticate() method.
        return Authenticate(userName, password);
    }
}
```

On the other hand, if you do want to return user data, you only need minor changes to your existing code. The next example shows how the DatabaseCredentialStore class can return an e-mail address, with only minor changes.

```
public bool Authenticate(string userName, string password,
  out string userData)
{
    userData = null;

    string passwordToCompare;
    if ((hashingAlgorithm != null) && (hashingAlgorithm != "Clear"))
    {
        // If a hashing algorithm is specified, hash the password.
        passwordToCompare =
          FormsAuthentication.HashPasswordForStoringInConfigFile(
          password, hashingAlgorithm);
    }
    else
    {
        // Otherwise, use the plain text of the password.
        passwordToCompare = password;
    }
```

```csharp
    // Retrieve the connection string from the configuration file.
    SqlConnection con = new SqlConnection(
      ConfigurationSettings.AppSettings[connectionSetting]);

    // Create a parameterized command to prevent SQL injection attacks.
    string query = "SELECT UserName, Password, EmailAddress" +
      "FROM Users WHERE UserName = @UserName";
    SqlCommand cmd = new SqlCommand(query, con);
    cmd.Parameters.Add("@UserName", userName);

    bool isAuthenticated = false;
    try
    {
        con.Open();
        SqlDataReader matchingUser =
          cmd.ExecuteReader(CommandBehavior.SingleRow);

        if (matchingUser.Read())
        {
            if (((string)matchingUser["Password"] == passwordToCompare)
             && ((string)matchingUser["UserName"] == userName))
            {
                userData = (string)matchingUser["emailAddress"];
                isAuthenticated = true;
            }
        }
        matchingUser.Close();
    }
    catch (Exception error)
    {
        return false;
    }
    finally
    {
        con.Close();
    }
    return isAuthenticated;
}

public bool Authenticate(string userName, string password)
{
    // Pass the call on to the other version of the
    // Authenticate() method.
    string ignoredUserData;
    return Authenticate(userName, password, out ignoredUserData);
}
```

Attaching User-Specific Data

The login code now requires a few minor modifications. It needs to retrieve the user data by using the overloaded version of the Authenticate() method that returns this information. It also needs to store this email address in the ticket for later use. As a result, you can't rely on the FormsAuthentication.RedirectFromLoginPage() method, because this doesn't give you the ability to modify the ticket. Instead, you must create a new FormsAuthenticationTicket object with the user data, encrypt it using FormsAuthentication.Encrypt(), attach it manually, and then redirect the user with FormsAuthentication.Redirect().

Here's the complete code you need to perform this task when the user logs in:

```
private void cmdLogin_Click(object sender, System.EventArgs e)
{
    if (Page.IsValid)
    {
        // Create the class that represents the credential store.
        ICredentialStore store = new DatabaseCredentialStore(
          "CredentialConnectionString", "SHA1");

        string userData;
        if (store.Authenticate(txtName.Text, txtPassword.Text,
          out userData))
        {
            // Create a new authentication ticket.
            FormsAuthenticationTicket ticket = new
             FormsAuthenticationTicket(
                1,                              // Version
                txtName.Text,                   // User name
                DateTime.Now,                   // Date issued
                DateTime.Now.AddMinutes(30),    // Date to expire
                false,                          // Persistent
                userData);                      // User data string

            // Encrypt the ticket.
            string encryptedTicket = FormsAuthentication.Encrypt(ticket);

            // Create the authentication cookie.
            HttpCookie formsCookie = new HttpCookie(
              FormsAuthentication.FormsCookieName, encryptedTicket);

            // Attach the cookie to the response.
            Response.Cookies.Add(formsCookie);

            // Redirect the user back to the original URL.
            Response.Redirect(FormsAuthentication.GetRedirectUrl(
              txtName.Text, false));
        }
        else
```

```
        {
            lblStatus.Text = "Try again.";
        }
    }
}
```

In order for this code to work, you must use the correct name for the
cookie with the authentication ticket. You can retrieve this name using the
FormsAuthentication.FormsCookieName property.

Now you can access the ticket and its user data in any request where the user is authenticated. Here's an example page that extracts and displays the ticket information:

```
if (Request.IsAuthenticated)
{
    if (User.Identity is FormsIdentity)
    {
        // Get the ticket.
        FormsAuthenticationTicket ticket =
         ((FormsIdentity)User.Identity).Ticket;

        // Get the user data.
        string email = Ticket.UserData;

        // (Display or use the data).
    }
}
```

Figure 15-7 shows the custom user data from the ticket.

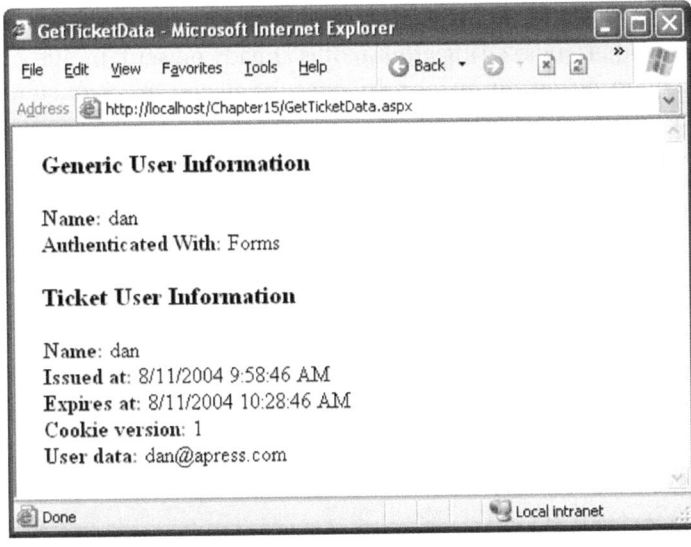

Figure 15-7. *The user data from the ticket*

The Limits of the UserData Property

The authentication ticket UserData property is not suitable for storing large amounts of data. This is because there is a limit on the size of cookies. This limit is imposed by browsers. If a cookie exceeds the size limit, the browser will simply reject it. The limit can vary from browser to browser. Internet Explorer and Netscape typically support cookies up to 4 KB in size.

It's important to ensure that you do not write too much information to the authentication ticket. If you do, the user's cookie will be rejected by some browsers and the user will not be authenticated. If you need to store more user-specific information, you should use a different state mechanism. For example, you could use session state, or add multiple cookies at once.

Cookie-Less Forms Authentication

One significant limitation of standard forms authentication is the requirement that the browser supports and is configured to accept cookies. Many mobile devices do not support cookies. Additionally, in some environments, users who are concerned about privacy may disable cookies in their browser. If you want to make forms authentication work for these types of user, you need to find a way to make forms authentication work without cookies. That means you need to find another way to persist the authentication ticket between requests.

ASP.NET includes part, but not all, of a possible solution. If the forms authentication cookie is not present, the FormsAuthenticationModule will automatically check the query string parameters in the URL, looking for a parameter with the same name that the authentication cookie should have. If you pass the encrypted authentication ticket in this parameter, the forms authentication module will pick it up and use it in exactly the same way as if the information had arrived in a cookie.

Setting this parameter in the login method is fairly straightforward. You can create the ticket by hand, as you've seen earlier, and encrypt it to a string. However, you won't add a cookie. Instead, the last step is to refer the user to the originally requested URL, with the ticket information appended to the end of the query string. The only complication is making sure that the URL is updated correctly if another query string argument is already present. In this case, you need to add an additional query string argument using the ampersand (&) character, rather than begin the query string using the question mark (?).

Here's the login code that accomplishes this task:

```
private void cmdLogin_Click(object sender, System.EventArgs e)
{
    if (Page.IsValid)
    {
        string userData;
        if (FormsAuthentication.Authenticate(txtName.Text,
          txtPassword.Text))
        {
            // Create an authentication ticket.
            FormsAuthenticationTicket ticket =
```

```
            new FormsAuthenticationTicket(txtName.Text, false, 30);

        // Encrypt it.
        string encryptedTicket = FormsAuthentication.Encrypt(ticket);

        // Create a string to hold the redirect URL.
        string destinationURL;

        // Get the original redirection URL.
        string originalURL =
          FormsAuthentication.GetRedirectUrl(txtName.Text,false);

        // Check whether the original URL has query parameters/
        if (originalURL.IndexOf("?") == -1)
        {
            // Add the encrypted authentication ticket as
            // the only parameter.
            destinationURL = originalURL + "?" +
              FormsAuthentication.FormsCookieName + "=" +
              encryptedTicket;
        }
        else
        {
            // Add the encrypted authentication ticket as
            // an additional parameter.
            destinationURL = originalURL + "&" +
              FormsAuthentication.FormsCookieName + "=" +
              encryptedTicket;
        }
        Response.Redirect(destinationURL);
    }
    else
    {
        lblStatus.Text = "Try again.";
    }
}
}
```

Now users will be automatically redirected to their original requested page after they log in, with the encrypted authentication ticket in a query string parameter. The forms authentication module will recognize the authentication ticket, decrypt it, and authenticate the user.

Figure 15-8 shows the originally requested page after logging in. You can see some of the encrypted authentication ticket in the Address box.

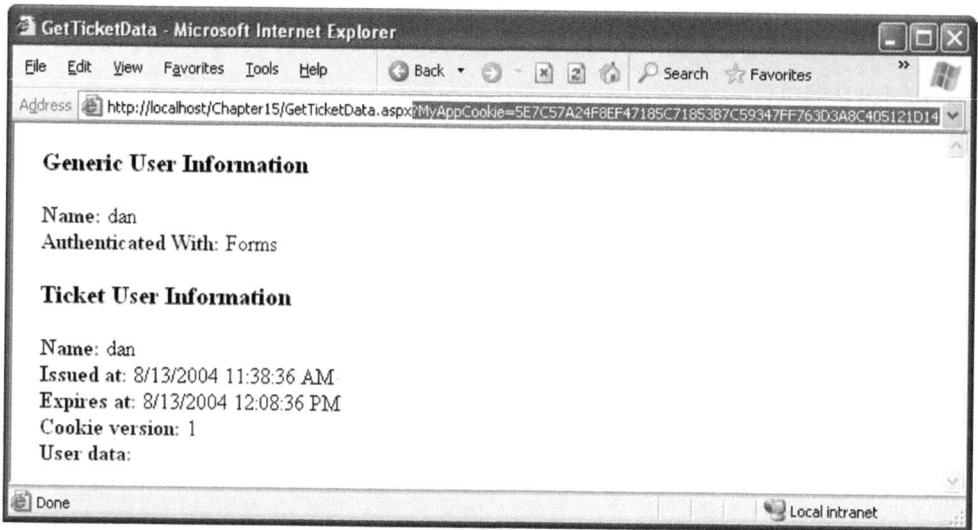

Figure 15-8. *A cookieliess authentication ticket*

On the surface, this seems like an ideal solution. However, there is a significant problem. If a user is authenticated by an encrypted authentication ticket in the URL and then clicks a link on the page to move to another restricted page on the site, the authentication ticket in the query string will be lost. As a result, the user will be immediately redirected to the login form and forced to enter user credentials again. This is clearly bad for usability.

There are number of work-arounds to this problem, but none are perfect. For example, when you use a Response.Redirect() statement, you can manually check for the current ticket, and dynamically add it to the target URL, as shown here:

```
string targetUrl = "newpage.aspx";
if (Page.Request.QueryString[FormsAuthentication.FormsCookieName] != null)
{
    // There is an authentication ticket. Add it to the target URL.
    if (targetUrl.IndexOf("?") == -1)
    {
        targetUrl += "?" + FormsAuthentication.FormsCookieName + "=" +
          Page.Request.QueryString[FormsAuthentication.FormsCookieName];
    }
    else
    {
        targetUrl += "&" + FormsAuthentication.FormsCookieName + "=" +
          Page.Request.QueryString[FormsAuthentication.FormsCookieName];
    }
}
Response.Redirect(targetUrl);
```

To make slightly cleaner code, you could create a generic method that loops through all the controls on a page, finds the HtmlAnchor and HyperLink objects, and adjusts their URLs using this approach. You could create this as a static method of a utility class, so you could use it in any page. The following class includes an UpdateHtmlAnchors() method that does exactly that.

Of course, this technique won't update links in other places in your web page HTML, including static <a> tags.

```
public class FixLinks
{
    public static void UpdateHtmlAnchors(ControlCollection controls)
    {
        // Scan the page.
        foreach (Control control in controls)
        {
            // Update all HtmlAnchor objects
            if (control is HtmlAnchor)
            {
                HtmlAnchor anchor = (HtmlAnchor)control;
                anchor.HRef = UpdateUrl(anchor.HRef);
            }
            else if (control is HyperLink)
            {
                HyperLink link = (HyperLink)control;
                link.NavigateUrl = UpdateUrl(link.NavigateUrl);
            }

            // Search the control tree recursively.
            if (control.Controls != null)
            {
                UpdateHtmlAnchors(control.Controls);
            }
        }
    }

    public static string UpdateUrl(string targetUrl)
    {
        HttpContext context = HttpContext.Current;
        if (context.Request.QueryString[
          FormsAuthentication.FormsCookieName] != null)
        {
            // There is an authentication ticket. Add it.
            if (targetUrl.IndexOf("?") == -1)
            {
                targetUrl += "?" + FormsAuthentication.FormsCookieName +
                  "=" + context.Request.QueryString[
                  FormsAuthentication.FormsCookieName];
            }
            else
            {
                targetUrl += "&" + FormsAuthentication.FormsCookieName +
                  "=" + context.Request.QueryString[
                  FormsAuthentication.FormsCookieName];
```

```
        }
    }
    return targetUrl;
  }
}
```

Next, to update the links in the page, you simply need to call the UpdateHtmlAnchors()
method when the page first loads, as shown here:

```
private void Page_Load(object sender, System.EventArgs e)
{
    FixLinks.UpdateHtmlAnchors(this.Page.Controls);
}
```

Another possible approach is to combine forms authentication and session state.
Because ASP.NET supports cookieless session state natively, session state is a good place to
store an authentication ticket. You would then need to retrieve the ticket from session state on
subsequent postbacks and apply it to the URL or current user security context. This requires
reacting to application events or building a custom HTTP module. Unfortunately, ASP.NET
does not include any intrinsic support for attaching authentication tickets to the URL of a
request, unlike its strong support for cookieless sessions.

Summary

In this chapter, you've seen how to use forms authentication to implement authentication
systems that simplify life and provide a great deal of flexibility. You've learned how to protect
passwords, use any data source for credential storage, and easily track user-specific
information. In the next chapter, you'll look at a different approach to validating user
identity—Windows authentication.

CHAPTER 16

Windows Authentication

Forms authentication is a great approach if you want to roll your own authentication system using a back-end database and a custom login page. But what if you are creating a web application for a smaller set of known users who already have Windows user accounts? In these situations, it makes sense to use an authentication system that can leverage the existing user and group membership information.

The solution is *Windows authentication*, which matches web users to Windows user accounts that are defined on the local computer or another domain on the network. In this chapter, you'll learn how to use Windows authentication in your web applications. You'll also learn how to apply impersonation to temporarily assume another identity.

Introducing Windows Authentication

Unlike forms authentication, Windows authentication isn't built into ASP.NET. Instead, Windows authentication hands over responsibility for authentication to Internet Information Services (IIS). IIS asks the browser to authenticate itself by providing credentials that map to a Windows user account. If the user is successfully authenticated, IIS allows the web-page request, and passes the user and role information onto ASP.NET so that your code can act on it in much the same way that it works with identity information in a forms authentication scenario.

Figure 16-1 shows the end-to-end flow.

Why Use Windows Authentication?

There are three main reasons why you would want to use Windows authentication:

- It involves little programming work on the developer's part.

- It allows you to use existing user logins.

- It allows you to use impersonation and Windows security.

The first reason is quite simple—using Windows authentication allows IIS and the client browser to take care of the authentication process so you don't need to create a login page, check a database, or write any custom code. Similarly, Windows already supports basic user account features like password expiry, account lockout, and group membership.

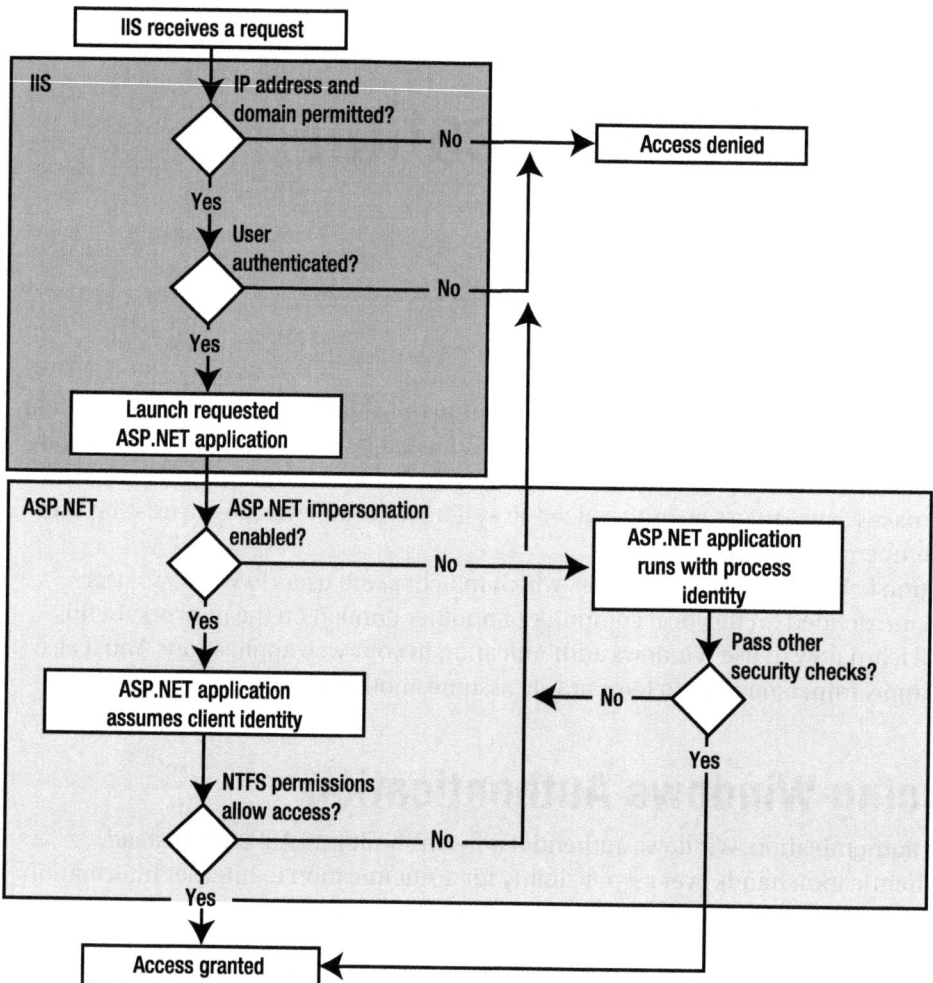

Figure 16-1. *The Windows authentication process*

The second, and most important, reason for using Windows authentication is that it allows you to leverage existing Windows accounts. Typically, you use Windows authentication for applications where the users are part of the same local network or intranet as your web server. That means you can authenticate users with the same credentials they use to log in to their computers. Best of all, depending on the settings you use and the network architecture, you may be able to provide "invisible" authentication that works without forcing a separate login step. Instead, the browser simply uses the logged-in identity of the current user.

The third reason you might want to use Windows authentication is that it allows you to take advantage of existing Windows security settings. For example, you can control access to files by setting Windows file-access permissions. However, it's important to remember that these permissions don't come into effect automatically. That's because by default your web application runs using a fixed account (typically ASPNET, as defined in the machine.config file). You can change this behavior by carefully using Windows authentication and imperson-ation, as described at the end of this chapter.

Why Would You *Not* Use Windows Authentication?

So why would you not want to use Windows authentication?

- It's tied to Windows users.

- It's tied to Windows client machines.

- It doesn't provide much flexibility or control, and can't be customized easily.

The first problem is that Windows authentication won't work unless the users you are authenticating already have valid Windows accounts. In a public website, this probably isn't the case. Even if you could create a Windows account for each visitor, it wouldn't be as efficient as a database-based approach for large numbers of users. There's also a potential security risk, because Windows user accounts can also have permissions to the web server computer or other network computers. You might not want to risk granting these abilities to your website users.

The second problem is that some of the authentication methods that IIS uses require users to have compatible software on their computers. This limits your ability to use Windows authentication for users who are using non-Microsoft operating systems or users who aren't using Internet Explorer.

The final main problem is that Windows authentication doesn't give you any control over the authentication process. There's also no easy way to add, remove, and manage Windows account information programmatically, or to store other user-specific information with the user credentials. As you learned in the last chapter, all of these features are easy to add to forms authentication, but they don't play any part in Windows authentication.

Mechanisms for Windows Authentication

When you use Windows authentication, IIS uses one of three possible authentication strategies to authenticate each request it receives:

- **Basic authentication.** The user name and password are passed as clear text. This is the only form of authentication supported by all browsers as part of the HTML standard.

- **Digest authentication.** The user name and password are not transmitted. Instead, a cryptographically secure hash with this information is sent.

- **Integrated Windows authentication.** The user name and password are not transmitted. Instead, the identity of a user already logged in to windows is passed automatically as a token. This is the only form of authentication that takes place transparently (without user intervention).

The following sections discuss these options.

Note There are other less commonly used protocols for Windows authentication. One example is certificate-based authentication. If you use this approach, you must distribute a digital certificate to each client, and map each certificate to the appropriate Windows account. Unfortunately, this technique is rife with administrative and deployment headaches. Additionally, IIS 6 includes support for advanced digest authentication (which works essentially the same as digest authentication, but stores the passwords more securely), and Passport authentication, which allows a user to log in using a Passport account that maps to a Windows user account.

Basic Authentication

The most widely supported authentication protocol is basic authentication. It's supported by almost all web browsers. When a website requests client authentication using basic authentication, the web browser displays a login dialog box for user and password, like the one shown in Figure 16-2.

Figure 16-2. *A login box for basic authentication*

After a user provides this information, the data itself is transmitted to the web server (in this case localhost). Once IIS receives the authentication data, it attempts to authenticate the user with the corresponding Windows account.

The key limitation of basic authentication is that it isn't secure—at least not on its own. User name and password credentials obtained via basic authentication are transmitted between the client and server as clear text. The data itself is encoded (not encrypted) into a Base64 string that eavesdroppers can easily read. For this reason, basic authentication should only be used in situations where there's no need to protect user credentials, or in conjunction with an HTTP wire encryption protocol such as Secure Sockets Layers (SSL). In this way, the data that would otherwise be clearly visible to any network sniffing utility will be encrypted using complex algorithms (as discussed in Chapter 14).

Digest Authentication

Digest authentication, like basic authentication, requires the user to provide account information using a login dialog box that is displayed by the browser. Unlike basic authentication, however, digest authentication passes a hash of the password, rather than the password itself. (Digest is another name for hash, which explains the name of this authentication scheme.) Because a hash is used, the password itself is never sent across the network, thereby preventing it from being stolen even if you aren't using SSL.

The process of authenticating a user with digest authentication works like this:

1. The unauthenticated client requests a restricted web page.

2. The server responds with an HTTP 401 response. This response includes a *nonce* value—a randomly generated series of bytes. The web server ensures that each nonce value is unique before it issues it.

3. The client uses nonce, the password, the user name, and some other values to create a hash. This hash value, known as the digest, is sent back to the server along with the plain text user name.

4. The server uses the nonce value, its stored password for the user name, and the other values to create a hash. It then compares this hash to the one provided by the client. If they match then the authentication succeeds.

Since the nonce value changes with each authentication request, the digest is not very useful to an attacker. The original password cannot be extracted from it. Similarly, because it incorporates a random nonce, the digest cannot be used for *replay attacks*, in which an attacker attempts to gain access at a later time by resending a previously intercepted digest.

In theory, digest authentication is a standard, and web servers and web browsers should all be able to use digest authentication to exchange authentication information. Unfortunately, Microsoft interpreted a part of the Digest authentication specification in a slightly different way than other organizations, such as the Apache Foundation (which provides the Apache web server) and the Mozilla project (which provides the Mozilla web browser). Currently, IIS digest authentication only works with Internet Explorer 5.0 or later.

Another limitation of Digest authentication in IIS is that it will only function when the virtual directory being authenticated is running on or controlled by a Windows Active Directory domain controller.

Integrated Windows Authentication

Integrated Windows authentication is the most convenient authentication standard for WAN-based LAN-based intranet applications, because it performs authentication without requiring any client interaction. When IIS asks the client to authenticate itself, the browser sends a token that represents the Windows user account of the current user. If the web server fails to authenticate the user with this information, a login dialog box is shown where the user can enter a different user name and password.

In order for integrated Windows authentication to work, both the client and the web server must be on the same local network or Intranet. That's because integrated Windows authentication doesn't actually transmit the user name and password information. Instead, it coordinates with the domain server or Active Directory instance where it is logged in, and gets that computer to send the authentication information to the web server. Integrated Windows authentication is extremely secure, but it's limited. It only works on Internet Explorer 2.0 or higher (integrated Windows authentication is not supported in non-Internet Explorer clients) and can't work across a proxy server.

Implementing Windows Authentication

In order to use Windows authentication in an ASP.NET application and have access to the user identity in ASP.NET, you need to take three steps:

- Configure the type of Windows authentication using IIS Manager.

- Configure ASP.NET to use the IIS authentication information using the web.config file.

- Restrict anonymous access for a web page, a subdirectory, or the entire application.

These steps are described in the following sections.

Configuring IIS

Before you can use Windows authentication, you need to choose the supported protocols by configuring the virtual directory. To do so, start IIS Manager (select Settings ➤ Control Panel ➤ Administrative Tools ➤ Internet Information Services). Then right-click a virtual directory or a subdirectory inside a virtual directory, and choose Properties. Select the Directory Security tab, which is shown in Figure 16-3.

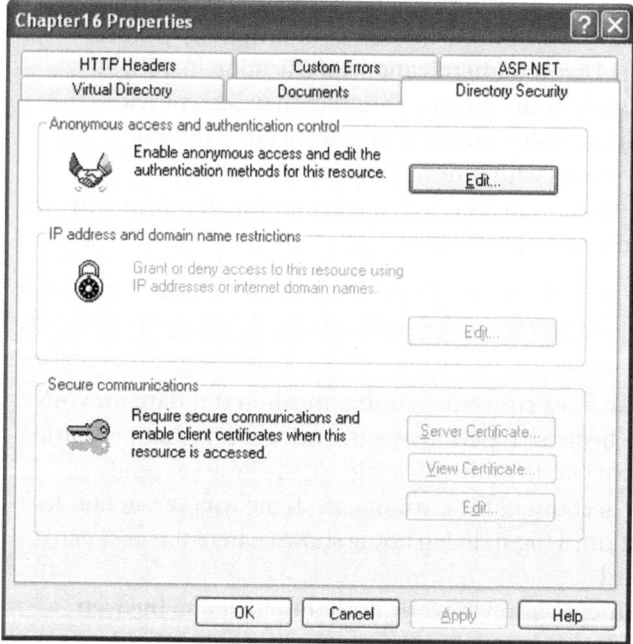

Figure 16-3. *Directory security settings*

Click the Edit button to modify the directory security settings. Enable the supported protocols in the Authenticated access box in the bottom half of the window. If you enable basic authentication, you can also set a default domain to use when interpreting the user credentials. (The user can also log in to a specific domain by supplying a user name in the format DomainName\UserName.) In the example in Figure 16-4, support is enabled for integrated Windows authentication and anonymous access.

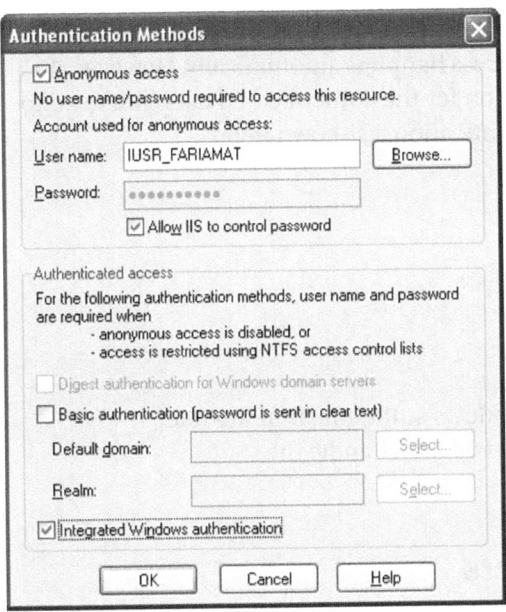

Figure 16-4. *Directory authentication methods*

■**Note** If you allow anonymous access, you can also set the Windows user account that IIS will use automatically. However, this user account has very little effect, and is mostly a holdover from classic ASP. In classic ASP, this account would be used to execute all code. In ASP.NET, a fixed account is used to execute code (typically ASPNET), because more privileges are required in order to successfully compile and cache web pages.

If you enable more than one authentication option, the client will use the strongest authentication method it supports as long as anonymous access is *not* enabled. If anonymous access is enabled, the client will access the website anonymously. That means if you want to force clients to log in, you need to take one of two steps:

- Remove the Anonymous access check box.

- Add authorization rules to the web.config file that explicitly deny anonymous users from accessing a specific page, subdirectory, or application.

Authorization rules are described briefly in this chapter, and in more detail in Chapter 17.

■**Note** If you remove integrated Windows authentication from your virtual directory, you won't be able to debug your web application. That's because Visual Studio .NET uses this protocol to authenticate you when you compile and run an application in the development environment.

Configuring ASP.NET

Once you've configured IIS, the authentication process happens automatically. However, if you want to be able to access the identity information for the authenticated user, you need to configure the web.config file to use Windows authentication, as shown here:

```
<configuration>
    <system.web>
        <!-- Other settings omitted. -->
        <authentication mode="Windows"/>
    </system.web>
</configuration>
```

This tells ASP.NET that you want to use the Windows authentication module. The WindowsAuthenticationModule HTTP module will then handle the Application_AuthenticateRequest event.

Denying Access to Anonymous Users

As described earlier, you can force users to log on by modifying IIS virtual directory settings, or by using authorization rules in the web.config file. The second approach is generally preferred. Not only does it give you more flexibility, but it also makes it easier to verify and modify authorization rules after the application is deployed to a production web server.

Authorization is described in detail in Chapter 17. For now, you'll only consider the simple technique of denying access to all unauthenticated users. To do this, you must use the <authorization> element of the web.config to add a new authorization rule, as follows:

```
<configuration>
    <system.web>
        <!-- Other settings omitted. -->
        <authorization>
            <deny users="?" />
        </authorization>
    </system.web>
</configuration>
```

The question mark (?) is a wildcard character that matches all anonymous users. By including this rule in your web.config file, you specify that anonymous users are not allowed. Every user must be authenticated using one of the configured Windows authentication protocols.

Accessing Windows User Information

One of the nice things about Windows authentication is that no login page is required. When the user requests a page that requires authentication, the browser transmits the credentials to IIS. Your web application can then retrieve information directly from the User property of the web page.

Here's an example that displays the currently authenticated user:

```
if (Request.IsAuthenticated)
{
    // Display generic identity information.
    lblInfo.Text = "<b>Name: </b>" + User.Identity.Name;
    lblInfo.Text += "<br><b>Authenticated With: </b>";
    lblInfo.Text += User.Identity.AuthenticationType;
}
```

This is the exact same code you could use to get information about the current identity when using forms authentication. However, you'll notice one slight difference. The user name is always in the form DomainName\UserName or ComputerName\UserName. Figure 16-5 shows an example with a user account named Matthew on the computer FARIAMAT.

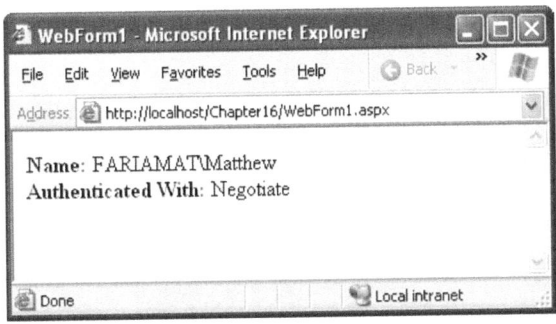

Figure 16-5. *Displaying user information*

The WindowsPrincipal Class

As you've learned in the past two chapters, the User property returns an IPrincipal object. When you use Windows authentication, this is an instance of the WindowsPrincipal class. The WindowsPrincipal class provides access to a WindowsIdentity object through the Identity property.

The WindowsPrincipal class implements three different overloads of IsInRole() that all check whether the user is in a specified Windows user group. The required IsInRole(string) overload is implemented so that it accepts the name of the user group to be checked. IsInRole(int) expects an integer Role Identifier (RID) that refers to a user group. Finally, an overload is provided that expects a member of the WindowsBuiltInRole enumeration, which provides a list of predefined Windows account types (like Guest, Administrator, and so on). The WindowsPrincipal, WindowsIdentity, and WindowsBuiltInRole types are all found in the System.Security.Principal namespace.

Here's a simple example that tests if the user is in a predefined Windows role:

```
if (Request.IsAuthenticated)
{
    lblInfo.Text = "<b>Name: </b>" + User.Identity.Name;
    WindowsIdentity principal = (WindowsPrincipal)User;
    lblInfo.Text += "<br><b>Power user? </b>";
    lblInfo.Text += principal.IsInRole(
        WindowsBuiltInRole.PowerUser).ToString();
}
```

Note that you must cast the User object to a WindowsPrincipal in order to access this Windows-specific functionality. Figure 16-6 shows the result.

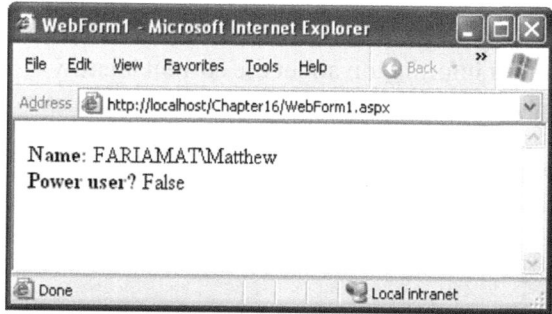

Figure 16-6. *Testing group membership*

Table 16-1 lists all the possible roles that are provided through the WindowsBuiltInRole enumeration. You can also test for membership with any arbitrary group you've created. This technique is discussed in Chapter 17.

Table 16-1. *Values for the WindowsBuiltInRole enumeration*

Role	Description
AccountOperator	Users with the special responsibility of managing the user accounts on a computer or domain.
Administrator	Users with complete and unrestricted access to the computer or domain.
BackupOperator	Users who can override certain security restrictions only as part of backing up or restoring operations.
Guest	Like the User role, but even more restrictive.
PowerUser	Similar to Administrator, but with some restrictions.
PrintOperator	Like a User, but with additional privileges for taking control of a printer.
Replicator	Like a User, but with additional privileges to support file replication in a domain.
SystemOperator	Similar to Administrator, with some restrictions. Generally, system operators manage a computer.

Role	Description
User	Users are prevented from making systemwide changes, and can only run *certified applications* (see http://www.microsoft.com/windows2000/server/ evaluation/business/certified.asp for more information).

The WindowsIdentity Class

You can also access some additional information about the currently authenticated user by casting the generic Identity object to a WindowsIdentity object. WindowsIdentity provides a number of additional members, as described in Table 16-2.

Table 16-2. *Additional Members of the WindowsIdentity Class*

Member	Description
IsAnonymous	This property returns true if the user is anonymous (has not been authenticated).
IsGuest	This property returns true if the user is using a Guest account. Guest accounts are designed for public access and do not confer very many privileges.
IsSystem	Returns true if the user account has the "act as part of the operating system" setting, which means it is a highly privileged system account.
Token	Returns the operating system token for the identity.
Impersonate()	This method instructs ASP.NET to run the following code under the corresponding Windows account. You'll learn much more about impersonation later in this chapter.
GetAnonymous()	This static method creates a WindowsIdentity that represents an anonymous user.
GetCurrent()	This static method creates a WindowsIdentity that represents the identity tied to the current security context (the user whose identity the current code is running under). If you use this method in an ASP.NET application, you'll retrieve the user account under which the code is running, *not* the user account that was authenticated by IIS and is provided in the User object.

The following code displays extra Windows-specific information about the user:

```
if (Request.IsAuthenticated)
{
    lblInfo.Text = "<b>Name: </b>" + User.Identity.Name;

    WindowsIdentity identity = (WindowsIdentity)User.Identity;
    lblInfo.Text += "<br><b>Token: </b>";
    lblInfo.Text += identity.Token.ToString();
    lblInfo.Text += "<br><b>Guest? </b>";
    lblInfo.Text += identity.IsGuest.ToString();
    lblInfo.Text += "<br><b>System? </b>";
    lblInfo.Text += identity.IsSystem.ToString();
}
```

Figure 16-7 shows the result.

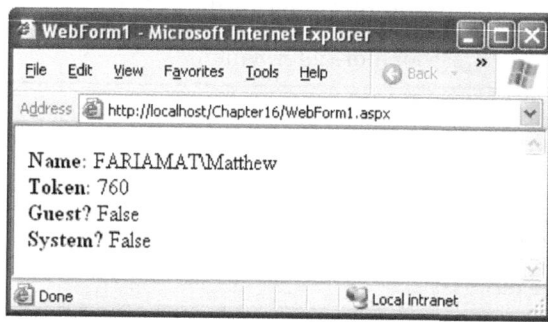

Figure 16-7. *Showing Windows-specific user information*

Impersonation

Everything that ASP.NET does is executed under a Windows account. By default, this identity is the account ASPNET (in IIS 5), but it can be configured through the machine.config file, as described in Chapter 2. As each page request is processed, the configured identity determines what ASP.NET can and cannot do.

Impersonation provides you with a way to make this system more flexible. Instead of using a fixed account for all users, web pages, and applications, you can temporarily change the identity that ASP.NET uses for certain tasks. This process of temporarily assuming the identity of another Windows account is impersonation.

One common reason to use impersonation is to differentiate the permissions given to different web applications on the same computer. In this case, you configure impersonation to use a specific, fixed account for each web application. Another potential reason to use impersonation is to make use of the permissions that are defined for the currently authenticated user. This means that the actions ASP.NET performs will be limited according to the person who is using the application. For example, your web server might be set up with a number of personalized directories, one for each user. By impersonating the user in your web application, you ensure that your application cannot inadvertently give the user access to any files except the ones in that user's directory. If you attempt to access a restricted file, the Windows operating system will intervene, and an exception will be raised in your code.

■**Note** Impersonation does not give you the ability to circumvent Windows security. You must still have the credentials for the user you wish to impersonate, whether you write them into your code or they are provided by a user at runtime.

There are two types of impersonation in ASP.NET. Configured (web.config) impersonation allows you to specify that page requests should be run under the identity of the user who is making the request. Programmatic impersonation gives you the ability to switch to another identity within the code and switch back to the original identity when a specific task is finished. You'll learn about both of these techniques in the following sections.

Impersonation in Windows 2000

In order to impersonate other users when running on Windows 2000, the account that does the impersonation must have the "act as part of the operating system" permission. This permission is not required on Windows XP or later.

In order to use impersonation, you must specifically add this permission to the ASPNET account. You can perform this administrative task using the Local Security Policy tool. Select Control Panel ➤ Administrative Tools, and select Local Security Policy. Then browse to the Local Policies ➤ User Rights Assignment node. You'll see a list of settings, as shown in Figure 16-8.

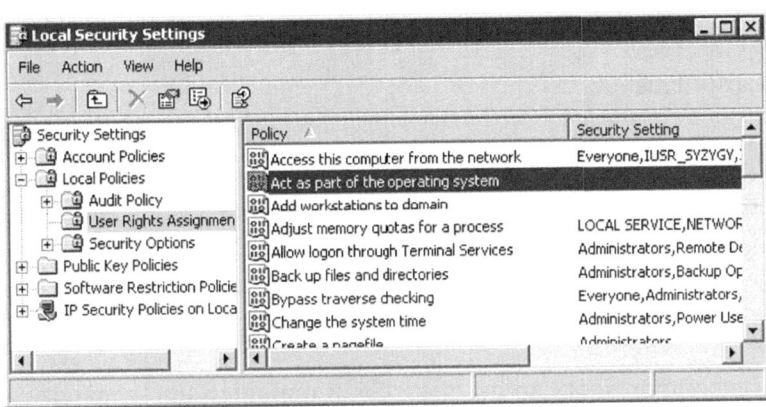

Figure 16-8. *Reviewing user rights assignments*

Double-click the Act as Part of the Operating System entry and select Add User or Group. This displays a dialog box where you can explicitly give this permission to an account. In the text box at the bottom of the window, enter the account name ASPNET, as shown in Figure 16-9.

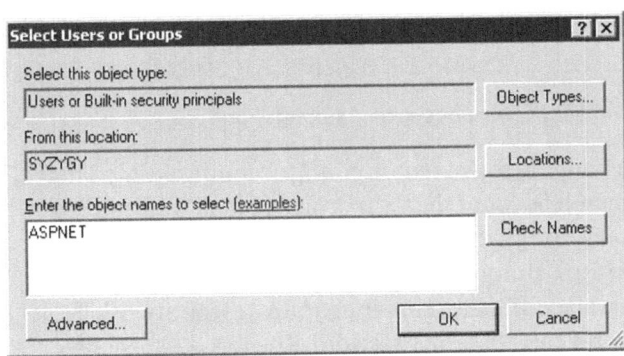

Figure 16-9. *Assigning the permission to ASPNET*

Finally, click OK to confirm your action and add this permission to the ASPNET account.

Tip This permission doesn't need to be assigned to the local system account, which always has it. As a result, if you've configured ASP.NET to use the local system account, no additional configuration steps are required.

Configured Impersonation

The simplest form of impersonation is configured impersonation, where you use the web.config file to define the impersonation behavior you want. You accomplish this by adding the <identity> element shown here:

```
<configuration>
    <system.web>
        <!-- Other settings omitted. -->
        <identity impersonate="true" />
    </system.web>
</configuration>
```

There is more than one way to configure the identity element, depending on the result you want. If you want to impersonate the IIS authenticated account, you should use this setting:

```
<identity impersonate="true">
```

Keep in mind that if you allow anonymous access, the IUSR_[ComputerName] account may be used. When using this approach, the impersonated account must have all the permissions required to run ASP.NET code, including read-write access to the c:\[WinDir]\ Microsoft.NET\Framework\[Version]\Temporary ASP.NET Files where the compiled ASP.NET files are stored. Otherwise, an error will occur and the page will not be served.

ASP.NET also provides the option to specifically set an account that will be used for running code. This technique is useful if you want different ASP.NET applications to execute with different, but fixed, permissions. In this case, the user's authenticated identity isn't used by the ASP.NET code. It just sets a base level of permissions you want your application to have. Here's an example:

```
<identity impersonate="true" userName="matthew" password="secret" >
```

This approach is more flexible than changing the machine.config account setting. The machine.config setting determines the default account that will be used for all web applications on the computer. The impersonation settings, on the other hand, override the machine.config setting for individual websites. Unfortunately, the password for the impersonated account cannot be encrypted in the web.config file. This constitutes a security risk if other users have access to the computer, and can read the password. The risk is especially severe if you are using impersonation with a highly privileged account.

Programmatic Impersonation

Configured impersonation allows you to impersonate a user for the entire duration of a request. If you want more control, such as the ability to impersonate a user for only part of the page request, you have to do the impersonation yourself in your code.

The key to impersonating a user programmatically is the WindowsIdentity.Impersonate() method. This method sets up impersonation for a specific account. You identify the account you want to impersonate by using its *account token*. Account tokens are what Windows uses to track users once their credentials are approved. If you have the token for a user, you can impersonate that user.

The general process is as follows:

1. Obtain an account token for the account you want to impersonate.

2. Use WindowsIdentity.Impersonate() to start impersonation. This method returns a WindowsImpersonationContext object.

3. Call the Undo() method of the WindowsImpersonationContext object to revert to the original identity.

Getting a Token

There are two main ways that you can get an account token. The most common approach is to retrieve the token for the currently authenticated user. You can access this token through the current security context, using the WindowsIdentity.Token property. Tokens are represented in .NET as IntPtr objects, which are representations of pointers to unmanaged memory locations. However, you never need to interact with this directly. Instead, you simply need to pass the token to the WindowsIdentity.Impersonate() method.

Here's an example that extracts the token for the current user:

```
IntPtr token = ((WindowsIdentity)User.Identity).Token;
```

The only other way to get a user token is to programmatically log in with a specific user name and password. Unfortunately, .NET does not provide managed classes for logging a user in. Instead, you must use the LogonUser() function from the unmanaged Win32 security API.

In order to use the LogonUser() function, you must first declare it as shown here:

```
[DllImport(@"c:\Windows\System32\advapi32.dll")]
public static extern bool LogonUser(string lpszUserName,
   string lpszDomain, string lpszPassword, int dwLogonType,
   int dwLogonProvider, out int phToken);
```

As you can see, the LogonUser() function exists in the advapi32.dll. It takes a user name, domain, password, logon type, and logon provider input parameters, along with an output parameter that allows you to access the token following a successful logon. The parameter names aren't important. In this example, the somewhat cryptic names from the Windows API reference are used. A Boolean result is returned to indicate whether the logon was successful.

■**Note** Windows XP and later operating systems impose restrictions on the use of blank passwords to prevent network-based attacks. As a result of these restrictions, you won't be able to use the LogonUser() function to impersonate an account with a blank password.

Once you have imported the LogonUser() function, you can use it in your code to log the user in, as shown here:

```
// Define required variables.
string user = "matthew";
string password = "secret";
string machine = "FARIAMAT";
int returnedToken;

// Try to log on.
if (LogonUser(user, machine, password, 3, 0, out returnedToken))
{
    // The attempt was successful. Get the token.
    IntPtr token = new IntPtr(returnedToken);
}
```

Not that you must convert the integer value returned by LogonUser() into an IntPtr in order to use it with the WindowsIdentity.Impersonate() method.

Performing the Impersonation

Once you have an account token, you can use the WindowsIdentity.Impersonate() method to start impersonating the corresponding identity. There are two ways to use the Impersonate() method. You can use the static version, which requires an account token. Alternatively, you can use the instance version, which impersonates the identity represented by the corresponding WindowsIdentity object. In either case, the Impersonate() method returns a WindowsImpersonationContext object that has a single function—it allows you to revert back to the original identity by calling its Undo() method.

Here's an example of programmatic impersonation at its simplest, using the static version of the Impersonate() method:

```
WindowsImpersonationContext impersonateContext;
impersonateContext = WindowsIdentity.Impersonate(token);

// (Now perform tasks under the impersonated ID.
// This code will not be able to perform any task
// that the user would not be allowed to do.)

impersonateContext.Undo()
```

At anytime, you can determine the identity that your code is currently executing under by calling the WindowsIdentity.GetCurrent() method. Here's a function that uses that technique to determine the current identity and display the corresponding user name in a label on a web page:

```
private void DisplayIdentity()
{
    // Get the identity under which the code is currently executing.
    WindowsIdentity identity = WindowsIdentity.GetCurrent();
    lblInfo.Text += "Executing as: " + identity.Name + "<br>";
}
```

Using the method, you can create a simple test that impersonates the authenticated IIS identity and then reverts to the standard identity:

```
private void Page_Load(object sender, System.EventArgs e)
{
    if (User is WindowsPrincipal)
    {
        DisplayIdentity();

        // Impersonate the IIS identity.
        WindowsIdentity id;
        id = (WindowsIdentity)User.Identity;
        WindowsImpersonationContext impersonateContext;
        impersonateContext = id.Impersonate();
        DisplayIdentity();

        // Revert to the original ID as shown here.
        impersonateContext.Undo();
        DisplayIdentity();
    }
    else
    {
        // User isn't Windows authenticated.
        // Throw an error or take other steps.
    }
}
```

Figure 16-10 shows the result.

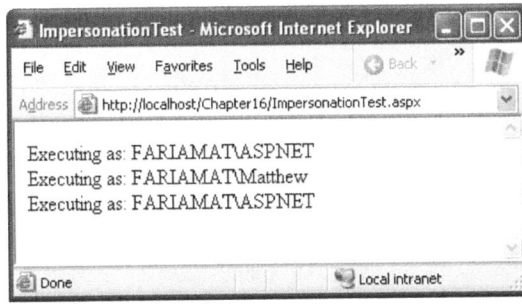

Figure 16-10. *Impersonating a user programmatically*

Summary

In this chapter, you've learned how to use Windows authentication with ASP.NET to let IIS validate user identities. You've learned about the different types of authentication, how to retrieve user information, and how to impersonate users so your code runs under a different Windows account. In the next chapter, you'll learn about using advanced authorization rules that apply to Windows authentication and forms authentication.

■ ■ ■

CHAPTER 17

Authorization

So far, you've seen how to confirm that users are who they say they are, and how to retrieve information about that authenticated identity. This gives your application the basic ability to distinguish between different users, but it's only a starting point. To create a truly secure web application, you need to act upon that identity at various points using *authorization*.

Authorization is the process of determining if an authenticated user has sufficient permissions to perform a given action. This action could be requesting a web page, accessing a resource controlled by the operating system (like a file or database), or performing an application-specific task (like placing an order or assigning a project). Some of these checks are performed automatically by Windows, and you can code others declaratively using the web.config file. There are still others that you'll need to perform directly in your code using the IPrincipal object.

In this chapter, you'll learn how ASP.NET authorization works, how to protect different resources, and how to implement your own role-based security.

URL Authorization

The most straightforward way to set security permissions is on individual web pages, web services, and subdirectories. Ideally, a web application framework should support resource-specific authorization without requiring you to change code and recompile the application. ASP.NET supports this requirement with declarative *authorization rules*, which you can define in the web.config file.

The rules you define are acted upon by UrlAuthorizationModule, a specific HTTP module. It examines these rules, and checks each request to make sure that users can't access resources you've specifically restricted. This type of authorization is called *URL authorization* because it considers only two details—the security context of the user, and the URL of the resource that the user's attempting to access. If the page is forbidden and you're using forms authentication, the user will be redirected to the login page. If the page is forbidden and you're using Windows authentication, the user will receive an "access denied" (HTTP 401) error page, as shown in Figure 17-1, or a more generic error message or custom error page, depending on the <customErrors> element.

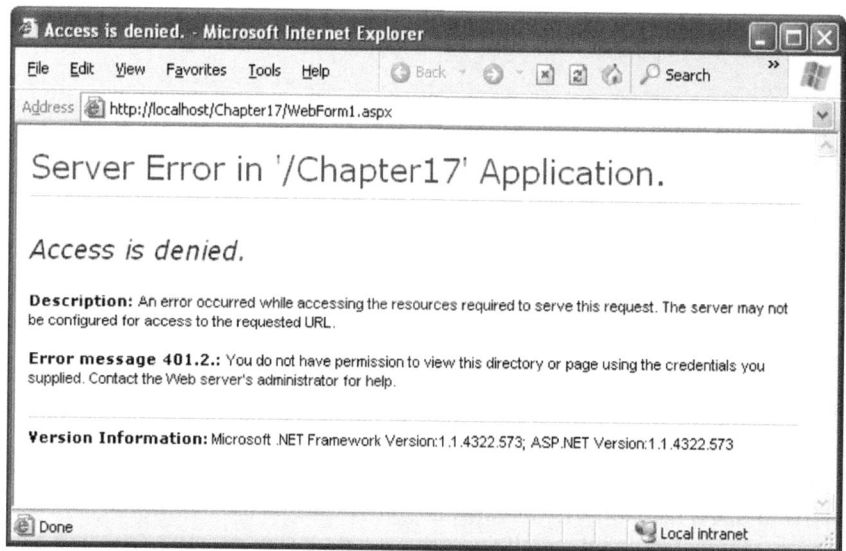

Figure 17-1. *Trying to request a forbidden web page*

Authorization Rules

You define the authorization rules in the <authorization> element of the web.config file.
The basic structure is shown here:

```
<authorization>
  <allow users="comma-separated list of users"
         roles="comma-separated list of roles"
         verbs="comma-separated list of verbs" />
  <deny  users="comma-separated list of users"
         roles="comma-separated list of roles"
         verbs="comma-separated list of verbs" />
</authorization>
```

In other words, there are two types of rules: allow and deny. You can add as many allow
and deny rules as you want. Each rule identifies one or more users or roles (groups of users).
In addition, you can use the verbs attribute to create a rule that only applies to specific types
of HTTP requests (GET, POST, HEAD, or DEBUG).

You've already seen the simplest example in the previous chapters. To deny access to all
anonymous users, you can use a <deny> rule like this:

```
<authorization>
  <deny users="?" />
</authorization>
```

In this case, the question mark (?) is a wildcard that represents all users with unknown
identities. This rule is almost always used in authentication scenarios. That's because you can't
specifically deny other, known users unless you first force all users to authenticate themselves.

There's one additional wildcard—the asterisk (*), which represents all users. For example,
the following <authorization> section allows access by authenticated and anonymous users:

```
<authorization>
  <allow users="*" />
</authorization>
```

This rule is rarely required, because it's already present in the machine.config file. After ASP.NET applies all the rules in the web.config file, it applies rules from the machine.config. As a result, any user who is explicitly denied access automatically gains access.

Now consider what happens if you add more than one rule in the authorization section:

```
<authorization>
    <allow users="*" />
    <deny users="?" />
</authorization>
```

When evaluating rules, ASP.NET scans through the list from top to bottom. As soon as it finds an applicable rule, it stops its search. Thus, in the previous case, it will determine that the rule <allow users="*"> applies to the current request, and will not evaluate the second line. That means these rules will allow all users, including anonymous users. Reversing the order of these two lines, however, will deny anonymous users (by matching the first rule) and allow all other users (by matching the second rule).

```
<authorization>
    <deny users="?" />
    <allow users="*" />
</authorization>
```

When you add authorization rules to the web.config file in the root directory of the web application, they automatically apply to all the web resources that are a part of that application. If you've denied anonymous users, ASP.NET will examine the authentication mode. If you've selected forms authentication, ASP.NET will direct the user to the login page. If you're using Windows authentication, IIS will request user credentials from the client browser, and a login dialog box may appear (depending on the protocols you've enabled).

In the following sections, you'll learn how to fine-tune authorization rules to give them a more carefully defined scope.

Controlling Access for Specific Users

The <allow> and <deny> rules don't need to use the asterisk or question mark wildcards. Instead, they can specifically identify a user name or a list of comma-separated user names. For example, the following authorization rule specifically restricts access from three users. These users will not be able to access the pages in this directory. All other authenticated users will be allowed.

```
<authorization>
  <deny users="?" />
  <deny users="dan" />
  <deny users="jenny" />
  <deny users="matthew" />
  <allow users="*" />
</authorization>
```

You can also use a comma-separated list to deny multiple users at once. Here's an equivalent version of the previous example that only uses two authorization rules:

```
<authorization>
  <deny users="?" />
  <deny users="dan,jenny,matthew" />
  <allow users="*" />
</authorization>
```

Note that in both these cases, the order in which the three users are listed is unimportant. However, it *is* important that these users are denied before you include the <allow> rule. For example, the following authorization rules won't affect jenny, because ASP.NET matches the rule allowing all users and doesn't read any further:

```
<authorization>
  <deny users="?" />
  <deny users="dan,matthew" />
  <allow users="*" />
  <deny users="jenny" />
</authorization>
```

When creating secure applications, it's often a better approach to explicitly allow specific users or groups, and then deny all others (rather than denying specific users, as in our examples so far). Here's an example of authorization rules that explicitly allow two users. All other user requests will be denied access, even if they are authenticated.

```
<authorization>
  <deny users="?" />
  <allow users="dan,matthew" />
  <deny users="*" />
</authorization>
```

There's one other detail to consider. The format of user names in these examples assumes forms authentication. In forms authentication, you assign a user name when you call the RedirectFromLoginPage() method. At this point, the UrlAuthorizationModule will use that name, and check it against the list of authorization rules. Windows authentication is a little different, because names are entered in the format DomainName\UserName or ComputerName\UserName. You need to use the same format when listing users in the authorization rules. For example, if you have the user accounts dan and matthew on a computer named FARIAMAT, you can use these authorization rules:

```
<authorization>
  <deny users="?" />
  <allow users="FARIAMAT\dan,FARIAMAT\matthew" />
  <deny users="*" />
</authorization>
```

■**Note** Make sure you specify the computer or domain name in the users attribute when you use Windows authentication. You can't use an alias like localhost, because this will not be successfully matched.

Controlling Access to Specific Directories

A common application design is to place files that require authentication into a separate directory. With ASP.NET configuration files, this approach is easy. Just leave <authorization> element in the normal parent directory empty, and add a web.config file that specifies stricter settings in the secured directory.

Remember that when you add the web.config file in the subdirectory, it shouldn't contain any of the application-specific settings. In fact, it should only contain the authorization information, as shown here:

```
<configuration>
  <system.web>
    <authorization>
      <deny users="?" />
    </authorization>
  </system.web>
</configuration>
```

■**Note** You cannot change the <authentication> tag settings in the web.config file of a subdirectory in your application. Instead, all the directories in the application must use the same authentication system. However, each directory can have its own authorization rules.

When using authorization rules in a subdirectory, ASP.NET still reads the authorization rules from the parent directory. The difference is that it applies the rules in the subdirectory *first*. This is important, because ASP.NET stops as soon as it matches an authorization rule. For example, consider an example in which the root virtual directory contains this rule:

```
<allow users="dan" />
```

and a subdirectory contains this rule:

```
<deny users="dan" />
```

In this case, the user dan will be able to access any resource in the root directory, but no resources in the subdirectory. If you reverse these two rules, dan will be able to access resources in the subdirectory but not the root directory.

To make life more interesting, ASP.NET allows an unlimited hierarchy of subdirectories and authorization rules. For example, it's quite possible to have a virtual directory with authorization rules, a subdirectory that defines additional rules, and then a subdirectory inside that subdirectory that applies even more rules. The easiest way to understand the authorization process in this case is to imagine all the rules as a single list, starting with the directory where the requested page is located. If all those rules are processed without a match, ASP.NET then begins reading the authorization rules in the parent directory, and then its parent directory, and so on, until it finds a match. If no authorization rules match, ASP.NET will ultimately match the <allow users="*"> rule in the machine.config file.

Controlling Access to Specific Files

Generally, setting file access permissions by directory is the cleanest and easiest approach. However, you also have the option of restricting specific files by adding <location> tags to your web.config file.

The location tags sit outside of the main <system.web> tag and are nested directly in the base <configuration> tag, as shown here.

```
<configuration>
    <system.web>
        <!-- Other settings omitted. -->
        <authorization>
            <allow users="*" />
        </authorization>
    </system.web>

    <location path="SecuredPage.aspx">
        <system.web>
            <authorization>
                <deny users="?" />
            </authorization>
        </system.web>
    </location>

    <location path="AnotherSecuredPage.aspx">
        <system.web>
            <authorization>
                <deny users="?" />
            </authorization>
        </system.web>
    </location>

</configuration>
```

In this example, all files in the application are allowed, except SecuredPage.aspx and AnotherSecuredPage.aspx, which have an access rule denying anonymous users.

Controlling Access for Specific Roles

To make website security easier to understand and maintain, users are often grouped into categories, called *roles*. If you need to manage an enterprise application that supports thousands of users, you can understand the value of roles. If you needed to define permissions for each individual user, it would be tiring, difficult to change, and nearly impossible to complete without error.

In Windows authentication, roles are automatically available and naturally integrated. In this case, roles are actually Windows groups. You might use built-in groups (like Administrator, Guest, PowerUser, and so on), or you can create your own to represent application-specific categories (like Manager, Contracter, Supervisor, and so on). Roles aren't provided intrinsically in forms authentication, but it's fairly easy to create your own system that slots users into appropriate groups based on their credentials. You'll learn about this technique later in this chapter.

Once roles have been defined, you can create authorization rules that act on these roles. In fact, these rules look essentially the same as the user-specific rules you've seen already.

For example, the following authorization rules deny all anonymous users, allow two specific users (dan and matthew), and allow two specific groups (Manager and Supervisor). All other users are denied.

```
<authorization>
  <deny users="?" />
  <allow users="FARIAMAT\dan,FARIAMAT\matthew" />
  <allow roles="FARIAMAT\Manager,FARIAMAT\Supervisor" />
  <deny users="*" />
</authorization>
```

Using role-based authorization rules is simple conceptually, but it can become tricky in practice. The issue is that when you use roles, your authorization rules can overlap. For example, consider what happens if you allow a group that contains a specific user, and then explicitly deny that user. Or consider the reverse—allowing a user by name, but denying the group to which the user belongs. In these scenarios, you might expect the more fine-grained rule (the rule affecting the user) to take precedence over the more general rule (the rule affecting the group). Or, you might expect the more restrictive rules to always take precedence, as in the Windows operating system. However, neither of these approaches is used in ASP.NET. Instead, ASP.NET simply uses the first matching rule. As a result, rule ordering can become very important.

Consider this example:

```
<authorization>
  <deny users="?" />
  <allow users="FARIAMAT\matthew" />
  <deny roles="FARIAMAT\Guest" />
  <allow roles="FARIAMAT\Manager" />
  <deny users="FARIAMAT\dan" />
  <allow roles="FARIAMAT\Supervisor" />
  <deny users="*" />
</authorization>
```

Here's how ASP.NET parses these rules:

- In this example, the user matthew is allowed, no matter what group he belongs to.

- All users in the Guest role are then denied. If matthew is a Guest, matthew is still allowed because the user-specific rule is matched first.

- Next, all users in the Manager group are allowed. The only exception is users who are in both the Manager and Guest group. The Guest rule occurs earlier in the list, so they would have already been denied.

- Next, the user dan is denied access. But if dan belongs to the allowed Manager group, dan will already have been allowed, because this rule won't be executed.

- Any users who are in the Supervisor group, and who haven't been explicitly allowed or denied by one of the preceding rules, are allowed.

- Finally, all other users are denied.

Keep in mind that these overlapping rules can also span multiple directories. For example, a subdirectory might deny a user while a parent directory allows a user in that group. In this example, when accessing files in the subdirectory, the user-specific rule is matched first.

File Authorization

URL authorization is one of the cornerstones of ASP.NET authorization. However, ASP.NET also uses another type of authorization that's often not recognized. This is file-based authorization, and it's implemented by the FileAuthorizationModule. File-based authorization only comes into effect if you're using Windows authentication. If you're using custom authentication or forms authentication, it's not used.

To understand file authorization, you need to understand how the Windows operating system enforces file-system security. If your file system uses the NTFS format, you can set ACLs (access control lists) that specifically identify users and roles that are allowed or denied access to individual files. The FileAuthorizationModule simply checks the Windows permissions for the file you're requesting. For example, if you request a web page, the FileAuthorizationModule checks that the currently authenticated IIS user has the permissions required to access the underlying .aspx file. If it doesn't, the page code is not executed, and the user receives an "access denied" message.

New ASP.NET users often wonder why file authorization needs to be implemented by a separate module—shouldn't it take place automatically at the hands of the operating system? To understand why the FileAuthorizationModule is required, you need to remember how ASP.NET executes code. Unless you've enabled impersonation, ASP.NET executes under a fixed user account, such as ASPNET. The Windows operating system will check that the ASPNET account has the permissions it needs to access the .aspx file, but it wouldn't perform the same check for the user authenticated by IIS. The FileAuthorizationModule fills the gap. It performs authorization checks using the security context of the current user. As a result, the system administrator can grant permissions to files or folders and use that to control access to portions of an ASP.NET application. Generally, it's clearer and more straightforward to use authorization rules in the web.config file. However, if you want to take advantage of existing Windows permissions in a local network or an intranet scenario, you can.

Authorization Checks in Code

With URL authorization and file authorization, you can only control access to individual web pages. The next step in ensuring a secure application is to build checks into your application before attempting specific tasks or allowing certain operations. In order to use these techniques, you'll need to write some code.

Using the IsInRole() Method

As you've seen in earlier chapters, all IPrincipal objects provide an IsInRole() method, which lets you evaluate whether a user is a member of a group. It accepts the role name as a string name, and returns true if the user is a member of that role.

For example, here's how you can check if the current user is a member of the Supervisors role:

```
if (User.IsInRole("Supervisors"))
{
    // Do nothing, the page should be accessed as normal because the
    // user has administrator privileges.
}
else
{
    // Don't allow this page. Instead, redirect to the home page.
    Response.Redirect("default.aspx");
}
```

Remember that when using Windows authentication you need to the format DomainName\GroupName or ComputerName\GroupName. Here's an example:

```
if (User.IsInRole(@"FARIAMAT\Supervisors"))
{ ... }
```

This approach works for custom groups that you've created, but not for built-in groups that are defined by the operating system. If you want to check if a user is a member of one of the built-in groups, you use this syntax:

```
if (User.IsInRole(@"BUILTIN\Administrators"))
{ ... }
```

Of course, you can also cast the User object to a WindowsPrincipal and use the overloaded version of IsInRole() that accepts the WindowsBuiltInRole enumeration, as described in Chapter 16.

Using the PrincipalPermission Class

.NET also includes another way to enforce role and user rules. Instead of checking with the IsInRole() method, you can use the PrincipalPermission class from the System.Security.Permissions namespace.

The basic strategy is to create a PrincipalPermission object that represents the user or role information you require. Then, invoke the PrincipalPermission.Demand() method. If the current user doesn't meet the requirements, a SecurityException will be thrown, which you can catch (or deal with using a custom error page).

The Demand() method takes two parameters—one for the user name, and one for the role name. You can omit either one of these parameters by supplying a null reference in its place. For example, the following code tests if the user is a Windows administrator:

```
try
{
    PrincipalPermission pp = new PrincipalPermission(null,
      @"BUILTIN\Administrators");
    pp.Demand();


    // If the code reaches this point, the demand succeeded.
    // The current user is an administrator.
}
catch (SecurityException err)
{
    // The demand failed. The current user isn't an administrator.
}
```

The advantage of this approach is that you don't need to write any conditional logic. Instead, you can simply demand all the permissions you need. This works particularly well if you need to verify that a user is a member of multiple groups. The disadvantage is that using exception handling to control the flow of your application is a slower approach. Often, PrincipalPermission checks are used in addition to web.config rules as a failsafe. In other words, you can call Demand() to ensure that even if a web.config file has been inadvertently modified, users in the wrong groups won't be allowed.

Merging PrincipalPermission Objects

The PrincipalPermission approach also gives you the ability to evaluate more complex authentication rules. For example, consider a situation where UserA and UserB, who belong to different groups, are both allowed to access certain functionality. If you use the IPrincipal object, you need to call IsInRole() twice. An alternate approach is to create multiple PrincipalPermission objects and merge them to get one PrincipalPermission object. Then you can call Demand() on just this object.

Here's an example that combines two roles:

```
try
{
    PrincipalPermission pp1 = new PrincipalPermission(null,
      @"BUILTIN\Administrators");
    PrincipalPermission pp2 = new PrincipalPermission(null,
      @"BUILTIN\Guests");

    // Combine these two permissions.
    PrincipalPermission pp3 = (PrincipalPermission)pp1.Union(pp2);
    pp3.Demand();
```

```
    // If the code reaches this point, the demand succeeded.
    // The current user is in one of these roles.
}
catch (SecurityException err)
{
    // The demand failed. The current user is in none of these roles.
}
```

This example checks that a user is a member of either one of the two Windows groups, Administrators or Guests. You can also ensure that a user is a member of *both* groups. In this case, use the PrincipalPermission.Intersect() method instead of PrincipalPermission.Union().

Using the PrincipalPermission Attribute

The PrincipalPermission attribute provides another way of validating the current user's credentials. It serves the same purpose as the PrincipalPermission class, but it's used declaratively. In other words, you attach it to a given class or method, and the CLR (common language runtime) checks it automatically when the corresponding code runs. Unlike the PrincipalPermission object, there's no way to catch the exception thrown by the PrincipalPermission attribute.

When you use a PrincipalPermission attribute, you can restrict access to a specific user or a specific role. Here's an example that prevents a web page being used by nonadministrators:

```
[PrincipalPermission(SecurityAction.Demand,
 Role=@"BUILTIN\Administrators")]
public class MyWebPage
{ ... }
```

And here's an example that restricts a particular method to a specific user:

```
[PrincipalPermission(SecurityAction.Demand, User=@"FARIAMAT\matthew")]
private void DoSomething()
{ ... }
```

PrincipalPermission attributes give you another way to safeguard your code. You won't use them to make decisions at runtime, but you might use them to ensure that even if web.config rules are modified or circumvented, a basic level of security remains.

Role-Based Authorization with Forms Authentication

Role-based authorization is a flexible and manageable approach to managing authorization. Unfortunately, with forms authentication there is no automatic way to assign a user to specific roles. There is no method that provides this functionality in the FormsAuthentication class and, and even if you store user credentials in the web.config file, there is no way to declare roles. However, if you plug in to the application event model, you can customize forms authentication and associate roles with all users.

The key step is to respond to the HttpApplication.AuthenticateRequest event in the global.asax file, which fires when the user logs in. At this point, you can create a new GenericPrincipal class using the current user information and the additional role information. You can attach that GenericPrincipal to the current security context by assigning it to the User property. That way it will be available for the remainder of the request processing.

Of course, in order to perform this task you need to have a way to determine the roles for each user. You can draw this information from any data store, including a file or a database. In the next example, you'll see how to extend the forms authentication example from Chapter 15 to support custom roles.

The basic steps are as follows:

- Add the role information to the user credential store.

- Add a method to the credential store class that can retrieve the roles for a user.

- Alter the login code so it calls this method, and adds the list of roles to the authentication cookie.

- Create a new GenericPrincipal for the user, with the roles, when the HttpApplication.AuthenticateRequest event fires.

Creating the Data Store

The first step is to change the structure of the back-end database. Roles and users have a many-to-many relationship. In other words, one user can belong to multiple roles, and one role can be applied to multiple users. For that reason, you need three tables—a table that lists roles, a table that lists users, and an intermediary table that links the two. Figure 17-2 shows the three tables and their relationships.

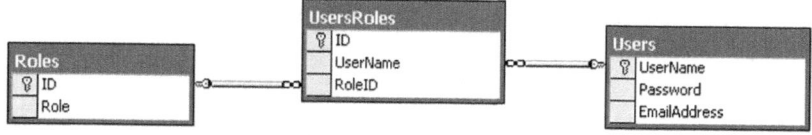

Figure 17-2. *Storing user roles in a database*

Each record in the UsersRoles table represents a pairing between one user and one role. Figure 17-3 shows some sample data. For example, you can see that the user jenny is a member of the Users role, while dan is a member of the Administrators role and the Supervisors roles.

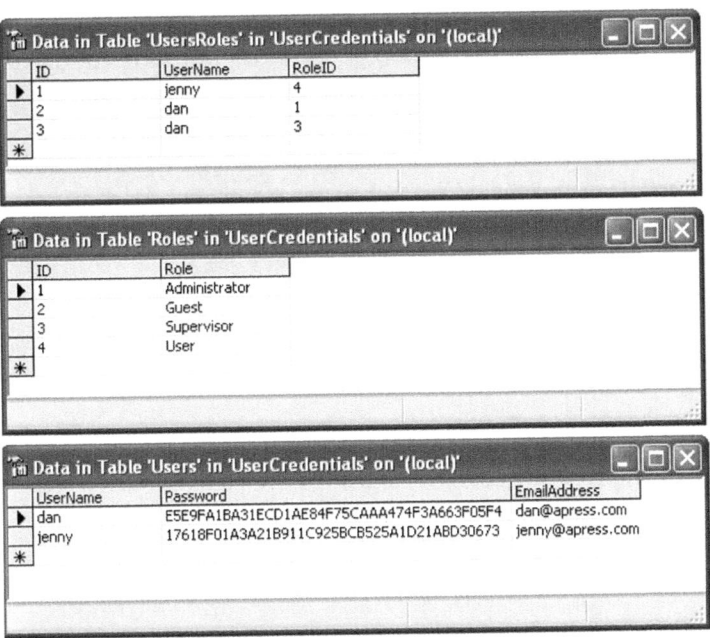

Figure 17-3. *Sample user and role data*

Now that you have the information in place, you're ready to work with it in your application.

Retrieving the Role Information

You now need to write the code that extracts the role information for a given user. It makes natural sense to add a dedicated method for this task to the DatabaseCredentialStore class developed in Chapter 15. This code simply needs to execute a database command that retrieves the list of roles and store them in some sort of object. In this example, the objects are filled into a dynamic ArrayList and then converted into an ordinary string array. (You can't use a string array from the start, because all arrays are fixed in size and you won't know how many matching roles there are until the reader is finished reading all the returned records.)

```
public string[] GetRoles(string userName)
{
    // Retrieve the connection string from the configuration file.
    SqlConnection con = new SqlConnection(
      ConfigurationSettings.AppSettings[connectionSetting]);

    // Create a parameterized command to prevent SQL injection attacks.
    string query = "SELECT Role FROM UsersRoles " +
      "INNER JOIN Roles ON UsersRoles.RoleID = Roles.ID " +
      "WHERE UserName = @UserName";
    SqlCommand cmd = new SqlCommand(query, con);
    cmd.Parameters.Add("@UserName", userName);
```

```
ArrayList roles = new ArrayList();
try
{
    con.Open();

    SqlDataReader reader = cmd.ExecuteReader();
    while (reader.Read())
    {
        roles.Add((string)reader["Role"]);
    }
    reader.Close();
}
catch (Exception error)
{
    // Don't return any roles.
    return new string[]{};
}
finally
{
    con.Close();
}
return (string[])roles.ToArray(typeof(string));
}
```

Note that if an error occurs, an empty array is returned with no roles.

Attaching the Roles

As explained earlier, you can only attach the role information in the
HttpApplication.AuthenticateRequest event. However, this event occurs on every request.
To ensure optimum performance, you don't want to query the database each time. Instead, a
better idea is to store the list of roles in the forms authentication ticket when the user logs.
You can then retrieve the list of roles from the authentication ticket when the
HttpApplication.AuthenticateRequest event fires.

Tip It's safe to store role names in the ticket, because this information is encrypted and validated (unless you've changed the protection attribute of the <forms> tag in the web.config file). It's computationally infeasible to decrypt or change this information successfully before the ticket expires.

The following code sample is the rewritten login code that retrieves the role information
and attaches it to the ticket. Remember, you can only add a single string of information to
the ticket, so the array of roles must be converted into a single piece of text. Fortunately, the
String.Join() method handles this task neatly. It combines the strings and adds a delimiter in
between each one so you can separate them later. Other than that, everything is the same as
in the example in Chapter 15 for storing user-specific data in the ticket.

```
private void cmdLogin_Click(object sender, System.EventArgs e)
{
    // Check if the control values are valid.
    if (Page.IsValid)
    {
        ICredentialStore store = new DatabaseCredentialStore(
          "CredentialConnectionString", "SHA1");
        if (store.Authenticate(txtName.Text, txtPassword.Text))
        {
            lblStatus.Text = "Logged in.";

            // Get the role information.
            string[] roles = store.GetRoles(txtName.Text);

            // Convert the roles to a single string,
            // so it can be attached to the cookie.
            string roleList = string.Join("%", roles);

            // Create a new authentication ticket.
            FormsAuthenticationTicket ticket =
              new FormsAuthenticationTicket(
              1,                             // Version
              txtName.Text,                  // User name
              DateTime.Now,                  // Date issued
              DateTime.Now.AddMinutes(30),   // Date to expire
              false,                         // Persistent
              roleList);                     // User data string

            // Encrypt the ticket.
            string encryptedTicket = FormsAuthentication.Encrypt(ticket);

            // Create the authentication cookie.
            HttpCookie authenticationCookie  = new HttpCookie(
              FormsAuthentication.FormsCookieName, encryptedTicket);

            // Attach the cookie to the response.
            Response.Cookies.Add(authenticationCookie);

            // Redirect the user back to their original URL.
            Response.Redirect(FormsAuthentication.GetRedirectUrl(
              txtName.Text, false));
        }
        else
        {
```

```
                    // Show an error message.
                    lblStatus.Text = "Try again.";
                }
            }
        }
    }
```

The final step is to extract the roles from the cookie when each request is authenticated and create a GenericPrincipal object with the roles. To do this, you need to respond to the HttpApplication.AuthenticateRequest event in the global.asax file. This code will then execute just after the forms authentication module performs its authentication (and before any authorization or page processing happens).

Here's the code you need:

```
protected void Application_AuthenticateRequest(Object sender, EventArgs e)
{
    // Check that the request has been authenticated.
    if (Request.IsAuthenticated)
    {
        // Get the roles from the ticket.
        string roleList = ((FormsIdentity)
          Context.User.Identity).Ticket.UserData;

        // Split the roles into an array.
        string[] roles = roleList.Split('%');

        // Create a new GenericPrincipal with this role information.
        GenericPrincipal newPrincipal =
          new GenericPrincipal(Context.User.Identity, roles);

        // Add the principal to the security context
        // (replacing the current GenericPrincipal).
        Context.User = newPrincipal;
    }
}
```

You can now use all the same authorization techniques with roles, including authorization rules in the web.config file, and programmatic tests with the IPrincipal.IsInRole() method and the PrincipalPermission.Demand() method.

Here's a simple example of web-page code that tests if the current user belongs to several different groups, and adds information to a StringBuilder accordingly:

```
if (User.IsInRole("Administrator"))
    htmlString.Append("This user is an administrator.<br>");
else
    htmlString.Append("This user is not an administrator.<br>");

if (User.IsInRole("Supervisor"))
    htmlString.Append("This user is a supervisor.<br>");
```

```
else
    htmlString.Append("This user is not a supervisor.<br>");

if (User.IsInRole("Guest"))
    htmlString.Append("This user is a guest.<br>");
else
    htmlString.Append("This user is not a guest.<br>");
```

Figure 17-4 shows a test page that uses this technique to check the role information of the user dan.

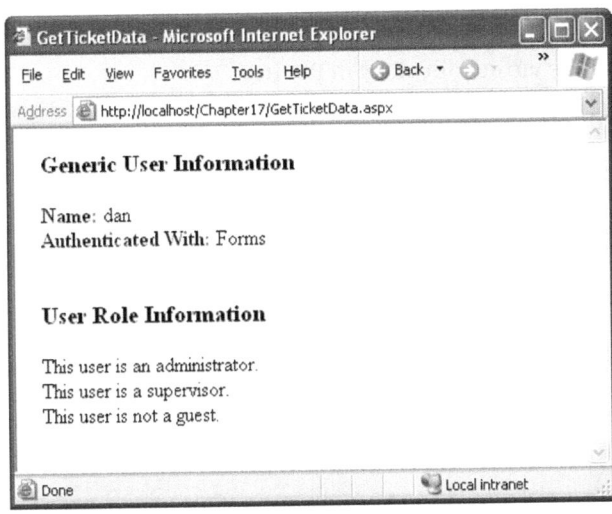

Figure 17-4. *Testing user roles*

Protecting Non-Web-Page Resources

There is one limitation of all the authorization and authentication systems you've learned so far—they only work on file types that ASP.NET handles. In other words, if a user requests a GIF file or HTML page from the same virtual directory, that user will completely bypass your authentication mechanisms. Depending on your security needs, this may be completely acceptable, simply irrelevant, or potentially dangerous.

This behavior is a result of the way IIS uses file mappings, which was first examined in Chapter 2. By default, ASP.NET is registered to deal with a small set of relevant files. These include files it needs to execute—like web pages and web services—and files it wants to protect—like source-code files, configuration files, and project files. If you want requests for other file types to filter through the ASP.NET request processing architecture and security models, you have to map those file types to the ASP.NET ISAPI filter.

Mapping additional file types to ASP.NET gives you some additional features. For example, it gives you the ability to deny anonymous user requests for image files. However, it can also add overhead, because files that would normally be served directly now require ASP.NET to perform some work. This overhead is fairly minimal if you aren't expecting users to request non-ASP.NET file types, and you're simply using this technique to provide a higher level of security.

Note If you're using Windows authentication, it is technically possible to force IIS to authenticate all requests, even those that are for non-ASP.NET files. To do so, you simply need to remove the Anonymous access option for the virtual directory. However, this option isn't as useful as it seems, because it doesn't allow you to enforce authentication for specific files or file types. As a result, you may find it more useful to allow anonymous access, but use the techniques described in this section to protect specific resources.

Adding a File Type Mapping

To add a file type mapping to IIS 5, follow these steps:

1. Launch IIS Manager, and browse to the virtual directory in the tree.

2. Right-click the virtual directory and select Properties.

3. Choose the Virtual Directory tab. Then click the Configuration button in the Application section of the Virtual Directory tab. The Application Configuration dialog box will appear, as shown in Figure 17-5.

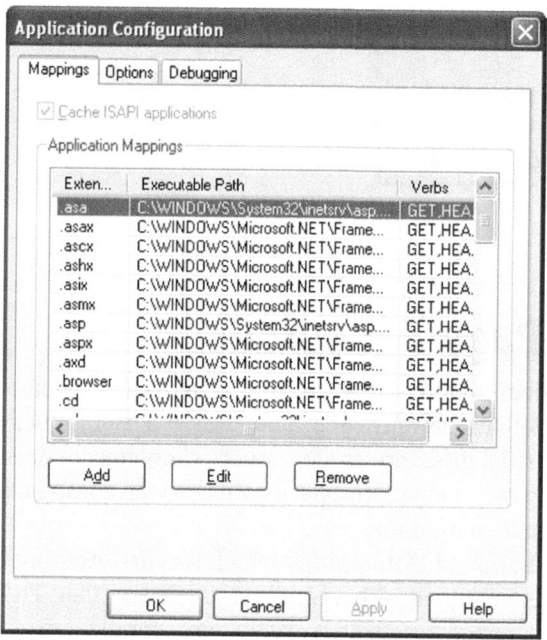

Figure 17-5. *Application mappings*

4. You need to add a new mapping for each file type you want to protect with forms authentication. This mapping will route requests for that file type to ASP.NET ISAPI DLL. Click the Add button to create a new mapping. You'll see the dialog box shown in Figure 17-6.

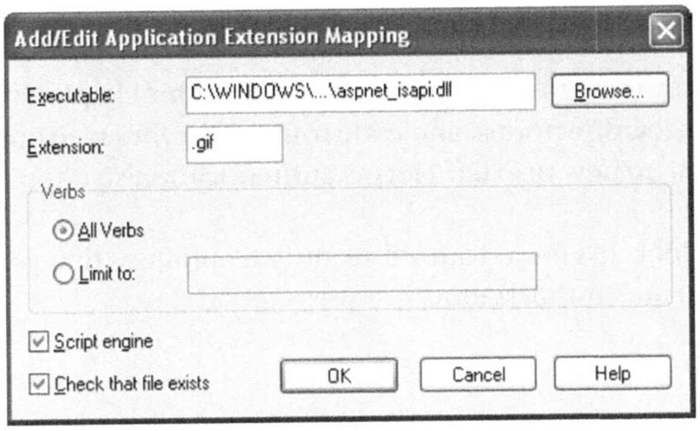

Figure 17-6. *Adding an application mapping*

5. The executable you want to use is aspnet_isapi.dll. The exact directory depends on the version of ASP.NET you have installed. In .NET 1.1, it's c:\[WinDir]\Microsoft.Net\Framework\v1.1.4322\aspnet_isapi.dll. You also need to enter the file extension you want to map. Finally, you should also specify that you want to perform this mapping for all verbs (a verb is a method for requesting the file from the server over HTTP, such as GET or POST).

6. Once you have taken these steps, click OK to add the extension.

PROBLEMS WITH SOME FILE TYPES

Developers have reported some problems when using forms authentication to protect Adobe Acrobat (PDF) files. It's possible that similar problems could affect other file types, especially if they require a web browser plug-in to be displayed.

With PDF files, the problems are caused by a combination of the ActiveX component that allows Internet Explorer to view Acrobat files and IIS. The problem is that PDF files are sent from the server to the client in chunks so that the user does not have to wait until the whole file has downloaded to start viewing it. For some reason, this system is adversely affected by redirections (for example, using the Response.Redirect() method). Redirecting to a PDF file causes the file to be reported as corrupted. This causes problems if you try to use forms authentication to protect PDF files. After the user logs in, the redirection back to the original PDF causes the file to be reported as corrupted or simply not displayed.

In order to solve this problem, you need to avoid using FormsAuthentication.RedirectFromLoginPage() or Response.Redirect() to send the user back to the PDF file. Fortunately, there is a technique that can help. You simply need to write an HTML that instructs the browser to redirect itself using the Response.AppendHeader() method. This header has the name refresh and takes the form 0;url=[originalUrl]. This causes the browser to immediately load the target URL (the 0 indicates a delay of 0 seconds).

Here's the code statement you need to use instead of the RedirectFromLoginPage() method:

```
Response.AppendHeader("refresh","0;url=" + url);
```

Remember that because you aren't using the RedirectFromLoginPage() method, you'll also need to create and attach the cookie before you perform the redirect.

Summary

Authorization provides an effective way to control access to resources. In this chapter, you've learned how to safeguard different pages, directories, and code routines in your web application using authorization. You've also seen how to extend forms authentication so it too can make use of role-based authorization.

In the next chapter, you'll take a look at a few advanced security techniques that you can use to extend ASP.NET authentication and authorization.

■ ■ ■

CHAPTER 18

Advanced Security

Over the last four chapters, you've learned how to verify user identities with forms and Windows authentication, and how to protect your application by building in various types of authorization rules. However, .NET has quite a bit more in store. It includes a rich API for a wide range of cryptographic tasks, and an extensible model that allows you to plug in to the authentication system and create your own IPrincipal and IIdentity classes. You'll see both of these techniques in this chapter, as well as some traditional problem solving that allows you to track the users accessing your application at any given time.

Encrypting Data

In Chapter 15 you learned how to use hashing to protect passwords. With hashing, you store a digital fingerprint of the original data, not the data itself. As a result, there's no way to reverse the hashing process to retrieve the original data. All you can do is hash new data and perform a comparison.

The hashing approach is the most secure practice for validating passwords. However, it's not much help if you want to protect other pieces of sensitive data that you need to decrypt later. For example, if you're creating an e-commerce application, you probably want to store a user's credit card information so it can be reused in later orders. In this scenario, your application needs to be able to retrieve the credit card details on its own. Hashing doesn't apply.

Often developers deal with these situations by storing sensitive data in clear text. They assume that because the data is kept in a secure server-side storage location, there's no need to go to the additional work of encrypting it. However, security experts know this is far from true. Without encryption, a malicious user only needs to gain access to the server for a matter of minutes or even seconds to retrieve the full list of passwords for every customer. Security breaches can occur from poor administrative policy, weak administrator passwords, or other exploitable software on the server. Problems can even occur from hardware maintenance, and dozens of companies have reported selling or discarding old server hard drives without properly erasing the sensitive customer data they contained. Finally, many organizations have a privacy policy that explicitly pledges to keep customer information confidential and encrypted at all times. If a security breach occurs and the company is forced to notify users that their data is at risk because it wasn't properly encrypted, the company can face significant embarrassment and loss of trust. In order to avoid these problems and ensure that data is safe, you need to take encryption into your own hands using the classes in the System.Security.Cryptography namespace.

Understanding the .NET Cryptography Classes

Before you can perform cryptography in .NET, you need to understand a little more about the underlying plumbing. The .NET encryption classes are divided into three layers. The first layer is a set of abstract base classes that represent an encryption task. These include the following:

- **AsymmetricAlgorithm.** This class represents asymmetric encryption, which uses a public/private key pair. Data encrypted with one key can only be decrypted with the other key.

- **SymmetricAlgorithm.** This class represents symmetric encryption, which uses a shared secret value. Data encrypted with the key can only be decrypted using exactly the same key.

- **HashAlgorithm.** This class represents hash generation and verification. You can use hashes to ensure that data is not tampered with.

The second level includes classes that represent a specific encryption algorithm. They derive from the encryption base classes, but they are also abstract classes. For example the DES algorithm class, which represents the DES (Data Encryption Standard) algorithm, derives from SymmetricAlgorithm.

The third level of classes is a set of encryption implementations. Each implementation class derives from an algorithm class. This means that a specific encryption algorithm like DES could have multiple implementation classes. In reality, there is only one provided out of the box in the .NET Framework: DESCryptoServiceProvider. However, it's quite conceivable that Microsoft or a third-party vendor could create another implementation that provides better performance in the future.

While some .NET Framework encryption classes are implemented entirely in managed code, most are actually thin wrappers over the CryptoAPI library, which is a part of the Windows operating system. The classes that wrap CryptoAPI functions have "CryptoServiceProvider" in the class name (for example, DESCryptoServiceProvider), while the managed classes typically have "Managed" in the name (for example, RijndaelManaged). Essentially, the managed classes perform all their work in the .NET world under the supervision of the CLR (common language runtime), while the unmanaged classes use calls to the unmanaged CryptoAPI library. This might seem like a limitation, but it's actually an efficient reuse of existing technology. CryptoAPI has never been faulted for its technology, just its awkward programming interface.

Figure 18-1 shows the classes in the System.Security.Cryptography namespace. This three-layer organization allows almost unlimited extensibility. You can create a new implementation for an existing cryptography class by deriving from an existing algorithm class. For example, you could create a class that implements the DES algorithm entirely in managed code by creating a new DESManaged class and inheriting from DESCryptoServiceProvider. Similarly, you can add support for a new encryption algorithm by adding an abstract algorithm class for it (for example, CAST128, which is similar to DES but is not provided in the framework), and a concrete implementation class (such as CAST128Managed).

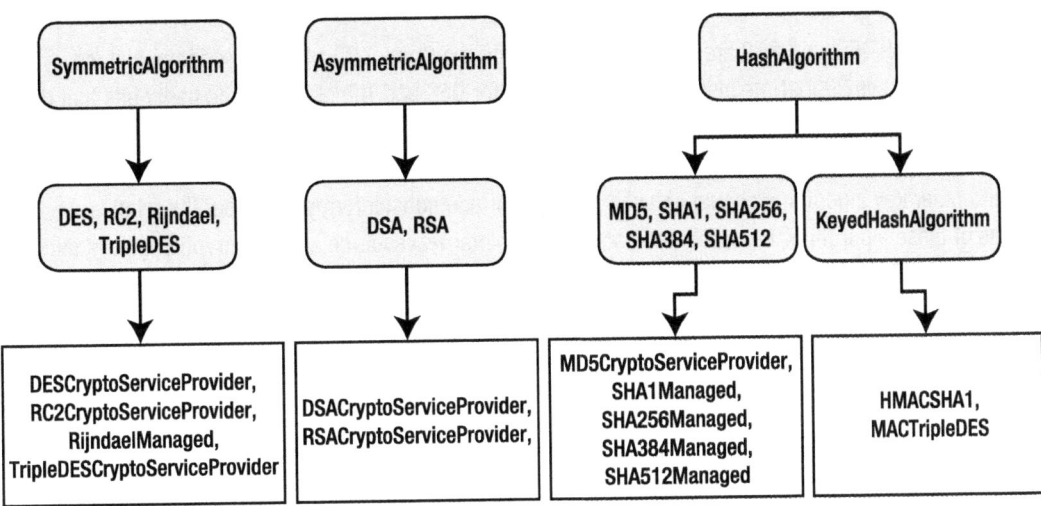

Figure 18-1. *The cryptographic class hierarchy*

■**Note** The encryption classes are one of the few examples in the .NET class library where the standard naming and case rules are not followed. This means, for example, that you'll find classes like TripleDES and RSA rather than TripleDes and Rsa.

The Symmetric Algorithms

Table 18-1 lists the symmetric algorithms provided by the .NET Framework.

Table 18-1. *Symmetric Algorithms in .NET*

Algorithm	Abstract Algorithm Class	Default Implementation Class	Valid Key Size	Default Key Size
DES	DES	DESCryptoServiceProvider	64	64
TripleDES	TripleDES	TripleDESCryptoServiceProvider	128, 192	192
RC2	RC2	RC2CryptServiceProvider	40–128	128
Rijndael	Rijndael	RijndaelManaged	128, 192, 256	256

The strength of the encryption corresponds with the length of the key. Keep in mind that the greater the key size, the harder it is for a brute-force attack to succeed, because there are far more possible key values to test. Of course, greater symmetric key sizes also lead to larger messages and slower encryption times. For most purposes, a good standard choice is Rijndael. It offers solid performance and support for large key sizes.

Note DES, TripleDES, and RC2 are all implemented using the CryptoAPI, and thus need the high encryption pack on Windows 2000. Note also that the key length for DES and TripleDES include parity bits that don't contribute to the strength of the encryption. Thus, TripleDES with a 192-bit key only uses 168 bits, while a 128-bit key uses 112 bits. In DES, the 64-bit key uses only 56 bits. For that reason, it's considered fairly weak, and other key algorithms should be used instead. For additional information about the relative strengths of these algorithms, consult a dedicated book or Internet resource about encryption theory, such as Bruce Schneier's *Applied Cryptography: Protocols, Algorithms, and Source Code in C* (Wiley, 1995).

The Abstract Encryption Classes

The abstract encryption classes actually serve two purposes. First, they define the basic members that encryption implementations need to support. They also provide some functionality that you can use directly without creating a class instance, through the static Create() method. This method allows you to create one of the concrete implementation classes without needing to know how it is implemented.

For example, consider the following line of code:

```
DES crypt = DES.Create();
```

The static Create() method returns an instance of the default DES implementation class. In this case, the class is DESCryptoServiceProvider. The advantage of this technique is that you can code generically, without creating a dependency on a specific implementation. Best of all, if Microsoft updates the framework and the default DES implementation class changes, your code will pick up the change seamlessly. This is particularly useful if you are using a CryptoAPI class, which could be replaced with a managed class equivalent in the future.

In fact, you can work at even higher-level if you like by using the static Create() method in one of the cryptographic task classes. For example, consider this code:

```
SymmetricAlgorithm crypt = SymmetricAlgorithm.Create();
```

This creates an instance of whatever cryptography class is defined as the default symmetric algorithm. In this case, it isn't DES, but Rijndael. The object returned is an instance of the RijndaelManaged implementation class.

Tip It is good practice to code generically using the abstract algorithm classes. This allows you to know which type of algorithm you use (and any limitations it may have), without worrying about the underlying implementation.

The ICryptoTransform Interface

.NET uses a stream-based architecture for encryption and decryption, which makes it easy to encrypt and decrypt different types of data from different types of sources. This architecture also makes it easy to perform multiple cryptographic operations in succession, on the fly, independent of the low-level details about the actual cryptography algorithm you're using (like the block size).

To understand how all this works, you need to consider the core types—the ICryptoTransform interface and the CryptoStream class. The ICryptoTransform interface represents blockwise cryptographic transformation. This could be an encryption, decryption, hashing, Base64 encoding/decoding, or formatting operation. To create an ICryptoTransform object for a given algorithm, you use the CreateEncryptor() and CreateDecryptor() methods (depending on whether you want to encrypt or decrypt data).

Here's a code snippet that creates an ICryptoTransform for encrypting with the DES algorithm:

```
DES crypt = DES.Create();
ICryptoTransform transform = crypt.CreateEncryptor();
```

The insight here is that various cryptographic tasks execute in the same way, even though the actual cryptographic function performing the transformation may be very different. Every cryptographic operation requires that data be subdivided into blocks of a fixed size before it can be processed. You can use an ICryptoTransform instance directly, but in most cases you'll take an easier approach and simply pass it to another class: the CryptoStream.

The CryptoStream Class

The CryptoStream wraps an ordinary stream, and uses an ICryptoTransform to perform its work behind the scenes. The key advantage is that the CryptoStream uses buffered access, thereby allowing you to perform automatic encryption without worrying about the block size required by the algorithm. The other advantage of the CryptoStream is that, because it wraps an ordinary .NET Stream-derived class, it can easily "piggyback" on another operation, like file access (through a FileStream), memory access (through a MemoryStream), low-level network calls (through a NetworkStream), and so on.

To create a CryptoStream you need three pieces of information: the underlying stream, the mode, and the ICryptoTransform you want to use. For example, the following code snippet creates an ICryptoTransform using the DES algorithm implementation class, and then uses it with an existing stream to create a CryptoStream.

```
DES crypt = DES.Create();
ICryptoTransform transform = crypt.CreateEncryptor();
CryptoStream cs = new CryptoStream(fileStream, transform,
  CryptoStreamMode.Write);

// (Now you can use cs to write encrypted information to the file.)
```

Note that the CryptoStream can be in one of two modes: read mode or write mode, as defined by the CryptoStreamMode enumeration. In read mode, the transformation is performed as it is retrieved from the underlying stream (as shown in Figure 18-2).

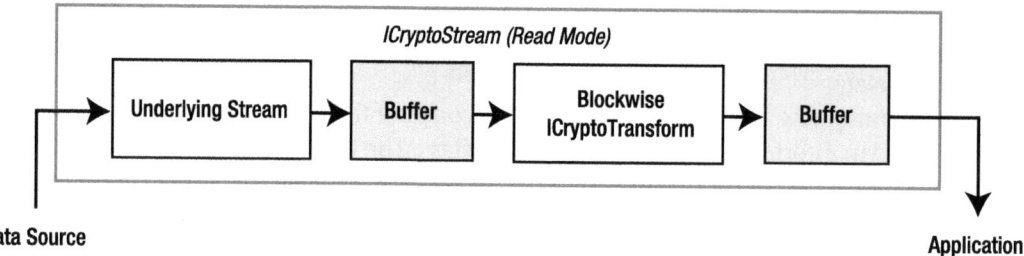

Figure 18-2. *Reading and decrypting data*

In write mode, the transformation is performed before the data is written to the underlying stream (as shown in Figure 18-3).

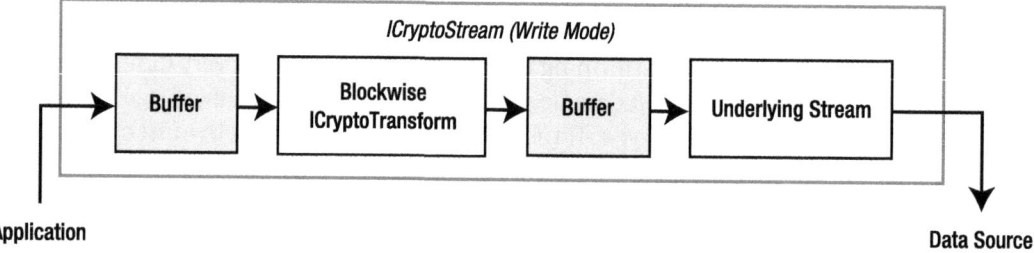

Figure 18-3. *Writing and encrypting data*

You cannot combine both modes to make a readable and writable CryptoStream (which would have no meaning anyway). Similarly, the Seek() method and Position property, which are used to move to different positions in a stream, are not supported for the CryptoStream(), and will throw a NotSupportedException if called. However, you can often use these members with the underlying stream.

Encrypting Sensitive Data

Now that you've taken an in-depth look at .NET cryptography, it's time to put it all together with an end-to-end example that securely stores credit card numbers.

Here are the steps you need to take:

- Choose an algorithm and prepare the database.

- Create and store the secret key.

- Write the code for encrypting and decrypting data.

- Create a test page to see it all in action.

Choosing an Algorithm

The first step is to choose the algorithm and key size you want to use, as this will determine the amount of storage space required for the encrypted data. In this example, we'll use the Rijndael algorithm with a 256-bit (32-byte) key size. As a result, one block of encrypted data will require 32 bytes of storage. Encrypted data will always use at least one block. In this example, we're encrypting credit cards, which include a very small amount of data. As a result, one 32-byte block of data will be sufficient to store the encrypted credit card number in the database.

> ■**Note** When encrypting data with Rijndael, one 16-byte block of raw data becomes a 32-byte block of encrypted data. (The last block is automatically padded to fill a complete block.) This means that one block gives a maximum length of 15 characters in the credit card (assuming the last byte is required to indicate the end of the string). You can use different encoding systems, but this one is easy to implement.

The next step is to create a field in a database table for storing the encrypted data. All encryption works on binary data—arrays of raw bytes. Although you can convert the encrypted data into a string representation (as the Encrypt() method of the FormsAuthentication class does), it's more efficient to store it in its binary format. Thus, you need to create a binary field in your table. Figure 18-4 shows the CreditCardData field you need. If you need the ability to store more than a block of data, make sure you use a varbinary field rather than a fixed-size binary field. Otherwise, the blank bytes added at the end of short values will confuse your decryption code (and waste space).

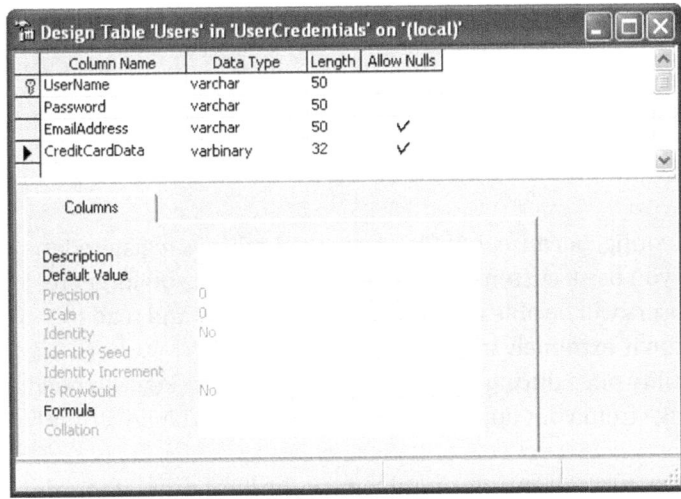

Figure 18-4. *Adding a binary field for encrypted data*

Creating the Key

Next, you need to create a key that will be used to encrypt and decrypt the data. Although ASP.NET defines a computer-specific key in the machine.config file, this key can't be directly retrieved through any .NET classes. There are a few other reasons you probably shouldn't use this key—including the fact that it is shared with all applications on the computer, and dynamically generated by default. As a result, if you change the key or deploy your application on another web server, you may suddenly discover that you can't retrieve any of the encrypted data!

A better approach is to create an application-specific key. In this example, the application key is stored in a file in the same virtual directory as the web application. To create a secure, random series of bytes to use from the key, you simply need to create an instance of the encryption class you want to use. You can then retrieve the key data.

Here's the code for a simple test page that generates and saves a key:

```
private void Page_Load(object sender, System.EventArgs e)
{
    // Don't overwrite an existing key.
    if (File.Exists(Server.MapPath("key.config")))
    {
        Response.Write("Key already exists in key.config.");
    }
    else
    {
        // Create the secret key.
        Rijndael crypt = Rijndael.Create();

        // Save the key.
        FileStream fs = File.OpenWrite(Server.MapPath("key.config"));
        fs.Write(crypt.Key, 0, crypt.Key.Length);

        // Save the initialization vector.
        fs.Write(crypt.IV, 0, crypt.IV.Length);
        fs.Close();

        Response.Write("Created key in file key.config");
    }
}
```

The key file uses the extension .config, because that file extension is always registered to ASP.NET and explicitly forbidden. If you use a custom extension (like .key) and you forget to set up the mappings in IIS, remote users will be able to request the file directly and read the raw key file data. Thus, this precaution is extremely important.

You only need to run this test utility once during development to create the key you need. After that, you should remove the page from your application so that users can't inadvertently access it.

To reduce the overhead of needing to read key information from the hard drive, it makes sense to load it into Application or Cache state when the application first starts. You can accomplish this with the following event handler in the global.asax file:

```
protected void Application_Start(Object sender, EventArgs e)
{
    // Retrieve the key.
```

```
    FileStream fs = File.OpenRead(Server.MapPath("key.config"));
    byte[] key = new byte[32];
    byte[] IV = new byte[16];
    fs.Read(key, 0, key.Length);
    fs.Read(IV, 0, IV.Length);
    fs.Close();

    // Create a new encryption class with this key.
    Rijndael crypt = Rijndael.Create();
    crypt.Key = key;
    crypt.IV = IV;

    // Store the key information in Application state.
    Application["Key"] = crypt;
}
```

Note Remember that your data is only as secure as your key! However, in order to get user credit cards, an attacker must now steal both the key and the lists of user records. Another danger is losing the key. If you do, you won't be able to retrieve any of the encrypted information in the database. In a large-scale application, the key won't be stored on the hard drive at all, but will be kept instead in a secure location (such as a specialized piece of hardware that's connected to the web server).

Creating the Encryption and Decryption Routines

Now that you have a key available, you can create the code for encrypting and decrypting credit card data. Your code needs to provide two methods, one that sets a credit card number for an existing customer, and another that retrieves an existing credit card number. Each of these tasks actually takes two steps—a cryptographic step and a data access step. The easiest way to code them is to split these steps into separate methods.

One place you can put this code is in the DatabaseCredentialStore class that was created in Chapter 15. This works well for a simple demonstration, but as you add additional methods for creating, updating, and deleting user records, you'll probably want to create a dedicate UsersDB class in addition to the DatabaseCredentialStore class.

This example uses two new classes. The first class is UsersDB, which contains the GetCreditCard() and SetCreditCard() methods that are used to retrieve and update the encrypted data in the database. A separate helper class named EncryptionUtil performs the actual decryption work with its EncryptString() and DecryptString() methods. This design is used because in .NET, the process for encrypting any string is the same. By making these routines relatively generic, you can reuse them for different purposes. You could even compile the EncryptionUtil class in a separate class library assembly and reuse it with different applications.

Here's the outline for the EncryptionUtil class:

```
using System.Security.Cryptography;
using System.IO;

public class EncryptionUtil
{
    public static byte[] EncryptString(string stringToEncrypt,
     SymmetricAlgorithm crypt)
    { ... }

    public static string DecryptToString(byte[] dataToDecrypt,
     SymmetricAlgorithm crypt)
    { ... }
}
```

Note that the EncryptString() and DecryptString() methods accept an encryption object, but it doesn't need to be an instance of the Rijndael class. Instead, they accept an instance of the base class SymmetricAlgorithm (which Rijndael derives from). This makes the EncryptionUtil class even more generic, giving your application the ability to support different algorithms with the same code. You'll also notice that both methods are marked static. This allows you to call these methods without calling an EncryptionUtil object.

The EncryptString() method takes a string with ordinary data and a key, and returns a byte of encrypted data. Here's the complete code:

```
public byte[] EncryptString(string stringToEncrypt,
 SymmetricAlgorithm crypt)
{
    // Create an in-memory stream for storing the encrypted data.
    MemoryStream ms = new MemoryStream();

    // Wrap the in-memory stream with an encrypting stream.
    CryptoStream cs = new CryptoStream(ms,
        crypt.CreateEncryptor(), CryptoStreamMode.Write);

    // Write the string to binary data with the help of a BinaryWriter.
    BinaryWriter w = new BinaryWriter(cs);
    w.Write(stringToEncrypt);

    // All the data has been written. Now make sure the last block
    // is properly padded. Failing to do this will cause an error
    // when you attempt to decrypt the data.
    cs.FlushFinalBlock();

    // Now move the encrypted data out of the stream,
    // and into an array of bytes.
    return ms.ToArray();
}
```

This code creates an in-memory stream where all the data can be written. The code uses a cryptographic stream so that as it writes the information to memory it's automatically encrypted. The last step is to convert the encrypted information in the stream to an array of bytes.

Now your data access code can rely on this routine to convert a user-supplied value into a blob of encrypted data. With this encryption problem solved, all you need is some straightforward ADO.NET code in the UsersDB class.

Here's the SetCreditCard() method for the UsersDB class, which commits the encrypted data to the database:

```
public void SetCreditCard(string userName, string cardNumber)
{
    byte[] encryptedData = EncryptionUtil.EncryptString(
     cardNumber, (Rijndael)HttpContext.Current.Application["Key"]);

    // Retrieve the connection string from the configuration file.
    SqlConnection con = new SqlConnection(
      ConfigurationSettings.AppSettings[connectionSetting]);

    // Create a parameterized command with placeholders.
    string SQL = "UPDATE Users SET CreditCardData = @CreditCardData " +
      "WHERE UserName = @UserName";
    SqlCommand cmd = new SqlCommand(SQL, con);

    // Add the @UserName parameter.
    cmd.Parameters.Add("@CreditCardData", encryptedData);
    cmd.Parameters.Add("@UserName", userName);

    try
    {
        // Update the record.
        con.Open();
        cmd.ExecuteNonQuery();
    }
    finally
    {
        con.Close();
    }
}
```

You can follow the same approach for coding the logic needed to retrieve and decrypt the credit card data. First, you'll need a generic routine that can decrypt a binary block of data that contains a single string:

```
public string DecryptToString(byte[] dataToDecrypt,
 SymmetricAlgorithm crypt)
{
    MemoryStream ms = new MemoryStream();
```

```
CryptoStream cs = new CryptoStream(ms,
  crypt.CreateDecryptor(), CryptoStreamMode.Write);

// Write the binary data to the memory stream.
cs.Write(dataToDecrypt, 0, dataToDecrypt.Length);
cs.FlushFinalBlock();

// Read the unencrypted data from the stream into a string
// with the help of the BinaryReader.
BinaryReader r = new BinaryReader(ms);
ms.Position = 0;
string decryptedData = r.ReadString();
r.Close();

return decryptedData;
}
```

The DecryptToString() method is essentially the reverse of the EncryptString() method. It creates an in-memory stream, and writes the decrypted data to that stream. Finally, it converts the binary information in the stream into the expected string.

The last step is to add the database code that can retrieve a user record and decrypt the credit card data using DecryptToString(). Here's the code you need in the UsersDB class:

```
public string GetCreditCard(string userName)
{
    // Retrieve the connection string from the configuration file.
    SqlConnection con = new SqlConnection(
      ConfigurationSettings.AppSettings[connectionSetting]);

    // Create a parameterized command with placeholders.
    string SQL = "SELECT CreditCardData FROM Users " +
      "WHERE UserName = @UserName";
    SqlCommand cmd = new SqlCommand(SQL, con);
    cmd.Parameters.Add("@UserName", userName);

    byte[] encryptedData;
    try
    {
        // Update the record.
        con.Open();
        SqlDataReader reader = cmd.ExecuteReader(
          CommandBehavior.SingleRow);
        reader.Read();
        encryptedData = (byte[])reader["CreditCardData"];
        reader.Close();
    }
    catch
    {
```

```
        return null;
    }
    finally
    {
        con.Close();
    }

    // Decrypt and return the credit card number.
    return DecryptToString(
     encryptedData, (Rijndael)HttpContext.Current.Application["Key"]);
}
```

If you plan to store multiple pieces of encrypted data, you'll probably build additional encryption methods to support different data types. You could even use the object serialization techniques described in Chapter 13 to convert an entire object to a stream of bytes, and then encrypt it. This code could work generically to encrypt any serializable object. Using techniques like these, you might want to develop a separate encryption component. However, in this application that level of detail isn't required.

Creating a Test Page

Figure 18-5 shows a simple test page that demonstrates how the whole system works. When you click Retrieve from Database, the page queries the database for the credit card number of the current user, and displays it. When you click Update Database, the page takes the current value of the text box, encrypts it, and updates the corresponding user record in the database.

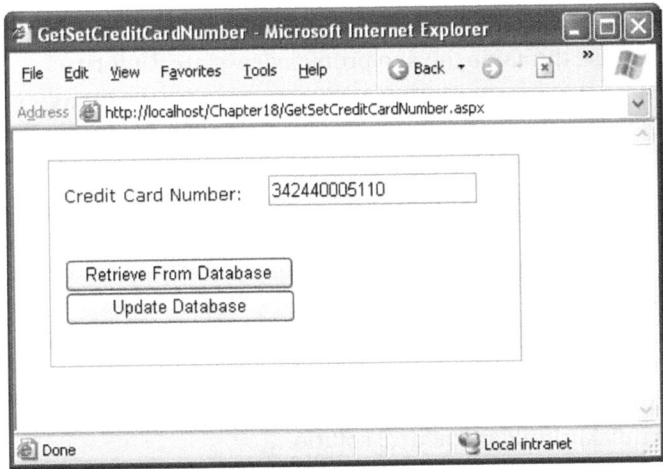

Figure 18-5. *Testing database encryption*

Here's the complete code for the test page:

```
public class GetSetCreditCardNumber : System.Web.UI.Page
{
    protected System.Web.UI.WebControls.TextBox txtCreditCard;
    protected System.Web.UI.WebControls.Button cmdSet;
```

```
protected System.Web.UI.WebControls.Button cmdGet;
// (Designer code omitted.)

private void cmdSet_Click(object sender, System.EventArgs e)
{
    UsersDB db = new UsersDB("CredentialConnectionString");
    db.SetCreditCard(User.Identity.Name, txtCreditCard.Text);
}

private void cmdGet_Click(object sender, System.EventArgs e)
{
    UsersDB db = new UsersDB("CredentialConnectionString");
    txtCreditCard.Text = db.GetCreditCard(User.Identity.Name);
}
}
```

As this page demonstrates, once you've created the underlying infrastructure, it doesn't take any extra effort to work with encrypted data. In fact, the web page has no way of knowing whether or not the credit card information is being encrypted (and what algorithms and key sizes are being used), because it's all neatly tucked away behind the scenes in the DBUsers and EncryptionUtil classes.

Encrypting the Query String

In this book, you've seen several examples in which ASP.NET security works behind the scenes to protect your data and ensure security. For example, in Chapter 15 you learned how ASP.NET uses encryption and hash codes to ensure that the data in the form cookie is always protected. In Chapter 7 you learned how you could use the same tools to protect view state. Unfortunately, ASP.NET doesn't provide a similar way to enable automatic encryption for the query string (which is the extra bit of information you add to URLs to transmit information from one page to another). In many cases, the URL query information corresponds to user-supplied data, and it doesn't matter if the user can see or modify it. In other cases, however, the query string contains information that should remain hidden from the user. In this case, the only option is to switch to another form of state management (which may have other limitations), or devise a system to encrypt the query string.

In the next example, you'll see the second approach—a simple way to tighten security by scrambling data before you place it in the query string. Once again, you can rely on the cryptography classes provided with .NET. In fact, you can leverage the EncryptionUtil class developed in the previous example to quickly build a practical solution.

Wrapping the Query String

The starting point is to build an EncryptedQueryString class. This class should accept a collection of string-based information (just like the query string), and allow you to retrieve it in another page. Behind the scenes, the EncryptedQueryString class needs to encrypt the data before it's placed in the query string, and decrypt it seamlessly on the way out.

Here's the starting point for the EncryptedQueryString class you need:

```
public class EncryptedQueryString:
 System.Collections.Specialized.StringDictionary
{
    SymmetricAlgorithm crypt;
    public EncryptedQueryString(SymmetricAlgorithm crypt)
    {
        this.crypt = crypt;
    }

    // (Remaining code omitted.)
}
```

There are two details you should notice immediately about the EncryptedQueryString class. First, it derives from the StringDictionary class, which represents a collection of strings indexed by strings. By deriving from StringDictionary, you gain the ability to use the EncryptedQueryString like an ordinary string collection. As a result, you can add information to the EncryptedQueryString in the same way that you add information to the Request.QueryString collection. Here's an example:

```
encryptedQueryString["value1"] = "Sample Value";
```

Best of all, you get this functionality for free, without needing to write any additional code.

The next important feature of the EncryptedQueryString class is the fact that it requires a SymmetricAlgorithm object in the constructor, which it then stores in a private member variable. This is the key that will be used for all the encryption and decryption operations. This is a slightly different approach than the one used for the EncryptionUtil class, which forced you to specify the key every time you called a method. That's because the EncryptedQueryString isn't stateless—instead, it represents a collection of data. For that reason, it makes sense to store the key you need to use in a member variable.

So with just this rudimentary class, you have the ability to store a collection of name/value strings. But how do you actually place this information into the query string? The EncryptedQueryString class provides a ToString() method that examines all the collection data, and combines it into a single encrypted string. The static EncryptionUtil.EncryptString() method performs the actual encryption, but the EncryptedQueryString.ToString() method still needs to take care of a few important details.

First, it needs to combine the separate collection values into a delimited string so that it's easy to split the string back into a collection on the destination page. In this case, the ToString() method uses the conventions of the query string, separating each value from the name with an equal sign (=), and separating each subsequent name/value pair with the ampersand (&). However, in order for this to work you need to make sure that the names and values of the actual item in the collection don't include these special characters. To solve this problem, the ToString() method uses the HttpServerUtility.UrlEncode() method to escape the strings before joining them together.

Here's the first portion of the ToString() method, which escapes and joins the collection settings into one string:

```
public override string ToString()
{
    // Build the query string.
    HttpServerUtility server = HttpContext.Current.Server;
    StringBuilder sb = new StringBuilder();
    foreach (DictionaryEntry item in this)
    {
        sb.Append(server.UrlEncode(item.Key.ToString()));
        sb.Append("=");
        sb.Append(server.UrlEncode(item.Value.ToString()));
        sb.Append("&");
    }

    // Remove the last &.
    sb.Remove(sb.Length-1, 1);
    ...
```

The next step is to use the EncryptionUtil class to encrypt the data. The EncryptString() method returns a byte array, so you need to take additional steps to convert the byte array to a string form that's suitable for the query string. One approach that seems reasonable is the static Convert.ToBase64String() method, which creates a Base64-encoded string. Unfortunately, Base64 strings can include symbols that aren't allowed in the query string (namely, the equals sign). Although you could create a Base64 string and then URL-encode it, this further complicates the decoding stage. The problem is that the ToBase64String() method may also introduce a series of characters that look like URL-encoded character sequences. These character sequences will then be incorrectly replaced when you decode the string.

A simpler approach is to use a different form of encoding. This example uses hex encoding, which replaces each character with an alphanumeric code. The methods for hex encoding aren't shown in this example, but they are available with the downloadable code.

```
    ...
    // Perform the encryption.
    byte[] encryptedData = EncryptionUtil.EncryptString(
      sb.ToString(), crypt);

    // Convert the encrypted byte array to a URL-legal string.
    // This would also be a good place to check that the data isn't
    // too large to fit in a typical 4 KB query string.
    return HexEncoding.ToString(encryptedData);
}
```

The string returned from EncryptedQueryString.ToString() can be placed directly into a query string using the Response.Redirect() method.

The destination page that receives the query data needs a way to deserialize and decrypt the string. The first step is to create a new EncryptedQueryString object, and supply the encrypted data. To make this step easier, it makes sense to add a new constructor to the

EncryptedQueryString class that accepts both a SymmetricAlgorithm object and the encrypted string:

```
public EncryptedQueryString(SymmetricAlgorithm crypt,
  string encryptedString)
{
    this.crypt = crypt;
    Deserialize(encryptedString);
}
```

This constructor also calls a private Deserialize() method. The Deserialize() method takes the encrypted information, and reverses all the steps from the ToString() method. In other words, it converts the data back to a byte array, decrypts it with the EncryptionUtil.DecryptToString(), un-encodes it, and then splits it into a collection of name/value settings, which are added to the internal dictionary.

Here's the complete Deserialize() code:

```
private void Deserialize(string encryptedString)
{
    HttpServerUtility server = HttpContext.Current.Server;

    // Decode the string back into a byte array.
    byte[] encryptedData =
      HexEncoding.GetBytes(server.UrlDecode(encryptedString));

    // Decrypt the string.
    string decryptedString = EncryptionUtil.DecryptToString(
      encryptedData, crypt);

    // Split the string into values.
    string[] values = decryptedString.Split('&');
    foreach (string val in values)
    {
        string[] nameValuePair = val.Split('=');
        base.Add(server.UrlDecode(
          nameValuePair[0]), server.UrlDecode(nameValuePair[1]));
    }
}
```

Now you have the entire infrastructure in place to create a simple test page, and transmit information from one page to another in a secure fashion.

Create a Test Page

To try out the EncryptedQueryString class, you need two pages—one that sets the query string and redirects the user, and another that retrieves the query string.

Here's the event-handling code for the first page, which provides a button and a text box. When the button is clicked, it sets two hard-coded values and one additional value by drawing the text from the text box:

```
private void cmdOK_Click(object sender, System.EventArgs e)
{
    EncryptedQueryString queryString = new
        EncryptedQueryString((Rijndael)HttpContext.Current.Application["Key"]);

    queryString["testValue1"] = "This is a sample string.";
    queryString["testValue2"] = "6171742";
    queryString["TextBox"] = txtData.Text;

    // Note that when redirecting, all the values become a single
    // encrypted query string argument.
    Response.Redirect("SecureQueryStringRecipient.aspx?data=" +
        queryString.ToString());
}
```

Notice that this page passes the encrypted query string information in a query string parameter named data. The page must manually add this parameter to the URL, although you don't need to perform any additional encoding step. This approach gives you the freedom to use more than one separately encrypted query string at the same time.

Figure 18-6 shows this page.

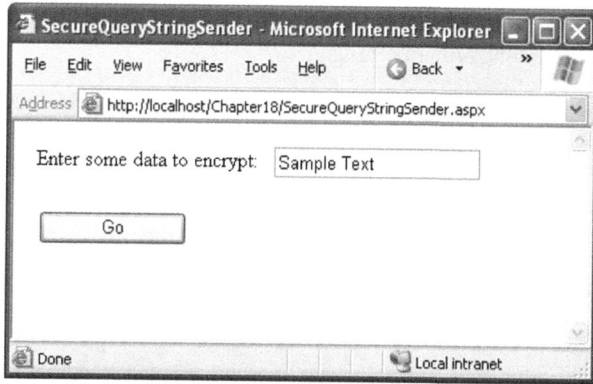

Figure 18-6. *Encrypting the query string*

The receiving page creates the EncryptedQueryString object using the information received in the data parameter. This single step decrypts the data and makes it available. The page can now retrieve a single value by name, or loop through all the values as in this example:

```
private void Page_Load(object sender, System.EventArgs e)
{
    EncryptedQueryString queryString = new EncryptedQueryString(
        (Rijndael)HttpContext.Current.Application["Key"],
        Request.QueryString["data"]);

    StringBuilder sb = new StringBuilder();
    foreach (DictionaryEntry item in queryString)
    {
```

```
            sb.Append("Found ");
            sb.Append(item.Key);
            sb.Append(" = ");
            sb.Append(item.Value);
            sb.Append("<br>");
        }
        lblInfo.Text = sb.ToString();
}
```

Figure 18-7 shows the recipient page. You can see some of the encrypted query string information in the URL.

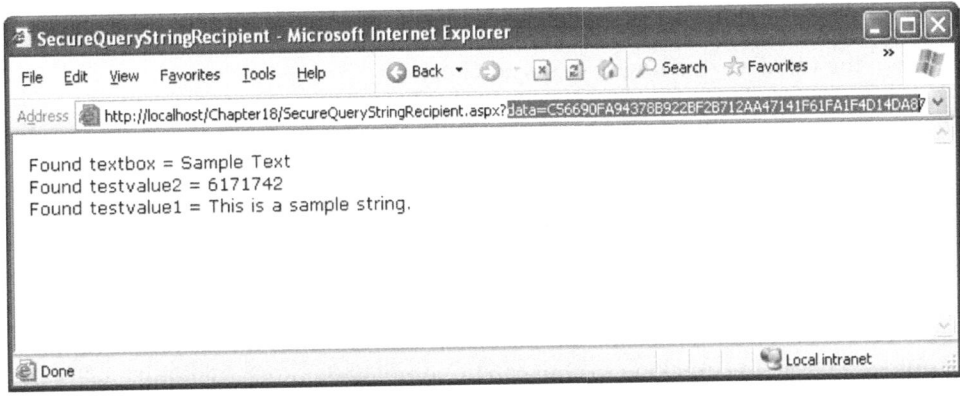

Figure 18-7. *Decrypting the query string*

As it stands, the EncryptedQueryString provides a good approach that provides solid security. However, there are still a number of features you can add to the EncryptedQueryString. For example, you could add a hash code to data before encrypting it, which would allow you to verify that no one has tampered with the query string. You could also add an expiry date, so that the query string data could be refused if a certain interval of time passes. This allows you to use query strings to provide a user ticket (like when signing in on the Microsoft Passport website), and it lets you give a time-limited trial page to users who are interested in a restricted portion of your website. Both of these features are quite easy to add to the existing EncryptedQueryString.

Tracking Logged-On Users

So far, this Chapter has focused exclusively on cryptography, one of the heavyweights of the security world. In the remainder of the chapter, the focus shifts to looking at how you can extend the .NET security framework with a few new features. The first topic you'll consider is how you can refine your login pages to incorporate user tracking.

Sometimes you may want to keep a list of which users are currently accessing your application. This may be for diagnostic or administrative purposes. For example, it could allow a system administrator to alert online users of scheduled downtime. Displaying a list of logged-in users can also be a great feature for community websites such as forum systems, because it allows users to see who else is active at a glance.

In order to create a user-listing system, you need to complete these steps:

1. Create a data structure to store the list of logged-in users. Typically, you'll store this in memory when the application starts (although you could also use a back-end database and the cache).

2. Add each user to the user list as the user logs in.

3. Remove each user from the user list when the user logs out.

You might also want to track anonymous users, that is, users who haven't authenticated themselves. This requires a few additional steps, as follows:

1. Create a variable to hold the number of anonymous users when the application starts.

2. Add one to the value when a new user session begins.

3. Deduct one from the value when a user session ends.

Tracking users isn't foolproof. You need to rely on certain events, like Session_End, which aren't fired immediately or in every scenario. You also need to assume that users who still have active sessions (in other words, users who have requested a page in the last 30 minutes) are still active. Of course, it's quite possible that a user will simply close the browser without signing out, in which case the user will remain in the user list until the session times out. Despite these minor quirks, a basic user-tracking system can be completed quite easily, and it will work fairly reliably.

Reacting to Application Events

The first step is to decide how to store the user information. Although you could create a specialized collection and store a collection of user information, a simple hashtable works well on its own. Using this hashtable, you can keep a list of user names indexed by session ID. The indexing is important—it allows you to quickly remove a user or check if a user already exists in the list.

When tracking anonymous users, you won't have user-specific information. A simple integer will work perfectly well. However, a good technique is to wrap this integer in a simple class. That way you can lock the class using the C# lock statement. This ensures that multiple worker threads can successfully update the counter without losing data. You can't create a lock on a simple value type like an integer, so a class is mandatory.

```
public class Counter
{
    public int Count = 0;

    public override string ToString()
    {
        return Count.ToString();
    }
}
```

Once you've chosen your data structures, you simply need to create them when the application first starts:

```
protected void Application_Start(Object sender, EventArgs e)
{
    // Track logged-in users.
    Application["CurrentUsers"] = new Hashtable();
    Application["AnonymousUsers"] = new Counter();
}
```

Now every time a session starts, you can register a new anonymous user:

```
protected void Session_Start(Object sender, EventArgs e)
{
    Counter anonymous = (Counter)Application["AnonymousUsers"];
    lock (anonymous)
    {
        anonymous.Count++;
    }
}
```

■**Tip** Using a lock statement is more efficient than relying on the Application.Lock() method. The lock statement locks just a single object, while the Application.Lock() method prevents all users from adding or modifying any items in the collection.

When a user logs in, you need to add the user information to the hashtable. At the same time, you need to decrement the anonymous user count, to reflect the fact that one user has gone from being anonymous to authenticated. That user's existence is now reflected in the hashtable collection.

Here's the code you need to use if the login process succeeds:

```
// Update the list of logged-in users.
Hashtable users = (Hashtable)Application["CurrentUsers"];
lock (users)
{
    users.Add(Session.SessionID, txtName.Text);
}

// Reduce the list of anonymous users.
Counter anonymous = (Counter)Application["AnonymousUsers"];
lock (anonymous)
{
    anonymous.Count--;
}
```

The final thing you need to deal with is the end of a user session. When you respond to this event, you can't simply decrement the number of anonymous users, because you don't know whether the user is anonymous or logged in. Instead, you need to first check the list of logged-in users, as shown here:

```
protected void Session_End(Object sender, EventArgs e)
{
    Hashtable users = (Hashtable)Application["CurrentUsers"];
    Counter anonymous = (Counter)Application["AnonymousUsers"];

    if (users.Contains(Session.SessionID))
    {
        lock (users)
        {
            users.Remove(Session.SessionID);
        }
    }
    else
    {
        lock (anonymous)
        {
            anonymous.Count--;
        }
    }
}
```

One of the nice things about this system is that users are removed automatically when the session ends. That means if you want to add a button that allows the user to log out, you don't need to change the user list. Instead, the list will be modified automatically, provided you release the session, as shown here:

```
if (Request.IsAuthenticated)
{
    Session.Abandon();
    FormsAuthentication.SignOut();
}
```

Creating a Test Page

With these event handlers and login code, you now have a system that will store the number of active anonymous users and the user names of logged-in users. All you need now is a way to display this information.

One option, which is demonstrated in the next example, is to use data binding to create a user list. In this case, the DataList makes perfect sense. You can fill the DataList with the logged-in users, and add the current anonymous user count in the footer. Here's the control tag you need:

```
<asp:DataList id="UsersDataList" runat="server" BorderColor="#999999"
 BorderStyle="Solid" ForeColor="Black" BackColor="White" CellPadding="3"
 GridLines="Vertical" BorderWidth="1px">
  <HeaderStyle Font-Bold="True" ForeColor="White"
   BackColor="Black"></HeaderStyle>
  <FooterStyle BackColor="#CCCCCC"></FooterStyle>
  <HeaderTemplate>
    Currently Logged In Users
  </HeaderTemplate>
  <FooterTemplate>
    Anonymous Users:<%# Application["AnonymousUsers"]%>
  </FooterTemplate>
  <ItemTemplate>
    <%#DataBinder.Eval(Container, "DataItem")%>
  </ItemTemplate>
</asp:DataList>
```

As you can see, the footer binds directly to the anonymous user count in the Application collection. To fill the DataList, you need to use this code when the page loads:

```
private void Page_Load(object sender, System.EventArgs e)
{
    Hashtable users = (Hashtable)Application["CurrentUsers"];
    if (users.Count > 0)
    {
        // Bind the list to the values in the users hashtable.
        UsersDataList.DataSource = users.Values;
    }
    else
    {
        // Bind the list to a string array with a single piece
        // of static text.
        string[] noUsers = {"No users logged in"};
        UsersDataList.DataSource = noUsers;
    }
    UsersDataList.DataBind();
}
```

Figure 18-8 shows an example with two logged-in users and one anonymous user.

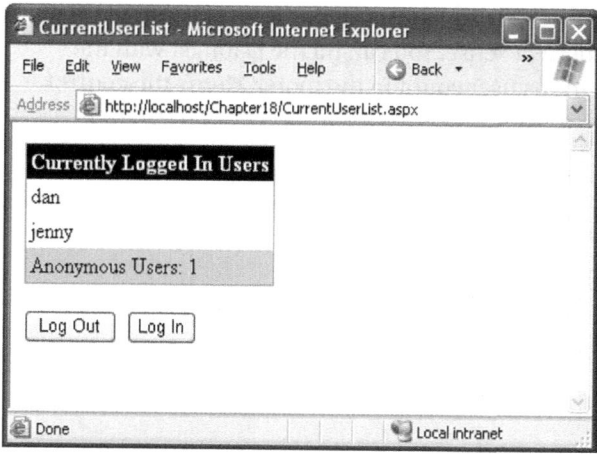

Figure 18-8. *Tracking current users*

Figure 18-9 shows the window after one of the users (jenny) logs out by clicking the Log Out button.

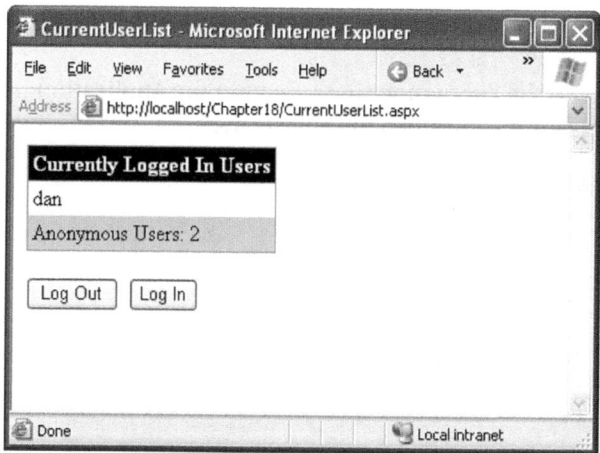

Figure 18-9. *One user logs out*

If you want to show the user list on multiple pages, you could place it into a user control, and host the user control on each page. You'll learn about user controls in more detail in the Part Four.

Extending ASP.NET Authentication

So far you've learned how you can implement a wide range of solutions using the built-in authentication services in ASP.NET. However, ASP.NET security isn't an all-or-nothing framework. If you want, you can create your own IPrincipal and IIdentity classes, and even roll your own custom authentication module.

Custom authentication systems are only limited by your own imagination. In this section, you'll consider two examples that show how you can extend the ASP.NET security framework. First, you'll look at generating your own IPrincipal and IIdentity classes. Then you'll see how to use application events to implement custom authentication.

Custom Identity and Principal Objects

Until this point, you've only considered three types of IIdentity objects—the WindowsIdentity (used by Windows authentication), the FormsIdentity (used by forms authentication), and the GenericIdentity (often used in customized authentication code). To make more specialized identity objects, you need to create a class that derives from GenericIdentity or implements IIdentity.

One reason you might want to take this step is to provide easier access to user-specific information. For example, forms authentication provides a ticket that allows you to access a single string with custom data. You can enter multiple settings in this string, but you'll need to complicate your web-page code with messy parsing logic. A neater solution is to replace the FormsIdentity with an identity object that provides strongly typed access to the information you want. You can replace the FormsIdentity object with your custom identity object when the HttpApplication.AuthenticateRequest event fires.

The first step to implement this approach is to create a custom identity class that implements IIdentity. When you implement IIdentity, you are responsible for supplying three key properties:

- **AuthenticationType.** This property returns a string variable containing the method of authentication that was used to authenticate the user. This value can be any string value you need to represent the authentication method you've employed. Of course, you'll want to provide some sort of logical name for the authentication type your application can use later on. If you only use one type of authentication, you can hardcode this value.

- **IsAuthenticated.** This property contains a Boolean value that's true if the use has been authenticated according to some scheme. If you don't create an identity object until a user is authenticated (the usual practice), this property can be hard-coded to return true.

- **Name.** This property returns a string with the user name. Like the other two properties, Name is read-only. You set it through the constructor when the identity object is instantiated.

In addition, the custom identity class in this example needs a property that can store e-mail address information. Here's the complete code for the custom identity class:

```
public class CustomIdentity : IIdentity
{
    public string AuthenticationType
    {
        get {return "CustomAuthenticationType";}
    }
```

```
    string name;
    public string Name
    {
        get {return name;}
    }

    string email;
    public string EmailAddress
    {
        get {return email;}
    }

    public bool IsAuthenticated
    {
        get {return true;}
    }

    public CustomIdentity(string name, string emailAddress)
    {
        this.name = name;
        this.email = emailAddress;
    }
}
```

Now that you've created a custom IIdentity class, you can also create a matching IPrincipal that uses this IIdentity class. However, you don't need to take this step, because the GenericPrincipal class can work with any type of identity object. The only reason you would create a custom principal (aside from making clearer code), is to change how role-based authorization works. For example, if you know that your system only supports three levels of authorization, you might want to add an additional UserInRole() method that works with a custom enumeration.

Now that you've created the custom identity class, you can bind it to the security context by reacting to the HttpApplication.AuthenticateRequest event. In this example, this is the point at which you must retrieve the user's email address from the ticket.

Here's the code you need:

```
protected void Application_AuthenticateRequest(Object sender, EventArgs e)
{
    // Check that the request has been authenticated.
    if (Request.IsAuthenticated)
    {
        if (Context.User.Identity is FormsIdentity)
        {
            // Get the e-mail address from the ticket.
            string email = ((FormsIdentity)
              Context.User.Identity).Ticket.UserData;
```

```
        // Create a new identity with this e-mail information.
        CustomIdentity identity = new
          CustomIdentity(Context.User.Identity.Name, email);

        // Create and attach a new principal (with no roles).
        GenericPrincipal newPrincipal =
          new GenericPrincipal(identity, new string[]{});
        Context.User = newPrincipal;
      }
    }
}
```

You can now retrieve the e-mail address from the strongly typed
CustomIdentity.EmailAddress property anywhere else in your web application code,
as shown here:

```
if (Request.IsAuthenticated)
{
    if (User.Identity is CustomIdentity)
    {
        string email = ((CustomIdentity)User.Identity).EmailAddress;
    }
}
```

■ **Note** Because the CustomIdentity object replaces the FormsIdentity object, you lose access to other
details that are specific to forms authentication, like the authentication ticket. If you need to access these
details, you could extend the CustomIdentity class accordingly.

Custom Authentication

ASP.NET also allows you to control the entire authentication process on your own. In most
cases, you won't need these more advanced features. Instead, you'll be able to customize the
existing forms authentication or Windows authentication technologies to suit your needs.
However, there are some cases where custom authentication becomes truly useful. Notable
examples are if you want to extend the ASP.NET request-processing architecture to work with
new protocols. For example, you might want to step outside the bounds of the web-page
model to build HTTP handlers and modules that perform proprietary request processing. In
this case, traditional forms authentication may not work, because there won't be an interac-
tive user using a web browser to log in.

To use custom authentication, you first set the authentication mode to None, as
shown here:

```
<configuration>
    <system.web>
        <!-- Other settings omitted. -->
        <authentication mode="None"/>
```

```
        <authorization>
          <deny users="?" />
        </authorization>
      </system.web>
    </configuration>
```

If you don't take any other steps, your web page will no longer function. When you request a page in the website, you'll be presented with a browser-based dialog box like the one used to authenticate users with Windows authentication. But no matter what credentials you enter, you'll receive an access denied error. In essence, ASP.NET has no way of authenticating any visitors, and since the application has been instructed to disallow anonymous access, all attempts at access will be denied!

To change this behavior, you need to respond to the event HttpApplication.AuthenticateRequest. You can do this in the global.asax file, or in a custom HTTP module that you've registered in the web.config file (as described in Chapter 6). As long as you attach an IIdentity with a user name other than an empty string (""), the request will be considered authenticated and page processing will continue. The only difference between this approach and the techniques you used earlier to extend authentication is that in this case, you first check that the current is *not* authenticated before you take any actions. (In the earlier examples, you began by checking that the user was authenticated, before tweaking the identity and principal objects.)

For example, the following event handler checks for a UserName value in the query string. If it exists, the code creates a new identity and allows the code to continue. If it doesn't, no action is taken, the user is not authenticated, and the user will receive an access denied message if your authorization rules prevent anonymous users.

```
protected void Application_AuthenticateRequest(Object sender, EventArgs e)
{
    if (Request.IsAuthenticated)
    {
        // Check for the UserName query string parameter.
        if (Context.Request.QueryString["UserName"] != null)
        {
            string user = Context.Request.QueryString["UserName"];

            // Create the new security context.
            Context.User = new GenericPrincipal(
              new GenericIdentity(user), new string[]{});
        }
    }
}
```

Obviously, more sophisticated checks are possible. For example, you might compare the user's IP address (available through the Request.UserHostAddress property) against a list of blocked or permitted addresses in a file or database. The important principle demonstrated in this example is that you can plug in your own logic to the ASP.NET authentication system in several ways. For example, you can choose to customize the existing forms authentication model, or you can replace it entirely with an authentication scheme you've built from the ground up.

Summary

In this chapter, you learned how take control of the .NET security with advanced techniques. You saw how to use stream-based encryption to protect stored data and the query string, and how to track users as they sign in and out of your application. Finally, you saw how to extend the ASP.NET authentication system with custom identity objects and authentication logic.

PART FOUR

■■■

Advanced User Interface

CHAPTER 19

■ ■ ■

User Controls

The core set of ASP.NET controls is broad and impressive. It includes controls that encapsulate basic HTML tags and controls that provide a rich higher-level model, like the AdRotator, Calendar, and the data bound lists. Of course, even the best set of controls can't meet the needs of every developer. Sooner or later, you'll want to get under the hood, start tinkering, and build your own user interface components.

In .NET, there are two different ways you can plug in to the web forms framework with your own controls. You can develop either of the following:

- **User controls.** A user control is a small section of a page that can include static HTML code and web server controls. The advantage of user controls is that once you create one, you can reuse it in multiple pages in the same web application. You can even add properties, events, and methods that encapsulate business logic.

- **Custom server controls.** Custom server controls are compiled classes that programmatically generate their own HTML. Unlike user controls (which are declared like web form pages in a plain text file), server controls are always precompiled into DLL assemblies. Depending on how you code the server control, you can render the content from scratch, inherit the appearance and behavior from an existing web control and extend its features, or build the interface by instantiating and configuring a group of constituent controls.

In this chapter, you'll explore the first option—user controls. User controls are a great way to standardize repeated content across all the pages in a website. For example, user controls are ideal when you need to build site headers and footers and navigational aids like a menu bar. User controls also work well if you want to group a set of commonly used input controls together and attach a few validator controls.

Tip In all of these examples, you could avoid user controls entirely and just copy and paste the code wherever you need. However, if you do you'll run into serious problems once you need to modify, debug, or enhance the controls in the future. Because multiple copies of the user interface code will be scattered throughout your website, you'll have the unenviable task of tracking down each copy and repeating your changes. Clearly, user controls provide a more elegant, object-oriented approach.

User Control Basics

User control (.ascx) files are very similar to ASP.NET web form (.aspx) files. Like web forms, user controls are composed of a user interface portion with control tags (the .ascx file), and can use inline script or a .cs code-behind file. User controls can contain just about anything a web page can, including static HTML content and ASP.NET controls, and they also receive the same events as the Page object (like Load and PreRender), and expose the same set of intrinsic ASP.NET objects through properties (like Application, Session, Request, and Response).

The only differences between user controls and web pages are as follows:

- User controls begin with a Control directive instead of a Page directive.

- User controls use the file extension .ascx instead of .aspx, and their code-behind files inherit from the System.Web.UI.UserControl class. In fact, the UserControl class and the Page class both inherit from the same TemplateControl class, which is why they share so many of the same methods and events.

- User controls can't be requested directly by a client. (ASP.NET will give a generic "that file type is not served" message to any user who tries.) Instead, user controls are embedded inside other web pages.

The following example is a user control named Header.ascx with static HTML. This HTML creates a header bar for all the web pages in a site.

```
<%@ Control %>
<table width="100%" border="0" bgcolor="blue">
    <tr>
        <td><font face="Verdana,Arial" size="6" color="yellow"><b>
            User Control Test Page</b></font>
        </td>
    </tr>
    <tr>
        <td align="right"><font size="3" color="white"><b>
            An Apress Creation © 2004</b></font>   
        </td>
    </tr>
</table>
```

In this example, the Control directive identifies that this is a user control, but it doesn't identify a code-behind class. That's because the simple header doesn't need any code to work.

Now to test the control, you need to place it on a web form. First, you need to tell the ASP.NET page that you plan to use that user control with the Register directive, as shown here:

```
<%@ Register TagPrefix="apress" TagName="Header" Src="Header.ascx" %>
```

This line identifies the source file that contains the user control using the Src attribute. It also defines a tag prefix and tag name that will be used to declare a new control on the page. In the same way that ASP.NET server controls have the <asp: ... > prefix to declare the controls (for example, <asp:TextBox>), you can use your own tag prefixes to help distinguish the controls you've created. This example uses a tag prefix of apress and a tag named Header. The full tag is shown in this page:

```
<%@ Page language="c#" Codebehind="HeaderHost.aspx.cs" AutoEventWireup="false"
    Inherits="UserControls.HeaderHost" %>
<%@ Register TagPrefix="apress" TagName="Header" Src="Header.ascx" %>
<HTML>
    <HEAD>
        <title>HeaderHost</title>
    </HEAD>
    <body MS_POSITIONING="GridLayout">
        <form id="Form1" method="post" runat="server">
            <apress:Header id="Header1" runat="server"></apress:Header>
        </form>
    </body>
</HTML>
```

At a bare minimum, when you add a user control to your page you should give it a unique ID and indicate that it runs on the server, as with all ASP.NET controls.

Figure 19-1 shows the results.

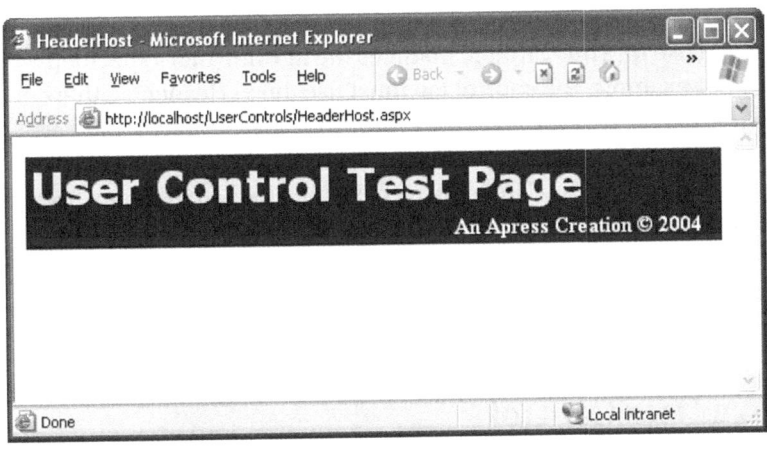

Figure 19-1. *Testing the header user control*

This is the simplest possible user control example, but it can already provide some realistic benefits. Think about what might happen if you had to manually copy the header's HTML code into all of your ASP.NET pages, and then you had to change the title, add a contact link, or something else. You would need to change and upload all the pages again. With a separate user control, you just update that one file. Best of all, you can combine any combination of HTML, user controls, and server controls on an ASP.NET web form.

User Controls in Visual Studio .NET

You can create a user control in Visual Studio .NET in much the same way that you add a web page. Just right-click the project in the Solution Explorer, and select Add ➤ Add User Control. If you aren't using Visual Studio .NET, you simply begin by creating an .ascx text file. You can design a user control in the same way that you design a web form, except that controls are always added in flow layout mode, because there's no way to position elements absolutely on a web page without knowing where your user control will appear. If you need more fine-grained control to position elements, consider adding a Grid Layout Panel (from the HTML tab in the Toolbox). You can then position other elements precisely inside the Panel.

In Visual Studio .NET, you don't need to code the Register directive by hand. Instead, once you've created your user control, simply select the .ascx in the Solution Explorer, and drag it onto the drawing area of a web form. Visual Studio .NET will automatically add the Register directive for you as well as an instance of the user control tag. However, Visual Studio .NET won't add a declaration for the user control to your code-behind class. This won't make a difference if your user control is simply a static block of HTML, but if you've added custom methods or properties that you want to access programmatically, you need a way to refer to the user control. The easiest solution is for you to add the declaration to the code-behind class. For example, to create a control reference for the Header user control, you would add this line:

```
public class HeaderHost : System.Web.UI.Page
{
    protected Header Header1;
    ...
}
```

Make sure that the name you use for your variable matches the id value that's specified for the user control *exactly*. In this example, the control tag must use the id Header1. Otherwise, Visual Studio .NET won't recognize that the control tag and your control declaration are really one and the same.

Finally, you'll also notice that Visual Studio .NET doesn't have the ability to render a user control at design time. (Or, more precisely, Visual Studio .NET makes no attempt to render user controls at design time, because it can't be certain they don't contain time-consuming code.) In the design environment, all user controls are displayed as a nondescript gray box (just like a Repeater or DataList without any templates).

Converting a Page to a User Control

Sometimes the easiest way to develop a user control is to put in a web page first, test it on its own, and then translate the page to a user control. Even if you don't follow this approach, you might still end up with a portion of user interface that you want to extract from a page and reuse in multiple places.

Overall, this process is a straightforward cut-and-paste operation. However, there are a few points you need to watch for. They are as follows:

- Remove all <html>, <body>, and <form> tags. These tags appear once in a page, so they can't be added to user controls (which might appear multiple times in a single page).

- If there is a Page directive, change it to an Control directive and remove the attributes that the Control directive does not support, namely: AspCompat, Buffer, ClientTarget, CodePage, Culture, EnableSessionState, EnableViewStateMac, ErrorPage, LCID, ResponseEncoding, Trace, TraceMode, and Transaction.

- If you aren't using the code-behind model, make sure you still include a class name in the Control directive by supplying the ClassName attribute. This way, the web page that consumes the control can be strongly typed, which allows it to access properties and methods you've added to the control.

- Change the file extension from .aspx to .ascx.

Adding Code to a User Control

The previous example didn't use any code. Instead, it simply provided a useful way to reuse a static block of web page UI. In many cases, however, you'll want to add some code to your user control creation, either to handle events or add functionality that the client can access. Just like a web form, you can add this code in a <script> block directly in the .ascx file (as you would with Web Matrix), or as a separate .cs code-behind file (which is the cleaner approach enforced by Visual Studio .NET).

Handling Events

To get a better idea of how this works, the next example creates a simple TimeDisplay user control with some event-handling logic. This user control encapsulates a single LinkButton control. Whenever the link is clicked, the time displayed in the link is updated. The time is also refreshed when the control first loads.

Here's the user control, using an inline script as you would with Web Matrix:

```
<%@ Control Language="C#" %>
<asp:LinkButton runat="server" ID="DateTimeLink" OnClick="lnkTime_Click"/>

<script language="C#" runat="server">
void Page_Load(object sender, EventArgs e)
{
    if (!Page.IsPostBack)
        RefreshTime();
}

void lnkTime_Click (object sender, EventArgs e)
{
    RefreshTime();
}

public void RefreshTime()
{
    lnkTime.Text = DateTime.Now.ToLongTimeString();
}
</script>
```

Note that the lnkTime_Click event handler calls a method named RefreshTime(). Because this method is public, the code on the hosting web form can trigger a label refresh programmatically by calling the method at any time. Figure 19-2 shows the resulting control.

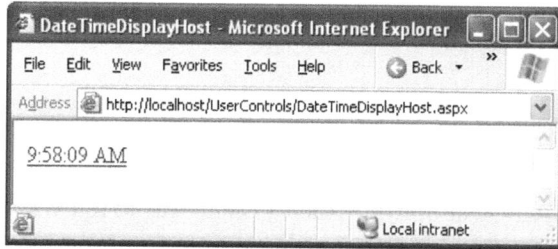

Figure 19-2. *A user control that handles its own events*

The code takes a turn for the better if you split it into a separate .ascx portion and a .cs code-behind file. In this case, the Control directive must specify the Src attribute with the name of the user control source-code file *or* the Inherits attribute with the name of the compiled class. User controls created in Visual Studio .NET are always compiled into the single DLL assembly that contains all the web-page code for the web application, and so you always use the Inherits attribute.

Here's an example with the Visual Studio .NET approach:

```
<%@ Control Language="c#" AutoEventWireup="false"
    Codebehind="DateTimeDisplay.ascx.cs" Inherits=" DateTimeDisplay" %>
<asp:LinkButton id="lnkTime" runat="server">LinkButton</asp:LinkButton>
```

And here's the corresponding code-behind class:

```
public class DateTimeDisplay : System.Web.UI.UserControl
{
    protected System.Web.UI.WebControls.LinkButton lnkTime;
    // (Designer code omitted.)

    private void Page_Load(object sender, System.EventArgs e)
    {
        if (!Page.IsPostBack)
            RefreshTime();
    }
    private void lnkTime_Click(object sender, System.EventArgs e)
    {
        RefreshTime();
    }
    public void RefreshTime()
    {
        lnkTime.Text = DateTime.Now.ToLongTimeString();
    }
}
```

Note that in this example, the user control receives and handles a Page.Load event. This event and event handler are completely separate from the Page.Load event that the web form can respond to (although they both are raised as a consequence of the same thing—a page being created). This makes it very easy for you to add initialization code to a user control.

Adding Properties

Currently, the TimeDisplay user control allows only limited interaction with the page that hosts it. All you can really do in your web form code is call RefreshTime() to update the display. To make a user control more flexible and much more reusable, developers often add properties.

The next example shows a revised TimeDisplay control that adds a public Format property. This property accepts a standard .NET format string, which is used to configure the format of the displayed date. The RefreshTime() method has been updated to take this information into account.

```
public class DateTimeDisplay : System.Web.UI.UserControl
{
    protected System.Web.UI.WebControls.LinkButton lnkTime;
    // (Designer code omitted.)

    private void Page_Load(object sender, System.EventArgs e)
    {
        if (!Page.IsPostBack)
            RefreshTime();
    }

    private string format;
    public string Format
    {
        get { return format; }
        set { format = value; }
    }

    private void lnkTime_Click(object sender, System.EventArgs e)
    {
        RefreshTime();
    }

    public void RefreshTime()
    {
        if (format == "")
        {
            lnkTime.Text = DateTime.Now.ToLongTimeString();
        }
        else
        {
            // This will throw an exception for invalid format strings,
```

```
                    // which is acceptable.
                    lnkTime.Text = DateTime.Now.ToString(format);
            }
        }
}
```

In the hosting page, you have two choices. You can set the Format property at some point in your code by manipulating the control object, as shown here:

```
TimeDisplay1.Format = "dddd, dd MMMM yyyy HH:mm:ss tt (GMT z)";
```

In this case, you need to make sure that the user control is declared in your code-behind class. Remember, Visual Studio .NET won't add this line directly. Here's what you need to add to the page class:

```
protected TimeDisplay TimeDisplay1;
```

Your second option is to configure the user control when it's first initialized by setting the value in the control tag, as shown here:

```
<apress:TimeDisplay id="TimeDisplay1"
  Format="dddd, dd MMMM yyyy HH:mm:ss tt (GMT z)" runat="server" />
<hr>
<apress:TimeDisplay id="TimeDisplay2" runat="server" />
```

In this example, two versions of the TimeDisplay control are created, one with a control that displays the date in the default format, and another one with a custom format applied. Figure 19-3 shows the resulting page on the browser.

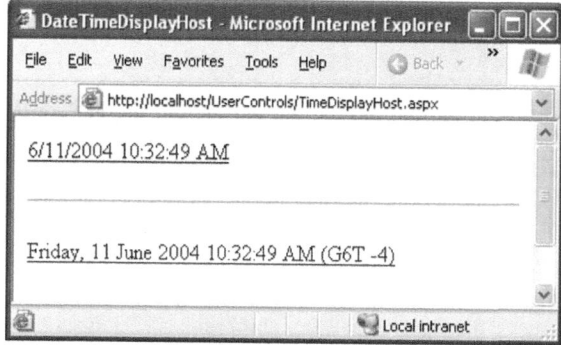

Figure 19-3. *Two instances of a dynamic user control*

Tip If you use simple property types like int, DateTime, float, and so on, you can still set them with string values when declaring the control on the host page. ASP.NET will automatically convert the string to the property type defined in the class.

When you begin adding properties to a user control, it becomes more important to understand the sequence of events. Essentially, page initialization follows this order:

1. The page is requested.

2. The user control is created. If you have any default values for your variables, or if you perform any initialization in a class constructor, it's applied now.

3. If any properties are set in the user control tag, these are applied now.

4. The Page.Load event in the page executes, potentially initializing the user control.

5. The Page.Load event in the user control executes, potentially initializing the user control.

Once you understand this sequence, you'll realize that you shouldn't perform user control initialization in the Page.Load event of the user control that might overwrite the settings specified by the client.

Using Custom Objects

Many user controls are designed to *abstract* away the details of common scenarios with a higher-level control model. For example, if you need to enter address information, you might group several TextBox controls into one higher-level AddressInput control. When you're modeling this sort of control, you'll need to use more complex data than individual strings and numbers. Often, you'll want to create custom classes designed expressly for communication between your web page and your user control.

To demonstrate this idea, the next example develops a LinkTable control that renders a set of hyperlinks in a formatted table. Figure 19-4 shows the LinkTable control.

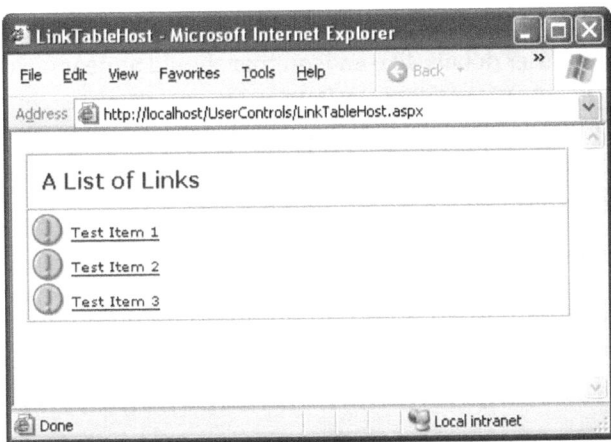

Figure 19-4. *A user control that displays a table of links*

In order to support this control, you need a custom class that defines the information needed for each link:

```
public class LinkTableItem
{
    private string text;
    public string Text
    {
        get { return text; }
        set { text = value; }
    }

    private string url;
    public string Url
    {
        get { return url; }
        set { url = value; }
    }

    // Default constructor.
    public LinkTableItem()
    {}

    public LinkTableItem(string text, string url)
    {
        this.text = text;
        this.url = url;
    }
}
```

This class could be expanded to include other details, like an icon that should appear next to the control. The LinkTable simply uses the same icon for every item.

Next, consider the code-behind class for the LinkTable. It defines a Title property that allows you to set a caption, and an Items collection that accepts an array of LinkTableItem objects, one for each link that you want to display in the table.

```
public class LinkTable : System.Web.UI.UserControl
{
    protected System.Web.UI.WebControls.DataList listContent;
    protected System.Web.UI.WebControls.Label lblTitle;
    // (Designer code omitted.)

    public string Title
    {
        get { return lblTitle.Text; }
        set { lblTitle.Text = value; }
    }
```

```
    private LinkTableItem[] items;
    public LinkTableItem[] Items
    {
        get { return items; }
        set
        {
            items = value;

            // Refresh the grid.
            listContent.DataSource = items;
            listContent.DataBind();
        }
    }
}
```

The control itself uses data binding to render most of its user interface. Whenever the Items property is set or changed, a DataList in the LinkTable control is rebound to the item collection. The DataList contains a single template that, for each link, displays each HyperLink control, which appears with an exclamation mark icon next to it.

```
<%@ Control Language="c#" AutoEventWireup="false" Codebehind="LinkTable.ascx.cs"
    Inherits="UserControls.LinkTable" %>
<table border="1" width="100%" cellspacing="0" cellpadding="2" height="43">
    <tr>
        <td width="100%" height="1">
          <asp:Label id="lblTitle" runat="server" ForeColor="#C00000"
            Font-Bold="True" Font-Names="Verdana" Font-Size="Small">
            [Title Goes Here]</asp:Label>
        </td>
    </tr>
    <tr>
        <td width="100%" height="1">
          <asp:DataList id="listContent" runat="server">
            <ItemTemplate>
              <img height="23" src="exclaim.gif"
                width="25" align="absMiddle" border="0">
              <asp:HyperLink id="HyperLink1"
                NavigateUrl='<%# DataBinder.Eval(Container.DataItem, "Url") %>'
                Font-Names="Verdana" Font-Size="XX-Small" ForeColor="#0000cd"
                Text='<%# DataBinder.Eval(Container.DataItem, "Text") %>'
                runat="server">
              </asp:HyperLink>
            </ItemTemplate>
          </asp:DataList>
        </td>
    </tr>
</table>
```

Finally, here's the typical web-page code you would use to define a list of links and display it by binding it to the LinkTable user control:

```
private void Page_Load(object sender, System.EventArgs e)
{
    // Set the title.
    LinkTable1.Title = "A List of Links";

    // Set the hyperlinked item list.
    LinkTableItem[] items = new LinkTableItem[3];
    items[0] = new LinkTableItem("Test Item 1", "http://www.apress.com");
    items[1] = new LinkTableItem("Test Item 2", "http://www.apress.com");
    items[2] = new LinkTableItem("Test Item 3", "http://www.apress.com");
    LinkTable1.Items = items;
}
```

Once it's configured, the web-page code never needs to interact with this control again. When the user clicks one of the links, the user is just forwarded on to the new destination without the need for any additional code. Another approach would be to design the LinkTable so that it raises a server-side click event. You'll see that approach in the next section.

Adding Events

Another way that communication can occur between a user control and a web page is through events. With methods and properties, the user control reacts to a change made by the web-page code. With events, the story is reversed—the user control notifies the web page about an action, and the web-page code responds.

Usually, you'll delve into events when you create a user control that the user can interact with. After the user takes a certain action—like clicking a button or choosing an option from a list—your user control intercepts a web control event, and then raises a new, higher-level event to notify your web page.

The first version of LinkTable control is fairly functional, but it doesn't use events. Instead, it simply creates the requested links. To demonstrate how events can be used, the next example revises the LinkTable so that it notifies the user when an item is clicked. Your web page can then determine what action to take based on which item was clicked.

The first step to implement this design is to define the events. Remember that to define an event you must use the event keyword with a delegate that represents the signature of the event. The .NET standard for events specifies that every event should use two parameters. The first one provides a reference to the control that sent the event, while the second one incorporates any additional information. This additional information is wrapped into a custom EventArgs object, which inherits from the System.EventArgs class. (If your event doesn't require any additional information, you can just use the generic System.EventArgs object, which doesn't contain any additional data. Many events in ASP.NET, such as Page.Load or Button.Click, follow this pattern.)

In the LinkTable example, it makes sense to transmit basic information about what link was clicked. To support this design, you can create the following EventArgs object, which adds a read-only property that has the corresponding LinkTableItem object:

```
public class LinkTableEventArgs : EventArgs
{
    private LinkTableItem selectedItem;
    public LinkTableItem SelectedItem
    {
        get { return selectedItem; }
    }

    private bool cancel = false;
    public bool Cancel
    {
        get { return cancel; }
        set { cancel = value; }
    }

    public LinkTableEventArgs(LinkTableItem item)
    {
        selectedItem = item;
    }
}
```

Notice that the LinkTableEventArgs defines two new details—a SelectedItem property that allows the user to get information about the item that was clicked, and a Cancel property that the user can set to prevent the LinkTable from navigating to the new page. One reason you might set Cancel is if you want to respond to the event in your web-page code and handle the redirect yourself. For example, you might want to show the target link in a server-side <iframe> or use it to set the content for an <img> rather than navigating to a new page.

Next, you need to create a new delegate that represents the LinkClicked event signature. Here's what it should look like:

```
public delegate void LinkClickedEventHandler(object sender,
    LinkTableEventArgs e);
```

Using the LinkClickedEventHandler, the LinkTable class defines a single event:

```
public event LinkClickedEventHandler LinkClicked;
```

In order to intercept the server click, you need to replace the HyperLink control with a LinkButton, because only the LinkButton raises a server-side event. (The HyperLink simply renders as an anchor that directs the user directly to the target when clicked.) Here's the new template you need:

```
<ItemTemplate>
  <img height="23" src="exclaim.gif"
   width="25" align="absMiddle" border="0">
  <asp:LinkButton id="HyperLink1" Font-Names="Verdana" Font-Size="XX-Small"
   ForeColor="#0000cd" runat="server"
   Text='<%# DataBinder.Eval(Container.DataItem, "Text") %>'
```

```
        CommandArgument='<%# DataBinder.Eval(Container.DataItem, "Url") %>'>
    </asp:LinkButton>
</ItemTemplate>
```

You can then intercept the server-side click event, and forward it along to the web page as a LinkClicked event. Here's the code that you need:

```
private void listContent_ItemCommand(object source,
    System.Web.UI.WebControls.DataListCommandEventArgs e)
{
    if (LinkClicked != null)
    {
        // Get the HyperLink object that was clicked.
        LinkButton link = (LinkButton)e.Item.Controls[1];

        // Construct the event arguments.
        LinkTableItem item = new LinkTableItem(link.Text, link.CommandArgument);
        LinkTableEventArgs args = new LinkTableEventArgs(item);

        // Fire the event.
        LinkClicked(this, args);

        // Navigate to the link if the event recipient didn't
        // cancel the operation.
        if (!args.Cancel)
        {
            Response.Redirect(item.Url);
        }
    }
}
```

Note that when you raise an event, you must first check to see if the event variable contains a null reference. If it does, it signifies that no event handlers are registered yet (perhaps the control hasn't been created). Trying to fire the event at this point will generate a null reference exception. If the event variable isn't null, you can fired the event by using the name and passing along the appropriate event parameters.

Consuming this event isn't quite as easy as it is for the standard set of ASP.NET controls. The problem is that user controls don't provide much in the way of design-time support. (Custom controls, which you'll look at next chapter, do provide design-time support.) As a result, you can't use the Properties window to wire up the event handler at design time. Instead, you need to write the event handler and the code that attaches it yourself

Here's an example of an event handler that has the required signature (as defined by the LinkClickedEventHandler):

```
private void LinkClicked(object sender, LinkTableEventArgs e)
{
    lblInfo.Text = "You clicked '" + e.SelectedItem.Text +
```

```
     "' but this page chose not to direct you to '" +
   e.SelectedItem.Url + "'.";
   e.Cancel = true;
}
```

And here's the code you need to use in the Page.Load event handler:

```
LinkTable1.LinkClicked += new LinkClickedEventHandler(LinkClicked);
```

Figure 19-5 shows the result when a link is clicked.

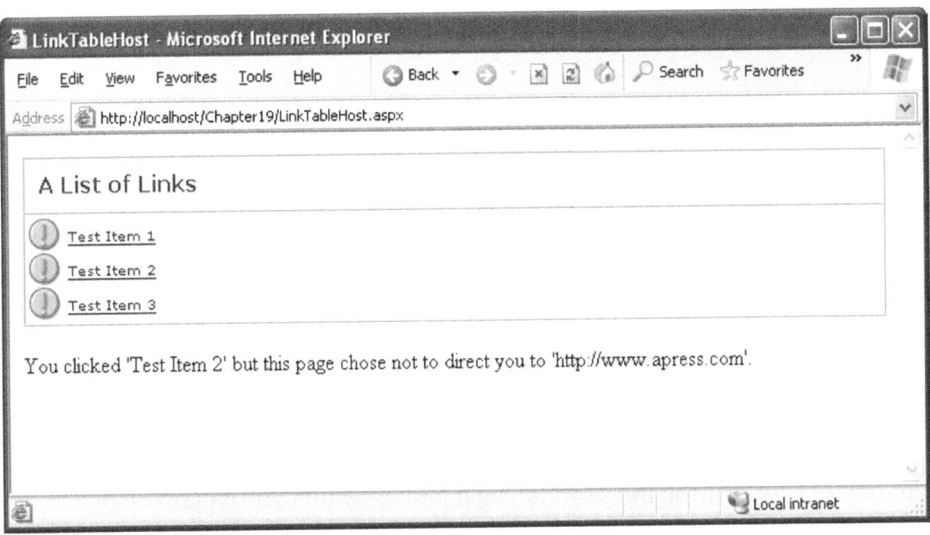

Figure 19-5. *A user control that fires an event*

Exposing the Inner Web Control

One important detail to remember is that the user control's constituent controls can only be accessed by the user control. That means the web page that hosts the user control can receive the events, set the properties, or call the methods of these contained controls. For example, in the TimeDisplay user control the web page has no ability to access the LinkButton control that it uses.

Usually, this behavior is exactly what you want. It means your user control can add public properties to expose specific details without giving the web page free rein to tamper with everything and potentially introduce invalid or inconsistent changes. For example, if you want to give the web page the ability to tweak the foreground color of the LinkButton control, you might add a ForeColor property to your user control. Here's an example:

```
public Color ForeColor
{
    get { return lnkTime.ForeColor; }
    set { lnkTime.ForeColor = value; }
}
```

To change the fore color in your web-page code, you would now use code like this:

```
TimeDisplay1.ForeColor = System.Drawing.Color.Green;
```

This example maps the lnkTime.ForeColor property to the ForeColor property of the user control. This trick is usually the best approach, but it can become tedious if you need to expose a large number of properties. For example, your user control might render a table and you might want to let the user configure the formatting of each of the individual table cells.

In this case, it might make sense to expose the complete control object. Here's an example that exposes the lnkTime control for the TimeDisplay user control:

```
public LinkButton InnerLink
{
    get { return lnkTime; }
}
```

Notice that you need to use a read-only property, because it's not possible for the web page to replace the control with something different.

Now this is how you would set the foreground color in the hosting page:

```
TimeDisplay1.InnerLink.ForeColor = System.Drawing.Color.Green;
```

Keep in mind that when you use this practice you expose *all* the details of the inner control. This means the web page can call methods and receive events from that control. This approach gives unlimited flexibility, but it reduces the reusability of the code. It also increases the chance that your web page will become tightly coupled to the internal details of the current implementation of your control, thereby making it less likely that you can revise or enhance the user control without disrupting the web pages that use it. As a general rule of thumb, it's always better to create dedicated methods, events, and properties to expose just the functionality you need, rather than opening a back door that could be used to create messy work-arounds.

Dynamically Loading User Controls

So far you've seen how you can add server controls to a page by registering the type of user control and adding the corresponding tag. You can also create user controls dynamically—in other words, create them on the fly using nothing but a little web-page code.

This technique is similar to the technique you used to add ordinary web controls dynamically (as described in Chapter 4). As with ordinary controls, you should do the following:

- Add user controls when the Page.Load event fires (so that your user control can properly restore its state and receive postback event).

- Use container controls and the PlaceHolder control to make sure the user controls end up exactly where you want.

- Give the user control a unique name by settings its ID property. You can use this information to retrieve a reference to the control when you need it with the Page.FindControl() method.

There's one additional wrinkle. You can't create a user control object directly, like you can with an ordinary control. That's because user controls aren't entirely based on code—they also require the control tags that are defined in the .ascx file. In order to use a user control, ASP.NET needs to process this file and initialize the corresponding child control objects.

In order to perform this step, you need to call the Page.LoadControl() method. When you call LoadControl(), you pass the filename of the .ascx user control markup file. LoadControl() returns a UserControl object, which you can then add to the page, and cast to the specific class type to access control-specific functionality.

Here's an example that loads the TimeDisplay user control dynamically and adds it to the page using a PlaceHolder control:

```
TimeDisplay ctrl = (TimeDisplay)Page.LoadControl("TimeDisplay.ascx");
PlaceHolder1.Controls.Add(ctrl);
```

Despite this slightly awkward detail, dynamically loading is a very powerful technique when used in conjunction with user controls. It's commonly used to create highly configurable portal frameworks.

Portal Frameworks

Although it takes a fair bit of boilerplate code to create a complete portal framework, you can see the most important principles with a simple example. Consider the page shown in Figure 19-6. It includes a panel that contains four controls—a DropDownList, a PlaceHolder, a Label, and a PlaceHolder control.

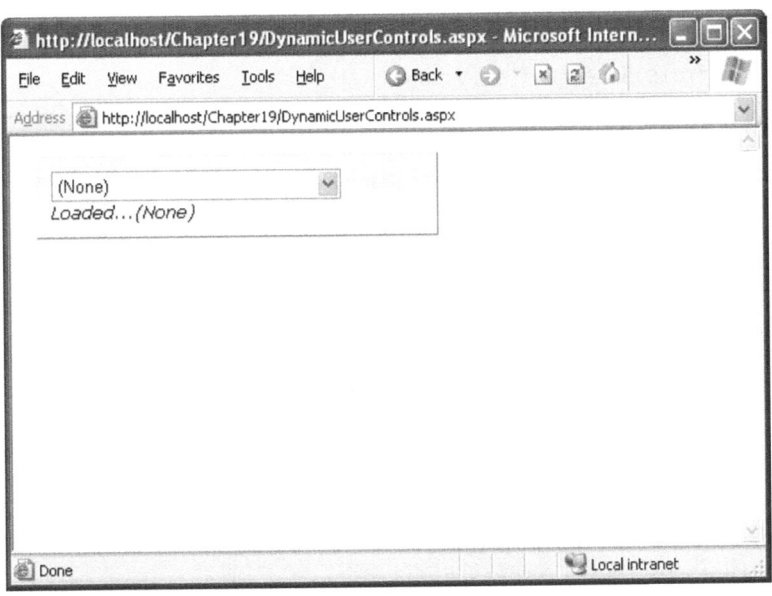

Figure 19-6. *A panel for holding user controls*

When the user selects an item from the drop-down list, the page posts back, and the appropriate user control is loaded dynamically and inserted into the placeholder. Figure 19-7 shows the result.

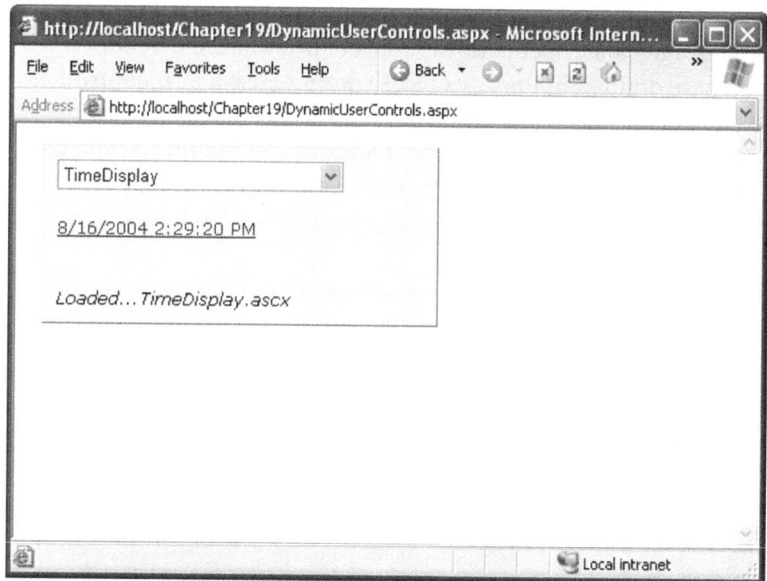

Figure 19-7. *A dynamically loaded user control*

Here's the code that loads the selected control:

```
private void Page_Load(object sender, System.EventArgs e)
{
    // Remember that the control must be loaded in the Page.Load event handler.
    // The DropDownList.SelectedIndexChanged event fires too late.
    string ctrlName = listControls.SelectedItem.Value;
    if (ctrlName.EndsWith(".ascx"))
    {
        placeHolder.Controls.Add(Page.LoadControl(ctrlName));
    }
    lbl.Text = "Loaded..." + ctrlName;
}
```

This example demonstrates a number of interesting features. First, because the PlaceHolder is stored in a formatted container, the user controls you load automatically acquire the container's font, background color, and so on (unless they explicitly define their own fonts and colors).

Best of all, because you're loading these controls when the Page.Load event fires, the control object is able to handle its own events. You can try this out by loading the TimeDisplay user control and then clicking the link to refresh the time.

■**Note** Because the TimeDisplay control isn't loaded until the page is posted back at least once, it won't show the time until you click the link at least once. Instead, it will start with the generic control name text. There's a number of ways you can solve this problem, including calling the RefreshTime() method from your web page when the control is loaded. An even better approach is to create an interface for all your user controls that defines certain basic methods, like InitializeControl(). That way, you can initialize any control generically. Most portal frameworks use interfaces to provide this type of standardization.

It's not too difficult to extend this example to provide an entire configurable web page. All you need to do is create more panels and organize them on your web page (possibly using tables and other panels to group them together). This might seem like a tedious task, but you can actually deal with it quite effectively by writing some generic code that deals with all the panels on your page. One option would be to create a user control that loads other user controls. Another approach is to a custom method, as shown here, which handles user control loading for three panels:

```
private void Page_Load(object sender, System.EventArgs e)
{
    LoadControls(DIV1);
    LoadControls(DIV2);
    LoadControls(DIV3);
}

private void LoadControls(Control container)
{
    DropDownList list = null;
    PlaceHolder ph = null;
    Label lbl = null;

    // Find the controls for this panel.
    foreach (Control ctrl in container.Controls)
    {
        if (ctrl is DropDownList)
        {
            list = (DropDownList)ctrl;
        }
        else if (ctrl is PlaceHolder)
        {
            ph = (PlaceHolder)ctrl;
```

```
        }
        else if (ctrl is Label)
        {
            lbl = (Label)ctrl;
        }
    }

    // Load the dynamic content into this panel.
    string ctrlName = list.SelectedItem.Value;
    if (ctrlName.EndsWith(".ascx"))
    {
        ph.Controls.Add(Page.LoadControl(ctrlName));
    }
    lbl.Text = "Loaded..." + ctrlName;
}
```

Figure 19-8 shows this example in action.

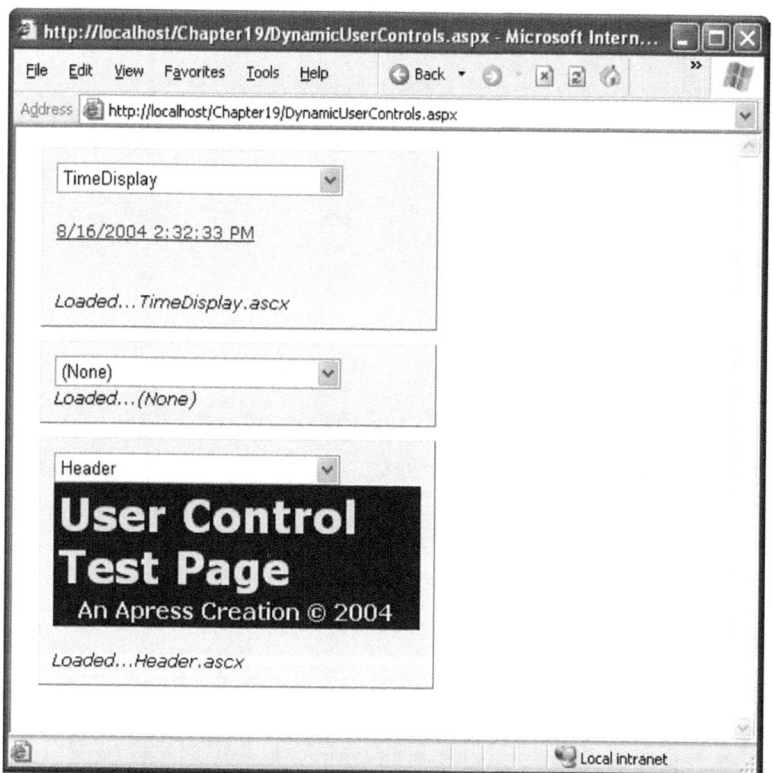

Figure 19-8. *A dynamic web page with multiple user controls*

If you want to learn more about portal frameworks, you'll find a wealth of resources on the Internet. One excellent example is provided by Microsoft's Portal Starter Kit, which you can download from www.asp.net. Best of all, you're free to redistribute and customize the Portal Starter Kit to suit your needs. The Portal Starter Kit builds its entire interface out of discrete modules. Different users can customize the interface to show just the modules they are interested in. These settings are stored in a back-end database. Another example is the ongoing DotNetNuke project. This application evolved from the Portal Starter Kit example, and it has expanded into a much larger and more ambitious open-source project. For more information, surf to `www.dotnetnuke.com`.

Partial Page Caching

In Chapter 7, you learned how you can cache a web page by adding the OutputCache directive to the .aspx page. This type of caching, called *output caching*, caches a rendered HTML version of the page, which ASP.NET can reuse automatically for future requests without executing any of your page code.

One of the drawbacks with response caching is that it works on an all-or-nothing basis. It doesn't work if you need to render a portion of your page dynamically. For example, you might want to cache a table that's filled with records read from a data source so that you can limit the round-trips to the database server, but you might still need to get a fresh output for the rest of the page. If that's your situation, user controls can provide exactly what you're looking for because they can cache their own output. This feature is called partial caching or *fragment caching*, and it works in almost the same way as output caching. The only difference is that you add the OutputCache directive to the user control, instead of the page.

To test this feature, add the following line to the .ascx portion of a user control like the TimeDisplay:

```
<%@ OutputCache Duration="10" VaryByParam="None" %>
```

Now in the hosting page you'll see that the displayed time won't change for ten seconds. Refreshing the page has no effect. The VaryByParam parameter has the same meaning as it did with web pages—it allows to you to generate and cache fresh HTML output when the parameters in the query string portion of the URL change.

Alternatively, you can enable caching by adding the following attribute to the declaration of your user control class:

```
[PartialCaching(10)]
public class MyUserControl
{ ... }
```

There's one caveat when using fragment caching. When a user control is cached, the user control essentially becomes a block of static HTML. As a result, the user control object won't be available to your web-page code. Instead, ASP.NET instantiates one of two more generic object types, depending on how the user control was created. If the user control was created declaratively (by adding a user tag to the web page), a StaticPartialCachingControl object is added. If the user control was created programmatically (using the LoadControl() method), a PartialCachingControl object is added. ASP.NET places the object into the logical position that a user control would occupy in the page's control hierarchy if it were not cached. However, these objects are just placeholders—they won't allow you to interact with the user control through its properties or methods. If you aren't sure if caching is in effect, you should test for a null reference before you attempt to use the user control object.

Summary

In this chapter, you learned how to create simple and more sophisticated user controls. You also saw how to load user controls dynamically, and how to cache them. Though user controls are easy to create, they don't solve every custom control challenge. In fact, user controls are quite limited in scope (they can't be easily shared across applications), and have limited design-time support (for example, you can't set events or properties in the Properties window or see how the control will look at design time). User controls also lack advanced features, and aren't well suited if you need to render HTML and JavaScript on the fly. To improve on this situation, you can step up to custom controls, which are much more sophisticated and quite a bit more complicated to create.

Note Although server controls are more powerful than user controls, most of the concepts you've learned in this chapter apply to server controls in the same way that they apply to user controls. For example, you can create server controls that include properties and methods, use custom objects, fire events, and expose child controls.

■■■

CHAPTER 20

Custom Server Controls

Each type of custom control has its own advantages and disadvantages. User controls are easier to create, but custom server controls are far more powerful. Server controls beat user controls in two key areas:

- Server controls give you complete control over the HTML you generate. In other words, you can create a control like the ASP.NET Calendar, which provides a single object interface but renders itself as a complex combination of elements.

- Server controls provide better design-time support. You can add them to the Toolbox in Visual Studio .NET and set properties and add event handlers at design time. You can even configure the description that Visual Studio .NET will show for each property, along with other design-time niceties.

All of ASP.NET's web controls are server controls. In this chapter, you'll learn how you can build your own.

Custom Server Control Basics

Server controls are .NET classes that derive from System.Web.UI.WebControls.WebControl (which itself derives from Control) or System.Web.UI.Control. The Control class provides properties and methods that are common across all server Controls (such as ID, ViewState, and the Controls collection). The WebControl class adds a few features that help you implement standard styles. These include properties like Font, ForeColor, and BackColor.

No matter what base class you choose, every server control is deployed as a compiled assembly. This model has several immediate consequences:

- Server controls can be easily shared among multiple different web applications. All you need to do is copy the control DLL into the Bin subdirectory of each application.

- Server controls can be written in any .NET language and can be reused in pages written in different languages. This is not possible with user controls, which require that the language used for the server-side code matches the language used in the hosting page.

- If you're using Visual Studio .NET, you need to create your server control in a separate project. This approach ensures that it's compiled separately, which allows you to add it to the Toolbox and add it to a web form at design time.

To get a better idea of how custom controls work, the following sections demonstrate a couple of simple examples.

Creating a Bare-Bones Custom Control

To create a basic custom control, you need to derive from the Control class and override the Render() method. The Render() method provides an HtmlTextWriter object that you use to generate the HTML for the control. The simplest approach is simply to call HtmlTextWriter.Write() to write a string of raw HTML to the page. (ASP.NET tags and other server-side content obviously won't work here.)

Here's an example control that generates a simple hyperlink using the HtmlTextWriter in the Render() method:

```
public class LinkControl : Control
{
    protected override void Render(HtmlTextWriter output)
    {
        output.Write(
          "<a href='http://www.apress.com'>Click to visit Apress</a>");
    }
}
```

The HtmlTextWriter class not only lets you write raw HTML, but it provides some helpful methods to help you manage style attributes and tags. Table 20-1 describes the key methods.

Table 20-1. *HtmlTextWriter Methods*

Method	Description
AddAttribute()	Adds any HTML attribute and its value to an HtmlTextWriter output stream. This attribute is automatically used for the next tag you create by calling RenderBeginTag(). Instead of using the exact attribute name, you can choose a value from the HtmlTextWriterAttribute enumeration.
AddStyleAttribute()	Adds an HTML style attribute and its value to an HtmlTextWriter output stream. This attribute is automatically used for the next tag you create by calling RenderBeginTag(). Instead of using the exact style name, you can choose a value from the HtmlTextWriterStyle enumeration, and it will be rendered appropriately depending on whether the browser is an up-level or down-level client.
RenderBeginTag()	Writes the start tag for the HTML element. For example, if you are writing an anchor tag, this writes <a>. Instead of using the exact tag name, you can choose a value from the HtmlTextWriterTag enumeration.
RenderEndTag()	Writes the end tag for the HTML element. For example, if you are in the process of writing an anchor tag, this writes the closing </a>. You don't need to specify the tag name.
WriteBeginTag()	This method is similar to the RenderBeginTag() method, except it doesn't write the closing > character for the start tag. That means you can add call WriteAttribute() to add more attributes to the tag.
WriteAttribute()	Writes an HTML attribute to the output stream. This must follow the WriteBeginTag() method.
WriteEndTag()	Writes the closing > character for the current HTML tag (the one that was last opened using the WriteBeginTag() method).

Using the HtmlTextWriter methods, you can modify the rendering code. The next example presents the same control, with a couple of minor differences. First, it renders the start tag and the end tag for the anchor separately, using the RenderBeginTag() and RenderEndTag() methods. Second, it adds style attributes that configure how the control will appear. Here's the complete code:

```
public class LinkControl : Control
{
    protected override void Render(HtmlTextWriter output)
    {
        // Specify the URL for the upcoming anchor tag.
        output.AddAttribute(HtmlTextWriterAttribute.Href,
          "http://www.apress.com");

        // Add the style attributes.
        output.AddStyleAttribute(HtmlTextWriterStyle.FontSize, "20");
        output.AddStyleAttribute(HtmlTextWriterStyle.Color, "Blue");

        // Create the anchor tag.
        output.RenderBeginTag(HtmlTextWriterTag.A);

        // Write the text inside the tag.
        output.Write("Click to visit Apress");

        // Close the tag.
        output.RenderEndTag();

        // (At this point, you could continue writing more tags and attributes.)
    }
}
```

There are a few important points to note in this example. First, to make life easier, several enumerations are used. These enumerations help avoid minor typographic mistakes that would cause unexpected problems. The enumerations include the following:

- **HtmlTextWriterTag.** This enumeration defines a large set of common HTML tag attributes like onClick, href, align, alt, and more.

- **HtmlTextWriterAttribute.** This enumeration defines dozens of HTML tags, like <a>, <p>, <font>, and many more.

- **HtmlTextWriterStyle.** This enumeration defines 14 style attributes, including BackgroundColor, BackgroundImage, BorderColor, BorderStyle, BorderWidth, Color, FontFamily, FontSize, FontStyle, FontWeight, Height, and Width. All of these pieces of information are joined in a semicolon-delimited list, which is used to set the style attribute.

When the Render() method executes, it begins by defining all the attributes that will be added to the upcoming tag. Then when the start tag is created (using the RenderBeginTag() method), all of these attributes are placed into the tag. The final rendered tag looks like this:

```
<a href="http://www.apress.com" style="font-size:20;color:Blue;">
Click to visit Apress</a>
```

Using a Custom Control

Before you can use a custom control, you need to compile it into an assembly. If you are coding by hand or using Web Matrix, you'll perform this step at the command line using the csc.exe C# compiler. This process is identical to the steps you need to take to precompile a code-behind file by hand, as shown here:

```
csc /r:System.dll /r:System.Web.dll /t:library LinkControl.cs
```

Once you've compiled the control, you need to copy it to the Bin directory of your web application. Then you can register the control and instantiate it using tags.

To register the control, you use the Register directive, just as you did with user controls in the last chapter. However, this time you need to indicate slightly different information. Not only must you include a TagPrefix, but also need to specify the assembly file (without the DLL extension) and the namespace where the control class is located. You don't need to specify the TagName, because the server control's class name is used automatically. Here's an example of the Register directive:

```
<%@ Register TagPrefix="apress" Namespace="CustomServerControlsLibrary"
  Assembly="CustomServerControlsLibrary" %>
```

Once you've registered the control, you can declare it with a standard control tag, as shown here:

```
<apress:LinkControl id="LinkControl1" runat="server"/>
```

Figure 20-1 shows the custom LinkControl in action.

Figure 20-1. *A bare-bones server control*

Custom Controls in Visual Studio .NET

In Visual Studio .NET, you need to develop your custom controls in a separate class library project. You can then compile the assembly into a DLL, and add a reference to the assembly in a new web project. Fortunately, it's still just as easy to use them in a web page and debug their code at runtime.

In many cases, you'll want to add the web control and the website that uses it to the same solution. This allows you to edit the source code for both the website and the control in the same Visual Studio .NET window. To add a new project to an existing solution, select File ➤ Add Project ➤ New Project. To simplify your life, choose the web control library project type (see Figure 20-2). A web control library project is identical to an ordinary class library project, except for the fact that it automatically includes references to some of the assemblies you'll need to use, like System.Web.dll.

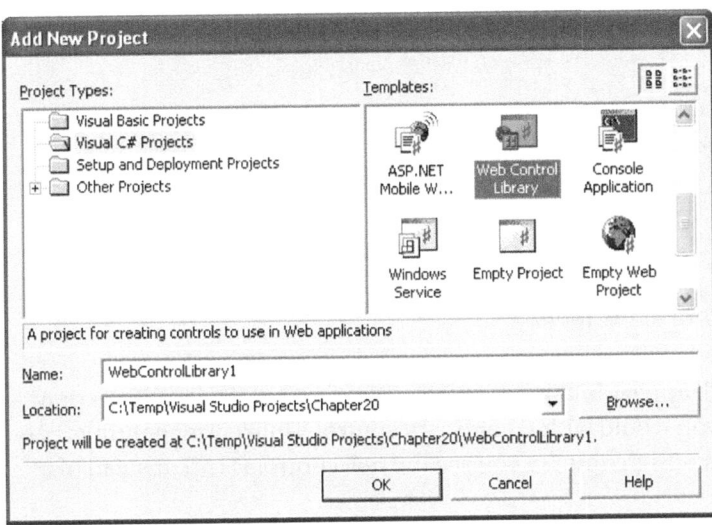

Figure 20-2. *Creating a class library project for web controls*

Now you can define your controls in the control library project. You develop this project in the same way that you work with any other DLL component. You can build the project at any time, but you can't start it directly because it isn't an actual application.

To test your controls, you need to use them in another application. There are two approaches you can use. First of all, you can add a reference in the same way that you add a reference to any other .NET assembly, by selecting Project ➤ Add Reference. However, although this step allows you to use the control classes in your code, it doesn't give you any design support (such as the ability to drag and drop controls onto your web form). To get these features, you need to add your custom controls to the Visual Studio .NET Toolbox.

■Note Before you can add your control to the Visual Studio .NET Toolbox, you must compile it. If you've added a new control but haven't yet recompiled your assembly, the new control won't appear as one of the classes you can add to the Toolbox.

Start by right-clicking the Toolbox, and choosing Add/Remove Items (or Customize Toolbox in Visual Studio .NET 2002). Next, click the .NET Framework Components tab, and then click the Browse button. Then choose the custom control assembly from the file browser. The controls will be added to the list of available .NET controls, as shown in Figure 20-3.

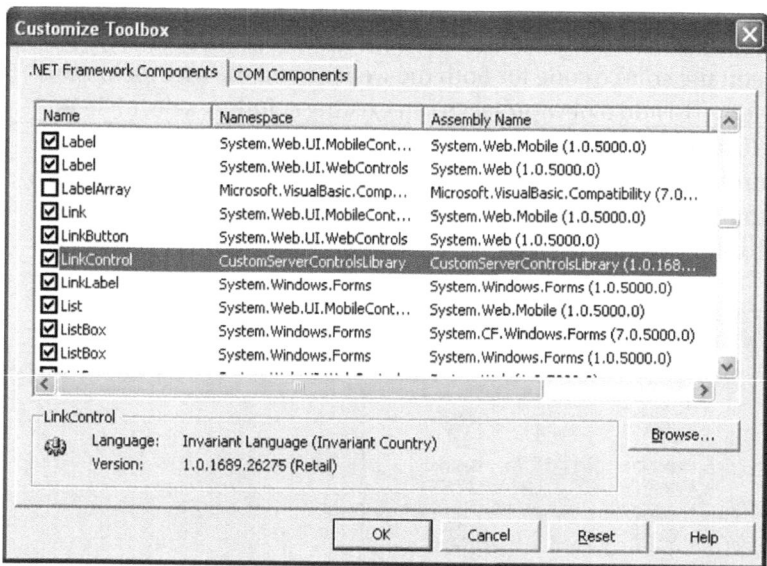

Figure 20-3. *Adding a custom control to the Toolbox*

All checkmarked controls will appear in the Toolbox (see Figure 20-4). You can then draw them on your web forms just as you would with an ordinary control. Unlike user controls, custom controls are fully rendered at design time, so you see the real control HTML instead of a gray placeholder box.

Note that controls aren't added on a per-project basis. Instead, they will remain in the Toolbox until you delete them. To remove a control, right-click it and select Delete. This action removes the icon only, not the referenced assembly.

■Tip As with any other type of reference in Visual Studio .NET, every time you compile your project, the most recent version of the referenced assembly is copied into your web application's Bin directory. This means that if you change and recompile a custom control after adding it to the Toolbox, there's no reason to remove and re-add it.

Visual Studio .NET gives you quite a bit of basic design-time support. For example, after you add a custom control to a web page, you can modify its properties in the Properties window (they will appear under the Misc group) and attach event handlers. In Chapter 21, you'll learn how you can further customize the design-time behavior and appearance of your control.

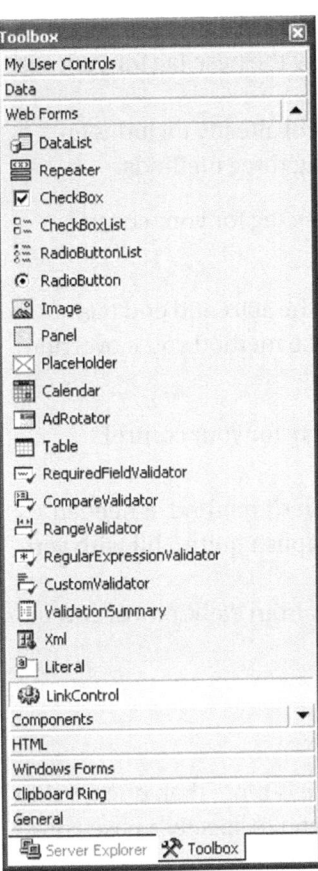

Figure 20-4. *The Toolbox with a custom control*

Creating a WebControl that Supports Style Properties

The previous custom control example doesn't allow you the web page to customize the control's appearance. The custom control doesn't provide any properties for setting foreground or background colors, the font, or other attributes of the HTML tag that you generate. To add support for these features, you need to explicitly add public properties that represent these values. You would then need to read these properties in the Render() method and generate the appropriate HTML code.

Of course, style properties are a basic part of infrastructure that many HTML controls need to take advantage of. Ideally, all controls should follow a single, streamlined model for style information, and not force custom control developers to write this generic functionality themselves. ASP.NET does exactly that with the WebControl base class (in the System.Web.UI.WebControls namespace). Every web control that's included with ASP.NET derives from WebControl, and you can derive your custom controls from it as well.

Not only does the WebControl class include basic style-related properties like Font, ForeColor, BackColor, and so on, but it also renders them automatically in the control tag. Here's how it works. The WebControl assumes that it should add the attributes to a single

HTML tag, called the *base tag*. If you're writing multiple elements, the attributes are added to the outermost element that contains the other elements. You specify the base tag for your web control in the constructor.

Finally, you don't override the Render() method. The WebControl already includes an implementation of Render() that farms the work out to the following three methods:

- **RenderBeginTag().** This method is called to write the opening tag for your control, along with the attributes you've specified.

- **RenderContents().** This method writes everything between the start and end tag, which can include text content or other HTML tags. This is the method you'll override most often to write your custom control content.

- **RenderEndTag().** This method is called to write the closing tag for your control.

Of course, you can change this behavior by overriding the Render() method, if needed. But if this basic framework suits your needs, you'll be able to accomplish quite a bit with very little custom code.

The next example demonstrates a new link control that derives from WebControl and thereby gains automatic support for style properties.

```
public class LinkWebControl : WebControl
{ ... }
```

The default constructor calls the WebControl constructor. There is more than one version of WebControl constructor—this code uses the version that allows you to specify a base control tag. In this example, the base control tag is the <a> anchor, as shown here:

```
public LinkWebControl() : base (HtmlTextWriterTag.A)
{}
```

The LinkWebControl constructor doesn't require any actual code. It's just important that you use this opportunity to call the WebControl constructor to set the base control tag. If you use the default (zero-parameter) WebControl constructor, a <span> tag is used automatically. You can then render additional HTML inside this <span> tag, which ensures that all elements will have the same style attributes.

The LinkWebControl also defines two properties, which allow the web page to set the text and the target URL:

```
private string text;
public string Text
{
    get {return text;}
    set {text = value;}
}

private string hyperLink;
public string HyperLink
{
```

```
    get {return hyperLink;}
    set
    {
        if (value.IndexOf("http://") == -1)
        {
            throw new ApplicationException("Specify HTTP as the protocol.");
        }
        else
        {
            hyperLink = value;
        }
    }
}
```

You could set the text and hyperLink variables to empty strings when you define them. However, this example overrides the OnInit() method to demonstrate how you can initialize a control programmatically:

```
protected override void OnInit(EventArgs e)
{
    base.OnInit(e);
    if (hyperLink == null)
        hyperLink = "http://www.apress.com";

    if (text == null)
        text = "Click here to visit Apress";
}
```

The LinkWebControl presents a minor challenge. To successfully create an <a> tag, you need to specify a target URL and some text. The text is placed between the start and end tags. However, the URL is added as an attribute (named href) to the start tag. As you've already learned, the WebControl manages the attributes for the start tag automatically. Fortunately, the WebControl class gives you the ability to add extra tags by overriding the method AddAttributesToRender(), as shown here:

```
protected override void AddAttributesToRender(HtmlTextWriter output)
{
    output.AddAttribute(HtmlTextWriterAttribute.Href, HyperLink);
    base.AddAttributesToRender(output);
}
```

Note that whenever a custom control overrides a method, it should call the base class implementation using the base keyword. This ensures that you don't inadvertently suppress any code that needs to run. Often, all the base method does is fire a related event, but that's not always the case. For example, if you override RenderBeginTag() and don't call the base implementation, the rendering code will fail with an unhandled exception because the tag isn't opened.

Finally, the RenderContents() method adds the text inside the anchor:

```
protected override void RenderContents(HtmlTextWriter output)
{
    output.Write(Text);
    base.RenderContents(output);
}
```

Note that none of the code uses the style properties. Instead, ASP.NET applies these automatically when it renders the base tag.

Now that you have created the control, you can use it in any ASP.NET web page. You can set the style properties in code or in the control tag. You can even use the Properties window. Here's an example:

```
<apress:LinkWebControl id="LinkWebControl1" runat="server"
  BackColor="#FFFF80" Font-Names="Verdana" Font-Size="Large"
  ForeColor="#C00000" Text="Click to visit Apress"
  HyperLink="http://www.apress.com"></apress:LinkWebControl>
```

The HyperLink and Text attributes are automatically mapped to the corresponding public properties of the custom control. The same is true of the style-related properties, which are defined in the base WebControl class.

Figure 20-5 shows this control in a web browser.

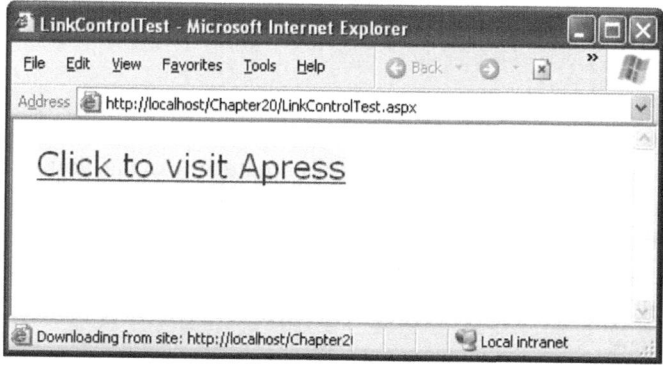

Figure 20-5. *A custom control that supports style properties*

Tip As a general guideline, you should derive from the WebControl class if your control needs to create any type of user interface. Of course, there are exceptions. For example, if you know you only want a subset of the UI features, or you want to combine multiple controls, which will each have their own specific style properties, you might want to derive from Control instead of WebControl. However, the basic rule of thumb that the .NET class library follows is always to derive from WebControl, even if some of the properties aren't relevant.

The Rendering Process

The previous example introduced several new rendering methods. Before going any further, it's a good idea to look at how they all work together.

The starting point for the rendering process is the RenderControl() method. The RenderControl() method is the public rendering method that ASP.NET uses to render each control on a web page to HTML. You can't override RenderControl(). Instead, RenderControl() calls the protected Render() method that starts the rendering process. You *can* override Render(), as demonstrated in the first example in this chapter. However, if you override Render() and don't call the base implementation of the Render() method, none of the other rendering methods will fire.

The base implementation of the Render() method calls RenderBeginTag(), RenderContents(), and then RenderEndTag(), as you saw in the previous example. However, there's one more twist. The base implementation of the RenderContents() method calls another rendering method—RenderChildren(). This method loops through the collection of child controls in the Controls collection, and calls the RenderControl() method for each individual control. By taking advantage of this behavior, you can easily build a control out of other controls. This approach is demonstrated later in this chapter with composite controls.

So which rendering method should you override? If you want to replace the entire rendering process with something new, or if you want to add HTML content *before* your base control tag (like a block of JavaScript code), you can override Render(). If you want to take advantage of the automatic style attributes, you should define a base tag and override RenderContents(). If you want to prevent child controls from being displayed or customize how they are rendered (for example, by rendering them in the reverse order), you can override RenderChildren().

Figure 20-6 summarizes the rendering process.

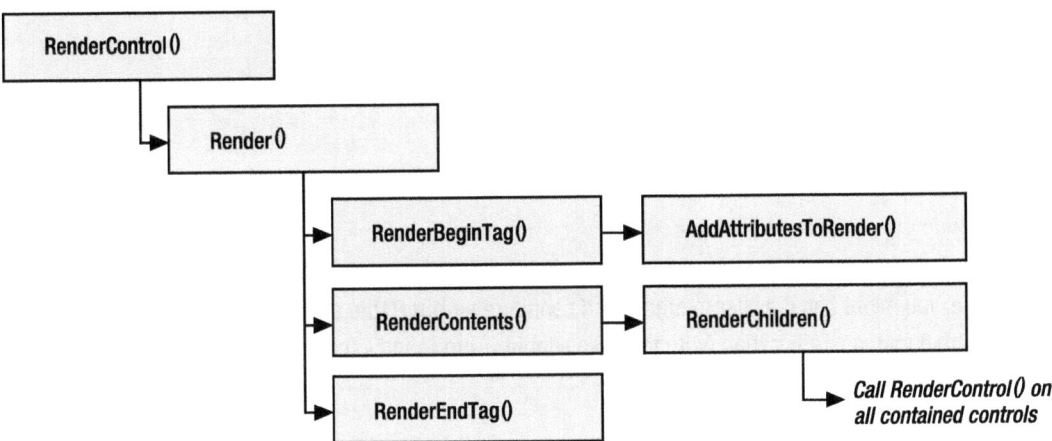

Figure 20-6. *The control rendering methods*

It's worth noting that you can call RenderControl() yourself to examine the HTML output for a control. In fact, this technique can be a convenient shortcut when debugging. Here's an example that gets the rendered HTML for a control and displays it in a label on a web page:

```
// Create the in-memory objects that will catch the rendered output.
StringWriter writer = new StringWriter();
HtmlTextWriter output = new HtmlTextWriter(writer);

// Render the control.
LinkWebControl1.RenderControl(output);

// Display the HTML (and encode it properly so that
// it appears as text in the browser).
lblHtml.Text = "The HTML for LinkWebControl1 is<br><blockquote>" +
  Server.HtmlEncode(writer.ToString()) + "</blockquote>";
```

Figure 20-7 shows the page with the control and its HTML.

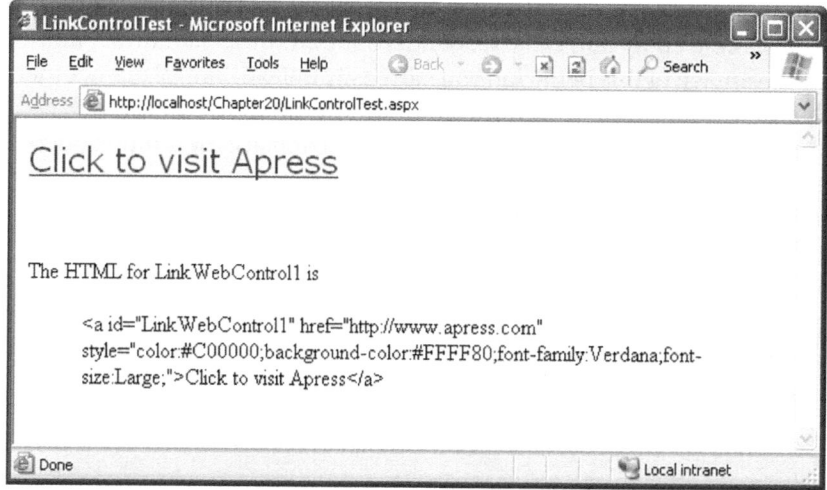

Figure 20-7. *Getting the HTML representation of a control*

■**Tip** This technique isn't just for debugging. You could also use it to simplify your rendering code. For example, you might find it easier to create and configure an HtmlTable control and then call its RenderControl() method, rather than write tags like <table>, <td>, and <tr> directly to the output stream.

Adaptive Rendering

Due to the wide range of variation in the number of features supported by different browsers, it's a challenge to create applications that work across all the browsers and still provide the best possible user experience. As a result, it's often necessary to detect browser configuration to determine the level of support offered for different types of page content. To accomplish this, you can use the Browser property of the HttpRequest object, which returns a reference to an HttpBrowserCapabilities object, as shown here:

```
HttpBrowserCapabilities browserCap = Page.Request.Browser;
```

When a client makes an HTTP request, an HttpBrowserCapabilities object is created and filled with information about the capabilities of the browser. The information provided in the HttpBrowserCapabilities class includes the kind of browser and its version, whether scripting support is available on the client-side, and so on. By detecting the capabilities of the browser, you can choose to customize your output to provide different behaviors on different browsers. This way, you can fully exploit the potential capabilities of up-level clients, without breaking down-level clients.

Table 20-2 summarizes the properties of HttpBrowserCapabilities class.

Table 20-2. *HttpBrowserCapabilities Properties*

Property	Description
Browser	Gets the browser string that was sent with the request in the user-agent header.
MajorVersion	Gets the major version number of the client browser. (For example, this returns 4 for version 4.5.)
MinorVersion	Gets the minor version number of the client browser. (For example, this returns 5 for version 4.5.)
Type	Gets the name and the major version number of the client browser.
Version	Gets the full version number of the client browser.
Beta	Returns true if the client browser is a beta release.
AOL	Returns true if the client is an AOL (America Online) browser.
Platform	Provides the name of the operating system platform that the client uses.
Win16	Returns true if the client is a Win16-based computer.
Win32	Returns true if the client is a Win32-based computer.
ClrVersion	Provides the highest version number of the .NET CLR (common language runtime) installed on the client computer. You can also use the GetClrVersions() method to retrieve information about all the installed CLR versions. This setting is only significant if you have embedded .NET Windows Forms controls in your web page. Client browsers don't need the CLR to run ordinary ASP.NET web pages.
ActiveXControls	Returns true if the client browser supports ActiveX controls.
BackgroundSounds	Returns true if the client browser supports background sounds.
Cookies	Returns true if the client browser supports cookies.
Frames	Returns true if the client browser supports frames.
Tables	Returns true if the client browser supports HTML tables.
JavaScript	Indicates whether the client browser supports JavaScript.
VBScript	Returns true if the client browser supports VBScript.
JavaApplets	Returns true if the client browser supports embedded Java applets.
EcmaScriptVersion	Gets the version number of ECMA script that the client browser supports.
MSDomVersion	Gets the version of Microsoft HTML DOM (Document Object Model) that the client browser supports.
Crawler	Returns true if the client browser is a web crawler search engine.

The following code snippet shows how to dynamically tailor rendered output based on the capabilities of the requesting browser. In this example, the code simply outputs different strings to indicate what it has detected. In a more realistic example, you would render different HTML or JavaScript based on the same information.

```
protected override void RenderContents(HtmlTextWriter writer)
{
    base.RenderContents(writer);

    if (Page.Request.Browser.JavaScript)
    {
        writer.Write("<i>You support JavaScript.</i><br>");
    }

    if (Page.Request.Browser.Browser == "IE")
    {
        writer.Write("<i>Output configured for IE.</i><br>");
    }
    else if (Page.Request.Browser.Browser == "Netscape")
    {
        writer.Write("<i>Output configured for Netscape.</i><br>");
    }
}
```

There is one glaring limitation with the HttpBrowserCapabilities class—it's limited to evaluating the built-in functionality of the browser. It does *not* evaluate the current state of a browser's functionality. For example, imagine you are evaluating the client-side JavaScript support provided by the browser. If the requesting browser is IE 5.5, this will return true since the browser supports client-side JavaScript support. However, if the user has the scripting capabilities turned off, the JavaScript property still returns true. In other words, you don't learn what the browser is capable of doing, just what it *should* be capable of doing. In fact, all ASP.NET really does is read the user-agent information that's passed from the browser to the server during the request, and compare this string against the predefined user-agent information in the machine.config file. It's the machine.config file that lists the corresponding browser capabilities, such as whether the browser supports scripting, styles, frames, and so on. Unfortunately, the client just doesn't send any information about how the browser is configured.

This situation leaves you with two options. You can rely on the HttpBrowserCapabilities class to tell you if certain browser features should be available, and base your programming logic on that information. In this case, you may need to tolerate the occasional error. If you need a more robust approach, you need to write your own code to actually test the support for the features you need. For example, with cookies you could (over two web pages) attempt to set a cookie and then attempt to read it. If the second test doesn't succeed, cookie support isn't enabled. You could use similar work-arounds to check for other features like JavaScript support. For example, you could add a piece of JavaScript code to the page that writes to a hidden form variable, and then check it on the server. These steps are awkward and messy, but they're the only way to be absolutely certain of specific browser features. Unfortunately, when creating custom controls you usually don't have the luxury of performing these tests.

Table 20-3 shows how some common browsers stack up with the HttpBrowserCapabilities class.

Table 20-3. *HttpBrowserCapabilities Properties for Common Browsers*

Browser	EcmaScriptVersion	MSDomVersion	W3CDomVersion	ClrVersion
IE6+	1.2	6.0	1.0	1.0.3705
NS6+	1.5	0.0	1.0	0.0
Opera6+	1.3	0.0	1.0	0.0

It's also worth asking how the ASP.NET rich controls distinguish between up-level and down-level browsers. Usually, they enforce the following requirements:

- ECMAScript (JScript, JavaScript) version 1.2

- HTML version 4.0

- MSDOM (Microsoft Document Object Model)

- CSS (Cascading Style Sheets)

Unfortunately, this definition of an up-level browser is clearly quite restricted because it requires support for MSDOM, which isn't provided by any browser other than ASP.NET. As a result, even though Netscape and Opera support JavaScript, rich controls like the ASP.NET validators don't emit client-side script for these browsers. However, when deciding what support to give your own controls, it's up to you what criteria you use.

Control State and Events

ASP.NET uses web controls to create an object-oriented layer of abstraction over the lower-level details of HTML and HTTP. Two cornerstones of this abstraction are view state (the mechanism that lets you store information between requests) and postback (the technique wherein a web page posts back to the same URL with a collection of form data). In order to create realistic server controls, you need to know how to create classes that plug into both of these parts of the web-page infrastructure.

ViewState Data

Controls need to store information in state just like your web pages. Fortunately, all controls provide a ViewState property that you can use to store and retrieve information just as you do with a web page. You'll need to use the ViewState collection to restore private information after a postback.

A common design pattern with web controls is to access the ViewState collection in your property procedures. For example, consider the LinkWebControl presented earlier. Currently, this control doesn't use view state, which means that if you change its Text and HyperLink properties programmatically, the changes will be lost in subsequent postbacks. (This isn't true of the style properties like Font, ForeColor, and BackColor, which are stored in view state automatically.) To change the LinkWebControl to ensure that state information is retained for the Text and HyperLink properties, you need to rewrite the property procedure code as shown here:

```
public string Text
{
    get {return (string)ViewState["Text"];}
    set {ViewState["Text"] = value;}
}

public string HyperLink
{
    get {return (string)ViewState["HyperLink"];}
    set
    {
        if (value.IndexOf("http://") == -1)
        {
            throw new ApplicationException("Specify HTTP as the protocol.");
        }
        else
        {
            ViewState["HyperLink"] = value;
        }
    }
}

protected override void OnInit(EventArgs e)
{
    base.OnInit(e);
    if (ViewState["HyperLink"] == null)
        ViewState["HyperLink"] = "http://www.apress.com";

    if (ViewState["Text"] == null)
        ViewState["Text"] = "Click here to visit Apress";
}
```

It's important to realize that the ViewState property of a control is separate from the ViewState property of the page. In other words, if you add an item in your control code, you can't access it in your web page, and vice versa. When the page is rendered to HTML, ASP.NET takes the view state of the page and all the combined controls, and merges it into a special tree structure.

Although view state is easy to use in a control, there are a couple of few considerations. First, you shouldn't store large objects because they will reduce page transmission times. For example, the ASP.NET controls that support data binding don't store the DataSource property in view state. They simply hold it in memory until you call the DataBind() method. This makes programming a little more awkward—for example, it forces you to rebind data controls after every postback—but it ensures that pages don't become ridiculously bloated.

Another consideration with view state is that it's at the mercy of the containing page. If the page sets the EnableViewState property of your control to false, all your view state information will be lost after each postback. Usually, it's the responsibility of the client to ensure that a control still works effectively without using view state. However, you shouldn't code your control in such a way that it depends on view state information. Instead, it should work even if view state information is missing, even if that means properties revert to their original values.

Note Even if the EnableViewState property is set to false, the ViewState collection will still work. The only difference is that the information you place in that collection will be discarded once the control is finished processing and the page is rendered.

Finally, keep in mind that you can't assume data is in the ViewState collection. If you try to retrieve an item that doesn't exist, you'll run into a NullReferenceException. To prevent this problem, you should check for null values, or set default view state information in the OnInit() method or the custom control constructor. For example, the LinkWebControl won't run into null references because it uses OnInit() to set initial view state values.

Note Although the WebControl provides a ViewState property, it doesn't provide properties like Cache, Session, and Application. However, if you need to use these objects to store or retrieve data, you can access them through the static HttpContext.Current property.

Occasionally, you might want more flexibility to customize how view state information is stored. You can take control by overriding the LoadViewState() and SaveViewState() methods. The SaveViewState() method is always called before a control is rendered to HTML. You can return a single serializable object from this method, which will be stored in view state. Similarly, the LoadViewState() is called when your control is re-created on subsequent postbacks. You receive the object you stored as a parameter, and you can now use it to configure control properties. In most simple controls, there's no reason to override these methods. However, there are cases in which it does become useful, such as when you've developed a more compact way of storing multiple pieces of information in view state using a single object, or when you're deriving from an existing control and you want to prevent it from saving its state. You also need this method when you're managing how a complex control saves the state of nested child controls. You'll see an example of this last technique at the end of this chapter. For more information about advanced control programming, you may want to consult a dedicated book about ASP.NET control programming, like *Developing Microsoft ASP.NET Server Controls and Components* (Microsoft Press, 2002).

Postback Data and Change Events

View state helps you keep track of control state, but it's not enough for input controls. That's because input controls have an additional ability—they allow users to change their data. For example, consider a text box that's represented as an <input> tag in a form. When the page posts back, the data from the <input> tag is part of the information in the control collection. The TextBox control needs to retrieve this information and update its state accordingly.

In order to process the data that's posted to the page in your custom control, you need to implement the IPostBackDataHandler interface. By implementing this interface, you indicate to ASP.NET that when a postback occurs, your control needs a chance to examine the post-back data. Your control will get this opportunity, regardless of which control actually triggers the postback.

The IPostBackDataHandler interface defines two methods:

- **LoadPostData().** ASP.NET calls this method when the page is posted back, before any control events are raised. It allows you to examine the data that's been posted back, and update the state of the control accordingly. However, you shouldn't fire change events at this point, because other controls won't be updated yet.

- **RaisePostDataChangedEvent().** After all the input controls on a page have been initialized, ASP.NET gives you the chance to fire a change event, if necessary, by calling the RaisePostDataChangedEvent() method.

The best way to understand how these methods work is to examine a basic example. The next control emulates the basic TextBox control. Here's the basic control definition:

```
public class CustomTextBox : WebControl, IPostBackDataHandler
{ ... }
```

As you can see, the control inherits from WebControl, and implements IPostBackDataHandler.

The control requires only a single property, Text. The Text is stored in view state, and initialized to an empty string in the control constructor. The constructor also sets the base tag to be <input>.

```
public CustomTextBox() : base(HtmlTextWriterTag.Input)
{
    Text = "";
}

public string Text
{
    get {return (string)ViewState["Text"];}
    set {ViewState["Text"] = value;}
}
```

Because the base tag is already set to <input>, there's very little extra rendering work required. You can handle everything by overriding the AddAttributesToRender() method, and adding a type attribute that indicates the <input> control represents a text box, and a value attribute that contains the text you want to display in the text box, as follows:

```
protected override void AddAttributesToRender(HtmlTextWriter output)
{
    output.AddAttribute(HtmlTextWriterAttribute.Type, "text");
    output.AddAttribute(HtmlTextWriterAttribute.Value, Text);
    output.AddAttribute("name", this.UniqueID);
    base.AddAttributesToRender(output);
}
```

You must also add the UniqueID for the control using the name attribute. That's because ASP.NET matches this string against the posted data. If you don't add the UniqueID, the LoadPostData() method will never be called, and you won't be able to retrieve posted data.

All that's left is to implement the IPostBackDataHandler methods to give the control the ability to respond to user changes.

First, you need to implement the LoadPostData() method. This method uses two parameters. The second parameter is a collection of values posted to the page. The first parameter is the key value that identifies the data for the current control. Thus, you can access the data for your control using syntax like this:

```
string newData = postData[postDataKey];
```

The LoadPostData() also needs to tell ASP.NET whether a change event is required. You can't fire an event at this point, because the other controls may not be properly updated with the posted data. However, you can tell ASP.NET that a change has occurred by returning true. If you return true, ASP.NET will call the RaisePostDataChangedEvent() method after all the controls are initialized. If you return false, ASP.NET will not call this method.

Here's the complete code for the LoadPostData() method in the CustomTextBox:

```
public bool LoadPostData(string postDataKey, NameValueCollection postData)
{
    // Get the value posted and the past value.
    string postedValue = postData[postDataKey];
    string val = Text;

    // If the value changed, then reset the value of the text property
    // and return true so the RaisePostDataChangedEvent will be fired.
    if (val != postedValue)
    {
        Text = postedValue;
        return true;
    }
    else
    {
        return false;
    }
}
```

The RaisePostDataChangedEvent() has the relatively simple task of firing the event. However, most ASP.NET controls use an extra layer, whereby the RaisePostDataChangedEvent()

calls an OnXxx() method, and the OnXxx() method actually raises the event. This extra gives other developers the ability to derive a new control from your control, and alter its behavior by overriding the OnXxx() method.

Here's the remaining code:

```
public event EventHandler TextChanged;

public void RaisePostDataChangedEvent()
{
    // Call the method to raise the change event.
    OnTextChanged(new EventArgs());
}

portected virtual void OnTextChanged(EventArgs e)
{
    // Check for at least one listener and then raise the event.
    if (TextChanged != null)
        TextChanged(this, e);
}
```

Figure 20-8 shows a sample page that tests the CustomTextBox control and responds to its event.

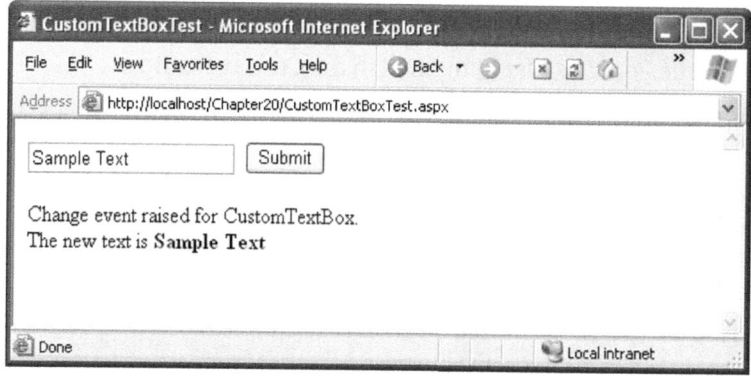

Figure 20-8. *Retreiving posted data in a custom control*

Triggering a Postback

By implementing IPostBackDataHandler, you're able to participate in every postback, and retrieve the posted data that belongs to your control. But what if you want to *trigger* a postback? The simplest example of such a control is the Button control, but many other rich web controls—including the Calendar and DataGrid—allow you to trigger a postback by clicking an element or a link somewhere in the rendered HTML.

There are two ways to trigger a postback. First, you could render an <input> tag for a submit button, which always posts back the form. Your other option is to call the JavaScript function called __doPostBack() that ASP.NET automatically adds to the page. The __doPostBack() function accepts two parameters: the name of the control that's triggering the postback, and a string representing additional postback data.

ASP.NET makes it easy to access the __doPostBack() function with the Page.GetPostBackEventReference() method. This method creates a reference to the client-side __doPostBack() function, which you can then render into your control. Usually, you'll place this reference in the onClick attribute of one of HTML elements in your control. That way, when that HTML element is clicked, the __doPostBack() function is triggered. Of course, JavaScript provides other attributes that you can make use of, some of which you'll see in Chapter 22.

The best way to see postbacks in action is to create a simple control. The following example demonstrates a clickable image. When clicked, the page is posted back, without any additional data.

This control is based on the <img> tag and requires just a single property:

```
public CustomImageButton() : base(HtmlTextWriterTag.Img)
{
    ImageUrl = "";
}


public string ImageUrl
{
    get {return (string)ViewState["ImageUrl"];}
    set {ViewState["ImageUrl"] = value;}
}
```

The only customization you need to make is to add a few additional attributes to render. These include the unique control name, the image URL, and the onClick attribute that wires the image up to the __doPostBack() function, as follows:

```
protected override void AddAttributesToRender(HtmlTextWriter output)
{
    output.AddAttribute("name", UniqueID);
    output.AddAttribute("src", ImageUrl);
    output.AddAttribute("onClick", Page.GetPostBackEventReference(this));
}
```

This is enough to trigger the postback, but you need to take additional steps in order to participate in the postback and raise an event. This time, you need to implement the IPostBackEventHandler interface. This interface defines a single method named RaisePostBackEvent():

```
public class CustomImageButton : WebControl, IPostBackEventHandler
{ ... }
```

When the page is posted back, ASP.NET determines which control triggered the postback (by looking at each control's UniqueID property) and, if that control implements

IPostBackEventHandler, ASP.NET then calls the RaisePostBackEvent() method with the event data. At this point, all the controls on the page have been initialized, and it's safe to fire an event, as shown here:

```
public event EventHandler ImageClicked;

public void RaisePostBackEvent(string eventArgument)
{
    OnImageClicked(new EventArgs());
}

protected virtual void OnImageClicked(EventArgs e)
{
    // Check for at least one listener and then raise the event.
    if (ImageClicked != null)
        ImageClicked(this, e);
}
```

Figure 20-9 shows a sample page that tests the CustomImageButton control and responds to its event.

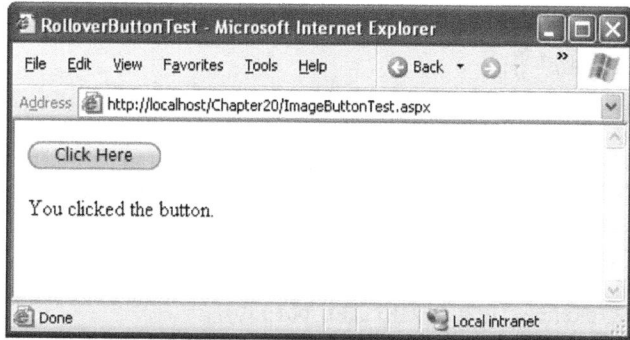

Figure 20-9. *Triggering a postback in a custom control*

This control doesn't offer any functionality you can't already get with existing ASP.NET web controls, like the ImageButton. However, it's a great starting point to building something that's much more useful. In Chapter 22, you'll see how to extend this control with JavaScript code to create a rollover button—something with no equivalent in the .NET class library.

Extending Existing Web Controls

In many situations, you don't need to create a new control from scratch. Some of the functionality might already exist in the basic set of ASP.NET web controls. Because all ASP.NET controls are ordinary classes, you can make use of their functionality with basic object-oriented practices like composition (creating a class that uses instances of other classes) and inheritance (creating a class that extends an existing class to change its functionality). In this section, you'll see how both tasks apply to custom control design.

Composite Controls

So far you've seen a few custom controls that programmatically generate all the HTML code they need (except for the style properties, which can be inherited from the WebControl class). If you want to write a series of controls, you need to output all the HTML tags, one after the other. Fortunately, ASP.NET includes a feature that can save you this work by allowing you to build your control class out of other, existing web controls.

The basic technique is to override the CreateChildControls() method. At this point, you can create one or more control objects, set their properties and event handlers, and finally add them to the Controls collection of the current control. The best part about this approach is that you don't need to customize the rendering code at all. Instead, the rendering work is delegated to the constituent server controls. You also don't need to worry about details like triggering postbacks and getting postback data, because the child controls will handle these details themselves.

The following example creates a TitledTextBox control that pairs a label (on the left) with a text box (on the right). Here's the class definition for the control:

```
public class TitledTextBox : WebControl, INamingContainer
{ ... }
```

You'll notice that the control implements the INamingContainer interface. This interface doesn't have any methods. It simply instructs ASP.NET to make sure all the child controls have unique ID values. ASP.NET does this by prepending the ID of the server control before the ID of the control. This ensures that there won't be any naming conflict, even if you add several instances of the TitleTextBox control to a web form.

Note You should use the INamingContainer interface whenever you deal with data bound or composite controls that programmatically create child controls.

To make life easier, you should track the constituent controls with member variables. This allows you to access them in any method in your control. However, you shouldn't create these controls yet, because that's the function of the CreateChildControls() method.

```
protected Label label;
protected TextBox textBox;
```

The web page won't be able to directly access either of these controls. If you want to allow access to certain properties, you need to add property procedures to your custom control class, as follows:

```
public string Title
{
    get {return (string)ViewState["Title"];}
    set {ViewState["Title"] = value;}
}
```

```
public string Text
{
    get {return (string)ViewState["Text"];}
    set {ViewState["Text"] = value;}
}
```

Note that these properties simply store information in view state—they don't directly access the child controls. That's because the child controls might not yet exist. These properties will be applied to the child controls in the CreateChildControls() method.

In the constructor, you should call the base WebControl constructor without specifying a base tag, as shown here:

```
public TitledTextBox() : base()
{
    Title = "";
    Text = "";
}
```

This means the base tag will automatically be <span>, which works well. It ensures that if the web page applies font, color, or position attributes to the TitledTextBox control, it will have the desired effect on all the child controls.

Now you can override the CreateChildControls() method to create the Label and TextBox control objects. These objects are separated with one additional control object—a LiteralControl, which simply represents a scrap of HTML. In this example, the LiteralControl wraps two nonbreaking spaces. Here's the complete code for the CreateChildControls() method:

```
protected override void CreateChildControls()
{
    // Add the label.
    label = new Label();
    label.EnableViewState = false;
    label.Text = Title;
    Controls.Add(label);

    // Add a space.
    Controls.Add(new LiteralControl("  "));

    // Add the text box.
    textBox = new TextBox();
    textBox.EnableViewState = false;
    textBox.Text = Text;
    textBox.TextChanged += new EventHandler(OnTextChanged);
    Controls.Add(textBox);
}
```

Note The CreateChildControls() method is not called in a deterministic way, so you can't be sure that it has been already called when you try to access a child control from another method or event handler. However, you shouldn't call CreateChildControls() on your own. Instead, if you need to set or retrieve a child control value, you should first call EnsureChildControls(). This makes sure that ASP.NET calls CreateChildControls() if it hasn't already called it. If you want to check if the controls have been created yet, you can examine the Boolean ChildControlsCreated property.

The CreateChildControls() code attaches an event handler to the TextBox.TextChanged event. When this event fires, your TitledTextBox should pass it along to the web page as the TitledTextBox.TextChanged event. Here's the code you need to implement the rest of this design:

```
public event EventHandler TextChanged;

protected virtual void OnTextChanged(object sender, EventArgs e)
{
    if (TextChanged != null)
        TextChanged(this, e);
}
```

Figure 20-10 shows a sample page that tests the TitledTextBox control and responds to its event.

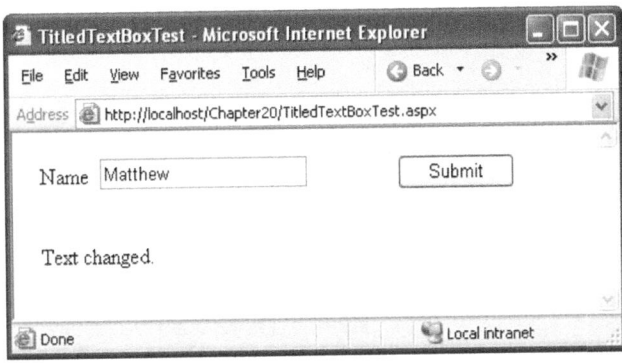

Figure 20-10. *Creating a composite control with a label and text box*

You may prefer to follow the earlier approach and use an HtmlTextWriter to get full control over the HTML markup you render. But if you want to handle postbacks and events and create complex controls (such as an extended DataGrid or a navigational aid), using composite controls can simplify your life dramatically.

Derived Controls

Another approach to creating controls is to derive a more specialized control from one of the existing control classes. You can then override or add just the functionality you need, rather than re-creating the whole control. This approach isn't always possible, because some controls keep key pieces of their infrastructure out of site in private methods you can't override. However, when it does work it can save a lot of work.

Sometimes, you might create a derived control so that you can preinitialize an existing control with certain styles or formatting properties. For example, you could create a custom Calendar or DataGrid that sets styles in the OnInit() method. That way, when you add this Calendar control, it's already formatted with exactly the look you need. In other cases, you might add entirely new functionality in the form of new methods or properties, as demonstrated in the following examples.

Creating a Higher-Level Calendar

In previous chapters, you've learned how to customize the DataGrid to add niceties like a summary row. You also learned how to use day-specific formatting in the Calendar. In order to implement either one of these changes, you need to handle a generic control event, and wait for the element you want to format. A more elegant solution would be to simply set a property, and let the control handle the task. You can add this extra layer of abstraction with a custom control.

For example imagine you want to provide an easy way to designate nonselectable days in a calendar. To accomplish this, you could create a custom calendar control that adds two properties, as shown here:

```
public class RestrictedCalendar : Calendar
{
    public bool AllowWeekendSelection
    {
        get {return (bool)ViewState["AllowWeekendSelection"];}
        set {ViewState["AllowWeekendSelection"] = value;}
    }

    public DateTimeCollection NonSelectableDates
    {
        get {return (DateTimeCollection)ViewState["NonSelectableDates"];}
        set {ViewState["NonSelectableDates"] = value;}
    }

    // (Other code omitted.)
}
```

The AllowWeekendSelection property indicates whether Saturday and Sunday should be selectable. The NonSelectableDates property provides a collection of exact dates that won't be selectable. The DateTimeCollection is a custom collection class defined in the control project. It works the same as an ordinary ArrayList, except that it's strongly typed to only accept DateTime values. This technique of creating a custom collection class was first introduced in Chapter 11. You can see the full collection code with the downloadable code sample.

Now when the calendar is rendered, you can take this information into account and automatically adjust any matching dates. This means you don't need to handle the DayRender event in your code. Instead, you can specify the restricted dates declaratively using the Properties window.

Here's the control code that handles the process:

```
protected override void OnDayRender(TableCell cell, CalendarDay day)
{
    if (day.IsWeekend && !AllowWeekendSelection)
    {
        day.IsSelectable = false;
    }
    else if (NonSelectableDates.Contains(day.Date))
    {
        day.IsSelectable = false;
    }

    // Let the base class raise this event.
    // The web page can respond to this event to perform further processing
    // (or even reverse the changes made here).
    base.OnDayRender(cell, day);
}
```

Note that your custom control doesn't handle the DayRender event. Instead, it overrides the corresponding OnDayRender() method. This gives a similar result without worrying about delegate code and event handlers. Although controls don't need to provide OnXxx() methods for every event, most do as a matter of convention. That makes it easier for you to customize the control.

The RestrictedCalendar control also uses the constructor to initialize some formatting-related properties:

```
public RestrictedCalendar()
{
    // Set default properties.
    AllowWeekendSelection = true;
    NonSelectableDates = new DateTimeCollection();

    // Configure the default appearance of the calendar.
    CellPadding = 8;
    CellSpacing = 8;
    BackColor = Color.LightYellow;
    BorderStyle = BorderStyle.Groove;
    BorderWidth = Unit.Pixel(2);
    ShowGridLines = true;

    // Configure the font.
    Font.Name = "Verdana";
    Font.Size = FontUnit.XXSmall;
```

```
    // Set calendar settings.
    FirstDayOfWeek = FirstDayOfWeek.Monday;
    PrevMonthText = "<--";
    NextMonthText = "-->";

    // Select the current date by default.
    SelectedDate = DateTime.Today;
}
```

This code also demonstrates how you can access the inherited properties of the Calendar control (like CellPadding and CellSpacing) just as easily as you access the new properties you've added (like AllowWeekendSelection).

This example allows the user to designate specific restricted dates in a specific month and year. You could also use a similar approach to allow the user to restrict specific years, months in any year, days in any month, and so on. In a sense, adding these sorts of properties complicates the calendar control and makes it less flexible. However, that isn't a problem if you want to tailor the control for a specific scenario.

Note The online code for the RestrictedCalendar adds quite a bit more logic to improve design-time support. This code ensures that you can set the restricted dates using the Properties window. You'll learn more about design-time support in Chapter 21.

Creating a Label for Specific Data

One common reason for creating customized controls is to fine-tune a control for specific types of data. For example, consider the Label. In its standard form, it's a flexible all-purpose tool that you can use to render text content and insert arbitrary HTML. However, in many situations it would be nice to have a higher-level way to output text that takes care of some of the encoding. The following example is designed for one of these scenarios. It shows how you can customize the rendering of a derived label control for a specific type of content.

In Chapter 5, you learned about the Xml control, which allows you to display XML content in a page using an XSLT stylesheet. However, the Xml control doesn't give you any way to show arbitrary XML. So what should you do if you want to duplicate the Internet Explorer behavior, which shows a color-coded tree of XML tags? You could implement this approach using an XSLT stylesheet. However, another interesting choice is to create a custom label control that's designed for XML content. This label control can apply the formatting you want automatically.

First, consider what happens if you try to display XML content *without* taking any extra steps. In this case, all the XML tags will be interpreted as meaningless HTML tags, and they won't be shown. The display will simply show a jumbled block of text that represents all the content of all elements from start to finish. You can improve upon this situation slightly by using the HttpServerUtility.HtmlEncode() method, which replaces all special HTML characters with the equivalent character entities. However, the XML display you'll create with this approach is still far from ideal. For one thing, all the whitespace will be collapsed, and all the line breaks will be ignored, leading to a long string of text that's not easy to interpret. Figure 20-11 shows this approach with the DvdList.xml document used in Chapter 12.

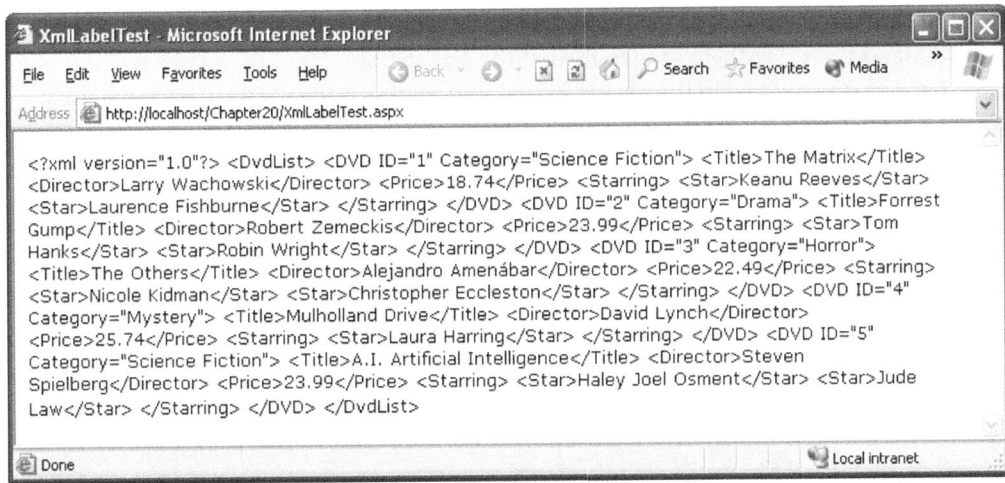

Figure 20-11. *Displaying XML data with HTML escaping*

The custom XmlLabel control solves this problem by applying formatting to XML start and end tags. This functionality is wrapped into a static method called ConvertXmlTextToHtmlText(), which accepts a string with XML content and returns a string with formatted HTML content. This functionality is implemented as a static method rather than an instance method so that you can call it to format text for display in other controls.

The ConvertXmlTextToHtmlText() method uses a regular expression to find all the XML tags in the string. Here's the expression you need:

```
<([^>]+)>
```

This expression matches the less than sign (<) that starts the tag, followed by a sequence of one or more characters that aren't greater than signs (>). The match ends as soon as a greater than (>) sign is found. This expression matches both start tags (like <DvdList>) and end tags (like </DvdList>).

Tip You might think you could use a simpler regular expression such as <.+> to match a tag. The problem is that regular expressions use *greedy matching*, which means they often match as much as possible. As a result, an expression like <.+> will match everything between the less than (<) sign of the first tag to the greater than sign (>) in the last tag at the end of document. In other words, you'll end up with a single match that obscures other embedded matches. To prevent this behavior, you need to create a regular expression that explicitly specifies what characters you *don't* want to match.

Once you have a match, the next step is to replace this text with the text you really want. The replacement expression is as follows:

<<b>$1></b>

This replacement uses the HTML entities for the less than and greater than signs (< and >), and it adds an HTML <b> tag to format the text in bold. The $1 is a *back reference* that refers to the bracketed text in the search expression. In this example, the bracketed text includes the full tag name—everything between the opening < and the closing >.

Once the tags are bolded, the last step is to replace the spaces in the string with the   character entity, so that whitespace will be preserved. At the same time, it makes sense to replace all the line feeds with an HTML <br>.

Here's the complete code for formatting the XML text:

```
public static string ConvertXmlTextToHtmlText(string inputText)
{
    // Replace all start and end tags.
    string startPattern = @"<([^>]+)>";
    Regex regEx = new Regex(startPattern);
    string outputText = regEx.Replace(inputText, "&lt;<b>$1&gt;</b>");

    outputText = outputText.Replace(" ", " ");
    outputText = outputText.Replace("\r\n", "<br>");
    return outputText;
}
```

The rest of the XmlLabel code is remarkably simple. It doesn't add any new properties. Instead, it simply overrides the RenderContents() to ensure that the formatted text is rendered instead of the ordinary text:

```
protected override void RenderContents(HtmlTextWriter output)
{
    string xmlText = XmlLabel.ConvertXmlTextToHtmlText(Text);
    output.Write(xmlText);
}
```

Note that this code doesn't call the base implementation of RenderContents(). That's because the goal of the XmlLabel control is to *replace* the rendering logic for the label text, not to supplement it.

Figure 20-12 shows what ordinary XML data looks like when displayed in the XmlLabel control. Of course, now that you have the basic framework in place there's a lot more you could do to perfect this output, including color-coding and automatic indenting.

■**Tip** You could use a similar technique to create a label that automatically converts mail addresses and URLs to links (wrapped by the <a> tag), formats multiple lines of text into a bulleted list, and so on.

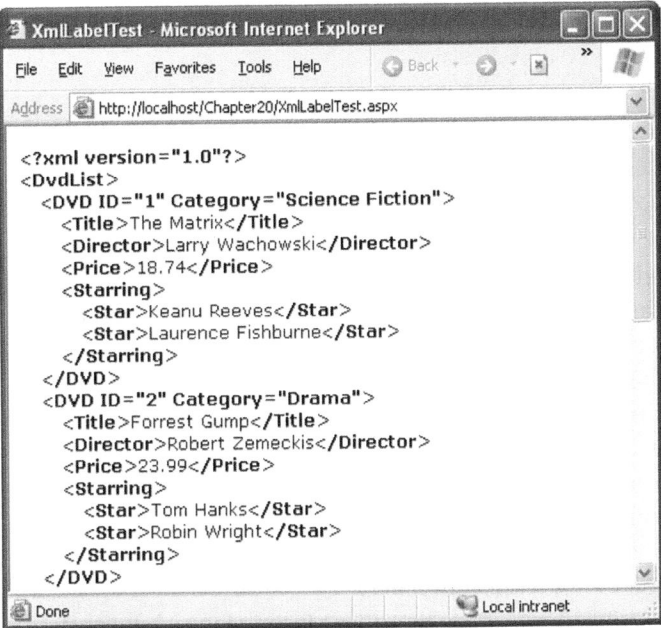

Figure 20-12. *Displaying formatted XML data*

Templated Controls

Up to this point, the controls you've seen have rendered themselves based on the logic and code within the control. The consumers of the control (the web pages that use it) do not have the ability to directly define the layout and style of the control's content.

Templated controls and styles allow you to create controls and add functionality without needing to lock users into a fixed layout. With templates, the control consumer provides a set of HTML tags that define the information and formatting used by the control. The templated control uses one or more templates to render portions of its interface. As a result, templated controls can be much more flexible than ordinary controls.

ASP.NET includes three controls that support templates: the Repeater, DataList, and DataGrid. In this section, you'll learn how to support templates in your own controls.

Creating a Templated Control

It's surprisingly easy to create a basic templated control. You start by creating a composite control. This control should derive from WebControl, and implement the INamingContainer interface to make sure that every child control has a unique name.

The next step is to create one or mote template containers. A template container allows the user to specify the template declaratively in the .aspx portion of the web page. In order to support a template, you just need a control property that accepts an ITemplate object, as shown here:

```
private ITemplate itemTemplate;

public ITemplate ItemTemplate
{
    get {return itemTemplate;}
    set {itemTemplate = value;}
}
```

Note that the template isn't stored in view state, because it's always retrieved from the .aspx file, and it doesn't change programmatically. That means you can store it in a private variable, and re-create it with each postback.

The ITemplate interface defines a single method, InstantiateIn(), which creates an instance of a template inside an existing control. Essentially, when the InstantiateIn() method is called, ASP.NET parses the template and creates controls based on the tags and code in the template. These controls are then added to the control container that's passed into the method. For example, if a template contains a single Label tag, then calling InstantiateIn() creates a Label control and adds it the Controls collection of the specified container. Your control uses the InstantiateIn() method to render its templates.

The final ingredient is the CreateChildControls() method. This is the place where you create the template using the InstantiateIn() method, and add it to the Controls collection.

To understand how this all works together, consider the following extremely simple templated control. It defines a single template, and an additional property that lets the user choose how many times the template should be repeated in the web page. Overall, it works more or less the same as the simple Repeater control (without any support for data binding). Here's the complete code:

```
public class SuperSimpleRepeater : WebControl, INamingContainer
{
    public SuperSimpleRepeater() : base()
    {
        RepeatCount = 1;
    }

    public int RepeatCount
    {
        get {return (int)ViewState["RepeatCount"];}
        set {ViewState["RepeatCount"] = value;}
    }

    private ITemplate itemTemplate;
    public ITemplate ItemTemplate
    {
        get {return itemTemplate;}
        set {itemTemplate=value;}
    }

    protected override void CreateChildControls()
    {
```

```
        // Clear out the control collection before starting.
        Controls.Clear();

        if ((RepeatCount > 0) && (itemTemplate!=null))
        {
            // Instantiate the template in a panel multiple times.
            for (int i = 0; i<RepeatCount; i++)
            {
                Panel container = new Panel();
                itemTemplate.InstantiateIn(container);
                Controls.Add(container);
            }
        }
        else
        {
            // Show an error message.
            Controls.Add(new LiteralControl(
              "Specify the record count and an item template"));
        }
    }
}
```

In order to use this control, you need to provide a template for the ItemTemplate property. You can do this declaratively by adding the HTML and control tags in an <ItemTemplate> tag. Here's an example:

```
<apress:SuperSimpleRepeater id="sample" runat="server" RepeatCount="10">
  <ItemTemplate>
    <div align="center">
      <hr>Creating templated controls is <b>easy</b> and <i>fun</i>.<br><hr>
    </div>
  </ItemTemplate>
</apress:SuperSimpleRepeater>
```

Figure 20-13 shows the rendered content, which copies the template HTML into the page ten times.

There's one additional detail this example has neglected. All template controls should use the PersistChildren attribute as shown here:

```
[PersistChildren(true)]
public class SuperSimpleRepeater : WebControl, INamingContainer
{ ... }
```

This tag indicates that all child elements in the control tag should be interpreted as properties. As a result, if you add an <ItemTemplate> tag inside the <SuperSimpleRepeater> tag, the ASP.NET parser will assume the <ItemTemplate> tag defines the content for the SuperSimpleRepeater.ItemTemplate property. If your control derives from WebControl, this is already the default behavior, so you don't need to take this step. However, it's still a good practice to include this attribute to explicitly indicate how the control deals with nested tags.

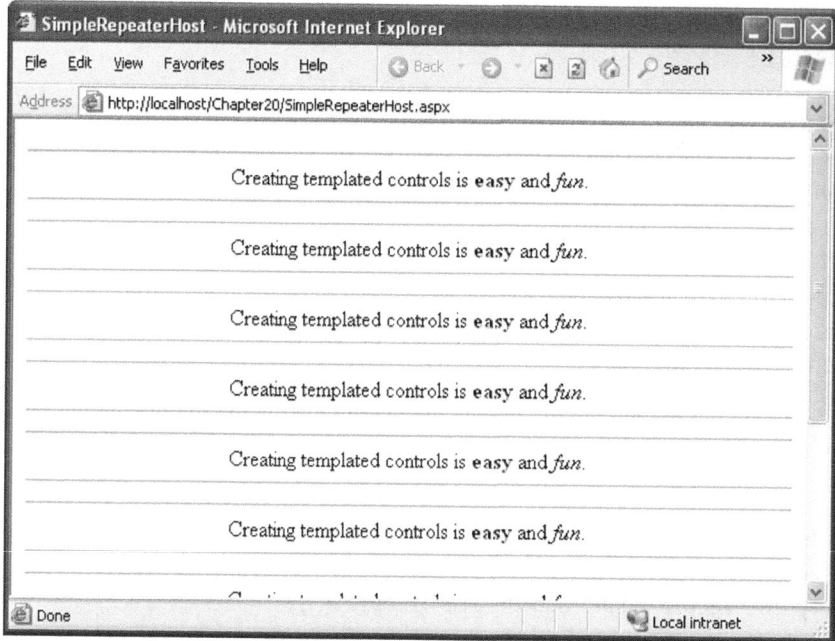

Figure 20-13. *Repeating a template*

If you apply the PersistChildren with an argument of false, the ASP.NET parser assumes that any nested tags are child controls. It then creates the corresponding control object, and passes it your control by calling the AddParsedSubObject() method. The default implementation of this method simply adds the child control to the Controls collection of the current control, although you can change this behavior by overriding this method.

Using Customized Templates

As you can see, creating a basic templated control isn't difficult and doesn't require much code. However, the previous example still lacks a few key features. For one thing, it doesn't allow you to access any information from the templated items. It would be much more useful if there were a way to access some basic information about each item. Using this information, you could write data-binding expressions in your template, as you can with templated controls like the Repeater and DataList.

In order to support this technique, you need to create a custom control class to use as a template container. This control needs to include properties that provide the information you're interested in. The following example shows a custom template container that provides two properties: an item number representing the index of the template in the series, and the total number of items:

```
public class SimpleRepeaterItem : WebControl, INamingContainer
{
    int index;
    public int Index
    {
        get {return index;}
```

```
    }

    int total;
    public int Total
    {
        get {return total;}
    }

    public SimpleRepeaterItem(int itemIndex, int totalCount)
    {
        index = itemIndex;
        total = totalCount;
    }
}
```

Note that because this control acts as a template container, it needs to implement the INamingContainer interface.

Now you need to adjust the CreateChildControls() method so that it creates instances of the SimpleRepeaterItem control, instead of an ordinary Panel control. Each instance of the SimpleRepeaterItem will then hold a single instance of the item template.

But before you get to this point, it's worth making the templated control a little more sophisticated. The next example adds a header and footer template, and an alternating item template. With these four templates the programmer will have much more control over the layout of the content. Here's the template code you need:

```
private ITemplate itemTemplate;
[TemplateContainer(typeof(SimpleRepeaterItem))]
public ITemplate ItemTemplate
{
    get {return itemTemplate;}
    set {itemTemplate=value;}
}

private ITemplate alternatingItemTemplate;
[TemplateContainer(typeof(SimpleRepeaterItem))]
public ITemplate AlternatingItemTemplate
{
    get {return alternatingItemTemplate;}
    set {alternatingItemTemplate=value;}
}

private ITemplate headerTemplate;
[TemplateContainer(typeof(SimpleRepeaterItem))]
public ITemplate HeaderTemplate
{
    get {return headerTemplate;}
    set {headerTemplate=value;}
}
```

```
private ITemplate footerTemplate;
[TemplateContainer(typeof(SimpleRepeaterItem))]
public ITemplate FooterTemplate
{
    get {return footerTemplate;}
    set {footerTemplate=value;}
}
```

Note that each template property uses the TemplateContainer attribute to indicate what type of container your control will use when it instantiates the template.

Now you can revise the CreateChildControls() method. The CreateChildControls() will create instances of the SimpleRepeaterItem container, and pass the current index and the total item count as constructor arguments. Then, it will add the SimpleRepeaterItem as a child control of the SuperSimpleRepeater.

```
protected override void CreateChildControls()
{
    Controls.Clear();

    if ((RepeatCount > 0) && (itemTemplate!=null))
    {
        // Start by outputing the header template (if supplied).
        if(headerTemplate != null)
        {
            SimpleRepeaterItem headerContainer =
              new SimpleRepeaterItem(0, RepeatCount);
            headerTemplate.InstantiateIn(headerContainer);
            Controls.Add(headerContainer);
        }

        // Output the content the specified number of times.
        for (int i = 0; i<RepeatCount; i++)
        {
            SimpleRepeaterItem container =
              new SimpleRepeaterItem(i+1, RepeatCount);

            if ((i%2 == 0) && (alternatingItemTemplate != null))
            {
                // This is an alternating item and there is an
                // alternating template.
                alternatingItemTemplate.InstantiateIn(container);
            }
            else
            {
                itemTemplate.InstantiateIn(container);
            }
            Controls.Add(container);
        }
```

```
        // Once all of the items have been rendered,
        // add the footer template if specified.
        if (footerTemplate != null)
        {
            SimpleRepeaterItem footerContainer =
              new SimpleRepeaterItem(RepeatCount, RepeatCount);
            footerTemplate.InstantiateIn(footerContainer);
            Controls.Add(footerContainer);
        }
    }
    else
    {
        // Show an error message.
        Controls.Add(new LiteralControl(
          "Specify the record count and an item template"));
    }
}
```

There's one additional caveat. In order for data binding to work with the new SuperSimpleRepeater control, you need to call the DataBind() method of the header, footer, and item containers. In order to make sure that this critical step takes place, you need to override the DataBind() method. By default, the DataBind() method binds all the child controls in the Controls collection. However, your overridden implementation needs to call EnsureChildControls() first to make sure all the template containers have been created before the control is bound. Here's the code you need:

```
public override void DataBind()
{
    // Make sure the template containers have been created.
    EnsureChildControls();

    // Bind all the child controls.
    base.DataBind();
}
```

You can now test the new SuperSimpleRepeater with the following control tag and templates:

```
<apress:SuperSimpleRepeater id="sample" runat="server" RepeatCount="10">
  <HeaderTemplate>
    <h2 style="Color:Red">Super Simple Repeater Strikes Again!</h2>
    Now showing <%# Container.Total %> Items for your viewing pleasure.
  </HeaderTemplate>
  <ItemTemplate>
    <div align="center">
    <hr>Item <%# Container.Index %> of <%# Container.Total%><br><hr>
    </div>
  </ItemTemplate>
```

```
  <AlternatingItemTemplate>
   <div align="center" style="border-right: fuchsia double; border-top: fuchsia
double; border-left: fuchsia double; border-bottom: fuchsia double">
   Item <%# Container.Index %> of <%# Container.Total%>
   </div>
  </AlternatingItemTemplate>
  <FooterTemplate>
   <i>This presentation of the Simple Repeater Control brought to you by the
   letter <b>W</b></i>
  </FooterTemplate>
</apress:SuperSimpleRepeater2>
```

Note how the <ItemTemplate> and <AlternatingItemTemplate> sections use data-binding expressions that refer to Container. These expressions are evaluated against the properties of the container object, which in this example is an instance of the SimpleRepeaterItem class. All your web page needs to do is call the SuperSimpleReader.DataBind() method when the page loads. You can call SuperSimpleReader.DataBind() directly, or indirectly through the Page.DataBind() method, as shown here:

```
private void Page_Load(object sender, System.EventArgs e)
{
    Page.DataBind();
}
```

Figure 20-14 shows the new repeater control in action. Odd items (1, 3, 5, and so on) use the normal item template, while even items (2, 4, 6, and so on) use the alternative item template with the double border.

Tip As you saw with templated controls like the Repeater and DataList), it is common practice to extend the container control to provide a DataItem property. When a data item is read from the data source, the data item is passed to the container, which then exposes it and allows the web page to bind to it. In this way, the templated control becomes ultimately flexible, because it doesn't need to know anything about the type or structure of the data that it's displaying.

Styles

In the templated examples that you've seen so far, it's up to the web page to supply HTML elements for the template *and* the style attributes that tailor their appearance. Many templated controls simplify this process through style objects. In ASP.NET, the System.Web.UI.WebControls.Style class represents the complete collection of style information including colors, fonts, alignment, borders, and spacing. Using this class, you can easily add style support to your templated controls.

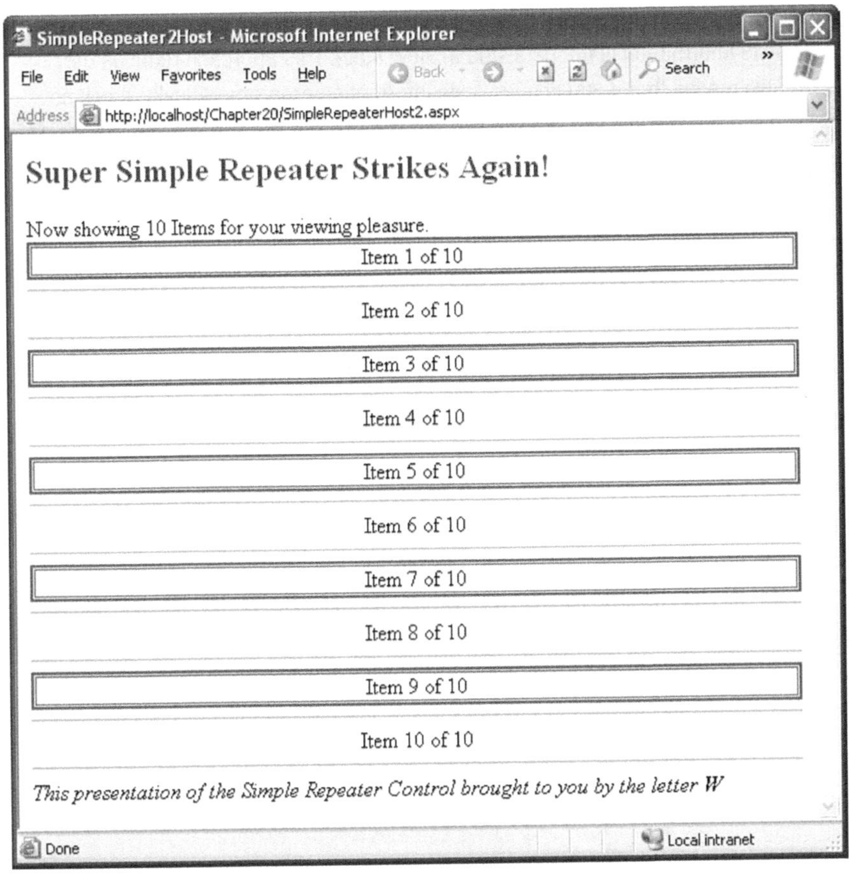

Figure 20-14. *Repeating more advanced templates*

For example, consider the SuperSimpleRepeater presented in the previous example, which uses four templates (item, alternating item, header, and footer). Using the Style class, you can define four corresponding style properties, one for each template.

Here's an example of the style property for the header:

```
private Style headerStyle
public Style HeaderStyle
{
    get
    {
        if (headerStyle == null)
        {
            headerStyle = new Style();
        }
        return headerStyle;
    }
}
```

Note In this example, the style information is not persisted in view state. This approach reduces the overall page size. However, it also means that if you change style information programmatically, it will be reset after every postback.

The Style class provides a collection of properties that you can set programmatically. Here's an example of how you could set the background color of the header using the SuperSimpleReader.HeaderStyle property:

```
repeater.HeaderStyle.BackColor = Color.Red;
```

Even more usefully, you can configure all the style properties using the Properties window. Just look for the style property, and click the plus sign next to it. A full list of subproperties will appear, each of which you can configure in the same way that you configure style information for an ordinary web control. Figure 20-15 shows this process at work with the SuperSimpleRepeater.

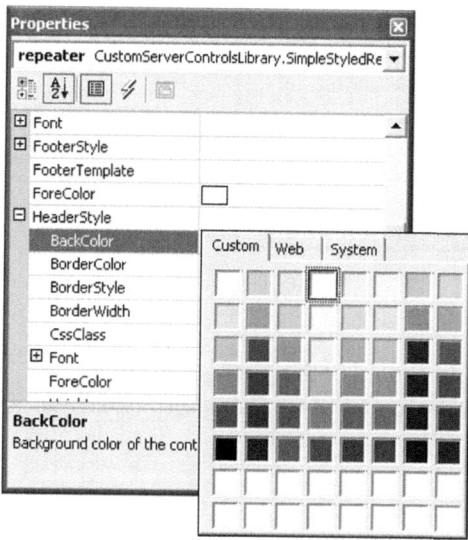

Figure 20-15. *Configuring a style property*

Of course, once you've added the properties for storing style information, you still need to adjust the control creation code to use these styles. The basic technique is the Control.ApplyStyle() method, which copies all the style information from a style object to a control. Here's how you can use this technique to set the style attributes for the header:

```
if (headerStyle != null)
{
    headerContainer.ApplyStyle(headerStyle);
}
```

The alternating item template is a special case. Usually, the alternating item will use the item style plus any styles that are redefined in the alternating item style. In this way, the user can just a few additional style settings for the alternating item, rather than redefining all the style settings from the item style.

To accomplish this behavior, you need the help of the CopyFrom() and MergeWith() methods of the Style class. The CopyFrom() method copies the styles from one style object to the calling style object, overwriting current values if they exist. The MergeWith() method combines the two styles so that if a value exists for the style attribute in the first style, this value will not be overwritten by the style value from the second style object.

Table 20-4 demonstrates how this works. The first two columns show the values for several style properties on two instances of the style class. The third column shows the updated values for the first style after calling CopyFrom() and passing in the second style. The last column shows the same values in Style1 after calling MergeWith() and passing Style2 as a parameter. Note that Style2 is not changed by either of these operations.

Table 20-4. *How Styles Are Copied and Merged*

	Style1 Before	Style2 Before	Style1 After CopyFrom(Style2)	Style1 After MergeWith(Style2)
BackColor	Black	White	White	Black
ForeColor	White	Black	Black	White
Height	25	[Not set]	25	25
Width	[Not set]	25	25	25

Here's how you can use the CopyFrom() and MergeWith() methods to create a style for alternating items:

```
Style altStyle = new Style();
altStyle.MergeWith(itemStyle);
altStyle.CopyFrom(alternatingItemStyle);
```

You can now apply that style when needed, just as with any other style:

```
container.ApplyStyle(altStyle);
```

With this revised version of the control, you can add style tags to the repeater. Here's an example of the style information that might be created after configuring the style properties in Visual Studio .NET:

```
<apress:SimpleStyledRepeater id="sample" runat="server" repeatcount="10">
  <AlternatingItemStyle Font-Bold="True" BorderStyle="Solid" BorderWidth="1px"
  ForeColor="White" BackColor="Red"></AlternatingItemStyle>
  <HeaderStyle Font-Italic="True" BackColor="#FFFFC0"></HeaderStyle>
  <AlternatingItemTemplate>
    Item <%# Container.Index %> of <%# Container.Total%>
  </AlternatingItemTemplate>
```

```
<ItemTemplate>
  <hr>Item <%# Container.Index %> of <%# Container.Total%><br><hr>
</ItemTemplate>
<HeaderTemplate>
  Now showing <%# Container.Total %> Items for your viewing pleasure.
</HeaderTemplate>
</apress:SimpleStyledRepeater>
```

Notice that the templates in this example are pared down so that they no longer apply formatting directly through HTML tags and style attributes. Instead, all the formatting is set using the styles. Figure 20-16 shows the result when you bind the SimpleStyledRepeater and show the page.

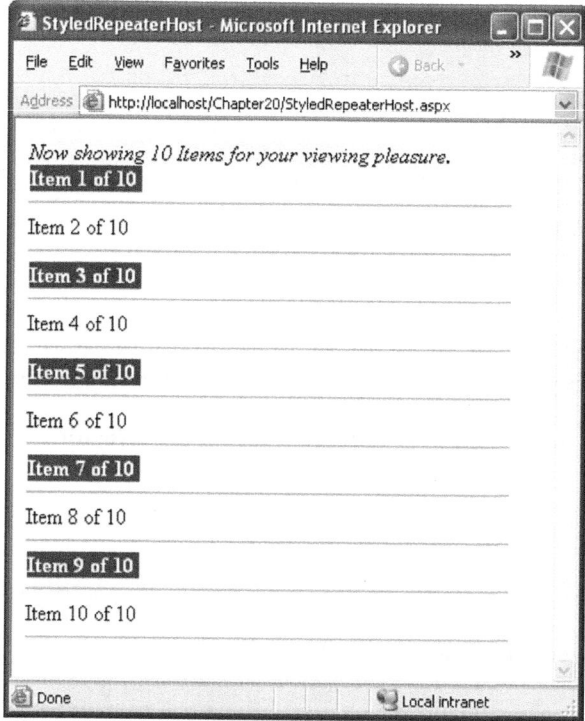

Figure 20-16. *Using styles with templates*

There's quite a bit more you can accomplish with templated controls, and it would take a significant amount of code (and a major investment of time) to duplicate the DataList or DataGrid. However, these examples show what you need to get started. Using them, you can create templated controls that are fine-tuned for your own custom data.

Creating Data Bound Controls

In the earlier chapters in this book, you studied data access and the ASP.NET data bound controls in great detail. In this section, you'll consider how you can apply data-binding techniques to your own custom controls.

Data bound controls come in two major flavors: simple and templated. Templated controls (such as the Repeater, DataList, and DataGrid) rely on your data-binding expressions. They use data source to determine how many instances of a given template to create and add to the control hierarchy. They then expose the data item from the data source through a property, which you can use to create data-binding expressions in a template.

Simple data bound controls consume the data you provide on their own. In the ASP.NET class library, most controls support some form of simple data binding, whether it's single-value data binding, or repeated-value data binding (as used by the list controls). For example, the DropDownList uses the data source it is provided with to populate the option items of an HTML <select> tag. Because of this direct interaction with the data object, simple data bound controls can be more difficult to create than templated controls.

In this section, you won't consider creating data bound templated controls. However, you will see an example of a simple repeated-value data bound control.

Data bound controls generally share a few common characteristics:

- They provide a DataSource property that can be assigned to some set of data.

- They include other properties like DataMember and DataTextField, which help you identify specific fields or properties in a data object.

- They provide a DataBind() method that, when invoked, binds the DataSource to the control.

Although this process sounds fairly simple, creating a generic, reusable data bound control often requires a fair bit of code. Some of the issues you confront include creating child controls, dealing with multiple different types of data objects, and making sure that the view state of the child objects is properly saved and restored over postbacks. Over the next few sections, you'll see an example with a simple data bound control that replicates the ASP.NET DropDownList control. You'll examine this custom control, named DbDropDown, piece by piece.

Figure 20-17 shows the DbDropDown in a web page. Clearly, it doesn't provide anything you can't already achieve with the DropDownList control. However, once you create this control you will have a class you can modify to show customized content. Using this control, you could easily tweak the rendering process to create different types of lists, including lists of links, lists with repeated icons, lists in a tabular format, and so on.

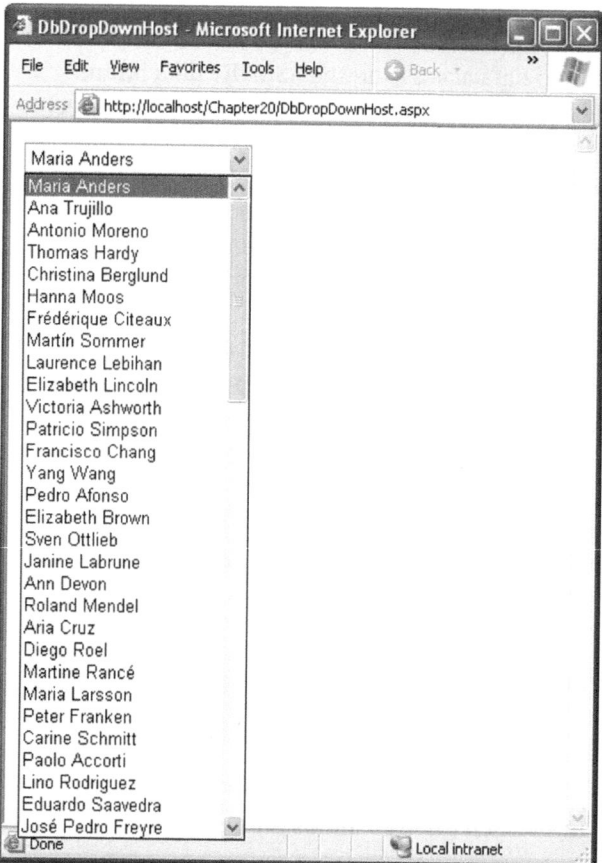

Figure 20-17. *Testing a custom data bound control*

The Data Items

One common aspect of data bound controls is that they are usually modeled as a composition of distinct items. For example, the RadioButtonList, CheckBoxList, and DropDownList are made up from a set of ListItems instances. The DataGrid is composed of a collection of DataGridItems. By convention, these items are usually themselves web controls (albeit controls that can't exist outside of their container control). This gives them the ability to take part in the rendering process.

In the DbDropDown list control, the container item class is DbListItem. It exposes the list text (Text), the value attribute (Value), and a Boolean property that indicates whether the item is selected (Selected). If you were planning to create a customized data item, you might want to add more properties. For example, you could use an IconLink property to point to an image you want to display next to the list item. Similarly, you could extend the DbListItem class to use a link, provide some JavaScript effect, or apply custom formatting on the data value.

Here's the data portion of the DbListItem:

```
public class DbListItem : System.Web.UI.WebControls.WebControl
{
    string text;
```

```
    public string Text
    {
        get {return text;}
        set {text = value;}
    }

    string itemValue;
    public string Value
    {
        get {return itemValue;}
        set {itemValue = value;}
    }

    bool selected;
    public bool Selected
    {
        get {return selected;}
        set {selected = value;}
    }

    public DbListItem(){}

    public DbListItem(string itemValue, string text, bool isSelected)
    {
        Text = text;
        Value = itemValue;
        Selected = isSelected;
    }

    // (Rendering and view state code omitted.)
}
```

You'll notice that the DbListItem control doesn't use view state in its property procedures. That's because you need to take more explicit control of view state in order to make sure the values are persisted and restored at the right time when the DbDropDown control is being created. In order to do this, you need to override the LoadViewState() and SaveViewState() methods. The following code shows the most efficient approach.

```
protected override object SaveViewState()
{
    // Create a new triplet with the three properties.
    Triplet tri = new Triplet(Text, Value, Selected);
    return tri;
}

protected override void LoadViewState(object state)
{
```

```
// Get the three properties out of the Triplet object that is in view state.
Triplet tri = (Triplet)state;
Text = (string)tri.First;
Value = (string)tri.Second;
Selected = (bool)tri.Third;
}
```

This code might seem a little unusual at first glance, because it uses the Triplet object. The Triplet represents three serializable pieces of information, which are written together in an efficient view state structure. Two other classes that are often used are the ArrayList and Pair.

In addition, the DbListItem control needs to render itself as part of the DbDropDown control. Here's the format of the HTML you need to generate:

```
<select>
  <option value="DataValueField">DataTextField</option>
  ...
</select>
```

The DbListItem doesn't need to worry about extracting this information from the data item, however, because the DbDropDown class takes care of that task. Instead, the DbListItem simply needs to examine its Text and Value properties, and render those to an option tag. Here's the Render() method that takes care of this step:

```
// Render the option tag using the properties of the control.
protected override void Render(HtmlTextWriter output)
{
    // Add the value attribute.
    output.AddAttribute(HtmlTextWriterAttribute.Value, Value);

    // If this item is selected, then add that attribute.
    if (Selected)
    {
        output.AddAttribute(HtmlTextWriterAttribute.Selected, "true");
    }

    // Render the option tag with the text in it.
    output.RenderBeginTag(HtmlTextWriterTag.Option);
    output.Write(Text);
    output.RenderEndTag();
}
```

The Data Source

Most data bound controls provide a DataSource property. This property usually has a type of IEnumerable, IList, or another collection interface. By using an interface for the DataSource property, the control can be more flexible by allowing for a larger variety of objects that can act as a data source. Each of these interfaces has its niche. For example, the IList interface provides indexed access to items in a collection, while the IEnumerable interface enables enumerating over the objects in the collection. ICollection provides everything in

IEnumerable plus members to provide synchronized access and a Count property. Many collection classes implement multiple interfaces to provide richer support for the typical actions that developers expect from collections.

In selecting the interface for your controls, the needs of your control will most likely dictate the interface type you use for the data source. For example, if your control design dictates that indexed access to the data source is a necessity, then the DataSource property for your control will most likely be IList or another interface that supports this type of access. If you need complete flexibility and plan to support several interfaces (as the ASP.NET data controls do), you might accept any object for the DataSource property, and then examine it to make sure it implements at least one of the interfaces you need. Choosing the supported data objects is one of the first decisions you make when creating a bindable control.

The DbDropDown control accepts data objects that implement IEnumerable. This includes ADO.NET classes like the DataView and DataReader, and collections like the ArrayList. That means you can bind the DbDropDown control to relational data extracted from a database, or a collection of custom data classes (like EmployeeDetails).

Here are the data-related properties for the DbDropDown control:

```
private IEnumerable dataSource;
public IEnumerable DataSource
{
    get {return dataSource;}
    set {dataSource=value;}
}

private string dataText;
public string DataTextField
{
    get {return dataText;}
    set {dataText=value;}
}

private string dataValue;
public string DataValueField
{
    get {return dataValue;}
    set {dataValue=value;}
}
```

The DbDropDown control also needs two member variables to store the number of items in the collection, and the index of the currently selected item. These member variables need to be exposed as read-only properties:

```
private int itemCount = -1;
public int ItemCount
{
    get {return itemCount;}
}
```

```
private int selectedIndex;
public int SelectedIndex
{
    get {return selectedIndex;}
}
```

These are also the only two pieces of information you need to store in view state. That's because on postbacks, the DbDropDown control needs to determine how many items are present in the list. It can then create the corresponding DbListItem control objects. Once the DbListItem objects are created, ASP.NET will retrieve their view state information and set the DbListItem properties.

Unfortunately, it's nearly impossible for ASP.NET to manage this process on its own. Instead, you need to take direct control of the view state serialization and deserialization process, as with the DbListItem control. In this case, the Triplet object is used again. It combines three pieces of information—the state of the base WebControl class (which includes details like style settings), the selected index, and the item count. Here's the complete code:

```
protected override object SaveViewState()
{
    // Create a new triplet with the base state and
    // the selected index and item count information.
    Triplet tri = new Triplet(base.SaveViewState(),selectedIndex, itemCount);
    return tri;
}

protected override void LoadViewState(object state)
{
    // Cast the state object to a triplet.
    Triplet tri = (Triplet)state;

    // Load the state for the base control.
    base.LoadViewState(tri.First);

    // Get the selected index and item count.
    selectedIndex = (int)tri.Second;
    itemCount = (int)tri.Third;
}
```

The Data Binding Process

The next step is to create the code that displays the bound data. This task unfolds over several steps. The easiest way to understand it, and the design decisions you need to make, is to consider the entire life cycle of the control:

1. Data is created or retrieved from a data source (by the web page) and placed into a data object.

2. The web page sets the DataSource, DataTextField, and DataValueField properties.

3. The web page calls the DataBind() method of the control.

4. The DataBind() method calls the control's OnDataBinding() method. This is where you place your custom code to manage the binding process.

5. The OnDataBinding() method calls the CreateControlHierarchy() method and passes a parameter of true. This indicates that the control hierarchy should be built using the data source.

6. The CreateControlHierarchy() method examines the properties of the data source object and creates the child data item controls. When this process is complete, the ChildControlsCreated property is set to true, so that ASP.NET will not call CreateChildControls().

This is the how the process works when a page is first requested, but it doesn't tell the whole story. When the user interacts with the page and initiates a postback, a different set of steps unfolds:

1. No data source is accessed and the DataBind() method is not called.

2. ASP.NET calls the CreateChildControls() method of the control.

3. The CreateChildControls() method calls the CreateControlHierarchy() method, and passes false indicating that the control should build its hierarchy from view state.

4. A dummy or generic data source is used to create the hierarchy using uninitialized controls.

5. The child controls are populated with the ViewState data.

As you can see, there are two different ways that the control hierarchy can be built. The first is that on the initial request for the page, at which point the DataBind() method is called and the control hierarchy is built from the data source. The second way is on postback, when the CreateChildControls() method is called and an empty control hierarchy is built so that the view state can be restored for each of the child controls. In each case, the structure of this hierarchy and the classes you use are the same.

It's also worth pointing out that the CreateControlHierarchy() method isn't a built-in control method. You need to create this method yourself. However, it's a recommended convention that you implement data binding using this method. It helps direct the organization of your control code so that you can rebuild your logic regardless of whether the control is being re-created from view state or bound directly from the data source.

OnDataBinding()

The first issue you have to address in a data bound control is handling the DataBind() command. In order to do this, you override the OnDataBinding() method. Within this method you do a number of things to prepare for the control creation, and then clean up after the child controls are created.

Most of the code in the OnDataBinding() method is just basic boilerplate. The actual work of examining the data source and creating the child controls is performed in the

CreateControlHierarchy() method, which OnDataBinding() calls. The first task you need to perform is to empty out the Controls collection and clear the view state of all child controls in order to ensure that there isn't anything left over from previous use of the control, as shown here:

```
protected override void OnDataBinding(EventArgs e)
{
    base.OnDataBinding(e);

    // Clear child controls and view state.
    Controls.Clear();
    if(HasChildViewState)
    {
        ClearChildViewState();
    }
    ...
```

Now you call CreateControlHierarchy() to perform the actual work, and supply a parameter of true to indicate that there is a data object available and waiting to be used:

```
    ...
    // Create controls from data.
    CreateControlHierarchy(true);
    ...
```

After you call CreateControlHierarchy(), it's time to finish the cleanup. You need to set the ChildControlsCreated property to true so that the ASP.NET runtime won't invoke your CreateChildControls() method. You also need to enable view state tracking. Here's the code you use:

```
    ...
    // Indicate that the controls have been created.
    ChildControlsCreated = true;

    // Turn on view state tracking.
    if(IsTrackingViewState)
    {
        TrackViewState();
    }
}
```

CreateControlHierarchy()

The CreateControlHierarchy() method contains the core of the data-binding code. It's at this point that you create all the child DbListItem objects, and add them to the DbDropDown control.

The first step is to get an enumerator for walking through the collection of data. In the DbDropDown control, you need to use the IEnumerator interface, because the data object is guaranteed to implement this interface. However, there's still one wrinkle. If the data source isn't present (because the control is being re-created as part of a postback), the enumerator is retrieved from a special helper object named DummyDataSource, not the actual bound data source object (which no longer exists). Here's the code that gets the enumerator:

```
protected void CreateControlHierarchy(bool useDataSource)
{
    IEnumerator items;

    // Set the enumerator to the data source or the item array.
    if (useDataSource)
    {
        items = dataSource.GetEnumerator();
    }
    else
    {
        items = new DummyDataSource(itemCount).GetEnumerator();
    }
    ...
```

Once you have the enumerator, you can begin looping through the items. Each time you find an item, the code creates a new DbListItem object. The process for creating this object depends on whether the bound source is available or not. If it is available, the DataTextField and DataValueField properties are retrieved from the object at the current position, as shown here:

```
    ...
    int count = 0;
    while (items.MoveNext())
    {
        DbListItem item;
        if (useDataSource)
        {
            // Create the new item with the object values.
            string itemText = (string)DataBinder.GetPropertyValue(
                items.Current, DataTextField);
            string itemValue = (string)DataBinder.GetPropertyValue(
                items.Current, DataValueField);
            item = new DbListItem(itemText, itemValue, false);

            // Start tracking view state.
            item.TrackViewState();
        }
        ...
```

This code is particularly interesting because it uses reflection. Essentially, the static DataBinder.GetPropertyValue() method extracts the value from a property in an object with a certain name. You only need to supply the name as a string. It doesn't matter whether you're retrieving the information from a custom class or a field from an ADO.NET data object like the DataRowView. Of course, if the properties doesn't exist, an exception will occur.

If you aren't binding to the data object, the code simply creates an empty DbListItem control. The values will be filled into this control automatically from the view state data, once it has been inserted into the control hierarchy. Here's the code that creates an empty DbListItem:

```
...
else
{
    // Create a new empty item.
    // It's values will be retrieved from view state.
    item = new DbListItem();
}
...
```

The last step is to add the DbListItem to the DbDropDown.Controls collection. When all the items have been added, you can store the total number of items in a private member variable named itemCount:

```
        ...
        // Add the item to the Controls collection
        Controls.Add(item);
        count++;
    }
    if (useDataSource)
    {
        // Store the number of items in a private member variable.
        itemCount = count;
    }
}
```

Rendering the Control

Once you've built the appropriate collection of child controls, it's easy to add the rendering logic. The DbListItem.Render() method already performs the work for adding the nested <option> tags. All you need to do is choose the <select> tag by calling the base constructor as shown here:

```
public DbDropDown() : base(HtmlTextWriterTag.Select)
{}
```

Then you can override AddAttributesToRender() to add the attributes you need, as follows:

```
protected override void AddAttributesToRender(HtmlTextWriter writer)
{
    base.AddAttributesToRender(writer);
    writer.AddAttribute(HtmlTextWriterAttribute.Id, UniqueID);
    writer.AddAttribute(HtmlTextWriterAttribute.Name, UniqueID);
}
```

That's it! The Render() method automatically calls RenderContents(), which calls the Render() method of each DbListItem child control to create the complete HTML output.

Dealing with Postbacks

So far you've seen the code that you need to bind and render the control. However, there's a little more work you need to ensure it's populated properly when the page is posted back. The missing ingredient is the CreateChildControls() method, which ASP.NET calls when re-creating your control. At this point, you need to clear any existing child controls, and then call the CreateControlHierarchy() method with a value of false to indicate that the collection of DbListItem objects will be built from the view state information. Here's the complete code for the CreateChildControls() method:

```
protected override void CreateChildControls()
{
    Controls.Clear();
    if (itemCount>0) CreateControlHierarchy(false);
}
```

The next step is to implement the IPostBackDataHandler interface so that the DbDropDown control receives notification when the page is posted back and can retrieve information about which item was selected:

```
public class DbDropDown : WebControl, IPostBackDataHandler
{ ... }
```

Now you can handle the postback with the LoadPostData, and retrieve the posted data:

```
public bool LoadPostData(string postDataKey, NameValueCollection postData)
{
    bool hasIndexChanged = false;

    // Get the posted value.
    string selectedValue = postData[postDataKey];

    // Make sure the DbListItem controls are created.
    // At this point, ASP.NET will call CreateChildControls()
    // if it hasn't been called yet.
    EnsureChildControls();
    ...
```

Next, you need to search the collection of child controls, and find the matching DbListItem. You can then mark that item as selected.

```
    ...
    // Loop through the controls selecting the appropriate one
    // and deselecting all the others.
    int currentIndex = 0;

    foreach(Control ctrl in Controls)
```

```
        {
            if (ctrl as DbListItem !=null)
            {
                if (((DbListItem)ctrl).Value == selectedValue)
                {
                    ((DbListItem)ctrl).Selected = true;

                    // If the index has changed, flip the flag to
                    // true so the event will be raised.
                    if (selectedIndex != currentIndex)
                    {
                        selectedIndex = currentIndex;
                        hasIndexChanged = true;
                    }
                }
                else
                {
                    ((DbListItem)ctrl).Selected = false;
                }
                currentIndex++;
            }
        }
    }
    return hasIndexChanged;
}
```

If the LoadPostData() method returns true, the RaisePostDataChangedEvent() method will be triggered next. The remainder of the code is the same as it is for any control that raises a change event:

```
public event EventHandler SelectedIndexChanged;
public void RaisePostDataChangedEvent()
{
    OnSelectedIndexChanged();
}


protected void OnSelectedIndexChanged()
{
    if (SelectedIndexChanged != null)
    {
        SelectedIndexChanged(this, EventArgs.Empty);
    }
}
```

This completes the walk-through of the DbListItem and DbDropDown classes. You can now create a simple test page. All you need to do is add the DbDropDown control to a web page, set the DataSource, DataTextValue, and DataFieldValue properties, and call DataBind(), just as you would with the ASP.NET DropDownList control. The downloadable code for this chapter provides a sample test page that you can use to bind the control and test its SelectedIndexChanged event.

Note There are a few other minor details in this control that aren't shown here, such as the dummy data source class definition. For all the details, refer to the downloadable code for this chapter.

Summary

In this chapter, you learned how to use a variety of techniques to create custom controls. In the next chapter, you'll continue your exploration by learning how to take control of the design-time representation of a control. In Chapter 22 and Chapter 23, you'll see examples of custom controls that use JavaScript and GDI+ for advanced solutions.

Even after you've read all these chapters, you still won't have learned everything there is to know about ASP.NET custom control creation. If you want to continue your exploration into the tricks, techniques, and idiosyncrasies of custom control programming, you might be interested in a dedicated book about the topic. One good resource is *Developing Microsoft ASP.NET Server Controls and Components* (Microsoft Press, 2002).

CHAPTER 21

■ ■ ■

Design-Time Support

Custom controls have two requirements. They need to interact with a web page (and your code) at runtime, and they need to interact with Visual Studio .NET at design time. These two tasks are related, but they can be refined and customized separately. Some of ASP.NET's most advanced controls (like the Calendar and DataList) include an impressive degree of design-time smarts, including the ability to configure complex properties and apply themes with the click of a mouse.

You've probably already noticed that Visual Studio .NET gives custom controls a high degree of design-time support automatically. For example, every custom control can be added to the toolbox, dragged onto a form, and moved and repositioned. Additionally, you can configure the properties of the control in the Properties window, and depending on how you've implemented the rendering logic, you may even see a design-time representation of the control's HTML. In this chapter, you'll learn how to extend this level of design-time support.

Many of the techniques you'll see are frills and niceties that make it easier to work with custom controls. For example, you might use design-time support to add descriptions that appear in the Properties window or render a more representative appearance for your control on the design surface. However, there are other cases where design-time support is required. For example, if you create a control that exposes complex objects as properties and you don't take any extra steps to add design-time support, the control will work erratically in the design-time environment. You might have trouble setting properties with the Properties window, or you might discover that when you do the nested child control tags are wiped out. These quirks are a result of how ASP.NET serializes your control properties, and you'll learn how to tackle these issues in this chapter.

Note This chapter talks about design-time control features as seen in Visual Studio .NET. However, the .NET Framework actually provides a generic design-time model that can be used by any editor, including Web Matrix and SharpDevelop.

Design-Time Attributes

The first level of design-time support consists of control *attributes*—declarative flags that are compiled into the metadata of your custom control assembly. Attributes give you a way to add information that's related to a piece of code without forcing you to change the code or create a separate file in an entirely different format.

Attributes are always placed in square brackets before the code element they modify. For example, here's how you can add an attribute that provide a description for the Text property of a control:

```
[Description("The text to be shown in the control")]
public string Text
{ ... }
```

In this case, the Description attribute *decorates* the Text property.

Note   All attributes are actually classes. By convention, the class name ends in "Attribute." For example, the Description attribute is actually represented by the DescriptionAttribute class. Although you can use the full class name, the C# compiler allows you to use a handy shortcut and omit the final "Attribute" word.

In .NET, attributes are used for a range of tasks. The key detail to understand about attributes is that they can be read and interpreted by different agents. For example, you can add attributes that give information to the CLR (common language runtime), the compiler, or a custom tool. This chapter focuses primarily on attributes that provide information to Visual Studio .NET, and tell it how to work with a control at design time. Later in this chapter, you'll also learn about some attributes that influence how the ASP.NET parser interprets control tags in the .aspx file.

Tip   Like many of the classes for design-time support, most of the attributes you'll learn about in this chapter are found in the System.ComponentModel namespace. Before applying these attributes, you should import that namespace into the code files for your custom controls.

The Properties Window

The simplest attributes influence how the properties of your control appear in the Properties window. For example, you've probably noticed that the core set of ASP.NET web controls group their properties into several categories. When you select a property, the Properties window shows a brief description. To add this information to your own control, you need to decorate each property with the Category and Description attribute, as shown here:

```
[Category("Appearance")]
[Description("The text to be shown in the control")]
public string Text
{
    get {return (string)ViewState["Text"];
    set {ViewState["Text"] = value;}
}
```

As you can see, both the Category and Description attribute accept a single string as an argument. Figure 21-1 shows the resulting display if you select the Text property in the Properties window.

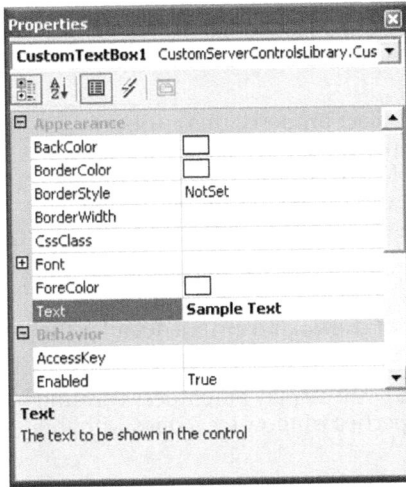

Figure 21-1. *A property with a description*

Table 21-1 lists the key attributes that influence the way a property is displayed in the Properties window.

Table 21-1. *Attributes for Control Properties*

Attribute	Description
Browsable(true|false)	If false, this property will not appear in the Properties window (although the programmer can still modify it in code or by manually adding the control tag attribute, as long as you include a Set property procedure). One reason you might use this attribute is to hide calculated or runtime properties that can't be changed at design time.
Category(string)	A string that indicates the category under which the property will appear in the Properties window.
Description(string)	A string that indicates the description the property will have when selected in the Properties window.
DefaultValue()	Sets the default value that will be displayed for the property in the Properties window. The default value is typically the initial value, in which case you don't need to use the DefaultValue attribute. However, using this attribute can sometimes allow the code generator to optimize the tags it generates by leaving out information if it matches the default.
ReadOnly(bool)	When true, this property is read-only in the Properties window at design time.

Continued

Table 21-1. *Continued*

Attribute	Description
DesignOnly(bool)	When set to true, this property is only available at design time. This is typically used with special properties that configure how a control behaves at design time, and don't correspond to a "real" piece of information about the control.
ImmutableObject(bool)	When set to true on an object property, this attribute ensures that the subproperties of this object are displayed as read-only. For example, if you apply this to a property that uses a Point object, the X and Y subproperty will be read-only.
MergableProperty(bool)	Configures how the Properties window behaves when more than one instance of this control are selected at once. If false, the property is not shown. If true (the default), the property can be set for all selected controls at once.
ParenthesizePropertyName(bool)	If true, Visual Studio .NET will display parentheses around this property in the Properties window (as it does with the ID property).
Bindable(bool)	If true, Visual Studio .NET will display this property in the DataBindings dialog box and allow it to be bound to a field in a data source.
RefreshProperties()	You use this attribute with a value from the RefreshProperties enumeration. It specifies whether the rest of the Properties window must be updated when this property is changed (for example, if one property procedure could change another property).

There are two attributes that can be applied to your custom control class declaration, rather than a specific property: DefaultEvent and DefaultProperty. Additionally, the TagPrefix attribute is used at the assembly level, and isn't attached to any code construct. Table 21-2 describes these attributes.

Table 21-2. *Attributes for Control Classes and Assemblies*

Attribute	Description
DefaultEvent(string)	Indicates the name of the default event. When you double-click the control in the design environment, Visual Studio .NET automatically adds an event handler for the default event.
DefaultProperty(string)	Indicates the name of the default property. The DefaultProperty is the property that is highlighted in the Properties window by default, the first time the control is selected.
TagPrefix(string, string)	Associates a namespace with a prefix, which will be used when adding control tags to an .aspx page.

As you learned in Chapter 20, every custom control has a prefix that's registered with the Register directive in the .aspx page. Visual Studio .NET adds this directive automatically when you insert the control. If you want to customize the prefix, you can use the TagPrefix attribute, which accepts two string parameters. The first string is the namespace your controls are in, and the second string is the tag prefix you want to use.

Here's an example that specifies that controls in the CustomServerControlsLibrary should use the apress tag prefix:

```
[assembly: System.Web.UI.TagPrefix("CustomServerControlsLibrary", "apress")]
```

Now if you add a control with the class name CustomTextBox from the CustomServerControlsLibrary namespace, this is the tag Visual Studio .NET uses:

```
<apress:CustomTextBox ... />
```

If you have controls in multiple namespaces, you need to use TagPrefix multiple times, once for each namespace. You can use the same prefix or different prefixes. Often, the TagPrefix attribute is placed in the AssemblyInfo.cs file.

Here's the simple CustomTextBox control from the previous chapter, with a full complement of attributes. The code has been left out.

```
[assembly: System.Web.UI.TagPrefix("CustomServerControlsLibrary", "apress")]
namespace CustomServerControlsLibrary
{
    [DefaultProperty("Text")]
    [DefaultEvent("TextChanged")]
    public class CustomTextBox : WebControl, IPostBackDataHandler
    {
        public CustomTextBox() : base(HtmlTextWriterTag.Input)
        { ... }

        [Category("Appearance")]
        [Description("The text to be shown in the control")]
        [DefaultValue("")]
        [MergableProperty(true)]
        public string Text
        { ... }

        protected override void AddAttributesToRender(HtmlTextWriter output)
        { ... }

        public bool LoadPostData(string postDataKey,
          NameValueCollection postData)
        { ... }

        public void RaisePostDataChangedEvent()
        { ... }

        public event EventHandler TextChanged;
        protected virtual void OnTextChanged(EventArgs e)
        { ... }
    }
}
```

Attributes and Inheritance

When you derive a control from a base class that has design-time attributes, the control inherits the design-time functionality of its parent, just like it inherits the methods and properties. If the parent class's implementation of the design-time attributes is sufficient for your control, you do not need to reapply them.

However, in some cases you might want to change the design-time behavior of an existing property. In this case, you must first override the property, and reapply the changed attributes or add the new ones.

Most of the properties in the base classes WebControl and Control are marked as virtual, which allows you to change their behavior. For example, if you wanted to hide the Height property of a custom control that derives from WebControl (maybe because it is calculated from the content rather than set by the developer), you could override the Height property and apply the Browsable attribute, as shown here:

```
[Browsable(false)]
public override Unit Height
{
  get {return base.Height;}
  set {base.Height = value;}
}
```

The Toolbox Icon

Adding a Toolbox icon is refreshingly easy. All you need to do is add a bitmap to your project and ensure that it has the same filename as your custom control class. This bitmap must meet a few basic criteria:

- It must be 16 by 16 pixels. Otherwise, it will be mangled when Visual Studio .NET attempts to scale it.

- It must use only 16 colors.

Once you add the file, use the Properties window to set the Build Action for it to Embedded Resource. Then recompile the control project. Figure 21-2 shows the required image for the CustomTextBox control.

When you add the control to a client project, the embedded bitmap appears in the Toolbox. Figure 21-3 shows an example with two custom controls. One has the generic gear icon, while the CustomTextBox uses the bitmap added to the control project.

If you're creating a simple control, all you may need to do is add a set of descriptive properties and a Toolbox icon. However, more complex controls often require other considerations. These range from code serialization issues (how the control tag is created when you use the Properties window), to control designers (advanced tools for customizing the design-time HTML your control renders). In the rest of the chapter, you'll take a look at these topics.

Figure 21-2. *Adding a Toolbox bitmap*

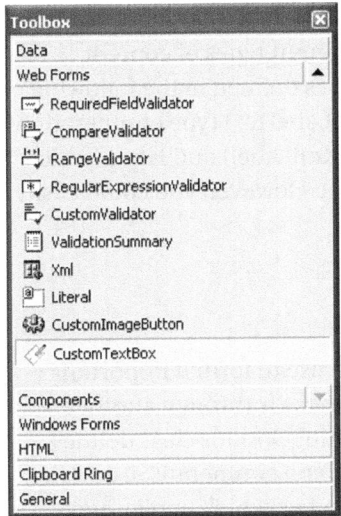

Figure 21-3. *A custom Toolbox bitmap*

Code Serialization

When you configure control properties in the Properties window, Visual Studio .NET needs to be able to create and modify the corresponding control tag in the .aspx file. This process is called *code serialization*, and it often works automatically. However, it can run into trouble if you use properties that are themselves complex types, or if you create a templated control or a control that supports child controls.

In the following sections, you'll learn about the different ingredients that affect control serialization, and what changes you need to make in order to resolve common problems.

Type Converters

The Properties window deals seamlessly with common data types. String data doesn't present a problem, but the Properties window can also convert strings to numeric types. For example, if you look at the Width property of a control, you'll see a value like 50 px. You can enter any characters in this field, but if you try to commit the change (by pressing Enter or moving to another field) and you've include characters that can't be interpreted as a unit, the change will be rejected.

This behavior is made possible by *type converters*, specialized classes that are designed for the sole purpose of converting a specialized data type to a string representation and back. Most of the core .NET data types have default type converters that work perfectly well. (You can find these type converters in the System.ComponentModel.TypeConverter namespace.) However, if you create your own structures or classes and use them as properties, you may also want to create custom type converters that allow them to work in the Properties window.

A Control with Object Properties

The next example uses a RichLabel control that's a slightly revised version of the XmlLabel control presented in Chapter 20. The difference is that while the XmlLabel is designed to show XML documents, the RichLabel control is designed to support different types of content.

Essentially, the RichLabel can support any type of content that's defined in the following RichLabelTextType enumeration. In this simple example, the RichLabelTextType enumeration only includes two options: Xml (which uses the same code as the XmlLabel) and Html (which treats the text as is, and doesn't perform any additional processing). However, you could easily add the rendering code for different types of text.

```
public enum RichLabelTextType
{Xml, Html}
```

The RichLabel also allows you to choose what tag you want to use to format important details (like the XML tags in XML rendering mode). The way this works is through another class, named RichLabelFormattingOptions. The RichLabelFormattingOptions class defines two properties: Type (which holds a value from the RichLabelTextType enumeration) and HighlightTag (which stores a tag name as a string, like b for the <b> tag, which applies bold formatting).

```
[Serializable()]
public class RichLabelFormattingOptions
{
    private RichLabelTextType type;
    public RichLabelTextType Type
    {
        get {return type;}
        set {type = value;}
    }

    private string highlightTag;
    public string HighlightTag
    {
```

```
        get {return highlightTag;}
        set {highlightTag = value;}
    }

    public RichLabelFormattingOptions(RichLabelTextType type,
      string highlightTag)
    {
        this.highlightTag = highlightTag;
        this.type = type;
    }
}
```

The RichLabel class includes a Format property, which exposes an instance of the custom RichLabelFormattingOptions class. The rendering logic in the RichLabel control uses this information to customize the HTML it generates.

Here's the code for the RichLabel control:

```
[DefaultProperty("RichText")]
public class RichLabel : WebControl
{
    public RichLabel() : base()
    {
        Text = "";
        // Default to XML text with tags formatted in bold.
        Format = new RichLabelFormattingOptions(RichLabelTextType.Xml, "b");
    }

    [Category("Appearance")]
    [Description("The content that will be displayed.")]
    public string Text
    {
        get {return (string)ViewState["Text"];}
        set {ViewState["Text"] = value;}
    }

    [Category("Appearance")]
    [Description("Options for configuring how text is rendered.")]
    public RichLabelFormattingOptions Format
    {
        get {return (RichLabelFormattingOptions)ViewState["Format"];}
        set {ViewState["Format"] = value;}
    }

    protected override void RenderContents(HtmlTextWriter output)
    {
        string convertedText = "";
        switch (Format.Type)
        {
```

```
            case RichLabelTextType.Xml:
                // Find and highlight the XML tags.
                convertedText = RichLabel.ConvertXmlTextToHtmlText(
                  Text, Format.HighlightTag);
                break;
            case RichLabelTextType.Html:
                // Keep the text as is.
                convertedText = Text;
                break;
            }
            output.Write(convertedText);
        }
    }

    public static string ConvertXmlTextToHtmlText(string inputText,
      string highlightTag)
    {
        // (Code omitted.)
    }
}
```

Alternative designs are possible. For example, you could add these two pieces of information (Type and HighlightTag) as separate properties in the RichLabel class, in which case you wouldn't need to take any extra steps to ensure proper serialization. However, there are a number of reasons why you might decide to group related properties together using a custom class. Perhaps you want the ability to reuse the RichLabelFormattingOptions class in order to specify text-formatting options for other controls. Or maybe you need to create a more complex control that accepts several different pieces of text, and can convert all of them using independent RichLabelFormattingOptions settings. In both of these situations, it becomes useful to group the properties together using the RichLabelFormattingOptions class.

However, the RichLabel control doesn't work well with Visual Studio .NET. When you try to modify this control at design time, you'll immediately notice the problem. The Properties window doesn't allow you to edit the RichLabel.Format property. Instead, it shows an empty edit box where you can't type anything. To solve this problem, you need to create a custom type converter, as explained in the next section.

Creating a Custom Type Converter

A custom type converter is a class that can convert from your proprietary data type (in this case, the RichLabelFormattingOptions class) to a string and back. In the following example, you'll see such a class, named RichLabelFormattingOptionsConverter.

The first step is to create a custom class that derives from the base class TypeConverter, as shown here:

```
public class RichLabelFormattingOptionsConverter : TypeConverter
{ ... }
```

By convention, the name of a type converter class is made up of the class type it converts, followed by the word "Converter".

Once you create the type converter, you have several methods to override. These include the following:

- **CanConvertFrom().** This method examines a data type, and returns true if the type converter can make the conversion from this data type to the custom data type.

- **ConvertFrom().** This method performs the conversion from the supplied data type to the custom data type.

- **CanConvertTo().** This method examines a data type, and returns true if the type converter can make the conversion from the custom object to this data type.

- **ConvertTo().** This method performs the conversion from the custom data type to the requested data type.

Remember that the key task of a type converter is to convert between your custom data type and a string representation. This example uses a string representation that includes both values from the RichLabelFormattingOptions object, separated by a comma and a space, and with angled brackets around the tag name. Here's what the string format looks like:

```
Type Name, <HighlightTag>
```

Here's an example with XML formatting and a <b> tag:

```
Xml, <b>
```

With that in mind, you can create two helper methods in the converter class to perform this conversion. The first is a ToString() method that builds the required string representation:

```
private string ToString(object value)
{
    RichLabelFormattingOptions format = (RichLabelFormattingOptions)value;
    return String.Format("{0}, <{1}>", format.Type, format.HighlightTag);
}
```

The second part is a FromString() method that decodes the string representation. If the string isn't in the format you need, the FromString() code raises an exception. Otherwise, it returns the new object instance:

```
private RichLabelFormattingOptions FromString(object value)
{
    string[] values = ((string)value).Split(',');
    if (values.Length != 2)
        throw new ArgumentException("Could not convert the value");

    try
    {
        // Convert the name of the enumerated value into the corresponding
        // enumerated value (which is actually an integer constant).
        RichLabelTextType type = (RichLabelTextType)Enum.Parse(
          typeof(RichLabelTextType), values[0], true);
```

```
        // Get rid of the spaces and angle brackets around the tag name.
        string tag = values[1].Trim(new char[]{' ','<','>'});
        return new RichLabelFormattingOptions(type, tag);
    }
    catch
    {
        throw new ArgumentException("Could not convert the value");
    }
}
```

Before attempting a conversion from a string to RichLabelFormattingOptions object, the Properties window will first query the CanConvertFrom() method. If it receives a true value, it will call the actual ConvertFrom() method. All the CanConvertFrom() method needs to is check that the supplied type is a string, as follows:

```
public override bool CanConvertFrom(ITypeDescriptorContext context,
  Type sourceType)
{
    if (sourceType == typeof(string))
    {
        return true;
    }
    else
    {
        return base.CanConvertFrom(context, sourceType);
    }
}
```

The ConvertFrom() method calls the conversion by calling the FromString() method shown earlier:

```
public override object ConvertFrom(ITypeDescriptorContext context,
  CultureInfo culture, object value)
{
    if (value is string)
    {
        return FromString(value);
    }
    else
    {
        return base.ConvertFrom(context, culture, value);
    }
}
```

Note It is good object-oriented programming practice to always give the base classes from which you inherit a chance to handle a message you are not going to support. In this case, any requests to perform a conversion from an unrecognized type are passed to the base class.

The exact same process occurs in reverse when converting a RichLabelFormattingOptions object to a string. First, the Properties window calls CanConvertTo(). If it returns true, the next step is to call the ConvertTo() method. Here's the code you need:

```
public override bool CanConvertTo(ITypeDescriptorContext context,
  Type destinationType)
{
    if (destinationType == typeof(string))
    {
        return true;
    }
    else
    {
        return base.CanConvertTo(context, destinationType);
    }
}

public override object ConvertTo(ITypeDescriptorContext context,
  CultureInfo culture, object value, Type destinationType)
{
    if (destinationType == typeof(string))
    {
        return ToString(value);
    }
    else
    {
        return base.ConvertTo(context, culture, value, destinationType);
    }
}
```

Now that you have a fully functioning type converter, the next step is to attach it to the corresponding property.

Attaching a Type Converter

To link a class to a type converter, you add the TypeConverter attribute to the property that uses it. When you use the TypeConverter, you need to specify the specific type that has the conversion logic. Here's an example:

```
[TypeConverter(typeof(RichLabelFormattingOptionsConverter))]
public RichLabelFormattingOptions Format
{ ... }
```

Now you can recompile the code and try using the RichLabel control in a sample web page. When you select a RichLabel, you'll see the current value of the RichLabel.Format property in the Properties window (shown in Figure 21-4), and you can edit it by hand.

> **Note** When changing details like type converter, control designer, and control builders, your changes will not appear immediately in the design environment after a recompile. Instead, you may need to close the solution with the test web pages and then reopen it.

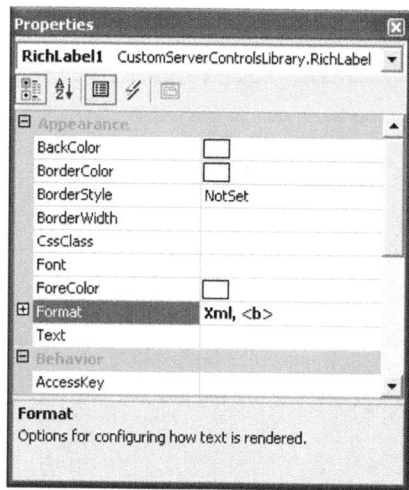

Figure 21-4. *A string representation of the RichLabelFormattingOptions object*

Of course, unless you enter the correct string representation, you'll receive an error message and your change will be rejected. In other words, the custom type converter shown here gives you the ability to specify a RichLabelFormattingOptions object as a string, but the process certainly isn't user-friendly. The next section shows you how to improve this level of support.

The ExpandableObjectConverter

There are a number of object properties that are supported by ASP.NET web controls. The best example is Font, which refers to a FontInfo object with properties like Bold, Italic, Name, and so on. When you set the Font property in the Properties window, you don't need to type all this information in a single, correctly formatted string. Instead, you can expand the Font property (by clicking the plus (+) box) and edit all of the FontInfo properties individually.

You can enable the same type of editing with your own custom object types—you simply need to create a custom type converter that derives from ExpandableObjectConverter class instead of the base TypeConverter class. For example, you could take the RichLabelFormattingOptionsConverter developed in the previous section, and change it as shown here:

```
public class RichLabelFormattingOptionsConverter : ExpandableObjectConverter
{ ... }
```

Now you can specify the Format property by typing in a string or expanding the property and modifying one of the two subproperties. Figure 21-5 shows the much more convenient interface that you'll see in the Properties window.

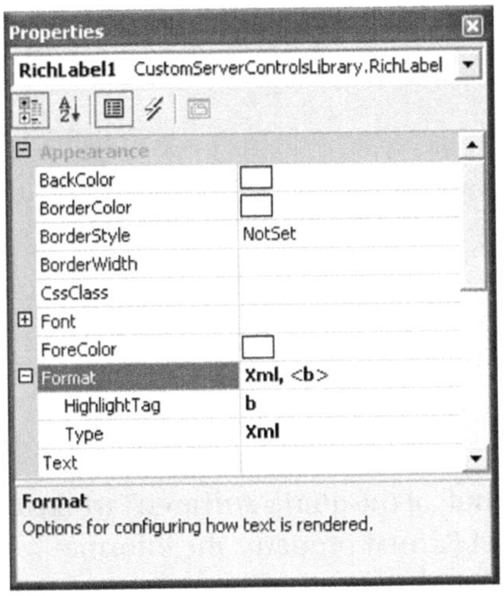

Figure 21-5. *Editing properties of the RichLabelFormattingOptions object*

This looks good at first pass, but there are still a few quirks. One problem is that when you change a subproperty (Type or HighlightTag), the string representation that's shown in the Format box isn't immediately updated. To solve this problem you need to apply the NotifyParentProperty and RefreshProperties attributes to the properties of the RichLabelFormattingOptions class. At the same time, you might also want to add a Description attribute to configure the text that will appear in the Properties window for this subproperty.

Here's the revised code for the RichLabelFormattingOptions class:

```
public class RichLabelFormattingOptions
{
    private RichLabelTextType type;

    [RefreshProperties(RefreshProperties.Repaint)]
    [NotifyParentProperty(true)]
    [Description("Type of content supplied in the text property")]
    public RichLabelTextType Type
    {
        get {return type;}
        set {type = value;}
    }

    private string highlightTag;

    [RefreshProperties(RefreshProperties.Repaint)]
    [NotifyParentProperty(true)]
    [Description(
     "The HTML tag you want to use to mark up highlighted portions.")]
    public string HighlightTag
    {
```

```
        get {return highlightTag;}
        set {highlightTag = value;}
    }

    public RichLabelFormattingOptions(RichLabelTextType type,
      string highlightTag)
    {
        this.highlightTag = highlightTag;
        this.type = type;
    }
}
```

This solves the synchronization and editing problems, but all the quirks *still* aren't worked out. The problem is that although you can edit the RichLabel.Format property, the information you set isn't persisted into the control tag. This means that the changes you make at design time are essentially ignored. To resolve this problem, you need to dig a little deeper into how .NET serializes control properties, as described in the next section.

Serialization Attributes

You can control how control properties are serialized into the .aspx file using attributes. There are two key attributes to consider—DesignerSerializationVisibility and PersistenceMode.

The DesignerSerializationVisibility attribute determines whether or not a property will be serialized. You have three choices:

- **Visible.** This is the default value. It specifies that the property should be serialized, and it works for simple data types, like strings, dates, enumerations, and the numeric data types.

- **Content.** Serializes the entire content of an object. You can use this value to serialize complex types with multiple properties, like a collection.

- **Hidden.** Specifies that a property shouldn't be serialized at all. For example, you might use this to prevent a calculated value from being serialized.

The PersistenceMode attribute allows you to specify *how* a property is serialized. You have the following choices:

- **Attribute.** This is the default option. The property will be serialized as an HTML attribute of the control.

- **InnerProperty.** The property will be persisted as a nested tag inside the control. This is the preferred setting to generate complex nested hierarchies of objects. An example is the Calendar or DataList control.

- **InnerDefaultProperty.** The property will be persisted inside the control tag. It will be the only content of the control tag. An example is the Text property of the Label control. When using a default property, the property name doesn't appear in the nested content.

- **EncodedInnerDefaultProperty.** This is the same as InnerDefaultProperty, except that the content will be HTML encoded before it is persisted.

To understand how these different options work, it's worth considering a few examples. The PersistenceMode.Attribute choice is the default option that you've seen with the core set of ASP.NET control tags. If you combine this attribute with DesignerSerializationVisibility.Content in a property whose type contains subproperties, ASP.NET uses the object-walker syntax, in the form Property-SubProperty="Value". You can see an example with the Font property, as shown here:

```
<apress:ctrl Font-Size="8pt" Font-Names="Tahoma" Bold="True" ... />
```

On the other hand, consider what happens if you create a custom control that overrides the persistence behavior of the Font property to use PersistenceMode.InnerProperty, as shown here:

```
[PersistenceMode(PersistenceMode.InnerProperty)]
public override FontInfo Font
{
    get {return base.Font;}
}
```

Now the persisted code for the Font property takes this form:

```
<apress:ctrl ... >
  <Font Size="8pt" Names="Tahoma" Bold="True"></Font>
</apress:ctrl>
```

To allow the RichLabel to serialize its Format property correctly, you need to apply both the PersistenceMode and DesignerSerializationVisibility attributes. The DesignerSerializationVisibility attribute will specify Content, because the Format property is a complex object. The PersistenceMode attribute will specify InnerProperty, which stores the Format property information as a separated, nested tag. Here's how you need to apply these two attributes:

```
[TypeConverter(typeof(RichLabelFormattingOptionsConverter))]
[DesignerSerializationVisibility(DesignerSerializationVisibility.Content)]
[PersistenceMode(PersistenceMode.InnerProperty)]
public RichLabelFormattingOptions Format
{
    get {return (RichLabelFormattingOptions)ViewState["Format"];}
    set {ViewState["Format"] = value;}
}
```

Now when you configure the Format property in the Properties window, ASP.NET will create a tag in this form:

```
<apress:RichLabel id="RichLabel1" runat="server">
  <Format Type="Xml" HighlightTag="b"></Format>
</apress:RichLabel>
```

The end result is that the RichLabel control works perfectly when inserted into a web page at runtime as well as when a developer is using it at design time.

There are two other related serialization properties that you apply at the class level—PersistChildren and ParseChildren. Both attributes control how ASP.NET deals with nested tags, and whether it supports child controls. When PersistChildren is true, child controls are persisted as contained tags. When PersistChildren is false, any nested tags designate properties. ParseChildren plays the same role when reading control tags. When ParseChildren is true, the ASP.NET parser interprets all nested tags as properties rather than controls.

When deriving from the WebControl class, the default is that PersistChildren is false and ParseChildren is true, in which case any nested tags are treated as property values. If you want child content to be treated as child controls in the control hierarchy, you need to explicitly set PersistChildren to true and ParseChildren is false. Because the RichLabel control isn't designed to hold other controls, this step isn't needed—the defaults are what you want.

Templated Controls

The RichLabel isn't the only control that needs the serialization attributes. In order to successfully use the templated controls described in Chapter 20 (like SuperSimpleRepeater), all the template properties need to use PersistenceMode.InnerProperty serialization.

Here's an example of a templated property that's correctly configured:

```
[PersistenceMode(PersistenceMode.InnerProperty)]
[TemplateContainer(typeof(SimpleRepeaterItem))]
public ITemplate ItemTemplate
{
    get {return itemTemplate;}
    set {itemTemplate=value;}
}
```

Otherwise, when you set other properties in the control, the template content will be wiped out.

Controls with Collections

Unfortunately, serialization can become a fair bit more complicated than the RichLabel example. One such case is the RestrictedCalendar control demonstrated in the previous chapter. The RestrictedCalendar stores a collection of dates the user isn't allowed to select in a NonSelectableDates property. Ordinarily, you would deal with the serialization of the NonSelectableDates property by adding the attributes shown here:

```
[DesignerSerializationVisibility(DesignerSerializationVisibility.Content)]
[PersistenceMode(PersistenceMode.InnerProperty)]
public DateTimeCollection NonSelectableDates
{
    get {return (DateTimeCollection)ViewState["NonSelectableDates"];}
    set {ViewState["NonSelectableDates"] = value;}
}
```

Everything seems fine at first. In fact, you don't even need to create a type converter for the NonSelectableDates property. That's because .NET automatically recognizes it as a collection, and uses the CollectionConverter. The CollectionConverter simply displays the text (Collection), as shown in Figure 21-6.

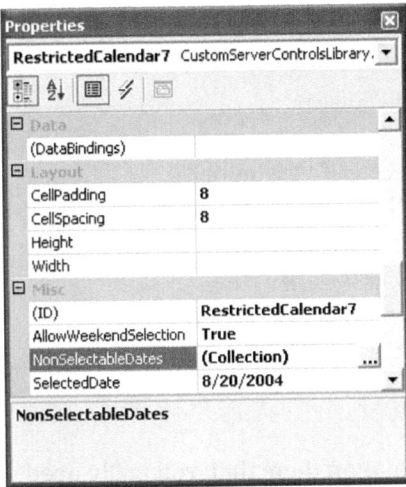

Figure 21-6. *A collection property*

You can click the ellipsis next to the property name to open a designer where you can add DateTime objects. You can even choose values for each date using a drop-down calendar, as shown in Figure 21-7. This graphical functionality is actually the work of another component, called a type editor. (You'll learn about type editors in the next section.)

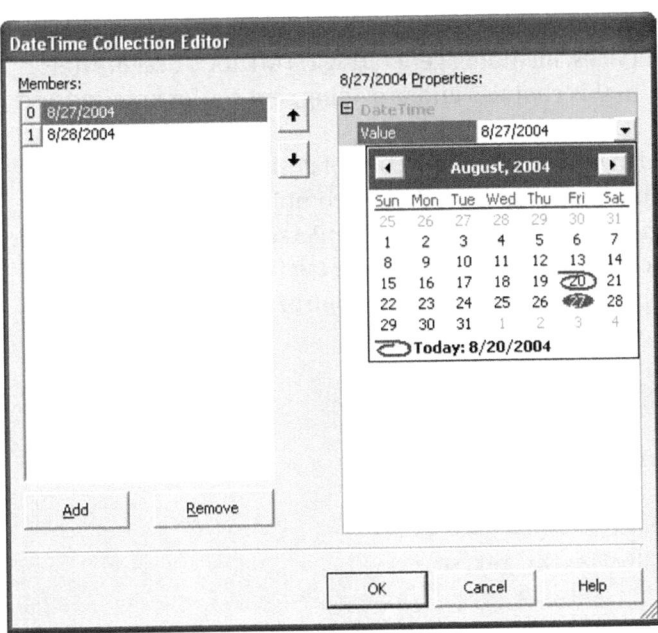

Figure 21-7. *Adding dates to a collection property*

This all works well enough. If you look at the generated HTML for the RestrictedCalendar after you add two dates, you'll see something like this:

```
<cc1:RestrictedCalendar id="RestrictedCalendar8" runat="server">
  <NonSelectableDates>
    <System.DateTime Year="2004" DayOfWeek="Friday" Second="0" Minute="0"
      TimeOfDay="00:00:00" Day="20" Millisecond="0" Date="2004-08-20" Hour="0"
      DayOfYear="233" Ticks="632285568000000000" Month="8"></System.DateTime>
    <System.DateTime Year="2004" DayOfWeek="Saturday" Second="0" Minute="0"
      TimeOfDay="00:00:00" Day="21" Millisecond="0" Date="2004-08-21" Hour="0"
      DayOfYear="234" Ticks="632286432000000000" Month="8"></System.DateTime>
  </NonSelectableDates>
</cc1:RestrictedCalendar>
```

This code raises two problems. First, there's more information there than you really need to store. The RestrictedCalendar is really only interested in the date portion of the DateTime object, and the time information is wasted space. A more serious problem is the fact that when you request this page, ASP.NET won't be able to re-create the DateTimeCollection that's exposed by the NonSelectableDates property. Instead, it will raise an error when attempting to deserialize the nested tags and set read-only properties like Year, Month, and Ticks.

In order to solve this problem, you need to plug in to the serialization and parsing infrastructure for your control. The first step is to customize the code that's serialized for each DateTime object in the NonSelectableDates collection. To accomplish this, you need to create a new class called a *control designer*. Control designers are complex components that can perform a whole variety of design-time services, including generating HTML for a design-time representation (a topic you'll see later in this chapter) and providing services for entering and editing templates at design time.

In this case, you're only interested in one aspect of the control designer—it's ability to control how the content inside the control tag is serialized. To accomplish this, you create a class that inherits from ControlDesigner, and you override the GetPersistInnerHtml() method. This method will read the list of restricted dates, and create a new tag for each DateTime object. This tag will then be added into the RestrictedCalendar control tag.

Here's the complete code:

```
public class RestrictedCalendarDesigner : ControlDesigner
{
    public override string GetPersistInnerHtml()
    {
        StringWriter sw = new StringWriter();
        HtmlTextWriter html = new HtmlTextWriter(sw);

        RestrictedCalendar calendar = this.Component as RestrictedCalendar;
        if (calendar != null)
        {
            // Create tags in the format:
            //    <DateTime Value='xxx' />
            foreach (DateTime date in calendar.NonSelectableDates)
            {
```

```
            html.WriteBeginTag("DateTime");
            html.WriteAttribute("Value", date.ToString());
            html.WriteLine(HtmlTextWriter.SelfClosingTagEnd);
        }
    }
    return sw.ToString();
    }
}
```

In order to tell the control to use this control designer, you need to apply a Designer attribute to the RestrictedCalendar class declaration. At the same time, you should also set ParseChildren to false so that the nested tags the ControlDesigner creates aren't treated as control properties.

```
[ControlBuilder(typeof(RestrictedCalendarBuilder))]
[ParseChildren(false)]
public class RestrictedCalendar : Calendar
{ ... }
```

This accomplishes half of the process. Now when you add restricted dates at design time, the control tag markup will be created in this format:

```
<cc1:RestrictedCalendar id="RestrictedCalendar1" runat="server">
  <DateTime Value="8/27/2004 " />
  <DateTime Value="8/28/2004 " />
</cc1:RestrictedCalendar>
```

The next step is to enable your control to read this custom HTML and regenerate the RestrictedDates collection at runtime. To make deserialization easier, you need to create a class that models the <DateTime> tag. In this case, the <DateTime> tag has only a single attribute named value. As a result, this following class works perfectly well:

```
public class DateTimeHelper
{
    private string val;
    public string Value
    {
        get {return val;}
        set {val = value;}
    }
}
```

Note how the public property of this class matches the serialized tag exactly. That means ASP.NET will be able to deserialize the tag into a DateTimeHelper without needing any extra help. However, you still need to take extra steps to instruct the ASP.NET parser to use the DateTimeHelper class for deserialization. Finally, you also need to write code that can examine the DateTimeHelper, and use it to configure a RestrictedCalendar instance.

In order to perform the first task of these two tasks, you need the help of a *control builder*. When ASP.NET parses a page, it enlists the help of a control builder to interpret the HTML and generate the control objects. The default control builder simply examines the ParseChildren attribute for the control, and then tries to interpret the nested tags as properties (if ParseChildren is true) or child controls (if ParseChildren is false). The custom control builder that the RestrictedCalendar will use overrides the GetChildControlType(), which is called every time the parser finds a nested tag.

The GetChildControlType() method examines a nested tag, and then returns a Type object that tells the parser what type of child object to create. In this case, your custom control builder should find a <DateTime> tag, and then inform the runtime to create a DateTimeHelper object.

Here's the complete control builder code:

```
public class RestrictedCalendarBuilder : ControlBuilder
{
    public override Type GetChildControlType(string tagName,
      IDictionary attribs)
    {
        if (tagName == "DateTime")
        {
            return typeof(DateTimeHelper);
        }
        return base.GetChildControlType (tagName, attribs);
    }
}
```

To associate this builder with the RestrictedCalendar control, you need to add a Designer attribute to class declaration:

```
[ControlBuilder(typeof(RestrictedCalendarBuilder))]
[ParseChildren(false)]
[Designer(typeof(RestrictedCalendarDesigner))]
public class RestrictedCalendar : Calendar
{ ... }
```

Your odyssey still isn't quite complete. Now the ASP.NET parser can successfully create the DateTimeHelper object, but it doesn't know what to do with it. Because you've set ParseChildren to false, the parser won't attempt to recognize it as a property. Instead, it will call the AddParsedSubObject() method of your control class, which will fail because the DateTimeHelper isn't a control and can't be added to the Controls collection. Fortunately, you can override the AddParsedSubObject() method to provide more suitable functionality. In this case, you need to take the supplied DataTimeHelper object, and use it to add a new DateTime to the NonSelectableDates collection, as shown here:

```
protected override void AddParsedSubObject(object obj)
{
    if (obj is DateTimeHelper)
    {
        DateTimeHelper date = (DateTimeHelper)obj;
        NonSelectableDates.Add(DateTime.Parse(date.Value));
    }
}
```

Now you've finished all the code required to both serialize and parse the custom HTML content. This process clearly wasn't easy, and it demonstrates that though basic design-time support is easy, advanced custom control design is a highly complex topic. To become an expert, you'll need to study the MSDN documentation, or continue your exploration with another dedicated book about server controls.

Type Editors

So far you've seen how type converters can convert various data types to strings for representation in the Properties window. But some data types don't rely on string editing at all. For example, if you need to set an enumerated value (like BorderStyle) you can choose from a drop-down list of all the values in the enumeration. More impressively, if you need to set a color you can choose from a drop-down color picker. And some properties have the ability to break out of the Properties window altogether. One example is the Columns property of the DataGrid. If you click the ellipsis next to the property name, a dialog box will appear where you can configure the column collection using a rich user interface. The RestrictedCalendar in the previous example showed a similar, but less impressive example with the collection editor for editing restricted dates.

These properties all rely on *UI type editors.* Type editors have a single task in life—they generate user interfaces that allow you to set control properties more conveniently. Certain data types (like collections, enumerations, and colors) are automatically associated with advanced type editors. In other cases, you might want to create your own type editor classes from scratch. All UI type editors are located in the System.Drawing.Design namespace.

Just as with type converters (and almost everything in the extensible architecture of .NET design-time support), creating a new type editor involves inheriting a base class (in this case UITypeEditor) and overriding desired members. The methods you can override include the following:

- **GetEditStyle().** Specifies whether the type editor is a DropDown (provides a list of specially drawn choices), Modal (provides a dialog box for property selection), or None (no editing supported).

- **EditValue().** This method is invoked when property is edited (for example, the ellipsis next to the property name is clicked in the Properties window). Generally, this is where you would create a special dialog box for property editing.

- **GetPaintValueSupported().** Use this to return true if you are providing a PaintValue() implementation.

- **PaintValue().** Invoked to paint a graphical thumbnail that represents the value in the property grid. For example, this is used to create the color box for color properties.

The code for UI type editors isn't overly complicated, but it can take a bit of getting used to for web developers. That's because it involves using the other user interface platform in .NET—Windows Forms. Although the topic of Windows Forms is outside the scope of this book, you can learn a lot from a basic example. Figure 21-8 shows a custom color editing control that allows you to set various components of a color independently using sliders. As you do, it displays the color in a box at the bottom of the control.

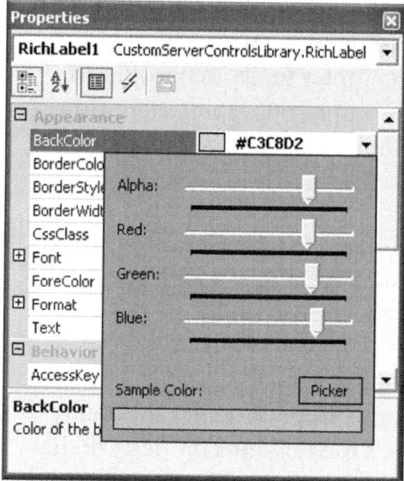

Figure 21-8. *Using a custom type editor*

The code for the actual control isn't shown here, but you can refer to the downloadable examples for this chapter to take closer look. However, the full code for the type editor that uses this control is as follows:

```
public class ColorTypeEditor : UITypeEditor
{
    public override UITypeEditorEditStyle GetEditStyle(
      ITypeDescriptorContext context)
    {
        // This editor appears when you click a drop-down arrow.
        return UITypeEditorEditStyle.DropDown;
    }

    public override object EditValue(ITypeDescriptorContext context,
      IServiceProvider provider, object value)
    {
        IWindowsFormsEditorService srv = null;

        // Get the editor service from the provider,
        // which you need to create the drop-down window.
        if (provider != null)
            srv = (IWindowsFormsEditorService)
        provider.GetService(typeof(IWindowsFormsEditorService));

        if (srv != null)
        {
            // Create an instance of the custom Windows Forms
            // color-picking control.
```

```
                    // Pass the current value of the color.
                    ColorTypeEditorControl editor =
                      new ColorTypeEditorControl((System.Drawing.Color)value,
                      context.Instance as WebControl);

                    // Show the control.
                    srv.DropDownControl(editor);

                    // Return the selected color information.
                    return editor.SelectedColor;
                }
                else
                {
                    // Return the current value.
                    return value;
                }
            }
        }

        public override bool GetPaintValueSupported(ITypeDescriptorContext context)
        {
            // This type editor will generate a color box thumbnail.
            return true;
        }

        public override void PaintValue(PaintValueEventArgs e)
        {
            // Fills the left rectangle with a color.
            WebControl control = e.Context.Instance as WebControl;
            e.Graphics.FillRegion(new SolidBrush(control.BackColor),
              new Region(e.Bounds));
        }
    }
}
```

To use this type editor, you need to attach it to a property that uses the Color data type. Most web controls already include color properties, but there's no reason you can't override one of them and apply a new Editor attribute.

Here's an example that does exactly that to attach the type editor to the BackColor property of the RichLabel control:

```
[Editor(typeof(ColorTypeEditor), typeof(UITypeEditor))]
public override Color BackColor
{
    get {return base.BackColor;}
    set {base.BackColor = value;}
}
```

Control Designers

You've probably noticed that custom controls aren't all treated the same on the design surface. ASP.NET tries to show a realistic design-time representation by running the rendering logic, but there are exceptions. For example, composite and templated controls aren't rendered at all in the design-time environment, which means you're left with nothing but a blank rectangle on your design surface.

To deal with these issues, controls often use custom control designers that produce basic HTML that's only intended for design-time display. This display can be a sophisticated block of HTML that's designed to reflect the real appearance of the control, a basic snapshot that shows a typical example of the control (as you'll see for a DataGrid that doesn't have any configured columns), or just a gray placeholder box with a message (as shown for the Repeater and DataList when they don't have any templates).

If you want to customize the design-time HTML for your control, you can derive a custom designer from the ControlDesigner base class, and override one of the following three methods:

- **GetDesignTimeHtml().** Returns the HTML that's used to represent the current state of the control at design time. The default implementation of this method simply returns the result of calling the RenderControl() method.

- **GetEmptyDesignTimeHtml().** Returns the HTML that's used to represent an empty control. The default implementation simply returns a string that contains the name of the control class and the ID.

- **GetErrorDesignTimeHtml().** Returns the HTML that's used if a design-time error occurs in the control. This HTML can provide information about the exception (which is passed as an argument to this method).

Of course, these methods only reflect a small portion of the functionality that's available through the ControlDesigner. There are many more methods you can override to configure different aspects of design-time behavior. In the following section, you'll see how to create a control designer that adds enhanced support for the SuperSimpleRepeater.

A Basic Control Designer

The next example develops a control designer that generates a reasonable representation for the SuperSimpleRepeater developed in the last chapter. Without a custom control designer, the design-time content of the SuperSimpleRepeater is an empty string.

The first step in creating a designer is to build a class that derives from the ControlDesigner namespace in the System.Web.UI.Design namespace.

```
public class SuperSimpleRepeaterDesigner : ControlDesigner
{ ... }
```

You can apply the designer to the control using the Designer attribute:

```
[Designer(typeof(SuperSimpleRepeaterDesigner))]
public class SuperSimpleRepeater : WebControl, INamingContainer
{ ... }
```

When creating a control designer, the first step is to create the GetEmptyDesignTimeHtml() method. This method simply needs to return a static piece of text. The ControlDesigner includes a helper method named CreatePlaceHolderDesignTimeHtml(), which generates a gray HTML box with a message that you specify (just like the Repeater control without any templates). You can use this method to simplify your rendering code, as shown here:

```
protected override string GetEmptyDesignTimeHtml()
{
    string text = "Switch to design view to add a template to this control.";
    return CreatePlaceHolderDesignTimeHtml(text);
}
```

Figure 21-9 shows the empty design-time view of the SuperSimpleRepeater control.

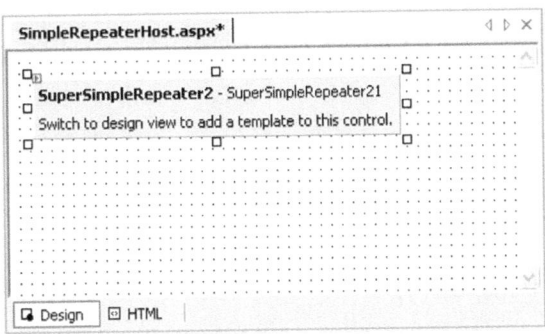

Figure 21-9. *The empty design-time HTML*

> ■**Note** Keep in mind that ASP.NET isn't able to decide when your control is empty. Instead, you'll need to call the GetEmptyDesignTimeHtml() method when needed. As you'll see in this example, the GetDesignTimeHtml() method calls GetEmptyDesignTimeHtml() if a template isn't present.

Coding the GetErrorDesignTimeHtml() method is just as easy. Once again, you can use the CreatePlaceHolderDesignTimeHtml() method, but this time you should supply the details about the exception that occurred.

```
protected override string GetErrorDesignTimeHtml(Exception e)
{
    string text = string.Format("{0}{1}{2}{3}",
      "There was an error and the control can't be displayed.",
      "<BR>", "Exception: ", e.Message);
    return CreatePlaceHolderDesignTimeHtml(text);
}
```

The final step is to build the GetDesignTimeHtml() method. This code retrieves the current instance of the SuperSimpleRepeater control from the ControlDesigner.Component property. It then checks for an item template. If no template is present, the empty HTML is shown. If a template is present, the control is data bound, and *then* the design-time HTML is displayed, as follows:

```
public override string GetDesignTimeHtml()
{
    try
    {
        SuperSimpleRepeater repeater = (SuperSimpleRepeater1)base.Component;
        if (repeater.ItemTemplate == null)
        {
            return GetEmptyDesignTimeHtml();
        }
        else
        {
            String designTimeHtml = String.Empty;
            repeater.DataBind();
            designTimeHtml = base.GetDesignTimeHtml();
            return designTimeHtml;
        }
        return base.GetDesignTimeHtml();
    }
    catch (Exception e)
    {
        return GetErrorDesignTimeHtml(e);
    }
}
```

This produces the vastly improved design-time representation shown in Figure 21-10, which closely resembles the actual runtime appearance of the SuperSimpleRepeater.

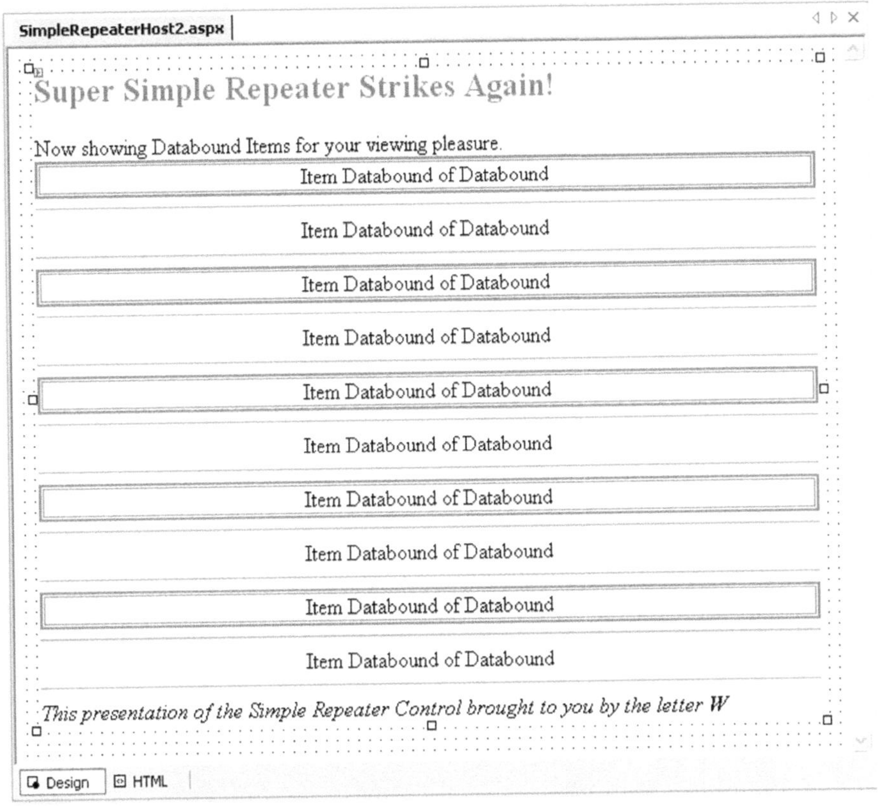

Figure 21-10. *The improved design-time representation*

Summary

In this chapter, you've taken a tour through some of the simple and complex aspects of the .NET design-time architecture. You've learned how to configure the way control properties are displayed in the Properties window, and how to take charge of control serialization and parsing. For many more advanced topics, like custom control designers, you can consult the MSDN documentation.

■ ■ ■

JavaScript

ASP.NET provides a rich server-based programming model. The postback architecture allows you to perform all your work with object-oriented programming languages on the server, which ensures that your code is secure and compatible with all browsers. However, the postback architecture has its weaknesses. Because there's always a small but noticeable over-head to post back the page, it's impossible to react efficiently to mouse movements and key presses. Additionally, there are some tasks—like showing pop-up windows, providing a real-time status message, and communicating between frames—that need browser interaction and just aren't possible with server-side programming.

To compensate for these problems, experienced ASP.NET developers sometimes use client-side programming to supplement their server-side web-page code. This client-side script allows you to make more responsive pages, and accomplish some feats that wouldn't otherwise be possible. Often, these considerations occur when creating custom controls that render rich user interface (like pop-up menus or rollover buttons). For the greatest browser compatibility, the client-side script language of choice is JavaScript.

JavaScript Essentials

JavaScript is an embedded language. That means that JavaScript code is inserted directly into another document—typically, an HTML web page. The code is downloaded to the client com-puter, and executed by the browser.

There are two ways to embed JavaScript code in a web page:

- You can embed the code directly in an event attribute for an HTML element. This is the most straightforward approach for small amounts of code.

- You can add a <script> tag that contains the JavaScript code. You can choose to run this code automatically when the page loads, or you can create a JavaScript function that will be called in response to a client-side event.

In many cases, you'll use both of these techniques at the same time. For example, you might define a function in a <script> block, and then wire this function up to a client-side event using an event attribute. ASP.NET follows this pattern when it performs automatic post-backs. The __doPostBack() function defines the code needed to set the appropriate event information for every control, and it's rendered inside a <script> block. The __doPostBack() function is then connected to different controls using JavaScript event attributes like onClick.

It's important to realize that whether you use <script> blocks, event attributes, or both, you have two choices. Your first option is to add static JavaScript code to the .aspx portion of your page. The second option is to add JavaScript code dynamically by using the methods of the Page class. This gives you the greatest flexibility, including the ability to tweak the JavaScript on the fly and decide what you want to render at runtime. When you create custom controls, the controls render the JavaScript they need in this way.

The followings sections explore the basic techniques for using JavaScript. You'll learn how to use JavaScript event attributes, script blocks, and the methods of the Page class for rendering JavaScript.

Note   You can also use VBScript if your web application exists on a company intranet where Internet Explorer is the standard. However, JavaScript is the only standard supported by a wide range of browsers.

JavaScript Events

JavaScript supports a rich set of client-side events. These events are listed in Table 22-1.

Table 22-1. *Commonly Supported JavaScript Events*

Event	Description	Applies To
onChange	Occurs when the user changes value in an input control. In text controls, this event fires after the user changes focus to another control.	select, text, text area
onClick	Occurs when the user clicks a control.	button, check box, radio, link, area
onMouseOver	Occurs when the user moves the mouse pointer over a control.	link, area
onMouseOut	Occurs when the user moves the mouse pointer away from a control.	link, area
onKeyUp	Occurs when the user presses a key.	text, text area
onKeyDown	Occurs when the user releases a pressed key.	text, text area
onSelect	Occurs when the user selects a portion of text in an input control.	text, text area
onFocus	Occurs when a control receives focus.	select, text, text area
onBlur	Occurs when focus leaves a control.	select, text, text area
onAbort	Occurs when the user cancels an image download.	image
onError	Occurs when an image can't be downloaded (probably due to an incorrect URL).	image
onLoad	Occurs when a new page finishes downloading.	window, location
onUnload	Occurs when a page is unloaded (typically just after a new URL has been entered or a link has been clicked, just before the new page is downloaded).	window

The combination of JavaScript and the HTML document model is called DHTML (Dynamic HTML). As usual in the world of the Web, not all browsers support the same level of DHTML. As a result, the events you can use, the elements you can manipulate, and the way events work vary from browser to browser. However, Table 22-1 lists a core set of events that is usually safe to use in any browser that supports JavaScript. As usual, if you are creating a web application for a large number of users, you must perform extensive testing.

Tip You can find event compatibility tables on the Internet (see for example www.quirksmode.org/js/ events_compinfo.html). For a comprehensive introduction to DHTML, you can refer to the MSDN website at http://msdn.microsoft.com/workshop/author/dhtml/dhtml.asp. A full JavaScript reference is provided by at http://devedge.netscape.com/library/manuals.

You can insert JavaScript code for any of the attributes listed in Table 22-1. For example, the following web page adds the onMouseOver attribute to two text box controls:

```
private void Page_Load(object sender, System.EventArgs e)
{
    TextBox1.Attributes.Add("onMouseOver",
      "alert('Your mouse is hovering on TextBox1.');");
    TextBox2.Attributes.Add("onMouseOver",
      "alert('Your mouse is hovering on TextBox2.');");
}
```

When the user moves the mouse over the appropriate text box, the event occurs, and the JavaScript alert() function is called, which shows a message box (as shown in Figure 22-1).

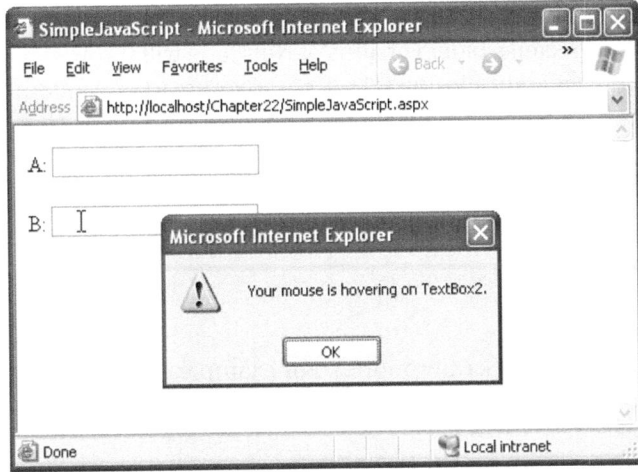

Figure 22-1. *Responding to a JavaScript event*

■Note Keep in mind that ASP.NET already uses the onChange event to enable automatic postback. If you add the onChange attribute and set the AutoPostBack property to true, ASP.NET is intelligent enough to add both your JavaScript and the __doPostBack() function call to the attribute. Your client-side JavaScript code will be executed first, followed by the __doPostBack() function.

Script Blocks

It's impractical to place a large amount of JavaScript code in an attribute, particularly if you need to use the same code for several controls. A more common approach is to place a JavaScript function in a <script> block, and then call that function using an event attribute.

The <script> tag can appear anywhere in the header or the body of an HTML document, and a single document can have any number of <script> tags in it. However, everything in the document is processed in the order in which it appears in the file, from top to bottom. In other words, if you need to call a function, that function must be defined in a <script> block before the event attribute that calls it.

The <script> tag takes a language attribute that specifies the language and version. Browsers will ignore <script> blocks for languages or language versions they don't support (although there are certain quirks).

A typical inline script looks like this:

```
<script language="JavaScript">
  <!--
  window.alert('This windows displayed through JavaScript.');
  // -->
</script>
```

In this case, the HTML comment markers (<!-- and -->) hide the content from browsers that don't understand script. Additionally, the closing HTML comment marker (-->) is preceded by a JavaScript comment (//). This is because older versions of Netscape will throw a JavaScript parsing exception when encountering the closing HTML comment marker. Modern browsers don't suffer from these problems, and most browsers now recognize the <script> tag (even if they don't support JavaScript).

You can also use the src attribute to reference an external file containing JavaScript, as shown here:

```
<script language="JavaScript" src="ExternalJavaScript.js">
</script>
```

This technique is often used with complex JavaScript routines. For example, the ASP.NET validation controls use a JavaScript file on the web server named WebUIValidation.js.

■Note Placing JavaScript in a separate file doesn't prevent users from retrieving it, examining it (and even modifying their local copy of the web page to use a tampered version of the script file). Therefore, you should never include any secret algorithms or information in your JavaScript code. You should also make sure that you repeat any JavaScript validation steps on the server, because the user can circumvent them.

Creating a JavaScript Page Processor

How many times have you clicked a web page just to watch that Internet Explorer globe spin for what seems like an eternity? Did your Internet connection go down? Was there any error connecting to a back-end system? Or is the system just that slow? These issues often compli-cate the deployment of new web-based solutions, particularly if you're moving from an internal forms-based system that may appear to be more responsive. In this situation, the easiest way to help get the users back on your side is by providing them with messages along the way to let them know that the system is currently working on their request.

One common way to give a status message is to use JavaScript to create a standard page processor. When the user navigates to a page that takes a long time to process, the page processor appears immediately, and shows a standard message (perhaps with scrolling text). At the same time, the requested page is downloaded in the background. Once the results are available, the page processor message is replaced by the requested page.

You can't solve the processing delay problem by adding JavaScript code to the target page, because this code won't be processed until the page has finished processing and the rendered HTML is returned to the user. However, you *can* create a generic page processor that can han-dle requests for any other page.

In order to create a page processor, you need to react to the onLoad and onUnload events. Here's a page that defines a table with the message text "Loading Page - Please Wait." The <body> element is wired up to two functions, which aren't shown here:

```
<HTML>
  <head>
    <title>LoadPage</title>
    <script> <!-- JavaScript functions go here. --> </script>
  </head>
  <body onLoad="javascript:BeginPageLoad();"
        onUnload="javascript:EndPageLoad();">
    <form id="frmPageLoader" method="post" runat="server">
      <table border="0" cellpadding="0" cellspacing="0"
       width="99%" height="99%" align="center" vAlign="middle">
        <tr>
          <td align="center" vAlign="center">
            <font color=Navy size=5>
            <span id="MessageText">Loading Page - Please Wait</span>
            <span id="ProgressMeter"
             style="width:25px;text-align:left;"></span>
            </font>
          </td>
        </tr>
      </table>
    </form>
  </body>
</HTML>
```

This page is saved as PageProcessor.aspx. In order to use the page processor, you request this page, and pass the desired page as a query string argument. For example, if you want to load TimeConsumingPage.aspx in the background, you would use this query string:

```
PageProcessor.aspx?Page=TimeConsumingPage.aspx
```

The page processor needs very little server-side code. In fact, all it does is retrieve the originally requested page from the query string and store it in a protected page class variable. This variable can then be accessed by data-binding expressions in the .aspx file. Here's the complete page code:

```
public class PageProcessor : System.Web.UI.Page
{
    // Designer code omitted.
    protected string PageToLoad;

    private void Page_Load(object sender, System.EventArgs e)
    {
        PageToLoad = Request.QueryString["Page"];
    }
}
```

The page is then rendered and sent to the client. The rest of the work is performed with client-side JavaScript. When the page processor first loads, the onLoad event fires, which calls the client-side BeginPageLoad() function. The BeginPageLoad() function keeps the current window open and begins retrieving the page that the user requested. In order to accomplish this, it uses the window.setInterval() method, which sets a timer that calls the custom UpdateProgressMeter() function periodically.

Here's the code for the BeginPageLoad() JavaScript function:

```
var iLoopCounter = 1;
var iMaxLoop = 6;
var iIntervalId;

function BeginPageLoad()
{
  /* Redirect the browser to another page while keeping focus */
  location.href = "<%=PageToLoad %>";
  /* Update progress meter every 1/2 second */
  iIntervalId = window.setInterval
      ("iLoopCounter=UpdateProgressMeter(iLoopCounter,iMaxLoop)", 500);
}
```

Notice that the page you want to download isn't hard-coded in the JavaScript code. Instead, it's extracted using the data-binding expression <%=PageToLoad %>. When the page is rendered on the server, ASP.NET automatically inserts the actual name of the page from the PageToLoad variable.

The BeginPageLoad() function is only part of the solution. You also need another custom JavaScript function in your web page, which is named UpdateProgressMeter().

The UpdateProgressMeter() function is called periodically on a timer. When it's triggered, it simply adds periods to the status message to make it look more like an animated progress meter. It cycles repeatedly from 0 to 5 periods.

Here's the JavaScript code for the UpdateProgressMeter() function:

```
function UpdateProgressMeter(iCurrentLoopCounter, iMaximumLoops)
{
  iCurrentLoopCounter += 1;
  if(iCurrentLoopCounter <= iMaximumLoops)
  {
    ProgressMeter.innerText += ".";
    return iCurrentLoopCounter
  }
  else
  {
    ProgressMeter.innerText = "";
    return 1;
  }
}
```

Finally, when the page is fully loaded, the client-side onUnload event fires, which triggers the EndPageLoad() JavaScript function. This function clears the progress message, and sets a temporary transfer message that disappears as soon as the new page is rendered in the browser. Here's the code:

```
function EndPageLoad()
{
  window.clearInterval(iIntervalId);
  ProgressMeter.innerText = "Page Loaded - Now Transfering";
}
```

No postbacks are made through the whole process. The end result is a progress message (see Figure 22-2) that remains until the target page is fully processed and loaded.

To test the page processor, you simply need to use a target page that takes a long time to execute on the server (because of the work performed by the code) or to be downloaded in the client (because of the size of the page). You can simulate a slow page by placing the following time delay code in the target page:

```
private void Page_Load(object sender, System.EventArgs e)
{
    // Simulate a slow page loading (wait ten seconds).
    System.Threading.Thread.Sleep(10000);
}
```

As you can see, with just a small amount of client-side JavaScript code, you can keep the user informed that a page is processing. By keeping users informed, the level of perceived performance increases.

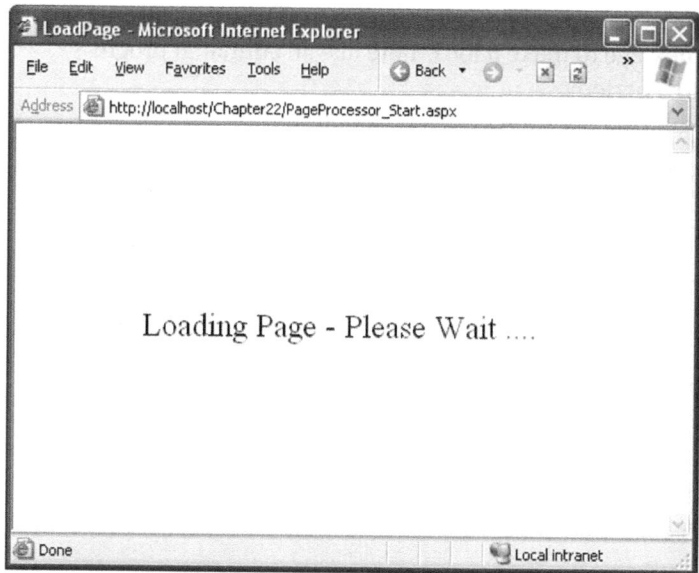

Figure 22-2. *An automated progress meter*

Using JavaScript to Download Images Asynchronously

The previous example demonstrated how JavaScript can help you create a more responsive interface. This advantage isn't limited to page processors. You can also use JavaScript to download time-consuming portions of a page in the background. Often, this requires a little more work, but it can provide a much better user experience.

For example, consider a case where you're displaying a list of records in a DataGrid. One of the fields displays a small image. This technique, which was demonstrated in Chapter 13, requires a dedicated page to retrieve the image and, depending on your design, it may require a separate trip to the file system or database for each individual record. In many cases you can optimize this design (for example, by preloading images in the cache before you bind the grid), but this won't be possible if the images are retrieved from a third-party source. This is exactly the case in the next example, which displays a list of books and retrieves the associated images from the Amazon website.

Rendering the full table can take a significant amount of time, especially if there are a large number of records. You can deal with this situation more effectively by using placeholder images that appear immediately. The actual images can be retrieved in the background and displayed once they're available. The time required to display the complete grid with all its pictures won't change, but the user will be able to start reading and scrolling through the data before the images have been downloaded, which makes the slowdown easier to bear.

The first step in this example is to create the page that displays the DataGrid. For the purposes of this example, the code fills a DataSet with a static list of books from an XML file:

```
private void Page_Load(object sender, System.EventArgs e)
{
    if (!Page.IsPostBack)
    {
```

```
        // Get data.
        DataSet ds = new DataSet();
        ds.ReadXml(Server.MapPath("Books.xml"));
        DataGrid1.DataSource = ds.Tables["Book"];
        DataGrid1.DataBind();
    }
}
```

Here's the content of the XML file:

```
<?xml version="1.0" encoding="utf-8" ?>
<Books>
    <Book Title="Expert C# Business Objects" isbn="1590593448"
     Publisher="Apress"></Book>
    <Book Title="C# and the .NET Platform" isbn="1590590554"
     Publisher="Apress"></Book>
    <Book Title="Beginning XSLT" isbn="1590592603"
     Publisher="Apress"></Book>
    <Book Title="SQL Server Security Distilled" isbn="1590592190"
     Publisher="Apress"></Book>
</Books>
```

As you can see, the XML data doesn't include any picture information. Instead, these details need to be retrieved from the Amazon website. The DataGrid binds directly to the columns that are available (Title, isbn, and Publisher) and then uses another page (named GetBookImage.aspx) to find the corresponding image for this ISBN.

Here's the DataGrid tag without the style information:

```
<asp:DataGrid id="DataGrid1" runat="server" AutoGenerateColumns="False">
  <Columns>
    <asp:BoundColumn DataField="Title" HeaderText="Title"/>
    <asp:BoundColumn DataField="isbn" HeaderText="ISBN"/>
    <asp:BoundColumn DataField="Publisher" HeaderText="Publisher"/>
    <asp:TemplateColumn>
      <HeaderTemplate>
        Book Cover
      </HeaderTemplate>
      <ItemTemplate>
        <img src="UnknownBook.gif"
          onerror="javascript:this.src='Unknownbook.gif'"
          onload=
      "javascript:this.src='GetBookImage.aspx?isbn=
      <%# DataBinder.Eval(Container.DataItem, "isbn") %>';">
      </ItemTemplate>
    </asp:TemplateColumn>
  </Columns>
</asp:DataGrid>
```

The innovative part is the last column, which contains an <img> tag. Rather than pointing this tag directly to GetBookImage.aspx, the src attribute is set to a local image file (UnknownBook.gif), which can be quickly downloaded and displayed. Then the onLoad event (which occurs as soon as the UnknownBook.gif image is first displayed) begins downloading the real image from the GetBookImage.aspx page, in the background. When the real image is retrieved, it's displayed, unless an error occurs during the download process. The onError event is handled in order to ensure that if an error occurs the UnknownBook.gif image remains (rather than the red X error icon).

The GetBookImage.aspx performs the time-consuming task of retrieving the image, which can involve contacting a web service or connecting to a database. In this case, it simply hands the work off to a dedicated class named FindBook. Once the URL is retrieved, it redirects the page:

```
private void Page_Load(object sender, System.EventArgs e)
{
    FindBook findBook = new FindBook();
    string imageUrl = findBook.GetImageUrl(Request.QueryString["isbn"]);
    Response.Redirect(imageUrl);
}
```

The FindBook class is more complex. It uses screen scraping to find the <img> tag for the picture on the Amazon website. Unfortunately, there is no clear naming convention for Amazon's image thumbnails that would allow you to retrieve the URL directly. However, based on the ISBN you can find the book detail page, and you can look through the HTML of the book detail page to find the image URL. That's the task the FindBook class performs.

There are two methods at work in the FindBook class. The GetWebPageAsString() method requests a URL, retrieves the HTML content, and converts it to a string, as shown here:

```
public string GetWebPageAsString(string url)
{
    // Create the request.
    WebRequest requestHtml = WebRequest.Create(url);

    // Get the response.
    WebResponse responseHtml = requestHtml.GetResponse();

    // Read the response stream.
    StreamReader r = new StreamReader(responseHtml.GetResponseStream());
    string htmlContent = r.ReadToEnd();
    r.Close();
    return htmlContent;
}
```

The GetImageUrl() method uses GetWebPageAsString(), and a little regular expression wizardry. Amazon image URLs take the form shown here:

```
http://images.amazon.com/images/P/" + [ISBN] + [some character sequence]
```

Using the regular expression, the code matches the full URL (with the ending character sequence, and returns it). Here's the complete code:

```
public string GetImageUrl(string isbn)
{
    try
    {
        // Find the pointer to the book cover image.
        // Amazon.com has the most cover images,
        // so go there to look for it.
        // Start with the book details page.
        isbn = isbn.Replace("-", "");
        string bookUrl = "http://www.amazon.com/exec/obidos/ASIN/" + isbn;

        // Now retrieve the HTML content of the book details page.
        string bookHtml = GetWebPageAsString(bookUrl);

        // Search the page for an image tag that has the requested ISBN.
        string imgTagPattern =
          "<img src=\"(http://images.amazon.com/images/P/" + isbn +
          "[^\"]+)\"";
        Match imgTagMatch = Regex.Match(bookHtml, imgTagPattern);
        return imgTagMatch.Groups[1].Value;
    }
    catch
    {
        return "";
    }
}
```

■**Note** Using the dedicated Amazon web service would obviously be a more flexible and robust approach, although it wouldn't change this example, which demonstrates the performance enhancements of a little JavaScript. Web services are dealt with in Part Five, and you can get information about Amazon's offerings at www.amazon.com/gp/aws/landing.html.

The end result is a page that initially loads with default images, as shown in Figure 22-3.

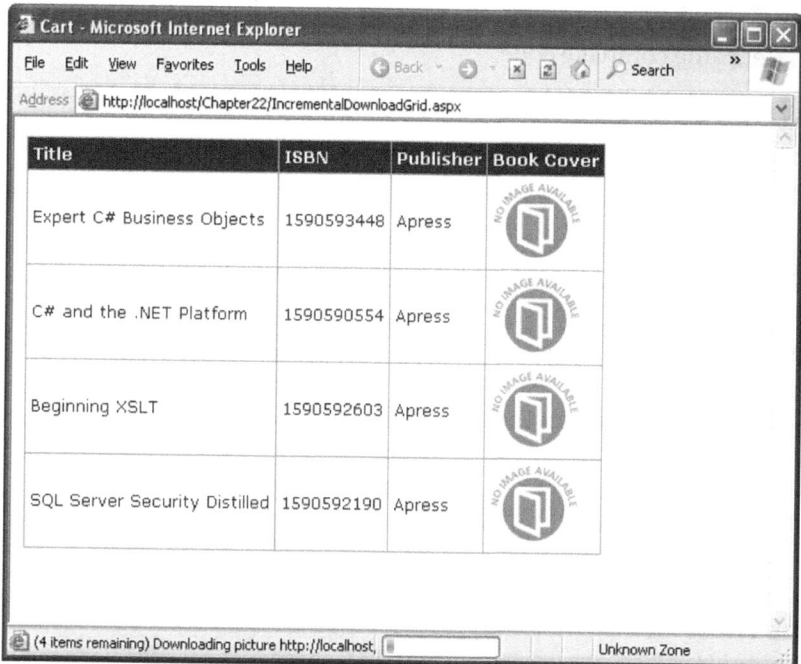

Figure 22-3. *The initial view of the page*

After a short delay, the images will begin to appear, as shown in Figure 22-4.

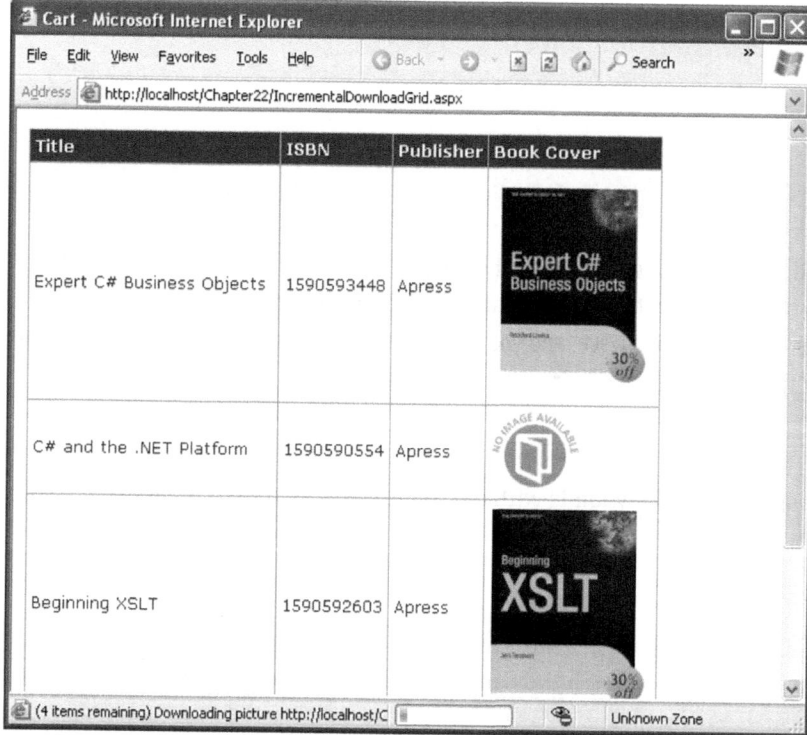

Figure 22-4. *The page with image thumbnails*

Once loaded, the real book images will load in the background, but the user can begin using the page immediately.

Tip This technique becomes particularly powerful when combined with a little DHTML know-how. For example, you could download a portion of a page in the background and insert it when it's available. Creating this effect is more work (and is notoriously difficult to support on different browsers), but it is an interesting technique.

Rendering Script Blocks

So far the examples you've seen have made use of static <script> blocks that are inserted directly in the .aspx portion of your page. However, it's often more flexible to render the script using the following two methods in the Page class:

- **RegisterClientScriptBlock().** Writes a script block at the beginning of the web form, right after the <form runat="server"> tag.

- **RegisterStartupScript().** Writes a script block at the beginning of the web form, right before the closing </form> tag.

These two methods perform the same task—they take a string input with the <script> block and add it to the rendered HTML. RegisterClientScriptBlock() is designed for functions that are called in response to JavaScript events. These <script> blocks can be placed anywhere in the HTML document. Placing them at the beginning of the web form is just a matter of convention, and makes them easy to find. The RegisterStartupScript() is meant to add JavaScript code that will be executed immediately when the page loads. This code might manipulate other controls on the page, so to be safe it should be placed at the end of the web form. Otherwise, it might try to manipulate elements that haven't been created yet.

When you use RegisterClientScriptBlock() and RegisterStartupScript(), you also specify a key name for the script block. For example, if your function opens a pop-up window, you might use the key name ShowPopUp. The actual key name isn't important as long as it's unique. The purpose is to ensure that ASP.NET doesn't add the same script function more than once. This scenario is most important when dealing with server controls that render JavaScript. For example, consider the ASP.NET validation controls. Every validation control requires the use of certain validation functions, but it doesn't make sense for each control to add a duplication <script> block. But because each control uses the same key name when it calls RegisterClientScriptBlock(), ASP.NET realizes they are duplicate definitions, and it only renders a single copy.

For example, the following code registers a JavaScript function named confirmSubmit(). This function displays a confirmation box and, depending on whether the user clicks OK or Cancel, either posts back the page or does nothing. This function is then attached to a button through the onClick attribute.

```
private void Page_Load(object sender, System.EventArgs e)
{
    string script = @"<script language='JavaScript'>
```

```
      function confirmSubmit() {
        var doc = document.forms[0];
        var msg = 'Are you sure you want to submit this data?';
        if (confirm(msg))
        {
          doc.submit();
        }
        else
        {
          // Do nothing.
        }
      }
    </script>";

    Page.RegisterClientScriptBlock("Confirm", script);
    cmdSubmit.Attributes.Add("onClick", "confirmSubmit();");
}
```

■**Note** To make it easier to define a JavaScript function over multiple lines, you can precede the string with the @ symbol. That way, all the characters are treated as string literals, and you can span multiple lines.

Figure 22-5 shows the result.

Figure 22-5. *Using a JavaScript confirmation message*

In the next section, you'll see a practical example that makes use of the RegisterStartupScript() method.

Using JavaScript to Set Control Focus

The ASP.NET web control model doesn't provide any feature that allows you to set which control has focus when the page is sent to the client. Although web controls provide a TabIndex property that allows you to set the tab order, this property only applies to Microsoft Internet Explorer.

This limitation is easily conquered with a little snippet of JavaScript code and the RegisterStartupScript() method. The basic approach is to create a snippet of JavaScript code that runs when the page first loads. This code can use the JavaScript focus() method of the corresponding element to set the focus.

Here's a server-side method that generalizes this task. It examines a control object, retrieves the corresponding client ID, and creates and registers the required startup <script> block.

```
private void SetFocus(Control ctrl)
{
    string script = @"<script language='JavaScript'>
      "document.getElementById("'" + ctrl.ClientID +
      "').focus();</script>";

    RegisterStartupScript("SetFocus", script);
}
```

You can use this method elsewhere in your page code to control which control will have the focus. You can even call this method more than once—because the key is the same, only the last version will be emitted into the page.

Here's an example that sets the control focus when the page first loads:

```
private void Page_Load(object sender, System.EventArgs e)
{
    if (!Page.IsPostBack)
    {
        // Make sure that the TextBox1 control is focused when the page
        // first loads.
        SetFocus(TextBox1);
    }
}
```

This example is a case in which static JavaScript just won't work. Instead, the RegisterStartupScript() method allows you to dynamically choose which client-side script you want to render in the page.

Custom Controls with JavaScript

JavaScript plays an important role in many advanced web controls. In an ideal world, the web-page developer never needs to worry about JavaScript at all. Instead, web-page developers program with neat object-oriented controls, which render the JavaScript they need to optimize their appearance and their performance. This gives you the best of both worlds—object-oriented programming on the server, and the client-side capabilities of JavaScript.

There's no end to the number of controls you can create with JavaScript and the HTML document model. Common examples include rich menus, trees, and lists, many of which are available (some for free) at Microsoft's www.asp.net community site. In this section, you'll consider two custom controls that use JavaScript—a pop-up window generator, and a rollover button.

Pop-Up Windows

For most people, pop-up windows are one of the Web's most annoying characteristics. Usually, they deliver advertisements, but sometimes they serve the more valid purpose of providing helpful information or inviting the user to participate in a survey or promotional offer. A related variant is the pop-under window, which displays the new window underneath the current window. This way, the advertisement doesn't distract the user until the original browser window is closed.

It's fairly easy to show a pop-up window by using the window.open() function in a JavaScript block. Here's an example:

```
<script language="javascript">
  window.open('http://www.apress.com', 'myWindow', 'toolbar=0, height=500,
              width=800, resizable=1, scrollbars=1')
  window.focus();
</script>
```

The window.open() function accepts several parameters. They include the link for the new page, and the frame name of the window (which is important if you want to load a new document into that frame later, through another link). The third parameter is a comma-separated string of attributes that configure the style and size of the pop-up window. These attributes can include any of the following:

- height and width, which are set to pixel values

- toolbar, menuBar, and scrollbars, which can be set to 1 or 0 (or yes or no) depending on if you want to display these elements

- resizable, which can be set to 1 or 0 depending on if you want a fixed or resizable window border

- scrollbars, which can be set to 1 or 0 depending on if you want to show scrollbars in the pop-up window

You can add a <script> block to your code to use the window.open() function, or you can use the window.open() function directly with a JavaScript event attribute. However, you may want to use the same functionality for several pages, and possibly tailor the pop-up URL based on user-specific information. For example, you might want to check whether the user has already seen this advertisement, or you might want to pass the user name in the query string to the new window so that it can be incorporated in a message. In these scenarios, you need some level of programmatic control, and it makes sense to create a component that wraps these details. The next example develops a PopUp control to fill this role.

By deriving this component from Control, you gain the ability to add it to the Toolbox and drop it on a web form at design time. Here's the definition for the PopUp control:

```
public class PopUp : Control
{ ... }
```

To ensure that the component is as reusable as possible, it provides properties like Scrollbars, Height, Width, Resizable, Pop, and Url, which allow you to configure the generated JavaScript. Here are the PopUp properties:

```
public bool PopUnder
{
    get {return (bool)ViewState["PopUnder"];}
    set {ViewState["PopUnder"] = value;}
}

public string Url
{
    get {return (string)ViewState["Url"];}
    set {ViewState["Url"] = value;}
}

public int WindowHeight
{
    get {return (int)ViewState["WindowHeight"];}
    set
    {
        if (value < 1)
        throw new ArgumentException("WindowHeight must be greater than 0");
        ViewState["WindowHeight"] = value;
    }
}

public int WindowWidth
{
    get {return (int)ViewState["WindowWidth"];}
    set
    {
        if (value < 1)
        throw new ArgumentException("WindowWidth must be greater than 0");
        ViewState["WindowWidth"] = value;
    }
}

public bool Resizable
{
    get {return (bool)ViewState["Resizable"];}
    set {ViewState["Resizable"] = value;}
}

public bool Scrollbars
```

```
{
    get {return (bool)ViewState["Scrollbars"];}
    set {ViewState["Scrollbars"] = value;}
}
```

Now that the control has defined these properties, it's time to put them to work in the Render() method, which writes the JavaScript to the page. The first step is to make sure that the browser supports JavaScript by examining the Page.Request.Browser.JavaScript property. If JavaScript is supported, the code uses a StringBuilder to build the script block. This code is fairly straightforward—the only unusual detail is that the Boolean Scrollbars and Resizable values need to be converted to integers and *then* to strings. That gives the required form scrollbars=1 rather than scrollbars=true (which is the text you end up with if you convert a Boolean value directly to a string).

Here's the complete rendering code:

```
protected override void Render(HtmlTextWriter writer)
{
    if (Page.Request.Browser.JavaScript)
    {
        StringBuilder javaScriptString = new StringBuilder();
        javaScriptString.Append("<script language='JavaScript'>");
        javaScriptString.Append("\n<!-- ");
        javaScriptString.Append("\nwindow.open('");
        javaScriptString.Append(Url + "', '" + ID);
        javaScriptString.Append("','toolbar=0,");
        javaScriptString.Append("height=" + (WindowHeight + ","));
        javaScriptString.Append("width=" + (WindowWidth + ","));
        javaScriptString.Append("resizable=" +
          Convert.ToInt16(Resizable).ToString() + ",");
        javaScriptString.Append("scrollbars=" +
          Convert.ToInt16(Scrollbars).ToString());
        javaScriptString.Append("');\n");
        if (PopUnder) javaScriptString.Append("window.focus();");
        javaScriptString.Append("\n-->\n");
        javaScriptString.Append("</script>\n");
        writer.Write(javaScriptString.ToString());
    }
    else
    {
        writer.Write( "<!-- This browser does not support JavaScript -->");
    }
}
```

Tip Usually, custom controls register JavaScript blocks in the OnPreRender() method, rather than writing it directly in the Render() method. However, the PopUp control bypasses this approach, and takes direct control of writing the script block. That's because you don't want the usual behavior of one script block for multiple PopUp controls. Instead, if the developer adds more than one PopUp control, you want to create a separate script block for each control. This gives the developer the ability to create pages that display multiple pop-up windows.

Figure 22-6 shows the PopUp control in action.

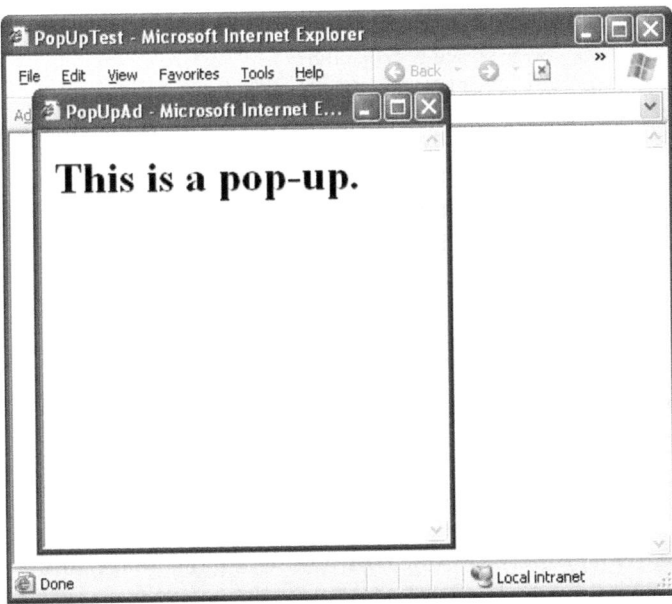

Figure 22-6. *Showing a pop-up window*

If you want to enhance the PopUp component you can add more properties. For example, you could add properties that allow you to specify the position where the window will be displayed. Some websites use advertisements that don't appear for several seconds. You could use this technique with this component by adding a JavaScript timer (and wrapping it with a control property that allows you to specify the number of seconds to wait). Once again, the basic idea is to give the page developer a neat object to program with, and use the rendering methods to generate the required JavaScript in the page.

Rollover Buttons

Another useful JavaScript trick that has no equivalent in the ASP.NET world is rollover buttons. A rollover button displays one image when it first appears and another image when the mouse hovers over it (and sometimes a third image when it's clicked).

To provide the rollover effect, a rollover button usually consists of an <img> tag that handles the onClick, onMouseOver, and onMouseOut JavaScript events. These events will call a function that swaps images for the current button, like this:

```
<script language='JavaScript'>
function swapImg(id, url) {
   elm = document.getElementById(id);
   if(elm) elm.src=url;
 }
</script>
```

A configured <img> tag would then look like this:

```
<img src="buttonOriginal.jpg"
 onMouseOver="swapImg('RollOverButton1', 'buttonMouseOver.jpg');"
 onMouseOut="swapImg('RollOverButton1', 'buttonOriginal.jpg');" />
```

Rollover buttons are a mainstay on the Web, and it's fairly easy to fill the gap in ASP.NET with a custom control. The easiest way to create this control is to derive from the WebControl class, and use <img> as the base tag. You also need to implement the IPostBackEventHandler to allow the button to trigger a server-side event when clicked.

Here's the declaration for the RollOverButton and its constructor:

```
public class RollOverButton : WebControl, IPostBackEventHandler
{
    public RollOverButton() : base(HtmlTextWriterTag.Img)
    { ... }
    // Other code omitted.
}
```

The RollOverButton class provides two properties—one URL for the original image, and another URL for the image that should be shown when the user moves the mouse over the button. Here are the property definitions:

```
public string ImageUrl
{
    get {return (string)ViewState["ImageUrl"];}
    set {ViewState["ImageUrl"] = value;}
}

public string MouseOverImageUrl
{
    get {return (string)ViewState["MouseOverImageUrl"];}
    set {ViewState["MouseOverImageUrl"] = value;}
}
```

The next step is to have the control emit the client-side JavaScript that can swap between the two pictures. In this case, it's quite likely that there will be multiple RollOverButton instances on the same page. That means you need to register the script block with a control-specific key so that no matter how many buttons you add there's only a single instance of the

function. By convention, this script block is registered by overriding the OnPreRender()
method, which is called just before the rendering process starts, as shown here:

```
protected override void OnPreRender(EventArgs e)
{
    if (!Page.IsClientScriptBlockRegistered("swapImg"))
    {
        string script =
          "<script language='JavaScript'> " +
          "function swapImg(id, url) { " +
          "elm = document.getElementById(id); " +
          "if(elm) elm.src=url; }" +
          "</script> ";
        Page.RegisterClientScriptBlock("swapImg", script);
    }
    base.OnPreRender (e);
}
```

This code explicitly checks whether the script block has been registered using the
IsClientScriptBlockRegistered() method. You don't actually need to test this property; as long
as you use the same key, ASP.NET will only render a single instance of the script block. However, you can use the IsClientScriptBlockRegistered() and the IsStartupScriptRegistered()
methods to avoid performing potentially time-consuming work. In this example, it saves the
minor overhead of constructing the script block string if you don't need it.

Remember that because RollOverButton derives from WebControl and uses <img> as the
base tag, it already has the rendering smarts to output an <img> tag. The only parts you need
to supply are the attributes like name and src. Additionally, you need to handle the onClick
event (to post back the page), and the onMouseOver and onMouseOut events to swap the
image. You can do this by overriding the AddAttributesToRender() method, as follows:

```
protected override void AddAttributesToRender(HtmlTextWriter output)
{
    output.AddAttribute("name", ClientID);
    output.AddAttribute("src", ImageUrl);
    output.AddAttribute("onClick", Page.GetPostBackEventReference(this));

    output.AddAttribute("onMouseOver",
      "swapImg('" + this.ClientID + "', '" + MouseOverImageUrl + "');");

    output.AddAttribute("onMouseOut",
      "swapImg('" + this.ClientID + "', '" + ImageUrl + "');");
}
```

The last ingredient is to create the RaisePostBackEvent() method, as required by the
IPostBackEventHandler interface, and use it to raise a server-side event, as shown here:

```
public void RaisePostBackEvent(string eventArgument)
{
    OnImageClicked(new EventArgs());
```

```
}

public event EventHandler ImageClicked;
protected virtual void OnImageClicked(EventArgs e)
{
    // Check for at least one listener and then raise the event.
    if (ImageClicked != null)
      ImageClicked(this, e);
}
```

Figure 22-7 shows a page with two rollover buttons.

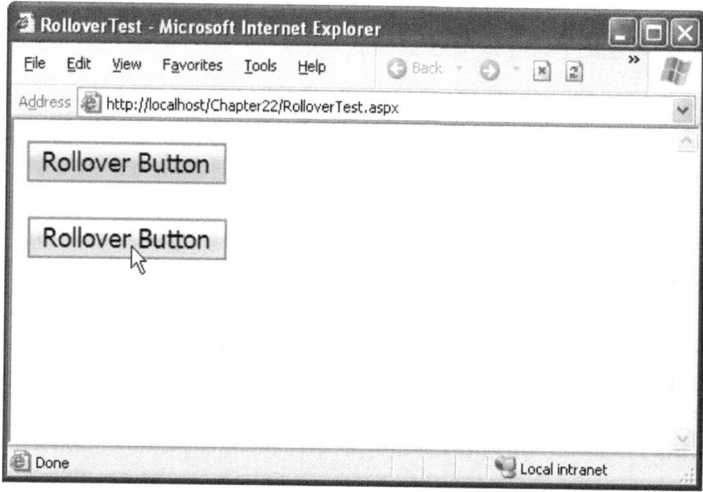

Figure 22-7. *Using a rollover button*

Frames

Another well-established feature of the Web is frames. *Frames* allow you to display more than one HTML document in the same browser window. Frames are commonly used to provide navigational controls (like a menu with links) that remain visible on every page. You could simulate the same effect by creating a user control for navigation and including it on every page. However, only by using frames can you ensure that the placement is exactly the same. Frames also give you the ability to independently scroll the content frame, while keeping the navigational controls fixed in place.

Tip For more information about frames, refer to the tutorial www.w3schools.com/html/html_frames.asp or the FAQ at www.htmlhelp.com/faq/html/frames.html. Frames, like JavaScript, are completely independent of ASP.NET. They are simply a part of the HTML standard.

Unfortunately, frames aren't always that easy to integrate into an ASP.NET page. Showing separate frames is easy—you simply need to create an HTML frames page that references the ASP.NET pages you want to show and defines their positioning. However, developers often want an action in one frame to have a result in another frame, and this interaction is not as straightforward. The problem is that each frame loads a different page, and from the point of view of the web server these pages are completely separate. That means that the only way you can interact between frames is on through the browser, using client-side script.

Frame Navigation

When you use frames for navigation, the user needs to be able to click a link in one frame and load a new page in the other frame. This task is more easily accomplished on the client than on the server.

For example, consider the following HTML page, which defines a frameset with two frames (a navigation frame on the left and a content frame on the right):

```
<html>
  <head>
    <title>Frame Test</title>
  </head>
  <frameset framespacing="1" cols="200,*">
    <frame name="menu" src="Frame1.aspx" scrolling="no" />
    <frame name="content" src="" scrolling="auto" />
    <noframes>
      <body>
        <p>This page uses frames, but your browser doesn't support them.</p>
      </body>
    </noframes>
  </frameset>
</html>
```

The left frame shows the Frame1.aspx page. In this page, you might want to add controls that set the content in the other frame. This is easy to do using static HTML, such as an anchor tag. For example, if a user clicks the following hyperlink, it will automatically load the target NewPage.aspx in the frame on the right, which is named content:

```
<a href="NewPage.aspx" target="content">Click here</a>
```

You can also perform the same feat when a JavaScript event occurs by setting the parent.[FrameName].location property. For example, you could add an <img> tag on the left frame and use it to set the content on the right frame as shown here:

```
<img src="ImgFile.gif" onClick="parent.content.location='NewPage.aspx'">
```

However, navigation becomes more complicated if you want to perform programmatic frame navigation in response to a server-side event. For example, you might want to log the user's action, examine security credentials, or commit data to a database, and then perform the frame navigation. The only way to accomplish frame navigation from the server side is to write a snippet of JavaScript that instructs the browser to change the location of the other frame when the page first loads on the client.

For example, imagine you add a button to the leftmost frame, as shown in Figure 22-8. When this button is clicked, the following server-side code runs. It defines the <script> block, and then registers it in the page. When the page is posted back, the script executes and redirects the rightmost frame to the requested page.

```
private void Button1_Click(object sender, System.EventArgs e)
{
    string url = "http://www.google.com";
    string frameScript = "<script language='javascript'>" +
        "window.parent.content.location='" + url + "';</script>";
    Page.RegisterStartupScript("FrameScript", frameScript);
}
```

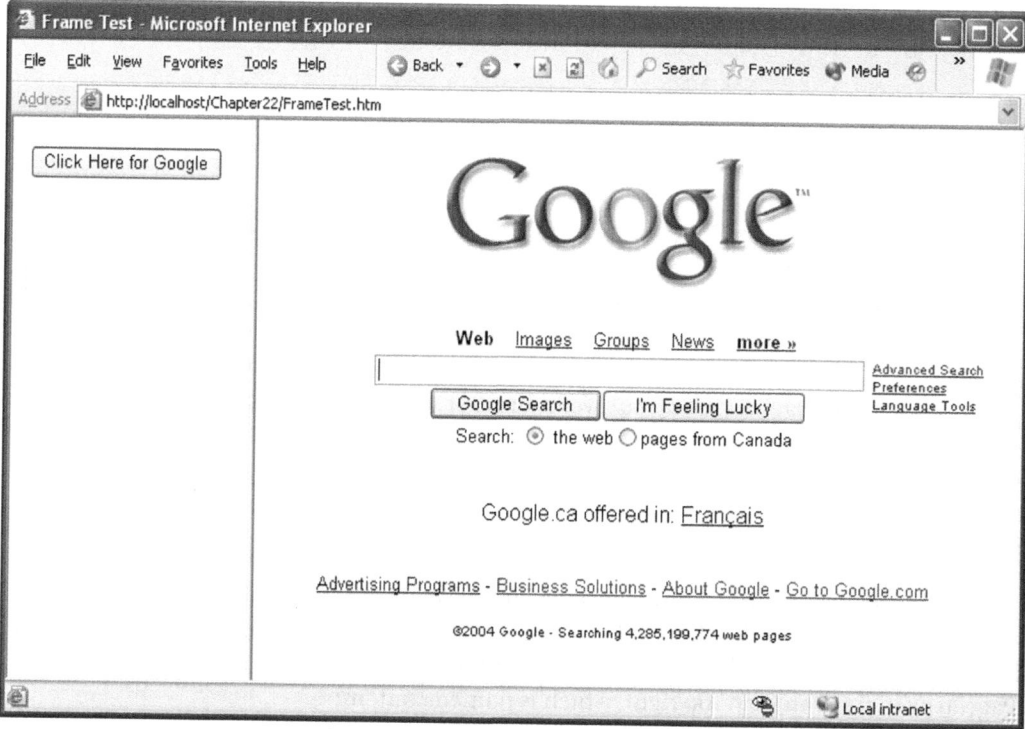

Figure 22-8. *Using server-side code to control frame navigation*

Tip Oddly enough, in this example the RegisterClientScriptBlock() method probably works slightly better than the RegisterStartupScript() block method. No matter how you implement this approach, there will be a slight delay before the new frame is refreshed. Because the script block doesn't depend on any of the controls on the page, you can render it immediately after the opening <form> tag using RegisterClientScriptBlock(), rather than at the end. This ensures that the JavaScript code that triggers the navigation is executed immediately, rather than after all the other content in the page has been downloaded.

Inline Frames

One solution that combines server-side programming with framelike functionality is the <iframe> tag (which is defined as part of the HTML 4.0 standard). The <iframe> in an inline, or embedded, frame that you can position anywhere inside an HTML document. Both the main document and the embedded page are treated as complete, separate documents.

Here's an example of an <iframe> tag:

```
<iframe src="page.aspx" width="40%" height="80" align="right">
</iframe>
```

The key problem with the <iframe> tag is that support is not universal across all browsers. Internet Explorer has supported it since version 3, but Netscape added in only in version 6. However, you can define static text that will be displayed in browsers that don't recognize the tag, as shown here:

```
<iframe src="page.aspx" width="40%" height="80" align="right">
  <p>See the content at <a href="page.aspx">page.aspx</a>.</p>
</iframe>
```

Once you've added an <iframe> to your page, you can define it in the code-behind to access it programmatically. ASP.NET doesn't have a control class that specifically represents the <iframe>, so you need to use the HtmlGenericControl. (In Visual Studio .NET, just right-click the control and choose Run As Server Control).

Here's the control declaration you need:

```
protected System.Web.UI.HtmlControls.HtmlGenericControl IFrame1;
```

Now you can set the src attribute at any point to redirect the frame:

```
IFrame1.Attributes["src"] = "page.aspx";
```

Of course, you can't actually interact with the page objects of the embedded page. In fact, the page isn't even generated in the same pass. Instead, the browser will request the page referenced by the src attribute separately and then display it in the frame. However, you can use a variety of techniques for passing information between the pages, including session state and the query string.

Figure 22-9 shows a page with two embedded frames, one of which has a border. The topmost <iframe> is using the page processor from earlier in this chapter, which indicates to the user that a part of the page is still being processed.

■**Tip** One common reason to use an <iframe> is to simulate a scrollable table (as in the previous example), which wouldn't otherwise be possible in HTML. To achieve this effect, point <iframe> to a page that contains the DataGrid, and set the marginHeight and marginWidth attributes of the <iframe> to 0.

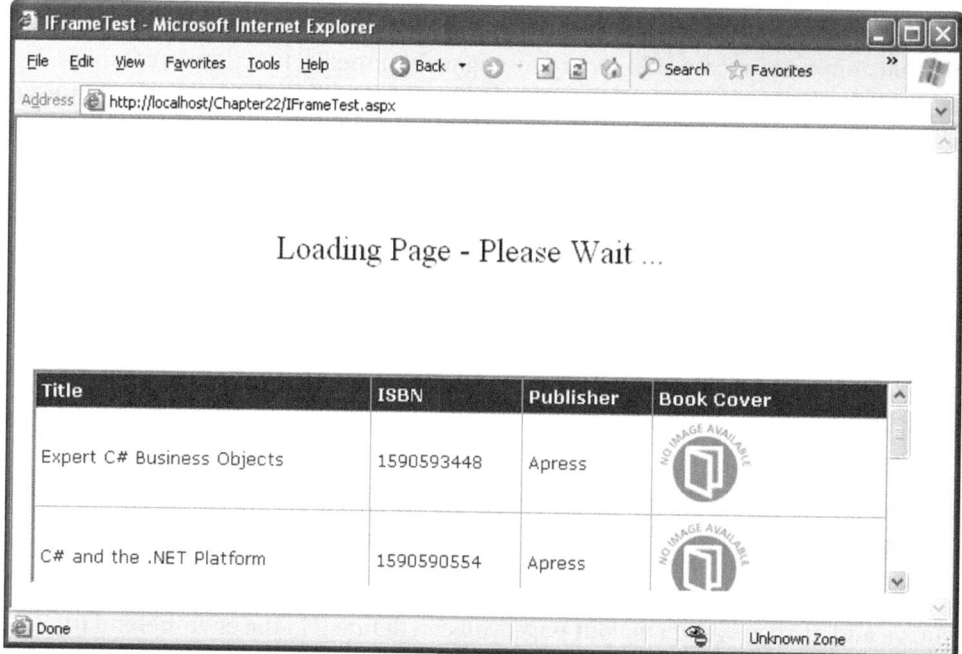

Figure 22-9. *Using inline frames*

Summary

In this chapter, you've seen how a bit of carefully chosen JavaScript code can extend your ASP.NET web pages with more responsive interfaces and more dynamic effects. Along the way, you've seen how to develop .NET solutions for some traditional HTML and JavaScript techniques, like page processors, pop-up windows, rollover buttons, and frames. There's a lot more you can do with the creative application of a little JavaScript. For more ideas, check out some of the custom controls available at Microsoft's www.asp.net community website.

■ ■ ■

CHAPTER 23

Dynamic Graphics with GDI+

The .NET Framework includes a new model for rendering dynamic graphics, called GDI+. GDI+ has a number of uses in .NET applications, including writing documents to the printer, displaying graphics in a Windows application, and rendering graphics in a web page.

In general, using GDI+ code to draw a graphic is slower than using a static image file. However, it gives you much more freedom, and enables a number of possibilities that weren't possible (or were prohibitively difficult) in earlier web development platforms, such as classic ASP. For example, you can create rich graphics that incorporate user-specific information, and render charts and graphs on the fly based on the records in a database.

In this chapter, you'll learn how to create graphics with GDI+, how to embed these graphics in a web page, and how to create custom controls that make use of GDI+.

GDI+ Basics

The heart of GDI+ programming is the System.Drawing.Graphics class. The Graphics class encapsulates a GDI+ drawing surface, whether it is a window, a print document, or an in-memory bitmap. ASP.NET developers rarely have the need to paint windows or print documents, so it's the last option that is the most practical.

To use GDI+ in ASP.NET, you need to follow a sequence of four steps:

1. Create the in-memory bitmap where you'll perform all your drawing.

2. Create a GDI+ graphics context for the image. This gives you the System.Drawing.Graphics object you need.

3. Perform the drawing using the methods of the Graphics object. You can draw and fill lines and shapes, and even copy bitmap content from existing files.

4. Write the binary data for the image to the browser, using the Response.OutputStream property.

In the following sections, you'll see several examples of web pages that use GDI+. Before continuing, you may want to ensure that the following namespaces are imported:

```
using System.Drawing;
using System.Drawing.Drawing2D;
using System.Drawing.Imaging;
```

The System.Drawing namespace defines many of the fundamental ingredients for drawing, including pens, brushes, and bitmaps. Visual Studio .NET adds this namespace import to all your web pages by default. The System.Drawing.Drawing2D namespace adds other useful details like the flexible GraphicsPath class, while System.Drawing.Imaging includes the ImageFormat namespace that lets you choose the graphics format in which your bitmap will be rendered when it's sent to the client.

Simple Drawing

The following example demonstrates the simplest possible GDI+ page. All the work is performed in the event handler for the Page.Load event.

The first step is to create the in-memory bitmap by creating an instance of the System.Drawing.Bitmap class. When you create this object, you need to specify the height and width of the image in pixels as constructor arguments. You should make the size as small as possible. Not only will a larger bitmap consume additional server memory while your code is executing, but the size of the rendered content you send to the client will also increase, slowing down the transmission time.

```
// Create the in-memory bitmap where you will draw the image.
// This bitmap is 300 pixels wide and 50 pixels high.
Bitmap image = new Bitmap(300, 50);
```

The next step is to create a GDI+ graphics context for the image, which is represented by the System.Drawing.Graphics object. This object provides the methods that allow you to draw content on the in-memory bitmap. To create a Graphics object from an existing Bitmap object, you just use the static Graphics.FromImage() method as shown here:

```
Graphics g = Graphics.FromImage(image);
```

Now comes the interesting part. Using the methods of the Graphics class, you can draw text, shapes, and image on the bitmap. In this example, the drawing code is exceedingly simple. First, it fills the graphic with a solid white background using the FillRectangle() method of the Graphics object.

```
// Draw a solid white rectangle.
// Start from point (1, 1).
// Make it 298 pixels wide and 48 pixels high.
g.FillRectangle(Brushes.White, 1, 1, 298, 48);
```

The FillRectangle() method requires several arguments. The first argument sets the color, the next two parameters set the starting point, and the final two parameters set the width and height. When measuring pixels, the point (0, 0) is the top-left corner of your image in (x, y) coordinates. The x coordinate increases as you go further to the right, and the y coordinate increases as you go further down. In the current example, the image is 300 pixels wide and 50 pixels high, which means the point (300, 50) is the bottom-right corner.

In this example, the FillRectangle() method doesn't quite fill the entire bitmap. Instead, it leaves a border one pixel wide all around. Because you haven't painted any content to this area, these pixels will have the default color (which, for a bitmap that you render to the GIF format, is black).

The next portion of the drawing code renders a static label message. In order to do this, you need to create a System.Drawing.Font object that represents the font you want to use. This shouldn't be confused with the FontInfo object you use with ASP.NET controls to specify the requested font for a web page. Unlike FontInfo, Font represents a single, specific font (including typeface, size, and style) that's installed on the current computer. When you create a Font object, you specify the font name, point size, and style, as shown here:

```
Font font = new Font("Impact", 20, FontStyle.Regular);
```

Tip Because this image is generated on the server, you can use any font that the server has installed when creating the graphic. The client won't need to have the same font, because the client receives the text as a rendered image.

To render the text, you use the DrawString() method of the Graphics object. As with the FillRectangle() object, you need to specify the coordinates where the drawing should begin. This point represents the top-left of the text block. In this case, the point (10, 5) is used, which gives a distance of 10 pixels from the left and 5 pixels from the top.

```
g.DrawString("This is a test.", font, Brushes.Blue, 10, 5);
```

Once the image is complete, you can send it to the browser using the Image.Save() method. Conceptually, you "save" the image to the browser's response stream. It then gets sent to the client, and is displayed in the browser. When you use this technique, your image replaces any other web page data and bypasses the web control model.

```
// Render the image to the output stream.
image.Save(Response.OutputStream,
   System.Drawing.Imaging.ImageFormat.Gif);
```

Tip You can save an image to any valid stream, including a FileStream. This technique allows you to save dynamically generated images to disk, so you can use them later in other web pages.

Finally, you should explicitly release your image and graphics context when you're finished, because both hold on to some unmanaged resources that won't be released right away if you don't. You release resources by calling the Dispose() method, as shown here:

```
g.Dispose();
image.Dispose();
```

Figure 23-1 shows the completed web page created by this code.

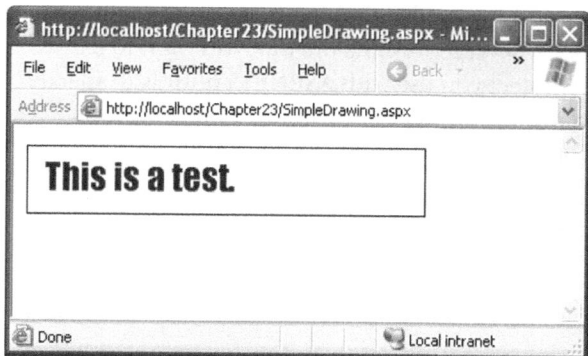

Figure 23-1. *A graphical label*

Image Format and Quality

When you save the image, you can also choose the format you want to use. JPEG offers the best color support and graphics, although it uses compression that can lose detail and make text look fuzzy. GIF is often a better choice for graphics containing text, but it doesn't offer good support for color. In .NET, every GIF uses a fixed palette with 256 generic colors. If you use a color that doesn't map to one of these presets, the color will be dithered, leading to a less-than-optimal graphic.

Alternatively, you can use PNG for an all-purpose format that always provides high quality. There are two quirks that you need to be aware of when using PNG. First, some older browsers (including Netscape 4.x) don't support PNG. Second, you can't use the Bitmap.Save() method as shown in the previous example.

Technically speaking, the problem is that you can't use the Save() method with a nonseekable stream. Response.OutputStream is a nonseekable stream, which means data must be written from beginning to end. Unfortunately, in order to create a PNG file .NET needs to be able to move back and forth in file, which means it requires a seekable stream. The solution is fairly simple. Instead of saving directly to Response.OutputStream, you can create a System.IO.MemoryStream object, which represents an in-memory buffer of data. The MemoryStream is always seekable, so you can save the image to this object. Once you've performed this step, you can easily copy the data from the MemoryStream to the Response.OutputStream. The only disadvantage is that this technique requires more memory because the whole graphic needs to be helped in memory at once. However, the graphics you use in web pages generally aren't that large, and so you probably won't observe any reduction in performance.

Here's the code you need to implement this solution, assuming you've imported the System.IO namespace:

```
Response.ContentType = "image/png";

// Create the PNG in memory.
MemoryStream mem = new MemoryStream();
image.Save(mem, System.Drawing.Imaging.ImageFormat.Png);

// Write the MemoryStream data to the output stream.
mem.WriteTo(Response.OutputStream);

// Clean up.
g.Dispose();
image.Dispose();
```

Quality isn't just determined by the image format. It also depends on the way you render the original bitmap. GDI+ allows you to choose between optimizing your drawing code for appearance or speed. When you choose to optimize for the best appearance, .NET uses extra rendering techniques like antialiasing to improve the drawing.

Antialiasing is a technique used to smooth out jagged edges in shapes and text. It works by adding shading at the border of an edge. For example, gray shading might be added to the edge of a black curve to make a corner look smoother. Technically, antialiasing blends a curve with its background. Figure 23-2 shows a close-up of an antialiased ellipse.

Figure 23-2. *Antialiasing with an ellipse*

To use smoothing in your applications, you set the SmoothingQuality property of the Graphics object. You can choose between None, HighSpeed (the default), AntiAlias, and HighQuality (which is similar to AntiAlias but uses other, slower optimizations that improve the display on LCD screens). The Graphics.SmoothingQuality property is one of the few stateful Graphics class members. That means that you set it before you begin drawing, and it applies to any text or shapes you draw in the rest of the paint session (until the Graphics object is disposed of).

```
g.SmoothingMode = Drawing.Drawing2D.SmoothingMode.AntiAlias;
```

■Tip Antialiasing makes the most difference when you're displaying curves. That means it will dramatically improve the appearance of ellipses, circles, and arcs, but it won't make any difference with straight lines, squares, and rectangles.

Antialiasing can also be used with fonts to soften jagged edges on text. You can set the Graphics.TextRenderingHint property to ensure optimized text. You can choose between SingleBitPerPixelGridFit (fastest performance and lowest quality), AntiAliasGridFit (better quality but slower performance), and ClearTypeGridFit (the best quality on an LCD display). Or you can use the SystemDefault value to use whatever font-smoothing settings the user has configured. SystemDefault is the default setting, and the default system settings for most computers enable text antialiasing. Even if you don't set this setting your dynamically rendered text will probably be drawn in high quality. However, because you can't necessarily control the system settings of the web server, it's a good practice to specify this setting explicitly if you need to draw text in an image.

The Graphics Class

The majority of the GDI+ drawing smarts is concentrated in the Graphics class. The Graphics class also provides a slew of methods for drawing specific shapes, images, and text. Table 23-1 describes these methods, many of which are used in the examples in this chapter.

Table 23-1. *Graphics Class Methods for Drawing*

Method	Description
DrawArc()	Draws an arc representing a portion of an ellipse specified by a pair of coordinates, a width, and a height.
DrawBezier() and DrawBeziers()	The infamous and attractive Bezier curve, which is defined by four control points.
DrawClosedCurve()	Draws a curve, and then closes it off by connecting the end points.
DrawCurve()	Draws a curve (technically, a cardinal spline).
DrawEllipse()	Draws an ellipse defined by a bounding rectangle specified by a pair of coordinates, a height, and a width.
DrawIcon() and DrawIconUnstreched()	Draws the icon represented by an Icon object, and (optionally) stretches it to fit a given rectangle.
DrawImage and DrawImageUnscaled()	Draws the image represented by an Image-derived object, and (optionally) stretches it to fit a given rectangle.
DrawLine() and DrawLines()	Draws a line connecting the two points specified by coordinate pairs.
DrawPath()	Draws a GraphicsPath object, which can represent a combination of curves and shapes.

Method	Description
DrawPie()	Draws a "piece-of-pie" shape defined by an ellipse specified by a coordinate pair, a width, and a height and two radial lines.
DrawPolygon()	Draws a multisided polygon defined by an array of points.
DrawRectangle() and DrawRectangles()	Draws an ordinary rectangle specified by a starting coordinate pair and width and height.
DrawString()	Draws a string of text in a given font.
FillClosedCurve()	Draws a curve, closes it off by connecting the end points, and fills it.
FillEllipse()	Fills the interior of an ellipse.
FillPath()	Fills the shape represented by a GraphicsPath object.
FillPie()	Fills the interior of a "piece-of-pie" shape.
FillPolygon()	Fills the interior of a polygon.
FillRectangle() and FillRectangles()	Fills the interior of a rectangle.
FillRegion()	Fills the interior of a Region object.

The DrawXxx() methods draw outlines (for example, the edge around a rectangle). The FillXxx() methods paint solid regions (for example, the actual surface inside the borders of a rectangle). The only exception is the DrawString() method, which draws filled-in text using a font you specify, and DrawIcon() and DrawImage(), which copy bitmap images onto the drawing surface.

If you want to create a shape that has both an outline in one color, and a fill in another color, you need to combine both a draw and a fill method. Here's an example that first paints a white rectangle, and then adds a green border around it:

```
g.FillRectangle(Brushes.White, 0, 0, 300, 50);
g.DrawRectangle(Pens.Green, 0, 0, 299, 49);
```

■ Note If you specify coordinates that are not in the drawing area, you won't receive an exception. However, the content you draw that's off the edge won't appear in the final image. In some cases, this means a partial shape may appear (which might be exactly the effect you want).

You'll notice that when you use a fill method, you need to specify a Brush object. When you use a draw method, you need to specify a Pen object. In this example, the code uses a prebuilt Pen and Brush object, which can be retrieved from the Pens and Brushes classes, respectively. Brushes retrieved in this way always correspond to solid colors. Pens retrieved in this way are always one pixel wide. Later in this chapter, you'll learn how to create your own custom pens and brushes for more exotic patterns.

Using the techniques you've learned, it's easy to create a simple web page that draws a more complex GDI+ image. The next example uses the Graphics class to draw an ellipse, a text message, and an image from a file.

Here's the code you'll need:

```
private void Page_Load(Object sender, EventArgs e)
{
    // Create the in-memory bitmap where you will draw the image.
    // This bitmap is 450 pixels wide and 100 pixels high.
    Bitmap image = new Bitmap(450, 100);
    Graphics g = Graphics.FromImage(image);

    // Ensure high-quality curves.
    g.SmoothingMode = SmoothingMode.AntiAlias;

    // Paint the background.
    g.FillRectangle(Brushes.White, 0, 0, 450, 100);

    // Add an ellipse.
    g.FillEllipse(Brushes.PaleGoldenrod, 120, 13, 300, 50);
    g.DrawEllipse(Pens.Green, 120, 13, 299, 49);

    // Draw some text using a fancy font.
    Font font = new Font("Harrington", 20, FontStyle.Bold);
    g.DrawString("Oranges are tasty!", font, Brushes.DarkOrange, 150, 20);

    // Add a graphic from a file.
    System.Drawing.Image orangeImage =
      System.Drawing.Image.FromFile(Server.MapPath("oranges.gif"));
    g.DrawImageUnscaled(orangeImage, 0, 0);

    // Render the image to the output stream.
    Response.ContentType = "image/png";
    MemoryStream mem = new MemoryStream();
    image.Save(mem, System.Drawing.Imaging.ImageFormat.Png);
    mem.WriteTo(Response.OutputStream);

    // Clean up.
    g.Dispose();
    image.Dispose();
}
```

Figure 23-3 shows the resulting web page.

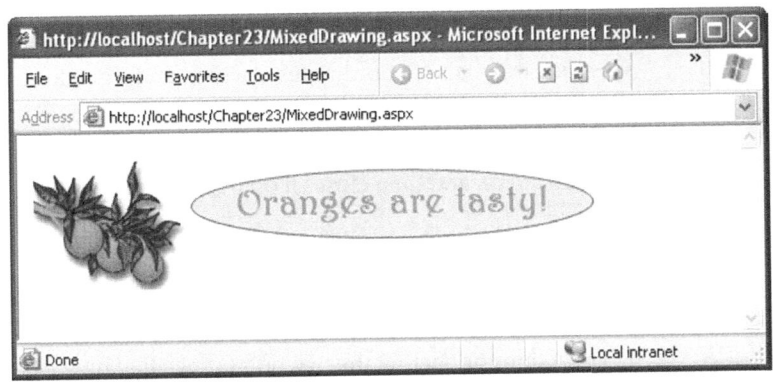

Figure 23-3. *Using multiple elements in a drawing*

Using a GraphicsPath

Two interesting methods that you haven't seen yet include DrawPath() and FillPath(), which work with the GraphicsPath class in the System.Drawing.Drawing2D namespace.

The GraphicsPath class encapsulates a series of connected lines, curves, and text. You used the GraphicsPath class in Chapter 5 to create a shaped form. To build a GraphicsPath object, you simply create a new instance, and use the methods in Table 23-2 to add all the required elements.

```
GraphicsPath path = new GraphicsPath();
path.AddEllipse(0, 0, 100, 50);
path.AddRectangle(New Rectangle(100, 50, 100, 50);
```

Optionally, you can also create a solid, filled figure out of separate line segments. To do this, you first call the StartFigure() method. Then you add the required curves and lines using the appropriate methods. When finished, you call the CloseFigure() method to close off the shape by drawing a line from the endpoint to the starting point. You can use these methods multiple times to add several closed figures to a single GraphicsPath object. Here's an example that draws a single figure based on an arc and a line:

```
GraphicsPath path = new GraphicsPath();
path.StartFigure();
path.AddArc(10, 10, 100, 100, 20, 50);
path.AddLine(20, 100, 70, 230);
path.CloseFigure();
```

Table 23-2. *GraphicsPath Methods*

Method	Description
AddArc()	Draws an arc representing a portion of an ellipse specified by a pair of coordinates, a width, and a height.
AddBezier() and AddBeziers()	The infamous and attractive Bezier curve, which is defined by four control points.
AddClosedCurve()	Draws a curve, and then closes if off by connecting the end points.
AddCurve()	Draws a curve (technically, a cardinal spline).
AddEllipse()	Draws an ellipse defined by a bounding rectangle specified by a pair of coordinates, a height, and a width.
AddLine() and AddLines()	Draws a line connecting the two points specified by coordinate pairs.
AddPath()	Adds another GraphicsPath object to this GraphicsPath object.
AddPie()	Draws a "piece-of-pie" shape defined by an ellipse specified by a coordinate pair, a width, a height, and two radial lines.
AddPolygon()	Draws a multisided polygon defined by an array of points.
AddRectangle() and AddRectangles()	Draws an ordinary rectangle specified by a starting coordinate pair and width and height.
AddString()	Draws a string of text in a given font.
StartFigure() and CloseFigure()	StartFigure() defines the start of a new closed figure. When you use CloseFigure(), the starting point will be joined to the end point by an additional line.
Transform(), Warp(), and Widen()	Applies a matrix transform, a warp transform (defined by a rectangle and parallelogram), or an expansion, respectively.

Pens

When you use the DrawXxx() methods from the Graphics class, the border of the shape or curve is drawn with the Pen object you supply. You can retrieve a standard pen using one of the static properties from the System.Drawing.Pens class. These pens all have a width of one pixel. They only differ in their color.

```
Pen myPen = Pens.Black;
```

You can also create a Pen object on your own, and configure all the properties described in Table 23-3. Here's an example:

```
Pen myPen = new Pen(Color.Red);
myPen.DashCap = DashCap.Triangle;
myPen.DashStyle = DashDotDot;
g.DrawLine(myPen, 0, 0, 10, 0);
```

Table 23-3. *Pen Members*

Member	Description
DashPattern	Defines a dash style for broken lines using an array of dashes and spaces.
DashStyle	Defines a dash style for broken lines using the DashStyle enumeration.
LineJoin	Defines how overlapping lines in a shape will be joined together.
PenType	The type of fill that will be used for the line. Typically this will be SolidColor, but you can also use a gradient, bitmap texture, or hatch pattern by supplying a brush object when you create the pen. You cannot set the PenType through this property, however, because it is read-only.
StartCap and EndCap	Determines how the beginning and ends of lines will be rendered. You can also define a custom line cap by creating a CustomLineCap object (typically by using a GraphicsPath), and then assigning it to the CustomStartCap or CustomEndCap property.
Width	The pixel width of lines drawn by this pen.

The easiest way to understand the different LineCap and DashStyle properties is to create a simple test page that loops through all the options, and displays a short line segment of each. The following web-page code creates a drawing that does exactly that:

```
private void Page_Load(object sender, System.EventArgs e)
{
    // Create the in-memory bitmap where you will draw the image.
    // This bitmap is 300 pixels wide and 50 pixels high.
    Bitmap image = new Bitmap(500, 400);
    Graphics g = Graphics.FromImage(image);

    // Paint the background.
    g.FillRectangle(Brushes.White, 0, 0, 500, 400);

    // Create a pen to use for all the examples.
    Pen myPen = new Pen(Color.Blue, 10);

    // The y variable tracks the current y (up/down) position
    // in the image.
    int y  = 60;

    // Draw an example of each LineCap style in the first column (left).
    g.DrawString("LineCap Choices", new Font("Tahoma", 15, FontStyle.Bold),
      Brushes.Blue, 0, 10);
    foreach (LineCap cap in System.Enum.GetValues(typeof(LineCap)))
    {
        myPen.StartCap = cap;
        myPen.EndCap = cap;
        g.DrawLine(myPen, 20, y, 100, y);
        g.DrawString(cap.ToString(), new Font("Tahoma", 8),
```

```
                Brushes.Black, 120, y - 10);
        y += 30;
    }


    // Draw an example of each DashStyle in the second column (right).
    y = 60;
    g.DrawString("DashStyle Choices", new Font("Tahoma", 15,
      FontStyle.Bold), Brushes.Blue, 200, 10);
    foreach (DashStyle dash in System.Enum.GetValues(typeof(DashStyle)))
    {
        // Configure the pen.
        myPen.DashStyle = dash;

        // Draw a short line segment.
        g.DrawLine(myPen, 220, y, 300, y);

        // Add a text label.
        g.DrawString(dash.ToString(), new Font("Tahoma", 8), Brushes.Black,
          320, y - 10);

        // Move down one line.
        y += 30;
    }

    // Render the image to the output stream.
    image.Save(Response.OutputStream,
      System.Drawing.Imaging.ImageFormat.Gif);

    g.Dispose();
    image.Dispose();
}
```

Figure 23-4 shows the resulting web page.

Brushes

Brushes are used to fill the space between lines. Brushes are used when drawing text or when using any of the FillXxx() methods of the Graphics class for painting the inside of a shape.

You can quickly retrieve a predefined solid brush using a static property from the Brushes class, as shown here:

```
Brush myBrush = Brushes.White;
```

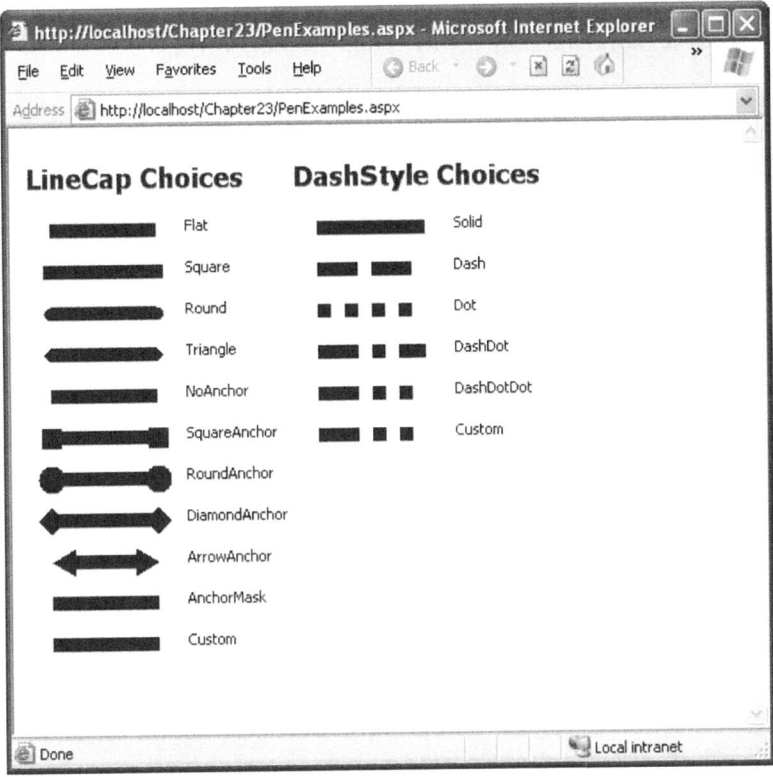

Figure 23-4. *Different pen options*

You can also create a custom brush. You need to decide what type of brush you are creating. Solid brushes are created from the SolidBrush class, while other classes allow fancier options:

- **HatchBrush.** A HatchBrush has a foreground color, a background color, and a hatch style that determines how these colors are combined. Typically, colors are interspersed using stripes, grids, or dots, but you can even select unusual pattern styles like bricks, confetti, weave, and shingles.

- **LinearGradientBrush.** The LinearGradientBrush allows you to blend two colors in a gradient pattern. You can choose any two colors (as with the hatch brush) and then choose to blend horizontally (from left to right), vertically (from top to bottom), diagonally (from the top-left corner to the bottom-right), or diagonally backward (from the top-right to the bottom-left). You can also specify the origin point for either side of the gradient.

- **TextureBrush.** The TextureBrush attaches a bitmap to a brush. The image is tiled in the painted portion of the brush, whether it is text or a simple rectangle.

You can experiment with all of these brush types in your applications. Here's an example of the drawing logic you need to test all the different styles of LinearGradientBrush:

```
private void Page_Load(object sender, System.EventArgs e)
{
    // Create the in-memory bitmap.
    Bitmap image = new Bitmap(300, 300);
    Graphics g = Graphics.FromImage(image);

    // Paint the background.
    g.FillRectangle(Brushes.White, 0, 0, 300, 300);

    // Show a rectangle with each type of gradient.
    LinearGradientBrush myBrush;
    int y = 20;
    foreach (LinearGradientMode gradientStyle in
      System.Enum.GetValues(typeof(LinearGradientMode)))
    {
        // Configure the brush.
        myBrush = new LinearGradientBrush(new Rectangle(20, y, 100, 60),
          Color.Violet, Color.White, gradientStyle);

        // Draw a small rectangle and add a text label.
        g.FillRectangle(myBrush, 20, y, 100, 60);
        g.DrawString(gradientStyle.ToString(), new Font("Tahoma", 8),
          Brushes.Black, 130, y + 20);

        // Move to the next line.
        y += 70;
    }

    // Render the image to the output stream.
    Response.ContentType = "image/png";
    MemoryStream mem = new MemoryStream();
    image.Save(mem, System.Drawing.Imaging.ImageFormat.Png);
    mem.WriteTo(Response.OutputStream);
    g.Dispose();
    image.Dispose();
}
```

Figure 23-5 shows the result.

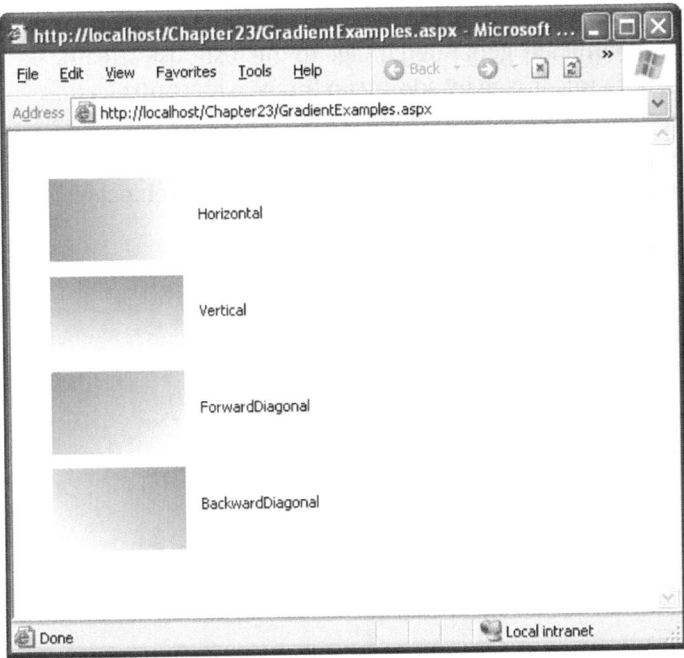

Figure 23-5. *Testing different gradient styles*

Tip You can also create a pen that draws using the fill style of a brush. This allows you to draw lines that are filled with gradients and textures. To do so, begin by creating the appropriate brush, and then create a new pen. One of the overloaded pen constructor methods accepts a reference to a brush—that's the one you need to use for a brush-based pen.

Embedding Dynamic Graphics in a Web Page

There is one problem with the Image.Save() approach that's been used in all the examples so far. When you save an image to the response stream, you overwrite whatever information ASP.NET would otherwise use. If you have a web page that includes other static content and controls, this content won't appear at all in the final web page. Instead, the dynamically rendered graphics will replace it.

Fortunately, there is a simple solution. You can link to a dynamically generated image using the HTML <img> tag or the Image web control. But instead of linking your image to a static image file, link it to the .aspx file that generates the picture.

For example, consider the graphic shown earlier in Figure 23-1. It's stored in a file named SimpleDrawing.aspx, and it writes a dynamically generated image to the response stream. In another page, you could show the dynamic image by adding an Image web control, and setting the ImageUrl property to SimpleDrawing.aspx. You could then add other controls, or even multiple Image controls that link to the same content. In fact, you'll even see the image appear in the Visual Studio .NET design-time environment before you run the web page.

Figure 23-6 shows an example that uses two <img> tags that point to SimpleDrawing.aspx, along with additional ASP.NET web controls in between.

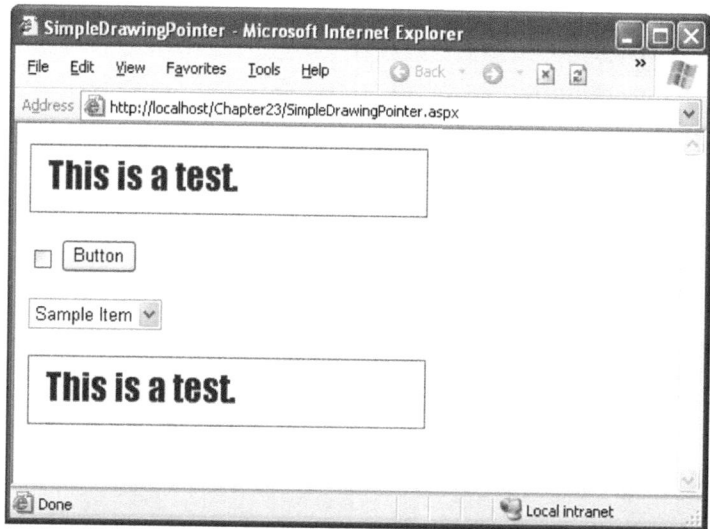

Figure 23-6. *Mixing dynamically drawn content and ordinary web controls*

■**Tip** Remember that creating a GDI+ drawing is usually an order of magnitude slower than serving a static image. As a result, it's probably not a good idea to implement graphical buttons and other elements that you'll repeat multiple times on a page using GDI+. (If you do, consider caching or saving the image file once you've generated it to increase performance.)

Passing Information to a Dynamic Images

When you use this technique to embed dynamic graphics in web pages, you also need to think about how the web page can send information to the dynamic graphic. For example, what if you don't want to show a fixed piece of text, but you want to generate a dynamic label that incorporates the name of the current user? (In fact, if you do want to show a static piece of text, it's probably better to create the graphic ahead of time and store it in a file, rather than generating it using GDI+ code each time the user requests the page.) One solution is to pass the information using the query string. The page that renders the graphic can then check for the query string information it needs.

The following example uses this technique to create a data bound list that shows a thumbnail of every bitmap in a given directory. Figure 23-7 shows the final result.

Figure 23-7. *A data bound thumbnail list*

This page needs to be designed in two parts: the page that contains the DataList, and the page that dynamically renders a single thumbnail. The DataList page will call the thumbnail page multiple times (using <img> tags) to fill the list.

It makes sense to design the page that creates the thumbnail first. In order to make this component as generic as possible, you shouldn't hardcode any information about the directory to use or the size of thumbnail. Instead, this information will be retrieved through three query string arguments. The first step that you need to perform is to check that all this information is supplied when the page first loads, as shown here:

```
private void Page_Load(object sender, System.EventArgs e)
{
    if ((Request.QueryString["X"] == null) ||
      (Request.QueryString["Y"] == null) ||
      (Request.QueryString["FilePath"] == null))
    {
        // There is missing data, so don't display anything.
        // Other options include choosing reasonable defaults
```

```
        // or returning an image with some static error text.
    }
    else
    {
        int x = Int32.Parse(Request.QueryString["X"]);
        int y = Int32.Parse(Request.QueryString["Y"]);
        string file = Server.UrlDecode(Request.QueryString["FilePath"]);
        ...
```

Once you have the basic set of data, you can create your Bitmap and Graphics object as always. In this case, the Bitmap dimensions should correspond to the size of the thumbnail, because you don't want to add any additional content:

```
    ...
    // Create the in-memory bitmap where you will draw the image.
    Bitmap image = new Bitmap(x, y);
    Graphics g = Graphics.FromImage(image);
    ...
```

Creating the thumbnail is easy. All you need to do is load the image (using the static Image.FromFile() method) and then draw it on the drawing surface. When you draw the image, you specify the starting point (0, 0), and the height and width. The height and width correspond to the size of the Bitmap object. The Graphics class will automatically scale your image to fit these dimensions, using antialiasing to create a high-quality thumbnail:

```
    ...
    // Load the file data.
    System.Drawing.Image thumbnail =
      System.Drawing.Image.FromFile(file);

    // Draw the thumbnail.
    g.DrawImage(thumbnail, 0, 0, x, y);
    ...
```

Lastly, you can render the image and perform the clean up, as follows:

```
        ...
        // Render the image.
        image.Save(Response.OutputStream, ImageFormat.Jpeg);
        g.Dispose();
        image.Dispose();
    }
}
```

The next step is to make use of this page (named ThumbnailViewer.aspx) in the page that contains the DataList. The basic idea is that the user will enter a directory path and click the submit button. At this point, your code can perform a little work with the System.IO classes. First, you need to create a DirectoryInfo object that represents the user's choice. Then you need to retrieve a collection of FileInfo objects that represent files in that directory using the

DirectoryInfo.GetFiles() method. To narrow the selection down so that it only includes bitmaps, the search expression *.bmp is used. Finally, the code binds the array of FileInfo objects to the DataList, as shown here:

```
private void cmdShow_Click(object sender, System.EventArgs e)
{
    // Get a string array with all the image files.
    DirectoryInfo dir = new DirectoryInfo(txtDir.Text);
    listThumbs.DataSource = dir.GetFiles("*.bmp");

    // Bind the string array.
    listThumbs.DataBind();
}
```

It's up to the DataList template to determine how the bound FileInfo objects are displayed. In this example, you need to show two pieces of information—the short name of the file, and the corresponding thumbnail. Showing the short name is straightforward. You simply need to bind to the FileInfo.Name property. Showing the thumbnail requires using an <img> tag to invoke the ThumbnailViewer.aspx page. However, constructing the right URL can be a little tricky, so the best solution is to hand the work off to a method in the web-page class called GetImageUrl().

Here's the complete DataList declaration with the template:

```
<asp:DataList id="listThumbs" runat="server">
  <ItemStyle Font-Size="X-Small" Font-Names="Verdana"></ItemStyle>
  <ItemTemplate>
    <img src=
    '<%# GetImageUrl(DataBinder.Eval(Container.DataItem, "FullName")) %>'/>
    <%# DataBinder.Eval(Container.DataItem, "Name") %>
    <hr>
  </ItemTemplate>
</asp:DataList>
```

The GetImageUrl() method examines the full file path, encodes it, and adds it to the query string so ThumbnailViewer.aspx can find the required file. At the same time, the GetImageUrl() method also chooses a thumbnail size of 50 by 50 pixels. Note that the file path is URL-encoded. That's because filenames commonly include characters that aren't allowed in URLs, like the space:

```
protected string GetImageUrl(object path)
{
    return "ThumbnailViewer.aspx?x=50&y=50&FilePath=" +
      Server.UrlEncode((string)path);
}
```

All in all, this solution demonstrates a fairly impressive result without much code required.

Custom Controls That Use GDI+

Based on everything you learned in Chapter 21 and Chapter 22, you're probably eager to use GDI+ to create your own well-encapsulated custom controls. Unfortunately, ASP.NET doesn't make it easy, because of the way you need to embed GDI+ images in a page.

As you've seen, if you want to use GDI+ you need to create a separate web page. You can then embed the content of this page in another page by using an <img> tag. As a result, you can't just drop a custom control that uses GDI+ onto a web page. What you *can* do is create a custom control that wraps an <img> tag. This control can provide a convenient programming interface, complete with properties, methods, and events. However, the custom control won't actually generate the image. Instead, it will collect the data from its properties, and use it to build the query string portion of a URL. The custom control will then render itself on the page as an <img> tag, which points to the page that performs the real work.

■**Tip** If you want, the custom control can also render other HTML elements above or below the <img> tag, such as a separating line, a title, and so on.

Essentially, the custom control provides a higher-level wrapper that abstracts the process of transferring information to your GDI+ page. Figure 23-8 shows how this process works with the example you'll consider next, which uses the custom control approach to create a simple label that renders with a gradient background. In this example, the custom control is named GradientLabel. The GDI+ code is found in a separate web page named GradientLabel.aspx. To see this example at work, you can request the GradientTest.aspx web page, which hosts a single instance of the GradientLabel control.

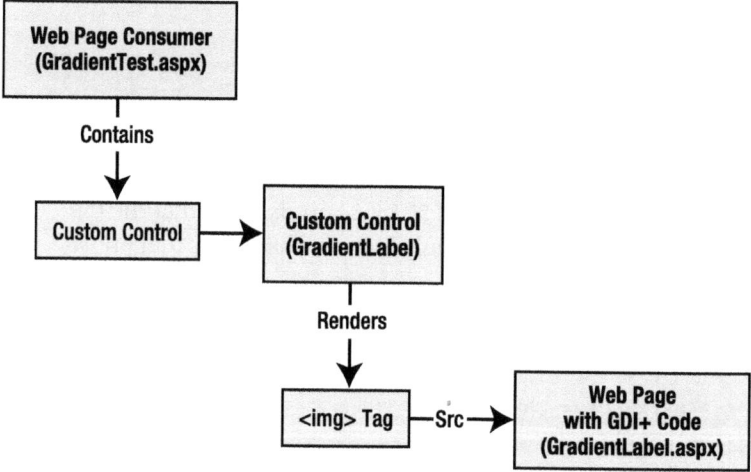

Figure 23-8. *Using custom controls with GDI+*

■**Tip** If you're worried about confusing your real web pages with the web pages you use to supply GDI+ drawing, consider using a custom HTTP handler to generate the image. With an HTTP handler, your image generators can have a custom extension, and use essentially the same code in the ProcessRequest() method. HTTP handlers were first demonstrated in Chapter 6.

The Custom Control Class

The first step is to create the control class. This class (named GradientLabel), derives from Control rather than WebControl. That's because it won't be able to support the rich set of style properties because it renders a dynamic graphic, not an HTML tag.

```
public class GradientLabel : Control
{ ... }
```

The GradientLabel class provides five properties, which allow the user to specify the text, the font size, and the colors that are used for the gradient and text, as follows:

```
public string Text
{
    get {return (string)ViewState["Text"];}
    set {ViewState["Text"] = value;}
}

public int TextSize
{
    get {return (int)ViewState["TextSize"];}
    set {ViewState["TextSize"] = value;}
}

public Color GradientColorA
{
    get {return (Color)ViewState["ColorA"];}
    set {ViewState["ColorA"] = value;}
}

public Color GradientColorB
{
    get {return (Color)ViewState["ColorB"];}
    set {ViewState["ColorB"] = value;}
}

public Color TextColor
{
    get {return (Color)ViewState["TextColor"];}
    set {ViewState["TextColor"] = value;}
}
```

The properties are set to some sensible defaults in the GradientLabel constructor, as shown here:

```
public GradientLabel()
{
    Text = "";
    TextColor = Color.White;
    GradientColorA = Color.Blue;
    GradientColorB = Color.DarkBlue;
    TextSize = 14;
}
```

The GradientLabel renders itself as an <img> tag that points to the GradientLabel.aspx page. It's the GradientLabel.aspx page that contains the actual GDI+ drawing code. When the GradientLabel is rendered, it reads the information from all the properties, and supplies the information in the query string.

```
protected override void Render(HtmlTextWriter writer)
{
    HttpContext context = HttpContext.Current;
    writer.Write("<img src='" + "GradientLabel.aspx?" +
      "Text=" + context.Server.UrlEncode(Text) +
      "&TextSize=" + TextSize.ToString() +
      "&TextColor=" + TextColor.ToArgb() +
      "&GradientColorA=" + GradientColorA.ToArgb() +
      "&GradientColorB=" + GradientColorB.ToArgb() +
      "'>");
}
```

The Rendering Page

The first step for the GradientLabel.aspx page is to retrieve the properties from the query string, as follows:

```
private void Page_Load(object sender, System.EventArgs e)
{
    string text = Server.UrlDecode(Request.QueryString["Text"]);
    int textSize = Int32.Parse(Request.QueryString["TextSize"]);
    Color textColor = Color.FromArgb(
      Int32.Parse(Request.QueryString["TextColor"]));
    Color gradientColorA = Color.FromArgb(
      Int32.Parse(Request.QueryString["GradientColorA"]));
    Color gradientColorB = Color.FromArgb(
      Int32.Parse(Request.QueryString["GradientColorB"]));
    ...
```

The GradientLabel.aspx has an interesting challenge. The text and font size are supplied dynamically, so it's impossible to use a fixed bitmap size without the risk of creating it too small (so that some text content is cut off) or too large (so that extra server memory is wasted and the image takes longer to send to the client). One way to try to resolve this problem is to create the Font object you want to use, and then invoke the Graphics.MeasureString() argument to determine how many pixels are required to display the desired text. The only caveat is that you need to be careful not to allow the bitmap to become too large. For example, if the user submits a string with hundreds of characters, you don't want to create a bitmap that's dozens of megabytes in size! To avoid this risk, the rendering code imposes a maximum height and width of 800 pixels.

Tip You can also use an alternative version of the DrawString() method that accepts a rectangle in which you want to place the text. This version of DrawString() automatically wraps the text if there's room for more than one line. You could use this approach to allow the display of large amounts of text over several lines.

Here's the portion of the drawing code that retrieves the query string information and measures the text:

```
...
// Define the font.
Font font = new Font("Tahoma", textSize, FontStyle.Bold);

// Use a test image to measure the text.
Bitmap image = new Bitmap(1, 1);
Graphics g = Graphics.FromImage(image);
SizeF size = g.MeasureString(text, font);
g.Dispose();
image.Dispose();

// Using these measurements, try to choose a reasonable bitmap size.
// Even if the text is large, cap the size at some maximum to
// prevent causing a serious server slowdown!
int width = (int)Math.Min(size.Width + 20, 800);
int height = (int)Math.Min(size.Height + 20, 800);
image = new Bitmap(width, height);
g = Graphics.FromImage(image);
...
```

You'll see that in addition to the size needed for the text, an extra 20 pixels are added to each dimension. This allows for a padding of 10 pixels on each side.

Finally, you can create the LinearGradientBrush, paint the drawing surface, and then add the text, as follows:

```
...
LinearGradientBrush brush = new LinearGradientBrush(
    new Rectangle(new Point(0,0), image.Size),
    gradientColorA, gradientColorB, LinearGradientMode.ForwardDiagonal);
```

```
// Draw the gradient background.
g.FillRectangle(brush, 0, 0, 300, 300);

// Draw the label text.
g.DrawString(text, font, new SolidBrush(textColor), 10, 10);

// Render the image to the output stream.
Response.ContentType = "image/png";
MemoryStream mem = new MemoryStream();
image.Save(mem, System.Drawing.Imaging.ImageFormat.Png);
mem.WriteTo(Response.OutputStream);
g.Dispose();
image.Dispose();
}
```

To test the label, you can create a control tag like this:

```
<cc1:gradientlabel id="GradientLabel1" runat="server"
  Text="Test String" GradientColorA="MediumSpringGreen"
  GradientColorB="RoyalBlue"></cc1:gradientlabel>
```

Figure 23-9 shows the rendered result.

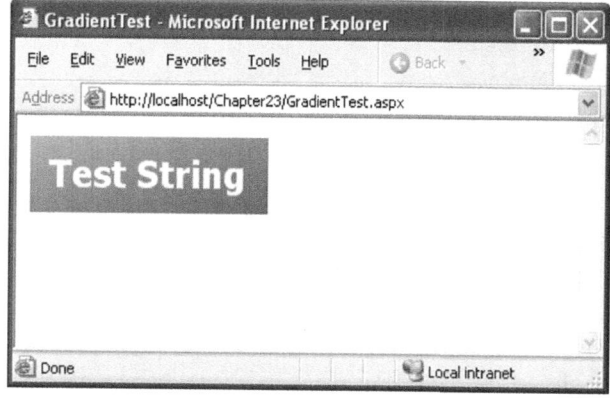

Figure 23-9. *A GDI+ label custom control*

This control still has many shortcomings. Notably, it can't size the drawing surface or wrap its text dynamically, and it doesn't allow the user to set the text font or the spacing between the text and the border. To complete the control, you would need to find a way to pass this extra information in the query string. Clearly, if you want to create a practical web control using GDI+, you have a significant amount of work to do.

Charting with GDI+

When the query approach works, it's a great, logical way to solve the problem of sending information from an ordinary page to a page that creates a dynamic graphic. However, it won't always work. One of the problems with the query string is that it's limited to a relatively small amount of string data. If you need to send something more complex, like an object or a block of binary data, you need to find another technique.

One realistic solution is to use the Session collection. This has more overhead, because everything you put in the Session collection uses server memory, but it allows you to transmit any type of data, including custom objects. To get a feel for why you might want to use the Session collection, it helps to consider a more advanced example.

The next example uses GDI+ to create a graphical pie chart. Because the pie chart is drawn dynamically, your code can build it according to information in a database or information supplied by the user. In this example, the user adds each slice of the pie using the web page, and the image is redrawn automatically. The slices are sent to the dynamic image page through the Session collection as special PieSlice objects.

To create this example, the first step is to create the PieSlice object. Each PieSlice includes a text label and a numeric value, as shown here:

```
public class PieSlice
{
    private float dataValue;
    public float DataValue
    {
        get {return dataValue;}
        set {dataValue = value;}
    }

    private string caption;
    public string Caption
    {
        get {return caption;}
        set {caption = value;}
    }

    public PieSlice(string caption, float dataValue)
    {
        Caption = caption;
        DataValue = dataValue;
    }

    public override string ToString()
    {
        return Caption + " (" + DataValue.ToString() + ")";
    }
}
```

The PieSlice class overrides the ToString() method to facilitate display in a data bound ListBox. When a ListBox contains custom objects, it calls the ToString() method to get the text to show. (Another approach would be to use a DataList with a custom template.)

The test page (shown in Figure 23-10), has the responsibility of letting the user create pie slices. Essentially, the user enters a label and a numeric value for the slice, and clicks the Add button. The PieSlice object is then created and shown in a ListBox.

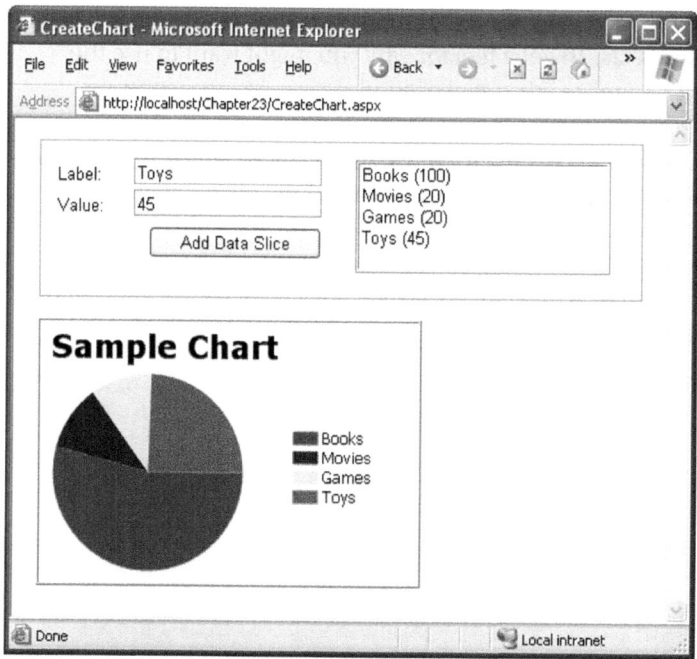

Figure 23-10. *A dynamic pie chart page*

The amount of code required is fairly small. The trick is that every time the page is finished processing (and the Page.PreRender event fires), all the PieSlice objects in the ListBox are stored in session state. Every time the page is requested (and the Page.Load event fires), any available PieSlice objects are retrieved from session state.

Here's the complete code for the test page:

```
public class CreateChart : System.Web.UI.Page
{
    protected System.Web.UI.WebControls.ListBox lstPieSlices;
    protected System.Web.UI.WebControls.Button cmdAdd;
    protected System.Web.UI.WebControls.TextBox txtLabel;
    protected System.Web.UI.WebControls.TextBox txtValue;

    // The data that will be used to create the pie chart.
    private ArrayList pieSlices = new ArrayList();

    private void Page_Load(object sender, System.EventArgs e)
    {
        // Retrieve the pie slices that are defined so far.
        if (Session["ChartData"] != null)
        {
            pieSlices = (ArrayList)Session["ChartData"];
```

```
        }
    }

    private void cmdAdd_Click(object sender, System.EventArgs e)
    {
        // Create a new pie slice.
        PieSlice pieSlice = new PieSlice(txtLabel.Text,
          Single.Parse(txtValue.Text));
        pieSlices.Add(pieSlice);

        // Bind the list box to the new data.
        lstPieSlices.DataSource = pieSlices;
        lstPieSlices.DataBind();
    }

    private void CreateChart_PreRender(object sender, System.EventArgs e)
    {
        // Before rendering the page, store the current collection
        // of pie slices.
        Session["ChartData"] = pieSlices;
    }
}
```

The pie drawing code is quite a bit more involved. It creates a new bitmap, retrieves the PieSlice objects, examines them, and draws the corresponding pie slices and legend.

The first step is to create the drawing surface and retrieve the chart data from session state, as follows:

```
private void Page_Load(object sender, System.EventArgs e)
{
    Bitmap image = new Bitmap(300, 200);
    Graphics g = Graphics.FromImage(image);
    g.FillRectangle(Brushes.White, 0, 0, 300, 200);
    g.SmoothingMode = SmoothingMode.AntiAlias;

    if (Session["ChartData"] != null)
    {
        // Retrieve the chart data.
        ArrayList chartData = (ArrayList)Session["ChartData"];
        ...
```

Next, the drawing code adds a title to the chart, as you can see here:

```
        ...
        // Write some text to the image.
        g.DrawString("Sample Chart",
          new Font("Verdana", 18, FontStyle.Bold),
          Brushes.Black, new PointF(5, 5));
        ...
```

The next step is to calculate the total of all the data points, as follows. This allows you to size each slice proportionately in the pie.

```
...
// Calculate the total of all data values.
float total = 0;
foreach (PieSlice item in chartData)
{
    total += item.DataValue;
}
...
```

Once you know the total, you can calculate the percentage of the pie that each slice occupies. Finally, you can multiply this percentage by the total angle width of a circle (360 degrees) to find the angle width required for that slice.

To draw each slice, you can use the Graphics.FillPie() method, and specify the starting and ending angle. When you draw each slice, you also need to ensure that you choose a new color that hasn't been used for a previous slice. This task is handled by a GetColor() helper method, which chooses the color from a short list based on the slice's index number:

```
...
// Draw the pie slices.
float currentAngle = 0, totalAngle = 0;
int i = 0;
foreach (PieSlice item in chartData)
{
    currentAngle = item.DataValue / total * 360;
    g.FillPie(new SolidBrush(GetColor(i)), 10, 40, 150, 150,
      (float)Math.Round(totalAngle),
      (float)Math.Round(currentAngle));
    totalAngle += currentAngle;
    i++;
}
...
```

The last drawing step is to render the legend. To create the legend, you need a rectangle that shows the slice color, followed by the pie slice label. Once again, the GetColor() method returns the correct color for the slice:

```
...
// Create a legend for the chart.
PointF colorBoxPoint = new PointF(200, 83);
PointF textPoint = new PointF(222, 80);

i = 0;
foreach (PieSlice item in chartData)
{
    g.FillRectangle(new SolidBrush(GetColor(i)), colorBoxPoint.X,
      colorBoxPoint.Y, 20, 10);
```

```
        g.DrawString(item.Caption, new Font("Tahoma", 10),
          Brushes.Black, textPoint);
        colorBoxPoint.Y += 15;
        textPoint.Y += 15;
        i++;
    }
    ...
```

Finally, you can render the image. In this case, GIF format is acceptable because the drawing code uses a fixed set of colors that are all in the basic 256-color GIF palette, as follows:

```
        image.Save(Response.OutputStream, ImageFormat.Gif);
    }
}
```

The only detail that's been omitted so far is the GetColor() method, which returns a color for each pie slice, as shown here:

```
private Color GetColor(int index)
{
    // Support six different colors. This could be enhanced.
    if (index > 5)
    {
        index = index % 5;
    }

    switch (index)
    {
        case 0:
            return Color.Red;
        case 1:
            return Color.Blue;
        case 2:
            return Color.Yellow;
        case 3:
            return Color.Green;
        case 4:
            return Color.Orange;
        case 5:
            return Color.Purple;
        default:
            return Color.Black;
    }
}
```

In its current implementation, GetColor() starts to return the same set of colors as soon as you reach the seventh slice, although you could easily change this behavior.

The end result is that both pages work together without a hitch. Every time a new slice is added, the image is redrawn seamlessly.

There's a fair bit you could do to improve this chart. For example, you could make it more generic so that it could render to different sizes, display larger amounts of data in the legend, and provide different labeling options. You could also render different types of charts, like line charts and bar graphs.

Tip To take a look at a more ambitious pie- and bar-chart renderer, you can download a free starter kit sample from Microsoft's ASP.NET website at `www.asp.net/ReportsStarterKit`. This sample is available in C# and VB .NET, and free to customize as you desire. Although it sports improved drawing logic, the mechanism used to transfer information is somewhat limited. Because it uses the query string, there's a limit to how much chart data you can specify. Of course, there's nothing to stop you from improving the example to support other options, like session state.

Summary

In this chapter, you've learned how to master basic and advanced GDI+. Although these techniques aren't right for every web page, they give you a set of features that can't be matched by many other web application programming frameworks.

PART FIVE

■■■

Web Services

CHAPTER 24

■ ■ ■

Creating Web Services

For years software developers and architects have tried to create software components that can be called remotely over local networks and the Internet. In the process, a number of new technologies and patched-together proprietary solutions have been created. Although some of these technologies have been quite successful running back-end systems on internal networks, none has met the challenges of the Internet—a wide, sometimes unreliable network of computers running on every type of hardware and operating system possible.

This is where XML web services enter the scene. To interact with a web service, you simply need to send an XML message over HTTP. Because every Internet-enabled device supports HTTP, and virtually every programming language has access to an XML parser, there are few limits on what types of applications can use web services. In fact, most programming frameworks include higher-level toolkits that make harnessing a web service as easy as calling a local function.

In this chapter, you'll learn about web services and the problems they solve. You'll also see how to create and consume web services using ASP.NET. However, you won't dive into the lower-level details of the underlying protocols just yet. Instead, you'll get started using a web service, and then learn to extend it in the next chapter.

Web Services Overview

While HTML pages (or the HTML output generated by ASP.NET web forms) are meant to be read by the end user, web services are used by other applications. They are pieces of business logic that can be accessed over the Internet. For example, an e-commerce site could use the web service of a shipping and packaging company to calculate the cost of the shipment. A news site could retrieve the news headlines and articles produced by external news providers, and expose them on its own pages in real time. A company could even provide the real-time value of their stock options, reading it from a specialized financial or investment site. With web services, you can reuse someone else's business logic instead of replicating it yourself, using just a few lines of code. This technique is similar to what programmers currently do with libraries of APIs, classes, and components. The main difference is that web services can be located remotely on another server, and managed by another company.

The History of Web Services

Even though web services are a new technology, there's a lot you can learn from recent history. Two of the major shifts in software development over the last couple of decades have been the development of object-oriented programming and component-based technology.

Object-oriented programming joined the mainstream in the early 1980s. Many saw object-oriented programming as the solution to the software crisis that resulted from the increasing complexity and size of software applications. Most projects were late and over budget, and the end result was often unreliable. The promise of object-oriented code was that by structuring code into objects, developers could create components that were more reusable, extensible, and maintainable.

The 1990s saw the birth of component technology, which made it possible to build applications by assembling components. Component technology is really an extension of object-oriented principles outside the boundaries of any one particular language so that it becomes a core piece of infrastructure that everyone can use. While object-oriented languages allowed developers to reuse objects in their applications, component-based technologies allowed developers to easily share compiled objects *between* applications. Two dominant component-based technologies emerged—COM (the Component Object Model) and CORBA (Common Object Request Broker Architecture). Since that time, other component technologies have appeared (like JavaBeans and .NET), but these are designed as proprietary solutions for specific programming frameworks.

Soon after COM and CORBA were created, these standards were applied to distributed components so that an application could interact between objects hosted on different computers in a network. Although both COM and CORBA have a great deal of technical sophistication, they are often difficult to set up and support in network environments, and they can't work together. These headaches became dramatically worse when the Internet appeared and developers began to apply these technologies to create distributed applications that spanned slower, less reliable, WANs (wide area networks). Because of their inherent complexity and proprietary nature, neither COM nor CORBA became truly successful in this environment.

Web services are a new technology that aims to answer these problems by extending component object technology to the Web. Essentially, a web service is a unit of application logic (a component) that can be remotely invoked over the Internet. Many of the promises of web services are the same as those of component technology—the aim is to make it easier to assemble applications from prebuilt application logic, share functionality between organizations and partners, and create more modular applications. Unlike earlier component technologies, web services are designed *exclusively* for this purpose. This means that as a .NET developer, you will still use the .NET component model to share compiled assemblies between .NET applications. However, if you want to share functionality between applications running on different platforms or hosted by different companies, web services fit perfectly.

Web services also place a much greater emphasis on interoperability. All software development platforms that allow programmers to create web services use the same bedrock of open XML-based standards. This ensures that you can create a web service using .NET and call it from a Java client, or create a Java web service and call it from a .NET application.

■**Note** Web services are not limited to the .NET Framework. The standards were defined before .NET was released, and they are exposed, used, and supported by vendors other than Microsoft. The .NET Framework is special because it hides all the plumbing code, and this makes it far easier to expose your own services over the Internet, or to access the services provided by other companies. As you'll see, you don't need to know all the details of XML and SOAP to successfully program web services (although, of course, some knowledge helps). ASP.NET abstracts the nitty-gritty stuff and generates wrapper classes that expose a simple object-oriented model to send, receive, and interpret the SOAP messages easily.

Distributed Computing and Web Services

To fully understand the importance of web services, you need to understand the requirements of *distributed computing*. Distributed computing is the partitioning of application logic into units that are executed on two or more computers in a network. The idea of distributed computing has been around a long time, and numerous communication technologies have been developed to allow the distribution and reuse of application logic.

There are many reasons for distributing application logic. Some of the most important include

- **High scalability.** By distributing the application logic, the load is spread out to different machines. This usually won't improve the performance of the application for individual users (in fact, it may slow it down), but it will almost always improve the scalability, thereby allowing the application to serve a much larger number of users at the same time.

- **Easy deployment.** Pieces of a distributed application may be upgraded without upgrading the whole application. A centrally located component can be updated without needing to update hundreds (or event thousands) of clients.

- **Improved security.** Distributed applications often span company or organization boundaries. For example, you might use distributed components to let a trading partner query your company's product catalog. It wouldn't be secure to let the trading partner connect directly to your company database. Instead, the trading partner needs to use a component running on your servers, which you can control and restrict appropriately.

The Internet has increased the importance and applicability of distributed computing. The simplicity and ubiquity of the Internet makes it a logical choice as the backbone for distributed applications.

Before web services, the dominant protocols were COM (which is called DCOM, or Distributed COM, when used on a network) and CORBA. Although CORBA and DCOM have a lot in common, they differ in the details, making it hard to get the protocols to interoperate. Table 24-1 summarizes some similarities and differences between CORBA, DCOM, and web services. It also introduces a slew of acronyms.

Table 24-1. *Comparing Different Distributed Technologies*

Characteristic	CORBA	DCOM	Web Services
RPC (Remote Procedure Call) mechanism	IIOP (Internet Inter-ORB Protocol)	DCE-RPC (Distributed Computing Environment Remote Procedure Call)	HTTP (Hypertext Transfer Protocol)
Encoding	CDR (Common Data Representation)	NDR (Network Data Representation)	XML (Extensible Markup Language)
Interface description	IDL (Interface Definition Language)	IDL (Interface Definition Language)	WSDL (Web Service Description Language)
Discovery	Naming service and trading service	Registry	UDDI (Universal Description, Discovery, and Integration)
Firewall friendly	No	No	Yes
Complexity of protocols	High	High	Low
Cross-platform	Partly	No	Yes

Both CORBA and DCOM allow for the invocation of remote objects. CORBA uses a standard called IIOP (Internet Inter-ORB Protocol), while DCOM uses a variation of a standard named DCE-RPC (Distributed Computing Environment Remote Procedure Call). The encoding of data in CORBA is based on a format named CDR (Common Data Representation). In DCOM, the encoding of data is based on a similar but incompatible format named NDR (Network Data Representation). These layers of standards make for significant complexity!

There are also differences between the languages that both protocols support. DCOM supports a wide range of languages (C++, Visual Basic, and so on), but was used primarily on Microsoft operating systems. CORBA supported different platforms, but mostly gained traction with Java-based applications. As a result, developers had two platforms that had the technical ability to support systems of distributed objects, but couldn't work together.

The Problems with Distributed Component Technologies

Interoperability is only part of the problem with CORBA and DCOM. Other technical challenges exist. Both protocols were developed before the Internet, and as such they aren't designed with the needs of a loosely coupled, sometimes unreliable, heavily trafficked network in mind. For example, both protocols are connection-oriented. That means a DCOM client holds on to a connection to the DCOM server to make multiple calls. The server-side DCOM component can also retain information about the client in memory. This provides a rich, flexible programming model, but it's a poor way to design large-scale applications that use the stateless protocols of the Internet. If the client simply disappears without properly cleaning up the connection, unnecessary resources are wasted. Similarly, if thousands of clients try to connect at once, the server can easily become swamped, running out of memory or connections.

Another problem is the fact that both protocols are exceedingly complex. They combine distributed-object technology with features for network security and lifetime management. Web services are so much easier to use in large part because they don't include this level of sophistication. However, that doesn't mean you can't create a secure web service. It just means that if you do, you'll need to rely on web services *and* another standard, such as SSL (as implemented by the web server), or WS-Security and XML Encryption (as implemented by the programming framework).

Note The danger here is that developers could be swamped by a proliferation of standards that aren't required for basic web services, but are required for sophisticated web service applications. However, this model still represents the best trade-off between complexity and simplicity. The advantage is that architects can develop new innovations for web services (like transactional support), without compromising the basic level of interoperability provided by the core web service standards.

The Benefits of Web Services

Web services are interesting from several perspectives. From a technological perspective, web services try to solve some problems faced when using tightly coupled technologies such as CORBA and DCOM. These are problems such as getting through firewalls, dealing with the complexities of lower-level transport protocols, and integrating heterogeneous platforms. Web services are also interesting from an organizational and economic perspective, because they open up doors for new ways of doing business and integrating systems between organizations.

DCOM and CORBA are fine for building enterprise applications with software running on the same platform and in the same closely administered local network. They are not fine, however, for building applications that span platforms, span the Internet, and need to achieve Internet scalability. They were simply not designed for this purpose.

This is where web services come in. Web services represent the next logical step in the evolution of component-based distributed technologies. Some key advantages include the following:

- **Web services are simple.** That simplicity means they can be easily supported on a wide range of platforms.

- **Web services are loosely coupled.** The web service may extend its interface and add new methods without affecting the clients as long as it still provides the old methods and parameters.

- **Web services are stateless.** A client makes a request to a web service, the web service returns the result, and the connection is closed. There is no permanent connection. This makes it easy to scale up and out to many clients and use a server farm to serve the web services. The underlying HTTP Protocol used by web services is also stateless. Of course, it is possible to provide some state by using additional techniques like the ones you use in ASP.NET web pages, including cookies. However, these techniques aren't standardized.

- **Web services are firewall-friendly.** Firewalls can pose a challenge for distributed object technologies. The only thing that almost always gets through firewalls is HTTP traffic on ports 80 and 443. Because web services use HTTP, they can pass through firewalls without explicit configuration.

Note It is still possible to use the firewall to block SOAP traffic. This is possible since the HTTP header of a web service message identifies it as a SOAP message, and an administrator may configure the firewall to stop SOAP traffic. For business-to-business scenarios, the firewall may only allow SOAP traffic from selected ranges of IP addresses.

Of course, the simplicity of web services does come with a cost. Namely, web services don't have all the features of more complex distributed component technologies. For example, there is no support for bidirectional communication, which means the web server cannot call back to a client after the client disconnects. In this respect, tightly coupled protocols such as DCOM and CORBA are more powerful than web services. The .NET Framework also has a new technology, *remoting*, which is ideal for communicating between distributed .NET applications in an internal network. Remoting is the successor to DCOM on the .NET platform. If you want to know more about remoting, you can read *Advanced .NET Remoting* (Apress, 2002) by Ingo Rammer. For information about whether you should use remoting instead of web services, refer to the sidebar "When to Use Web Services."

WHEN TO USE WEB SERVICES

Microsoft suggests two rules of thumb for deciding whether or not to use web services. If you need to cross *platform boundaries* (for example, communicate between a .NET and a Java application) or *trust boundaries* (for example, communicate between two different companies), web services make great sense. Web services are also a good choice if you want to make use of built-in ASP.NET features like caching, or IIS features like SSL security or Windows authentication. They also make sense if you want to leave yourself open to third-party integration in the future.

However, if you simply want to share functionality between two .NET applications, web services can be overkill—and they may introduce unnecessary overhead. For example, if you simply want web applications to have access to specific business logic, a much better approach is to create a class library assembly (which is compiled to a DLL) and use it in both applications. This avoids the overhead of out-of-process or network communication, which can be significant.

Finally, if you want to distribute functionality so it can be accessed remotely, but both the client and server are built using the .NET Framework, you might want to consider using .NET remoting instead. Remoting doesn't provide the same level of support for open standards like SOAP, but it does give you the freedom to use different types of communication, proprietary .NET data types, stateful objects, and faster TCP/IP communication. In short, remoting offers more features and the possibility to enhance performance for .NET-only solutions.

Making Money with Web Services

A new technology is doomed if it does not give new opportunities for the people concerned with making money. From a businessperson's perspective, web services open up new possibilities for the following reasons:

- By centralizing information and services, new payment structures may be used. The user of a web service can pay a subscription fee for using the service. One example may be the news feed from Associated Press. Another possibility is a pay-per-view, or *micro payment* model. A provider of a credit verification service, for instance, may charge per request.

- Web services enable real-time interaction and collaboration. Today, data is typically replicated and used locally. Web services enable real-time queries to remote data. An example is an e-commerce site selling computer games. The e-commerce site may hook up to a warehouse to get the number of items in stock in real time. This enables the e-commerce site to provide a better service. Nothing is more frustrating than buying something over the Internet just to learn the next day that the product you wanted is out of stock.

- There is a potential for aggregated services. A web service may aggregate other web services, screen-scraped websites, legacy components exposed using proprietary protocols, and so on. A typical example of an aggregated service is a comparative service giving you the best deal on products. Another type of service is one that groups related services. For example, imagine you're moving to a new home. Someone could provide you with a service that can update your address at the post office, find the transportation company to move all your possessions, and so on.

Web services are by no means the only technology that can provide these solutions. Many similar solutions are available today using existing technology. However web services have the momentum and standards to make these kinds of services generally available.

The Web Service Stack

The key to the success of web services is that they are based on open standards *and* that major vendors such as Microsoft, IBM, and Sun are behind these standards. Still, open standards do not automatically lead to interoperability. First, the vendors must implement all the standards. Furthermore, they must implement the standards in a compatible way.

There are several specifications that are used when building web services. Figure 24-1 shows the web service stack as it exists today.

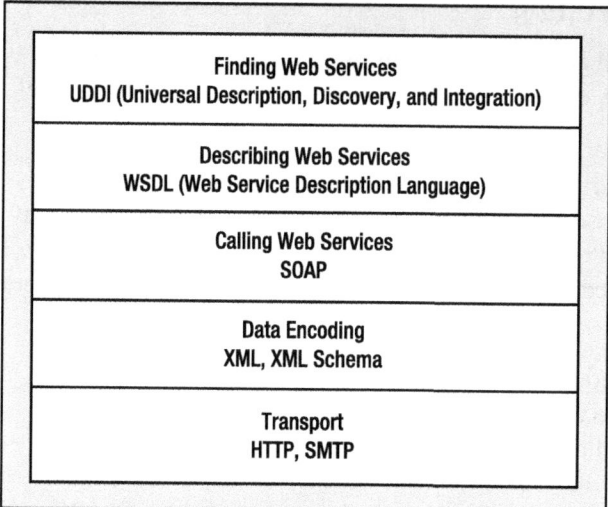

Figure 24-1. *The web service technology stack*

You'll learn much more about the SOAP, WSDL, and UDDI Protocols that support web services in the next chapter. However, before you get started creating and using web services, it's important to get a basic understanding of the role these standards play. Table 24-2 summarizes these standards, and the next few sections fill in some of the details. You'll get into much more detail in the next chapter.

Table 24-2. *Web Service Standards*

Standard	Description
WSDL	The Web Service Description Language tells a client what methods are present in a web service, what parameters and return values each method uses, and how to communicate with them.
SOAP	The preferred way to encode information (such as data values) before sending it to a web service.
HTTP	The protocol over which all web service communication takes place. For example, SOAP messages are sent over HTTP channels.
DISCO	The discovery standard that contains links to web services or can be used to provide a dynamic list of web services in a specified path.
UDDI	The business registry that lists information about companies, the web services they provide, and the corresponding URLs for DISCO files or WSDL contracts. Unfortunately, it's still too new to be widely accepted and useful.

Finding Web Services

In a simple application, you may already know the URL of the web service you want to use. If so, you can hardcode it or place it in a configuration file. No other steps are required.

In other situations, you might want to search for the web service you need at runtime. For example, you might use a standardized service that's provided by different hosting companies, and is not always available at the same URL. Or, you may just want an easy way to find all the web services provided by a trading partner. In both of these situations, you need to use *discovery* to programmatically locate the web services you need.

There are two specifications that help in the discovery of a web service:

- **DISCO** (an abbreviation of discovery). The DISCO standard is used to create a single file that groups together a list of related web services. A company can publish a DISCO file on its server that contains links to all the web services it provides. Then clients simply need to request this file to find all the available web services. This is useful when the client already knows the company, and that it's offering services, and wants to see what web services they expose and find links to the details of their services. It's not very useful for search for new web services over the Internet, but it may be very helpful for local networks where a client connects to the server and can see what and where services are available.

- **UDDI** (Universal Description, Discovery, and Integration). UDDI is a centralized directory where web services are published by a group of companies. It's also the place where potential clients can go and search for their specific needs. Different organizations and groups of companies may use different UDDI registries. To retrieve information from a UDDI directory or register your components, you use a web service interface.

Discovery is one of the newest and least mature parts of the web service protocol stack. DISCO is only supported by Microsoft, and is slated to be replaced by a similar more general standard named WS-Inspection in future .NET releases. UDDI is designed for web services that are intended to be shared publicly or among a consortium of companies or organizations. It's not yet incorporated into the .NET Framework, although you can download a separate .NET component to search UDDI directories and register your components. Because there aren't yet any well-established UDDI directories, and because many web services are simply designed for use in a single company or between a small set of known trading partners, it's likely that most web services will not be published in UDDI.

Describing a Web Service

In order for a client to know how to access a web service, it must know what methods are available, what parameters each method uses, and what the data type of each parameter is. The WSDL (Web Service Description Language) is an XML-based language that describes all these details. It describes the request message a client needs to submit to the web service, and the response message the web service returns. It also defines the transport protocol you need to use (typically HTTP) and the location of the web service.

WSDL is a complex standard. But as you'll see in this chapter, there are tools that consume WSDL information and automatically generate helper classes that hide the low-level plumbing required to interact with web services.

The Wire Format

To communicate with a web service, you need a way to create request and response messages that can be parsed and understood on any platform. SOAP (formerly Simple Object Access Protocol, but no longer considered an acronym) is the XML-based language that you use to create these messages.

It's important to understand that SOAP defines the messages you use to exchange data (the message format), but it doesn't describe how you send the message (the transport protocol). With ASP.NET web services, the transport protocol is HTTP. In other words, in order to communicate with a web service, a client opens an HTTP connection, and sends a SOAP message.

.NET also supports HTTP GET and HTTP POST, two simpler approaches for interacting with web services that aren't as standardized and don't offer the same rich set of features. In both these cases, an HTTP channel is used for communication, data is sent as a simple collection of name/value pairs, not as a full-blown SOAP message. The only place you're likely to see this simpler approach used in the .NET environment is in the simple browser-based test page ASP.NET provides for testing your web services. In fact, by default the ASP.NET 1.1 machine.config file only allows HTTP POST requests from the local computer, and disables HTTP GET support entirely.

Figure 24-2 summarizes the web service life cycle. First, the web service consumer finds the web service, either by going directly to the web service URL, or by using a UDDI server or DISCO file. Next, the client retrieves the web service WSDL document, which describes how to interact with the web service. Both of these tasks are performed at design time. When you run the application and actually interact with the web service, the client sends a SOAP message to trigger to the appropriate web method.

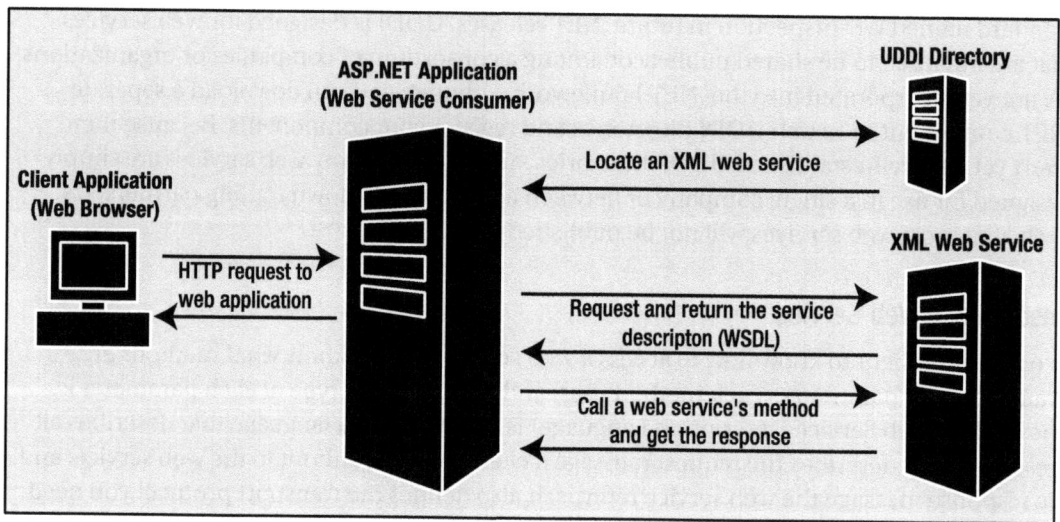

Figure 24-2. *The web service life cycle*

Building a Basic Web Service

In this section, you'll see how to build a web service with ASP.NET and how to test it in a browser. In this example, you'll develop a web service called EmployeesService, which will count and return the number of employees for a specific city (or the total of all employees) by querying the Employees table in SQL Server's sample Northwind database.

The Web Service Class

A web service begins as a stateless class with one or more methods. It's these methods that the remote clients call to invoke your code.

The EmployeeService is designed to allow remote clients to retrieve information about the employees in a company. It provides a GetEmployees() method that returns a DataSet with the full set of employee information. It also provides a GetEmployeesCount() method, which simply returns the number of employees in the database. In order to provide these methods, you need nothing more than some basic ADO.NET code. Here's the full class listing:

```
public class EmployeesService
{
    private string connectionString =
      "Data Source=localhost;Initial Catalog=Northwind;Integrated Security=SSPI";

    public int GetEmployeesCount()
    {
        SqlConnection con = new SqlConnection(connectionString);
        string sql = "SELECT COUNT(*) FROM Employees";
        SqlCommand cmd = new SqlCommand(sql, con);

        // Open the connection and get the value.
        cmd.Connection.Open();
        int numEmployees = -1;
        try
        {
            numEmployees = (int)cmd.ExecuteScalar();
        }
        finally
        {
            cmd.Connection.Close();
        }
        return numEmployees;
    }
```

```
public DataSet GetEmployees()
{
    // Create the command and the connection.
    string sql = "SELECT EmployeeID, LastName, FirstName, Title, " +
      "TitleOfCourtesy, HomePhone FROM Employees";
    SqlConnection con = new SqlConnection(connectionString);
    SqlDataAdapter da = new SqlDataAdapter(sql, con);
    DataSet ds = new DataSet();

    // Fill the DataSet.
    da.Fill(ds, "Employees");
    return ds;
}
}
```

Both GetEmployees() and GetEmployeesCount() are public methods, which means that the class can be used from any web page in the same project. (Or, if you compile this class into a separate DLL, in any project that references this assembly.) However, there are a few extra steps you need to take to make this class ready for a web service.

Web Service Requirements

Before you transform your class into a web service, you need to make sure it's compatible with the requirements of the underlying XML-based standards (which you'll learn more about in the next chapter). Because web services are executed by ASP.NET, which hosts the CLR (common language runtime), you can use any valid .NET code. That means you can use .NET classes to access data with ADO.NET or validate data with regular expressions. As with any back-end business component, you can't show any user interface, but other than that your code has no restrictions.

However, there *are* limitations on what information your code can accept (in the form of parameters) and return (in the form of a return value). That's because web services are built on XML-based standards for exchanging data. As a result, the set of data types they can use is limited to the set of data types recognized by the XML Schema standard. That means that you can use simple data types like strings and numbers, but you can't send proprietary .NET objects like a FileStream, an Image, or an EventLog. This restriction makes a lot of sense. Clearly, other programming languages have no way to interpret these more complex classes, so even if you could devise a way to send them over the wire the client might not be able to interpret them, which would thwart interoperability. (.NET remoting is an example of a distributed component technology that *does* allow you to use .NET-specific types. However, the cost of this convenience is the fact that it won't support non-.NET clients.)

Table 24-3 lists the supported web service data types.

Table 24-3. *Web Service Data Types for Parameters and Return Values*

Data Type	Description
The Basics	Simple C# data types such as integers (short, int, long), unsigned integers (ushort, uint, ulong), nonintegral numeric types (float, double, decimal), and a few other miscellaneous types (bool, string, char, byte, and DateTime).
Arrays	You can use arrays of any supported type. You can also use an ArrayList (which is simply converted into an array), but you can't use more specialized collections like the Hashtable. You can also use binary data through byte arrays. Binary data is automatically Base64 encoded so that it can be inserted into an XML web service message.
Custom Objects	You can pass any object you create based on a custom class or structure. The only limitation is that only public data members are transmitted, and all public members and properties must use one of the other supported data types. If you use a class that includes custom methods, these methods will not be transmitted to the client, and they will not be accessible to the client.
Enumerations	Enumerations types (defined in C# with the enum keyword) are supported. However, the web service uses the string name of the enumeration value (not the underlying integer).
XmlNode	Objects based on System.Xml.XmlNode are representations of a portion of an XML document. You can use this to send arbitrary XML.
DataSets	You can use the DataSet to return information from a relational database. Other ADO.NET data objects, like DataTables and DataRows, aren't supported. When you use a DataSet, it's automatically converted to XML in a similar way as if you used the GetXml() or WriteXml() methods of the DataSet.

■**Note** The supported web service data types are based on the types defined by the XML Schema standard. These map fairly well to the basic set of C# data types.

The EmployeesServices class follows these rules. The only data types it uses for parameters and return values are int and DataSet, both of which are supported. Of course, some web service programmers prefer to steer clear of the DataSet (see the sidebar in this section), but it's still a reasonable, widely used approach.

One other requirement is that your web services need to be stateless. In fact, the web service architecture works in the exact same way as the web-page architecture—a new web service object is created at the beginning of the request, and the web service object is destroyed as soon as the request has been processed and the response has been returned. The EmployeesServices class fits well with this model, because it doesn't retain any state in class member variables. The only exception is the connectionString variable, which is initialized with the required value every time the class is created.

THE DATASET AND XML WEB SERVICES

You'll notice that the DataSet is one of the few specialized .NET classes that is supported by web services. That's because the DataSet has the ability to automatically serialize itself to XML. However, this support comes with a significant caveat—even though non-.NET clients can use a web service that returns a DataSet, they might not be able to do anything useful with the DataSet XML! That's because other languages won't be able to automatically convert the DataSet into a manageable objects. Instead, they will be forced to use their own XML programming APIs. Although these work in theory, they can be tedious in practice, especially with complex, proprietary XML. For that reason, developers usually avoid the DataSet when creating web services that need to support clients on a wide range of different platforms.

It's worth noting that Microsoft could have used the DataSet approach with many other .NET classes in order to allow them to automatically serialize themselves as XML. However, Microsoft wisely restrained itself from adding these features, realizing that they would make it far too easy for programmers to create applications that used web service standards but weren't practical in cross-platform scenarios. (Not so long ago, Microsoft might have pursued exactly this "embrace and extend" philosophy, but fortunately they've recognized the need to foster integration and broad compatibility between applications.)

So that still leaves the question of why Microsoft decided to support the DataSet in their web services toolkit. The reason is because the DataSet enables one of the most common uses of web services—returning a snapshot of information from a relational database. The benefit of adding this feature seemed worth the cost of potential interoperability headaches for developers who don't consider their web service architecture carefully.

Exposing a Web Service

Now that you've verified that the EmployeesService class is ready for the Web, it's time to convert it to a web service. The crucial first step is to add the System.Web.Services.WebMethod attribute to each method you want to expose as part of your web service. This web service instructs ASP.NET to make this method available for inspection and remote invocation.

Here's the revised class with two web methods:

```
public class EmployeesService
{
    private string connectionString =
      "Data Source=localhost;Initial Catalog=Northwind;Integrated Security=SSPI";

    [WebMethod()]
    public int GetEmployeesCount()
    {
        SqlConnection con = new SqlConnection(connectionString);
        string sql = "SELECT COUNT(*) FROM Employees";
        SqlCommand cmd = new SqlCommand(sql, con);

        // Open the connection and get the value.
        cmd.Connection.Open();
        int numEmployees = -1;
        try
```

```
    {
        numEmployees = (int)cmd.ExecuteScalar();
    }
    finally
    {
        cmd.Connection.Close();
    }
    return numEmployees;
}


[WebMethod()]
public DataSet GetEmployees()
{
    // Create the command and the connection.
    string sql = "SELECT EmployeeID, LastName, FirstName, Title, " +
      "TitleOfCourtesy, HomePhone FROM Employees";
    SqlConnection con = new SqlConnection(connectionString);
    SqlDataAdapter da = new SqlDataAdapter(sql, con);
    DataSet ds = new DataSet();

    // Fill the DataSet.
    da.Fill(ds, "Employees");
    return ds;
}
}
```

These two simple changes complete the transformation from your class into a web service. However, the client still has no entry point into your web service—in other words, there's no way for another application to trigger your web methods. To allow this, you need to create an .asmx file that exposes the web service.

■Note In this example, the web service contains the data access code. However, if you plan to use the same code in a web application, it's worth adding an extra layer using database components. To implement this design, you would first create a separate database component (as described in Part Two), and then use that database component directly in your web pages and your web service.

ASP.NET implements web services as files with the .asmx extension. As with a web page, the code for a web service can be placed directly in the .asmx, or in a class in a code-behind file that the .asmx file references (which is the Visual Studio .NET approach).

For example, you could create a file named EmployeesService.asmx and link it to your EmployeesService class. Every .asmx file begins with a WebService directive that declares the server-side language used in the file and the class. It can optionally declare other information, such as the code-behind file, and whether or not you want to generate debug symbols during the compilation. In this respect it is similar to the Page directive for .aspx files.

Here's an example .asmx file with the EmployeesService:

```
<%@ WebService Language="C#" Class="EmployeesService" %>
```

In this case, you have two choices. You can insert the class code immediately after the WebService attribute, or you can compile it into one of the assemblies in the Bin directory. If you've added the EmployeesService class to a Visual Studio .NET project, it will automatically be compiled as part of the web application DLL, so you don't need to include anything else in the .asmx file.

At this point, you're finished. Your web service is complete, available, and ready to be used in other applications.

Tip There's no limit to how many web services you add to a single web application, and you can freely mingle web services and web pages.

Web Services in Visual Studio

If you're using Visual Studio .NET, you probably won't go through the process of creating a class, converting it a web service, and then adding an .asmx file. Instead, you'll create the .asmx file and the code-behind in one step, by selecting Project ➤ Add Web Service from the menu.

When you take this step, you won't actually be able to see or edit the .asmx file in Visual Studio .NET. However, if you open it in a text editor like Notepad you'll see the same WebService directive described earlier, with one additional detail—a CodeBehind attribute that tells Visual Studio .NET what file contains the source code for the corresponding web service class.

Note that when you create a web service in Visual Studio .NET, the class contains a few additional details. For example, you'll see initialization code in a collapsed region labeled "Component Designer generated code." This code is similar to the design code in a Visual Studio .NET web page. In most cases, it doesn't perform any function, but if you drag-and-drop components onto the design surface of your web service, Visual Studio .NET will add the code to this region to create and configure these objects. For example, rather than creating a DataSet by hand, you could drag it onto your web service from the toolbox, and then use it in your web service code. Although this approach works perfectly well, some developers (myself included) find that it makes code less readable and makes it difficult to separate the functionality of distinct web methods.

There are also two additional details in the web service that you haven't used yet. First, the web service class inherits from System.Web.Services.WebService, and second, a WebService attribute is applied to the class declaration. Neither of these details is required, but you'll consider their role in the following sections.

Deriving from the WebService Class

When you create a web service in Visual Studio .NET, your web service class automatically derives from the base WebService class, as shown here:

```
public class EmployeesService : System.Web.Services.WebService
{ ... }
```

Inheriting from the WebService class is a convenience that allows you to access the built-in ASP.NET objects (such as Application, Session, and User) just as easily as you can in a web form. These objects are provided as properties of the WebService class, which your web service acquires through inheritance. If you don't need to use any of these objects (or if you're willing to go through the static HttpContext.Current property to access them), you don't need to inherit.

Here's how you would access Application state in a web service if you derive from the base WebService class:

```
// Store a number in session state.
Session["Counter"] = 10;
```

Here's the equivalent code you would need to use if your web service class doesn't derive from WebService:

```
// Store a number in session state.
HttpContext.Current.Session["Counter"] = 10;
```

Table 24-4 lists the properties you receive by inheriting from WebService.

Table 24-4. *WebService Properties*

Property	Description
Application	An instance of the HttpApplicationState class that provides access to the global application state of the web application.
Context	An instance of the HttpContext class for the current request.
Server	An instance of the HttpServerUtility class.
Session	An instance of the HttpSessionState class that provides access to the current session state.
User	An IPrincipal object that allow you to examine user credentials and roles, if the user has been authenticated.

Since the .NET Framework only supports single inheritance, inheriting from WebService means that your web service class cannot inherit from other classes. This is really the only reason not to inherit from WebService.

■Note An interesting point with inheriting from WebService is that WebService is derived from the System.MarshalByRefObject class. This class is the base class used for .NET remoting. As a result, when you create a class that derives from WebService, you gain the ability to use your class in several ways. You can use it as any other local class (and access it directly in your web pages), you can expose it as part of a web service, or you can expose it as a distributed object in a .NET remoting host. To learn more about .NET remoting, refer to *Advanced .NET Remoting* (Apress, 2002) by Ingo Rammer.

Documenting a Web Service

Web services are self-describing, which means that ASP.NET automatically provides all the information the client needs about what methods are available and what parameters they require. This is provided by the XML-based standard called WSDL, which you'll explore in the next chapter. However, although a WSDL document describes the mechanics of the web service, it doesn't describe its purpose or the meaning of the information supplied to and returned from each method. Most web services will provide this information in separate developer documents. However, you can (and should) include a bare minimum of information with your web service by using the WebMethod and WebService attributes.

You can add descriptions to each method through the Description property of the WebMethod attribute and to the entire web service as a whole using the Description property of the WebService attribute. You can also apply a descriptive name to the web service using the Name property of the WebService attribute. Here's an example of how you might insert this information in the EmployeesService:

```
[WebService(Name="Employees Service",
 Description="Retrieve the Northwind Employees")]
public class EmployeesService : System.Web.Services.WebService
{
    [WebMethod(Description="Returns the total number of employees.")]
    public int GetEmployeesCount()
    { ... }

    [WebMethod(
     Description="Returns the full list of employees.")]
    public DataSet GetEmployees()
    { ... }
}
```

These custom descriptions are added to the WSDL document that describes your service. It's also shown in the automatically generated test page that you'll use in the next section.

There's one other detail you should supply for your web service—a unique XML namespace. This allows your web service (and the XML messages it generates) to be uniquely identified. XML namespaces were first introduced in Chapter 12. By default, ASP.NET web services use the default XML namespace http://tempuri.org/, which is only suitable for testing. If you don't set a custom namespace, you'll see a warning message in the test page advising you to use something more distinctive. Note that the XML namespace has no relationship to the concept of .NET namespaces. It doesn't affect how your code works, or how the client uses your web service. Instead, the XML namespace is simply used to identify your web service. XML namespaces usually look like URLs. However, they don't need to correspond to a valid Internet location.

Ideally, the namespace you use will refer to a URL address that you control. Often, this will incorporate your company's Internet domain name as part of the namespace. For example, if your company uses the website http://www.mycompany.com, you might give the Employees web service a namespace like http://www.mycompany.com/EmployeesService.

The namespace is specified through the WebService attribute, as shown here.

```
[WebService (Name="Employees Service",
 Description="Retrieve the Northwind Employees",
 Namespace="http://www.apress.com/ProASP.NET/")]
public class EmployeesService : System.Web.Services.WebService
{ ... }
```

Testing a Web Service

Now that you've seen how to create a simple web service, you're ready to test it. Fortunately, you don't need to write a client application to test it because .NET includes a test web page that ASP.NET uses automatically when you request the URL of an .asmx file in a browser. This page uses reflection to read and show information about the web services, such as the names of the methods it provides.

To try out the test page, request the EmployeesService.asmx file in your browser. (In Visual Studio .NET, you simply need to set this as the start page for your application and then run it.) Figure 24-3 shows the test page you'll see.

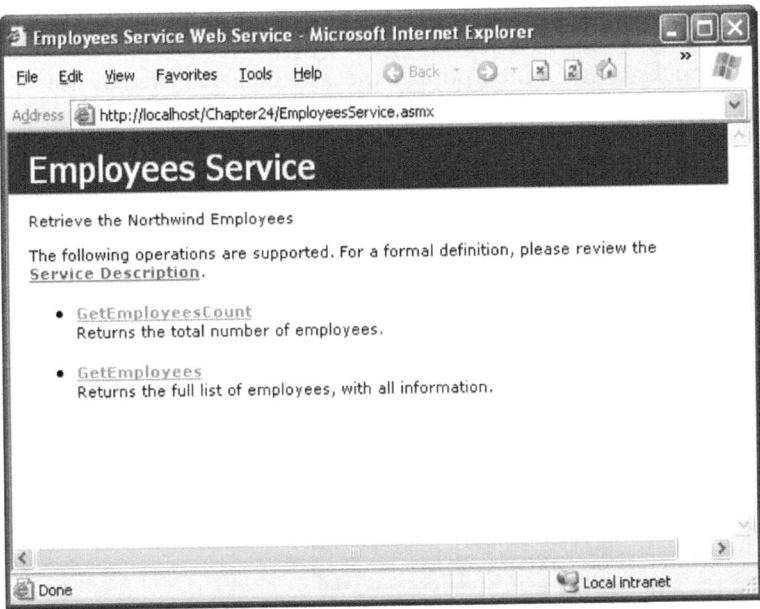

Figure 24-3. *The web service test page*

Note that the page displays the two web methods with their descriptions, and the page's title is the name of the web service. If you click one of the methods, you'll see a page that allows you to test the method (and supply the data for any method parameters). Figure 24-4 shows the page that allows you to test the GetEmployeesCount() method.

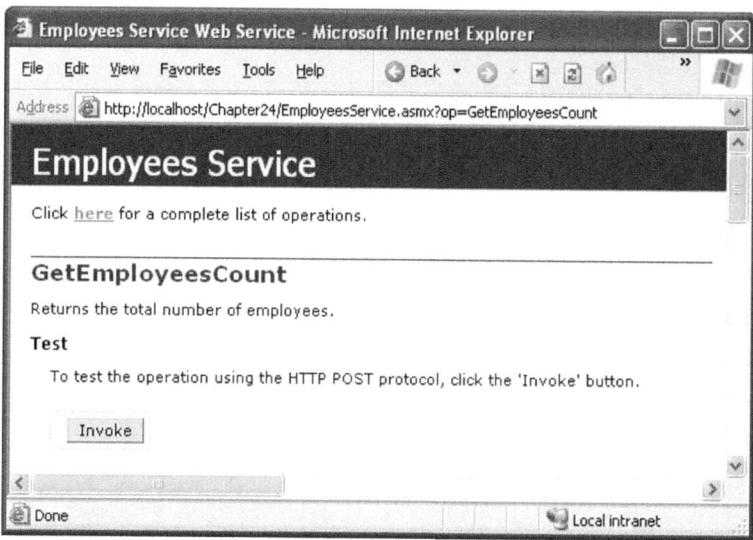

Figure 24-4. *Testing a web method*

When you click the Invoke button, a new web page appears with an XML document that contains the requested data. Looking at Figure 24-5, you can see that there are nine employee records. If you look at the URL, you'll see that it incorporates the .asmx file, followed by the web service method name.

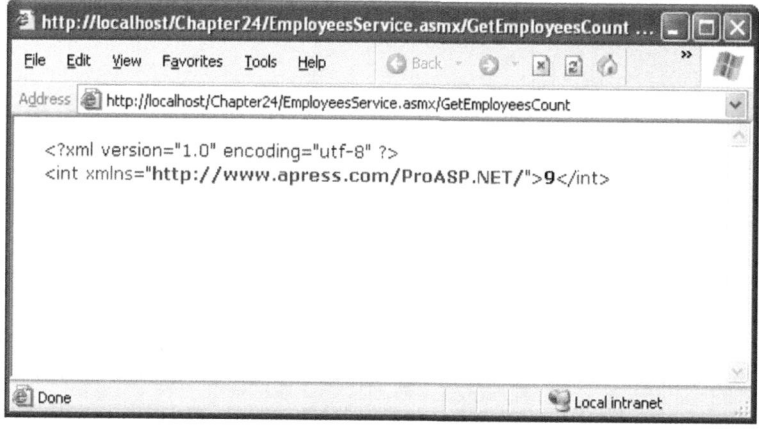

Figure 24-5. *The results for GetEmployeesCount()*

You can repeat this process to invoke GetEmployees(), in which case you'll see the much more detailed XML that represents the entire DataSet contents (as shown in Figure 24-6).

As you can see, thanks to this helper page, testing a basic web service is quite straightforward and doesn't require you to build a client.

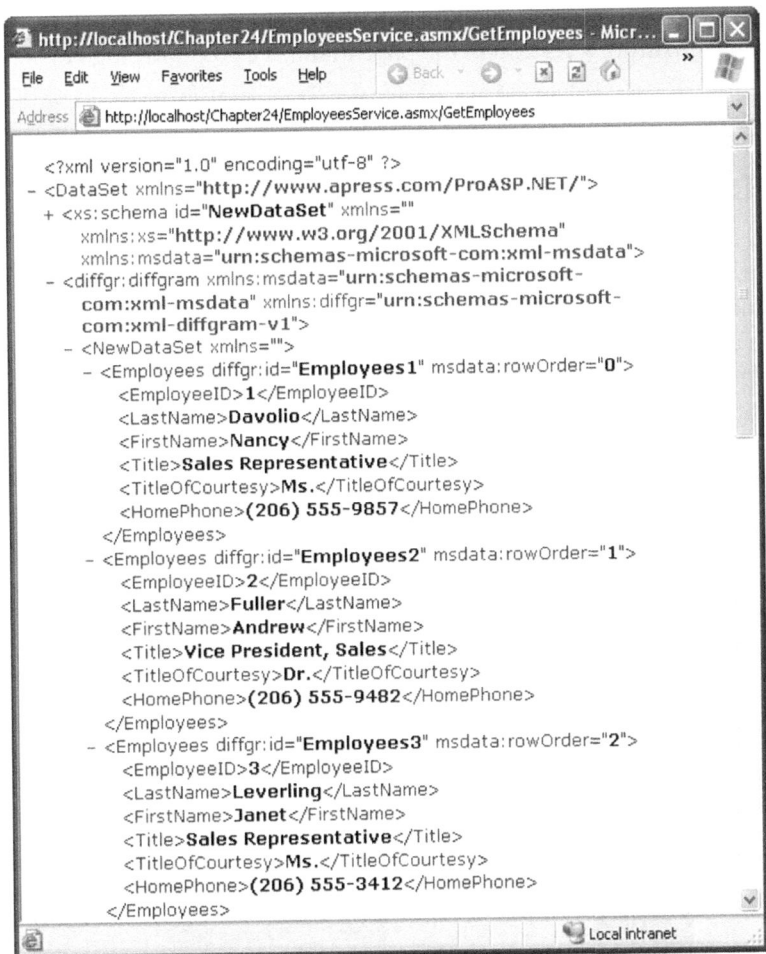

Figure 24-6. *The results for GetEmployees()*

The test pages aren't a part of the web services standards; they're just a frill provided by ASP.NET. In fact, the test page is rendered by ASP.NET on the fly using the web page c:\[WinDir]\Microsoft.NET\Framework\[Version]\Config\DefaultWsdlHelpGenerator.aspx. In some cases, you may want to modify the appearance or behavior of this page. If so, you simply need to copy the DefaultWsdlHelpGenerator.aspx file to your web application directory, modify it, and then change the web.config file for the application to point to the new rendering page by adding the <wsdlHelpGenerator> element, as shown here:

```
<configuration>
  <system.web>
    <webServices>
      <wsdlHelpGenerator href="MyWsdlHelpGenerator.aspx"/>
    </webServices>
    <!-- Other settings omitted. -->
  </system.web>
</configuration>
```

This technique is most commonly used to change the look of the test page. For example, you might use this technique to substitute a version of the page that has a company logo or copyright notice.

Consuming a Web Service

In order for a client to make use of the web service it has to be able to create, send, receive, and understand XML-based messages. This process is easy in principle, but fairly tedious in practice. If you had to implement it yourself, you would need to write the same low-level infrastructure code again and again.

Fortunately, .NET provides a solution with a dedicated component called a *proxy class*, which performs the heavy lifting for your application. The proxy class wraps the calls to the web service's methods. It takes care of generating the correct SOAP message format and managing the transmission of the messages over the network (using HTTP). When it receives the response message, it also converts the results back to the corresponding .NET data types.

This process is graphically represented in Figure 24-7. In this example, a browser is running an ASP.NET web page, which is using a web service from another server behind the scenes. The ASP.NET web page uses the proxy class to contact this external web service.

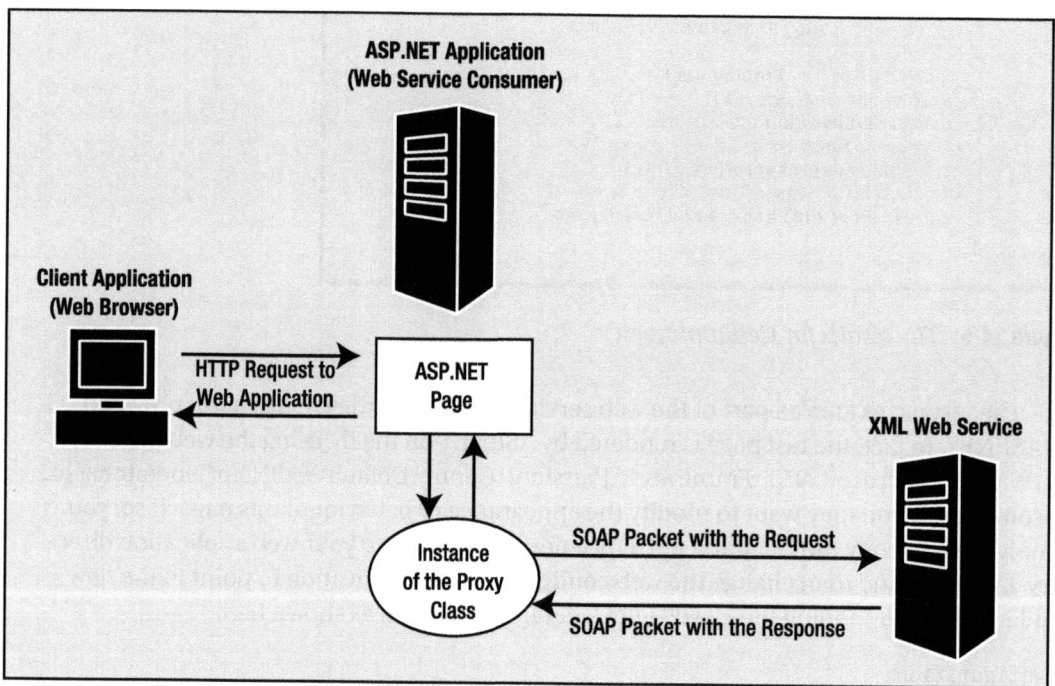

Figure 24-7. *The web service proxy class*

■**Note** Thanks to the proxy class, you can call a method in a web service as easily as you call a method in a local component. Of course, this behavior isn't always a benefit. Web services have different characteristics than local components. For example, it takes a nontrivial amount of time to call a web method because every call needs to be converted to XML and sent over the network. The danger is that the more this reality is hidden from developers, the less likely they are to take it into account and design their applications accordingly.

There are two ways to create a proxy class in .NET:

- You can use the wsdl.exe command-line tool.

- You can use the Visual Studio .NET web reference feature.

Both of these approaches produce essentially the same result, because they use the same classes in the .NET Framework to perform the actual work. In fact, you can even harness these classes (which are found in the System.Web.Services namespaces) to generate your own proxy classes programmatically, although this approach isn't terribly practical.

In the following sections, you'll learn how to use wsdl.exe and Visual Studio .NET to create proxy classes. You'll learn how to consume a web service in three types of clients—an ASP.NET web page, a Windows application, and a classic ASP page.

Generating the Proxy Class with Wsdl.exe

The wsdl.exe tool takes a web service and generates the source code of the proxy class in either VB .NET or C#. The name WSDL stems from the web service standard (Web Services Description Language) that's used to describe the functionality provided by a web service. You'll learn more about WSDL in the next chapter.

You can find the wsdl.exe file in the .NET Framework directory, which is typically in a path similar to c:\Program Files\Microsoft.NET\FrameworkSDK\Bin. Visual Studio .NET users have the WSDL.exe utility in the c:\Program Files\Microsoft Visual Studio .NET\ FrameworkSDK\Bin directory. This file is a command-line utility, so it's easiest to use by opening a command prompt window.

The WSDL document can be passed by specifying the URL or the web service plus the ?WSDL parameter, or it can be a file containing the text. The minimum syntax to generate the class is the following:

```
wsdl http://localhost/Chapter24/EmployeesService.asmx
```

By default the generated class is in the C# language, but you can change it by adding the /language parameter, as follows:

```
wsdl /language:VB http://localhost/Chapter24/EmployeesService.asmx
```

By default the generated file also has the same name as the web service (specified in the Name property of the WebService attribute). You can change it by adding a /out parameter to the wsdl.exe command, and you can use a /namespace parameter to change the namespace for the generated class. Here's an example (split over two lines to fit the page margins):

```
wsdl /namespace:ApressServices /out:EmployeesProxy.cs
  http://localhost/Chapter24/EmployeesService.asmx
```

Table 24-5 shows the full list of supported parameters.

Table 24-5. *Wsdl.exe Parameters*

Parameter	Description
<url or path>	A URL or path to a WSDL contract, an XSD schema, or a .discomap document.
/nologo	Suppresses the banner.
/language:<language>	The language to use for the generated proxy class. Choose from CS, VB, JS, or provide a fully qualified name for a class implementing System.CodeDom.Compiler.CodeDomProvider. The default is C#. Short form is /l.
/server	Generate an abstract class for a web service implementation based on the contracts. The default is to generate client proxy classes.
/namespace:<namespace>	The namespace for the generated proxy or template. The default namespace is the global namespace. Short form is /n.
/out:<fileName>	The filename for the generated proxy code. The default name is derived from the service name. Short form is /o.
/protocol:<protocol>	Override the default protocol to implement. Choose from SOAP, HTTP-GET, HTTP-POST, or custom protocol as specified in the configuration file.
/username:<username> /password:<password> /domain:<domain>	The credentials to use when connecting to a server that requires authentication. Short forms are /u, /p, and /d.
/proxy:<URL>	The URL of the proxy server to use for HTTP requests. The default is to use the system proxy setting.
/proxyusername:<username> /proxypassword:<password> /proxydomain:<domain>	The credentials to use when connecting to a proxy server that requires authentication. Short forms are /pu, /pp, and /pd.
/appsettingurkey:<key>	The configuration key to use in the code generation to read the default value for the URL property. The default is to not read from the config file. Short form is /urlkey.
/appsettingbaseurl:<baseURL>	The base URL to use when calculating the URL fragment. The appsettingurlkey option must also be specified. The URL fragment is the result of calculating the relative URL from the appsettingbaseurl to the URL in the WSDL document. Short form is /baseurl.

Before you can use this class in an ASP.NET application, you'll need to compile the file. Assuming that it's a C# file, you must use the csc.exe compiler included with the .NET Framework. For example, to turn your EmployeeProxy class into a DLL, use the following statement in the command prompt window:

```
csc /t:library /out:EmployeeProxy.dll /r:System.Web.Services.dll EmployeeProxy.cs
```

You can now use it with other applications. For example, to use it with an ASP.NET client, simply copy the DLL file to the Bin directory of your ASP.NET client application.

Generating the Proxy Class with Visual Studio .NET

In Visual Studio .NET, you create the proxy class by adding a web reference in the client project. Web references are similar to ordinary references, but instead of pointing to assemblies with ordinary .NET types, they point to a web service URL with a WSDL contract.

To create a web reference, follow these steps:

1. Right-click the client project in the Solution Explorer, and select Add Web Reference.

2. The Add Web Reference window opens, as shown in Figure 24-8. This window provides options for searching web registries or entering a URL directly. There's also a link that allows you to browse all the web services on the local computer or search a UDDI registry.

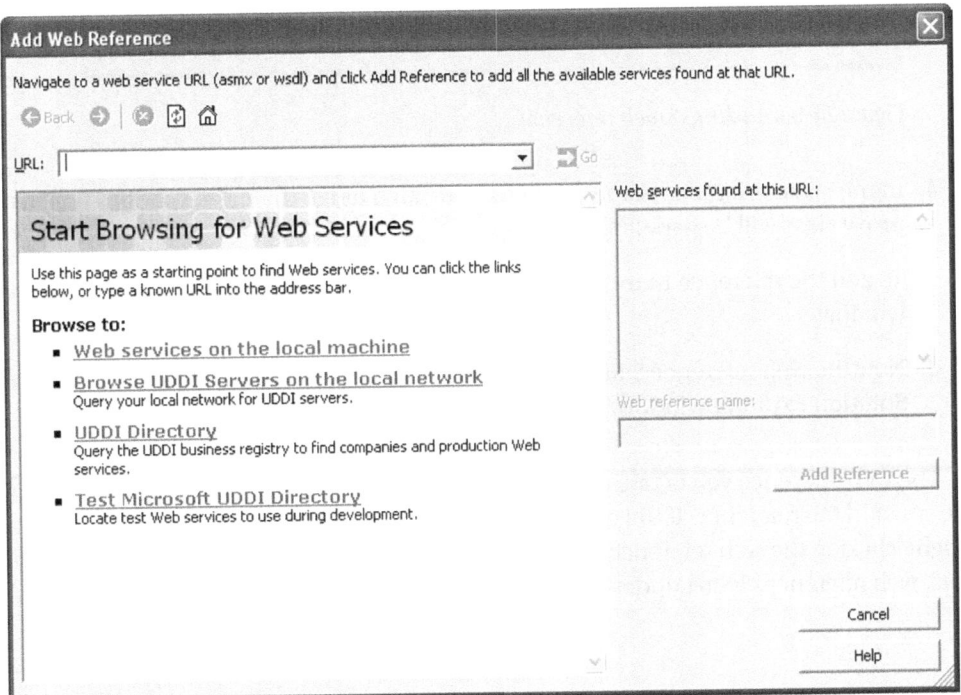

Figure 24-8. *The Add Web Reference window*

3. You can browse directly to your web service by entering a URL that points to the .asmx file. The test page will appear in the window (as shown in Figure 24-9), and the Add Reference button will be enabled.

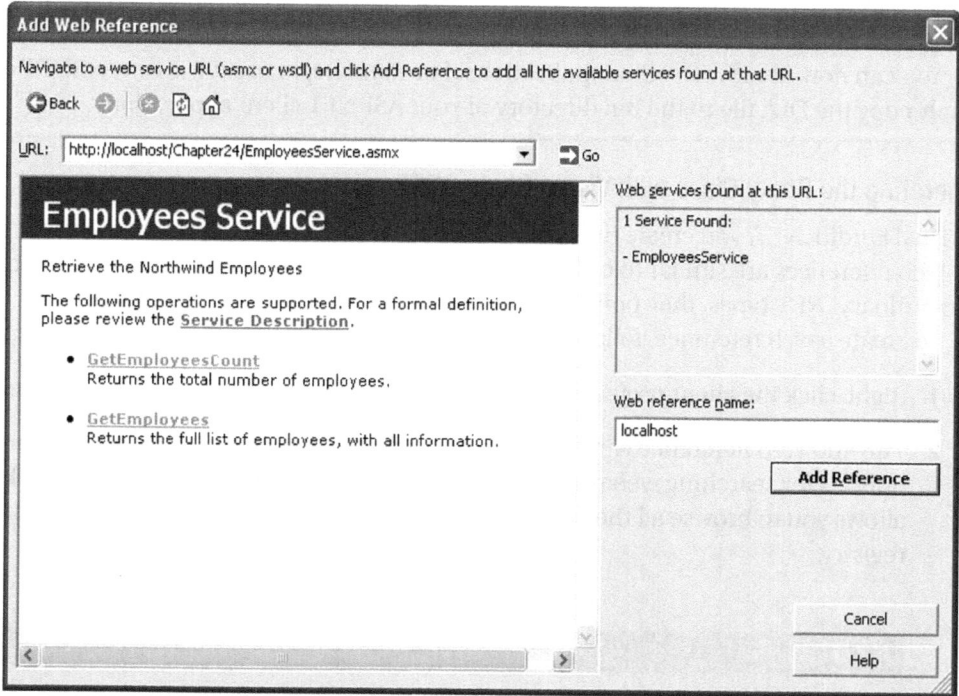

Figure 24-9. *Adding a web reference*

4. In the "Web reference name" text box you can change the namespace in which the proxy class will be generated.

5. To add the reference to this web service, click Add Reference at the bottom of the window.

6. Now the web reference will appear in the Web References group for your project in the Solution Explorer window.

The web reference you create uses the WSDL contract and information that exists at the time you add the reference. If the web service is changed, you'll need to update your proxy class by right-clicking the web reference and choosing Update Web Reference. Unlike local components, web references aren't updated automatically when you recompile the application.

Tip When developing and testing a web service in Visual Studio .NET, it's often easiest to add both the web service and the client application to the same solution. This allows you to test and change both pieces at the same time. You can even use the integrated debugger to set breakpoints and step through the code in both the client and the server, as though they were really a single application. To choose which application you want Visual Studio .NET to launch when you click Start, right-click the appropriate project name in the Solution Explorer and select Set As StartUp Project.

When you add a web reference, Visual Studio .NET creates a proxy class for you automatically. By default, this class is hidden from view. To see it, select Project ➤ Show All Files. You'll find a copy of the corresponding discovery document and WSDL contract under the corresponding web reference (see Figure 24-10). You'll also see a file named Reference.cs. This file contains the proxy class code that's used to interact with the web service.

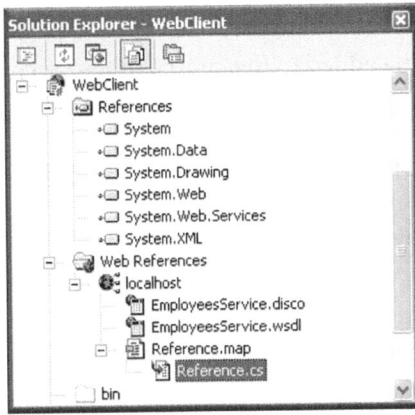

Figure 24-10. *The WSDL contract and proxy class*

Dynamic URLs

By default, when you create a proxy class the web service URL is hard-coded in the class constructor. However, you can change this behavior so that the proxy class reads the URL from a configuration file. That way, you can change the URL by modifying the configuration file, rather than regenerating the proxy class and recompiling your application. This is useful if you plan to change the location of the web service when you deploy the application, and you don't want to regenerate the proxy class.

To use a dynamic URL with Visual Studio .NET, you need to select the web reference, and change the URL Behavior option in the Properties window to Dynamic, as shown in Figure 24-11.

Figure 24-11. *Configuring a dynamic web service URL*

When you make this change, the web service URL will be added to the <appSettings> section of the client's configuration file. If the client is a web application, this information will be added to the web.config file. If you're creating a different type of client application, like a Windows application, the configuration file will have a name in the format [AppName].exe.config. For example, if your application is named SimpleClient.exe, the configuration file will be SimpleClient.exe.config. You must follow this naming convention.

Tip Visual Studio .NET uses a little sleight of hand with named configuration files. In the design environment, the configuration file will have the name App.config. However, when you build the application, this file will be copied to the build directory and given the appropriate name (to match the executable file). The only exception is if the client application is a web application. All web applications use a configuration file named web.config, no matter what file names you use. That's what you'll see in the design environment as well.

An example of the automatically generated configuration file setting is shown here:

```xml
<?xml version="1.0" encoding="utf-8"?>
<configuration>
  <appSettings>
    <add key="AppName.ServerName.ServiceName"
     value="http://www.myserver.com/ws/Employees.asmx"/>
  </appSettings>
  <!-- Other settings omitted. -->
</configuration>
```

The code in the proxy class is modified so that it attempts to read whatever information is in the configuration file. If it doesn't find the required value, it defaults to the URL that was used during development. Here's the code that's placed in the constructor:

```
string urlSetting =
  ConfigurationSettings.AppSettings("AppName.ServerName.ServiceName");

if (urlSetting != null)
{
    this.Url = urlSetting;
}
else
{
    this.Url = "http://localhost/Chapter24/EmployeesService.asmx";
}
```

To use a dynamic URL with the wsdl.exe utility, you need to use the /appsettingurlkey. For example, you could use this command line:

```
wsdl http://localhost/Chapter24/EmployeesService.asmx /appsettingurlkey:WsUrl
```

In this case, the key is stored with the key WsUrl in the <appSettings> section, as follows:

```
<?xml version="1.0" encoding="utf-8" ?>
<configuration>
  <appSettings>
    <add key="WsUrl" value="http://www.myserver.com/ws/Employees.asmx"/>
  </appSettings>
  <!-- Other settings omitted. -->
</configuration>
```

The Proxy Class

Once you create the proxy class, it's worth taking a closer look at the generated code to see how it works.

The proxy class has the same name as the web service class. It inherits from SoapHttpClientProtocol, which has properties such as Credentials, Url, and Timeout, which you'll learn about later in this chapter. Here's the declaration for the proxy class that provides communication with the EmployeesService:

```
public class EmployeesService :
 System.Web.Services.Protocols.SoapHttpClientProtocol
{ ... }
```

The proxy class contains a copy of each method in the web service. However, the version in the proxy class doesn't contain the business code. (In fact, there's no way for the client to get any information about the internal workings of your web service code—if it could, that would constitute a serious security breach.) Instead, the proxy class contains the code needed to query the remote web service and convert the results. For example, here's the GetEmployeesCount() method in the proxy class:

```
[System.Web.Services.Protocols.SoapDocumentMethodAttribute()]
public int GetEmployeesCount()
{
```

```
    object[] results = this.Invoke("GetEmployeesCount", new object[0]);
    return ((int)(results[0]));
}
```

This method calls the base SoapHttpClientProcotol.Invoke() to actually create the SOAP message, and start waiting for the response. The second line of code converts the returned object into an integer.

The proxy also has two other methods, called BeginGetEmployeesCount() and EndGetEmployeesCount(), which are there to support asynchronous calls to the web methods. The client can call BeginGetEmployeesCount() and continue performing other tasks while the proxy class waits for the web service response. You'll learn more about asynchronous calls and see practical examples of how to use them Chapter 26.

Here's an example of the asynchronous proxy class methods:

```
public System.IAsyncResult BeginGetEmployeesCount(
 System.AsyncCallback callback, object asyncState)
{
    return this.BeginInvoke("GetEmployeesCount", new object[0],
     callback, asyncState);
}


public int EndGetEmployeesCount(System.IAsyncResult asyncResult)
{
    object[] results = this.EndInvoke(asyncResult);
    return ((int)(results[0]));
}
```

The proxy class concludes with the proxy code for the GetEmployees() method. You'll notice that this code is nearly identical to the code used for the GetEmployeesCount() method—the only difference is the method name that's passed to the Invoke() method, and the fact that the return value is converted to a DataSet rather than an integer.

```
[System.Web.Services.Protocols.SoapDocumentMethodAttribute()]
public System.Data.DataSet GetEmployees()
{
    object[] results = this.Invoke("GetEmployees", new object[0]);
    return ((System.Data.DataSet)(results[0]));
}


public System.IAsyncResult BeginGetEmployees(
 System.AsyncCallback callback, object asyncState)
{
    return this.BeginInvoke("GetEmployees", new object[0],
     callback, asyncState);
}
```

```
public System.Data.DataSet EndGetEmployees(System.IAsyncResult asyncResult)
{
    object[] results = this.EndInvoke(asyncResult);
    return ((System.Data.DataSet)(results[0]));
}
```

Creating an ASP.NET Client

Now that you have a web service and proxy class, it's quite easy to develop a simple web page client. If you're using Visual Studio .NET, the first step is to create a new web project and add a web reference to the web service. If you're using another tool, you'll need to compile a proxy class first using wsdl.exe, and then place it in the new web application Bin directory.

The following example uses a simple web page with a button and a DataGrid. When the user clicks the button, the web page posts back, creates the proxy class, retrieves the DataSet of employees from the web service, and then displays the result by binding it to the grid.

Before you add this code, it helps to import the proxy class namespace. In Visual Studio .NET, the namespace is automatically the namespace of the current project, plus the namespace you specified in the Add Web Reference dialog box (which is localhost by default). Assuming your project is named WebClient, the web service is on the local computer, and you didn't make any changes in the Add Web Reference dialog box, you'll use this namespace:

```
using WebClient.localhost;
```

Now you can add the code that uses the proxy class to retrieve the data:

```
private void cmdGetData_Click(object sender, System.EventArgs e)
{
    // Create the proxy.
    EmployeesService proxy = new EmployeesService();

    // Call the web service and get the results.
    DataSet ds = proxy.GetEmployees();

    // Bind the results.
    DataGrid1.DataSource = ds.Tables[0];
    DataGrid1.DataBind();
}
```

Because the proxy class has the same name as the web service class, when the client instantiates the proxy class it seems as though the client is actually instantiating the web service. To help emphasize the difference, this code names the object variable proxy.

If you run the page, you'll see the page shown in Figure 24-12.

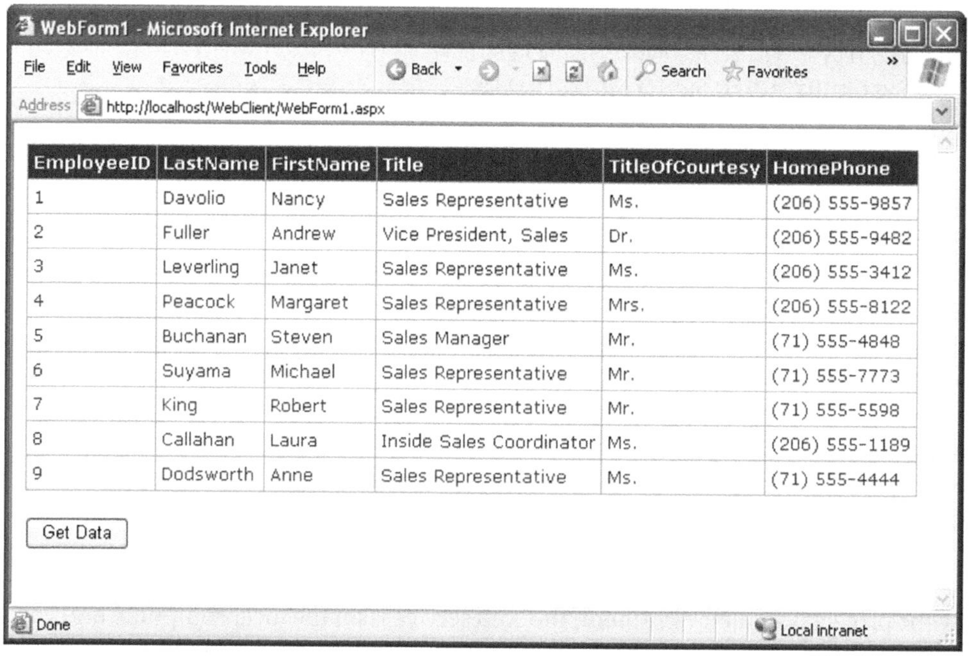

Figure 24-12. *Displaying data from a web service in a web page*

From the point of view of your web-page code, there's no difference between calling a web service and using an ordinary stateless class. However, you must remember that the web service that actually implements the business logic could be on a web server on the other side of the world. As a result, you need to reduce the number of times you call it, and be prepared to handle exceptions resulting from network problems and connectivity errors.

Timeouts

The proxy class includes a Timeout property that allows you to specify the maximum amount of time you're willing to wait, in milliseconds. By default, the timeout is 100,000 milliseconds (10 seconds).

When using the Timeout property, you need to include error handling. If the Timeout period expires without a response, an exception will be thrown, giving you the chance to notify the user about the problem.

Here's how you could rewrite the ASP.NET web-page client to use a timeout of three seconds:

```
private void cmdGetData_Click(object sender, System.EventArgs e)
{
    // Create the proxy.
    EmployeesService proxy = new EmployeesService();
```

```csharp
// This timeout will apply to all web service method calls.
proxy.Timeout = 3000;   // 3,000 milliseconds is 3 seconds.

DataSet ds = null;
try
{
    // Call the web service and get the results.
    ds = proxy.GetEmployees();
}
catch (System.Net.WebException err)
{
    if (err.Status == WebExceptionStatus.Timeout)
    {
        lblResult.Text = "Web service timed out after 3 seconds.";
    }
    else
    {
        lblResult.Text = "Another type of problem occurred."
    }
}

// Bind the results.
if (ds != null)
{
    DataGrid1.DataSource = ds.Tables[0];
    DataGrid1.DataBind();
}
}
```

You can also set the timeout to -1 to indicates that you'll wait as long as it takes. However, this will make your web application unacceptably slow if you attempt to perform a number of operations with an unresponsive web service.

Connecting Through a Proxy

The proxy class also has some built-in intelligence that allows you to reroute its HTTP communication with special Internet settings. By default the proxy class uses the Internet settings on the current computer. In some networks, this may not be the best approach. You can override these settings by using the Proxy property of the web service proxy class.

■**Tip** In this case, "proxy" is being used in two different ways: as a proxy that manages communication between a client and a web service, and as a proxy server in your organization that manages communication between a computer and the Internet.

For example, if you need to connect through a computer called ProxyServer using port 80, you could use the following code before you called any web service methods:

```
// Create the web service proxy.
EmployeesService proxy = new EmployeesService();

// Specify a proxy server for network communication.
WebProxy connectionProxy = new WebProxy("ProxyServer", 80);
proxy.Proxy = connectionProxy;
```

There are many other options for the WebProxy class that allow you to configure connections and set authentication information in more complicated scenarios.

Creating a Windows Forms Client

One of the main advantages of web services is the way they allow you to web-enable local applications, like rich client applications. Using a web service, you can create a desktop application that gets up-to-the-minute data from a web server. The process is almost entirely transparent. In fact, as high-speed access becomes more common, you may not even be aware of which portions of functionality depend on the Internet and which ones don't.

You can use web service functionality in a Windows application in exactly the same way that you would use it in an ASP.NET application. First, you create the proxy class using Visual Studio .NET or the wsdl.exe utility. Next, you add code to create an instance of the proxy class and call a web method. The only difference is the user interface the application uses.

If you haven't explored desktop programming with .NET yet, you'll be happy to know that you can reuse much of what you've learned in ASP.NET development. Many web controls (such as labels, buttons, text boxes, and lists) closely parallel their .NET desktop equivalents, and the code you write to interact with them can often be transferred from one environment to the other with very few changes. In fact, the most significant difference between desktop programming and web programming in .NET is the extra steps you need to take in web applications to preserve information between postbacks and when transferring the user from one page to another.

To begin creating your Windows client in Visual Studio .NET, create a new Windows Application project, and then add the web reference. Web projects start with a single startup form, which you can design in much the same way you design a web page. For this example, you simply need to drag and drop a button and a DataGrid from the Toolbox. (Keep in mind the Button and DataGrid classes used in a Windows application aren't the same as their ASP.NET counterparts. Even though they use the same class name and expose a similar programming, they're stored in different namespaces, and their plumbing is completely different.)

Once again, begin by importing the namespace you need at the top of the form class file, as you did in the ASP.NET page:

```
using WindowsClient.localhost;
```

Next, add the event-handling code for the button. This code retrieves the DataSet and displays it in the form. Data binding works slightly differently in a Windows application—for example, there's no need to call an explicit DataBind() method after you set the data source.

This code also introduces one refinement—it explicitly sets the application to use an hourglass cursor while the web service call is underway, so the user knows that the operation is in progress. Other than that, the code is identical:

```
private void cmdGetData_Click(object sender, System.EventArgs e)
{
    this.Cursor = Cursors.WaitCursor;

    // Create the proxy.
    EmployeesService proxy = new EmployeesService();

    // Call the web service and get the results.
    DataSet ds = proxy.GetEmployees();

    // Bind the results.
    DataGrid1.DataSource = ds.Tables[0];

    this.Cursor = Cursors.Default;
}
```

Figure 24-13 shows what you'll see when you run the Windows client and click the button to retrieve the web service data.

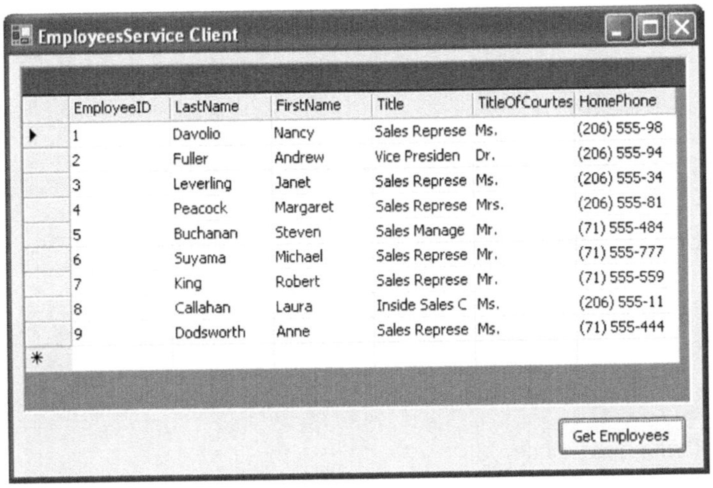

Figure 24-13. *Displaying data from a web service in a Windows form*

Of course, Windows development contains many other possibilities, which are covered in many other excellent books. The interesting part from your vantage point is the way that a Windows client can interact with a web service just like an ASP.NET application does. This raises a world of new possibilities for integrated Windows and web applications. For example, you could extend this Windows application so that it allows the user to modify the employee data. You could then add methods to the EmployeesService that allow the client to submit the changed data, and commit the changes to the back-end database.

It's important to understand that what you do to consume your sample web service is exactly what you would do to consume any other third-party web service. Web service providers don't need to distribute their proxy classes, because programming platforms like .NET include the tools to generate them automatically.

Tip If you'd like to try consuming some non-.NET web services, you can search the web service catalog at XMethods (www.xmethods.com). Or, for more practice with genuinely useful web services, Microsoft's MapPoint (http://msdn.microsoft.com/library/en-us/dnanchor/html/anch_mappointmain.asp) is an interesting example that enables you to access high-quality maps and geographical information. There's also Microsoft's TerraService (http://terraservice.net/webservices.aspx), which is based on the hugely popular TerraServer site where web surfers can view topographic maps and satellite photographs of the globe. Using TerraService you can query information about different locations on the globe and even download tiles with satellite photography of specific regions.

Creating an ASP Client with MSXML

It's also interesting to demonstrate how a web service can be called by a legacy application of any type and platform. The following example shows a bare-bones approach to displaying data in a legacy ASP page:

```
<SCRIPT LANGUAGE="VBScript" RUNAT="Server">
Option Explicit

Dim URL
URL = "http://localhost/Chapter24/EmployeesService.asmx/GetEmployeesCount"
Dim objHTTP
Set objHTTP = CreateObject("Microsoft.XMLHTTP")

' Send an HTTP POST command to the URL.
objHTTP.Open "POST", URL, False
objHTTP.Send

' Read and display the value of the root node.
Dim numEmp
numEmp = objHTTP.responseXML.documentElement.Text
Response.Write(numEmp & " employee(s) in London")
</SCRIPT>
```

This code simply sets the URL to point to the web method in the web service. It then uses the Microsoft.XMLHTTP class (from the Microsoft XML Parser, a COM component that provides classes to manipulate XML data, send HTTP commands and receive the respective responses) to open an HTTP connection and to send the command in a synchronous manner. In this case, the code is accessing the service through an HTTP POST command, which ASP.NET web services only support on the local computer. When the send method returns, the response text is saved in the responseXML property. It's provided as an MSXML2.DOMDocument object with a documentElement property that points to the root node of the returned XML data. Using this object, you can navigate the XML of the response. In this case, because the data simply contains an integer result, you can use the text property to read the value of that element. Figure 24-14 shows the result.

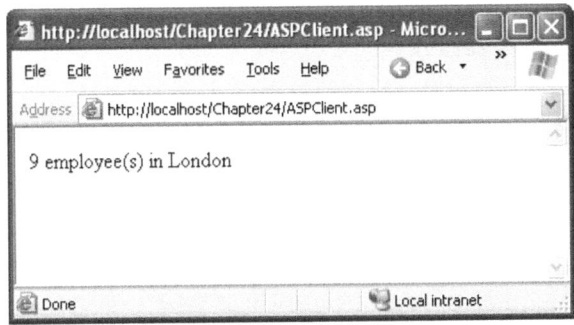

Figure 24-14. *Displaying data from a web service in an ASP page*

The interesting part of this example is that it uses the Microsoft XML library, which has classes to send commands via HTTP, receive the response text, and parse XML. That's all you need. If you don't already have this common component, you can download it from `http://msdn.microsoft.com/library/en-us/xmlsdk/html/xmmscxmlinstallregister.asp`. Note that the previous code, with minor modifications, can be used in any VBScript or VBA application, including a Microsoft Office macro or a WSH (Windows Scripting Host) client.

Now consider a more complex example—the GetEmployees() web method that returns a complete DataSet. To interact with this data, you need to dig through the XML response. Here's the code that loops through the <Employees> tags and extracts several pieces of information about each employee to create a list:

```
<SCRIPT LANGUAGE="VBScript" RUNAT="Server">
Option Explicit

Dim URL
URL = "http://localhost/Chapter24/EmployeesService.asmx/GetEmployeesCount"
Dim objHTTP
Set objHTTP = CreateObject("Microsoft.XMLHTTP")

' Send an HTTP POST command to the URL.
objHTTP.Open "POST", URL, False
objHTTP.Send

' Retrieve the XML response.
Dim Doc
Set Doc = objHTTP.responseXML
```

```
' Dig into the XML DataSet structure.
' Skip down one node to get past the schema. Then go one level deeper
' to the root DataSet element.
' Finally, loop through the contained tags, each of which
' represents an employee.
Dim Child
For Each Child In Doc.documentElement.childNodes(1).childNodes(0).childNodes
    ' The first node is the ID.
    Response.Write(Child.childNodes(0).Text + "<br>")
    ' The second node is the first name.
    Response.Write(Child.childNodes(1).Text)
    ' The third node is the last name.
    Response.Write(Child.childNodes(2).Text + "<br><br>")
Next
</SCRIPT>
```

Creating an ASP Client with the SOAP Toolkit

The previous example showed the lowest common denominator for web service invocation—posting a message over HTTP and parsing the returned XML by hand. Most clients have access to more robust toolkits that directly support SOAP. One example is the Microsoft SOAP Toolkit, which is a COM component that you can use to call any type of web service that provides a valid WSDL document. Thus, the SOAP Toolkit supports .NET web services, and web services created on other platforms. You can use the SOAP Toolkit to use web services in COM-based applications like those created in Visual Basic 6, Visual C++ 6, and ASP. To download the latest version of the Microsoft SOAP Toolkit, refer to http://msdn.microsoft.com/webservices/building/soaptk.

In order to use the Microsoft SOAP Toolkit, you need to know the location of the WSDL for the service you want to use. Using this WSDL document, the SOAP Toolkit will dynamically generate a proxy. You can't see the proxy (because it's created at runtime), but you can use it to have access the same higher-level web services model.

The following example rewrites the ASP page to use the SOAP Toolkit. In this case, the WSDL document is retrieved directly from the web server. In order to improve performance, it's recommended that you save a local copy of the WSDL file, and use that to configure the SoapClient object.

```
<SCRIPT LANGUAGE="VBScript" RUNAT="Server">
Option Explicit

Dim SoapClient
Set SoapClient = CreateObject("MSSOAP.SoapClient"

' Generate a proxy.
Dim WSDLPath
WSDLPath = "http://localhost/Chapter24/EmployeesService.asmx?WSDL"
SoapClient.MSSoapInit WSDLPath
```

```
' Read the number of employees.
Dim numEmp
numEmp = SoapClient.GetEmployeesCount()
Response.Write(numEmp & " employee(s) in London")
</SCRIPT>
```

Notice that in this example, there's no need to read any XML. Instead, the client calls the GetEmployeesCount() method directly using the SoapClient object. However, this approach still won't help you manipulate a DataSet, because there is no COM equivalent for this class. Instead, you'll need to fall back on parsing XML, as shown in the previous example.

Of course Java, C++, Delphi, and so on have their own components, libraries, and APIs to establish HTTP connections, send commands, and parse XML text, but the essential approach is the same.

Refining a Web Service

So far you've seen how to create a basic web service with a couple of methods, and create a web page and Windows application that use it. However, there are a number of web service features that you haven't touched on yet. For example, a web method can cache data, use session state, and perform transactions. In the remainder of this chapter, you'll take a look at how you can use these techniques.

The secret to applying these features is the WebMethod attribute. So far the examples you've seen have used the WebMethod attribute to mark the methods you want to expose as part of a web service, and to attach a description (using the Description property). However, there are actually several additional WebMethod properties, as described in Table 24-6.

Table 24-6. *Properties of the WebMethod Attribute*

Argument	Description
Description	The method's description.
MessageName	The alias name for the method, which is used if you have overloaded versions of the method, or if you want to expose the method with a different name.
CacheDuration	This is the number of seconds that the method's response will be maintained in cache. The default is zero, meaning it's not cached.
EnableSession	Gets or sets whether the method can access information in the Session collection.
BufferResponse	Gets or sets whether the method's response is buffered. It is true by default, and it should be set to false only if you know that the request will take long to complete, and you want to send sections of data earlier.
TransactionOption	Gets or sets whether the method supports transaction, and of what type. Allowed values are disabled, NotSupported, Supported, Required, RequiresNew. Due to the stateless nature of web services, they can only participate as the root object of a transaction.

MessageName

When you expose a method, the name of the web method is, by default, the same as the name of the method in the web service class. However, there are cases when you might want to give the web method a different name than the class method. One example is with overloaded methods.

Both C# and VB .NET allow overloaded methods. However, the WSDL standard, which is used to describe web services, does not. If you try to use a web service with overloaded methods you'll receive an error page.

One solution is to simply rename one of the methods so that they have different names. However, in some situations you might want to keep the use of overload methods (perhaps so that other code in the same web application can use it directly), while changing how it appears in a web service. You can accomplish this using the MessageName property of the WebMethod attribute.

The following example disambiguates two versions of the GetEmployees() method using the MessageName property. One accepts a city parameter and returns a smaller set of matching rows, while the other returns the full DataSet. In this example, the version that takes the parameter is renamed to the web method GetEmployeesByCityName().

```
[WebMethod(Description="Returns the full list of employees.")]
public DataSet GetEmployees()
{
    // Create the command and the connection.
    string sql = "SELECT EmployeeID, LastName, FirstName, Title, " +
      "TitleOfCourtesy, HomePhone FROM Employees";
    SqlConnection con = new SqlConnection(connectionString);
    SqlDataAdapter da = new SqlDataAdapter(sql, con);
    DataSet ds = new DataSet();

    // Fill the DataSet.
    da.Fill(ds, "Employees");
    return ds;
}


[WebMethod(Description="Returns the full list of employees by city.",
  MessageName="GetEmployeesByCity")]
public DataSet GetEmployees(string city)
{
    // Create the command and the connection.
    string sql = "SELECT EmployeeID, LastName, FirstName, Title, " +
      "TitleOfCourtesy, HomePhone FROM Employees " +
      "WHERE City LIKE '%'+ @City + '%'";
    SqlConnection con = new SqlConnection(connectionString);
    SqlDataAdapter da = new SqlDataAdapter(sql, con);
    da.SelectCommand.Parameters.Add("@City", city);
    DataSet ds = new DataSet();
```

```
    // Fill the DataSet.
    da.Fill(ds, "Employees");
    return ds;
}
```

The new name will appear in the browser test page. However, the wsdl.exe tool and the Visual Studio .NET web reference feature are both smart enough to recognize overloaded methods. When it generates the proxy class, it will create two GetEmployees() methods, each with a different signature. This means that .NET client applications will be able to call the methods using the overloaded method name defined in the web service class. The proxy class will automatically invoke the GetEmployeesByCity() web method when the client calls the overloaded version of GetEmployees() that takes a city argument.

CacheDuration

As you learned in Chapter 7, ASP.NET has built-in support for two types of caching: output caching, and data caching. Web services can use both these forms of caching, as you'll see in the following sections.

Output Caching

The simplest kind of web service caching is output caching. Output caching works with web services in the same way that it does with web pages: identical requests (in this case, requests for the same method and with the same parameters) will receive identical responses from the cache, until the cached information expires. This can greatly increase performance in heavily trafficked sites, even if you only store a response for a few seconds.

Output caching should only be used for straightforward information retrieval or data-processing functions. It should not be used in a method that needs to perform other work, such as changing session items, logging usage, or modifying a database. This is because subsequent calls to a cached method will receive the cached result, and the web method code will not be executed.

To enable caching for a function, you use the CacheDuration property of the WebMethod attribute. Here's an example with the GetEmployees() method:

```
[WebMethod(CacheDuration=30)]
public DataSet GetEmployees()
{ ... }
```

This example caches the employee DataSet for 30 seconds. Any user who calls the GetProducts() method in this time span will receive the same DataSet, directly from the ASP.NET output cache.

Output caching becomes more interesting when you consider how it works with methods that require parameters. For example, consider the overloaded GetEmployees() method that takes a city parameter, as demonstrated in the previous section. Here's an example that caches this web method for ten minutes:

```
[WebMethod(CacheDuration=600), MessageName="GetEmployeesByCity")]
public DataSet GetEmployees(string city)
{ ... }
```

In this case, ASP.NET is a little more intelligent. It only reuses requests that supply the same city value. For example, here's how three web service requests might unfold:

1. A client calls GetEmployees() with the city parameter of London. The web method calls, contacts the database, and stores the result in the web service cache.

2. A client calls GetEmployees() with the city parameter of Kirkland. The web method calls, contacts the database, and stores the result in the web service cache. The previously cached DataSet is not reused, because the city parameter differs.

3. A client calls GetEmployees() with the city parameter of London. Assuming ten minutes haven't elapsed since the request in step 1, ASP.NET automatically reuses the first cached result. No code is executed.

Whether or not it makes sense to cache this version of GetEmployees() really depends on how much traffic your web service receives, and how many different cities there are. If there are only a few different city values, this approach may make sense. If there are dozens and your web server memory is limited, it's guaranteed to be inefficient.

Data Caching

ASP.NET also supports data caching, which allows you to store full-fledged objects in the cache. As with all ASP.NET code, you can use data caching through the Cache object (which is available through the Context.Cache property in your web service code). This object can temporarily store information that is expensive to create so that the web method can reuse it for other calls by other clients. In fact, the data can even be reused in other web services or web pages in the same application.

Data caching makes a lot of sense in the version of the EmployeesService that provides two GetEmployees() methods, one of which accepts a city parameter. To ensure optimum performance but cut down on the amount of data in the cache, you can store a single object in the cache: the full employee DataSet. Then, when a client calls the version of GetEmployees() that requires a city parameter, you simply need to filter out the rows for the city the client requested.

The following code shows this pattern at work. The first step is to create a private method that uses the cache, called GetEmployeesDataSet(). If the DataSet is available in the cache, GetEmployeesDataSet() uses that version and bypasses the database. Otherwise, it creates a new DataSet and fills it with the full set of employee records. Here's the complete code:

```
private DataSet GetEmployeesDataSet()
{
    DataSet ds;

    if (Context.Cache["EmployeesDataSet"] != null)
    {
        // Retrieve it from the cache
        ds = (DataSet)Context.Cache["EmployeesDataSet"];
    }
    else
    {
```

```csharp
        // Retrieve it from the database.
        string sql = "SELECT EmployeeID, LastName, FirstName, Title, " +
          "TitleOfCourtesy, HomePhone, City FROM Employees";
        SqlConnection con = new SqlConnection(connectionString);
        SqlDataAdapter da = new SqlDataAdapter(sql, con);
        ds = new DataSet();
        da.Fill(ds, "Employees");

        // Track when the DataSet was created. You can
        // retrieve this information in your client to test
        // that caching is working.
        ds.ExtendedProperties.Add("CreatedDate", DateTime.Now);

        // Store it in the cache for ten minutes.
        Context.Cache.Insert("EmployeesDataSet", ds, null,
          DateTime.Now.AddMinutes(10), TimeSpan.Zero);
    }
    return ds;
}
```

Both versions of the GetEmployees() method can use the private GetEmployeesDataSet() method. The difference is that the version that accepts a city argument loops through the records and manually removes each record that doesn't match the supplied city name. Here are both versions:

```csharp
[WebMethod(Description="Returns the full list of employees.")]
public DataSet GetEmployees()
{
    return GetEmployeesDataSet();
}


[WebMethod(Description="Returns the full list of employees by city.",
 MessageName="GetEmployeesByCity")]
public DataSet GetEmployees(string city)
{
    // Copy the DataSet.
    DataSet dsFiltered = GetEmployeesDataSet().Copy();

    // Remove the rows manually.
    // This is a good approach (rather than using the
    // DataTable.Select() method) because it is impervious
    // to SQL injection attacks.
    foreach (DataRow row in dsFiltered.Tables[0].Rows)
    {
        // Perform a case-insensitive compare.
        if (String.Compare(row["City"].ToString(), city.ToUpper(), true) != 0)
        {
            row.Delete();
```

```
        }
    }

    // Remove these rows permanently.
    dsFiltered.AcceptChanges();

    return dsFiltered;
}
```

Generally, you should determine the amount of time to cache information depending on how long the underlying data will remain valid. For example, if a stock quote were being retrieved, you would use a much smaller number of seconds than you might for a weather forecast. If you were storing a piece of information that seldom changes, like the results of a yearly census poll, your considerations would be entirely different. In this case, the information is almost permanent, but the amount of returned information will be larger than the capacity of ASP.NET's output cache. Your goal in this situation would be to limit the cache duration enough to ensure that only the most popular requests are stored.

Of course, caching decisions should also be based on how long it will take to re-create the information and how many clients will be using the web service. You may need to perform substantial real-world testing and tuning to achieve perfection. For more information on data caching, refer to Chapter 7.

Tip The data cache is global to an entire application (on a single web server). That means you can store information in the cache in a web service, and retrieve it in a web page in the same web application, and vice versa.

EnableSession

The best practice for ASP.NET web services is to disable session state. In fact, by default, web services do not support session state. Most web services should be designed to be stateless in order to achieve high scalability. There are cases, however, where you might decide to use state management to retain user-specific information or optimize performance in a specialized scenario. In this case, you need to use the EnableSession property, as shown here:

```
[WebMethod(EnableSession=true)]
public DataSet StatefulMethod()
{ ... }
```

What happens when you have a web service that enables session state management for some methods but disables it for others? Essentially, disabling session management just tells ASP.NET to ignore any in-memory session information and withhold the Session collection from the current procedure. It doesn't cause existing information to be cleared out of the collection (that will only happen when the session times out). The only performance benefit you're receiving is from not having to look up session information when it isn't required. You don't need to take the same steps to allow your code to use Application state—this global state collection is always available.

Session state handling is not a part of the SOAP specification. As a result, you must rely on the support of the underlying infrastructure. ASP.NET relies on HTTP cookies to support session state. The session cookie stores a session ID and ASP.NET uses the session ID to associate the client with the session state on the server. However, when you use a stateful web service, there's no guarantee that the client will support cookies. In fact, many will not. If the client doesn't support cookies, ASP.NET state management won't work, and a new session will be created with each new request. Unfortunately, your code has no way to identify this error condition.

To try out session state (and observe the potential problems), you can create the simple web service shown here. It stores a single piece of personalized information (the user name), and allows you to retrieve it later.

```
public class StatefulService : System.Web.Services.WebService
{
    [WebMethod(EnableSession=true)]
    public void StoreName(string name)
    {
        Session["Name"] = name;
    }

    [WebMethod(EnableSession=true)]
    public string GetName()
    {
        if (Session["Name"] == null)
        {
            return "";
        }
        else
        {
            return (string)Session["Name"];
        }
    }
}
```

When you test the StoreName() and GetName() web methods using the ASP.NET test page, you get the expected behavior. When you call GetName(), you receive whatever string you supplied the last time you called StoreName(). That's because web browsers support cookies without a hitch.

By default, the proxy class doesn't share this ability. To see this problem in action, add a reference to the StatefulService in the Windows client. Then add a new button with the following event-handling code:

```
private void cmdTestState_Click(object sender, System.EventArgs e)
{
    // Create the proxy.
    StatefulService proxy = new StatefulService();
```

```
    // Set a name.
    proxy.StoreName("John Smith");

    // Try to retrieve the name.
    MessageBox.Show("You set: " + proxy.GetName());
}
```

Unfortunately, this code doesn't work as you might expect. When you run it, you'll see the empty string shown in Figure 24-15.

Figure 24-15. *A failed stateful service*

To resolve this problem, you need to explicitly prepare the web service proxy to accept the session cookie by creating a cookie container (an instance of the System.Net.CookieContainer class).

To correct this code, you can create the cookie container as a form-level variable, as shown here. This ensures that it lives as long as the enclosing class (the form) and can be reused in multiple methods in the same form, without losing the current web service session:

```
public class Form1 : System.Windows.Forms.Form
{
    private System.Net.CookieContainer cookieContainer =
      new System.Net.CookieContainer();
    ...
}
```

Now you simply need to attach this cookie container to the proxy class before you call any web method:

```
private void cmdTestState_Click(object sender, System.EventArgs e)
{
    StatefulService proxy = new StatefulService();
    proxy.CookieContainer = cookieContainer;

    proxy.StoreName("John Smith");
    MessageBox.Show("You set: " + proxy.GetName());
}
```

Now both web method calls use the same session, and the user name appears in the message box, as shown in Figure 24-16.

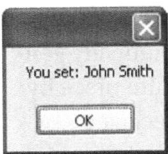

Figure 24-16. *A successful stateful service*

You need to keep the cookie container around as long as you need to keep the session cookie. For example, if your client is a web application and you want to be able to perform web service operations after every postback without losing the session, you'll need to store the session cookie in the session state of the current page. Note that the session state of the web application is different from the session state of the web service. Not only are they separate applications, but they are also probably running on completely separate web servers.

By now, you're probably seeing a hint of the complexity of trying to use sessions with web services. Because web services are destroyed after every method call, they don't provide a natural mechanism for storing state information. You can use the Session collection to compensate for this limitation, but this approach raises the following complications:

- Session state will disappear when the session times out. The client will have no way of knowing when the session times out, which means the web service may behave unpredictably.

- Session state is tied to a specific user, not to a specific class or object. This can cause problems if the same client wants to use the same web service in two different ways or creates two instances of the proxy class at once.

- Session state is only maintained if the client preserves the session cookie. The state management you use in a web service won't work if the client fails to take these steps.

For these reasons, web services and state management don't offer a natural fit.

BufferResponse

The BufferResponse property allows you to control when the data returned from the web service is sent to the client. By default the BufferResponse property is set to true. This means that the entire result is serialized before it is sent to the client. By setting this property to false (as follows), ASP.NET will start returning output as it is serialized.

```
[WebMethod(BufferResponse=false)]
public byte[] GetLargeStreamOfData()
{ ... }
```

The web service method will always finish executing before anything is returned. The BufferResponse setting applies to the serialization that takes place *after* the method has executed. With buffering turned off, the first part of the result is serialized and sent. Then the next part of the result is serialized and sent, and so on.

Setting BufferResponse to false only makes sense when the web service returns a large amount of data. Even then, it probably makes little difference, because the automatically generated .NET proxy class doesn't have the ability to start processing the returned data piece by piece. This means that the proxy class will still wait for all the information to be received before it passes it back to your application. However, you could use lower-level .NET classes to take more direct control of the SOAP stream and change this behavior, although it's unlikely to be worth the considerable effort required.

TransactionOption

Web services, like any other piece of .NET code, can initiate ADO.NET transactions. Additionally, web services can easily participate in COM+ transactions. COM+ transactions are interesting because they allow you to perform a transaction that spans multiple different data sources (for example, a SQL Server database and an Oracle database). COM+ transactions also commit or rollback automatically. However, there's a price that you must pay for these added features and convenience—because COM+ transactions use a two-state commit protocol, they are always slower than using ADO.NET client-initiated transactions or stored procedure transactions.

The support for COM+ transactions in a web service is also somewhat limited. Because of the stateless nature of HTTP, web service methods can only act as the root object in a transaction. That means that a web service method can start a transaction and use it to perform a series of related tasks, but multiple web services cannot be grouped into one transaction. As a result, you may have to put in some extra thought when you're creating a transactional web service. For example, it won't make sense to create a financial web service with a separate DebitAccount() and CreditAccount() methods, because they won't be able to be grouped into a transaction. Instead, you can make sure both tasks are executed as a single unit using a transactional TransferFunds() method.

To use a transaction in a web service, you first have to add a reference to the System.EnterpriseServices assembly. In order to do this in Visual Studio .NET, right-click References in the Solution Explorer, select Add Reference, and choose System.EnterpriseServices. You should then import the corresponding namespace so that the types you need (TransactionOption and ContextUtil) are at your fingertips:

```
using System.EnterpriseServices;
```

To start a transaction in a web service method, set the TransactionOption property of the WebMethod attribute. TransactionOption is an enumeration that provides several values that allow you to specify whether a code component uses or requires transactions. Because web services must be the root of a transaction, most of these options don't apply. To create a web service method that starts a transaction automatically, use the following attribute:

```
[WebMethod(TransactionOption=TransactionOption.RequiresNew)]
public DataSet TransactionMethod()
{ ... }
```

The transaction is automatically committed when the web method completes. The transaction is rolled back if any unhandled exception occurs or if you explicitly instruct the transaction to fail using the following code:

```
ContextUtil.SetAbort();
```

Most databases support COM+ transactions. The moment you use these databases in a transactional web method, they will automatically be enlisted in the current transaction. If the transaction is rolled back, the operations you perform with these databases (like adding, modifying, or removing records) will be automatically reversed. However, some operations (like writing a file to disk) aren't inherently transactional. That means that these operations will not be rolled back if the transaction fails.

Now consider the following web method, which takes two actions: It deletes records in a database and then tries to read from a file. However, if the file operation fails and the exception isn't handled, the entire transaction will be rolled back, and the deleted records will be restored. Here's the transactional code:

```
[WebMethod(TransactionOption=TransactionOption.RequiresNew)]
public void UpdateDatabase()
{
    // Create ADO.NET objects.
    SqlConnection con = new SqlConnection(connectionString);
    SqlCommand cmd = new SqlCommand("DELETE * FROM Employees", con);

    // Apply the update. This will be registered as part of the transaction.
    using (con)
    {
        con.Open();
        cmd.ExecuteNonQuery();
    }

    // Try to access a file. This generates an exception that isn't handled.
    // The web method will be aborted and the changes will be rolled back.
    FileStream fs = new FileStream("does_not_exist.bin", IO.FileMode.Open);

    // (If no errors have occurred, the database changes
    // are committed here when the method ends).
}
```

Another way to handle this code is to catch the error, perform any cleanup that's required, and then explicitly roll back the transaction, if necessary:

```
[WebMethod(TransactionOption=TransactionOption.RequiresNew)]
public void UpdateDatabase()
{
    // Create ADO.NET objects.
    SqlConnection con = new SqlConnection(connectionString);
    SqlCommand cmd = new SqlCommand("DELETE * FROM Employees", con);

    // Apply the update.
    try
    {
        con.Open();
        cmd.ExecuteNonQuery();
```

```
      FileStream fs = new FileStream("does_not_exist.bin",
        IO.FileMode.Open);
    }
    catch
    {
        if (con.State != ConnectionState.Closed) con.Close();
        ContextUtil.SetAbort();
    }
    finally
    {
        con.Close();
    }
}
```

Does a web service need to use COM+ transactions? It all depends on the situation. If multiple updates are required in separate data stores, you may need to use transactions to ensure your data's integrity. If, on the other hand, you're only modifying values in a single database (such as SQL Server 2000), you can probably make use of the data provider's built-in transaction features instead, as described in Chapter 13.

Note In the future, other emerging standards, like XLANG and WS-Transaction may fill in the gaps by defining a cross-platform standard that will let different web services participate in a single transaction. However, this goal is still a long way from being realized.

Summary

In this chapter, you've learned what web services are, and why they are important for businesses. You've also taken your first look at how to create and consume web services in .NET, and test web services with nothing but a browser. In the next two chapters, you'll dig in to the underlying standards and learn how to extend the web service infrastructure.

■ ■ ■

CHAPTER 25

Web Service Standards and Extensions

In the previous chapter, you learned how .NET hides the low-level plumbing of web services, allowing you to create and consume sophisticated web services without needing to know anything about the low-level details of the protocols you're using. This higher level abstraction is a general theme of modern programming—for example, few Windows developers worry about the individual pixels in their business applications, and ASP.NET developers rarely need to write raw markup to the output stream. Of course, there *are* situations where high-level frameworks aren't quite enough. For example, Windows developers creating real-time games just might need to work with low-level video hardware, and web developers creating custom controls will probably need to immerse themselves in a thorny tangle of JavaScript and HTML.

The same principle is true of web services. In most cases, the high-level web services model in .NET is all you need. It ensures fast, productive, error-proof coding. Sometimes, however, you need to dig a little deeper. This is particularly true if you need to send complex objects to non-.NET clients or build extensions that plug into the .NET web services model. In this chapter, you'll take a look at this lower level, and learn more about the underlying SOAP and WSDL protocols.

SOAP

SOAP is a cross-platform standard used to format the messages sent between web services and client applications. The beauty of SOAP is its flexibility. Not only can you use SOAP to send any type of XML data (including your own proprietary XML tags), you can also apply SOAP to transport protocols other than HTTP, including FTP and SMTP (although .NET only includes support for the most common use of SOAP, which is SOAP over HTTP).

Note SOAP was originally considered an acronym (Simple Object Access Protocol). However, in the latest version of the SOAP standard, this is no longer the case. For the detailed SOAP specifications, surf to www.w3.org/TR/soap.

SOAP is a fairly straightforward standard. The first principle is that every SOAP message is an XML document. This XML document has a single root element that is the SOAP envelope. The rest of the data for the message is stored inside the envelope, which includes a header section and a body. Essentially, web services use two types of SOAP messages. The client sends a *request message* to a web service to trigger a web method. When processing is complete, the web service sends back a *response message*. Both of these messages have the same format, which is shown in Figure 25-1.

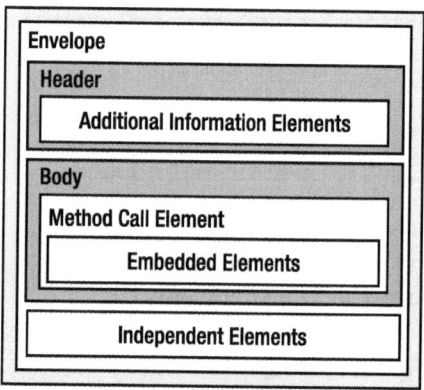

Figure 25-1. *The SOAP message*

Keep in mind that unlike some other *routed* messaging and distributed access protocols, SOAP provides no means for encoding source and destination information into the envelope. The envelope is simply a neat and tidy package containing information. It's up to the underlying infrastructure to decide where the SOAP message should be sent, and how it should be sent there.

SOAP Encoding

There are actually two different (but closely related) styles of SOAP. *Document-style* SOAP views the data exchanged as documents. In other words, each SOAP message you send or receive contains an XML document in its body. *RPC-style* SOAP views the data exchange as method calls on remote objects. The remote object may be a Java object, a COM component, a .NET object, or something else entirely. In RPC-style SOAP, the outermost element in the request is named after the method and there is an element for each parameter on that method. In the response, the outermost element has the same name as the method with the text "Response" appended.

Seeing as .NET web services embrace the object-oriented RPC model, you might assume that .NET web services use RPC-style SOAP. However, this isn't the case. The simple reason is that document-style SOAP is more flexible, and is emerging as the standard of choice. However, even though .NET uses document-style SOAP, it formats messages in a very similar way to RPC-style, using many of the same conventions.

To make life even more interesting, there are two ways in which data in a SOAP message can be encoded: literal and SOAP section 5. *Literal encoding* means that the data is encoded according to a specific XML schema. With *SOAP section 5 encoding*, data is encoded according to the similar, but more restricted rules set out in section 5 of the SOAP specification (this is also called *encoded* style). In fact, these rules are a bit of a throwback. The underlying reason that they exist is because SOAP was developed before the XML Schema standard was finalized. Today, most web services use literal encoding, and .NET is no exception. However, it's important to note that when a web service uses RPC-style SOAP, it must use SOAP section 5 encoding. If the web service uses document-style SOAP, it can use either type of encoding.

At this point, you might wonder why you need to know any of these lower-level SOAP details. In most cases, you don't. However, there are times when you might want to change the overall encoding of your web service. One reason might be that you need to expose a web method that needs to be called by a client that only supports RPC-style SOAP. Although this scenario is becoming less and less common, it can still occur.

ASP.NET has two attributes (both of which are found in the System.Web.Services.Protocols namespace) that you can use to control the overall encoding of all methods in a web service:

- **SoapDocumentService.** Use this to make every web service use document-style SOAP (which is already the default). However, you can use the SoapBindingUse parameter to specify SOAP section 5 encoding instead of document encoding.

- **SoapRpcService.** Use this to make every web service use RCP style SOAP with SOAP section 5 encoding.

You can also use the following two attributes on individual web methods:

- **SoapDocumentMethod.** Add this attribute to use document-style SOAP for a single web method. You can specify the encoding to use.

- **SoapRpcMethod.** Add this attribute to use RPC-style SOAP for a single web method.

This is useful if you want to expose two methods in a web service that perform a similar function but support a different type of SOAP encoding. However, in this chapter you'll focus on understanding the SOAP message style that .NET uses by default (document/literal).

Tracing SOAP Messages

Before looking at the SOAP standard in detail, it's worth exploring how you can take a look at the SOAP messages sent to and from a .NET web service. Unfortunately, .NET doesn't include any tools for tracing or debugging SOAP messages. However, it's fairly easy to take a look at the underlying SOAP using other tools.

The first approach is to use the browser test page. As you know, the browser test page doesn't use SOAP—instead, it uses the scaled-down HTTP POST protocol that encodes data as name/value pairs. However, the test page does include an example of what a SOAP message should look like for a particular web method.

For example, consider the EmployeesService developed in the previous chapter. If you load the test page, click the link for the GetEmployeesCount() method, and scroll down the page, you'll see a sample request and response message with placeholders where the data values should go. Figure 25-2 shows part of this data example. You can also scroll further down the page to see the format of the simpler HTTP POST messages.

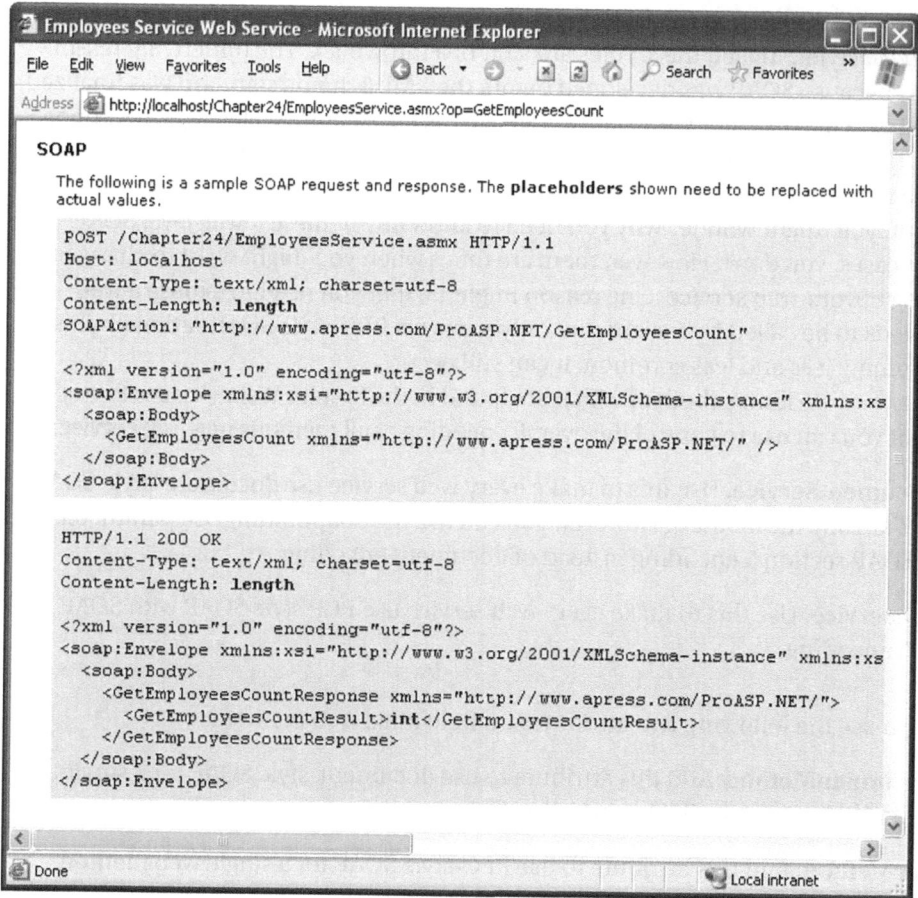

Figure 25-2. *Sample SOAP messages for GetEmployeesCount()*

These examples can help you understand the SOAP standard, but they aren't as useful if you want to see live SOAP messages, perhaps to troubleshoot an unexpected compatibility problem between a .NET web service and another client. Fortunately, there is an easy way to capture real SOAP messages as they flow across the wire, but you need to use another tool. This is the Microsoft SOAP Toolkit, a COM library that includes objects that allow you to consume web services in COM-based languages like Visual Basic 6 and Visual C++ 6. Along with these tools, the SOAP Toolkit also includes an indispensable tracing tool for peeking under the covers at SOAP communication.

To download the SOAP Toolkit, surf to `http://msdn.microsoft.com/webservices/building/soaptk`. Once you've installed the SOAP Toolkit, you can run the trace utility by selecting Microsoft SOAP Toolkit ➤ Trace Utility from the Start menu. Once the trace utility loads, select File ➤ New ➤ Formatted Trace. You'll see the window shown in Figure 25-3.

The default settings indicate that the trace utility will listen for communication on port 8080, and forward all messages to port 80 (which is where the IIS web server is listening for unencrypted HTTP traffic, including GET and POST requests and SOAP messages). Click OK to accept these settings.

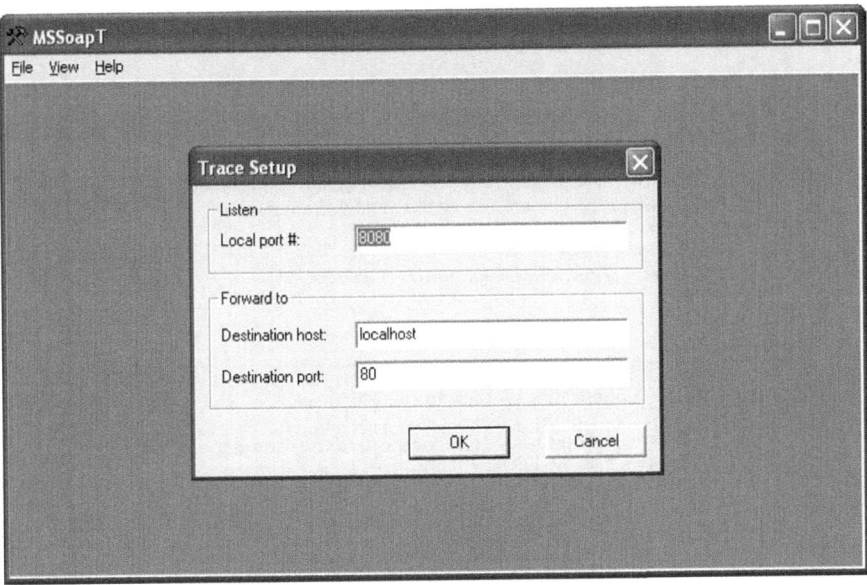

Figure 25-3. *Starting a new SOAP trace*

There's one additional detail you need. By default, your web service clients will bypass the tracing tool by sending their SOAP messages directly to port 80, not 8080. You need to tweak your client code so that it sends the SOAP messages to port 8080 instead. To do this, you simply need to use a URL that specifies the port, as shown here:

```
http://localhost:8080/MyWebSite/MyWebService.asmx
```

To change the URL, you simply need to modify the Url property of the proxy class before you invoke any of its methods. Rather than hard-coding a new URL, you can use the code shown here, which uses the System.Uri class to generically redirect any URL to port 8080:

```
// Create the proxy.
EmployeesService proxy = new EmployeesService();

Uri newUrl = new Uri(proxy.Url);
proxy.Url = newUrl.Scheme + "://" + newUrl.Host + ":8080" + newUrl.AbsolutePath;

// Call the web service and get the results.
DataSet ds = proxy.GetEmployeesCount();
```

You don't need to make a similar change to the web service, because it automatically sends its response message back to the port where the request message originated—in this case 8080. The trace utility will then log the response message, and forward it back to the client application.

Once you've finished calling the web service, you can expand the tree in the trace utility to look at the request and response messages. Figure 25-4 shows the result of running the previous code snippet. In the top window is the request message for the GetEmployeesCount() method. In the bottom window is the response with the current number of employees in the table (nine). As you invoke more web methods, additional nodes will be added to the tree.

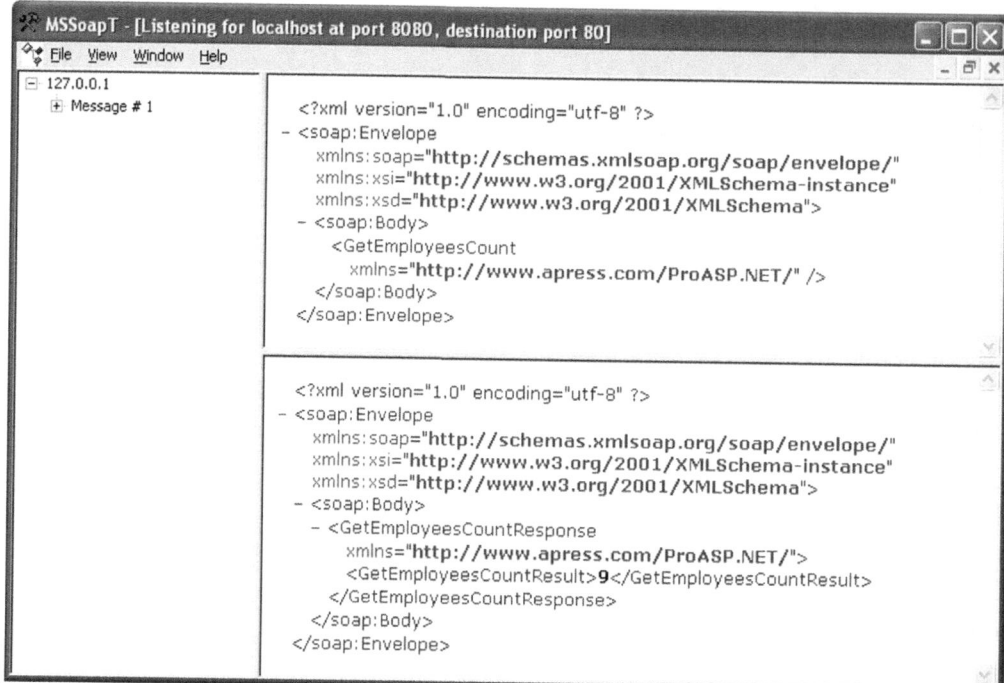

Figure 25-4. *Capturing SOAP messages*

The SOAP trace tool is a powerful tool for looking at SOAP messages, particularly if you want to see how an unusual data type is serialized, test a custom extension, or troubleshoot an interoperability problem. Best of all, you don't need to install any special software on the web server. Instead, you simply need to forward the client's messages to the local trace utility.

In the following sections, you'll take a closer look at the SOAP format. You may want to use the SOAP trace utility to test these examples, and take a look at the underlying SOAP messages for yourself.

The SOAP Envelope

Every SOAP message is enclosed in a root <Envelope> element. Inside the envelope, there is an optional <Header> element, and a required <Body> element. Here's the basic skeleton:

```
<soap:Envelope xmlns:soap="http://schemas.xmlsoap.org/soap/envelope/" >
  <soap:Header>
  </soap:Header>
  <soap:Body>
  </soap:Body>
</soap:Envelope>
```

Notice that the <Envelope>, <Body>, and <Header> elements all exist in the SOAP envelope namespace. This is a requirement.

The <Body> element contains the message payload. It's here that you place the actual data, such as the parameters in a request message or the return value in the response message. You can also specify fault information to indicate an error condition, and *independent elements*, which define the serialization of complex types.

Request Messages

With automatically generated .NET web services, the first element in the <Body> element identifies the name of the method you are invoking. For example, here's a complete SOAP message for calling the GetEmployeesCount() method:

```
<soap:Envelope xmlns:soap="http://schemas.xmlsoap.org/soap/envelope/" >
  <soap:Body>
    <GetEmployeesCount xmlns="http://www.apress.com/ProASP.NET/" />
  </soap:Body>
</soap:Envelope>
```

In this example, all you need is an empty <GetEmployeesCount> element. However, if the method requires any information (in the form of parameters), these are encoded in the <GetEmployeesCount> element with the appropriate parameter name. For example, the following SOAP represents a call to GetEmployeesByCity() that specifies a city name of London:

```
<soap:Envelope xmlns:soap="http://schemas.xmlsoap.org/soap/envelope/" >
  <soap:Body>
    <GetEmployeesByCity xmlns="http://www.apress.com/ProASP.NET/">
      <city>London</city>
    </GetEmployeesByCity>
  </soap:Body>
</soap:Envelope>
```

You'll notice that in both these examples, the data inside the <Body> element is given the namespace of the web service (in this example, `http://www.apress.com/ProASP.NET/`) The SOAP protocol is actually flexible enough to allow any XML markup in the <Body> element. This means that rather than treating SOAP as a protocol for remote method invocation, you can also use it as a way to exchange complex XML documents. In a business-to-business scenario, different parts of this document might be created by different companies in an automated workflow, and they might even include digital signatures. Unfortunately, the .NET programming model makes it hard to work in this way, because it wraps the SOAP and WSDL details with an object-oriented abstraction. However, leading web service developers are challenging this approach, and it's likely that future versions of ASP.NET will include increased flexibility.

Note At this point, you may be wondering if there's the possibility to create incompatible versions of SOAP. For example, .NET web services use the name of a method for the first element in the <Body>, but other web service implementations may not follow this convention. The solution to these challenges is WSDL, a standard that you'll consider later in this chapter. It allows .NET to define the message format for your web services in great detail. In other words, it doesn't matter if the naming and organization of a .NET SOAP message is slightly different than that of a competitor's platform, because the non-.NET platform will read the rules in the WSDL document to determine how it should interact with the web service.

Response Messages

After sending a request message, the client waits to receive the response from the web server (as with any HTTP request). This response message uses a similar format to the request message. By .NET convention (again, not a requirement of the SOAP specification), the first child element in the <Body> element has the name of the method with the suffix "Response" appended. For example, after calling the GetEmployeesCount() method, you might receive a response like this:

```
<soap:Envelope xmlns:soap="http://schemas.xmlsoap.org/soap/envelope/" >
  <soap:Body>
    <GetEmployeesCountResponse xmlns="http://www.apress.com/ProASP.NET/">
      <GetEmployeesCountResult>9</GetEmployeesCountResult>
    </GetEmployeesCountResponse>
  </soap:Body>
</soap:Envelope>
```

As with the request message, the response message is namespace-qualified using the namespace of the web service. Inside the <GetEmployeesCountResponse> element is an element with the return value named <GetEmployeesCountResult>. By .NET convention, this has the name of the web method, followed by the suffix "Result." Interestingly, this isn't the only piece of information you can find in the <XxxResponse> element. If the method uses ref or out parameters, the data for those parameters will also be included. This allows the client to update its parameter values after the method call completes, which gives the same behavior as when you use out or ref parameters with a local method call.

Fault Messages

The SOAP standard also defines a way to represent error conditions. If an error occurs on the server, a message is sent with a <Fault> element as the first element inside the <Body> element. Fortunately, .NET follows this standard and applies it automatically. If an unhandled exception occurs while a web method is running, .NET sends a SOAP fault message back to the client. When the proxy class receives the fault message, it throws a client-side exception to notify the client application. However, as you'll see, this process of converting a web service exception to a client application exception isn't entirely seamless.

Consider, for example, what happens if you call the GetEmployeesCount() method when the database server isn't available. A SqlException is thrown on the web server side and caught by ASP.NET, which returns the following (somewhat abbreviated) fault message:

```
<soap:Envelope xmlns:soap="http://schemas.xmlsoap.org/soap/envelope/" >
  <soap:Body>
    <soap:Fault>
      <faultcode>soap:Server</faultcode>
      <faultstring>System.Web.Services.Protocols.SoapException: Server was unable
to process request. ---> System.Data.SqlClient.SqlException: SQL Server does not
exist or access denied. at ... </faultstring>
      <detail />
    </soap:Fault>
  </soap:Body>
</soap:Envelope>
```

In general the Fault element contains a <faultcode>, <faultstring>, and <detail> element. The <faultcode> takes one of several predefined values, including ClientFaultCode (there was a problem with the client's SOAP request), MustUnderstandFaultCode (a required part of the SOAP message was not recognized), ServerFaultCode (an error occurred on the server), and VersionMismatchFaultCode (an invalid namespace was found). The <faultstring> element contains a full description of the problem. The optional <detail> element can be used to store additional information about the error that occurred (although it's empty in this example).

The problem is that the <Fault> element doesn't map directly to the .NET exception class. When the proxy receives this message, it can't identify the original exception object (and it has no way of knowing if that exception class is even available on the client). As a result, the proxy class simply throws a generic SoapException with the full <faultstring> details.

To understand how this works, consider what happens if you write the following code in your client:

```
EmployeesService proxy = new EmployeesService();

int count = -1;
try
{
    count = proxy.GetEmployeesCount();
}
catch (SqlException err)
{ ... }
```

In this case, the exception will never be caught, because it's a SoapException, not a SqlException (even though the root cause of the problem and the original exception object *is* a SqlException). Even if you catch the SqlException in the web method and manually throw a different exception object, it will still be converted into a SoapException on the client. That makes it difficult for the client to distinguish between different types of error conditions. The client can only catch a System.Net.WebException (which represents a timeout or a general network problem) or a System.Web.Services.Protocols.SoapException (which represents any .NET exception that occurred in the web service).

There is one other option. You can catch the exception in the web method on the server side, and throw the supported SoapException yourself. The advantage of this approach is that before your web service throws the SoapException object, you can configure it by inserting additional XML in the <detail> element. The client can then read the content and use it to programmatically determine what really happened.

For example, here's a faulty version of the GetEmployeesCount() method that uses this approach to add the original exception type name to the SoapException using a custom <ExceptionType> element. You could extend this approach to add any combination of elements, attributes, and data.

```
[WebMethod()]
public int GetEmployeesCountError()
{
    SqlConnection con = null;
    try
    {
        con = new SqlConnection(connectionString);
```

```
                    // Make a deliberately faulty SQL string
                    string sql = "INVALID_SQL COUNT(*) FROM Employees";
                    SqlCommand cmd = new SqlCommand(sql, con);

                    con.Open();
                    return (int)cmd.ExecuteScalar();
                }
                catch (Exception err)
                {
                    // Create the detail information
                    // an <ExceptionType> element with the type name.
                    XmlDocument doc = new XmlDocument();
                    XmlNode node = doc.CreateNode(XmlNodeType.Element,
                      SoapException.DetailElementName.Name,
                      SoapException.DetailElementName.Namespace);
                    XmlNode child = doc.CreateNode(XmlNodeType.Element,
                      "ExceptionType", SoapException.DetailElementName.Namespace);
                    child.InnerText = err.GetType().ToString();
                    node.AppendChild(child);

                    // Create the custom SoapException.
                    // Use the message from the original exception,
                    // and add the detail information.
                    SoapException soapErr = new SoapException(err.Message,
                      SoapException.ServerFaultCode, Context.Request.Url.AbsoluteUri, node);

                    // Throw the revised SoapException.
                    throw soapErr;
                }
                finally
                {
                    con.Close();
                }
            }
```

The client application can read the <ExceptionType> element to get the additional information you've added. Here's an example that displays the exception name in a Windows message box (see Figure 25-5):

```
EmployeesService proxy = new EmployeesService();
try
{
    int count = proxy.GetEmployeesCountError();
}
catch (SoapException err)
{
    MessageBox.Show("Original error was: " + err.Detail.InnerText);
}
```

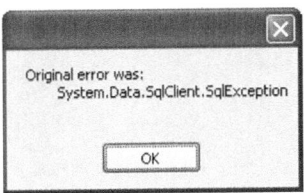

Figure 25-5. *Retreiving additional SOAP fault information*

The SOAP Header

SOAP also defines a <Header> section where you can place out-of-band information. This is typically information that doesn't belong in the message payload. For example, a SOAP header might contain user authentication credentials or a session ID. These details might be required for processing the request, but they aren't directly related to the method you're calling. By separating these two portions, you achieve two improvements:

- **The method interface is simpler.** For example, you don't need to create a version of the GetEmployees() method that accepts a user name and password as parameters. Instead, that information is passed in the header, keeping the method less cluttered.

- **The service is more flexible.** For example, if you add an authentication service using a SOAP header, you have the freedom to change how that service works and what information it requires without changing the interface of your web methods.

As in all types of programming, loosely coupled solutions are almost always preferable. The <Header> element is optional, and it allows for an unlimited number of child elements to be placed within the header. To define new headers for use with a .NET web service, you create classes that derive from System.Web.Services.Protocols.SoapHeader.

Note There is a potentially confusing difference in the way Microsoft uses the term SOAP header, and the use of the same term in the SOAP specification. The SOAP specification refers to *the* SOAP header as the <Header> element, meaning there is a single header portion with compound information. Microsoft considers *a* SOAP header to be a single child element within the <Header> element.

For example, imagine you want to design a better way to support state in a web service. Instead of trying to use the session cookie (which requires an HTTP cookie, and can't be defined in the WSDL document), you could pass the session ID as a header with every SOAP message. The following sections implement this design.

The Custom Header

The first step to implement this design is to create a custom class that derives from SoapHeader and includes the information you want to transmit as public properties.

Here's an example:

```
public class SessionHeader: SoapHeader
{
    public string SessionID;

    public SessionHeader(string sessionID)
    {
        SessionID = sessionID;
    }

    // A default constructor is required for automatic deserialization.
    public SessionHeader()
    {}
}
```

The SoapHeader class is really nothing more than a data container that can be serialized in and out of the <Header> element in a SOAP message. The custom SessionHeader adds a string SessionID variable with the session key.

Linking the Header to a Web Service

To use the SessionHeader in the web service, you need to create a public member variable in the web service for the header, as shown here:

```
public class SessionHeaderService : System.Web.Services.WebService
{
    public SessionHeader CurrentSessionHeader;
    ...
}
```

When you build a proxy class for this web service, it automatically includes a CurrentSessionHeader property. You can read or set the session header using this property. The definition for the custom SessionHeader class is also added to the proxy class file.

Headers are linked to individual methods using the SoapHeader attribute. For example, if you want to use the SessionHeader service in a web method named DoSomething(), you would apply the WebMethod and SoapHeader attributes like this:

```
[WebMethod()]
[SoapHeader("CurrentSessionHeader")]
public void DoSomething()
{}
```

Note that SoapHeader attribute takes the name of the public member variable where you want .NET to store the SOAP header. In the DoSomething() method, the SoapHeader attributes tells ASP.NET to create a new SessionHeader object using the header information that's been received from the client, and store it in the public CurrentSessionHeader member variable of the web service. ASP.NET uses reflection to find this member variable at runtime. If it's not present, an error will occur.

The SoapHeader attribute can also accept two named properties: Direction and Required. Direction specifies whether the SOAP header will be sent from the client to the web service, from the web service to the web client, or both. Required specifies whether the SOAP header must be supplied by the client. However, the Required property is considered obsolete and will be removed from future versions of .NET, because this restriction isn't defined in the SOAP standard itself.

The following example shows how you can use the session header to create a simple system for storing state. First, a CreateSession() web method allows the client to initiate a new session. At this point, a new session ID is generated for a new SessionHeader object. Next, a new Hashtable collection is created in the Application collection, indexed under the session ID. Because the session ID uses a GUID (globally unique identifier), it's statistically guaranteed to be unique among all users.

```
[WebMethod()]
[SoapHeader("CurrentSessionHeader", Direction=SoapHeaderDirection.Out)]
public void CreateSession()
{
    // Create the header.
    CurrentSessionHeader = new SessionHeader(Guid.NewGuid().ToString());

    // From now on, all session data will be indexed under that key.
    Application[CurrentSessionHeader.SessionID] = new Hashtable();
}
```

This Hashtable will be used to store the additional session information. This isn't the best approach (for example, the Application collection isn't shared between computers in a web farm, doesn't persist if the web application restarts, and isn't scalable with large numbers of users). However, you could easily extend this approach to use a combination of a back-end database and caching. That solution would be much more scalable, and it would use the same system of session headers that you see in this example.

You'll also notice that the CreateSession() method uses the direction SoapHeaderDirection.Out, because it creates the header and sends it back to the client. Here's the interesting part. When the client receives the custom header, it's stored in the CurrentSessionHeader property of the proxy class. The best part is that from that point on, whenever the client application calls a method in the web service that requires the header, it's submitted with the request. In fact, as long as the client uses the same proxy class, the headers are automatically transmitted and the session management system is completely transparent.

To test this out, you need to add two more methods to the web service. The first method, SetSessionData(), accepts a DataSet and stores it in the Application slot for the current user's session.

```
[WebMethod()]
[SoapHeader("CurrentSessionHeader", Direction=SoapHeaderDirection.In)]
public void SetSessionData(DataSet ds)
{
    Hashtable session = (Hashtable)Application[CurrentSessionHeader.SessionID];
    session.Add("DataSet", ds);
}
```

■**Note** You don't need to lock the Application collection in this example. That's because no two clients use the same session ID, and so there's no possibility for two users to attempt to change that slot of the Application collection at the same time.

Next, you can use a GetSessionData() method to retrieve the DataSet for the current user's session and return it:

```
[WebMethod()]
[SoapHeader("CurrentSessionHeader", Direction=SoapHeaderDirection.In)]
public DataSet GetSessionData()
{
    Hashtable session = (Hashtable)Application[CurrentSessionHeader.SessionID];
    return (DataSet)session["DataSet"];
}
```

Consuming a Web Service That Uses a Custom Header

When a web method requires a SOAP header, there's no way to test it using the simpler HTTP GET or HTTP POST protocols. As a result, you can't test the code in the browser test page. (In fact, the Invoke button won't even appear on this page.) Instead, you need to create a simple client.

The following code shows an example test. It creates the session (at which point it receives the SOAP header), stores a new, empty DataSet on the server, and then retrieves it:

```
SessionHeaderService proxy = new SessionHeaderService();
proxy.CreateSession();
proxy.SetSessionData(new DataSet("TestDataSet"));
DataSet ds = proxy.GetSessionData();
```

The SOAP message used for the call to CreateSession() is similar to the previous examples:

```
<soap:Envelope xmlns:soap="http://schemas.xmlsoap.org/soap/envelope/" >
  <soap:Body>
    <CreateSession xmlns="http://www.apress.com/ProASP.NET/" />
  </soap:Body>
</soap:Envelope>
```

The response message includes the SOAP header:

```
<soap:Envelope xmlns:soap="http://schemas.xmlsoap.org/soap/envelope/" >
  <soap:Header>
    <SessionHeader xmlns="http://tempuri.org/">
      <SessionID>bbc0bfed-c3c2-4552-b70e-dfa5564447fd</SessionID>
    </SessionHeader>
  </soap:Header>
  <soap:Body>
    <CreateSessionResponse xmlns="http://www.apress.com/ProASP.NET/" />
```

```
    </soap:Body>
</soap:Envelope>
```

Now, subsequent method invocations also have the SOAP header automatically included, as shown here:

```
<soap:Envelope xmlns:soap="http://schemas.xmlsoap.org/soap/envelope/" >
  <soap:Header>
    <SessionHeader xmlns="http://tempuri.org/">
      <SessionID>bbc0bfed-c3c2-4552-b70e-dfa5564447fd</SessionID>
    </SessionHeader>
  </soap:Header>
  <soap:Body>
    <GetSessionData xmlns="http://www.apress.com/ProASP.NET/" />
  </soap:Body>
</soap:Envelope>
```

The result, in this example, is a web service that provides an alternate session state mechanism that uses SOAP headers instead of less reliable HTTP cookies. However, you can also use SOAP headers for many more web service extensions. In fact, in the next chapter you'll see how they allow you to leverage new and emerging web service standards with Microsoft's Web Services Enhancements component.

Encoding Complex Data Types

As you learned last chapter, the SOAP specification supports all the data types defined by the XML Schema standard. These are considered *simple types*. Additionally, SOAP supports *complex types*, which are structures built out of an arrangement of simple types. Complex types can be used for a web method return value or as a parameter. However, if a web method requires complex type parameters, you can only interact with it using SOAP. The simpler HTTP GET and HTTP POST mechanisms won't work, and the browser test page won't allow you to invoke the web method.

You've already used one example of a complex type: the DataSet. When you call the GetEmployees() method in the EmployeesService, .NET returns an XML document that describes the schema of the DataSet and its contents. Here's a partial listening of the SOAP response message:

```
<soap:Envelope xmlns:soap="http://schemas.xmlsoap.org/soap/envelope/" >
  <soap:Body>
    <GetEmployeesResponse xmlns="http://www.apress.com/ProASP.NET/">
      <GetEmployeesResult>
        <xs:schema id="NewDataSet" xmlns=""
         xmlns:xs="http://www.w3.org/2001/XMLSchema"
         xmlns:msdata="urn:schemas-microsoft-com:xml-msdata">
        <!-- Schema omitted. -->
        </xs:schema>
        <diffgr:diffgram xmlns:msdata="urn:schemas-microsoft-com:xml-msdata"
         xmlns:diffgr="urn:schemas-microsoft-com:xml-diffgram-v1">
        <EmployeesDataSet xmlns="">
```

```
            <Employees diffgr:id="Employees1" msdata:rowOrder="0">
              <EmployeeID>1</EmployeeID>
              <LastName>Davolio</LastName>
              <FirstName>Nancy</FirstName>
              <Title>Sales Representative</Title>
              <TitleOfCourtesy>Ms.</TitleOfCourtesy>
              <HomePhone>(206) 555-9857</HomePhone>
            </Employees>
            <Employees diffgr:id="Employees2" msdata:rowOrder="1">
              <EmployeeID>2</EmployeeID>
              <LastName>Fuller</LastName>
              <FirstName>Andrew</FirstName>
              <Title>Vice President, Sales</Title>
              <TitleOfCourtesy>Dr.</TitleOfCourtesy>
              <HomePhone>(206) 555-9482</HomePhone>
            </Employees>
            ...
          </EmployeesDataSet></diffgr:diffgram>
        </GetEmployeesResult>
      </GetEmployeesResponse>
    </soap:Body>
</soap:Envelope>
```

You can also use your own custom classes with .NET web services. In this case, when you build the proxy, a copy of the custom class will automatically be added to the client (in the appropriate language of the client).

The process of converting objects to XML is known as serialization, and the process of reconstructing the objects from XML is know as deserialization. The component that performs the serialization is the System.Xml.Serialization.XmlSerializer class. This class shouldn't be confused with the serialization classes you learned about in Chapter 13, such as the BinaryFormatter and SoapFormatter. These classes perform .NET-specific serialization that works with proprietary .NET objects, so long as they are marked with the Serializable attribute. Unlike the BinaryFormatter and SoapFormatter, the XmlSerializer works with any class, but it's much more limited than the BinaryFormatter and SoapFormatter, and can only extract public data.

In order to use the XmlSerializer and send your custom objects to and from a web service, you need to be aware of a few restrictions:

- Any code you include will be ignored in the client. That means the client's copy of the custom class won't include methods, constructor logic, or property procedure logic. Instead, these details will be stripped out automatically.

- Any properties you use will be converted to public member variables in the client class. It's usually best to avoid using property procedures altogether to help keep this fact in mind.

- Your class must have a default zero-argument constructor. This allows .NET to create a new instance of this object when it deserializes a SOAP message that contains the corresponding data.

- Read-only class properties are not serialized. In other words, if a property only has a get accessor and not a set accessor, it cannot be serialized. Similarly, private properties and private member variables are ignored.

Clearly, the need to serialize a class to a piece of cross-platform XML imposes some strict limitations. If you use custom classes in a web service, it's best to think of them as simple data containers, rather than true participants in object-oriented design.

Creating a Custom Class

To see the XmlSerializer in action, you need to create a custom class and a web method that uses it. In the next example, we'll use the database component first developed in Chapter 8. This database component doesn't use the disconnected DataSet objects. Instead, it returns the results of a query using the custom EmployeeDetails class.

Here's what the EmployeeDetails class looks like currently, without any web service-related enhancements:

```
public class EmployeeDetails
{
    private int employeeID;
    public int EmployeeID
    {
        get {return employeeID;}
        set {employeeID = value;}
    }

    private string firstName;
    public string FirstName
    {
        get {return firstName;}
        set {firstName = value;}
    }

    private string lastName;
    public string LastName
    {
        get {return lastName;}
        set {lastName = value;}
    }

    private string titleOfCourtesy;
    public string TitleOfCourtesy
    {
        get {return titleOfCourtesy;}
        set {titleOfCourtesy = value;}
    }

    public EmployeeDetails(int employeeID, string firstName, string lastName,
```

```
        string titleOfCourtesy)
    {

        this.employeeID = employeeID;
        this.firstName = firstName;
        this.lastName = lastName;
        this.titleOfCourtesy = titleOfCourtesy;
    }
}
```

The EmployeeDetails class uses property procedures instead of public member variables. However, you can still use it because the XmlSerializer will perform the conversion automatically. The EmployeeDetails class doesn't have a default zero-parameter constructor, so before you can use it in a web method you need to add one, as shown here:

```
public EmployeeDetails(){}
```

Now the EmployeeDetails class is ready for a web service scenario. To try it out, you can create a web method that returns an array of EmployeeDetail objects. The next example shows one such method—a GetEmployees() web method that calls the EmployeeDB.GetEmployees() method in the database component. (For the full code for this method, you can refer back to Chapter 8 or consult the downloadable code.)

Here's the web method you need:

```
[WebMethod(Description="Returns the full list of employees.")]
public EmployeeDetails[] GetEmployees()
{
    EmployeeDB db = new EmployeeDB();
    return db.GetEmployees();
}
```

Generating the Proxy

When you generate the proxy (either using wsdl.exe or adding a web reference), you'll end up with two classes. The first class is the proxy class used to communicate with the web service. The second class is the definition for EmployeeDetails in a much more compact form. Here's what it looks like:

```
public class EmployeeDetails
{
    public int EmployeeID;
    public string FirstName;
    public string LastName;
    public string TitleOfCourtesy;
}
```

The version of EmployeeDetails that's declared in the client doesn't preserve the non-default constructor, and it replaces all the public properties with public member variables. All the other details are discarded.

Testing the Custom Class Web Service

The next step is to write the code that calls the GetEmployees() method. Because the client now has a definition of the EmployeeDetails class, this step is easy:

```
EmployeesServiceCustomDataClass proxy = new EmployeesServiceCustomDataClass();
EmployeeDetails[] employees = proxy.GetEmployees();
```

The response message includes the employee data in the <GetEmployeesResult> element. By default, the XmlSerializer creates a structure of child elements based on the class name (EmployeeDetails) and the public property or variable names (EmployeeID, FirstName, LastName, TitleOfCourtesy, and so on). Interestingly, this default structure looks quite a bit like the XML used to model the DataSet, without the schema information.

Here's a somewhat abbreviated example of the response message:

```
<soap:Envelope xmlns:soap="http://schemas.xmlsoap.org/soap/envelope/" >
  <soap:Body>
    <GetEmployeesResponse xmlns="http://www.apress.com/ProASP.NET/">
      <GetEmployeesResult>
        <EmployeeDetails>
          <EmployeeID>1</EmployeeID>
          <FirstName>Nancy</FirstName>
          <LastName>Davolio</LastName>
          <TitleOfCourtesy>Ms.</TitleOfCourtesy>
        </EmployeeDetails>
        <EmployeeDetails>
          <EmployeeID>2</EmployeeID>
          <FirstName>Andrew</FirstName>
          <LastName>Fuller</LastName>
          <TitleOfCourtesy>Dr.</TitleOfCourtesy>
        </EmployeeDetails>
      </GetEmployeesResult>
      ...
    </GetEmployeesResponse>
  </soap:Body>
</soap:Envelope>
```

When the client receives this message, the XML response is converted into an array of EmployeeDetails objects, using the client-side definition of the EmployeeDetails class.

There's a significant limitation to the client application in this example. Because the EmployeeDetails class doesn't use properties, you can't bind it to a data-bound control like a DataGrid. There's no elegant way around this limitation. One solution is to delete the EmployeeDetails class from the proxy file and copy the original, complete EmployeeDetails into the project. In this case, you need to make sure the EmployeeDetails class is in the exact same namespace as the proxy class. This approach solves the problem (and is demonstrated in the downloadable samples), but it has one flaw. Every time you refresh the web reference, a duplicate, stripped-down EmployeeDetails class will be added to your proxy, which you must delete before recompiling the application.

■**Note** As you've seen, because the proxy class doesn't include property procedures, it won't work in data binding scenarios without a slightly awkward workaround. This limitation is corrected in .NET 2.0, which supports property procedure generation for proxy classes (although it obviously still ignores any code you may have added).

Shaping the XML of Complex Data Types

Sometimes, you may want to customize the XML representation of a custom class. This approach is most useful in cross-platform programming scenarios when a client expects XML in a certain form. For example, you might have an existing schema that expects EmployeeDetails to use an EmployeeID attribute instead of a nested <EmployeeID> tag. .NET provides an easy way to apply these rules, using attributes. The basic idea is that you apply attributes to your data classes (like EmployeeDetails). When the XmlSerializer creates a SOAP message, it reads these attributes and uses them to tailor the XML payload it generates.

The System.Xml.Serialization namespace contains a number of attributes that can be used to control the shape of the XML. There are two sets of attributes: one where the attributes are named XmlXxx and another where the attributes are named SoapXxx. Which attributes you use depends on how the parameters are encoded.

As discussed earlier in this chapter, there are two types of SOAP serialization: literal and SOAP section 5 encoding. The XmlXxx attributes apply when you use literal style parameters. As a result, they apply in the following cases:

- When you use a web service with the default encoding (In other words, you haven't changed the encoding by adding any attributes.)

- When you use the HTTP GET or HTTP POST protocols to communicate with a web service

- When you use the SoapDocumentService or SoapDocumentMethod attribute with the Use property set to SoapBindingUse.Literal

- When you use the XmlSerializer on its own (outside of a web service)

The SoapXxx attributes apply when you use encoded style parameters. That occurs in the following cases:

- When you use the SoapRpcService or SoapRpcMethod attributes

- When you use the SoapDocumentService or SoapDocumentMethod attribute with the Use property set to SoapBindingUse.Encoded

A class member may have both the SoapXxx and the XmlXxx attributes applied at the same time. Which one is used depends on the type of serialization being performed.

Table 25-1 lists most of the available attributes. Most of the attributes contain a number of properties. Some properties are common to most attributes, such as the Namespace property (used to indicate the namespace of the serialized XML) and the DataType property (used to indicate a specific XML Schema data type that might not be the one the XmlSerializer would choose by default). For a complete reference that describes all the attributes and their properties, refer to the MSDN Help.

Table 25-1. *Attributes to Control XML Serialization*

Xml Attribute	SOAP Attribute	Description
XmlAttribute	SoapAttribute	Used to make fields into XML attributes instead of elements.
XmlElement	SoapElement	Used to name the XML elements. Can also be used with arrays to list array elements without being nested under a common element.
XmlArray		Used to name arrays.
XmlIgnore	SoapIgnore	Used to prevent fields from being serialized.
XmlInclude	SoapInclude	Used with derived classes.
XmlRoot		Used to name the top-level element.
XmlText		Used to serialize fields directly in the XML text without elements.
XmlEnum	SoapEnum	Used to give the members of an enumeration a name different from the name used in the enumeration.
XmlType	SoapType	Used to control the name of types in the WSDL file.

To see how SOAP serialization works, you can apply these attributes to the EmployeeDetails. For example, consider the following modified class declaration that uses several serialization attributes:

```
public class EmployeeDetails
{
    [XmlAttribute("id")]
    public int EmployeeID
    {
        get {return employeeID;}
        set {employeeID = value;}
    }

    [XmlElement("First")]
    public string FirstName
    {
        get {return firstName;}
        set {firstName = value;}
    }

    [XmlElement("Last")]
    public string LastName
    {
        get {return lastName;}
```

```
        set {lastName = value;}
    }


    [XmlIgnore()]
    public string TitleOfCourtesy
    {
        get {return titleOfCourtesy;}
        set {titleOfCourtesy = value;}
    }

    // (Constructors and private data omitted.)
}
```

Here's what a serialized EmployeeDetails will look like in the SOAP message:

```
<soap:Envelope xmlns:soap="http://schemas.xmlsoap.org/soap/envelope/" >
  <soap:Body>
    <GetEmployeesResponse xmlns="http://www.apress.com/ProASP.NET/">
      <GetEmployeesResult>
        <EmployeeDetails id="1">
          <First>Nancy</First>
          <Last>Davolio</Last>
          </EmployeeDetails>
        <EmployeeDetails id="2">
          <First>Andrew</First>
          <Last>Fuller</Last>
          </EmployeeDetails>
        ...
    </GetEmployeesResponse>
  </soap:Body>
</soap:Envelope>
```

■ **Tip** If you want to experiment with different serialization attributes, you can also use the XmlSerializer class directly. Just create an instance of the XmlSerializer, and pass the type of the object you want to serialize as a constructor parameter. You can then use the Serialize() method to convert the object to XML and write the data to a stream or a TextWriter object. You can use Deserialize() to read the XML data from a stream or TextReader and re-create the original object. You can also use a command line tool called xsd.exe that's included with the .NET Framework to generate C# class definitions based on XML schema documents. The class declaration will automatically include the appropriate serialization attributes.

SOAP Extensions

ASP.NET web services provide high-level access to SOAP. As you've seen, you don't need to know much about SOAP in order to create and call web services. If, however, you are a developer with a good understanding of SOAP and you want to get your hands dirty with low-level access to SOAP messages, the .NET Framework allows that too. In this section, you'll see how to intercept SOAP messages and manipulate them.

SOAP extensions are an extensibility mechanism. They allow third-party developers to create components that plug into the web service model and provide other services. For example, you could create a SOAP extension to automatically encrypt or compress SOAP messages before they are sent over the network from the client. Of course, you would also need to run a matching SOAP extension on the server to decrypt or decompress the message after it's received but before it's deserialized.

To create a SOAP extension, you need to create a class that derives from the System.Web.Services.Protocols.SoapExtension class. The SoapExtension class includes a ProcessMessage() method that's triggered automatically as the SOAP message passes through several stages. For example, if you run a SOAP extension on a web server, the following four stages will occur:

- **SoapMessageStage.BeforeDeserialize** occurs immediately after the web server receives the SOAP request message.

- **SoapMessageStage.AfterDeserialize** occurs after the raw SOAP message is translated to .NET data types but just before the web method code runs.

- **SoapMessageStage.BeforeSerialize** occurs after the web method code runs but before the return value is translated into a SOAP message.

- **SoapMessageStage.AfterSerialize** occurs after the return data is serialized into a SOAP response message but before it is sent to the client application.

At each stage, you can retrieve various bits of information about the SOAP message. In the BeforeDeserialize or AfterSerialize stage, you can retrieve the full SOAP message text.

You can also implement a SOAP extension on the client. In this case, the same four stages occur. Except now, the message is being received, deserialized, and acted upon by the proxy class, not the web service. Figure 25-6 shows the full process.

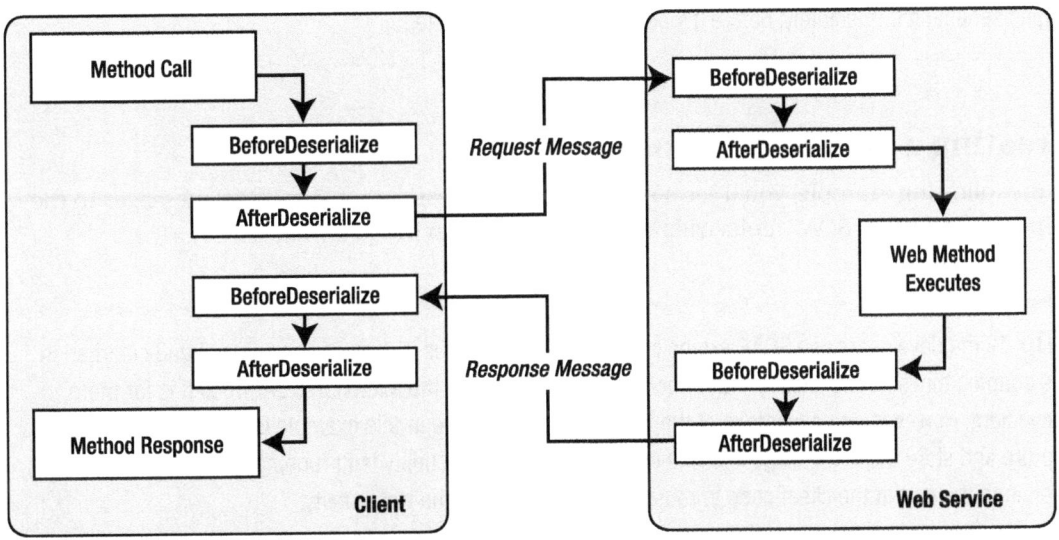

Figure 25-6. *SOAP processing on the client and server*

Creating production-level SOAP extensions is not easy. There are a number of serious challenges:

- SOAP extensions often need to be executed on both the server and client. That means you need to worry about distributing and managing another component, which can be exceedingly complex in a large distributed system.

- SOAP extensions make your web services less compatible. Third-party clients may not realize they need to install and run a SOAP extension to use your service, as this information isn't added in the WSDL document. If the clients are running non-.NET platforms, they won't be able to use the SoapExtension class you've created, and you may need to find another way to extend the SOAP processing pipeline, which can range from difficult to impossible depending on the environment.

- Creating production-level SOAP extensions is not easy. For example, the Internet abounds with examples of SOAP extensions that apply encryption in a very poor, insecure fashion. The flaws include insecure key management, no ability to perform a key exchange, and slow performance due to a reliance on asymmetric encryption instead of symmetric encryption. A much better choice is to use a SSL through IIS, which is bullet-proof.

In most cases, creating SOAP extensions is a task that's best left to the architects at Microsoft, who are focused on the issues and challenges of developing enterprise-level plumbing. In fact, Microsoft implements several newer, less mature web service standards using SOAP extensions in a freely downloadable component called the Web Services Enhancements (WSE). You'll learn more about WSE in the next chapter.

Note SOAP extensions only work over SOAP. When you test a web method through the browser test page, they won't be invoked. Also, SOAP messages won't work if you set the BufferResponse attribute of the WebMethod attribute to false. In this case, the SOAP extension can't act on the SOAP data, because ASP.NET begins sending it immediately, before it's been completely generated.

Creating a SOAP Extension

In the following example, you'll see a sample SOAP extension that logs SOAP messages to the Windows event log. SOAP faults will be logged as errors in the event log.

Tip Some developers use SOAP extensions for tracing purposes. However, as you've already learned in this chapter, that's not necessary—the trace utility included with the Microsoft SOAP Toolkit is far more convenient. However, one advantage of the SOAP logger you'll see in this example is that you could use it to capture and store SOAP messages permanently, even if the trace utility isn't running. You also don't need to change the port in the client code to route messages through the trace utility.

All SOAP extensions consist of two ingredients: a custom class that derives from System.Web.Services.Protocols.SoapExtension and a custom attribute that you apply to a web method to indicate that your SOAP extension should be used. The custom attribute is the simpler of the two ingredients.

The SoapExtension Attribute

The SoapExtension attribute allows you to link specific SOAP extensions to the methods in a web class. When you create your SoapExtension attribute, you derive from the System.Web.Services.Protocols.SoapExtensionAttribute, as shown here:

```
[AttributeUsage(AttributeTargets.Method)]
public class SoapLogAttribute : System.Web.Services.Protocols.SoapExtensionAttribute
{ ... }
```

Note that the attribute class bears another attribute—the AttributeUsage attribute. It indicates where you can use your custom attribute. SOAP extension attributes are always applied to individual method declarations, much like the SoapHeader and WebMethod attributes. Thus, you should use AttributeTargets.Method to prevent the user from applying it to some other code construct (like a class declaration). You should use AttributeUsage anytime you need to create a custom attribute—it isn't limited to web service scenarios.

Every SoapExtension attribute needs to override two abstract properties: Priority and ExtensionType. Priority is used to set the order that SOAP extensions work if you have multiple extensions configured. However, it's not needed in simpler extensions like the one in this example. The ExtensionType property returns a Type object that represents your custom SoapExtension class, and it allows .NET to attach your SOAP extension to the method. In this example, the class name of the SOAP Extension is SoapLog, although we haven't considered the code yet.

```
private int priority;
public override int Priority
{
    get { return priority; }
    set { priority = value; }
}


public override Type ExtensionType
{
    get { return typeof(SoapLog); }
}
```

In addition, you can add properties that will supply extra bits of initialization information to your SOAP extension. The following example adds a Name property, which stores the source string that will be used when writing event log entries, and a Level property, which configures what types of messages will be logged. If the level is 1, the SoapLog extension will only log error messages. If the level is 2 or greater, the SoapLog extension will write all types of messages. If the level is 3 or greater, the SoapLog extension will add an extra piece of information to each message that records the stage when the log entry was written.

```
private string name = "SoapLog" ;
public string Name
{
    get { return name;}
    set { name = value; }
}

private int level = 1;
public int Level
{
    get { return level;}
    set { level = value; }
}
```

You can now apply this custom attribute to a web method, and set the Name and Level properties. Here's an example that uses the log source name EmployeesService.GetEmployeesCount and a log level of 3:

```
[SoapLog(Name="EmployeesService.GetEmployeesCount", Level=3)]
[WebMethod()]
public int GetEmployeesCount()
{ ... }
```

Now, whenever the GetEmployeesCount() method is called with a SOAP message, the SoapLog class is created, initialized, and executed. It has the chance to process the SOAP request message before the GetEmployeesCount() method receives it, and it has the chance to process the SOAP response message after the GetEmployeesCount() method returns a result.

The SoapExtension

The SoapExtension class that we'll use to log messages is fairly long, although much of the code is basic boilerplate that every SOAP extension uses. We'll examine it piece by piece.

The first detail to notice is that the class derives from the abstract base class SoapExtension. This is a requirement. The SoapExtension class provides many of the methods you need to override, including the following:

- **GetInitializer() and Initialize().** These methods are used to pass initial information to the SOAP extension when it's first created.

- **ProcessMessage().** This is where the actual processing takes place, allowing your extension to take a look at (and modify) the raw SOAP.

- **ChainStream().** This method is a basic piece of infrastructure that every web service should provide. It allows you to gain access to the SOAP stream without disrupting other extensions.

Here's the class definition:

```
public class SoapLog : System.Web.Services.Protocols.SoapExtension
{ ... }
```

ASP.NET calls the GetInitializer() method the first time your extension is used for a particular web method. It gives you the chance to initialize and store some data that will be used
when processing SOAP messages. You store this information by passing it back as the return
value from the GetInitializer() method.

When the GetInitializer() method is called, you receive one important piece of information—the custom attribute that was applied to the corresponding web method. In the case of
the SoapLog, this is an instance of the SoapLogAttribute class, which provides the Name and
Level property. To store this information for future use, you can return this attribute from the
GetInitializer() method as shown here:

```
public override object GetInitializer(LogicalMethodInfo methodInfo,
 SoapExtensionAttribute attribute)
{
    return attribute;
}
```

There are actually two versions of the GetInitializer() method. Only one is invoked, and it
depends on whether the SOAP extension is configured through an attribute (as in this example) or through a configuration file. If applied through a configuration file, the SOAP extension
automatically runs for every method of every web service.

Even if you don't plan to use the configuration file to initialize a SOAP extension, you still
need to implement the other version of GetInitializer(). In this case, it makes sense to return a
new SoapLogAttribute instance, so that the default Name and Level settings are available later:

```
public override object GetInitializer(Type obj)
{
    return new SoapLogAttribute();
}
```

GetInitializer() is only called the first time your SOAP extension is executed for a
method. However, every time the method is invoked, the Initialize() method is triggered. If
you returned an object from the GetInitializer() method, ASP.NET provides this object to the
Initialize() method every time it's called. In the SoapLog extension, this is a good place to
extract the Name and Level information and store it in member variables so it will be available
for the remainder of the SOAP processing work. (You couldn't store this information in the
GetInitialize() method, because that method won't be called every time the SOAP extension is
executed.)

```
private int level;
private string name;

public override void Initialize(object initializer)
{
    name = ((SoapLogAttribute)initializer).Name;
    level = ((SoapLogAttribute)initializer).Level;
}
```

The workhorse of the extension is the ProcessMessage() method, which ASP.NET
calls at various stages of the serialization process. A SoapMessage object is passed to the
ProcessMessage() method, and you can examine this method to retrieve information about

the message, like its stage and the message text. The SoapLog extension only reads the full message in the AfterSerialize and BeforeDeserialize stages, because these are the only stages when you can retrieve the full XML of the SOAP message. However, if the level is 3 or greater, a basic log entry will be created in the BeforeSerialize and AfterDeserialize stages that simply records the name of the stage.

Here's the full ProcessMessage() code:

```
public override void ProcessMessage(SoapMessage message)
{
    switch (message.Stage)
    {
        case System.Web.Services.Protocols.SoapMessageStage.BeforeSerialize:
            if (level > 2 )
                WriteToLog(message.Stage.ToString(),
                  EventLogEntryType.Information);
            break;
        case System.Web.Services.Protocols.SoapMessageStage.AfterSerialize:
            LogOutputMessage(message);
            break;
        case System.Web.Services.Protocols.SoapMessageStage.BeforeDeserialize:
            LogInputMessage(message);
            break;
        case System.Web.Services.Protocols.SoapMessageStage.AfterDeserialize:
            if (level > 2 )
                WriteToLog(message.Stage.ToString(),
                  EventLogEntryType.Information);
            break;
    }
}
```

The ProcessMessage() method doesn't contain the actual logging code. Instead, it calls other private methods like WriteLogLog(), LogOutputMessage(), and LogInputMessage(). The WriteToLog() is the final point at which the log entry is created using the System.Diagnostics.EventLog class. If needed, this code creates a new event log, and a new log source using the name that was set in the Name property of the custom extension attribute.

Here's the complete code for the WriteToLog() method:

```
private void WriteToLog(string message, EventLogEntryType type)
{
    // Create a new log named Web Service Log, with the event source
    // specified in the attribute.
    EventLog log;
    if (!EventLog.SourceExists(name))
      EventLog.CreateEventSource(name, "Web Service Log");

    log = new EventLog();
    log.Source = name;
    log.WriteEntry(message, type);
}
```

When the SOAP message is in the BeforeSerialize or AfterDeserialize stage, the WriteToLog() method is called directly, and the name of the stage is written. When the SOAP message is in the AfterSerialize or BeforeDeserialize stage, you need to perform a little more work to retrieve the SOAP message.

Before you can build these methods, you need another ingredient—the CopyStream() method. That's because the XML in the SOAP message is contained in a stream. The stream has a pointer that indicates the current position in the stream. The problem is that as you read the message data from the stream (for example, to log it), you move the pointer. This means that if the log extension reads a stream that is about to be deserialized, it will move the pointer to the end of the stream. In order for ASP.NET to property deserialize the SOAP message, the pointer must be set back to the beginning of the stream. If you don't take this step, a deserialization error will occur.

To make this process easier, you can use a private CopyStream() method. This method copies the contents of one stream to another stream. After this method is executed, both streams will be positioned at the end.

```
private void CopyStream(Stream fromstream, Stream tostream)
{
    StreamReader reader = new StreamReader(fromstream);
    StreamWriter writer = new StreamWriter(tostream);
    writer.WriteLine(reader.ReadToEnd());
    writer.Flush();
}
```

Another ingredient you need is the ChainStream() method, which the ASP.NET plumbs calls before serialization or deserialization takes place. Your SOAP extension can override the ChainStream() method to insert itself into the processing pipeline. At this point, the extension can cache a reference to the original stream and create a new in-memory stream, which is then returned to the next extension in the chain.

```
private Stream oldStream;
private Stream newStream;

public override Stream ChainStream(Stream stream)
{
    oldStream = stream;
    newStream = new MemoryStream();
    return newStream;
}
```

Of course, this is only part of the story. It's up to the other methods to either read data out of the old stream or write data into the new stream, depending on what stage the message is in. This is accomplished by calling the CopyStream() method. Once you've implemented this somewhat confusing design, the end result is that every SOAP extension has a chance to modify the SOAP stream without overwriting each other's changes. For the most part, the ChainStream() and CopyStream() methods are basic pieces of SOAP extension architecture that are identical in every SOAP extension you'll see.

The LogInputMessage() and LogOutputMessage() have the task of extracting the message information and logging it. Both methods use the CopyStream() method. When deserializing, the input stream contains the XML to deserialize and the pointer is at the beginning of the stream. The LogInputMessage() method copies the input stream into the memory stream buffer, and logs the contents of the stream. It sets the pointer to the beginning of the memory stream buffer so that the next extension can get access to the stream.

```
private void LogInputMessage(SoapMessage message)
{
    CopyStream(oldStream, newStream);
    message.Stream.Seek(0, SeekOrigin.Begin);
    LogMessage(message, newStream);
    message.Stream.Seek(0, SeekOrigin.Begin);
}
```

When serializing, the serializer writes to the memory stream created in ChainStream(). When the LogOutputMessage() function is called after serializing, the pointer is at the end of the stream. The LogOutputMessage() function sets the pointer to the beginning of the stream so that the extension can log the contents of the stream. Before returning, the content of the memory stream is copied to the outgoing stream and the pointer is then back at the end of both streams.

```
private void LogOutputMessage(SoapMessage message)
{
    message.Stream.Seek(0, SeekOrigin.Begin);
    LogMessage(message, newStream);
    message.Stream.Seek(0, SeekOrigin.Begin);
    CopyStream(newStream, oldStream);
}
```

Once they've moved the stream to the right position, both LogInputMessage() and LogOutputMessage() extract the message data from the SOAP stream, and write a log message entry with that information. The function also checks whether the SOAP message contains a fault. In that case, the message is logged in the event log as an error.

```
private void LogMessage(SoapMessage message, Stream stream)
{
    StreamReader reader = new StreamReader(stream);
    eventMessage = reader.ReadToEnd();

    string eventMessage;
    if (level > 2)
        eventMessage = message.Stage.ToString() +"\n" + eventMessage;
    if (eventMessage.IndexOf("<soap:Fault>") > 0)
    {
        // The SOAP body contains a fault.
```

```
        if (level > 0)
            WriteToLog(eventMessage, EventLogEntryType.Error);
    }
    else
    {
        // The SOAP body contains a message.
        if (level > 1)
            WriteToLog(eventMessage, EventLogEntryType.Information);
    }
}
```

This completes the code for the SoapLog extension.

Using the SoapLog Extension

To test the SoapLog extension, you need to apply the SoapLogAttribute to a web method, as shown here:

```
[SoapLog(Name="EmployeesService.GetEmployeesCount", Level=3)]
[WebMethod()]
public int GetEmployeesCount()
{ ... }
```

You then need to create a client application that calls that method. When you run the client and call the method, the SoapLog extension will run and create the event log entries.

■**Note** In order for the SoapLog extension to successfully write to the event log, the ASP.NET worker process (typically, the account ASPNET) must have permission to access the Windows event log. Otherwise, no entries will be written. Note that if a SOAP extension fails and generates an exception at any point, it will simply be ignored. Your client code and web service methods will not be notified.

To verify that the entries appear, run the Event Viewer (choose Programs ➤ Administrative Tools ➤ Event Viewer from the Start menu). Look for the log named Web Service Log. Figure 25-7 shows the event log entries that you'll see after calling GetEmployessCount() twice with a log level of 3.

You can look at individual entries by double-clicking them. The Description field shows the full event log message, with the XML data from the SOAP message, as shown in Figure 25-8.

The SoapLog extension is a useful tool when developing or monitoring web services. However, you should use it judiciously. If you track even a single method, the number of event log entries could quickly grow into the thousands. As the event log fills, old messages are automatically discarded. You can configure these properties by right-clicking an event log in the Event Viewer and choosing Properties.

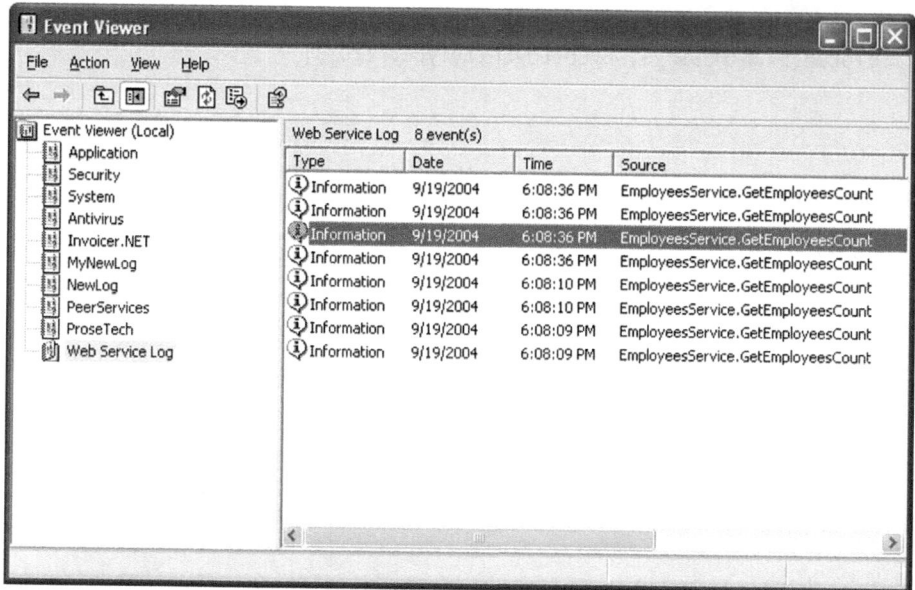

Figure 25-7. *The event log entries for the SOAP extension*

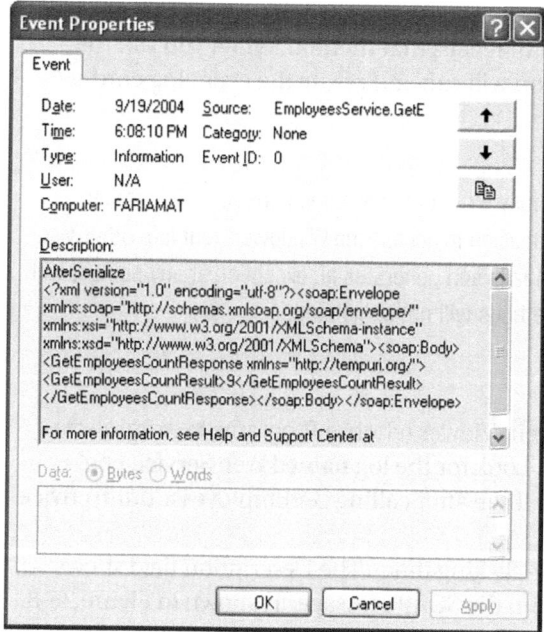

Figure 25-8. *A SOAP message in an event log entry*

WSDL

WSDL (Web Service Description Language) is an XML-based language used to describe the public interface of a web service, and the communication protocols it supports. A WSDL document is essentially a contract that tells the client what it needs to know in order to interact with a web service. Essentially, a WSDL document plays the same role as a type library for a COM component. (There's no direct analog to a type library in the .NET world, because all the descriptive type information you need is embedded into the compiled assembly as metadata.)

SOAP provides the ability to communicate with a web service. However, it doesn't tell you how to format your messages. Without WSDL, it would be up to you to document and explain the XML format your web services expect in the SOAP envelope. After locating a web service, the client developers would need to understand this information and handcraft the SOAP request and response messages accordingly. If this sort of human intervention was required in order to access every new service, the move towards web services would certainly be inhibited.

WSDL fills in the gaps by describing the supported protocols and expected message formats used by a web service. The power of WSDL is that it is not tied to any particular platform or object model. It is an XML language that provides an interface to web services across all platforms.

The full WSDL standard can be found at www.w3.org/TR/wsdl. The standard is fairly complex, but its underlying logic is hidden from the developer in ASP.NET programming, just as ASP.NET web controls abstract away the messy details of HTML tags and attributes.

Viewing the WSDL for a Web Service

Once you've created a web service, you can easily get ASP.NET to generate the corresponding WSDL document. All you need to do is request the web service .asmx file, and add ?WSDL to the end of the URL. (Another option is to click the Service Description link on the browser test page, which requests this URL.) Figure 25-9 shows part of the WSDL document you'll see for the EmployeesService developed in the previous chapter.

WSDL is keenly important because it allows the designers of programming frameworks like .NET to create tools that can create proxy classes programmatically. When you add a web reference in Visual Studio .NET (or use wsdl.exe), you point it to the WSDL document for the web service. (If it's a .NET web service, you can save a step by pointing it to the .asmx web service file, because both tools are smart enough to add the ?WSDL to the end of the query string to get a WSDL document for a .NET web service.) The tool then scans the WSDL document, and creates a proxy class that uses the same methods, parameters, and data types. Other languages and programming platforms provide tools that work similar magic.

Figure 25-9. *A WSDL document for the EmployeesService*

■**Note** The WSDL document contains information for communication between a web service and client. It doesn't contain any information that has anything to do with the code or implementation of your web service methods—that is unnecessary and would compromise security. Remember, when you add a web reference, all you need is the WSDL document. Neither Visual Studio .NET nor the wsdl.exe tool have the ability to examine web service code directly.

WSDL documents tend to be extremely long, and take more work to navigate than a simple SOAP message. In the next few sections, you'll examine a sample WSDL document for the EmployeesService.

The Basic Structure

WSDL documents consist of five main elements that combine to describe a web service. The first three of these are abstract and define the messaging. The last two are concrete and define the protocol and address information.

The three abstract elements, the <types>, <message>, and <portType> elements, combine to define the interface of the web service. They define the methods, parameters, and the properties of a web service. The two concrete elements, the <binding> element and the <port> element, combine to provide the protocol (SOAP over HTTP) and address information (the URI) of a web service. Separating the message definition elements from the location and protocol information provides the flexibility to reuse a common set of messages and data types within different protocols. It makes WSDL documents quite a bit more complicated than they would be otherwise, but it also gives unlimited flexibility for the future. For example, in the future WSDL documents could be used to describe how to interact with web services of SMTP, FTP, or some entirely different network-based protocol.

The WSDL 1.1 specification comes with SOAP over HTTP, HTTP GET, HTTP POST, and MIME extensions layered on top of the base specification. ASP.NET supports all of these except the MIME extension. Since WSDL is most commonly implemented utilizing SOAP over HTTP and since that is the default in ASP.NET, this chapter will focus on WSDL in relation to SOAP and HTTP. SOAP is really dominant and there seems to be no real competitor to it at this point. Microsoft seems to be more interested in supporting raw SOAP over TCP, a transfer protocol known as Direct Internet Message Encapsulation (DIME), and building work abounds to the HTTP request response structure, than they are in supporting MIME.

The <definitions> element is the root element of a WSDL document. It is where most of the namespaces are defined. Inside the <definitions> element are five main elements—one of which, <message>, commonly occurs multiple times.

Here's the basic structure of a WSDL document:

```
<?xml version="1.0" encoding="utf-8" ?>
<definitions>
  <types></types>
  <message></message>
  <message></message>
  <portType></portType>
  <binding></binding>
  <service></service>
</definitions>
```

Here is an overview of the main elements of a WSDL document:

- **Types.** This section is where all the web service data types are defined. This includes custom data types and the message formats.

- **Messages.** This section provides details about the request and response messages used to communicate with the web service.

- **PortType.** This section groups messages in input/output pairs. Each pair represents a method.

- **Binding.** This section provides information about the transport protocols supported by the web service.

- **Service.** This section provides the endpoint (URI address) for the web service.

The following sections examine these elements.

Types Section

The <types> section is where the web service data types are defined. The <types> element is actually an embedded XML schema, and all data types defined in the XML Schema standard are valid. Other type systems can be added through extensibility if required.

In a .NET web service, every message is defined as a complex type. The complex type definition describes the method name, its parameters, the minimum and maximum times the element can occur, and the data types. For example, consider the GetEmployeesCount() method. The request message needs no data, and is defined using XML schema syntax, like this:

```
<s:element name="GetEmployeesCount">
  <s:complexType />
</s:element>
```

The response message returns in integer (the int type from the XML Schema standard). It's defined like this:

```
<s:element name="GetEmployeesCountResponse">
  <s:complexType>
    <s:sequence>
      <s:element minOccurs="1" maxOccurs="1" name="GetEmployeesCountResult"
        type="s:int" />
    </s:sequence>
  </s:complexType>
</s:element>
```

The <types> section will typically be quite lengthy, because it defines two complex types for each web method.

A more interesting example is the web service that returns a custom object. For example, consider the GetEmployees() method developed earlier in this chapter that returns an array of EmployeeDetails objects. If you look in the <types> section for this web service, you'll find that the request message is unchanged:

```
<s:element name="GetEmployees">
  <s:complexType />
</s:element>
```

However, the response refers to another complex type, named ArrayOfEmployeeDetails:

```
<s:element name="GetEmployeesResponse">
  <s:complexType>
    <s:sequence>
      <s:element minOccurs="0" maxOccurs="1" name="GetEmployeesResult"
```

```
        type="s0:ArrayOfEmployeeDetails" />
    </s:sequence>
  </s:complexType>
</s:element>
```

This ArrayOfEmployeeDetails is a complex type that's generated automatically. It represents a list of 0 or more EmployeeDetails objects, as shown here:

```
<s:complexType name="ArrayOfEmployeeDetails">
  <s:sequence>
    <s:element minOccurs="0" maxOccurs="unbounded" name="EmployeeDetails"
      nillable="true" type="s0:EmployeeDetails" />
  </s:sequence>
</s:complexType>
```

The EmployeeDetails data class is also defined as a complex type in the <types> section. It's made up of an EmployeeID, FirstName, LastName, and TitleOfCourtesy, as shown here:

```
<s:complexType name="EmployeeDetails">
  <s:sequence>
    <s:element minOccurs="1" maxOccurs="1" name="EmployeeID" type="s:int" />
    <s:element minOccurs="0" maxOccurs="1" name="FirstName" type="s:string" />
    <s:element minOccurs="0" maxOccurs="1" name="LastName" type="s:string" />
    <s:element minOccurs="0" maxOccurs="1" name="TitleOfCourtesy"
      type="s:string" />
  </s:sequence>
</s:complexType>
```

Another ingredient that will turn up in the <types> section is the definition for any SOAP headers you use. For example, the stateful web service test developed earlier in this chapter defines the following type to represent the data in the session header:

```
<s:element name="SessionHeader" type="s0:SessionHeader" />
<s:complexType name="SessionHeader">
  <s:sequence>
    <s:element minOccurs="0" maxOccurs="1" name="SessionID" type="s:string" />
  </s:sequence>
</s:complexType>
```

Message Section

Messages represent the information exchanged between a web service method and a client. When you request a stock quote from the simple web service, ASP.NET sends a message, and the web service sends a different message back. The definition for these messages is found in the <message> section of the WSDL document. Here's an example:

```
<message name="GetEmployeesCountSoapIn">
  <part name="parameters" element="s0:GetEmployeesCount" />
</message>
<message name="GetEmployeesCountSoapOut">
```

```
    <part name="parameters" element="s0:GetEmployeesCountResponse" />
</message>
```

In this example, you'll notice that ASP.NET creates both a GetEmployeesCountSoapIn and a GetEmployeesCountSoapOut message. The naming is a matter of convention, but it underscores the fact that a separate message is required for input (sending parameters and invoking a web service method) and output (retrieving a return value from a web service method).

The data used in these messages is defined in terms of the information in the <types> section. For example, the GetEmployeesCountSoapIn request message uses the GetEmployeesCount message, which is defined as an empty complex type in the <types> section.

PortType Section

The information in the <portType> section of the WSDL document provides a catalog of the functionality available in a web service. Unlike the <message> element just discussed, which contained independent elements for the input and output messages, these operations are tied together in a request-response grouping. The operation name is the name of the method. The <portType> is a collection of operations, as shown here:

```
<portType name="EmployeesServiceSoap">
  <operation name="GetEmployeesCount">
    <documentation>Returns the total number of employees.</documentation>
    <input message="s0:GetEmployeesCountSoapIn" />
    <output message="s0:GetEmployeesCountSoapOut" />
  </operation>
  <operation name="GetEmployees">
    <documentation>Returns the full list of employees.</documentation>
    <input message="s0:GetEmployeesSoapIn" />
    <output message="s0:GetEmployeesSoapOut" />
  </operation>
</portType>
```

Additionally, you'll see a <documentation> tag with the information added through the Description property of the WebMethod attribute.

Note There are four types of operations: one-way, request-response, solicit-response, and notification. The current WSDL specification defines only bindings for the one-way and request-response operation types. The other two can have bindings defined via binding extensions. The latter two are simply the inverse of the first two; the only difference is whether the endpoint in question is on the receiving or sending end of the initial message. HTTP is a two-way protocol, so the one-way operations will work only with MIME (which is not supported by ASP.NET) or with another custom extension.

Binding Section

The <binding> elements link the abstract data format to the concrete protocol used for transmission over an Internet connection. So far, the WSDL document has specified the data type used for various pieces of information, the required messages used for an operation, and the structure of each message. With the <binding> element, the WSDL document specifies the low-level communication protocol that you can use to communicate with a web service. It links this to an <operation> from the <portType> section.

Although we won't go into all the details of SOAP encoding, here's an example that defines how SOAP communication should work with the GetEmployeesCount() method of the EmployeesService:

```
<binding name="EmployeesServiceSoap" type="s0:EmployeesServiceSoap">
  <soap:binding transport="http://schemas.xmlsoap.org/soap/http"
   style="document" />
  <operation name="GetEmployeesCount">
    <soap:operation
     soapAction="http://www.apress.com/ProASP.NET/GetEmployeesCount"
     style="document" />
    <input>
      <soap:body use="literal" />
    </input>
    <output>
      <soap:body use="literal" />
    </output>
  </operation>
```

If your method uses a SOAP header, that information is added as a <header> element. Here's an example with the CreateSession() method from the custom state web service developed earlier in this chapter. The CreateSession() method doesn't require the client to submit a header, but it does return one. As a result, only the output message references the header:

```
<operation name="CreateSession">
  <soap:operation soapAction="http://tempuri.org/CreateSession"
   style="document" />
  <input>
    <soap:body use="literal" />
  </input>
  <output>
    <soap:body use="literal" />
    <soap:header message="s0:CreateSessionSessionHeader"
     part="SessionHeader" use="literal" />
  </output>
</operation>
```

Service Section

The <service> section defines the entry points into your web service, as one or more <port> elements. Each <port> provides address information or a URI. Here's an example from the WSDL for the EmployeesService:

```
<service name="EmployeesService">
  <documentation>Retrieve the Northwind Employees</documentation>
  <port name="EmployeesServiceSoap" binding="s0:EmployeesServiceSoap">
    <soap:address location="http://localhost/Chapter24/EmployeesService.asmx" />
  </port>
</service>
```

The <service> section also includes a <documentation> element with the Description property of the WebService attribute, if it's set.

Summary

In this chapter, you took an in-depth look at the two most important web service protocols: SOAP and WSDL. SOAP is an incredibly lightweight protocol for messaging. WSDL is a flexible, extensible protocol for describing web services. Together, they ensure that web services can be created and consumed on virtually any programming platform for years to come.

■ ■ ■

CHAPTER 26

Advanced Web Services

In the past two chapters, you've taken a close look at how web services work with ASP.NET. Using the techniques you've learned already, you can create web services that expose data to other applications and organizations, and you can consume .NET and non-.NET web services on the Internet.

However, the story doesn't end there. In this chapter, you'll learn how to extend your web service skills with specific techniques that are often important in real-world web service scenarios. You'll focus on three different topic areas, as follows:

- **Calling web services asynchronously.** Web service calls take time, especially if the web server is located across the globe and connected by a slow network connection. By using asynchronous calls, you can keep working while you wait for a response.

- **Securing web services.** In Part Three you learned how you can secure web pages to prevent anonymous users. You can apply some of the same techniques to protect your web services.

- **Extending web services with the WSE.** Since .NET first hit the scene, new standards have been developed. Some of these are integrated into a new WSE (Web Services Enhancements) component that's available from Microsoft. You'll see how to use the WSE in the two most useful ways—to efficiently send a large block of binary data, and to pass authentication credentials.

All of these topics build on the concepts you've learned in the past two chapters.

Asynchronous Calls

As you learned in Chapter 24, the .NET Framework shields the programmer from the complexities of calling a web service by providing your applications with a proxy class. The code that uses the proxy class looks the same whether the web service is on the same computer, a local network, or across the Internet.

Despite superficial similarities, the underlying plumbing used to invoke a web service is very different from an in-process function call. Not only must the call be packaged into a SOAP message, it also needs to be transmitted across the network using HTTP. Because of the inherent nature of the Internet, the time it takes to call a web service can vary greatly from one call to the next. Although there's no way your client can speed up a web method invocation, it can choose not to sit idle while waiting for the response. Instead, it can continue to perform calculations, read from the file system or a database, and even call additional web services. This asynchronous design pattern is more difficult to implement, but in certain situations it can reap significant benefits.

There are two general cases where asynchronous processing makes sense:

- If you're creating a Windows application. In this case, an asynchronous call allows the user interface to remain responsive.

- If you have other computationally expensive work to do, or you have to access other resources that have a high degree of latency. By performing the web service call asynchronously, you can carry out this work while waiting for the response. A special case is when you need to call several independent web services. In this situation, you can call them all asynchronously, collapsing your total waiting time.

It's just as important that you realize when you should *not* use the asynchronous pattern. Asynchronous calls won't speed up the time taken to receive a response. That means that in most web applications that use web services, there's no reason to call the web service asynchronously, because your code still needs to wait for the response to be received before it can render the final page and send it back to the client. However, if there's a number of web services you need to call at once, or there are other tasks you can perform while waiting, you may shave a few milliseconds off the total request processing time.

In the following sections, you'll see asynchronous calls used to save time with a web client and provide a more responsive user interface with a Windows client.

The Proxy Class

There are several ways to create new threads in .NET. All delegates provide BeginInvoke() and EndInvoke() methods that allow you to trigger them on one of the threads in the CLR thread pool. Additionally, you can use the System.Threading.Thread class to explicitly create a new thread, with complete control over its priority and lifetime. However, when using .NET web services you don't need to resort to these approaches. Instead, the automatically generated proxy class has support for basic asynchronous use built in.

To understand how this works, it helps to take another look at the proxy class. When you generate the proxy class, it automatically includes *three* methods for each web method. For example, consider the GetEmployees() method in the EmployeesService developed in Chapter 24. When you build the proxy class for this web method, it will include a GetEmployees(), BeginGetEmployees(), and EndGetEmployees() method. The GetEmployees() method is the ordinary, synchronous version that calls the web service and waits for the response, blocking your code. It uses the inherited SoapHttpClientProtocol.Invoke() method. The other two methods invoke the web method asynchronously using the inherited SoapHttpClientProtocol.BeginInvoke() and SoapHttpClientProtocol.EndInvoke() methods. The BeginGetEmployees() starts an asynchronous operation that returns immediately. The EndGetEmployees() retrieves the results from the asynchronous operation after it's complete.

```
[System.Web.Services.Protocols.SoapDocumentMethodAttribute()]
public System.Data.DataSet GetEmployees()
{
    object[] results = this.Invoke("GetEmployees", new object[0]);
```

```
    return ((System.Data.DataSet)(results[0]));
}

public System.IAsyncResult BeginGetEmployees(AsyncCallback callback,
  object asyncState)
{
    return this.BeginInvoke("GetEmployees", new object[0], callback, asyncState);
}

public System.Data.DataSet EndGetEmployees(IAsyncResult asyncResult)
{
    object[] results = this.EndInvoke(asyncResult);
    return ((System.Data.DataSet)(results[0]));
}
```

You'll notice that the BeginXxx() method always provides two extra parameters. For example, if the GetEmployees() web method requires two parameters, BeginGetEmployees() will have four. The last two parameters are used to define a callback method, which can notify your code automatically when the method is complete. Additionally, the BeginXxx() method always returns an IAsyncResult object. You can use this object to track the current state of an ongoing asynchronous operation. You'll see both of these techniques in the following sections.

A Simple Asynchronous Call

The simplest way to perform an asynchronous operation is to call the BeginXxx() method to send your request, perform whatever work you need to perform in the meantime, and then call the EndXxx() method to retrieve the result. If you use this pattern, you won't necessarily retrieve the result as soon as it's available. However, this doesn't cause a problem. If the response is received before you call EndXxx(), .NET will simply hold onto it until you're ready. If the response still is not received by the time you call EndXxx(), your code will wait, effectively becoming synchronous for the remainder of the call duration.

Here's an example:

```
// Send the request. (This method returns immediately.)
IAsyncResult handle = proxy.BeginGetEmployees(null, null);

// Pick up the response (and wait if needed).
DataSet ds = proxy.EndGetEmployees(handle);
```

The BeginXxx() returns an IAsyncResult object that you need to keep track of the asynchronous operation. For example, you can examine the IsCompleted property to determine if the response has been received and processed before you call EndGetEmployee().

The following example demonstrates the difference between synchronous and asynchronous code. In order to test the example, you need to slow down your code artificially to simulate heavy load conditions or time-consuming tasks. First of all, add this line to the GetEmployees() method in the web service to add a delay of four seconds:

```
System.Threading.Thread.Sleep(4000);
```

The next step is to create a web page that uses the web service. This web page also defines a private method that simulates a time-consuming task, again using the Thread.Sleep() method. Here's the code you need to add to the web page:

```
private void DoSomethingSlow()
{
    System.Threading.Thread.Sleep(3000);
}
```

In your page, you need to execute both methods. Using a simple piece of timing code, you can compare the synchronous approach with the asynchronous approach. Depending on which button the user clicks, you will perform the two operations synchronously (one after the other), or asynchronously at the same time.

Here's how you would execute the two tasks synchronously:

```
private void cmdSynchronous_Click(object sender, System.EventArgs e)
{
    // Record the start time.
    DateTime startTime = DateTime.Now;

    // Get the web service data.
    EmployeesService proxy = new EmployeesService();
    try
    {
        DataGrid1.DataSource = proxy.GetEmployees();
    }
    catch (Exception err)
    {
        lblInfo.Text = "Problem contacting web service.";
        return;
    }

    DataGrid1.DataBind();

    // Perform some other time-consuming tasks.
    DoSomethingSlow();

    // Determine the total time taken.
    TimeSpan timeTaken = DateTime.Now.Subtract(startTime);
    lblInfo.Text = "Synchronous operations took " + timeTaken.TotalSeconds +
        " seconds.";
}
```

And here's how you could start the web service first, so that the operations overlap:

```
private void cmdAsynchronous_Click(object sender, System.EventArgs e)
{
    // Record the start time.
    DateTime startTime = DateTime.Now;
```

```
// Start the web service.
EmployeesService proxy = new EmployeesService();
IAsyncResult handle = proxy.BeginGetEmployees(null, null);

// Perform some other time-consuming tasks.
DoSomethingSlow();

// Retrieve the result. If it isn't ready, wait.
try
{
    DataGrid1.DataSource = proxy.EndGetEmployees(handle);
}
catch (Exception err)
{
    lblInfo.Text = "Problem contacting web service.";
    return;
}
DataGrid1.DataBind();

// Determine the total time taken.
TimeSpan timeTaken = DateTime.Now.Subtract(startTime);
lblInfo.Text = "Asynchronous operations took " + timeTaken.TotalSeconds +
  " seconds.";
}
```

Notice that the exception handler wraps the EndGetEmployee() method, but not the BeginGetEmployee() method. That's because if any errors occur while processing the request (whether due to network problems or a server-side exception), your code won't receive it until you call the EndXxx() method.

When you run these two examples, you'll find that the synchronous code takes between 7 and 8 seconds, while the asynchronous code only takes between 4 and 5 seconds. Figure 26-1 shows the web page with the time reading at the bottom.

■**Tip** Remember, the advantage of threading depends on the type of operations. In this example, the full benefit of threading is realized because the operations aren't CPU bound—they are simply waiting idly. This is similar to the behavior you'll experience contacting external web services or databases. However, if you try to use threading to simultaneously run two tasks that make use of the CPU on the *same* computer, you won't see any advantage, because both tasks will get about half the CPU resources, and will take about twice as long to execute. That's why threading is so ideal for web services, but not nearly as useful for the rest of your business code.

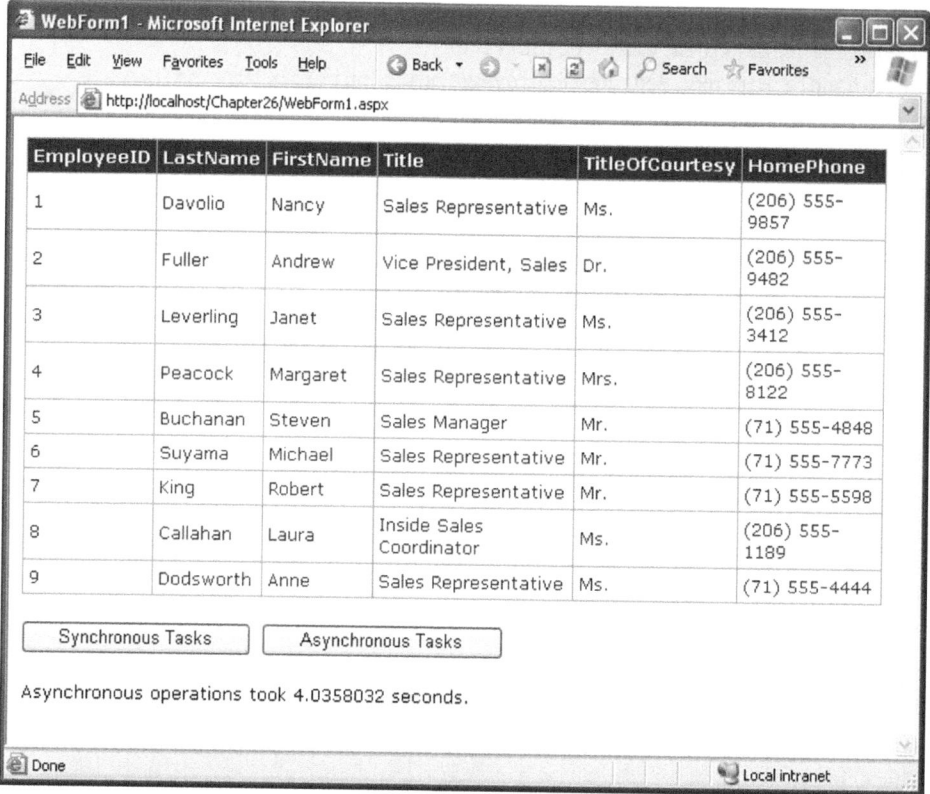

Figure 26-1. *Testing an asynchronous method call*

Concurrent Asynchronous Calls

The IAsyncState object gives you a few other options that are useful when calling multiple web methods at once. The key is the IAsyncState.WaitHandle object, which returns a System.Threading.WaitHandle object. Using this object, you can call WaitAll() to wait until all your asynchronous operations are complete. The following example uses this technique to call the GetEmployees() method three times at once:

```
private void cmdMultiple_Click(object sender, System.EventArgs e)
{
    // Record the start time.
    DateTime startTime = DateTime.Now;

    EmployeesService proxy = new EmployeesService();

    // Call three methods asynchronously.
    IAsyncResult async1 = proxy.BeginGetEmployees(null, null);
    IAsyncResult async2 = proxy.BeginGetEmployees(null, null);
    IAsyncResult async3 = proxy.BeginGetEmployees(null, null);

    // Create an array of WaitHandle objects.
```

```
    WaitHandle[] waitHandles = {async1.AsyncWaitHandle,
      async2.AsyncWaitHandle, async3.AsyncWaitHandle};

    // Wait for all the calls to finish.
    WaitHandle.WaitAll(waitHandles);

    // You can now retrieve the results.
    DataSet ds1 = proxy.EndGetEmployees(async1);
    DataSet ds2 = proxy.EndGetEmployees(async2);
    DataSet ds3 = proxy.EndGetEmployees(async3);

    // Merge all the results into one table and display it.
    DataSet dsMerge = new DataSet();
    dsMerge.Merge(ds1);
    dsMerge.Merge(ds2);
    dsMerge.Merge(ds3);
    DataGrid1.DataSource = dsMerge;
    DataGrid1.DataBind();

    // Determine the total time taken.
    TimeSpan timeTaken = DateTime.Now.Subtract(startTime);
    lblInfo.Text = "Calling three methods took " + timeTaken.TotalSeconds +
      " seconds.";
}
```

This technique doesn't actually improve performance when compared against the basic asynchronous approach shown in the previous section. Instead of using a wait handle, you could launch the three asynchronous calls by calling BeginXxx() three times, and then call the three EndXxx() methods immediately after. In this case, your code would wait if required. However, using a wait handle clarifies your code.

You can also use one of the overloaded versions of the WaitAll() method that accepts a timeout value. If this amount of time passes without the calls completing, an exception will be thrown. However, it's usually best to rely on the Timeout property of the proxy instead, which will end the call if a response isn't received in the designated amount of time.

You can also instruct a wait handle to block the thread until any one of the method calls has finished using the static WaitHandle.WaitAny() method with an array of WaitHandle objects. The WaitAny() method returns as soon as at least *one* of the asynchronous calls completes. This can be a useful technique if you need to process a batch of data from different sources, and the order that you process it is not important. It allows you to begin processing the results from one method before the others are complete. However, it also complicates your code, because you'll need to test the IsCompleted property of each IAsyncResult object, and call WaitAny() multiple times (usually in a loop) until all the methods have finished.

Responsive Windows Clients

In a Windows client, the threading code you use is a little different. Typically, you'll want to allow the application to continue unhindered while the operation is taking place. When the call is complete, you might simply want to refresh the display with updated information.

The best way to code this model is to pass a callback to the BeginXxx() method. As soon as the response is received and deserialized, .NET will call this method to notify your application. You can then retrieve the results.

To try this pattern out, you can modify the Windows client developed in Chapter 24 to use an asynchronous call. The first step is to create a method that can handle the callback in the form class. This method needs to have no return value and take a single IAsyncResult parameter. This method signature is defined by the AsyncCallback delegate. Here's an example:

```
private void Callback(IAsyncResult asyncResult)
{ ... }
```

When the user clicks the Get Employees button, the code will use the BeginGetEmployees() method to start the process. It will also pass a delegate that points to the Callback() method as the first parameter for BeginGetEmployees(). This ensures that the callback will be triggered once the call is complete. The code will also submit the proxy object as the second parameter for the BeginGetEmployees() method. This ensures the proxy object will be retained for the duration of the call and passed to the callback. Using the proxy object, you can easily complete the call by calling its EndGetEmployees() method.

Here's the code that starts the asynchronous call:

```
private void cmdGetEmployees_Click(object sender, System.EventArgs e)
{
    // Disable the button so that only one asynchronous
    // call will be permitted at a time.
    cmdGetEmployees.Enabled = false;

    // Create the proxy.
    EmployeesService proxy = new EmployeesService();

    // Create the callback delegate.
    AsyncCallback callback = new AsyncCallback(Callback);

    // Call the web service asynchronously and
    // pass the callback and the proxy object.
    // There is no need to store the IAsyncResult object,
    // because this example doesn't check the state.
    proxy.BeginGetEmployees(callback, proxy);
}
```

When the operation is finished, the proxy class calls the Callback() method to notify your code. The Callback() method retrieves the proxy object, and uses it to get the DataSet that was returned from the web service.

```
private void Callback(IAsyncResult asyncResult)
{
    // Retrieve the proxy from state.
    EmployeesService proxy = (EmployeesService)asyncResult.AsyncState;
```

```
    // Complete the call.
    DataSet ds = proxy.EndGetEmployees(asyncResult);
}
```

Unfortunately, there's one catch. When the callback fires, it won't be on the same thread as your client application. That means it isn't safe to update the Windows user interface. Although updating a piece of user interface from another thread won't usually cause a problem, it can introduce subtle and mysterious problems that appear at the worst times. For example, under certain situations data binding to a DataGrid from the wrong thread can freeze the application. To avoid these headaches, you need to explicitly marshal your code back to the user interface thread where it can finish its work. This crucial extra step complicates the callback pattern.

In order to solve the problem, you need to create another private method in the form that updates the grid. Here's an example that binds the retrieved DataSet and also enables the cmdGetEmployees button so the user can call the web service again:

```
private void UpdateGrid(DataSet newDataSet)
{
    // Bind the results.
    dataGrid1.DataSource = newDataSet.Tables[0];

    // Re-enabled the button for another refresh.
    cmdGetEmployees.Enabled = true;
}
```

Next, you need to define a delegate for the UpdateGrid() method that defines its signature. This is a necessity, because in order to call UpdateGrid() on the right thread, you'll need to use a delegate.

```
private delegate void UpdateGridDelegate(DataSet newDataSet);
```

Now the final step is to update the Callback() method so that it calls UpdateGrid(). Of course, it can't call UpdateGrid() directly, or the call would still execute on the wrong thread. Instead, it needs to use the Control.Invoke() method and pass a delegate that points to the UpdateGrid() method. Control.Invoke() then executes the code on the correct user interface thread. In this method, you can use the Invoke() method of any control on the form (including the DataGrid, Button, or Form), because they are all tied to the same thread.

Here's the updated Callback() method:

```
private void Callback(IAsyncResult asyncResult)
{
    // Retrieve the proxy from state.
    EmployeesService proxy = (EmployeesService)asyncResult.AsyncState;

    // Complete the call.
    DataSet ds = proxy.EndGetEmployees(asyncResult);

    // Update the user interface on the right thread.
    this.Invoke(new UpdateGridDelegate(UpdateGrid), new object[]{ds});
}
```

If you run this example and click the Get Employees button, the button will become disabled, but the application will remain responsive. You can drag and resize the window, click other buttons to execute more code, and so on. Finally, when the results have been received, the callback will be triggered, and the DataGrid will be refreshed automatically.

Note Remember, .NET gives you even more threading options with the Thread class. For example, if you need to call a series of web services in a specific order as part of a long-running background service in a Windows application, the Thread class offers the best solution. For more information about multithreading, consult a book that explores advanced Windows programming techniques.

Asynchronous Services

So far, you've seen several examples that allow clients to call web services asynchronously. But in all these examples, the web method still runs synchronously from start to finish. What if you want a different behavior that allows the client to trigger a long-running process and then connect later to pick up the results?

Unfortunately, .NET doesn't directly support this model. Part of the problem is that all web service communication must be initiated by the client. There's currently no way for the web server to initiate a call back to the client to tell them when a task is complete. And even if standards evolve to fill this gap, it's unlikely that this solution will gain widespread use because of the nature of the architecture of the Web. Many clients connect from behind proxy servers or firewalls that don't allow incoming connections or hide location information like the IP address. As a result, the client needs to initiate every connection.

Of course, there are still some innovative solutions that can provide some of the functionality you want. For example, there's no reason that a client can't reconnect periodically to poll the server, and see if a task is complete. You could use this design if a web server needs to perform extremely time-consuming tasks, like rendering complex graphics. However, there's still one missing ingredient. In these situations, you need a way for a client to start a web method without waiting for the web method to finish executing. ASP.NET makes this behavior possible with *one-way methods*.

With one-way methods (also known as fire-and-forget methods), the client sends a request message but the web service never responds. That means the web method returns immediately and closes the connection. The client doesn't need to spend any time waiting. However, there are also a few drawbacks with one-way methods. Namely, the web method can't provide a return value or use a ref or out parameter. Similarly, if the web method throws an unhandled exception, it won't be propagated back to the client.

To create a fire-and-forget XML Web service method, you need to apply a SoapDocumentMethod attribute to the appropriate web method and set the OneWay property to true, as shown here:

```
[SoapDocumentMethod(OneWay = true)]
[WebMethod()]
public DataSet GetEmployees()
{ ... }
```

The client doesn't need to take any special steps to call a one-way method asynchronously. Instead, the method always returns immediately.

Of course, there are some reasons you might not want to use one-way methods. The most important limitation is that you can't return any information. For example, a common asynchronous server-side pattern is for the server to return some sort of unique automatically generated ticket to the client when the client submits a request. The client can then submit this ticket to other methods to check the status or retrieve the results. With a one-way method, there's no way to return a ticket to the client or notify the client if an error occurs. Another problem is the fact that one-way methods still use ASP.NET worker threads. If the task is extremely long, and there are many ongoing tasks, other clients might not be able to submit new requests, which is far from ideal.

The only practical way to deal with long-running, asynchronous tasks in a heavily trafficked website is to combine web services with another .NET technology—*remoting*. For example, you could create an ordinary, synchronous web method that returns a ticket, and then calls a method in a server-side component using remoting. The remoting component could then begin its processing task asynchronously. This technique of using a web service as a front-end to a full-fledged, continuously running server-side component is a more complex hallmark of distributed design. To learn more, you may want to consult a dedicated book about distributed programming, like *Microsoft .NET Distributed Applications* (Matthew MacDonald, Microsoft Press, 2003), or a book about .NET remoting, like *Advanced .NET Remoting* (Ingo Rammer, Apress, 2002). Of course, if you don't need this flexibility, you're better off to avoid it completely, because it introduces significant complexity and extra work.

Securing Web Services

In an ideal world, you could treat a web service as a class library of functionality, and not worry about coding user authentication or security logic. However, in order to create subscription-based or micro-payment web services, you need to determine who is using it. And even if you aren't selling your logic to an audience of eager web developers, you may still need to use authentication to protect sensitive data and lock out malicious users, especially if your web service is exposed over the Internet.

You can use some of the same techniques you use to protect web pages to defend your web services. For example, you can use IIS to enforce SSL (just direct your clients to a web service URL starting with https://). You can also use IIS to apply Windows authentication, although there are a few additional steps you need to apply, as you'll learn in the next section. Finally, you can create your own custom authentication system using SOAP headers.

Windows Authentication

Windows authentication works with a web service in much the same way that it works with a web page. The difference is that a web service is executed by another application, not directly by the browser. For that reason, there's no built-in way to prompt the user for a user name and password. Instead, the application that's using the web service needs to supply this information. The application might read this information from a configuration file or database, or might prompt the user for this information before contacting the web service.

For example, consider the following web service, which provides a single TestAuthenticated() method. This method checks whether the user is authenticated. If the user is authenticated, it returns the user name (which will be a string in the form DomainName\UserName or ComputerName\UserName).

```
public class SecuredService : System.Web.Services.WebService
{
    [WebMethod()]
    public string TestAuthenticated()
    {
        if (!User.Identity.IsAuthenticated)
        {
            return "Not authenticated.";
        }
        else
        {
            return "Authenticated as: " + User.Identity.Name;
        }
    }
}
```

The web service can also examine role membership, although this web service doesn't take this step.

In order to submit user credentials to this service, the client needs to modify the NetworkCredential property of the proxy class. You have two options:

- You can create a new NetworkCredential object, and attach this to the NetworkCredential property of the proxy object. When you create the NetworkCredential object, you'll need to specify the user name and password that you want to use. This approach works with all forms of Windows authentication.

- If the web service is using integrated Windows authentication, you can automatically submit the credentials of the current user by using the static DefaultCredentials property of the CredentialCache class, and applying that to the NetworkCredential property of the proxy object.

Both the CredentialCache and NetworkCredential classes are found in the System.Net namespace. Thus, before continuing, you should import this namespace:

```
using System.Net;
```

The following code shows a web page with two text boxes and two buttons (see Figure 26-2). One button performs an unauthenticated call, while the other submits the user name and password that have been entered in the text boxes.

The unauthenticated call will fail if you've disabled anonymous users. Otherwise, the unauthenticated call will succeed, but the TestAuthenticated() method will return a string informing you that authentication wasn't performed. The authenticated call will always succeed as long as you submit credentials that correspond to a valid user on the web server.

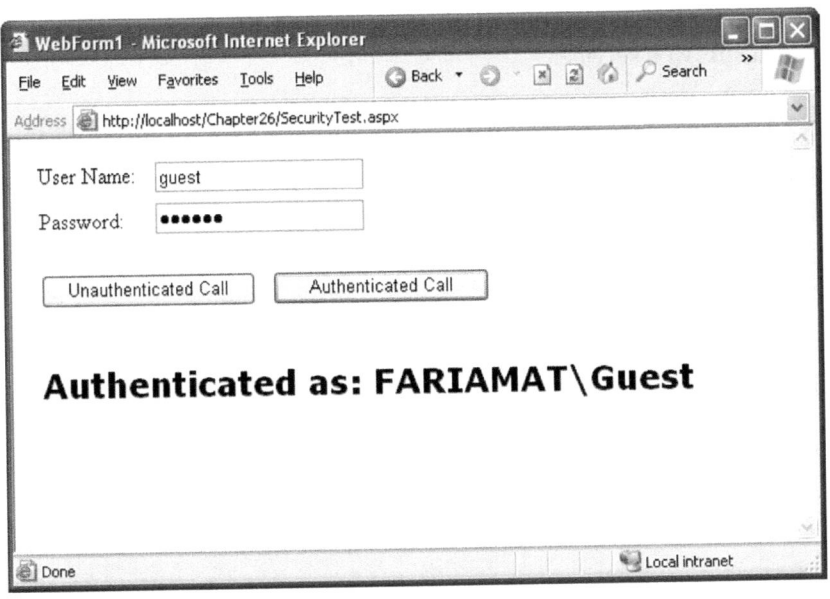

Figure 26-2. *Succesful authentication through a web service*

Here's the complete web page code:

```
public class TestSecuredService : Page
{
    protected Button cmdUnauthenticated;
    protected Button cmdAuthenticated;
    protected Label lblInfo;

    // (Initialization code omitted.)

    private void cmdUnauthenticated_Click(Object sender, EventArgs e)
    {
        SecuredService proxy = new SecuredService();
        lblInfo.Text = proxy.TestAuthenticated();
    }

    private void cmdAuthenticated_Click(Object sender, EventArgs e)
    {
        SecuredService proxy = new SecuredService();

        // Supply some user credentials for the web service.
        NetworkCredential credentials = new NetworkCredential(
          txtUserName.Text, txtPassword.Text);
        proxy.Credentials = credentials;

        lblInfo.Text = proxy.TestAuthenticated();
    }
}
```

To try this out, you can add the following <location> tag to the web.config file to restrict access to the SecureService.asmx web service:

```
<configuration>
    <system.web>
        <!-- Other settings omitted. -->
        <authorization>
            <allow users="*" />
        </authorization>
    </system.web>

    <location path="SecureService.asmx">
        <system.web>
            <authorization>
                <deny users="?" />
            </authorization>
        </system.web>
    </location>
</configuration>
```

If you wanted to use the credentials of the currently logged-in account with Integrated Windows authentication, you would use this code instead:

```
SecuredService proxy = new SecuredService();
proxy.Credentials = CredentialCache.DefaultCredentials;
lblInfo.Text = proxy.TestAuthenticated();
```

In this example (as in all web pages), the current user account will be the account that ASP.NET is using, not the user account of the remote user who is requesting the web page. If you use the same technique in a Windows application, you'll submit the account information of the user who is running the application.

Custom Ticket-Based Authentication

Windows authentication is a good solution for web services when you have a small set of users that have existing Windows accounts. However, it doesn't work as well for large-scale public web services. When working with ASP.NET web pages, you usually turn to forms authentication to fill the gaps. However, forms authentication won't work with a web service because there's no way for a web service to direct the user to a web page. In fact, the web service might not even be accessed through a browser—it might be used by a Windows application or even an automated Windows service. Forms authentication is also cookie-based, which is an unnecessary restriction to place on web services, which might use protocols that don't support cookies or clients that don't expect them.

The usual solution is to roll your own authentication system. In this model, users will call a specific web method in the web service to log in, at which point they will supply credentials (like a user name and password combination). The login method will register the user session and create a new, unique ticket. From this point on, the user can reconnect to the web service by supplying the ticket to every other method.

A properly designed ticket system has a number of benefits. As with forms authentication, it provides complete flexibility. It also optimizes performance and ensures scalability, because you can cache the ticket in memory. On subsequent requests, you can verify the ticket rather than authenticating the user against the database. Finally, it allows you to take advantage of SOAP headers, which make the ticket management and authorization process transparent to the client.

The following sections take you through the process of creating a custom authentication system for web services based on SOAP headers. To develop this example, you need the back-end Users, Roles, and UsersRoles tables that supported role-based forms authentication in Chapter 17.

Tracking the User Identity

To use custom security, the first step is to decide what user-specific information you want to cache in memory. You need to create a custom class that represents this information. This class can include information about the user (name, e-mail address, and so on), and his or her permissions. It should also include the ticket.

Here's a basic example that stores a user name, ticket, and array of roles:

```
public class TicketIdentity
{
    private string userName;
    public string UserName
    {
        get { return userName; }
    }

    private string[] roles;
    public string Roles
    {
        get { return roles; }
    }

    private string ticket;
    public string Ticket
    {
        get { return ticket; }
    }

    public TicketIdentity(string userName, string[] roles)
    {
        this.userName = userName;
        this.roles = roles;

        // Create the ticket GUID.
        Ticket = Guid.NewGuid().ToString();
    }
}
```

Note You've probably noticed that this identity class doesn't implement IIdentity. That's because this approach doesn't allow you to plug into the .NET security model in the same way you could with custom web page authentication. Essentially, the problem is that you need to perform the authentication *after* the User object is already created. And you can't get around this problem using the global.asax class, because the application event handlers won't have access to the web method parameters and SOAP header you need to perform the authentication and authorization.

Once you have the user identity class, you need to create a SOAP header. This header tracks a single piece of information—the user ticket. Because the ticket is a randomly generated GUID, it's not practically possible for a malicious user to "guess" what ticket value another user has been issued.

```
public class TicketHeader : SoapHeader
{
    public string Ticket;

    public TicketHeader(string ticket)
    {
        Ticket = ticket;
    }

    public TicketHeader()
    {}
}
```

You must then add a member variable for the TicketHeader to your web service:

```
public class SoapSecurityService : WebService
{
    public TicketHeader Ticket;
    ...
}
```

Authenticating the User

The next step is to create a dedicated web method that logs the user in. The user needs to submit user credentials to this method (such as a login and password). Then, the method will retrieve the user information, create the TicketIdentity object, and issue the ticket.

In this example, the web service allows the user to choose the type of encryption for user credentials. There are three options, as defined by the following HashAlgorithm enumeration:

```
public enum HashAlgorithm
{
    SHA1, MD5, Clear
}
```

This gives the user the flexibility to supply unencrypted user credentials (for example, if the client doesn't have access to the required encryption library on their platform) or transmit them securely. Of course, if the client opts for clear text, it should use an SSL connection to prevent eavesdroppers from stealing the user name and password information.

The Login() web method checks the user credentials by calling a private Authenticate() method, and then retrieves the role information. A new ticket is constructed with the role information, and stored in a user-specific slot in the Application collection. At the same time, a new SOAP header is issued with the ticket so that the user can access other methods.

Here's the complete code for the Login() method:

```
[WebMethod()]
[SoapHeader("Ticket", Direction = SoapHeaderDirection.Out)]
public void Login(string userName, string password, HashAlgorithm hashAlgorithm)
{
    if (Authenticate(userName, password, hashAlgorithm))
    {
        // Get the user roles.
        string[] roles = GetRoles(userName);

        // Create a new ticket.
        TicketIdentity ticket = new TicketIdentity(userName, roles);

        // Add this ticket to Application state.
        Application[ticket.Ticket] = ticket;

        // Create the SOAP header.
        Ticket = new TicketHeader(ticket.Ticket);
    }
    else
    {
        throw new SecurityException("Invalid credentials.");
    }
}
```

This code doesn't show the Authenticate() or GetRoles() methods, because they were already used in the custom forms-based authentication examples in Chapter 17. For the complete data access code, refer to the downloadable samples.

■**Tip** This Login() method uses the HashPasswordForStoringInConfigFile() method of the FormsAuthentication class behind the scenes. That means the client can choose to send a SHA1 or MD5 password hash, rather than clear text (which would only be appropriate if you are logging in over an SSL connection).

Note that in this example, the TicketIdentity object is stored in the Application collection, which is global to all users. However, you don't need to worry about one user's ticket overwriting another. That's because the tickets are indexed using the unique GUID. Every user has a separate ticket GUID, and hence a separate slot in the Application collection.

The Application collection has certain limitations, including no support for web farms, and poor scalability to large numbers of users. The tickets will also be lost if the web application restarts. To improve this solution, you could store the information in two places: the Cache object, and a back-end database. That way, your code can check the Cache first, and if a matching TicketIdentity is found, no database call is required. But if the TicketIdentity isn't present, the information can still be retrieved from the database. It's important to understand that this enhancement still uses the same SOAP header with the ticket and the same TicketIdentity object. The only difference is how the TicketIdentity is stored and retrieved in between requests.

Authorizing the User

Once you have the Login() method in place, it makes sense to create a private method that can be called to verify that a user is present. You can then call this method from other web methods in your web service.

The following AuthorizeUser() method checks for a matching ticket and returns the TicketIdentity if it's found. If not, an exception is thrown, which will be returned to the client.

```
private TicketIdentity AuthorizeUser(string ticket)
{
    TicketIdentity ticketIdentity = (TicketIdentity)Application[ticket];
    if (ticket != null)
    {
        return ticketIdentity;
    }
    else
    {
        throw new SecurityException("Invalid ticket.");
    }
}
```

In addition, this overloaded version of AuthorizeUser() verifies that the user has a ticket and is a member of a specific role:

```
private TicketIdentity AuthorizeUser(string ticket, string role)
{
    TicketIdentity ticketIdentity = AuthorizeUser(ticket);
    if (Array.IndexOf(ticketIdentity.Roles, role) == -1)
    {
        throw new SecurityException("Insufficient permissions.");
    }
    else
    {
        return ticketIdentity;
    }
}
```

Using these two helper methods, you can build other web service methods that test a user's permissions before performing certain tasks or returning privileged information.

Testing the SOAP Authentication System

Now you simply need to create a test web method that uses the AuthorizeUser() method to check that the user has the required permissions. Here's an example that checks that the client is an administrator before allowing them to retrieve the DataSet with the employee list:

```
[WebMethod()]
[SoapHeader("Ticket", Direction = SoapHeaderDirection.In)]
public DataSet GetEmployees()
{
    AuthorizeUser(Ticket.Ticket, "Administrator");

    ...

}
```

Now you can create a client that tests this. In this case, we use a web page that provides two text boxes for the user to supply a user name and password (see Figure 26-3). This information is passed to the Login() method, and then the GetEmployees() method is called to retrieve the data. This method succeeds for a user with the Administrator role, but fails for everyone else. Here's the web page code:

```
private void cmdCall_Click(object sender, System.EventArgs e)
{
    SoapSecurityService proxy = new SoapSecurityService();

    try
    {
        proxy.Login(txtUserName.Text, txtPassword.Text, HashAlgorithm.SHA1);
        DataGrid1.DataSource = proxy.GetEmployees();
        DataGrid1.DataBind();
    }
    catch (Exception err)
    {
        lblInfo.Text = err.Message;
    }
}
```

The best part is that the client doesn't need to be aware of the ticket management. That's because the Login() method issues the ticket, and the proxy class maintains it. As long as the client uses the same instance of the proxy class, the same ticket value will be submitted automatically, and the user will be authenticated.

Tip In the next section, you'll see another way to implement custom security—with the WSE. Although the WSE presents the road of the future, you might still prefer to use the custom approach in today's applications, at least until the WSE becomes a more mature, standardized part of the .NET Framework.

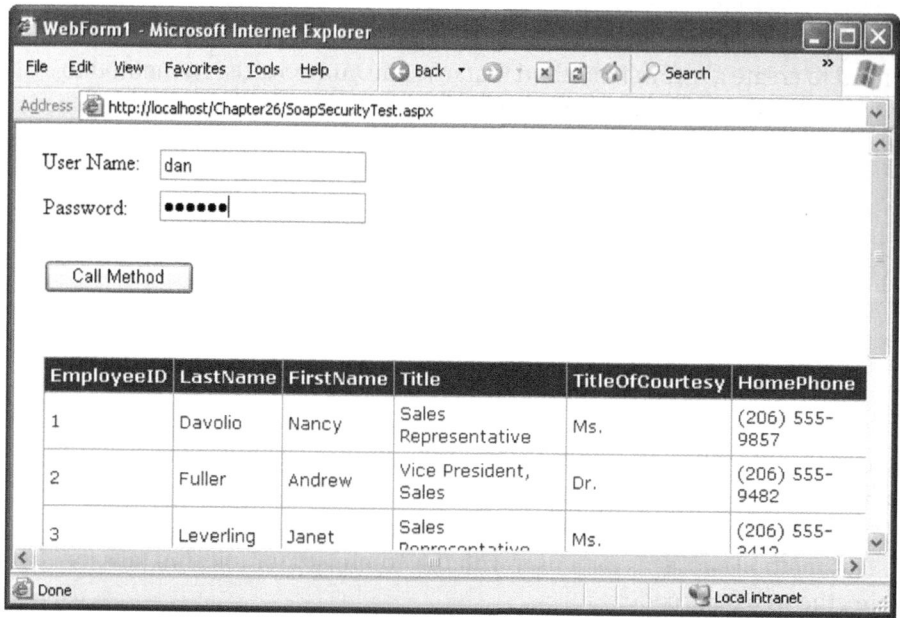

Figure 26-3. *Testing a web method that uses ticket-based authorization*

The Web Services Enhancements

In the months since .NET 1.0 first appeared, the world of web service standards hasn't been quiet. In fact, numerous standards, in various degrees of testing, revision, and standardization, are continuously being developed and put to the developer community. In future versions of .NET, many of these additions will be fused into the class library. As these standards are still fairly new and subject to change, they aren't ready yet. However, you can download another Microsoft tool—the free WSE 2.0 toolkit—to gain support for a slew of new web service standards today.

To install the WSE (or just read about it), browse to `http://msdn.microsoft.com/webservices/building/wse`. The WSE provides a class library assembly with a set of useful .NET classes. Behind the scenes, the WSE uses SOAP extensions, which you learned about in Chapter 25, to adjust the web service messages. That means that your code interacts with a set of helper objects, and behind the scenes the WSE implements the appropriate SOAP standards. There are two key disadvantages of using the WSE. First, the toolkit is subject to change, and already version 2.0 is completely incompatible with the earlier, more limited version 1.0. Second, you need to use WSE on both the client and web server. In other words, if you want to use a web service that uses WSE to gain a new feature, your application must also use the WSE (if it's a .NET client), or another toolkit that supports the same standards (if it's not).

Many of the features in the WSE are implemented through a special SoapContext class. Your code interacts with the SoapContext object. Then, when you send the message, various filters (SOAP extensions) examine the properties of the SoapContext and, if warranted, add SOAP headers to the outgoing message. Figure 26-4 illustrates this process.

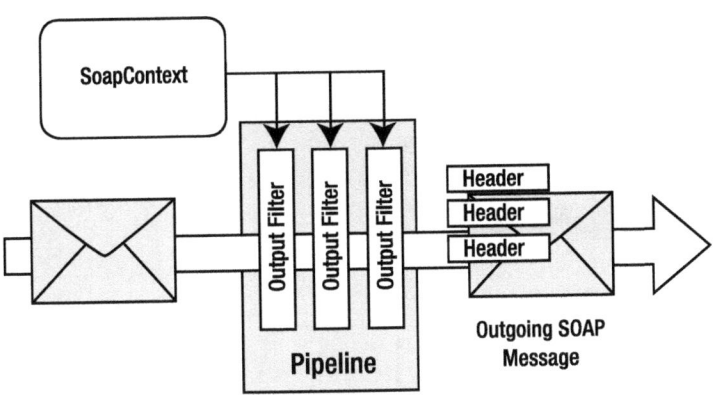

Figure 26-4. *Processing an outgoing SOAP message*

The idea behind the filters is that they can be plugged in only when they are needed. For example, if you don't need a security header, then you can leave the security header filter out of the processing pipeline by tweaking the configuration settings. Additionally, because each filter works by adding a distinct SOAP header, you have the freedom to combine as many (or as few) extensions as you need at once.

When a SOAP message is received, the same process happens in reverse. In this case, the filters look for specific SOAP headers, and use the information in them to configure the SoapContext object. This processing model is shown in Figure 26-5.

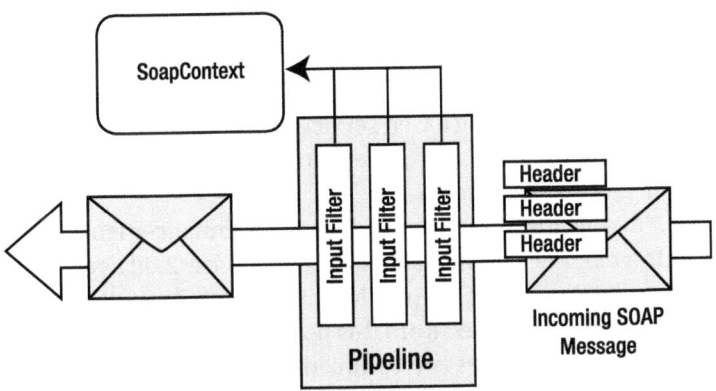

Figure 26-5. *Processing an incoming SOAP message*

So what are the standards supported by the WSE? The full list is available with the WSE documentation, but it includes support for authentication and message encryption, establishing trust, message routing, attachments, and interoperability. WSE also allows you to use SOAP messages for direct communication over a TCP connection (no HTTP required).

In this chapter, you'll see how to use two of the most practical WSE features, as follows:

- Perform automatic authentication with WS-Security.

- Send large blocks of data efficiently with WS-Attachments and DIME.

Installing the WSE

Before considering either of these examples, you need to download and install the WSE. When you run the setup program, choose Visual Studio Developer if you have Visual Studio .NET 2003 installed, as this enables project support (see Figure 26-6).

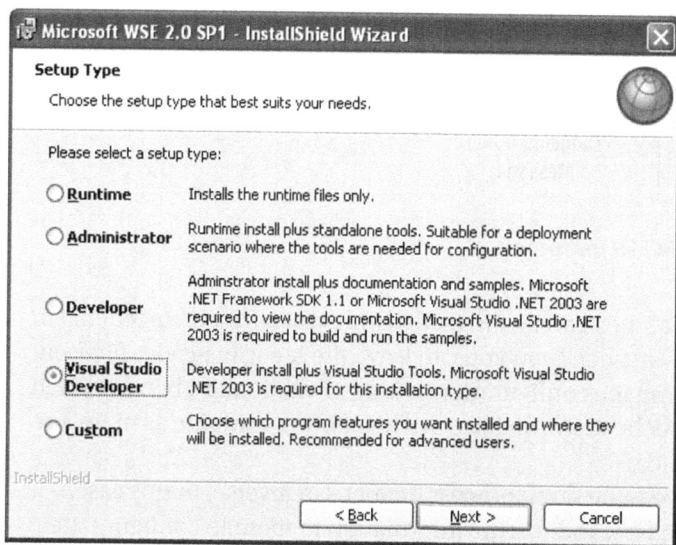

Figure 26-6. *Installing WSE*

To use WSE in a project, you need to take an additional step. In Visual Studio .NET, right-click the project name in the Solution Explorer, and select WSE Settings from the bottom of the menu. You'll see two check boxes. If you're creating a web service, select both settings, as shown in Figure 26-7. If you're creating a client application, select only the first setting, which is labeled "Enable this project for Web Services Enhancements."

When you select the first option, "Enable this project for Web Services Enhancements," Visual Studio .NET automatically adds a reference to the Microsoft.Web.Services2.dll assembly and modifies the web.config for the application to add support for the WSE configuration handler. In addition, any web references that are created from this point on will include WSE support in the proxy class. However, the web references you've already created won't have WSE support until you update them.

When you enable the second option, "Enable Microsoft Web Services Enhancements SOAP Extensions," Visual Studio .NET modifies the web.config file to register the SOAP extension that adds support for your web services. This option is only required for ASP.NET web services that use the WSE.

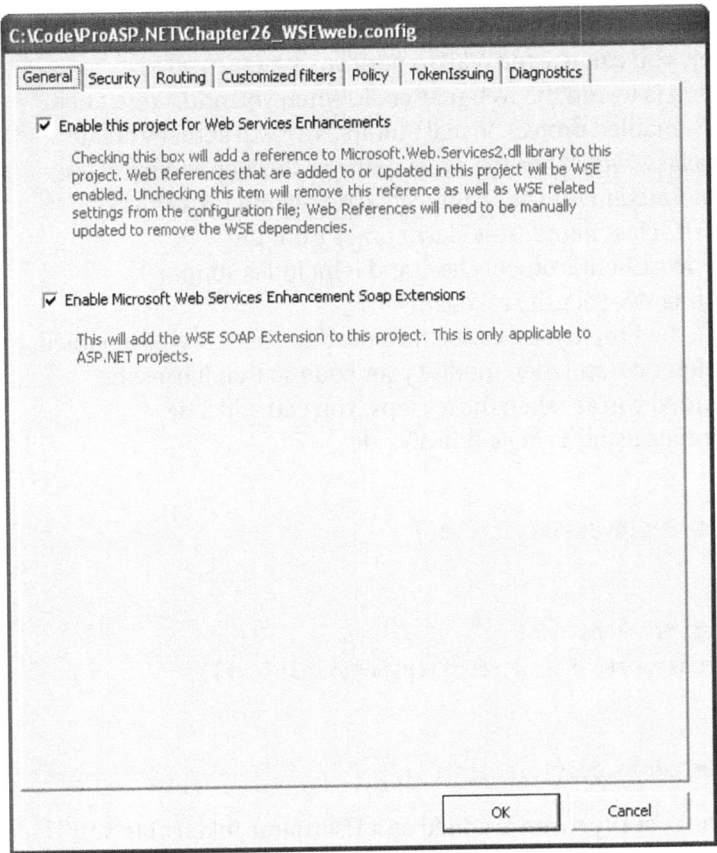

Figure 26-7. *Enabling WSE for a project*

Performing Authentication with the WSE

Many of the WSE classes support security standards. One of the most simple and straightforward of these classes is the UsernameToken class, which represents user credentials.

The UsernameToken information is added to the message as a SOAP header. However, it's added in a way that's conformant with the WS-Security standard, which would be quite laborious to implement on your own. The benefit is that by implementing this more general security model, you can add authentication without developing a proprietary approach that could make it more difficult for third-party and cross-platform use of your web service. Also, it's very likely that ASP.NET and WS-Security can provide a more secure, robust approach than one that an individual developer or organization could develop without investing considerable time and effort.

At the present, the security infrastructure in WSE has a few holes, and doesn't fully deliver on its promise. However, it's easy to use and extend. To see how it works, it's helpful to consider a simple example.

Setting Credentials in the Client

In the next example, you'll see how you can use the WSE to perform a secure call to the EmployeesService. The first step is to add the web reference. When you add a reference to the EmployeesService in a WSE-enabled project, Visual Studio .NET will actually create *two* proxy classes. The first proxy class (which has the same name as the web service class) is the same as the web service generated in non-WSE projects. The second proxy class has the suffix "WSE" appended to its class name. This class comes from the Microsoft.Web.Services2.WebServicesClientProtocol class, and it includes support for WSE features (in this case, adding WS-Security tokens).

Thus, to use WS-Security with the EmployeesService, you need to create a WSE-enabled project, add or refresh the web reference, and then modify your code so that it uses the EmployeeServiceWSE proxy. Provided you've taken those steps, you can add a new UsernameToken with your credentials using a single line of code:

```
// Create the proxy.
EmployeesServiceWse proxy = new EmployeesServiceWse();

// Add the WS-Security token.
proxy.RequestSoapContext.Security.Tokens.Add(
    new UsernameToken(userName, password, PasswordOption.SendPlainText));

// Bind the results.
dataGrid1.DataSource = proxy.GetEmployees().Tables[0];
```

As this code demonstrates, the security token is added as a UsernameToken object. It's inserted in the Security.Tokens collection of the RequestSoapContext, which is a SoapContext object that represents the request message you're about to send.

In order to use this code as written, you need to import the following namespaces:

```
using Microsoft.Web.Services2;
using Microsoft.Web.Services2.Security;
using Microsoft.Web.Services2.Security.Tokens;
```

Note Notice that the WSE namespaces incorporate the number 2, which indicates the second version of the WSE toolkit. This is because the second version is not backward compatible with the first. In order to prevent a conflict with partially upgraded applications, the WSE classes are separated into distinct name-spaces by version. This is part of the messy reality of working with emerging web service standards.

The constructor for the UsernameToken class accepts three parameters: a string with the user name, a string with the password, and the hashing option you would like to use. Unfortunately, if you want to use the default authentication provider in the WSE (which uses Windows authentication), you *must* choose PasswordOption.SendPlainText. As a result, this code is extremely insecure and subject to network spying unless you send the request over an SSL connection.

Although this example only adds two additional details to the request, the SOAP message actually becomes much more complex due to the way the WS-Security standard is structured. It defines additional details such as an expiration date (used to prevent replay attacks) and a *nonce* (a random value that can be incorporated in the hash to increase security). Here's a slightly shortened example of the SOAP request message:

```
<soap:Envelope xmlns:soap="http://schemas.xmlsoap.org/soap/envelope/"
 xmlns:wsa="http://schemas.xmlsoap.org/ws/2004/03/addressing"
 mlns:wsse="http://docs.oasis-open.org/wss/2004/01/..."
 xmlns:wsu="http://docs.oasis-open.org/wss/2004/01/...">
  <soap:Header>
    <wsa:Action>http://www.apress.com/ProASP.NET/GetEmployees</wsa:Action>
    <wsa:MessageID>uuid:5b1bc235-7f81-40c4-ac1e-e4ea81ade319</wsa:MessageID>
      <wsa:ReplyTo>
        <wsa:Address>http://schemas.xmlsoap.org/ws/2004/03/...</wsa:Address>
      </wsa:ReplyTo>
      <wsa:To>http://localhost:8080/Chapter26_WSE/EmployeesService.asmx</wsa:To>
      <wsse:Security soap:mustUnderstand="1">
      <wsu:Timestamp wsu:Id="Timestamp-dc0d8d9a-e385-438f-9ff1-2cb0b699c90f">
        <wsu:Created>2004-09-21T01:49:33Z</wsu:Created>
        <wsu:Expires>2004-09-21T01:54:33Z</wsu:Expires>
      </wsu:Timestamp>
      <wsse:UsernameToken xmlns:wsu="http://docs.oasis-open.org/wss/2004/01/..."
        wsu:Id="SecurityToken-8b663245-30ac-4178-b2c8-724f43fc27be">
        <wsse:Username>guest</wsse:Username>
        <wsse:Password
          Type="http://docs.oasis-open.org/wss/2004/01/...">secret</wsse:Password>
        <wsse:Nonce>9m8UofSBhw+XWIqfO83NiQ==</wsse:Nonce>
        <wsu:Created>2004-09-21T01:49:33Z</wsu:Created>
      </wsse:UsernameToken>
    </wsse:Security>
  </soap:Header>
  <soap:Body>
    <GetEmployees xmlns="http://www.apress.com/ProASP.NET/" />
  </soap:Body>
</soap:Envelope>
```

Reading Credentials in the Web Service

The WSE-enabled service examines the supplied token and validates it immediately. The default authentication provider that's included with WSE uses Windows authentication, which means it extracts the user name and password from the SOAP header and uses it to log the user in under a Windows account. If the token doesn't map to a valid Windows account, an error message is returned to the client. However, if no token is supplied, no error occurs. It's up to you to check for this condition on the web server in order to restrict access to specific web methods.

Unfortunately, the WSE isn't integrated in such a way that it can use the User object. Instead, you need to retrieve the tokens from the current context. The WSE provides a RequestSoapContext. Using the RequestSoapContext.Current property, you can retrieve an instance of the SoapContext class that represents the last received message. You can then examine the SoapContext.Security.Tokens collection.

To simplify this task, it helps to create a private method like the one shown here. It checks that a token exists, and throws an exception if it doesn't. Otherwise, it returns the user name.

```
private string GetUsernameToken()
{
    // Although there may be many tokens, only one of these
    // will be a UsernameToken.
    foreach (UsernameToken token in RequestSoapContext.Current.Security.Tokens)
    {
        return token.Username;
    }
    throw new SecurityException("Missing security token");
}
```

You could call the GetUsernameToken() is method at the beginning of a web method to ensure that security is in effect. Overall, this is a good approach to enforce security. However, it's important to keep its limitations in mind. First of all, there is no support for hashing or encrypting the user credentials. There's no support for more advanced Windows authentication protocols like digest authentication and integrated Windows authentication. That's because the authentication is implemented by the WSE extensions, not by IIS. Similarly, the client always needs to submit a password and user name. There's no way for the client to automatically submit the credentials of the current user, as demonstrated earlier in this chapter with the CredentialCache object. In fact, the Credentials property of the proxy is ignored completely.

Fortunately, you aren't limited to the scaled-down form of Windows authentication provided by the default WSE authentication service. You can also create your own authentication logic, as described in the next section.

Custom Authentication

By creating your own authentication class, you can perform authentication against any data source, including an XML file or a database. To create your own authenticator, you simply need to create a class that derives from UsernameTokenManager and overrides the AuthenticateToken() method. In this method, your code needs to look up the user who is trying to become authenticated, and return the password for that user. ASP.NET will then compare this password against the user credentials and decide whether authentication fails or succeeds.

Creating this class is quite straightforward. Here's an example that simply returns hard-coded passwords for two users. This provides a quick-and-easy test, although a real-world example would probably use ADO.NET code to get the same information.

```
public class CustomAuthenticator : UsernameTokenManager
{
    protected override string AuthenticateToken(UsernameToken token)
    {
```

```
        string username = token.Username;

        if (username == "dan")
            return "secret";
        else if (username == "jenny")
            return "opensesame";
        else
            return "";
    }
}
```

The reason that you don't perform the password test on your own is because the type of comparison depends on how the credentials are encoded. For example, if they are passed in clear text, you need to perform a simple string comparison. If they are hashed, you need to create a new password hash using the same, standardized algorithm, which must take the same data into account (including the random nonce from the client message). However, WSE can perform this comparison task for you automatically, which dramatically simplifies your logic. The only potential problem is that you need to have the user's password stored in a retrievable form on the web server. If you're only storing password hashes in a back-end database, you won't be able to pass the original password to ASP.NET, and it won't be able to recreate the credential hash it needs to authenticate the user.

Once you've created your authentication class, you still need to tell WSE to use it for authenticating user tokens by registering your class in the web.config file. To accomplish this, right-click the project name in the Solution Explorer and select WSE Settings. Next, select the Security tab (shown in Figure 26-8).

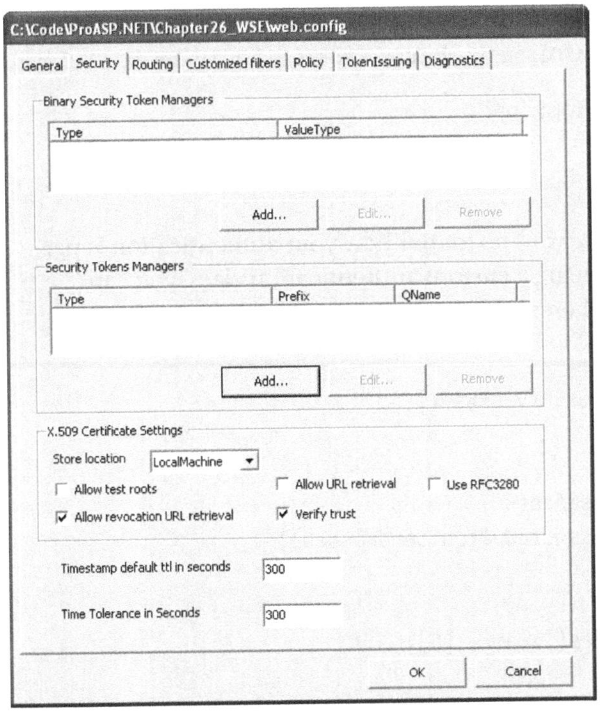

Figure 26-8. *Security settings*

In the Security Tokens Managers section, click the Add button. This displays the SecurityToken Manager dialog box (see Figure 26-9).

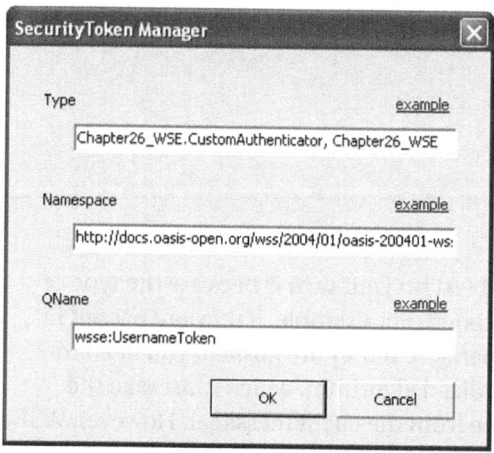

Figure 26-9. *Configuring a new UsernameTokenManager*

In the SecurityTokenManager dialog box you need to specify three pieces of information:

- **Type.** Enter the fully qualified class name, followed by a comma, followed by the assembly name (without the .dll extension). For example, if you have a web project named MyProject with an authentication class named CustomAuthenticator, this string should be MyProject.CustomAuthenticator, MyProject.

- **Namespace.** Enter the following hard-coded string:

  http://docs.oasis-open.org/wss/2004/01/oasis-200401-wss-wssecurity-secext-1.0.xsd

- **QName.** Enter the following hard-code string:

  wsse:UsernameToken

The client is built in essentially the same way, no matter how your authentication is performed on the server. However, when you create a custom authentication class, you can choose to use hashed passwords, as shown here:

```
// Create the proxy.
EmployeesServiceWse proxy = new EmployeesServiceWse();

// Add the WS-Security token.
proxy.RequestSoapContext.Security.Tokens.Add(
  new UsernameToken("dan", "secret", PasswordOption.SendHashed));

// Bind the results.
dataGrid1.DataSource = proxy.GetEmployees().Tables[0];
```

The best part is the fact that you don't need to manually hash or encrypt the user password. Instead, WSE hashes it automatically based on your instructions, and performs the hash comparison on the server side. It even incorporates a random nonce value to prevent replay attacks.

Sending a Web Service Attachment

Web services support binary data through the byte data type. There's no reason you can't create web methods that accept or return blocks of binary data as byte arrays. However, this approach is terribly inefficient for large amounts of data. The problem is that the binary data needs to be completely serialized to XML when creating the SOAP message, which incurs needless overhead. A better approach would be to send the binary data *after* the SOAP message, as a binary attachment the client can read and process after parsing the SOAP message.

WSE supports attachments according to the WS-Attachments and DIME standards. WS-Attachments defines how to associate an attachment with a message. The DIME format uses explicitly-sized chunks to encode the attachment. Each chunk has a record number and a size associated with it. The advantage of DIME over MIME is that the recipient of a DIME-formatted attachment can move efficiently from one attachment to the next, without searching for the boundaries.

The following example uses WSE to create a web method that accepts a large file and saves it to the web server.

Retrieving an Attachment

If you wanted to create a method that accepts an attachment without the WSE, you would create a method that accepts a binary array, as shown here:

```
[WebMethod()]
public void UploadFile(string fileName, byte[] fileData)
{ ... }
```

However, when creating a web method that accepts a binary attachment, you don't include the attachment as one of the parameters. Instead, the attachment is sent immediately following the message. To access the attachment, you use the Attachments collection of the current SoapContext. The client can send multiple attachments at once, and each attachment is provided a .NET stream.

Here's an example that ensures there is only a single attachment, and then writes the data from the stream to a file with the requested name:

```
[WebMethod()]
public void UploadFile(string fileName)
{
    if (RequestSoapContext.Current.Attachments.Count != 1)
    {
        throw new ArgumentException("Only upload one file at a time.");
    }
    else
    {
```

```
        // Ensure that the supplied file name doesn't include a path
        // (so the application can't be tricked into using anything
        // other than the designated directory).
        fileName = Path.GetFileName(fileName);

        // Note that there's still no guarantee this file is unique,
        // so you might want to use randomly generated data in the name
        // (like a GUID) or a user-specific directory.

        // Save the file using the name provided.
        string fullPath = HttpContext.Current.Server.MapPath(fileName);
        FileStream fs = File.Create(fullPath);

        Stream stream = RequestSoapContext.Current.Attachments[0].Stream;
        while (stream.Position < (stream.Length-1))
        {
            // Write one byte at a time.
            // You could also grab larger chunks to be more efficient.
            fs.WriteByte((byte)stream.ReadByte());
        }
        fs.Close();
    }
}
```

In order to use this code as written, you'll need to import the core WSE namespace:

```
using Microsoft.Web.Services2;
```

Sending the Attachment

Any WSE-enabled client can send an attachment, including both web applications and Windows applications. The following example uses a web page that allows users to upload a file through the HtmlInputFile control (as shown in Figure 26-10). When the page is posted back with the file, the web page code creates a new attachment with the data and calls the web method UploadFile().

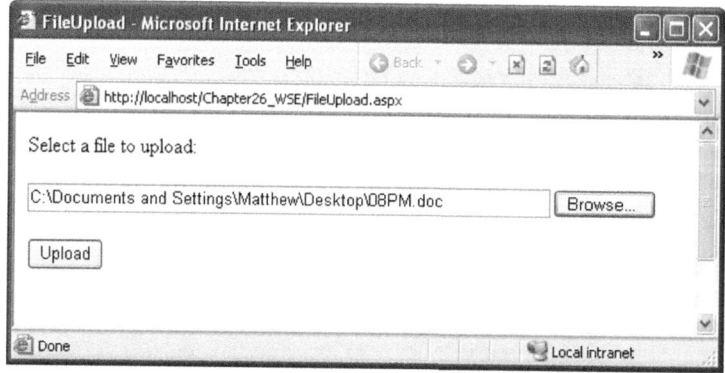

Figure 26-10. *Sending a file as a DIME attachment*

The code for the Upload button is as follows:

```
private void cmdUpload_ServerClick(object sender, System.EventArgs e)
{
    // Check if a file was submitted.
    if (Uploader.PostedFile.ContentLength != 0)
    {
        try
        {
            UploadServiceWse proxy = new UploadServiceWse();

            // Create the attachment.
            // You can use either a file path or an open stream.
            string fileName = Path.GetFileName(Uploader.PostedFile.FileName);
            DimeAttachment attachment = new DimeAttachment(
                fileName, TypeFormat.MediaType, Uploader.PostedFile.InputStream);
            proxy.RequestSoapContext.Attachments.Add(attachment);

            // Call the web method and upload the attachment.
            proxy.UploadFile(fileName);
            lblStatus.InnerText = "Thanks for submitting your file";
        }
        catch (Exception err)
        {
            lblStatus.InnerText = err.Message;
        }
    }
}
```

In order to use this code as written, you need to import the following namespace to get easy access to the DimeAttachment class:

```
using Microsoft.Web.Services2.Dime
```

Note that you must make sure your code doesn't close the stream with the attachment data. If you do, the information won't be accessible and an exception will occur. Instead, you can rely on the WSE proxy to close the stream after it has sent the attachment. The DimeAttachment class also provides a constructor that accepts the path of a file you want to send. You can use this in a Windows application to quickly send a file that a user has chosen using a control like the OpenFileDialog.

Summary

In this chapter, you learned a variety of advanced SOAP techniques, including how to call web services asynchronously, how to enforce security, and how to gain support for new SOAP standards with the freely downloadable WSE toolkit. The world of web services is sure to continue to evolve in the future, so look for new standards and increasingly powerful capabilities to appear in future versions of the .NET Framework. For a more complete examination of the WSE, refer to Jeffrey Hasan's book *Expert Service-Oriented Architecture in C#: Using the Web Services Enhancements 2.0* (Apress, 2004).

Index